FILE

About Island Press

Island Press is the only nonprofit organization in the United States whose principal purpose is the publication of books on environmental issues and natural resource management. We provide solutions-oriented information to professionals, public officials, business and community leaders, and concerned citizens who are shaping responses to environmental problems.

In 2001, Island Press celebrates its seventeenth anniversary as the leading provider of timely and practical books that take a multidisciplinary approach to critical environmental concerns. Our growing list of titles reflects our commitment to bringing the best of an expanding body of literature to the environmental community throughout North America and the world.

Support for Island Press is provided by The Bullitt Foundation, The Mary Flagler Cary Charitable Trust, The Nathan Cummings Foundation, Geraldine R. Dodge Foundation, Doris Duke Charitable Foundation, The Charles Engelhard Foundation, The Ford Foundation, The George Gund Foundation, The Vira I. Heinz Endowment, The William and Flora Hewlett Foundation, W. Alton Jones Foundation, The John D. and Catherine T. MacArthur Foundation, The Andrew W. Mellon Foundation, The Charles Stewart Mott Foundation, The Curtis and Edith Munson Foundation, National Fish and Wildlife Foundation, The New-Land Foundation, Oak Foundation, The Overbrook Foundation, The David and Lucile Packard Foundation, The Pew Charitable Trusts, Rockefeller Brothers Fund, The Winslow Foundation, and other generous donors.

The Wellbeing
of Nations

la vida buena es cara,
hay otra mas barata,
pero ya no es vida

[the good life is dear,
there's another that is cheaper,
but it's no life]

Spanish maxim

The Wellbeing
of Nations

A Country-by-Country Index
of Quality of Life and the Environment

Robert Prescott-Allen

in cooperation with
International Development Research Centre
IUCN – The World Conservation Union
International Institute for Environment and Development
Food and Agriculture Organization of the United Nations
Map Maker Ltd
UNEP World Conservation Monitoring Centre

ISLAND PRESS
Washington • Covelo • London

Library of Congress Cataloging-in-Publication Data

Prescott-Allen, Robert, 1942–
    The wellbeing of nations : a country-by-country index of quality of
life and the environment / Robert Prescott-Allen.
        p. cm.
    Includes bibliographical references and index.
    ISBN 1-55963-830-3 (cloth : alk. paper) — ISBN 1-55963-831-1 (pbk.
: alk. paper)
    1. Environmental quality. 2. Environmental indicators. I. Title.

GE140 .P74 2001
363.7—dc21
                                                    2001004282

Printed on recycled, acid-free paper

British Cataloguing-in-Publication Data available.

Manufactured in the United States of America
10 9 8 7 6 5 4 3 2 1

Contents

Appendix A. Monetary and physical accounts   269

Appendix B. Wellbeing Assessment   277

List of Maps, Figures, and Tables

Maps

Figures

Data Sources

Major Sources

Food and Agriculture Organization of the United Nations
Global Environmental Monitoring System
International Telecommunication Union
IUCN—The World Conservation Union
United Nations Development Programme
United Nations Educational, Scientific, and Cultural Organization
United Nations Environment Programme
UNEP World Conservation Monitoring Centre
United Nations Population Division
World Bank
World Health Organization

Other Important Sources

BirdLife International
Carbon Dioxide Information Analysis Center
Conservation International
Freedom House
International Institute for Strategic Studies
International Labour Office
International Livestock Research Institute
International Monetary Fund
International Soil Reference and Information Centre
Inter-Parliamentary Union
Organisation for Economic Co-operation and Development
Transparency International
United Nations Children's Fund
United Nations Crime Prevention and Criminal Justice Division
United Nations Economic Commission for Europe
United Nations Energy Statistics Unit
World Energy Council
World Meteorological Organization
World Resources Institute
World Wildlife Fund (USA)

Acknowledgments

I could not have written this book without the help of two people. First, Christine, my wife and super editor, who scrutinized each draft for clarity and readability, and wrote improvements. Any part of this book that is expressed compellingly I owe to her; any that is turgid or obscure is due to my obstinacy in the face of her counsel. Above all, she sustained me with love throughout the four years it has taken me to bring this labor of love to fruition.

Second, Eric Dudley, the extraordinary polymath who invented and continues to develop Map Maker, the GIS program I used for all the maps in this book. He gave me new versions of Map Maker, taught me to use it, wrote a subprogram so that I could manipulate land quality data, wrote the Combo program for calculating and combining indicator scores, and has been a regular source of sage advice.

Many people contributed intellectually to the Barometer of Sustainability and Wellbeing Assessment method used by the book. The Barometer of Sustainability was inspired by the Human Development Index, which was devised by the late Mahub ul Haq and his colleagues at the Human Development Report Office of the United Nations Development Programme. The Barometer's early development was helped by the experience of Albert Adriaanse with his Environmental Pressure Index, and by advice from my colleagues on the IUCN International Assessment Team: Ashoke Chatterjee, Eric Dudley, Alejandro Imbach, Tony Hodge, Diana Lee-Smith, and Adil Najam. Tony Hodge, Alejandro Imbach, and Diana Lee-Smith also made major contributions to the Wellbeing Assessment method. Two people at IUCN's Regional Office for Southern Africa made specific improvements: Carmel Lue-Mbizvo urged the inclusion of global as well as local impacts on the ecosystem; Emmanuel Guveya sim-plified the method of calculating indicator scores. I have benefited greatly from discussions with Edgar Gutiérrez-Espeleta, Director of the Development Observatory at the University of Costa Rica; Manuel Winograd at the Land Management Unit of the Centro Internacional de Agricultura Tropical (CIAT) in Colombia; Ali Qadir, IUCN Pakistan; and Alex Moiseev and Irene Gujit.

I learned much from Tony Hodge during our assessment of the sustainability of British Columbia, and Tony has continued to feed me ideas and information. I have been immeasurably helped by those who have tested the Barometer of Sustainability: Ashok Kumar and his colleagues at Development Alternatives in Karnataka, India (watershed assessment in Tumkur District); Isabel Adriana Gutiérrez Montes at the Centro Agronomico Tropical de Investigación y Enseñanza (CATIE) and the IUCN Regional Office for Meso America (rural sustainable development assessment in Nicaragua); Peter Hardi and Lazlo Pinter at the International Institute for Sustainable Development (IISD) (assessment of the Prairie Ecozone in Manitoba); Stephen Owen, Stuart Gale, Linda Hannah, Justin Longo, Linda Michaluk, and Risa Smith, who shared the assessment of British Columbia's sustainability; Misael Kokwe, Emmanuel Guveya, and Freddie Kachote at the IUCN Regional Office for Southern Africa (wellbeing assessment of Mangisai, Nyevera, and Sedeya communities in Zimuto communal lands, Zimbabwe); and the great team of people who worked on district environmental action plans in Zimbabwe—Sam Chimbuya, Elliot Mhaka, Cephas Chidenga, Douglas Chimhande, Joseph Chizororo, Peter Gambara, Davison Haukozi, Carmel Lue-Mbizvo, Zii Masiye, John Mbetu, Peter Mfumu, John Mupingo, Constantine Mushure, Aaron Tshabangu, and Unity Tshabangu.

I owe a special debt to Nancy MacPherson, who coordinated the IUCN/IDRC project on assessing progress toward sustainability and who gave me the invaluable opportunity to co-develop and test the Wellbeing Assessment method as part of that project; and to Diana Lee-Smith and Alejandro Imbach, with whom I worked closely for much of the project.

IDRC, IUCN, IIED, IISD, and Island Press arranged for previous drafts to be independently reviewed. The comments of the anonymous reviewers made for a much better book.

The organizations who generously gave data are listed under "Data Sources" and acknowledged specifically in the notes to chapters and tables. Many individuals helped me to obtain information and advised on how to use it:

Food and Agriculture Organization of the United Nations: Sustainable Development Department—H. Carsalade, Linda Collette, Dominique Lantieri, J. S. Latham, and in particular Jeff Tschirley and Stephanie Vertecchi; Fisheries Department—Serge M. Garcia, Richard J. R. Grainger, John F. Caddy, Purwito Martosubroto, H. C. F. Naeve, Rolf Willmann; Forestry Department—Lennart S. Ljungman, Christel Palmberg-Lerche, Robert R. Davis, R. Michael Martin, Froylan Castañeda, Klaus Janz, Christian Pilegaard Hansen, So Thirong Patrick, P. Vantomme; Land and Water Development Division—W. G. Sombroek, Jean-Marc Faurès, G. G. Appelgren, José Benites, Mathieu Bousquet, Arumugam Kandiah, A. P. Koohafkan, Freddy Nachtergaele; Animal Production and Health Division—Keith Hammond, Beate Scherf; Commodities and Trade Division—M. De Nigris, A. Gürkan; Statistics Division—Sam Zarqua, Giulia Cimino, E. D. Gillin, Richard Hoad, L. O. Larson, Jorge Mernies, L. Naiken, Martha Neundorfer, Jean Viseur; Information Division—Jean-Philippe Decraene, Tony Loftas.

Global Environmental Monitoring System: Andrew S. Fraser (National Water Research Institute, UNEP and WHO GEMS/Water Collaborating Centre).

International Telecommunication Union: Michael R. Minges, Dalia Mendiluce, Linda O'Driscoll.

IUCN–The World Conservation Union: Adrian Phillips, Wendy Strahm, Simon Stuart.

United Nations Development Programme: Sakiko Fukuda-Parr and Selim Jahan.

United Nations Educational, Scientific and Cultural Organization: Chu Shiu-Kee, Lynda Bellaiche, Karl Hochgesand, Takeo Jimbow, Geraldo Nascimento.

United Nations Environment Programme: G. M. Bankobeza, Franklin G. Cardy, Arthur Lyon Dahl, Michael Graber, Miriam Schomaker, Veerle Vandweerd.

UNEP World Conservation Monitoring Centre: Mark Collins, Gillian Bunting, Harriet Gillett, Michael J. B. Green, Brian Groombridge, Jeremy (Jerry) Harrison, James Paine, Julie Reay, Tony Turner.

United Nations Population Division: Joseph Chamie, Joseph-Alfred Grinblat, Mary Beth Weinberger.

World Bank: John Dixon, Abdolreza Farivari, M. H. Saeed Ordoudabi, William C. Prince.

World Health Organization: Monika Blössner, Tord Kjellström, Doris Ma Fat, Dieter Schwela, the late Sylvère Siméant.

BirdLife International: Colin Bibby, Martin Sneary, Alison Stattersfield.

Carbon Dioxide Information Analysis Center: Tom Boden and Karen Gibson.

Conservation International: Lee Hannah and Silvio Olivieri.

Freedom House: Charles Braybow.

International Institute for Strategic Studies: Digby Waller.

International Labour Office: Magali Imbert-Luccioni and Brigitte du Jeu.

International Monetary Fund: Tom Nordman.

International Soil Reference and Information Centre: Roel Oldeman and Hans van Baren.

Organisation for Economic Co-operation and Development: Joke Waller-Hunter and Christian Avérous.

United Nations Children's Fund: Gareth Jones.

United Nations Economic Commission for Europe: G. de Bellis, Radovan Chrást, Andreas Kahnert, Kit Prins.

United Nations Energy Statistics Unit: Eszter Horváth and Gordon Telesford.

World Energy Council: Julian Chisholm.

World Resources Institute: Dan Tunstall and Eric Rodenburg.

World Wildlife Fund (USA): William M. (Bill) Eichbaum and David M. Olson.

United Nations Centre for Human Settlements: Christine Auclair.

United Nations Statistics Division: Peter Bartelmus, Cristina Hannig, Jan W. van Tongeren.

Equilibrium: Nigel Dudley.

International Journal of Hydropower & Dams: Alan Manchester.

This book could not have been published in full color without generous contributions to the cost of doing so by the International Development Research Centre (IDRC), IUCN–The World Conservation Union, and the International Institute for Environment and Development (IIED). I am especially grateful for the support of:

IDRC: Maureen O'Neil, President; Pierre Beemans, David Brooks, Terry Smutylo, Bill Carman, and in particular Fred Carden.

IUCN: David McDowell, former Director General; Jeff McNeely, Javed Ahmad, Mark Halle, Elaine Shaughnessy, Estelle Viguet, John Waugh.

IIED: Richard Sandbrook, former Executive Director, and Nigel Cross, current Executive Director.

Last but not least, I acknowledge Tom Lovejoy, who encouraged Island Press to publish *The Wellbeing of Nations;* and to everyone involved at Island Press for doing so.

My heartfelt thanks to all.

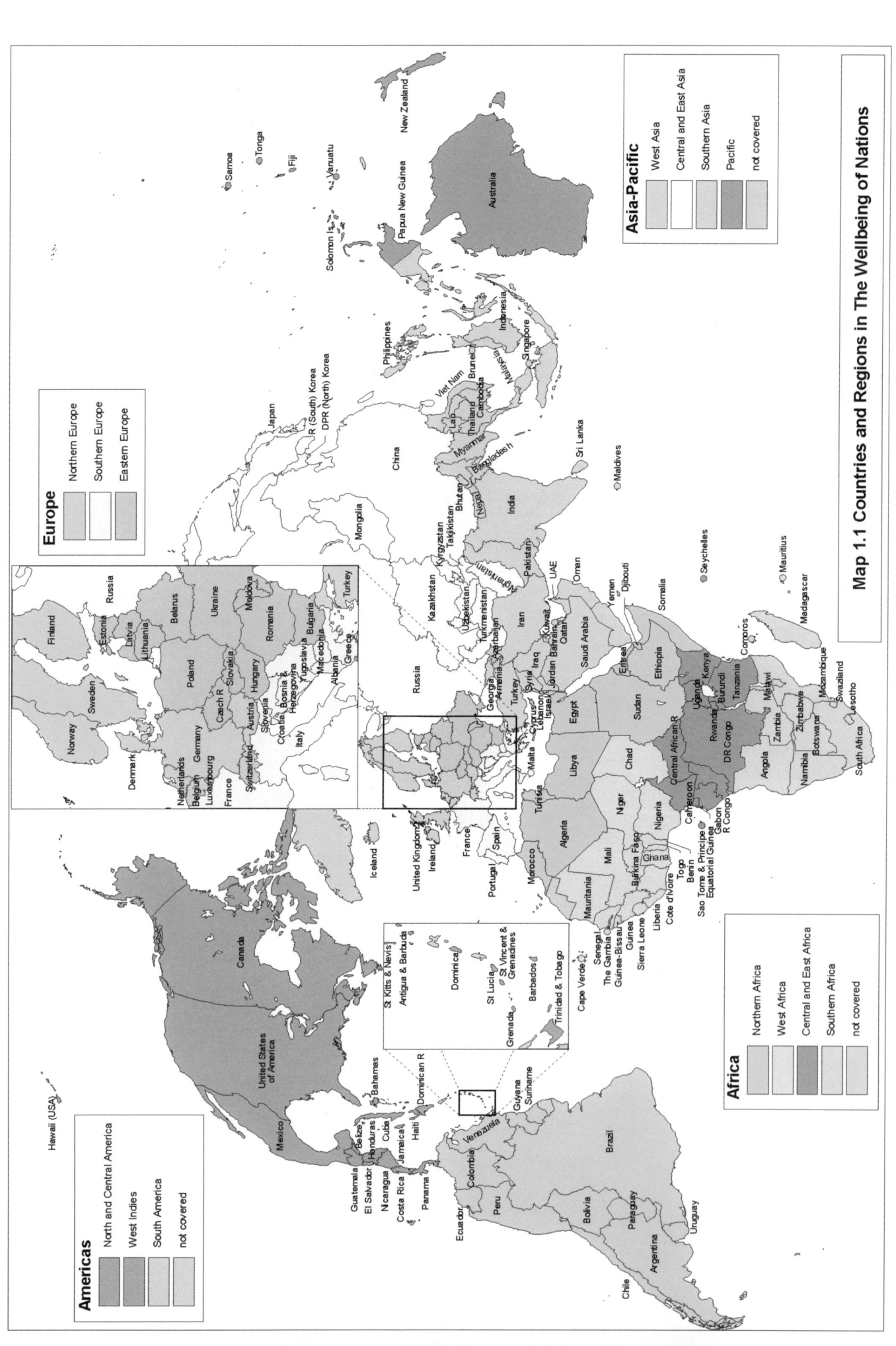

Map 1.1 Countries and Regions in The Wellbeing of Nations

1. The Quest for Wellbeing and Sustainability

How Far to the Good Life?

The Chinese seek the five blessings of long life, riches, health, love of virtue, and a natural death in old age. The French desire liberty, equality, and fraternity. Indians aspire to power, pleasure, morality, and emancipation from the world. The English hope for health, wealth, and wisdom. Americans uphold life, liberty, and the pursuit of happiness.

However envisaged, the good life has always been a demanding goal. Today, it is becoming increasingly difficult to achieve for more than a minority and even harder to sustain. As human populations and economies have grown, it has become impossible to improve one's own wellbeing without affecting other people's. Through trade, money markets, and environmental change, the ripple of interactions, dependencies, and impacts among communities and nations has steadily widened. The scope of self-interest has expanded from the individual and his or her society to all societies. Our one Earth has become one world.

At the same time, people have become a shaping force in the planet's evolution, extending the scope of self-interest still further, from humanity to all life. Many views of the good life have regarded nature's bounty as a given. Today, pollution, resource shortages, and the declining diversity of plants and animals are signs that too much of that bounty is being taken. Henceforth, to sustain their own wellbeing, people need to look after the wellbeing of the ecosystem: the system of land, water, air, and living creatures that embraces and supports them.

This dramatic change in the human condition impels the growing concern for sustainable development. People still need ways of living that correspond to their views of the good life. But now these ways of life must also be equitable—both within and among societies and between present and future generations—and they must safeguard the diversity, productivity, and resilience of the ecosystem.

Nobody knows how to meet these new demands. There is no proven recipe for success. In fact, no one has a clear sense of what success would be. Making progress toward ways of living that are desirable, equitable, and sustainable is like going to a country we have never been to before with a sense of geography and the principles of navigation but without map or compass. We do not know what the destination will be like, we cannot tell how to get there, we are not even sure which direction to take.

However, if we had some navigational tools, we could define a starting point, check our position along the way, and so determine our direction. Then if we designed our actions so that we learned as we went along, we could make course corrections before going too far astray.

The most informative navigational aid is a wellbeing assessment that societies—from countries to communities—could undertake regularly. To enable each society to set a baseline, keep track of progress, and learn from its actions, the assessment would ask three questions:

- How well are people?
- How well is the ecosystem?
- How are people and the ecosystem affecting each other?

By exploring and measuring the three questions together, societies can learn what combinations of human and ecosystem wellbeing are sustainable, and make their own decisions about how to achieve them.

Until they do, the good life will recede into the unattainable distance. At present, no country is sustainable or even close. Nations with a high standard of living impose excessive pressure on the global environment. Nations with low demands on the ecosystem are desperately poor. No country knows how to be green without going into the red.

We have been unable to see this dichotomy so clearly before because there has been no way to compare human conditions with the state of the environment. To fill this gap, *The Wellbeing of Nations* presents a new method of measuring human and ecosystem wellbeing, together with a first assessment of 180 countries and four indices. The Human Wellbeing Index (HWI) and Ecosystem Wellbeing Index (EWI) are comprehensive measures of the quality of life and the environment. The Wellbeing Index (WI) juxtaposes them so that they can be compared. The Wellbeing/Stress Index (WSI) shows how much human wellbeing each nation obtains for the amount of ecosystem stress it causes. In the majority of countries, ecosystem stress is higher than human wellbeing, a clear sign that most people's efforts to improve their lot are inefficient and overexploit the environment.

The 180 countries are ranked in terms of the HWI, EWI, WI, and WSI. The first two rankings differ significantly from equivalents produced by other methods due to differences in scope, choice of issues and indicators, and the way in which the indicators are combined. The other two indices are unique to the Wellbeing Assessment method used in *The Wellbeing of Nations*.

The rankings themselves are not as important as what the indices say about each country and what they reveal about the strengths and weaknesses of the various methods as measures of performance. To explore the differences, the HWI is compared with the Human Development Index, and the EWI with the Ecological Footprint.[1]

Why New Indices?

The four indices, and the Wellbeing Assessment method that produces them, provide several essentials for improving human and environmental conditions:

- A clearly stated goal.
- A way of measuring progress toward the goal.
- An analytical tool for deciding priority actions.
- A process to keep the goal constantly in mind and to help people learn how to reach it.

The first two essentials go together. A measurable goal is a more attainable goal. If gross domestic product

(GDP) and its constituent indicators did not exist, the world would lack both a measurement of the market economy and a sense of economic growth as a realizable goal. The goal and the measurement emerged together, each reinforcing the other. The goal made the index significant, a measurement worth paying attention to. The index made the goal possible since no one will adopt an objective whose achievement cannot be recognized.

The same goes for equitable and sustainable ways of living. The HWI, EWI, WI, and WSI are the means by which societies can measure the overall conditions of people and the environment, thereby making it possible for them to adopt better human and ecosystem wellbeing as an achievable goal. The four indices act as beacons, signaling a society's wellbeing and sustainability and reminding it of the need to reach them.

By breaking down the indices into major components (e.g., land, water, air, biological diversity, energy, health, wealth, knowledge, community, equity), societies can identify the factors most responsible for their current levels of human and ecosystem wellbeing. This is the starting point for analyzing policies realistically and deciding which actions to take first.

It is fairly easy to forge consensus around the vague idea of sustainable development. It is much harder to get competing interest groups to agree on specific policies on (for instance) carbon dioxide emissions or terms of trade. Wellbeing assessments can facilitate consensus building by providing a logical progression from the goal, through objectives for particular themes or sectors, to standards of achievement for indicators. They also provide a much-needed mental bridge between the short term and the long term. The hurly burly of immediate demands and sudden events can overwhelm long-term goals and sharply reduce their influence over the daily decisions of households, businesses, and governments. Wellbeing assessments can offset this danger (to some extent at least) by providing a mechanism to link the practical realities of the present to people's vision of a desirable future.

The Wellbeing Assessment Difference

The two main approaches to measuring sustainability are accounts and assessments. Accounts are constructed from raw data and are designed to be as complete as possible. Hence they excel at tracking the economy or the flow of materials and energy because these fields produce abundant statistics.

The most widely used method of measuring progress is the System of National Accounts, which records the transactions of national economies and sums them into monetary indicators such as the GDP. The GDP is enormously influential and is relied on by politicians, the business community, the media, and the public as a sign of prosperity and wellbeing. It is nothing of the kind. GDP measures the output of the market economy and is not designed to do anything more. Its narrow focus neglects completely many aspects of the economy (from income distribution to unpaid work and the black economy) and all nonmonetary contributors to human fulfillment (including health, education, freedom, security, and peace). It ignores the state of the ecosystem and either omits environmental and social costs (such as pollution, resource depletion, cancer, and crime) or counts them as benefits if they cause money to change hands.

Attempts at less distorted accounts include the System of Integrated Environmental and Economic Accounting, the Index of Sustainable Economic Welfare (or Genuine Progress Indicator), and the World Bank's estimates of national wealth and genuine saving. These green accounts are unlikely to provide a satisfactory measure of wellbeing because they use money as their measure, and money cannot measure everything. No matter how meticulous the calculation, dollars trivialize much of what people value most: fresh air, a species' existence, good health, security, a human life, or freedom. The price of liberty is eternal vigilance, not $4.99. (For more on accounts, see Appendix A.)

Assessments make no attempt to be complete but rely instead on measuring representative aspects, or indicators. Because they can be selective, they are better equipped than accounts to cover the wide array of issues necessary for an adequate portrayal of human and environmental conditions. Stimulated by the World Commission on Environment and Development's call for sustainable development in 1987 and the United Nations Conference on Environment and Development in 1992, major innovations in methods of assessing sustainable development have been made in the last decade or so. They include the pressure-state-response framework for environmental indicators, the Human Development Index, the Environmental Pressure Index, and the Ecological Footprint.[2]

Despite these advances, assessments continue to lag behind accounts in influencing national policies. They have yet to cover the full extent of human and environmental concerns and distill them into an index as power-

ful as the GDP. Among the major global assessments (Table 1.1), few combine their indicators into an index, so it is extremely difficult to extract the big picture from the details. Almost all of them focus either on people or on the environment. Few cover both, and none treats them as equals.

By contrast, the main features of *The Wellbeing of Nations* and the Wellbeing Assessment method are that they:

- Cover both people and the ecosystem, and give them equal weight.
- Assess the condition of people and the environment through a broad range of indicators chosen to represent widely shared values and key properties of human societies and the ecosystem.
- Combine the indicators into four indices.

The HWI is a more realistic measure of socioeconomic conditions than narrowly monetary indicators such as the GDP and covers more aspects of human wellbeing than the Human Development Index. The EWI is an equally broad measure of the state of the environment,

Table 1.1. Global assessments and reports, showing their coverage of people and the ecosystem (✓ = major, ✗ = minor) and whether they combine indicators into an index (✓ = yes, ✗ = no). Agenda 21 refers to the set of sustainable development indicators of the United Nations Commission on Sustainable Development (United Nations 1996). Ecological Footprint: Wackernagel et al. (2000). Environmental Sustainability Index: Global Leaders for Environment Tomorrow Task Force (2001). Global Environment Outlook: United Nations Environment Programme (1999). Human Development Report (includes the human development index): United Nations Development Programme (1990–1999). Living Planet Report: Loh et al. (1999). State of the World's Children: UNICEF (1999b). World Development Report: World Bank (2000a). World Resources Report: World Resources Institute et al. (1998).

Assessment or Report	People	Ecosystem	Index
Wellbeing of Nations	✓	✓	✓
Agenda 21	✓	✓	✗
Ecological Footprint	✗	✓	✓
Environmental Sustainability Index	✗	✓	✓
Global Environment Outlook	✗	✓	✗
Human Development Report	✓	✗	✓
Living Planet Report	✗	✓	✓
State of the World's Children	✓	✗	✗
World Development Report	✓	✗	✗
World Resources Report	✗	✓	✗

with a fuller treatment of national conditions than other global indices except the Environmental Sustainability Index, which (unlike the EWI) is muddled by the inclusion of human indicators. The WI and WSI break new ground in measuring people and the ecosystem together to compare their conditions, show the impact of one on the other, and shine a spotlight on the improvement of both.

Guide to This Book

The Wellbeing of Nations assesses 180 independent countries for which data could be obtained on at least half the indicators.[3] The countries are organized into 4 continental groups and 14 regions (Map 1.1):

Americas (35 countries)
North and Central America (10 countries)
West Indies (13 countries)
South America (12 countries)

Africa (53 countries)
Northern Africa (10 countries)
West Africa (17 countries)
Central and East Africa (13 countries)
Southern Africa (13 countries)

Europe (37 countries)
Northern Europe (13 countries)
Southern Europe (12 countries)
Eastern Europe (12 countries)

Asia–Pacific (55 countries)
West Asia (18 countries)
Russia, Central and East Asia (12 countries)
Southern Asia (17 countries)
Pacific (8 countries)

Chapter 2 assesses human wellbeing and Chapter 3 ecosystem wellbeing for all the countries. Each chapter is divided into six sections. The first section presents the HWI (Chapter 2) or EWI (Chapter 3). The remaining sections show how the index was obtained. Each section covers a dimension, or set of major features of wellbeing. Every dimension section starts with an overview of the elements that make up the dimension and a synthesis and index of the state of that dimension. Then the elements and their indicators are covered in turn. World maps for each index and most indicators summarize the performance of all the countries.

The map projection is the Dudley equal area projection, chosen because it shows countries' true areas with little distortion of their shapes and makes very efficient use of space. Its sole disadvantage is that north is not always straight up the page, so the orientation of some countries is unusual. Antarctica has been omitted to save space.[4]

Chapter 4 combines the results into the overall WI and WSI. It examines the patterns of national performance that the indices reveal and analyzes the scope for improvement. It discusses the relationships between ecosystem stress and human wellbeing, income, and resource consumption. Finally, it suggests the main changes needed for countries to progress toward satisfying and sustainable ways of life.

The rest of this chapter discusses why people and the ecosystem are treated equally and explains enough of the method for readers to follow the other chapters. A full description of the Wellbeing Assessment method is given in Appendix B.

Equal Treatment of People and the Ecosystem

The underlying hypothesis of Wellbeing Assessment is that sustainable development is a combination of human wellbeing and ecosystem wellbeing (defined in Box 1.1). Human wellbeing is a requirement for sustainability because no rational person would want to perpetuate a low standard of living. Ecosystem wellbeing is a requirement because the ecosystem supports life and makes possible any standard of living. Although trade-offs between the needs of people and the needs of the ecosystem are unavoidable, they must be limited. For a while, human progress may be won at the expense of the natural environment. It may be necessary to turn forests and wetlands into farms, and farms into towns. But people will not prosper or even survive for long unless the ecosystem is healthy, productive, and diverse. At the same time, it does not matter how well the ecosystem is if people cannot meet their needs. A robust economy and flourishing community are as vital for people's health, wealth, and happiness as a rich and resilient ecosystem. Ultimately, human and ecosystem wellbeing are equally important, and a sustainable society needs to achieve both together.

The hypothesis is expressed in the metaphor of the Egg of Wellbeing (Figure 1.1). The ecosystem surrounds and supports people much as the white of an egg surrounds and supports the yolk. Just as an egg can be good only if both the yolk and white are good, so a society can

Box 1.1. Human and ecosystem wellbeing defined

Human wellbeing: a condition in which all members of society are able to determine and meet their needs and have a large range of choices to meet their potential.

Ecosystem wellbeing: a condition in which the ecosystem maintains its diversity and quality—and thus its capacity to support people and the rest of life—and its potential to adapt to change and provide a wide range of choices and opportunities for the future.

be well and sustainable only if both people and the ecosystem are well.

To compare human development and ecosystem conservation and to keep the focus on improving both, the wellbeing of people and the ecosystem are considered together but measured separately. Information is organized into two subsystems: people (human communities, economies, and artifacts) and ecosystem (ecological communities, processes, and resources). Interactions between the two are recorded under the receiving subsystem. Human stresses on the ecosystem (such as pollution and resource depletion)—as well as benefits to it from conser-

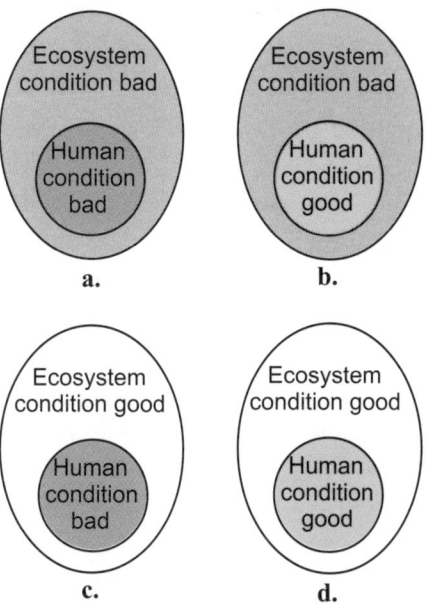

Figure 1.1. The Egg of Wellbeing. A society is obviously unwell and unsustainable if people are suffering and the ecosystem is degraded (a). It is also unwell and unsustainable if either the ecosystem condition is bad (b) or the human condition is bad (c). Only condition (d) is sustainable.

vation—are recorded under *ecosystem*. Benefits from the ecosystem to people (from the supply of resources to spiritual comfort) are recorded under *people*, along with environmental stresses on people (such as the effects of natural disasters). For example, the impact of agriculture and fisheries on the land, water, air, and organisms is measured as part of ecosystem wellbeing; their impact on food supply, incomes, employment, health, and community stability is measured as part of human wellbeing.

Choosing What to Measure

Since it is impossible to measure human or ecosystem wellbeing directly, assessments must select indicators of the main features of each. (An indicator is something that represents a particular attribute, characteristic, or property of a system.[5]) Knowing the essential role of indicators, it is tempting to jump right in and choose them at once. However, it is seldom clear at the start of an assessment how well a given set of indicators represents a desirable combination of human and environmental conditions, what aspects are left out, how much the indicators overlap, or how they relate to each other. Since indicators require the collection and analysis of often large amounts of data, choosing the wrong ones can be a costly mistake.

Consequently, it is necessary first to take apart the concepts of human and ecosystem wellbeing to identify the features that need to be measured and then to unpack each feature to reveal aspects that are both representative and measurable.

Wellbeing Assessment does this by going down the hierarchy in Figure 1.2, which provides a series of increasingly specific stepping stones from system and goal to indicators and performance criteria (standards of achievement).

The system is whatever is being assessed, and the goals provide the basis for deciding what will be measured. In *The Wellbeing of Nations,* the system is the people and ecosystem of 180 countries, and the proposed goal for the system is sustainable and equitable combinations of human and ecosystem wellbeing. Goals for people and the ecosystem are defined in Chapters 2 and 3.

Five human dimensions and five ecosystem dimensions have been identified to provide a common framework for all assessments using the Wellbeing Assessment method (Figure 1.3). The dimensions are designed to combine a wide range of topics into a few major groups of roughly equal importance. They are

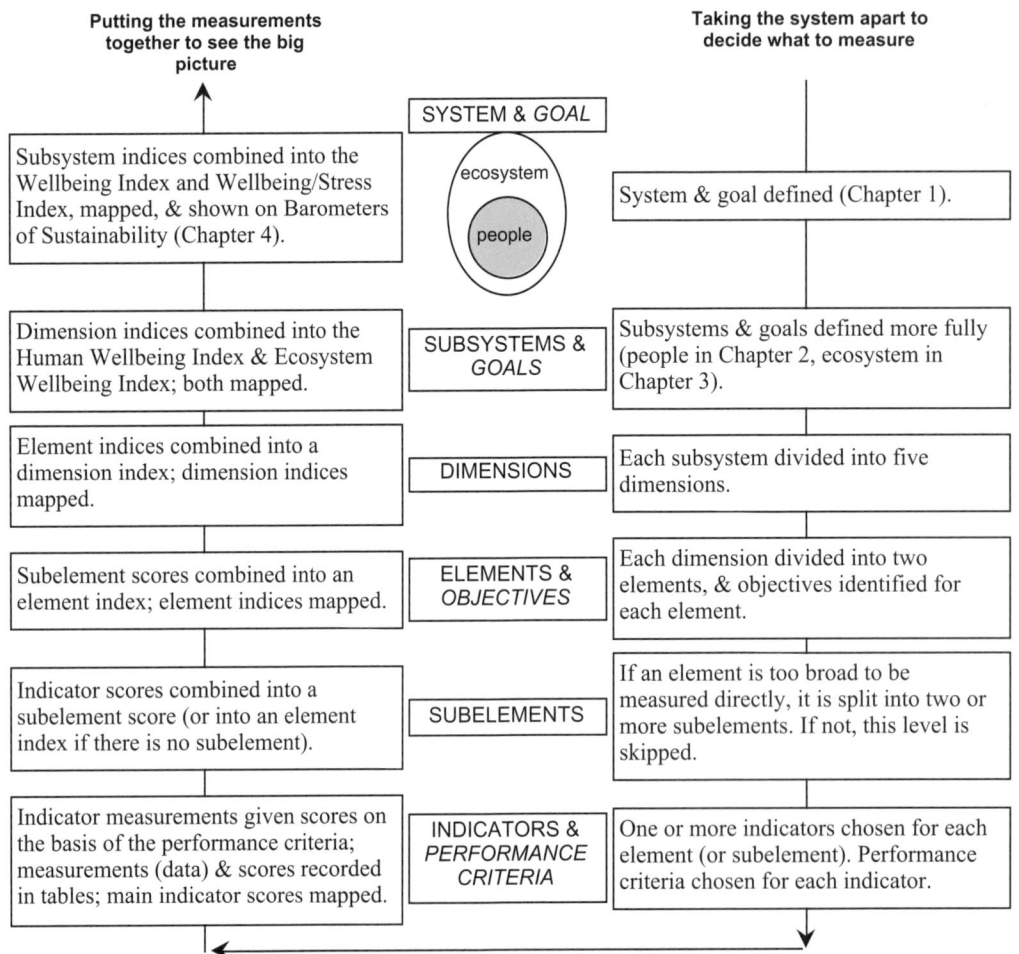

Figure 1.2. The procedure for selecting and combining indicators used in *The Wellbeing of Nations*.

comprehensive enough to accommodate most of the concerns of most societies: any issue regarded as significant for wellbeing and sustainable development has a place in one of them. The remaining levels of the hierarchy (from elements and objectives through indicators and performance criteria) may vary from assessment to assessment.

The dimensions are subdivided into elements: key subjects or concerns that must be considered to get an adequate sense of the condition of people or the ecosystem. (If an element is too broad to measure directly, it is split into subelements; otherwise, the subelement level is skipped.) For example, I have divided the wealth dimension into two elements—household wealth and national wealth—and household wealth into two subelements: needs and income (Figure 1.4). An objective is defined for each element to aid the selection of indicators and performance criteria. The objective for household wealth

is "enough material goods and income to secure basic needs and decent livelihoods."

One or more indicators are chosen for each element (or subelement) on the basis of how fully the indicator represents the element or subelement concerned and how reliable and feasible it is (Box 1.2). *The Wellbeing of Nations* relies entirely on indicators for which data can be obtained from international sources. If an otherwise suitable indicator has insufficient data, a substitute is used. If none can be found, the indicator, subelement, or element is excluded, in which case its absence is clearly shown. For example, several indicators of food sufficiency are used because none is available for all countries, but there is no indicator of shelter because the data are too sparse (Figure 1.4). The details of choosing indicators are discussed in Appendix B.

Performance criteria are then chosen for each indicator. Their purpose is explained next.

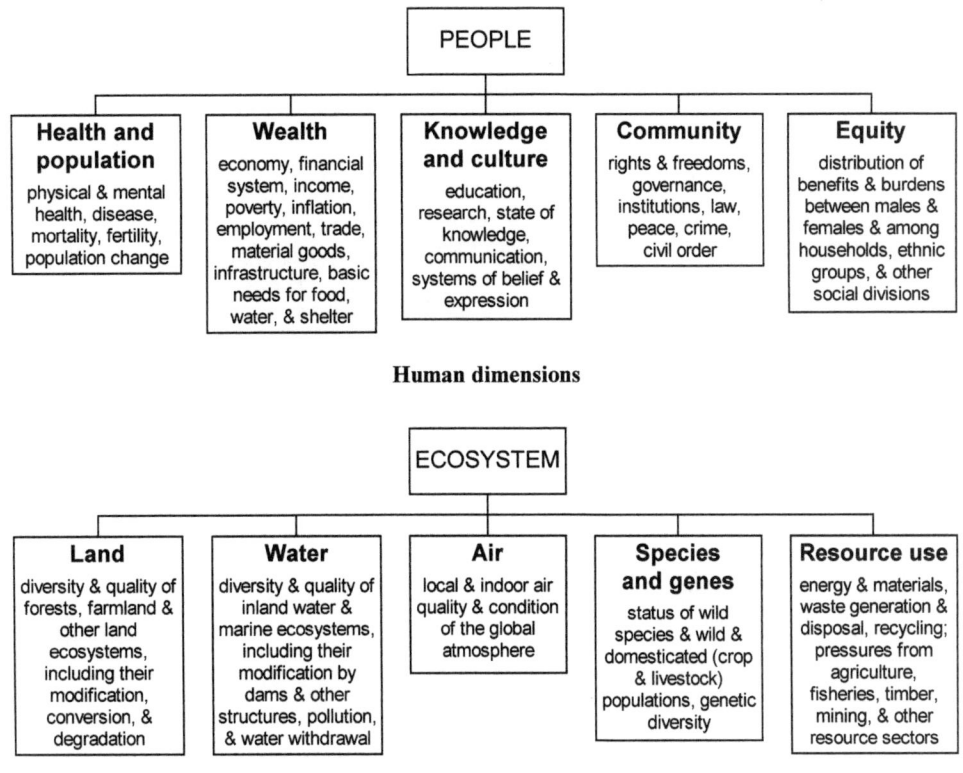

Figure 1.3. Common framework of dimensions. The dimensions (in **bold**) are fixed, but the elements covered under each dimension may change depending on the assessment. The lists here are examples to illustrate the scope of the dimensions. The elements identified for *The Wellbeing of Nations* are described in Chapters 2 (people) and 3 (ecosystem).

Combining the Measurements

A large number of indicators is inevitable, given the broad scope of human and ecosystem wellbeing, but presents an enormous communication problem. Every indicator sends a signal. The more indicators, the more signals—a perplexing cacophony of good, bad, and somewhere-in-between news. Moreover, each indicator conveys information about the particular element or subelement it represents but not about the system as a whole.

The problem is overcome by combining the indicators into indices. How to do this raises other obstacles, however, because a typical set of indicators is a mess of incompatible measurements: land condition in hectares, water pollution in milligrams per liter, carbon dioxide emissions in metric tons of carbon, species diversity in percentages of threatened species, health in years of life expectancy and death rates, income in money, education in school enrollment rates, freedom in the observation of rights, and so on.

Combining such different indicators mixes apples and oranges. To do this successfully requires finding a common unit that does not distort their qualities as apples or oranges ("citrus units" would favor oranges, "pome units"

Box 1.2. The ideal indicator is . . .

Representative: it covers the most important aspects of the element concerned; and shows trends over time and differences between places and groups of people.

Reliable: it directly reflects how far the objective concerned is met; and is well founded, accurate, and measured in a standardized way with sound and consistent sampling procedures.

Feasible: it depends on data that are readily available or obtainable at reasonable cost.

Indicator selection is often a matter of balancing these qualities.

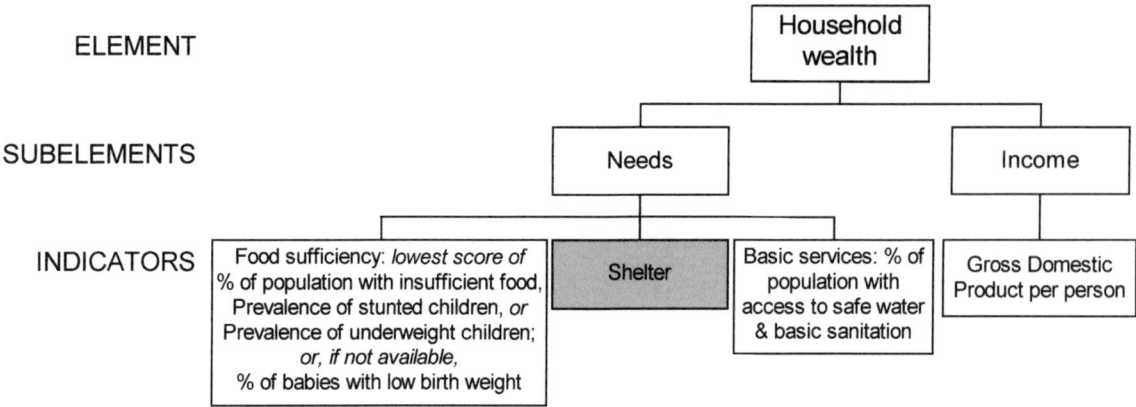

Figure 1.4. Indicator chart for household wealth. The absence of an indicator for shelter is shown by the shaded box.

would favor apples). The common unit may be a physical unit, money, or a performance score. Wellbeing Assessment uses performance scores.

Physical units can combine only a limited range of things. Materials can be combined on the basis of their weight, but this does not account for their different impacts: a ton of arsenic is more of a problem than a ton of old lace. Pollutants with similar effects can be combined according to their potential for that effect: greenhouse gas emissions can be combined according to the contribution of each gas to global warming, and heavy metals on the basis of their toxicity. But pollutants with different effects cannot be combined in this way.

Money is standard in all economic accounts, but it too has serious weaknesses. It reflects the market price of apples and oranges, not their taste, nutritional content, or cultural value. It can measure the value of things that are traded in the market, but it distorts the value of anything that is not traded. The less tradable the item, the greater the distortion. Since most items in an assessment of wellbeing and sustainability have no market price, nonmarket values have to be estimated from contingent values (asking people how much they would pay for a benefit or how much compensation they would accept if deprived of the benefit) or from expenditures on avoiding and treating damage. Using these methods together is like combining real apples (market values), fake apples (contingent values), real oranges (actual expenditures), and fake oranges (hypothetical expenditures).

The advantage of a performance score is that it measures how good an orange is at being an orange and how good an apple is as an apple—the distance between a standard level of performance and the actual performance recorded by an indicator measurement. On a 0–100 scale, best performance is 100 and worst 0. A given apple or orange would receive a score according to how good it was in relation to best and worst. Performance criteria for apples and oranges may be very different, but because their scores are calculated in the same way on the same scale, the scores can be combined.

Wellbeing Assessment uses the Barometer of Sustainability (Figure 1.5) because it is the only performance scale designed to measure human and ecosystem wellbeing together without submerging one in the other. The Barometer's unique features are:

- Two axes: one for human wellbeing, the other for ecosystem wellbeing. This enables each set of indicators to be combined* independently, keeping them separate to allow analysis of people–ecosystem interactions.

- The axis with the lower score overrides the other axis. This prevents a high score for human wellbeing from offsetting a low score for ecosystem wellbeing (or vice versa), reflecting the view that people and the ecosystem are equally important and that sustainable development must improve and maintain the wellbeing of both.

- Each axis is divided into five bands. This allows users to define not just the end points of the scale but intermediate points as well, for greater flexibility and control of the scale.

The performance criteria enable indicator measurements to be given a score by converting them to the scale

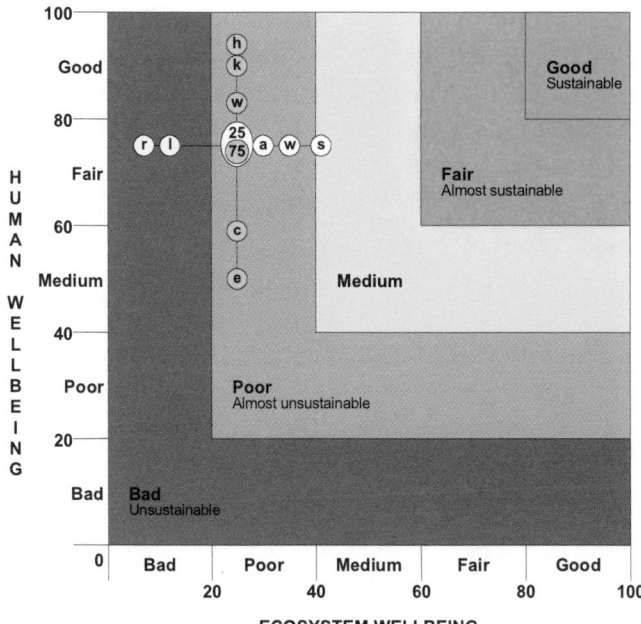

Figure 1.5. Barometer of Sustainability. The Wellbeing Index (WI) of a hypothetical country is shown on the Barometer. The Human Wellbeing Index (HWI) is in the yolk of the egg. The Ecosystem Wellbeing Index (EWI) is in the white. The WI is where the HWI and EWI intersect. Yellow circles (vertical axis) show the points on the scale of the human dimensions: c = community, e = equity, h = health and population, k = knowledge, w = wealth. White circles (horizontal axis) show the points of the ecosystem dimensions: a = air, l = land, r = resource use, s = species and genes, w = water.

of the Barometer. They define the rate of exchange between the indicator and the scale—the level of performance that is worth a given number of points (Table 1.2).

Performance criteria require a great deal of thought. They are guided by the range of actual*performance, the objective of the element that the indicator represents, and

Table 1.2. The five bands of the Barometer of Sustainability.

Band	Points Range	Top	Definition
Good	100–81	100	Desirable performance, objective fully met
Fair	80–61	80	Acceptable performance, objective almost or barely met
Medium	60–41	60	Neutral or transitional performance
Poor	40–21	40	Undesirable performance
Bad	20–1	20	Unacceptable performance
Base	0	0	Base of scale

Table 1.3 Performance criteria for food sufficiency indicators. Performance is good (81–100 points) if less than 10% of the population lacks enough food.

Band	Top Point on Scale	% of Population with Insufficient Food
Good	100	0
Fair	80	10
Medium	60	20
Poor	40	35
Bad	20	50
Base	0	100

factors such as estimated sustainable rates, observed thresholds, international standards or targets, expert opinion, and the performance criteria of related indicators. For example, the World Health Organization has set international targets for three of the four food sufficiency indicators: less than 20% for prevalence of stunting in children, no more than 10% for prevalence of underweight children, and no more than 10% for babies with low birth weight. These targets strongly influenced my definition of good performance in food sufficiency as less than 10% of population undernourished, fair as 10–19%, and bad performance as 50% or more (Table 1.3 and Figure 1.6).

Performance criteria are displayed graphically on maps of the indicators, given in full in the tables in the Data section, and summarized in Appendix C. The technicalities of choosing them are discussed in Appendix B, which also explains the straightforward procedure for calculating scores.

To prevent high scores resulting merely from lack of data, a good score is allowed only if it is based on all applicable components (e.g., data in an indicator, indicators in an element, elements in a dimension) and a fair score only if it is based on at least half the components. Potentially good scores based on more than half but not all the applicable components are reduced to 80 (the top of fair). Potentially good or fair scores based on fewer than half the applicable components are reduced to 60 (the top of medium). For example, the needs score has two components: food sufficiency and basic services (Figure 1.4). Malta has a score of 88 (good) for food sufficiency but no data on basic services, so its score for needs is not 88 but 80.

The main indicators are mapped on the basis of their scores. Maps and analyses are in Chapters 2 and 3, and indicator measurements and scores are given in the Data section.

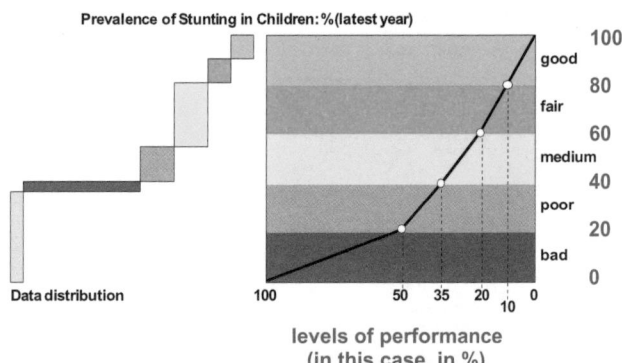

Figure 1.6 How performance criteria are graphically displayed in this book. In the square graphic on the right, the vertical axis is the scale of the Barometer of Sustainability and never changes: 0 is the base of the scale, and 20, 40, 60, 80, and 100 are the top points of, respectively, the bad, poor, medium, fair, and good bands. The horizontal axis shows levels of performance. It is specific to the indicator in question and is expressed in the measurement units of the indicator (in this case, percentages). The numbers along this axis represent levels of performance, from worst (on the left) to best (on the right). In this example, 100% corresponds to the base of the scale, 50% to the top point of the bad band, 35% to the top of poor, 20% to the top of medium, 10% to the top of fair, and 0% to the top of good. Note that the labels in red do not appear in the usual picture but are shown here to assist explanation. The staircase graphic on the left is explained in the text.

Throughout *The Wellbeing of Nations,* performance is mapped by color, the colors matching the bands of the Barometer of Sustainability (Figure 1.5): green always represents good performance; blue, fair; yellow, medium; pink, poor; and red, bad. Gray stands for no data. Seven territories excluded for general lack of data are also mapped in gray.[6]

Every indicator map includes a pair of graphics: a square graphic (explained in the caption to Figure 1.6) showing the performance criteria used to convert the indicator measurements to a score, and a staircase graphic showing the distribution of the data.

In the staircase graphic, the height of each step represents the number of countries whose performance (scored on the basis of the criteria specified in the square graphic) falls within that band. In the example of the prevalence of stunting in children (Figure 1.6), the largest number of countries has no data (gray), followed by medium (yellow) performance, then poor (pink), then fair (blue), then good (green), then bad (red).

The width of each step in the staircase graphic repre-

sents the proportion of the performance scale that falls within that band. In stunting in children, the good (green) and fair (blue) steps are narrowest because they include spans of only 10 percentage points. The bad (red) step is widest, comprising a 50-point spread. In between are the medium (yellow) and poor (pink) steps, each covering 15 percentage points.

Once the indicators have been given a score, they can be combined back up the hierarchy (Figure 1.2), from indicators to system: indicator scores are combined into a subelement score, subelement scores into an element index, element indices into a dimension index, and dimension indices into a subsystem index. Combining involves taking either the average or the lower of the scores. In Figure 1.4, for example, the needs (subelement) score is the lower score of the food sufficiency and basic services indicators; the household wealth (element) index is the average of the needs score and the income score. Dimensions are given equal weight, but elements, subelements, and indicators are sometimes given different weights: for example, the knowledge (element) index is the average of the education and communication scores, with education given twice the weight of communication.

The combining procedure used is stated in a panel at the start of each section of Chapters 2 and 3. A full description of combining procedures is given in Appendix B, and all index calculations are summarized in Appendix D.

A Disclaimer and an Invitation

It is extremely difficult to take a clear and easily communicated snapshot of something as complex and poorly understood as human societies, the ecosystem, and interactions between them. There is no perfect or even best way to do it. All methods entail hard choices about what to focus on and are bound to omit aspects that somebody considers important. Problems of data quality and conflicting values mean that crucial parts of the picture are blurred and open to alternative interpretations.

Hence no method can provide a definitive assessment, and Wellbeing Assessment is no exception. Rather, the method provides a framework for reflection and debate about the relationship between people and the ecosystem, the factors that are crucial for ecosystem wellbeing and human wellbeing, the indicators that best represent these factors, and performance criteria for each indicator. The Wellbeing Assessment method is meant to be easy to use and is fully described in Appendix B. All data, assumptions, and judgments are in the tables and Appendices C and D. They are there so that readers with different views on the elements, indicators, and performance criteria may test them for themselves.

The Wellbeing of Nations is offered as both a contribution to the debate and a first approximation of national conditions. Because international statistics take several years to collect and process, global reviews are always a few years behind the times. Most of the data for this review are for 1996–1999. They provide a perspective of where countries were at the end of one millennium and a baseline so that they can assess their progress from 2001 onward. The data record national averages, which mask the often great differences that exist among groups and places within countries. I hope that countries and communities will expose and explore these differences themselves by using the method to undertake their own more detailed assessments.

Notes

1. Human Development Index: United Nations Development Programme (1990–2000). Ecological Footprint: Wackernagel et al. (2000).
2. World Commission on Environment and Development (1987). United Nations Conference on Environment and Development: United Nations (1992). Pressure–state–response framework: Organisation for Economic Co-operation and Development (1994). Environmental Pressure Index: Adriaanse (1993) and Appendix B. The Human Development Index (United Nations Development Programme 1990–2000) is described in Chapter 2 and Appendix B. The Ecological Footprint (Wackernagel & Rees 1996) is described in Chapter 3 and Table 9 in the Data section.
3. The following countries and territories were excluded for lack of data. *Americas:* Anguilla, Aruba, Bermuda, British Virgin Islands, Cayman Islands, Falkland Islands (Malvinas), French Guiana, Greenland, Guadeloupe, Martinique, Montserrat, Netherlands Antilles, Puerto Rico, St Pierre and Miquelon, Turks and Caicos Islands, United States Virgin Islands. *Africa:* Mayotte, Réunion, St Helena and dependencies, Western Sahara. *Europe:* Andorra, Channel Islands, Faeroe Islands, Liechtenstein, Isle of Man, San Marino. *Asia–Pacific:* American Samoa, Cook Islands, East Timor, French Polynesia, Guam, Kiribati, Marshall Islands, Micronesia, Nauru, New Caledonia, Niue, Northern Mariana Islands, Palau, Palestine (Gaza Strip and West Bank), Tokelau, Tuvalu, Wallis and Futuna Islands.
4. All maps were made with Map Maker Pro, described in Appendix E.
5. Gallopín (1997).
6. Falkland Islands (Malvinas), French Guiana, Greenland, Guadeloupe, Martinique, New Caledonia, and Western Sahara.

$2.$ Human Wellbeing

Human Wellbeing Index

Human Wellbeing Index (HWI) (Map 2.1)

What it is: Average of indices of health and population, wealth, knowledge, community, and equity *or* average of indices of health and population, wealth, knowledge, and community, *whichever is lower.*

Country results: 3 good (2%), 34 fair (19%), 52 medium (29%), 51 poor (28%), 40 bad (22%).

Highlights:

- Two-thirds of the world's people live in countries with a poor or bad HWI, and less than one-sixth in countries with a fair or good HWI.

- The gap between the best and worst off is huge: the median HWI of the top 10% of countries is almost eight times that of the bottom 10%.

- Even the top performers need to do better. Only Norway, Denmark, and Finland have a good HWI. The rest are merely fair, pulled down by flaws (such as debt, unemployment, and crime) and inequities—10 countries have a standard of living as high as the top three's but not as evenly shared.

Measuring Human Wellbeing

Human wellbeing is a condition in which all members of society are able to determine and meet their needs and have a large range of choices and opportunities to fulfill their potential.

This definition builds on the idea of human development promoted by the United Nations Development Programme (UNDP) in its *Human Development Report:* that development is a process of enlarging choices. A long and

healthy life, education, and an adequate income are essential features of this process, and UNDP includes them in its Human Development Index (HDI). Other features are self-respect, opportunities for being creative and productive, security against crime and violence, guaranteed human rights, and political, economic, and social freedom. UNDP excludes these from the HDI largely because they are hard to measure.[1] They also spark disagreement over the balance between personal and community interests and between material and nonmaterial values.

Yet people are both spiritual and physical, social and individual. Assessments of human wellbeing must include all these aspects, despite the technical and political challenges they pose. To ensure that as many as possible of the main features are covered, Wellbeing Assessment divides human wellbeing into 5 dimensions, which I have further split into 10 elements (Figure 2.1). They are described in the remaining sections of this chapter, and distilled into a short statement here:

Health	People enjoy long lives in good health
Population	while keeping their numbers within the bounds of human and natural resources.
Household wealth	Individuals and households have the material goods and income to secure basic needs and decent livelihoods,
National wealth	and the community has the resources to support enterprise and maintain prosperity.
Knowledge	People have the knowledge to innovate and cope with change, live well and sustainably, and fulfill their potential,
Culture	with avenues for spiritual growth, creativity, and self-expression.

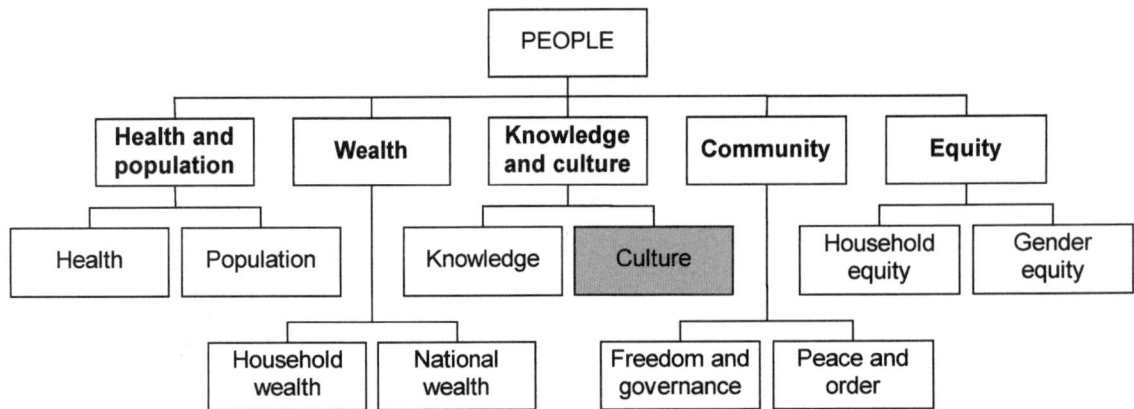

Figure 2.1. Human dimensions and elements. The five dimensions are in **bold**, the 10 elements in normal type. Culture (shaded box) is not covered due to lack of a suitable indicator.

Freedom and governance	Human rights are fully respected, and individuals are free to choose how decisions are made and who should make them. Decision-making bodies are open, clean, and effective.
Peace and order	Communities coexist peacefully and protect their members from crime and violence.
Household equity	Benefits and burdens are shared fairly among households and groups
Gender equity	and between males and females.

The resulting Human Wellbeing Index (HWI) measures progress toward a proposed goal of a high level of human wellbeing, based on all of these elements except culture (for which I could not identify a suitable indicator).

Few Nations Well, Many Unwell

The HWI of all countries is shown in Map 2.1. Table 2.1 gives a regional summary. Figure 2.2 displays patterns of performance. Full scores are in Table 1, and rankings in Table 25, in the Data section.

To achieve a good HWI, a country must perform well in all dimensions. Only Norway, Denmark and Finland manage to do this. Norway enjoys a life expectancy of 79 years including 72 in full health, a fertility rate just below replacement, gross domestic product (GDP) per person over $26,000 (all dollars are international purchasing power parity dollars),[2] inflation below 3%, unemployment below 4%, public debt down to a third of GDP, 100% enrollment through secondary school, a large university population, well-developed communications, strong political rights and civil liberties, and negligible corruption. Even in its weakest

Table 2.1. Human Wellbeing Index (HWI), showing the number of countries at each level by continental group and region. Most of the Americas has a medium HWI. The widest gaps are in the West Indies (Barbados with a fair HWI, Haiti with a bad HWI). Africa and Europe are the reverse of each other: Africa with poor or bad HWIs except for five countries with a medium HWI (Tunisia, Cape Verde, Seychelles, Mauritius, South Africa); Europe with good, fair, or medium HWIs except for Albania and Bosnia and Herzegovina (poor). Asia–Pacific has mainly poor or medium HWIs, but differences in performance are extreme within Asian regions.

Region and Continental Group	Fair or Good	Medium	Poor	Bad	Total
North and Central America	2	4	4	0	10
West Indies	1	10	1	1	13
South America	1	9	2	0	12
Americas	*4*	*23*	*7*	*1*	*35*
Northern Africa	0	1	4	5	10
West Africa	0	1	4	12	17
Central and East Africa	0	1	1	11	13
Southern Africa	0	2	7	4	13
Africa	*0*	*5*	*16*	*32*	*53*
Northern Europe	13	0	0	0	13
Southern Europe	7	3	2	0	12
Eastern Europe	7	5	0	0	12
Europe	*27*	*8*	*2*	*0*	*37*
West Asia	1	8	7	2	18
Russia, Central and East Asia	2	2	7	1	12
Southern Asia	1	4	8	4	17
Pacific	2	2	4	0	8
Asia-Pacific	*6*	*16*	*26*	*7*	*55*
WORLD	37	52	51	40	180

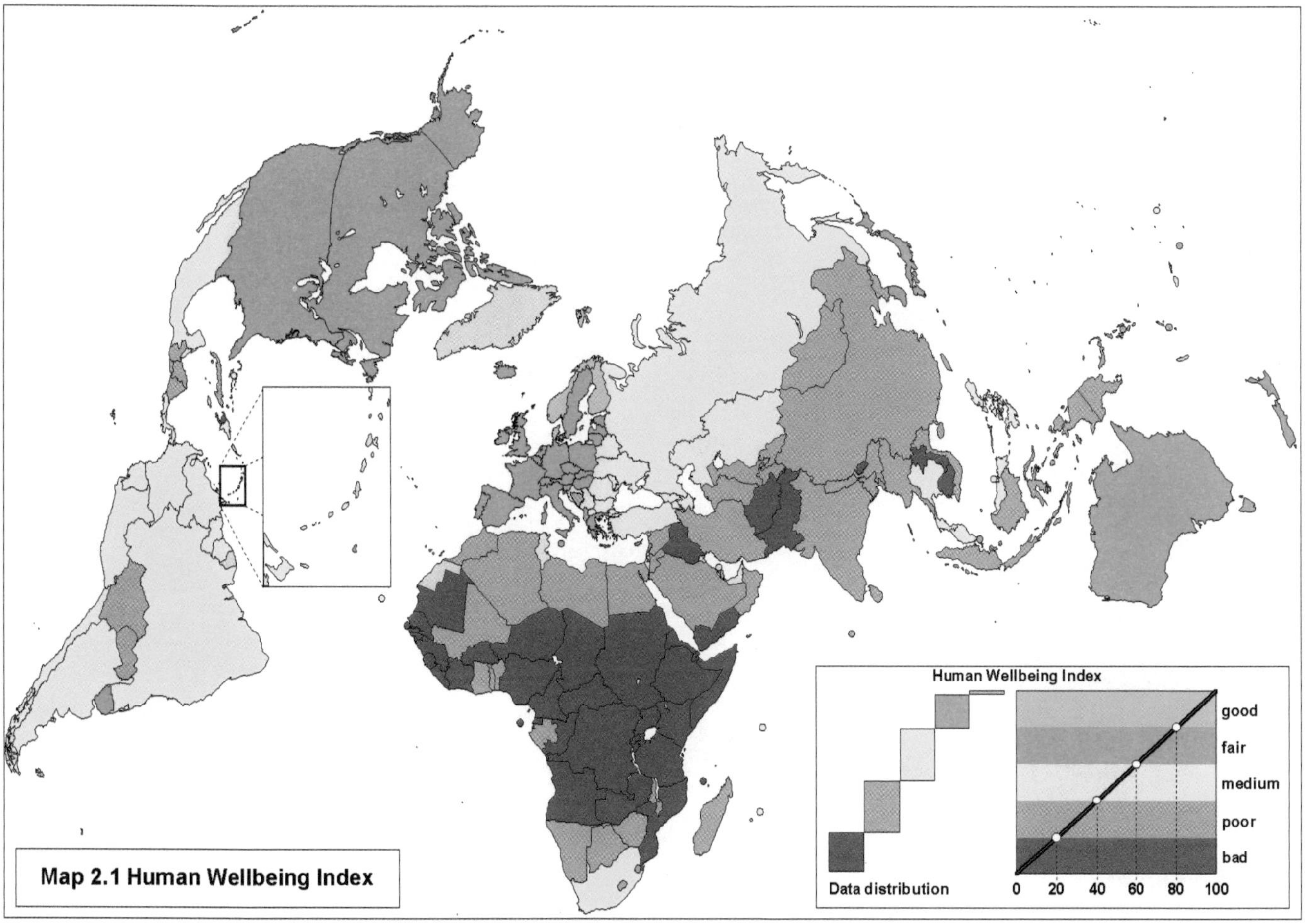

Map 2.1 Human Wellbeing Index

Human Wellbeing Index

good
fair
medium
poor
bad

Data distribution   0 20 40 60 80 100

areas—crime, peace, and gender equity—Norway does better than most: over 180 assaults per 100,000 people (but low murder and rape rates), little more than 2% of the budget spent on the military, no less than one-third of parliamentary seats held by women, and school enrollment of males only 9% lower than that of females.

Thirty-four countries with 16% of the world population enjoy a fair HWI. Most deny themselves a good HWI by subpar showings in equity and one other dimension. The stellar economy of the United States is offset by the high incidence of violent crime and a wide gap between rich and poor. In other countries, the weakest areas (besides equity) are unemployment and debt, followed by inflation, crime, and peace.

Fifty-two countries—the largest group, with the second biggest share of the global population (17%)—have a medium HWI. Their performance is a bewildering mixture of highs, lows, and in between, unlike the predominantly fair scores of countries in the groups above them or mainly poor scores of those below. Russia's strongest area is education, but it is overwhelmed by corruption, war in Chechnya, high inflation and unemployment, and

a life expectancy of only 61 years, seven of which are lost to ill health.

Several medium countries are prevented from rising to a fair HWI or falling to a poor one by an especially high or low score in one dimension. Bulgaria does moderately well in knowledge and health and population, and could attain

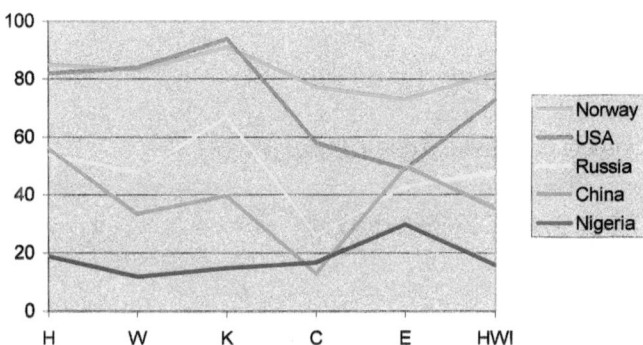

Figure 2.2 Comparison of five countries at each level of the Human Wellbeing Index (HWI) (green = good, blue = fair, yellow = medium, pink = poor, red = bad) and for each dimension (H = health and population, W = wealth, K = knowledge, C = community, E = equity).

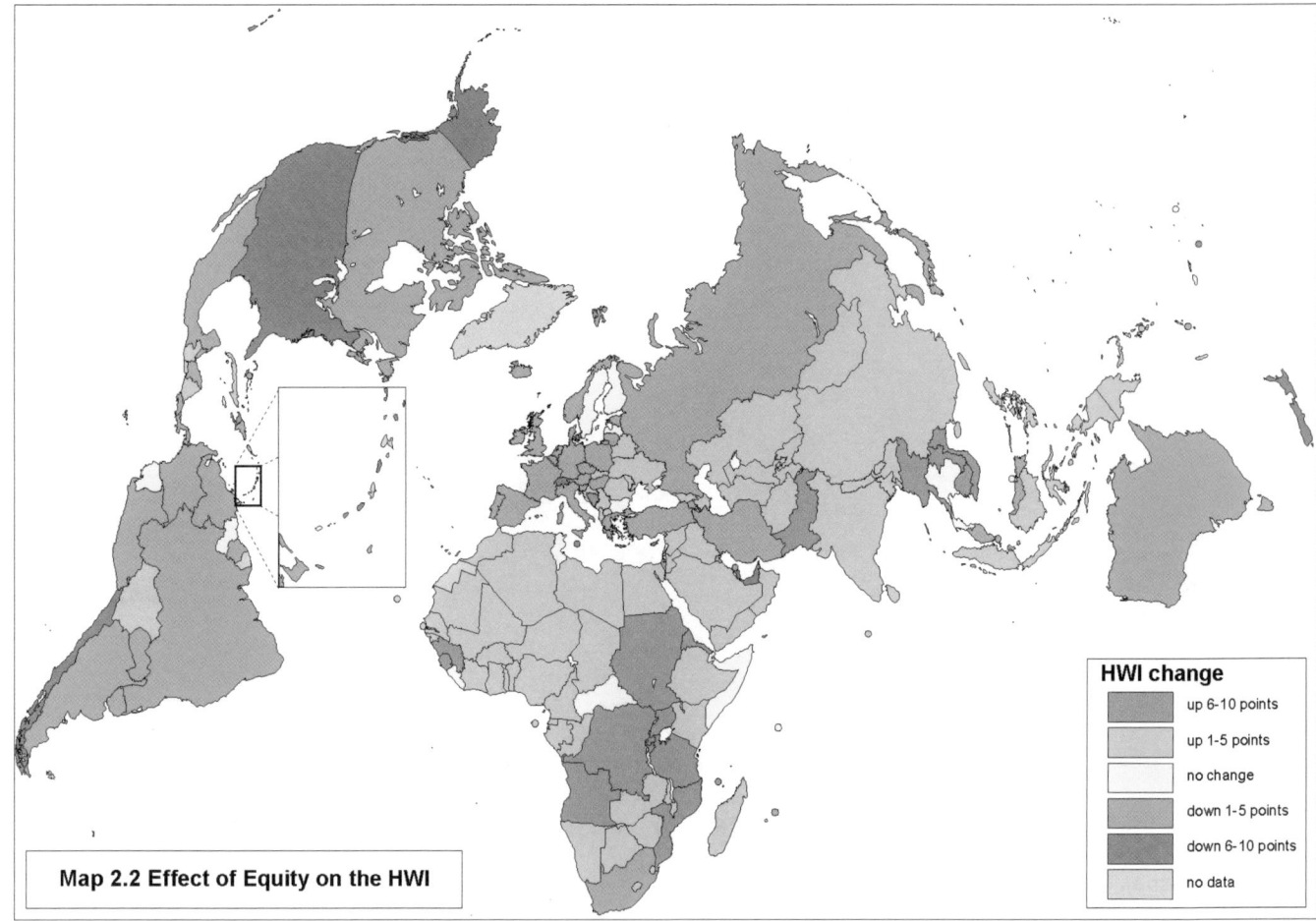

Map 2.2 Effect of Equity on the HWI

HWI change

up 6-10 points

up 1-5 points

no change

down 1-5 points

down 6-10 points

no data

a fair HWI but for its low income of $4,810 per person, double-digit inflation and unemployment, and burdensome external debt. By contrast, South Africa's 95% enrollment through secondary school offsets the declining health (life expectancy 49 years and dropping) and persistent violence that otherwise would reduce it to a poor HWI.

Fifty-one countries, with 54% of the world's people, have a poor HWI. They tend to have bright spots overshadowed by bigger areas of deficient performance. China's plusses are health (life expectancy of 70 years, much reduced child and maternal mortality rates), a subreplacement fertility rate, low unemployment (around 3%), moderate debt, and a low violent crime rate (at least officially). But its minuses are widespread poverty (34% of children are stunted by lack of food, only 24% of people have basic sanitation, and GDP per person is only $3,105), inadequate tertiary education, primitive communications (under nine main telephone lines and mobile phones per 100 people), denial of political rights and civil liberties, high levels of corruption, armed conflict in Xinjiang, and more than 5% of the budget spent on the military.

The 40 countries with a bad HWI represent 12$\frac{1}{2}$%

of the world population. All have poor or bad scores for health and population, wealth, knowledge, and (except for Burkina Faso) community. They are trapped in the vicious synergy of underdevelopment as illness and illiteracy cripple livelihoods, debt stifles the economy, and governments fail to lead. Nigeria has emerged from 16 years of military dictatorship with life expectancy a mere 50 years, a fertility rate of five children per woman, 43% of children stunted, half the households without safe water, GDP per person under $800, and institutions in ruins.

The Equity Effect

The effect of equity on the HWI is illustrated in Map 2.2 and Figure 2.3 and summarized in Table 2.2. Full details are in Table 1 in the Data section.

Equity is *included* in the HWIs of 65 countries (36%) where it lowers the HWI. The high standard of living revealed by the other dimensions is unevenly distributed. Equity is therefore included to give a more realistic picture of national conditions. With the inclusion of equity,

Qatar's HWI drops from medium to poor, Chile's from fair to medium, and Switzerland's from good to fair. Nine other countries (Australia, Austria, Belgium, Canada, Iceland, Ireland, Luxembourg, Japan, and Netherlands) also fall from a good to a fair HWI. Nations with the biggest reductions in HWI are concentrated in the West Indies, West Asia and Northern Europe.

Conversely, equity is *excluded* from the HWI of 96 countries (53%) where its inclusion would have raised the HWI. Many of them are in Africa. In all but one of these countries (Slovakia), human development is inadequate throughout society, so what is being shared is misery. Accordingly, equity is excluded to avoid making conditions look rosier than they are. Haiti's HWI is thereby prevented from rising from bad to poor, and Libya's from poor to medium.

Equity has no effect on the HWIs of 19 countries (11%), such as Thailand and Samoa.[3]

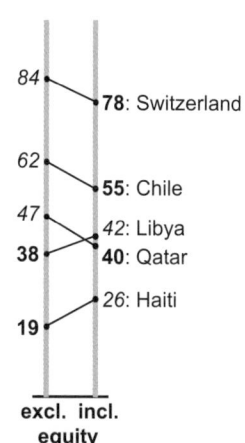

Figure 2.3. The equity effect: HWIs excluding and including equity. The final HWI is the lower score (in **bold**).

nance. The close matches among dimensions and between dimensions and the HWI are probably due to two factors. First, health, wealth, knowledge, and freedom and governance reinforce each other, good performance in one fostering good performance in the others. Second, income plays a crucial role in them all, paying for health services and material necessities; for research, education and communication; and for such ingredients of freedom as free and fair elections, an honest and efficient judiciary and police force, and a clean and competent bureaucracy.

Not surprisingly, therefore, income is highly correlated both with the HWI and with health and knowledge. All of the 25 richest economies have a good or fair HWI, except for Israel, Kuwait, and United Arab Emirates (with medium HWIs), and Qatar (poor HWI). At the other end of the scale, all of the 25 poorest economies have a poor or bad HWI. Among countries with a good or fair HWI, Latvia's GDP per person of $5,730 is the lowest, but in 84% of the group it is above $10,000. While the income of countries with a poor or bad HWI ranges from $460 (Sierra Leone) to $20,985 (Qatar), in 91% it is below $5,000.

Income is not the only building block of a high standard of living. Health, population stability, education, and freedom and good governance are just as important. All but four countries with a good or fair HWI have high scores for all these elements (the exceptions are Estonia, Latvia, and Lithuania, with subpar health; and Singapore, with a medium rating for freedom and governance).[4]

It's the Economy, and It's Not

Four of the five human dimensions—health and population, wealth, knowledge, and community—are highly correlated with the HWI, and the fifth (equity) is moderately correlated. Health and population, wealth, and knowledge are also strongly linked with each other and to a lesser extent community, especially freedom and gover-

How Far from Having Nothing—Or How Close to Having It All?

The Human Development Index (HDI), the only other international index of human wellbeing currently produced, is shown in Map 2.3 and compared with the HWI in Table 2.3. Full details are in Table 1 in the Data section.

The HDI is consistently higher than the HWI.[5] Taking the 173 countries they have in common,

- 44 countries have a good HDI; only three a good HWI.

- Twice as many countries have a fair HDI as have a fair HWI.

Table 2.2. Number of countries whose HWI is changed by the inclusion of equity, according to size of change and level of the HWI before the inclusion of equity.

HWI Change	Good	Fair	Medium	Poor	Bad	Total
Up 6–10 points	0	0	0	3	16	19
Up 1–5 points	0	1	12	41	20	74
UP SUBTOTAL	*0*	*1*	*12*	*44*	*36*	*93*
NO CHANGE	*1*	*2*	*11*	*1*	*4*	*19*
Down 1–5 points	10	18	22	3	0	53
Down 6–10 points	2	6	6	1	0	15
DOWN SUBTOTAL	*12*	*24*	*28*	*4*	*0*	*68*
TOTAL	13	27	51	49	40	180

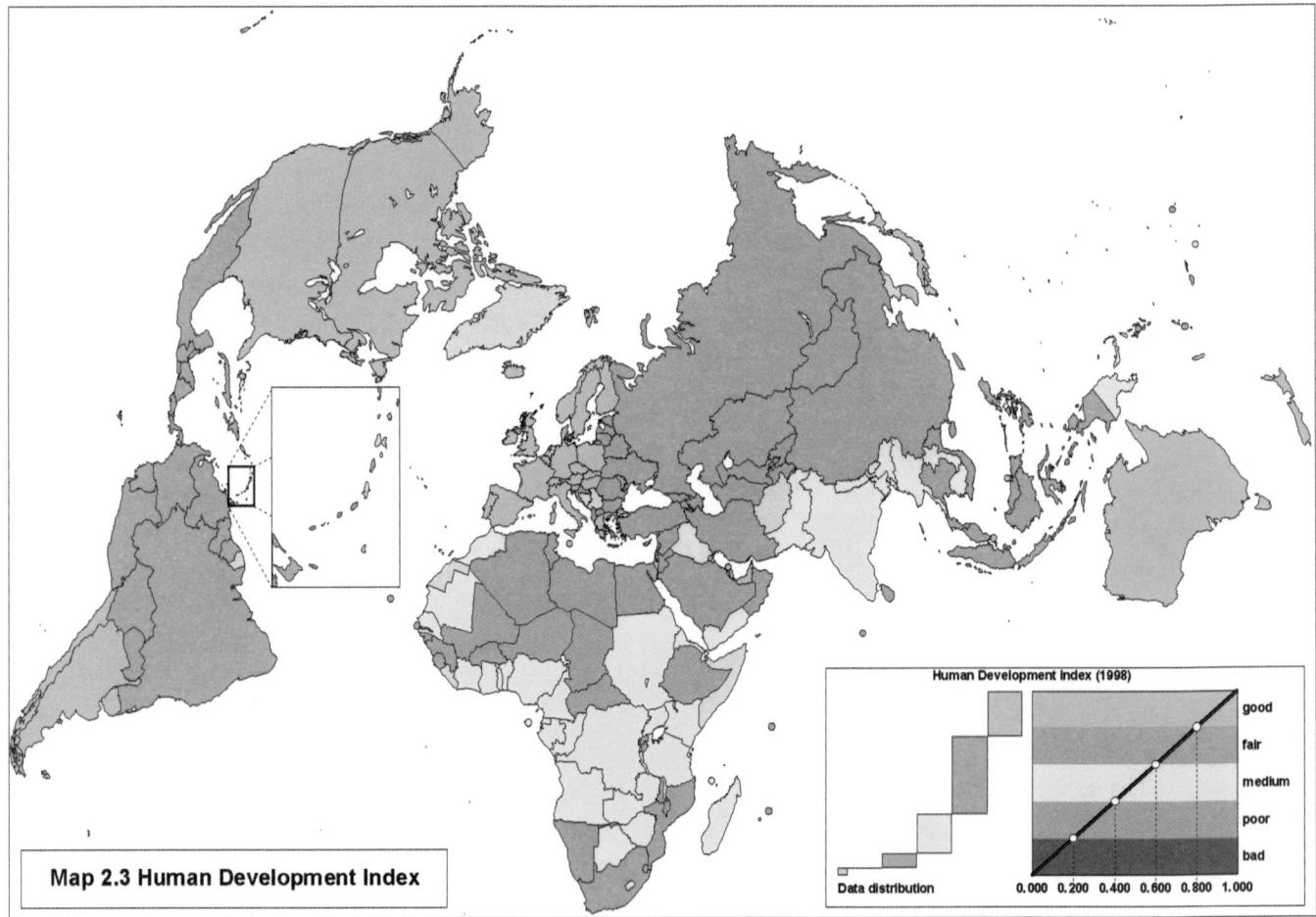

Map 2.3 Human Development Index

Human Development Index (1998)

good
fair
medium
poor
bad

Data distribution   0.000 0.200 0.400 0.600 0.800 1.000

- No country has a bad HDI; 37 have a bad HWI.

- Individual country scores are from 10 points (Denmark) to 51 points (Maldives) higher in the HDI than in the HWI.

These differences are due to contrasting aims and approaches. The two poles of human aspiration are escape from deprivation and fulfillment of potential. The primary

Table 2.3. Performance of 173 countries rated by the Human Wellbeing Index (HWI) and the Human Development Index (HDI).

Band	HWI	HDI
Good	3	44
Fair	34	76
Medium	51	38
Poor	48	15
Bad	37	0
Total	173	173

aim of the HDI is to measure distance from deprivation: how far societies are from having nothing. The HWI tries to measure distance from fulfillment: how close societies are to the good life. This is not to pander to greed but to recognize that people have a wide range of needs whose satisfaction is a legitimate and compelling goal.

Because the HWI measures progress toward a high level of human wellbeing, it cannot omit such major concerns as freedom, violence, or equity. It therefore covers 9 elements represented by 36 indicators. The HDI, with the less onerous task of showing progress away from poverty, need address only a few issues, and thus is based on three elements represented by four indicators: health (life expectancy), wealth (income), and knowledge (literacy and school enrollment). It is easier for countries to do well on three elements than on nine.

However, with so few indicators, the HDI is more susceptible to distortion by missing data, forcing its compilers to provide their own estimates. For example, in 22 developed countries where adult literacy is not measured, they assume the rate to be 99%, further elevating those countries' scores. With its larger number of indicators, the HWI is robust enough for missing data to be left blank.

Consistent with its less demanding goal, the performance criteria chosen for each indicator are less stringent for the HDI than for the HWI. Consequently, an income of $12,000 receives a score of 80 in the HDI, 64 in the HWI; a life expectancy of 55 years scores 50 in the HDI, 33 in the HWI.

The HDI also conveys a sense of international equity that the HWI contradicts:

- In the HDI, the score of top-ranked Canada (93) is almost 4 times that of bottom-ranked Sierra Leone (25). In the HWI, the score of first-place Norway (82) is more than 27 times that of last-place Somalia (3).

- In the HDI, the median score of the top 10% of countries (92) is about two and a half times that of the bottom 10% (37). In the HWI, the median score of the top 10% of countries (78) is almost eight times that of the bottom 10% (10).

Again, these discrepancies are due to scope and performance criteria. As one of four indicators, life expectancy has a much stronger influence on the HDI than on the HWI (where it is one of 36). In addition, its inherently restricted range—the longest life expectancy is little more than double the shortest—also limits any separation between rich and poor. The HDI further narrows the gap between haves and have-nots by compressing the span of scores for income: in the HDI, $5,000 scores 65 and $20,000 scores 88, a difference of only 23 points; in the HWI, they score 40 and 80 respectively, a 40-point difference.

The HDI and HWI present two contrasting views of the world. According to the HDI, most countries are pretty well off, and disparities among them are modest. From the HWI's perspective, a fortunate few are close to the good life (albeit with economic and social flaws), and the gap between them and the rest of the world is enormous.

Health and Population

Health and Population Index (Map 2.4)

What it is: Lower of health index and population index.

Country results: 26 good (14%), 22 fair (12%), 49 medium (27%), 34 poor (19%), 49 bad (27%).

A sustainable society would provide its members with the conditions for a long and healthy life. At the same time, its members would freely choose to limit family size so that their longevity and health did not result in population growth.

A long life is widely valued because it increases a person's opportunity to pursue goals, develop abilities, and fulfill potential. This is all the more so if the life can be lived in excellent health, with diseases and accidents few and far between and with an effective health service to overcome them when they occur.

As people's health improves and life spans lengthen, populations grow. Most people want children, and

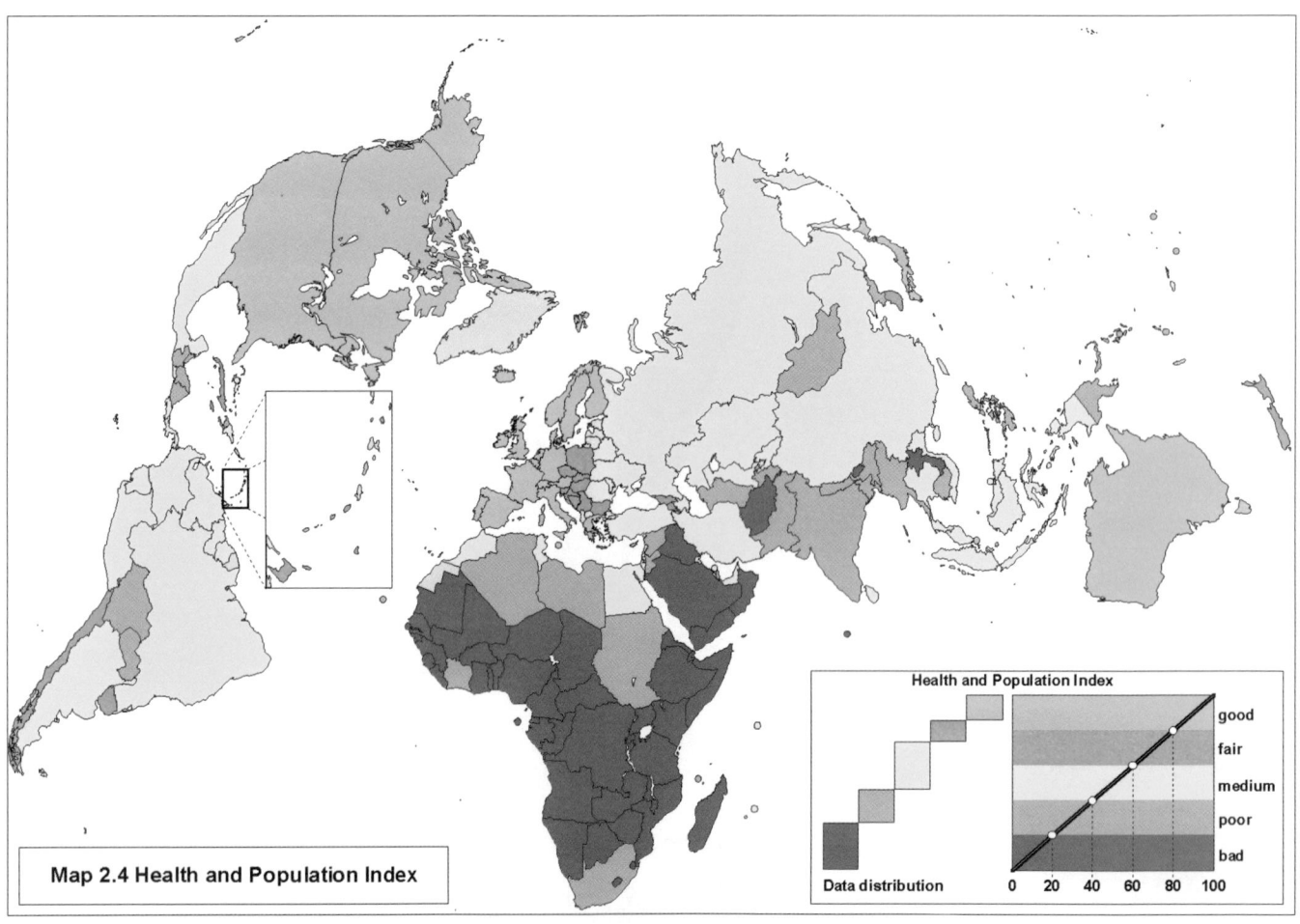

Map 2.4 Health and Population Index

Health and Population Index

good
fair
medium
poor
bad

Data distribution   0 20 40 60 80 100

more people mean more workers and consumers, so some regard population growth as an unambiguous good. But large populations, especially if they consume a lot, place enormous demands on the ecosystem. Rapidly growing populations also impose pressures on economies, infrastructure, and institutions, straining a society's capacity to provide adequate education, health services, and jobs.

Since good health does not compensate for high population growth or low fertility for poor health, the health and population index was obtained from whichever element (health or population) had the lower score.

Countries with a good index have populations that are long-lived, healthy, and stable or declining. The best performer is Japan, with an index of 91. Most countries with a fair index have good scores for population but merely fair scores for health (the rest have fair scores for both). By contrast, the majority of countries with a poor or bad health and population index have poor or bad scores for both elements. Most African and some Asian nations are typical of this group, including the worst performer, Sierra Leone (with an index of 2).

The largest gaps between high population and lower health scores are in Eastern Europe, Russia, North Korea, Myanmar, China, Thailand, and Seychelles. In the last three countries, they may mean only that health programs lag behind successful population policies. Elsewhere, they are signs of trouble. The health scores of Russia and Eastern Europe stem from a fall in living standards, a rise in alcoholism in men, and the decay of health services, which cut life expectancies in the late 1980s and early 1990s; their population scores reflect very low fertility rates, perhaps because of pessimism about the future. Despair may also be the cause of low fertility in North Korea and Myanmar. North Korea's low health score is due to famine, which doubled death rates between 1995 and 1997; Myanmar's, to spreading AIDS, malaria, and malnutrition.[6]

West Asia has the biggest gaps between high health and lower population scores. For example, Saudi Arabia has a health score of 62 but a population score of 16 due to a high total fertility rate of 5.6 children per woman. Improved health has failed to influence fertility patterns because one or both of two other essential factors are missing: economic security and access by women to education and wealth.

For all data and scores for health and population, together with details of the indicators, performance criteria, and combining procedures, see Table 2 in the Data section.

Health

> ### Health Index (Map 2.5)
> **What it is:** One indicator, healthy life expectancy at birth (Figure 2.4).
>
> **Objective:** Long lives in good health.
>
> **Country results:** 27 good (15%), 32 fair (18%), 59 medium (33%), 31 poor (17%), 31 bad (17%).

The health index measures healthy life expectancy at birth: the average number of years that a child born in a given year—in this case, 1999—could expect to live in good health. Total life expectancy at birth takes account of all causes of death, and the death rates from those causes, that a typical person would be exposed to in his or her lifetime. *Healthy* life expectancy is total life expectancy at birth adjusted for the number of years likely to be lost to disease and injury. The number is based on estimates of the prevalence, duration, and severity of communicable and noncommunicable illnesses, neuropsychiatric disorders, and intentional and unintentional injuries. As such it serves as an indicator of overall health, the healthfulness of living conditions (diet, clean water, sanitation, and clean air), and the availability and effectiveness of health services.

World average total life expectancy at birth (both sexes combined) in 1999 was 64.5 years, a rise of almost six years over the last two decades. Progress has not been uniform, however, and the gap between the longest and shortest life spans has widened. People in the top five countries (Japan, Sweden, Australia, Switzerland, France) live more than twice as long as

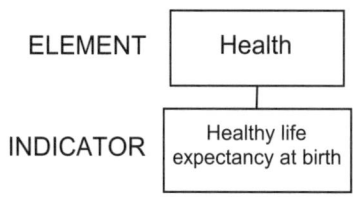

Figure 2.4. Indicator chart for health.

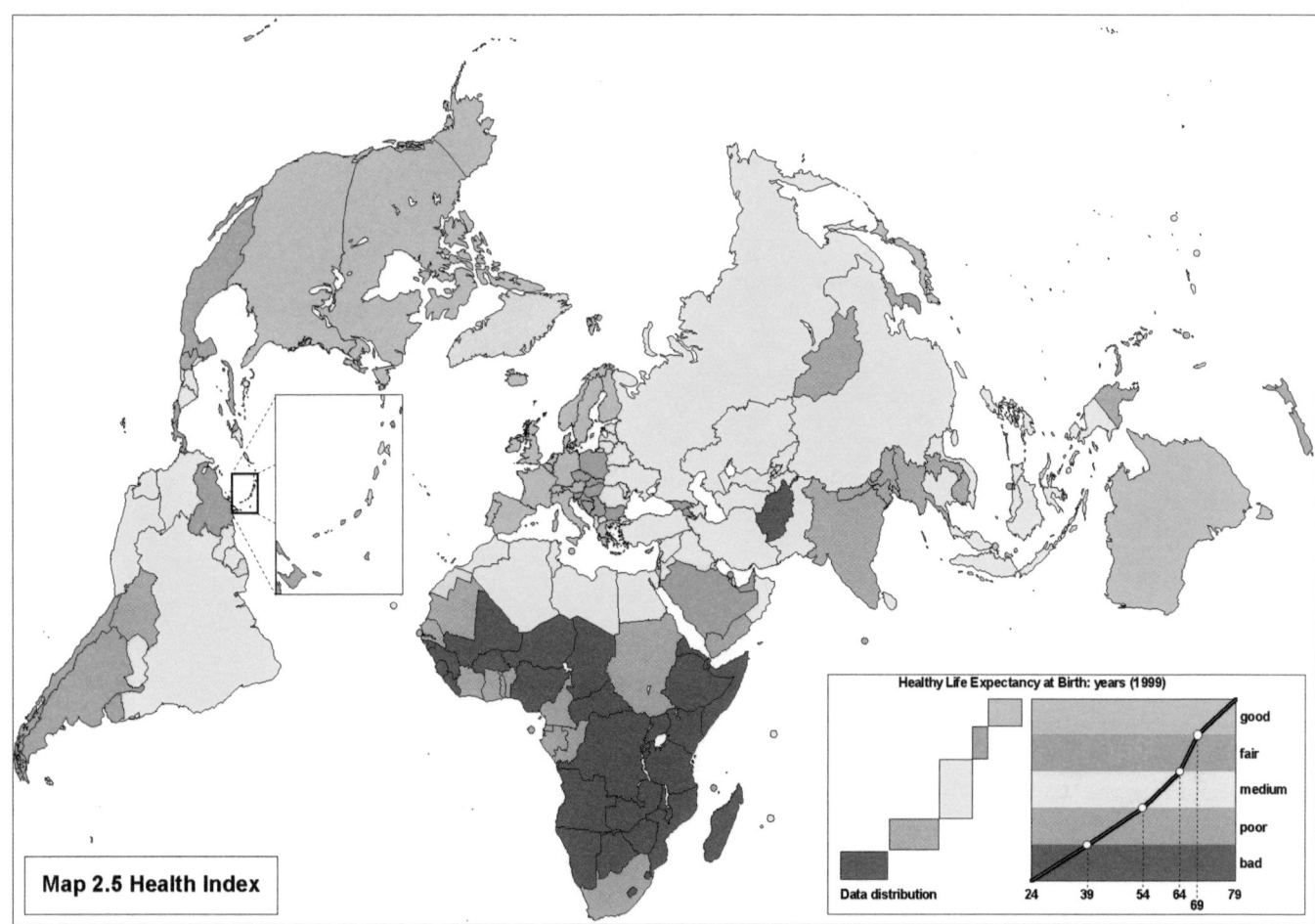

Map 2.5 Health Index

Healthy Life Expectancy at Birth: years (1999)

good
fair
medium
poor
bad

Data distribution   24   39   54   64   79
69

people in the bottom five (Botswana, Niger, Zambia, Malawi, Sierra Leone). Disparities in child survival (child death rates below 1% in industrialized countries, above 10% in Africa) are compounded by even greater disparities in adult survival, chiefly due to HIV/AIDS, which has cut life expectancies by 1–10 years in 39 countries (32 in Africa, four in the Americas, three in Asia) and by 11–20 years in Botswana, Lesotho, Kenya, Namibia, Swaziland, Zambia, and Zimbabwe. AIDS killed 300,000 Africans in 1989, 2.2 million in 1999. Where it is most prevalent, 55–60% of survivors to age 15 will die before age 60.

World average healthy life expectancy at birth in 1999 was 56.8 years, 7.7 years lower than total life expectancy. Although people who live longer have a greater opportunity to acquire nonfatal disabilities as they grow older, they spend less of their lives in ill health than people with short life spans. Years of disability account for 9% of life expectancy in countries with average life spans longer than 75 years; 18% in those with average life spans of 60 years or less. The

spread among healthy life expectancies is even wider than among total life expectancies: 46.6 years separate the total life expectancies of 80.9 years in Japan and 34.3 years in Sierra Leone; 48.6 years separate their healthy life expectancies of 74.5 and 25.9 years.

Patterns of disease also differ greatly. Among countries with a good health index, the top four causes of loss of healthy life expectancy are ischemic heart disease, depression (especially among women), cerebrovascular disease, and alcohol dependence. Among those with a bad health index, the top four causes are HIV/AIDS, malaria, acute lower respiratory infections, and diarrhoeal diseases.[7]

United Nations' targets are that all countries should have total life expectancies of at least 60 years by 2000, more than 70 years by 2005, and more than 75 years by 2015. I lowered these by six years to provide corresponding targets for healthy life expectancy—respectively, 54, 64, and 69 years—which define the top points of the poor, medium, and fair bands (as shown in the performance graph in Map 2.5).[8]

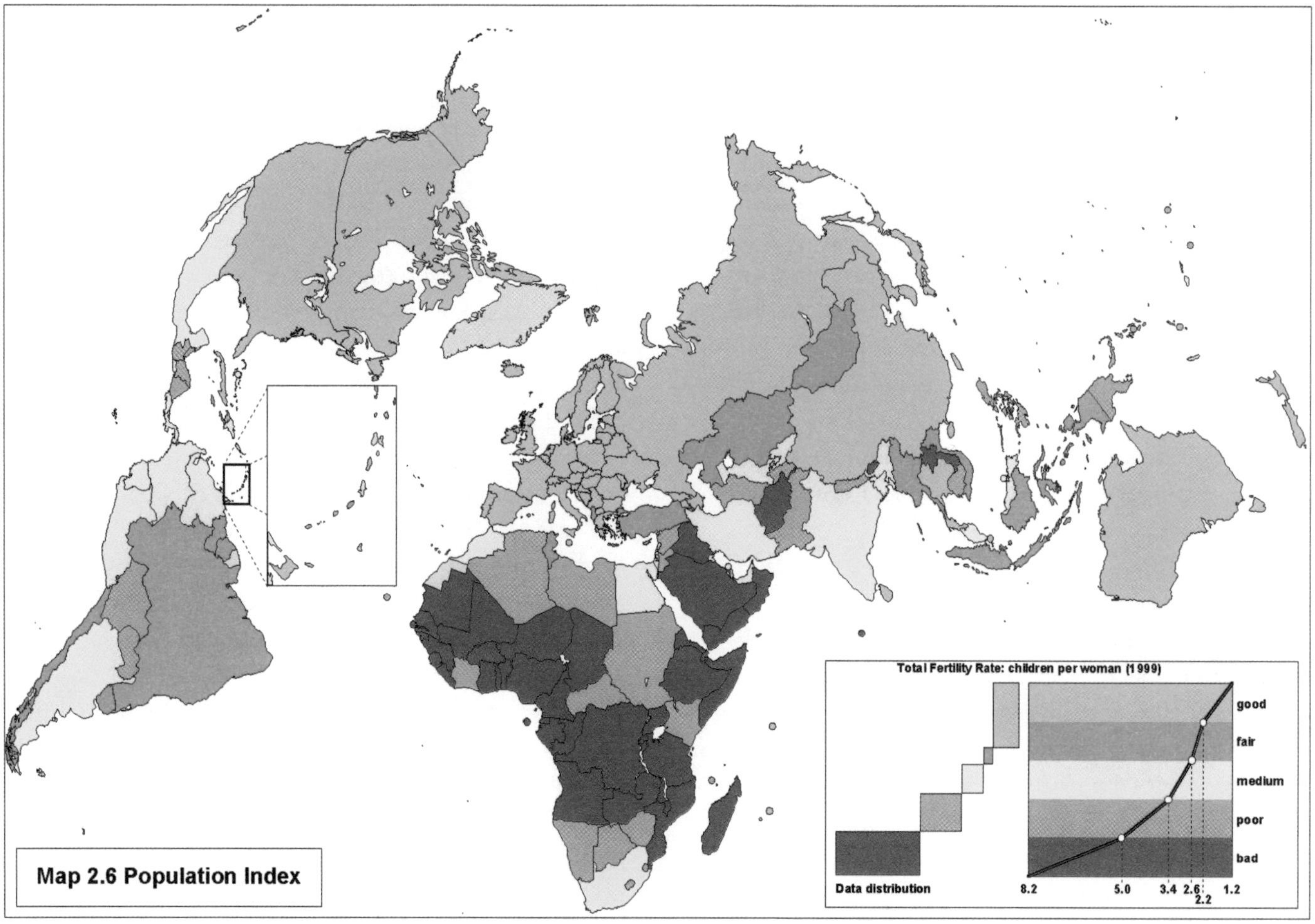

Total Fertility Rate: children per woman (1999)

good
fair
medium
poor
bad

Data distribution

8.2   5.0   3.4 2.6   1.2
2.2

Map 2.6 Population Index

Population

Population Index (Map 2.6)

What it is: One indicator, total fertility rate (Figure 2.5).

Objective: A stable population.

Country results: 60 good (33%), 16 fair (9%), 27 medium (15%), 35 poor (19%), 42 bad (23%).

The total fertility rate (TFR) is the average number of children born alive by a woman in her lifetime. It is an indicator of family size, birth rates, birth control practices and services, and other factors that act together to determine family size (such as family income and security, women's status in society, and religious and cultural influences).

Because it directly reflects choices about family size, TFR is a good indicator of population stability. (Population growth rate may be a more direct measure, but

because it includes migration it is not as clear a sign of what is going on within the society.)

TFRs range from 7.4 children per woman (Yemen) to 1.1 children (Spain). A sustainable rate would be the replacement rate, which (with average sex ratios) is 2.1.[9] The good band was therefore defined as 2.1 or below, and the fair band as less than half a child above replacement (see the performance graph in Map 2.6).

Rates below replacement are not sustainable, but the excessively high scores they get have little effect on the health and population index because they are usually offset by lower health scores. For example, although countries with a TFR of 1.1 or 1.2 receive a score of 100 for

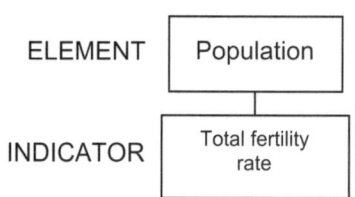

Figure 2.5. Indicator chart for population.

population, their health and population index ranges from 87 (Italy and Spain) to as low as 57 (Romania) due to their lower health scores.

Countries with a good population index (fertility rates at or below replacement) include 44% of the world's people. They cover all Europe (except Albania) and major parts of Asia and the Americas. The populations of half these countries—including Germany, Russia, and Japan—will fall between 1998 and 2050, their declines ranging from 1% of the 1998 population in Yugoslavia to 35% in Estonia. The populations of the other half—including the United States, China, and Thailand—will continue to rise due to immigration and higher proportions of young people. Regionally, the sharpest declines will be in Eastern and Southern Europe, which by 2050 will be reduced to, respectively, 18% and 20% of their 1998 sizes.

Countries with a fair or medium population index (slightly to moderately above replacement) represent respectively 10% and 28% of the global population, mostly in the Americas and Southern Asia.

Nations with a poor or bad population index have TFRs well above replacement and account for 20% of the world's people. The majority are in Africa (47

countries), followed by Asia–Pacific (22). These fast-growing populations place an increasingly heavy strain on environmental resources and on their abilities to lift themselves out of poverty.

Even so, falling populations are becoming almost as much of a concern as growing ones. In many developed countries fertility has stayed below replacement levels for at least 20 years. A generation ago a TFR of 1.3 children or below was considered highly unlikely. Now it is found in 11 countries. The chief worry is that declining fertility coupled with longer life expectancy is aging the world's population. In Europe the proportions of children (below 15 years) and elders (60 years or over) were roughly equal in 1998. By 2050, elders are expected to outnumber children by two and a half times, and one in every three people will be 60 years or older. Higher proportions of the elderly could mean that a smaller labor force has a larger body of retired people to support and a bigger health care bill to pay. But as elders look forward to more years of active life, retirement patterns are beginning to change. In Japan, for instance, older people are returning to work to seek new sources of personal growth as well as income to supplement inadequate pensions.[10]

Wealth

Wealth Index (Map 2.7)

What it is: Average of household wealth index and national wealth index.

Country results: 8 good (4%), 29 fair (16%), 45 medium (25%), 48 poor (27%), 50 bad (28%).

Wealth is the material component of human wellbeing: the goods and income that enable people to survive and develop opportunities. The wealth index measures whether individuals and households can meet basic needs and gain secure livelihoods and whether the nation has the resources to support enterprise and maintain prosperity.

The richest economies—those with a good wealth index (United States, Denmark, Iceland, Luxembourg, Netherlands, Norway, Switzerland, and Singapore)—meet the basic needs of almost all their people and have incomes above $20,000 per person, low rates of inflation and unemployment, and limited debt.

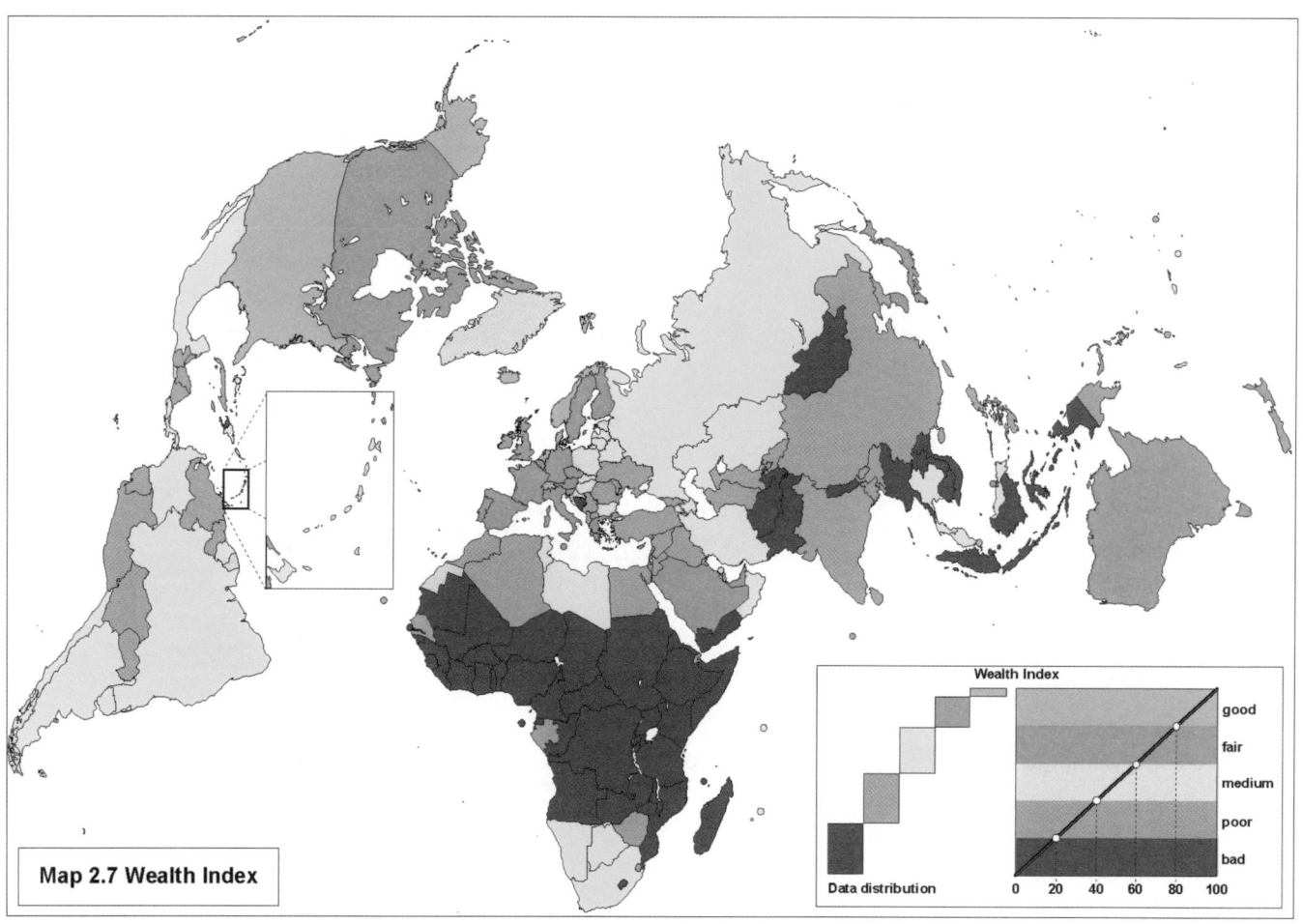

Map 2.7 Wealth Index

Wealth Index

good
fair
medium
poor
bad

Data distribution

0 20 40 60 80 100

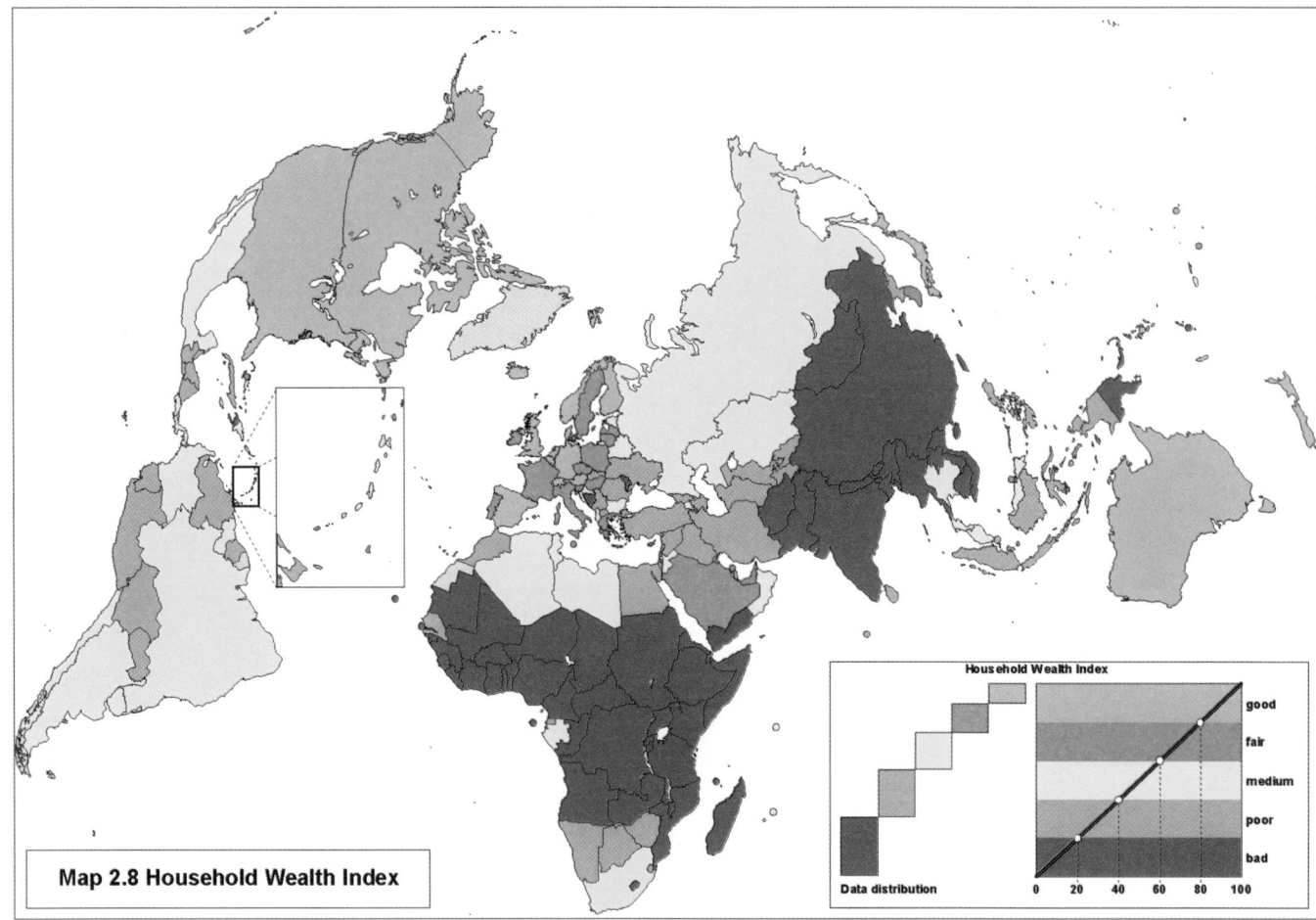

Map 2.8 Household Wealth Index

In general, countries with a fair wealth index (mainly in Northern and Southern Europe and West Asia) have lower incomes. A few have incomes as high as the top economies but are not as strong in other aspects (such as public debt in Belgium and unemployment in France).

Countries with a medium index are concentrated in South America, the West Indies, and Eastern Europe. They tend to have moderately healthy household economies but weaker national economies.

Most economies with a poor index are in Asia–Pacific, with clusters in Northern Africa, Eastern Europe, and Central America. Indonesia is typical: 42% of children are stunted by poor diet, little more than half the population has basic sanitation, income per person is $2,650, and the economy is struggling to recover from its collapse in 1997.

In countries with a bad index, almost entirely in Africa and Southern Asia, households are desperately poor and national economies crippled by debt.

For all data and scores, together with details of the indicators, performance criteria, and combining procedures, see Table 3 (wealth index, household wealth) and Table 4 (national wealth) in the Data section.

Household Wealth

Household Wealth Index (Map 2.8)

What it is: Average of needs and income scores (Figure 2.6).

Objective: Enough material goods and income to secure basic needs and decent livelihoods.

Country results: 19 good (11%), 27 fair (15%), 34 medium (19%), 44 poor (24%), 56 bad (31%).

The household wealth index is partly a poverty index, showing the extent to which people lack the essentials for survival. Needs include food, safe water, and basic sanita-

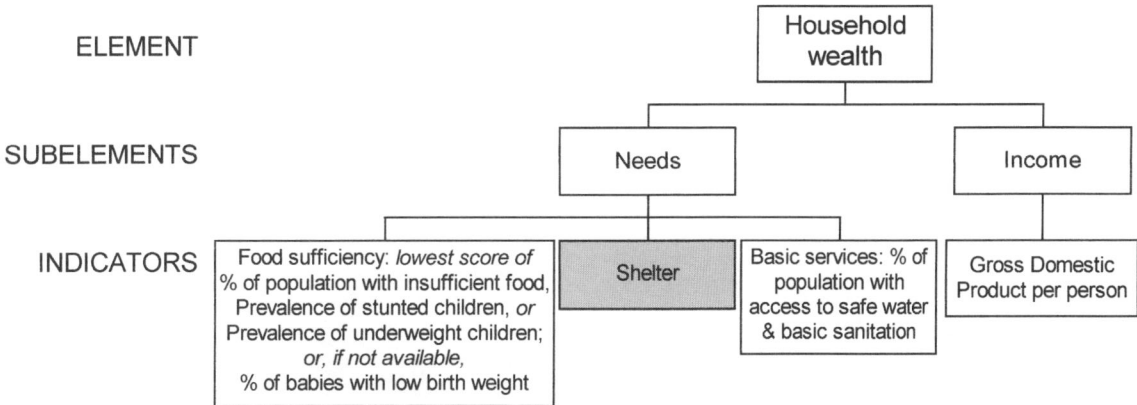

Figure 2.6. Indicator chart for household wealth. Shelter (shaded box) is not covered because of lack of a suitable indicator.

tion (shelter could not be covered due to data deficiencies). Income provides the resources required to meet these needs, provide a degree of security, acquire conveniences, and enjoy leisure.

At least half the population is acutely poor in countries with a bad index and at least a third in those with a poor index. In countries with a medium index, poverty afflicts more than a fifth of the population. A tenth to a fifth of the population is poor in countries with a fair or good index, possibly less in some of the latter. (However, poverty measurements change radically depending on the indicator, and the ones used here give only a rough approximation.)

Needs

> ### Needs (Map 2.9)
> **What it is:** The lower score of a food sufficiency indicator (Map 2.10) and a basic services indicator (Map 2.11). The latter is based on water or sanitation, whichever is less available.
> **Country results:** 16 good (9%), 47 fair (26%), 31 medium (17%), 23 poor (13%), 58 bad (32%), 5 no data (3%).

Food and basic services (water and sanitation) are essential for health and survival, and people's needs are not met if they lack either. Hence the needs score is based on whichever is in shorter supply. For the same reason, the basic services score is based on water or sanitation, depending on which is less available. For example, North

Korea's needs score reflects food sufficiency, Zambia's water, and Moldova's sanitation (Figure 2.7). A good score for needs indicates that more than 90% of the population has adequate food, water and sanitation (e.g., Tonga); a fair score means that all are available to more than 80%. Conversely, a bad score means that 50% or more of the population lacks at least one of these necessities, be it food or either of the basic services.

In most countries, fewer people have access to basic services than to enough food: 65 countries have a good score for food but only 23 for water and sanitation; 19 countries have a bad score for food, 52 for basic services (Figure 2.8). These numbers explain why so few countries have a good score for needs and so many a bad score. Of

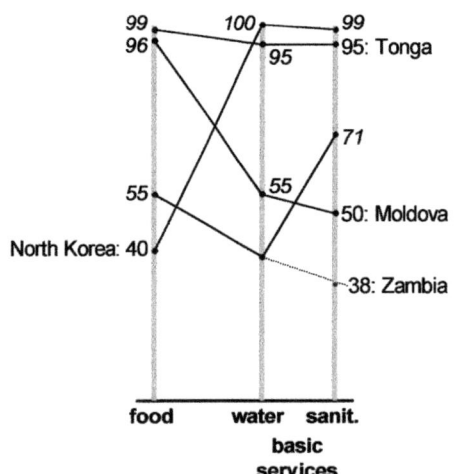

Figure 2.7. Percentages of the population with sufficient food and basic services (water and sanitation). The needs score is based on the lowest percentage.

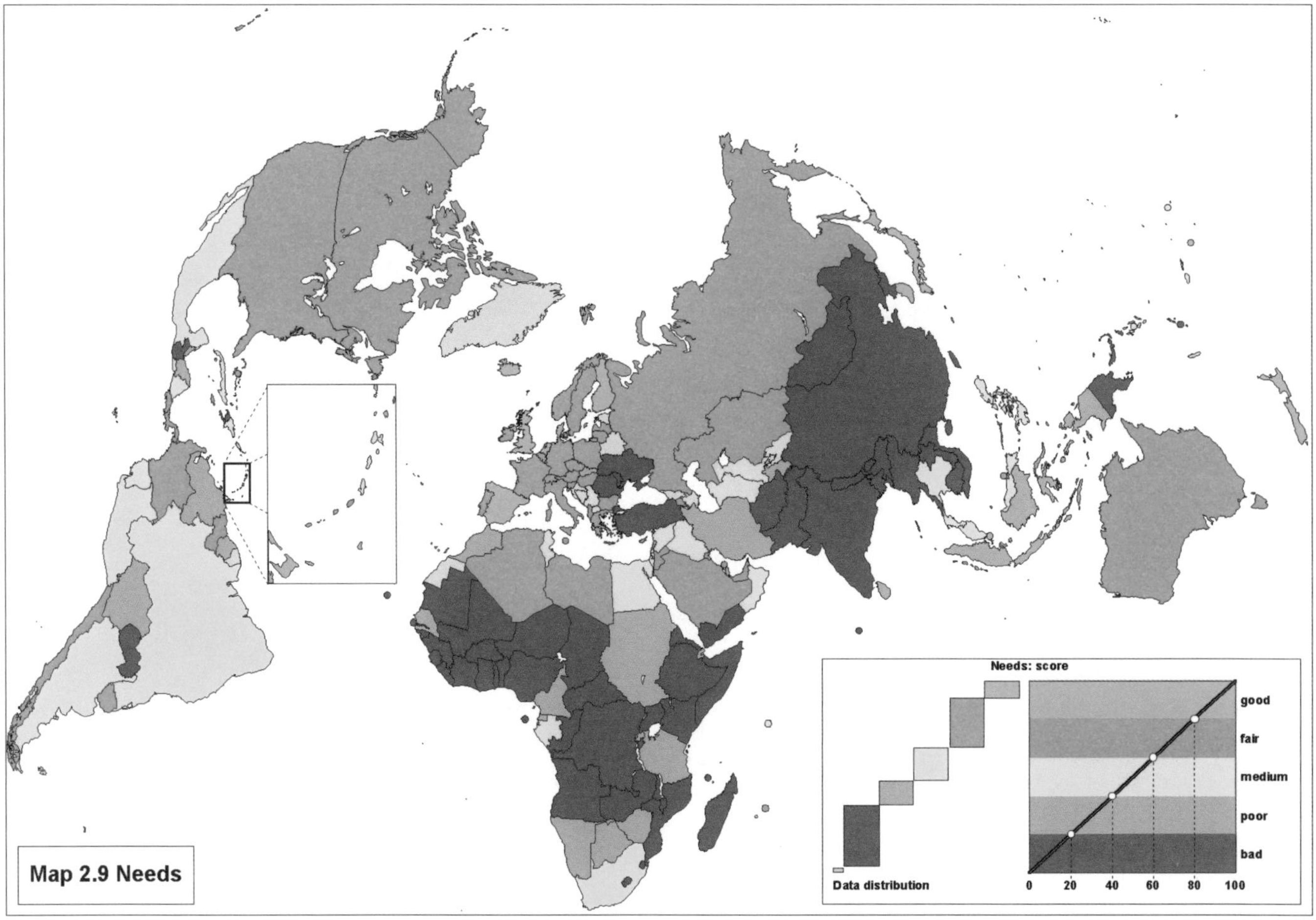

Map 2.9 Needs
Needs: score
good
fair
medium
poor
bad
Data distribution
0
20
40
60
80
100

those with a high score for food, only 16 rate as well for basic services. Most are like Moldova, where 96% of the people have enough food but many fewer (only 50%) have access to basic services. Lack of water or sanitation is also the sole or main contributing factor in all but six of the countries with a bad score for needs.

Within basic services, sanitation is more neglected than water supply. In two out of three countries, fewer people have access to adequate sanitation than to safe water, casting doubt on how safe the water really is. Of the 52 countries with a bad score for basic services, access to both services is the deficient factor in 20, water in 9, and sanitation in 23. Zambia is unusual in providing more people with sanitation than with clean water or sufficient food (Figure 2.7).

The information required to assess needs is often missing or suspect. Food sufficiency is represented by one of four indicators because none covers all countries. The most direct is the percentage of the population that is undernourished, but the survey covers only the bigger developing countries. Of the alternatives—percentage of children who are stunted (short for their age), percentage of underweight children, and percentage of babies with low birth weight—the first two are preferable because they are less influ-

70
60
50
40
30
20
10
0
countries
good
fair
medium
poor
bad
no data
Food sufficiency
Basic services

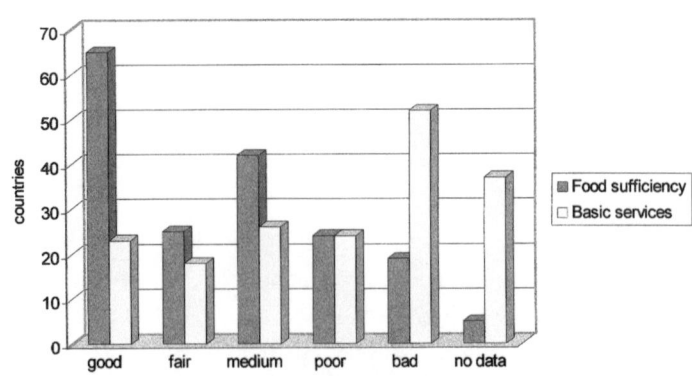

Figure 2.8. Country performance for food sufficiency and basic services.

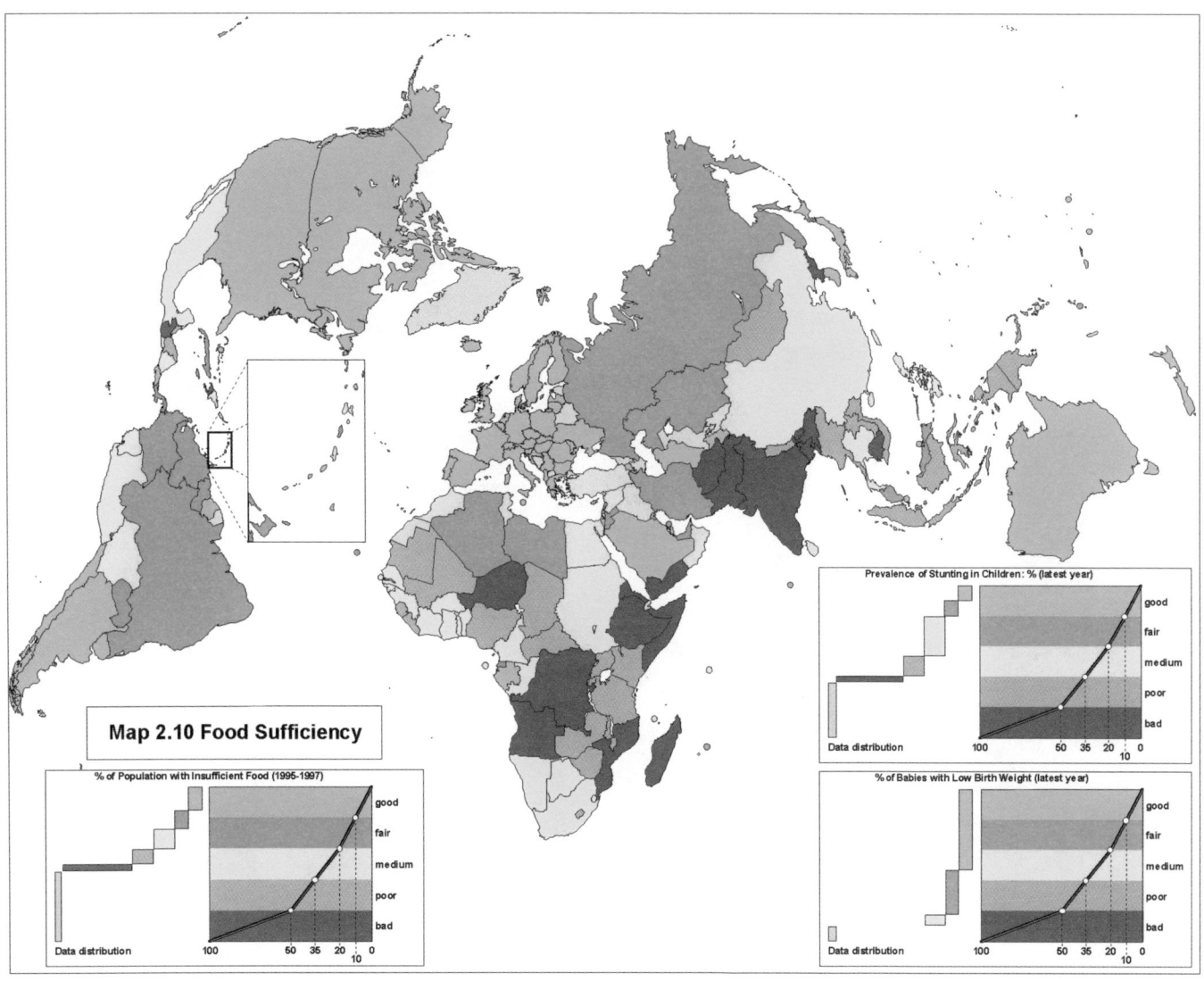

Map 2.10 Food Sufficiency

% of Population with Insufficient Food (1995-1997)

Prevalence of Stunting in Children: % (latest year)

% of Babies with Low Birth Weight (latest year)

enced by factors other than prolonged lack of food (such as malaria).

Statistics on water and sanitation are available for fewer countries (Figure 2.4), and they are not as trustworthy. Government reports are sometimes more sanitized than the water, and surveys vary widely in thoroughness of coverage and standards of water safety, adequacy of sanitation, and accessibility. Accessible water may come from a standpipe at the far end of the street, and the sanitation may be as basic as a poorly maintained outhouse.

Relying on the most conservative of several indicators can offset these deficiencies to some extent. Independent estimates of food sufficiency in North Korea (40%) probably give a more realistic sense of the overall satisfaction of needs than official reports on basic services (99%).

The World Health Organization has set targets of less than 20% for prevalence of stunting in children and no more than 10% for prevalence of low birth weight babies and underweight children (no target exists for the percentage of the population that is undernourished). The United Nations' target for access to safe water and basic sanitation is 100%. These targets were used to define the good and fair bands of all the indicators. Performance on food sufficiency ranges from 73% of the population with not enough food (Afghanistan) to 1% (South Korea) and from 64% of children stunted (Ethiopia) to 1% (Croatia and Tonga). Performance on basic services ranges from 3% of the population with safe water and basic sanitation (Malawi) to 100% (several countries, including Barbados, Finland, Cyprus, and Singapore).[11]

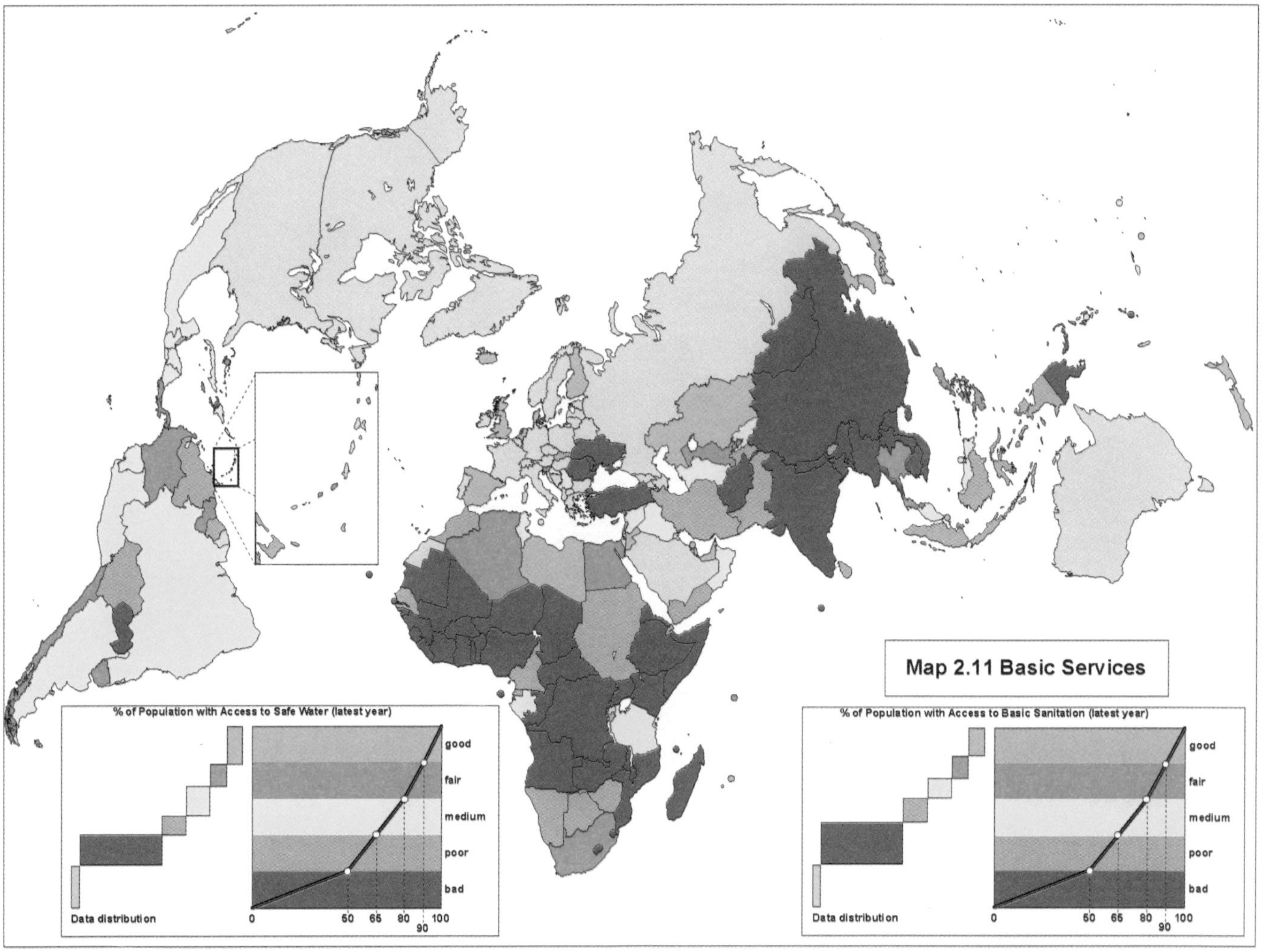

Map 2.11 Basic Services

% of Population with Access to Safe Water (latest year)

good
fair
medium
poor
bad

Data distribution

0   50 65   80   100
                  90

% of Population with Access to Basic Sanitation (latest year)

good
fair
medium
poor
bad

Data distribution

0   50 65   80   100
                  90

Income/Size of Economy

Income/Size of Economy (Map 2.12)

What it is: One indicator, gross domestic product (GDP) per person (in international purchasing power parity dollars)—"income," for short.[12] The indicator is counted twice: under household wealth (income) and under national wealth (size of economy).

Country results: 21 good (12%), 19 fair (11%), 35 medium (19%), 47 poor (26%), 58 bad (32%).

Most countries with incomes that are good (above $20,000) or fair (above $10,000) are in Europe (21), followed by Asia–Pacific (12, largely in West Asia), the Americas (6), and Africa (Seychelles).

The definitions of good and fair incomes beg the question, How much money is enough? The answer is that small increases in income are sufficient to escape from poverty, but it takes much more money to acquire the resources associated with high levels of human wellbeing. It is possible for countries to provide more than 90% of the people with adequate food and basic services at incomes as low as $4,280 (Tonga). But only at incomes above $10,000 (for food) and $14,000 (for basic services) do countries that meet 90% of their people's needs outnumber those that do not.

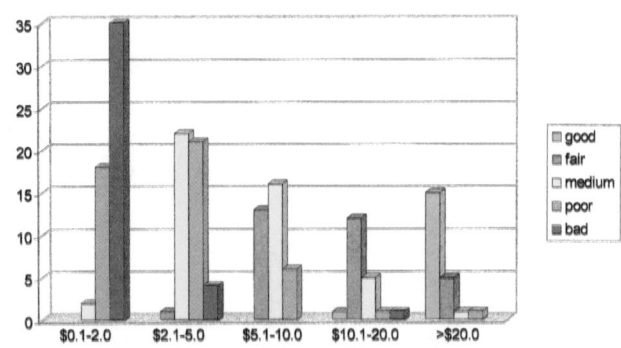

Figure 2.9. Number of countries with good, fair, medium, poor, or bad scores for a combination of health and population, knowledge, and community at different income levels ($000s).

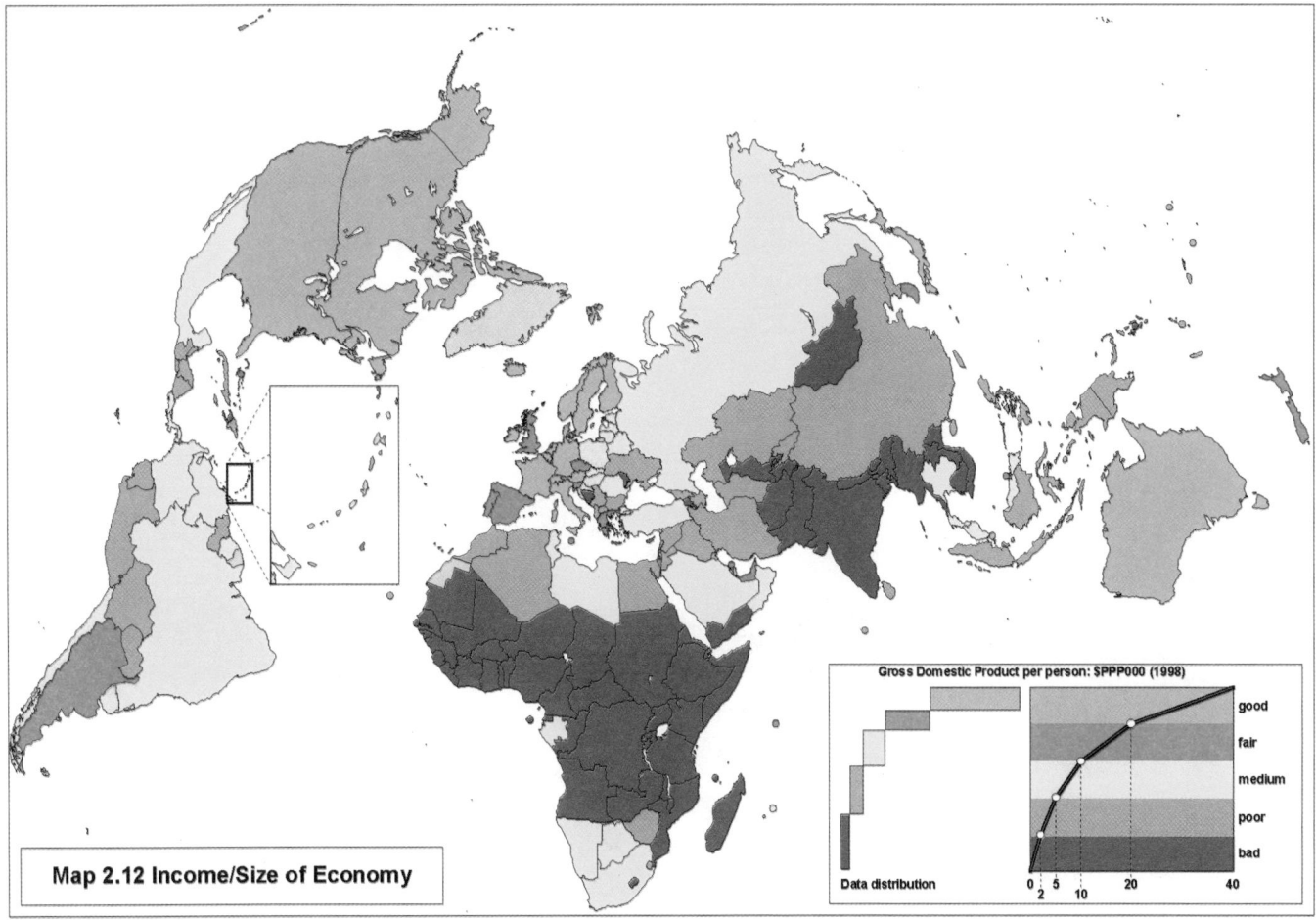

Map 2.12 Income/Size of Economy

Gross Domestic Product per person: $PPP000 (1998)

good
fair
medium
poor
bad

Data distribution

0 2 5 10 20 40

Securing the added benefits of human wellbeing takes higher incomes, as shown by comparing income with a combined score for health and population, knowledge, and community (Figure 2.9). Good scores predominate among countries with incomes above $20,000, fair scores above $10,000, and medium scores above $5,000. Only nine countries (five of which are in West Asia) have incomes above $10,000 but scores below fair. Almost all nations with incomes of $2,000 or less have poor or bad scores.[13]

National Wealth

National Wealth Index (Map 2.13)

What it is: Weighted average scores for three subelements [weights in brackets]: size of economy [2], inflation and unemployment [1], and debt [1] (Figure 2.10).

Objective: Sufficient resources to promote enterprise and maintain prosperity.

Country results: 6 good (3%), 23 fair (13%), 47 medium (26%), 54 poor (30%), 50 bad (28%).

Size of economy (GDP per person) is the main indicator of national wealth. Inflation was included to show whether real incomes are being eroded by rising prices, unemployment to measure the social impact of policies to control inflation, and debt to indicate if countries are living within their means. These additional indicators produce some dramatic shifts, demoting some countries from good to fair (high public debt and unemployment in Italy), fair to medium (the same in Greece and Argentina), and medium to poor (high inflation and public and external debt in Turkey); and promoting others from bad to poor (low inflation and unemployment in Bangladesh; moderate external and public debt in Bhutan) and poor to medium (low inflation and unemployment and moderate external debt in China). (Growth is not a separate indicator but can be measured by annual changes in the size of economy indicator or in the national wealth index.)

The financial crisis that blitzed Pacific Asia in 1997 and spread to Russia, South Africa, and Latin America in 1998 demonstrated that institutional and social factors are just as vital for a strong economy as strictly economic

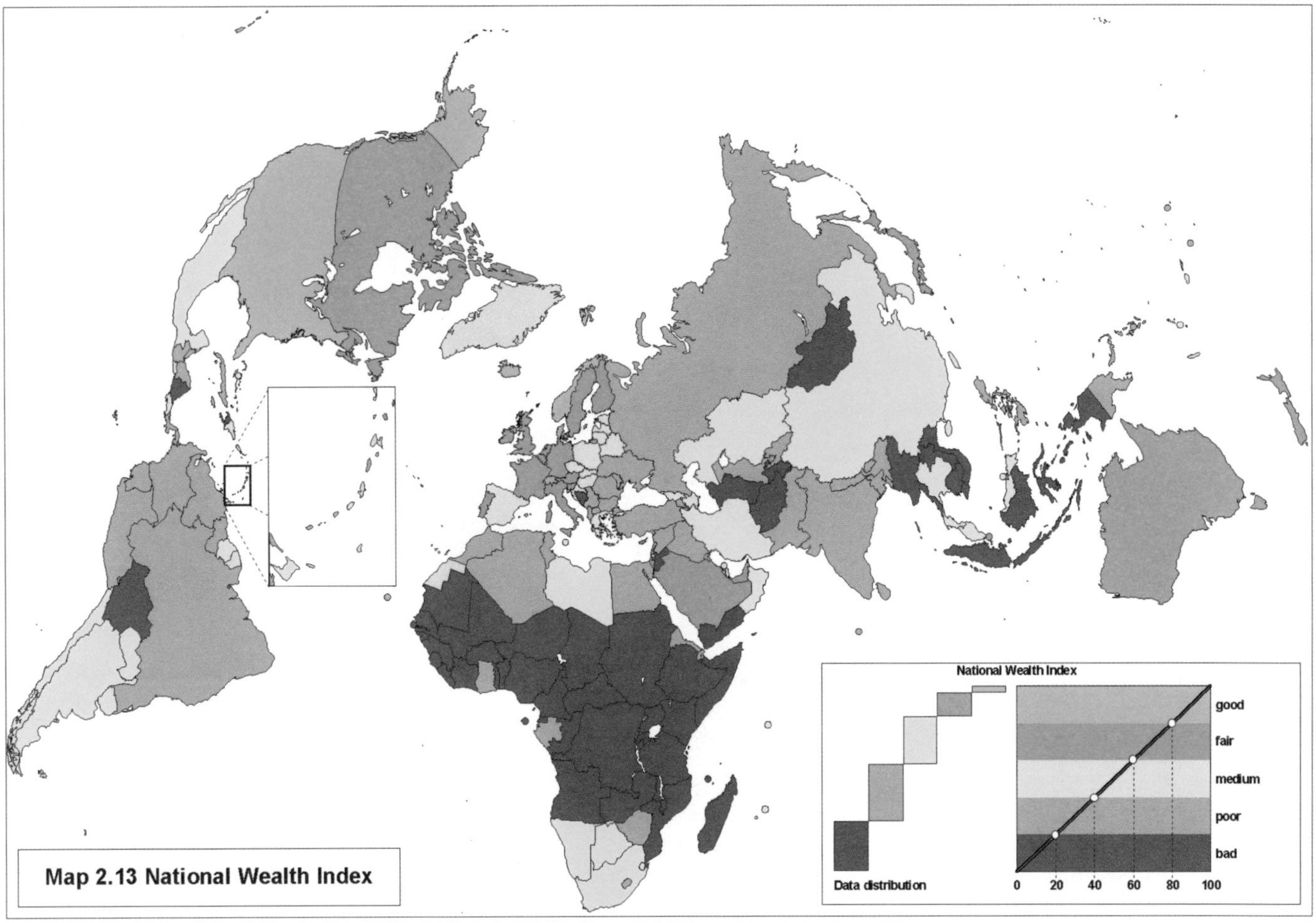

Map 2.13 National Wealth Index

National Wealth Index

good
fair
medium
poor
bad

Data distribution   0   20   40   60   80   100

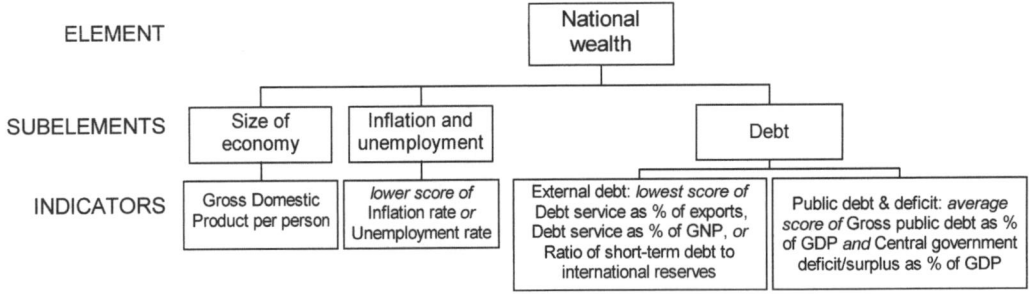

Figure 2.10. Indicator chart for national wealth.

ones: adequate regulation of the financial sector, separation of big business and government, open decision making and a free and vigilant press to give people confidence in markets and regulatory bodies, an education and research system that equips people to innovate, and a political system that can maintain social harmony while coping with economic shocks. To the extent possible, these are covered later in this chapter, under the dimensions of knowledge and community.

Inflation and Unemployment

Inflation and Unemployment (Map 2.14)

What it is: Lower score of inflation rate and unemployment rate.

Country results: 13 good (7%), 19 fair (11%), 29 medium (16%), 28 poor (16%), 13 bad (7%), 78 no data (43%).

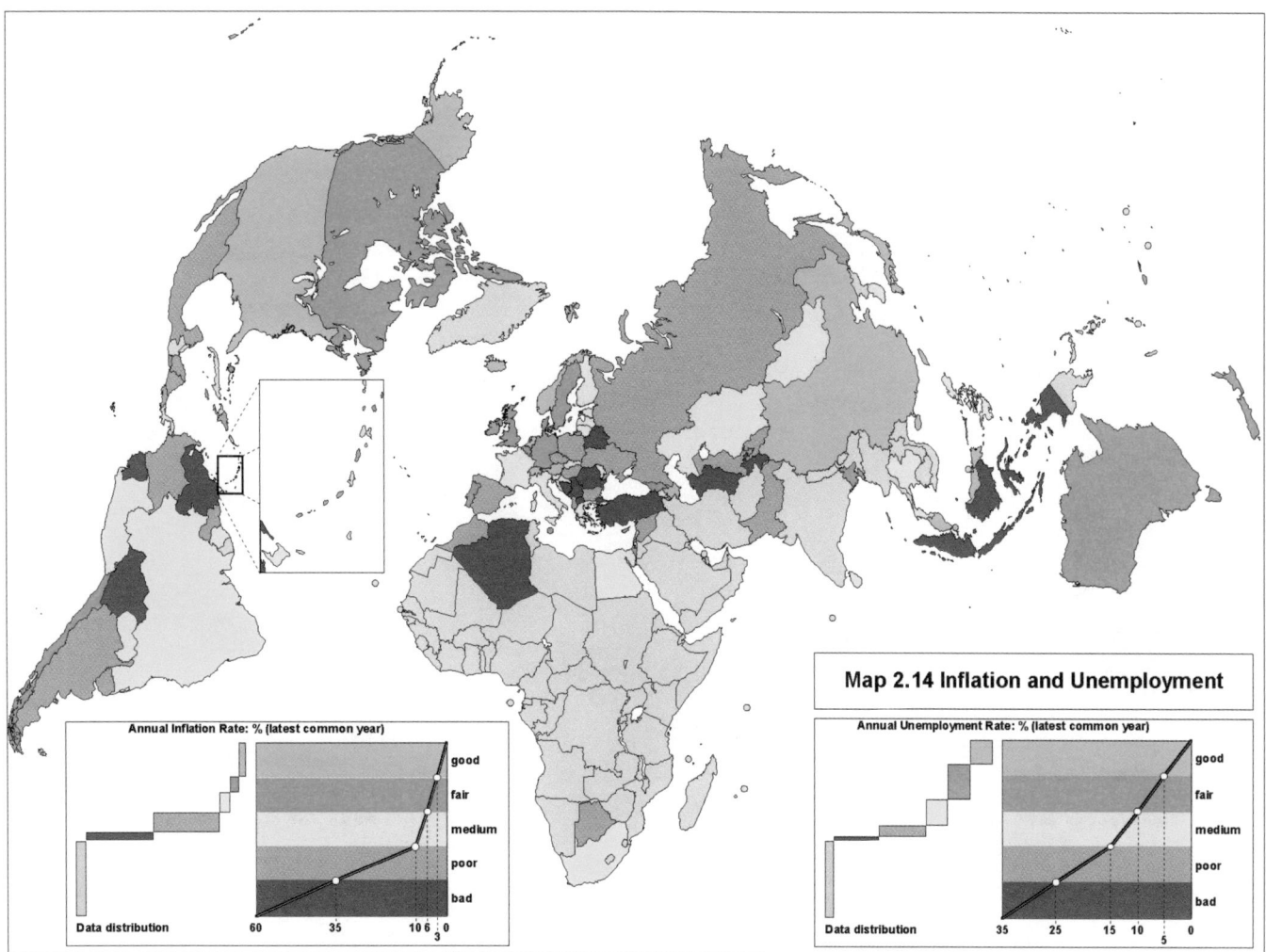

Map 2.14 Inflation and Unemployment

Annual Inflation Rate: % (latest common year)

good
fair
medium
poor
bad

Data distribution   60   35   10 6 0
                                      3

Annual Unemployment Rate: % (latest common year)

good
fair
medium
poor
bad

Data distribution   35   25   15 10   0
                                        5

In countries that record both, the annual inflation rate in the late 1990s ranged from 1,005% (Turkmenistan) to –0.8% (Azerbaijan and China) and the annual unemployment rate from 72.5% (Bosnia and Herzegovina) to 0.4% (Uzbekistan).

High inflation causes uncertainty about the future, which reduces investment and the real return on saving, shrinking future growth. Double-digit inflation is unquestionably harmful. Low inflation provides a predictable economic environment for households and businesses. However, negative inflation (deflation) signals a contracting economy, and even extremely low inflation (below 1%) may increase unemployment. Although economists debate how low inflation should be, central bank targets are from 3% to 0%.

Unemployment causes hardship, undermines self-esteem, wastes potential, and is socially divisive. Rates above 10% are generally regarded as undesirable, but rates much below 3% are probably impossible to sustain without driving up prices.

Inflation and unemployment used to be thought of as ends of a seesaw: if one goes down, the other goes up. But the worst of both worlds is possible (high inflation producing high unemployment, as in Ecuador and Russia), and so is the best: low inflation can stabilize output and jobs. Low inflation plus low unemployment are most likely when output is both potentially and actually high (as in the United States during the 1990s). Excluding deflationary economies (such as Azerbaijan), Luxembourg has the best combination of low inflation (1.0%) and low unemployment (2.5%), followed by Switzerland, Norway, Cyprus, and the United States.[14]

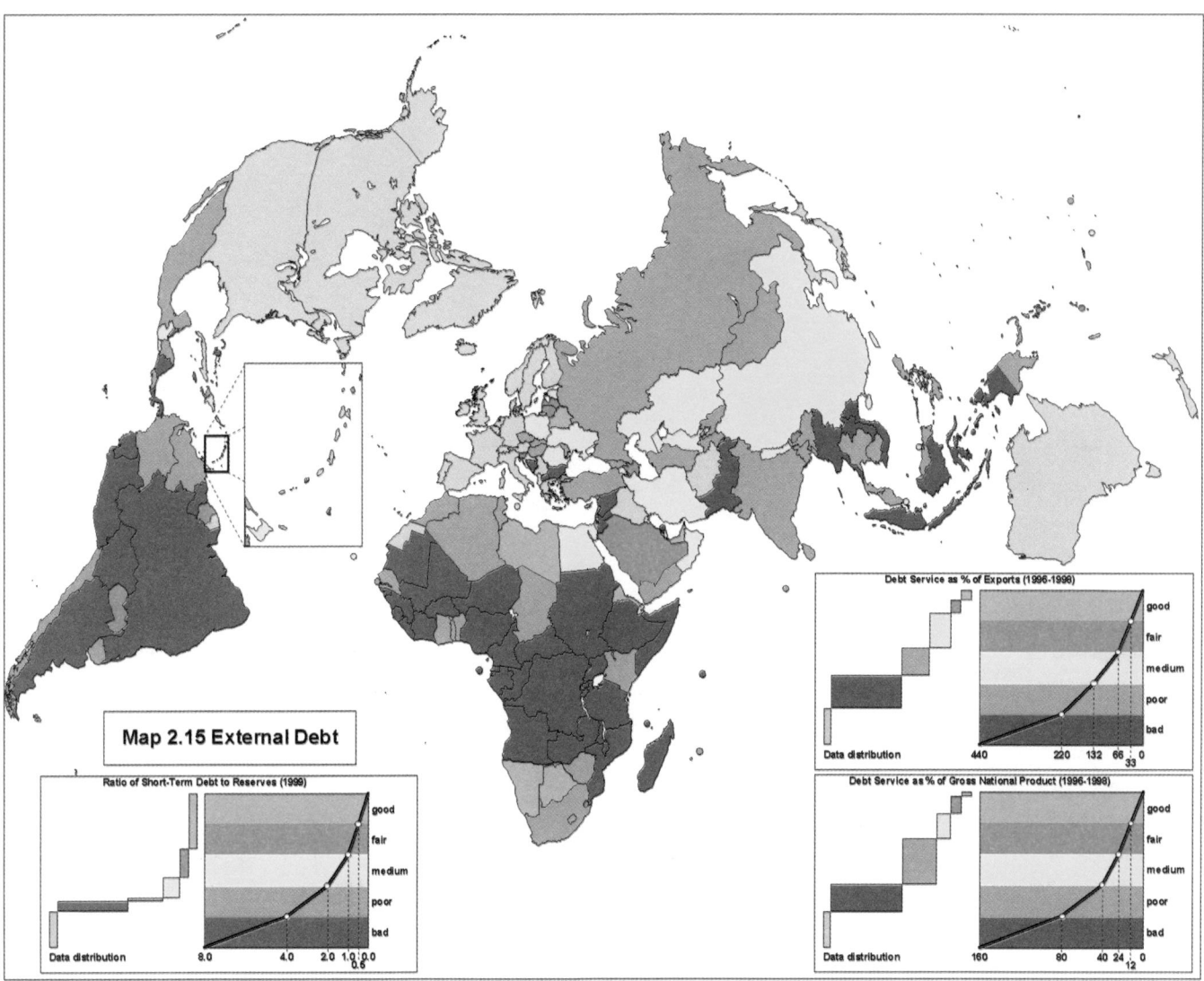

Map 2.15 External Debt

Debt

Of the 58 countries with a bad score, 54 are for external debt, 3 for public debt and deficit (Malta, Lebanon, and Mongolia), and 1 for both (Brazil).

External debt is public and private debt to other countries or to international bodies. It is not recorded for industrialized countries. Debt service as percentages of exports and gross national product (GNP) compare a country's outstanding obligations with its power to pay for them. They are the two main indicators used by the World Bank to classify indebtedness, and the poor and bad performance bands match the World Bank's definitions of moderately and severely indebted, respectively.

The ratio of short-term debt to international reserves emerged during the Asian financial crisis as a key sign of a country's vulnerability to creditor panic. When the ratio exceeds 1.0, international creditors are inclined to

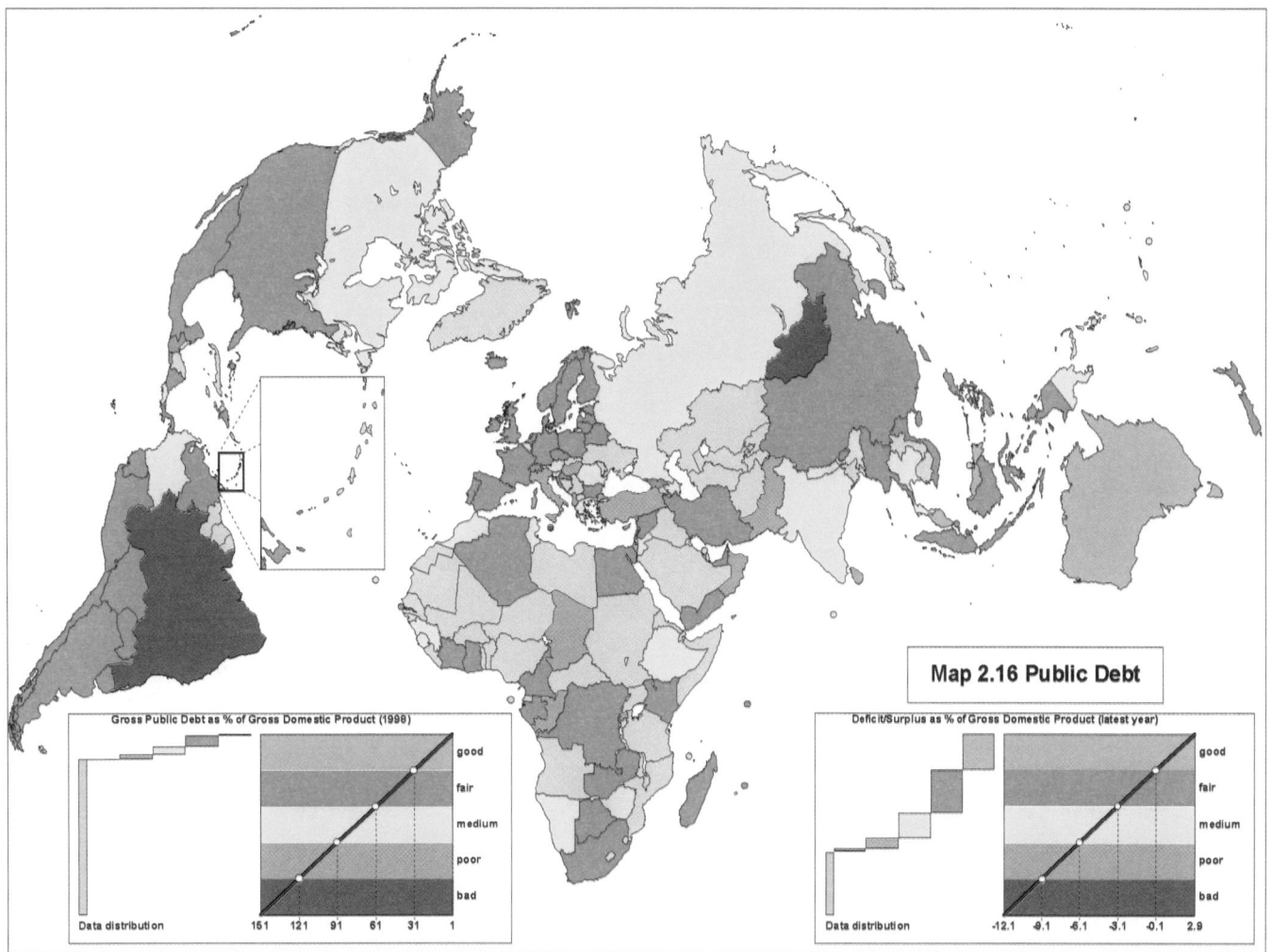

Map 2.16 Public Debt

bolt, which in Pacific Asia led to the runaway depletion of foreign exchange reserves. Short-term debt is more likely to be a practical problem for countries (such as South Korea) that borrow heavily from private sources than for those (such as Cameroon) where most of the debt is owed to much less skittish governments and international bodies. Since economies with open and well regulated access to global capital markets can manage ratios of short-term debt to reserves that are higher than 1.0, some of the more open economies (such as the Bahamas and Singapore) may be unduly penalized by this indicator.

Of the 55 countries with a bad score for external debt, 43 (mostly in Africa) received it for debt service, 6 for short-term debt, and 6 for both.[15]

Public debt consists of the gross financial liabilities of governments and is compiled only for industrialized countries. The public deficit indicator records the central government budget balance and is collected for a variety of countries. The bottom of the fair band corresponds to the standards for an acceptable public debt (60% of GDP) and deficit (3% of GDP) set by the European Union's Treaty of Maastricht.[16]

Of the 33 countries with a good or fair score for debt, 17 were rated for public debt and deficit (the United States, Australia, New Zealand, and 14 European nations), 7 for external debt and public deficit, and 9 for external debt alone.[17]

Knowledge and Culture

Knowledge Index (Map 2.17)

What it is: Weighted average [weights in brackets] of education score [2] and communication score [1] (Figure 2.11).

Objective: Better knowledge to equip people to innovate and cope with change, live well and sustainably, and fulfill their potential.

Country results: 24 good (13%), 26 fair (14%), 56 medium (31%), 24 poor (13%), 50 bad (28%).

Culture (a society's systems of belief and expression) could not be covered here for lack of a suitable indicator.

Knowledge helps people to lead more fulfilling and satisfying lives, deepening their understanding and enjoyment of the world and equipping them with the information and skills required to live well and sustainably. Knowledge is now the most important means of production in post-industrial economies, in the form of knowledge assets (discoveries, patents, and licenses) and market information (what to produce and how, what to sell and when), and as

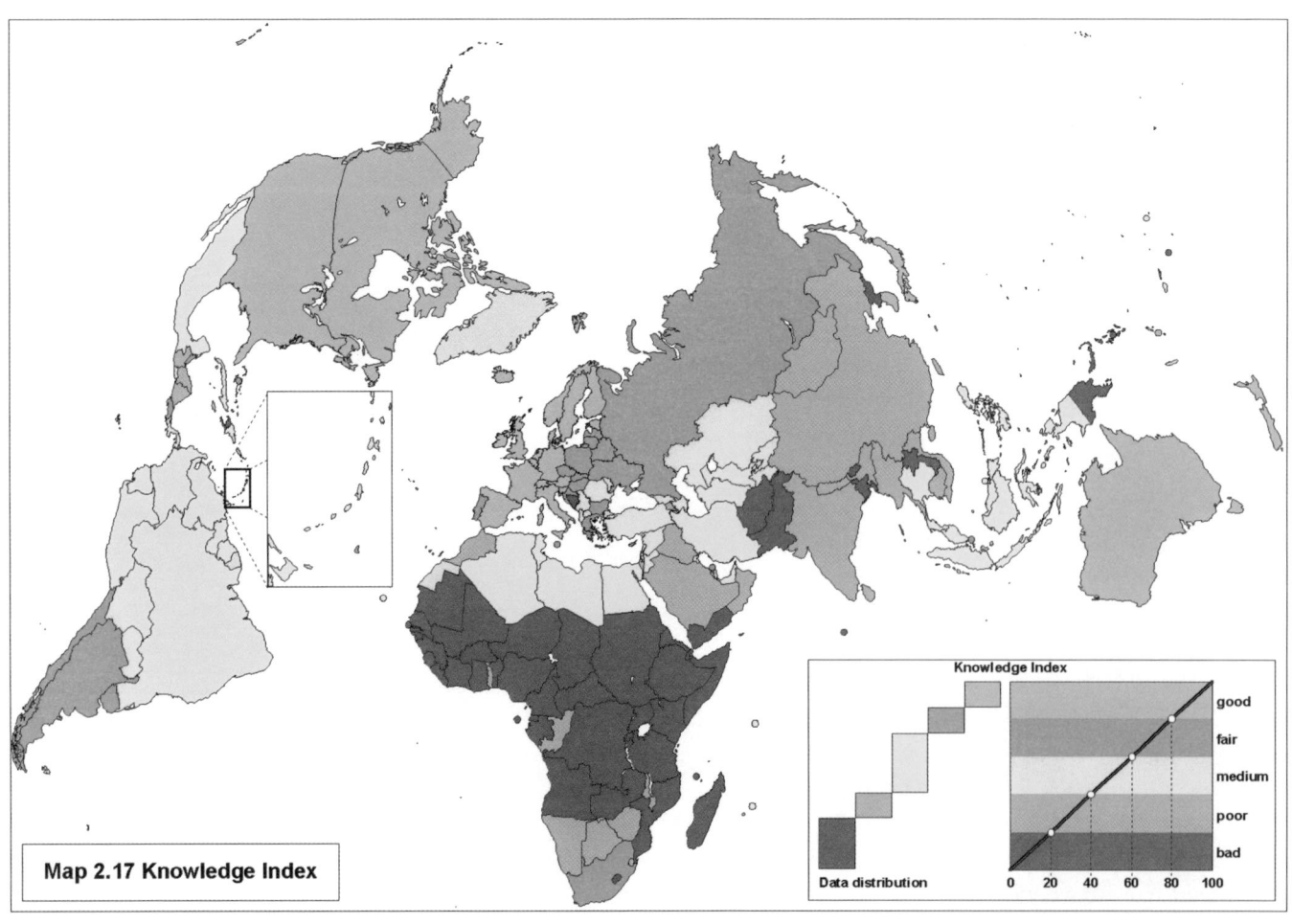

Map 2.17 Knowledge Index

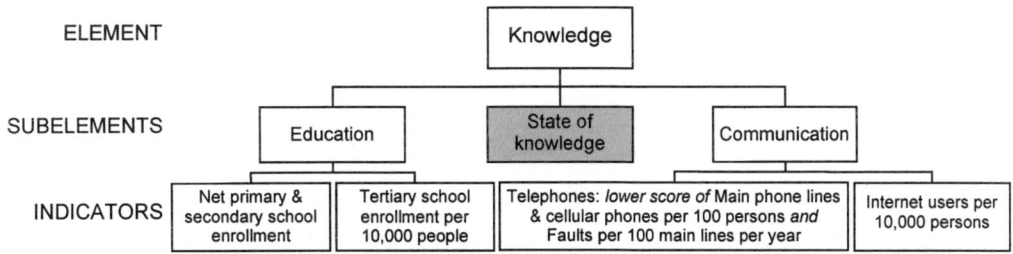

Figure 2.11. Indicator chart for knowledge. State of knowledge (shaded box) is not covered because of lack of a suitable indicator.

the resource of such growth industries as electronics, finance, medicine, communication, and entertainment.[18]

In the absence of a satisfactory way to measure the state of knowledge, the knowledge index gauges education and communication—the formal and informal means of transmitting and sharing knowledge. Countries with a good index have high levels of education and well-developed, widely shared communication systems. Those with a poor or bad index have medium or low scores for education and even lower ones for communication. The performance of countries with a fair or medium index is more mixed. Most (such as Kazakhstan) have a moderately to highly educated population but an underachieving communication sector. A few (such as United Arab Emirates) have an advanced communication system but not the education to make it fully productive.

For all data and scores, together with details of the indicators, performance criteria, and combining procedures, see Table 5 (knowledge) in the Data section.

Education

Education (Map 2.18)

What it is: Average score of two indicators: primary and secondary school enrollment (average score of the net primary and net secondary school enrollment rates) and tertiary school enrollment (students per 10,000 people; Figure 2.11). (The net enrollment rate is the percentage of children of primary or secondary school age who are enrolled in school at the level appropriate for their age.)

Country results: 27 good (15%), 52 fair (29%), 36 medium (20%), 21 poor (12%), 30 bad (17%), 14 no data (8%).

All countries with a good education score have primary enrollment rates above 95%, all but five (Belarus, Esto-

nia, Iceland, Portugal, and Russia) have secondary enrollment rates above 90%, and all but three (Czech Republic, Germany, and Libya) have tertiary enrollment rates above 280 students per 10,000 people. High enrollment rates from primary school to university are signs not just of participation in education but also of educational attainment. Although it is possible for semiliterate individuals to reach and graduate from university, the percentages of children who enter secondary school and then a college or university are a reasonably reliable measure of successful completion of the levels below.

A more direct guide to a nation's level of education would be functional literacy: the ability to understand and use the information required to function effectively in a knowledge-dependent society. This includes the capacity to understand and use information from printed texts, to locate and use information in different formats (such as maps, tables, and charts), and to use and calculate numbers. However, functional literacy has been measured in few countries: one of the most thorough assessments, the International Adult Literacy Survey (IALS), covers only 12. The widely available adult literacy rate is an unsuitable gauge of educational attainment because its reliability is questionable and it does not measure functional literacy. Often the censuses and other household surveys that obtain the data merely ask people whether they are literate (or household heads how many in the household are literate). Literacy is usually defined in its narrowest sense, as the ability to read and write a simple statement about everyday life. Consequently, the adult literacy rate can show how many people are on the literacy ladder but not how far up they have gone. Thus Poland's adult literacy rate is reported to be 99.7%, although the IALS found that a mere 57.4% of the adult population has a level of prose literacy adequate for reading the dosage on a medicine bottle (i.e., above level 1 in Figure 2.12).[19]

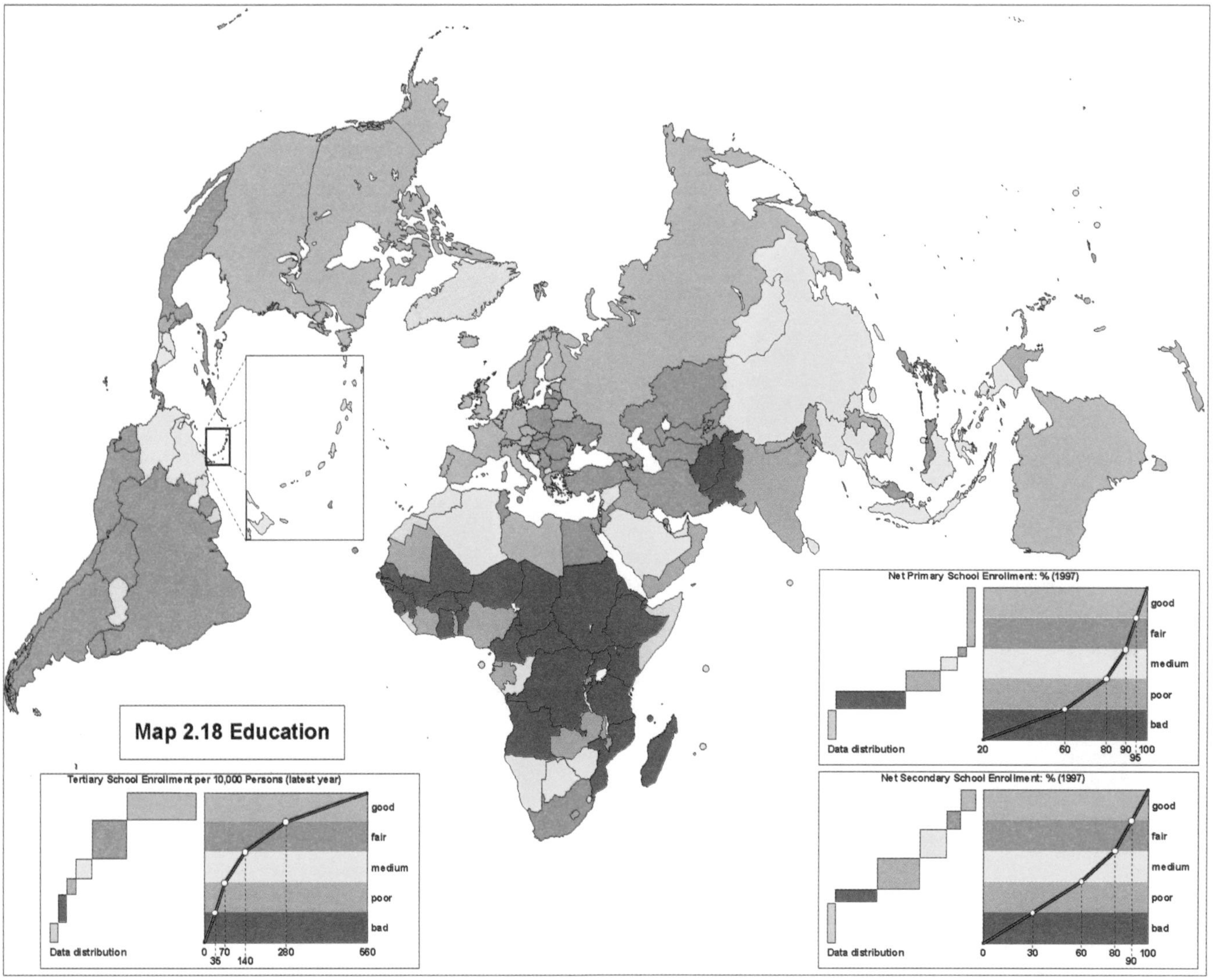

Map 2.18 Education
Tertiary School Enrollment per 10,000 Persons (latest year)
good
fair
medium
poor
bad
Data distribution
0 35 70 140 280 560
Net Primary School Enrollment: % (1997)
good
fair
medium
poor
bad
Data distribution
20 60 80 90 95 100
Net Secondary School Enrollment: % (1997)
good
fair
medium
poor
bad
Data distribution
0 30 60 80 90 100

Without assessing different levels of literacy, it is impossible to tell what proportions of the so-called literate population are scarcely literate, highly literate, or in between. The IALS found that the percentages at each literacy level vary greatly: Poland has a high percentage of scarcely literate (42.6%) and a low percentage of highly literate (3.1%); Sweden the reverse (7.5% and 32.4%, respectively); Germany has low percentages of both (14.4% and 13.4%); the United States high percentages of both (20.7% and 21.1%).

Net primary school enrollment ranges from 13% (Bhutan) to almost 100% (50 countries), net secondary enrollment from 8% (Rwanda) to virtually 100% (eight countries), and tertiary enrollment from 3 students per 10,000 people (Djibouti) to 611 students (South Korea). Enrollment drops—often sharply—from primary to secondary school in all countries except the Republic of Congo, where it rises from 78% to 84%, and the eight countries

100
90
80
70
60
%
50
40
30
20
10
0
adult literacy rate
level 1
level 2
level 3
levels 4-5

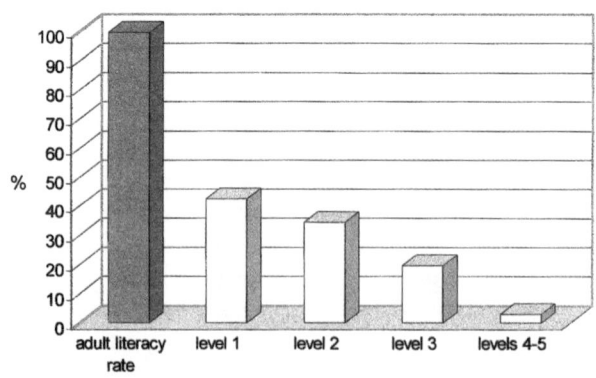

Figure 2.12. Poland's adult literacy rate (blue) compared with levels of functional literacy (yellow). Level 1 = scarcely literate (may be unable to read the dosage on a medicine bottle); level 2 = borderline literate (can deal only with simple messages); level 3 = adequately literate (minimum desirable threshold in many countries); levels 4 and 5 = highly literate (able to integrate several sources of information or solve more complex problems).

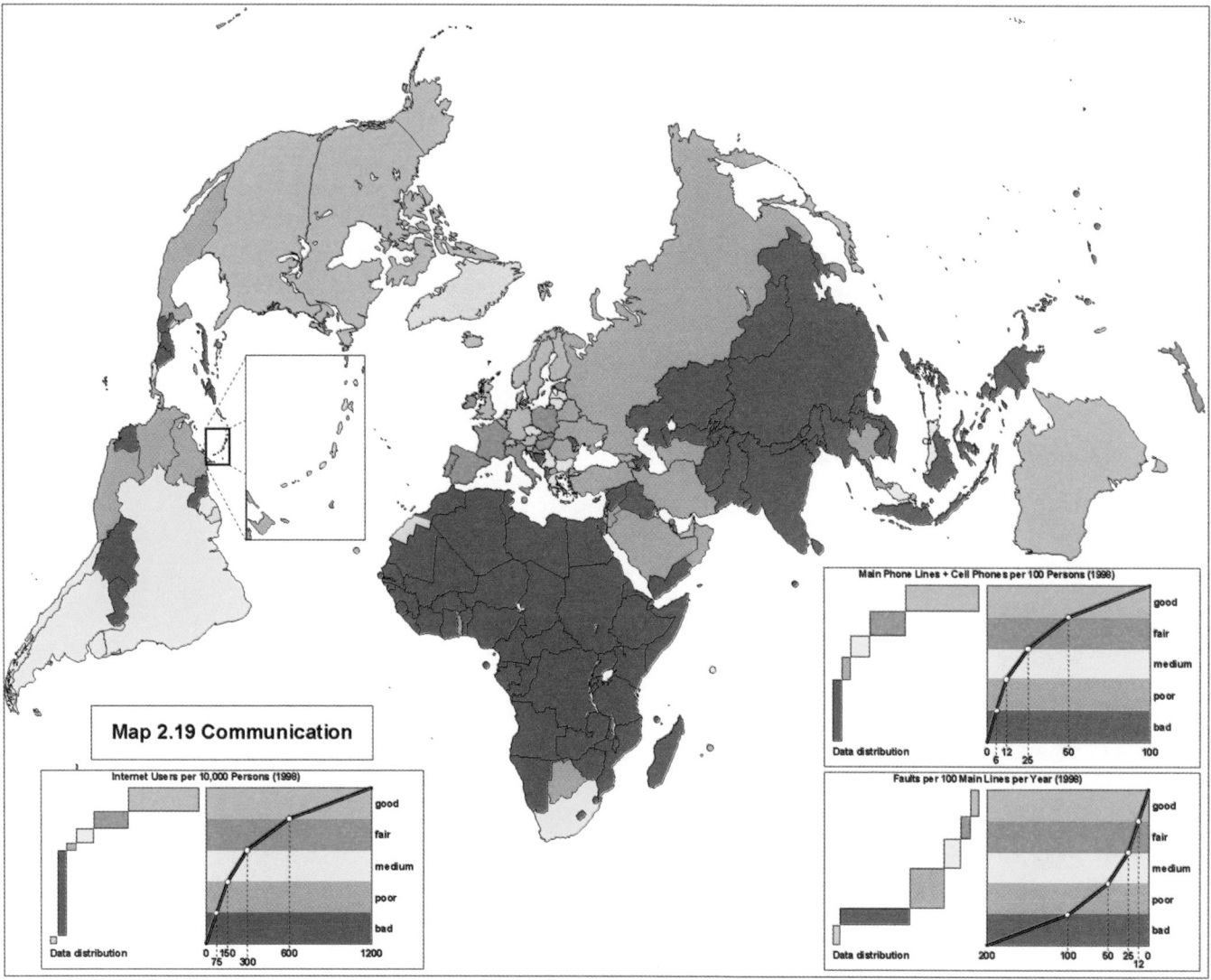

Map 2.19 Communication

Internet Users per 10,000 Persons (1998)

Data distribution

good
fair
medium
poor
bad

0 150 300   600   1200
   75

Main Phone Lines + Cell Phones per 100 Persons (1998)

Data distribution

good
fair
medium
poor
bad

0 12 25   50   100
   6

Faults per 100 Main Lines per Year (1998)

Data distribution

good
fair
medium
poor
bad

200   100   50 25 0
                    12

with almost 100% in both. Tertiary enrollment seldom matches the primary and secondary rates. This is partly because the former is measured as a proportion of the total population and the latter as percentages of the primary and secondary school-age populations. But large discrepancies reflect real differences in the numbers of children who go on from high school to university. They are much lower than expected in Southern Africa and Southern Asia (Mauritius has a 68% secondary enrollment rate but only 57 tertiary students per 10,000 people; Cambodia, a 39% secondary enrollment rate and a mere eight tertiary students per 10,000 people) and much higher than expected in Central America (Panama has 302 tertiary students per 10,000 people, despite a 71% secondary enrollment rate).

The performance criteria for the indicators reflect United Nations' targets for universal primary education and literacy (interpreting the latter as functional literacy). The countries with the largest proportions of highly literate adults (Sweden, Canada, and the United States) have tertiary enrollment rates of 312, 595, and 534 students per 10,000 people, respectively. The good band for tertiary enrollment was set to include the lowest of these rates.[20]

Communication

Communication (Map 2.19)

What it is: Average score of telephone indicator and Internet users per 10,000 persons; the telephone indicator is the lower score of main telephone lines and cellular phone subscribers per 100 persons and faults per 100 main lines per year.

Country results: 20 good (11%), 20 fair (11%), 23 medium (13%), 26 poor (14%), 91 bad (51%).

Communication includes all media from puppet shows to books. But the focus here is on the telephone and Internet because together they provide people with an independent means of talking to each other, revolutionary access to information, and a cheap and convenient way to tell their stories and sell their wares.

Not surprisingly, telecommunication development and Internet use go together. Countries with a good communication score have advanced and reliable telephone systems and large numbers of Internet users. Those with a bad score have meager and unreliable phone systems and few people on the Internet. The number of countries with a bad score rises from 78 based on the telephone indicators alone to 91 including Internet use (more than for any other indicator), suggesting that the knowledge revolution is widening the gap between the haves and have-nots. Most of Africa and much of Southern Asia have under three main lines and mobile phone subscribers per 100 people, and fewer than 10 Internet users per 10,000.

The 69 countries with neither a good nor bad score have contradictory mixtures of performance. Internet use is lower than expected from the medium to fair state of the phone network in 19 countries (such as Barbados and Hungary) and higher than expected, given the frustrations of faulty lines, in 20 (such as Uruguay and Latvia).[21]

Community

A desirable community upholds the freedom and rights of its members, has an open and clean government, is peaceful, and is safe from violence and crime. Only Switzerland and Austria seem able to find the required balance of personal autonomy and social harmony and have a good community index. The rest of the world falls short in one aspect or another—a little in countries with a fair index, a lot in those with a poor or bad index.

Countries with a fair index fall into three groups, represented by Japan, Canada, and Benin (Figure 2.13). Japan (and Hungary, Malta, and Slovakia) are just as peaceful as Switzerland and Austria but not as free or as unblemished by corruption. Canada (along

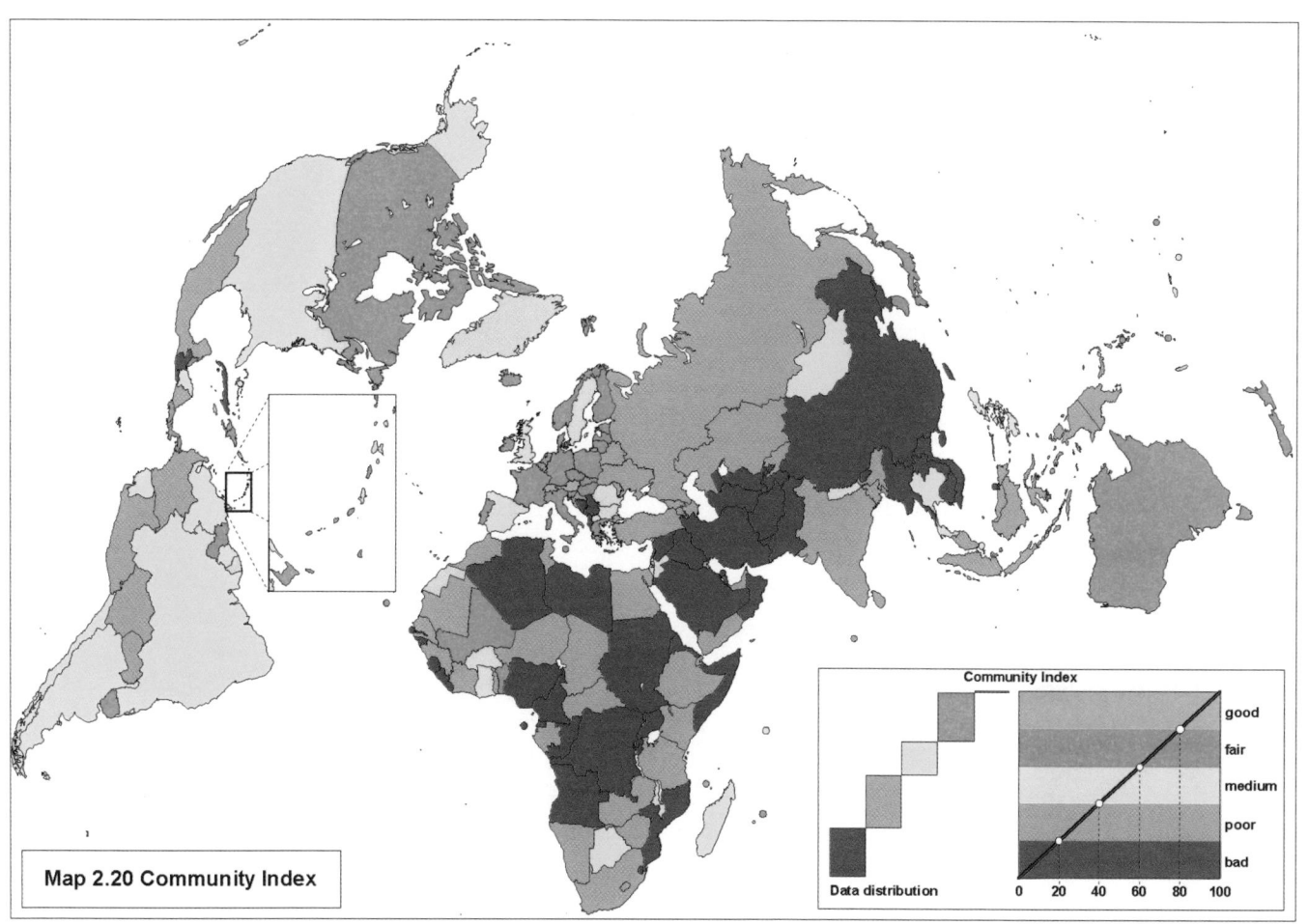

Map 2.20 Community Index

Community Index

good
fair
medium
poor
bad

Data distribution

0   20   40   60   80   100

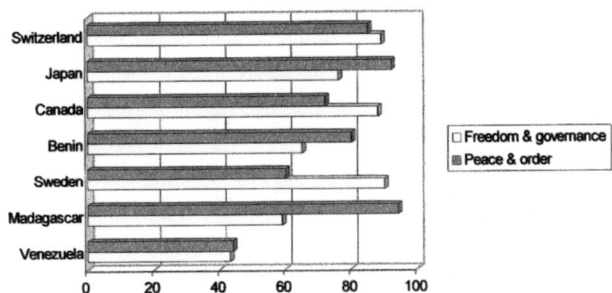

Figure 2.13. Community indices from medium to good. The index is the lower of the two scores (medium = 41–60, fair = 61–80, good = 81–100).

with Australia, New Zealand, and much of Northern Europe) are as free and well governed but have lower scores for peace and order. Benin (and the remaining fair index countries) have fair scores for both elements.

Countries with a medium index also fall into three groups, represented by Sweden, Madagascar, and Venezuela. Most have a high score for peace and order but a medium grade for freedom and governance due to corruption (the majority), limited civil liberties (e.g., Madagascar), or a restricted press (e.g., Nepal). Some have the reverse, their flaws being high crime rates (Sweden, the United States, Chile, Bahamas, Jamaica, Botswana) or armed conflict (Spain and the United Kingdom). Venezuela (and Ecuador, Suriname, Israel, Philippines, and Tonga) have medium scores for both elements.

Countries with a poor or bad index have almost uniformly low scores for both elements. Only 23 of the 100 have a fair score for peace and order—and half of these have no data on crime, so their high ratings may be false. A mere six (Bolivia, St Vincent and Grenadines, Namibia, São Tomé and Principe, South Africa, and Papua New Guinea) have a fair score for freedom and governance. More than a third (37) endure wretched mixtures of oppression, corruption, and violence, with poor or bad ratings across the board. Most (32) are in Africa and Asia, including all of Northern Africa, almost all of Central and East Africa, and West and Central Asia.

For all data and scores, together with details of the indicators, performance criteria, and combining procedures, see Table 6 (community index, freedom and governance, peace) and Table 7 (crime) in the Data section.

Freedom and Governance

> ### Freedom and Governance Index (Map 2.21)
>
> **What it is:** Average score of four indicators: political rights rating, civil liberties rating, press freedom rating (Map 2.22), and corruption perceptions index (Map 2.23) (Figure 2.14).
>
> **Objective:** Human rights fully respected; people free to choose how decisions are made and who should make them; decision-making bodies open, clean, and effective.
>
> **Country results:** 15 good (8%), 48 fair (27%), 36 medium (20%), 47 poor (26%), 34 bad (19%).

Freedom and governance are strongest in Northern Europe (all countries good or fair), followed by North and Central America and the Pacific (all countries good, fair, or medium). Close behind are the West Indies, South America, Eastern and Southern Europe, and Southern Africa, where only a handful of countries have a poor or bad index—in contrast to the rest of Africa and all Asia, where they are still in the majority.

The four indicators overlap to some extent but together produce more consistent results than if any were omitted. Freedom House's political rights rating (PRR) and civil liberties rating (CLR) provide comprehensive measurements of freedom. The PRR assesses

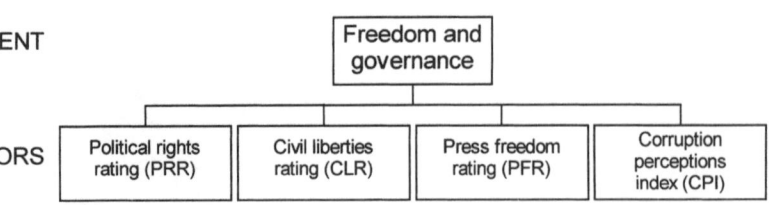

Figure 2.14. Indicator chart for freedom and governance.

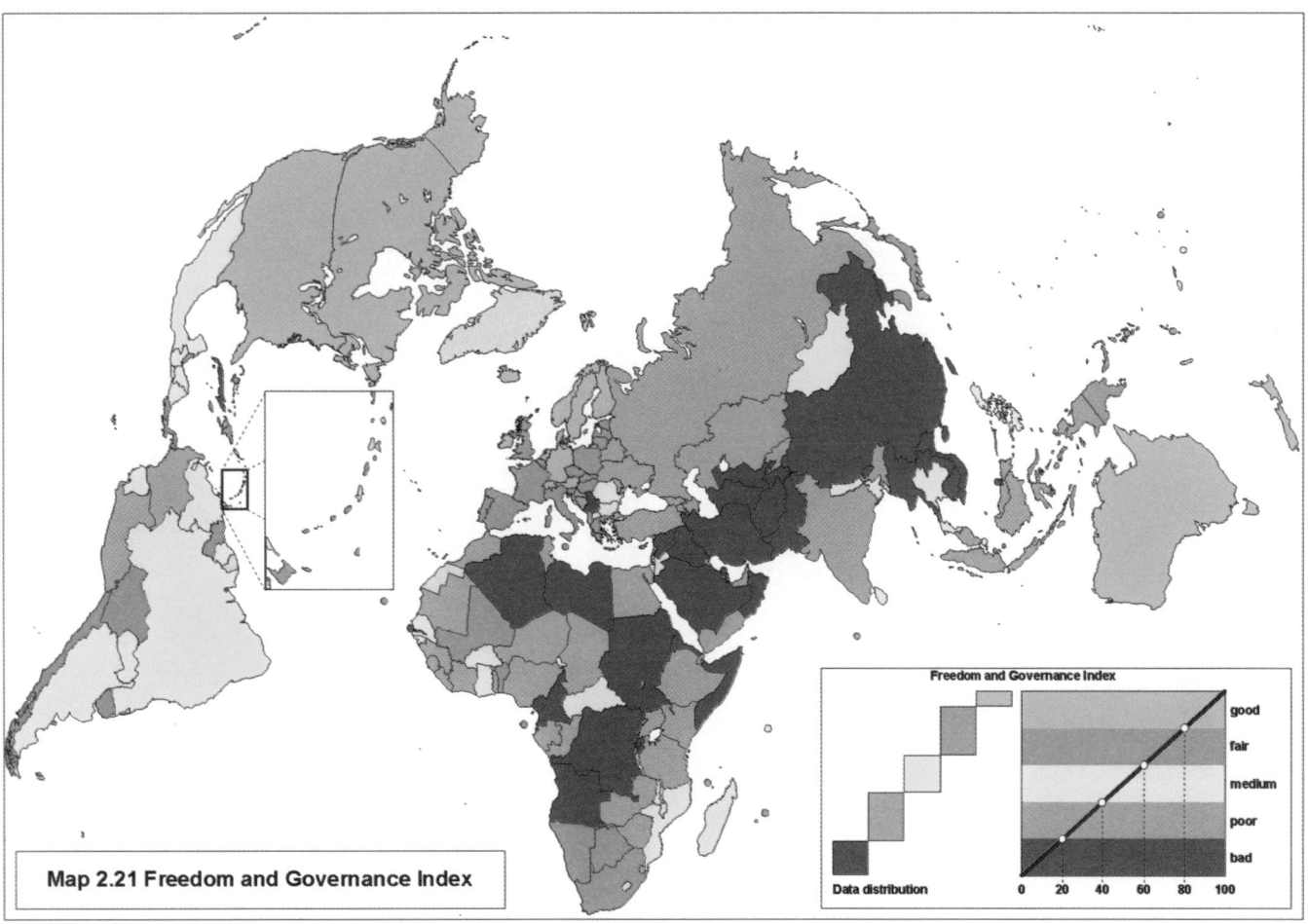

Map 2.21 Freedom and Governance Index

Freedom and Governance Index

good
fair
medium
poor
bad

Data distribution   0 20 40 60 80 100

whether all members of society have the right to choose their decision-making system and select who makes decisions. The CLR measures the practice of economic freedoms (e.g., secure property rights and free collective bargaining), freedoms of belief and expression (including religious tolerance and freedom of assembly), personal freedoms (such as freedom of movement and residence), and the rule of law (an independent judiciary, equal treatment under the law, fair and public hearings, direct civilian control of the police, and protection from political terror, unjustified imprisonment, exile, or torture).

All countries with a good or fair index are electoral democracies, as are 80% of those with a medium index but only a quarter of those with a poor index and none with a bad. Of the 70 countries with undemocratic regimes, 35 have a higher CLR than PRR, but civil liberties are higher only because political rights are so low.

Among the 100 electoral democracies, only 6 (Australia, Cyprus, St Vincent and Grenadines, and the struggling democracies of Indonesia, Nigeria, and Paraguay) have a higher CLR than PRR. This reflects both their more consistent commitment to political rights and the difficulty of upholding the complex array of civil liberties to the fullest extent. Even the most democratic societies are tested by antidemocratic forces: hostility is growing toward immigrants in Norway, anti-Semitism persists in Switzerland (an estimated tenth of the population is against Jews), Nazis are welcome in Austria's Freedom Party, and neo-Nazi groups exploit Denmark's tradition of tolerance.

The other two indicators—Freedom House's press freedom rating (PFR) and Transparency International's corruption perceptions index (CPI)—focus on a specific aspect of freedom and governance, respectively. The PFR (Map 2.22) gauges legal, administrative, political, and

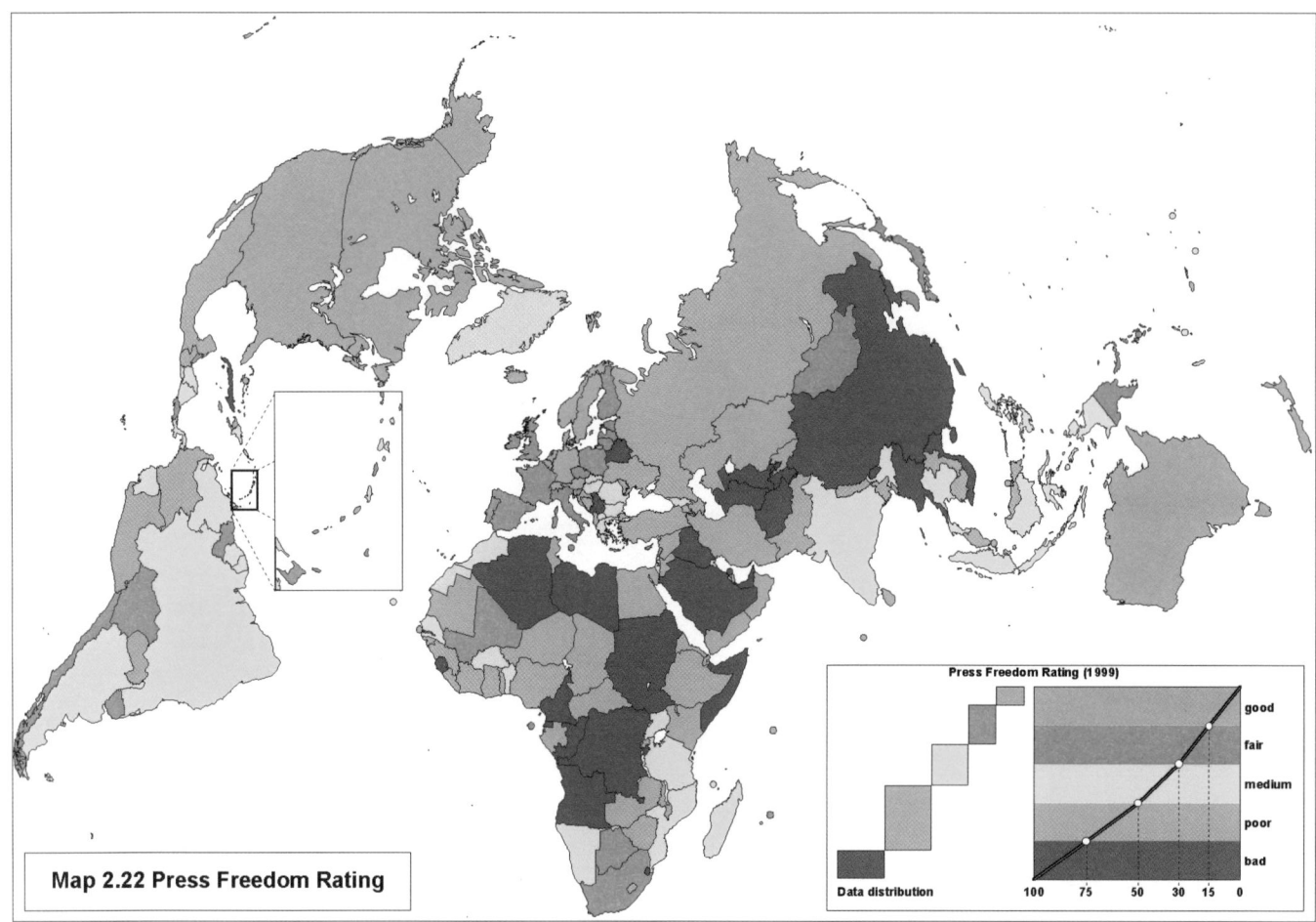

Map 2.22 Press Freedom Rating

Press Freedom Rating (1999)

good
fair
medium
poor
bad

Data distribution   100   75   50   30   15   0

economic influences on media content, as well as violations of press freedoms, such as censorship, harassment, assaults, and murder. The CPI (Map 2.23) measures the level of corruption (the abuse of public office for private gain) among public officials and politicians within a country, as perceived by businesspeople, risk analysts, and the general public.

Press freedom ranges from the total restrictions of Myanmar (where two journalists were tortured to death after their newspaper published an article critical of a military officer) and North Korea (where criticism of the regime or its head may be punished by imprisonment in a labor camp or execution) to the almost unfettered openness of Norway (with a variety of independent national and local newspapers and broadcasting stations, no government interference in the editorial content of state radio and television, and many newspapers subsidized by the state to promote political pluralism).

Among the 100 countries rated between 1997 and 2000, Nigeria and Yugoslavia are the most corrupt and Finland and Denmark the least. A free press is one of the forces that keeps a nation honest, and countries with the freest media usually have the cleanest governments. Most countries with a good or fair PFR also have a good or fair CPI, and most with a poor or bad CPI also have a poor or bad PFR. True to form, the media criticize the government freely and with impunity in Denmark, while journalists in Nigeria are regularly harassed, assaulted, and threatened with death. But there are some striking exceptions. Singapore is one of the least corrupt countries in the world (with the best CPI in Asia–Pacific after New Zealand), but the government tightly controls the media, censors Internet use, and does not tolerate reports of such corruption that exists. In South Korea, corruption is pervasive, although press freedom is growing and news broadcasting in particular is increasingly independent and diverse.[22]

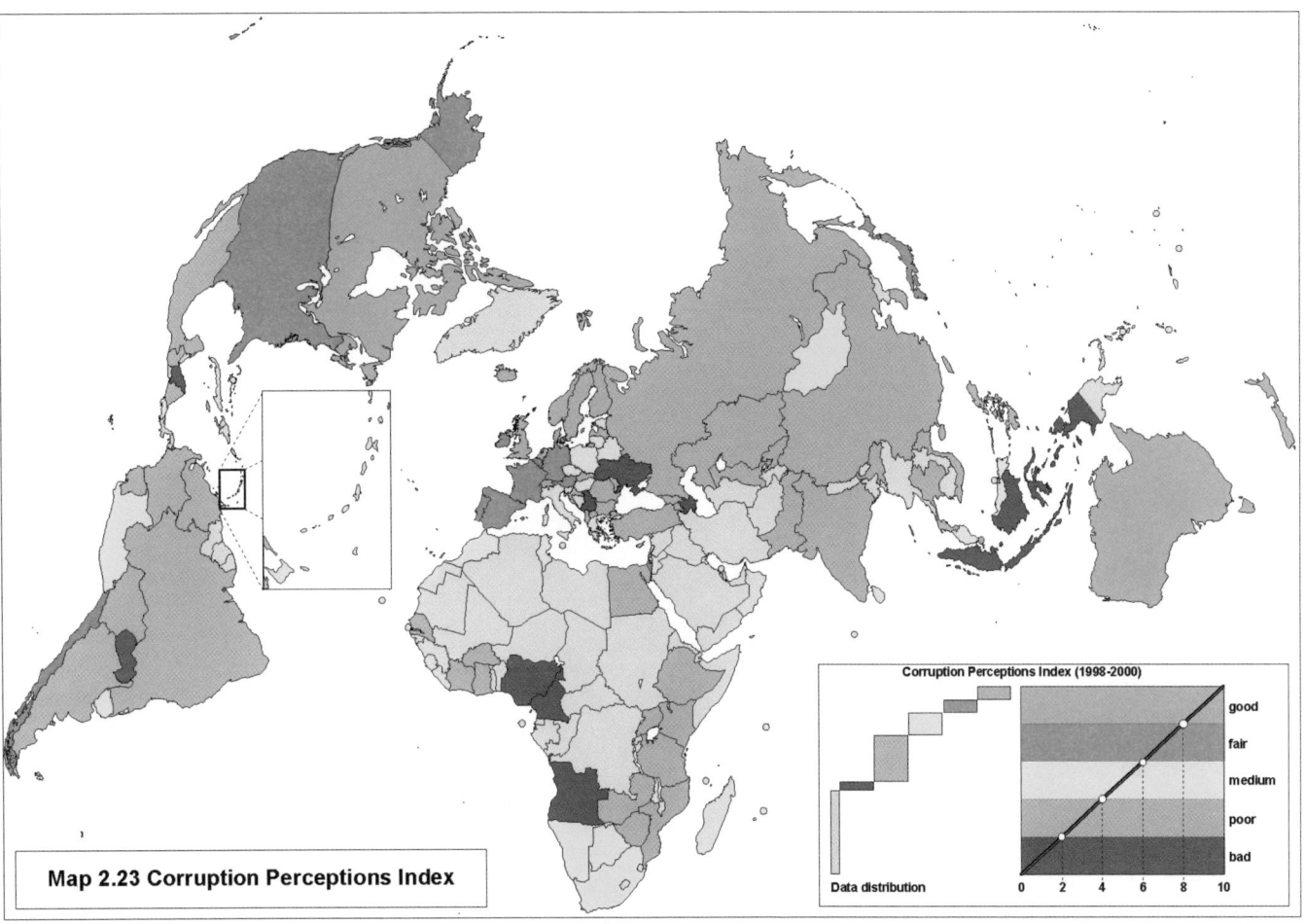

Map 2.23 Corruption Perceptions Index

Corruption Perceptions Index (1998-2000)

Data distribution

good
fair
medium
poor
bad

0   2   4   6   8   10

Peace and Order

Peace and Order Index (Map 2.24)

What it is: Average of peace score and crime score (Figure 2.15).

Objective: Peaceful communities, protected from crime and violence.

Country results: 7 good (4%), 77 fair (43%), 36 medium (20%), 30 poor (17%), 25 bad (14%), 5 no data (3%).

A good or fair peace and order index should mean that the country is not engaged in any armed conflict (apart from peacekeeping missions), military expenditure is a small percentage of GDP, and the violent crime rate is low. This is probably true of countries with a good index, which were assessed on all these aspects. But 33 of those with a fair index may not merit it. Four (St Kitts and Nevis, Maldives, Samoa, and Vanuatu) had

no peace data, and the rest could not be rated on crime: 15 in Africa (all except Egypt, Mauritius, Morocco, and Seychelles), 7 in the Americas (Argentina, Antigua and Barbuda, Belize, Brazil, Dominican Republic, Guyana, and Honduras), 6 in Asia–Pacific (Lao, Mongolia, Turkmenistan, Viet Nam, Fiji, and New Zealand), and Ireland. Europe has the most countries with a good or fair index based on both peace and crime (5 good, 22 fair).

Peace

Peace (Map 2.25)

What it is: Lower score of deaths from armed conflicts per year and military expenditure as a percentage of gross domestic product.

Country results: 39 good (22%), 36 fair (20%), 16 medium (9%), 36 poor (20%), 40 bad (22%), 13 no data (7%).

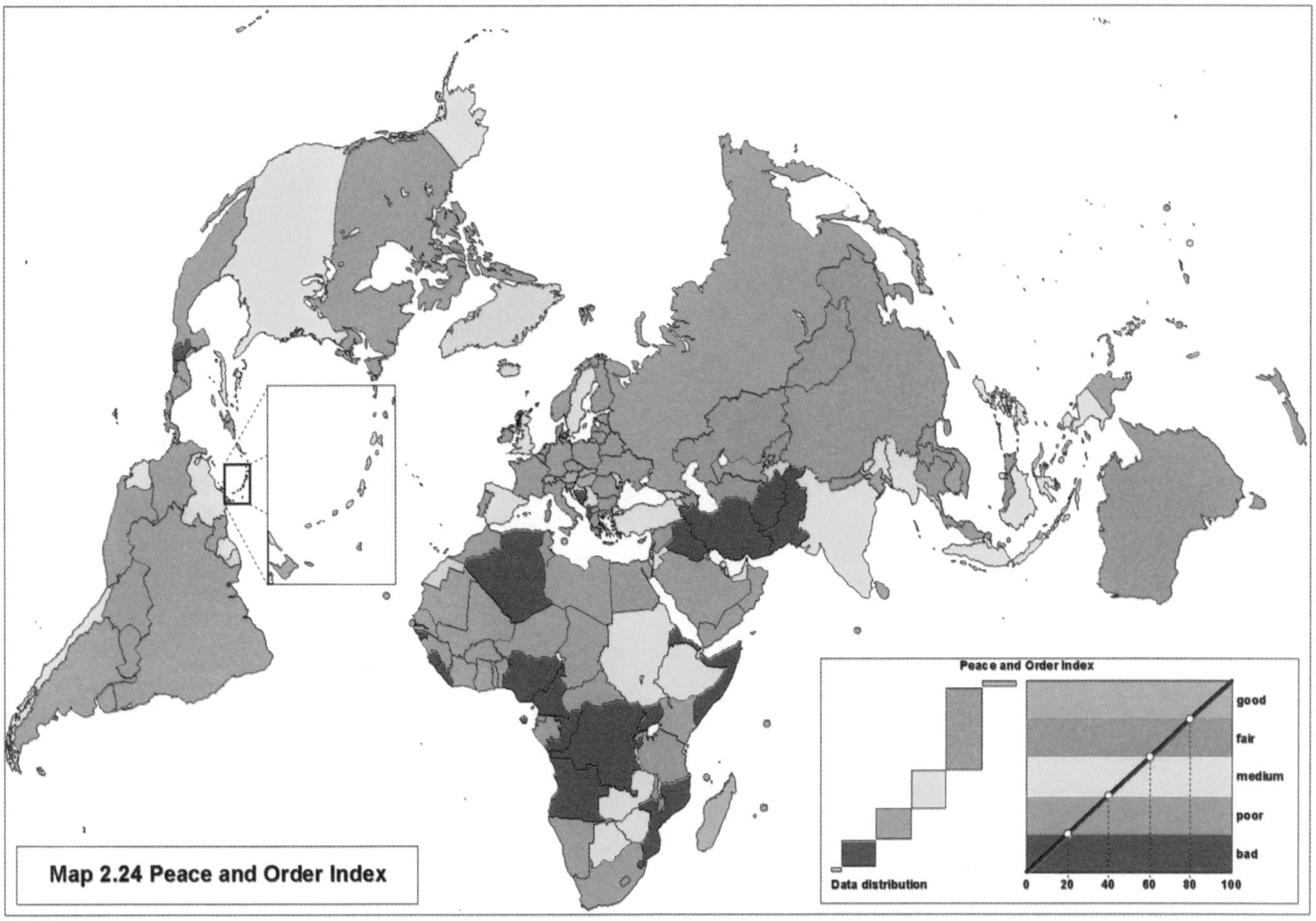

Map 2.24 Peace and Order Index

None of the countries with a good, fair, or medium score for peace is involved in armed conflict (other than international peacekeeping). They differ only in the amount of GDP they devote to the military.

All countries with a bad score and all but six with a poor score have incurred deaths from border and territorial conflicts, internal conflicts, or terrorism between 1995 and 1999. The exceptions (Armenia, Kuwait, Oman, Qatar, Saudi Arabia, and North Korea) have a poor score because their military expenditure exceeds 8% of GDP.

Although required for national defense, military expenditure—which ranges from 0.5% of GDP (Barbados) to 36% of GDP (Eritrea)—is a potentially destructive use of resources that competes with health, education, and other essentials for a prosperous peace. A country isn't necessarily bellicose if it buys guns and pays people to shoot them, but the likelihood of warfare rises with the priority given to fighting: the proportion of countries engaged in conflict increases from 29% (of those spending less than 2% of GDP) to 33% (2–3.9% of GDP) to 61% (4% and above).

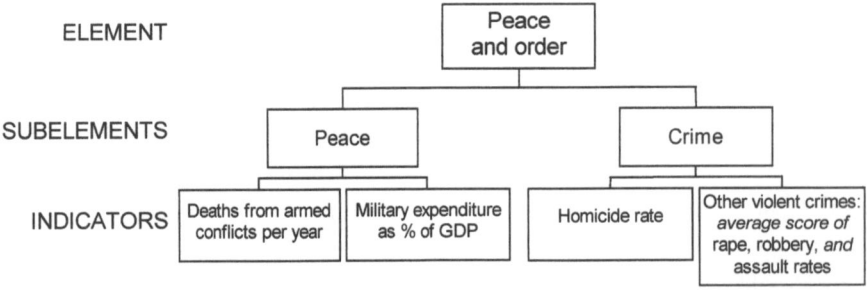

Figure 2.15. Indicator chart for peace and order.

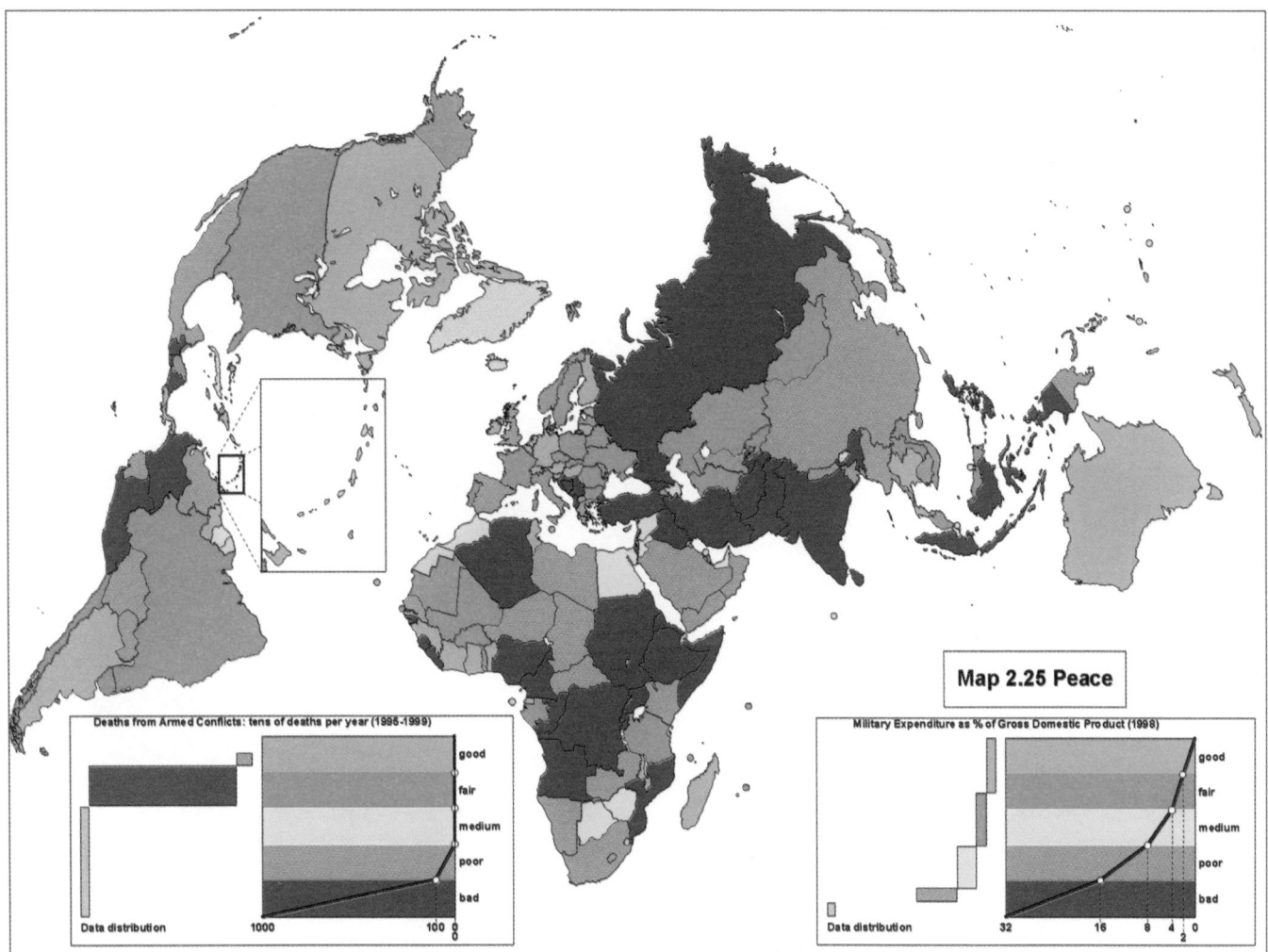

Average annual military and civilian deaths from armed conflicts range from 10 or below in countries subject to sporadic terrorism (such as Paraguay and Uzbekistan) to 84,000 in Rwanda, which has been at war internally since 1990 and in neighboring Democratic Republic of Congo since 1998. Even if a cease fire or peace accord is now in force (such as in Mozambique), all conflicts that occurred in any year between 1995 and 1999 were counted. Average death rates were estimated from the year each conflict started.[23]

Crime

Crime (Map 2.26)

What it is: Average of scores for homicide rate and for other violent crimes (average score for rape, robbery, and assault rates).

Country results: 23 good (13%), 42 fair (23%), 21 medium (12%), 7 poor (4%), 3 bad (2%), 84 no data (47%).

The focus here is on violent crimes because they are more harmful than other offenses and are recorded less erratically. Homicide is further distinguished from the other violent crimes because it is the most serious and is reported more consistently. Crime statistics reflect a combination of actual crime rates and the diligence of the police. If the justice system is weak, records will show unrealistically low rates. This problem is evident in the international data, which for several countries show utopian crime rates.

Homicide rates range from 142 per 100,000 people (São Tomé and Principe) to 0.4 (Madagascar), robbery rates from 688 (Bahrain) to 0.1 (Ethiopia and Syria), and assault rates from 1,487 (Trinidad and Tobago) to 0.2 (Egypt). The rates for rape range from 199 per 100,000 people (Estonia) to essentially 0 (Egypt). However, since women are often blamed if they are raped, victimized by the justice system, and ostracized by their communities, rape is commonly underreported. The data undoubtedly reflect this.

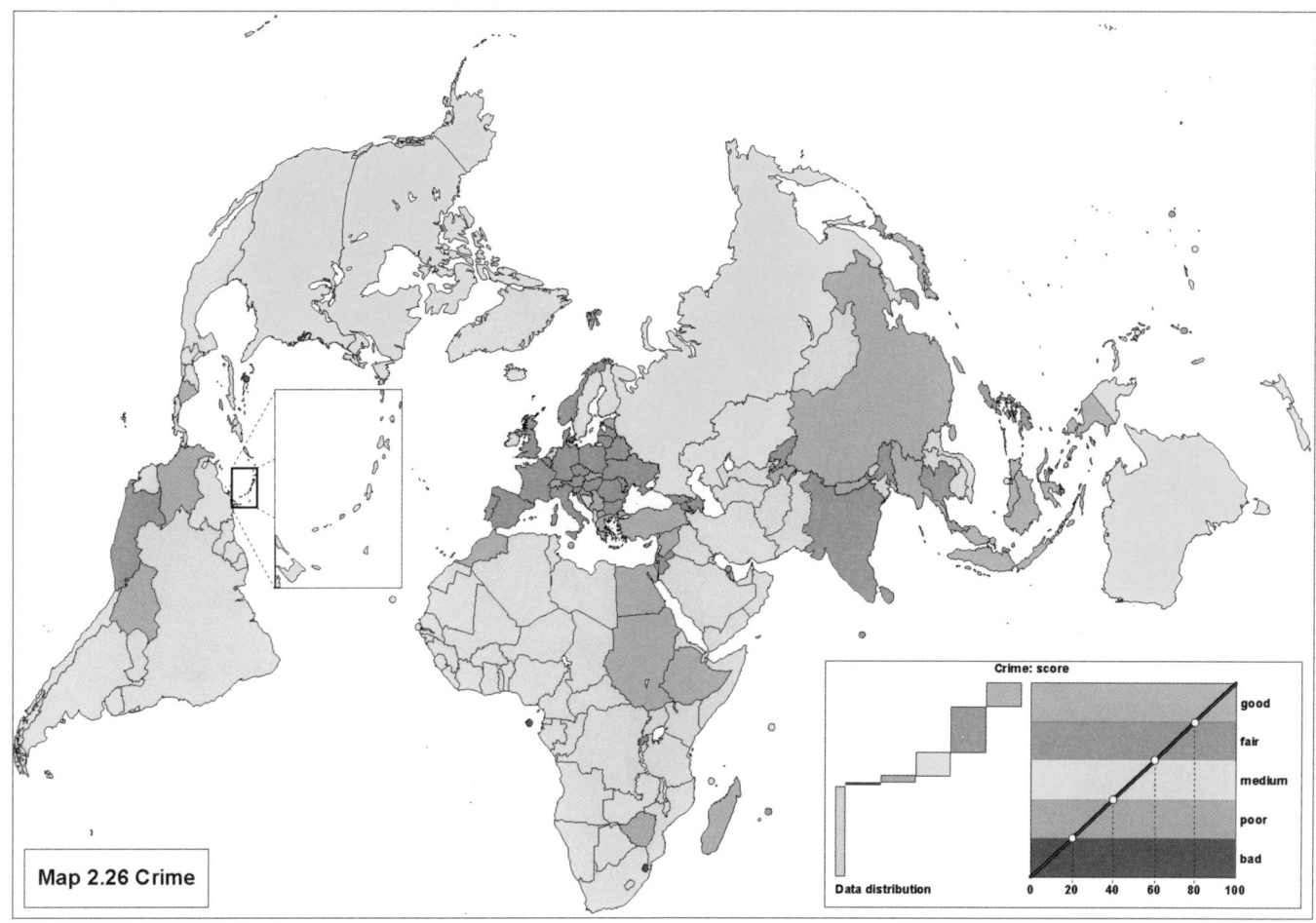

Map 2.26 Crime

In general, countries with a good score for crime report consistently low violent crime rates: homicides below 5 per 100,000 people (except Ethiopia, 7.6, and Yugoslavia, 5.5), rapes below 10, robberies below 40 (except Qatar, 66), and assaults below 80 (except Cyprus, 133). The performance of countries with a fair or medium score is often mixed. Sweden has medium homicide, rape, and robbery rates but a very high assault rate (611). Canada has the widest gap between its scores for homicides (94) and for other violent crimes (18) because it has one of the lowest homicide rates (1.8) but rape and assault rates of 84 and 737, respectively. Bahrain has the highest robbery rate but the fourth lowest homicide rate, and Kuwait has the fifth highest homicide rate but the third lowest rape rate. While almost all countries with a poor or bad score have homicide rates above 20 and robbery rates above 80, their rape and assault rates vary.[24]

Equity

The equity index measures the distribution of wealth and other benefits within the general population of a country (household equity) and between males and females (gender equity). Since health, wealth, knowledge, freedom, peace, and other goods are widely valued, it is right that they be widely shared. The cost of achieving them should also be fairly shared. A society is not well if only a few groups in it enjoy power, privilege, and high levels of the opportunities and benefits that make up wellbeing, while others are weak, disadvantaged, and poor. Large disparities are both unjust and destabilizing.

Of all the human dimensions, equity is unique in having no country with a good index and the fewest with a bad index. The majority of the 69 countries assessed on gender equity alone have medium or poor

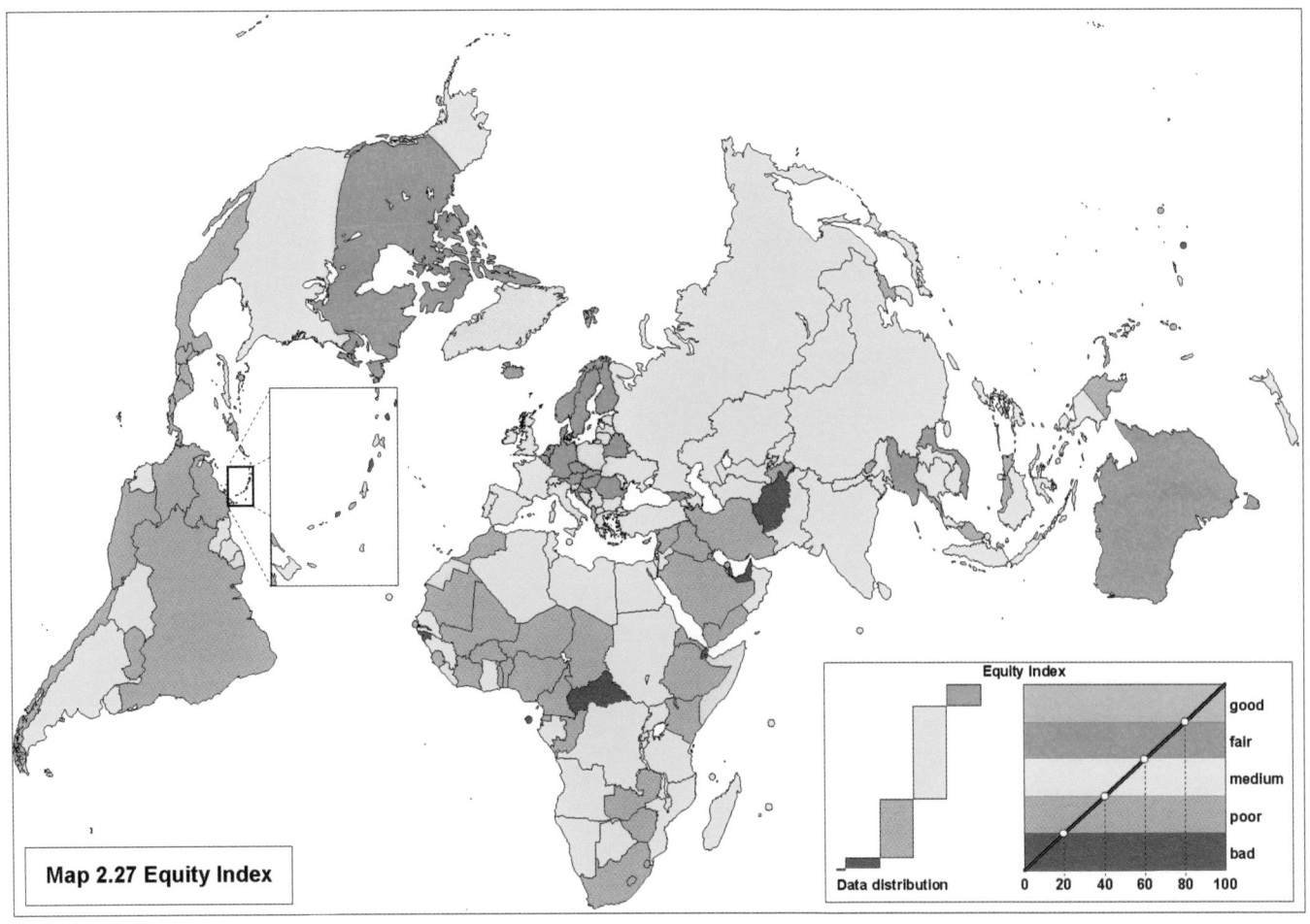

Map 2.27 Equity Index

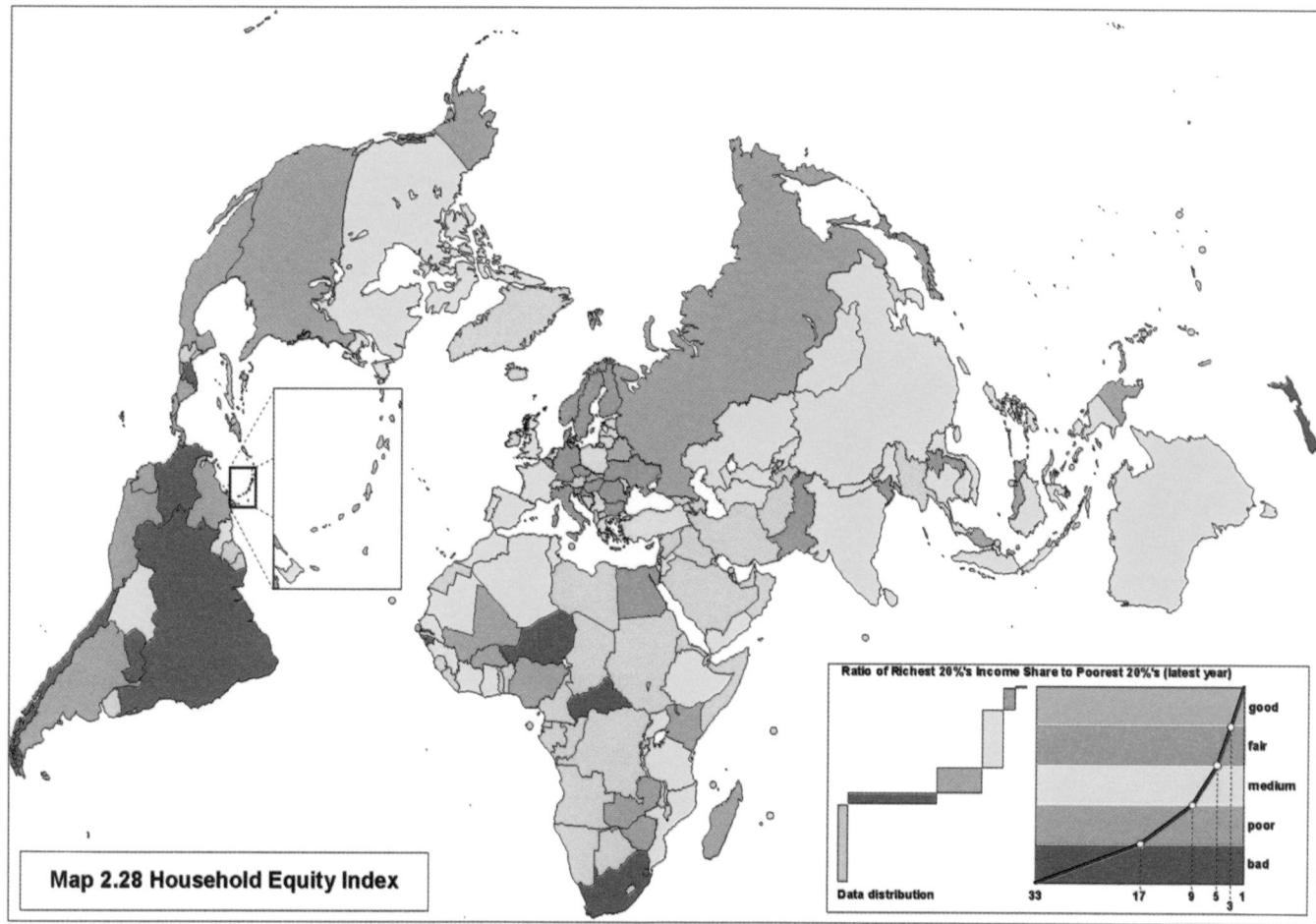

Map 2.28 Household Equity Index

Ratio of Richest 20%'s Income Share to Poorest 20%'s (latest year)

good
fair
medium
poor
bad

Data distribution   33   17   9   5   3   1

scores. Performance by the 109 countries rated on both gender and household equity is more erratic. A mere 8 (all in Europe) achieve good or fair scores in both, and 14 (mostly in Africa) get poor or bad scores in both.[25] Most of the rest do markedly worse in one than in the other.

The household divide is wider than the gender gap by more than 5 points in 43 countries, including much of the Americas and Southern Africa: South Africa has a 52-point difference between fair gender and bad household equity, and Colombia a 41-point gap (gender medium, household bad). Gender discrimination exceeds inter-household disparities by more than 5 points in another 43 countries, including much of Northern Africa, Eastern Europe, and Southern Asia: in Egypt, Bangladesh, and Pakistan, household equity is at least 30 points higher than gender equity.

For all data and scores for equity, together with details of the indicators, performance criteria, and combining procedures, see Table 8 in the Data section.

Household Equity

Household Equity Index (Map 2.28)

What it is: One indicator, ratio of richest 20%'s income share to poorest 20%'s (Figure 2.16).

Objective: Equitable distribution of benefits and burdens among households and societal groups.

Country results: 2 good (1%), 20 fair (11%), 52 medium (29%), 24 poor (13%), 11 bad (6%), 71 no data (39%).

The ratio of the income share of the richest fifth of the population to that of the poorest fifth shows how much more money the rich get than the poor. Because the data are gathered by national surveys, which tend to miss the poorest households, the reported ratios are likely to be underestimates. They range from 32.5:1 in the Central African Republic to 2.6:1 in Slovakia. Average national incomes have no effect on the gap between rich and poor. Yemen and Zambia both have incomes per person of $720,

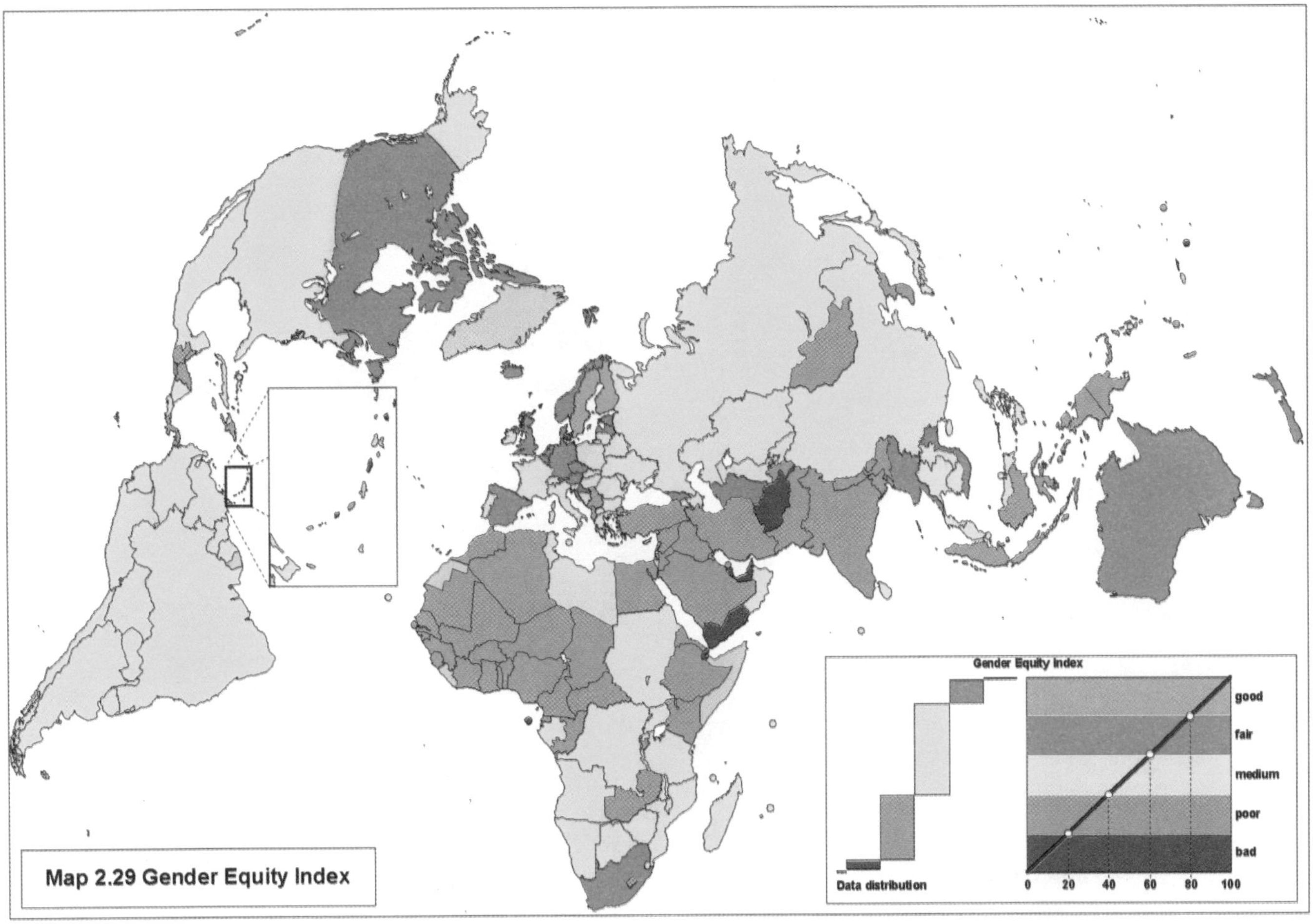

Map 2.29 Gender Equity Index

Gender Equity Index

good
fair
medium
poor
bad

Data distribution

0   20   40   60   80   100

ELEMENT — Household equity

INDICATOR — Ratio of richest 20%'s income to poorest 20%'s

Figure 2.16. Indicator chart for household equity.

but Yemen's ratio is 8:1, Zambia's 13:1. Viet Nam and France, with the same ratios of 5.6:1, have incomes of $1,690 and $21,175, respectively.

Poor and bad ratios are mainly in the Americas and West and Southern Africa; medium and fair in Europe, Asia, and Northern Africa. Income disparities have risen in most Eastern European countries since their embrace of capitalism, so Belarus and Slovakia, the only countries in the good band, may not be there for long. During the 1990s, the income gap between rich and poor also widened in the Bahamas, China, and Thailand but narrowed in Jamaica and Brazil.[26]

Income share is the best available indicator of household equity but does not necessarily reflect other areas of potential disparity such as health, knowledge, power, or freedom. Ideally, the index would cover these as well.

Gender Equity

> **Gender Equity Index (Map 2.29)**
>
> **What it is:** Average of gender and wealth, gender and knowledge, and gender and community scores (Figure 2.17).
>
> **Objective:** Equal distribution of benefits and burdens between males and females.
>
> **Country results:** 2 good (1%), 22 fair (12%), 84 medium (47%), 60 poor (33%), 10 bad (6%), 2 no data (1%).

Maps 2.30–2.32 show that the number of countries with major inequities increases sharply from wealth (income) to knowledge (education) to community (government). Almost half the countries have a medium gender equity

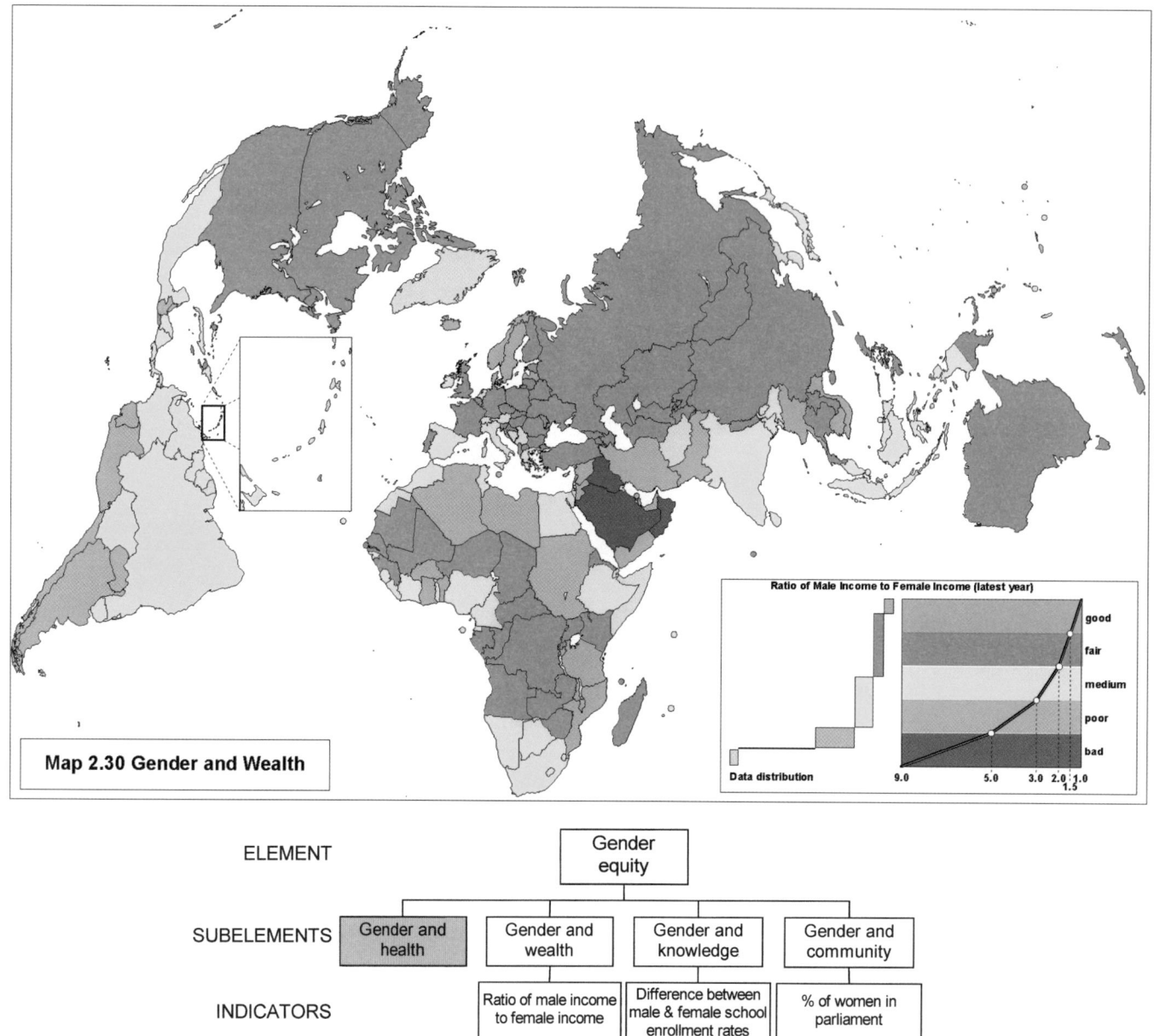

Map 2.30 Gender and Wealth

Ratio of Male Income to Female Income (latest year)

good
fair
medium
poor
bad

Data distribution   9.0   5.0   3.0   2.0 1.0
                                            1.5

ELEMENT

Gender equity

SUBELEMENTS

Gender and health | Gender and wealth | Gender and knowledge | Gender and community

INDICATORS

Ratio of male income to female income | Difference between male & female school enrollment rates | % of women in parliament

Figure 2.17. Indicator chart for gender equity. Gender and health (shaded box) is not covered due to lack of a suitable indicator (difference between male and female life expectancy is not used because it is hard to tell whether greater equality means men are doing better or women worse).

index, often because gains in wealth or knowledge are offset by subpar scores for community. Sweden, Finland, and only three of the countries with a fair index (Denmark, Germany, and Norway) have good or fair scores across the board. Others with a fair index are inconsistent. The door to gender parity opens in one room only to shut in another, and in countries with a poor or bad index most doors are still locked.

Gender and Wealth

Gender and Wealth (Map 2.30)

What it is: One indicator, ratio of male income to female income.

Country results: 16 good (9%), 68 fair (38%), 54 medium (30%), 22 poor (12%), 3 bad (2%), 17 no data (9%).

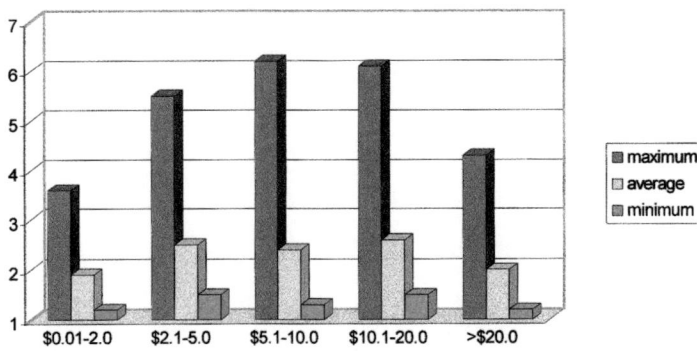

Figure 2.18. Maximum, average, and minimum ratios of male income to female income in each of five GDP groups ($000s per person).

Males earn more than females everywhere, and income differences are wide, ranging from negligible (1.2:1 in Sweden and Cambodia) to more than six times (6.2:1 in Oman). The size of the difference is unrelated to a country's gross domestic product per person, except that it is smallest in both the richest and poorest countries (Figure 2.18). Income share between the sexes is least equal where average incomes are between $2,100–$20,000 per person, with males earning on average two and a half times as much as females. Once incomes are below $2,000 or above $20,000, the incomes of males are about double those of females.

The best-performing regions are Eastern Europe, where all countries have good or fair scores (men's income less than double women's), and Central and East Asia, where two-thirds do. The worst are West Asia, where almost two-thirds (61%) have bad or poor scores (men's income at least triple women's), and South America (42% with a poor score). Lower ratios in these regions, such as Turkey's 1.7:1 and Colombia's 2.0:1, demonstrate that such blatant inequities are avoidable.

The indicator does not show if women have equal access to high-paying jobs or are paid the same rate as equally qualified men. It also ignores situations in which men dominate wage earning but women maintain the unpaid economy, running the home, growing food, and fetching fuel and water.[27]

Gender and Knowledge

> ## Gender and Knowledge (Map 2.31)
>
> **What it is:** One indicator, difference between male and female school enrollment rates (average of net primary, net secondary, and tertiary differences).
>
> **Country results:** 27 good (15%), 37 fair (21%), 40 medium (22%), 32 poor (18%), 24 bad (13%), 20 no data (11%).

Education is essential for personal and economic development, and makes a crucial contribution to overall gender equity. Therefore the United Nations target is for all countries to achieve 0% difference in school enrollment and literacy by 2005.

Taking only those countries with data on all three levels (primary, secondary, and tertiary), the average difference in enrollment ranges from more than double (United Arab Emirates) to near parity (Australia). The smallest differences are in the Americas and Europe; the biggest are in Africa and West and Southern Asia.

While males always have more wealth and power than females, they sometimes have less education. Male enrollment is higher in about 60% of countries, especially in Africa and Southern Asia. Female enrollment is higher in the other 40%, notably in South America and Southern and Eastern Europe.

Inequality between male and female enrollment tends to shrink as overall enrollment improves (Figure 2.19). Of 77 countries with good or fair education scores, 20 have good

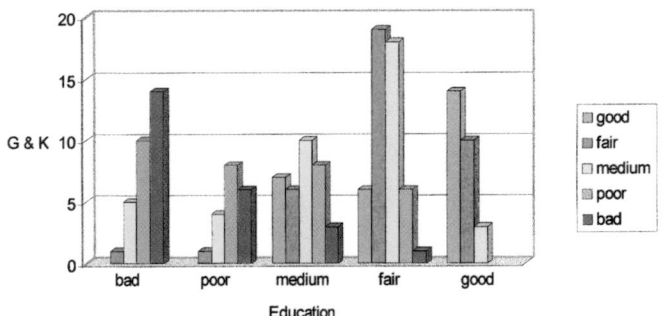

Figure 2.19. Gender parity is high (good or fair gender and knowledge [G and K] scores) where overall enrollment is high (good or fair education scores) and low where overall enrollment is low. Scale shows number of countries.

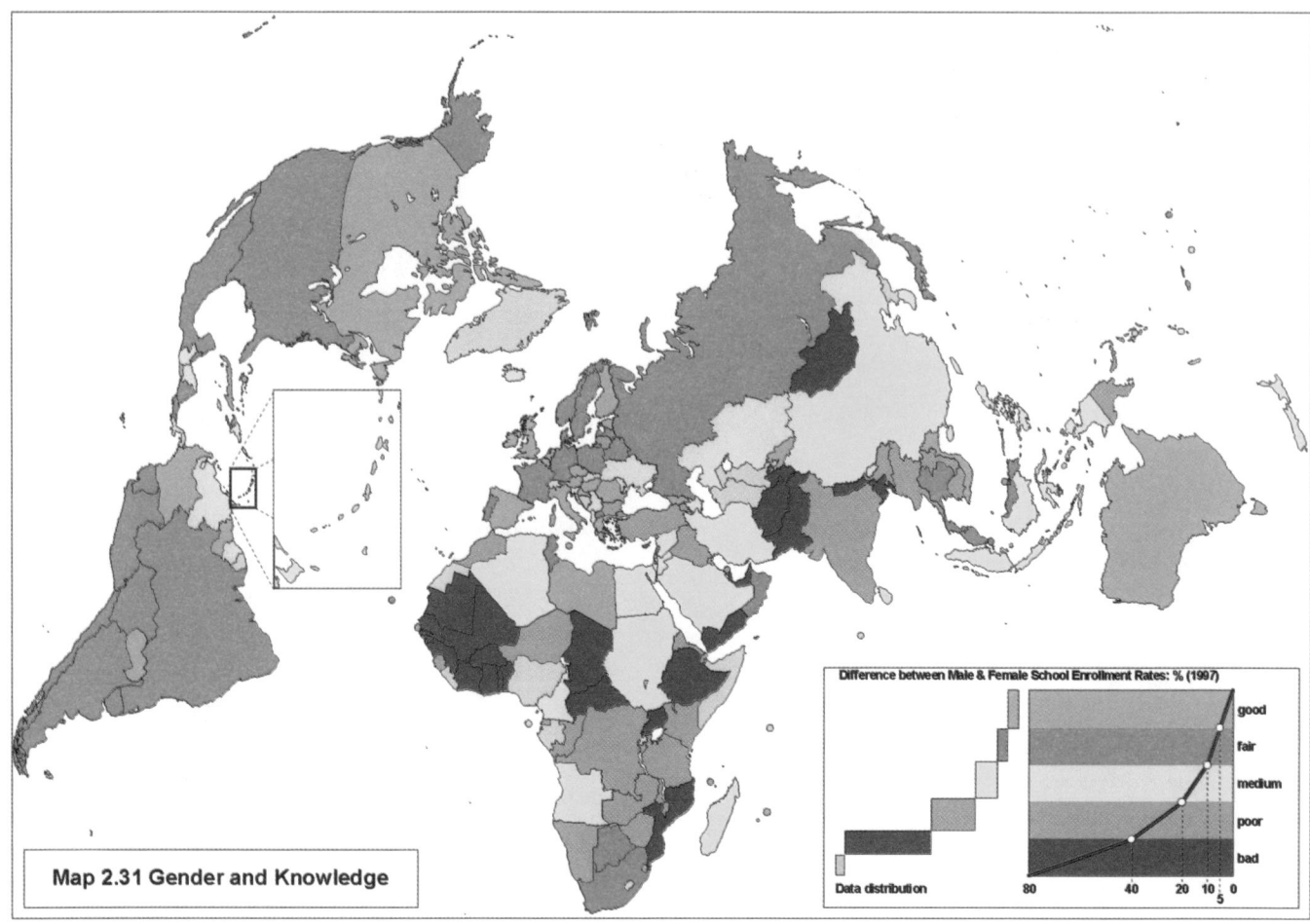

Map 2.31 Gender and Knowledge

Difference between Male & Female School Enrollment Rates: % (1997)

good
fair
medium
poor
bad

Data distribution   80   40   20 10   0
5

equity scores (female–male enrollment differences below 5%), and 29 have fair scores (differences below 10%). By contrast, of 49 countries with poor or bad education scores, 38 get poor or bad equity scores (differences of 20% or more).[28]

Gender and Community

Gender and Community (Map 2.32)

What it is: One indicator, percentage of seats in the national parliament held by women.

Country results: 1 good (1%), 6 fair (3%), 19 medium (11%), 53 poor (29%), 87 bad (48%), 14 no data (8%).

The proportion of seats held by women in national parliaments is a sign of the opportunities open to women for political office and of society's willingness to be represented by them. It ranges from 0% (Djibouti, Jordan, Kuwait, United Arab Emirates, Tonga, and Vanuatu) to

42.7% (Sweden). In almost half the countries it is no higher than 10%.

Sweden and the 6 countries with a fair score (parliaments with more than 30% women) are also among the 16 freest and most democratic nations. But 4 of the others with good a freedom and governance index (Austria, Switzerland, Australia, and New Zealand) have only 21–30% parliamentary representation by women, and the rest (Canada, United States, Ireland, Portugal, and Luxembourg) fail to reach even this level. More than a third of countries with a fair freedom and governance index get a bad score for the percentage of women in parliament, including Greece (6.3%), Japan (4.6%), Papua New Guinea (1.8%), and Vanuatu (0%).

On the other side of the aisle, having women in parliament is no guarantee of freedom: five undemocratic regimes (Cuba, China, Lao, Turkmenistan, and Viet Nam) have parliaments with more than 20% women.

Low representation in parliament tends to translate into smaller percentages of ministerial or subministerial

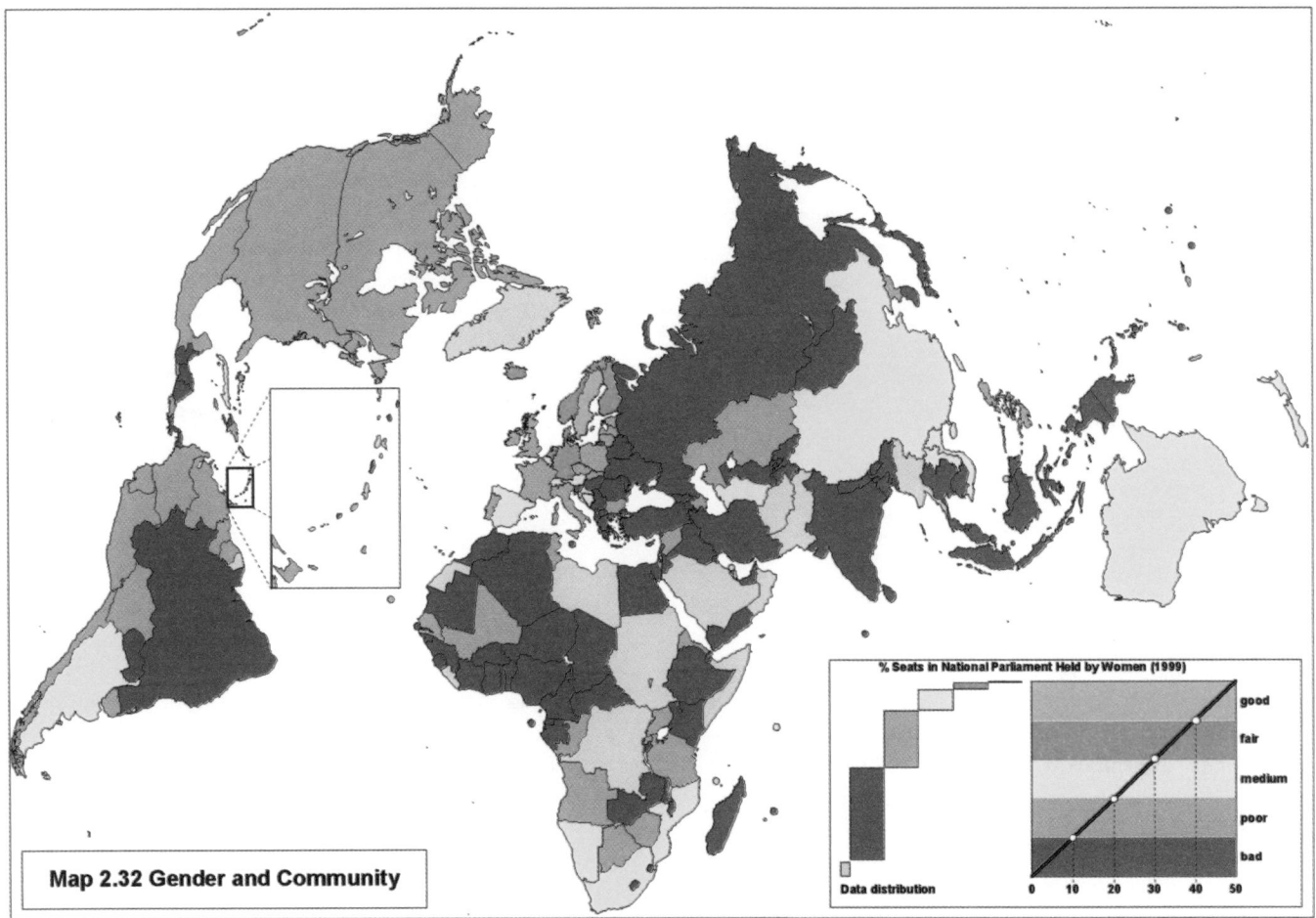

Map 2.32 Gender and Community

% Seats in National Parliament Held by Women (1999)

good
fair
medium
poor
bad

Data distribution

posts in government, although the data are less current and not strictly comparable. In half the countries, women have roughly the same proportions of senior posts as parliamentary seats. In just under a third, they have many fewer, as in Iceland (34.9% in parliament, 8.2% in government) and Turkmenistan (26% in parliament, 2.2% in government). Only in about a fifth do women have many more ministerial positions, as in the United States (13.3% in parliament, 33.1% women in government) and Haiti (3.6% in parliament, 22.2% in government).[29]

Notes

1. United Nations Development Programme (1990). In other years, UNDP experimented with a human freedom index—a modification of Charles Humana's *World Human Rights Guide* (Humana 1992)—and proposed a political freedom index (United Nations Development Programme 1991, 1992).
2. International purchasing power parity dollars (PPP$) avoid distortion by exchange rates and national differences in purchasing power. PPP$ are estimated from the local costs of a common set of goods and services. Essentially they are U.S. dollars adjusted for the difference in cost of living between the United States and the country concerned.
3. Equity is an integral part of the Human Wellbeing Index because its inclusion provides a more realistic portrayal of conditions. It is treated as a separate dimension, rather than integrated into the other dimensions, to reveal clearly the impact of equity on each country's overall performance. By comparison, the World Bank's estimates of national wealth and genuine saving acknowledge the importance of distribution but do not cover it (Kunte et al. 1998; World Bank staff 1997). The Genuine Progress Indicator fully incorporates equity by adjusting its figure for personal consumption expenditure to reflect disparities in income (Cobb, Halstead, & Rowe 1995a). Since 1995, UNDP has published a gender-related development index (GDI) and a gender empowerment measure (GEM). It prefers to keep the GDI and GEM separate from the Human Development Index (HDI) to maintain the continuity of the HDI and show clearly the differences between it and the gender-adjusted indicators (United Nations

Development Programme 1995). UNDP has also experimented with a distribution-adjusted HDI (United Nations Development Programme 1991, 1992, 1993).

4. These findings support the thesis of Landes (1999) that good governance and freedom to innovate and to own the fruits of one's labor are key conditions for wealth.

5. The HDI is for 1998 and is from United Nations Development Programme (2000). The HDI was converted to a score by multiplying it by 100 and rounding to the nearest whole number.

6. Russia, Eastern Europe, North Korea, Myanmar: Lopez et al. (2000); Mathers et al. (2000).

7. Indicator description and data: Lopez et al. (2000); Mathers et al. (2000); World Health Organization (2000).

8. UN targets are from the International Conference on Population and Development, Cairo, 1994, and the World Summit for Social Development, Copenhagen, 1995 (United Nations Population Division 1997; Office of the UN System Support and Services 1996). The reduction by six years lowers the targets for healthy life expectancy from 7.1% to 20.0% below those for life expectancy, close to the range of the percentages of lifespan lost to disability (from 7.0% in Greece to 25.1% in Niger). See also Table 2.

9. Indicator description: United Nations (1996); United Nations Population Division (1998a). Data: UNICEF (1999b); United Nations Population Division, personal communication (1998).

10. Fertility decline and aging: United Nations Population Division (1998a). At present the oldest country in the world is Italy, with 1.6 elders per child. By 2050 it will be Spain, with 3.6 elders per child. Africa is the youngest continent, with 43% children and 4% elders in 1998. By 2050 it will still be the youngest, but with only twice as many children as elders. Uganda is the world's youngest country, with only one in every 31 persons aged 60 or over.

11. Undernourished percentage of population (does not have enough food to meet minimum daily energy requirements), indicator description: Food and Agriculture Organization of the United Nations (1996a); data: Food and Agriculture Organization of the United Nations (1999b). Stunting and underweight children, indicator descriptions and targets: Onis & Blössner (1997), Visschedjik & Siméant (1998); World Health Organization (1998b); data: Onis & Blössner (1997), UNICEF (1999b). Percentage of babies with low birth weight: indicator description and target, United Nations (1996); data: UNICEF (1999b), World Health Organization (1996–1998a).

   Safe water and basic sanitation, indicator descriptions and limitations: United Nations (1996); data: UNICEF (1999b), World Health Organization (1996–1998a). UN target is from the International Conference on Population

and Development, Cairo, 1994; the World Summit for Social Development, Copenhagen, 1995; the Fourth World Conference on Women, Beijing, 1995; and the Second World Conference on Human Settlements (Habitat II), Istanbul, 1996 (United Nations Population Division 1997; Office of the UN System Support and Services 1996).

12. Purchasing power parity dollars: see note 2.

13. Income data: United Nations Development Programme (2000). Relationships of income to provision of needs and to health and population, knowledge, and community: analysis of Tables 2, 4, 6, and 7, summarized in Table 3b in the Data section. The nine countries with incomes above $10,000 but scores below fair are Bahamas, St Kitts and Nevis, Seychelles, Brunei Darussalam, Bahrain, Kuwait, Qatar, Saudi Arabia, and United Arab Emirates.

14. Inflation data: International Monetary Fund (2000); International Institute for Strategic Studies (1999a). Indicator method: Table 4. Central bank inflation targets (central banks of Australia, Canada, England, the Euro area, New Zealand, and Sweden) (*The Economist* 1999). Unemployment data: International Labour Office (2000). Indicator method: Table 4.

15. External debt indicator description: United Nations (1996). External debt service data and World Bank classification of indebtedness, World Bank (1999b, 2000b). Impact of short-term debt ratio to international reserves: Sachs & Woo (1999). Description of reverse indicator, ratio of international reserves to short-term debt: IMF Policy Development and Review Department (2000). Data on short-term debt and international reserves: BIS/IMF/OECD/World Bank (2000).

16. Public debt indicator description: World Bank (1999a). Public debt data: Eurostat (2000); International Institute for Strategic Studies (1999a); World Bank (1999a, 2000a). Treaty of Maastricht standards: Black (1997).

17. Countries with fair debt scores not rated for public debt: Paraguay, Botswana, Belarus, Latvia, Lithuania, Bhutan, and United Arab Emirates. Countries with fair debt scores not rated for public debt and deficit (rated for external debt only): Antigua and Barbuda, Suriname, Eritrea, Libya, Swaziland, Slovenia, Saudi Arabia, Solomon Islands, and Vanuatu.

18. Knowledge in postindustrial economies: Chichilnisky (1997, 1998).

19. Adult literacy rate indicator description and limitations: United Nations (1996); data: UNESCO (1999a). International Adult Literacy Survey (IALS), including IALS data in figure and following paragraph: Organisation for Economic Co-operation and Development, Human Resources Development Canada & Statistics Canada (1997).

20. School enrollment indicator description: United Nations (1996); data: UNESCO (1999b, 1999c); UN target from the World Summit for Social Development, Copenhagen, 1995, and the Fourth World Conference on Women, Beijing, 1995: United Nations Population Division (1997); Office of the UN System Support and Services (1996).

21. Indicator descriptions: International Telecommunication Union (1997); data: International Telecommunication Union (1997, 1998, 1999, 2000). The number of main lines and cellular phones per 100 persons ranges from less than 0.1 (Democratic Republic of Congo) to 113.8 (Sweden). Luxembourg has the highest density of main lines (69.2) and Finland of mobile phone subscribers (57.2), who now outnumber main lines. Faults per 100 main telephone lines per year range from 761.0 (Tonga) to 1.1 (United Arab Emirates). The number of Internet users per 10,000 people ranges from almost 0 (Somalia) to 3,953 (Sweden).

22. Political rights rating, civil liberties rating, and press freedom rating descriptions and data: Freedom House (1999b, 2000a, 2000b). Corruption perceptions index description and data: Transparency International (1999, 2000).

23. Indicator description and data: International Institute for Strategic Studies (1999a, 1999b).

24. Indicator definitions and data: United Nations Crime Prevention and Criminal Justice Division (1997, 1999).

25. Good or fair scores in both household and gender equity: Belgium, Croatia, Czech Republic, Denmark, Finland, Germany, Norway, and Sweden. Poor or bad scores in both: Dominican Republic, Honduras, Panama, St Lucia, Burkina Faso, Central African Republic, Gambia, Guinea–Bissau, Kenya, Mali, Niger, Nigeria, Zambia, and Papua New Guinea.

26. Indicator description and data: World Bank (1998, 2000a).

27. Indicator description and data: United Nations Development Programme (1999, 2000). Dollars are purchasing power parity dollars (see note 2).

28. Indicator description: United Nations (1996); data: UNESCO (1999a, 1999b). UN target from the World Summit for Social Development, Copenhagen, 1995, and the Fourth World Conference on Women, Beijing, 1995: United Nations Population Division (1997); Office of the UN System Support and Services (1996).

29. Indicator description and data: Inter-Parliamentary Union (2000).

3. Ecosystem Wellbeing

Ecosystem Wellbeing Index

Ecosystem Wellbeing Index (EWI) (Map 3.1)

What it is: Average of indices of land, water, air, species and genes, and resource use, *or* average of indices of land, water, air, and species and genes, *whichever is lower.*

Country results: 0 good (0%), 27 fair (15%), 81 medium (45%), 68 poor (38%), 4 bad (2%).

Highlights:

• Countries with a poor or bad EWI cover almost half (48.4%) of the planet's land and inland water surface; those with a medium EWI, 43%. Countries with a fair EWI occupy a mere 8.6%.

• Many countries with a fair or medium EWI would probably have lower ratings if their environments were better monitored. Air quality, water quality, and the state of aquatic ecosystems are especially neglected.

• The way for most countries to raise their EWI is to restore and maintain habitats, expand protected areas, conserve agricultural diversity, and improve water quality. Industrialized countries also need to cut greenhouse gases.

Measuring Ecosystem Wellbeing

Ecosystem wellbeing is a condition in which the ecosystem maintains its diversity and quality—and thus its capacity to support people and the rest of life—and its potential to adapt to change and provide a wide range of choices and opportunities for the future.

The global ecosystem consists of layers of smaller ecosystems: communities of plants, animals, and other creatures, together with their physical environments.

These are the building blocks of life. They maintain the planet's chemical balance and such life-supporting processes as the capture, storage, and transfer of energy and the cycling of nutrients and water. They moderate climate, filter and neutralize pollutants, and renew soil. They provide the resources that keep people alive and sustain economies, and their beauty and intricacy enrich mind and spirit.

Diversity includes the pattern (or type, size, and distribution) of these communities in the landscape and seascape, their species composition, the size and structure of component populations, and the connections and interactions among and within communities. The apparent overabundance—even redundancy and inefficiency—of this diversity is necessary to provide a range of responses to change (so that if one fails others can take its place) and to give people plenty of choices for the future.[1]

The quality of ecosystems includes their capacity to maintain themselves through cycles of growth, maturity, death, and renewal; their productivity; and the chemical and physical integrity of soil, water, and the atmosphere.

The opposite condition to ecosystem wellbeing is ecosystem stress, in which the ecosystem loses its diversity and quality and so becomes less able to support people and other life. The five main pressures people place on the ecosystem are:

• *Conversion and occupation of ecosystems.* Land ecosystems are converted to farmland and pasture or replaced by built systems, such as settlements, infrastructure, and mines. Dams and dikes alter the flow of rivers. Docks, jetties, breakwaters, and quays restructure coasts and shores. Habitat destruction due to ecosystem conversion is by far the biggest cause of losses of diversity (followed by resource extraction, translocation of species, and pollution).[2]

- *Resource extraction.* Plant and animal products, water, fossil fuels, and minerals are taken from the ecosystem, reducing the size of stocks and populations and modifying ecosystems; for instance, logging and grazing change the structure of vegetation, and fishing alters the structure of fish stocks by leaving fewer individuals of breeding age. The collapse of fisheries, such as Atlantic cod, throws people out of work and denies many their only source of income (other than social assistance). Reductions in fuelwood supplies add to the time and effort women must expend to seek fuel and carry it home. Exhaustion of accessible and easily extracted oil, gas, and ore increases the cost of producing energy and minerals.

- *Translocation of species.* Organisms are moved from their native habitat to new habitats, both deliberately (as in the stocking of nonnative fishes for recreational fishing and aquaculture) and accidentally (as in the entry of many diseases, pests, and weeds as stowaways on ships and imported farm produce). Such introduced species prey on native species or compete with them for food and space and are the agents of major outbreaks of disease among crops, livestock, and people.

- *Emissions and waste disposal.* Much of the material extracted from the ecosystem is returned to it as physical, chemical, and biological waste and pollution, usually in forms and at rates to which it is not adapted. The consequences include increased disease and death rates, lowered air and water quality, and disrupted atmosphere and climate.

- *Soil degradation.* Cultivation, grazing, and logging often degrade soils through erosion (above natural rates), loss of nutrients and organic matter, salinization, and physical damage such as compaction. This reduces the productivity of the land and harms aquatic ecosystems, polluting water, silting up reservoirs and channels, and smothering habitats such as coral reefs.

Singly and in concert these pressures reduce diversity and carrying capacity (the capacity of an ecosystem to support healthy organisms while maintaining its productivity, adaptability, and capability of renewal). Humans use energy, industry, and agriculture to enlarge their share of this capacity, but in doing so they encroach on the share of other species, shrinking diversity even more. As a result, people now consume, destroy, or control a quarter of the planet's terrestrial and aquatic plant energy, the ultimate source of food for virtually all nonplant life.[3]

The implications of reduced carrying capacity are that the Earth will support fewer people well, or more people less well, or a world of sharply increased disparities (a few people well, a great many poorly). It is also likely that climatic and environmental events will become more capricious, leading to a rise in so-called natural disasters: more frequent and severe storms, floods, droughts, and plagues.

To ensure full coverage of the diversity and quality of the ecosystem and of the main pressures on them, Wellbeing Assessment divides ecosystem wellbeing into 5 dimensions, which I have further split into 10 elements (Figure 3.1). They are described in the remaining sections of this chapter and distilled into a short statement here:

Land diversity	All major land ecosystems are maintained or restored in large units with minimal loss of the habitats and communities within them.
Land quality	Soil degradation on cultivated and modified lands is kept close to degradation rates on natural lands.
Inland waters	All major aquatic ecosystems, both inland and
Sea	marine, are maintained or restored in large units with minimal loss of the communities and habitats within them and minimal stress from pollution and water uses.
Global atmosphere	Pollutants that disrupt the chemical balance of the global atmosphere are eliminated or substantially reduced.
Local air quality	Local air pollutants are below levels that affect people or the ecosystem.
Wild diversity	All native wild species are maintained, and extinctions are reduced to background rates.
Domesticated diversity	As much as possible of the heritage of crop varieties and livestock breeds is maintained.
Energy and materials	Consumption of energy and materials and
Resource sectors	extraction and production of resources are within the carrying capacity of the ecosystem.

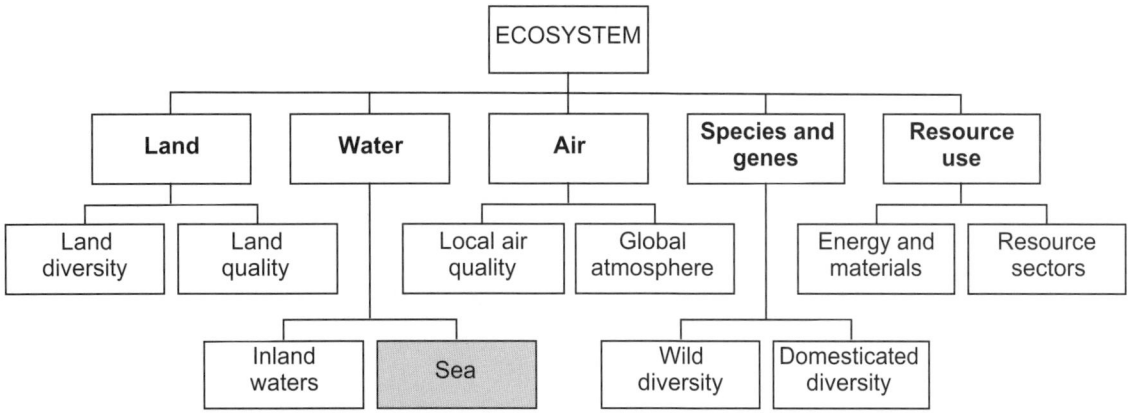

Figure 3.1. Ecosystem dimensions and elements. The 5 dimensions are in **bold**; the 10 elements are in normal type. Sea (shaded box) is not covered due to lack of adequate data.

The resulting Ecosystem Wellbeing Index (EWI) measures progress toward the proposed goal of a high level of ecosystem wellbeing, based on all these elements except the sea (on which data are inadequate). The goal might be stated better as a low level of ecosystem stress since we know more about the pressures that cause ecosystem stress than we do about the levels of diversity and quality required for ecosystem wellbeing.

The pressures a country places on the ecosystem often extend well beyond its borders. Pollutants are carried over long distances by winds and currents. Greenhouse gases and the chemicals that deplete the stratospheric ozone layer damage the atmosphere, which spans the entire planet. Dams and water withdrawals from rivers can have impacts all the way downstream. Importers of raw materials and processed goods reap the benefits while exporters incur the ecosystem stress caused by their extraction and manufacture. I have tried to account for such cross-border effects by:

- Including issues that portray global impacts (global atmosphere, energy and materials) and giving them the same weight as the corresponding national issues (local air quality, resource sectors).

- Factoring in the proportion of national food supply that is met by domestic production.

- Adding imports to domestic timber production and summing them as a percentage of national supply.

Thus, as far as possible, the EWI measures each country's stress on the ecosystem as a whole, not just on the area within the country's jurisdiction.

Most of the Planet is Poor or Mediocre

The EWI of all countries is shown in Map 3.1. Table 3.1 gives a regional summary. Figure 3.2 displays patterns of performance. Full scores are in Table 9, and rankings in Table 25, in the Data section.

To achieve a good EWI, a country must perform well in all dimensions. None does so. Twenty-seven countries, occupying less than 9% of Earth's land and inland water surface, have a fair EWI, but not one of them was assessed on water quality or local air quality. Had they been, it is likely that many would have dropped to a medium EWI. Benin's EWI of 71 (the second highest, after the Republic of Congo's 72) is partly due to its low impact on inland waters and the global atmosphere: its rivers are largely undammed, it uses only 1.5% of its water supply, and it emits negligible amounts of the chemicals that damage the atmosphere. Not being rated on water quality or local air quality (factors that contribute to the poor EWI of nearby Ghana), its scores for water and air are high. These are buttressed by fairly low threats to wild and domesticated species: as far as is known, 4% of the country's mammals—but less than 1% of its flowering plants and no birds or livestock breeds—are at risk of extinction. Benin does moderately well even in its weakest element, land quality, with soil degradation

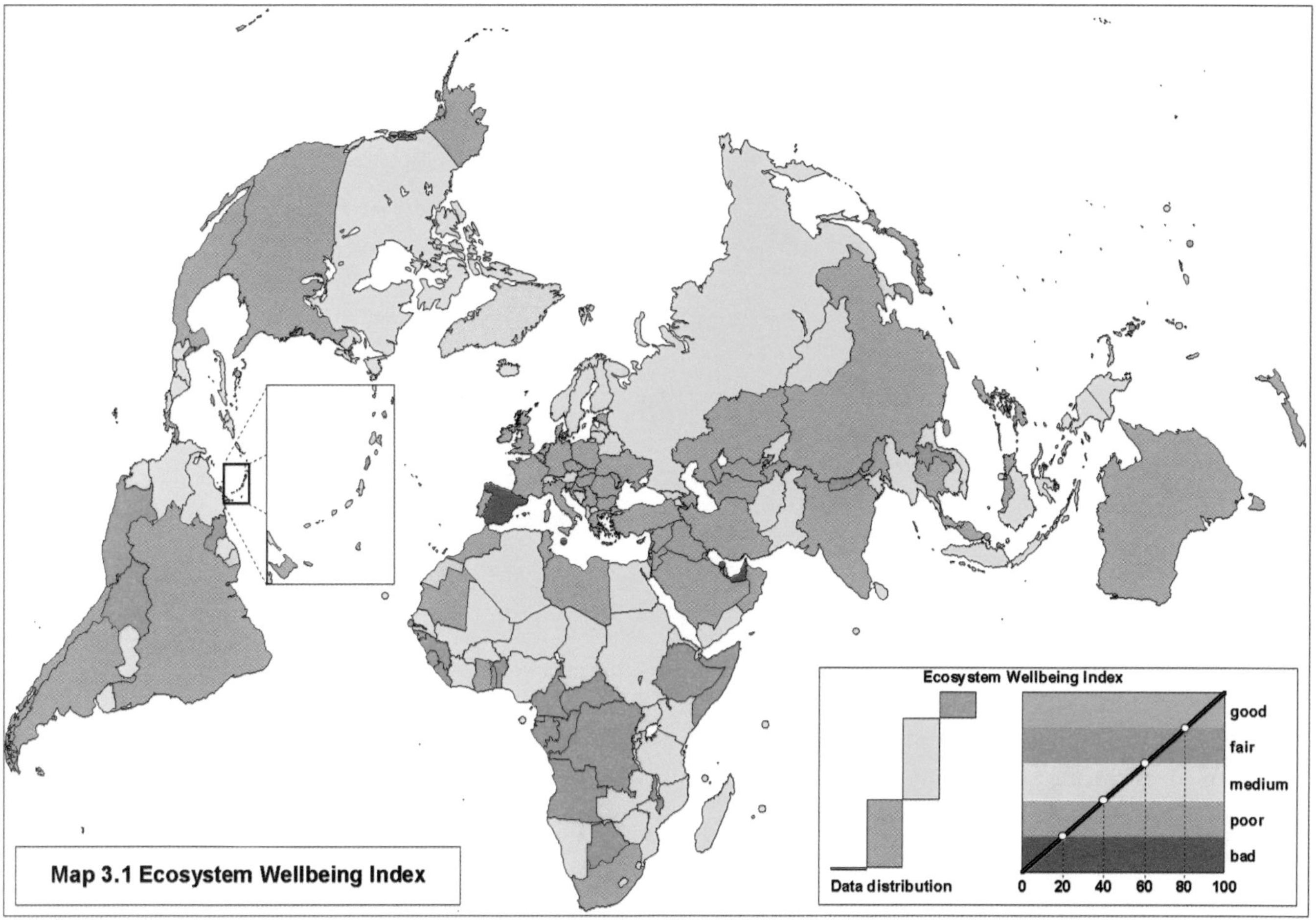

Map 3.1 Ecosystem Wellbeing Index

Ecosystem Wellbeing Index

Data distribution

good
fair
medium
poor
bad

0   20   40   60   80   100

affecting no more than 19% of its cultivated and modi-fied land area.

Eighty-one countries, covering 43% of the planet's land and inland water surface, have a medium EWI. Colombia's performance is a typical mixture of strength in some aspects and weakness in others. Only about 10% of its land area has been converted to settlements and cultivation and 29% modified by logging, ranching, or other human activities. Although almost a third of the cultivated and modified area is degraded, most of the degradation is light and easily remedied. Water quality is a different story: the Magdalena, the country's largest river basin, is heavily contaminated with nutrients and fecal coliforms. Emissions to the global atmosphere are low (local air quality was not rated), and pressure from energy use, farming, and logging is also low. Despite this and the positive state of the land, many of Colombia's wild species are threatened, notably 10% of its mammals and 55% of its gymnosperms (plants such as conifers).

The 68 countries with a poor EWI occupy 48% of the Earth's land and inland water area. They tend to be better monitored than countries with a fair or medium

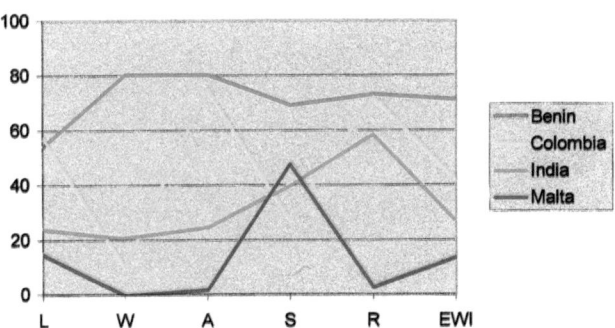

Figure 3.2. Comparison of four countries at each level of the Ecosystem Wellbeing Index (EWI) (blue = fair, yellow = medium, pink = poor, red = bad) and for each dimension (L = land, W = water, A = air, S = species and genes, R = resource use). No country has a good EWI.

Table 3.1. Ecosystem Wellbeing Index (EWI), showing the number of countries at each level by continental group and region. Most of the Americas has a medium or poor EWI. Asia–Pacific is similar, except that more countries have a poor EWI, especially in West Asia. As with the Human Wellbeing Index, Africa and Europe are the reverse of each other, except in this case Africa is the better performer: most EWIs are poor in Europe, medium or fair in Africa. In Central and East Africa, the strongest region, all countries have a fair or medium EWI.

Region and Continental Group	Fair	Medium	Poor	Bad	Total
North and Central America	1	6	3	0	10
West Indies	1	7	5	0	13
South America	3	6	3	0	12
Americas	*5*	*19*	*11*	*0*	*35*
Northern Africa	2	5	3	0	10
West Africa	7	8	2	0	17
Central and Eastern Africa	6	7	0	0	13
Southern Africa	3	9	1	0	13
Africa	*18*	*29*	*6*	*0*	*53*
Northern Europe	0	6	7	0	13
Southern Europe	0	3	7	2	12
Eastern Europe	0	3	9	0	12
Europe	*0*	*12*	*23*	*2*	*37*
West Asia	0	3	13	2	18
Russia, Central and East Asia	0	5	7	0	12
Southern Asia	3	9	5	0	17
Pacific	1	4	3	0	8
Asia–Pacific	*4*	*21*	*28*	*2*	*55*
WORLD	27	81	68	4	180

EWI and to show a pattern of satisfactory results in a few elements but subpar performance in most. India has lost 98% of its natural land, more than 40% of its cultivated and modified land is degraded, rivers and even groundwater are polluted with nutrients and bacteria, city air is dense with particulates, and 8% of the country's flowering plants, 6% of its birds, and 24% of its mammals are at risk of extinction. India's best dimension is resource use, with moderate pressure from farming and fisheries balanced by low rates of energy consumption.

The four countries with a bad EWI—Spain, Malta, Bahrain, and United Arab Emirates (UAE)—cover 0.4% of the planet's land and inland water area. Spain has high proportions of threatened species and livestock breeds. The others have bad scores for water, air, and resource use, consuming many times their renewable supplies of water (Malta 3 times, UAE 14 times, Bahrain 60 times) and large amounts of ozone-depleting substances, and depending heavily on other countries for food and timber.

The Resource Use Effect

The effect of resource use on the EWI is illustrated in Map 3.2 and Figure 3.3 and summarized in Table 3.2. Full details are in Table 9 in the Data section.

The resource use indicators measure parts of the consumption process whose impacts on the ecosystem may not be adequately covered by the other dimensions. Also, by factoring in imports, they may reveal pressures on the global ecosystem omitted by the mainly national indicators of land, water, air, and species and genes. If the other dimensions do not account for these pressures, resource use will lower the EWI and so is included to ensure that the EWI better reflects the actual state of the ecosystem. If they do account for them, resource use will leave the EWI unchanged or will increase it, and so is excluded to prevent double-counting. In 32 countries (18%), resource use lowers the EWI and is *included*. As a consequence, Lesotho's EWI falls from fair to medium. Resource use is *excluded* from the EWI of 138 countries (77%) where inclusion would have raised it. Spain's EWI is thereby prevented from rising from bad to poor, the EWIs of Panama and 11 other countries from poor to medium, and those of Cambodia and six others from medium to fair. Resource use has no effect on the EWIs of 10 countries (6%) such as Belize and Austria.

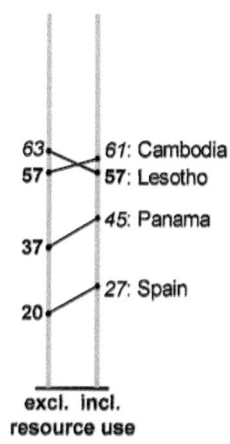

Figure 3.3. The resource use effect: EWIs excluding and including resource use. The final EWI is the lower score (in **bold**).

Map 3.2 Effect of Resource Use on the EWI

EWI change

up 6-10 points
up 1-5 points
no change
down 1-5 points
down 6-10 points
no data

Table 3.2. Number of countries whose EWI is changed by the inclusion of resource use, according to size of change and level of the EWI before the inclusion of resource use.

EWI Change	Fair	Medium	Poor	Bad	Total
Up 6–10 points	0	17	24	1	42
Up 1–5 points	23	45	28	0	96
UP SUBTOTAL	23	62	52	1	138
NO CHANGE	3	5	2	0	10
Down 1–5 points	1	13	13	3	30
Down 6–10 points	1	0	1	0	2
DOWN SUBTOTAL	2	13	14	3	32
Total	28	80	68	4	180

Biodiversity and Environmental Quality

The five ecosystem dimensions are much less closely matched with the EWI or with each other than are human dimensions with the HWI. Only two, water and air, are highly correlated with the EWI. Resource use and land are moderately related to it (land much less so than resource use) and species and genes hardly at all. Air and resource use are strongly associated with each other, primarily due to the close link between energy consumption and carbon emissions. By the same token, local air quality and pressure on the global atmosphere are inversely correlated, rich countries controlling urban air pollution better than poor ones, but emitting more carbon dioxide.

Ecosystem dimensions are weakly linked because ecosystem wellbeing is more complex than human wellbeing, reflecting both the interplay of ecological processes and human impacts on them. Hence, representative indicators are more difficult to identify and reliable data harder to obtain.

Biodiversity (the diversity of ecological communities, species, and genetic variants) and environmental quality are the keys to ecosystem wellbeing. Indicators of the former are in the land, water, and species and genes dimensions; indicators of the latter are in the land, water, and air dimensions. Botswana is the one country that performs well across the board, with good or fair scores for all biodiversity components and for the two environmen-

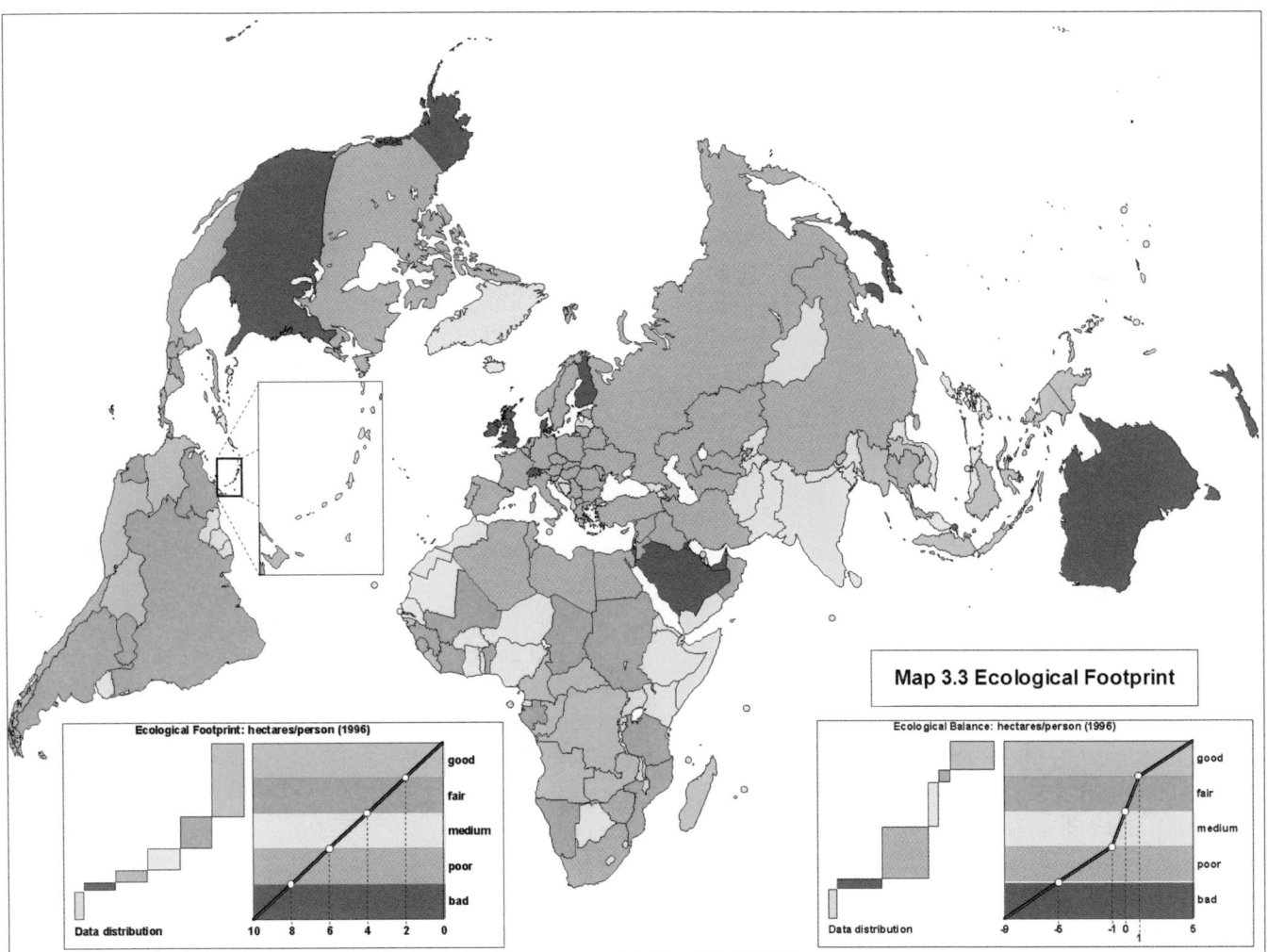

Map 3.3 Ecological Footprint

Ecological Footprint: hectares/person (1996)

Data distribution

good
fair
medium
poor
bad

10 8 6 4 2 0

Ecological Balance: hectares/person (1996)

Data distribution

good
fair
medium
poor
bad

-9 -5 -1 0 1 5

tal quality indicators on which it reports (land degradation and global atmosphere). Benin, Republic of Congo, and Namibia are the only other countries with good or fair scores for a majority of the indicators. Benin has no bad or poor scores. The others have one or two flaws (land protection in the Congo, animal breeds and inland water quality in Namibia).

Globally (excluding "no data" countries), the strongest performance areas, with the highest proportions of good or fair scores and the lowest of poor or bad scores, are river conversion (by dams), land quality, and global atmosphere. The weakest, with the fewest high scores and most low scores, are inland water quality, animal species, animal breeds, and land protection.

Among the 40 countries that could be rated on all biodiversity and environmental quality components, Sweden has the highest EWI (49), followed by Cuba (45), Finland and Lithuania (44), Canada, Norway, and Switzerland (43), and Austria (42). The EWIs of the rest

are poor. The group's strengths and weaknesses match those of the global set, except that due to the predominance of developed countries, local air quality is a strength and global atmosphere a major weakness.

Hence the way for most countries to raise their EWI is to restore and maintain habitats, increase the area of protected ecosystems, conserve agricultural diversity, improve water quality, and (chiefly industrialized countries) reduce greenhouse gases.

The Size of the Foot—or Where It's Put?

No environmental equivalent of the Human Development Index exists with which to compare the EWI. The Environmental Sustainability Index is compromised as a measurement of the state of the environment because it includes human indicators and indicators of environmental policies and practices (rather than of actual environmental stresses and conditions). The Ecological Footprint (EF), an index of consumption pressure, provides a more informative contrast. It is shown in Map 3.3 and compared with the EWI in Table 3.3. Full details are in Table 9 in the Data section.

The EF combines the quantities of energy and renewable resources (minerals excluded) a society consumes by converting them to a common unit of area: the area of productive land and sea required to supply the resources and absorb the carbon dioxide from fossil fuels. This area is a society's ecological footprint. Of the 151 countries covered by the EF and the EWI, 73 have a footprint that exceeds the world average share of productive capacity of 2.2 hectares per person. The EF also estimates a country's ecological balance: if its footprint is bigger than its national area of productive land and sea, it has a deficit; if it is smaller, it has a surplus. In translating the EF into a score, I have defined the good band as a footprint smaller than both the world average share of productive capacity and the national productive area. The EF score is the lower of the footprint score and the balance score.

Eighteen countries have an EF score that is more than 10 points lower than the EWI. Forty-seven have an EF score that is more than 10 points higher. The main reason for these differences is that the EWI attempts to measure the actual state of the ecosystem, whereas the EF is a gauge of pressures whose effect on the ecosystem depends on how they are applied and where. A liter of gasoline burned without pollution controls in a confined space contaminates the air more than a liter of clean fuel burned in the open.[4]

Singapore has a footprint of 12.3 hectares per person and an ecological deficit of 13.8 hectares per person,

Table 3.3. Performance of 151 countries rated by the Ecosystem Wellbeing Index (EWI) and the Ecological Footprint (EF).

Band	EWI	EF
Good	0	19
Fair	22	19
Medium	65	43
Poor	62	55
Bad	2	15
Total	151	151

reflecting its small size and booming consumption. The EWI reflects these factors as well, with bad scores for air and resource use and a poor score for land. But it also takes account of mitigating performance: less than 4% of animal species and less than 2% of plant species threatened. Indonesia has a footprint of 1.5 hectares per person and an ecological surplus of 1.5 hectares per person. In line with this low pressure, the EWI includes fair scores for global atmosphere and resource use. But forest loss, high percentages of threatened mammals and birds, and severe water pollution reduce its overall EWI to medium.

To the extent that they are comparable, the gap between the EF and the EWI is the difference between the expected stress (EF) and the actual stress (EWI) caused by the consumption process. One is the size of the foot, the other what the foot treads on. Singapore and others with an EF score lower than the EWI damage the ecosystem less than expected from the amount they consume. Indonesia and others with a higher EF score harm it more than expected.

Land

Land Index (Map 3.4)

What it is: Lower of land diversity index and land quality index.

Country results: 0 good (0%), 11 fair (6%), 63 medium (35%), 88 poor (49%), 18 bad (10%).

To achieve a good or fair land index, a country must conserve or restore the diversity of its natural land ecosystems and maintain the quality of the ecosystems it develops. Land diversity matters because it is the foundation of

ecosystem health: loss, fragmentation, or structural modification of natural land ecosystems changes nutrient and water cycles, alters the chemistry of the atmosphere, menaces the survival of species, provokes outbreaks of pests and diseases, and reduces the ability of the environment to recover from disturbances.[5] Land quality—keeping cultivated and modified land in good heart—is vital to sustain yields of crops, livestock, and timber. Land diversity and land quality are quite different conditions, and success in one does not compensate for failure in the other. Diversity loss determines the index of most countries in all regions

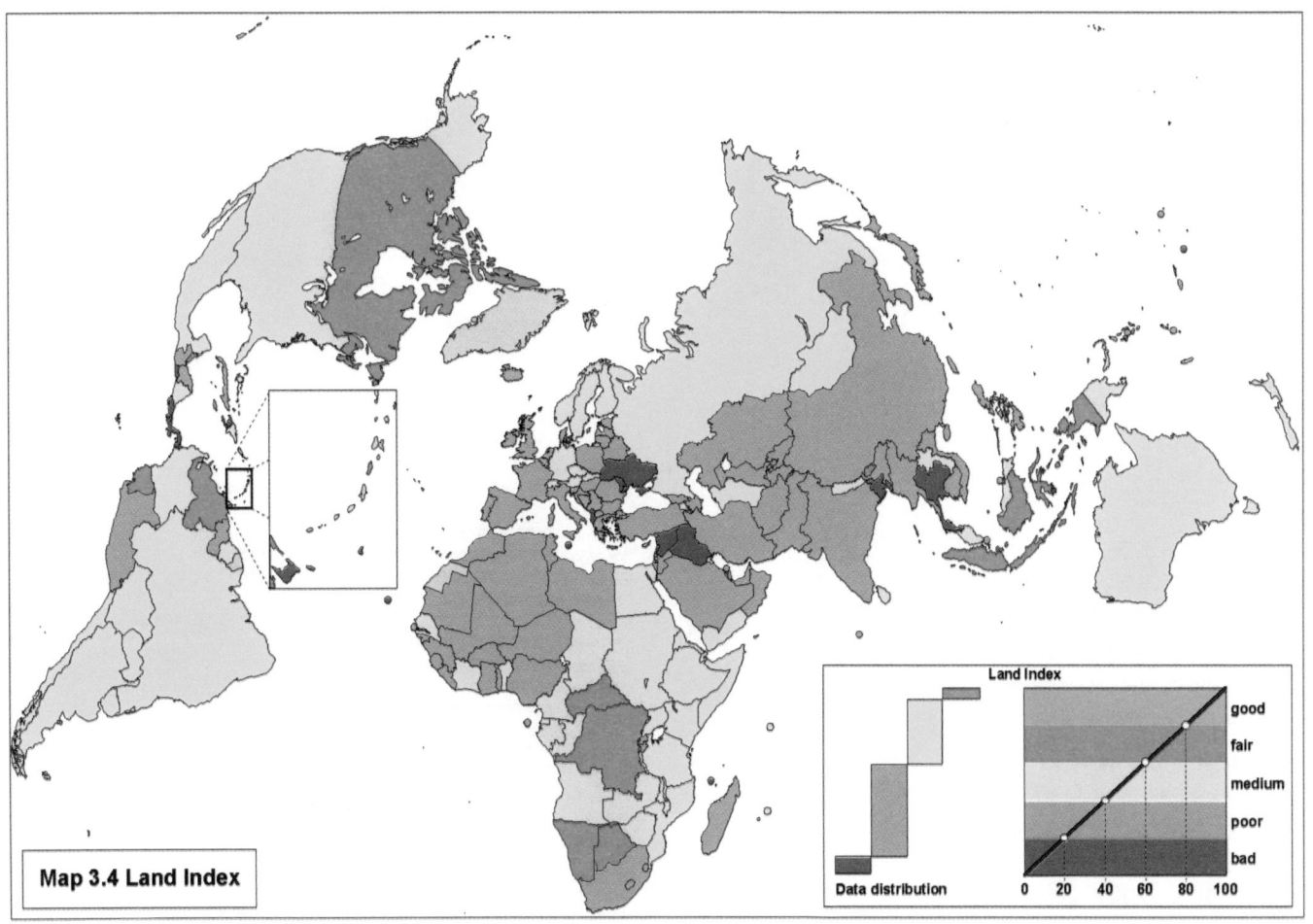

Map 3.4 Land Index

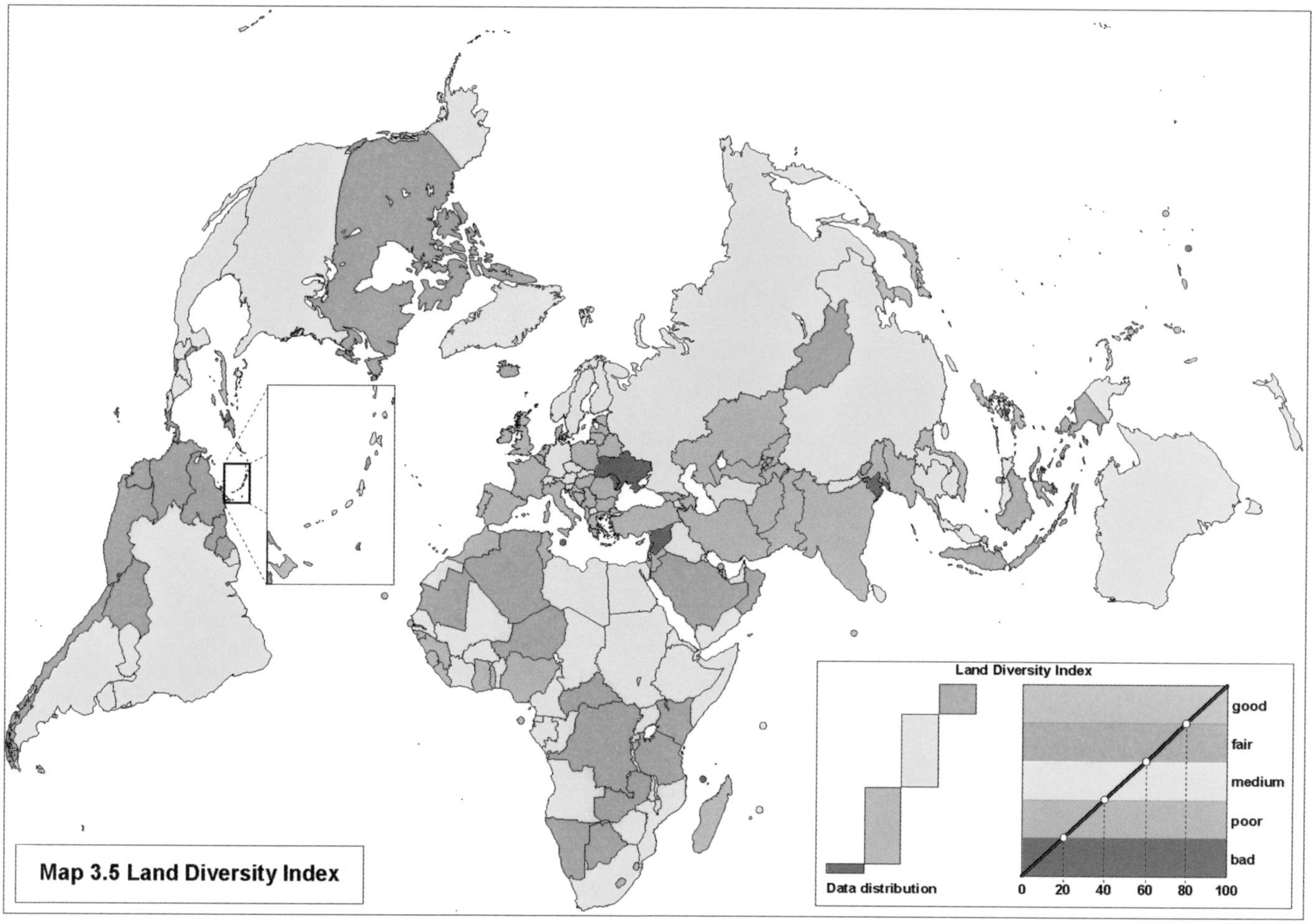

Map 3.5 Land Diversity Index

Land Diversity Index

good
fair
medium
poor
bad

Data distribution   0 20 40 60 80 100

except North, Central, and South America, where land degradation is the more frequent determinant (Figure 3.4).

For all data and scores, together with details of the indicators, performance criteria, and combining procedures, see Table 10 (land index, basic data, native forest change), Table 11 (natural, modified, cultivated, and built land), Table 12 (land protection), and Table 13 (land quality) in the Data section.

Land Diversity

Land Diversity Index (Map 3.5)

What it is: Weighted average [weights in brackets] of land modification and conversion score [2] and land protection score [1] (Figure 3.5).

Objective: All major land ecosystems maintained or restored in large units with minimal loss of the habitats and communities within them.

Country results: 0 good (0%), 30 fair (17%), 69 medium (38%), 70 poor (39%), 11 bad (6%).

The land diversity index measures how much land has been converted to cultivated and built areas, how much of the unconverted remainder is natural (negligibly to lightly human-influenced), and how much of the land is protected.[6]

The proportions of the land that are converted, modified (moderately to heavily human-influenced but not

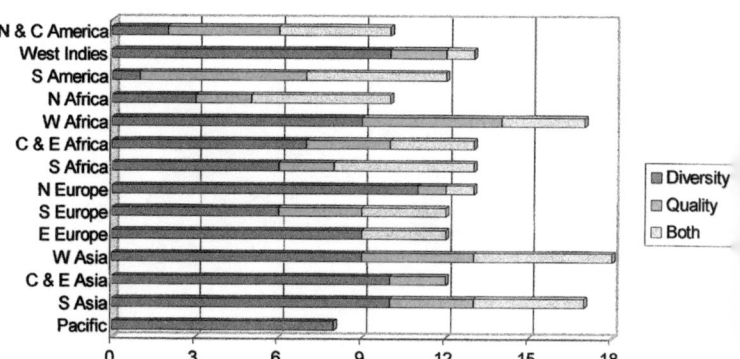

Figure 3.4. Number of countries whose land index is determined by land diversity, land quality, or both. Both elements are considered determinants if their scores are in the same performance band.

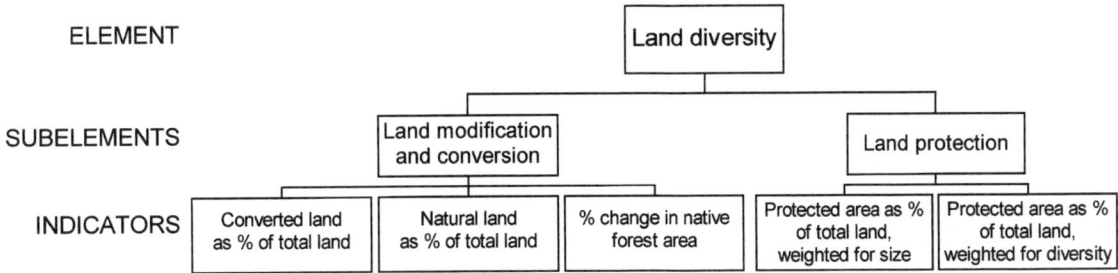

Figure 3.5. Indicator chart for land diversity.

cultivated or built), and natural reveal the scale and rate of a society's overall impact on the ecosystem, both within and beyond its borders. A nation that conserves its natural and modified lands is an ecological donor, helping to maintain the support system of the entire planet. A nation whose territory is largely cultivated and built is an ecological debtor, dependent on other countries for the services that natural and modified areas provide.

The select club of ecological donors—countries with a fair land diversity index—is a motley group, ranging in land area from 922-million-hectare Canada to 75,000-hectare-Dominica and in income per person from $25,110 Iceland to $480 Tanzania. One explanation of their performance is low population pressure: 83% of them (all except Dominica, Dominican Republic, Kenya, Brunei Darussalam, and Indonesia) have a land availability (land area divided by population) of 2 hectares or more per person, compared with 19% of those with a poor or bad land diversity index. Another explanation is low agricultural pressure: only six (20%) of the countries (Canada, Chile, Colombia, Guyana, Panama, and Venezuela) meet much of their needs from their land, achieving good or fair scores for both food sufficiency and food production as a percentage of supply. The others depend heavily on imports for food, are ill fed, or (in the cases of Mauritania and Mongolia) both.

Yet the American countries show that it is possible to maintain land diversity while producing enough from the land to meet most domestic needs. Chile's performance is particularly impressive. Less than 10% of its land is converted, 50% is still natural, and more than 18% is protected. At the same time, the country produces 85% of its food supply and meets the food needs of 95% of its people. Even Dominica, whose land availability is a globally more typical 1.1 hectares per person (compared

with Chile's 4.9), performs fairly well on both fronts. Although a quarter of the island's land area has been converted, almost 43% is still natural, 9% is protected, and the area of native forest is stable. The island produces 63% of its food supply (not enough, but respectable for its size) and achieves a fair score for food sufficiency.

The vastly more numerous ecological debtors (countries with a poor or bad land diversity index) tend to have a long history of land transformation and little land per person. Even in the best circumstances, restoring natural conditions would take many centuries. It is feasible only in nations with large proportions of unconverted land and land availability that is high (say 4 hectares or more per person) or, if low, stable or increasing.

None of the countries with a bad index qualifies. Among those with a poor index, more than half the land is unconverted in 53 of them, but only 17 meet the other criteria. Kazakhstan, Kyrgyzstan, Solomon Islands, and Vanuatu have 4 hectares or more per person; Trinidad and Tobago, Azerbaijan, Georgia, and 10 countries in Europe have less (from 0.4 to 3.0 hectares per person), but land availability is stable or increasing.[7]

Most countries with a poor index are burdened with large proportions of converted land, high population densities, or high growth rates. They will be lucky to hang onto the scraps of natural area they have left. If they fail to do so, their only way to offset their ecological debt will be to perform correspondingly better in other ecosystem elements, such as global atmosphere and species and genes.

Countries with a medium land diversity index are lesser debtors and could improve their positions fairly easily. All but Mauritius, Rwanda, and the Czech Republic have converted less than half their land

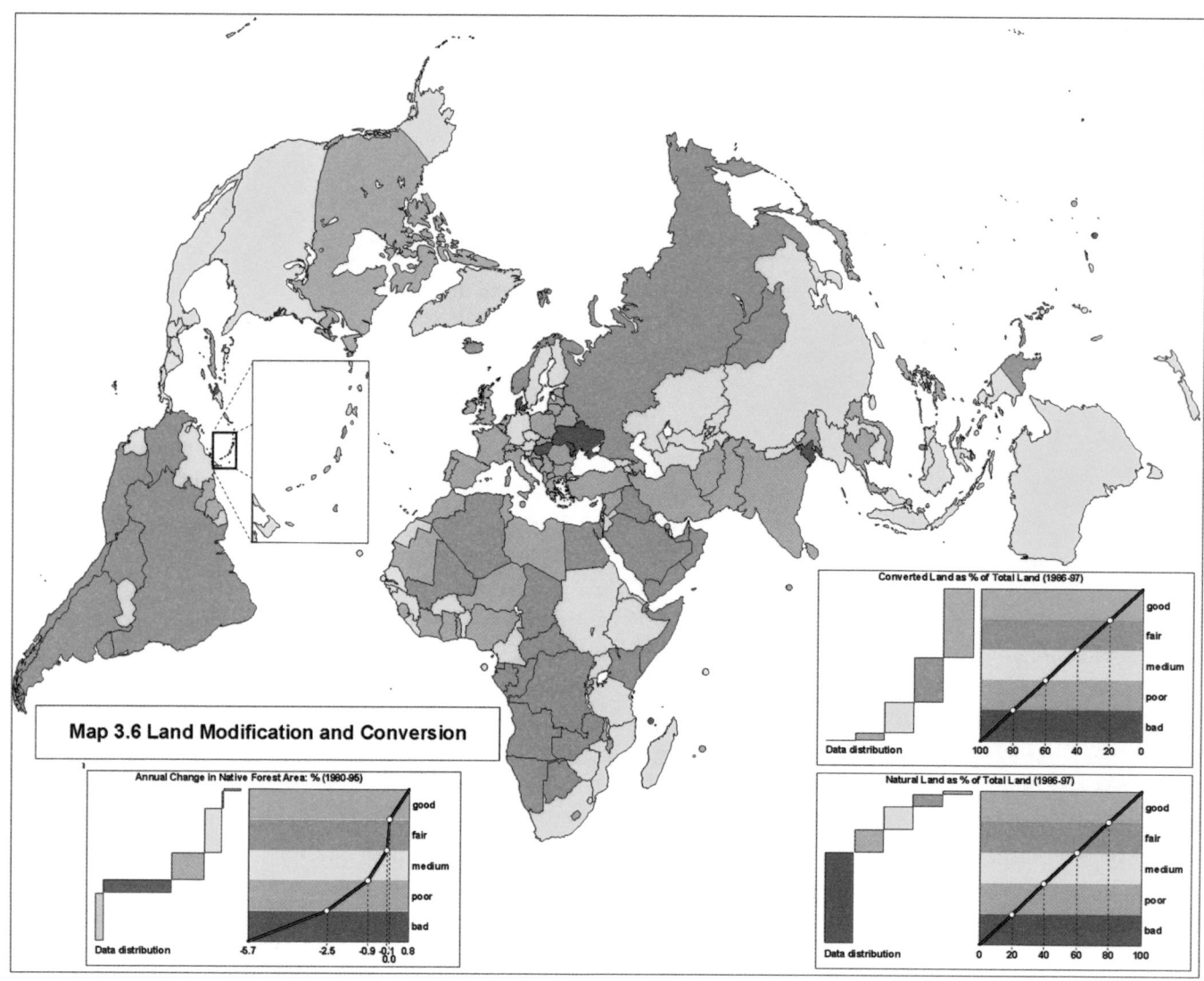

Map 3.6 Land Modification and Conversion

area. Land availability is over 4 hectares per person in 23 of them; among the 46 with less land, it is rising or stable in St Kitts and Nevis, Austria, Slovakia, and Slovenia.

The best way to maintain or restore a high percentage of natural land is to expand the system of protected areas. A large proportion of protected land shows a society's commitment to conserving its heritage of different landscapes. However, because protected designations may not be upheld in practice, the protection score was given half the weight of the modification and conversion score. Hence the land diversity index approximates the latter score, except where protection is much stronger or much weaker. In 21 countries, stronger protection raises the index to a higher performance band: Belize, Dominican Republic,

Ecuador, Panama, Venezuela, Tanzania, Bhutan, and Indonesia go from medium to fair; 11 countries from poor to medium (4 in Africa, 3 each in Europe and Asia, and St Lucia); and Denmark and Hungary go from bad to poor. In 53 countries, weaker protection drops the index to a lower band: Canada, Guyana, Suriname, Niger, and Mauritania go from good to fair; Libya from good to medium; 19 countries from fair to medium (9 in Africa, 5 in Asia–Pacific, 3 in South America, Norway, and Russia); 23 from medium to poor (13 in Asia–Pacific, 8 in Africa, 2 in the Americas); and Barbados, El Salvador, Malta, Lebanon, and Syria go from poor to bad.

Note that this index shows not how diverse each country is but how well it maintains the diversity it has. Some of the poor scorers—including India,

Nicaragua, and Madagascar—are also among the world's most biologically diverse.[8] They may have more land diversity left than some of the fair scorers (such as Iceland, Algeria, and Mongolia) that are less varied naturally.

Land Modification and Conversion

> ### Land Modification and Conversion (Map 3.6)
>
> **What it is:** Average of scores for converted land as percentage of total land, natural land as percentage of total land, and percentage average annual change in native forest area.
>
> **Country results:** 6 good (3%), 36 fair (20%), 69 medium (38%), 61 poor (34%), 8 bad (4%).

In most countries with a good or fair score, no more than 10% of the land has been converted to cultivated and built areas, and more than 40% of the land is natural. However, the area of native (nonplanted) forest is stable in only nine (Canada, Dominica, Djibouti, Libya, Mauritania, Niger, Iraq, Mongolia, and Yemen). The rest—except Iceland and Norway (no data) and Egypt, Kuwait, Oman, and United Arab Emirates (no forest)—are losing their native forests to agriculture, settlement, and infrastructure. The majority of nations with a poor or bad score have converted more than 30% of their land, less than 5% remains natural, and native forests are shrinking in all but one (Mauritius) of the 32 countries with data.

Overall, the percentage of converted land ranges from 75.4% (Bangladesh) to 0.6% (Suriname), and of natural land from 0% (several countries) to 94% (Suriname). Annual change in native forest area ranges from a decline of 7.4% (Jamaica) to an increase (through natural regeneration) of 0.7% (Dominican Republic). The percentages of converted and natural land are correlated with each other but, surprisingly, not with forest change—probably because the data were derived in incompatible ways, often requiring leaps of extrapolation. All three indicators are influenced by land availability: 76% of the good and fair scores occur above 4 hectares per person (86% above 2 hectares per person); all the poor and bad scores are below 4 hectares per person (93% below 2 hectares per person).[9]

Land Protection

> ### Land Protection (Map 3.7)
>
> **What it is:** Weighted average [weights in brackets] of protected area size score [2] and protected area diversity score [1].
>
> **Country results:** 9 good (5%), 39 fair (22%), 45 medium (25%), 27 poor (15%), 60 bad (33%).

Good and fair scores go to countries that keep substantial proportions of their various land and inland water ecosystems in large totally protected areas. The international target is full protection of 10% of each biome or major ecological region. Totally protected areas score higher than partially protected areas because they are likely to support a wider range of ecological communities. Within the totally protected category, large areas score higher than small ones because the bigger the area, the more it can buffer human activities and allow ecological communities to persist and evolve "naturally."[10] Areas qualify as large on a sliding scale depending on the size of the country: an 8,000-hectare protected area in a 75,000-hectare country (such as Dominica) is just as valuable as an 8-million-hectare protected area in a 75-million-hectare country (such as Zambia). Although protecting a country's ecosystem diversity matters as much as the size of the protected areas, the diversity score was given less weight because the indicator is less reliable. Note that both indicators measure protection on paper, not necessarily on the ground.

Only in North and Central America and Central and East Africa do more countries have good or fair scores than poor or bad. Performance is unrelated to land availability or to biological diversity: Central African Republic and Gabon are similar in both respects, but the former fully protects 5% of its land (4.5% in million-hectare areas), the latter 0.1%. Among countries with good or fair scores, 15 have less than a hectare of land per person; among those with bad scores, 11 have more than 4 hectares per person. Of the 45 countries with the most plant and animal species, 19 have a good or fair score, and 13 have a bad or poor score.[11]

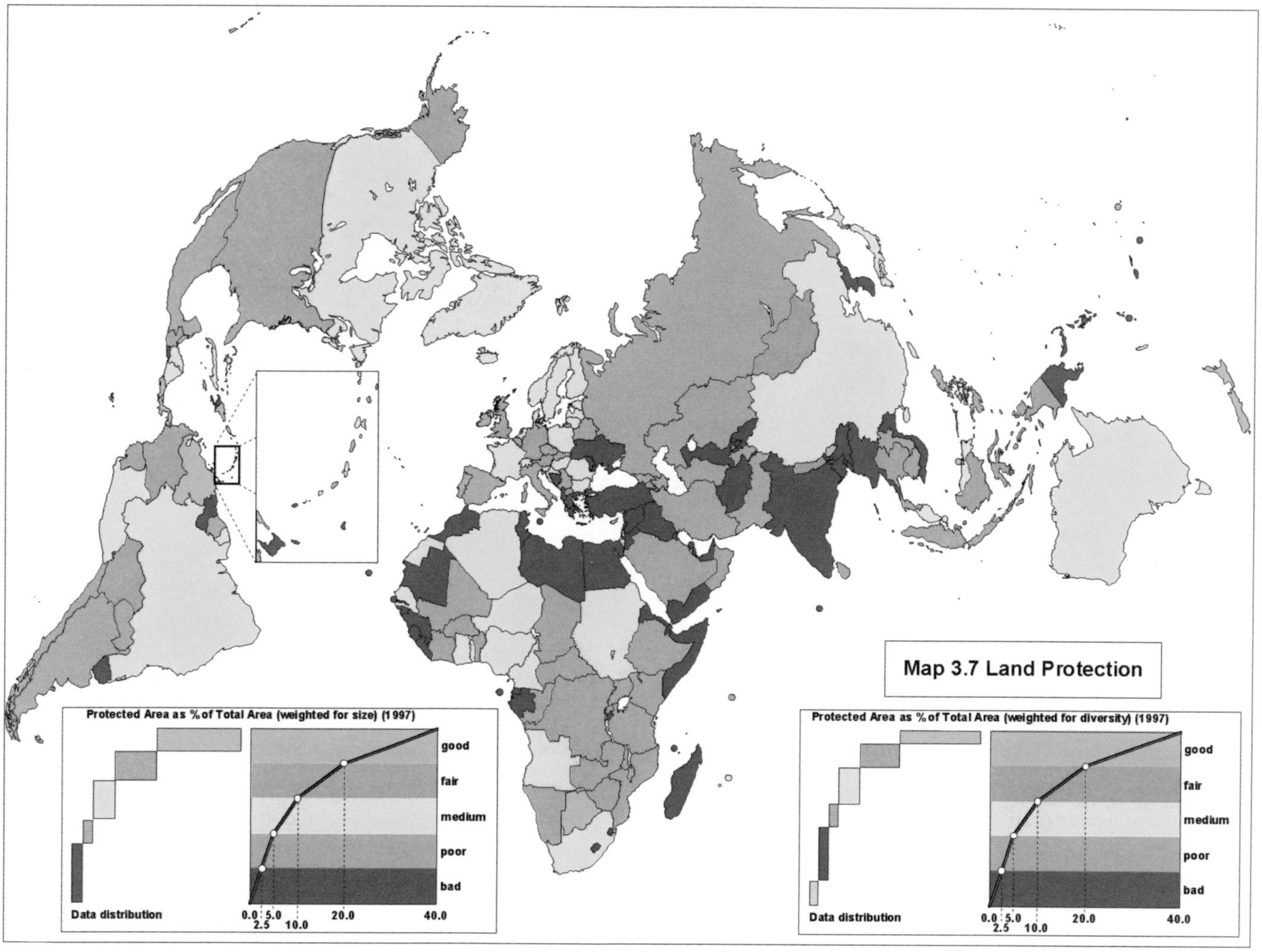

Map 3.7 Land Protection
Protected Area as % of Total Area (weighted for size) (1997)
good
fair
medium
poor
bad
Data distribution
0.0 5.0 2.5 10.0 20.0 40.0
Protected Area as % of Total Area (weighted for diversity) (1997)
good
fair
medium
poor
bad
Data distribution
0.0 5.0 2.5 10.0 20.0 40.0

Land Quality

> **Land Quality Index (Map 3.8)**
>
> **What it is:** One indicator, degraded land as percentage of cultivated and modified land, weighted according to the severity of degradation (Figure 3.6).
>
> **Objective:** Soil degradation close to background rates.
>
> **Country results:** 37 good (21%), 39 fair (22%), 44 medium (24%), 38 poor (21%), 9 bad (5%), 13 no data (7%).

Production of crops, livestock, and timber depends on the quality of cultivated and modified land but can impair it through erosion, depletion of nutrients and organic matter, salinization, and physical deterioration (such as compaction). Soils may also be degraded by acid rain and chemical pollution. Erosion is a natural phenomenon; only human-caused erosion above background or natural rates is counted here as degradation.

In some of the countries with poor or bad scores, much of the productive land is arid or semiarid and highly vulnerable to degradation (66% in Mexico, 99% in Pakistan, and 100% in Cape Verde, Eritrea, Libya, Niger, and Tunisia). In others, such as China, large areas are naturally erosive, and high rates of soil loss are extremely hard to prevent. Excessive production and pro-

ELEMENT
Land quality
INDICATOR
Degraded land as % of cultivated + modified land

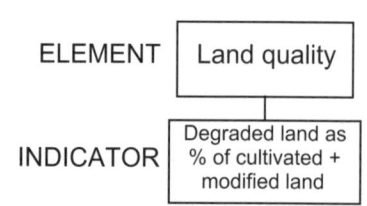

Figure 3.6. Indicator chart for land quality.

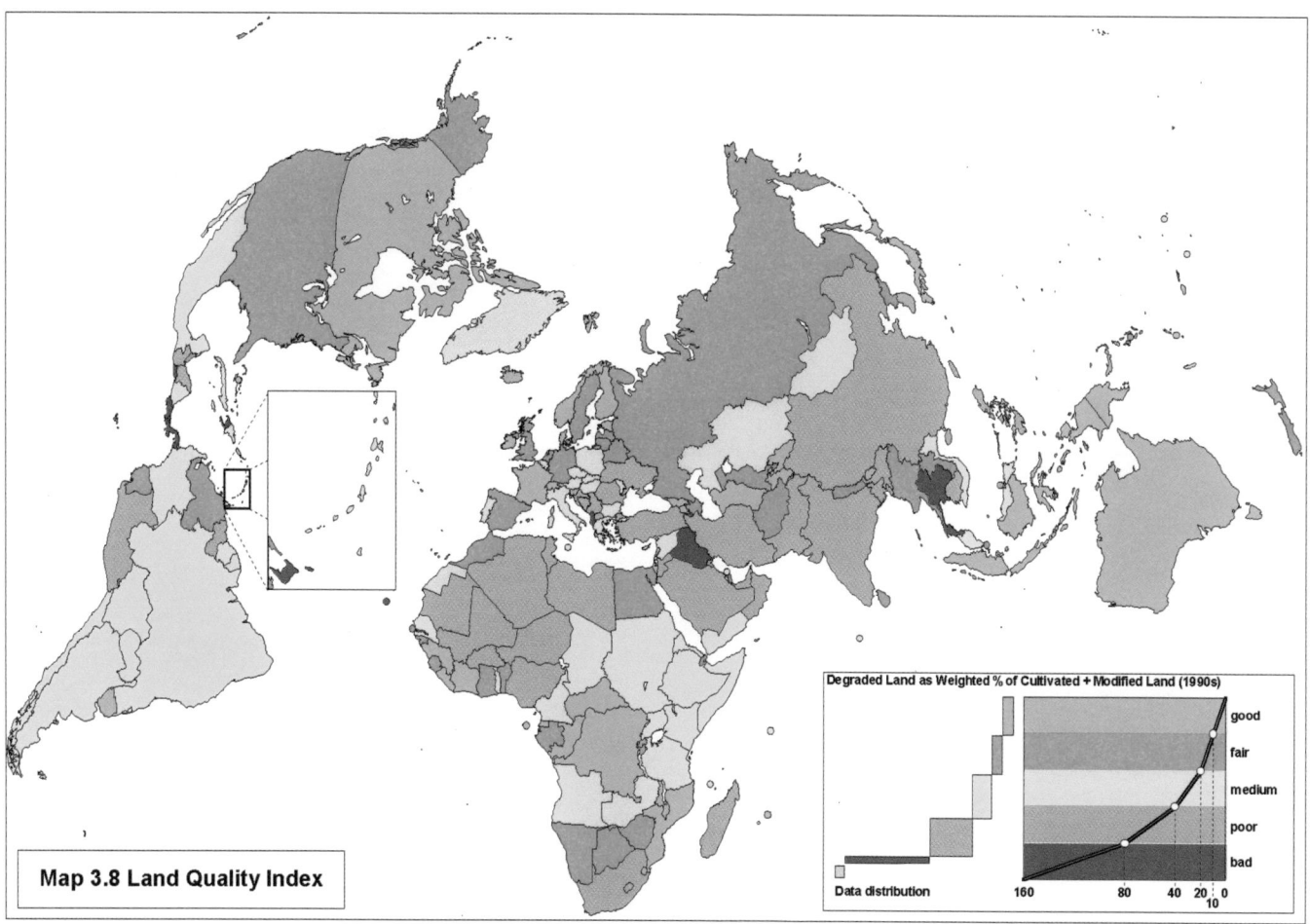

Map 3.8 Land Quality Index

Degraded Land as Weighted % of Cultivated + Modified Land (1990s)

good
fair
medium
poor
bad

Data distribution   160   80   40   20   0
10

duction of unsuitable crops are also factors: in Thailand, cassava raised for export as livestock feed has reduced nutrient levels on many small farms.

Except for East and Southern Asia, the estimates of degradation come from a large-scale review (the Global Assessment of Soil Degradation), which may be inaccu-rate for countries smaller than 10 million hectares (the size of Iceland): too high for some small countries with bad scores (such as Costa Rica, Haiti, Panama, Cape Verde, and Albania) and too low for others with good scores (such as Bahamas, Liberia, Malawi, Denmark, Georgia, Israel, Lebanon, and Fiji).[12]

Water

Inland Waters Index (Map 3.9)

What it is: Lowest of river conversion, water quality, and water withdrawal scores (Figure 3.7).

Objective: All major aquatic ecosystems maintained or restored in large units with minimal loss of the communities and habitats within them and minimal stress from pollution and water uses.

Country results: 0 good (0%), 46 fair (26%), 42 medium (23%), 32 poor (18%), 52 bad (29%), 8 no data (4%).

The sea could not be covered here for lack of adequate data.

This index measures the three main threats to inland water ecosystems: river conversion, pollution, and water withdrawal. River conversion—the construction of dams, banks, channels, dikes, and embankments—destroys habitats or degrades them by disrupting flows. Pollution harms people and aquatic life: so much wastewater enters rivers each year that its adequate dilution takes two-thirds of the world's reliable runoff. Water withdrawal, by reducing flow volumes, can intensify the effects of conversion and pollution.[13]

Rivers and lakes are even less well monitored than

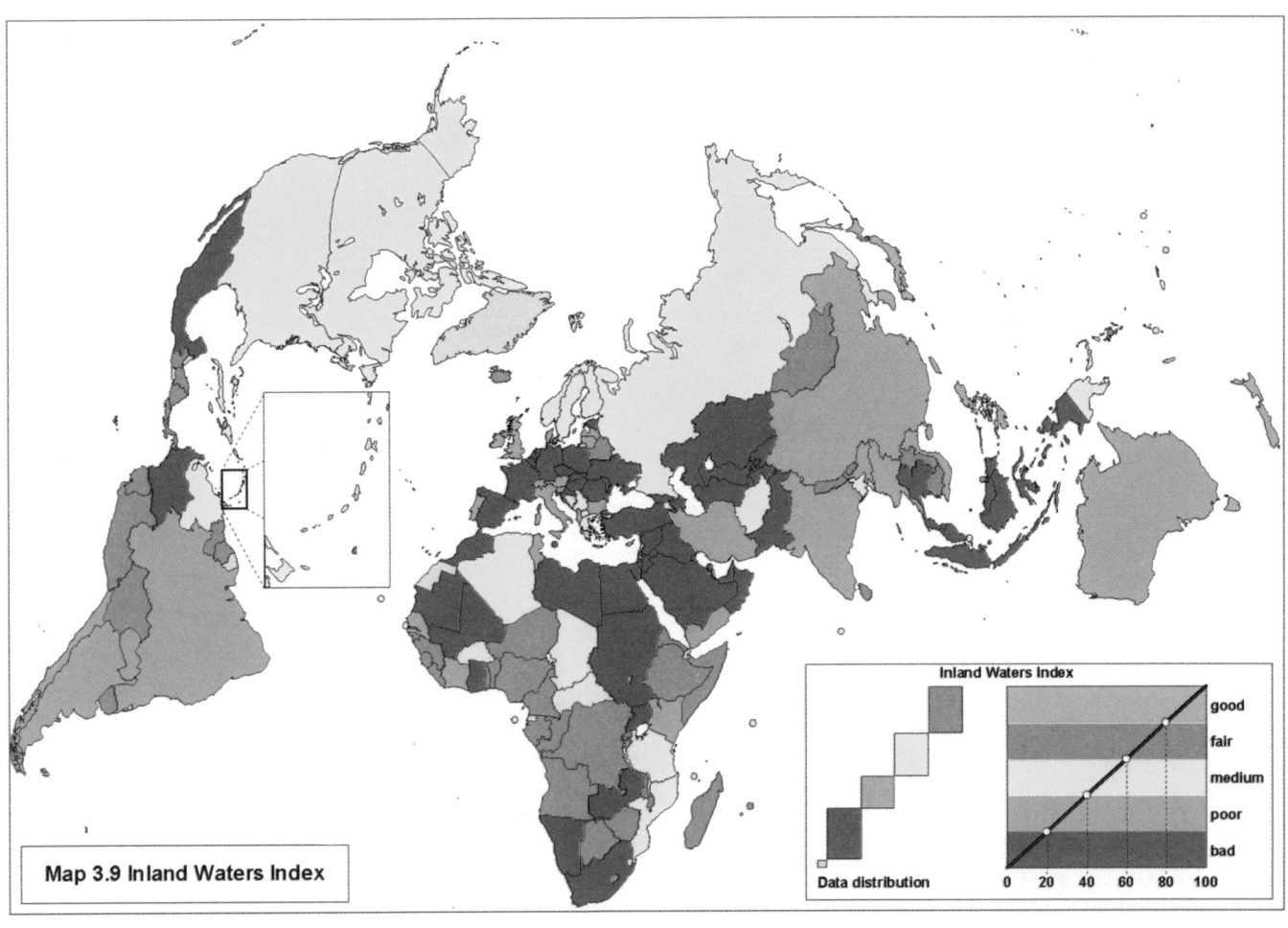

Map 3.9 Inland Waters Index

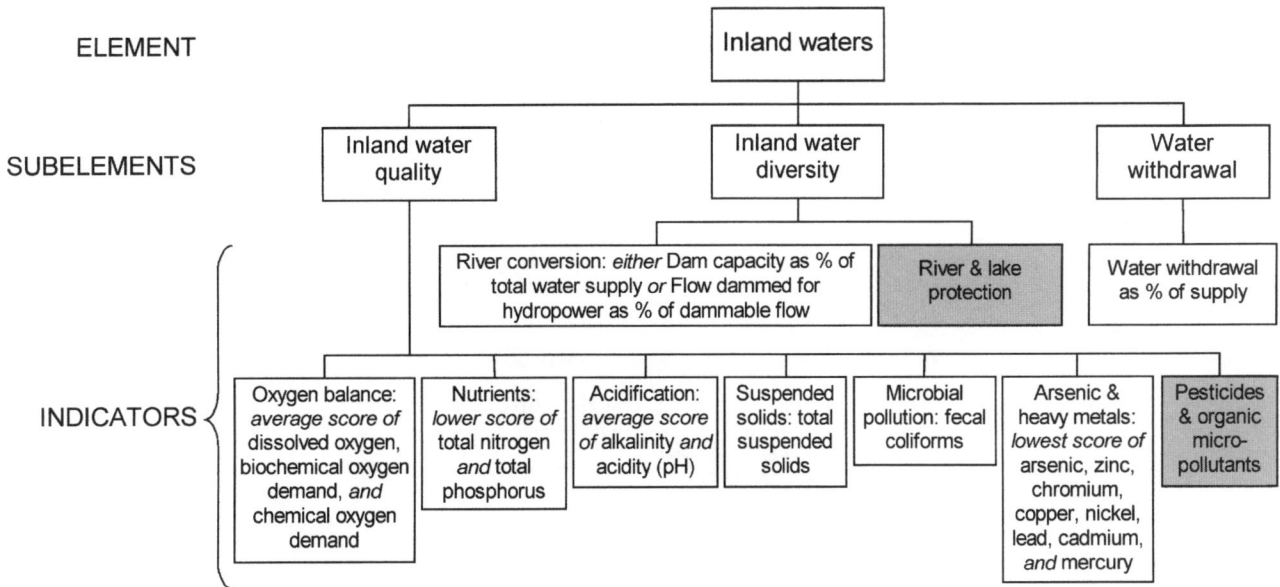

Figure 3.7. Indicator chart for inland waters. River and lake protection and pesticides and organic micropollutants (shaded boxes) are not covered due to lack of data.

land ecosystems but are probably in worse shape. Water quality is the weakest aspect, with data on a mere 72 countries, most of which do badly or poorly (Figure 3.8). No country with a fair index and only 11 with a medium index (Canada, Cuba, United States, Tanzania, Finland, Greece, Norway, Sweden, Russia, Bangladesh, and Papua New Guinea) could be rated on water quality. But it was the determining factor in two-thirds of the countries with a poor or bad index.

For all data and scores, together with details of the indicators, performance criteria, and combining procedures, see Table 14 (water index, river conversion, water withdrawal), Table 15 (inland water quality: score, oxygen balance, nutrients, and acidification), and Table 16 (inland water quality: suspended solids, microbial pollution, and arsenic and heavy metals) in the Data section. The classification of drainage basins used to organize water quality data is in Appendix F.

Inland Water Quality

> ### Inland Water Quality (Map 3.10)
>
> **What it is:** Average score of drainage basins in each country, each basin score being the lowest score of six indicators: oxygen balance, nutrients, acidification, suspended solids, microbial pollution, and arsenic and heavy metals.
>
> **Country results:** 0 good (0%), 0 fair (0%), 12 medium (7%), 26 poor (14%), 34 bad (19%), 108 no data (60%).

Deliberately or inadvertently, societies still treat water bodies as the ultimate receptacles for most of their wastes. Consequently, water quality is neither good nor fair in any country. In most, it is bad or poor.

The water quality indicator includes six major pollution concerns. *Oxygen balance* is critical for aquatic life and the biogeochemical processes that reduce pollutant loads in rivers. *Nutrients* (nitrogen and phosphorus) from farmland and municipal waste pollute drinking water, contaminate fisheries, reduce diversity, and stimulate blooms of algae that consume oxygen when they rot. *Acidification* by sulfuric and nitric acids, originating largely from fossil fuel combustion, reduces aquatic productivity and diversity. *Sus-*

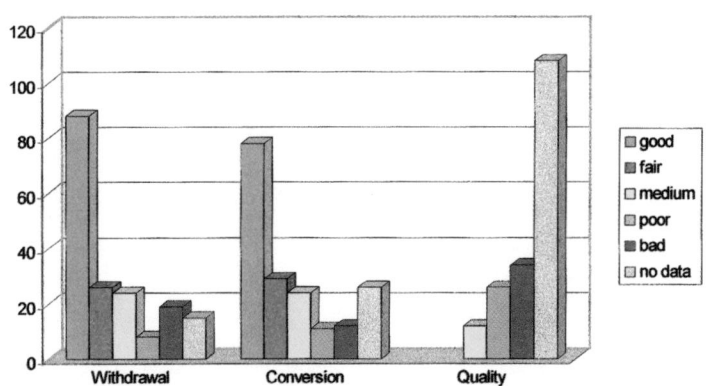

Figure 3.8. Number of countries by performance band for water withdrawal, river conversion, and water quality.

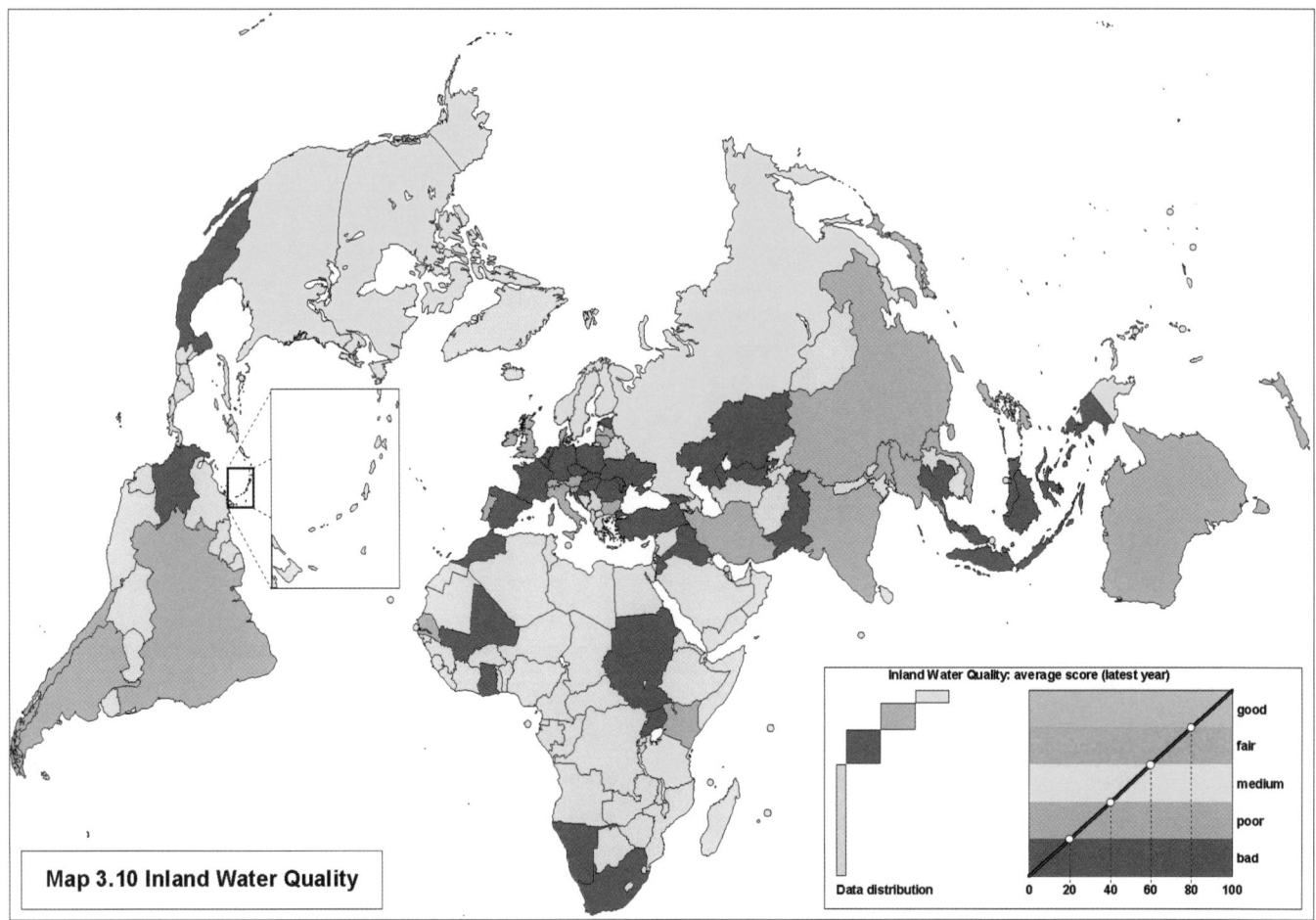

Map 3.10 Inland Water Quality

pended solids (particles carried in the water column, mostly from erosion) can destroy fish habitat, limit light penetration, reduce reservoir life through sedimentation, and are the main carriers of pollutants that accumulate in the food chain. *Microbial pollutants* (human and animal feces) carry pathogens that cause 5 million human deaths a year worldwide. *Arsenic and heavy metals* (cadmium, chromium, copper, lead, mercury, nickel, and zinc) are highly toxic and can kill or deform people and aquatic life.[14]

To be healthy, rivers and lakes must be well oxygenated, sparingly nourished (not excessively enriched with nutrients), close to neutral in acidity, only lightly burdened with suspended solids and bacteria, and negligibly contaminated by poisons such as heavy metals. Failure to meet any of these criteria is cause for concern. Thus the River Kiso in Japan was rated on the basis of its poor score for fecal coliforms, despite medium to good scores for oxygen balance, nutrients, acidity, suspended solids, and heavy metals.

Nutrients are the leading cause of low water quality scores in all regions except Southern Asia (where fecal coliforms figure as frequently) and South America

(where heavy metals are the main culprit). The next most common cause of low scores is heavy metals in West Africa, Northern Europe, and Central and East

Table 3.4. Countries reporting on most indicators for most basins. Number of basins (total); number with at least one report on oxygen balance (O_2), nutrients (NP), acidification (pH), suspended solids (SS), fecal coliforms (FC), arsenic and heavy metals (HM); and mean percentage (%).

Country	Total	O_2	NP	pH	SS	FC	HM	%
Bangladesh	3	3	2	3	3	3	0	78
Hungary	2	1	2	2	1	2	1	75
Morocco	4	3	3	3	2	3	3	71
Japan	10	7	7	7	7	7	7	70
United Kingdom	6	5	5	5	5	0	5	69
Ghana	3	2	2	2	2	2	2	67
Belgium	3	2	2	2	2	2	2	67
Poland	4	2	3	3	2	2	2	58
Finland	4	3	3	3	2	0	2	54
Mexico	12	7	7	7	7	7	2	51

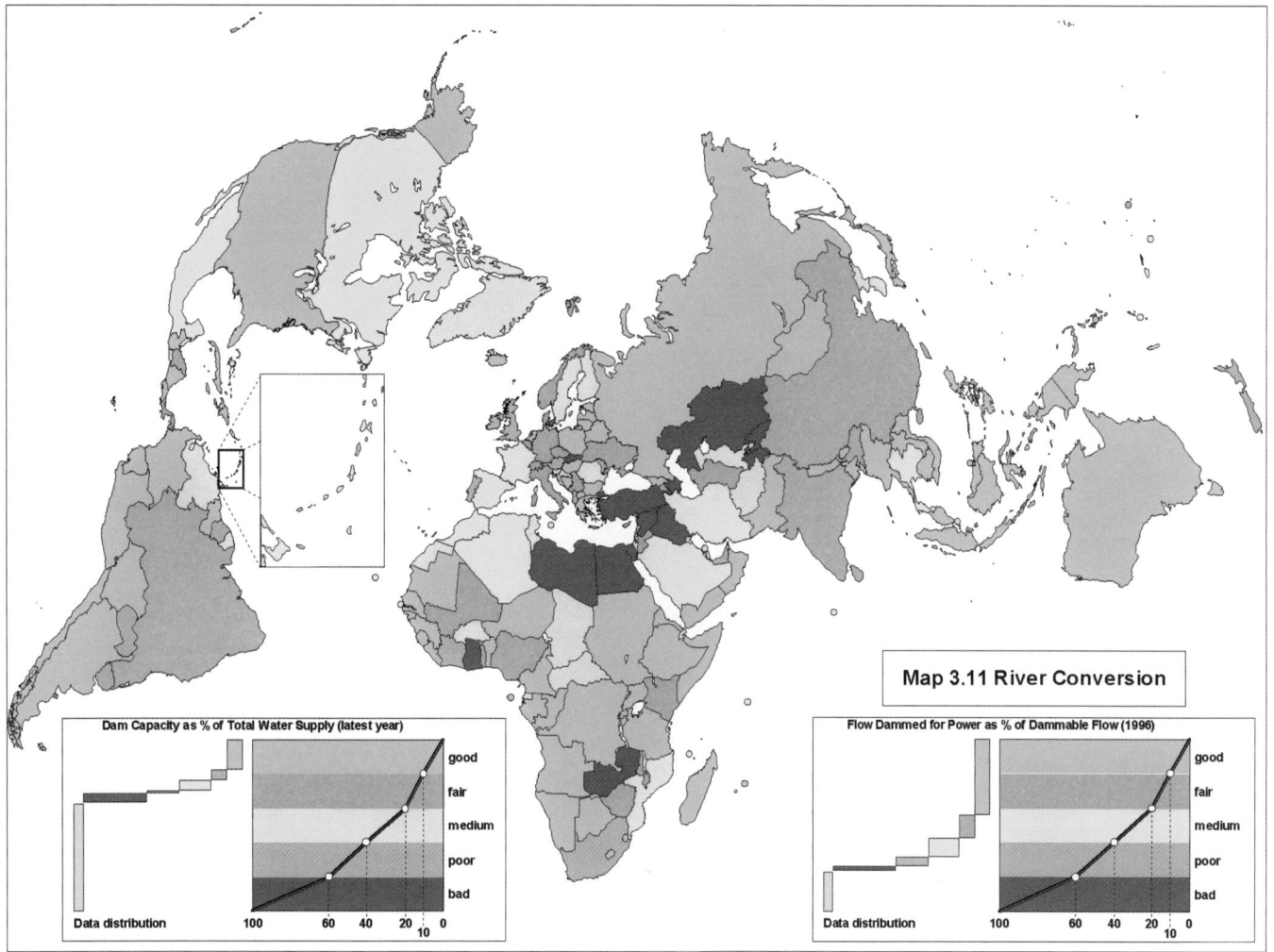

Map 3.11 River Conversion

Dam Capacity as % of Total Water Supply (latest year)

good
fair
medium
poor
bad

Data distribution   100   60   40   20   0
                                                10

Flow Dammed for Power as % of Dammable Flow (1996)

good
fair
medium
poor
bad

Data distribution   100   60   40   20   0
                                                10

Asia, and fecal coliforms in the Americas and Northern Africa.

A problem with measuring national water quality is how to translate data from an economical number of monitoring stations into a reading that is valid for the whole country. My approach was to divide the world into basins (Appendix F), defining a basin as an area of at least 100,000 square kilometers drained by a single river system or a group of smaller drainages. I chose a station at the mouth or downstream frontier of each country-basin (the part of a basin within one country) since a downstream point is fairly representative of the area that drains to that point. If possible, additional stations were chosen for large basins where conditions can change dramatically from one subbasin to another and for long coasts fed by many short rivers (as in Norway and New Zealand). Groundwater was treated as one basin. The number of country-basins so defined ranges from 32 in Russia to 2 in small islands and nations drained by one river system, such as Hungary (drained by the Danube).

No country reports on all indicators for all its basins. Table 3.4 lists the few with more than 50% coverage. They include only 2 (Bangladesh and Finland) of the 12 countries with medium scores. Bangladesh's omission of arsenic casts doubt on its score because high levels of arsenic have been found in its groundwater.[15] Inferior coverage reduces the reliability of other medium scores, notably those of Cuba, Tanzania, Albania, Norway, and Papua New Guinea, where coverage is especially sparse.

River Conversion

River Conversion (Map 3.11)

What it is: Dam capacity as percentage of total water supply or, if unavailable, flow dammed for hydropower as percentage of dammable flow.

Country results: 78 good (43%), 29 fair (16%), 24 medium (13%), 11 poor (6%), 12 bad (7%), 26 no data (14%).

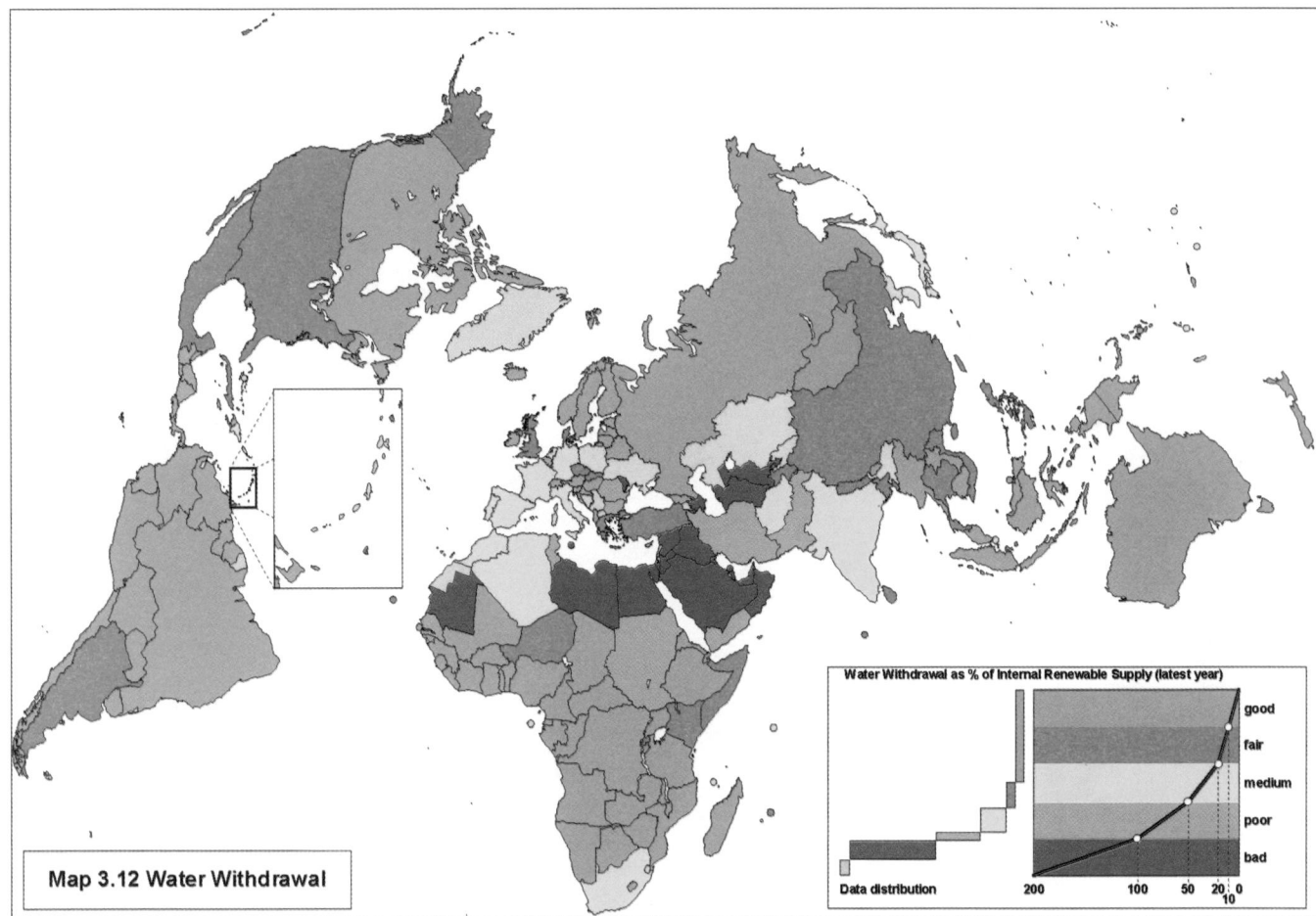

Map 3.12 Water Withdrawal

Water Withdrawal as % of Internal Renewable Supply (latest year)

good
fair
medium
poor
bad

Data distribution   200   100   50   20 0
                                          10

Much as for the land, the proportions of rivers that are natural, modified, or built (dammed, embanked, or channeled) reveal a society's overall impact on aquatic ecosystems. Dams and dikes can harm species, habitats, fisheries, and people by drowning some areas, denying water to others, changing the timing and volume of flow, increasing the salinity of coastal waters, trapping sediments, and starving downstream wetlands of nutrients and silt.[16] As flow control increases, wild rivers are converted into a series of artificial lakes.

Dams affect less than 20% of river flow in more than half the countries surveyed. Countries where 40% or more of the flow is controlled by dams are largely in regions that are arid (Northern Africa, Southern Africa, West Asia) or densely populated (Europe).

Most countries in Africa and Asia were assessed on the basis of dam capacity as percentage of total water supply. Other countries were assessed on the basis of the hydropower indicator, which can result in underestimates since it omits dams used exclusively for water storage and irrigation.

Both indicators would give different results if they measured each country's basins and subbasins separately

rather than treating them as a single homogeneous entity. Zambia gets a bad score because its dam capacity is almost double its total water supply. But the dams are concentrated on the Kafue River, one of six major subbasins (four of the Zambezi, two of the Congo). The other subbasins are largely undammed, and the entire upper Zambezi above Victoria Falls is essentially wild. An average of the six subbasins would be more meaningful.[17]

Water Withdrawal

Water Withdrawal (Map 3.12)

What it is: One indicator, water withdrawal as a percentage of internal renewable supply. (Withdrawal is the total gross volume of ground and surface water extracted annually for domestic, agricultural, and industrial uses, including losses during transport. Internal renewable supply is the amount of water available each year from precipitation.)

Country results: 88 good (49%), 26 fair (14%), 24 medium (13%), 8 poor (4%), 19 bad (11%), 15 no data (8%).

Water withdrawal as a percentage of supply shows pressure on water bodies, the degree of water scarcity, and the likelihood of competition and conflict among different water uses and users. High rates of water withdrawal threaten aquatic species and ecosystems. Increases in water withdrawal, especially in dry lands and coastal areas, add to salinization and other water quality problems. In many countries, overuse of groundwater has led to land sinkage, salt water intrusion, or reduced river flow.

Water withdrawal ranges from 54,000% of internal renewable supply in Kuwait to close to 0% in eight countries. Countries with poor or bad scores are in dry regions of Africa and Asia or at the downstream end of rivers in Europe, where competition is high. A poor score means that the country uses at least half the internal renewable supply; a bad score that it uses all of it or more. The former situation puts great pressure on freshwater ecosystems. The latter is obviously unsustainable since water must be obtained from river flows of other countries (making the supply vulnerable to damming, pollution, and removal by upstream users), from fossil groundwater supplies (which are nonrenewable and eventually will disappear), or from desalinization.[18]

Good scores are good for the ecosystem but may be bad for the people. In Africa and Asia, they are often a sign that water use is too low to meet domestic and agricultural needs. Gabon is the only African country with a good score for water withdrawal that does not have a bad or poor score for food sufficiency or basic services (water and sanitation). And Brunei Darussalam and Malaysia are alone in Southern Asia to win on low water use without losing on basic needs.

Air

Air Index (Map 3.13)

What it is: Lower of global atmosphere index and local air quality index.

Country results: 0 good (0%), 82 fair (46%), 27 medium (15%), 42 poor (23%), 28 bad (16%); 1 no data (1%).

The global atmosphere provides essential conditions for the existence of life as we know it today. It regulates climate and the distribution of solar energy, maintaining the moisture and temperature regimes to which humans and other organisms are adapted. It lets in enough sunlight for plant production while blocking harmful solar and cosmic rays. It cleanses itself and prevents the ecosystem from suffocating in its own wastes by destroying the wastes or converting them to a form that the ecosystem can reuse. Rising levels of greenhouse gases, the weakening ozone shield, and reductions in the atmosphere's cleansing capacity are signs that human activities are disrupting the chemical balance on which these functions depend.[19]

Local air pollution damages human health, economic resources, and the ecosystem on a wide scale. Many cities

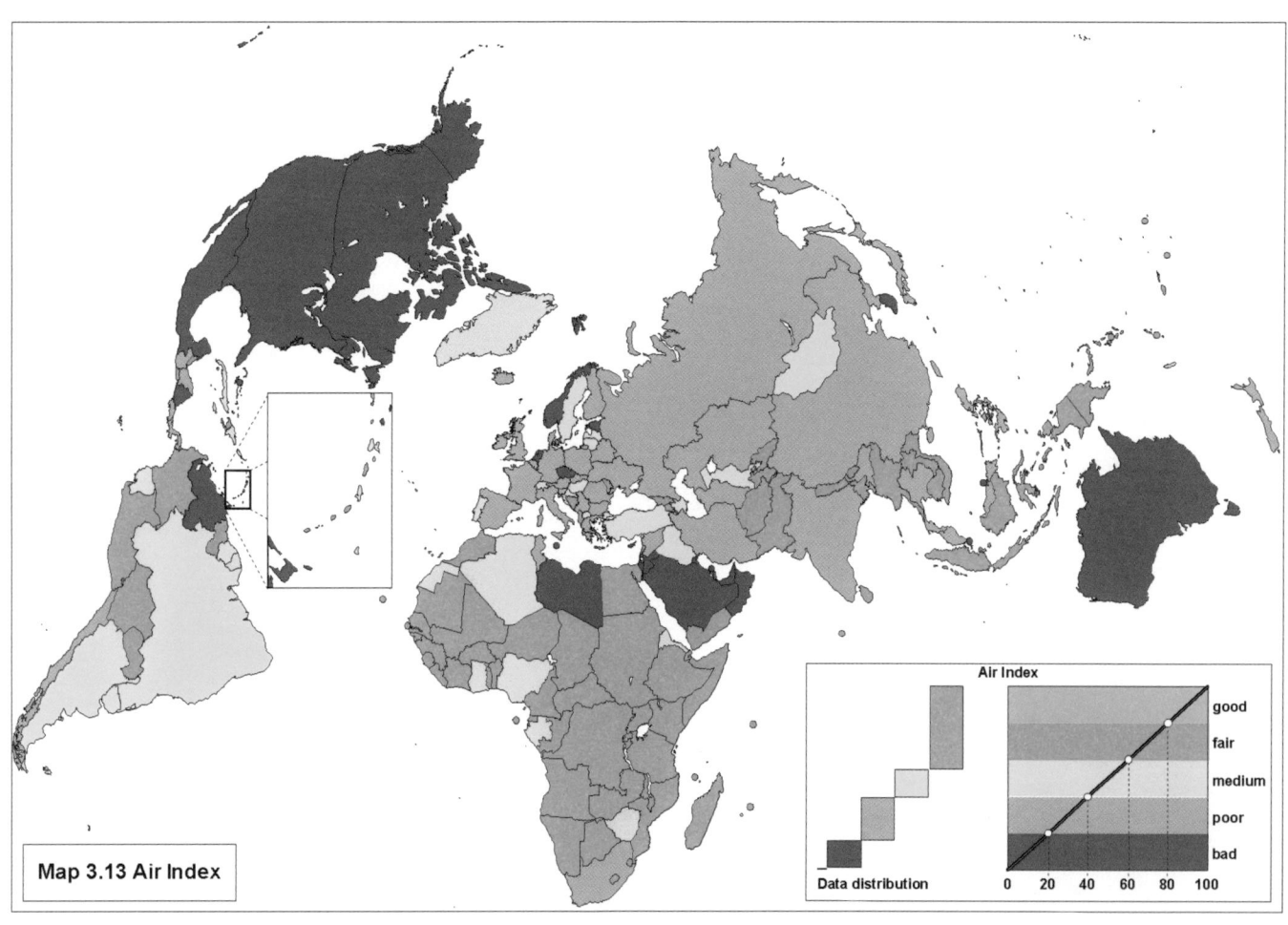

Map 3.13 Air Index

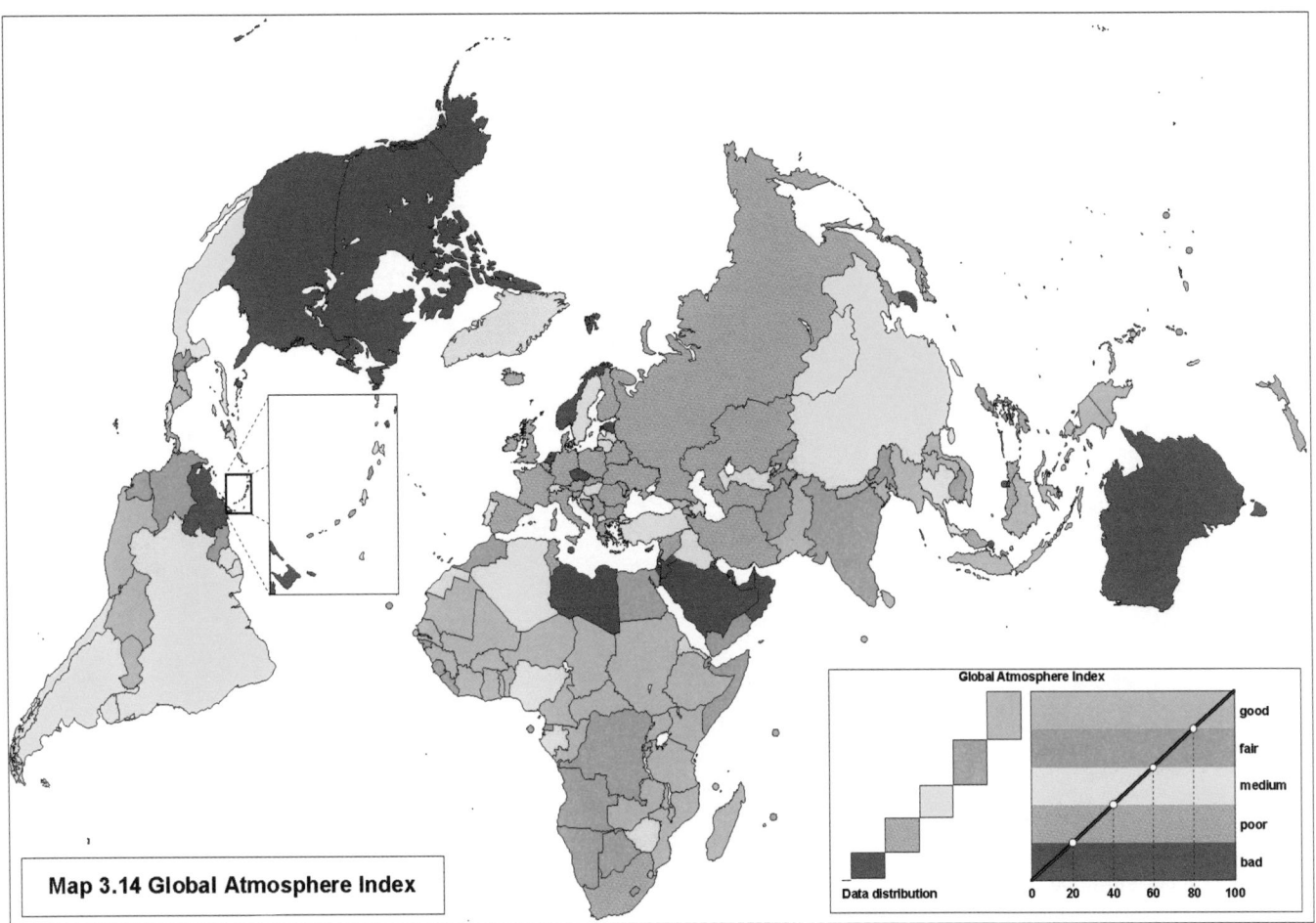

Map 3.14 Global Atmosphere Index

often choke in vehicle emissions. Smoke from burning vegetation is a major blight in rural areas that spreads into city air as well.

Because of a lack of data on local air quality, all countries with a fair air index and 15 with a medium index were assessed on global atmosphere alone (Argentina, Brazil, Cuba, Ecuador, Ghana, Croatia, Hungary, Lithuania, Portugal, Sweden, Switzerland, and Turkey were assessed on both). Among countries with a poor or bad index, 29 were rated only on global atmosphere, 41 on both elements. Among the latter, the weaker element is global atmosphere in South Africa, South Korea, and 25 industrialized nations; local air quality in 10 developing countries in the Americas and Asia. Panama, Italy, Bulgaria, and Kuwait have poor or bad scores for both.

For all data and scores, together with details of the indicators, performance criteria, and combining procedures, see Table 17 (air index; global atmosphere) and Table 18 (local air quality) in the Data section.

Global Atmosphere

Global Atmosphere Index (Map 3.14)

What it is: Lower of greenhouse gases score and ozone depleting substances score (Figure 3.9).

Objective: Elimination or sharp reduction of pollutants that disrupt the chemical balance of the atmosphere.

Country results: 46 good (26%), 43 fair (24%), 30 medium (17%), 34 poor (19%), 26 bad (14%), 1 no data (1%).

Greenhouse gases are so called because they allow the sun's rays to reach the Earth but prevent much of the heat from radiating away. The effects of rising concentrations of these gases are likely to include changes in rainfall patterns and in the timing and length of seasons, more frequent and severe storms, flooding of low-lying islands and coastal areas, the spread of insect-borne diseases, major disruptions to food supplies, and global warming. Global annual temperatures increased between 1910 and

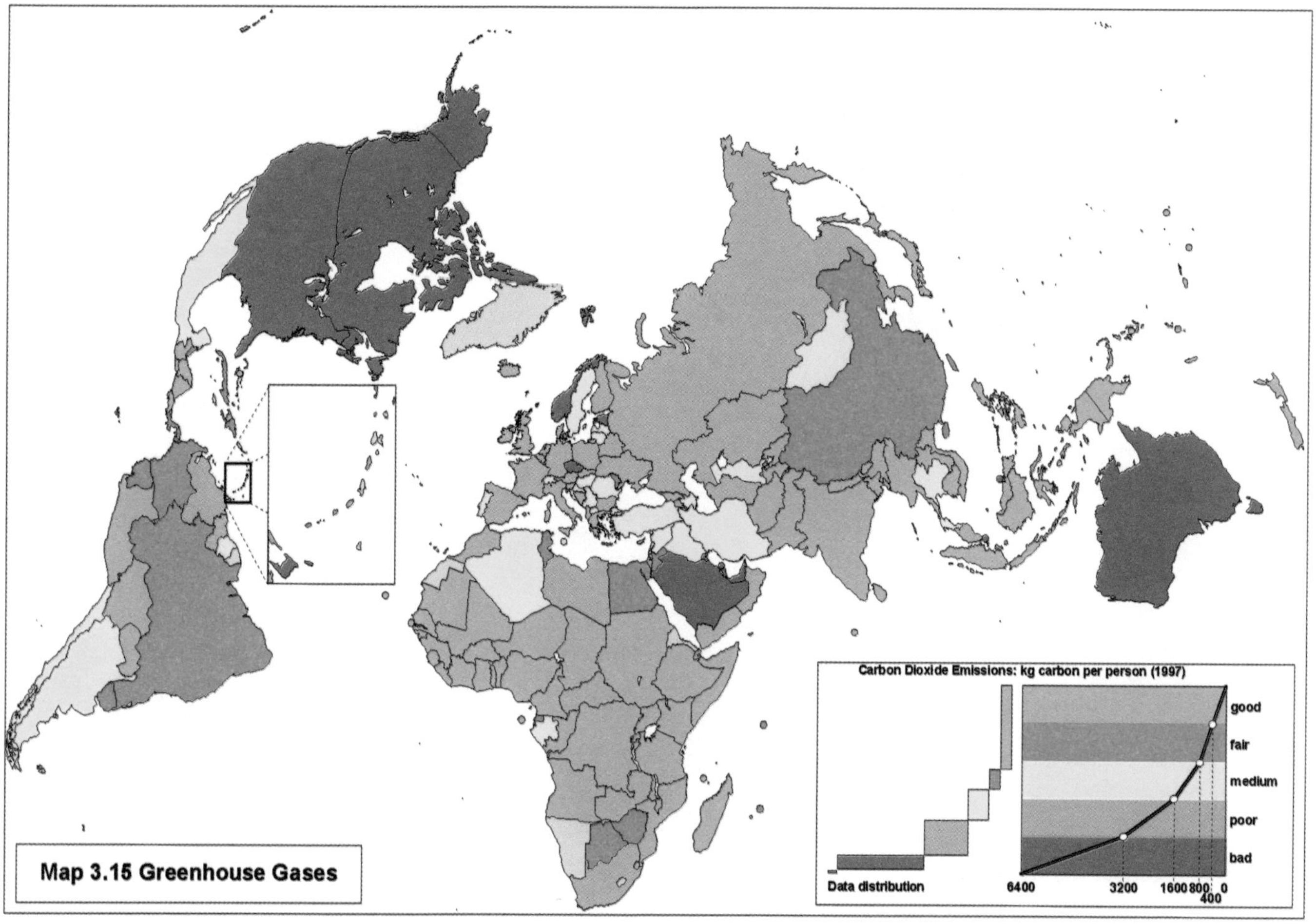

Map 3.15 Greenhouse Gases

Carbon Dioxide Emissions: kg carbon per person (1997)

good
fair
medium
poor
bad

Data distribution   6400   3200   1600 800 0
                                              400

ELEMENT

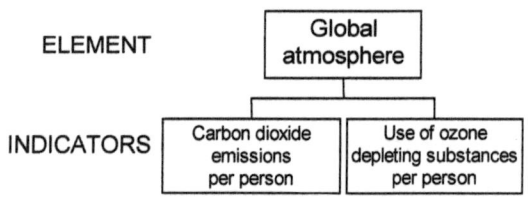

Figure 3.9. Indicator chart for global atmosphere.

1940 and stabilized until 1980. From then on they have risen rapidly, bringing the 11 warmest years since 1860.[20]

Ozone in the stratosphere filters out ultraviolet-B (UVB) rays from the sun. UVB rays reduce the productivity of the seas, damage crops and other plants, suppress human immunity to disease, and cause eye damage and skin cancer. Globally, in each decade since 1979, the stratospheric ozone layer has become 4–6% thinner in middle latitudes and 10–12% thinner in higher latitudes.[21]

Countries with a good index do well on both indicators. Those with a fair index include 24 (over half in Africa) rated on only one of the indicators. Among countries with a poor or bad index, carbon dioxide was the determining factor in

27, ozone depletion in 11, and 21 had poor or bad scores for both (Kazakhstan was not assessed on ozone depletion).

Greenhouse Gases

Greenhouse Gases (Map 3.15)

What it is: One indicator, carbon dioxide emissions per person.

Country results: 79 good (44%), 20 fair (11%), 29 medium (16%), 34 poor (19%), 15 bad (8%), 3 no data (2%).

This indicator is limited to carbon dioxide (CO_2) because it is the most important greenhouse gas, accounting for 64% of the increased greenhouse effect (methane accounts for 19%, nitrous oxide 6%, and halocarbons 11%). The chief human sources of CO_2 are burning of fossil fuels (coal, oil, and gas), cement manufacture, gas flaring, burning of wood and vegetation, and forest loss.[22]

The scientific consensus is that dangerous climate change will probably occur if the concentration of CO_2 in

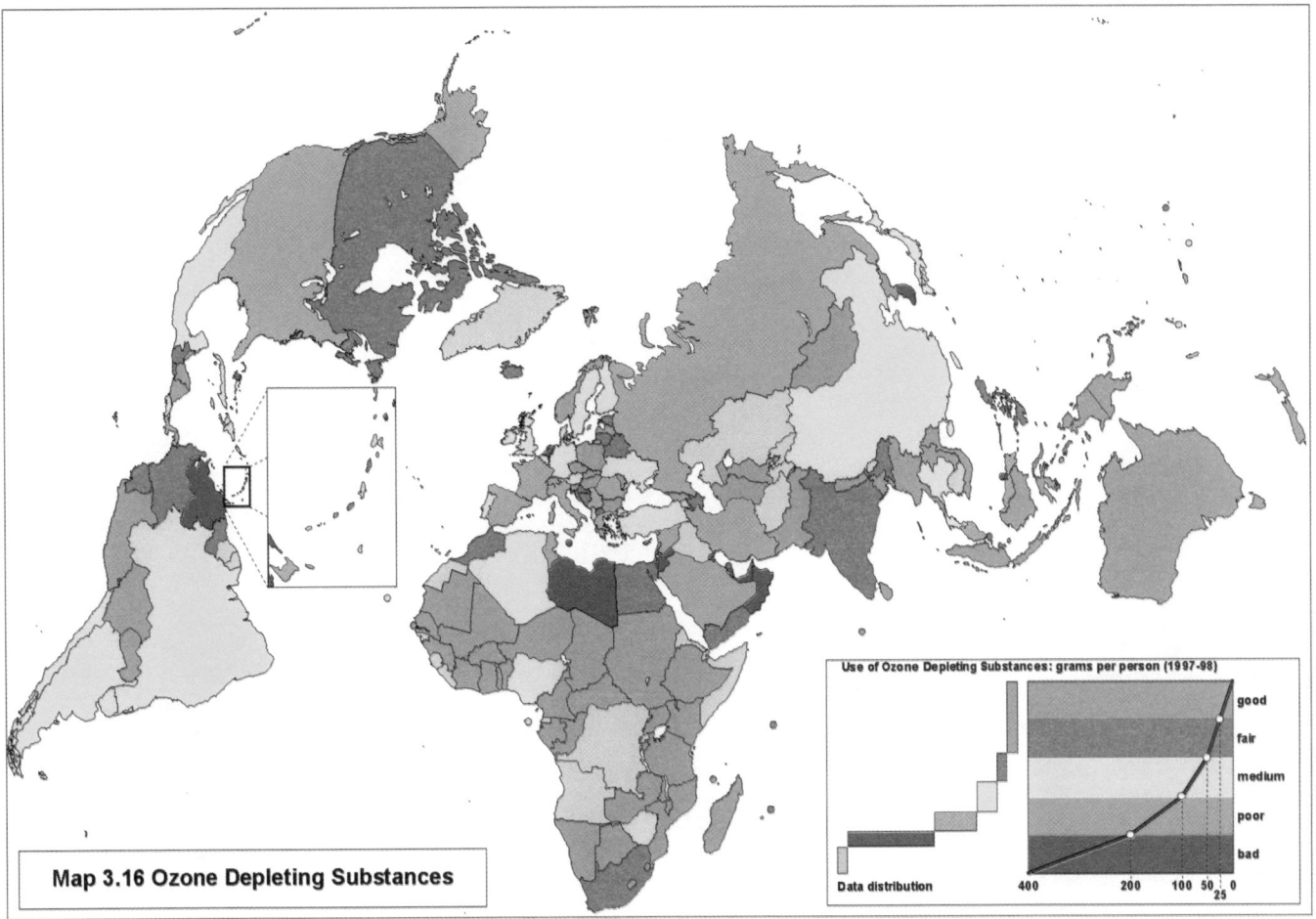

Map 3.16 Ozone Depleting Substances

the atmosphere rises to more than twice the preindustrial level. To stay below this level, global emissions would have to be cut from 6.6 billion metric tons of carbon in 1997 to between 3.7 and 4.9 billion metric tons. If the intermediate amount of 4.3 billion were shared equally by the world population of 10.8 billion projected for 2050 (United Nations medium variant projection), each person would have an emissions allowance of just under 400 kilograms.[23]

Countries with a good score achieve this target—but as a side effect of a low standard of living: only Botswana, Costa Rica, and St Lucia have a gross domestic product (GDP) above $5,000 per person; and only 14 have a medium HWI, the rest being poor or bad. Countries with a fair score emit up to twice the target amount and tend to be better off. Nine have medium incomes (GDP per person of $5,100–$10,000), and 11 low incomes ($5,000 or less). Eleven have a medium HWI; 8 a poor or bad HWI. Uniquely, Uruguay has both a fair score for CO_2 emissions and a fair HWI. At the other end of the spectrum, all countries with incomes above $20,000 have poor or bad

scores for CO_2 (except Switzerland), as do all countries with a fair HWI except for Uruguay, Barbados, Hungary, Latvia, Malta, Portugal, Sweden, and Switzerland.

Until the links between economic performance, transport, and fossil fuel consumption can be broken, countries will continue to balk at limiting—let alone substantially cutting—greenhouse gas emissions.

Ozone Depleting Substances

Ozone Depleting Substances (Map 3.16)

What it is: One indicator, use of ozone depleting substances per person (use is production or consumption, whichever is higher).

Country results: 67 good (37%), 27 fair (15%), 28 medium (16%), 17 poor (9%), 15 bad (8%), 26 no data (14%).

The protective stratospheric ozone shield is being weakened by gases known as ozone depleting substances (ODSs), such as chlorofluorocarbons (CFCs). They are

Map 3.17 Local Air Quality Index

produced exclusively by people for use in air conditioners, refrigerators, fire extinguishers, solvents, and plastic foams and as aerosol propellants.[24]

Most countries have agreed to phase out and eventually end ODS emissions. However, even if international targets are met, the ozone shield will take more than a century to recover. CFCs are likely to persist in the atmosphere for up to 50 years after emissions cease. Since the late 1980s, ODS consumption has dropped sharply in all industrialized countries and in Argentina, Brazil, Colombia, Egypt, South Africa, and Singapore. But it continues to rise in many developing countries, such as Venezuela, Nigeria, and India. In addition, phaseouts of production by the United States and Europe are being partly offset by illegal imports.

Since the aim is to eliminate use of ODSs, the best performance is 0 grams per person. Countries with a good score are within striking distance of this target. While most in this group are poor, they include a number with midrange incomes (largely in Eastern Europe) and four with high incomes (Norway, Switzerland, Australia, and New Zealand).

All countries were rated on consumption, except for those where production exceeds consumption (Mexico,

United States, Venezuela, France, Greece, Italy, Netherlands, Spain, United Kingdom, Russia, China, India, Israel, and Japan). These countries were rated on production because consumption data understate their reliance on ODSs and also ignore the problem of illegal trade. All have a poor or bad score except for India (fair) and Mexico, United Kingdom, China, and Japan (medium). Poor and bad scores among nonproducing countries are concentrated in West Asia.[25]

Local Air Quality

Local Air Quality Index (Map 3.17)

What it is: Average score of cities in each country, each city score being the lowest score of six indicators—sulfur dioxide, nitrogen dioxide, ground-level ozone, carbon monoxide, particulates (tiny solid or liquid particles that damage health and reduce visibility), and lead (Figure 3.10).

Objective: Minimal air pollution.

Country results: 0 good (0%), 12 fair (7%), 27 medium (15%), 12 poor (7%), 2 bad (1%), 127 no data (71%).

ELEMENT

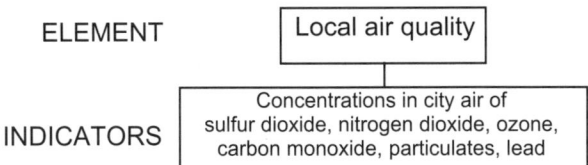

Local air quality

INDICATORS

Concentrations in city air of
sulfur dioxide, nitrogen dioxide, ozone,
carbon monoxide, particulates, lead

Figure 3.10. Indicator chart for local air quality.

All six pollutants included in the local air quality index are hazards to health. Sulfur dioxide, nitrogen dioxide, and ozone also damage vegetation and aquatic life. Of the 160 cities analyzed, nitrogen dioxide determined the air quality score of 103 (64%) and particulates of 40 (25%). The former is the dominant pollutant in five of the seven regions where at least 10 cities were assessed, the latter in the other two regions—South America and Southern Asia (Figure 3.11). The main source of these contaminants is road transport, which needs to be better regulated everywhere.

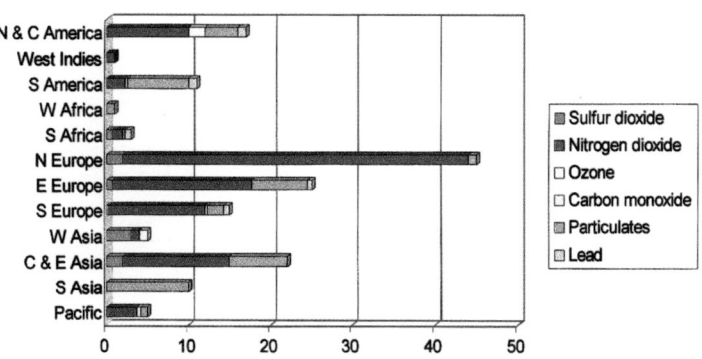

Figure 3.11. Number of cities covered in each region, and the determining pollutant for their air quality scores.

The fair scores should be treated cautiously since none reflects measurement of all six pollutants in a representative sample of cities.[26]

Species and Genes

Species and Genes Index (Map 3.18)

What it is: Weighted average [weights in brackets] of wild diversity index [2] and domesticated diversity index [1].

Country results: 0 good (0%), 19 fair (11%), 89 medium (49%), 60 poor (33%), 12 bad (7%).

Wild diversity is the linchpin of natural and modified ecosystems, the basis of their resilience and adaptability. Wild species have intrinsic worth and are the source of all biological wealth, supplying food, raw materials, medicines, recreation, and a store of other goods and services worth many billions of dollars per year. Although it is natural for species to come and go, the background (or natural) rate of extinction is extremely low (less than 0.01% per century). The rising number of plant and animal species threatened with extinction foretells an irreparable and unprecedented loss. Wild species are more threatened today than since the extinction of the dinosaurs 65 million years ago.[27]

Domesticated diversity is the key to sustainable use of

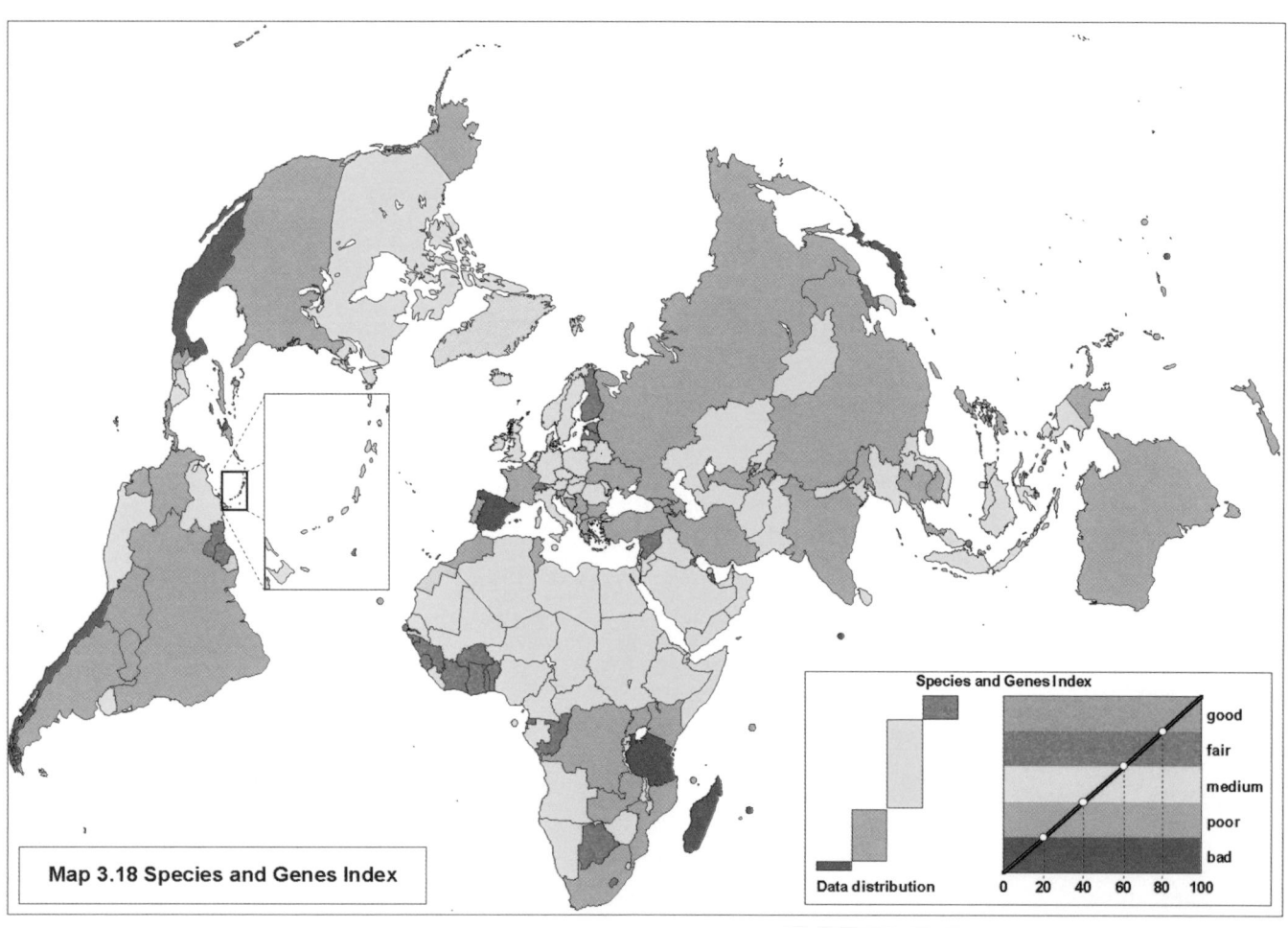

Map 3.18 Species and Genes Index

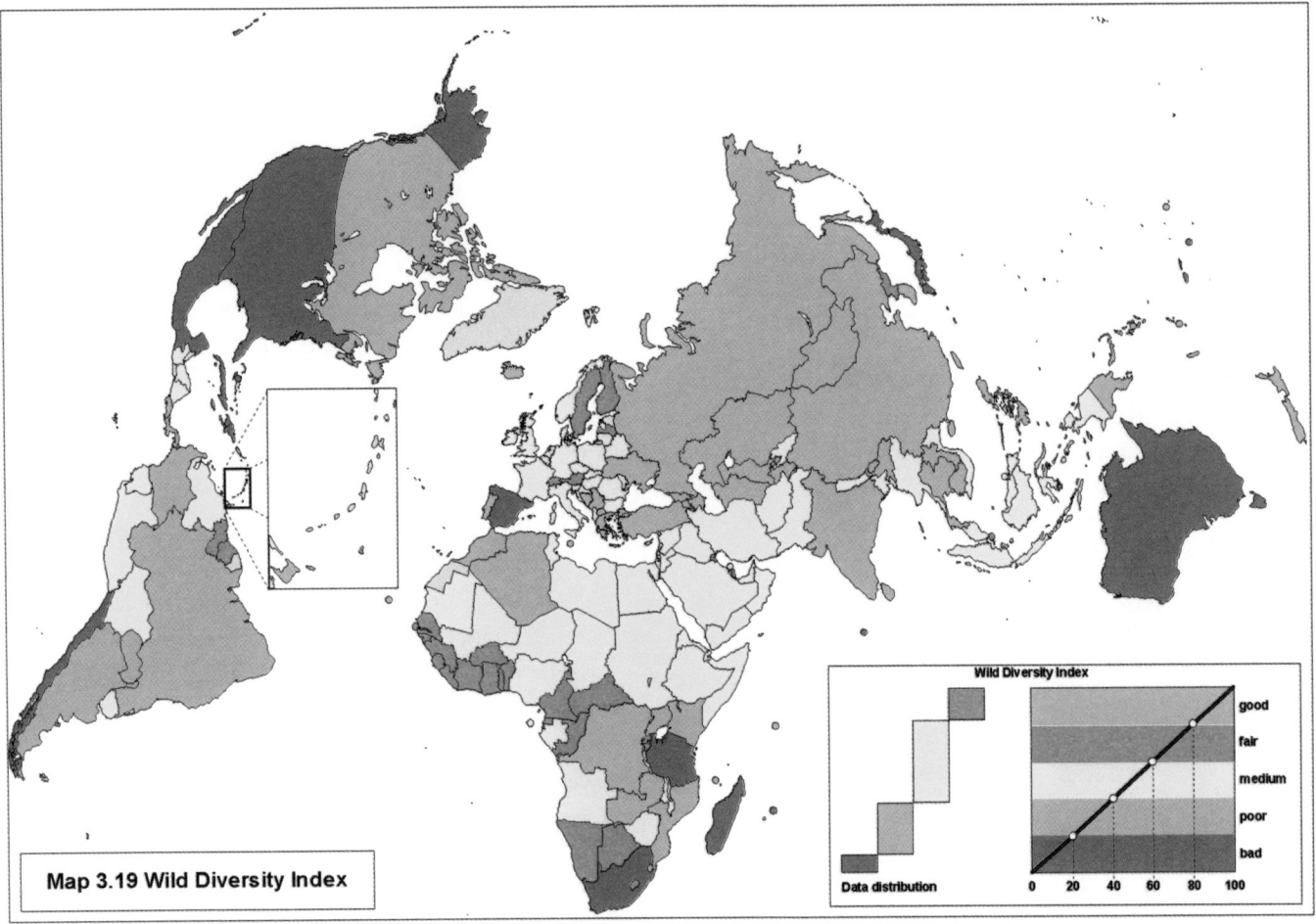

Map 3.19 Wild Diversity Index

modified and cultivated ecosystems. Many heirloom crops and ancient breeds represent centuries of selection to harmonize cultural preferences with ecosystem capacities. Locally adapted strains of livestock produce food, fiber, and income from places that are too cold, dry, wet, or barren to grow crops. The genetic material within crop varieties, livestock breeds, and domesticated strains of microorganisms provides essential traits for improving food and fiber production and developing biotechnologies. These traits—including yield, disease resistance, hardiness, marketability, and culturally desirable qualities such as flavor and color—are constantly in demand to cope with changing markets and environmental conditions.

Since the extinction of an entire species is more drastic than the loss of a breed or variety, wild diversity was given more weight than domesticated diversity. As a result, the species and genes index stays in the same performance band as the wild diversity rating in all but 36 countries. In 19 (such as Turkmenistan), high scores for domesticated diversity raise the index; in the other 17

(such as Austria), domesticated diversity is much more at risk than wild diversity and lowers the index.

For all data and scores, together with details of the indicators, performance criteria, and combining procedures, see Table 19 (species and genes index, wild species rank, wild plant species), Table 20 (wild animal species, domesticated diversity), and Table 21 (domesticated diversity continued) in the Data section.

Wild Diversity

Wild Diversity Index (Map 3.19)

What it is: Average of wild plant species score and wild animal species score (Figure 3.12).

Objective: Maintenance of all native wild species and reduction of extinctions to background rates.

Country results: 0 good (0%), 28 fair (16%), 77 medium (43%), 55 poor (31%), 20 bad (11%).

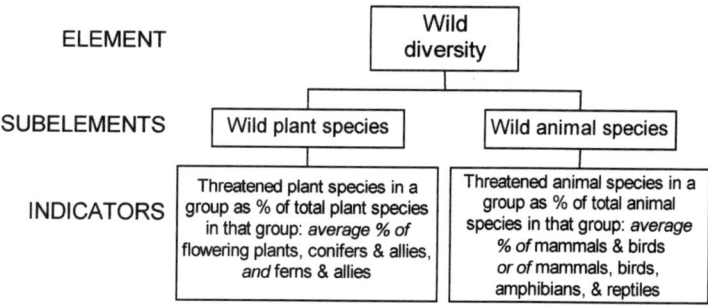

Figure 3.12. Indicator chart for wild diversity.

Most countries with a fair wild diversity index are modestly endowed with plant and animal species. Only four—Guyana, Suriname, Cameroon, and Côte d'Ivoire—rank among the top 45 nations in numbers of species. By contrast, 23 countries with a poor or bad index are in the top 45, including China, Mexico, Australia, and Madagascar.[28]

A species is threatened with extinction when it is reduced to a few small populations or restricted to such a small area that it could be wiped out by habitat change, disease outbreak, fire, pollution accident, building development, series of bad weather years, or other catastrophe. The aim is to maintain viable populations of all wild species, but since it is impossible to identify all species, let alone track what is happening to them, the indicators focus on groups whose numbers have been estimated and whose status is monitored.

Assessing species diversity maintenance on the basis of the percentage of threatened species per class (or other large group) accomplishes two things. First, it makes the numbers more meaningful: knowing that Rwanda and Mauritius both have nine threatened bird species says little about the performance of these countries without the information that Rwanda is home to 513 breeding bird species and Mauritius to 27. Second, it recognizes that

Table 3.5. The species hierarchy. Genetic loss increases up the hierarchy.

Kingdom (e.g., Animals [Animalia])
 Phylum (e.g., chordates [Chordata])
  Class (e.g., mammals [Mammalia])
   Order (e.g., even-toed ungulates [Artiodactyla])
    Family (e.g., antelope, buffalos, cattle, goats, and sheep [Bovidae])
     Genus (e.g., banteng, cattle, gaur, kouprey, yak [*Bos*])
      Species (e.g., cattle [*Bos primigenius*])
       Subspecies, type (e.g., humpless cattle)
        Breed group (e.g., Brown Swiss group)
         Breed (e.g., Braunvieh, Brune des Alpes, Rendena)

the higher an extinction is in the species hierarchy (Table 3.5), the more serious the genetic loss. Knowing only that 9% of Haiti's mammals, birds, reptiles, and amphibians are threatened masks the most alarming aspect: that all of its mammals are threatened, boding the disappearance of an entire class.

Habitat destruction is the main threat to species, so there ought to be a link between the land diversity index (LDI), which measures how much land is converted, natural, or protected, and the wild diversity index (WDI). Yet in only 57 countries (32%) do performances in the two indices fall in the same band: 4 fair (Suriname, Botswana, Central African Republic, and Namibia), 31 medium, 20 poor, and 2 bad (Haiti and Tonga).

In 40 countries (22%), the LDI and WDI differ by as much as two performance bands, with the WDI lower in 13 and higher in 27. Countries where the WDI is markedly lower tend to be medium-sized to large: all except Bhutan and Dominican Republic have a land area of more than 10 million hectares. The mismatch between the WDI and LDI may be due to the uneven occurrence of species: some parts of a country may have many species and others few. The species-rich habitats may be small or rare, whereas large or common habitats may be species-poor. In Chile, which has the most extreme spread between a bad WDI of 16 and a fair LDI of 67, the greatest number of species is concentrated in just 2 of the country's 12 ecoregions: the winter rain forests and the matorral (Mediterranean climate zone scrub). These also happen to be the most modified and least protected ecoregions. In Algeria (with a poor WDI of 34 and a fair LDI of 67), 83% of the natural land and 12% of the protected area is species-poor desert. The richest nondesert remnants are precisely the areas at greatest risk of conversion or modification. Thus the LDI can be an effective predictor of threats to species only if it is differentiated by ecoregion or major habitat, which at present it is not.[29]

Most (70%) of the countries where the WDI is much higher than the LDI are smaller than 10 million hectares. In the smallest, Barbados (with a fair WDI of 66 and a bad LDI of 17), 58% of the land area has been converted to settlements and cultivation, only 9% is natural or seminatural, and a mere 40 hectares is protected. Its most endangered animal group is reptiles, with two species threatened out of nine. But none of its mammal, breeding bird, or amphibian

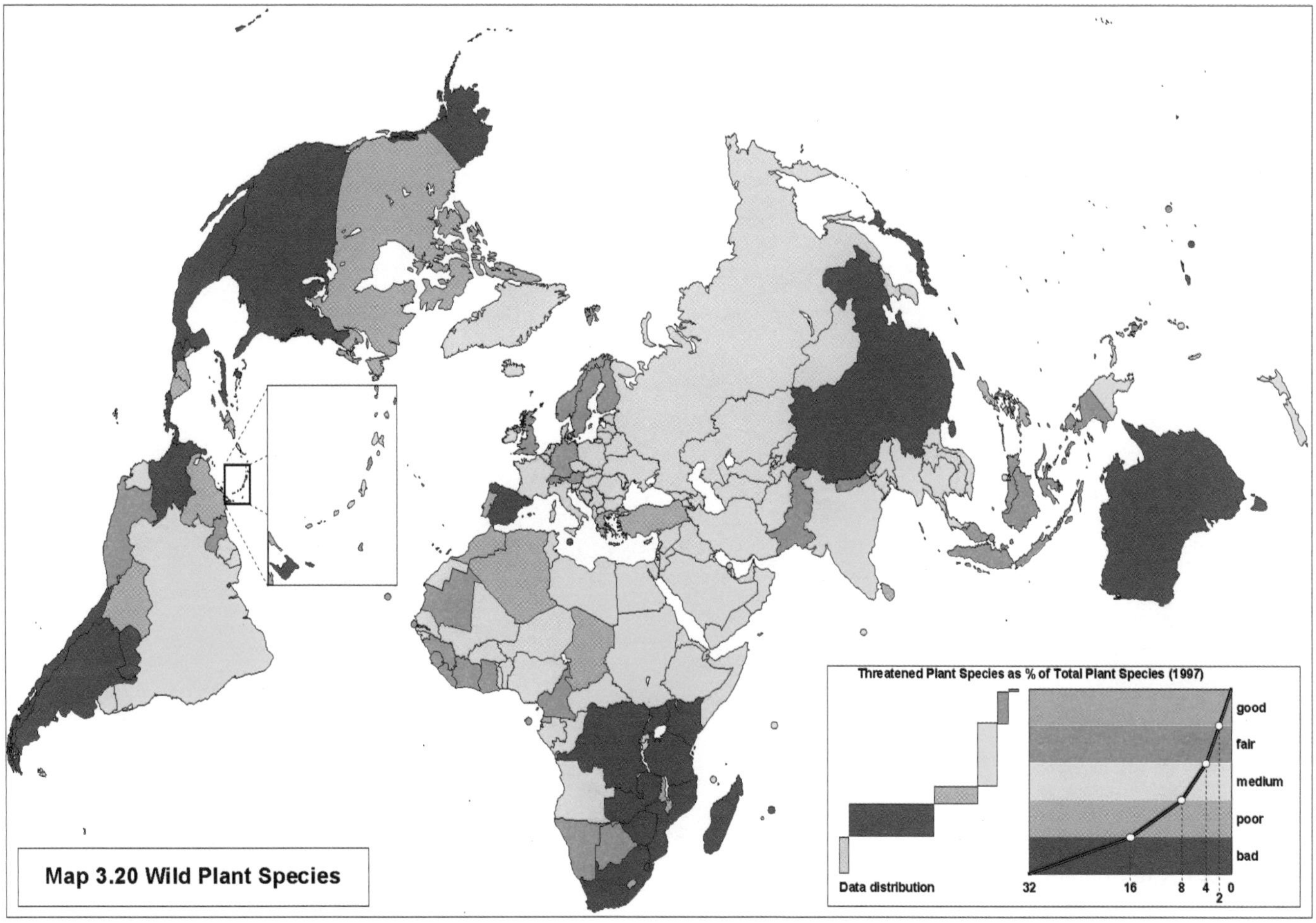

Map 3.20 Wild Plant Species

Threatened Plant Species as % of Total Plant Species (1997)

good
fair
medium
poor
bad

Data distribution   32   16   8 4 2 0

species is threatened, and only 2 (0.4%) of the 542 flowering plant species are at risk. One explanation may be that the main impact of land conversion and modification was in the past, and mostly common and resilient species remain. Another may be that concentrations of species are as easy to maintain as they are to lose.

Wild Plant Species

Wild Plant Species (Map 3.20)

What it is: Score of threatened plant species in a group as percentage of total species in that group (average percentage of three groups: flowering plants, gymnosperms [conifers, cycads, gnetophytes], and ferns and allies).

Country results: 2 good (1%), 31 fair (17%), 61 medium (34%), 18 poor (10%), 32 bad (18%), 36 no data (20%).

The plant species results are strongly influenced by the distribution of gymnosperms. Although they never make up more than 2% of the plant species in a country, the

percentage of gymnosperms that is threatened is generally high—up to 100%—compared with flowering plants (up to 51%) and ferns (up to 28%). High percentages (8% or above) of gymnosperms are threatened in 58 of the 64 countries for which there are data, but few countries have high percentages of threatened flowering plants or ferns (Figure 3.13). Among countries with a poor or bad score

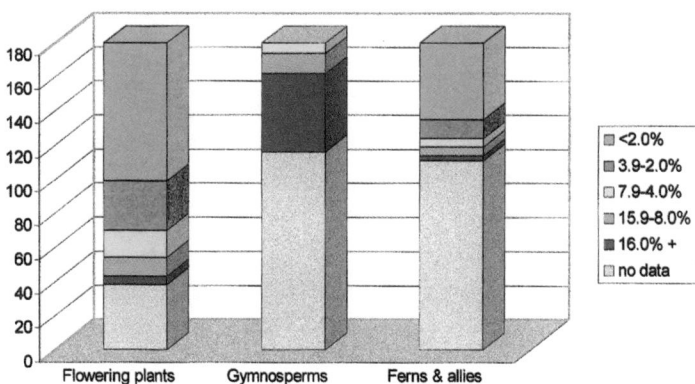

Figure 3.13. Number of countries with various percentages of threatened flowering plants, gymnosperms, and ferns and allies.

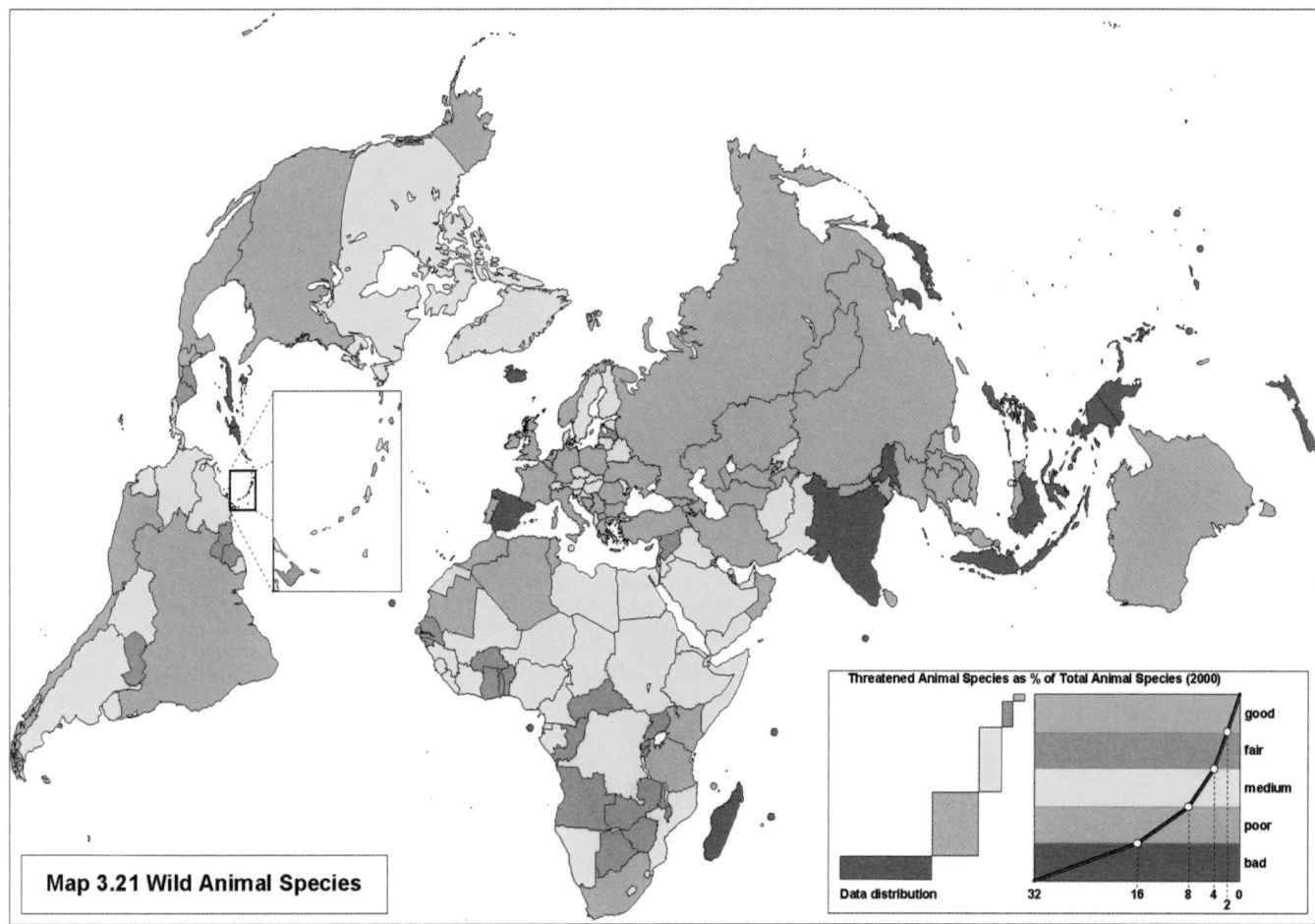

Map 3.21 Wild Animal Species

for plants, Canada, United States, Portugal, Spain, Japan, and Australia have high proportions of threatened species in all three groups. The rest have high percentages of threatened gymnosperms, except for Burkina Faso, Guinea–Bissau, Niger, and Mauritius, which lack these species, and Chad, Turkey, and Sri Lanka, which were not assessed on them.

The definition of a good percentage of threatened species (below 2%) is based on the estimated natural rate of extinction of less than 0.01% per century.

Coverage is fairly complete for flowering plants but much less for gymnosperms and ferns (Figure 3.13). Countries with no information on the status of gymnosperms, including 16 with a fair score and 47 with a medium score, may look better than they are. In fact, missing data probably distort the results of many more. A mere 46 countries cover all their plant groups, none of them in Northern Africa, Northern Europe, or West Asia and just one each in West Africa and Southern Asia. The only regions where coverage is complete for more than a third of the countries are North and Central America (80%), South America

(67%), Pacific (62%), Southern Africa (54%), and West Indies (46%). Significantly, these regions have the highest percentages of countries with bad or poor scores: 100%, 50%, 38%, 62%, and 46%, respectively.[30]

Wild Animal Species

Wild Animal Species (Map 3.21)

What it is: Score of threatened animal species in a group as percentage of total species in that group (average percentage of either two groups [mammals and birds] or four [mammals, birds, reptiles, and amphibians]).

Country results: 3 good (2%), 22 fair (12%), 54 medium (30%), 73 poor (41%), 28 bad (16%).

Mammal and bird data are more reliable than the data on reptiles and amphibians, and ideally the indicator would be based on these two classes alone. However, information on reptiles and amphibians is no worse than on plants, and excluding them would give misleadingly high

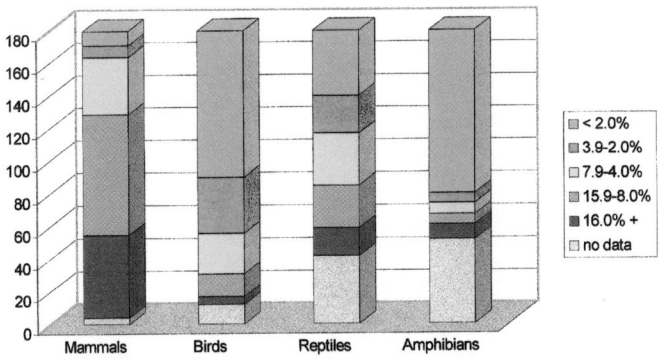

Figure 3.14. Number of countries with various percentages of threatened mammals, birds, reptiles, and amphibians.

scores to several countries. For example, Antigua and Barbuda and St Kitts and Nevis have no threatened mammals and only one threatened bird (2.7% and 3.1%, respectively, of their native bird species), but a third of their reptiles are threatened. Scores are based on mammals and birds alone in 160 countries, and on the four classes in 20 (10 in the Americas, 4 in Asia, 4 in Europe, and 2 in Africa).

High percentages (8% or above) of mammals are threatened in 107 countries, many more than the other classes (Figure 3.14). The mammals exclude ocean-dwelling whales and dolphins because they cannot be assigned to particular countries. The birds include only breeding species because of widely differing standards in recording vagrants, accidentals, and irregular migrants.

All countries with a bad score are islands, reflecting a high incidence of endemic species (species found nowhere else). The only islands with a fair score are Trinidad and Tobago.[31]

Domesticated Diversity

Domesticated Diversity Index (Map 3.22)

What it is: Average score of two indicators—number of not-at-risk breeds per million head of a species and ratio of threatened breeds to not-at-risk breeds of a species—based on three livestock species (Figure 3.15).

Objective: Maintenance of as much as possible of the heritage of livestock breeds.

Country results: 2 good (1%), 22 fair (12%), 78 medium (43%), 36 poor (20%), 13 bad (7%), 29 no data (16%).

Good and fair scores mean that domesticated animal stocks consist of a variety of different breeds, few of which are at risk of extinction. Poor and bad scores indicate that livestock diversity is low, many breeds are threatened, or both. As far as possible, only established breeds have been counted, excluding recent imports, experimental lines, and breeds under development. Nations were rated on the basis of up to three livestock species: the most numerous—cattle and kin (Bali cattle, mithun, yak) in 49 countries, sheep in 49, pig in 31, goat in 22—and the next most numerous or most fully assessed of these species plus water buffalo, Bactrian camel, dromedary, ass, horse, llama, and alpaca. Few countries have assessed their livestock species comprehensively. With better knowledge, they may prove to be more diverse and to have higher or lower proportions of threatened breeds.[32]

The two nations with a good score are Togo and the Republic of Congo. The latter has few breeds in total but many in relation to its livestock numbers: one breed per 285,000 goats (3.5 per million), one per 115,000 sheep (8.7 per million), and two per 75,000 head of cattle (26.7 per million). None is threatened, giving it an average of 13 not-at-risk breeds per million head, the highest of all countries rated on three species.

The lowest diversity is 0.1 breeds per million head, found in Argentina, Brazil, Mexico, Paraguay, Madagascar, and Saudi Arabia. Brazil's not-at-risk breeds are extremely few in relation to its vast stocks: 13 per 163 million cattle, 1 per 27 million pigs, and 3 per 18 million sheep. Four breeds of cattle, seven of pigs, and two of sheep are threatened. They include Crioulo Lageano cattle (noted for being good mothers) and the Canastrão pig of Rio de Janeiro and Minas Gerais, a fat Celtic type that once contributed to feijoada and dobradinha, pork dishes emblematic of those states.[33]

The most common threat to breeds is population decline, due to replacement by more popular types, industrialization of farming, abandonment of marginal lands, and war. The Holstein–Friesian, which accounts for more than a third of the world's dairy cows, has ousted many low-maintenance local breeds solely because of its unrivalled ability to fill up milk buckets. Intensive production systems leave free-range virtuosos out in the cold. As a result, formerly abundant breeds are now rare, such as the British Gloucester Old Spot, a pig capable of yielding excellent meat from foraging on windfall apples and being served low-cost feed such as whey. Sheep and

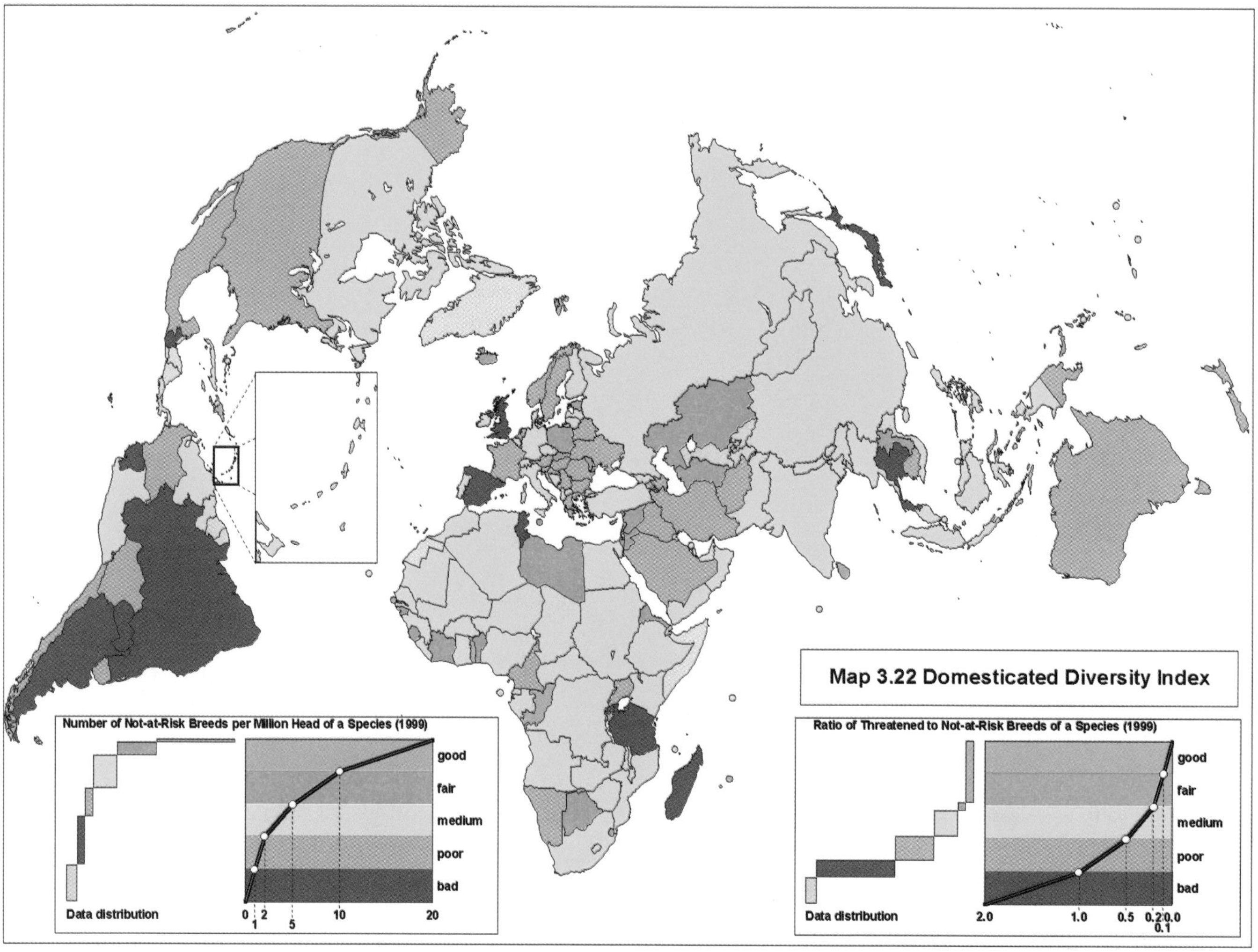

Map 3.22 Domesticated Diversity Index

Number of Not-at-Risk Breeds per Million Head of a Species (1999)

good
fair
medium
poor
bad

Data distribution   0 2 5   10   20
                      1

Ratio of Threatened to Not-at-Risk Breeds of a Species (1999)

good
fair
medium
poor
bad

Data distribution   2.0   1.0   0.5 0.2 0.0
                                        0.1

cattle breeds adapted to mountains, marshes, and semi-desert have been abandoned as the people who raised them died out or fled to the cities. Wars slaughter live-stock as well as people and are decimating African cattle breeds such as the Serere of Uganda and the Bashi of the Democratic Republic of Congo.[34]

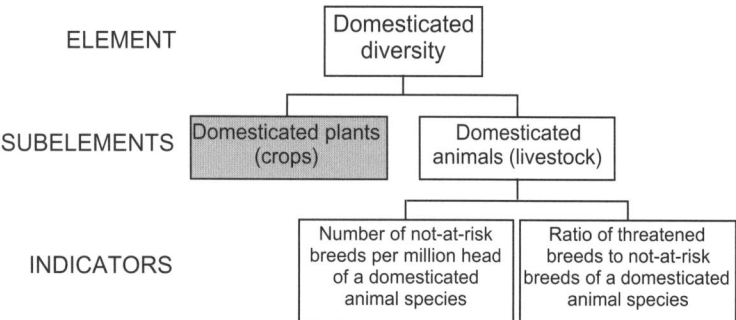

ELEMENT

SUBELEMENTS

INDICATORS

Domesticated diversity

Domesticated plants (crops)

Domesticated animals (livestock)

Number of not-at-risk breeds per million head of a domesticated animal species

Ratio of threatened breeds to not-at-risk breeds of a domesticated animal species

Figure 3.15. Indicator chart for domesticated diversity.
Crops (shaded box) are not covered due to lack of data.

The other major threats are deliberate crossbreeding and accidental interbreeding, which swamp a breed with the genes of another, obliterating its distinctive character-istics. They account for 30% of the risk to Europe's threatened cattle and horses and contribute to the endan-germent of 32 of Africa's 43 threatened cattle breeds. Namibia's Damara cattle breed has become less Damara-like, losing its beautifully arched and twisted horns; and the Manjaca cattle breed of Guinea–Bissau has been entirely absorbed by the more abundant N'dama. Bolivia's Criollo goat has so much exotic blood that it is no longer recognizable as Criollo. Pakistan's sheep and goat diversity is being eroded as local breeds mate and merge with the flocks of refugees from Afghanistan.[35]

If breeds disappear, so will their unique combinations of genes. The genes provide both the adaptations neces-sary for production in diverse environments and the raw material required to meet the constant and changing demands of breeding programs. For example, China's highly prolific Taihu breeds are being used by the pork industry to increase the number of young produced by European pigs. The technology does not exist today, nor will it in the foreseeable future, to create these evolving genetic packages artificially.[36]

Local breeds are part of a country's cultural heritage. Navajo Churro sheep are integral to Navajo life in the arid southwestern United States, providing the people with milk, meat, and a two-textured, naturally colored wool esteemed by tribal rug and blanket weavers. Several of Tanzania's zebu cattle breeds are named for the tribes that raise them and the colors they favor: Iringa Red, Mkalama Dun, Singida White, and Ugogo Grey (the first three are threatened). Local breeds are also well attuned to the vagaries of their environments, and despite their often limited production potential they provide more secure sources of food and income than do nonlocal breeds.[37]

It is possible to reap the benefits of breeding without losing breeds, conserving domesticated diversity while increasing agricultural productivity. Kenya raises both indigenous Boran cattle and Improved Boran, upgraded by selection rather than with exotic blood. Denmark continues to use crossbreeding to better its Danish Red and Danish Friesian dairy cattle but also maintains purebred lines to preserve the traditional types. Financial incentives to raise local breeds can be boosted by linking the breeds to value-added products such as premium cheeses and meats. In Spain, for example, Ibérica pigs are the source of prestigious dried hams. In Italy, Pecorino Sardo cheese is produced specifically from the milk of Sarda sheep and Fontina cheese from the milk of three Valdostana cattle breeds.[38]

Resource Use

Resource Use Index (Map 3.23)

What it is: Average of energy and materials index and resource sectors index.

Country results: 18 good (10%), 76 fair (42%), 55 medium (31%), 19 poor (11%), 12 bad (7%).

All people stress the ecosystem by producing and consuming goods and services. The consumption process uses materials throughout and is fueled by energy: the more energy and materials consumed, the heavier the pressure on the environment. Resource sectors (primarily agriculture, fisheries, timber, mining, oil, and gas) are a more specific source of pressure: the greater their demands on arable land, the seas, inland waters, forests, and mineral deposits, the higher the risk of their depleting resources, degrading habitats, and threatening species.

The resource use index reflects energy consumption (materials use could not be assessed) more than the performance of resource sectors. Countries with a good index have a good score for energy and a good or fair score for resource sectors. Of those with a fair index, all

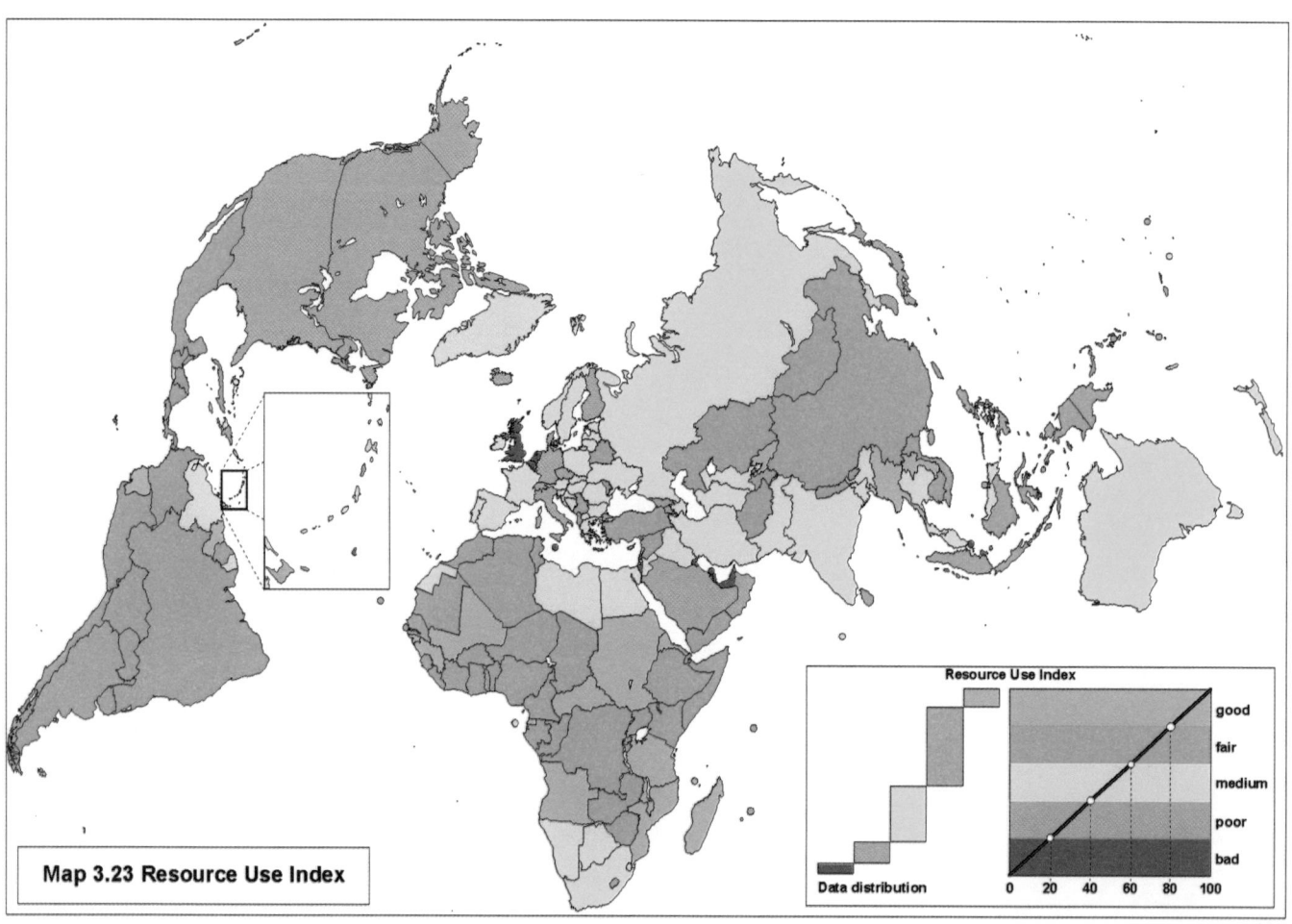

Map 3.23 Resource Use Index

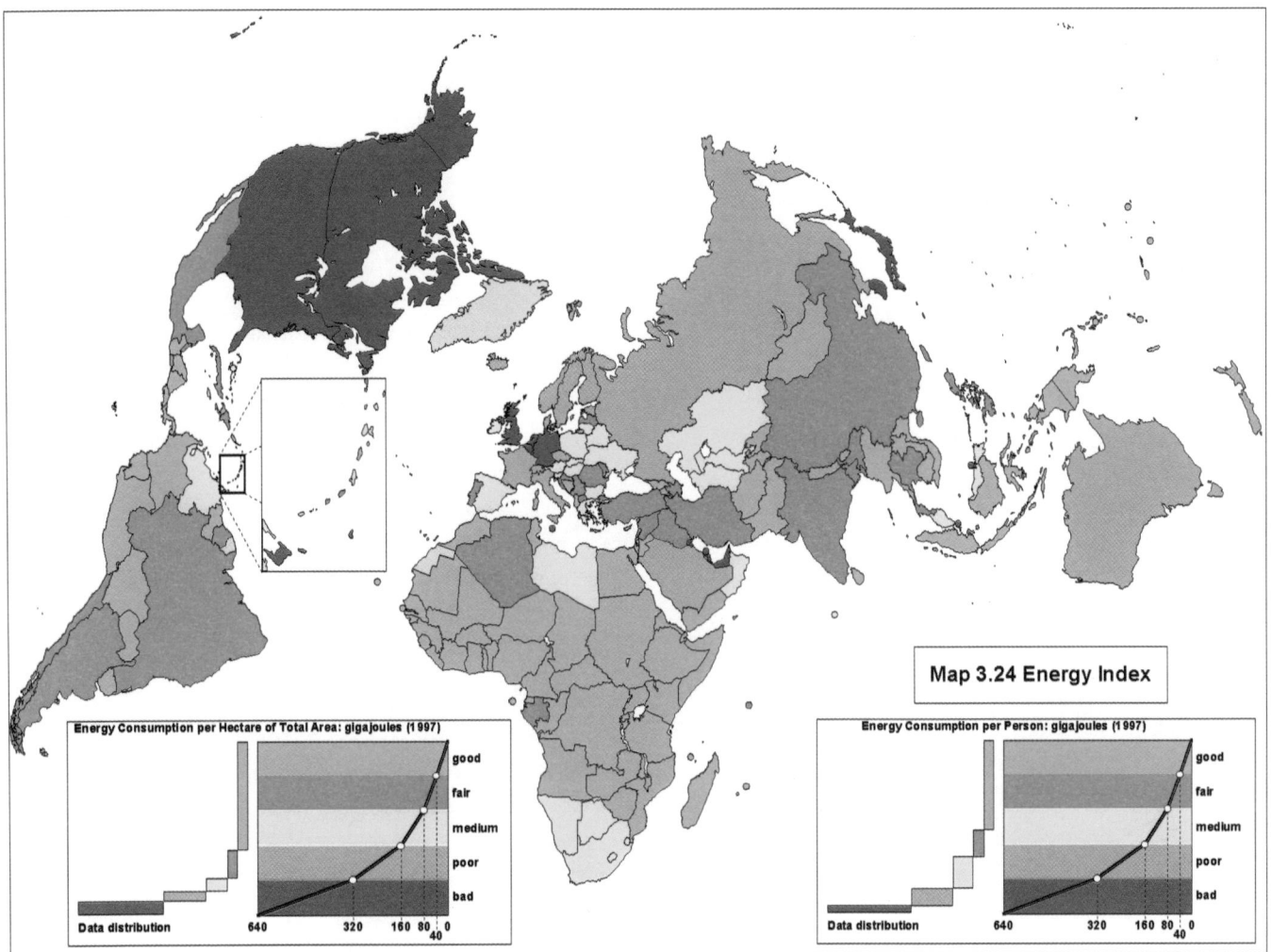

Map 3.24 Energy Index

except Kazakhstan have a good or fair energy score, but their scores for resource sectors range from fair (28 countries) through medium (41) to poor (Djibouti, Gambia, Niger, Nigeria, Rwanda, Somalia, and Yemen). Among nations with a poor or bad index, all except Lesotho, Cyprus, and Oman have a poor or bad energy score.

The pressures on the ecosystem summed in the resource use index are a direct result of the material benefits measured by the wealth index (Map 2.7). Most countries that do well in one do poorly in the other: of the 94 nations with a good or fair resource use index, 77 have a poor or bad wealth index and 17 a medium wealth index. Of the 37 with a good or fair wealth index, the resource use index is bad or poor in 24, medium in 13.

For all data and scores, together with details of the indicators, performance criteria, and combining procedures, see Table 22 (resource use index, energy, timber), Table 23

(agriculture, fish and seafood self-reliance), and Table 24 (fisheries) in the Data section.

Energy and Materials

Energy Index (Map 3.24)

What it is: Lower score of annual energy consumption per hectare of total area and annual energy consumption per person (Figure 3.16).

Objective: Energy consumption within the carrying capacity of the ecosystem.

Country results: 81 good (45%), 32 fair (18%), 30 medium (17%), 19 poor (11%), 18 bad (10%).

Energy consumption includes commercial energy (solid fuels, liquid fuels, gases, and electricity) and traditional fuels such as fuelwood, charcoal, and animal and plant waste. Although energy use is undoubtedly a source of

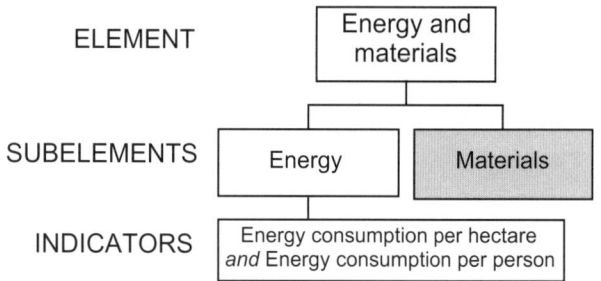

Figure 3.16. Indicator chart for energy and materials. Materials (shaded box) are not covered due to lack of data on total material requirement and waste generation.

environmental pressure (because of its central role in the consumption of all goods and services), no one knows how much pressure can be attributed to it alone. Hence it is not known what level of use might be sustainable or even what would be the most appropriate measure of pressure from energy use. Energy consumption per hectare of total area is valid if the effects of a country's energy use are absorbed largely by the ecosystems within its borders. Energy consumption per person is more defensible if national energy use has a global impact. Since either may be the case, both indicators are employed here.

All countries with a good index use low amounts of energy, however measured. Among those with a fair index, 13 do better per hectare than per person, 8 the reverse, and 11 have fair scores for both. Only 13 of the medium, poor, and bad scorers are in the same performance band for both indicators. Canada has the biggest discrepancy: 10 gigajoules (GJ) per hectare (score of 95), 344 GJ per person (score of 18).

Energy is essential for human wellbeing, but how much is enough? Among countries with a good or fair

Human Wellbeing Index, consumption per hectare ranges from 6 GJ (Australia) to 16,726 GJ (Singapore), and consumption per person from 36 GJ (Uruguay) to 350 GJ (United States). Austria, France, Hungary, Portugal, Slovakia, and Slovenia have roughly the same levels of consumption per hectare and per person. The rest show wide differences between the two, with use per person higher in large countries and use per hectare higher in small or densely populated nations.

Portugal has the best combination of high human wellbeing (HWI of 72) and moderate energy use, both per hectare (75 GJ) and per person (70 GJ). As such it provides the benchmark for the fair performance band. Ireland, Spain, and Cyprus have similar levels of achievement: HWIs of 76, 73, and 67, respectively; fair scores for energy use per hectare; and medium scores for energy use per person.[39]

Resource Sectors

Resource Sectors Index (Map 3.25)

What it is: Average of agriculture, fisheries, and timber scores (Figure 3.17).

Objective: Resource production within the carrying capacity of the ecosystem.

Country results: 3 good (2%), 53 fair (29%), 76 medium (42%), 36 poor (20%), 12 bad (7%).

Sustainable resource production means that crops, livestock, fish, and timber are produced in ways that limit ecosystem conversion and modification, maintain the resources on which production depends (soil, fish stocks, and forests), and have low impacts on the rest of the

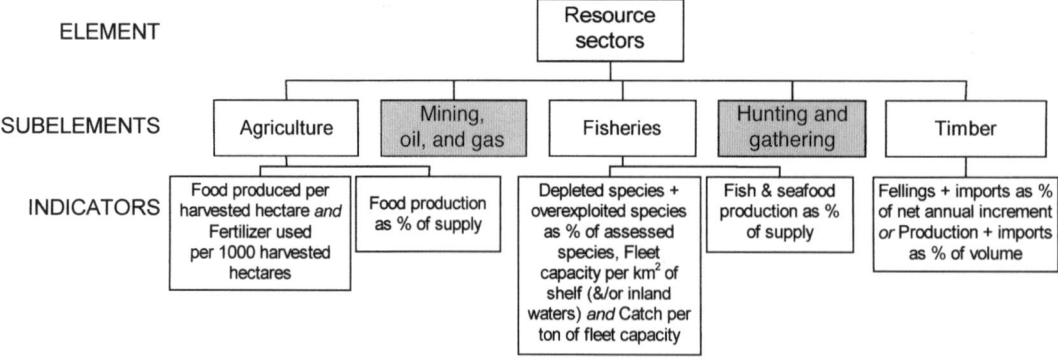

Figure 3.17. Indicator chart for resource sectors. Mining, oil, and gas and hunting and gathering (shaded boxes) are not covered due to lack of suitable indicators.

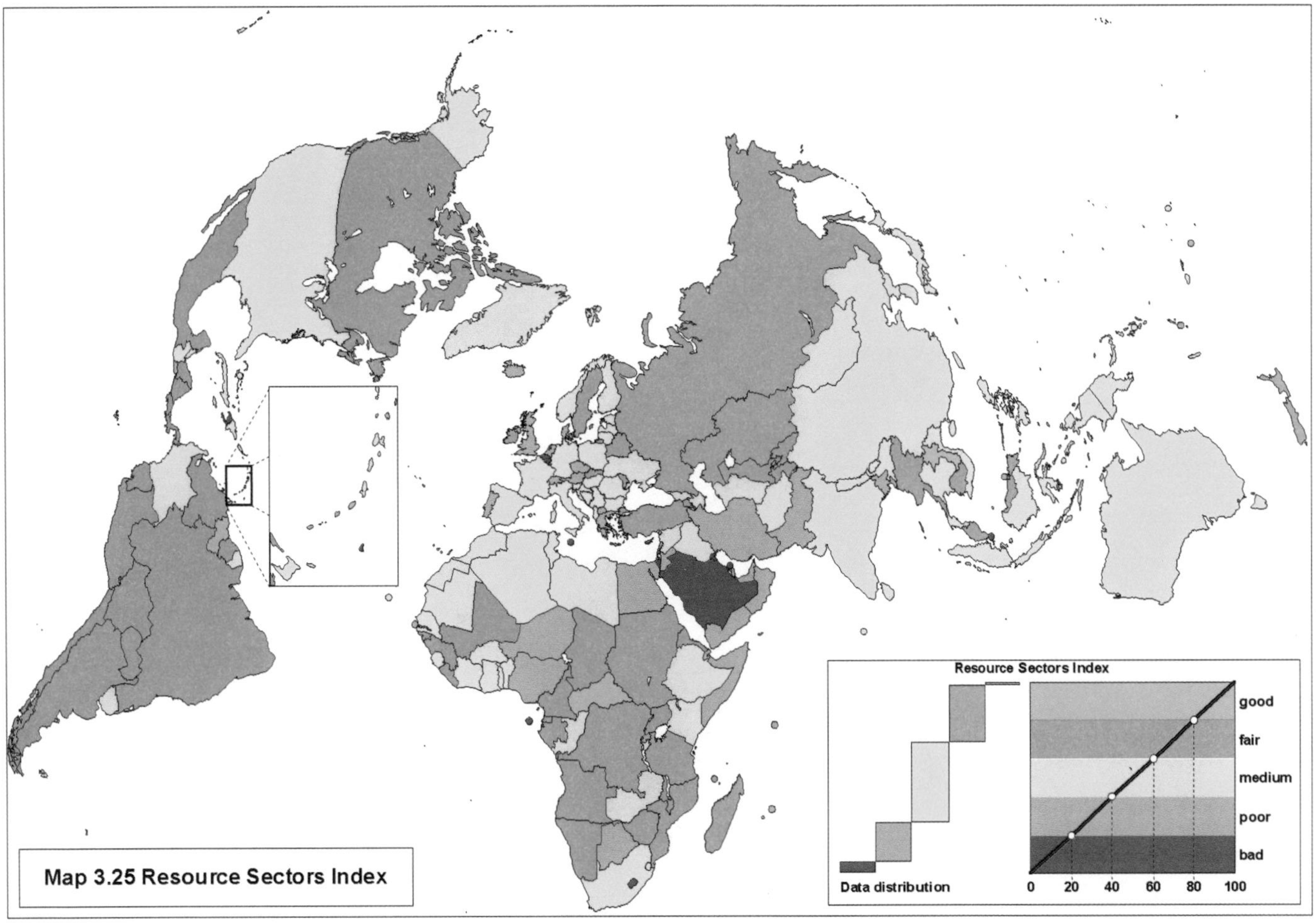

Map 3.25 Resource Sectors Index

Resource Sectors Index

good
fair
medium
poor
bad

Data distribution   0   20   40   60   80   100

ecosystem. Some of these factors are measured by other ecosystem indices, such as the land diversity index, the land quality index, and the domesticated diversity index. The resource sectors index should be interpreted in conjunction with them.

The three resource sectors tend to counterbalance each other. Only the countries with a good index (Guyana, Central African Republic, and Lao), and eight countries with a fair index (Costa Rica, Ecuador, Angola, Guinea, Madagascar, Malawi, Mozambique, and Tanzania) have high scores for all sectors. Only three countries with a poor index (St Lucia, Mauritius, and United Kingdom) and five with a bad index (Barbados, Lesotho, Malta, Kuwait, and Saudi Arabia) have low scores for all sectors.

Medium scores predominate in agriculture, poor and bad scores in fisheries, and good and fair scores in the timber sector (Figure 3.18). The fisheries results are not unexpected because excessively large and powerful fleets are chasing after declining stocks of fish. However, the absence of good performance in agriculture is surprising, and the timber picture looks too good to be true. Yet

both portrayals may fairly reflect what the indicators are intended to measure. The agriculture indicators measure productivity and self-reliance, which tend to offset each other because many of the most self-reliant countries are only moderately productive. The timber indicator measures the pressure of logging on wood supply, not its impact on the diversity and quality of forests or the loss of forests to agriculture and settlement (included in the land diversity index).

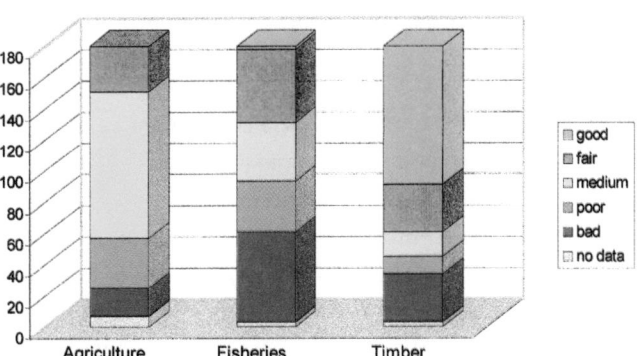

Figure 3.18. Number of countries by performance band for agriculture, fisheries, and timber.

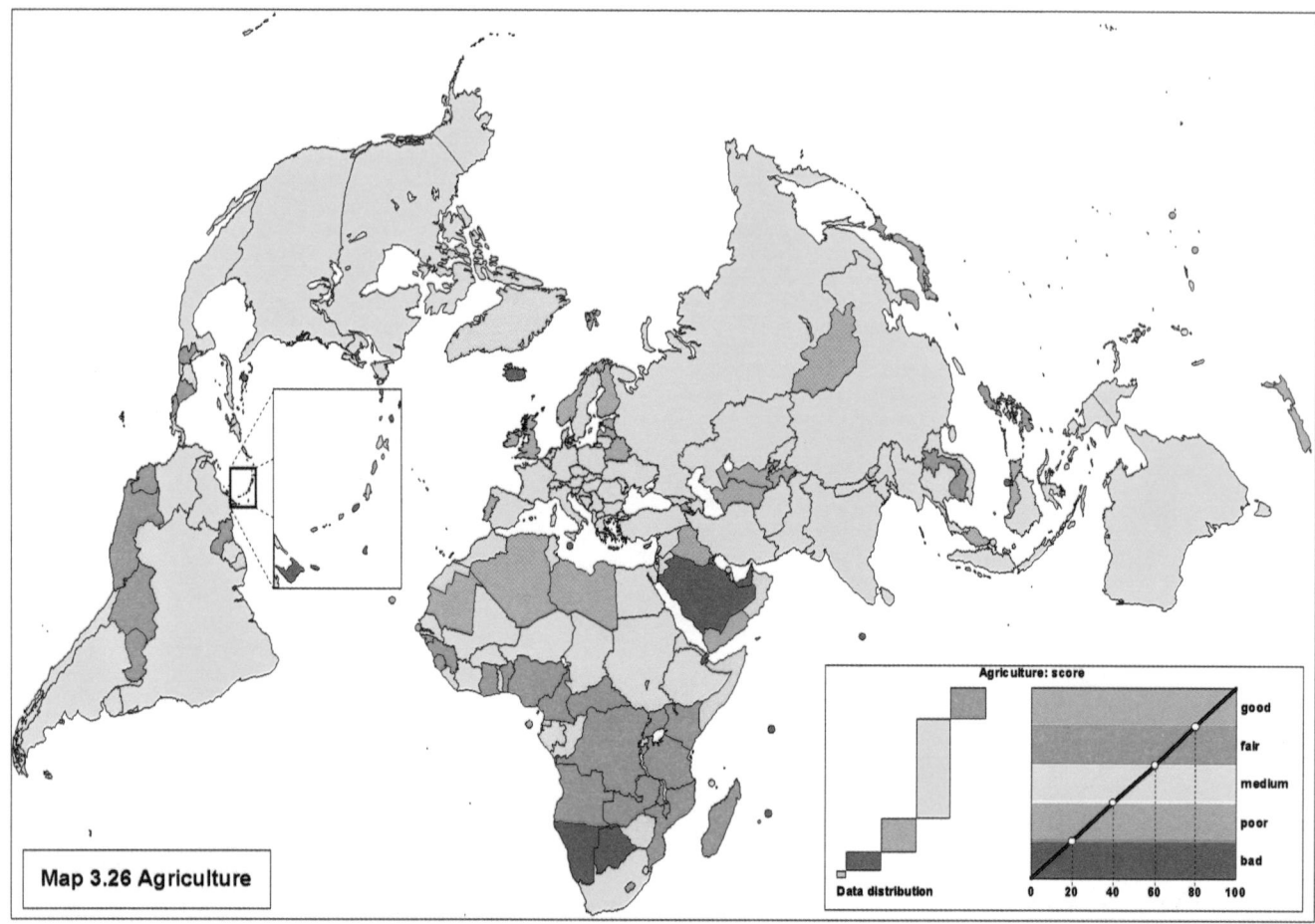

Map 3.26 Agriculture

Agriculture

Agriculture (Map 3.26)

What it is: Lower of agricultural productivity score and agricultural self-reliance score. Agricultural productivity (not shown as a separate map) is the average score of food produced per harvested hectare and fertilizer used per 1,000 harvested hectares. Agricultural self-reliance (Map 3.27) is one indicator, food production as percentage of supply.

Country results: 0 good (0%), 29 fair (16%), 94 medium (52%), 32 poor (18%), 18 bad (10%), 7 no data (4%).

High productivity per unit of land helps to prevent agriculture from putting natural and seminatural habitats to the plow. Land productivity can be increased by more efficient techniques, better control of pests and diseases, and the addition of fertilizer. High productivity per unit of fertilizer curbs excessive reliance on chemical inputs, which can pollute water and hurt the health of humans and other species.

High productivity is key to agricultural self-reliance, which matters for several reasons. First, it increases the security of the food supply, including control over the quality and safety of food and the manner in which it is produced. Second, it reduces the risk of environmental damage due to transport. Third, it ensures that countries bear the ecosystem stress resulting from food production rather than shift it to others.

The self-reliance indicator was calculated as the mean of eight food groups: cereals, starchy roots, sugar and sweeteners, plant oils and nuts, pulses and vegetables, fruit, meat and eggs, and dairy products. This checks distortion by surpluses of a few export crops. For example, Barbados produces a surplus of sugar but only 3% of its cereals; Botswana, a surplus of meat but less than half its supply of any other food group.[40]

The picture presented in Map 3.26 largely reflects the productivity score, which determined the agriculture rating in all countries in the fair band and 81 of those in the medium band.[41] Poor scores are a mixture: 16 were determined by self-reliance, 10 by productivity, and 6 by both factors.[42] All bad ratings reflect the self-reliance score, except for Namibia's (where productivity is bad and self-reliance poor).

Low food production (no more than 2 metric tons) per harvested hectare is the more common type of inferior pro-

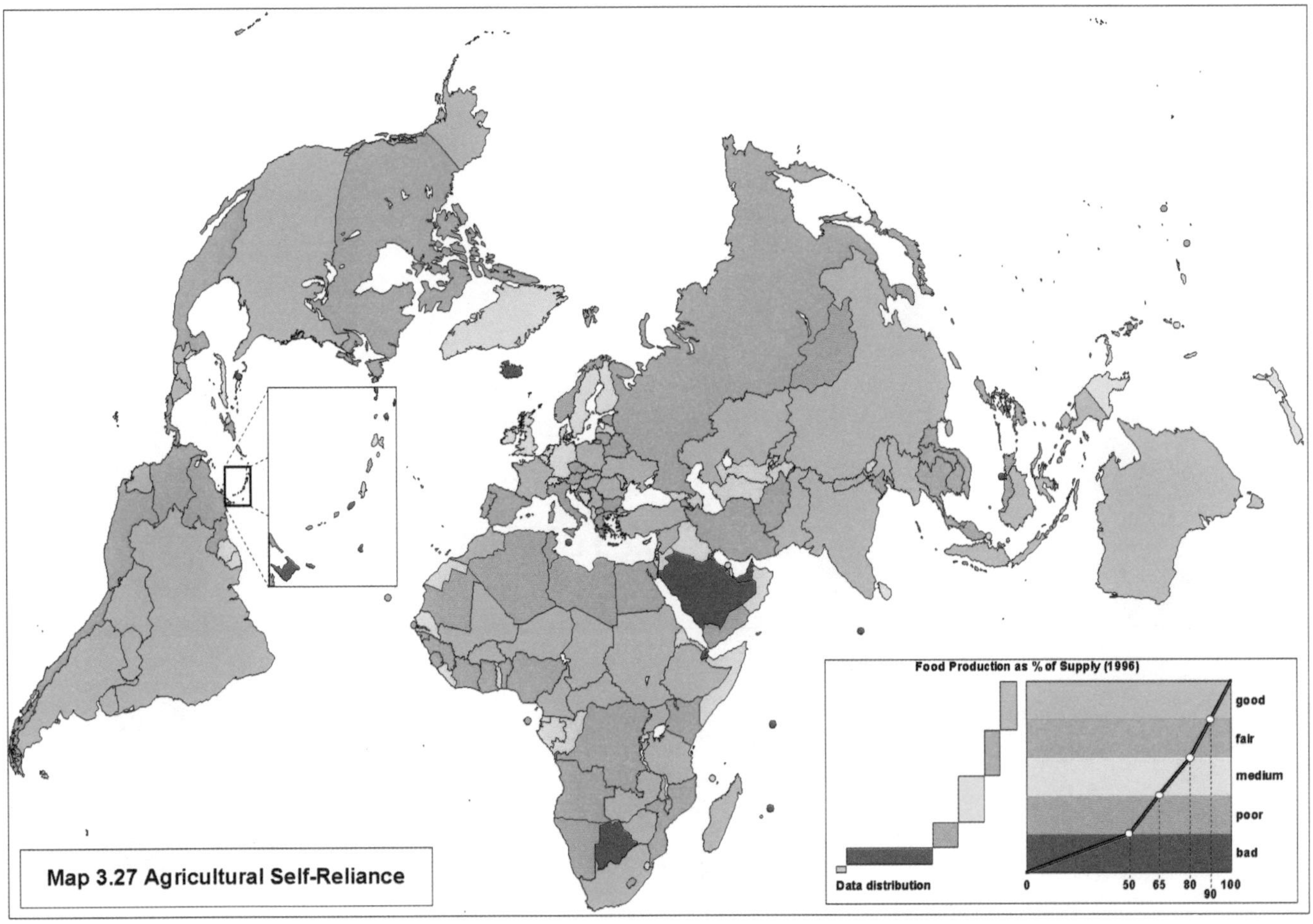

Map 3.27 Agricultural Self-Reliance

Food Production as % of Supply (1996)

good

fair

medium

poor

bad

Data distribution

0   50 65 80   100
90

ductivity in Africa (especially West Africa) and Central Asia. High fertilizer use (at least 80 metric tons of fertilizer per 1,000 harvested hectares) is the more frequent culprit in North and South America, Europe (notably Northern Europe), East Asia, and the developed Pacific. Excess fertilizer usually ends up in rivers, lakes, and the sea. Of 30 countries with high rates of fertilizer use that were also assessed on water quality, 20 have a poor or bad water quality score wholly or largely due to nutrient pollution. They include China, Japan, South Korea, Australia, New Zealand, eight countries in Northern Europe, four in Eastern Europe, and three in Southern Europe.[43]

All countries with a bad score for self-reliance and most with a poor score have small harvested areas in relation to their population (less than a quarter of a hectare per person). The exceptions produce scant amounts from their harvested area (St Vincent and Grenadines, São Tomé and Principe, Portugal, Malaysia, and Solomon Islands) or depend heavily on fertilizer (Dominica). The one inexplicable case is Estonia, which has almost a third of a hectare of harvested area per person and is moderately productive yet grows only 60% of its food supply.

The countries with a fair agriculture score—18 African, 8 American, and 3 Asian—place little agricultural pressure on the ecosystem, producing more than 80% of their food supply using modest amounts of land and fertilizer. However, the food supply is generally too small to meet the nutritional needs of their

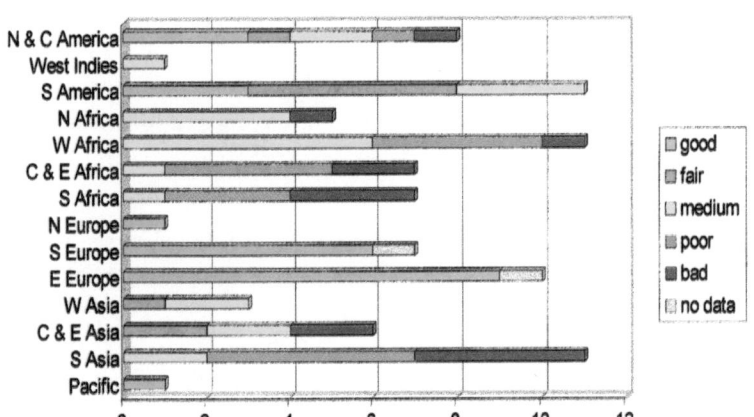

Figure 3.19. Regional breakdown of the 89 countries with a good or fair score for agricultural self-reliance by performance band for food sufficiency.

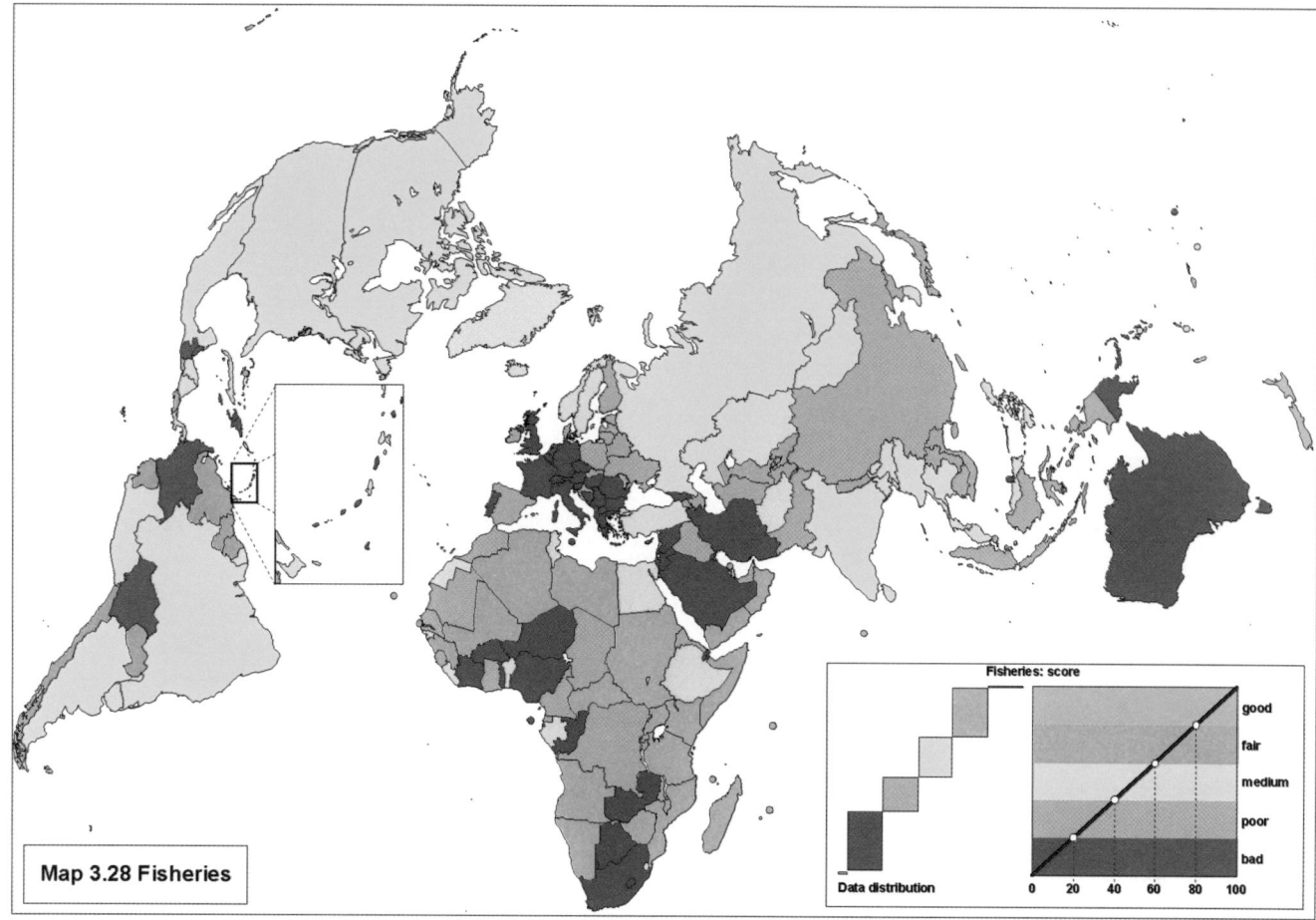

Map 3.28 Fisheries

people: only Costa Rica, Guyana, and Paraguay have high scores for food sufficiency, while Guatemala, Afghanistan, Cambodia, Lao, and 13 African countries have poor or bad scores (see the Wealth section in Chapter 2). In fact, self-reliance is consistently matched by food sufficiency only in Europe (Figure 3.19). In Africa and much of Asia, self-reliance often means a lack of money to buy desperately needed imports.

To what extent productivity and self-reliance affect actual ecosystem and human conditions depends on ecological practice and social policy, as the Philippines and Malaysia illustrate. The two countries are about the same size and have similar climates, but their performances are dramatically different. The Philippines' scores for productivity and self-reliance are both fair. Its land productivity is a modest 3.8 metric tons (mt) per hectare, but its fertilizer use is a respectably low 33.1 mt per 1,000 hectares. It produces surpluses of plant oils and fruit and more than 90% of its supply of all other food groups except cereals (88%) and dairy products (2%). Malaysia has a medium score for productivity and a poor score for self-reliance. High fertilizer productivity (only 12.2 mt of fertilizer used per 1,000 hectares) is negated by exceptionally low food production

per hectare (a scant 0.7 mt), perhaps due to the dominance of oil palm. Like the Philippines, it produces surpluses of plant oils and fruit but only half of its supply of starchy roots, a third of its vegetables, and a quarter of its cereals.

Theoretically, agriculture in the Philippines should have less of an impact on the land, and the people should be better fed than in Malaysia. Not so. A third of the Philippines' land area has been converted to cultivation, a quarter of Malaysia's. Land quality is poor in Malaysia but even worse in the Philippines, where soil degradation is extensive and severe. Almost a quarter (22%) of the population of the Philippines lacks sufficient food, compared with 2% in Malaysia, where undernutrition among children is also lower.

Fisheries

> ### Fisheries (Map 3.28)
>
> **What it is:** Lower of fishing pressure score and fish and seafood self-reliance score.
>
> **Country results:** 2 good (1%), 47 fair (26%), 38 medium (21%), 32 poor (18%), 58 bad (32%), 3 no data (2%).

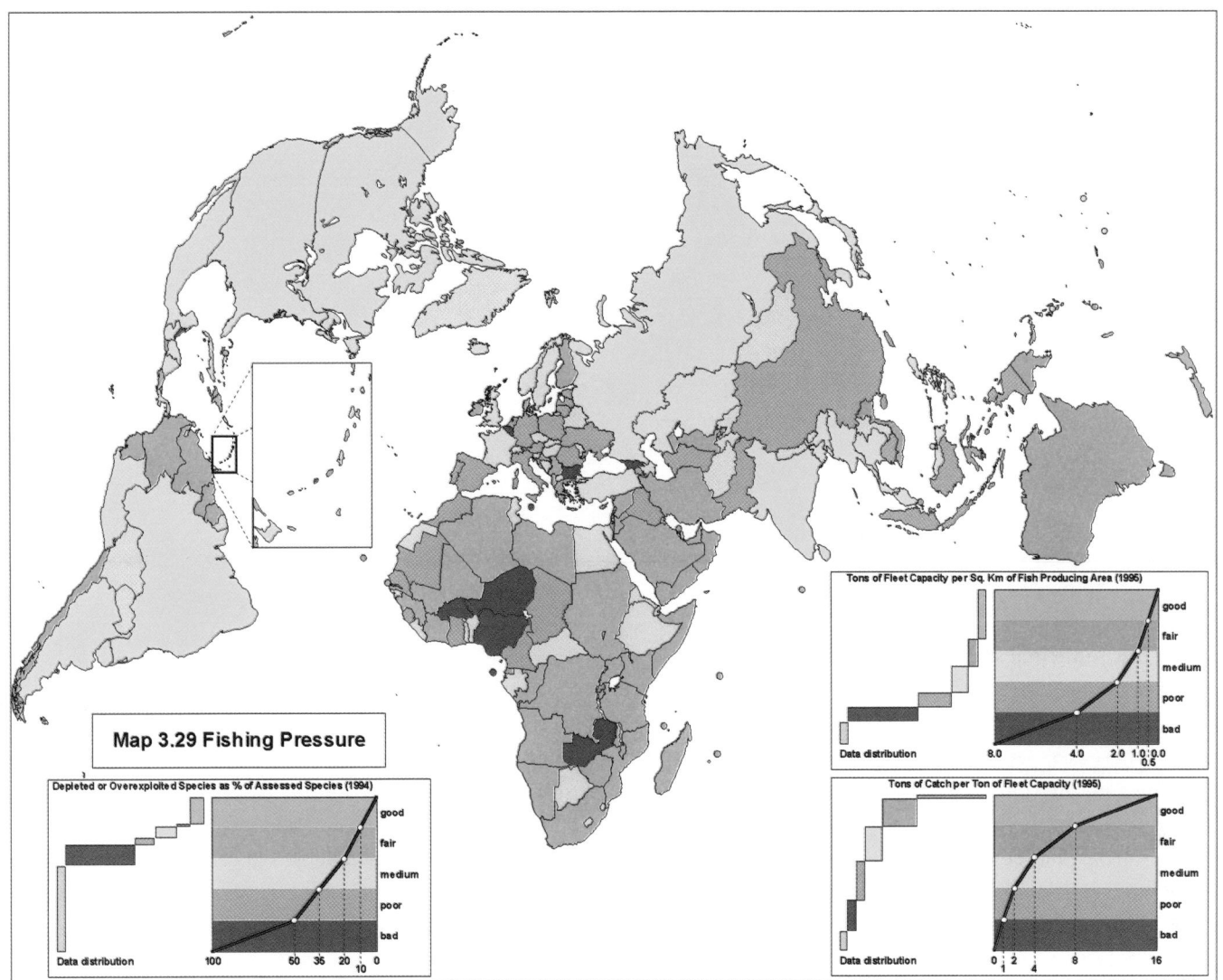

Map 3.29 Fishing Pressure

The two good scorers—Maldives and New Zealand—put little pressure on fisheries while producing their entire supply of seafood. Countries with a fair score produce more than 80% of their supply without imposing excessive stress on the fisheries. The rest perform modestly to badly in one aspect or the other.

Poor and bad scores are determined by fishing pressure in 31 countries (especially in West Africa, Eastern Europe, and Southern Asia), low self-reliance in 41 (particularly in the West Indies, Southern Africa, and West Asia), and both factors in 18 (notably in Southern and Northern Europe). Australia and 14 other countries dive from fair scores for pressure to bad scores for self-reliance. But Belize takes the biggest plunge, from good (self-reliance) to bad (pressure).

Fishing Pressure (Map 3.29)

What it is: Average score of three indicators: depleted and overexploited species as percentage of assessed species, fish-catching capacity per unit of fish-producing area, and weight of catch per unit of fish-catching capacity.

Country results: 2 good (1%), 55 fair (31%), 51 medium (28%), 38 poor (21%), 11 bad (6%), 23 no data (13%).

Together, the three indicators provide an adequate if rough measure of fishing pressure. None can do so alone. Data on the first indicator (depleted and overexploited species) are available for a minority of the marine species fished by just 80 countries. Moreover, some species classified as depleted succumb to other stresses besides overfishing. In the Black Sea, for example, stocks of anchovy and sprats failed because of predation by an introduced ctenophore (a jellyfish-like animal); shads and sturgeons declined because of rising salt levels in estuaries as dams and water withdrawals reduced river flows; and turbot fisheries collapsed because excessive nutrients from the Danube and other rivers cut oxygen levels in seawater.

Fishing has exacerbated these changes. Thirteen of the species fished by Ukraine are well enough known for the Food and Agriculture Organization of the United Nations (FAO) to assess their condition: nine are lightly to fully exploited, and four are depleted or overexploited, including three Black Sea species (Pontic shad, Azov Sea sprat, and European sprat).[44]

Countries are disposed to overfish if their fleet can catch more than their national waters can produce. The second indicator—catching capacity (the total tonnage of a country's fishing fleet) per unit of fish-producing area—measures this relationship. The fish-producing area is the country's continental shelf for marine fisheries and its inland water area for freshwater fisheries. Eighteen land-locked countries were rated on the basis of their fresh-water fisheries, 93 countries on their marine fisheries, and 46 (where marine and inland water fleets could not be distinguished) on both.

Countries that concentrate their fishing on their own areas tend to do better with this indicator than those with large distant water fleets. Turkey fishes only the Black Sea and Mediterranean and has a low 0.9 tons of fleet capacity per square kilometer of shelf. Ukraine's fleet has a very high 5.5 tons of capacity for every square kilometer of shelf because its fleet is active both in the Black Sea and in every ocean but the Arctic.[45]

The second indicator takes no account of differences in productivity and so may penalize countries with small but rich fish-producing areas. The third indicator, catch per unit of catching capacity, corrects this distortion by comparing the fishing power of the fleet with the amount of fish it catches. For example, Peru's fleet is large for its narrow shelf (1.5 tons per square kilometer). But highly productive upwellings, which bring nutrients from the ocean depths to the surface, support an exceptionally bountiful fishery. As a result, Peru catches a phenomenally high 44 tons of fish per ton of capacity.

Because of weak data, the second and third indica-

tors seldom accord with the first. Of 33 countries where 35% or more of assessed species are depleted or overexploited, only 18 have a correspondingly low score for capacity per area or catch per capacity. The indicators match in most of Northern and West Africa, Southern and Eastern Europe, and West Asia but in none of South America or Central Africa. Allowing for this flaw, pressure is highest in Eastern Europe (all assessed countries have poor or bad scores), Southern Europe (60% poor or bad), and West Africa (53%). Pressure is lowest in Southern Africa (82% have fair scores; few species are overexploited or depleted), East Africa (67% fair), and West Asia (53% fair).

Fish and Seafood Self-Reliance (Map 3.30)

What it is: One indicator, fish and seafood production as a percentage of supply.

Country results: 82 good (46%), 15 fair (8%), 15 medium (8%), 9 poor (5%), 50 bad (28%), 9 no data (5%).

Countries that produce more than 90% of their supply of fish and seafood are in a position to control the stress their consumption puts on fisheries. Those producing 50% or less are not. The most self-reliant regions, with the highest proportions of good scores, are North and Central America, Central and East Asia, and Southern Asia. The least self-reliant, with the highest frequency of bad scores, are Southern Europe, West Indies, and Northern Europe. Few self-reliant countries live up to their promise, however. Only 34 with high (good or fair) scores also have high marks for fishing pressure. The strongest regions are Southern Africa, where seven of the eight nations with high scores for self-reliance have high marks for pressure as well (Zambia is the exception); and East Africa and South America, each having five countries with high scores for both.[46]

Eighty countries perform consistently, achieving either good or fair, medium, or poor or bad scores in both fish and seafood and agricultural self-reliance. In the other 91, scores differ widely. Among the 59 nations with good or fair grades in both types of self-reliance, only 17 also have high ratings for food self-sufficiency: 6 in South America, 4 in North and Central America, 4 in Eastern Europe, and Croatia, Russia, and Kazakhstan.[47]

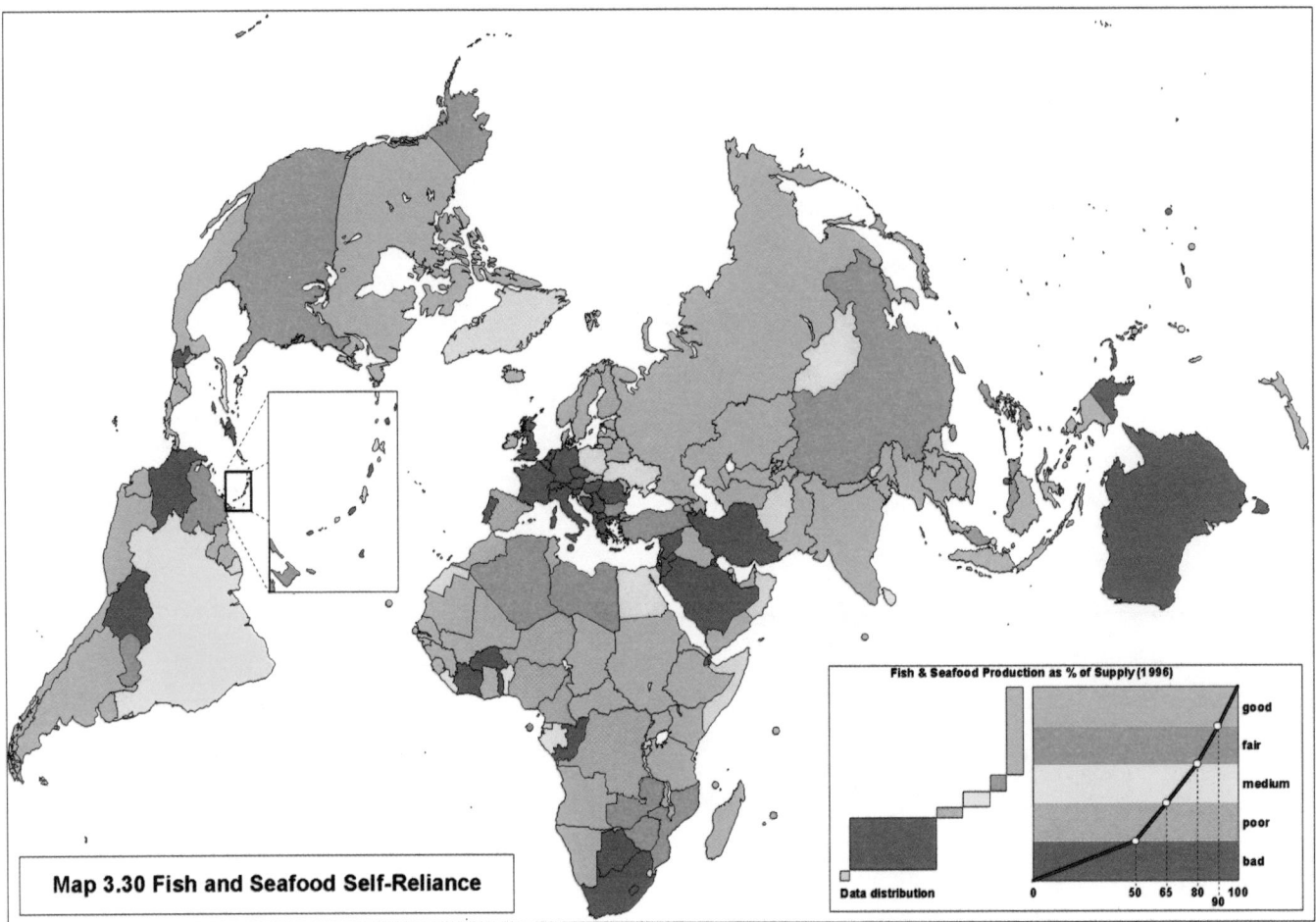

Map 3.30 Fish and Seafood Self-Reliance

Fish & Seafood Production as % of Supply (1996)

good
fair
medium
poor
bad

Data distribution

0   50 65 80   100
                90

Timber

Timber (Map 3.31)

What it is: One indicator, timber fellings plus imports as percentage of net annual increment or, if unavailable, timber production plus imports as percentage of volume.

Country results: 89 good (49%), 30 fair (17%), 16 medium (9%), 11 poor (6%), 31 bad (17%), 3 no data (2%).

The timber indicator shows whether countries are extracting wood within the forest's rate of renewal. It does not show whether logging is sustainable because it does not cover impacts on forest diversity and quality.

Europe, Canada, the United States, Russia, Japan, Kazakhstan, Tajikistan, Turkmenistan, Australia, New Zealand, and six West Asian countries—52 countries in all—were assessed with the first indicator: fellings plus imports as a percentage of net annual increment (NAI,

the amount the forest grows each year, less natural losses).[48] At 100% of NAI or less, logging is within the forest's rate of renewal; at 80% or less it is well within it. At more than 100%, the stock is being depleted. The 30 countries with a good score obtained from this indicator are using forests conservatively, and the 8 with a fair score are using them close to but within their rate of renewal. Three medium, 1 poor, and 10 bad scorers are putting slight to severe pressure on their own timber resources or those of other countries.

The rest of the world was assessed with the other indicator. This is much less reliable because the relationship between the volume of wood in a forest and its NAI depends on its age, species composition, and productivity. The 59 countries with a good score are probably using forests within their rate of renewal, and the 22 with fair scores are possibly doing so.

Imports are added to fellings or production because some countries relieve pressure on their own forests by importing timber. Belgium, Denmark, Luxembourg,

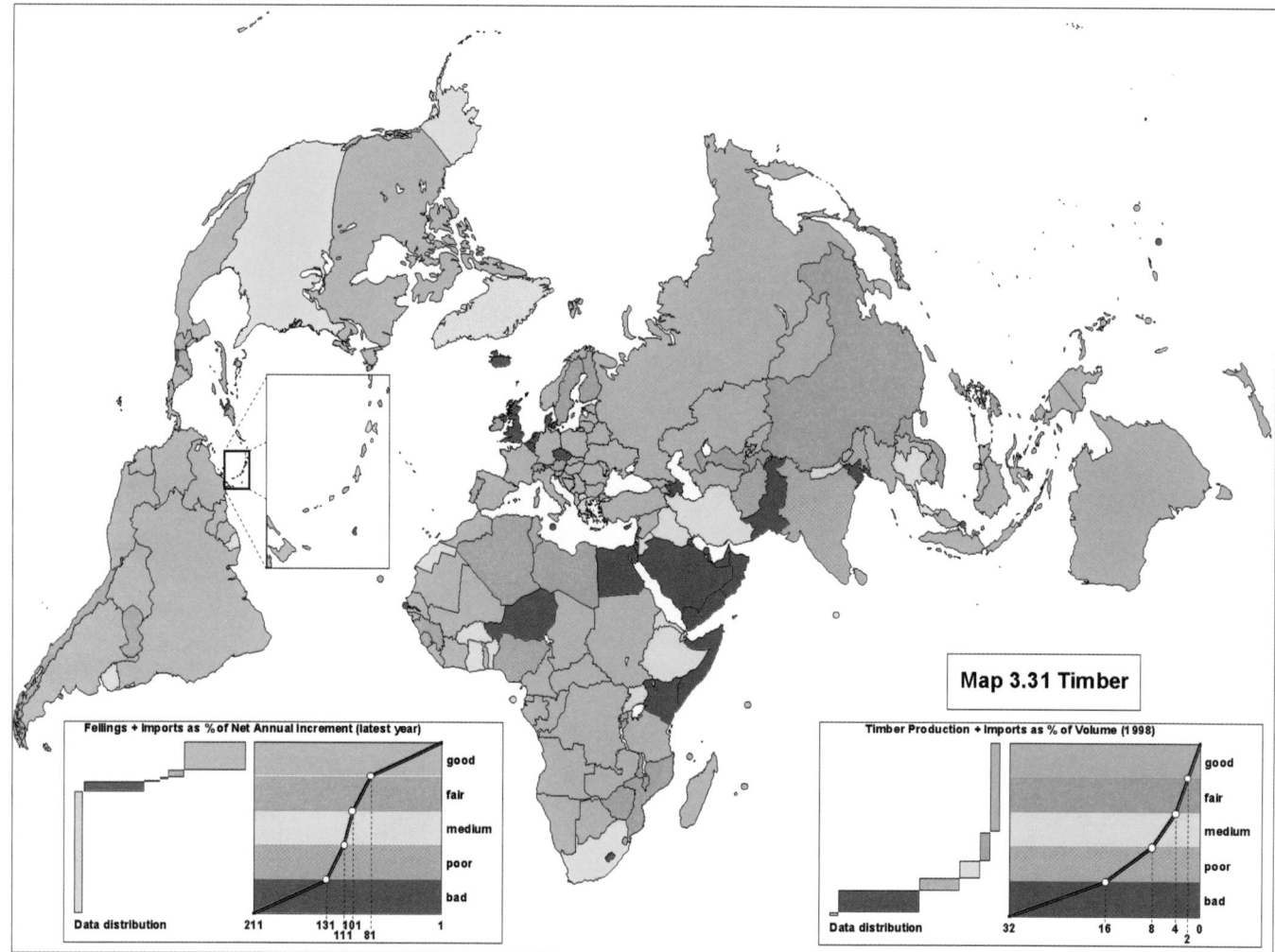

Map 3.31 Timber

Netherlands, United Kingdom, Cyprus, and Israel could achieve fair scores by keeping fellings at current rates and cutting imports. Eight other countries with poor or bad scores could achieve medium scores by limiting imports.[49]

Notes

1. Holling (1995).
2. Collar, Crosby, & Stattersfield (1994); World Conservation Monitoring Centre (1992).
3. This amounts to almost 40% if just land plant energy is considered (Vitousek et al. 1986). Ecosystem conversion accounts for about 37% of the plant energy that is destroyed or consumed, use of converted (cultivated and built) ecosystems for 29%, resource extraction and ecosystem modification for 26%, and soil degradation for 8% (my analysis of Vitousek et al. 1986 in Annex 1 of IUCN/UNEP/WWF 1991). IUCN/UNEP/WWF (1991) is also the source of the definition of carrying capacity.

4. Ecological Footprint description: Wackernagel et al. (2000). Data are for 1996 and are from Wackernagel et al. (2000). Seven of the eighteen countries with an EF score more than 10 points lower than the EWI are in Northern Europe, 3 are in West Asia, and the others are Canada, United States, Gambia, Zimbabwe, Belarus, Singapore, Australia, and New Zealand. Nineteen of the 47 countries with an EF score more than 10 points higher than the EWI are in Africa, 13 are in the Americas, and 9 in Southern Asia; the others are Bosnia and Herzegovina, Croatia, Georgia, Syria, China, and Papua New Guinea.
5. Levin (1995); O'Neill et al. (1995).
6. Ideally, the index would be differentiated by major ecosystem (rather than treating each country's land area as ecologically homogeneous) and would also measure how much each ecosystem has been fragmented into separate patches, but this information is not available.
7. The 10 European countries are Albania, Belarus, Croatia, Estonia, France, Greece, Latvia, Spain, United Kingdom, and Yugoslavia.
8. Based on the average of separate ranks for total species of

flowering plants, gymnosperms, pteridophytes, mammals, breeding birds, reptiles, and amphibians (see Table 19).

9. Indicator description: Table 11. Data: many sources (see Tables 11 and 12). Estimates of natural, modified, and converted land areas came from several sources, which often differed greatly. Many were derived from global and regional maps, resulting in large errors when translated into national statistics, and some were extrapolations.

10. Reid & Miller (1989).

11. Indicator description: United Nations (1996). Data: IUCN World Commission on Protected Areas & World Conservation Monitoring Centre (1998); World Conservation Monitoring Centre (1997); Iremonger, Ravilious, & Quinton (1997). The international target comes from IUCN/UNEP/WWF (1991) and Recommendation 16 of the 4th World Congress on National Parks and Protected Areas (McNeely 1993).

12. Indicator description: Oldeman (1993); van Lynden & Oldeman (1997). Data from GLASOD: Oldeman (1993); Oldeman, Hakkeling, & Sombroek (1991); UNEP/ISRIC (1990). Data from other studies: Baitullin & Bekturova (1997); FAO, UNDP, & UNEP (1994); van Lynden & Oldeman (1997).

13. Shiklomanov (1997).

14. Water quality concerns: National Water Research Institute (1996); Shiklomanov (1997). An additional major concern is salinization, not covered due to lack of data. Indicator descriptions: Table 15; National Water Research Institute (1996). Data: Eurostat et al. (1995); National Water Research Institute (1996); Organisation for Economic Co-operation and Development (1997, 1999); UNEP & WHO GEMS/Water Collaborating Centre (1988–1990, 1991–1993, 1999); OECD Centre for Co-operation with the Economies in Transition (1996). Performance criteria: United Nations Economic Commission for Europe (1990).

15. Arsenic in Bangladesh: Bangladesh Bureau of Statistics (1999).

16. Pernetta & Elder (1993); Welcomme (1985).

17. Indicator description: Table 14. Data: Food and Agriculture Organization of the United Nations (1995a, 1997b, 1997c, 1997d, 1999c, 2000b); World Energy Council (1999).

18. Impacts of water withdrawal: Shiklomanov (1997). Indicator description: United Nations (1996). Data: Eurostat, European Commission, & the European Environment Agency (1998); Food and Agriculture Organization of the United Nations (1995a, 1997b, 1997c, 1997d, 1999c, 2000b); Instituto Nacional de Estadística, Geografía e Informática (1998); Organisation for Economic Co-operation and Development (1999); World Resources Institute et al. (1998); Shiklomanov (1997).

19. Andreae & Dickinson (1995).

20. Intergovernmental Panel on Climate Change, Working Group 1 (1996).

21. World Meteorological Organization (1995).

22. Intergovernmental Panel on Climate Change, Working Group 1 (1996). The indicator is limited to burning of fossil fuels (coal, oil, gas), cement manufacture, and gas flaring because they are measured consistently for almost all countries, whereas forest loss and burning of wood and vegetation are not.

23. Indicator description: United Nations (1996). Data: Marland et al. (2000). Need to cut global CO_2 emissions by 60–80% of 1990 level (3.7–4.9 billion metric tons): Corner House (1997). Projected world population in 2050: United Nations Population Division (1998b).

24. World Meteorological Organization (1995); Ozone Secretariat, United Nations Environment Programme (1997).

25. Illegal trade: United Nations Environment Programme (1996); World Resources Institute et al. (1998). Indicator description: United Nations (1996). Data: Ozone Secretariat, United Nations Environment Programme (1999); United Nations Environment Programme (1998).

26. Health and environmental effects: World Health Organization (1998c); World Resources Institute et al. (1998). Indicator description: World Health Organization (1998c). Data: World Health Organization (1998c); Organisation for Economic Co-operation and Development (1999). Performance criteria: World Health Organization (1998d); Junker & Schwela (1998).

27. Background extinction rate: Reid & Miller (1989). Species more threatened today than since the dinosaurs: IUCN/UNEP/WWF (1991).

28. The top 45 countries are Indonesia, China, Mexico, Colombia, Brazil, Peru, India, United States, Ecuador, Venezuela, Australia, Papua New Guinea, Bolivia, Thailand, South Africa, Malaysia, Panama, Argentina, Tanzania, Democratic Republic of the Congo, Guatemala, Myanmar, Costa Rica, Kenya, Nicaragua, Viet Nam, Philippines, Angola, Uganda, Honduras, Cameroon, Nepal, Zimbabwe, Paraguay, Russia, Guyana, Suriname, Mozambique, Sudan, Nigeria, Japan, Ethiopia, Côte d'Ivoire, Malawi, and Madagascar (Table 19).

29. Chile: Dinerstein et al. (1995). Algeria: my analysis.

30. Indicator description: United Nations (1996). Data: World Conservation Monitoring Centre (1998a).

31. Indicator description: United Nations (1996). Data: IUCN Species Survival Commission (2000); BirdLife International (2000); World Conservation Monitoring Centre (1998b).

32. Also excluded are wild relatives, which are covered by the wild animal species indicator, and feral populations (descendants of domesticated stock now living in the wild)

because they are often a threat to wild species and natural ecosystems. Poultry were dropped because assessments include high proportions of nonestablished breeds. Indicator description: Table 20. Data: FAO Initiative for Domesticated Animal Diversity (1998, 1999); Rege (1999).

33. Characteristics of Crioulo Lageano cattle and Canastrão pig: FAO Initiative for Domesticated Animal Diversity (1998); Porter (1993). Pork dishes of Rio de Janeiro and Minas Gerais: Leroux (1980).

34. Holstein–Friesian cattle: Cunningham & Syrstad (1987). Gloucester Old Spot pig: Alderson (1989). War and African cattle breeds: Rege (1999); Rege & Tawah (1999).

35. Impact of crossbreeding and interbreeding on European cattle and horses: Simon (1999). African cattle: Rege (1999); Rege, Aboagye, & Tawah (1994); Rege & Tawah (1999). The Criollo goat: FAO Initiative for Domesticated Animal Diversity (1998). Pakistan's sheep and goats: Hasnain (1985).

36. Taihu pigs: Porter (1993).

37. Navajo Churro sheep: Bixby et al. (1994). Tanzanian cattle: Rege (1999); Rege & Tawah (1999).

38. Kenyan Boran cattle: Porter (1991); Rege & Tawah (1999). Danish Red and Danish Friesian cattle: FAO Initiative for Domesticated Animal Diversity (1998). Ibérica pigs: FAO Initiative for Domesticated Animal Diversity (1998); Porter (1993). Pecorino Sardo: Accademia Italiana della Cucina (1995). Fontina: Associazione Nazionale Allevatori Bovini Razza Valdostana (1995).

39. Indicator description: United Nations (1996). Data: United Nations Energy Statistics Unit (2000).

40. Data for all agricultural indicators: FAO (1998a).

41. Inferior self-reliance reduced 13 relatively productive countries to a medium rating (Belize, Cuba, Jamaica, Republic of Congo, Gabon, Rwanda, Comoros, Swaziland, Albania, Bosnia and Herzegovina, Fiji, Papua New Guinea, and Vanuatu).

42. Self-reliance was sole determinant of poor scores in Dominica, Grenada, St Vincent and Grenadines, Algeria, Gambia, Lesotho, Mauritania, Estonia, Portugal, Armenia, Japan, Malaysia, Mongolia, Yemen, Samoa, and Tonga; productivity in Finland, Ireland, United Kingdom, Belarus, Latvia, Iraq, Tajikistan, Turkmenistan, Uzbekistan, and New Zealand; and both factors in Libya, Cape Verde, São Tomé and Principe, Norway, South Korea, and Solomon Islands.

43. Northern Europe: Austria, Belgium, Denmark, Germany, Ireland, Luxembourg, Switzerland, United Kingdom. Eastern Europe: Czech Republic, Latvia, Lithuania, Poland. Southern Europe: Croatia, France, Slovenia.

44. Indicator description and data, including examples in this and previous paragraph: FAO Marine Resources Service, Fishery Resources Division (1997).

45. Second and third indicators (capacity per area and catch per capacity), description: Table 24. Data: FAO (1998b); FAO Fishery Information, Data and Statistics Unit (1998); FAO Fishery Resources Division, personal communication (1996).

46. Indicator data: FAO (1998a).

47. South America: Argentina, Chile, Guyana, Paraguay, Uruguay, and Venezuela. North and Central America: Canada, Costa Rica, Panama, and United States. Eastern Europe: Bulgaria, Lithuania, Moldova, and Slovakia.

48. The six West Asian countries are Armenia, Azerbaijan, Cyprus, Georgia, Israel, and Turkey.

49. Indicator data: FAO (1993, 1995c, 2000a); Pandey (1995); UNECE & FAO (2000). The eight countries that could achieve medium scores by cutting imports are St Lucia, Iceland, Mauritius, Kuwait, Saudi Arabia, Singapore, United Arab Emirates, and Yemen.

4. Combining Human and Ecosystem Wellbeing

Distances to Sustainability

This section introduces the Wellbeing Index (WI) and Wellbeing/Stress Index (WSI), two indices that combine human and ecosystem wellbeing, and then discusses the main combinations.

Highlights

- No country is sustainable or even close to sustainability.

- The leaders—Sweden, Finland, Norway, Iceland, and Austria—have good or fair human wellbeing but only medium ecosystem wellbeing.

- 37 *ecosystem deficit* countries (including the five leaders) have high standards of living but excessive impacts on the global environment.

- 27 *human deficit* countries have fairly low demands on the ecosystem but are desperately poor.

- The remaining 116 are *double deficit* countries, combining weak environmental performance and inadequate development.

- In 141 countries, ecosystem stress is higher than human wellbeing, a clear sign that most people's efforts to improve their lot are inefficient and overexploit the environment.

- A high quality of life can be attained for a low environmental price. Increases in human wellbeing do not necessarily result in greater impacts on the environment, which are less the product of the *level* of human wellbeing than of the *way* human wellbeing is pursued.

- The key conditions for combining high human wellbeing and low ecosystem stress are freedom, sound governance, and education.

Wellbeing Index

Wellbeing Index (WI)
(Figure 4.1 and Map 4.1)

What it is: The point on the Barometer of Sustainability where the Human Wellbeing Index (HWI) and the Ecosystem Wellbeing Index (EWI) intersect.

Country results: 0 good (0%), 5 fair (3%), 86 medium (48%), 89 poor (49%), 0 bad (0%).

*The main combinations of human and ecosystem wellbeing that make up the WI are shown in Figure 4.1 (examples) and Map 4.1 (all countries). The WI of all countries is given in Table 25 in the Data section. Nations **bold** in the text are shown in Figure 4.1.*

The Wellbeing Index (WI) displays the HWI and EWI together, combining the quality of human life and the environment without submerging one in the other (Figure 4.1). The closer a country is to the top right corner of the Barometer, the nearer it is to achieving a high quality of life for a low environmental price. A single number does not do justice to the WI, whether it be the lower of the HWI and EWI or the average. The lower number ignores half the picture: either the state of the environment or the condition of people. For example, **Australia, China,** and **Gabon** would end up with identical scores of 28, despite Australia's much higher human wellbeing and Gabon's superior ecosystem wellbeing. The average also masks differences in human and ecosystem wellbeing: **Croatia, Russia,** and **Gabon** have the same average of 45.0, although Croatia is impeded by poor ecosystem wellbeing, Gabon by inferior human wellbeing, and Russia is weak in both.

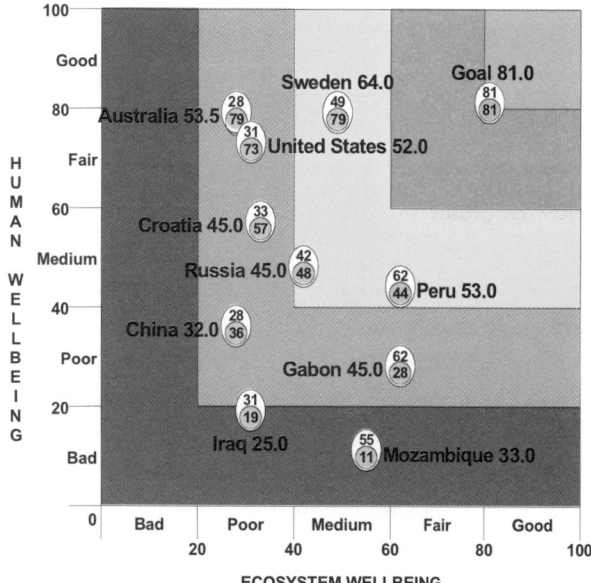

Map 4.1 Wellbeing Index

HWI/EWI combination

- HWI good or fair, EWI medium
- HWI medium, EWI fair
- HWI fair, EWI poor or bad
- HWI poor or bad, EWI fair
- Both medium
- HWI medium, EWI poor or bad
- HWI poor or bad, EWI medium
- Both poor or bad

Figure 4.1. Main combinations of human and ecosystem wellbeing. The Human Wellbeing Index (HWI) is in the yolk of the egg, the Ecosystem Wellbeing Index (EWI) in the white. The Wellbeing Index (WI), expressed as the average of the HWI and EWI, is next to the name of the country.

The merit of the average is that it expresses the distance a society has to go to achieve sustainability: Croatia, Russia, and Gabon are equally far from a sustainable WI of 81.0. Hence, when a single number is needed (such as to rank countries), the average is used. But it should be borne in mind that the true WI is the juxtaposition of human and ecosystem wellbeing shown on the Barometer of Sustainability.

A sustainable WI would combine a good HWI and a good EWI. In a close to sustainable WI, both parts would be fair or a mixture of good and fair. No country has achieved either. Instead, the 180 nations fall into eight combinations of human and ecosystem wellbeing in three major sets:

Ecosystem deficit (HWI good or fair, EWI below fair): 37 countries

Moderate ecosystem deficit (HWI good or fair, EWI medium), 10 countries: 6 in Northern Europe (e.g.,

Sweden with the highest WI in the world); 2 in Eastern Europe; Canada; Uruguay.

High ecosystem deficit (HWI fair, EWI poor or bad), 27 countries: 7 each in Northern and Southern Europe; 5 in Eastern Europe; 2 in Central and East Asia; 2 in the Pacific (e.g., **Australia**); **United States;** Barbados; Cyprus; Singapore.

Human deficit (HWI below fair, EWI fair): 27 countries

Moderate human deficit (HWI medium, EWI fair), 4 countries: Belize; Dominica; Guyana and **Peru.**

High human deficit (HWI poor or bad, EWI fair), 23 countries: 7 in West Africa; 6 in Central and East Africa (e.g., **Gabon**); 3 each in Southern Africa and Southern Asia; 2 in Northern Africa; Bolivia; Solomon Islands.

Double deficit (HWI and EWI both below fair): 116 countries

Moderate double deficit (HWI and EWI both medium), 21 countries: 5 in the West Indies; 4 in South America; 2 each in West Asia and the Pacific; Costa Rica; Cape Verde; Seychelles; Mauritius; FYR Macedonia; Belarus; **Russia;** Brunei Darussalam.

High double deficit, ecosystem worse (HWI medium, EWI poor or bad), 27 countries: 6 in West Asia; 4 each in the West Indies and Eastern Europe; 3 each in South America and Southern Asia; 2 in North and Central America; 2 in Southern Europe (e.g., **Croatia**); Tunisia; South Africa; Kazakhstan.

High double deficit, people worse (HWI poor or bad, EWI medium), 50 countries: 8 each in Southern Africa (e.g., **Mozambique**) and Southern Asia; 7 in West Africa; 6 in Central and East Africa; 5 in Northern Africa; 4 in North and Central America; 4 in Central and East Asia; 2 each in the West Indies, Southern Europe, and the Pacific; Paraguay; Yemen.

Extreme double deficit (HWI and EWI both poor or bad), 18 countries: 8 in West Asia (e.g., **Iraq** with

the lowest WI in the world); 4 in Central and East Asia (e.g., **China**); 2 each in Northern Africa and West Africa; India; Tonga.

In general, human deficits are more pronounced than ecosystem deficits. As a result, human deficit nations tend to have lower WIs and to be farther from sustainability than their ecosystem deficit counterparts. In addition, their environmental ratings may not be as fair as they seem, since they do not include the quality of inland waters and local air. If they did, the countries might have lower EWIs and drop to double deficits.

Wellbeing/Stress Index

Wellbeing/Stress Index (WSI) (Map 4.2)

What it is: The ratio of human wellbeing to ecosystem stress (derived by subtracting the EWI from 100 to obtain an Ecosystem Stress Index [ESI] and then dividing the HWI by the ESI). (Ecosystem stress is the opposite of ecosystem wellbeing, and the ESI is the reverse of the EWI.)

Country results: 0 good (0%), 0 fair (0%), 37 medium (21%), 84 poor (47%), 59 bad (33%).

The WSI and WSI score of all countries are given in Table 25 in the Data section.

Combining high levels of human and ecosystem wellbeing calls for an economy that gets a bigger buck for the bang. The buck is income, jobs, and other benefits. The bang is pressure on the ecosystem: the quantity of resources extracted, the amount and effect of wastes returned, the extent and degree of modification of the land, and impacts on biodiversity.

The Wellbeing/Stress Index (WSI) compares the socioeconomic benefits of development with its environmental costs, showing how much human wellbeing a society obtains for the amount of stress it places on the environment. A country with an HWI and EWI of 81 would have a WSI above 4.0, a level of human wellbeing more than four times higher than its level of ecosystem stress. Hence a good WSI is more than 4.0 and a fair

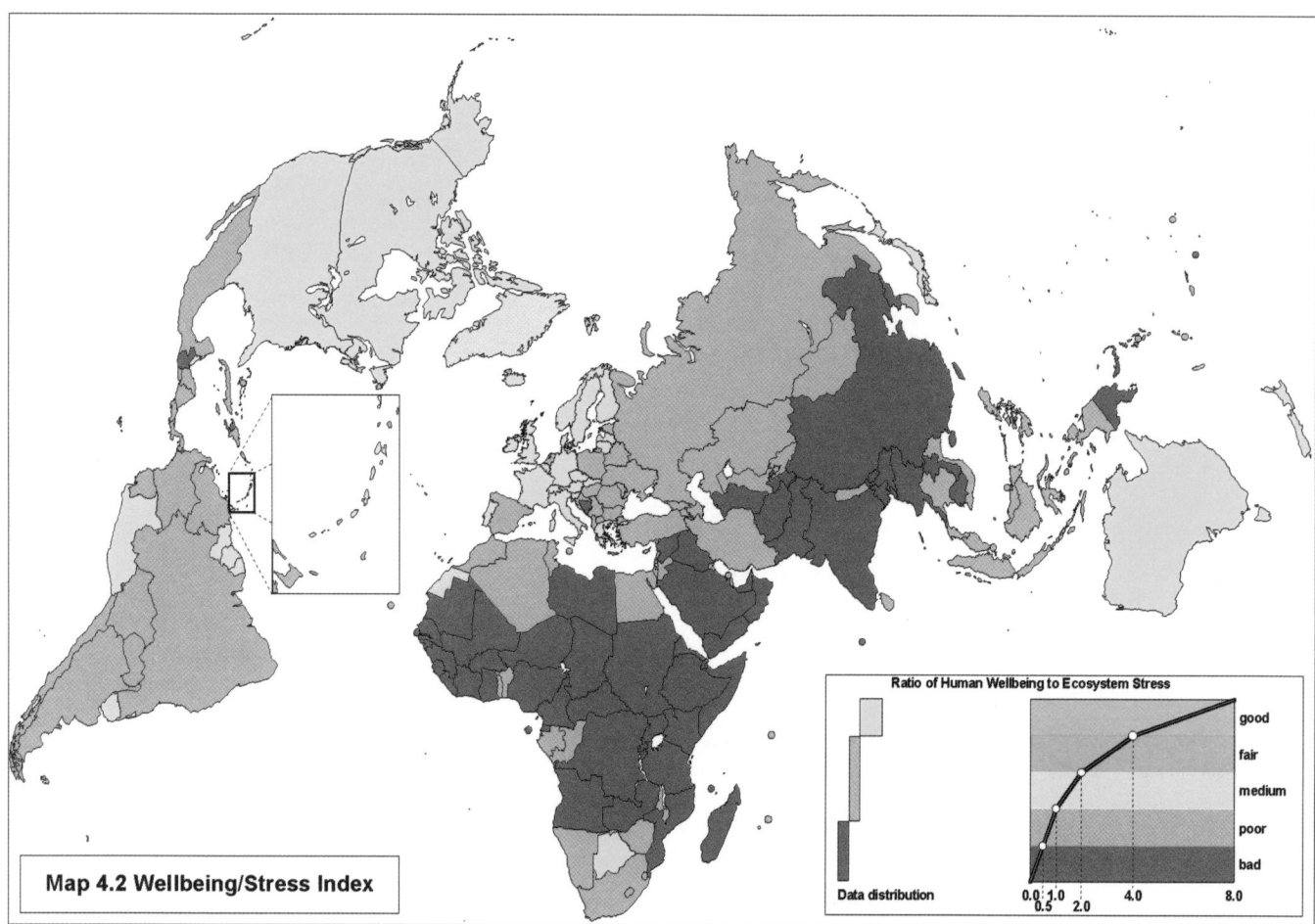

Map 4.2 Wellbeing/Stress Index

WSI more than 2.0 (human wellbeing twice the amount of ecosystem stress).

No country comes close. Among those rated on all human and ecosystem subelements, Sweden has the highest WSI: 1.55. Only 37 nations, more than half of them in Europe, have WSIs above 1.0 (that is, higher human wellbeing than ecosystem stress); 17 of the 37 edge above 1.0 by less than a tenth of a point (Table 4.2).

The Netherlands and Armenia head the poor scorers with WSIs of exactly 1.0, human wellbeing equaling ecosystem stress. In the other 141 nations, ecosystem stress is greater than human wellbeing, exceeding it by double or more in the 59 with a bad score—all in Africa and Asia–Pacific except for Guatemala, Haiti, and Bosnia and Herzegovina. Somalia has the lowest WSI (0.08), its limited impact on the environment far outweighed by the severity of human deprivation.

Table 4.1. Number of countries in each performance group. HW/EW combination = combination of human and ecosystem wellbeing. 1 through 5 are combinations of the Wellbeing Index (WI) and Wellbeing/Stress Index (WSI): 1 = fair WI/medium WSI; 2 = medium WI/medium WSI; 3 = medium WI/poor or bad WSI; 4 = poor WI/poor WSI; 5 = poor WI/bad WSI.

	WI/WSI Group				
HW/EW Combination	1	2	3	4	5
Moderate ecosystem deficit	5	5			
Moderate human deficit		4			
Moderate double deficit		4	17		
High ecosystem deficit		18	9		
High human deficit		1	9		13
High double deficit, ecosystem worse			10	16	1
High double deficit, people worse			9	9	32
Extreme double deficit				6	12
TOTAL	5	32	54	31	58

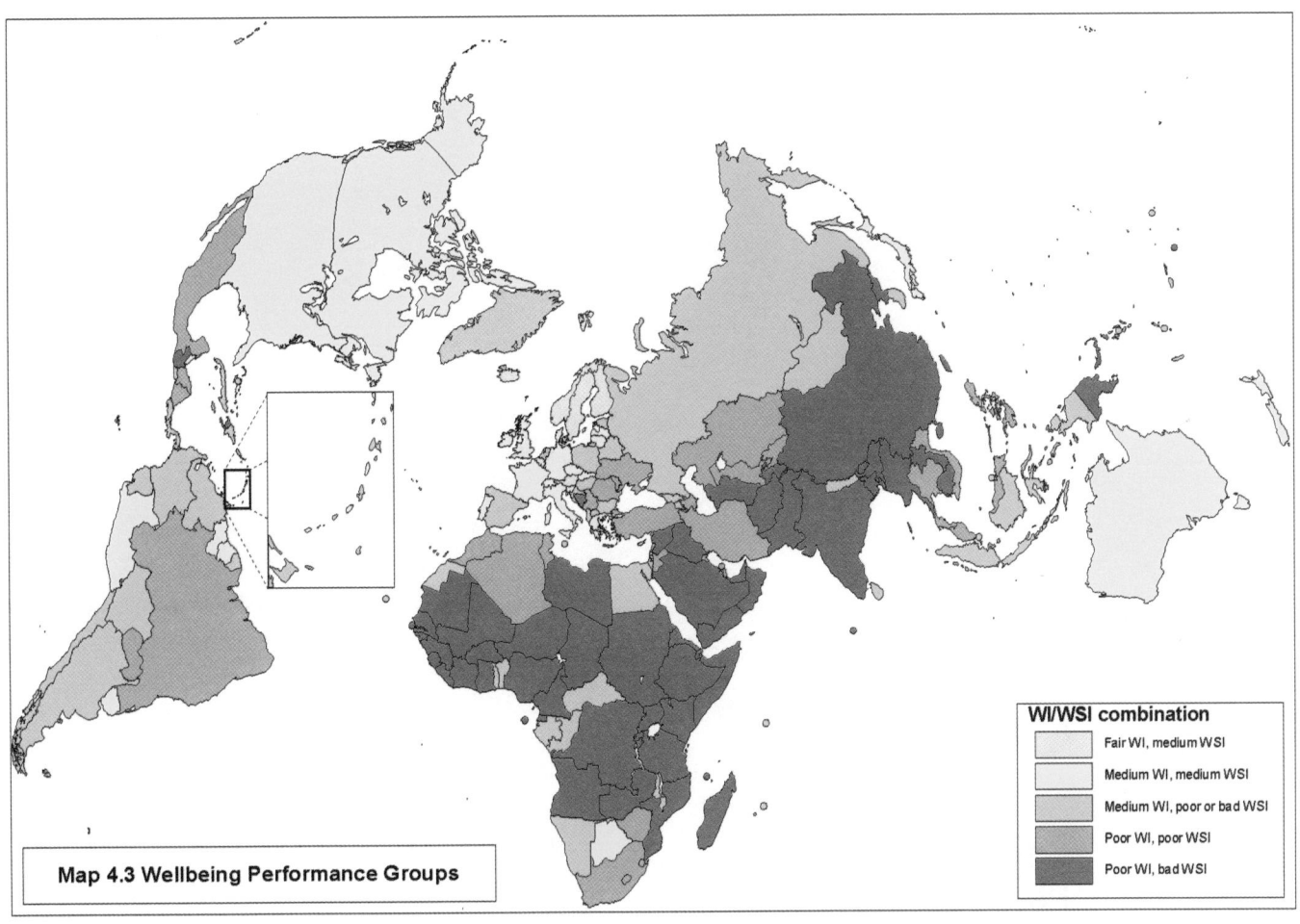

Map 4.3 Wellbeing Performance Groups

WI/WSI combination

Fair WI, medium WSI

Medium WI, medium WSI

Medium WI, poor or bad WSI

Poor WI, poor WSI

Poor WI, bad WSI

Wellbeing Performance Groups

Wellbeing Performance Groups (Map 4.3)

What they are: Combinations of Wellbeing Index (WI) and Wellbeing/Stress Index (WSI).

Country results: 5 fair WI/medium WSI (3%), 32 medium WI/medium WSI (18%), 54 medium WI/poor or bad WSI (30%), 31 poor WI/poor WSI (17%), 58 poor WI/bad WSI (32%).

The main performance groups are shown in Map 4.3, summarized in Table 4.1, and given in detail in Table 26 in the Data section. The top countries, ranked by WI, are in Table 4.2; all countries, in Table 27 in the Data section.

Together the WI and WSI show how well and sustainable societies are overall, revealing a world that is largely unwell and unsustainable, much of it severely so. Only 37 countries, with WIs above 50.0 and WSIs above 1.0, have gone more than half the distance toward sustainability. The other 143 have a much longer road ahead.

The five leaders—Sweden, Finland, Norway, Iceland, and Austria—are all moderate ecosystem deficit countries with fair WIs and medium WSIs. They enjoy high human wellbeing but at the cost of low-medium ecosystem wellbeing. Their clear priority is to raise the latter to fair.

The 32 runners-up, with medium WIs and medium WSIs, are a mixture of ecosystem deficit, human deficit, and double deficit countries. In the ecosystem deficit group, Canada, Switzerland, Uruguay, Latvia, and Lithuania have medium EWIs and moderate deficits; the rest have poor EWIs and high deficits. While the priority for this group is the same as for the leaders—to better environmental conditions—Uruguay, Latvia, and Lithuania, with barely acceptable human wellbeing, also need to ele-

Table 4.2. The 37 countries with a Wellbeing Index (WI) above 50.0. HWI = Human Wellbeing Index, EWI = Ecosystem Wellbeing Index, ESI = Ecosystem Stress Index, WSI = Wellbeing/Stress Index. Countries with the same WI were ranked by WSI. Those with the same three-digit WSI were differentiated by taking the WSI to four digits. * Country not rated on all 30 human and ecosystem subelements. *Countries in italics were rated on less than two-thirds of the human or ecosystem indicators.*

Rank	Country	HWI	EWI	ESI	WI	WSI
1	Sweden	79	49	51	64.0	1.55
2	Finland	81	44	56	62.5	1.45
3	Norway	82	43	57	62.5	1.44
4	Iceland*	80	43	57	61.5	1.40
5	Austria*	80	42	58	61.0	1.38
6	*Dominica**	*56*	*65*	*35*	*60.5*	*1.60*
7=	Canada	78	43	57	60.5	1.37
7=	Switzerland	78	43	57	60.5	1.37
9	Belize*	50	64	36	57.0	1.39
10	Guyana*	51	63	37	57.0	1.38
11	Uruguay*	61	52	48	56.5	1.27
12	Germany	77	36	64	56.5	1.20
13	Denmark	81	31	69	56.0	1.17
14	New Zealand*	73	38	62	55.5	1.18
15	Suriname*	52	58	42	55.0	1.24
16	Latvia*	62	46	54	54.0	1.15
17	Ireland*	76	32	68	54.0	1.12
18	Australia	79	28	72	53.5	1.10
19	Peru*	44	62	38	53.0	1.16
20	Slovenia*	71	35	65	53.0	1.09
21	*St Kitts and Nevis**	*52*	*53*	*47*	*52.5*	*1.11*
22	Lithuania	61	44	56	52.5	1.09
23	Cyprus*	67	38	62	52.5	1.08
24	Japan	80	25	75	52.5	1.07
25	*St Lucia**	*53*	*51*	*49*	*52.0*	*1.08*
26	*Grenada**	*55*	*49*	*51*	*52.0*	*1.08*
27	United States	73	31	69	52.0	1.06
28	Italy	74	30	70	52.0	1.06
29	France	75	29	71	52.0	1.06
30=	Czech Republic*	70	33	67	51.5	1.04
30=	Greece	70	33	67	51.5	1.04
32	Portugal	72	31	69	51.5	1.04
33	United Kingdom	73	30	70	51.5	1.04
34	Belgium	80	23	77	51.5	1.04
35	Botswana*	34	68	32	51.0	1.06
36	Slovakia*	61	40	60	50.5	1.02
37	Luxembourg*	77	24	76	50.5	1.01

vate their HWIs. The human deficit countries (Belize, Dominica, Guyana, Peru, and Botswana) face the task of lifting their standard of living while maintaining ecosystem quality and diversity, more so in Botswana (poor HWI) than in the others (medium HWIs). The double deficit nations (Grenada, St Kitts and Nevis, St Lucia, and Suriname) need to improve on both fronts.

Twenty of the 37 leaders and runners-up were not rated on all 30 human and ecosystem subelements and might fall to a lower rank if they were.

The middle of the pack consists of the 54 countries with medium WIs but poor WSIs (or in one case, Central African Republic, a bad WSI). They are similar to the runners-up, except that all human or ecosystem deficits are high (none is moderate), as are more than half the double deficits. Hence they have the same targets as the runners-up, but are further from achieving them.

At the back of the pack are the 89 countries with poor WIs and poor or bad WSIs. Thirteen (Bhutan and 12 in Africa) have high human deficits and need to greatly improve their HWIs, all of which are well below 20. The rest have high or extreme double deficits—moderately to heavily stressed environments without the development to show for it. Theirs is the most demanding challenge: both to accelerate development and to upgrade the ecosystem.

Human Wellbeing and Ecosystem Stress: Signs of a Way Forward

Correlations and other supporting data are in Table 25 in the Data section.

A striking feature of the pattern of deficits is that countries with higher human than ecosystem wellbeing generally have a higher WI than those where human conditions are worse than the state of the environment. For example, the average WI of the moderate ecosystem deficit countries (which include the five leaders) is 59.6, compared with 56.9 among the moderate human deficit countries. The separation is still greater between the two high-deficit groups: an average WI of 50.9 for the high ecosystem deficit countries and 41.3 for the high human deficit countries. A similar disparity is found among high double deficit countries.[1]

Underlying these patterns are differences in the ratio of human wellbeing to ecosystem stress. Among

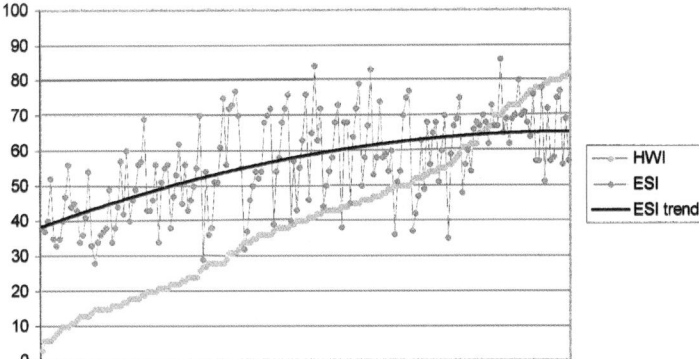

Figure 4.2. Ecosystem stress is only moderately related to human wellbeing. The Ecosystem Stress Index (ESI) rises less steeply than the Human Wellbeing Index (HWI), and individual country performance often is much better or worse than the trendline. The 180 countries are in ascending order of HWI. Where an ESI is below the HWI, human wellbeing exceeds ecosystem stress. Where an ESI is above the HWI, ecosystem stress exceeds human wellbeing.

ecosystem deficit countries, the WSI is medium in 28, poor in 9, bad in none. Among human deficit countries, the WSI is medium in 5, poor in 8, bad in 14. Among high double deficit countries, all but one (United Arab Emirates) have a poor WSI where the ecosystem is worse off, most (64%) a bad WSI where people are worse off.

These differences reflect two aspects of the relationship between human wellbeing and ecosystem stress. One is that even when countries with a bad or poor HWI put little pressure on the ecosystem, that pressure is high in relation to the benefits they derive from it. The other, more broadly significant aspect is that the state of the environment is only moderately tied to human conditions: ecosystem stress rises with human wellbeing, but not as much, and many countries perform much better or worse than the trendline (Figure 4.2). Some of this variation is due to disparities in indicator coverage, but when countries are grouped by completeness of coverage, the conclusions are the same for each group:

- Increases in human wellbeing do not necessarily result in greater ecosystem stress.

- One country can achieve the same quality of life for a smaller environmental price than another (Figure 4.3).

The flexibility of the link between human wellbeing

and ecosystem stress is due to the contrasting characteristics of each. Human wellbeing is consistent and predictable: several human elements (health, population, wealth, education, communication, and freedom and governance) reinforce each other, have similar scores, and are highly correlated with the HWI (Chapter 2, page 17). Ecosystem stress is much less consistent or predictable: only air and water are highly correlated with the EWI, and only air and resource use with each other (Chapter 3, page 64).

Income plays a major role in many more human than ecosystem elements and corresponds much more closely to the HWI than to the ESI. While the impact of rising incomes on human wellbeing is generally positive, on ecosystem wellbeing it may be negative (energy consumption tends to increase and pressure on the global atmosphere to worsen) or positive (local air quality tends to improve).

The inconsistency of ecosystem stress and the vari-

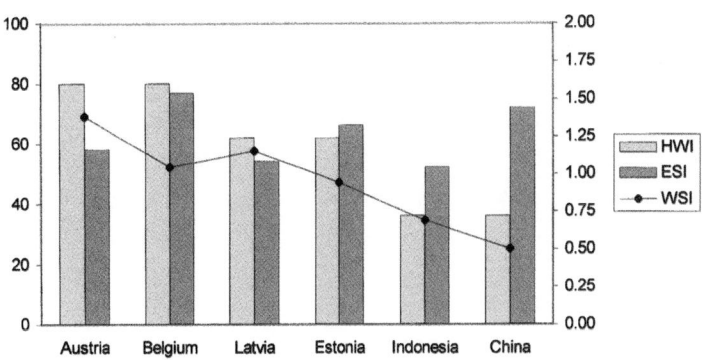

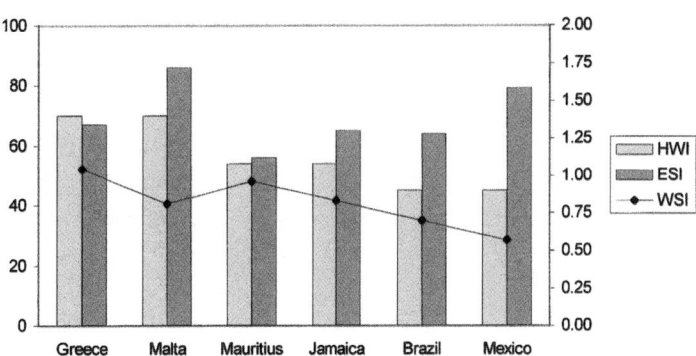

Figure 4.3. Same quality of life, different environmental price. Each pair of countries has the same Human Wellbeing Index (HWI), but the country on the left has a lower Ecosystem Stress Index (ESI) and hence a better Wellbeing/Stress Index (WSI). HWI and ESI scale on the left; WSI scale on the right.

able role of income result from the different effects of three factors. The first is consumption dependency. Higher incomes are more likely to increase ecosystem stress if they rely heavily on the consumption of energy and other resources. Among the country pairs in Figure 4.3, Estonia is more consumption dependent than Latvia—consuming 35.2 gigajoules of energy per $1,000 of income, in contrast to Latvia's 19.7 gigajoules—and has a bigger environmental impact.[2]

The second factor is ecological vulnerability. Some countries' environments are inherently more vulnerable than others. Densely populated areas are more likely to lose their ecosystems to settlements, infrastructure, and cultivation. Densely speciated areas—regions rich in species and habitats—are harder to develop without reducing diversity. Malta, with 12.16 people and 30.34 species per hectare, is ecologically more vulnerable than Greece (0.81 people and 0.41 species per hectare), and its level of ecosystem stress is higher.[3]

Consumption dependency and ecological vulnerability act in different ways. The former tends to influence environmental quality, the latter biodiversity (notably the diversity of land ecosystems and species and genes). But their indicators (energy/income, population/area, species/area) are approximate and may counteract each other. All three conform with the level of ecosystem stress in two of the six pairs in Figure 4.3 (Austria–Belgium and Brazil–Mexico), but in the others, one or two of the indicators are contradictory: Greece is more consumption dependent than Malta, Estonia has slightly fewer people per hectare than Latvia, species density is higher in Indonesia than in China, and both human and species densities are higher in Mauritius than in Jamaica.

Such contradictions undoubtedly reflect the third factor: the individual, local, and national decisions people make about their goals and how to achieve them. It is clear from the patterns revealed by this global assess-ment that the environmental price of development is not fixed, and much of the relationship between human wellbeing and ecosystem stress is a matter of choice. Ecosystem stress is a result not so much of the *level* of human wellbeing but of the *way* in which human well-being is pursued. A country's ecological vulnerability determines the minimum possible level of ecosystem stress. Consumption dependency and people's decisions determine how close the actual level of stress is to that minimum.

The opportunity and capacity to make sound decisions is crucial. Significantly, the WSI is highly correlated with the combination of freedom and governance plus education (more than with either of these alone or with income). This makes sense because the combination of freedom, good governance, and education provides people with both the opportunity and the capacity to make decisions that promote sus-tainability. Attaining high levels of human and ecosys-tem wellbeing requires organization, consensus, the rule of law, knowledge, and an awareness of being part of a wider community (extending beyond the confines of ethnic group, corporation, or nation, and ahead to future generations). These conditions do not guarantee that decisions will be right, but if they are made in ignorance, usurped by a minority, cloaked in secrecy, or influenced by bribes, decisions are much more likely to be wrong.

At present, all levels of human wellbeing cause too much damage to the environment, but they need not do so. High human wellbeing and low ecosystem stress—a win–no lose rather than a win–win situation—is an attainable combination. Countries with high standards of living can lead the way by reducing and eventually elimi-nating their ecosystem deficits. The rest of the world may feel that development is challenge enough without both-ering with conservation—but for all societies, real progress depends on both.

Regional Reviews

This section explores national performance patterns in the 14 regions, identifying common features and steps toward wellbeing and sustainability.

Highlights

- Northern Europe is the strongest region, with 12 countries in the top 40, including the 5 leaders.

- West Asia is the weakest, with 9 countries in the bottom 40 and the most with high or extreme double deficits.

- In the West Indies, South America, Northern and Eastern Europe, and West and Southern Asia, particularly wide differences in ecosystem wellbeing occur among nations with similar levels of human wellbeing.

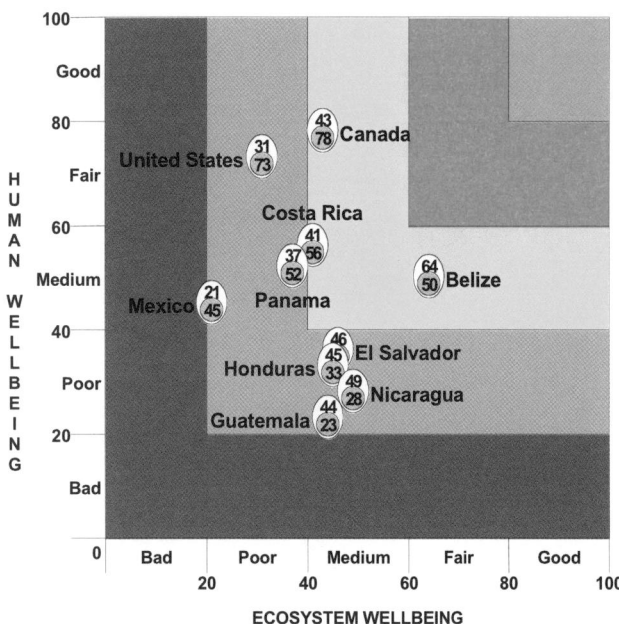

Figure 4.4. Wellbeing of North and Central America. Human Wellbeing Index (HWI) in yolk of egg, Ecosystem Wellbeing Index (EWI) in white. El Salvador's HWI is 36 and EWI 46.

Table 4.3. North and Central America: Wellbeing Index (WI), Wellbeing/Stress Index (WSI), performance group, and number (#) of subelements covered (out of 30). 1 = fair WI/medium WSI; 2 = medium WI and WSI; 3 = medium WI/poor WSI; 4 = poor WI and WSI; 5 = poor WI/bad WSI; mod. = moderate; def. = deficit, e = ecosystem worse; p = people worse. Country order is by performance group and then by WI.

Country	WI	WSI	Performance Group	#
Canada	60.5	1.37	2: mod. ecosystem def.	30
Belize	57.0	1.39	2: mod. human def.	24
United States	52.0	1.06	2: high ecosystem def.	30
Costa Rica	48.5	0.95	3: mod. double def.	28
Panama	44.5	0.83	3: high double def. e	28
El Salvador	41.0	0.67	3: high double def. p	26
Honduras	39.0	0.60	4: high double def. p	27
Nicaragua	38.5	0.55	4: high double def. p	28
Mexico	33.0	0.57	4: high double def. e	29
Guatemala	33.5	0.41	5: high double def. p	26

Most of North and Central America (Figure 4.4 and Table 4.3) shows the backward climb (from the bottom right to the top left of the Barometer) of conventional development: ecosystem wellbeing declines as human wellbeing improves, from Nicaragua's poor HWI and medium EWI to the United States' fair HWI and poor EWI. Mexico and Guatemala are extreme examples of this tendency, with

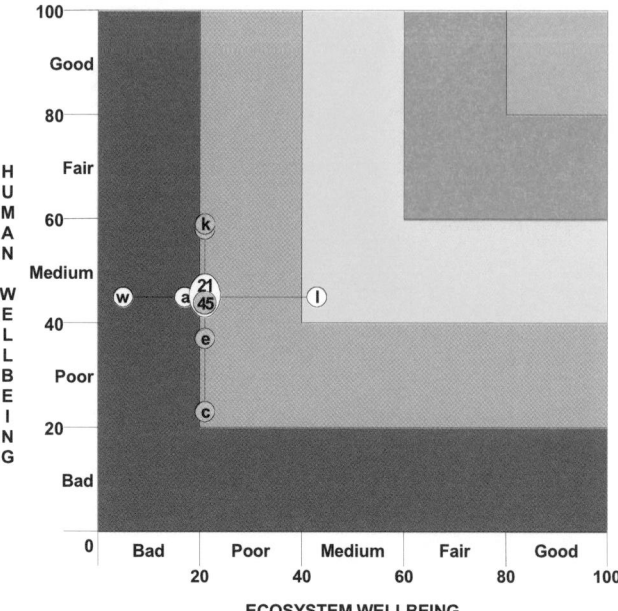

Figure 4.5. Structure of wellbeing: Mexico. Yellow circles show the points on the scale of the human dimensions: c = community; e = equity; h = health and population; k = knowledge; w = wealth. White circles show the points of the ecosystem dimensions: a = air; l = land; r = resource use; s = species and genes; w = water. Some dimensions are hidden by the egg (wealth, species and genes) or behind another dimension (health and population is behind knowledge). Mexico's EWI excludes resource use, which otherwise would have increased it artificially.

Guatemala's very poor HWI and low-medium EWI reversed into Mexico's very poor EWI and low-medium HWI.

Canada and Belize seem to have broken out of the trap and to be moving toward the top right corner of the Barometer. However, Belize may not be in as sound a position as it looks since it was not assessed on crime, household equity, river conversion, water quality, local air quality, or domesticated diversity. If Belize had the Central American average score for local air quality (30) and the same score as Mexico for water quality (5), its EWI would fall to 37. In fact, none of the Central American countries was rated for water quality. Fuller assessments would probably reduce their scores for the environment and shift their ecosystem positions on the Barometer toward Mexico. However, it is unlikely that their human positions would change significantly because coverage of human indicators is fairly complete.

Thus, while Mexico bridges North and Central America geographically, in terms of wellbeing it is entirely Central American. Its weakest human dimensions are community, equity, and wealth (Figure 4.5). The poor score for community (only El Salvador's and Guatemala's are worse) is due to conflicts in the states of Chiapas and Guerrero,

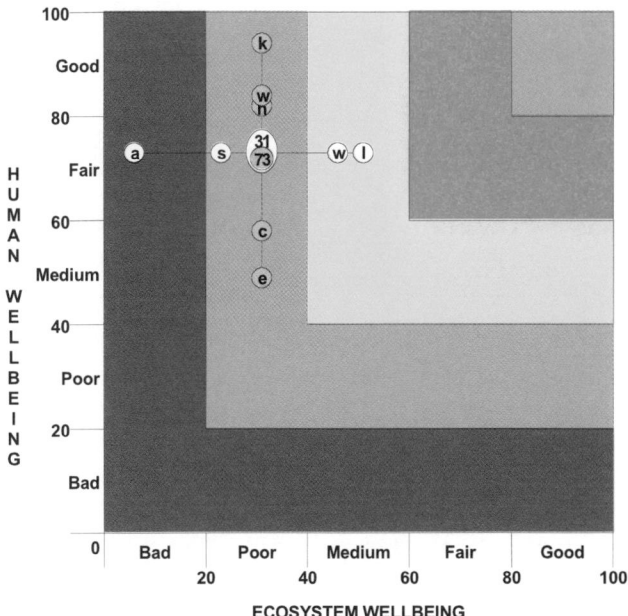

Figure 4.6. Structure of wellbeing: United States. See Figure 4.5 for key. The United States' EWI excludes resource use, which otherwise would have increased it artificially.

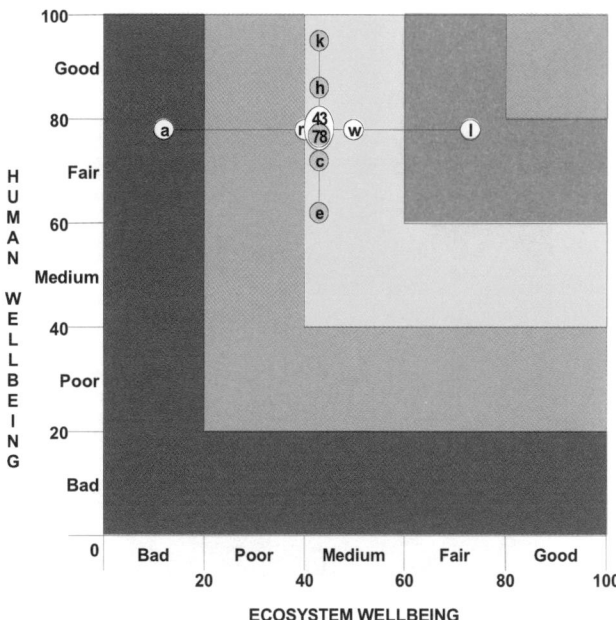

Figure 4.7. Structure of wellbeing: Canada. See Figure 4.5 for key. Some dimensions are hidden by the egg (wealth, species and genes, resource use).

which have caused an average of 830 deaths a year since 1994. Underlying such conflicts is the wide gap between a well-educated middle- and upper-class minority and a largely rural majority living in poverty (71% of the population),[4] a gap reflected in the poor score for equity. Inequities are exacerbated by corruption, a weak and politicized judicial system, and repression and human rights abuses in poor urban areas and throughout the countryside.

Political freedom has steadily increased since 1997, and the 2000 presidential election was the fairest in Mexico's history. This progress could provide the momentum to build the social infrastructure of human wellbeing: establishing the rule of law, professionalizing the bureaucracy, and extending economic and educational opportunities to rural areas.

These measures are also needed to increase ecosystem wellbeing. After Canada and the United States, Mexico is the least ecologically vulnerable country in the region,[5] yet it has the highest percentages of threatened wild species (10% of mammals and breeding birds, 36% of plants), and (apart from El Salvador) the lowest percentage of protected area—hence the poor score for species and genes and the low-medium score for land. Only stronger habitat protection coupled with improved rural living conditions can turn this around. And only better physical and social infrastructure, including societywide respect for regulations, can end the severe pollution of rivers, groundwater, and urban air behind the bad scores for air and water.

If human wellbeing were assessed solely on health and

population, wealth, and knowledge, the United States (Figure 4.6) and Canada (Figure 4.7) would have the same HWI. Their knowledge ratings are close, and the stronger economy of the United States offsets Canada's longer life spans and better health. Instead, community and equity make the difference. Canada has better scores for both elements of community: freedom and governance because corruption is lower; peace and order because it spends less on the military (1.1% of GDP versus 3.2%) and has lower homicide and robbery rates (but not lower rape or assault rates). The United States' equity score is lower largely because the income share of the richest households is nine times the share of the poorest (in Canada, it is five times).

The United States has a more pronounced ecosystem deficit than Canada, with lower scores for all dimensions (though in water only by a drop). The structure (pattern of dimensions) of each deficit is similar, however, and the same program is called for to reduce it: raise the scores for air and resource use by reducing carbon emissions and energy consumption; improve the species and genes rating by expanding habitat protection for wild species (in Canada 15% of plant species are threatened; in the United States 28% of plant species and 9% of animal species) and conserving agricultural diversity; and increase the water score by enhancing water quality and restoring the diversity of aquatic ecosystems. Probably the easiest elements to boost quickly are agricultural diversity (currently given scant support) and water quality.

West Indies

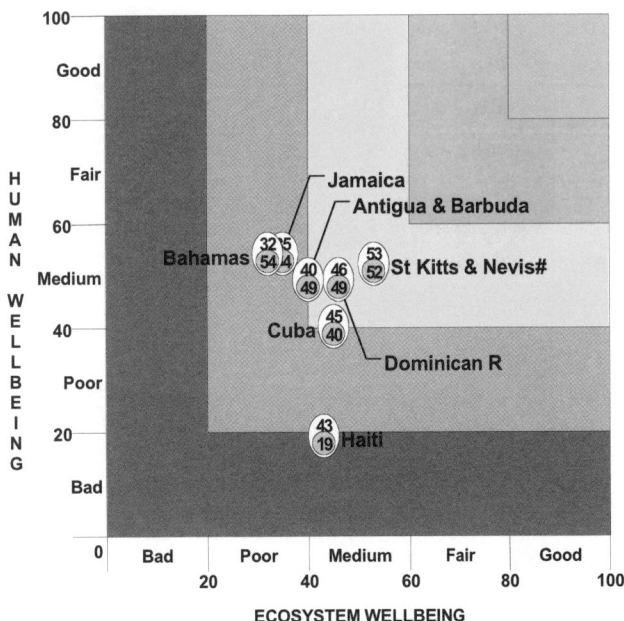

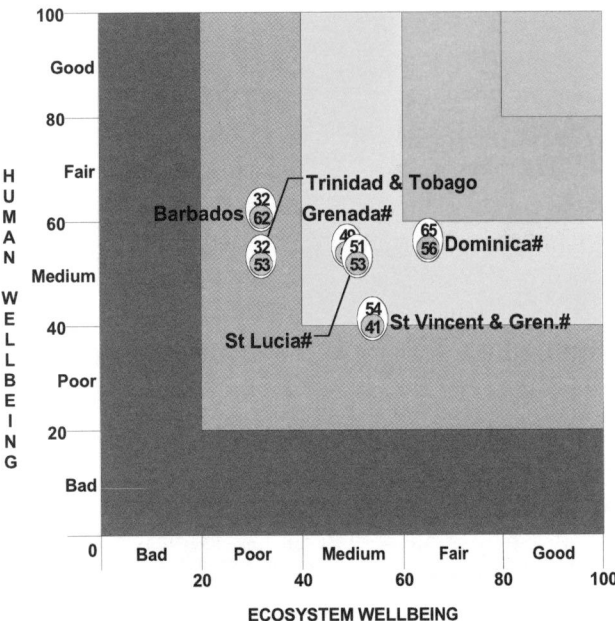

Figure 4.8. Wellbeing of the West Indies: northern islands above, southern islands below. Human Wellbeing Index (HWI) in yolk of egg, Ecosystem Wellbeing Index (EWI) in white. Jamaica's HWI is 54 and EWI 35; Grenada's HWI is 55 and EWI 49. # Dominica and Grenada were assessed on less than two-thirds of the human subelements; St Kitts and Nevis, St Lucia, and St Vincent and Grenadines on less than two-thirds of the ecosystem subelements.

In general, the smaller island states (under 100,000 hectares) seem to be closer to sustainability than the larger ones (Figure 4.8 and Table 4.4). Five of the top six countries in the region are small islands; the bottom seven, except for Antigua and Barbuda, are relatively

large. Unfortunately, apart from Barbados, the ratings of the small islands are marred by numerous data gaps. This is especially tantalizing because small island states face the same problem of sustainable development as cities—how to have a high quality of life without living beyond the ecological means of a restricted area—but the flow of people, goods, and services in and out of an independent country is easier to monitor. Some of the islands rated on the basis of the same indicators already show interesting differences. Dominica, for example, has an HWI 1 point higher than Grenada's but an EWI 12 points higher, probably helped by its lower ecological vulnerability (0.95 people and 17.44 species per hectare versus Grenada's 2.76 people and 33.88 species) and lower consumption dependency (3.3 gigajoules of energy per $1,000 of gross domestic product, half Grenada's 6.6 gigajoules).

Barbados (Figure 4.9) has the highest scores in the region for health, population, education, basic needs, and peace, and among the highest for freedom and governance. Its chief human weaknesses are crime (668 assaults and 130 robberies per 100,000 people), unemployment (almost 17%), and a riskily high (4.96) ratio of short-term debt to foreign exchange reserves. The lackluster equity rating is due

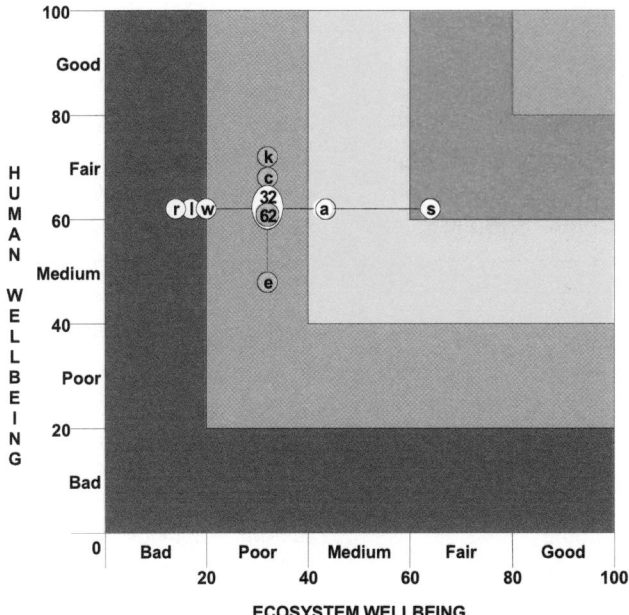

Figure 4.9. Structure of wellbeing: Barbados. Yellow circles show the points on the scale of the human dimensions: c = community; e = equity; h = health and population; k = knowledge; w = wealth. White circles show the points of the ecosystem dimensions: a = air; l = land; r = resource use; s = species and genes; w = water. Some dimensions are hidden by the egg (community, health and population, wealth).

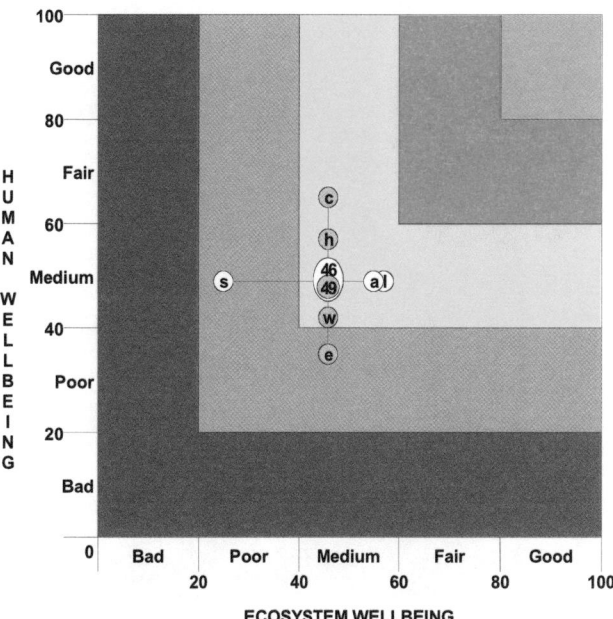

Figure 4.10. Structure of wellbeing: Dominican Republic. See Figure 4.9 for key. Some dimensions are hidden by the egg (knowledge, water) or behind another dimension (land is behind air). The Dominican Republic's EWI excludes resource use, which otherwise would have increased it artificially.

to underrepresentation of males in tertiary school and females in primary and secondary schools and in politics (women hold less than 11% of the seats in parliament).

Barbados has the highest population density in the region (6.28 people per hectare), which partly accounts for its extremely low scores for land, water, and resource use. Over half of its land area is either built or cultivated, less than a tenth is still more or less natural, and only 40 hectares are protected. Water withdrawal equals the renewable supply, the country depends on imports for food and timber, and its exploitation of fisheries is intense. Despite the evident pressure on land and water, few species are threatened: under 1% of plants and no mammals, breeding birds, amphibians, or land reptiles (two marine turtle species are at risk). Barbados could raise its EWI to medium by maintaining wild and domesticated diversity, increasing land protection, accelerating the phaseout of ozone depleting substances (consumption of which accounts for the low-medium score for air), holding energy use at current levels, increasing domestic food production without degrading the environment, and reducing fishing pressure.

Among the larger countries (Bahamas, Cuba, Dominican Republic, Haiti, Jamaica, and Trinidad and Tobago), the Dominican Republic (Figure 4.10) ranks fourth in human wellbeing, first in ecosystem wellbeing, and first

overall. Its strongest human dimension is community (surpassed only by Trinidad and Tobago): freedoms of expression, organization, and religion are generally respected, but elections are marred by violence and the judiciary is corrupt (crime was not rated). Its fair grade for education (only the Bahamas is better) is offset by mute communications: nine main telephone lines and three mobile phone subscribers per 100 people and even fewer Internet users (weaknesses shared by all countries in the group except the Bahamas). Incomes under $5,000 per person, and inflation and unemployment rates of 8% and 16%, reduce its wealth to low-medium, albeit the highest in the group after the Bahamas. With the Bahamas, its equity is the lowest: men have three times the income of women but less education (male enrollment drops from 95% of female enrollment at primary level to barely 80% at tertiary level).

On the environmental side, the Dominican Republic is the opposite of Barbados, with medium grades for land and water yet a poor score for species and genes. Its rates of land conversion and degradation are moderate, and 25% of the land is protected, including 14% in strictly protected areas bigger than 100,000 hectares. Yet, as in all the larger countries, many of its wild species are threatened: 20% of its mammals, 15% of the plants, and 10% of its reptiles and breeding birds. Since a major threat to many of the species is habitat loss, these percentages imply that land protection is better on paper than in practice.

119

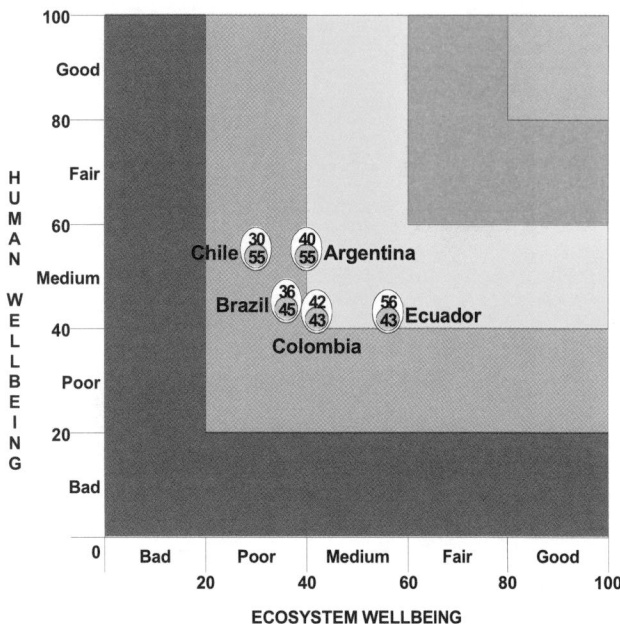

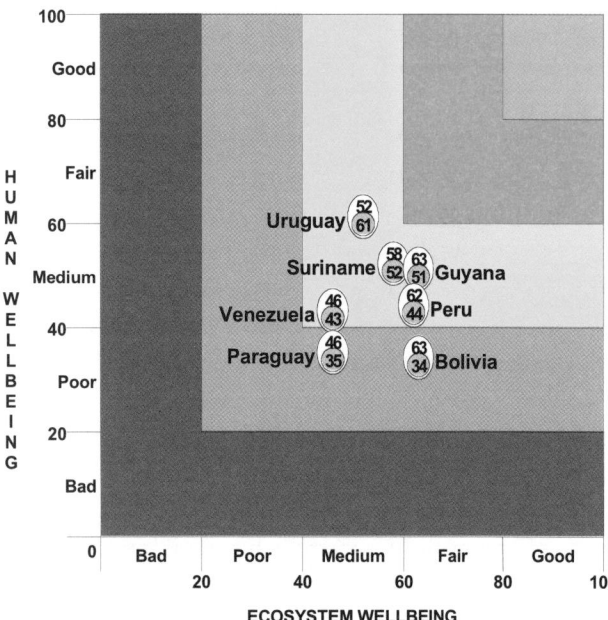

Figure 4.11. Wellbeing of South America. Human Wellbeing Index (HWI) in yolk of egg, Ecosystem Wellbeing Index (EWI) in white. The countries in the upper Barometer are the most fully assessed. Those in the lower Barometer were rated on fewer subelements (see Table 4.5).

South America provides several contrasting combinations of human and ecosystem wellbeing (Figure 4.11 and Table 4.5). Among the less fully assessed countries (lower Barometer of Figure 4.11), Peru and Venezuela have virtually the same HWI but quite different EWIs. Peru, with 0.20 people and 0.16 species per hectare against Venezuela's 0.27 people and 0.25 species, is somewhat less vulnerable ecologically. This advantage is borne out by a

Table 4.5. South America: Wellbeing Index (WI), Wellbeing/Stress Index (WSI), performance group, and number (#) of subelements covered (out of 30). 1 = fair WI/medium WSI; 2 = medium WI and WSI; 3 = medium WI/poor WSI; 4 = poor WI and WSI; 5 = poor WI/bad WSI; mod. = moderate; def. = deficit; e = ecosystem worse; p = people worse. Country order is by performance group and then by WI.

Country	WI	WSI	Performance Group	#
Guyana	57.0	1.38	2: mod. human def.	27
Peru	53.0	1.16	2: mod. human def.	28
Uruguay	56.5	1.27	2: mod. ecosystem def.	27
Suriname	55.0	1.24	2: mod. double def.	25
Ecuador	49.5	0.98	3: mod. double def.	29
Venezuela	44.5	0.80	3: mod. double def.	28
Colombia	42.5	0.74	3: mod. double def.	29
Bolivia	48.5	0.92	3: high human def.	28
Argentina	47.5	0.92	3: high double def. e	29
Chile	42.5	0.79	3: high double def. e	30
Brazil	40.5	0.70	4: high double def. e	29
Paraguay	40.5	0.65	4: high double def. p	27

higher score for species and genes and much lower rates of land conversion and forest loss. However, Venezuela fully protects 21% of its land area, compared with Peru's 2%; and only a tenth of its modified and cultivated land is moderately to strongly degraded, versus two-fifths in Peru. These differences raise Venezuela's land score to 71 and cut Peru's to 38. Peru ends up with a higher EWI because of superior performance in water and air, specifically river conversion and the global atmosphere (neither country was rated on inland water or local air quality). The decisive factor is Venezuela's greater consumption dependency: it consumes over three times more energy per dollar of GDP than Peru, has dammed a much higher proportion of its hydropower capacity (24% versus less than 1%), and emits 6 times more carbon dioxide and 19 times more ozone depleting substances per person. Reducing consumption dependency is clearly the key to raising Venezuela's EWI and would also improve its HWI by boosting economic efficiency.

Uruguay and Guyana have almost identical average WIs but trade places in almost every respect. Uruguay has fair human and medium ecosystem wellbeing, Guyana the reverse. Uruguay has the highest human wellbeing in the region—thanks to fair performance in health and population, knowledge, and community—and leads Guyana in every human dimension except community (it is penalized for high robbery and assault rates, whereas Guyana was not assessed on crime). Guyana has one of the two best EWIs in the region—with fair performance

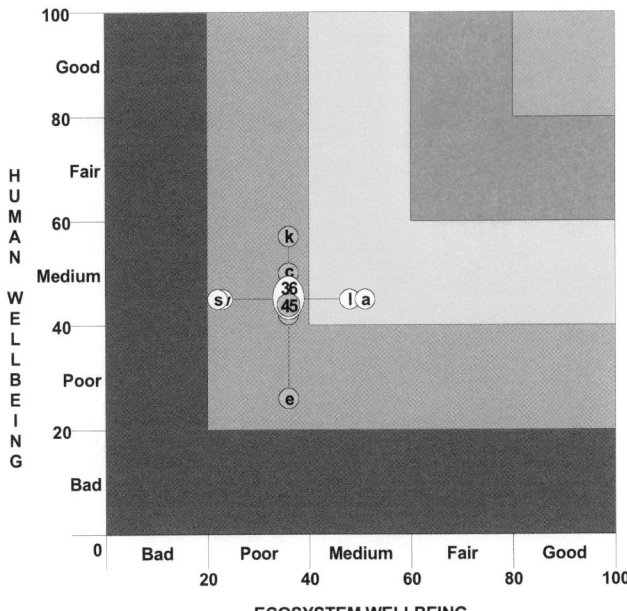

Figure 4.12. Structure of wellbeing: Brazil. Yellow circles show the points on the scale of the human dimensions: c = community; e = equity; h = health and population; k = knowledge; w = wealth. White circles show the points of the ecosystem dimensions: a = air; l = land; r = resource use; s = species and genes; w = water. Some dimensions are hidden by the egg (wealth) or behind another dimension (health and population is behind community, water behind species and genes). Brazil's EWI excludes resource use, which otherwise would have increased it artificially.

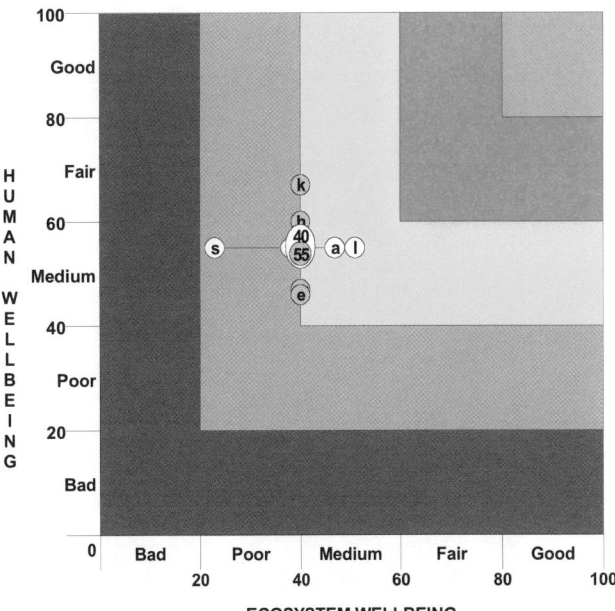

Figure 4.13. Structure of wellbeing: Argentina. See Figure 4.12 for key. Some dimensions are hidden by the egg (community, water) or behind another dimension (wealth is behind equity). Argentina's EWI excludes resource use, which otherwise would have increased it artificially.

in water, air, and species and genes—and is ahead of Uruguay in every ecosystem dimension except land (its cultivated land area, though much smaller, is more degraded). Uruguay's consumption dependency and species density are lower than Guyana's, and it could match the latter's EWI by greatly increasing the protected area (currently a tiny 0.3%), improving conservation of wild and domesticated diversity, and reducing consumption of ozone depleting substances. Guyana needs major improvements in income, health, education, and communication to equal Uruguay's HWI.

Of the countries in the upper Barometer of Figure 4.11, only Argentina, Brazil, and Chile were rated on air and water quality (Colombia lacks data on local air quality, Ecuador on water quality). If Ecuador had the average water quality of the other four countries, its EWI would fall to 42; if Colombia had the average air quality of the other four, its EWI would drop to 34.

Brazil (Figure 4.12) and Argentina (Figure 4.13) provide a more reliable contrast. Argentina is within reach of a fair HWI, but Brazil needs as big an effort to achieve a high-medium HWI. In both countries, the priority dimensions are wealth, equity, and community. Both are mired in debt and plagued by high unemployment, and

in both a quarter of the population lacks clean water and basic sanitation. Incomes are much lower in Brazil ($6,625 per person versus Argentina's $12,015) and even less fairly shared: in Argentina, the richest fifth of the population has 11 times the income share of the poorest fifth; in Brazil, 26 times. Rights and freedoms are more fully upheld in Argentina, but the judicial system is venal and inefficient. Brazil's is worse, and its police are among the world's most violent and corrupt. Brazil also trails Argentina in health and education.

Both countries could achieve an EWI above 50 by raising their medium scores in land and air to fair and their poor scores in water and species and genes to medium. The former would entail stabilizing land conversion, expanding the protected area system (more so in Argentina), making moderate improvements in the quality of cultivated land and urban air, and cutting ozone depleting substances. Brazil would also need to hold the line on carbon emissions, and Argentina (which emits more than twice as much per person) to reduce them. Water and species and genes present a tougher problem. Attaining medium scores requires cleaning up pollution (notably in Argentina's Paraná basin and the coastal drainages of Brazil), greatly enhancing species protection (better protected areas would help to secure the 24% of Argentina's plant species and 20% of Brazil's mammals at risk), and conserving domesticated diversity.

Northern Africa

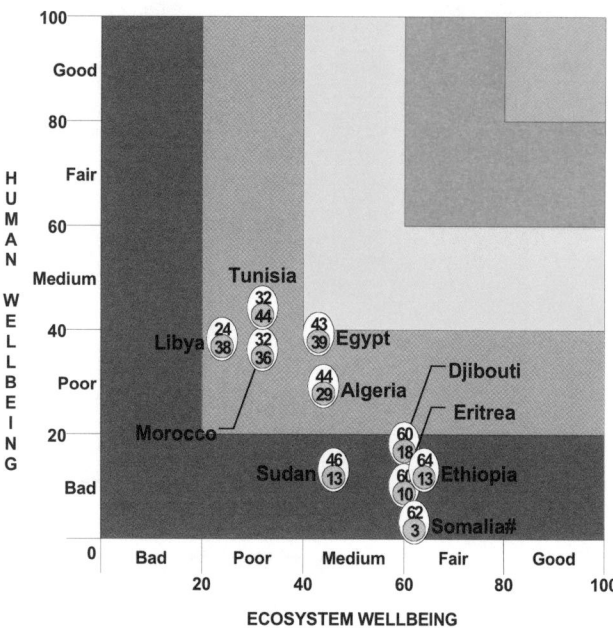

Figure 4.14. Wellbeing of Northern Africa. Human Wellbeing Index (HWI) in yolk of egg, Ecosystem Wellbeing Index (EWI) in white. Eritrea's EWI is 60. # Somalia was assessed on less than two-thirds of the human subelements.

Table 4.6. Northern Africa: Wellbeing Index (WI), Wellbeing/Stress Index (WSI), performance group, and number (#) of subelements covered (out of 30). 1 = fair WI/medium WSI; 2 = medium WI and WSI; 3 = medium WI/poor WSI; 4 = poor WI and WSI; 5 = poor WI/bad WSI; mod. = moderate; def. = deficit; e = ecosystem worse; p = people worse. Within each subregion, country order is by performance group and then by WI. *Somalia was rated on less than two-thirds of the human subelements.*

Country	WI	WSI	Performance Group	#
Northeast Africa				
Ethiopia	38.5	0.36	5: high human def.	27
Somalia	*32.5*	*0.08*	*5: high human def.*	*19*
Djibouti	39.0	0.45	5: high double def. p	23
Eritrea	35.0	0.25	5: high double def. p	22
Sudan	29.5	0.24	5: high double def. p	26
North Africa				
Egypt	41.0	0.68	3: high double def. p	28
Algeria	36.5	0.52	4: high double def. p	27
Tunisia	38.0	0.65	4: high double def. e	26
Morocco	34.0	0.53	4: extreme double def.	29
Libyan Arab J	31.0	0.50	5: extreme double def.	24

In Northeast Africa, ecosystem stress is more than double the level of human wellbeing because living standards are so low (Figure 4.14 and Table 4.6). Ethiopia (Figure 4.15) is typical in almost every human dimension: life expectancy 42 years, healthy life expectancy 33.5 years, rapid population growth (6.2 children per woman), less than half the popula-

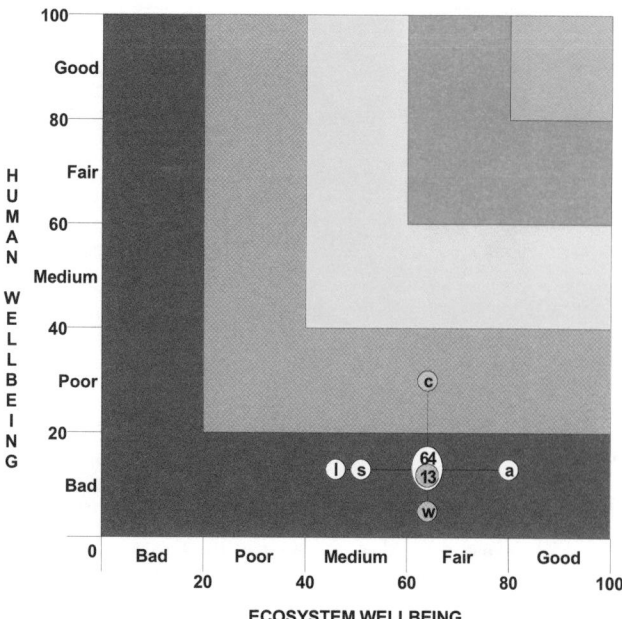

Figure 4.15. Structure of wellbeing: Ethiopia. Yellow circles show the points on the scale of the human dimensions: c = community; e = equity; h = health and population; k = knowledge; w = wealth. White circles show the points of the ecosystem dimensions: a = air; l = land; r = resource use; s = species and genes; w = water. Some dimensions are hidden by the egg (health and population) or behind another dimension (knowledge is behind wealth, water behind air). Ethiopia's HWI excludes equity and its EWI excludes resource use, which otherwise would have increased them artificially.

tion with enough food, less than a fifth with adequate water and sanitation, GDP per person $575, debt service payments bigger than GDP and nine times the value of exports, a mere third of primary-age children in primary school and a quarter of secondary-age children in secondary school, less than one main telephone line per 100 people, and a solitary Internet user per 100,000 people.

Despite these abysmal conditions, Ethiopia and its neighbors waste themselves on war: Djibouti, Somalia, and Sudan spend 5% of their GDP on the military, Ethiopia 6%, and Eritrea 36%. In the late 1990s, all but Djibouti have battled each other (border disputes among Eritrea, Ethiopia, and Sudan, between Ethiopia and Somalia, and between Sudan and Uganda) and internally (Somalia, northern and southern Sudan, and the Oromo area of Ethiopia). These conflicts have killed an average of 52,000 people a year since they began, and reveal a persistent refusal to set aside differences in favor of better lives for their people. (Ethiopia's score for community would be as bad as its co-combatants' but is lifted to poor by an astonishingly low reported crime rate.)

Endemic conflict also bodes ill for ecosystem wellbeing, which requires as great a commitment to the good

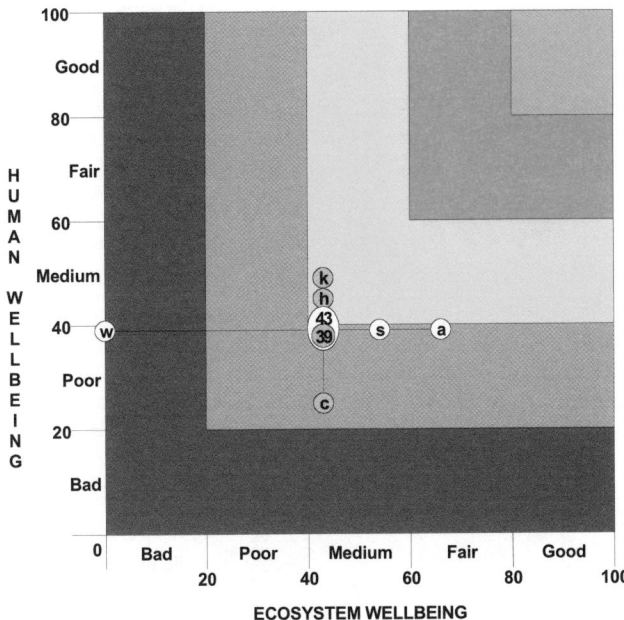

Figure 4.16. Structure of wellbeing: Egypt. See Figure 4.15 for key. Some dimensions are hidden by the egg (wealth) or behind another dimension (land is behind species and genes). Egypt's HWI excludes equity and its EWI excludes resource use, which otherwise would have increased them artificially.

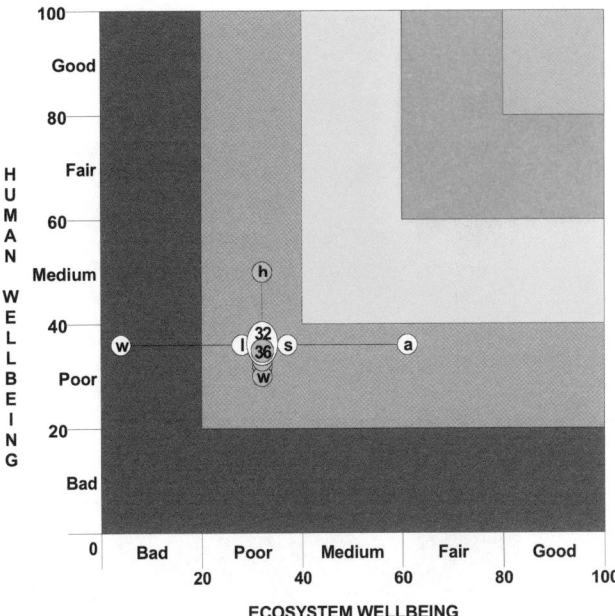

Figure 4.17. Structure of wellbeing: Morocco. See Figure 4.15 for key. Some dimensions are hidden by the egg (community, knowledge). Morocco's HWI excludes equity and its EWI excludes resource use, which otherwise would have increased them artificially.

of the community as does progress in health and education. The real EWIs of Ethiopia and its eastern neighbors are probably closer to Sudan's since it alone includes water quality (bad; in the Khartoum area, both the Blue and White Nile are bloated with heavy loads of nutrients). The chief concerns (besides water pollution) are land degradation, habitat loss, and the declining diversity of livestock breeds.

Human conditions are better in North Africa, but the state of the ecosystem is worse. Although the ratio of human wellbeing to ecosystem stress is higher than in Northeast Africa, the drift to the left of the Barometer is an ominous sign that the region is regressing environmentally almost as much as it is developing socioeconomically.

This need not be. Egypt, Morocco, and Libya have similar HWIs but quite dissimilar EWIs, showing that the environmental price of the quality of life is as flexible in North Africa as anywhere else. Egypt gets a zero score for water (Figure 4.16) because it extracts 80% of the flow of the Nile and 30 times more water than it receives from rain. Yet it manages to achieve a medium EWI, thanks to medium grades for land and species and genes and a fair rating for air (based on global atmosphere only). Morocco's water score also plumbs the depths (Figure 4.17): it takes a more frugal 37% of its supply (all from rainfall) but then fouls rivers and groundwater with nutrients, fecal coliforms, and heavy

metals. Its air score is close to Egypt's (and also does not count local air quality). Where it lags behind is in land and species and genes: 30% of land built or cultivated (Egypt 7%) and 13% of plant species threatened (Egypt 4%). Morocco could boost its EWI by cleaning up its water, curbing threats to wild and domesticated diversity, and expanding protected areas (which cover less than 1% of the land). Egypt's water problems are harder to fix, but it could raise its EWI further by strengthening habitat protection (its protected area coverage is also less than 1%).

Egypt's weakest human dimension is community, followed by wealth and health and population. Progress in one depends on advances in the others: Open and accountable government is needed to encourage enterprise, enterprise to raise incomes, economic opportunity and education (especially for females) to lower fertility rates, and population stability to relieve pressure on social services and the labor market.

Morocco also rates poorly in community, but corruption is lower than in Egypt, press freedom is higher, and attention is being paid to judicial reform and human rights. However, wealth and knowledge warrant just as much attention. The main needs are to extend safe water and sanitation to all, increase employment and incomes, cut external debt, and enhance access to primary and secondary education.

West Africa

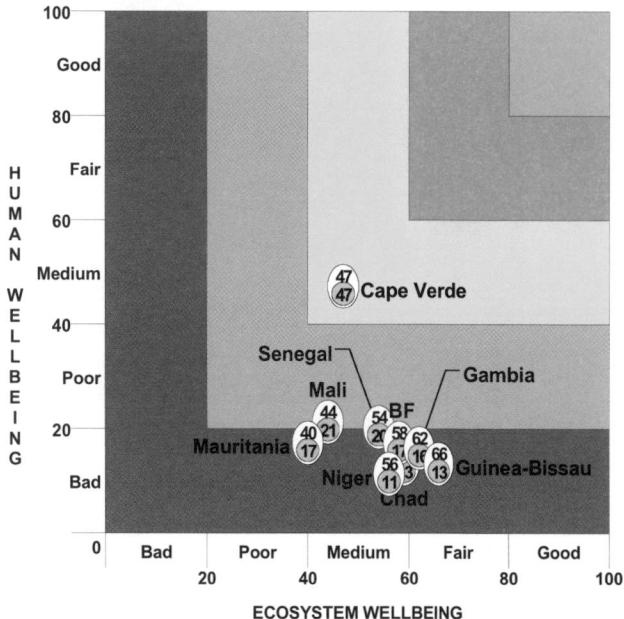

HUMAN WELLBEING (vertical axis): 0, 20 (Bad), 40 (Poor), 60 (Medium/Fair), 80 (Good), 100

ECOSYSTEM WELLBEING (horizontal axis): Bad (20), Poor (40), Medium (60), Fair (80), Good (100)

Cape Verde 47/47
Senegal, Mali, BF, Gambia
Mauritania 40/17, 44/21, 54/21, 58/11, 62/16, 66/13
Niger 56/11, Chad 3, Guinea-Bissau

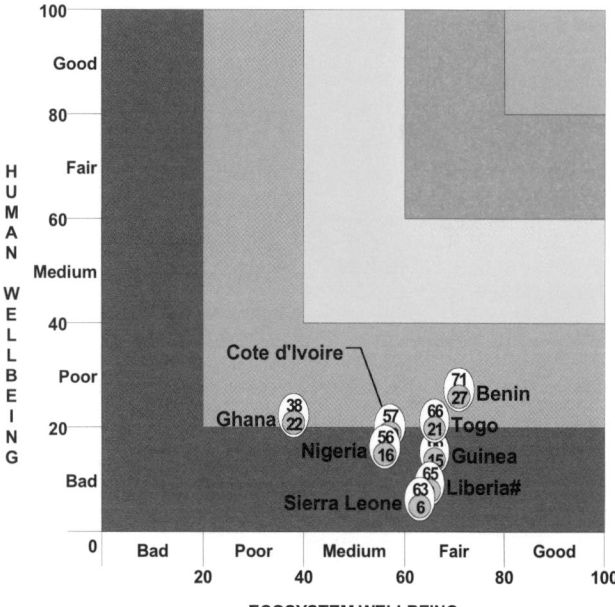

HUMAN WELLBEING (vertical axis): 0, 20 (Bad), 40 (Poor/Medium), 60 (Fair), 80, 100 (Good)

ECOSYSTEM WELLBEING: Bad (20), Poor (40), Medium (60), Fair (80), Good (100)

Cote d'Ivoire, Benin 71/27
Ghana 38/22, 57/56, Togo 66/21
Nigeria 16, Guinea 45
Sierra Leone 65, Liberia# 63/6

Figure 4.18. Wellbeing of West Africa: Sahelian West Africa above, Coastal West Africa below. Human Wellbeing Index (HWI) in yolk of egg, Ecosystem Wellbeing Index (EWI) in white. The HWI of Burkina Faso (BF) is 17; Chad's HWI is 14 and EWI 60; Côte d'Ivoire's HWI is 20; Guinea's EWI is 66; Liberia's HWI is 9. # Liberia was assessed on less than two-thirds of the human subelements.

Sahelian West Africa consists of the member countries of the Permanent Inter-State Committee to Combat Drought in the Sahel.[6] Coastal West Africa includes the remaining countries, which are generally less arid (although parts extend into the geographical Sahel).

Table 4.7. West Africa: Wellbeing Index (WI), Wellbeing/Stress Index (WSI), performance group, and number (#) of subelements covered (out of 30). 1 = fair WI/medium WSI; 2 = medium WI and WSI; 3 = medium WI/poor WSI; 4 = poor WI and WSI; 5 = poor WI/bad WSI; mod. = moderate; def. = deficit; e = ecosystem worse; p = people worse. Within each subregion, country order is by performance group and then by WI. *Liberia was rated on less than two-thirds of the human subelements.*

Country	WI	WSI	Performance Group	#
Sahelian				
Cape Verde	47.0	0.89	3: mod. double def.	23
Guinea-Bissau	39.5	0.38	5: high human def.	25
Gambia	39.0	0.42	5: high human def.	25
Burkina Faso	37.5	0.40	5: high double def. p	25
Senegal	37.0	0.43	5: high double def. p	27
Chad	36.0	0.32	5: high double def. p	24
Niger	33.5	0.25	5: high double def. p	25
Mali	32.5	0.38	5: high double def. p	27
Mauritania	28.5	0.28	5: extreme double def.	26
Coastal				
Benin	49.0	0.93	3: high human def.	25
Togo	43.5	0.62	3: high human def.	25
Guinea	40.5	0.44	5: high human def.	26
Liberia	*37.0*	*0.26*	*5: high human def.*	*21*
Sierra Leone	34.5	0.16	5: high human def.	25
Côte d'Ivoire	38.5	0.47	5: high double def. p	26
Nigeria	36.0	0.36	5: high double def. p	25
Ghana	30.0	0.35	5: extreme double def.	28

The Sahelian group crowds the bottom of the Barometer, with Cape Verde a clear standout (Figure 4.18 and Table 4.7). It leads in every human dimension—performing especially well in education, freedom and governance, and peace—to achieve an HWI 26 points higher than the next highest (Mali). Its medium EWI omits several subelements and is much less meaningful.

Mali (Figure 4.19) is, with Senegal, the best assessed. Its HWI is pulled up by community and down by the other dimensions. In the 1990s, Malians chose their national and local governments freely and fairly, and political debate is open. The human rights record is positive overall but marred by violent clashes between communities and instances of police brutality and torture by security forces. Press freedom is the highest in Africa after Mauritius and South Africa: state-run media, 40 independent newspapers, and 60 independent radio and television stations provide a variety of viewpoints in all regional languages.[7]

In all other respects, Malians are poorly served: GDP

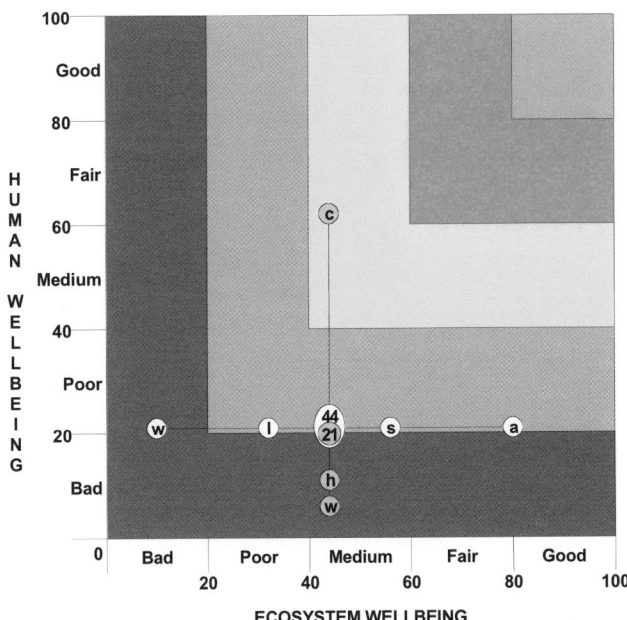

Figure 4.19. Structure of wellbeing: Mali. Yellow circles show the points on the scale of the human dimensions: c = community; e = equity; h = health and population; k = knowledge; w = wealth. White circles show the points of the ecosystem dimensions: a = air; l = land; r = resource use; s = species and genes; w = water. One dimension is behind another (knowledge is behind wealth). Mali's HWI excludes equity and its EWI excludes resource use, which otherwise would have increased them artificially.

per person is $680 and falling, only 6% of the population has adequate sanitation, 30% of children are stunted and 40% underweight from lack of food, and the child mortality rate is an appalling 236 per 1,000 live births. The knowledge revolution is a mirage: just 38% of primary-age children attend primary school, 18% of secondary-age children attend secondary school, and a mere 0.3% of the population has a main line or cell phone. Similarly, most of the other Sahelian countries combine low levels of health and population, wealth, and knowledge with better performance in community—from a little better but still poor in Chad, Mauritania, Niger, and Senegal to a lot better (medium) in Burkina Faso.

Raising Mali's standard of living is hampered by pressures on the ecosystem, particularly on water and land, which undermine the environmental foundations of health and wealth. Nutrient levels are dangerously high in groundwater and the Niger River. And although only 7% of the land is cultivated or built, barely 3% is protected, while 1% of forest is lost every year. Most seriously, 40% of the cultivated and modified land area is moderately to strongly degraded, risking declines in the already low agricultural productivity.

Coastal West Africa also crowds the floor of the

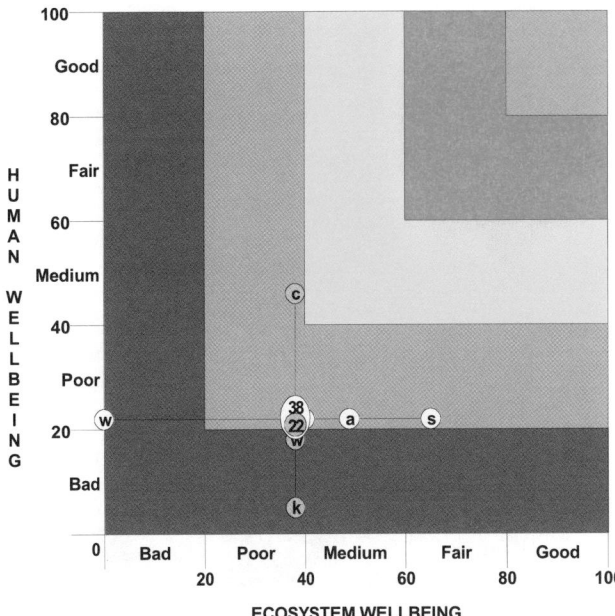

Figure 4.20. Structure of wellbeing: Ghana. See Figure 4.19 for key. Some dimensions are hidden by the egg (health and population, wealth, land). Ghana's HWI excludes equity and its EWI excludes resource use, which otherwise would have increased them artificially.

Barometer (Figure 4.18). Benin is separated from the pack by its human performance, lifted by a standard of freedom and governance higher than Mali's. Ghana (Figure 4.20) stands out for its inferior state of environment—but Ghana is also alone in being rated on all ecosystem subelements. Its poor land and fair species and genes scores are close to those of most of the other coastal countries: 28% of the land is cultivated or built, not much (5%) is protected, the forest is shrinking fast, but the threatened proportion of the inadequately assessed flora and fauna seems to be fairly small. However, Ghana's medium rating for air, which includes the air quality of Accra, is well below the fair and good grades of the rest of West Africa (except Nigeria), which count only pressure on the global atmosphere. So is its low mark for water, a result of severe pollution by heavy metals and the impact of dams on the Volta River—a degree of river conversion much greater than anywhere else in the region.

The pattern of human wellbeing on the Coast is the same as in the Sahel: very poor health and population, wealth, and knowledge; marginally better community in Côte d'Ivoire, Guinea, Niger, and Togo; much better community in Ghana, although nowhere near the level of Benin, where political rights are more fully observed and the press is freer.

Community levels in Benin, Mali, and Cape Verde show that high standards are achievable in West Africa. The rest of the region needs to match them, and all countries to make equivalent progress in health, education, income, and environmental quality.

Central and East Africa

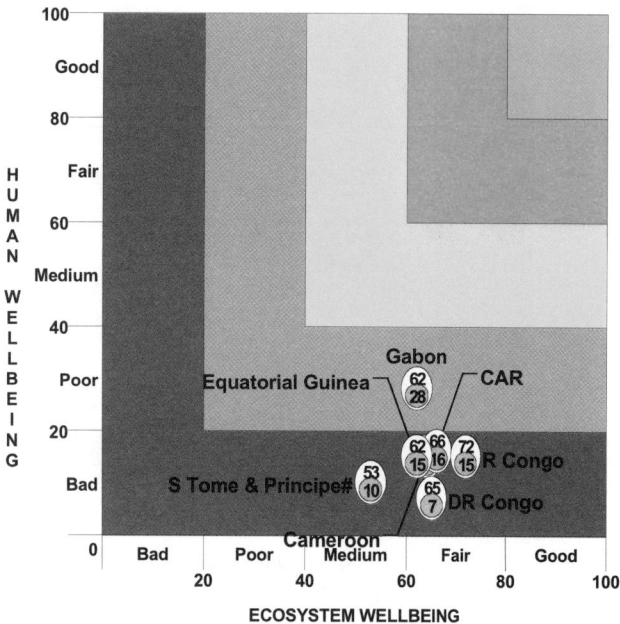

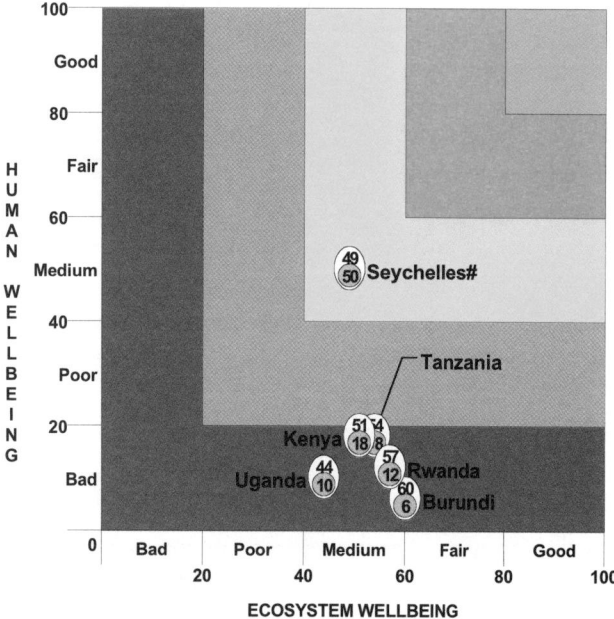

Figure 4.21. Wellbeing of Central and East Africa: Central Africa above, East Africa below. Human Wellbeing Index (HWI) in yolk of egg, Ecosystem Wellbeing Index (EWI) in white. Cameroon's HWI is 15 and EWI 64; the HWI of the Central African Republic (CAR) is 16; Tanzania's HWI is 18 and EWI 54. # São Tomé and Principe was assessed on less than two-thirds of the human subelements, Seychelles on less than two-thirds of the ecosystem subelements.

All but one of the Central African countries have high human deficits, combining fair ecosystem wellbeing and poor or bad (mostly bad) human wellbeing. By contrast, all but one of the East African countries have high double

Table 4.8. Central and East Africa: Wellbeing Index (WI), Wellbeing/Stress Index (WSI), performance group, and number (#) of subelements covered (out of 30). 1 = fair WI/medium WSI; 2 = medium WI and WSI; 3 = medium WI/poor or bad WSI; 4 = poor WI and WSI; 5 = poor WI/bad WSI; mod. = moderate; def. = deficit; e = ecosystem worse; p = people worse. Within each subregion, country order is by performance group and then by WI. *São Tomé and Principe was rated on less than two-thirds of the human subelements, Seychelles on less than two-thirds of the ecosystem subelements.*

Country	WI	WSI	Performance Group	#
Central Africa				
Gabon	45.0	0.74	3: high human def.	24
Congo, R	43.5	0.54	3: high human def.	25
Central African R	41.0	0.47	3: high human def.	25
Cameroon	39.5	0.42	5: high human def.	25
Equatorial Guinea	38.5	0.39	5: high human def.	23
Congo, DR	36.0	0.20	5: high human def.	24
São Tomé and Principe	*31.5*	*0.21*	*5: high double def. p*	*19*
East Africa				
Seychelles	*47.0*	*0.90*	*3: mod. double def.*	*20*
Tanzania	36.0	0.39	5: high double def. p	27
Kenya	35.5	0.40	5: high double def. p	27
Rwanda	34.5	0.28	5: high double def. p	24
Burundi	33.0	0.15	5: high double def. p	24
Uganda	27.0	0.18	5: high double def. p	27

deficits, combining medium ecosystem wellbeing and bad human wellbeing (Figure 4.21 and Table 4.8). Central Africa's environment scored better partly because it was less fully assessed and partly because more land is still natural or seminatural, less land is degraded, smaller percentages of wild species are threatened, and domesticated diversity is less at risk.

Gabon's air score (Figure 4.22) is relatively low because, like other oil producers, it uses fuel carelessly and emits large amounts of carbon. In most other environmental respects, Gabon is fairly typical of Central Africa. Just 4% of the land has been converted to farms and settlements, and 65% remains in a natural or seminatural state. Forest loss is well below 1% a year, and only 8% of cultivated and modified land is moderately degraded. Small percentages of flowering plant species (1.4%) and mammal and bird species (3.5%) are threatened. But the status of wild and domesticated diversity is poorly known, and the protected area system covers just 2.7% of the land area. The other countries in the subregion depart from this picture in different ways: Cameroon has much less natural land, land degradation

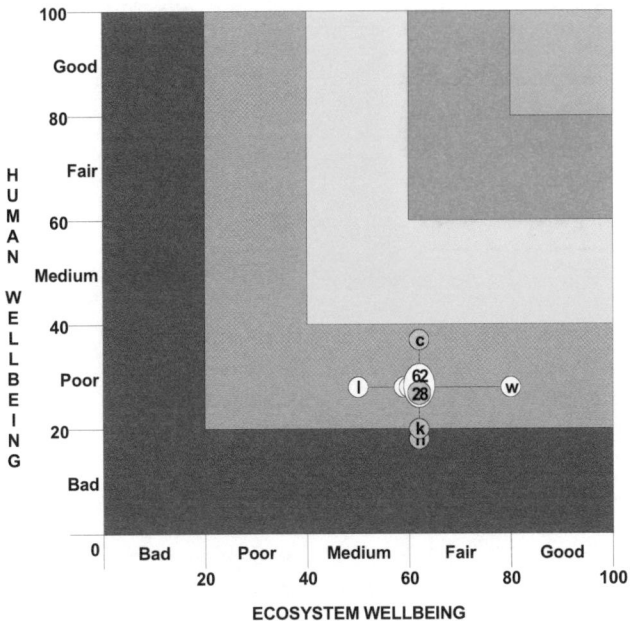

Figure 4.22. Structure of wellbeing: Gabon. Yellow circles show the points on the scale of the human dimensions: c = community; e = equity; h = health and population; k = knowledge; w = wealth. White circles show the points of the ecosystem dimensions: a = air; l = land; r = resource use; s = species and genes; w = water. Some dimensions are hidden by the egg (air, species and genes) or behind another dimension (health and population is behind knowledge, wealth is behind community). Gabon's HWI excludes equity and its EWI excludes resource use, which otherwise would have increased them artificially.

is extensive, and its heritage of livestock breeds is both better known and greatly at risk; the Central African Republic has an adequate system of protected areas; in the Democratic Republic of Congo 22% of plant species are threatened; and São Tomé and Principe has lost all but a patch of its natural land and is in danger of losing 26% of its mammals and birds.

Like much of East Africa, Tanzania (Figure 4.23) has retained a fair amount (40%) of natural land, but almost 13% of its cultivated and modified land is moderately to strongly degraded. The high point of its land performance is the system of parks and reserves, which cover an impressive 27% of the land—3% in strictly protected areas bigger than a million hectares. Inland water quality, while apparently almost fair, is erratically monitored. The weakest dimension is species and genes: a third of Tanzania's plant species is threatened, and almost two-thirds of its cattle breeds are at risk. Elsewhere in East Africa, land degradation is more widespread and severe (except possibly in the Seychelles, which lacks data); Burundi, Rwanda, and Seychelles have negligible natural land, and only scraps of Burundi are protected; livestock diversity is less at risk in

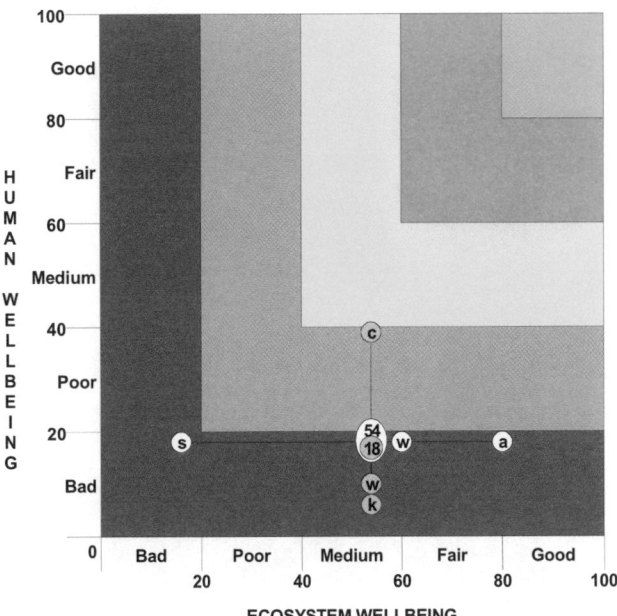

Figure 4.23. Structure of wellbeing: Tanzania. See Figure 4.22 for key. Some dimensions are hidden by the egg (health and population) or behind another dimension (land is behind water). Tanzania's HWI excludes equity and its EWI excludes resource use, which otherwise would have increased them artificially.

Kenya; and water pollution is worse in Kenya and Uganda (the only other countries where it was assessed).

Human conditions are virtually the same in Central and East Africa. All countries have poor or medium scores for equity (except Central African Republic and São Tomé and Principe, bad) and bad or poor scores for the other dimensions (except Seychelles, medium). Gabon's oil earnings translate into a regionally high GDP of $6,355 per person and higher percentages of people whose basic needs are met than anywhere else in the region except Seychelles (92% with enough food, 67% with safe water and basic sanitation) but not into better health or education. A high ratio (32.6) of short-term debt to reserves reduces its wealth score to poor.

Tanzania's knowledge, wealth, and health and population scores are bad because under half of primary-age children attend primary school; telecommunications barely function (more faults than main lines and cell phones combined); 40% of the population lacks sufficient food, 34% safe water; the economy is weak and heavily indebted; life expectancy at birth is 45 years, healthy life expectancy 36 years; and the total fertility rate exceeds five children per woman. Rapid improvements in these conditions depend on raising community standards from poor to medium or better: at present, corruption is rampant, the judiciary politically controlled, press freedom restricted, and elections tainted by fraud.

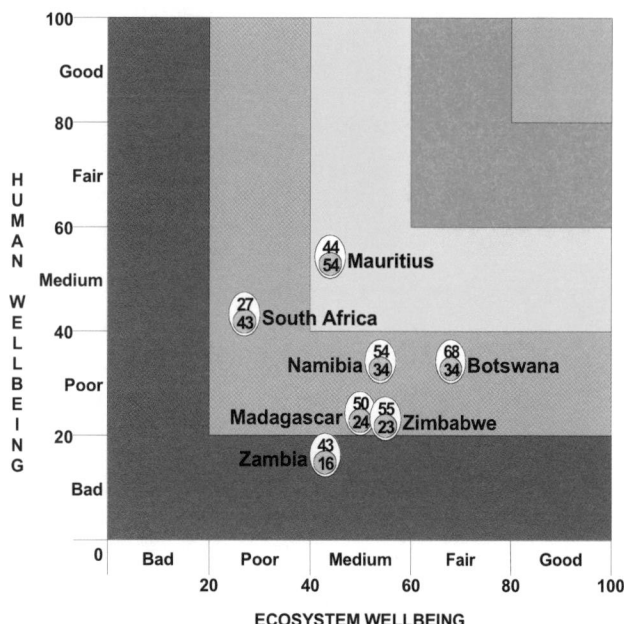

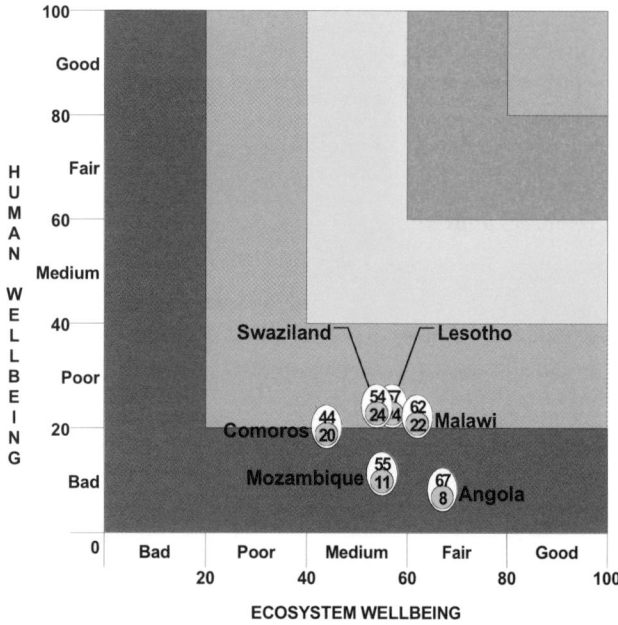

Figure 4.24. Wellbeing of Southern Africa. Human Wellbeing Index (HWI) in yolk of egg, Ecosystem Wellbeing Index (EWI) in white. The countries in the upper Barometer are the most fully assessed. Those in the lower Barometer were rated on fewer subelements (see Table 4.9). Lesotho's HWI is 24 and EWI 57.

Southern Africa is in a better position to advance toward sustainability than the other African regions (Figure 4.24 and Table 4.9). It has more countries with a WI above 40.0 (four) apart from Central and East Africa (also four); more with a WSI above 0.50 (eight), including the only one (Botswana) with a WSI above 1.00; more coun-

Table 4.9. Southern Africa: Wellbeing Index (WI), Wellbeing/Stress Index (WSI), performance group, and number (#) of subelements covered (out of 30). 1 = fair WI/medium WSI; 2 = medium WI and WSI; 3 = medium WI/poor WSI; 4 = poor WI and WSI; 5 = poor WI/bad WSI; mod. = moderate; def. = deficit; e = ecosystem worse; p = people worse. Country order is by performance group and then by WI.

Country	WI	WSI	Performance Group	#
Botswana	51.0	1.06	2: high human def.	27
Mauritius	49.0	0.96	3: mod. double def.	28
Namibia	44.0	0.74	3: high double def. p	26
Malawi	42.0	0.58	3: high human def.	25
Lesotho	40.5	0.56	3: high double def. p	25
Swaziland	39.0	0.52	4: high double def. p	25
Zimbabwe	39.0	0.51	4: high double def. p	27
South Africa	35.0	0.59	4: high double def. e	29
Angola	37.5	0.24	5: high human def.	25
Madagascar	37.0	0.48	5: high double def. p	27
Mozambique	33.0	0.24	5: high double def. p	26
Comoros	32.0	0.36	5: high double def. p	21
Zambia	29.5	0.28	5: high double def. p	27

tries with fair or medium education (six: Botswana, Mauritius, Namibia, South Africa, Swaziland, and Zimbabwe); and more with fair or medium freedom and governance (eight: Botswana, Lesotho, Madagascar, Malawi, Mauritius, Mozambique, Namibia, and South Africa).

Botswana (Figure 4.25) enjoys medium scores for wealth and community, thanks to a GDP per person of $6,105, one of the lightest debt loads in the world, limited corruption (the least among the African countries rated by Transparency International), the longest continuous multiparty democracy in Africa (governments have been freely and fairly elected since independence in 1966), and a start to restoring the land rights of the Basarwa ("Bushmen").

All is not well, however. GDP per person is falling (down from $7,690 the previous year), and poverty is widespread: 45% of the population lacks basic sanitation and 25% enough food. Primary and secondary school enrollment rates are quite high, but few children go on to university (59 per 10,000 people), and although more people have access to telephones and the Internet than in most other countries in Africa, they are still a small minority. But the main drag on the HWI is the poor score for health and population, largely due to HIV/AIDS. Currently infecting one of every four adults, AIDS has sliced life expectancy to 39 years and healthy life expectancy to 32 years.

Environmentally, Botswana has much to build on. Air, water, land, and species and genes are fair (but the first

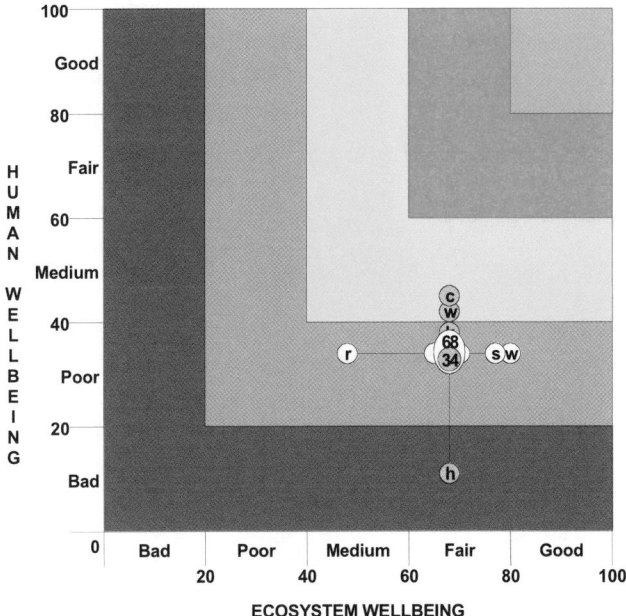

Figure 4.25. Structure of wellbeing: Botswana. Yellow circles show the points on the scale of the human dimensions: c = community; e = equity; h = health and population; k = knowledge; w = wealth. White circles show the points of the ecosystem dimensions: a = air; l = land; r = resource use; s = species and genes; w = water. Some dimensions are hidden by the egg (knowledge, air, land). Botswana's HWI excludes equity, which otherwise would have increased it artificially.

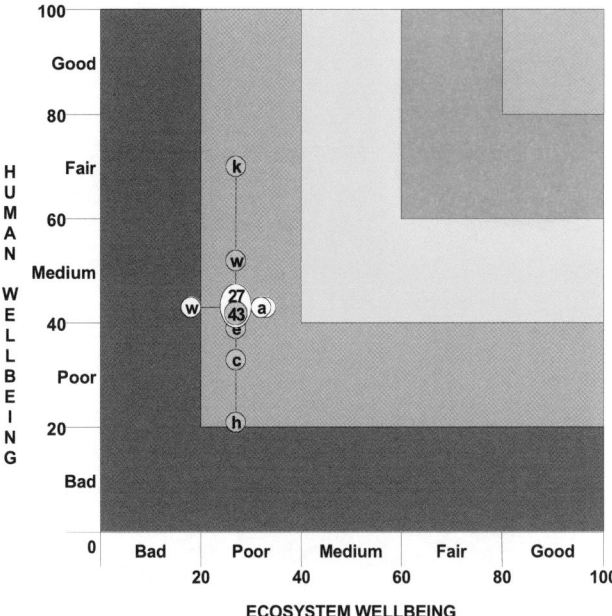

Figure 4.26. Structure of wellbeing: South Africa. See Figure 4.25 for key. Some dimensions are hidden by the egg (equity, species and genes) or behind another dimension (health and population is behind community, land is behind air). South Africa's EWI excludes resource use, which otherwise would have increased it artificially.

two do not include water quality or local air pollution). The main land concern is soil degradation (almost 14% of the modified and cultivated land area is moderately to strongly degraded), but more than 40% of the total land area is undisturbed, and more than 18% is protected, mostly in units of a million hectares or more. Few species are threatened (3% of mammals, 1% of breeding birds, 0.3% of flowering plants), and apparently little of the country's livestock diversity is at risk (except that local cattle types are lumped into the Tswana "breed" and may be disappearing). However, this modest pressure on the land may be a side effect of low self-reliance: Botswana imports most of its food, growing only a third of its supply of cereals and roots (hence the medium score for resource use).

South Africa's clear strength is knowledge (Figure 4.26): primary school enrollment virtually 100%, secondary enrollment 95%, 184 tertiary students per 10,000 people, and a moderately developed communication system (Africa's best along with those of Mauritius and the Seychelles). Wealth signals are mixed: GDP per person $8,490 and growing, but short-term debt more than double foreign exchange reserves; a low (for Africa) 13% of the population without safe water and basic sanitation, but 23% of children stunted by lack of food. The most

pressing weaknesses are health (as in the rest of the region, AIDS is whittling life expectancy) and community. South Africa's transition to democracy is being consolidated, the press has been unshackled, and the judiciary and other institutions that enforce the highly progressive constitution and protect human rights have established their independence. But these advances are compromised by a plague of violence, fueled by inequities and thwarted expectations: for example, the richest fifth of the population has 22 times the income share of the poorest fifth.

South Africa's struggle to spread the benefits of development is bound up with the state of the environment. More than a third of its extraordinarily rich plant diversity and 13% of its mammal species are at risk. Carbon dioxide emissions are high (2,232 kg per person), and dams control half the national water flow. Severe soil loss—accounting for both the poor score for land and the bad score for water—reduces the productivity of almost 40% of cultivated and modified land and burdens the waters of the Orange River basin (covering 47% of the country) with heavy loads of silt. One answer is to enhance habitat protection; another is to increase the resource efficiency of the economy. But improving the living conditions of the rural poor is also vital since much of the degraded area is land they depend on for survival.

Northern Europe

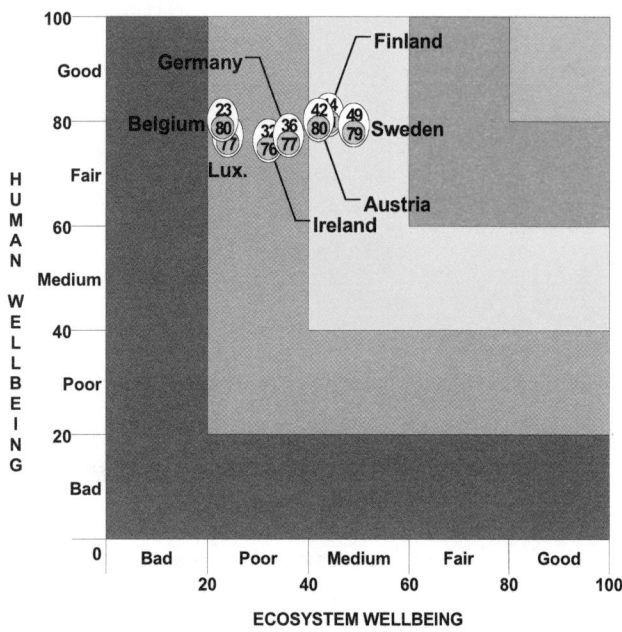

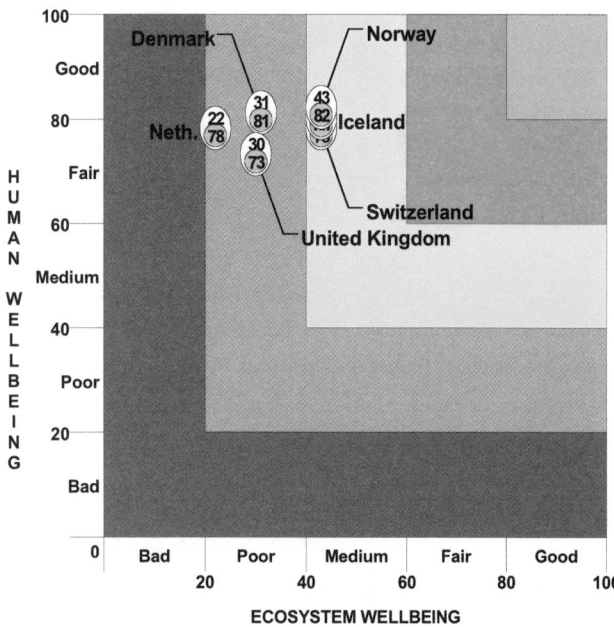

Figure 4.27. Wellbeing of Northern Europe. Human Wellbeing Index (HWI) in yolk of egg; Ecosystem Wellbeing Index (EWI) in white. Lux. = Luxembourg; Neth. = Netherlands. Finland's HWI is 81 and EWI 44; Luxembourg's HWI is 77 and EWI 24; Iceland's HWI is 80 and EWI 43; Switzerland's HWI is 77 and EWI 43.

Northern Europe spreads across the upper left eighth of the Barometer (Figure 4.27 and Table 4.10), with moderate ecosystem deficit countries to the right of high ecosystem deficit ones. HWIs are within 10 points of each other, and scores are similar for health and population (all good), wealth (good or high fair), and knowledge (good except for Luxembourg, capped at high fair because of lack of data).

Table 4.10. Northern Europe: Wellbeing Index (WI), Wellbeing/Stress Index (WSI), performance group, and number (#) of subelements covered (out of 30). 1 = fair WI/medium WSI; 2 = medium WI and WSI; 3 = medium WI/poor WSI; 4 = poor WI and WSI; 5 = poor WI/bad WSI; mod. = moderate; def. = deficit; e = ecosystem worse; p = people worse. Country order is by performance group and then by WI and WSI.

Country	WI	WSI	Performance Group	#
Sweden	64.0	1.55	1: mod. ecosystem def.	30
Finland	62.5	1.45	1: mod. ecosystem def.	30
Norway	62.5	1.44	1: mod. ecosystem def.	30
Iceland	61.5	1.40	1: mod. ecosystem def.	26
Austria	61.0	1.38	1: mod. ecosystem def.	29
Switzerland	60.5	1.37	2: mod. ecosystem def.	30
Germany	56.5	1.20	2: high ecosystem def.	30
Denmark	56.0	1.17	2: high ecosystem def.	30
Ireland	54.0	1.12	2: high ecosystem def.	28
United Kingdom	51.5	1.04	2: high ecosystem def.	30
Belgium	51.5	1.04	2: high ecosystem def.	30
Luxembourg	50.5	1.01	2: high ecosystem def.	28
Netherlands	50.0	1.00	3: high ecosystem def.	30

However, community performance ranges from good (Switzerland and Austria) to medium (Sweden and the United Kingdom; Sweden is hampered by relatively high crime rates, especially assaults, and the United Kingdom by the conflict in Northern Ireland) and equity from high fair (Sweden, Norway, Finland, Denmark, Belgium) to medium (Switzerland, Luxembourg, Ireland, United Kingdom).

While there is still room to improve human wellbeing, the more pressing need is to eliminate ecosystem deficits. This will be easier for Sweden (Figure 4.28), with no poor or bad dimension; harder for the other moderate-deficit countries and Germany and Ireland, with one to three weak dimensions; and most demanding for the remaining high-deficit countries (including the Netherlands, Figure 4.29), which have low scores for four dimensions. Countries could go far by emulating the regional leaders in land protection (Austria and Germany), land quality (Ireland and Norway), local air quality (Sweden), fisheries (Ireland), and timber (Germany and Norway), but they also need to advance dramatically in the other elements.

Species & genes (Finland and Switzerland fair; the rest medium). The status of wild mammal and bird species goes from bad in Iceland (27.3% threatened) to medium in Switzerland (4.3%). That of wild plant species seems to be good (from 1.8% threatened in Ireland to 0.1% in Belgium and the Netherlands), but no country reports on all plant groups.[8] Livestock breeds are more at risk, especially in Austria and the United Kingdom, where threat-

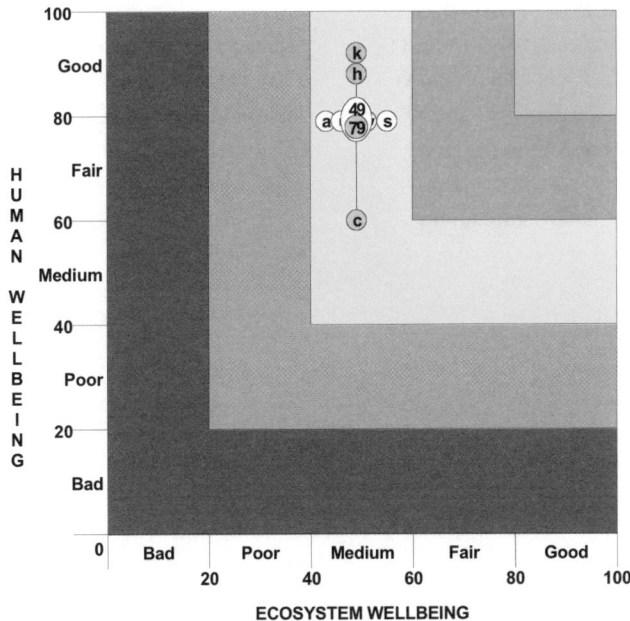

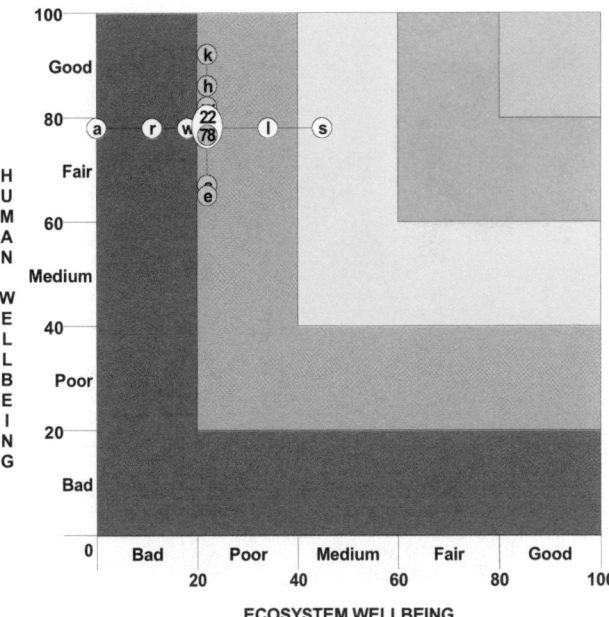

Figure 4.28. Structure of wellbeing: Sweden. Yellow circles show the points on the scale of the human dimensions: c = community; e = equity; h = health and population; k = knowledge; w = wealth. White circles show the points of the ecosystem dimensions: a = air; l = land; r = resource use; s = species and genes; w = water. Some dimensions are hidden by the egg (equity, wealth, land, water, resource use).

Figure 4.29. Structure of wellbeing: Netherlands. See Figure 4.28 for key. Some dimensions are hidden by the egg (wealth) or behind another dimension (community is behind equity).

ened breeds outnumber those whose survival is secure. The United Kingdom has pioneered livestock conservation but has the most breeds (120) to conserve.

Land (Austria, Finland, Germany, Norway, Sweden, and Switzerland medium; the rest poor). Finland, Norway, Sweden, Iceland, Austria, and Switzerland have converted less than a quarter of their land to buildings and cultivation, and the first four retain large tracts of natural land. Elsewhere, settlements and farmland occupy from 36% of the country in Ireland to 71% in Denmark, and natural land is scarce. Native forests are expanding in Austria and Germany, which also lead the region by protecting 28% and 25% of their respective land areas. Land quality is good or fair, except in Austria and Belgium (medium) and Iceland (poor due to overgrazing and plant removal).

Water (Iceland fair; Finland, Norway, and Sweden medium; the rest poor or bad). Iceland's fair score omits water quality, which is no better than medium in Finland, Norway, and Sweden (the latter two report patchily). Elsewhere, it is bad or poor, largely due to pollution by nutrients and heavy metals. Additional pressures on inland waters are high rates of extraction in Belgium (58% of rainfall) and Germany (41%) and dams in Austria, Ireland, Luxembourg, and the United Kingdom.

Air (Sweden and Switzerland medium; Luxembourg, Netherlands, and Norway bad; the rest poor). Local air

quality, which drops from Sweden's breathable 73 score to the United Kingdom's almost acceptable 55 score, is way above the grades for global atmosphere. Sweden and Switzerland, the region's lowest emitters of carbon dioxide, respectively discharge 1,462 and 1,531 kg of carbon per person, almost double the level that would get a fair score (below 800 kg). Most emit two to four times this amount, Norway exceeds it more than fivefold, and Luxembourg more than sixfold. Ozone depleting substances (ODSs) are a problem only where they are produced. Switzerland has cut consumption to an exemplary 1 gram per person. European Union members (all but Switzerland, Norway, and Iceland) consume 55 grams per person, but this is dwarfed by the almost 1,100 grams per person produced by the Netherlands, Europe's biggest manufacturer of ODSs.

Resource use (Austria, Ireland, Norway, and Sweden medium; the rest poor or bad). All countries consume too much energy, Belgium and the Netherlands the most (per hectare), Austria and Ireland the least. Many also consume more than their sustainable supply of farm produce (Iceland, Norway), seafood (Belgium, Germany), or timber (Netherlands, United Kingdom). Denmark and Ireland are self-reliant in seafood, and their fishing capacities are commensurate with their catches and fish-producing areas. Germany, Norway, Sweden, Finland, and Ireland keep their timber fellings plus imports well below the annual increment of their domestic forests (from 90% in Ireland to as low as 65% in Germany).

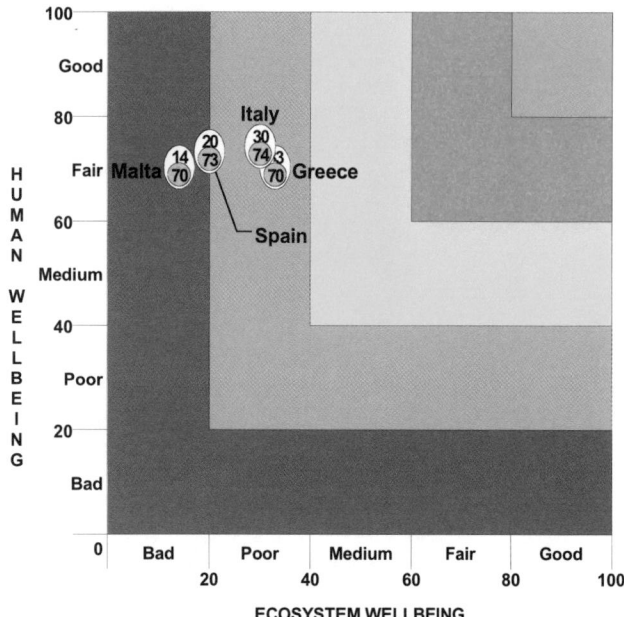

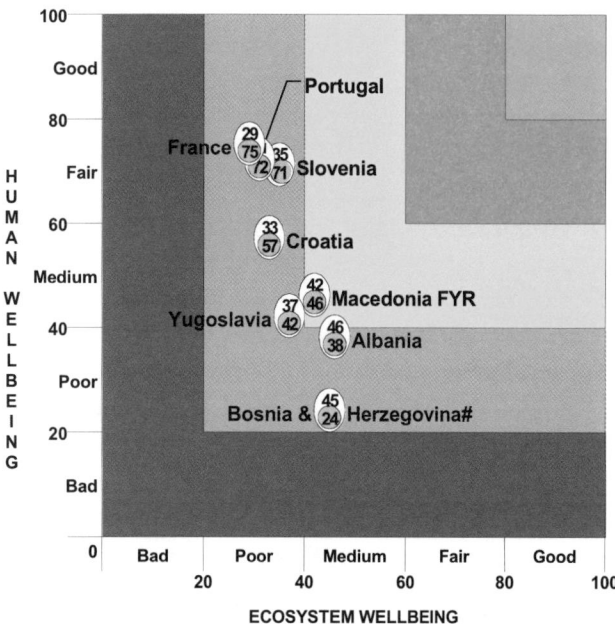

Figure 4.30. Wellbeing of Southern Europe. Human Wellbeing Index (HWI) in yolk of egg, Ecosystem Wellbeing Index (EWI) in white. Macedonia FYR = the Former Yugoslav Republic of Macedonia. Greece's EWI is 33; Portugal's HWI is 72 and EWI 31; Slovenia's HWI is 71 and EWI 35. # Bosnia and Herzegovina was assessed on less than two-thirds of the human subelements.

In Southern as in Northern Europe, most countries have high ecosystem deficits, clustering in the top left of the Barometer (Figure 4.30 and Table 4.11). A minority, consisting of Albania and the former Yugoslav republics except Slovenia, has double deficits. Those of Albania, Bosnia and Herzegovina, Macedonia, and Yugoslavia may

Table 4.11. Southern Europe: Wellbeing Index (WI), Wellbeing/Stress Index (WSI), performance group, and number (#) of subelements covered (out of 30). 1 = fair WI/medium WSI; 2 = medium WI and WSI; 3 = medium WI/poor WSI; 4 = poor WI and WSI; 5 = poor WI/bad WSI; mod. = moderate; def. = deficit, e = ecosystem worse; p = people worse. Country order is by performance group and then by WI. *Bosnia and Herzegovina was rated on less than two-thirds of the human subelements.*

Country	WI	WSI	Performance Group	#
Slovenia	53.0	1.09	2: high ecosystem def.	28
Italy	52.0	1.06	2: high ecosystem def.	30
France	52.0	1.06	2: high ecosystem def.	30
Greece	51.5	1.04	2: high ecosystem def.	30
Portugal	51.5	1.04	2: high ecosystem def.	30
Spain	46.5	0.91	3: high ecosystem def.	30
Malta	42.0	0.83	3: high ecosystem def.	26
Macedonia, FYR	44.0	0.79	3: mod. double def.	24
Croatia	45.0	0.85	3: high double def. e	29
Albania	42.0	0.70	3: high double def. p	27
Yugoslavia	39.5	0.67	4: high double def. e	24
Bosnia and Herzegovina	*34.5*	*0.44*	*5: high double def. p*	*20*

be worse than shown: Albania's EWI does not include local air quality, and the EWIs of the others omit water quality and water withdrawal as well.

Croatia (Figure 4.31) leads the five double deficit countries in all human dimensions except community, falling well behind Macedonia in freedom and governance (medium in Macedonia, bad in Yugoslavia, poor in the rest). It is healthier (healthy life expectancy drops from 66.9 years in Croatia to 59.9 years in Albania), wealthier, and has better developed education and communication systems than the others. Land is in a sorry state in all five countries: natural land has almost entirely disappeared, and large areas of modified and cultivated land are moderately to strongly degraded (from 41% in Macedonia to 72% in Albania). Croatia's water quality is bad (nutrients). Albania consumes less energy and emits less carbon dioxide than the other countries and has fewer threatened animal species (2.4% of mammals and birds, versus 6.6% in Croatia and 13–14% in the others).

The seven high ecosystem deficit countries enjoy levels of human wellbeing far above the double deficit group's and show the rewards of better governance and commitment to peace and democracy. Their human dimension scores are as high as Northern Europe's except for health and population in Slovenia; wealth in Greece, Malta, and Slovenia; knowledge in Greece, Malta, and Portugal; and community in Spain. Slovenia has the lowest healthy life expectancy in the group (68.4 years), and

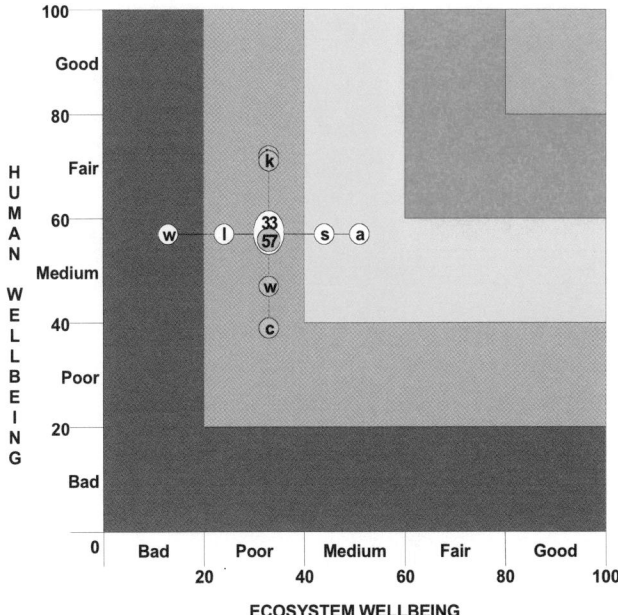

Figure 4.31. Structure of wellbeing: Croatia. Yellow circles show the points on the scale of the human dimensions: c = community; e = equity; h = health and population; k = knowledge; w = wealth. White circles show the points of the ecosystem dimensions: a = air; l = land; r = resource use; s = species and genes; w = water. One dimensions is behind another (health and population is behind knowledge). Croatia's HWI excludes equity and its EWI excludes resource use, which otherwise would have increased them artificially.

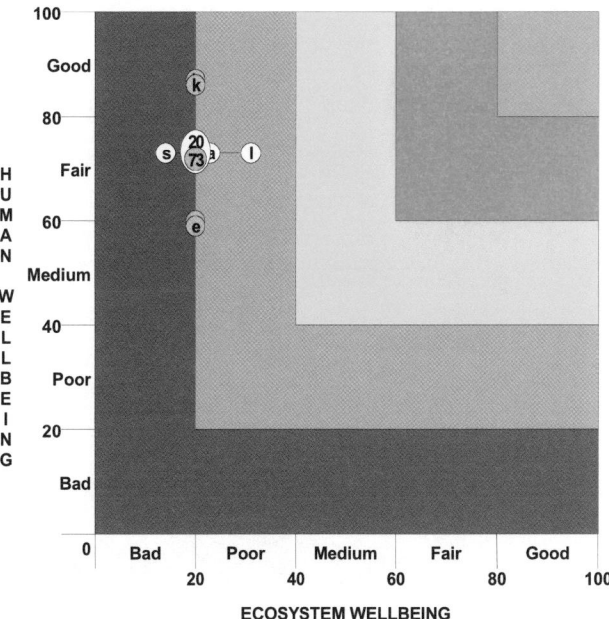

Figure 4.32. Structure of wellbeing: Spain. See Figure 4.31 for key. Some dimensions are hidden by the egg (wealth, air) or behind another dimension (community is behind equity, health and population behind knowledge, water behind species and genes). Spain's EWI excludes resource use, which otherwise would have increased it artificially.

its economy is sapped by inflation. Greece is the least prosperous (GDP per person $13,945), and its communication system needs upgrading; so does Portugal's. Malta's economy is flawed by high budget deficits, and it has the lowest education performance in the group. Spain's score for community is reduced by Basque separatist terrorism. Mediocre equity drags down the HWIs of all seven. Improving these aspects is the clear human priority.

Ecosystem stress is severe in all the high ecosystem deficit countries but especially in Malta and Spain, where it is higher than human wellbeing. Malta consumes more water, ozone depleting substances (ODSs), energy, food, and timber than its small, arid, and densely populated ecosystem can support. Spain has more room (room for almost 1,600 Maltas) but still causes an unusual degree of environmental damage, mostly to water, air, and species and genes (Figure 4.32).

Water quality is bad in Spain (nutrients and cadmium) and France (nutrients, heavy metals, and fecal coliforms), poor in Portugal, Slovenia, and Italy, medium in Greece (Malta not rated). Local air quality is medium except in Italy (poor) and Slovenia and Malta (not rated). However, all but Portugal have poor scores for global

atmosphere (and hence for air) because of their carbon dioxide emissions (over twice the amount of carbon that would qualify for a fair score), and four of them (Spain, France, Italy, and Greece) make large quantities of ODSs. Portugal does not produce ODSs, uses less energy (per person, hectare, and dollar of GDP), and emits a medium-scoring 1,370 kg of carbon per person.

Spain has the only bad score for species and genes (poor in France, Greece, Portugal, and Slovenia; medium in Italy and Malta). Despite having the fewest people and (after France) species per hectare, it has the most threatened plants (20%), mammals (29%), and breeding birds (2.2%). Like France and Italy, Spain has a rich heritage of livestock breeds, much of which has been lost already. While many of the survivors are in danger of disappearing in all three countries, more are on the brink in Spain: for every breed not at risk, almost two are threatened (compared with 0.75 each in France and Italy). Land scores are poor throughout (except Malta, bad) because of widespread loss of natural land and inadequate protection.

As in Northern Europe, a practical strategy for environmental progress in Southern Europe would be to emulate the regional leaders in some aspects (France in land quality, Portugal in energy) and to raise the bar in others (land protection, water quality, global atmosphere, local air quality, and wild and domesticated diversity).

133

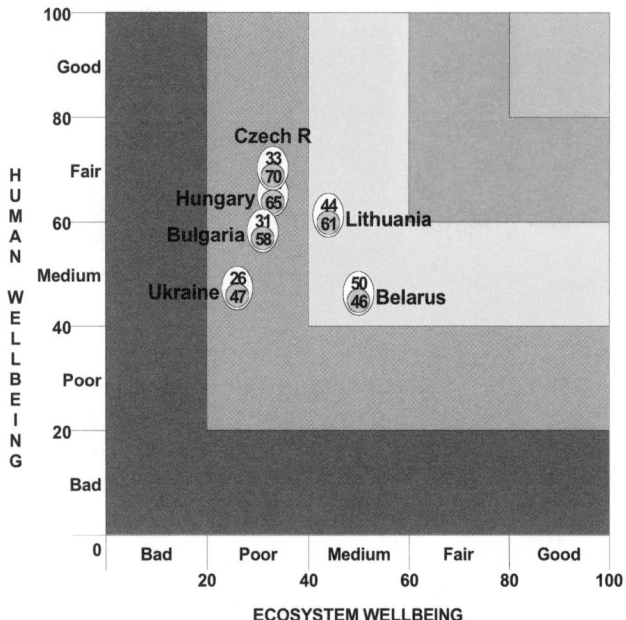

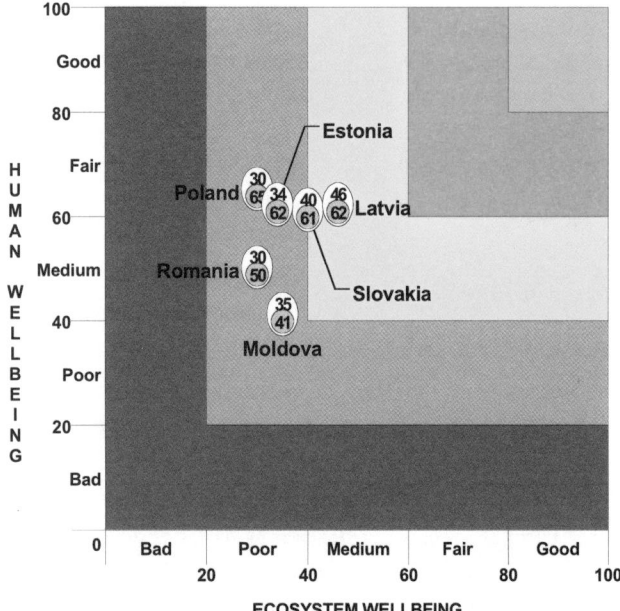

Figure 4.33. Wellbeing of Eastern Europe. Human Wellbeing Index (HWI) in yolk of egg, Ecosystem Wellbeing Index (EWI) in white. Hungary's EWI is 33.

Table 4.12. Eastern Europe: Wellbeing Index (WI), Wellbeing/Stress Index (WSI), performance group, and number (#) of subelements covered (out of 30). 1 = fair WI/medium WSI; 2 = medium WI and WSI; 3 = medium WI/poor WSI; 4 = poor WI and WSI; 5 = poor WI/bad WSI; mod. = moderate; def. = deficit; e = ecosystem worse; p = people worse. Country order is by performance group and then by WI.

Country	WI	WSI	Performance Group	#
Latvia	54.0	1.15	2: mod. ecosystem def.	28
Lithuania	52.5	1.09	2: mod. ecosystem def.	30
Czech R	51.5	1.04	2: high ecosystem def.	29
Slovakia	50.5	1.02	2: high ecosystem def.	29
Hungary	49.0	0.97	3: high ecosystem def.	30
Estonia	48.0	0.94	3: high ecosystem def.	28
Poland	47.5	0.93	3: high ecosystem def.	30
Belarus	48.0	0.92	3: mod. double def.	27
Bulgaria	44.5	0.84	3: high double def. e	30
Romania	40.0	0.71	4: high double def. e	30
Moldova	38.0	0.63	4: high double def. e	28
Ukraine	36.5	0.64	4: high double def. e	28

and Poland have HWIs within 4 points of each other but EWIs separated by up to 16 points.

The leaders in human wellbeing (Czech Republic, Hungary, Poland, Estonia, Latvia, Lithuania, and Slovakia) have a median HWI of 62, well below the Southern European vanguard's 72 and Northern Europe's 79 but well above the rest of Eastern Europe's 46. The leaders need to improve all human dimensions (except equity) to catch up with Northern Europe, and the laggards need to do likewise to catch up with their regional leaders. Healthy life expectancy at birth ranges from 61.5 years in Moldova to 68 years in the Czech Republic (in Northern Europe from 69 to 73 years). GDP per person rises from $1,945 in Moldova to $12,360 in the Czech Republic, far below Northern Europe's range of $20,335 to $33,505. Eastern European economies are also prone to high inflation, unemployment, or both and are more indebted. While all of Northern Europe (except Ireland) has a good score for communication, the most wired countries in Eastern Europe (Estonia, Slovakia, Hungary, and Poland) are no better than fair, although they are chatterboxes compared with Ukraine, Moldova, and Romania (19 main phone lines and cell phones per 100 people) and Belarus (7 Internet users per 10,000). The leaders with fair HWIs have fair scores for freedom and governance, falling short of the good scores of their northern neighbors (apart from Belgium and the United Kingdom), mainly because of greater corruption and restrictions on civil liberties. Freedoms are more limited in Bulgaria and Romania and still more so in Ukraine, Moldova, and authoritarian Belarus.

Eastern Europe clearly shows the breakability of the link between human wellbeing and ecosystem stress (Figure 4.33 and Table 4.12). The state of the environment is poor in 9 of the 12 countries, but development levels slide from comfortably fair in the Czech Republic, Hungary, and Poland to barely medium in Moldova. By the same token, nations with similar standards of living differ widely in ecosystem wellbeing: Belarus performs better than Ukraine; and Latvia, Lithuania, Slovakia, Estonia,

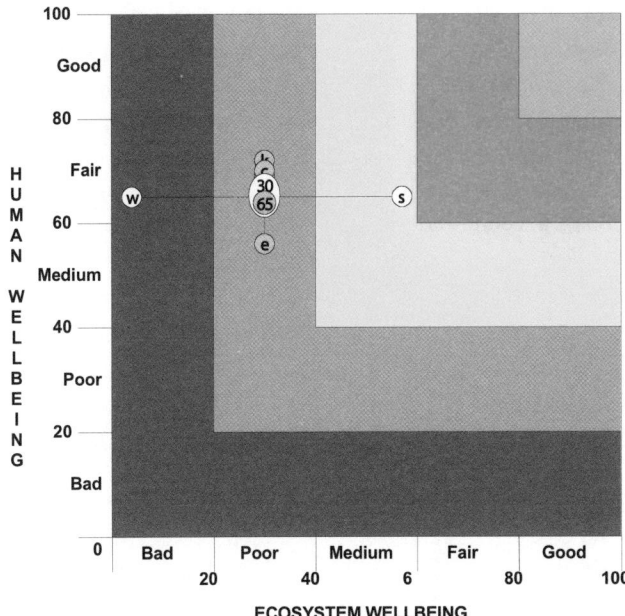

Figure 4.34. Structure of wellbeing: Poland. Yellow circles show the points on the scale of the human dimensions: c = community; e = equity; h = health and population; k = knowledge; w = wealth. White circles show the points of the ecosystem dimensions: a = air; l = land; r = resource use; s = species and genes; w = water. Some dimensions are hidden by the egg (air, land) or behind another dimension (health and population is behind community, wealth is behind equity). Poland's EWI excludes resource use, which otherwise would have increased it artificially.

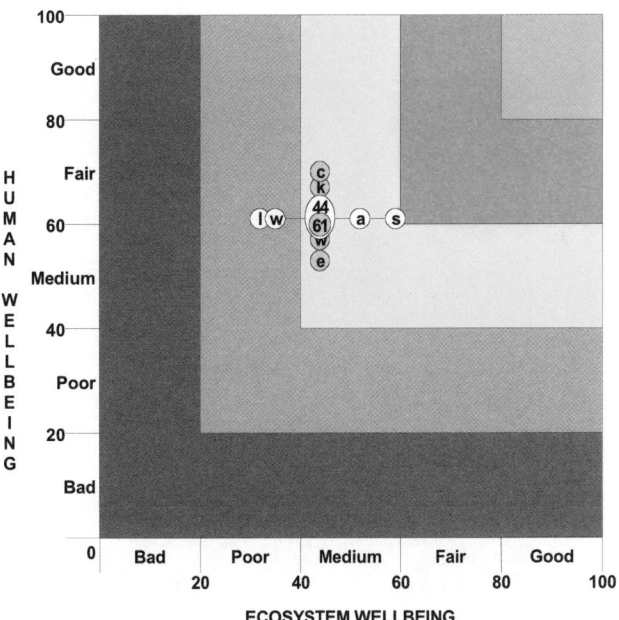

Figure 4.35. Structure of wellbeing: Lithuania. See Figure 4.34 for key. One dimension is hidden by the egg (health and population). Lithuania's EWI excludes resource use, which otherwise would have increased it artificially.

The state of the environment is better in Belarus than Ukraine in almost every respect. Less land has been converted to cultivation and settlement (35% versus 72%); less of the cultivated and modified land is degraded (3% moderately versus 34% moderately and 3% extremely); less of the water supply is controlled by dams or extracted (5% and 7% versus 13% and 49%); and fewer bird and mammal species are threatened (4% versus 9%). Belarus's local air quality is medium, Ukraine's water quality bad (neither was rated on both). Agriculture is the one aspect in which Ukraine outperforms Belarus, being both more productive and more self-reliant, advantages that will vanish unless soil quality is restored.

Latvia and Estonia, by contrast, have almost identical scores for land and species and genes. What separates them is their impacts on water and air. Latvia's rivers are overloaded with nutrients, but Estonia's are even more burdened. Estonia also emits 3,559 kg of carbon per person, almost four times Latvia's 904 kg (neither was assessed on local air quality). The pair's economic and social performance also differs, but not enough to explain the environmental discrepancies. Estonia's education and communication systems are stronger, but Latvia has a

higher community rating because of fewer violent crimes. Latvia has the better score for wealth (57 versus 50) because of lower debt, but incomes are higher in Estonia (GDP per person $7,680 versus $5,730). Estonia also consumes over twice as much energy (per person) and uses it less efficiently, requiring 35 gigajoules (GJ) per $1,000 of GDP, compared with Latvia's 20 GJ. (While all of Eastern Europe uses energy inefficiently, only Ukraine is more profligate than Estonia.)

Poland (Figure 4.34) and Lithuania (Figure 4.35) share similar levels and patterns of human wellbeing; the chief differences are that healthy life expectancy in Poland is two years longer and its knowledge score is slightly higher. Yet they diverge environmentally along the same lines as Estonia and Latvia: scores are practically the same for land and species and genes; dramatically different for water and air. Poland grossly contaminates rivers and groundwater with nutrients, fecal coliforms, and heavy metals. In Lithuania, nutrient and heavy metal pollution of inland waters is also serious but not as extreme. Local air quality is medium in both countries, but Poland's carbon dioxide emissions are more than double Lithuania's even though they use almost the same amount of energy per person and Poland is more efficient (17 versus 24 GJ per $1,000 of GDP). The difference is that Lithuania consumes mostly liquid fuels, which are low in carbon compared with the coal that Poland burns in huge quantities.

135

West Asia

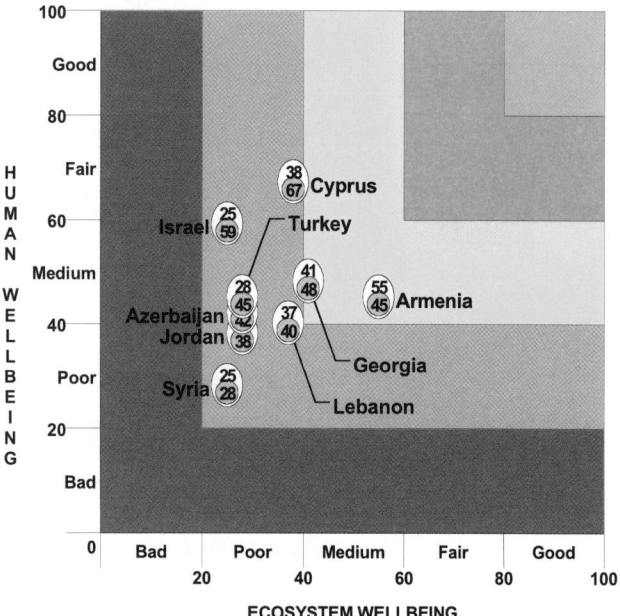

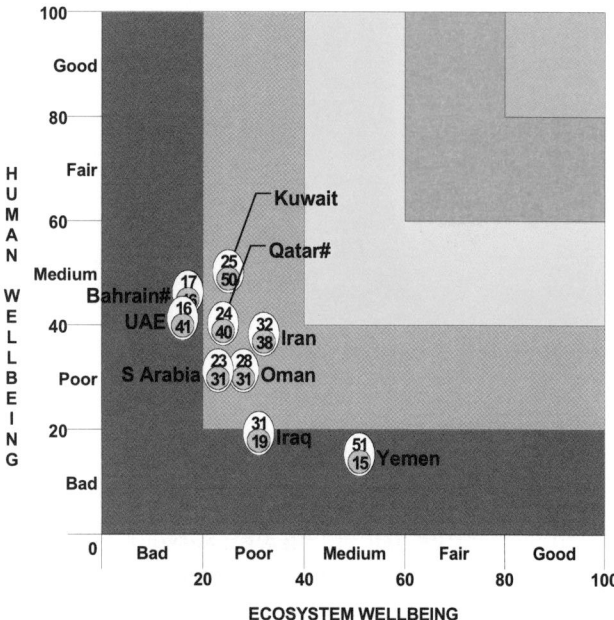

Figure 4.36. Wellbeing of West Asia: northwest above, southwest below. Human Wellbeing Index (HWI) in yolk of egg, Ecosystem Wellbeing Index (EWI) in white. Azerbaijan's HWI is 42 and EWI 28. Jordan's EWI is 28. Bahrain's HWI is 46. # Bahrain and Qatar were assessed on less than two-thirds of the ecosystem subelements.

West Asia presents the bleakest picture: most countries cluster in the bottom left corner of the Barometer (Figure 4.36), and it has the highest proportion of nations with high or extreme double deficits—all except Cyprus, Armenia, and Georgia—reflecting the widespread combination of environmental degradation, resource depletion, and depressed living standards (Table 4.13).

Table 4.13. West Asia: Wellbeing Index (WI), Wellbeing/Stress Index (WSI), performance group, and number of subelements covered (out of 30). 1 = fair WI/medium WSI; 2 = medium WI and WSI; 3 = medium WI/poor WSI; 4 = poor WI and WSI; 5 = poor WI/bad WSI; mod. = moderate; def. = deficit; e = ecosystem worse; p = people worse. Within each subregion, country order is by performance group and then by WI. *Bahrain and Qatar were rated on less than two-thirds of the ecosystem subelements.*

Country	WI	WSI	Performance Group	#
Northwest Asia				
Cyprus	52.5	1.08	2: high ecosystem def.	27
Armenia	50.0	1.00	3: mod. double def.	26
Georgia	44.5	0.81	3: mod. double def.	26
Israel	42.0	0.79	3: high double def. e	27
Turkey	36.5	0.63	4: high double def. e	30
Azerbaijan	35.0	0.58	4: high double def. e	26
Lebanon	38.5	0.63	4: extreme double def.	25
Jordan	33.0	0.53	4: extreme double def.	28
Syrian Arab R	26.5	0.37	5: extreme double def.	27
Southwest Asia				
Kuwait	37.5	0.67	4: high double def. e	25
Bahrain	*31.5*	*0.55*	*4: high double def. e*	*20*
Iran	35.0	0.56	4: extreme double def.	26
Qatar	*32.0*	*0.53*	*4: extreme double def.*	*20*
Yemen	33.0	0.31	5: high double def. p	26
United Arab Emirates	28.5	0.49	5: high double def. e	23
Oman	29.5	0.43	5: extreme double def.	23
Saudi Arabia	27.0	0.40	5: extreme double def.	24
Iraq	25.0	0.28	5: extreme double def.	24

The region is sharply divided between rich and poor: Incomes range from $720 per person in Yemen to more than $25,000 per person in Kuwait. Scores for wealth are poor for just under half the countries (Georgia, Iraq, Jordan, Lebanon, Syria, Turkey, and Yemen), fair for most of the other half (Cyprus, Israel, Kuwait, Qatar, Saudi Arabia, and United Arab Emirates). Armenia, Azerbaijan, Bahrain, Iran, and Oman have medium levels of wealth.

All but two countries have poor or bad ratings for freedom and governance, preventing their citizens from freely choosing how and by whom they will be governed, denying basic human rights, and shackling the press. Israel's score is medium, the average of a fair score in Israel proper (no better than fair because Arab Israelis are second-class citizens in education, housing, and social services) and poor in the West Bank and East Jerusalem. Cyprus is fair (rather than good) because of the division between Greek and Turkish Cypriots and limited political rights in Turkish Cyprus. Most nations also have poor or bad scores for peace, some because of ongoing conflicts

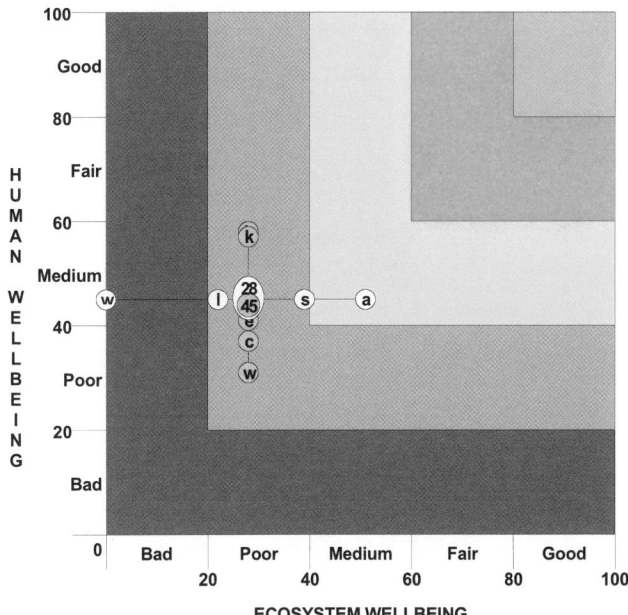

Figure 4.37. Structure of wellbeing: Turkey. Yellow circles show the points on the scale of the human dimensions: c = community; e = equity; h = health and population; k = knowledge; w = wealth. White circles show the points of the ecosystem dimensions: a = air; l = land; r = resource use; s = species and genes; w = water. Some dimensions are hidden by the egg (equity) or behind another dimension (health and population is behind knowledge). Turkey's EWI excludes resource use, which otherwise would have increased it artificially.

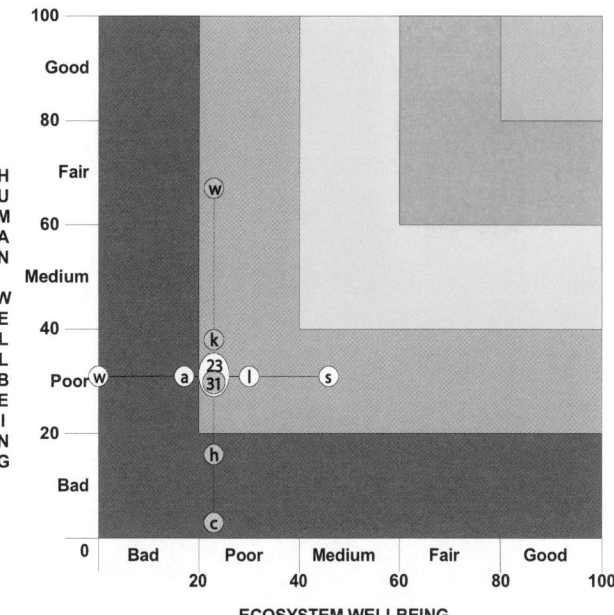

Figure 4.38. Structure of wellbeing: Saudi Arabia. See Figure 4.37 for key. One dimension is hidden by the egg (resource use). Saudi Arabia's HWI excludes equity, which otherwise would have increased it artificially.

with neighbors or groups inside their borders (Georgia, Iran, Iraq, Lebanon, Turkey, and Yemen), others because they devote 8% or more of their GDP to the military (Armenia, Kuwait, Oman, Qatar, and Saudi Arabia), Israel because of both.

Wealth is generally higher in Southwest Asia, but health and population, knowledge, and overall human wellbeing are higher in Northwest Asia. Turkey (Figure 4.37) and Saudi Arabia (Figure 4.38) typify their regions in this respect. Turkey's low wealth is due to inadequate infrastructure (only half the population has safe water), feverish inflation rates, and reckless deficits. Saudi Arabia's inferior health and population score reflects a fertility rate of almost six children per woman; its low grade for knowledge results from poor primary and secondary school attendance (a scant 63% of boys and 56% of girls) and negligible access to the Internet (one person in a thousand).

Damage to land, air, and water are widespread symptoms of wasteful consumption and disregard for the public good. The countries with fair scores for wealth emit excessive amounts of carbon dioxide and ozone depleting substances (ODSs). Several poorer nations (Iran, Jordan, Lebanon, and Syria) are heavy

users of ODSs. Yet Turkey sets an example with moderate impacts on the global atmosphere and medium local air quality. Eleven countries extract more than their renewable water supply: Azerbaijan, Israel, Jordan, and Syria in Northwest Asia, and all of Southwest Asia except Iran and Yemen (which use 55% and 72%, respectively). Turkey withdraws a restrained 18% but dams more than its total supply and severely pollutes rivers with nutrients, lead, and cadmium.

Turkey has the same HWI as Armenia, but Armenia's EWI is higher (by 27 points), partly because it was not rated on water quality, use of ODSs, or local air quality, but also because—despite being more densely populated—it is better at conserving land. Turkey has converted 46% of its land to buildings and cultivation, and the area of fairly natural land has shrunk to 2%. Armenia has converted 30%, and an estimated 13% is natural. Turkey protects less than 2%, Armenia 7%. As much as 42% of Turkey's agricultural land is moderately to strongly degraded, compared with 5% of Armenia's. However, scores for species and genes are almost identical because, although Turkey has higher percentages of threatened wild species (12% of plants, 15% of mammals), its livestock breeds are less at risk. Assuming Armenia's water quality is as bad as Georgia's (19 score) and its local air quality and ODS consumption are the same as Turkey's, Armenia would still have an EWI of 39 (11 points above Turkey's).[9]

Russia and Central and East Asia

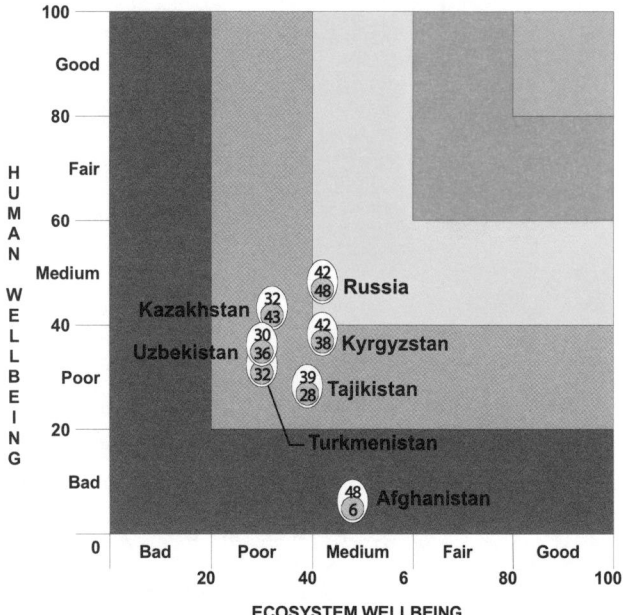

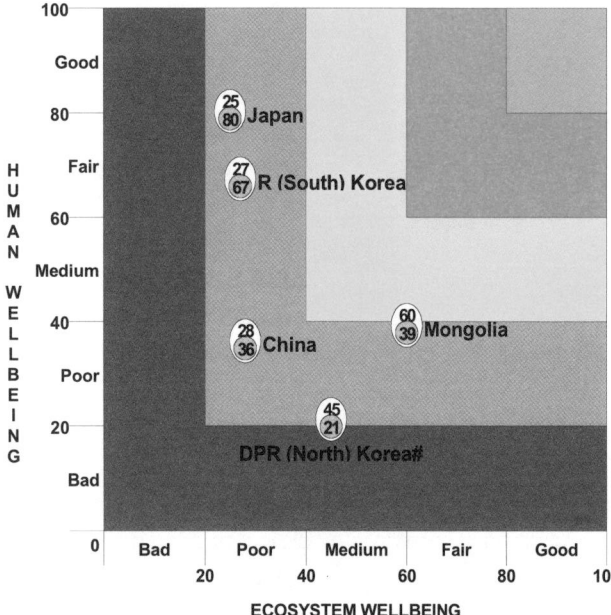

Figure 4.39. Wellbeing of Russia and Central and East Asia: Russia and Central Asia above, East Asia below. Human Wellbeing Index (HWI) in yolk of egg, Ecosystem Wellbeing Index (EWI) in white. Turkmenistan's EWI is 30. # Afghanistan and North Korea (DPR = Democratic People's Republic) were assessed on less than two-thirds of the human subelements.

Central Asian nations (Figure 4.39 and Table 4.14) differ in their ills, but oppression is common to all. In the most democratic, Kyrgyzstan, freedoms of expression and organization are upheld capriciously, and elections are tainted by ballot box stuffing and inflation of voter turnouts. In the least, Turkmenistan is ruled by a dictator, and Afghanistan is 10% fought over and 90% run by the

Table 4.14. Russia and Central and East Asia: Wellbeing Index (WI), Wellbeing/Stress Index (WSI), performance group, and number (#) of subelements covered (out of 30). 1 = fair WI/medium WSI; 2 = medium WI and WSI; 3 = medium WI/poor WSI; 4 = poor WI and WSI; 5 = poor WI/bad WSI; mod. = moderate; def. = deficit; e = ecosystem worse; p = people worse. Within each subregion, country order is by performance group and then by WI. *Afghanistan and DPR Korea were rated on less than two-thirds of the human subelements.*

Country	WI	WSI	Performance Group	#
Russia				
Russian Federation	45.0	0.83	3: mod. double def.	29
Central Asia				
Kyrgyzstan	40.0	0.66	3: high double def. p	27
Kazakhstan	37.5	0.63	4: high double def. e	28
Uzbekistan	33.0	0.51	4: extreme double def.	26
Afghanistan	*27.0*	*0.12*	*5: high double def. p*	*20*
Tajikistan	33.5	0.46	5: extreme double def.	26
Turkmenistan	31.0	0.46	5: extreme double def.	25
East Asia				
Japan	52.5	1.07	2: high ecosystem def.	30
Mongolia	49.5	0.98	3: high double def. p	26
Korea, R	47.0	0.92	3: high ecosystem def.	30
Korea, DPR	*33.0*	*0.38*	*5: high double def. p*	*18*
China	32.0	0.50	5: extreme double def.	30

Taliban, which shirks the duties of government but ruthlessly imposes religious dogma. The result: one of the world's worst records for disease, poverty, illiteracy, and abuse of women. Life is not nearly as grim elsewhere, but only Kazakhstan achieves medium scores for all human dimensions except community (poor). Ecosystem conditions are poor (the medium EWIs of Afghanistan and Kyrgyzstan are misleading since they do not count air and water quality), the main defects being skimpy land protection (all countries), massive river conversion (Kazakhstan, Kyrgyzstan, and Tajikistan) and overconsumption of water (Turkmenistan and Uzbekistan).

Continent-sized, sparsely populated Russia (Figure 4.40) has converted just 10% of its land to buildings and cultivation, and an estimated 66% is still natural. This includes 94% of native forest that is claimed to be undisturbed, implying that logging has affected a tree-huggingly small 6%.[10] Assuming that large tracts of natural forest do remain, they will not for long unless rampant cutting is curbed and the protected area (a meager 3%) is at least quadrupled. Rivers are extremely polluted in places—such as the Irtysh at Krasnyi Jar and the Kuban where it enters the Azov Sea—but on average water quality is medium. The main problems are acidification, heavy metals, and

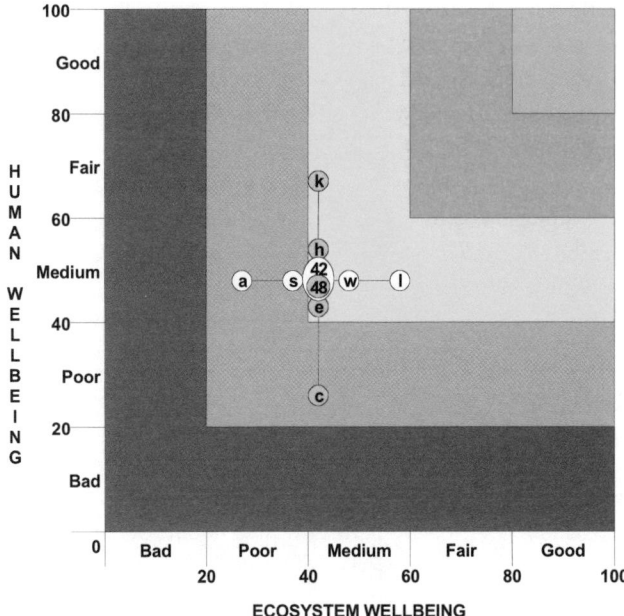

Figure 4.40. Structure of wellbeing: Russia. Yellow circles show the points on the scale of the human dimensions: c = community; e = equity; h = health and population; k = knowledge; w = wealth. White circles show the points of the ecosystem dimensions: a = air; l = land; r = resource use; s = species and genes; w = water. One dimension is hidden by the egg (wealth). Russia's EWI excludes resource use, which otherwise would have increased it artificially.

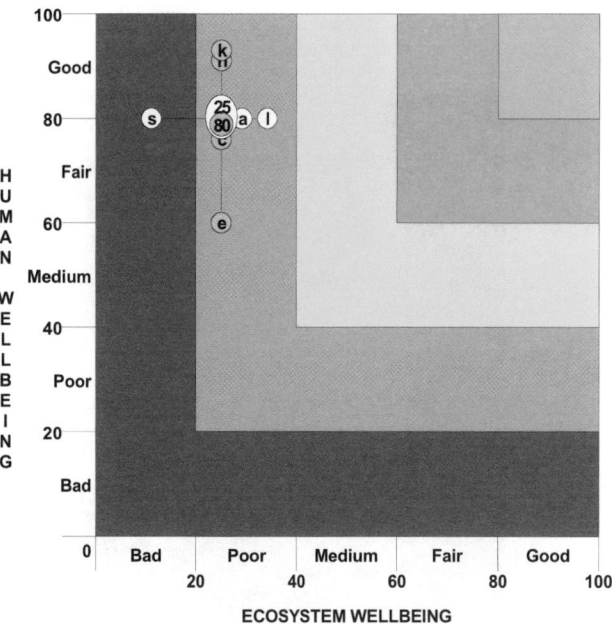

Figure 4.41. Structure of wellbeing: Japan. See Figure 4.40 for key. Some dimensions are hidden by the egg (community, wealth, water) or behind another dimension (health and population is behind knowledge). Japan's EWI excludes resource use, which otherwise would have increased it artificially.

excess nutrients, although this last lessened during the 1990s as agriculture stagnated and fertilizer use declined. Average local air quality is also medium, but Russia's air rating is poor because of high outputs of carbon dioxide and ozone depleting substances.

The chief obstacle to improving the environment is poor governance. The state has randomized into an arbitrary force, moved largely by corruption, that uses its power more to intimidate the media, coerce the judiciary, and make war on Chechnya than to create a fair arena for enterprise, provide high-quality social services, and uphold the rule of law. While education is still good, communications are backward, health is deteriorating, and infrastructure decaying. The economy is overdependent on consumption (38 gigajoules of energy per $1,000 of GDP) and short-changes citizens with double-digit unemployment, rising prices, and mediocre incomes (GDP $6,460 per person).

China's strength is health and population—a healthy life expectancy of 62 years and a fertility rate of 1.8 children per woman—but it is weak in most other aspects. Incomes are low (GDP $3,105 per person), three-quarters of the population lacks basic sanitation, university education is limited to a small minority, corruption is rife, and civil and political rights are ignored. The ecosystem is respected even less: 21% of farmland is moderately to strongly degraded;

rivers are laden with bacteria, toxics, and silt; and 17% of plants and 13% of mammals and birds are at risk.

In North Korea and Mongolia, almost half the people lack sufficient food. North Korea is poorer than China in all human dimensions; Mongolia, in all but community (thanks to huge advances in democracy). Their EWIs are better because neither was rated on air or water quality, both have less degraded land, and much of Mongolia's land is still fairly natural.

Japan (Figure 4.41) is among the world's leaders in every human dimension except equity (flawed by the obstacles women face in business and government). However, it needs to greatly improve every ecosystem dimension. Rivers and groundwater are polluted with nutrients, fecal coliforms, and heavy metals. Energy consumption is high, and carbon dioxide emissions three times the level that would get a fair score. The country's fisheries produce only 55% of its seafood supply, yet overexploit a fourth of major fish species. Well over half the land is built or cultivated, but less than 9% is protected—not enough to secure agricultural diversity or the 20% of plants and 18% of birds and mammals that are threatened.

South Korea has fewer species and livestock breeds at risk but protects less land and pollutes rivers as much and the global atmosphere more. Its task is to raise its EWI while elevating every human dimension except knowledge to catch up with Japan.

Southern Asia

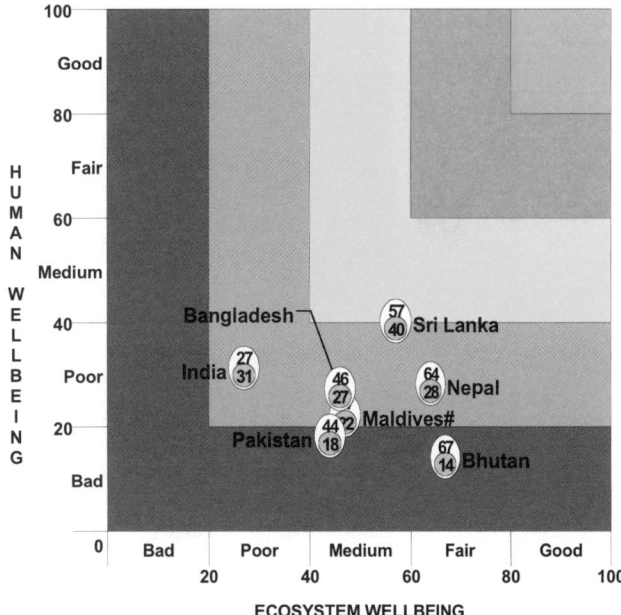

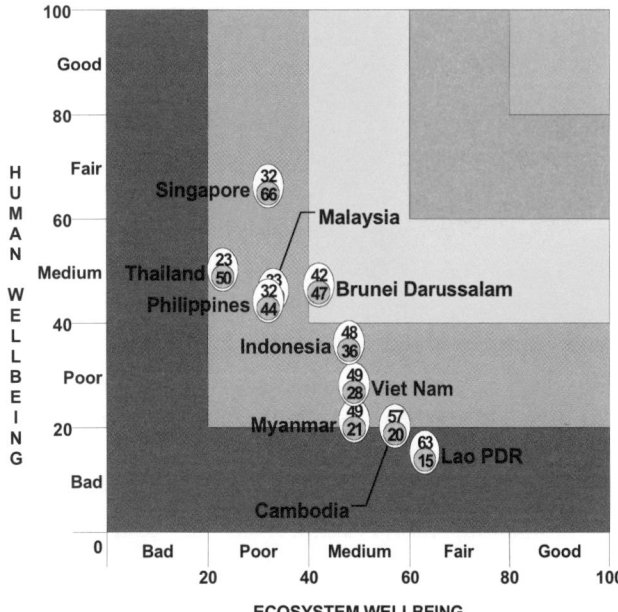

Figure 4.42. Wellbeing of Southern Asia: South Asia above, Southeast Asia below. Human Wellbeing Index (HWI) in yolk of egg, Ecosystem Wellbeing Index (EWI) in white. Lao PDR = Lao People's Democratic Republic. Maldives' HWI is 22 and EWI 47. Malaysia's HWI is 46 and EWI 33. # Maldives was assessed on less than two-thirds of the ecosystem subelements.

Most of South Asia is strung across the bottom of the Barometer, separated more by environmental than by socioeconomic performance (Figure 4.42 and Table 4.15). The exception is Sri Lanka, with a markedly higher quality of life thanks to superior health and population (Figure 4.43). Its healthy life expectancy of 62.8 years is well above the subregion's span of 49.4 years in Nepal to 55.9 years in

Table 4.15. Southern Asia: Wellbeing Index (WI), Wellbeing/Stress Index (WSI), performance group, and number (#) of subelements covered (out of 30). 1 = fair WI/medium WSI; 2 = medium WI and WSI; 3 = medium WI/poor WSI; 4 = poor WI and WSI; 5 = poor WI/bad WSI; mod. = moderate; def. = deficit; e = ecosystem worse; p = people worse. Within each subregion, country order is by performance group and then by WI. *Maldives was rated on less than two-thirds of the ecosystem subelements.*

Country	WI	WSI	Performance Group	#
South Asia				
Sri Lanka	48.5	0.93	3: high double def. p	28
Nepal	46.0	0.78	3: high human def.	27
Bhutan	40.5	0.42	5: high human def.	23
Bangladesh	36.5	0.50	5: high double def. p	28
Maldives	*34.5*	*0.42*	*5: high double def. p*	*19*
Pakistan	31.0	0.32	5: high double def. p	27
India	29.0	0.42	5: extreme double def.	29
Southeast Asia				
Singapore	49.0	0.97	3: high ecosystem def.	24
Brunei Darussalam	44.5	0.81	3: mod. double def.	22
Indonesia	42.0	0.69	3: high double def. p	29
Malaysia	39.5	0.69	4: high double def. e	29
Philippines	38.0	0.65	4: high double def. e	30
Thailand	36.5	0.65	4: high double def. e	30
Viet Nam	38.5	0.55	4: high double def. p	27
Lao PDR	39.0	0.41	5: high human def.	25
Cambodia	38.5	0.47	5: high double def. p	25
Myanmar	35.0	0.41	5: high double def. p	26

Pakistan, and its replacement-level fertility rate of 2.1 children per woman is well below the 3.0 of India and Bhutan's 5.4. These advances partly compensate for the depressed wealth, knowledge, and community that Sri Lanka shares with the rest of South Asia. GDP per person ranges from $1,155 in Nepal to $4,085 in the Maldives (Sri Lanka $2,980), and many in each nation go without the essentials for survival: 37% lack enough food in Bangladesh, 43% safe water in Sri Lanka, 84% basic sanitation in Nepal. Many are also deprived of the basic tools for intellectual development and economic betterment: primary school enrollment drops from 100% of primary-age children in Sri Lanka to 13% in Bhutan, tertiary enrollment from a low 64 per 10,000 people in India to 30 in Pakistan (47 in Sri Lanka); extremely small minorities have phones and access to the Internet. Restricted freedom, corruption, violence, armed conflict, or a mixture of these reduce community scores, which are medium in Nepal, bad in Bhutan and Pakistan, and poor in the rest—the key failing in Sri Lanka's case being the civil war with the Tamils.

The wide range of EWIs, from India's 27 to Bhutan's

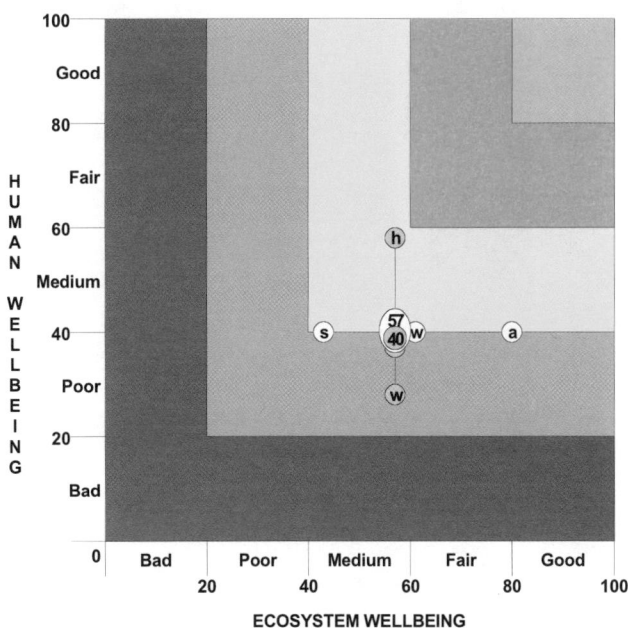

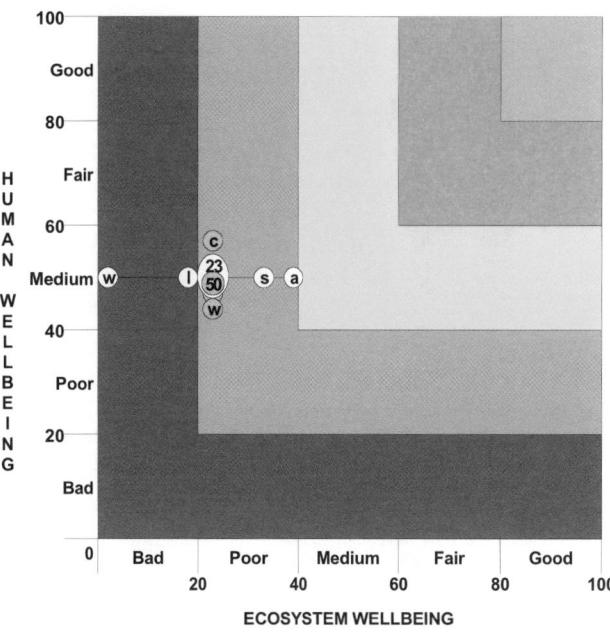

Figure 4.43. Structure of wellbeing: Sri Lanka. Yellow circles show the points on the scale of the human dimensions: c = community; e = equity; h = health and population; k = knowledge; w = wealth. White circles show the points of the ecosystem dimensions: a = air; l = land; r = resource use; s = species and genes; w = water. Some dimensions are hidden by the egg (community, knowledge) or behind another dimension (land is behind species and genes). Sri Lanka's HWI excludes equity and its EWI excludes resource use, which otherwise would have increased them artificially.

67, is due to two factors. First, differences in land diversity: lowest where most of the land is built or cultivated (Bangladesh and India), 5% or less is protected (Bangladesh, India, Maldives, and Pakistan), or forest loss is more than 2% a year (Bangladesh and Pakistan); highest where much of the land is natural (Nepal 21%, Bhutan 71%). Second, differences in coverage: local air quality was rated only in India, water quality in Bangladesh, India, and Pakistan. Sri Lanka's air score would be 25 if its city air is as poor as India's, its water score 29 if its rivers are as polluted as India's Coromandel Coast.

Southeast Asia climbs backwards from the bad HWI and fair EWI of Lao to the fair HWI and poor EWI of Singapore. Singapore could raise its HWI further by opening itself to political diversity and the free flow of information, giving women greater access to positions of power, and improving primary and secondary education. Cutting resource use is the key to boosting its EWI: energy consumption is the world's highest per hectare and ninth highest per person; carbon dioxide emissions are eight times the maximum fair level and rising fast.

While Thailand tackles its economic debt, its social and

Figure 4.44. Structure of wellbeing: Thailand. See Figure 4.43 for key. Some dimensions are hidden by the egg (equity, health and population, knowledge). Thailand's EWI excludes resource use, which otherwise would have increased it artificially.

ecosystem deficits are mounting (Figure 4.44). Incomes have fallen since the Asian financial crisis (GDP per person is $5,455), poverty has spread (24% lack enough food), and disparities have sharpened (the richest fifth has nine times the income share of the poorest). Efforts to increase wealth are impoverishing the environment. Air quality is poor, rivers are clogged with nutrients and fecal coliforms, almost 80% of farm and grazing land is moderately degraded, and 8% of mammals and birds are at risk, along with much agricultural diversity. Feeding people sustainably and boosting health depend on protecting diversity and restoring land, air, and water quality. Combining this with building the economy requires better education, communication, and governance: freedoms are generally respected, and elections are being cleaned up, but corruption is common among officials, the police, and the judiciary.

The three next best assessed countries have lower HWIs and higher EWIs. Malaysia is wealthier, with better-developed communications, but its fertility rate is higher and it is only partly free. The Philippines is more educated, but fertility, poverty, and corruption are higher. Indonesia is weaker in all human dimensions. On the environmental side, Malaysia has less degraded land and fewer threatened species; the Philippines has less extreme land degradation and water pollution; Indonesia is stronger in all ecosystem dimensions except water, which is just as contaminated.

Pacific

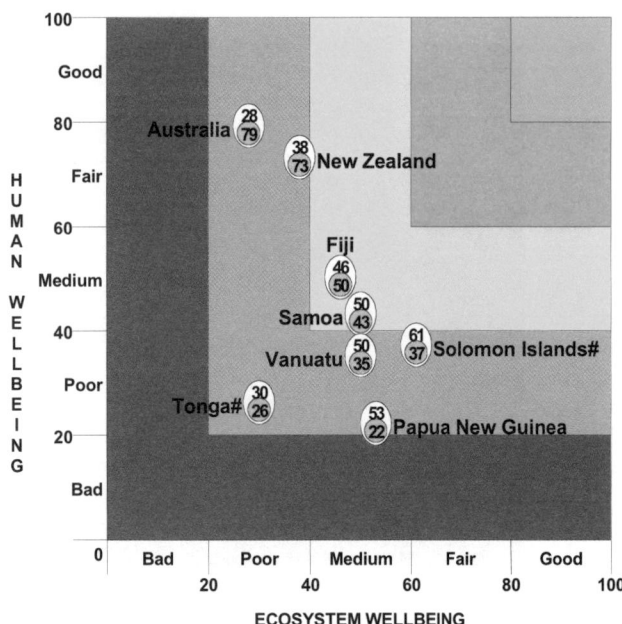

Figure 4.45. Wellbeing of the Pacific. Human Wellbeing Index (HWI) in yolk of egg, Ecosystem Wellbeing Index (EWI) in white. # Tonga was assessed on less than two-thirds of the human and ecosystem subelements; Solomon Islands on less than two-thirds of the human subelements.

Table 4.16. Pacific: Wellbeing Index (WI), Wellbeing/Stress Index (WSI), performance group, and number (#) of subelements covered (out of 30). 1 = fair WI/medium WSI; 2 = medium WI and WSI; 3 = medium WI/poor WSI; 4 = poor WI and WSI; 5 = poor WI/bad WSI; mod. = moderate; def. = deficit; e = ecosystem worse; p = people worse. Country order is by performance group and then by WI. *Tonga was rated on less than two-thirds of the human and ecosystem subelements, Solomon Islands on less than two-thirds of the human subelements.*

Country	WI	WSI	Performance Group	#
New Zealand	55.5	1.18	2: high ecosystem def.	29
Australia	53.5	1.10	2: high ecosystem def.	30
Solomon Islands	*49.0*	*0.95*	*3: high human def.*	*22*
Fiji	48.0	0.96	3: mod. double def.	26
Samoa	46.5	0.86	3: mod. double def.	22
Vanuatu	42.5	0.70	3: high double def. p	21
Papua New Guinea	37.5	0.47	5: high double def. p	27
Tonga	*28.0*	*0.37*	*5: extreme double def.*	*18*

Papua New Guinea (PNG) and the small island nations of the Pacific face the challenge of creating prosperous, democratic societies that protect their environments and respect their cultural traditions (Figure 4.45 and Table 4.16). Although PNG is better endowed with resources than its

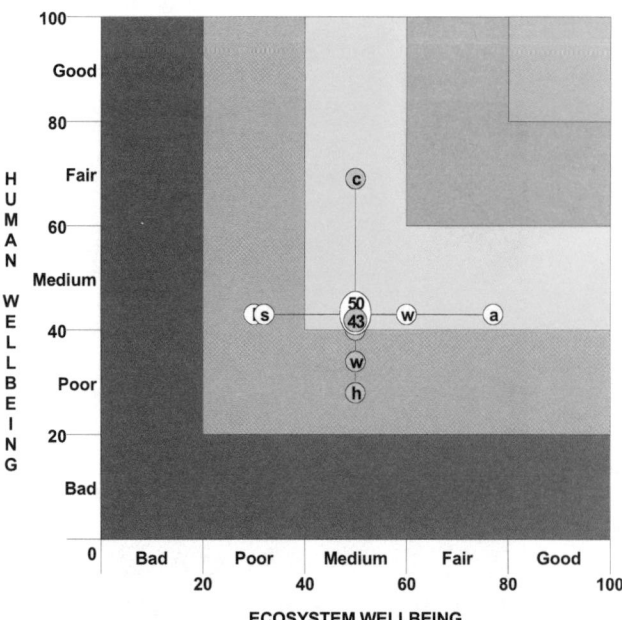

Figure 4.46. Structure of wellbeing: Samoa. Yellow circles show the points on the scale of the human dimensions: c = community; e = equity; h = health and population; k = knowledge; w = wealth. White circles show the points of the ecosystem dimensions: a = air; l = land; r = resource use; s = species and genes; w = water. Some dimensions are hidden by the egg (equity, knowledge) or behind another dimension (land is behind species and genes). Samoa's EWI excludes resource use, which otherwise would have increased it artificially.

smaller colleagues, it performs poorly in all human dimensions. Fiji is wealthier, more educated, and has a lower fertility rate than the others, but healthy lifespans are longer in Samoa and Tonga, and Fiji has yet to establish a political system that satisfies both indigenous and Indian Fijians. Underachievement in several dimensions pulls down the HWIs of the others, despite Tonga's medium scores for community and wealth and fair scores for community by Vanuatu, the Solomon Islands, and Samoa (Figure 4.46).

Samoa's community score reflects low rates of violent crime (except assaults) and acceptable, if flawed, freedom and governance. Its mixture of parliamentary democracy, chiefs, and village councils balances community norms and individual freedoms fairly well. However, corruption is growing, and the independent press has been victimized for exposing it. Incomes are low (GDP per person $3,830), 32% of the population lacks safe water, and the fertility rate exceeds 4 children per woman. Education, wealth, and power are also poorly shared in Samoa: fewer boys than girls have a secondary education, and women earn less than a third of the income and occupy just 8% of the seats in parliament.

The EWIs of PNG and its small island colleagues are distorted by lack of data on air and water quality. Land

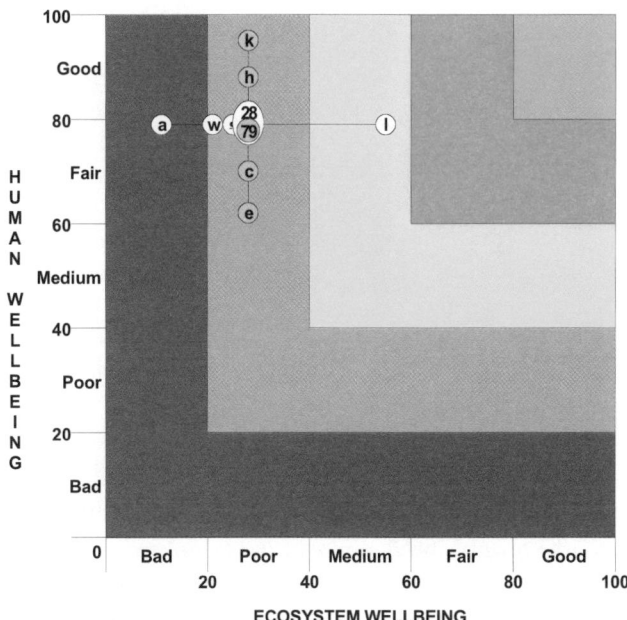

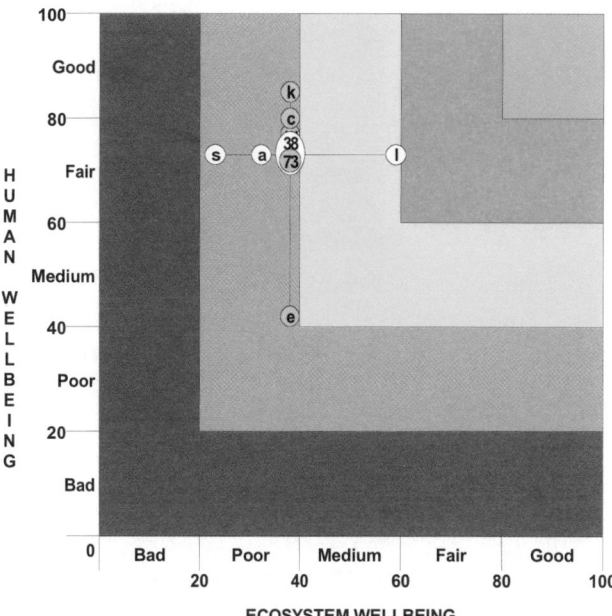

Figure 4.47. Structure of wellbeing: Australia. See Figure 4.46 for key. Some dimensions are hidden by the egg (wealth, species and genes). Australia's EWI excludes resource use, which otherwise would have increased it artificially.

Figure 4.48. Structure of wellbeing: New Zealand. See Figure 4.46 for key. Some dimensions are hidden by the egg (wealth, water) or behind another dimension (health and population is behind community). New Zealand's EWI excludes resource use, which otherwise would have increased it artificially.

and species and genes paint a more realistic picture. In Samoa, half the land is built or cultivated, natural land has shrunk to scraps, barely over 4% is protected, and 57% of mammals and birds face extinction. Elsewhere, the converted area ranges from 74% in Tonga to 2% in PNG, the natural area from 0% (Tonga) to 63% (PNG). The percentages of mammals and birds at risk are high throughout—58% in Fiji, 54% in Tonga, 26% in the Solomons, 22% in Vanuatu, 16% in PNG—and protected area coverage is tiny (from 0% in the Solomons and Tonga to 2% in PNG). Since communities will not give up their land, conservation depends on setting up protected areas that provide opportunities for development and are community owned.

Australia (Figure 4.47) and New Zealand (Figure 4.48) enjoy Northern European levels of human wellbeing. New Zealand's health and population and knowledge scores are below Australia's due to a shorter healthy life expectancy (69 versus 73 years), lower tertiary enrollment, and an unreliable telephone system (Australia does not report its phone line faults). Australia's lesser score for community includes crime; New Zealand's does not. The latter's subpar equity rating reflects large disparities in wealth: the richest fifth of the population has 17 times the income share of the poorest fifth (compared with 7 times in Australia).

New Zealand's better EWI reflects differences in

water (inland water quality) and air (global atmosphere)—poor in New Zealand, worse in Australia. New Zealand reports on oxygen balance, nutrient levels, and acidity in all large and many smaller rivers: phosphorus levels are high in most of them, probably because of inefficient use of fertilizers. Australia reports on just three rivers (Murray–Darling, Burdekin, and Derwent), which carry extreme loads of silt and nutrients. While both countries have dramatically cut their use of ozone depleting substances, they emit increasing amounts of carbon dioxide: New Zealand 2,258 kg and Australia 4,709 kg of carbon per person, respectively almost three and six times the maximum level defined as fair. Fossil fuel consumption is excessive, with solid fuels the main culprit in Australia, liquid fuels in New Zealand.

Scores for land and species and genes are close. Although New Zealand has converted more of its land to buildings and cultivation (25% versus Australia's 8%), it also protects more (20% versus 8%). Domesticated diversity is low in both countries, and very high percentages of wild species are threatened: 19% of plants and 15% of birds and mammals in Australia, 7% of plants and 61% of birds and mammals in New Zealand.

Better management of transport and industry is needed to curb fossil fuel use, and of land outside protected areas to conserve wild species, increase agricultural diversity, and restore water quality.

Aiming for Human and Ecosystem Wellbeing

Highlights

- The main reasons why no country combines high levels of human and ecosystem wellbeing are that it is inherently difficult to do and, more importantly, no country is committed to doing it.
- Six initiatives are needed for countries to achieve ways of living that are desirable, equitable, and sustainable:
  - Commitment to human and ecosystem wellbeing as a national goal
  - Regular wellbeing assessments to build support for the goal, analyze how to achieve it, and track progress
  - National information systems on human and ecosystem wellbeing and coverage of all aspects of wellbeing by the news media
  - Replacement of most, if not all, existing taxes with taxes on energy and materials
  - Wellbeing areas (Slow Zones) to maintain cultural heritage, wild and domesticated biodiversity, and a high quality of life in mixed built–cultivated–wild landscapes
  - Regional wellbeing alliances, so that existing and new groups of nations can harmonize their efforts to achieve sustainability; and partnerships between rich ecosystem deficit and poor human deficit countries to exchange development support for ecosystem capacity

Commitment to Human and Ecosystem Wellbeing

The combination of even fair levels of human and ecosystem wellbeing is obviously difficult to achieve, but the degree of difficulty is unknown because no society has consciously aimed for it.

The widespread espousal of international and national sustainable development agendas has not translated into equal commitments to raise the quality of human life and secure the quality and diversity of the environment. It is one thing to insert sustainability into policy documents and quite another to make the sweeping changes that the term implies. All aspects of wellbeing must be addressed together, but many—such as equity, the global atmosphere, and biodiversity—are poorly understood and fail to command more than fleeting political attention. The grand idea of people and the ecosystem in unison is reduced to pages of discrete prescriptions that tend to reflect the limited and often contradictory objectives of particular interest groups, from expanding trade to saving wilderness. These aims could contribute to sustainability if balanced by the other constituents of wellbeing but will obstruct it if pursued alone. Countries would have a better chance of forging them into a coherent agenda for sustainability if they made an explicit commitment to high levels of both human and ecosystem wellbeing as a national goal.

Regular Wellbeing Assessments

National and local wellbeing assessments provide three essentials for transforming the vision of sustainable development into reality:

- A means of making the goal achievable and measuring progress toward it.
- An analytical tool for deciding priority actions.
- A process to keep the goal constantly in mind and to help people learn how to reach it.

As noted in Chapter 1, a goal that is measurable is attainable. The HWI, EWI, WI, and WSI provide the means by which societies can measure the overall conditions of people and the environment, thereby making it possible for them to adopt better human and ecosystem wellbeing as an achievable goal. Each society can then set targets for itself, deciding how much it wants to raise its

HWI and EWI (and hence its WI and WSI) in a given period.

By breaking down the indices into major components, societies can identify the factors most responsible for their current levels of human and ecosystem wellbeing. The regional reviews illustrated how the Barometer of Sustainability shows instantly what dimensions of wellbeing most need attention. These dimensions can be examined in detail to determine critical features and their relationships with other socioeconomic and environmental factors. Then on the basis of this analysis, societies can consider practical policy options and decide priority actions.

Wellbeing assessments can facilitate the task of building consensus on (or at least majority support for) policies and actions by providing a logical progression from the goal, through objectives for particular elements or sectors, to performance criteria for indicators. They also provide a much-needed mental bridge between the short term and the long term. The hurly-burly of immediate demands and sudden events can overwhelm long-term goals and sharply reduce their influence over the daily decisions of households, businesses, and governments. Wellbeing assessments can offset this danger (to some extent at least) by providing a mechanism to link the practical realities of the present to people's vision of a desirable future.

Sustainable development is fraught with uncertainty. What is a desirable human condition? What makes a resilient and supportive ecosystem? What combinations of human and ecosystem wellbeing would be equitable and durable? Regular wellbeing assessments provide a means of learning from experience, testing the assumptions behind policies and programs, analyzing their impacts, and providing the information needed to do better.

Information and Communication on Human and Ecosystem Wellbeing

Most countries suffer from a glut of data but a dearth of understanding of human and environmental conditions and interactions. Tsunamis of facts, suppositions, opinions, and beliefs swamp the flow of useful information for decision making. Technologies to disseminate data have outstripped the capacities of societies to assemble and analyze the wide range of information needed to combine high levels of human and ecosystem wellbeing.

These capacities are often fragmented between a statistical agency and many usually tiny and underresourced departmental units responsible for monitoring and reporting on the economy, individual sectors, and international agreements. Such fragmentation has three consequences. First, data on the same topic may be gathered by more than one organization, using different methods and measurements and yielding incompatible results. Second, data are hard to find and are sometimes lost. Third, information is used inefficiently—assembled and analyzed for a particular purpose (say, for an impact assessment), then forgotten or poorly stored, then reassembled and reanalyzed for some other purpose (such as reporting on a treaty).

Lack of data prevented *The Wellbeing of Nations* from covering culture, the seas, and several subelements (state of knowledge, crop diversity, and consumption of materials). Other elements were limited to a small minority of countries or were marred by inferior indicators and inconsistent and unreliable data. Table 4.17 summarizes an informal evaluation of the quality of data on 30 elements and subelements, based on how well the data represented the element (or subelement) concerned, their reliability, and the number of countries for which the data were available. Only 9 of these elements and subelements had adequate data (good or fair rating); for 16, the data were poor or bad.

Environmental information lags well behind data on human conditions. While figures are regularly compiled on many aspects of health, education, and the economy, no one produces equivalent statistics on the status of ecosystems, species, or populations. Adequate environmental monitoring is difficult and expensive but would be far advanced if half the labor and money spent on ad hoc reports, one-time surveys, university theses, and conservation publicity were spent on systematic classification, mapping, and assessment of major ecosystems and groups of species and populations. Publicly and privately funded environmental projects and impact assessments could also contribute substantially to building a wellbeing information system in the countries concerned by standardizing and sharing their data and analyses.

Each country needs an information system on human and ecosystem wellbeing to ensure that essential data for decision making, education, and communication are collected, stored, analyzed, and shared efficiently. The system would turn existing information units into a network, fill the main information gaps, and organize data to facilitate assessments.

Table 4.17. Informal evaluation of the quality of data on human and ecosystem elements and subelements reviewed for *The Wellbeing of Nations*. Elements are in CAPITALS; subelements are in lowercase. *Elements and subelements dropped for lack of data are listed in italics.*

Rating	Human Wellbeing Number and Names of ELEMENTS and Subelements	Ecosystem Wellbeing Number and Names of ELEMENTS and Subelements
Good	3: POPULATION, income and size of economy, peace	0
Fair	3: HEALTH, debt, education	3: water withdrawal, global atmosphere, energy
Medium	4: inflation and unemployment, communication, FREEDOM AND GOVERNANCE, GENDER EQUITY	1: land protection
Poor	3: needs, crime, HOUSEHOLD EQUITY	5: LAND QUALITY, inland water quality, WILD DIVERSITY, domesticated animals, RESOURCE SECTORS
Bad	2: *state of knowledge, CULTURE*	6: land modification and conversion, inland water diversity, *SEA,* local air quality, *domesticated plants, materials*
Total	15	15

At the same time, wellbeing needs to be fully and widely communicated. Television, radio, magazines, newspapers, and the Internet are the main sources of information about what is happening outside a person's immediate family, neighborhood, and workplace. What people hear and read inevitably conditions their concerns and influences political priorities. If news media reported regularly on the wellbeing of their society and fully covered all aspects of human life and the state of the environment, they would expand the set of issues that citizens and their governments feel compelled to address.

Sustainable Wealth

Practical action hinges on wealth: how to gain enough of it for human wellbeing, how to spend it to enhance human wellbeing, and how to gain and spend it in ways that are compatible with ecosystem wellbeing. Wealth generation, resource use, and trade have the biggest impacts on human and environmental conditions, and the pace of progress toward high levels of wellbeing depends on the development of sustainable forms of these activities. One imperative is to equip the poorest societies to support themselves and obtain greater wealth from their local ecosystem in ways that restore the ecosystem's productivity and diversity. Another is for wealthier societies both to consume less and to pay more of the costs of consumption. Key steps:

- Take full account of the environmental and social costs of energy and resource production. Encourage the production methods that cost least and discourage those that cost most, if necessary by subsidizing the former and taxing (or removing subsidies from) the latter. Apply similar incentives to adopt technologies that increase the productivity of energy and materials. Many examples are brilliantly described in the book *Factor Four: Doubling Wealth, Halving Resource Use.*[11]

- Replace value-added (goods and services) taxes, sales taxes, and possibly income taxes with taxes on energy and raw materials. This step would increase the amount of value obtained from resources, raise economic efficiency, reduce consumption dependency, and reward enterprises that produce the greatest benefit for the least amount of damage to the environment. (Value-added taxes do the opposite—penalizing timber companies, for instance, for increasing the income from a log rather than rewarding them for using less wood.) Energy and raw materials taxes would be cheaper to collect than other taxes, and as long as the other taxes were cut by the same amount would not increase the total tax burden.

- Incorporate wellbeing assessments and conservation programs in resource production (food and agriculture, timber and forests, water and hydropower, energy and transport) strategies. This would provide resource sectors with a mechanism for increasing or maintaining the socioeconomic benefits of their activities while reducing their environmental costs.

- Protect ecologically sound products and practices from competition by ecologically damaging ones. Countries have the right and duty to ensure that their resources and environment are used sustainably and to protect responsible traders from being undercut by competitors whose prices do not include the full costs of production. This would be easier to achieve (and would not constitute a restraint of trade) by adopting energy and materials taxes and applying them equally to domestically produced goods and services and to imports.

- Provide consumers with simply expressed and quickly grasped statements of the social and environmental impacts of products and services so that they can make informed choices.

Wellbeing Areas (Slow Zones)

Nature reserves and other strictly protected areas are unlikely to cover more than a small proportion of each country—too small to secure its wild diversity. Moreover, they are not designed to maintain domesticated diversity or mixed built–cultivated–wild landscapes that express long-lived but vulnerable marriages between a society and its ecosystem. Wellbeing areas are proposed to fill this gap. They would be dedicated to maintaining cultural and biological diversity, including wildlife habitats; food production methods that respect land and water and maintain local crop varieties and livestock breeds; cities, towns, and villages that provide decent and attractive living spaces and maintain architectural heritage; and transport systems that ease the movement of people and goods without bludgeoning the landscape or clogging towns with noise and pollutants.

Wellbeing areas would be protected landscapes, with an emphasis on maintaining genetic as well as landscape diversity, urban as well as rural heritage, and practices that express the bond between a society and its ecosystem (such as local cuisines and sustainable use of local resources). I call them Slow Zones after the Italian concepts of Slow Cities (towns that provide a quality of life in harmony with their environment) and Slow Food (food produced, cooked, and eaten with respect for nature and culture, in opposition to fast food). Each would be managed by the residents of the area, in ways that reflect its particular social and environmental context, within a common framework of standards.

Wellbeing Alliances and Partnerships

In almost all regions, countries differ in size, population, cultures, environments, and human and ecosystem conditions. These differences bring their own sets of advantages and disadvantages. For example, Singapore has the highest human wellbeing in Southeast Asia but, being small and crowded, will find it harder than, say, Indonesia to improve its low ecosystem wellbeing. Groups of nations could pool their wellbeing by forming regional sustainable development blocs, possibly based on existing economic and political alliances, such as the Association of Southeast-Asian Nations, the Economic Community of West African States, the European Union, Mercosur (the common market of southern South America), and the North American Free Trade Agreement.

Countries with relatively diverse ecosystems could serve as reservoirs of diversity for countries whose environments are already heavily altered. In return, countries with stronger human development could assist in raising their environmental partners' standard of living.

Similarly, the practice of twinning municipalities could be expanded to twinning wealthy ecosystem deficit states or provinces with poor human deficit states or provinces (or even countries), exchanging development support for ecosystem capacity. This would supplement, not replace, good faith efforts by the well off to reduce ecosystem stress and by the disadvantaged to improve human conditions.

Regional groups of countries could also help each other by harmonizing their efforts to achieve sustainability. They could share information and expertise, adopt common legislation and incentive programs, and avoid any unfair competition that might arise if some countries act more slowly than others.

Wealthy countries have won much of their high human wellbeing at the cost of stress on the environments of other countries (via trade) or on the global ecosystem (notably impacts on the global atmosphere). Since they leave such a large ecological footprint, they should help to look after the places where they tread.

High human deficit and high and extreme double deficit countries will need a lot of help, including:

- Removal of tariffs on any goods they produce sustainably.
- Debt relief.
- Increased assistance with social and economic development and environmental protection.

This support should be extended to countries that commit themselves to improving human wellbeing (especially health, education, water and sanitation, equity, and democratic institutions) and ecosystem wellbeing. Attaching conditions to aid may be politically incorrect, but donors do it all the time, and it is necessary to ensure that the support gets results.

Several of these actions are on every do-gooder's wish list. Little is done about them because the constituencies that demand them are small and badly organized. This amplifies the importance of wellbeing assessments, for by engaging people in evaluations of their own conditions and prospects they can help to build constituencies for a high quality of life and a diverse and healthy environment. When we know what's going on, we can do something about it.

Notes

1. High double deficit countries have an average WI of 39.3 where the state of the environment is worse, 36.6 where human conditions are worse.
2. Energy consumption is a fairly reliable guide to resource consumption in general. The correlation between energy consumption per person and the more comprehensive Ecological Footprint (pages 65–66 and Table 9 in the Data section) is high: 0.922.
3. Species per hectare was calculated on the basis of the esti-
mated total number of species of higher plants (angiosperms, gymnosperms, and pteridophytes), mammals, breeding birds, reptiles, and amphibians, and the total surface area (land and inland waters) of the country.
4. Boltvinik & Hernández Laos (1999).
5. Mexico has 0.50 people and 0.14 species per hectare.
6. Comité Permanent Inter-Etats de Lutte Contre la Sécheresse au Sahel (CILSS).
7. Freedom House (2000a, 2000b).
8. Percentages of threatened species are lower than those reported in Organisation for Economic Co-operation and Development (1999) and elsewhere (e.g., Eurostat 1997) because national reports are not consistent with each other or with the international standards of IUCN-The World Conservation Union. Some count subspecies as species, and most include species that are nationally threatened regardless of their global status, whereas IUCN counts only full species that are globally at risk.
9. Armenia's EWI would then be the same as Georgia's, except that Georgia's ODS use and local air quality were not assessed either. If they, too, are the same as Turkey's, Georgia's EWI would be 34.
10. The estimated 66% natural is close to the 69% of ecologically similar Canada. But only 51% of Canada's native forest is estimated to be undisturbed (UNECE & FAO 2000).
11. Weizsäcker, Lovins, & Lovins (1997).

Data Tables

The following tables contain the data and scores for the indicators and indices used in *The Wellbeing of Nations:*

Countries are in alphabetical order within continental groups (the Russian Federation is treated as a continent). The sequence of groups is roughly west to east: Americas, Africa, Europe, Russian Federation, Asia, Pacific. Notes at the end of each table explain the data, performance criteria and combining procedures, and give sources.

-- = no data

Table 1. Human Wellbeing Index

Country	Health & pop	Wealth	Know-ledge	Com-munity	Equity	HWI + equity	HWI - equity	Equity diff	HWI	HDI	HDI score	HDI diff
AMERICAS												
Antigua & Barbuda	67	68	51	50	11	49	59	-10	49	0.833	83	34
Argentina	60	47	67	55	46	55	57	-2	55	0.837	84	29
Bahamas	50	58	71	54	39	54	58	-4	54	0.844	84	30
Barbados	64	60	72	68	48	62	66	-4	62	0.858	86	24
Belize	39	32	65	74	40	50	52	-2	50	0.777	78	28
Bolivia	30	22	48	37	43	36	34	2	34	0.643	64	30
Brazil	50	42	57	50	26	45	50	-5	45	0.747	75	30
Canada	86	77	95	72	62	78	82	-4	78	0.935	93	16
Chile	70	55	62	60	30	55	62	-7	55	0.826	83	28
Colombia	58	46	48	25	36	43	44	-1	43	0.764	76	33
Costa Rica	55	49	61	74	40	56	60	-4	56	0.797	80	24
Cuba	78	35	44	2	51	42	40	2	40	0.783	78	38
Dominica	81	43	58	80	19	56	65	-9	56	0.793	79	23
Dominican R	57	42	47	65	35	49	53	-4	49	0.729	73	24
Ecuador	50	28	50	46	43	43	43	0	43	0.722	72	29
El Salvador	48	42	43	12	42	37	36	1	36	0.696	70	34
Grenada	38	50	53	79	53	55	55	0	55	0.785	78	23
Guatemala	23	30	28	11	35	25	23	2	23	0.619	62	39
Guyana	52	34	43	74	53	51	51	0	51	0.709	71	20
Haiti	26	16	8	28	51	26	19	7	19	0.440	44	25
Honduras	31	27	32	45	29	33	34	-1	33	0.653	65	32
Jamaica	70	39	49	57	53	54	54	0	54	0.735	73	19
Mexico	58	47	59	23	37	45	47	-2	45	0.784	78	33
Nicaragua	29	26	33	24	38	30	28	2	28	0.631	63	35
Panama	60	42	54	70	32	52	56	-4	52	0.776	78	26
Paraguay	31	34	43	40	25	35	37	-2	35	0.736	74	39
Peru	51	35	59	36	40	44	45	-1	44	0.737	74	30
St Kitts & Nevis	55	63	56	61	27	52	59	-7	52	0.798	80	28
St Lucia	64	48	44	80	30	53	59	-6	53	0.728	73	20
St Vincent & Grenadines	70	42	47	37	10	41	49	-8	41	0.738	74	33
Suriname	57	42	58	59	46	52	54	-2	52	0.766	77	25
Trinidad & Tobago	62	42	50	70	43	53	56	-3	53	0.793	79	26
United States	82	84	94	58	49	73	79	-6	73	0.929	93	20
Uruguay	70	52	66	66	53	61	63	-2	61	0.825	82	22
Venezuela	53	34	49	43	34	43	45	-2	43	0.770	77	34
AFRICA												
Algeria	36	39	43	0	41	32	29	3	29	0.683	68	39
Angola	10	13	6	4	56	18	8	10	8	0.405	40	33
Benin	16	13	13	65	36	29	27	2	27	0.411	41	14
Botswana	11	42	38	45	51	37	34	3	34	0.593	59	25
Burkina Faso	11	11	4	42	37	21	17	4	17	0.303	30	13
Burundi	13	7	4	0	49	15	6	9	6	0.321	32	26
Cameroon	19	15	14	13	38	20	15	5	15	0.528	53	38
Cape Verde	39	27	49	74	51	48	47	1	47	0.688	69	22
Central African R	16	10	7	30	17	16	16	0	16	0.371	37	21
Chad	14	11	5	22	28	16	13	3	13	0.367	37	24
Comoros	24	13	8	37	46	26	20	6	20	0.510	51	31
Congo, DR	12	6	11	0	47	15	7	8	7	0.430	43	36
Congo, R	14	9	29	9	39	20	15	5	15	0.507	51	36
Côte d'Ivoire	21	14	19	27	40	24	20	4	20	0.420	42	22
Djibouti	18	21	4	30	16	18	18	0	18	0.447	45	27
Egypt	45	37	49	25	50	41	39	2	39	0.623	62	23
Equatorial Guinea	17	18	18	6	29	18	15	3	15	0.555	55	41
Eritrea	16	19	7	0	39	16	10	6	10	0.408	41	31
Ethiopia	13	5	5	30	38	18	13	5	13	0.309	31	18
Gabon	18	37	20	37	44	31	28	3	28	0.592	59	31
Gambia	19	16	13	18	33	20	16	4	16	0.396	40	24
Ghana	20	18	5	46	48	27	22	5	22	0.556	56	34
Guinea	18	15	6	23	41	21	15	6	15	0.394	39	24
Guinea-Bissau	16	7	11	20	18	14	13	1	13	0.331	33	20
Kenya	20	15	14	22	38	22	18	4	18	0.508	51	33
Lesotho	17	19	19	40	35	26	24	2	24	0.569	57	33
Liberia	13	7	0	18	--	9	9	0	9	--	--	--
Libyan Arab J	36	58	54	3	58	42	38	4	38	0.760	76	38
Madagascar	17	9	10	59	43	28	24	4	24	0.483	48	24
Malawi	7	6	25	50	42	26	22	4	22	0.385	38	16

150

Country	Health & pop	Wealth	Know-ledge	Com-munity	Equity	HWI + equity	HWI - equity	Equity diff	HWI	HDI	HDI score	HDI diff
Mali	11	6	6	62	35	24	21	3	21	0.380	38	17
Mauritania	18	13	15	24	39	22	17	5	17	0.451	45	28
Mauritius	57	54	43	72	46	54	56	-2	54	0.761	76	22
Morocco	50	30	32	33	38	37	36	1	36	0.589	59	23
Mozambique	13	8	5	17	50	19	11	8	11	0.341	34	23
Namibia	15	41	40	40	49	37	34	3	34	0.632	63	29
Niger	7	7	2	30	25	14	11	3	11	0.293	29	18
Nigeria	19	12	15	17	30	19	16	3	16	0.439	44	28
Rwanda	12	12	14	12	57	21	12	9	12	0.382	38	26
São Tomé & Principe	13	12	7	9	18	12	10	2	10	0.547	55	45
Senegal	18	22	12	30	41	25	20	5	20	0.416	42	22
Seychelles	50	49	50	53	47	50	50	0	50	0.786	79	29
Sierra Leone	2	3	7	12	36	12	6	6	6	0.252	25	19
Somalia	6	7	0	0	--	3	3	0	3	--	--	--
South Africa	21	52	70	33	39	43	44	-1	43	0.697	70	27
Sudan	25	13	10	4	45	19	13	6	13	0.477	48	35
Swaziland	19	36	36	6	30	25	24	1	24	0.655	65	41
Tanzania	16	10	6	39	48	24	18	6	18	0.415	41	24
Togo	14	16	28	27	25	22	21	1	21	0.471	47	26
Tunisia	55	43	50	29	45	44	44	0	44	0.703	70	26
Uganda	8	12	7	14	47	18	10	8	10	0.409	41	31
Zambia	8	8	15	35	35	20	16	4	16	0.420	42	26
Zimbabwe	12	24	31	25	34	25	23	2	23	0.555	55	33
EUROPE												
Albania	52	39	45	18	40	39	38	1	38	0.713	71	33
Austria	85	79	91	81	66	80	84	-4	80	0.908	91	11
Belarus	55	43	64	22	67	50	46	4	46	0.781	78	32
Belgium	85	74	90	78	71	80	82	-2	80	0.925	92	13
Bosnia & Herzegovina	64	15	16	0	57	30	24	6	24	--	--	--
Bulgaria	62	45	70	57	56	58	58	0	58	0.772	77	19
Croatia	72	47	71	39	69	60	57	3	57	0.795	79	23
Czech R	76	61	76	70	69	70	71	-1	70	0.843	84	14
Denmark	81	83	89	74	76	81	82	-1	81	0.911	91	10
Estonia	58	50	81	62	60	62	63	-1	62	0.801	80	18
Finland	83	80	93	70	77	81	81	0	81	0.917	92	11
France	88	75	86	69	58	75	79	-4	75	0.917	92	17
Germany	83	76	85	75	64	77	80	-3	77	0.911	91	14
Greece	87	66	79	63	54	70	74	-4	70	0.875	87	18
Hungary	61	58	75	69	61	65	66	-1	65	0.817	82	17
Iceland	82	84	86	80*	70	80	83	-3	80	0.927	93	13
Ireland	81	78	85	80	55	76	81	-5	76	0.907	91	15
Italy	87	71	84	69	60	74	78	-4	74	0.903	90	16
Latvia	56	57	68	67	60	62	62	0	62	0.771	77	15
Lithuania	60	57	67	70	53	61	63	-2	61	0.789	79	18
Luxembourg	84	89	80*	78	55	77	83	-6	77	0.908	91	14
Macedonia, FYR	59	28	48	50	50	47	46	1	46	0.763	76	30
Malta	83	68	73	80	45	70	76	-6	70	0.865	86	16
Moldova	55	24	52	34	53	44	41	3	41	0.700	70	29
Netherlands	86	82	92	67	65	78	82	-4	78	0.925	92	15
Norway	85	83	91	77	73	82	84	-2	82	0.934	93	11
Poland	69	56	72	70	56	65	67	-2	65	0.814	81	16
Portugal	81	72	79	71	56	72	76	-4	72	0.864	86	14
Romania	57	32	55	56	63	53	50	3	50	0.770	77	27
Slovakia	70	45	69	61	69	63	61	2	61	0.825	82	22
Slovenia	78	68	81	71	59	71	74	-3	71	0.861	86	15
Spain	87	71	86	60	59	73	76	-3	73	0.899	90	17
Sweden	88	78	92	60	78	79	79	0	79	0.926	93	14
Switzerland	87	81	82	85	53	78	84	-6	78	0.915	91	13
Ukraine	58	31	62	38	54	49	47	2	47	0.744	74	27
United Kingdom	85	80	90	52	59	73	77	-4	73	0.918	92	19
Yugoslavia	69	27	56	18	44	43	42	1	42	--	--	--
RUSSIAN FEDERATION	54	48	67	26	43	48	49	-1	48	0.771	77	29
ASIA												
Afghanistan	9	6	8	3	14	8	6	2	6	--	--	--
Armenia	71	41	40	31	42	45	46	-1	45	0.721	72	27
Azerbaijan	59	43	46	21	52	44	42	2	42	0.722	72	30
Bahrain	58	60	70	12	29	46	50	-4	46	0.820	82	36
Bangladesh	35	24	15	36	44	31	27	4	27	0.461	46	19

Country	Health & pop	Wealth	Know-ledge	Com-munity	Equity	HWI + equity	HWI - equity	Equity diff	HWI	HDI	HDI score	HDI diff
Bhutan	18	24	2	11	40	19	14	5	14	0.483	48	34
Brunei Darussalam	58	68	44	17	47	47	47	0	47	0.848	85	38
Cambodia	26	13	23	20	47	26	20	6	20	0.512	51	31
China	56	34	40	13	50	39	36	3	36	0.706	71	35
Cyprus	82	74	69	69	41	67	73	-6	67	0.886	89	22
Georgia	69	35	53	35	61	51	48	3	48	0.762	76	28
India	39	21	26	39	44	34	31	3	31	0.563	56	25
Indonesia	51	20	42	31	48	38	36	2	36	0.670	67	31
Iran	53	42	49	19	29	38	41	-3	38	0.709	71	33
Iraq	19	32	25	1	22	20	19	1	19	0.583	58	39
Israel	60	62	81	43	51	59	61	-2	59	0.883	88	29
Japan	91	79	93	76	60	80	85	-5	80	0.924	92	12
Jordan	24	34	52	42	43	39	38	1	38	0.721	72	34
Kazakhstan	45	48	54	25	50	44	43	1	43	0.754	75	32
Korea, DPR	38	29	16	0	40	25	21	4	21	--	--	--
Korea, R	64	67	93	63	49	67	72	-5	67	0.854	85	18
Kuwait	55	78	52	37	27	50	55	-5	50	0.836	84	34
Kyrgyzstan	44	33	47	28	52	41	38	3	38	0.706	71	33
Lao PDR	16	14	18	14	59	24	15	9	15	0.484	48	33
Lebanon	53	29	59	19	40	40	40	0	40	0.735	73	33
Malaysia	48	54	59	33	38	46	48	-2	46	0.772	77	31
Maldives	19	31	13	24	42	26	22	4	22	0.727	73	51
Mongolia	40	18	39	60	47	41	39	2	39	0.628	63	24
Myanmar	37	13	34	0	62	29	21	8	21	0.585	58	37
Nepal	29	16	21	46	43	31	28	3	28	0.474	47	19
Oman	16	55	36	18	46	34	31	3	31	0.730	73	42
Pakistan	21	20	13	17	47	24	18	6	18	0.522	52	34
Philippines	39	35	57	46	48	45	44	1	44	0.744	74	30
Qatar	38	71	59	20	13	40	47	-7	40	0.819	82	42
Saudi Arabia	16	67	38	3	36	32	31	1	31	0.747	75	44
Singapore	81	81	79	44	46	66	71	-5	66	0.881	88	22
Sri Lanka	58	28	37	39	49	42	40	2	40	0.733	73	33
Syrian Arab R	34	28	44	7	34	29	28	1	28	0.660	66	38
Tajikistan	33	19	49	12	30	29	28	1	28	0.663	66	38
Thailand	52	44	47	57	51	50	50	0	50	0.745	74	24
Turkey	58	31	57	37	41	45	46	-1	45	0.732	73	28
Turkmenistan	39	28	56	4	55	36	32	4	32	0.704	70	38
United Arab Emirates	43	73	60	21	8	41	49	-8	41	0.810	81	40
Uzbekistan	43	31	57	13	52	39	36	3	36	0.686	69	33
Viet Nam	48	16	37	11	67	36	28	8	28	0.671	67	39
Yemen	5	13	17	24	29	18	15	3	15	0.448	45	30
PACIFIC												
Australia	88	80	95	70	62	79	83	-4	79	0.929	93	14
Fiji	51	45	49	56	47	50	50	0	50	0.769	77	27
New Zealand	80	77	85	80	42	73	80	-7	73	0.903	90	17
Papua New Guinea	26	22	19	22	32	24	22	2	22	0.542	54	32
Samoa	28	34	43	69	40	43	43	0	43	0.711	71	28
Solomon Is	24	34	10	80	44	38	37	1	37	0.614	61	24
Tonga	33	49	2	48	0	26	33	-7	26	--	--	--
Vanuatu	30	30	21	65	29	35	36	-1	35	0.623	62	27

Notes

The Human Wellbeing Index (**HWI**) is the lower of the HWI including equity (HWI + equity) and the HWI excluding equity (HWI – equity). The former is the unweighted average of indices of health and population, wealth, knowledge, community, and equity. The latter is the unweighted average of indices of health and population, wealth, knowledge, and community. Taking the lower version of the HWI prevents equity from offsetting poor performance in the other human dimensions.

    Health & pop = health and population index (Table 2).

    Wealth = wealth index (Table 3).

    Knowledge = knowledge index (Table 5).

    Community = community index (Table 6).

    Equity = equity index (Table 8).

    HWI + equity = HWI including equity.

    HWI - equity = HWI excluding equity.

    Equity diff = equity difference = difference in points between the HWI excluding equity and the HWI including equity (minus means that inclusion of equity lowers the HWI).

    HDI = Human Development Index for 1998 (United Nations Development Programme 2000).

    HDI score = HDI score obtained by placing the HDI directly on the Barometer scale (multiplying the HDI by 100 and rounding to the nearest whole number).

    HDI diff = difference between the HDI score and the HWI.

    Correlations between the HWI, its main components (dimensions and elements) and income are shown in Table 1a.

	HWI	income	health	pop	Health & pop	h'hold wealth	national wealth	Wealth	Know-ledge	freedom & gov	peace & order	Com-munity	Equity
HWI	1												
income	**0.824**	1											
health	**0.902**	*0.749*	1										
population	**0.851**	0.598	**0.827**	1									
Health & population	**0.925**	*0.740*	**0.940**	**0.927**	1								
household wealth	**0.895**	**0.880**	**0.851**	*0.712*	**0.815**	1							
national wealth	**0.871**	**0.901**	**0.811**	*0.684*	*0.782*	**0.895**	1						
Wealth	**0.903**	**0.914**	**0.852**	*0.712*	**0.816**	**0.977**	**0.968**	1					
Knowledge	**0.948**	*0.795*	**0.868**	**0.816**	**0.879**	**0.871**	**0.835**	**0.874**	1				
freedom & governance	*0.740*	0.571	0.545	0.507	0.583	0.585	0.565	0.583	0.593	1			
peace & order	0.560	0.366	0.405	0.433	0.450	0.388	0.390	0.395	0.444	0.471	1		
Community	*0.782*	0.556	0.577	0.554	*0.613*	0.590	0.573	0.589	*0.609*	**0.908**	*0.705*	1	
Equity	0.531	0.358	0.412	0.528	0.495	0.324	0.364	0.345	0.508	0.315	0.325	0.363	1

Table 1a. Correlations between the HWI, human dimensions and elements, and income (GDP per person). Correlations of 0.8 and above are shown in **bold**; those between 0.6 and 0.8 are shown in *italic*.

* A score with an asterisk has been reduced in accordance with the insufficient data rule. To prevent high scores resulting merely from lack of data, a good score is allowed only if it is based on all applicable components (data in an indicator, indicators in an index), and a fair score only if it is based on at least half the components. Good and fair scores (100-61) based on fewer than half the applicable components have been reduced to 60. Good scores (100-81) based on more than half but not all the applicable components have been reduced to 80.

Table 2. Health and Population

Country	Pop. (000s)	Child mort./k	Disabled % LE F	M	ave.	Female LE	yrsdis	HLE	Male LE	yrsdis	HLE	Average LE	yrsdis	HLE	H score	TFR	P score	H&P index
AMERICAS																		
Antigua & Barbuda	68	c 20	11.1	11.2	11.1	76.8	8.5	68.3	71.4	8.0	63.4	74.10	8.25	65.85	67	1.7	90	67
Argentina	37032	25	10.6	9.6	10.1	77.8	8.2	69.6	70.6	6.8	63.8	74.20	7.50	66.70	71	2.6	60	60
Bahamas	307	18	16.3	15.4	15.9	73.6	12.0	61.6	67.0	10.3	56.7	70.30	11.15	59.15	50	2.6	60	50
Barbados	270	14	13.1	14.2	13.6	77.8	10.2	67.6	72.7	10.3	62.4	75.25	10.25	65.00	64	1.5	94	64
Belize	241	37	15.5	15.9	15.7	74.9	11.6	63.3	69.6	11.1	58.5	72.25	11.35	60.90	54	3.5	39	39
Bolivia	8329	88	13.1	13.6	13.3	62.2	8.1	54.1	60.8	8.3	52.5	61.50	8.20	53.30	39	4.2	30	30
Brazil	170115	48	12.3	13.3	12.8	71.7	8.8	62.9	63.7	8.5	55.2	67.70	8.65	59.05	50	2.2	80	50
Canada	31147	7	9.6	8.1	8.9	81.8	7.8	74.0	76.2	6.2	70.0	79.00	7.00	72.00	86	1.6	92	86
Chile	15211	15	10.8	10.1	10.4	79.9	8.6	71.3	73.4	7.4	66.0	76.65	8.00	68.65	79	2.4	70	70
Colombia	42321	39	11.6	11.5	11.5	74.1	8.6	65.5	68.1	7.8	60.3	71.10	8.20	62.90	58	2.7	58	58
Costa Rica	4023	15	13.7	12.1	12.9	78.9	10.8	68.1	74.2	9.0	65.2	76.55	9.90	66.65	71	2.8	55	55
Cuba	11201	12	10.3	8.4	9.4	77.4	8.0	69.4	73.6	6.2	67.4	75.50	7.10	68.40	78	1.6	92	78
Dominica	71	c 20	10.0	9.2	9.6	80.3	8.0	72.3	74.0	6.8	67.2	77.15	7.40	69.75	81	1.9	86	81
Dominican R	8495	46	13.6	12.9	13.3	72.8	9.9	62.9	71.3	9.2	62.1	72.05	9.55	62.50	57	2.7	58	57
Ecuador	12646	60	11.6	11.1	11.4	70.3	8.2	62.1	67.4	7.5	59.9	68.85	7.85	61.00	54	3.0	50	50
El Salvador	6276	41	11.6	12.4	12.0	73.0	8.5	64.5	66.9	8.3	58.6	69.95	8.40	61.55	55	3.1	48	48
Grenada	94	c 28	9.7	9.7	9.7	75.9	7.4	68.5	69.1	6.7	62.4	72.50	7.05	65.45	66	3.6	38	38
Guatemala	11385	61	12.8	13.4	13.1	64.7	8.3	56.4	60.2	8.1	52.1	62.45	8.20	54.25	40	4.8	23	23
Guyana	861	78	12.3	12.9	12.6	72.2	8.9	63.3	65.5	8.4	57.1	68.85	8.65	60.20	52	2.3	75	52
Haiti	8222	105	17.8	16.2	17.0	55.0	9.8	45.2	50.6	8.2	42.4	52.80	9.00	43.80	26	4.3	29	26
Honduras	6485	49	12.0	12.0	12.0	70.8	8.5	62.3	68.2	8.2	60.0	69.50	8.35	61.15	54	4.1	31	31
Jamaica	2583	27	12.3	11.2	11.7	77.4	9.5	67.9	75.2	8.4	66.8	76.30	8.95	67.35	73	2.4	70	70
Mexico	98881	38	12.4	12.2	12.3	77.2	9.6	67.6	71.0	8.6	62.4	74.10	9.10	65.00	64	2.7	58	58
Nicaragua	5074	58	13.0	13.0	12.9	68.8	8.9	59.9	64.8	8.4	56.4	66.80	8.65	58.15	48	4.3	29	29
Panama	2856	28	11.4	10.7	11.0	75.8	8.6	67.2	72.7	7.8	64.9	74.25	8.20	66.05	68	2.6	60	60
Paraguay	5496	48	11.8	12.9	12.3	74.1	8.8	65.3	69.6	8.9	60.7	71.85	8.85	63.00	58	4.1	31	31
Peru	25662	65	11.9	11.6	11.7	69.0	8.2	60.8	65.6	7.6	58.0	67.30	7.90	59.40	51	2.9	53	51
St Kitts & Nevis	38	c 37	9.5	9.7	9.6	71.2	6.8	64.4	65.0	6.3	58.7	68.10	6.55	61.55	55	2.4	70	55
St Lucia	154	c 21	9.8	9.4	9.6	74.9	7.3	67.6	68.9	6.5	62.4	71.90	6.90	65.00	64	2.3	75	64
St Vincent & Grenadines	114	c 23	9.8	9.5	9.7	75.2	7.4	67.8	71.8	6.8	65.0	73.50	7.10	66.40	70	1.9	86	70
Suriname	417	33	11.3	11.6	11.4	73.5	8.3	65.2	68.1	7.9	60.2	70.80	8.10	62.70	57	2.2	80	57
Trinidad & Tobago	1295	16	9.5	8.5	9.1	73.4	7.0	66.4	68.7	5.9	62.8	71.05	6.45	64.60	62	1.6	92	62
United States	278357	9	8.8	8.6	8.7	79.6	7.0	72.6	73.8	6.3	67.5	76.70	6.65	70.05	82	2.0	84	82
Uruguay	3337	20	10.2	9.1	9.6	77.8	7.9	69.9	70.5	6.4	64.1	74.15	7.15	67.00	72	2.4	70	70
Venezuela	24170	25	11.8	11.4	11.6	76.1	9.0	67.1	71.0	8.1	62.9	73.55	8.55	65.00	64	2.9	53	53
AFRICA																		
Algeria	31471	51	11.7	8.4	10.1	68.8	8.1	60.7	68.2	5.7	62.5	68.50	6.90	61.60	55	3.7	36	36
Angola	12878	208	20.7	20.0	20.4	49.1	10.2	38.9	46.3	9.3	37.0	47.70	9.75	37.95	19	6.6	10	10
Benin	6097	133	20.1	18.4	19.2	53.3	10.7	42.6	51.3	9.4	41.9	52.30	10.05	42.25	24	5.7	16	16
Botswana	1622	107	18.0	18.2	18.1	39.3	7.1	32.2	39.5	7.2	32.3	39.40	7.15	32.25	11	4.2	30	11
Burkina Faso	11937	171	21.9	19.9	20.9	45.7	10.0	35.7	44.1	8.8	35.3	44.90	9.40	35.50	15	6.4	11	11
Burundi	6695	179	21.1	19.9	20.5	43.8	9.2	34.6	43.2	8.6	34.6	43.50	8.90	34.60	14	6.1	13	13
Cameroon	15085	114	17.3	16.9	17.1	52.0	9.0	43.0	49.9	8.4	41.5	50.95	8.70	42.25	24	5.2	19	19
Cape Verde	428	64	15.5	15.0	15.3	71.8	11.2	60.6	64.2	9.6	54.6	68.00	10.40	57.60	47	3.5	39	39
Central African R	3615	157	18.7	17.7	18.3	44.9	8.4	36.5	43.3	7.7	35.6	44.10	8.05	36.05	16	4.8	23	16
Chad	7651	174	19.8	18.4	19.1	50.1	9.9	40.2	47.3	8.7	38.6	48.70	9.30	39.40	20	5.9	14	14
Comoros	694	106	18.3	17.7	18.0	58.1	10.6	47.5	56.0	9.9	46.1	57.05	10.25	46.80	30	4.7	24	24
Congo, DR	51654	139	22.1	19.3	20.7	46.5	10.3	36.2	45.1	8.7	36.4	45.80	9.50	36.30	16	6.3	12	12
Congo, R	2943	132	16.9	17.4	17.1	55.2	9.3	45.9	53.6	9.3	44.3	54.40	9.30	45.10	28	5.9	14	14
Côte d'Ivoire	14786	136	10.3	10.8	10.6	48.3	5.0	43.3	47.3	5.1	42.2	47.80	5.05	42.75	25	4.9	21	21
Djibouti	638	174	15.5	16.2	15.9	45.1	7.0	38.1	45.0	7.3	37.7	45.05	7.15	37.90	18	5.2	19	18
Egypt	68470	65	11.4	8.8	10.1	65.8	7.5	58.3	64.2	5.6	58.6	65.00	6.55	58.45	49	3.2	45	45
Equatorial Guinea	453	177	17.9	16.7	17.3	55.3	9.9	45.4	51.4	8.6	42.8	53.35	9.25	44.10	27	5.5	17	17
Eritrea	3850	146	20.6	17.5	19.1	46.5	9.6	36.9	46.7	8.2	38.5	46.60	8.90	37.70	18	5.6	16	16
Ethiopia	62565	184	22.1	19.1	20.6	43.0	9.5	33.5	41.4	7.9	33.5	42.20	8.70	33.50	13	6.2	13	13
Gabon	1226	135	14.8	14.6	14.7	57.5	8.5	49.0	54.6	8.0	46.6	56.05	8.25	47.80	32	5.3	18	18
Gambia	1305	203	16.1	15.7	15.9	58.9	9.5	49.4	56.0	8.8	47.2	57.45	9.15	48.30	32	5.1	19	19
Ghana	20212	101	17.2	16.9	17.1	55.6	9.6	46.0	54.2	9.2	45.0	54.90	9.40	45.50	29	5.0	20	20
Guinea	7430	207	21.2	19.9	20.6	48.9	10.4	38.5	46.2	9.2	37.0	47.55	9.80	37.75	18	5.4	18	18
Guinea-Bissau	1213	203	20.2	18.1	19.2	47.0	9.5	37.5	45.0	8.2	36.8	46.00	8.85	37.15	17	5.6	16	16
Kenya	30080	104	17.6	17.7	17.7	48.1	8.5	39.6	47.4	8.4	39.0	47.75	8.45	39.30	20	4.2	30	20

Country	Pop. (000s)	Child mort./k	Disabled % LE			Female			Male			Average			H score	TFR	P score	H&P index
			F	M	ave.	LE	yrsdis	HLE	LE	yrsdis	HLE	LE	yrsdis	HLE				
Lesotho	2153	130	17.7	17.0	17.4	45.2	8.0	37.2	44.1	7.5	36.6	44.65	7.75	36.90	17	4.7	24	17
Liberia	3154	174	23.8	20.4	22.2	44.9	10.7	34.2	42.5	8.7	33.8	43.70	9.70	34.00	13	6.2	13	13
Libyan Arab J	5605	32	12.1	8.2	10.2	67.0	8.1	58.9	65.0	5.3	59.7	66.00	6.70	59.30	51	3.7	36	36
Madagascar	15942	116	22.9	19.0	20.9	47.7	10.9	36.8	45.0	8.5	36.5	46.35	9.70	36.65	17	5.3	18	17
Malawi	10925	220	23.3	21.3	22.5	38.4	9.0	29.4	37.3	8.0	29.3	37.85	8.50	29.35	7	6.6	10	7
Mali	11234	236	23.8	21.0	22.5	44.0	10.5	33.5	41.3	8.7	32.6	42.65	9.60	33.05	12	6.4	11	11
Mauritania	2670	148	19.7	18.8	19.3	53.0	10.5	42.5	49.5	9.3	40.2	51.25	9.90	41.35	23	5.4	18	18
Mauritius	1158	18	10.4	11.6	10.9	74.0	7.7	66.3	66.7	7.7	59.0	70.35	7.70	62.65	57	1.9	86	57
Morocco	28351	68	11.0	9.8	10.5	66.8	7.4	59.4	65.1	6.4	58.7	65.95	6.90	59.05	50	2.9	53	50
Mozambique	19680	183	20.3	19.3	19.8	44.0	8.9	35.1	41.8	8.1	33.7	42.90	8.50	34.40	14	6.1	13	13
Namibia	1726	122	17.7	17.4	17.5	43.0	7.6	35.4	43.3	7.5	35.8	43.15	7.55	35.60	15	4.8	23	15
Niger	10730	190	25.8	24.3	25.1	40.6	10.5	30.1	37.1	9.0	28.1	38.85	9.75	29.10	7	6.7	9	7
Nigeria	111506	147	20.2	18.5	19.4	48.1	9.7	38.4	46.8	8.7	38.1	47.45	9.20	38.25	19	5.0	20	19
Rwanda	7733	202	22.6	20.3	21.5	42.3	9.6	32.7	41.3	8.4	32.9	41.80	9.00	32.80	12	6.0	14	12
São Tomé & Principe	147	c 77	15.5	16.1	15.8	64.9	10.1	54.8	62.1	10.0	52.1	63.50	10.05	53.45	39	6.1	13	13
Senegal	9481	115	18.8	18.7	18.8	56.2	10.6	45.6	53.5	10.0	43.5	54.85	10.30	44.55	27	5.4	18	18
Seychelles	77	c 18	11.9	13.0	12.4	70.5	8.4	62.1	64.8	8.4	56.4	67.65	8.40	59.25	50	2.0	84	50
Sierra Leone	4854	263	26.7	22.4	24.6	35.5	9.5	26.0	33.2	7.4	25.8	34.35	8.45	25.90	2	5.9	14	2
Somalia	10097	204	17.4	18.6	18.0	44.7	7.8	36.9	44.1	8.2	35.9	44.40	8.00	36.40	16	7.2	6	6
South Africa	40377	87	17.6	18.4	18.0	49.8	8.8	41.0	47.3	8.7	38.6	48.55	8.75	39.80	21	3.2	45	21
Sudan	29490	112	20.5	19.8	20.1	54.7	11.2	43.5	53.1	10.5	42.6	53.90	10.85	43.05	25	4.5	26	25
Swaziland	1008	100	17.9	17.5	17.7	46.8	8.4	38.4	45.8	8.0	37.8	46.30	8.20	38.10	19	4.6	25	19
Tanzania	33517	130	20.8	19.1	20.0	45.6	9.5	36.1	44.4	8.5	35.9	45.00	9.00	36.00	16	5.3	18	16
Togo	4629	129	18.6	18.2	18.4	50.8	9.4	41.4	48.9	8.9	40.0	49.85	9.15	40.70	22	5.9	14	14
Tunisia	9586	37	10.6	7.4	9.0	67.9	7.2	60.7	67.0	5.0	62.0	67.45	6.10	61.35	55	2.5	65	55
Uganda	21778	173	23.4	21.4	22.4	42.4	9.9	32.5	41.9	9.0	32.9	42.15	9.45	32.70	12	7.0	8	8
Zambia	9169	147	21.3	21.1	21.2	39.0	8.3	30.7	38.0	8.0	30.0	38.50	8.15	30.35	8	5.4	18	8
Zimbabwe	11669	117	18.9	18.4	18.7	40.0	7.6	32.4	40.9	7.5	33.4	40.45	7.55	32.90	12	3.7	36	12
EUROPE																		
Albania	3113	43	12.8	13.3	13.0	72.7	9.3	63.4	65.1	8.6	56.5	68.90	8.95	59.95	52	2.4	70	52
Austria	8211	7	7.4	7.5	7.5	80.4	6.0	74.4	74.4	5.6	68.8	77.40	5.80	71.60	85	1.4	96	85
Belarus	10236	28	9.9	9.9	9.9	74.5	7.3	67.2	62.4	6.2	56.2	68.45	6.75	61.70	55	1.4	96	55
Belgium	10161	8	8.2	7.8	8.0	81.3	6.7	74.6	74.5	5.8	68.7	77.90	6.25	71.65	85	1.6	92	85
Bosnia & Herzegovina	3972	17	11.5	11.0	11.3	75.0	8.6	66.4	71.3	7.9	63.4	73.15	8.25	64.90	64	1.4	96	64
Bulgaria	8225	20	9.4	9.3	9.4	74.8	7.1	67.7	67.5	6.3	61.2	71.15	6.70	64.45	62	1.2	100	62
Croatia	4473	12	8.6	8.7	8.6	77.2	6.6	70.6	69.3	6.0	63.3	73.25	6.30	66.95	72	1.6	92	72
Czech R	10244	8	9.5	8.8	9.2	78.3	7.5	70.8	71.5	6.3	65.2	74.90	6.90	68.00	76	1.2	100	76
Denmark	5293	9	8.4	7.9	8.1	78.1	6.6	71.5	72.9	5.7	67.2	75.50	6.15	69.35	81	1.7	90	81
Estonia	1396	25	9.5	9.8	9.7	75.3	7.2	68.1	64.4	6.3	58.1	69.85	6.75	63.10	58	1.3	98	58
Finland	5176	6	8.6	8.4	8.6	80.7	7.0	73.7	73.4	6.2	67.2	77.05	6.60	70.45	83	1.7	90	83
France	59080	8	8.0	7.5	7.8	83.6	6.7	76.9	74.9	5.6	69.3	79.25	6.15	73.10	88	1.7	90	88
Germany	82220	6	8.3	8.6	8.4	80.1	6.6	73.5	73.7	6.3	67.4	76.90	6.45	70.45	83	1.3	98	83
Greece	10645	9	7.4	6.7	7.0	80.5	5.9	74.6	75.5	5.0	70.5	78.00	5.45	72.55	87	1.3	98	87
Hungary	10036	12	9.6	9.0	9.3	75.1	7.2	67.9	66.3	5.9	60.4	70.70	6.55	64.15	61	1.3	98	61
Iceland	281	6	10.0	9.0	9.5	80.4	8.1	72.3	76.0	6.8	69.2	78.20	7.45	70.75	83	2.1	82	82
Ireland	3730	8	8.4	8.0	8.2	78.3	6.6	71.7	73.3	5.8	67.5	75.80	6.20	69.60	81	1.9	86	81
Italy	57298	8	8.2	7.1	7.7	82.1	6.7	75.4	75.4	5.4	70.0	78.75	6.05	72.70	87	1.2	100	87
Latvia	2357	25	9.9	10.2	10.1	74.6	7.4	67.2	63.6	6.5	57.1	69.10	6.95	62.15	56	1.3	98	56
Lithuania	3670	24	13.3	9.5	11.6	77.9	10.4	67.5	67.0	6.4	60.6	72.45	8.40	64.05	60	1.4	96	60
Luxembourg	431	8	8.8	8.7	8.8	81.4	7.2	74.2	74.5	6.5	68.0	77.95	6.85	71.10	84	1.7	90	84
Macedonia, FYR	2024	26	11.5	11.4	11.5	74.1	8.5	65.6	69.8	8.0	61.8	71.95	8.25	63.70	59	2.1	82	59
Malta	389	9	10.3	9.6	10.0	80.8	8.3	72.5	75.7	7.3	68.4	78.25	7.80	70.45	83	1.9	86	83
Moldova	4380	32	10.3	9.7	10.0	71.9	7.4	64.5	64.8	6.3	58.5	68.35	6.85	61.50	55	1.7	90	55
Netherlands	15786	8	8.2	7.2	7.8	81.1	6.7	74.4	75.0	5.4	69.6	78.05	6.05	72.00	86	1.5	94	86
Norway	4465	6	9.2	8.4	8.8	82.2	7.6	74.6	75.1	6.3	68.8	78.65	6.95	71.70	85	1.9	86	85
Poland	38765	16	8.5	8.2	8.4	76.6	6.5	70.1	67.9	5.6	62.3	72.25	6.05	66.20	69	1.5	94	69
Portugal	9875	11	8.6	8.4	8.5	79.5	6.8	72.7	72.0	6.1	65.9	75.75	6.45	69.30	81	1.4	96	81
Romania	22326	33	10.4	9.8	10.1	73.4	7.6	65.8	65.2	6.4	58.8	69.30	7.00	62.30	57	1.2	100	57
Slovakia	5387	13	9.1	7.8	8.5	76.7	7.0	69.7	68.9	5.4	63.5	72.80	6.20	66.60	70	1.4	96	70
Slovenia	1986	8	9.6	9.4	9.5	79.5	7.6	71.9	71.6	6.7	64.9	75.55	7.15	68.40	78	1.3	98	78
Spain	39630	8	7.7	7.3	7.6	82.1	6.4	75.7	75.3	5.5	69.8	78.70	5.95	72.75	87	1.1	100	87
Sweden	8910	6	8.5	7.7	8.1	81.9	7.0	74.9	77.1	5.9	71.2	79.50	6.45	73.05	88	1.6	92	88
Switzerland	7386	9	9.1	8.1	8.6	83.0	7.5	75.5	75.6	6.1	69.5	79.30	6.80	72.50	87	1.5	94	87
Ukraine	50456	25	9.3	9.1	9.2	74.4	6.9	67.5	64.3	5.8	58.5	69.35	6.35	63.00	58	1.4	96	58
United Kingdom	58830	8	7.5	6.7	7.1	79.7	6.0	73.7	74.7	5.0	69.7	77.20	5.50	71.70	85	1.7	90	85
Yugoslavia	10640	26	10.8	10.6	10.7	76.3	8.2	68.1	71.8	7.6	64.2	74.05	7.90	66.15	69	1.8	88	69

Country	Pop. (000s)	Child mort./k	Disabled % LE			Female			Male			Average			H score	TFR	P score	H&P index
			F	M	ave.	LE	yrsdis	HLE	LE	yrsdis	HLE	LE	yrsdis	HLE				
RUSSIAN FEDERATION	146934	22	10.3	10.5	10.4	74.0	7.6	66.4	62.7	6.6	56.1	68.35	7.10	61.25	54	1.4	96	54
ASIA																		
Afghanistan	22720	257	17.9	18.9	18.3	47.1	8.4	38.7	45.2	8.5	36.7	46.15	8.45	37.70	18	6.7	9	9
Armenia	3520	33	11.4	10.1	10.8	77.1	8.8	68.3	72.3	7.3	65.0	74.70	8.05	66.65	71	1.7	90	71
Azerbaijan	7734	50	11.4	10.6	11.0	75.3	8.6	66.7	67.8	7.2	60.6	71.55	7.90	63.65	59	2.0	84	59
Bahrain	617	22	11.8	9.7	10.7	73.6	8.7	64.9	70.7	6.8	63.9	72.15	7.75	64.40	62	2.7	58	58
Bangladesh	129155	111	14.3	12.9	13.6	58.1	8.3	49.8	57.5	7.4	50.1	57.80	7.85	49.95	35	3.0	50	35
Bhutan	2124	96	14.2	13.8	14.0	60.9	8.7	52.2	59.6	8.2	51.4	60.25	8.45	51.80	37	5.4	18	18
Brunei Darussalam	328	11	18.0	14.6	16.4	79.7	14.3	65.4	74.3	10.9	63.4	77.00	12.60	64.40	62	2.7	58	58
Cambodia	11168	134	14.2	15.8	15.1	55.4	7.9	47.5	52.2	8.3	43.9	53.80	8.10	45.70	29	4.5	26	26
China	1284958	48	11.2	10.2	10.7	71.3	8.0	63.3	68.1	6.9	61.2	69.70	7.45	62.25	56	1.8	88	56
Cyprus	786	9	10.0	8.2	9.1	78.8	7.9	70.9	74.8	6.1	68.7	76.80	7.00	69.80	82	2.0	84	82
Georgia	4968	23	9.5	9.1	9.3	76.7	7.3	69.4	69.4	6.3	63.1	73.05	6.80	66.25	69	1.9	86	69
India	1013662	89	12.5	11.3	12.0	61.2	7.7	53.5	59.6	6.8	52.8	60.40	7.25	53.15	39	3.0	50	39
Indonesia	212107	63	12.2	11.7	11.9	69.0	8.4	60.6	66.6	7.8	58.8	67.80	8.10	59.70	51	2.5	65	51
Iran	67702	52	11.9	8.2	10.1	67.9	8.1	59.8	66.8	5.5	61.3	67.35	6.80	60.55	53	2.7	58	53
Iraq	23115	116	12.2	10.0	11.2	62.8	7.7	55.1	61.6	6.2	55.4	62.20	6.95	55.25	42	5.1	19	19
Israel	6217	10	10.4	9.3	9.9	79.9	8.3	71.6	76.3	7.1	69.2	78.10	7.70	70.40	83	2.6	60	60
Japan	126714	6	8.4	7.3	7.9	84.3	7.1	77.2	77.6	5.7	71.9	80.95	6.40	74.55	91	1.4	96	91
Jordan	6669	31	12.1	8.4	10.3	67.5	8.2	59.3	66.3	5.6	60.7	66.90	6.90	60.00	52	4.7	24	24
Kazakhstan	16223	41	12.4	12.3	12.4	69.9	8.7	61.2	58.7	7.2	51.5	64.30	7.95	56.35	45	2.2	80	45
Korea, DPR	24039	26	12.5	11.3	12.0	60.7	7.6	53.1	58.0	6.6	51.4	59.35	7.10	52.25	38	2.0	84	38
Korea, R	46844	13	10.9	9.3	10.2	76.0	8.3	67.7	68.7	6.4	62.3	72.35	7.35	65.00	64	1.7	90	64
Kuwait	1972	15	15.8	12.4	14.1	75.3	11.9	63.4	71.9	8.9	63.0	73.60	10.40	63.20	58	2.8	55	55
Kyrgyzstan	4699	50	14.3	13.3	13.9	69.0	9.9	59.1	61.6	8.2	53.4	65.30	9.05	56.25	44	3.1	48	44
Lao PDR	5433	150	16.7	16.6	16.7	56.6	9.5	47.1	54.0	9.0	45.0	55.30	9.25	46.05	29	5.6	16	16
Lebanon	3282	35	10.7	7.7	9.2	67.3	7.2	60.1	66.3	5.1	61.2	66.80	6.15	60.65	53	2.6	60	53
Malaysia	22244	15	11.9	9.4	10.6	69.9	8.3	61.6	67.6	6.3	61.3	68.75	7.30	61.45	55	3.1	48	48
Maldives	286	66	14.9	14.0	14.5	62.6	9.3	53.3	63.3	8.9	54.4	62.95	9.10	53.85	40	5.2	19	19
Mongolia	2662	73	13.1	13.0	13.1	64.8	8.5	56.3	59.0	7.7	51.3	61.90	8.10	53.80	40	2.5	65	40
Myanmar	45611	113	12.4	12.1	12.3	59.3	7.4	51.9	58.5	7.1	51.4	58.90	7.25	51.65	37	2.3	75	37
Nepal	23930	117	14.3	13.7	14.1	57.8	8.3	49.5	57.3	7.9	49.4	57.55	8.10	49.45	34	4.3	29	29
Oman	2542	30	13.1	12.2	12.7	73.8	9.7	64.1	70.4	8.6	61.8	72.10	9.15	62.95	58	5.7	16	16
Pakistan	156483	106	12.6	12.1	12.4	65.0	8.2	56.8	62.6	7.6	55.0	63.80	7.90	55.90	44	4.9	21	21
Philippines	75966	44	12.5	11.0	11.8	69.4	8.7	60.7	64.2	7.1	57.1	66.80	7.90	58.90	50	3.5	39	39
Qatar	599	23	15.8	10.3	13.1	74.6	11.8	62.8	71.6	7.4	64.2	73.10	9.60	63.50	59	3.6	38	38
Saudi Arabia	21607	27	12.0	8.2	10.1	72.7	8.7	64.0	70.9	5.8	65.1	71.80	7.25	64.55	62	5.6	16	16
Singapore	3567	6	11.8	10.2	11.1	80.8	9.6	71.2	75.1	7.7	67.4	77.95	8.65	69.30	81	1.7	90	81
Sri Lanka	18827	21	9.7	9.9	9.8	73.4	7.1	66.3	65.8	6.5	59.3	69.60	6.80	62.80	58	2.1	82	58
Syrian Arab R	16125	40	12.3	8.9	10.6	67.1	8.2	58.9	64.6	5.8	58.8	65.85	7.00	58.85	50	3.9	34	34
Tajikistan	6188	81	15.2	15.5	15.3	70.0	10.6	59.4	67.6	10.1	55.1	67.60	10.35	57.25	46	4.0	33	33
Thailand	61399	35	11.8	11.6	11.7	70.4	8.3	62.1	66.0	7.6	58.4	68.20	7.95	60.25	52	1.7	90	52
Turkey	66591	60	11.6	8.2	9.9	69.9	8.1	61.8	69.7	5.7	64.0	69.80	6.90	62.90	58	2.4	70	58
Turkmenistan	4459	77	13.2	14.9	14.0	65.3	8.6	56.7	61.0	9.1	51.9	63.15	8.85	54.30	41	3.5	39	39
United Arab Emirates	2441	19	13.0	10.0	11.6	75.6	9.8	65.8	72.3	7.3	65.0	73.95	8.55	65.40	66	3.3	43	43
Uzbekistan	24318	63	12.6	11.7	12.1	71.2	8.9	62.3	65.7	7.7	58.0	68.45	8.30	60.15	52	3.3	43	43
Viet Nam	79832	56	13.3	12.3	12.9	68.8	9.2	59.6	64.7	8.0	56.7	66.75	8.60	58.15	48	2.5	65	48
Yemen	18112	113	14.3	13.2	13.8	58.0	8.3	49.7	57.3	7.6	49.7	57.65	7.95	49.70	34	7.4	5	5
PACIFIC																		
Australia	18886	7	8.1	7.8	8.0	82.2	6.7	75.5	76.8	6.0	70.8	79.50	6.35	73.15	88	1.8	88	88
Fiji	817	23	11.7	9.8	10.8	69.2	8.1	61.1	64.0	6.3	57.7	66.60	7.20	59.40	51	2.7	58	51
New Zealand	3862	8	10.2	9.2	9.7	79.3	8.1	71.2	73.9	6.8	67.1	76.60	7.45	69.15	80	2.0	84	80
Papua New Guinea	4807	84	14.3	14.7	14.5	56.6	8.1	48.5	53.3	7.8	45.5	54.95	7.95	47.00	31	4.5	26	26
Samoa	180	27	11.9	10.2	11.1	70.7	8.4	62.3	65.4	6.7	58.7	68.05	7.55	60.50	53	4.4	28	28
Solomon Is	444	27	13.7	12.2	12.9	64.0	8.7	55.3	62.0	7.5	54.5	63.00	8.10	54.90	42	4.7	24	24
Tonga	99	c 23	11.8	10.0	10.9	72.9	8.6	64.3	68.2	6.8	61.4	70.55	7.70	62.85	58	4.0	33	33
Vanuatu	190	48	13.7	12.7	13.1	63.0	8.6	54.4	58.7	7.4	51.3	60.85	8.00	52.85	38	4.2	30	30

Notes

The health and population index (**H&P index**) is the lower of a health index (**H score**) and a population index (**P score**). The lower score was chosen to avoid a high score for population offsetting a low score for health, and vice versa.

The health index is represented by a single indicator: healthy life expectancy at birth. All data are for 1999 and are from World Health Organization (2000), except for the child mortality data. Life expectancy at birth is one of four basic indicators of health endorsed by the United Nations Statistical Commission for its "minimum national social data set" (United Nations Statistical Division 1997). (The other three are the infant mortality rate, child mortality rate, and maternal mortality rate.) *Healthy* life expectancy at birth (HLE)—or disability-adjusted life expectancy at birth (DALE)—is a better indicator of a long and healthy life but until recently was compiled in only a few countries. In 2000, the World Health Organization adopted DALE as its sole indicator of the overall health of a population, and published estimates of DALE for 191 countries (Mathers *et al.* 2000; World Health Organization 2000). Life expectancy at birth is the average number of years that a child born in a given year could expect to live. It is calculated from the death rates of specific age groups—commonly 0-1, 1-5, and then 5-year groups for ages above 5. It reflects all the causes of death (including vehicle and other travel accidents, murders and suicides), and the death rates from those causes, that a typical person would be exposed to as she or he passes through each age group. HLE/DALE is life expectancy at birth minus the number of years that the new-born child could expect to live with various degrees of disability. It incorporates the likely incidence, duration and severity of disability. Disability includes a wide range of diseases and injuries, including neuro-psychiatric disorders. As such HLE/DALE is an excellent indicator of overall health, the healthfulness of living conditions, and the availability and effectiveness of health services. Nevertheless, it is subject to large uncertainties (actual HLE may be several years higher or lower than estimated HLE). Uncertainty ranges for each country are given in Mathers *et al.* (2000) and World Health Organization (2000).

Pop 000s = population estimates for the year 2000 in thousands of persons. Data are from United Nations Population Division (1998b).

Child mort./k = child mortality rate = deaths of children under 5 years of age per 1000 live births. Data are estimates and projections for 1995-2000 by United Nations Population Division (1998b), unless marked "c" which are for 1998 and are from UNICEF (1999b). Data and performance criteria (Table 2a) are given here as background information. The top of the medium band matches the UN target set by the International Conference on Population and Development (Cairo, 1994) and the World Summit for Social Development (Copenhagen, 1995) that all countries should have a child mortality rate below 45 per 1,000 live births by 2015 (United Nations Population Division 1997; Office of the UN System Support and Services 1996).

Disabled % LE = expected percentage of lifespan lived with disability:

    F = females

    M = males

    ave = average

Female/Male/Average:

    LE = life expectancy at birth in years

    yrsdis = expectation of disability at birth in years

    HLE = healthy life expectancy (LE minus yrsdis) in years

H score = health index, the score for healthy life expectancy. The performance criteria are shown in Table 2a. They are derived from performance criteria for life expectancy at birth unadjusted for disability. The base of the scale (24 years) and the top point of the good band (79 years) encompass the current range of healthy life expectancy (from 25.8 years for males in Sierra Leone to 77.2 years for females in Japan), and are six years below the corresponding points for unadjusted life expectancy (for which the range is from 33.2 years for males in Sierra Leone to 80.9 years for females in Japan). The top points of the poor, medium and fair bands for healthy life expectancy (HLE) were set at six points below the corresponding points for unadjusted life expectancy (LE). The latter were based on United Nations targets adopted by the International Conference on Population and Development (Cairo, 1994) and the World Summit for Social Development (Copenhagen, 1995) that all countries should have life expectancies of at least 60 years by 2000, more than 70 years by 2005, and more than 75 years by 2015 (United Nations Population Division 1997; Office of the UN System Support and Services 1996). These targets defined the top points of, respectively, the poor, medium, and fair bands for LE. Performance criteria for HLE are from 7.1% to 20.0% lower than those for LE, close to the range of percentages of lifespan lost to disability (7.0% to 25.1%).

The population index is represented by a single indicator: the total fertility rate—the average number of children born alive by a woman in her lifetime—derived from age-specific fertility rates (or sometimes surveys) (United Nations 1996, United Nations Population Division 1998a).

TFR = total fertility rate. Data are for 1999 and are from World Health Organization (2000).

P score = population index, the score for the total fertility rate. The performance criteria are shown in Table 2a. The top of the fair band is a point above 2.1, which (with average sex ratios) is the replacement rate—a rate that can be sustained indefinitely without the population increasing or declining. Thus the good band is 2.1 or below. The fair band was set to less than half a child above replacement. Rates below replacement are not sustainable, but the excessively high scores they get have little effect on the health and population index because they are usually offset by lower health scores.

band	top point on scale	child deaths per 1,000 live births	life expectancy [LE] (years)	healthy life expectancy [HLE] (years)	difference between HLE & LE	total fertility rate (children/woman)
good	100	0	85	79	-7.1%	1.2
fair	80	22	75	69	-8.0%	2.2
medium	60	45	70	64	-8.6%	2.6
poor	40	90	60	54	-10.0%	3.4
bad	20	180	45	39	-13.3%	5.0
base	0	360	30	24	-20.0%	8.2

Table 2a. Performance criteria for health and population indicators.

Table 3. Wealth Index; Household Wealth

Country	Food note	Low food %	Stunt %	Under wt %	Low b wt %	Food score	Basic note	% with water	% with sanit.	Basic score	Need score	GDP/pers PPP$	Inc. score	HW score	NW score	W index
AMERICAS																
Antigua & Barbuda	--c	--	--	--	8	84	-c	--	96	92	84	9277	57	70	66	68
Argentina	hhc	1	4.7	1.9	7	91	cc	71	68	44	44	12013	64	54	41	47
Bahamas	--h	--	--	--	h 7	86	cc	94	82	64	64	14614	69	66	50	58
Barbados	hhc	--	7.0	5.9	10	86	cc	100	100	100	86	12001	64	75	46	60
Belize	-hc	--	--	6.2	4	88	cc	83	57	29	29	4566	37	33	31	32
Bolivia	hcc	23	26.8	10	5	51	cc	80	65	40	40	2269	22	31	13	22
Brazil	hhc	10	10.5	5.7	8	79	cc	76	70	47	47	6625	46	46	39	42
Canada	--c	--	--	--	6	88		--	--	--	80*	23582	84	82	72	77
Chile	hhc	5	2.4	0.9	5	90	ch	91	83	66	66	8787	55	60	51	55
Colombia	hhc	12	15.0	8.4	9	70	cc	85	85	70	70	6006	44	57	35	46
Costa Rica	-hc	7	--	2.2	7	86	cc	96	84	68	68	5987	44	56	42	49
Cuba	-cc	19	--	9	7	62	cc	93	66	41	41	3967	33	37	33	35
Dominica	--c	--	--	--	10	80	cc	96	80	60	60	5102	40	50	36	43
Dominican R	ccc	26	11	6	13	52	cc	79	85	59	52	4598	37	44	41	42
Ecuador	hhc	5	34.0	16.5	13	41	cc	68	76	44	41	3003	27	34	23	28
El Salvador	hhc	10	23.1	11.2	11	56	cc	66	90	41	41	4036	34	37	47	42
Grenada	--c	--	--	--	9	82		--	--	--	80*	5838	43	61	39	50
Guatemala	hhc	17	49.7	26.6	15	20		68	87	44	20	3505	30	25	35	30
Guyana	ccc	16	10	12	15	68		91	88	76	68	3403	29	48	21	34
Haiti	hhc	61	31.9	27.5	15	16		37	25	10	10	1383	14	12	20	16
Honduras	hhc	21	39.6	18.3	9	34		78	74	52	34	2433	23	28	27	27
Jamaica	hhc	11	9.6	10.2	10	78		86	89	72	72	3389	29	50	29	39
Mexico	hhc	6	22.8	14.2	7	56		85	72	49	49	7704	51	50	44	47
Nicaragua	chc	31	25	11.9	9	45		78	85	57	45	2142	21	33	20	26
Panama	hcc	17	9.9	7	8	66		93	83	66	66	5249	41	53	31	42
Paraguay	chc	13	17	3.7	5	66		60	41	16	16	4288	35	25	43	34
Peru	hhc	19	25.8	7.8	11	52		67	72	43	43	4282	35	39	32	35
St Kitts & Nevis	--c	--	--	--	9	82		100	100	100	82	10672	61	71	56	63
St Lucia	--c	--	--	--	8	84		85	--	70	70	5183	41	55	41	48
St Vincent & Grenadines	--c	--	--	--	8	84		89	98	78	78	4692	38	58	26	42
Suriname	--c	9	--	--	13	82	hh	72	56	28	28	5161	41	34	50	42
Trinidad & Tobago	hhc	11	4.8	6.7	10	78	ch	97	56	28	28	7485	50	39	46	42
United States	hhc	--	2.1	1.4	7	96		--	--	--	80*	29605	90	85	83	84
Uruguay	ccc	4	8	5	8	84	hh	83	82	64	64	8623	54	59	45	52
Venezuela	hhc	15	13.2	4.5	9	70		79	59	32	32	5808	43	37	32	34
AFRICA																
Algeria	hhc	5	18.3	12.8	9	63		90	91	80	63	4792	39	51	28	39
Angola	ccc	43	53	42	19	19		31	40	12	12	1821	18	15	12	13
Benin	hh-	15	25.0	29.2	--	48		56	27	11	11	867	9	10	17	13
Botswana	ccc	25	29	17	11	48		90	55	27	27	6103	44	35	49	42
Burkina Faso	cc	30	29	30	21	47		42	37	15	15	870	9	12	11	11
Burundi	ch-	63	43	37.5	--	15		52	51	21	15	570	6	10	4	7
Cameroon	ccc	32	29	22	13	44		54	89	25	25	1474	15	20	10	15
Cape Verde	ccc	--	16	14	9	68		65	27	11	11	3233	28	19	35	27
Central African R	ccc	42	34	27	15	31		38	27	11	11	1118	11	11	10	10
Chad	cch	46	40	39	h 20	25		54	27	11	11	856	9	10	13	11
Comoros	hhc	--	33.8	25.8	8	42		53	23	9	9	1398	14	11	15	13
Congo, DR	hhc	55	45.2	34.4	15	18		42	18	7	7	822	8	7	5	6
Congo, R	rural;hhc	34	27.5	23.9	16	41		34	69	14	14	995	10	12	7	9
Côte d'Ivoire	hhc	15	24.4	23.8	12	54		42	39	16	16	1598	16	16	13	14
Djibouti	ccc	--	26	18	11	52		90	55	27	27	1266	13	20	23	21
Egypt	chc	4	25	12.4	10	53		87	88	74	53	3041	27	40	34	37
Equatorial Guinea	--h	--	--	--	h 12	76		95	54	25	25	1817	18	21	15	18
Eritrea	hhc	67	38.4	43.7	13	13		22	13	5	5	833	8	6	32	19
Ethiopia	rural;hhc	51	64.2	47.7	16	14		25	19	8	8	574	6	7	4	5
Gabon	---	8	--	--	--	84	ch	67	76	43	43	6353	45	44	30	37
Gambia	cc-	25	30	26	--	47		69	37	15	15	1453	14	14	18	16
Ghana	hhc	11	25.9	27.3	8	50		65	32	13	13	1735	17	15	22	18
Guinea	c-c	31	29	--	13	45		46	31	12	12	1782	18	15	16	15
Guinea-Bissau	--c	--	--	--	20	60		43	46	17	17	616	6	11	4	7
Kenya	hhc	41	33.6	22.5	16	32		44	85	18	18	980	10	14	17	15
Lesotho	ccc	28	44	16	11	28		62	38	15	15	1626	16	15	24	19
Liberia	---	42	--	--	--	31		46	30	12	12	843	8	10	5	7
Libyan Arab J	hhc	1	15.1	4.7	7	70		97	98	94	70	6697	47	58	58	58
Madagascar	hcc	39	49.8	40	5	20		40	40	16	16	756	8	12	7	9
Malawi	hhc	37	48.3	29.9	20	22		47	3	1	1	523	5	3	10	6
Mali	hhc	29	30.1	40.0	16	33		66	6	2	2	681	7	4	8	6

158

Country	Food note	Low food %	Stunt %	Under wt %	Low b wt %	Food score	Basic note	% with water	% with sanit.	Basic score	Need score	GDP/pers PPP$	Inc. score	*HW score*	*NW score*	**W index**
Mauritania	hhc	13	44.0	23.0	11	28		37	57	15	15	1563	16	15	12	13
Mauritius	hcc	6	9.7	16	13	68		98	100	96	68	8312	53	60	49	54
Morocco	chc	5	23	9.5	9	56		65	58	31	31	3305	29	30	31	30
Mozambique	ccc	63	36	26	20	15		46	34	14	14	782	8	11	5	8
Namibia	hhc	30	28.5	26.2	16	47		83	62	36	36	5176	41	38	44	41
Niger	ccc	39	41	50	15	20		61	19	8	8	739	7	7	8	7
Nigeria	hcc	8	42.7	36	16	30		49	41	16	16	795	8	12	12	12
Rwanda	ccc	37	42	27	17	31		--	--	--	31	660	7	19	5	12
São Tomé & Principe	hhc	--	25.9	16.6	7	52		82	35	14	14	1469	15	14	10	12
Senegal	hhc	17	24.7	22.2	4	54		81	65	40	40	1307	13	26	18	22
Seychelles	chc	--	23	5.7	10	56	hh96	83	98	66	56	10600	61	58	41	49
Sierra Leone	hhc	43	34.7	28.7	11	29		34	11	4	4	458	5	4	3	3
Somalia	--c	73	--	--	16	11		31	43	12	11	712	7	9	5	7
South Africa	hh-	--	22.8	9.2	--	56		87	87	74	56	8488	54	55	49	52
Sudan	hhc	20	34.3	33.9	15	41		73	51	21	21	1394	14	17	9	13
Swaziland	hhc	14	30.3	9.7	10	46		50	59	20	20	3816	32	26	47	36
Tanzania	ccc	40	42	27	14	31		66	86	41	31	480	5	18	3	10
Togo	hhc	23	29.2	24.5	20	48		55	37	15	15	1372	14	14	18	16
Tunisia	hhc	1	22.5	9.0	8	57		98	80	60	57	5405	42	49	38	43
Uganda	hhc	28	38.3	25.5	13	36		46	57	18	18	1074	11	14	11	12
Zambia	hhc	45	42.4	23.5	13	27		38	71	15	15	719	7	11	5	8
Zimbabwe	chc	39	32	15.5	10	35		79	52	23	23	2669	24	23	26	24
EUROPE																
Albania	--c	--	--	--	7	86		--	--	--	80*	2804	25	52	26	39
Austria	--c	--	--	--	6	88		--	--	--	80*	23166	83	81	77	79
Belarus	---	--	--	--	--	--		--	--	--	--	6319	45	45	41	43
Belgium	--c	--	--	--	6	88		--	--	--	80*	23223	83	81	68	74
Bosnia & Herzegovina	---	--	--	--	--	--		--	--	--	--	# 1720	17	17	13	15
Bulgaria	--c	--	--	--	6	88		--	--	--	80*	4809	39	59	31	45
Croatia	hh-	--	0.8	0.6	--	98	hh	96	68	44	44	6749	47	45	49	47
Czech R	hhc	--	1.9	1.0	6	96		--	--	--	80*	12362	65	72	51	61
Denmark	--c	--	--	--	6	88	hh	100	100	100	88	24218	84	86	81	83
Estonia	---	--	--	--	--	--		--	--	--	--	7682	51	51	50	50
Finland	--c	--	--	--	4	92	hh	100	100	100	92	20847	81	86	74	80
France	--c	--	--	--	5	90		--	--	--	80*	21175	81	80	70	75
Germany	--h	--	--	--	h 6	88		--	--	--	80*	22169	82	81	72	76
Greece	--c	--	--	--	6	88		--	--	--	80*	13943	68	74	59	66
Hungary	hhc	--	2.9	2.2	9	94		--	--	--	80*	10232	60	70	46	58
Iceland	--h	--	--	--	h 3	94	-h	--	95	90	90	25110	85	87	82	84
Ireland	--c	--	--	--	4	92		--	--	--	80*	21482	81	80	77	78
Italy	--c	--	--	--	5	90		--	--	--	80*	20585	81	80	63	71
Latvia	--h	--	--	--	h 5	90		--	--	--	80*	5728	43	61	53	57
Lithuania	--h	--	--	--	h 4	92		--	--	--	80*	6436	46	63	51	57
Luxembourg	--h	--	--	--	h 4	92		--	--	--	80*	33505	93	86	93	89
Macedonia, FYR	---	--	--	--	--	--		--	--	--	--	4254	35	35	22	28
Malta	--h	--	--	--	h 6	88		--	--	--	80*	16447	73	76	60	68
Moldova	--c	--	--	--	4	92		55	50	20	20	1947	19	19	30	24
Netherlands	--h	--	--	--	h 4	92	hh	100	100	100	92	22176	82	87	78	82
Norway	--c	--	--	--	4	92		--	--	--	80*	26342	86	83	84	83
Poland	--h	--	--	--	h 8	84		--	--	--	80*	7619	50	65	47	56
Portugal	--c	--	--	--	5	90		--	--	--	80*	14701	69	74	70	72
Romania	hhc	--	7.8	5.7	7	84	-h	--	49	20	20	5648	43	31	34	32
Slovakia	--h	--	--	--	h 6	88	-h	--	51	21	21	9699	59	40	51	45
Slovenia	--h	--	--	--	h 6	88	-h	--	89	78	78	14293	69	73	63	68
Spain	--c	--	--	--	4	92	hh	99	97	94	92	16212	72	82	60	71
Sweden	--c	--	--	--	5	90		--	--	--	80*	20659	81	80	76	78
Switzerland	--c	--	--	--	5	90		--	--	--	80*	25512	85	82	81	81
Ukraine	--h	--	--	--	h 6	88	hh	96	49	20	20	3194	28	24	39	31
United Kingdom	--c	--	--	--	7	86	hh	100	96	92	86	20336	80	83	78	80
Yugoslavia	hh-	--	6.8	1.6	--	86		76	69	45	45	# 2300	22	33	21	27
RUSSIAN FEDERATION	hhc	--	12.7	3.0	6	75		--	--	--	75	6460	46	60	37	48
ASIA																
Afghanistan	ccc	62	52	48	20	15		6	10	2	2	800	8	5	8	6
Armenia	--c	--	--	--	7	86		--	--	--	80*	2072	20	50	32	41
Azerbaijan	hhc	--	22.2	10.1	6	57		--	--	--	57	2175	21	39	48	43
Bahrain	hcc	--	9.9	9	6	80		94	97	88	80	13111	66	73	48	60
Bangladesh	hhc	37	54.6	56.3	50	17		95	43	17	17	1361	14	15	33	24
Bhutan	hh-	--	56.1	37.9	--	18		58	70	31	18	1536	15	16	32	24
Brunei Darussalam	--h	--	--	--	h 5	90		--	--	--	80*	16765	73	76	60*	68
Cambodia	cch	33	56	52	h 18	18		30	19	8	8	1257	13	10	17	13

159

Country	Food note	Low food %	Stunt %	Under wt %	Low b wt %	Food score	Basic note	% with water	% with sanit.	Basic score	Need score	GDP/pers PPP$	Inc. score	HW score	NW score	W index
China	ccc	13	34	16	9	41		67	24	10	10	3105	27	18	50	34
Cyprus	--h	--	--	--	h 9	82		100	--	100	82	17482	75	78	70	74
Georgia	---	--	--	--	--	--		--	--	--	--	3353	29	29	41	35
India	hhc	22	52.0	53.4	33	19		81	29	12	12	2077	20	16	26	21
Indonesia	hhc	6	42.2	34.0	8	30		74	53	24	24	2651	24	24	17	20
Iran	hhc	6	18.9	15.7	10	62		95	64	39	39	5121	40	39	46	42
Iraq	ccc	15	31	23	15	45		81	75	53	45	3197	28	36	28	32
Israel	--c	--	--	--	7	86	hh	99	70	47	47	17301	75	61	63	62
Japan	--c	--	--	--	7	86		97	--	94	86	23257	83	84	74	79
Jordan	hcc	3	15.8	5	10	68		97	99	94	68	3347	29	48	20	34
Kazakhstan	hhc	--	15.8	8.3	9	68		93	99	86	68	4378	36	52	44	48
Korea, DPR	cc-	48	60	60	--	16		100	99	98	16	4058	34	25	34	29
Korea, R	--c	1	--	--	9	98		93	100	86	86	13478	67	76	59	67
Kuwait	hhc	3	12.2	6.4	7	76		--	--	--	76	25314	85	80	76	78
Kyrgyzstan	ccc	--	25	11	6	53		79	100	59	53	2317	22	37	30	33
Lao PDR	hhc	33	47.3	40.0	18	24		44	18	7	7	1734	17	12	17	14
Lebanon	hhc	2	12.2	3.0	10	76		94	63	37	37	4326	35	36	23	29
Malaysia	-cc	2	--	19	8	62		78	94	57	57	8137	52	54	54	54
Maldives	ccc	--	27	43	13	29		60	44	18	18	4083	34	26	36	31
Mongolia	ccc	48	22	10	7	23		45	87	18	18	1541	15	16	20	18
Myanmar	hcc	7	44.6	39	24	27		60	43	17	17	1199	12	14	12	13
Nepal	hh-	21	48.8	46.9	--	22		71	16	6	6	1157	12	9	23	16
Oman	ccc	--	23	23	8	56		85	78	57	56	9960	60	58	52	55
Pakistan	hhc	19	49.6	38.2	25	20		79	56	28	20	1715	17	18	23	20
Philippines	ccc	22	30	28	9	47		85	87	70	47	3555	30	38	33	35
Qatar	hh-	--	8.1	5.5	--	84	hc	100	97	94	84	20987	81	82	60*	71
Saudi Arabia	--c	4	--	--	7	92		--	--	--	80*	10158	60	70	64	67
Singapore	--c	--	--	--	7	86	hh	100	100	100	86	24210	84	85	78	81
Sri Lanka	hcc	25	23.8	34	25	41		57	63	29	29	2979	26	27	30	28
Syrian Arab R	ccc	1	21	13	7	59		86	67	43	43	2892	26	34	23	28
Tajikistan	--h	--	--	--	h 8	84	ch	60	62	33	33	1041	10	21	18	19
Thailand	ccc	24	16	19	6	55		81	96	62	55	5456	42	48	41	44
Turkey	hhc	2	20.5	10.4	8	59		49	80	20	20	6422	46	33	29	31
Turkmenistan	--c	--	--	--	5	90		74	91	52	52	2550	24	38	18	28
United Arab Emirates	ccc	1	17	14	6	66		97	92	84	66	17719	75	70	76	73
Uzbekistan	hh-	--	31.3	18.8	--	45		90	100	80	45	2053	20	32	30	31
Viet Nam	ccc	19	44	41	17	28		45	29	12	12	1689	17	14	18	16
Yemen	ccc	37	52	46	19	19		61	66	35	19	719	7	13	13	13
PACIFIC																
Australia	--c	--	--	--	6	88		--	--	--	80*	22452	82	81	79	80
Fiji	hhc	--	2.7	7.9	12	84		77	92	56	56	4231	35	45	46	45
New Zealand	--c	--	--	--	6	88		97	--	94	88	17288	75	81	74	77
Papua New Guinea	rural;hhc	24	43.2	29.9	23	29		41	83	16	16	2359	22	19	25	22
Samoa	--c	--	--	--	6	88		68	--	44	44	3832	32	38	31	34
Solomon Is	hhc	--	27.3	21.3	20	50		--	--	--	50	1940	19	34	35	34
Tonga	h-c	--	1.3	--	2	97		95	95	90	90	w 4281	35	62	37	49
Vanuatu	hhc	--	19.1	19.7	7	61		77	28	11	11	3120	27	19	42	30

Notes

The wealth index (**W index**) is the unweighted average of a household wealth index (*HW score*) and a national wealth index (*NW score*). The household wealth index is shown here. The national wealth index is shown in Table 4.

The household wealth index is the average of two unweighted indicators (column heading in parentheses):

Needs (Need score), the lower score of two indicators—

Food sufficiency (Food score), represented by the percentage of population with insufficient food (Low food %), prevalence of stunting in children under five years of age (Stunt %), prevalence of low weight-for-age in children under five years (Under wt %), whichever gave the lowest score. If data were not available on these indicators, percentage of babies whose birth weight is less than 2500 grams (Low b wt %) was used instead.

Basic services (Basic score), represented by the percentage of population with access to safe water (% with water) or the percentage of population with access to basic sanitation (% with sanit), whichever gave the lower score.

Income (Inc score), represented by Gross Domestic Product per person, in current international purchasing-power-parity dollars ($PPP).

The food sufficiency indicators are not strictly comparable. The percentage of the population with insufficient food is a measure of food supply. The other indicators are measures of physiological condition, and are influenced by health and sanitation as well as food supply. The percentage of babies with low birth weight is especially affected by other factors.

Food note = sources and other notes for the Stunt % (left letter), Under wt % (center letter), and Low b wt % (right letter) columns.

Low food % = percentage of the population with insufficient food. Insufficient food means food consumption below minimum energy requirement. Data are for 1995-1997 and are from FAO (1999b). They were estimated from food supply data (derived from production and trade data) and household surveys (FAO 1996a).

Stunt % = prevalence of stunting = percentage of children under five years with low height-for-age. Data are for the latest year available and are from Onis & Blössner (1997), if indicated by the letter h in the Food note column, or UNICEF (1999b), if indicated by the letter c. The World Health Organization (WHO) regards height-for-age as the best indicator for monitoring child growth, because it measures cumulative deficient growth associated with long term factors, including chronic insufficient daily food intake, frequent infection, and poor feeding practices (Visschedjik & Siméant 1998; World Health Organization 1998b).

Under wt % = prevalence of low weight-for-age in children under five years. Data are for the latest year available and are from Onis & Blössner (1997), if indicated by the letter h in the Food note column, or UNICEF (1999b), if indicated by the letter c.

Low b wt % = babies whose birth weight is less than 2500 grams, as a percentage of babies born alive. Data are for the latest year in the period 1990-1997 and are from UNICEF (1999b), if indicated by the letter c in the Food note column, or World Health Organization (1996-1998a), if indicated by the letter h.

Food score = food sufficiency score. The performance criteria for the food indicators are shown in Table 3a. For insufficient food, the top of the fair band corresponds to the 1996 World Food Summit target to halve the number of hungry people by 2015, from 20% of the total population of developing countries to under 10% (FAO 1999b). For stunting, the top of the medium band corresponds to the WHO target of less than 20% in all countries by 2010 (World Health Organization 1998b; Visschedjik & Siméant 1998). For low weight-for-age children and low birth-weight babies, the top of the fair band corresponds to the general target of WHO's General Strategy for Health of no more than 10% (United Nations 1996). The criteria for percentage of the population with insufficient food match those for the other food indicators.

Basic note = sources for % with water (left) and % with sanit. (right) columns, if not the main source.

% with water = percentage of population with access to safe water. Data are for the latest year in the period 1990-1998 and are from UNICEF (1999b), except those marked with the letter h in the Basic note column, which are for a single year in the period 1991-1993 or for the year in the Basic note column, and are from World Health Organization (1996-1998a).

% with sanit. = percentage of population with access to basic sanitation. Data are for the latest year in the period 1990-1998 and are from UNICEF (1999b), except those marked with the letter h in the Basic note column, which are for a single year in the period 1991-1993 or for the year in the Basic note column, and are from World Health Organization (1996-1998a).

Basic score = basic services score = the lower of the water and sanitation scores. The performance criteria are shown in Table 3a. The top of the good band matches the UN target of 100% set by the International Conference on Population and Development (Cairo, 1994), the World Summit for Social Development (Copenhagen, 1995), the Fourth World Conference on Women (Beijing, 1995), and the Second World Conference on Human Settlements (Habitat II, Istanbul, 1996) (United Nations Population Division 1997; Office of the UN System Support and Services 1996).

Need score = needs score, the lower of the food sufficiency and basic services scores.

GDP/pers $PPP = Gross Domestic Product per person, in current international purchasing power parity dollars, except where marked with the symbol #, which is in current US dollars. GDP is the total economic activity of a country, regardless of who owns the productive assets (*The Economist* 1997). Data are for 1998 and are from United Nations Development Programme (2000), except where marked with the symbol #, which are for 1997 and are from United Nations Statistical Division (1999), or the letter w, which are for 1999 Gross National Product and are from World Bank (2000a).

Inc score = income score. The performance criteria are shown in Table 3a. The bands are based on the relationship between income and performance on health and population, knowledge, and community, as described in the section on income in Chapter 2 and shown in Table 3b.

band	top point on scale	% population with not enough food	prevalence of stunting in children under 5 (%)	prevalence of underweight children under 5 (%)	prevalence of babies with low birth-weight (%)	% population with safe water & basic sanitation	Gross Domestic Product per person $PPP
good	100	0	0	0	0	100	40,000
fair	80	10	10	10	10	90	20,000
medium	60	20	20	20	20	80	10,000
poor	40	35	35	35	35	75	5,000
bad	20	50	50	50	50	50	2,000
base	0	100	100	100	100	0	0

Table 3a. Performance criteria for indicators of food sufficiency, basic services, and income (GDP per person).

income group	good	fair	medium	poor	bad
PPP$20.1-40.0	15	5	1	1	0
PPP$10.1-20.0	1	12	5	1	1
PPP$5.1-10.0	0	13	16	6	0
PPP$2.1-5.0	0	1	22	21	4
PPP$0.1-2.0	0	0	2	18	35

Table 3b. Numbers of countries with good, fair, medium, poor or bad scores for a combination of health and population, knowledge, and community in different income groups (GDP per person in PPP$000s).

* A score with an asterisk has been reduced in accordance with the insufficient data rule. To prevent high scores resulting merely from lack of data, a good score is allowed only if it is based on all applicable components (data in an indicator, indicators in an index), and a fair score only if it is based on at least half the components. Good and fair scores (100-61) based on fewer than half the applicable components have been reduced to 60. Good scores (100-81) based on more than half but not all the applicable components have been reduced to 80.

Table 4. National Wealth

Country	Size score	IU note	Inflation %	Unem-ployed %	IU score	Debt note	Debt serv % export	Debt serv % GNP	ST debt: reserve	Pub debt % GDP	Def/sur % GDP	Debt score	NW score
AMERICAS													
Antigua & Barbuda	57	91	4.5	6.0	70	--	--	--	0.11	--	--	80*	66
Argentina	64	96	0.2	16.3	37	96-98;97	424	53	1.65	--	-1.5	1	41
Bahamas	69	97	0.5	9.8	61	s98	--	--	40.15	--	-1.9	0	50
Barbados	64	97	3.6	14.5	42	96-98	44	29	4.96	--	--	15	46
Belize	37	97	1.1	12.7	49	96-98;95	88	48	18.86	--	-5.0	0	31
Bolivia	22	96	89.1	4.2	0	96-98;98	336	63	1.68	--	-2.3	9	13
Brazil	46	97	6.9	7.8	55	96-98;93	347	28	1.22	--	-9.4	8	39
Canada	84	98	1.0	8.3	67	98	--	--	--	89.8	0.3	55	72
Chile	55	98	5.1	7.2	66	96-98;98	179	53	0.50	--	0.4	29	51
Colombia	44	98	18.7	15.0	33	96-98;98	215	32	0.70	--	-4.7	21	35
Costa Rica	44	98	11.7	5.6	39	96-98;96	63	40	0.77	--	-3.8	40	42
Cuba	33	s98	2.7	--	--	--	--	--	--	--	--	--	33
Dominica	40	97	2.4	23.1	24	96-98	56	35	1.91	--	--	42	36
Dominican R	37	97	8.3	15.9	38	96-98;97	51	30	1.44	--	0.4	51	41
Ecuador	27	98	36.1	11.5	19	96-98;94	228	79	0.71	--	0.0	19	23
El Salvador	34	97	4.5	8.0	68	96-98;96	84	29	0.56	--	-0.5	54	47
Grenada	43	96	2.8	17.0	36	96-98;95	95	52	0.41	--	2.3	34	39
Guatemala	30	98	6.6	--	--	96-98;97	117	25	1.10	--	-0.7	44	35
Guyana	29	92	28.2	11.7	25	96-98	151	163	0.24	--	--	0	21
Haiti	14	98	10.0	--	--	96-98	171	19	--	--	--	31	20
Honduras	23	98	13.7	3.9	37	96-98	147	72	0.37	--	--	24	27
Jamaica	29	99	6.3	15.8	38	96-98	91	80	1.44	--	--	20	29
Mexico	51	98	15.9	2.3	35	96-98;97	121	44	0.90	--	-1.1	38	44
Nicaragua	21	98	13.1	13.3	37	96-98;95	601	313	0.25	--	-0.6	0	20
Panama	41	98	0.6	13.9	44	96-98;98	71	82	12.97	--	0.2	0	31
Paraguay	35	96	9.8	8.2	41	96-98;93	48	23	0.69	--	1.2	62	43
Peru	35	98	7.3	7.7	53	96-98;98	380	55	0.76	--	-0.2	5	32
St Kitts & Nevis	61	98	3.6	--	--	96-98;94	65	36	0.04	--	1.1	45	56
St Lucia	41	97	0.0	20.5	29	96-98	42	29	0.95	--	--	54	41
St Vincent & Grenadines	38	91	5.5	19.8	30	96-98;98	248	139	10.86	--	-8.2	0	26
Suriname	41	97	7.2	10.5	54	--	--	--	0.84	--	--	66	50
Trinidad & Tobago	50	98	5.7	14.2	43	96-98;95	73	39	1.21	--	0.2	41	46
United States	90	98	1.6	4.5	82	s98	--	--	--	57.4	0.9	70	83
Uruguay	54	98	10.9	10.1	39	96-98;98	162	38	1.81	--	-0.8	33	45
Venezuela	43	97	50.0	11.4	8	96-98;98	150	46	0.41	--	-2.8	36	32
AFRICA													
Algeria	39	97	5.7	28.7	13	96-98;96	206	66	0.48	--	2.9	23	28
Angola	18	98	107.4	--	--	96-98	236	276	--	--	--	0	12
Benin	9	98	5.8	--	--	96-98	159	48	0.27	--	--	34	17
Botswana	44	95	10.5	21.5	27	96-98;96	14	9	0.00	--	8.4	80*	49
Burkina Faso	9	98	5.0	--	--	96-98	274	33	0.35	--	--	15	11
Burundi	6	98	12.5	--	--	96-98;97	806	69	1.13	--	-5.5	0	4
Cameroon	15	98	0.0	--	--	96-98;95	356	97	321.75	--	0.2	0	10
Cape Verde	28	98	4.4	--	--	96-98	75	32	0.32	--	--	50	35
Central African R	11	98	-1.9	--	--	96-98	358	56	0.27	--	--	7	10
Chad	9	98	4.4	--	--	96-98;91	211	40	0.19	--	-7.1	22	13
Comoros	14	98	1.0	--	--	96-98	268	67	0.19	--	--	16	15
Congo, DR	8	98	29.2	--	--	96-98;97	774	678	--	--	-0.8	0	5
Congo, R	10	98	1.8	--	--	96-98;97	286	84	16.41	--	-8.6	0	7
Côte d'Ivoire	16	98	4.5	--	--	96-98;98	246	129	2.17	--	-1.3	8	13
Djibouti	13	98	2.0	--	--	96-98	85	38	0.99	--	--	42	23
Egypt	27	95	9.4	11.3	43	96-98;97	129	32	0.33	--	-2.0	41	34
Equatorial Guinea	18	98	3.0	--	--	96-98	72	73	6.00	--	--	10	15
Eritrea	8	98	16.6	--	--	96-98	27	11	--	--	--	80*	32
Ethiopia	6	98	3.7	--	--	96-98;93	898	140	0.09	--	-5.9	0	4
Gabon	45	98	2.3	--	--	96-98;91	143	94	32.56	--	-1.7	0	30
Gambia	14	98	1.1	--	--	96-98;93	111	68	0.25	--	3.7	26	18
Ghana	17	98	19.3	--	--	96-98;93	172	57	1.86	--	-2.6	31	22
Guinea	18	98	5.1	--	--	96-98;98	306	68	0.83	--	-4.1	12	16
Guinea-Bissau	6	98	8.0	--	--	96-98	1733	299	0.60	--	--	0	4
Kenya	10	98	6.6	--	--	96-98;96	174	51	1.05	--	-0.9	30	17
Lesotho	16	98	7.8	--	--	96-98;98	73	41	0.30	--	-4.1	39	24
Liberia	8	s97	11.0	--	--	95-97	388	121	4914.0	--	--	0	5
Libyan Arab J	47	98	7.0	--	--	--	--	--	0.04	--	--	80*	58
Madagascar	8	98	6.2	--	--	96-98;96	396	90	0.79	--	-1.3	4	7
Malawi	5	98	29.8	--	--	96-98	226	62	0.19	--	--	19	10
Mali	7	98	4.1	--	--	96-98	322	85	0.42	--	--	11	8

Country	Size score	IU note	Inflation %	Unem-ployed %	IU score	Debt note	Debt serv % export	Debt serv % GNP	ST debt: reserve	Pub debt % GDP	Def/sur % GDP	Debt score	NW score
Mauritania	16	98	8.0	--	--	96-98	318	141	0.69	--	--	5	12
Mauritius	53	95	6.1	9.8	59	96-98;98	92	60	1.43	--	0.9	30	49
Morocco	29	96	3.0	17.8	34	96-98;95	157	55	0.44	--	-4.4	32	31
Mozambique	8	98	0.6	--	--	96-98	539	85	0.44	--	--	0	5
Namibia	41	98	6.2	--	--	93	--	--	0.19	--	-4.5	51	44
Niger	7	98	4.6	--	--	96-98	340	58	0.85	--	--	9	8
Nigeria	8	98	10.0	--	--	96-98	184	81	0.14	--	--	20	12
Rwanda	7	98	6.8	--	--	96-98;93	554	39	0.22	--	-7.4	0	5
São Tomé & Principe	15	98	42.1	--	--	96-98	1268	375	1.09	--	--	0	10
Senegal	13	98	2.5	--	--	96-98	187	60	0.75	--	--	27	18
Seychelles	61	98	1.0	--	--	96-98;98	47	33	17.00	--	1.4	0	41
Sierra Leone	5	98	35.5	--	--	96-98;97	745	105	0.21	--	-6.0	0	3
Somalia	7	s98	16.0	--	--	95-97	3090	341	--	--	--	0	5
South Africa	54	96	7.4	5.1	53	96-98;98	66	17	2.31	--	-2.9	37	49
Sudan	14	98	17.1	--	--	96-98	2448	195	1.68	--	--	0	9
Swaziland	32	98	8.1	--	--	96-98	17	14	0.14	--	--	77	47
Tanzania	5	98	12.6	--	--	96-98	484	81	0.22	--	--	0	3
Togo	14	98	1.0	--	--	96-98	143	68	0.98	--	--	26	18
Tunisia	42	98	3.1	--	--	96-98;96	118	57	0.83	--	-3.1	31	38
Uganda	11	98	5.8	--	--	96-98	311	37	0.10	--	--	12	11
Zambia	7	98	24.5	--	--	96-98;96	438	166	2.07	--	0.7	0	5
Zimbabwe	24	98	32.3	--	--	96-98;97	140	55	3.12	--	-5.0	29	26
EUROPE													
Albania	25	u98	20.7	17.6	31	96-98;98	79	22	0.12	--	-8.5	24	26
Austria	83	98	0.8	4.2	83	e99	--	--	--	65.2	-2.1	60	77
Belarus	45	98	73.0	2.3	0	96-98;98	14	5	0.46	--	-0.9	75	41
Belgium	83	98	0.9	9.1	64	e99	--	--	--	116.1	-0.7	41	68
Bosnia & Herzegovina	17	u97	14.0	72.5	0	95-97	234	38	--	--	--	19	13
Bulgaria	39	u98	22.3	12.2	30	96-98;98	150	91	0.13	--	0.0	17	31
Croatia	47	98	5.7	11.4	54	96-98;98	74	33	0.51	--	0.6	49	49
Czech R	65	98	10.6	7.5	39	96-98;98	77	46	0.44	--	-1.6	37	51
Denmark	84	98	1.8	5.5	78	e99	--	--	--	52.6	2.8	77	81
Estonia	51	98	8.2	9.6	49	96-98;98	18	14	1.53	--	-0.1	49	50
Finland	81	98	1.3	11.3	55	e99	--	--	--	46.6	1.9	78	74
France	81	98	0.7	11.8	53	e99	--	--	--	58.9	-1.8	64	70
Germany	82	98	0.6	9.7	61	e99	--	--	--	61.1	-1.4	64	72
Greece	68	97	5.4	10.3	59	e99	--	--	--	104.6	-1.8	43	59
Hungary	60	98	14.3	7.8	37	96-98;98	118	64	0.65	--	-6.1	28	46
Iceland	85	98	1.7	3.9	84	s98;97	--	--	--	48.3	0.4	73	82
Ireland	81	98	2.2	7.8	69	e99	--	--	--	50.1	1.9	76	77
Italy	81	98	1.8	12.2	51	e99	--	--	--	115.1	-1.9	39	63
Latvia	43	98	4.7	13.8	45	96-98;98	24	12	0.37	--	0.1	80*	53
Lithuania	46	98	5.1	13.5	46	96-98;98	37	20	0.57	--	-0.4	67	51
Luxembourg	93	98	1.0	2.5	90	e99	--	--	--	6.0	4.4	98	93
Macedonia, FYR	35	u98	-0.1	41.4	0	96-98	148	84	0.21	--	--	19	22
Malta	73	97	3.1	5.0	79	95-97;97	30	29	0.95	--	-9.8	15	60
Moldova	19	u98	7.7	1.9	51	96-98	93	53	0.14	--	--	33	30
Netherlands	82	98	2.0	4.4	82	e99	--	--	--	62.9	1.0	68	78
Norway	86	98	2.3	3.3	85	s98;97	--	--	--	33.4	0.7	80	84
Poland	50	98	11.8	10.5	39	96-98;98	103	30	0.32	--	-1.0	49	47
Portugal	69	98	2.2	5.0	80	e99	--	--	--	55.8	-2.0	64	70
Romania	43	98	59.1	6.3	1	96-98;97	97	28	0.54	--	-3.9	51	34
Slovakia	59	98	6.7	11.9	52	96-98	75	47	0.63	--	--	36	51
Slovenia	69	98	8.0	7.7	50	95-97	36	21	0.24	--	--	65	63
Spain	72	98	1.8	18.8	32	e99	--	--	--	63.7	-1.1	63	60
Sweden	81	98	-0.1	6.5	74	e99	--	--	--	65.7	1.9	69	76
Switzerland	85	98	0.1	3.6	86	s98;97	--	--	--	48.0	-1.3	70	81
Ukraine	28	98	10.6	11.3	39	96-98	64	24	0.92	--	--	60	39
United Kingdom	80	98	2.7	6.1	76	e99	--	--	--	45.7	1.3	76	78
Yugoslavia	22	su97	9.0	25.6	19	--	--	--	--	--	--	--	21
RUSSIAN FEDERATION	46	98	27.7	13.3	26	96-98;95	166	45	1.43	--	-4.7	32	37
ASIA													
Afghanistan	8	s98	14.0	--	--	--	--	--	--	--	--	--	8
Armenia	20	98	8.7	9.3	46	96-98	121	33	0.17	--	--	43	32
Azerbaijan	21	98	-0.8	1.1	96	96-98;98	54	15	0.09	--	-3.9	55	48
Bahrain	66	98	-0.4	--	--	98	--	--	5.60	--	-5.8	12	48
Bangladesh	14	96	4.5	2.5	70	96-98	151	24	0.17	--	--	36	33
Bhutan	15	98	7.0	--	--	96-98;98	56	21	0.01	--	-0.4	65	32
Brunei Darussalam	73	s98	0.0	--	--	--	--	--	--	--	--	--	60*
Cambodia	13	98	14.8	--	--	96-98	202	58	0.11	--	--	24	17

Country	Size score	IU note	Inflation %	Unem-ployed %	IU score	Debt note	Debt serv % export	Debt serv % GNP	ST debt: reserve	Pub debt % GDP	Def/sur % GDP	Debt score	NW score
China	27	98	-0.8	3.1	88	96-98;97	67	15	0.15	--	-1.5	60	50
Cyprus	75	98	2.2	3.3	85	97	--	--	1.67	--	-5.3	45	70
Georgia	29	u98	3.6	4.2	76	96-98;98	170	26	--	--	-2.5	31	41
India	20	98	13.2	--	--	96-98;98	147	20	0.30	--	-5.2	37	26
Indonesia	24	98	58.0	5.5	2	96-98;98	238	84	0.79	--	-2.4	18	17
Iran	40	98	20.0	--	--	96-98;98	71	13	--	--	0.3	58	46
Iraq	28	s98	45.0	--	--	--	--	--	--	--	--	--	28
Israel	75	98	5.4	8.6	64	w96;98	--	--	0.19	118.8	-1.2	38	63
Japan	83	98	0.6	4.1	84	s98;93	--	--	--	99.9	-1.5	46	74
Jordan	29	98	3.1	--	--	96-98;97	145	150	0.30	--	-3.3	2	20
Kazakhstan	36	98	7.3	13.7	45	96-98	74	25	0.41	--	--	58	44
Korea, DPR	34	s98	5.0	--	--	--	--	--	--	--	--	--	34
Korea, R	67	98	7.5	6.8	52	96-98;97	83	31	0.62	--	-1.3	51	59
Kuwait	85	98	0.5	--	--	--	--	--	1.09	--	--	58	76
Kyrgyzstan	22	u98	10.3	3.1	40	96-98	133	48	0.27	--	--	36	30
Lao PDR	17	98	81.0	--	--	96-98	246	70	0.10	--	--	18	17
Lebanon	35	98	4.6	--	--	96-98;98	159	44	0.42	--	-15.1	0	23
Malaysia	52	97	2.7	2.5	82	96-98;97	54	55	0.30	--	2.9	32	54
Maldives	34	98	5.0	--	--	96-98;98	29	42	0.22	--	-5.3	39	36
Mongolia	15	98	9.4	5.7	43	96-98;98	86	49	0.19	--	-10.8	9	20
Myanmar	12	98	10.0	--	--	96-98;97	309	3	0.61	--	-0.9	12	12
Nepal	12	98	8.4	--	--	96-98;98	118	31	0.05	--	-4.7	44	23
Oman	60	98	-0.9	--	--	96-98;98	49	23	1.25	--	-6.6	37	52
Pakistan	17	97	11.8	6.1	39	96-98;98	220	42	1.79	--	-6.3	20	23
Philippines	30	98	9.7	9.6	41	96-98;97	102	57	0.69	--	0.1	31	33
Qatar	81	98	2.9	--	--	--	--	--	--	--	--	--	60*
Saudi Arabia	60	98	-0.2	--	--	--	--	--	0.73	--	--	71	64
Singapore	84	98	-0.3	3.2	87	w97;97	--	--	1.04	74.2	11.7	59	78
Sri Lanka	26	98	9.4	10.6	43	96-98;98	97	43	0.59	--	-8.0	27	30
Syrian Arab R	26	91	19.0	6.8	33	96-98;97	349	129	--	--	-0.2	8	23
Tajikistan	10	u98	43.2	2.9	13	96-98	122	42	--	--	--	39	18
Thailand	42	98	8.1	3.4	49	96-98;98	116	58	0.48	--	-3.5	31	41
Turkey	46	98	84.6	6.2	0	96-98;97	176	52	1.06	--	-8.4	25	29
Turkmenistan	24	u95	1005.2	3.0	0	96-98	186	67	--	--	--	26	18
United Arab Emirates	75	98	2.0	--	--	98	--	--	0.46	--	-0.3	79	76
Uzbekistan	20	u98	29.0	0.4	25	96-98	81	13	--	--	--	55	30
Viet Nam	17	98	7.8	--	--	96-98;98	181	81	0.36	--	-1.1	20	18
Yemen	7	98	11.2	--	--	96-98;98	91	69	0.13	--	-2.6	25	13
PACIFIC													
Australia	82	98	0.9	8.0	68	s98;98	--	--	--	37.0	2.8	84	79
Fiji	35	95	5.2	5.4	65	96-98;96	15	10	0.04	--	-4.9	48	46
New Zealand	75	98	1.6	7.5	70	s98;98	--	--	--	38.7	0.5	78	74
Papua New Guinea	22	98	13.6	--	--	96-98;94	94	56	1.01	--	-4.1	32	25
Samoa	32	98	2.2	--	--	96-98	84	59	0.53	--	--	30	31
Solomon Is	19	98	12.4	--	--	96-98	30	19	0.18	--	--	68	35
Tonga	35	98	2.9	--	--	96-98;91	83	23	0.08	--	-5.8	42	37
Vanuatu	27	98	3.2	--	--	96-98	24	16	0.63	--	--	73	42

Notes

The national wealth index (*NW score*) is the average of three weighted indicators (column heading in parentheses) [weight in brackets]:

Size of the economy (Size score) [2], represented by Gross Domestic Product (GDP) per person.

Inflation and unemployment (IU score) [1], represented by the annual inflation rate or the annual unemployment rate for the same period, whichever gives the lower score.

Debt (Debt score) [1], represented by an external debt indicator or a public debt indicator, whichever gives the lower score.

Size was given a higher weight than the other indicators, because it is more comprehensive.

Size score = size of economy score, based on GDP/person, in current international purchasing power parity dollars (or, exceptionally, in current US dollars). Data are in Table 3. Performance criteria are the same as for income and are given in Table 3a.

IU note = the applicable year for the inflation and unemployment data. Where both indicators are available, the latest common year was chosen. Where only inflation data are available, the year is usually 1998.

Inflation % = the annual percentage change in the consumer price index (CPI), the cost to the average consumer of buying a fixed basket of goods and services. Because the basket varies from country to country (as does household and income group coverage), the CPI may not be as reliable an indicator for international comparisons of inflation as the GDP deflator (annual GDP at current prices divided by the value of GDP at constant prices), which reflects changes in prices in all components of GDP (such as government consumption, capital formation, and international trade) and not just private consumption. However, the CPI is the inflation measurement used for monetary policy and is more suitable for comparison with the unemployment rate. It is also more familiar than the GDP deflator. Data are from International Monetary Fund (2000), except where marked with the letter s in the IU note column, which are from International Institute for Strategic Studies (1999a).

Unemployed % = total unemployment as a percentage of the total labor force. Data are from International Labour Office (ILO 2000), except where marked with the letter u in the IU note column, which are from United Nations Economic Commission for Europe (UNECE 2000). ILO data are usually from national labor force surveys. UNECE data are from national employment office statistics and usually cover only registered unemployment, which tends to be less than total unemployment.

IU score = the lower of the inflation and unemployment scores. The performance criteria are shown in Table 4a. For inflation, the tops of the good and fair bands match the lowest and highest rates respectively in the range of inflation targets of the central banks of Australia, Canada, England, the Euro area, New Zealand, and Sweden; and the top of poor reflects the general view that inflation of 10% or more is harmful (*The Economist* 1999). Negative inflation (deflation) signals a contracting economy, and very low rates of inflation are a symptom of stagnation. However, stagnation and contraction are generally accompanied by increasing unemployment, which usually would prevent a country from getting a high score. It is harder to achieve low rates of unemployment than of inflation, and zero unemployment is probably impossible. High employment drives up prices, and during the 1990s only ten countries have achieved rates of inflation *and* unemployment below 4.0% (Azerbaijan, China, Cyprus, Iceland, Japan, Luxembourg, Malaysia, Norway, Singapore, Switzerland). Accordingly, the performance criteria for unemployment are less stringent than for inflation: the tops of the fair and medium bands are slightly above those for inflation.

Debt note = the applicable year for the debt data. A range of years refers to debt service data; a single year to public debt and deficit/surplus data.

Debt serv % export = the present value of debt service (the sum of principal repayments and interest payments on total external debt) as a percentage of exports of all goods and services. The present value of debt service is the discounted sum of all debt service payments due over the life of existing loans (discount rates are the rates charged by OECD countries for officially supported export credits). Total external debt is the sum of all disbursed and outstanding (at year-end) public and publicly guaranteed long-term debt, private non-guaranteed long-term debt, the use of IMF credit, and short-term debt due by all borrowers in a country to all non-resident creditors. Data for the period 1996-1998 are from World Bank (2000b); data for 1995-1997 are from World Bank (1999b).

Debt serv % GNP = the present value of debt service (the sum of principal repayments and interest payments on total external debt) as a percentage of Gross National Product. Data for the period 1996-1998 are from World Bank (2000b); data for 1995-1997 are from World Bank (1999b).

ST debt: reserve = the ratio of short-term debt to international reserves. Short-term debt is defined as external debt with an original maturity of one year or less, plus repayments due within the next 12 months on debt with an original maturity of over a year, plus arrears. It comprises liabilities to banks, debt securities (money market instruments, bonds and notes) issued in international markets by both public and private sector borrowers, and official and officially-guaranteed non-bank export credits. Because liabilities to banks and debt securities overlap, short-term debt may be overestimated. International reserves are gross reserves and comprise special drawing rights, reserves of International Monetary Fund (IMF) members held by the IMF, and holdings of foreign exchange under the control of monetary authorities. Reserves may be underestimated because they exclude monetary gold. Data are for 1999 and are from BIS/IMF/OECD/World Bank (2000).

Pub debt % GDP = gross public debt (general government gross financial liabilities) as a percentage of GDP. Data are for the year indicated in the Debt note column and are from the source indicated in the same column: e = Eurostat (2000); s = International Institute for Strategic Studies (1999a); w = World Bank (1999a).

Def/sur % GDP = central government overall budget deficit or surplus (current and capital revenue and official grants received, less total expenditure and lending minus repayments) as a percentage of the Gross Domestic Product in the national currency. Data are for the year indicated in the Debt notes column and are from World Bank (2000a), except where the year is preceded by the letter e, which are from Eurostat (2000).

Debt score = the lower of the external debt and public debt scores. The external debt score is of the lowest score of present value of external debt service as a % of exports of goods and services, or present value of external debt service as a % of GNP, or the ratio of short-term debt to international reserves. The public debt score is the weighted average [weights in brackets] of the scores for gross public debt as % of GDP [2] and annual central government deficit/surplus as % of GDP [1]. The performance criteria are shown in Table 4a. For the two debt service indicators, the tops of bad and poor match the points at which the World Bank classifies a country as severely and moderately indebted respectively (World Bank 2000b). For the ratio of short-term debt to international reserves, the top of medium is the benchmark suggested by IMF Policy Development and Review Department (2000) for the reverse indicator—the ratio of international reserves to short-term debt. The benchmark is less applicable to economies (such as those of industrialized countries), in which much of the private sector has unrestricted access to international capital markets, and which typically have ratios that would qualify as poor or bad according to these criteria. In less open or well regulated markets, the benchmark (a ratio of 1.0) matches the point above which a country is vulnerable to creditor panic, according to Sachs & Woo (1999). For the public debt and deficit indicators, the top of medium matches the Treaty of Maastricht's criteria of no more than 60% for an acceptable ratio of government debt to GDP and no more than 3% for an acceptable budget deficit (Black 1997).

band	top point on scale	inflation rate (%)	unemploy-ment rate (%)	debt service as % of exports	debt service as % of GNP	ratio of short-term debt to reserves	public debt as % of GDP	deficit/ surplus as % of GDP
good	100	0	0	0	0	0.0	1	2.9
fair	80	3	5	33	12	0.5	31	-0.1
medium	60	6	10	66	24	1.0	61	-3.1
poor	40	10	15	132	48	2.0	91	-6.1
bad	20	35	25	220	80	4.0	121	-9.1
base	0	60	35	440	160	8.0	151	-12.1

Table 4a. Performance criteria for indicators of inflation, unemployment, and debt.

* A score with an asterisk has been reduced in accordance with the insufficient data rule. To prevent high scores resulting merely from lack of data, a good score is allowed only if it is based on all applicable components (data in an indicator, indicators in an index), and a fair score only if it is based on at least half the components. Good and fair scores (100-61) based on fewer than half the applicable components have been reduced to 60. Good scores (100-81) based on more than half but not all the applicable components have been reduced to 80.

Table 5. Knowledge

Country	Ed note	1st net %	2nd net %	1st2nd score	3rd/ 10k	3rd score	E score	Tel note	Main lines/ 100	Cell subs/ 100	Phone total	Ph score	Fault/ 100 l/yr	Fault score	Tel score	Internet users/ 10k	I net score	C score	K index
AMERICAS																			
Antigua & Barbuda		--	--	--	--	--	--	s96	46.80	1.89	48.69	79	59.0	36	36	412.94	67	51	51
Argentina	t94	99.9	76.9	78	311.7	82	80	f97	20.27	7.81	28.08	62	19.7	68	62	83.05	22	42	67
Bahamas	t95	94.6	84.6	73	233.1	73	73		35.23	2.67	37.90	70	--	--	70	405.41	67	68	71
Barbados	t95	97.4	85.7	80	253.5	76	78	f95	42.40	4.48	46.88	77	9.6	84	77	186.57	45	61	72
Belize	--	99.9	63.6	72	--	--	72		13.75	1.49	15.24	45	69.5	32	32	434.78	69	50	65
Bolivia	t91	97.4	40.0	58	212.2	70	64	t97 f93	6.88	2.74	9.62	32	28.0	58	32	12.57	3	17	48
Brazil	t96	97.1	65.9	67	142.4	60	63	f97	12.05	4.68	16.73	47	3.8	94	47	180.89	44	45	57
Canada	t95	99.9	95.2	95	595.3	100	97		63.39	17.56	80.95	92	--	--	80*	2475.21	100	90	95
Chile	t97	90.3	85.2	65	260.2	77	71		20.55	6.50	27.05	62	52.0	39	39	202.37	47	43	62
Colombia	t96	89.4	76.4	57	164.0	63	60		17.35	4.91	22.26	56	56.0	38	38	46.32	12	25	48
Costa Rica	t94	91.8	55.8	52	283.0	80	66		17.18	2.83	20.01	52	42.1	46	46	260.35	55	50	61
Cuba	t96	99.9	69.9	75	101.3	49	62		3.49	0.04	3.53	12	14.3	76	12	22.49	6	9	44
Dominica	--	--	--	--	--	--	--	tf96	25.23	0.86	26.09	61	12.0	80	61	264.03	55	58	58
Dominican R	t96	91.3	78.5	61	222.3	72	66	f92	9.28	3.11	12.39	41	133.2	13	13	24.30	6	9	47
Ecuador	t90	99.9	50.9	67	201.2	69	68		7.83	2.53	10.36	34	82.0	27	27	12.32	3	15	50
El Salvador	t96	89.1	36.4	41	193.5	68	54	f96	8.00	1.76	9.76	32	36.7	51	32	49.73	13	22	43
Grenada	--	--	--	--	--	--	--		26.28	1.35	27.63	62	9.0	85	62	191.26	45	53	53
Guatemala	t95	73.8	34.9	28	80.4	43	35	t97 f93	4.08	1.03	5.11	17	45.2	44	17	46.29	12	14	28
Guyana	t96	92.8	74.9	63	107.1	51	57		7.05	0.17	7.22	24	--	--	24	23.53	6	15	43
Haiti	--	19.4	34.2	11	--	--	11	tf97	0.80	--	0.80	3	108.0	18	3	0.82	0	1	8
Honduras	t94	87.5	36.0	39	98.5	48	43		3.81	0.53	4.34	14	36.0	51	14	27.49	7	10	32
Jamaica	t95	95.6	69.8	66	76.8	42	54	t97 s96 f93	16.57	2.17	18.74	50	70.0	32	32	197.01	46	39	49
Mexico	t96	99.9	66.1	73	173.9	65	69	f95	10.36	3.50	13.86	43	4.6	92	43	140.87	38	40	59
Nicaragua	t97	78.6	50.5	36	120.9	54	45	f94	3.13	0.45	3.58	12	7.0	88	12	33.58	9	10	33
Panama	t96	89.9	71.3	55	302.5	82	68	f95	15.13	2.89	18.02	49	97.0	21	21	108.42	29	25	54
Paraguay	t96	96.3	61.1	63	94.8	47	55		5.53	4.12	9.65	32	--	--	32	19.15	5	18	43
Peru	t97	93.8	83.9	71	269.9	79	75	f97	6.67	3.00	9.67	32	33.6	53	32	80.65	21	26	59
St Kitts & Nevis	t95	--	--	--	102.4	49	49	t97	41.83	1.07	42.90	74	--	--	74	364.52	64	69	56
St Lucia	t95	--	--	--	72.5	41	41		26.79	1.29	28.08	62	--	--	62	135.64	36	49	44
St Vincent & Grenadines	--	--	--	--	--	--	--	f93	18.79	0.67	19.46	51	16.3	73	51	178.57	44	47	47
Suriname	t90	99.9	--	80*	112.4	52	66		15.23	1.36	16.59	47	47.5	42	42	163.71	42	42	58
Trinidad & Tobago	t96	99.9	71.5	75	78.7	42	58	f97	20.58	2.05	22.63	56	75.0	30	30	155.88	41	35	50
United States	t95	99.9	96.3	96	534.1	98	97	f97	66.13	25.60	91.73	97	13.4	78	78	2219.16	100	89	94
Uruguay	t96	94.3	83.8	72	245.8	75	73	f97	25.04	5.96	31.00	65	95.3	22	22	699.30	83	52	66
Venezuela	t91	82.5	48.9	39	275.7	79	59	f97	11.67	8.67	20.34	53	3.5	94	53	21.51	6	29	49
AFRICA																			
Algeria	t95	96.0	68.5	66	123.8	55	60		5.32	0.06	5.38	18	50.0	40	18	0.66	0	9	43
Angola	t91	34.7	31.2	14	6.6	4	9	f97	0.60	0.08	0.68	2	7.0	88	2	2.07	1	1	6
Benin	t96	67.6	28.2	23	25.6	15	19	f95	0.66	0.11	0.77	3	76.0	30	3	3.46	1	2	13
Botswana	t96	80.1	88.8	59	58.7	33	46	f97	6.50	1.46	7.96	26	37.2	50	26	63.69	17	21	38
Burkina Faso	96	32.3	12.8	7	8.3	5	6		0.36	0.02	0.38	1	70.9	32	1	0.88	0	0	4
Burundi	t92	35.6	17.1	9	7.4	4	6		0.29	0.01	0.30	1	32.4	54	1	0.23	0	0	4
Cameroon	t90	61.7	39.8	24	28.9	16	20	tsf97	0.54	0.03	0.57	2	73.0	31	2	1.40	0	1	14
Cape Verde	--	99.9	36.6	62	--	--	62		9.80	0.25	10.05	33	39.7	48	33	49.02	13	23	49
Central African R	t91	46.2	19.0	13	12.2	7	10	f96	0.27	0.02	0.29	1	61.9	35	1	0.57	0	0	7
Chad	t95	47.9	17.9	13	5.1	3	8	f97	0.12	--	0.12	0	80.2	28	0	0.46	0	0	5
Comoros	t95	50.1	35.7	19	5.7	3	11		0.95	--	0.95	3	84.8	26	3	3.04	1	2	8
Congo, DR	t94	58.2	37.1	22	21.2	12	17	ts97 f95	0.04	0.02	0.06	0	7.0	88	0	0.04	0	0	11
Congo, R	t92	78.3	84.1	53	58.7	33	43	f90	0.79	0.12	0.91	3	60.5	36	3	0.36	0	1	29
Côte d'Ivoire	t94	58.3	34.1	21	56.8	32	26		1.19	0.64	1.83	6	99.0	20	6	7.00	2	4	19
Djibouti	t96	31.9	19.6	9	2.6	1	5		1.27	0.04	1.31	4	98.0	21	4	8.03	2	3	4
Egypt	t95	95.2	75.1	68	189.5	67	67		6.02	0.14	6.16	20	--	--	20	15.16	4	12	49
Equatorial Guinea	t90	79.3	68.5	43	16.4	9	26		1.29	0.07	1.36	4	62.0	35	4	10.90	3	3	18
Eritrea	t97	29.3	37.9	15	9.0	5	10		0.67	--	0.67	2	64.0	34	2	0.84	0	1	7
Ethiopia	t96	35.2	24.8	12	7.4	4	8	f97	0.28	--	0.28	1	187.0	3	1	1.01	0	0	5
Gabon	t90	--	--	--	44.9	26	26	tsf97	3.27	0.83	4.10	14	67.0	33	14	17.14	5	9	20

Country	Ed note	1st net %	2nd net %	1st2nd score	3rd/10k	3rd score	E score	Tel note	Main lines/100	Cell subs/100	Phone total	Ph score	Fault/100 l/yr	Fault score	Tel score	Internet users/10k	I net score	C score	K index
Gambia	t94	65.9	33.3	24	14.8	8	16	f96	2.08	0.41	2.49	8	76.0	30	8	20.34	5	6	13
Ghana	t90	--	--	--	12.6	7	7	sf97	0.75	0.12	0.87	3	86.0	26	3	3.13	1	2	5
Guinea	t96	45.6	14.6	11	11.2	6	8		0.48	0.28	0.76	2	70.7	32	2	0.65	0	1	6
Guinea-Bissau	--	52.3	24.1	16	--	--	16		0.71	--	0.71	2	33.3	53	2	2.65	1	1	11
Kenya	t90	65.0	61.1	33	14.2	8	20	tsf97	0.92	0.02	0.94	3	192.7	1	1	5.17	1	1	14
Lesotho	t96	68.6	72.9	41	23.4	13	27		0.97	0.48	1.45	5	--	--	5	0.97	0	2	19
Liberia	--	--	--	--	--	--	--	tf97	0.22	--	0.22	1	144.0	11	1	0.38	0	0	0
Libyan Arab J	t91	99.9	99.9	100	161.0	63	81	f92	8.36	0.33	8.69	29	230.0	0	0	--	--	0	54
Madagascar	t96	58.7	--	19	18.8	11	15		0.29	0.08	0.37	1	91.9	23	1	1.83	0	0	10
Malawi	t95	98.5	72.6	73	5.8	3	38		0.35	0.10	0.45	1	--	--	1	1.86	0	0	25
Mali	t97	38.1	17.9	10	13.3	8	9		0.25	0.04	0.29	1	--	--	1	0.94	0	0	6
Mauritania	t95	62.9	--	23	36.5	21	22		0.58	--	0.58	2	138.0	12	2	3.95	1	1	15
Mauritius	t97	96.5	68.0	67	56.7	32	49		21.37	5.27	26.64	61	64.0	34	34	108.85	29	31	43
Morocco	t96	76.6	37.7	31	118.0	54	42	f97	5.44	0.42	5.86	19	46.0	43	19	14.35	4	11	32
Mozambique	t96	39.6	22.4	12	4.0	2	7		0.40	0.04	0.44	1	61.0	36	1	1.85	0	0	5
Namibia	t95	91.4	80.7	63	73.5	41	52	f96	6.86	1.17	8.03	27	76.0	30	27	30.12	8	17	40
Niger	t91	24.4	9.4	4	5.6	3	3	f93	0.18	0.01	0.19	1	327.0	0	1	0.30	0	0	2
Nigeria	t93	--	--	--	41.0	23	23	f92	0.38	0.02	0.40	1	--	--	1	0.38	0	0	15
Rwanda	p97 s91	78.3	8.0	21	--	--	21		0.16	0.08	0.24	1	17.0	72	1	1.21	0	0	14
São Tomé & Principe	--	--	--	--	--	--	--		2.21	--	2.21	7	67.0	33	7	28.37	8	7	7
Senegal	t94	59.5	19.8	16	29.7	17	16		1.55	0.25	1.80	6	23.4	62	6	8.33	2	4	12
Seychelles	--	--	--	--	--	--	--	f95	24.35	4.89	29.24	63	43.0	46	46	256.90	54	50	50
Sierra Leone	t90	44.0	--	12	11.9	7	9		0.38	--	0.38	1	23.0	63	1	10.95	3	2	7
Somalia	--	--	--	--	--	--	--		0.14	--	0.14	0	--	--	0	0	0	0	0
South Africa	t95	99.9	94.9	95	184.1	66	80		11.46	5.64	17.10	48	48.8	41	41	285.75	58	49	70
Sudan	t90	--	--	--	27.2	15	15		0.57	0.03	0.60	2	12.0	80	2	0.18	0	1	10
Swaziland	t96	94.6	81.5	70	63.0	36	53	f95	3.05	0.49	3.54	12	189.0	2	2	10.50	3	2	36
Tanzania	t97	47.4	--	14	5.7	3	8	f96	0.38	0.12	0.50	2	175.0	5	2	0.93	0	1	6
Togo	t96	82.3	58.3	42	31.5	18	30		0.71	0.17	0.88	3	60.0	36	3	170.57	43	23	28
Tunisia	t96	99.9	74.3	77	134.1	58	67		8.06	0.42	8.48	28	48.0	42	28	10.71	3	15	50
Uganda	t96	--	--	--	17.9	10	10		0.28	0.15	0.43	1	80.0	28	1	7.30	2	1	7
Zambia	t94	72.4	42.2	30	23.8	14	22		0.88	0.06	0.94	3	139.2	12	3	3.42	1	2	15
Zimbabwe	t96	93.1	59.2	55	66.1	38	46	tf97	1.72	0.43	2.15	7	223.0	0	0	7.88	2	1	31
EUROPE																			
Albania	p95 t96	96.0	--	80*	108.7	51	65		3.05	0.15	3.20	11	14.0	77	11	2.72	1	6	45
Austria	t96	99.9	97.3	97	298.8	81	89	f97	49.10	28.17	77.27	91	7.2	88	88	1351.35	100	94	91
Belarus	p95 t96	97.0	--	80*	316.8	83	81		24.14	0.12	24.26	59	8.2	86	59	7.27	2	30	64
Belgium	t95	99.9	99.9	100	355.1	85	92		50.02	17.32	67.34	87	4.7	92	87	788.88	86	86	90
Bosnia & Herzegovina	--	--	--	--	--	--	--		9.07	0.69	9.76	32	--	--	32	1.29	0	16	16
Bulgaria	t96	97.9	77.6	75	311.0	82	78	f97	32.89	1.52	34.41	67	5.9	90	67	179.94	44	55	70
Croatia	t96	99.9	72.4	76	191.1	67	71	f97	34.77	4.07	38.84	71	12.9	79	71	446.33	70	70	71
Czech R	t96	99.9	99.9	100	200.9	69	84		36.39	9.39	45.78	77	32.4	54	54	389.03	66	60	76
Denmark	t95	99.9	94.8	95	334.9	84	89		65.97	36.44	102.41	100	--	--	80*	1887.04	100	90	89
Estonia	t96	99.9	86.1	86	296.5	81	83		34.29	16.99	51.28	80	26.4	59	59	1031.75	94	76	81
Finland	t96	99.9	95.4	95	441.8	92	93		55.39	57.18	112.57	100	8.4	86	86	2857.97	100	93	93
France	t96	99.9	98.7	98	354.1	85	91	f96	56.97	18.78	75.75	90	5.9	90	90	335.10	62	76	86
Germany	t96	99.9	95.3	95	260.3	77	86	f95	56.68	16.97	73.65	89	8.7	85	85	731.38	84	84	85
Greece	t96	99.9	91.4	91	344.8	85	88		52.22	19.41	71.63	89	27.0	58	58	330.19	62	60	79
Hungary	t95	97.5	96.9	92	190.3	67	79	f97	33.59	10.50	44.09	75	16.8	73	73	294.35	59	66	75
Iceland	t96	99.9	87.5	87	291.8	81	84		64.65	33.14	97.79	99	--	--	80*	3623.19	100	90	86
Ireland	t96	99.9	99.9	100	370.3	86	93	f92	43.47	25.70	69.17	88	38.0	50	50	815.00	87	68	85
Italy	t96	99.9	95.0	95	329.9	84	89		45.07	35.53	80.60	92	16.2	73	73	520.29	75	74	84
Latvia	t96	99.9	80.6	80	224.9	72	76		30.16	6.81	36.97	70	56.8	37	37	406.77	67	52	68
Lithuania	t96	--	--	--	225.1	72	72		29.96	7.23	37.19	70	21.8	65	65	215.98	49	57	67
Luxembourg	--	--	--	--	--	--	--		69.17	30.80	99.97	100	10.1	83	83	1180.08	99	91	80*
Macedonia, FYR	p95 s95 t96	85.0	51.0	42	155.7	62	52	t97 f96	19.87	1.53	21.40	54	21.3	66	54	100.05	27	40	48
Malta	t96	99.9	85.2	85	218.3	71	78		49.88	5.87	55.75	82	35.1	52	52	520.83	75	63	73
Moldova	t96	--	--	--	214.3	71	71		15.02	0.16	15.18	45	79.0	28	28	7.51	2	15	52
Netherlands	t96	99.9	99.9	100	301.8	82	91		59.31	21.29	80.60	92	2.7	95	92	1016.37	94	93	92
Norway	t96	99.9	95.0	97	423.9	90	93	f97	66.01	47.39	113.40	100	14.0	77	77	2249.21	100	88	91
Poland	t95	99.4	86.5	85	186.5	67	76		22.76	4.98	27.74	62	26.0	59	59	408.34	67	63	72
Portugal	t95	99.9	89.7	89	324.2	83	86	f97	41.35	30.89	72.24	89	35.9	51	51	602.57	80	65	79

Country	Ed note	1st net %	2nd net %	1st2nd score	3rd/10k	3rd score	E score	Tel note	Main lines/100	Cell subs/100	Phone total	Ph score	Fault/100 l/yr	Fault score	Tel score	Internet users/10k	I net score	C score	K index
Romania	t96	99.9	75.8	78	181.9	66	72	f96	16.24	2.86	19.10	51	88.3	25	25	66.74	18	21	55
Slovakia	t96	--	--	--	189.7	67	67		28.63	8.65	37.28	70	27.3	58	58	929.89	91	74	69
Slovenia	p95 t96	99.9	--	80*	265.7	78	79		37.48	8.36	45.84	77	--	--	77	1003.51	93	85	81
Spain	t96	99.9	91.9	92	425.4	90	91		41.37	17.91	59.28	84	1.2	98	84	440.17	69	76	86
Sweden	t96	99.9	99.9	100	311.6	82	91	f95	67.37	46.40	113.77	100	8.4	86	86	3952.87	100	93	92
Switzerland	t95	99.9	83.7	83	207.2	70	76	f95	67.54	23.52	91.06	96	8.1	86	86	1406.15	100	93	82
Ukraine	t95	--	--	--	299.6	81	80*	f97	19.07	0.23	19.30	51	42.5	46	46	29.49	8	27	62
United Kingdom	t96	99.9	91.8	92	323.7	83	87	f97	55.69	25.23	80.92	92	3.7	94	92	1357.17	100	96	90
Yugoslavia,	t96	--	--	--	162.5	63	63		21.81	2.26	24.07	59	--	--	59	94.03	25	42	56
RUSSIAN FED.	t94	99.9	87.6	87	300.6	81	84		19.66	0.51	20.17	53	38.4	49	49	67.71	18	33	67
ASIA																			
Afghanistan	t90	49.7	21.9	15	16.5	9	12		0.14	--	0.14	0	--	--	0	--	--	0	8
Armenia	t96	--	--	--	99.6	48	48		15.72	0.20	15.92	46	20.0	68	46	11.31	3	24	40
Azerbaijan	t96	--	--	--	151.3	62	62		8.87	0.85	9.72	32	75.0	30	30	1.24	0	15	46
Bahrain	t93	98.2	87.2	83	144.4	61	72		24.55	14.34	38.89	71	18.0	71	71	311.45	61	66	70
Bangladesh	t90	75.1	21.6	24	39.7	23	23		0.30	0.06	0.36	1	17.3	72	1	0.10	0	0	15
Bhutan	--	13.2	--	0	--	--	0	f93	1.64	--	1.64	5	67.0	33	5	--	--	5	2
Brunei Darussalam	t95	87.9	81.9	60	51.6	29	44		24.68	15.60	40.28	72	86.2	25	25	317.46	61	43	44
Cambodia	t97	99.9	38.8	63	8.5	5	34	f97	0.23	0.57	0.80	3	35.1	52	3	0.67	0	1	23
China	t97	99.9	70.0	75	48.8	28	51		6.96	1.90	8.86	29	--	--	29	24.79	7	18	40
Cyprus	p95 s95 t96	96.0	93.0	85	132.3	58	71		58.51	16.83	75.34	90	23.2	63	63	433.71	69	66	69
Georgia	t96	89.0	75.9	57	314.9	82	69	f92	11.55	1.10	12.65	41	43.1	45	41	9.18	2	21	53
India	t96	77.2	59.7	38	63.8	36	37	f97	2.20	0.12	2.32	8	174.0	5	5	5.09	1	3	26
Indonesia	t96	99.2	56.1	67	115.7	53	60	f97	2.70	0.52	3.22	11	13.2	78	11	14.54	4	7	42
Iran	t96	90.0	81.2	61	176.3	65	63		11.18	0.59	11.77	39	2.6	96	39	15.21	4	21	49
Iraq	--	74.6	42.9	32	--	--	32		3.10	--	3.10	10	--	--	10	--	--	10	25
Israel	t95	--	--	--	357.1	85	80*	f95	47.11	35.88	82.99	93	12.0	80	80	752.01	85	82	81
Japan	t94	99.9	99.9	100	313.1	82	91	f95	50.26	37.38	87.64	95	1.7	97	95	1323.42	100	97	93
Jordan	p95 t94	89.0	--	58	213.6	70	64		8.55	1.18	9.73	32	58.0	37	32	101.81	27	29	52
Kazakhstan	t95	--	--	--	285.9	80	80	f95	10.36	0.17	10.53	35	405.0	0	0	11.67	3	1	54
Korea, DPR	--	--	--	--	--	--	--	f93	4.71	--	4.71	16	50.0	40	16	--	--	16	16
Korea, R	t97	99.9	99.9	100	610.6	100	100	f97	43.27	30.19	73.46	89	15.0	75	75	668.32	82	78	93
Kuwait	t96	65.2	63.2	34	174.0	65	49		23.59	13.80	37.39	70	30.0	56	56	331.31	62	59	52
Kyrgyzstan	t95	99.5	77.8	78	108.8	51	64	f94	7.64	0.03	7.67	26	37.0	50	26	5.41	1	13	47
Lao PDR	t96	73.0	63.4	38	26.0	15	26		0.55	0.12	0.67	2	--	--	2	--	--	2	18
Lebanon	t95	76.1	--	36	271.2	79	57		19.43	15.67	35.10	68	--	--	68	313.38	61	64	59
Malaysia	t95	99.9	64.0	72	104.8	50	61	f97	19.76	9.92	29.68	64	39.0	49	49	360.66	64	56	59
Maldives	--	--	--	--	--	--	--		7.05	0.56	7.61	25	69.6	32	25	5.93	2	13	13
Mongolia	t97	85.1	55.9	43	200.9	69	56	tsf97	3.66	0.08	3.74	12	18.0	71	12	5.03	1	6	39
Myanmar	t94	99.3	54.2	66	59.0	34	50		0.52	0.02	0.54	2	169.0	6	2	--	--	2	34
Nepal	t96	78.4	54.6	37	48.5	28	32	f94	0.85	--	0.85	3	200.0	0	0	5.69	1	0	21
Oman	t97	67.7	66.6	37	69.5	40	38	f96	9.23	4.33	13.56	42	1.8	97	42	83.96	22	32	36
Pakistan	t91	--	--	--	30.1	17	17		1.94	0.14	2.08	7	98.6	21	7	4.35	1	4	13
Philippines	t95	99.9	77.8	79	295.8	81	80	f97	3.70	2.19	5.89	20	5.2	91	20	20.56	5	12	57
Qatar	t96	83.3	73.3	50	151.8	62	56	f97	25.99	11.36	37.35	70	15.5	75	70	345.42	63	66	59
Saudi Arabia	t96	60.1	58.7	29	145.5	61	45		14.26	3.11	17.37	48	2.8	95	48	9.91	3	25	38
Singapore	t96	91.4	75.6	61	273.0	79	70		56.20	34.60	90.80	96	4.3	93	93	2370.79	100	96	79
Sri Lanka	t95	99.9	76.0	78	47.4	27	52	f97	2.84	0.94	3.78	13	15.2	75	13	10.84	3	8	37
Syrian Arab R	t94	94.7	42.3	53	155.9	62	57		9.54	--	9.54	32	50.0	40	32	6.52	2	17	44
Tajikistan	t96	--	--	--	189.5	67	67		3.68	0.01	3.69	12	121.8	16	12	--	--	12	49
Thailand	t96	88.0	47.6	44	225.2	72	58		8.35	3.25	11.60	39	26.4	59	39	33.17	9	24	47
Turkey	t96	99.9	58.4	69	230.1	73	71		25.41	5.25	30.66	64	56.1	38	38	67.43	18	28	57
Turkmenistan	t90	--	--	--	207.2	70	70		8.22	0.07	8.29	28	46.3	43	28	--	--	28	56
United Arab Emirates	t96	82.0	77.8	51	80.1	43	47	f93	38.90	20.96	59.86	84	1.1	98	84	849.98	88	86	60
Uzbekistan	t91	--	--	--	304.8	82	80*	f97	6.47	0.07	6.54	22	104.2	19	19	4.21	1	10	57
Viet Nam	t96	99.9	55.1	68	67.8	39	53		2.58	0.24	2.82	9	--	--	9	1.29	0	4	37
Yemen	t96	--	--	--	41.9	24	24	t97 f93	1.34	0.11	1.45	5	20.0	68	5	2.37	1	3	17
PACIFIC																			
Australia	t97	99.9	96.0	96	568.2	100	98		51.21	28.55	79.76	92	--	--	80*	1603.51	100	90	95
Fiji	t91	99.9	84.2	84	107.9	51	67		9.68	1.01	10.69	36	153.0	9	9	62.81	17	13	49

168

Country	Ed note	1st net %	2nd net %	1st2nd score	3rd/ 10k	3rd score	E score	Tel note	Main lines/ 100	Cell subs/ 100	Phone total	Ph score	Fault/ 100 l/yr	Fault score	Tel score	Internet users/ 10k	I net score	C score	K index
New Zealand	t97	99.9	92.9	93	451.1	92	92		47.91	20.26	68.17	87	46.0	43	43	1538.86	100	71	85
Papua New Guinea	t95	78.9	--	39	31.8	18	28	ts96 f95	1.14	0.07	1.21	4	10.1	83	4	0.12	0	2	19
Samoa	p97 s95	96.5	45.0	58	--	--	58		4.87	1.72	6.59	22	29.0	57	22	22.99	6	14	43
Solomon Is	--	--	--	--	--	--	--		1.89	0.17	2.06	7	5.0	92	7	47.96	13	10	10
Tonga	--	--	--	--	--	--	--	tsf96	7.90	0.31	8.21	27	761.0	0	0	16.24	4	2	2
Vanuatu	--	71.3	42.8	29	--	--	29	f95	2.84	0.12	2.96	10	56.0	38	10	5.75	1	5	21

Notes

The knowledge index (**K index**) is the average of two weighted indicators (column heading in parentheses) [weight in brackets]: an education score (*E score*) [2]; and a communication score (*C score*) [1]. Education has a higher weight than communication because the quality of communication depends on education.

The education score is the average of two unweighted indicators:

Primary and secondary school enrollment (1st2nd score), the unweighted average score of the net primary school enrollment rate and the net secondary enrollment rate.

Tertiary school enrollment per 10,000 population (3rd score).

Enrollment rates are more reliable than other available indicators of education, notably the adult literacy rate (the percentage of adults aged 15 years and over who are literate)—see the section on education in Chapter 2. Net enrollment rates are preferable to gross enrollment rates because the latter include late entrants and repeaters. A gross enrollment rate of 100% can mean good or not good performance depending on how much late entry and repetition is involved.

Ed note = education note: a year after the letter p or s is the year of the primary or secondary enrollment data other than 1997; a year after the letter t is the year of the tertiary enrollment data.

1st net % = net primary school enrollment rate = the percentage of children of primary school-age who are enrolled in primary school. Data are for 1997, except where noted otherwise in the Ed note column, and are from UNESCO (1999b).

2nd net % = net secondary school enrollment rate = the percentage of children of secondary school-age enrolled in secondary school. Data are for 1997, except where noted otherwise in the Ed note column, and are from UNESCO (1999b).

1st 2nd score = the average of the scores for the net primary and net secondary enrollment rates. The performance criteria are shown in Table 5a. The United Nations' target is for universal primary education by 2015 (World Summit for Social Development [Copenhagen 1995] and the Fourth World Conference on Women [Beijing 1995] [United Nations Population Division 1997; Office of the UN System Support and Services 1996]). Hence the top of the good band was set at 100% and the top of fair at 95%. No UN target exists for secondary education, but since it is almost as basic as primary, the top of the good band was set at 100%, with progressively lower standards for the other bands.

3rd/10k = tertiary school students per 10,000 population. Data are for the year given in the Ed note column (after the letter t) and are from UNESCO (1999c).

3rd score = tertiary enrollment score. The performance criteria are shown in Table 5a. They have been set so that the good band includes the lowest rates of countries with the largest proportions of highly literate adults (Sweden, Canada and the United States).

The communication score is the average score of two unweighted indicators:

A telephone indicator (Tel score), represented by the lower score of main telephone lines + cellular phone subscribers per 100 persons (Ph score), and Faults per 100 main telephone lines per year (Fault score).

Internet users per 10,000 persons (I net score).

Tel note: a year after the letter f is the year of the faults data (if not 1998); a year after the letter s, the year of the cell phone data (if not 1998); a year after the letter t, the year of the main line data (if not 1998).

Main lines/100 = main telephone lines per 100 persons. Data are for 1998 [unless noted otherwise in the Tel note column] and are from International Telecommunication Union (1997, 1998 & 2000).

Cell subs/100 = cellular mobile phone subscribers per 100 persons. Data are for 1998, unless noted otherwise in the Tel note column, and are from International Telecommunication Union (1997, 1998 & 2000).

Ph score = phone score. The performance criteria are shown in Table 5a. The top of fair is the point where (in general) 95% of households have a main line.

Fault/100 l/yr = faults per 100 main telephone lines per year. Data are for 1998, unless noted otherwise in the Tel note column, and are from International Telecommunication Union (1997, 1998 & 1999).

Fault score. The performance criteria are shown in Table 5a. The top of bad was set at one fault per main line per year.

Internet users/10k = Internet per 10,000 persons. Data are for 1998 and are from International Telecommunication Union (2000).

I net score = Internet score. The performance criteria are shown in Table 5a. They encompass the range of performance of 92% of countries but otherwise are arbitrary.

band	top point on scale	net primary school enrollment (%)	net secondary school enrollment (%)	tertiary school enrollment per 10,000 population	main telephone lines + cellular phones per 100 persons	faults per 100 main telephone lines	Internet users per 10,000 population
good	100	100	100	560	100	0	1200
fair	80	95	90	280	50	12	600
medium	60	90	80	140	25	25	300
poor	40	80	60	70	12	50	150
bad	20	60	30	35	6	100	75
base	0	20	0	0	0	200	0

Table 5a. Performance criteria for indicators of education and communication.

* A score with an asterisk has been reduced in accordance with the insufficient data rule. To prevent high scores resulting merely from lack of data, a good score is allowed only if it is based on all applicable components (data in an indicator, indicators in an index), and a fair score only if it is based on at least half the components. Good and fair scores (100-61) based on fewer than half the applicable components have been reduced to 60. Good scores (100-81) based on more than half but not all the applicable components have been reduced to 80.

Table 6. Community Index; Freedom and Governance; Peace

Country	F&G note	PRR	CLR	PFR	CPI	F&G score	Armed conflicts	Def% GDP	Peace score	Crime score	P&O score	C index
AMERICAS												
Antigua & Barbuda		45	60	44	--	50		0.6	94	--	80*	50
Argentina		75	60	49	35	55		1.8	82	--	80*	55
Bahamas		90	90	91	--	80*		0.6	94	14	54	54
Barbados		90	90	79	--	80*		0.5	95	42	68	68
Belize		90	90	67	--	80*		2.6	74	--	74	74
Bolivia		90	60	71	27	62	T[98-] ?	1.8	40	35	37	37
Brazil		60	45	57	39	50		3.2	68	--	68	50
Canada		90	90	81	92	88		1.1	89	55	72	72
Chile		75	75	64	74	72		3.7	63	58	60	60
Colombia		45	45	33	32	39	[63-] 1190 + [94-95] ?	3.2	20	31	25	25
Costa Rica		90	75	79	54	74		0.7	93	55	74	74
Cuba		0	0	5	--	2		5.3	53	--	53	2
Dominica		90	90	79	--	80*		--	--	--	--	80
Dominican R		75	60	60	--	65		1.1	89	--	80*	65
Ecuador		75	60	46	26	52	[95-98] ?	2.6	40	52	46	46
El Salvador		75	60	50	41	56	[79-95] 4410	1.7	12	--	12	12
Grenada		90	75	73	--	79		--	--	--	--	79
Guatemala	CPI99	60	45	37	32	43	[68-96] 5170	1.2	11	--	11	11
Guyana		75	75	71	--	74		1.0	90	--	80*	74
Haiti		30	30	34	--	31	[91-95] 600	2.4	28	--	28	28
Honduras	CPI99	60	60	42	18	45		2.0	80	--	80	45
Jamaica	CPI99	75	75	85	38	68		0.9	91	24	57	57
Mexico		60	45	40	33	44	[94-] 830	1.0	23	--	23	23
Nicaragua	CPI99	60	60	50	31	50	[82-98] 1770	1.1	18	31	24	24
Panama		90	75	60	--	75		1.3	87	53	70	70
Paraguay	CPI99	45	60	39	20	41	T[99-] ?	1.4	40	--	40	40
Peru		30	45	26	44	36	[81-95] 2000 + [95-98] ? + T[95-] ?	1.6	18	62	40	36
St Kitts & Nevis		90	75	76	--	80		--	--	61	61	61
St Lucia		90	75	83	--	80*		--	--	--	--	80
St Vincent & Grenadines		75	90	79	--	80*		--	--	37	37	37
Suriname		60	60	59	--	60		4.2	59	--	59	59
Trinidad & Tobago		90	75	63	--	76		0.7	93	47	70	70
United States	CL: Northern Marianas	90	75	83	78	81		3.2	68	49	58	58
Uruguay	CPI99	90	75	61	44	67		2.3	77	55	66	66
Venezuela		45	45	56	27	43	[94-95] ?	1.5	40	48	44	43
AFRICA												
Algeria		15	30	14	--	20	[92-] 10000	4.8	0	--	0	0
Angola		15	15	16	17	16	[92-] 1880 + [97-] 1670 + [98-] 4500	11.7	4	--	4	4
Benin		75	60	60	--	65		1.4	86	--	80*	65
Botswana		75	75	63	60	68		6.5	47	44	45	45
Burkina Faso		45	45	50	30	42		2.5	75	--	75	42
Burundi		15	15	14	--	15	[93-] 29430	7.2	0	--	0	0
Cameroon		0	15	18	20	13	[94-95] 2500	2.9	17	--	17	13
Cape Verde		90	75	58	--	74		1.6	84	--	80*	74
Central African R		60	45	32	--	46	[96-97] 500	4.7	30	--	30	30
Chad		15	30	22	--	22	[94-] 170 + T[98-] ?	5.6	37	--	37	22
Comoros		15	45	50	--	37	[97-] ?	--	40	--	40	37
Congo, DR		0	15	8	--	8	[96-] 21000 + [97-] 1670 + [98-] 4500	6.6	0	--	0	0
Congo, R		15	30	18	--	21	[98-] 6000	3.9	9	--	9	9
Côte d'Ivoire		15	45	21	27	27		0.9	91	--	80*	27
Djibouti		45	15	30	--	30		5.1	54	--	54	30
Egypt		15	30	25	31	25		4.1	59	97	78	25
Equatorial Guinea		0	0	18	--	6		1.5	85	--	80*	6
Eritrea		0	30	26	--	19	[95-]? + [98-] 8000	35.8	0	--	0	0
Ethiopia		30	30	30	32	30	[98-] 8000 + [97-] 670 + T[96-] ?	6.0	3	84	43	30
Gabon		30	45	36	--	37		2.2	78	--	78	37
Gambia		0	30	24	--	18		3.6	64	--	64	18
Ghana		60	60	31	35	46		1.4	86	--	80*	46
Guinea		15	30	23	--	23		1.8	82	--	80*	23
Guinea-Bissau		60	30	35	--	42	[98-99] 1000	5.5	20	--	20	20
Kenya		15	30	24	21	22	T[96-] 250	3.1	35	--	35	22
Lesotho		45	45	35	--	42	[98-] ?	3.5	40	--	40	40
Liberia		45	30	26	--	34	[89-96] 1880	3.9	18	--	18	18

Country	F&G note	PRR	CLR	PFR	CPI	F&G score	Armed conflicts	Def % GDP	Peace score	Crime score	P&O score	C index
Libyan Arab J		0	0	8	--	3	T[96-]	5.3	40	--	40	3
Madagascar		75	45	58	--	59		0.9	91	98	94	59
Malawi		60	60	38	41	50		1.2	88	--	80*	50
Mali		60	60	65	--	62		2.0	80	--	80	62
Mauritania		15	30	26	--	24		2.2	78	--	78	24
Mauritius		90	75	77	47	72		2.1	79	66	72	72
Morocco	PR;CL: Western Sahara	15	30	41	47	33		4.6	57	86	71	33
Mozambique		60	45	42	22	42	[76-95] 2500	3.9	17	--	17	17
Namibia		75	60	56	54	61	T[99] ?	3.6	40	--	40	40
Niger		30	30	30	--	30	[91-96] ? + T[99-] ?	1.5	40	--	40	30
Nigeria		45	60	38	12	39	[94-95] 2500 + T[96-] ?	4.3	17	--	17	17
Rwanda		0	15	22	--	12	[90-] 81100 + [97-] 3000	6.9	0	61	30	12
São Tomé & Principe		90	75	64	--	76		--	--	9	9	9
Senegal		45	45	57	35	45	[98-] 500	1.7	30	--	30	30
Seychelles		60	60	40	--	53		2.9	71	56	63	53
Sierra Leone		60	30	12	--	34	[91-99] 4440	3.3	12	--	12	12
Somalia		0	0	10	--	3	[91-] 39440 + [97-] 670	4.7	0	--	0	0
South Africa		90	75	67	50	70	T[94-] 330 + T[98-] ?	1.6	33	--	33	33
Sudan		0	0	12	--	4	[83-] 2940 + [95-] 1000 + [95-] 200	4.8	13	86	49	4
Swaziland		15	30	18	--	21		--	--	6	6	6
Tanzania		45	45	41	25	39		3.7	63	--	63	39
Togo		30	30	21	--	27		2.4	76	--	76	27
Tunisia		15	30	21	52	29		1.8	82	--	80*	29
Uganda		30	30	50	23	33	[95-] 200 + [93-] 430 + [97-] 3000	3.1	14	--	14	14
Zambia		30	45	30	34	35	T[99-] ?	1.9	40	55	47	35
Zimbabwe		15	30	26	30	25		5.0	55	38	46	25
EUROPE												
Albania	CPI99	45	30	35	23	33	[97] 2000	6.6	18	--	18	18
Austria		90	90	84	77	85		0.8	92	71	81	81
Belarus		15	15	16	41	22		3.2	68	66	67	22
Belgium		90	75	88	61	78		1.5	85	74	79	78
Bosnia & Herzegovina		30	30	35	--	32	[92-95] 22500	8.1	0	--	0	0
Bulgaria		75	60	60	35	57		3.7	63	64	63	57
Croatia		45	45	30	37	39	[91-95] 2000	8.3	18	79	48	39
Czech R		90	75	73	43	70		2.1	79	73	76	70
Denmark		90	90	88	98	91		1.6	84	65	74	74
Estonia		90	75	73	57	74		1.3	87	38	62	62
Finland		90	90	80	100	90		1.5	85	56	70	70
France	PR: New Caledonia	75	75	68	67	71		2.8	72	67	69	69
Germany		90	75	83	76	81		1.5	85	65	75	75
Greece		90	60	60	49	65	T[75-] ?	4.8	40	86	63	63
Hungary		90	75	60	52	69		1.4	86	76	81	69
Iceland		90	90	84	91	89		--	--	--	--	80*
Ireland		90	90	72	72	81		1.0	90	--	80*	80
Italy		90	75	64	46	69		2.0	80	78	79	69
Latvia		90	75	68	34	67		2.5	75	62	68	67
Lithuania		90	75	73	41	70		1.3	87	67	77	70
Luxembourg		90	90	87	86	88		0.9	91	65	78	78
Macedonia, FYR	CPI99	60	60	48	33	50	T[97-] ?	9.9	35	89	62	50
Malta		90	90	77	--	80*		0.9	91	90	90	80
Moldova	PR;CL: Transdniester	45	30	34	26	34	[92-97] 170	4.3	37	69	53	34
Netherlands	PR: Aruba; CL: Netherlands Antilles	82	82	81	89	83		1.8	82	52	67	67
Norway		90	90	93	91	91		2.2	78	76	77	77
Poland		90	75	75	41	70		2.2	78	77	77	70
Portugal		90	90	77	64	80		2.3	77	65	71	71
Romania		75	75	46	29	56		2.3	77	77	77	56
Slovakia		75	75	60	35	61		2.0	80	82	81	61
Slovenia		90	75	64	55	71		1.7	83	74	78	71
Spain		90	75	76	70	78	T[59-] 20	1.3	40	80	60	60
Sweden		90	90	85	94	90		2.5	75	46	60	60
Switzerland		90	90	89	86	89		1.4	86	85	85	85
Ukraine		60	45	32	15	38		2.9	71	68	69	38
United Kingdom	PR;CL: Northern Ireland	75	67	73	87	75	T[69-] 100	2.8	38	67	52	52
Yugoslavia	PR;CL: Kosovo	22	22	15	13	18	[98-99] 7500 + [99] 1000	9.1	3	82	42	18

171

Country	F&G note	PRR	CLR	PFR	CPI	F&G score	Armed conflicts	Def % GDP	Peace score	Crime score	P&O score	C index
RUSSIAN FEDERATION	PR;CL: Chechnya	30	22	32	21	26	[94-96] 11670 + [91-96] 170 + T[96-] ?	5.2	0	53	26	26
ASIA												
Afghanistan		0	0	8	--	3	[92-] 8250	14.5	4	--	4	3
Armenia	PR;CL: Nagorno-Karabakh; CPI 99	37	30	34	25	31		8.4	39	76	57	31
Azerbaijan	CL: Nagorno-Karabakh	15	30	24	15	21		4.6	57	80	68	21
Bahrain		0	15	20	--	12		6.7	46	63	54	12
Bangladesh		60	45	32	--	46	[82-98] 180	1.9	36	--	36	36
Bhutan		0	15	19	--	11		4.5	57	--	57	11
Brunei Darussalam		0	30	21	--	17		6.9	45	--	45	17
Cambodia		15	15	31	--	20	[97-98] 500	4.2	30	--	30	20
China	CL: Tibet	0	7	16	31	13	T[91-] 110	5.3	38	92	65	13
Cyprus	ave. Greek & Turk	67	82	79	--	76		5.5	52	87	69	69
Georgia	PR;CL: Abkhazia	37	37	43	23	35	[92-94] 2000 + [90-96] 140	2.5	17	73	45	35
India	PR;CL: Kashmir	45	37	48	28	39	[89-] 2000 + [84-] 60 + T[89-] 270 + T[96-] ?	3.0	17	74	45	39
Indonesia	PR; CL: West Papua	30	37	41	17	31	[75-] 8000 + [65-] 860 + [97-] 1330 + T[91-] 220 + T[98-] ?	2.6	0	97	48	31
Iran		15	15	26	--	19	[79-] 710 + [79-] 620	6.5	19	--	19	19
Iraq		0	0	2	--	1	[88-] 5000 + [91-] 3440 + T[93-] ?	7.3	3	--	3	1
Israel	PR;CL: Israeli-administered territories	52	52	60	66	57	[78-] 1320 + T[93-] ?	11.6	19	68	43	43
Japan		90	75	75	64	76		1.0	90	94	92	76
Jordan		45	45	34	46	42		7.7	41	74	57	42
Kazakhstan		15	30	26	30	25		2.2	78	58	68	25
Korea, DPR		0	0	0	--	0		14.3	24	--	24	0
Korea, R		75	75	64	40	63		3.1	69	72	70	63
Kuwait		45	30	42	--	39		12.9	28	46	37	37
Kyrgyzstan	CPI99	30	30	31	22	28		3.6	64	64	64	28
Lao PDR		0	15	27	--	14		3.7	63	--	63	14
Lebanon		15	30	31	--	25	[78-] 1320	3.6	19	--	19	19
Malaysia		30	30	24	48	33		3.7	63	88	75	33
Maldives		15	30	28	--	24		--	--	73	73	24
Mongolia	CPI99	75	60	61	43	60		2.1	79	--	79	60
Myanmar		0	0	0	--	0	[85-] 600	6.8	28	87	57	0
Nepal		60	45	33	--	46	T[97-] 330	0.7	33	94	63	46
Oman		15	15	23	--	18		13.6	26	--	26	18
Pakistan	CPI99	0	30	29	22	20	[89-] 2000 + [84-] 60 + T[90-] 100 + T[98-] ?	6.5	17	--	17	17
Philippines		75	60	60	28	56	[68-97] 2500	2.3	17	75	46	46
Qatar		15	15	30	--	20		12.0	30	82	56	20
Saudi Arabia		0	0	8	--	3		15.7	21	--	21	3
Singapore		30	30	27	91	44		5.0	55	89	72	44
Sri Lanka		60	45	24	--	43	[83-] 3410	6.1	15	63	39	39
Syrian Arab R		0	0	22	--	7		7.3	43	97	70	7
Tajikistan		15	15	5	--	12	[92-97] 8500	8.3	3	90	46	12
Thailand		75	60	60	32	57		1.5	85	74	79	57
Turkey		45	30	34	38	37	[84-] 2440 + T[77-] ?	4.4	17	89	53	37
Turkmenistan		0	0	11	--	4		2.8	72	--	72	4
United Arab Emirates		15	30	19	--	21		6.5	47	--	47	21
Uzbekistan		0	15	14	24	13	T[99-] ?	5.4	40	--	40	13
Viet Nam		0	0	20	25	11		3.4	66	--	66	11
Yemen		30	15	26	--	24	T[98-] ?	6.6	40	--	40	24
PACIFIC												
Australia	PR;CL: Christmas I	75	82	87	83	82		1.9	81	59	70	70
Fiji		75	60	34	--	56		1.6	84	--	80*	56
New Zealand	CL: Cook Is	90	82	89	94	89		1.5	85	--	80*	80
Papua New Guinea		75	60	63	--	66	[88-98] 910	1.0	22	--	22	22
Samoa		75	75	56	--	69		--	--	76	76	69
Solomon Is		90	75	76	--	80		--	--	--	--	80
Tonga		30	60	54	--	48		--	--	49	49	48
Vanuatu		90	60	46	--	65		--	--	68	68	65

Notes

The community index (**C index**) is the lower of a freedom and governance index (**F&G score**) and a peace and order index (**P&O score**).

The freedom and governance index is the average of four unweighted indicators (column heading in parentheses):

Political rights rating (PRR).

Civil liberties rating (CLR).

Press freedom rating (PFR).

Corruption perceptions index (CPI).

The PFR and CPI overlap with the CLR, which includes press freedom and corruption. However, all four indicators are used because each has its own strengths. The PRR and CLR together cover almost all aspects of human rights and freedoms, but the basis of each rating is not disclosed. The PFR and CPI cover only one aspect each, but the basis of each rating is fully described.

The peace and order index is the average of two unweighted indicators:

Peace (Peace score), represented by deaths from armed conflicts per year or military expenditure as a percentage of Gross Domestic Product, whichever gives the lower score.

Crime (Crime score), represented by the unweighted average of the homicide rate and other violent crimes. Crime data and scores are shown in Table 7.

F&G note = notes on adjustments to the PRR and CLR and on different years for the CPI. Countries with a PR or CL note here have had their PRR or CLR reduced because of a lower rating for a related or disputed territory. The reduced rating is the average of the country's rating and the territory's rating. The territory concerned is indicated after PR, CL or both. For example—PR;CL: Christmas I. Countries with a CPI note here have a CPI for 1997-1999 rather than 1998-2000.

PRR = Freedom House's political rights rating for 1999 (Freedom House 2000a). Freedom House converts raw points to ratings of 1-7. In general, it classifies ratings of 1 or 2 as "free", 3, 4 or 5 as "partly free", and 6 or 7 as "not free". The ratings were converted to the Barometer scale (Table 6a) as follows: 1=90; 2=75; 3=60; 4=45; 5=30; 6=15; 7=0.

CLR = Freedom House's civil liberties rating for 1999 (Freedom House 2000a). Freedom House converts raw points to ratings of 1-7. In general, it classifies ratings of 1 or 2 as "free", 3, 4 or 5 as "partly free", and 6 or 7 as "not free". The ratings were converted to the Barometer scale (Table 6a) as follows: 1=90; 2=75; 3=60; 4=45; 5=30; 6=15; 7=0.

PFR = Freedom House's press freedom rating for 1999 (Freedom House 2000b). Freedom House gives separate ratings for the print and broadcast media, with respect to laws and regulations that influence media content, political pressures and controls on media content, economic influences over media content, and repressive actions (killing journalists, physical violence, censorship, self-censorship, arrests, etc.). The resulting total number of points can range from 0 (complete freedom) to 100 (complete repression). Freedom House classifies 0-30 points as "free", 31-60 points as "partly free", and 61-100 points as "not free". The performance criteria in Table 6a were based on this classification.

CPI = Transparency International's corruption perceptions index. The index is for 1998-2000 and from Transparency International (2000), unless noted CPI99 in the F&G note column, in which case it is for 1997-1999 and from Transparency International (1999). Transparency International used 17 surveys from 10 independent institutions to assess a country's performance for its 1999 CPI (Transparency International 1999), and 16 surveys for its 2000 CPI (Transparency International 2000). At least three surveys were required for a country to be included in the 1999 or 2000 CPI. The CPI reflects perceptions of the degree of corruption as seen by business people, risk analysts and the general public and ranges from 10 (highly clean) to 0 (highly corrupt). The 10 to 0 scale was placed directly onto the Barometer scale (Table 6a).

Armed conflicts = international or internal armed conflict in at least one year in the period 1995-1999. The number in brackets is the year or years. The number outside the brackets is the average number of deaths per year since the conflict started (which may have been before 1995). ? = number of deaths not estimated. T = active terrorism. Data are from International Institute for Strategic Studies (1999b).

Def % GDP = defence expenditure as a percentage of Gross Domestic Product. Defence expenditure = military expenditure = the cash outlays of central or federal government to meet the costs of national armed forces. Armed forces include strategic land, naval, air, command, administration and support forces, and also paramilitary forces such as the *gendarmerie*, customs service and border guard if these are trained in military tactics, equipped as a military force and operate under military authority in the event of war. Costs include operating costs, procurement and construction, and research and development. Data are for 1998 and are from International Institute for Strategic Studies (1999a).

Peace score = the lower of the armed conflicts and military expenditure scores. If more than one armed conflict is recorded for a country, the armed conflicts score is based on the total number of deaths per year. If the number of deaths has not been estimated (that is, if the only entry is ?), it is assumed to be 10. Otherwise, a ? is ignored. For example— Uzbekistan: ? = 10; but Turkey: 2440 + ? = 2440. The performance criteria are shown in Table 6a.

Crime score: see Table 7 for data. The performance criteria are shown in Table 6a.

band	top point on scale	political rights rating	civil liberties rating	press freedom rating	corruption perceptions index	deaths from armed conflicts per year	military expenditure as % of GDP	homicides per 100,000 population	rapes per 100,000 population	robberies per 100,000 population	assaults per 100,000 population
good	100	100	100	0	10	--	0	0	0	0	0
fair	80	80	80	15	8	--	2	5	10	20	40
medium	60	60	60	30	6	--	4	10	20	40	80
poor	40	40	40	50	4	0	8	20	40	80	160
bad	20	20	20	75	2	1000	16	40	80	160	320
base	0	0	0	100	0	10000	32	80	160	320	640

Table 6a. Performance criteria for indicators of freedom and governance and peace and order.

* A score with an asterisk has been reduced in accordance with the insufficient data rule. To prevent high scores resulting merely from lack of data, a good score is allowed only if it is based on all applicable components (data in an indicator, indicators in an index), and a fair score only if it is based on at least half the components. Good and fair scores (100-61) based on fewer than half the applicable components have been reduced to 60. Good scores (100-81) based on more than half but not all the applicable components have been reduced to 80.

Table 7. Crime

Country	Year	Homicides (ho)			Rapes (ra)			Robberies (ro)			Assaults (as)			OVC score	Crime score
		number	rate	score	number	rate	score	number	rate	score	number	rate	score		
AMERICAS															
Antigua & Barbuda	--	--	--	--	--	--	--	--	--	--	--	--	--	--	--
Argentina	--	--	--	--	--	--	--	--	--	--	--	--	--	--	--
Bahamas	94asm	227	82.8	0	215	78.5	21	544	198.5	15	335	122.3	49	28	14
Barbados	90	30	11.5	57	71	27.3	53	339	130.4	27	1736	667.7	0	27	42
Belize	--	--	--	--	--	--	--	--	--	--	--	--	--	--	--
Bolivia	94	1687	23.3	37	2261	31.2	49	11543	159.5	20	--	--	--	34	35
Brazil	--	--	--	--	--	--	--	--	--	--	--	--	--	--	--
Canada	98	555	1.8	93	25493	84.1	19	28952	95.6	36	223260	736.8	0	18	55
Chile	94	626	4.5	82	961	6.9	86	72058	514.9	0	45383	324.3	20	35	58
Colombia	94	27130	78.6	1	1930	5.6	89	28486	82.5	39	28748	83.3	59	62	31
Costa Rica	94	298	9.7	61	294	9.6	81	16067	523.2	0	2052	66.8	67	49	55
Cuba	--	--	--	--	--	--	--	--	--	--	--	--	--	--	--
Dominica	--	--	--	--	--	--	--	--	--	--	--	--	--	--	--
Dominican R	--	--	--	--	--	--	--	--	--	--	--	--	--	--	--
Ecuador	94	2073	18.5	43	935	8.3	83	21814	194.4	16	2958	26.4	87	62	52
El Salvador	--	--	--	--	--	--	--	--	--	--	--	--	--	--	--
Grenada	--	--	--	--	--	--	--	--	--	--	--	--	--	--	--
Guatemala	--	--	--	--	--	--	--	--	--	--	--	--	--	--	--
Guyana	--	--	--	--	--	--	--	--	--	--	--	--	--	--	--
Haiti	--	--	--	--	--	--	--	--	--	--	--	--	--	--	--
Honduras	--	--	--	--	--	--	--	--	--	--	--	--	--	--	--
Jamaica	94	743	29.8	30	1070	42.9	38	5461	218.8	13	13855	555.1	5	19	24
Mexico	--	--	--	--	--	--	--	--	--	--	--	--	--	--	--
Nicaragua	94	1128	25.6	34	1323	30.1	50	13325	302.8	2	8991	204.3	34	29	31
Panama	94	323	12.5	55	290	11.2	78	3662	141.8	25	2763	107.0	53	52	53
Paraguay	--	--	--	--	--	--	--	--	--	--	--	--	--	--	--
Peru	90	1289	6.0	76	--	--	--	54130	250.7	9	5738	26.6	87	48	62
St Kitts & Nevis	90	2	5.0	80	19	47.5	36	4	10.0	90	236	590.0	3	43	61
St Lucia	--	--	--	--	--	--	--	--	--	--	--	--	--	--	--
St Vincent & Grenadines	94asm	16	14.4	51	123	110.8	12	44	39.6	60	1163	1047.7	0	24	37
Suriname	--	--	--	--	--	--	--	--	--	--	--	--	--	--	--
Trinidad & Tobago	90	94	7.6	70	220	17.7	65	3116	251.3	9	18435	1486.7	0	25	47
United States	97	18210	6.8	73	96120	35.9	44	497950	186.1	17	1022490	382.0	16	26	49
Uruguay	94hoi	186	5.9	76	--	--	--	3072	97.0	36	6981	220.4	32	34	55
Venezuela	90	2474	12.7	55	2928	15.0	70	38728	198.6	15	29621	151.9	42	42	48
AFRICA															
Algeria	--	--	--	--	--	--	--	--	--	--	--	--	--	--	--
Angola	--	--	--	--	--	--	--	--	--	--	--	--	--	--	--
Benin	--	--	--	--	--	--	--	--	--	--	--	--	--	--	--
Botswana	90	152	11.9	56	614	48.0	36	523	40.9	60	10414	813.6	0	32	44
Burkina Faso	--	--	--	--	--	--	--	--	--	--	--	--	--	--	--
Burundi	--	--	--	--	--	--	--	--	--	--	--	--	--	--	--
Cameroon	--	--	--	--	--	--	--	--	--	--	--	--	--	--	--
Cape Verde	--	--	--	--	--	--	--	--	--	--	--	--	--	--	--
Central African R	--	--	--	--	--	--	--	--	--	--	--	--	--	--	--
Chad	--	--	--	--	--	--	--	--	--	--	--	--	--	--	--
Comoros	--	--	--	--	--	--	--	--	--	--	--	--	--	--	--
Congo, DR	--	--	--	--	--	--	--	--	--	--	--	--	--	--	--
Congo, R	--	--	--	--	--	--	--	--	--	--	--	--	--	--	--
Côte d'Ivoire	--	--	--	--	--	--	--	--	--	--	--	--	--	--	--
Djibouti	--	--	--	--	--	--	--	--	--	--	--	--	--	--	--
Egypt	94	871	1.5	94	9	0.0	100	375	0.6	99	108	0.2	100	100	97
Equatorial Guinea	--	--	--	--	--	--	--	--	--	--	--	--	--	--	--
Eritrea	--	--	--	--	--	--	--	--	--	--	--	--	--	--	--
Ethiopia	90	3601	7.6	70	289	0.6	99	33	0.1	100	2955	6.2	97	99	84
Gabon	--	--	--	--	--	--	--	--	--	--	--	--	--	--	--
Gambia	--	--	--	--	--	--	--	--	--	--	--	--	--	--	--
Ghana	--	--	--	--	--	--	--	--	--	--	--	--	--	--	--
Guinea	--	--	--	--	--	--	--	--	--	--	--	--	--	--	--
Guinea-Bissau	--	--	--	--	--	--	--	--	--	--	--	--	--	--	--
Kenya	--	--	--	--	--	--	--	--	--	--	--	--	--	--	--
Lesotho	--	--	--	--	--	--	--	--	--	--	--	--	--	--	--
Liberia	--	--	--	--	--	--	--	--	--	--	--	--	--	--	--
Libyan Arab J	--	--	--	--	--	--	--	--	--	--	--	--	--	--	--
Madagascar	94	63	0.4	98	50	0.3	99	31	0.2	100	1158	8.1	96	98	98
Malawi	--	--	--	--	--	--	--	--	--	--	--	--	--	--	--
Mali	--	--	--	--	--	--	--	--	--	--	--	--	--	--	--

Country	Year	Homicides (ho)			Rapes (ra)			Robberies (ro)			Assaults (as)			OVC score	Crime score
		number	rate	score	number	rate	score	number	rate	score	number	rate	score		
Mauritania	--	--	--	--	--	--	--	--	--	--	--	--	--	--	--
Mauritius	94	36	3.3	87	34	3.1	94	767	69.5	45	12862	1165.0	0	46	66
Morocco	94	472	1.8	93	932	3.5	93	--	--	--	2396	9.0	95	80*	86
Mozambique	--	--	--	--	--	--	--	--	--	--	--	--	--	--	--
Namibia	--	--	--	--	--	--	--	--	--	--	--	--	--	--	--
Niger	--	--	--	--	--	--	--	--	--	--	--	--	--	--	--
Nigeria	--	--	--	--	--	--	--	--	--	--	--	--	--	--	--
Rwanda	90	926	13.2	54	721	10.3	79	2747	39.3	61	4762	68.1	66	69	61
São Tomé & Principe	94hoi	178	142.4	0	--	--	--	--	--	--	414	331.2	19	19	9
Senegal	--	--	--	--	--	--	--	--	--	--	--	--	--	--	--
Seychelles	90	5	7.1	72	32	45.7	37	11	15.7	84	584	834.3	0	40	56
Sierra Leone	--	--	--	--	--	--	--	--	--	--	--	--	--	--	--
Somalia	--	--	--	--	--	--	--	--	--	--	--	--	--	--	--
South Africa	--	--	--	--	--	--	--	--	--	--	--	--	--	--	--
Sudan	94asm	1002	3.5	86	610	2.1	96	846	2.9	97	17836	61.6	69	87	86
Swaziland	90	874	118.1	0	558	75.4	22	1514	204.6	14	9183	1240.9	0	12	6
Tanzania	--	--	--	--	--	--	--	--	--	--	--	--	--	--	--
Togo	--	--	--	--	--	--	--	--	--	--	--	--	--	--	--
Tunisia	--	--	--	--	--	--	--	--	--	--	--	--	--	--	--
Uganda	--	--	--	--	--	--	--	--	--	--	--	--	--	--	--
Zambia	94asm	1456	15.8	48	337	3.7	93	3287	35.7	64	22056	239.8	30	62	55
Zimbabwe	94	1779	16.0	48	3091	27.7	52	12378	111.0	32	67598	606.3	2	29	38
EUROPE															
Albania	--	--	--	--	--	--	--	--	--	--	--	--	--	--	--
Austria	94	283	3.5	86	553	6.9	86	2442	30.4	70	33667	419.2	14	57	71
Belarus	94	1029	9.9	60	672	6.5	87	7013	67.7	46	3221	31.1	84	72	66
Belgium	94	343	3.4	86	899	8.9	82	1448	14.4	86	33329	330.6	19	62	74
Bosnia & Herzegovina	--	--	--	--	--	--	--	--	--	--	--	--	--	--	--
Bulgaria	94	948	11.2	58	903	10.7	79	6597	78.1	41	1079	12.8	94	71	64
Croatia	94	367	8.1	68	94	2.1	96	389	8.6	91	1168	25.9	87	91	79
Czech R	90	--	--	--	890	8.6	83	3855	37.4	63	--	--	--	73	73
Denmark	94	263	5.1	80	481	9.2	82	4880	93.8	36	9881	189.8	36	51	65
Estonia	94	385	25.7	34	2981	198.9	0	--	--	--	411	27.4	86	43	38
Finland	94	533	10.5	59	387	7.6	85	2122	41.6	59	19836	389.3	16	53	56
France	94hoiasm	2696	4.7	81	6526	11.3	77	73310	127.0	28	63435	109.8	53	53	67
Germany	FRG90	2995	4.9	80	5112	8.3	83	35111	57.3	51	213481	348.1	18	51	65
Greece	94	298	2.9	88	258	2.5	95	812	7.8	92	7566	72.6	64	84	86
Hungary	94	477	4.6	82	828	8.1	84	2570	25.0	75	11077	108.0	53	71	76
Iceland	--	--	--	--	--	--	--	--	--	--	--	--	--	--	--
Ireland	--	--	--	--	--	--	--	--	--	--	--	--	--	--	--
Italy	94	3040	5.3	79	869	1.5	97	29981	52.4	54	20873	36.5	82	78	78
Latvia	94	412	16.2	48	129	5.1	90	1142	44.8	58	1059	41.6	79	76	62
Lithuania	94	560	15.0	50	165	4.4	91	806	21.7	78	956	25.7	87	85	67
Luxembourg	90	--	--	--	28	7.4	85	23	6.1	94	1452	382.1	16	65	65
Macedonia, FYR	94	80	3.7	85	38	1.8	96	132	6.2	94	527	24.6	88	93	89
Malta	94	11	3.0	88	10	2.7	95	33	9.1	91	83	22.8	89	92	90
Moldova	94	414	9.5	62	267	6.1	88	2288	52.6	54	1291	29.7	85	76	69
Netherlands	90	2206	14.8	50	1321	8.8	82	11946	79.9	40	22079	147.7	43	55	52
Norway	90	128	3.0	88	376	8.9	82	1047	24.7	75	7949	187.4	37	65	76
Poland	90	--	--	--	1840	4.8	90	16217	42.5	59	14350	37.6	81	77	77
Portugal	90	725	7.3	71	315	3.2	94	4709	47.7	56	26621	269.7	26	59	65
Romania	94	1732	7.6	70	1391	6.1	88	4161	18.3	82	6733	29.6	85	85	77
Slovakia	94	205	3.8	85	213	4.0	92	1244	23.3	77	--	--	--	80	82
Slovenia	94	111	5.7	77	240	12.4	75	294	15.1	85	1816	93.5	57	72	74
Spain	94hoi	641	1.6	94	1211	3.1	94	55678	142.2	24	12129	31.0	84	67	80
Sweden	94	1050	12.0	56	1812	20.6	59	5331	60.7	50	53665	611.2	2	37	46
Switzerland	94hoi	161	2.3	91	275	3.9	92	1954	27.9	72	3612	51.6	74	79	85
Ukraine	94asm	5008	9.6	62	1715	3.3	93	32553	62.7	49	17091	32.9	83	75	68
United Kingdom	94	1180	2.0	92	5844	10.0	80	66629	114.5	31	219861	377.7	16	42	67
Yugoslavia	90	559	5.5	78	364	3.6	93	509	5.0	95	6128	60.3	70	86	82
RUSSIAN FEDERATION	94as90	34302	23.2	37	13956	9.4	81	148546	100.4	35	16514	11.2	94	70	53
ASIA															
Afghanistan	--	--	--	--	--	--	--	--	--	--	--	--	--	--	--
Armenia	90	238	7.1	72	34	1.0	98	371	11.1	89	--	--	--	80*	76
Azerbaijan	94	667	8.9	64	77	1.0	98	295	3.9	96	418	5.6	97	97	80
Bahrain	90as89	5	1.0	96	18	3.7	93	3372	688.2	0	3050	622.4	1	31	63
Bangladesh	--	--	--	--	--	--	--	--	--	--	--	--	--	--	--
Bhutan	--	--	--	--	--	--	--	--	--	--	--	--	--	--	--
Brunei Darussalam	--	--	--	--	--	--	--	--	--	--	--	--	--	--	--
Cambodia	--	--	--	--	--	--	--	--	--	--	--	--	--	--	--

Country	Year	Homicides (ho)			Rapes (ra)			Robberies (ro)			Assaults (as)			OVC score	Crime score
		number	rate	score	number	rate	score	number	rate	score	number	rate	score		
China	90	23199	2.0	92	50331	4.4	91	105132	9.1	91	57498	5.0	97	93	92
Cyprus	94	12	1.6	94	7	1.0	98	14	1.9	98	976	133.0	47	81	87
Georgia	94	788	14.4	51	49	0.9	98	328	6.0	94	573	10.5	95	96	73
India	94	72543	7.9	68	13208	1.4	97	23933	2.6	97	--	--	--	80*	74
Indonesia	94hoi	1517	0.8	97	1678	0.9	98	6777	3.5	96	10062	5.2	97	97	97
Iran	--	--	--	--	--	--	--	--	--	--	--	--	--	--	--
Iraq	--	--	--	--	--	--	--	--	--	--	--	--	--	--	--
Israel	94	389	7.2	71	550	10.2	80	450	8.4	92	15351	285.2	24	65	68
Japan	94	1746	1.4	94	1616	1.3	97	2684	2.2	98	24032	19.3	90	95	94
Jordan	94	298	5.7	77	36	0.7	99	500	9.6	90	14946	287.5	24	71	74
Kazakhstan	94	2664	15.6	49	1862	10.9	78	11919	70.0	45	6088	35.8	82	68	58
Korea, DPR	--	--	--	--	--	--	--	--	--	--	--	--	--	--	--
Korea, R	94asm	4514	10.2	60	6173	13.9	72	4580	10.3	90	5495	12.4	94	85	72
Kuwait	94	940	58.0	11	9	0.6	99	162	10.0	90	1523	94.0	56	82	46
Kyrgyzstan	94	564	12.3	55	400	8.7	83	1987	43.2	58	1790	38.9	80	74	64
Lao PDR	--	--	--	--	--	--	--	--	--	--	--	--	--	--	--
Lebanon	--	--	--	--	--	--	--	--	--	--	--	--	--	--	--
Malaysia	94hoi	377	1.9	92	965	5.0	90	6072	31.2	69	2846	14.6	93	84	88
Maldives	90	14	6.4	74	2	0.9	98	28	12.7	87	474	215.4	33	73	73
Mongolia	--	--	--	--	--	--	--	--	--	--	--	--	--	--	--
Myanmar	90	1786	4.3	83	780	1.9	96	384	0.9	99	16244	38.9	80	92	87
Nepal	90	484	2.5	90	112	0.6	99	183	0.9	99	1141	5.9	97	98	94
Oman	--	--	--	--	--	--	--	--	--	--	--	--	--	--	--
Pakistan	--	--	--	--	--	--	--	--	--	--	--	--	--	--	--
Philippines	94asm	6338	9.5	62	2494	3.7	93	9169	13.7	86	17883	26.7	87	89	75
Qatar	94ro90	12	2.2	91	14	2.6	95	315	65.6	47	222	41.1	79	74	82
Saudi Arabia	--	--	--	--	--	--	--	--	--	--	--	--	--	--	--
Singapore	94	51	1.7	93	81	2.8	94	812	27.7	72	601	20.5	90	85	89
Sri Lanka	90	2353	13.7	53	369	2.1	96	5702	33.1	67	15093	87.6	58	74	63
Syrian Arab R	94	174	1.3	95	100	0.7	99	18	0.1	100	72	0.5	100	100	97
Tajikistan	90	177	3.3	87	123	2.3	95	738	13.9	86	289	5.5	97	93	90
Thailand	90	5586	10.0	60	2514	4.5	91	3396	6.1	94	21752	39.1	80	88	74
Turkey	94	1794	2.9	88	503	0.8	98	1542	2.5	97	32245	52.7	74	90	89
Turkmenistan	--	--	--	--	--	--	--	--	--	--	--	--	--	--	--
United Arab Emirates	--	--	--	--	--	--	--	--	--	--	--	--	--	--	--
Uzbekistan	--	--	--	--	--	--	--	--	--	--	--	--	--	--	--
Viet Nam	--	--	--	--	--	--	--	--	--	--	--	--	--	--	--
Yemen	--	--	--	--	--	--	--	--	--	--	--	--	--	--	--
PACIFIC															
Australia	94asm90	875	4.9	80	14027	78.2	21	14370	80.1	40	17963	106.4	53	38	59
Fiji	--	--	--	--	--	--	--	--	--	--	--	--	--	--	--
New Zealand	--	--	--	--	--	--	--	--	--	--	--	--	--	--	--
Papua New Guinea	--	--	--	--	--	--	--	--	--	--	--	--	--	--	--
Samoa	94	10	6.1	76	9	5.5	89	2	1.2	99	242	147.6	43	77	76
Solomon Is	--	--	--	--	--	--	--	--	--	--	--	--	--	--	--
Tonga	90	24	24.0	36	11	11.0	78	3	3.0	97	433	433.0	13	63	49
Vanuatu	90	1	0.7	97	30	20.0	60	--	--	--	530	353.3	18	39	68

Notes

The crime score is the average of two unweighted indicators: homicide rate (homicide score); and other violent crimes (OVC score)—the unweighted average of scores for the rape rate, robbery rate, and assault rate. Homicides are distinguished from other violent crimes because they are more serious and are reported less inconsistently. Homicides include intentional homicides (murder) and unintentional homicides (manslaughter, except as a result of traffic accidents). Rape is sexual intercourse without valid consent. Robbery is the use of force or the threat of force to steal property. Assault is physical attack against the body of another person, other than rape or robbery. All data are from United Nations Crime Prevention and Criminal Justice Division (1997 & 1999), except for Canada, which are from Canadian Centre for Justice Statistics (1999), and the United States which are from Federal Bureau of Investigation (1999). Rates are per 100,000 population. Performance criteria for the scores are shown in Table 6a.

Year = the applicable year. A year following the code—as (assaults), ho (homicides), ra (rapes) or ro (robberies)—indicates a different year for that category; asm = major assaults only; hoi = intentional homicides only; FRG = the former Federal Republic of Germany (West Germany).

* A score with an asterisk has been reduced in accordance with the insufficient data rule. To prevent high scores resulting merely from lack of data, a good score is allowed only if it is based on all applicable components (data in an indicator, indicators in an index), and a fair score only if it is based on at least half the components. Good and fair scores (100-61) based on fewer than half the applicable components have been reduced to 60. Good scores (100-81) based on more than half but not all the applicable components have been reduced to 80.

Table 8. Equity

Country	HE year	H inc ratio	HE score	G inc ratio	G&W score	1st F%M	2nd F%M	3rd F%M	F or M	Ave diff	G&K score	F % govt	F % parl	G&C score	GE score	E index
AMERICAS																
Antigua & Barbuda	--	--	--	--	--	--	--	--	--	--	--	26.7	5.3	11	11	11
Argentina	#92	10.8	35	3.4	36	100.0	107.7	--	=f-	3.9	80*	5.2	28.0	56	57	46
Bahamas	#93	13.4	29	1.5	80	113.0	130.3	--	ff=	21.7	38	30.3	15.0	30	49	39
Barbados	--	--	--	1.6	76	94.6	94.1	137.7	mmf	16.3	47	25.5	10.7	21	48	48
Belize	--	--	--	4.3	27	100.0	97.1	--	=m-	1.5	80*	6.0	6.9	14	40	40
Bolivia	90	8.6	42	2.7	46	95.0	86.5	--	mm-	9.3	63	7.3	11.5	23	44	43
Brazil	96	25.5	9	2.5	50	94.4	103.4	115.9	mff	8.3	67	13.7	5.7	11	43	26
Canada	94	5.2	59	1.6	76	100.0	98.3	111.7	=mf	4.5	82	17.7	19.9	40	66	62
Chile	94	17.4	19	3.4	36	97.5	104.8	83.6	mfm	7.9	68	10.3	10.8	22	42	30
Colombia	96	20.3	16	2.0	60	100.0	104.7	105.3	=ff	3.3	87	20.5	11.8	24	57	36
Costa Rica	96	12.9	30	2.8	44	101.6	103.8	81.7	ffm	7.9	68	27.2	19.3	39	50	40
Cuba	--	--	--	2.1	58	100.0	108.0	152.1	=ff	20.0	40	9.1	27.6	55	51	51
Dominica	--	--	--	--	--	--	--	--	--	--	--	25	9.4	19	19	19
Dominican R	96	12.5	31	2.9	42	105.1	109.3	139.9	fff	18.1	44	9.8	16.1	32	39	35
Ecuador	95	9.2	39	4.1	29	100.0	101.4	--	=f-	0.7	80*	3.4	17.4	35	48	43
El Salvador	96	16.6	21	1.9	64	100.0	101.7	97.2	=fm	1.5	94	26.8	16.7	33	64	42
Grenada	--	--	--	--	--	--	--	--	--	--	--	22.5	26.7	53	53	53
Guatemala	--	--	--	3.3	37	90.9	83.4	--	mm-	12.9	54	16.7	7.1	14	35	35
Guyana	93	7.4	48	2.7	46	100.4	104.1	100.4	fff	1.6	94	14.6	18.5	37	59	53
Haiti	--	--	--	1.8	68	105.3	94.6	--	fm-	5.4	78	22.2	3.6	7	51	51
Honduras	96	17.1	20	2.9	42	102.5	110.8	79.3	ffm	11.3	57	14.1	9.4	19	39	29
Jamaica	96	6.3	53	1.6	76	100.2	106.7	72.5	ffm	11.5	57	14.3	13.3	27	53	53
Mexico	95	16.2	22	2.8	44	100.0	93.8	89.6	=mm	5.5	78	7.5	18.2	36	53	37
Nicaragua	93	13.1	30	2.4	52	104.2	108.5	109.6	fff	7.4	70	17.4	9.7	19	47	38
Panama	97	14.7	26	2.4	52	100.7	101.1	149.1	fff	17.0	46	9.4	9.7	19	39	32
Paraguay	95	27.1	7	3.1	39	101.4	96.8	106.0	fmf	3.5	86	4.3	2.5	5	43	25
Peru	96	11.6	33	3.1	39	99.0	93.5	--	mm-	3.8	80*	13.2	10.8	22	47	40
St Kitts & Nevis	--	--	--	--	--	--	--	--	--	--	--	16.7	13.3	27	27	27
St Lucia	95	9.3	39	--	--	--	--	--	--	--	--	5.0	11.1	22	22	30
St Vincent & Grenadines	--	--	--	--	--	--	--	--	--	--	--	19.2	4.8	10	10	10
Suriname	--	--	--	2.7	46	100.0	--	--	=--	0.0	60*	11.3	15.7	31	46	46
Trinidad & Tobago	92	8.3	43	2.6	48	100.0	102.1	71.9	=fm	10.1	60	13.8	11.1	22	43	43
United States	97	8.9	40	1.6	76	100.0	99.6	121.3	=mf	7.2	71	33.1	13.3	27	58	49
Uruguay	--	--	--	2.0	60	101.1	112.1	--	ff-	6.6	74	13.7	12.1	24	53	53
Venezuela	96	14.4	26	2.5	50	102.7	123.7	--	ff-	13.2	54	14.5	12.1	24	43	34
AFRICA																
Algeria	95	6.1	54	3.6	34	93.3	87.9	68.2	mmm	16.9	46	4.8	3.2	6	29	41
Angola	--	--	--	1.5	80	96.6	81.6	--	mm-	10.9	58	4.9	15.5	31	56	56
Benin	--	--	--	1.4	84	59.4	47.8	22.7	mmm	56.7	12	14.9	6.0	12	36	36
Botswana	--	--	--	2.3	54	106.3	105.8	86.5	ffm	8.5	66	13.5	17.0	34	51	51
Burkina Faso	94	10.0	37	1.4	84	64.3	58.0	29.5	mmm	49.4	15	11.5	8.1	16	38	37
Burundi	92	5.3	58	1.4	84	85.9	69.8	33.9	mmm	36.8	23	5.4	6.0	12	40	49
Cameroon	--	--	--	2.3	54	91.9	77.3	--	mm-	15.4	49	4.5	5.6	11	38	38
Cape Verde	--	--	--	2.5	50	100.0	93.9	--	=m-	3.1	80*	11.1	11.1	22	51	51
Central African R	93	32.5	1	1.6	76	69.0	49.6	16.2	mmm	55.1	12	4.9	7.3	15	34	17
Chad	--	--	--	1.7	72	58.1	36.5	14.4	mmm	63.7	8	4.3	2.4	5	28	28
Comoros	--	--	--	1.9	64	83.0	82.4	40.2	mmm	31.5	28	2.7	--	--	46	46
Congo, DR	--	--	--	1.8	68	69.8	62.6	--	mm-	33.8	26	3.4	--	--	47	47
Congo, R	--	--	--	1.8	68	93.8	78.8	21.8	mmm	35.2	25	6.5	12.0	24	39	39
Côte d'Ivoire	95	6.2	54	2.7	46	76.0	53.0	30.5	mmm	46.8	17	7.1	8.0	16	26	40
Djibouti	--	--	--	--	--	75.3	66.1	76.7	mmm	27.3	33	0.9	0.0	0	16	16
Egypt	95	4.0	70	2.8	44	90.7	87.7	63.5	mmm	19.4	41	4.0	2.0	4	30	50
Equatorial Guinea	--	--	--	2.5	50	102.0	90.0	14.0	fmm	32.7	27	4.9	5.0	10	29	29
Eritrea	--	--	--	1.9	64	90.6	82.9	15.2	mmm	37.1	23	7.8	14.7	29	39	39
Ethiopia	95	6.7	51	2.0	60	62.1	54.7	25.4	mmm	52.6	14	8.9	2.0	4	26	38
Gabon	--	--	--	1.7	72	--	--	--	--	--	--	7.7	8.3	17	44	44
Gambia	92	12.0	32	1.7	72	79.1	60.3	55.2	mmm	35.1	25	18.9	2.0	4	34	33
Ghana	97	5.0	60	1.3	88	--	--	26.6	--m	73.4	3	9.6	9.0	18	36	48
Guinea	94	7.4	48	1.5	80	57.5	31.1	12.1	mmm	66.4	7	13.0	8.8	18	35	41
Guinea-Bissau	91	28.0	6	2.1	58	59.0	51.3	--	mm-	44.9	17	11.9	7.8	16	30	18
Kenya	94	10.0	37	1.6	76	105.0	88.6	38.5	fmm	26.0	34	5.8	3.6	7	39	38
Lesotho	--	--	--	2.3	54	117.7	122.2	115.2	fff	18.4	43	14.6	3.8	8	35	35
Liberia	--	--	--	--	--	--	--	--	--	--	--	7.0	--	--	--	--
Libyan Arab J	--	--	--	4.3	27	100.0	100.0	92.2	==m	2.6	90	3.4	--	--	58	58
Madagascar	93	10.2	37	1.7	72	102.1	--	80.4	f-m	10.9	58	1.8	8.0	16	49	43
Malawi	--	--	--	1.4	84	102.5	59.4	42.0	fmm	33.7	26	4.3	8.3	17	42	42
Mali	94	12.2	32	1.6	76	69.5	56.3	24.2	mmm	50.0	15	6.2	12.2	24	38	35

177

Country	HE year	H inc ratio	HE score	G inc ratio	G&W score	1st F%M	2nd F%M	3rd F%M	F or M	Ave diff	G&K score	F % govt	F % parl	G&C score	GE score	E index
Mauritania	95	7.4	48	1.8	68	91.0	--	20.7	m-m	44.2	18	5.4	3.8	8	31	39
Mauritius	#91	8.4	43	2.8	44	100.2	105.6	100.5	fff	2.1	92	9.8	7.6	15	50	46
Morocco	98--	7.2	49	2.5	50	78.4	73.5	69.9	mmm	26.1	34	0.9	0.6	1	28	38
Mozambique	96-97	7.2	49	1.4	84	76.4	61.7	31.1	mmm	43.6	18	12.8	25.2	50	51	50
Namibia	--	--	--	2.0	60	105.7	108.4	153.7	fff	22.6	37	11.4	25.0	50	49	49
Niger	95	20.5	16	1.7	72	60.9	52.8	100.0	mm=	28.8	31	10.9	1.2	2	35	25
Nigeria	96-97	12.7	31	2.3	54	--	--	--	--	--	--	6.2	2.5	5	29	30
Rwanda	--	--	--	1.5	80	101.0	77.8	--	fm-	11.6	57	10.7	17.1	34	57	57
São Tomé & Principe	--	--	--	--	--	--	--	--	--	--	--	7.7	9.1	18	18	18
Senegal	95	7.5	47	1.9	64	82.1	64.6	32.3	mmm	40.3	20	5.6	12.1	24	36	41
Seychelles	--	--	--	--	--	--	--	--	--	--	--	20.8	23.5	47	47	47
Sierra Leone	--	--	--	2.4	52	79.0	--	--	m--	21.0	39	5.9	8.8	18	36	36
Somalia	--	--	--	--	--	--	--	--	--	--	--	0.0	--	--	--	--
South Africa	93-94	22.3	13	2.3	54	100.0	104.3	89.7	=fm	4.9	80	7.0	30.0	60	65	39
Sudan	--	--	--	3.3	37	--	--	86.9	--m	13.1	54	1.7	--	--	45	45
Swaziland	94	23.9	11	2.4	52	101.6	93.5	99.1	fmm	3.0	88	7.5	3.1	6	49	30
Tanzania	93	6.7	51	1.4	84	101.9	--	23.9	f-m	39.0	21	9.6	16.4	33	46	48
Togo	--	--	--	2.1	58	74.4	52.2	20.6	mmm	50.9	14	3.0	1.2	2	25	25
Tunisia	90	7.8	46	2.9	42	100.0	95.0	82.1	=mm	7.6	70	7.9	11.5	23	45	45
Uganda	92-93	7.0	50	1.5	80	--	--	49.2	--mm	50.8	15	8.9	17.9	36	44	47
Zambia	96	13.0	30	1.7	72	98.1	70.8	39.4	mmm	30.6	29	8.4	10.1	20	40	35
Zimbabwe	90-91	15.6	23	1.7	72	98.1	90.5	41.1	mmm	23.4	37	11.6	14.0	28	46	34
EUROPE																
Albania	--	--	--	1.8	68	102.1	--	136.7	f-f	19.4	41	11.8	5.2	10	40	40
Austria	--	--	--	2.2	56	100.0	99.5	91.3	=mm	3.1	88	6.8	26.8	54	66	66
Belarus	98	2.9	81	1.6	76	96.9	--	110.3	m-f	6.7	73	6.6	4.5	9	53	67
Belgium	92	3.6	74	1.9	64	100.0	100.0	95.6	==m	1.5	94	6.6	23.3	47	68	71
Bosnia & Herzegovina	--	--	--	--	--	--	--	--	--	--	--	2.8	28.6	57	57	57
Bulgaria	95	4.4	66	1.6	76	102.6	94.7	151.4	fmf	19.8	40	14.6	10.8	22	46	56
Croatia	98	3.9	71	1.8	68	100.0	101.7	96.7	=fm	1.7	93	19.0	20.5	41	67	69
Czech R	96	3.5	75	1.6	76	100.0	100.0	89.1	==m	3.6	86	10.6	15.0	30	64	69
Denmark	92	3.6	74	1.4	84	100.0	101.3	114.4	=ff	5.2	79	13.9	37.4	75	79	76
Estonia	95	6.7	51	1.6	76	100.0	102.9	101.8	=ff	1.6	94	14.3	17.8	36	69	60
Finland	91	3.6	74	1.5	80	100.0	101.8	106.4	=ff	2.7	89	20.4	37.0	74	81	77
France	95	5.6	57	1.6	76	100.0	99.9	116.1	=mf	5.4	78	10.8	10.9	22	59	58
Germany	94	4.7	63	1.9	64	100.0	99.3	80.2	=mm	6.8	73	6.1	30.9	62	66	64
Greece	93	5.4	58	2.1	58	100.0	103.6	89.3	=fm	4.8	81	8.9	6.3	13	51	54
Hungary	96	4.5	65	1.8	68	98.5	102.7	104.4	mff	2.9	88	6.9	8.3	17	58	61
Iceland	--	--	--	1.3	88	100.0	101.4	142.0	=ff	14.5	51	8.2	34.9	70	70	70
Ireland	--	--	--	2.6	48	100.0	100.0	105.2	==f	1.7	93	11.7	12.0	24	55	55
Italy	95	4.2	68	2.3	54	100.0	102.0	110.7	=ff	4.2	83	7.1	11.1	22	53	60
Latvia	98	5.3	58	1.3	88	100.0	99.6	124.8	=mf	8.4	66	17.6	17.0	34	63	60
Lithuania	96	5.2	59	1.6	76	--	--	130.4	--f	30.4	30	7.3	17.5	35	47	53
Luxembourg	94	3.9	71	2.6	48	--	--	--	--	--	--	17.8	16.7	33	40	55
Macedonia, FYR	--	--	--	1.8	68	97.7	102.0	119.5	mff	7.9	68	20.0	7.5	15	50	50
Malta	--	--	--	3.7	33	100.0	95.7	106.8	=mf	3.7	85	3.0	9.2	18	45	45
Moldova	92	6.0	55	1.5	80	--	--	111.4	--f	11.4	57	4.3	8.9	18	52	53
Netherlands	94	5.5	57	2.0	60	100.0	100.0	91.0	==m	3.0	88	16.7	36.0	72	73	65
Norway	95	3.7	73	1.4	84	100.0	100.8	126.1	=ff	9.0	64	24.1	36.4	73	74	73
Poland	96	5.3	58	1.6	76	99.8	104.6	123.3	mff	9.4	62	9.8	13.0	26	55	56
Portugal	94-95	5.9	55	1.9	64	100.0	102.9	120.6	=ff	7.8	69	17.1	18.7	37	57	56
Romania	94	4.2	68	1.7	72	100.0	101.3	108.7	=ff	3.3	87	3.3	7.3	15	58	63
Slovakia	92	2.6	84	1.5	80	--	--	96.1	--m	3.9	60*	15.6	12.7	25	55	69
Slovenia	95	4.2	68	1.6	76	99.0	--	119.5	m-f	10.3	59	16.9	7.8	16	50	59
Spain	90	5.4	58	2.4	52	100.0	102.3	107.5	=ff	3.3	87	15.4	21.6	43	61	59
Sweden	92	3.6	74	1.2	92	100.0	100.0	123.9	==f	8.0	68	30.8	42.7	85	82	78
Switzerland	92	5.8	56	2.0	60	100.0	92.4	59.0	=mm	16.2	48	7.1	23.0	46	51	53
Ukraine	96	4.8	62	1.8	68	--	--	111.4	--f	11.4	57	1.7	7.8	16	47	54
United Kingdom	91	6.5	52	1.7	72	100.0	103.0	103.3	=ff	2.1	92	6.9	18.4	37	67	59
Yugoslavia	#90	5.3	58	--	--	--	--	115.0	--f	15.0	50	7.3	5.1	10	30	44
RUSSIAN FEDERATION	98	12.2	32	1.6	76	100.0	107.2	111.4	=ff	6.2	75	2.6	7.7	15	55	43
ASIA																
Afghanistan	--	--	--	--	--	49.7	45.8	47.3	mmm	52.4	14	0.0	--	--	14	14
Armenia	--	--	--	1.5	80	--	--	121.0	--f	21.0	39	2.1	3.1	6	42	42
Azerbaijan	--	--	--	1.7	72	--	--	94.1	--m	5.9	60*	7.1	12.0	24	52	52
Bahrain	--	--	--	4.0	30	101.2	108.2	187.4	fff	32.3	28	0.0	--	--	29	29
Bangladesh	95-96	4.9	61	2.6	48	86.6	57.6	19.8	mmm	45.3	17	1.9	9.1	18	28	44
Bhutan	--	--	--	2.0	60	87.9	--	--	m--	12.1	56	5.3	2.0	4	40	40
Brunei Darussalam	--	--	--	2.2	56	101.4	104.8	155.9	fff	20.7	39	2.3	--	--	47	47
Cambodia	97	6.9	50	1.2	92	100.0	66.3	22.5	=mm	37.1	23	2.4	8.2	16	44	47

Country	HE year	H inc ratio	*HE score*	G inc ratio	G&W score	1st F%M	2nd F%M	3rd F%M	F or M	Ave diff	G&K score	F % govt	F % parl	G&C score	*GE score*	E index
China	98	7.9	45	1.5	80	100.0	87.5	53.6	=mm	19.6	41	4.3	21.8	44	55	50
Cyprus	--	--	--	2.5	50	100.0	103.3	125.2	=ff	9.5	62	5.3	5.4	11	41	41
Georgia	--	--	--	1.6	76	99.1	98.6	97.8	mmm	1.5	94	3.4	7.2	14	61	61
India	97	5.7	56	2.7	46	85.5	68.0	60.9	mmm	28.5	31	5.8	9.0	18	32	44
Indonesia	96	5.6	57	2.0	60	98.7	90.8	53.3	mmm	19.1	42	1.9	8.0	16	39	48
Iran	--	--	--	3.8	32	98.2	87.8	59.5	mmm	18.2	44	0.4	4.9	10	29	29
Iraq	--	--	--	5.5	18	87.5	65.5	--	mm-	23.5	36	0.0	6.4	13	22	22
Israel	92	6.2	54	2.0	60	--	--	108.0	--f	8.0	60*	10.6	11.7	23	48	51
Japan	93	3.4	76	2.3	54	100.0	100.0	75.8	==m	8.1	68	9.3	4.6	9	44	60
Jordan	97	5.8	56	3.7	33	100.0	--	--	=--	0.0	60*	3.4	0.0	0	31	43
Kazakhstan	96	6.3	53	1.6	76	--	--	118.1	--f	18.1	44	2.1	10.4	21	47	50
Korea, DPR	--	--	--	--	--	--	--	--	--	--	--	0.8	20.1	40	40	40
Korea, R	93	5.2	59	2.2	56	100.0	100.0	61.2	==m	12.9	54	1.0	3.7	7	39	49
Kuwait	--	--	--	2.7	46	96.4	100.2	169.4	mff	24.4	36	4.9	0.0	0	27	27
Kyrgyzstan	97	7.5	47	1.5	80	99.7	102.5	105.6	mff	2.8	89	11.4	1.4	3	57	52
Lao PDR	92	4.2	68	1.5	80	90.3	71.8	43.9	mmm	31.3	29	3.7	21.2	42	50	59
Lebanon	--	--	--	3.4	36	97.0	--	92.2	m-m	5.4	78	0.0	2.3	5	40	40
Malaysia	95	12.0	32	2.6	48	100.4	114.5	90.6	ffm	8.1	68	8.1	7.3	15	44	38
Maldives	--	--	--	1.7	72	--	--	--	--	--	--	13.0	6.0	12	42	42
Mongolia	95	5.6	57	1.5	80	105.7	132.2	215.8	fff	51.2	14	1.7	7.9	16	37	47
Myanmar	--	--	--	1.4	84	98.6	95.7	155.5	mmf	20.4	40	0.0	--	--	62	62
Nepal	95-96	5.9	55	1.9	64	67.1	58.2	31.6	mmm	47.7	16	0.0	5.9	12	31	43
Oman	--	--	--	6.2	14	97.2	95.6	91.3	mmm	5.3	79	3.6	--	--	46	46
Pakistan	96-97	4.3	67	3.3	37	--	--	58.5	--m	41.5	19	2.6	--	--	28	47
Philippines	97	7.6	47	1.8	68	100.0	101.8	133.2	=ff	11.7	57	22.8	12.4	25	50	48
Qatar	--	--	--	4.3	27	102.9	96.6	531.3	fmf	145.9	0	0.0	--	--	13	13
Saudi Arabia	--	--	--	6.1	15	93.1	82.4	109.4	mmf	11.3	57	0.0	--	--	36	36
Singapore	--	--	--	2.0	60	98.0	97.9	80.7	mmm	7.8	69	7.2	4.3	9	46	46
Sri Lanka	95	5.3	58	2.1	58	100.0	108.8	69.2	=fm	13.2	54	10.2	4.9	10	41	49
Syrian Arab R	--	--	--	3.7	33	91.8	87.2	71.6	mmm	16.5	47	3.9	10.4	21	34	34
Tajikistan	--	--	--	1.7	72	--	--	46.8	--m	53.2	13	3.8	2.8	6	30	30
Thailand	98	7.6	47	1.6	76	102.6	97.1	111.1	fmf	5.5	78	2.1	5.6	11	55	51
Turkey	94	8.2	44	1.7	72	98.2	72.0	55.5	mmm	24.9	35	5.0	4.2	8	38	41
Turkmenistan	98	7.8	46	1.6	76	--	--	--	--	--	--	2.2	26.0	52	64	55
United Arab Emirates	--	--	--	4.6	24	98.3	105.4	608.5	fmm	171.9	0	0.0	0.0	0	8	8
Uzbekistan	93	5.5	57	1.5	80	--	--	--	--	--	--	1.3	6.8	14	47	52
Viet Nam	98	5.6	57	1.4	84	100.0	97.0	--	=m-	1.5	94	5.3	26.0	52	77	67
Yemen	92	7.6	47	3.6	34	--	--	14.4	--m	85.6	0	0.0	0.7	1	12	29
PACIFIC																
Australia	94	7.0	50	1.5	80	100.0	100.0	101.9	==f	0.6	98	22.6	22.4	45	74	62
Fiji	--	--	--	3.1	39	100.0	100.4	--	=f-	0.2	80*	14.5	11.3	23	47	47
New Zealand	91	17.4	19	1.5	80	100.0	102.3	130.2	=ff	10.8	58	26.4	29.2	58	65	42
Papua New Guinea	96	12.6	31	1.7	72	85.0	--	49.8	m-m	32.6	27	4.3	1.8	4	34	32
Samoa	--	--	--	3.4	36	101.0	114.3	--	ff-	7.7	69	9.1	8.2	16	40	40
Solomon Is	--	--	--	1.4	84	--	--	--	--	--	--	0.0	2.0	4	44	44
Tonga	--	--	--	--	--	--	--	--	--	--	--	--	0.0	0	0	0
Vanuatu	--	--	--	--	--	94.5	83.6	--	mm-	11.0	58	0.0	0.0	0	29	29

Notes

The equity index (**E index**) is the unweighted average of a household equity index (**HE score**) and a gender equity index (**GE score**).

The household equity index consists of a single indicator: the ratio of the richest 20%'s income share to the poorest 20%'s. This indicator is used instead of the Gini index because it is easier for the layperson to grasp, and the Gini index does not distinguish between inequality among the rich, inequality among the poor, or inequality between rich and poor.

The gender equity index is the average of three unweighted indicators:

Gender and wealth, represented by the ratio of male income to female income.

Gender and knowledge, represented by the average difference between the male and female school enrollment rates (average of the differences in net primary enrollment rate, net secondary enrollment rate, and tertiary enrollment rate).

Gender and community, represented by the percentage of women in the national parliament.

HE year = the year of the household equity data.

H inc ratio = household income ratio = the ratio of the income share of the richest fifth of the population to that of the poorest fifth. Data are from World Bank (2000a), except where marked # in the HE year column which are from World Bank (1998). Income means either income or consumption expenditure.

HE score = household equity index = household income ratio score. The performance criteria are shown in Table 8a.

G inc ratio = gender income ratio = the ratio of male income to female income. Income is represented by Gross Domestic Product per person in international purchasing power parity dollars. Data are for the latest year available (usually 1998) and are from United Nations Development Programme (2000). The indicator has several drawbacks. First, it ignores the pivotal role of women in maintaining the unpaid economy—for example, in rural Africa where women run households, fetch fuel and water, work in fields and gardens (but men dominate wage earning). Second, even within the context of the wage economy, the indicator does not show whether women have equal access to high paying jobs or are paid the same rate as equally qualified men. Third, the information is derived from data on the ratio of the average female wage to the average male wage and the female and male proportions of the economically active population aged 15 above, using complex manipulation to try to overcome the many data gaps.

G&W score = gender and wealth score. The performance criteria are shown in Table 8a.

1st F%M = the female net primary school enrollment rate as a percentage of the male net primary school enrollment rate. Data are for 1997 (except New Caledonia which are for 1991) and are from UNESCO (1999b).

2nd F%M = the female net secondary school enrollment rate as a percentage of the male net secondary school enrollment rate. Data are for 1997 (except Rwanda and New Caledonia which are for 1991) and are from UNESCO (1999b).

3rd F%M = the female tertiary school enrollment rate as a percentage of the male tertiary school enrollment rate. The rate is defined as the number of students per 100,000 population. Data are for the latest year available (years are shown in Table 5) and are from UNESCO (1999c).

F or M = whether the enrollment rates are equal (=), the female rate is higher (f), or the male rate is higher (m), shown in order of primary, secondary, and tertiary.

Ave diff = the average percentage difference between the female and male enrollment rates.

G&K score = gender and knowledge score, based on the average percentage difference between the female and male school enrollment rates. The performance criteria are shown in Table 8a. The top of good matches the United Nations' target of 0% difference by 2005 (World Summit for Social Development [Copenhagen 1995] and the Fourth World Conference on Women [Beijing 1995] [United Nations Population Division 1997; Office of the UN System Support and Services 1996]).

F % govt = percentage of women in ministerial or subministerial posts in the central or federal government. Data are for 1996 and are from United Nations Division for the Advancement of Women (1996). The indicator is not used here because it is not as representative of a society's attitudes and practices as the percentage of women in parliament, and the data are not as current. It is included in the table for comparison with the parliamentary indicator.

F % parl = percentage of women in the national parliament (lower or single house). Data are for 1999 and are from Inter-Parliamentary Union (2000).

G&C score = gender and community score. The performance criteria are shown in Table 8a.

band	top point on scale	ratio of richest 20%'s income share to poorest 20%'s	ratio of male income to female income	average % difference between male & female school enrollment rates	% of seats held by women in the national parliament
good	100	1:1	1:1	0	50
fair	80	3:1	1.5:1	5	40
medium	60	5:1	2:1	10	30
poor	40	9:1	3:1	20	20
bad	20	17:1	5:1	40	10
base	0	33:1	9:1	80	0

Table 8a. Performance criteria for indicators of equity.

* A score with an asterisk has been reduced in accordance with the insufficient data rule. To prevent high scores resulting merely from lack of data, a good score is allowed only if it is based on all applicable components (data in an indicator, indicators in an index), and a fair score only if it is based on at least half the components. Good and fair scores (100-61) based on fewer than half the applicable components have been reduced to 60. Good scores (100-81) based on more than half but not all the applicable components have been reduced to 80.

Table 9. Ecosystem Wellbeing Index

Country	Land	Water	Air	Spp & genes	Res use	EWI + RU	EWI - RU	RU diff	EWI	Foot ha/p	Foot score	Ebal ha/p	Ebal score	EF score	EF diff
AMERICAS															
Antigua & Barbuda	55	60*	0	47	44	41	40	1	**40**	--	--	--	--	--	--
Argentina	51	38	47	23	69	46	40	6	**40**	3.8	62	0.8	76	62	22
Bahamas	50	--	20	27	57	38	32	6	**32**	--	--	--	--	--	--
Barbados	17	20	43	64	14	32	36	-4	**32**	--	--	--	--	--	--
Belize	67	60*	76	52	66	64	64	0	**64**	--	--	--	--	--	--
Bolivia	52	80*	80*	39	77	66	63	3	**63**	1.3	87	11.8	100	87	24
Brazil	48	23	51	22	74	44	36	8	**36**	2.6	74	8.6	100	74	38
Canada	73	50	12	41	40	43	44	-1	**43**	7.7	23	2.4	87	23	-20
Chile	59	21	23	18	65	37	30	7	**30**	3.4	66	-1.8	36	36	6
Colombia	57	10	75	27	72	48	42	6	**42**	1.9	81	3.5	92	81	39
Costa Rica	10	80*	40	33	74	47	41	6	**41**	2.8	72	-1.0	40	40	-1
Cuba	38	60	55	29	67	50	45	5	**45**	2.1	79	-1.3	38	38	-7
Dominica	71	60*	77	51	70	66	65	1	**65**	--	--	--	--	--	--
Dominican R	57	47	55	25	63	49	46	3	**46**	1.4	86	-0.5	50	50	4
Ecuador	64	80*	47	33	81	61	56	5	**56**	2.3	77	1.4	82	77	21
El Salvador	13	47	74	49	47	46	46	0	**46**	1.5	85	-1.1	39	39	-7
Grenada	40	33	73	53	47	49	50	-1	**49**	--	--	--	--	--	--
Guatemala	26	80*	33	37	68	49	44	5	**44**	1.4	86	0.2	64	64	20
Guyana	30	80*	72	71	85	68	63	5	**63**	--	--	--	--	--	--
Haiti	2	80*	80	11	52	45	43	2	**43**	0.8	92	-0.6	48	48	5
Honduras	27	72	35	47	77	52	45	7	**45**	1.4	86	0.6	72	72	27
Jamaica	28	58	45	9	45	37	35	2	**35**	2.7	73	-2.3	33	33	-2
Mexico	43	5	17	20	67	30	21	9	**21**	2.7	73	-1.4	38	38	17
Nicaragua	41	80*	18	57	79	55	49	6	**49**	1.3	87	2.8	89	87	38
Panama	20	77	25	27	75	45	37	8	**37**	2.4	76	1.5	82	76	39
Paraguay	47	33	80*	24	80	53	46	7	**46**	2.8	72	2.3	86	72	26
Peru	38	80*	80*	51	80	66	62	4	**62**	1.3	87	7.7	100	87	25
St Kitts & Nevis	60	--	40	59	57	54	53	1	**53**	--	--	--	--	--	--
St Lucia	46	--	68	42	49	51	52	-1	**51**	--	--	--	--	--	--
St Vincent & Grenadines	42	--	80*	43	53	54	55	-1	**54**	--	--	--	--	--	--
Suriname	45	78	45	64	70	60	58	2	**58**	--	--	--	--	--	--
Trinidad & Tobago	15	60*	11	46	29	32	33	-1	**32**	2.4	76	-2.0	35	35	3
United States	51	46	6	23	35	32	31	1	**31**	12.3	0	-8.4	3	0	-31
Uruguay	44	64	53	47	66	55	52	3	**52**	4.9	51	-0.4	52	51	-1
Venezuela	71	56	15	43	57	48	46	2	**46**	2.9	71	2.6	88	71	25
AFRICA															
Algeria	31	50	56	41	66	49	44	5	**44**	1.8	82	-1.5	37	37	-7
Angola	56	80*	80	54	87	71	67	4	**67**	0.8	92	1.8	84	84	17
Benin	54	80*	80*	69	73	71	71	0	**71**	1.0	90	0.4	68	68	-3
Botswana	65	80*	70	77	48	68	73	-5	**68**	1.7	83	0.0	60	60	-8
Burkina Faso	31	55	80*	65	68	60	58	2	**58**	0.9	91	-0.2	56	56	-2
Burundi	23	80*	80*	56	71	62	60	2	**60**	0.8	92	-0.4	52	52	-8
Cameroon	46	80*	80*	52	77	67	64	3	**64**	0.9	91	3.2	91	91	27
Cape Verde	10	60*	80	40	71	52	47	5	**47**	--	--	--	--	--	--
Central African R	65	60*	80*	60	88	71	66	5	**66**	1.1	89	13.2	100	89	23
Chad	53	60*	80*	44	79	63	59	4	**59**	0.8	92	0.7	74	74	15
Comoros	11	--	80*	40	82	53	44	9	**44**	--	--	--	--	--	--
Congo, DR	62	80*	80	37	79	68	65	3	**65**	0.7	93	6.2	100	93	28
Congo, R	56	80*	80*	74	69	72	72	0	**72**	1.2	88	18.7	100	88	16
Côte d'Ivoire	48	31	80*	68	74	60	57	3	**57**	1.0	90	0.9	78	78	21
Djibouti	43	60*	80	58	66	61	60	1	**60**	--	--	--	--	--	--
Egypt	54	0	66	54	58	46	43	3	**43**	1.7	83	-1.3	38	38	-5
Equatorial Guinea	43	60*	80	66	86	67	62	5	**62**	--	--	--	--	--	--
Eritrea	42	80*	--	59	81	65	60	5	**60**	0.3	97	-0.2	56	56	-4
Ethiopia	46	80*	80*	51	76	67	64	3	**64**	0.9	91	-0.3	54	54	-10
Gabon	50	80*	60	59	64	63	62	1	**62**	2.1	79	31.4	100	79	17
Gambia	34	60*	80*	75	66	63	62	1	**62**	1.0	90	-0.7	46	46	-16
Ghana	40	0	49	65	73	45	38	7	**38**	1.1	89	-0.1	58	58	20
Guinea	39	80*	80*	67	83	70	66	4	**66**	0.8	92	0.6	72	72	6
Guinea-Bissau	31	80*	80	74	84	70	66	4	**66**	0.8	92	2.0	85	85	19
Kenya	54	36	80*	36	66	54	51	3	**51**	1.2	88	-0.7	46	46	-5
Lesotho	32	80*	80	61	33	57	63	-6	**57**	0.7	93	-0.3	54	54	-3
Liberia	39	80*	80	60	79	68	65	3	**65**	1.2	88	3.8	94	88	23
Libyan Arab J	22	0	16	60	53	30	24	6	**24**	4.4	56	-4.4	23	23	-1
Madagascar	37	80*	80*	4	85	57	50	7	**50**	0.9	91	1.9	84	84	34
Malawi	47	70	80*	51	81	66	62	4	**62**	0.9	91	-0.2	56	56	-6

181

Country	Land	Water	Air	Spp & genes	Res use	EWI + RU	EWI - RU	RU diff	EWI	Foot ha/p	Foot score	Ebal ha/p	Ebal score	EF score	EF diff
Mali	32	10	80*	56	81	52	44	8	44	0.9	91	0.3	66	66	22
Mauritania	22	0	80*	59	71	46	40	6	40	1.2	88	-0.8	44	44	4
Mauritius	41	67	68	13	33	44	47	-3	44	2.5	75	-0.5	50	50	6
Morocco	28	4	61	37	76	41	32	9	32	1.6	84	-0.8	44	44	12
Mozambique	50	59	80*	31	82	60	55	5	55	0.8	92	0.3	66	66	11
Namibia	68	18	80	52	59	55	54	1	54	0.7	93	1.1	80	80	26
Niger	21	71	80*	53	61	57	56	1	56	1.0	90	-0.7	46	46	-10
Nigeria	36	78	59	53	65	58	56	2	56	1.3	87	-0.6	48	48	-8
Rwanda	24	76	80	49	61	58	57	1	57	0.9	91	-0.6	48	48	-9
São Tomé & Principe	29	60*	80	44	54	53	53	0	53	--	--	--	--	--	--
Senegal	46	31	80*	60	75	58	54	4	54	1.1	89	-0.3	54	54	0
Seychelles	59	--	64	25	64	53	49	4	49	--	--	--	--	--	--
Sierra Leone	27	80*	80	67	76	66	63	3	63	0.7	93	0.6	72	72	9
Somalia	41	73	80	54	67	63	62	1	62	1.0	90	-0.4	52	52	-10
South Africa	33	18	32	27	50	32	27	5	27	4.0	60	-3.2	29	29	2
Sudan	50	0	80*	55	84	54	46	8	46	1.1	89	0.5	70	70	24
Swaziland	40	57	80*	45	49	54	55	-1	54	--	--	--	--	--	--
Tanzania	60	60	80*	16	84	60	54	6	54	1.0	90	0.2	64	64	10
Togo	38	75	80*	73	72	68	66	2	66	0.8	92	-0.1	58	58	-8
Tunisia	27	25	39	37	65	39	32	7	32	2.3	77	-1.4	38	38	6
Uganda	41	19	80*	35	80	51	44	7	44	0.9	91	0.0	60	60	16
Zambia	52	0	80*	39	71	48	43	5	43	1.2	88	2.9	89	88	45
Zimbabwe	56	75	42	47	75	59	55	4	55	1.5	85	-1.0	40	40	-15
EUROPE															
Albania	17	37	80	52	72	52	46	6	46	1.9	81	-0.7	46	46	0
Austria	57	23	34	55	41	42	42	0	42	5.4	46	-2.0	35	35	-7
Belarus	33	80*	40	49	62	53	50	3	50	5.3	47	-2.5	32	32	-18
Belgium	30	5	25	48	9	23	27	-4	23	6.1	39	-4.6	22	22	-1
Bosnia & Herzegovina	21	60*	73	31	42	45	46	-1	45	1.3	87	-0.1	58	58	13
Bulgaria	29	29	28	37	52	35	31	4	31	3.8	62	-2.3	33	33	2
Croatia	24	13	51	44	60	38	33	5	33	2.4	76	-0.5	50	50	17
Czech R	49	17	20	50	29	33	34	-1	33	6.3	37	-4.2	24	24	-9
Denmark	29	22	23	50	37	32	31	1	31	10.5	0	-6.3	13	0	-31
Estonia	40	19	18	61	43	36	34	2	34	7.1	29	-4.1	24	24	-10
Finland	52	45	23	63	38	44	46	-2	44	8.4	16	0.2	64	16	-28
France	35	12	29	40	41	31	29	2	29	7.3	27	-4.0	25	25	-4
Germany	54	17	25	55	31	36	38	-2	36	6.3	37	-4.6	22	22	-14
Greece	23	43	34	33	46	36	33	3	33	5.5	45	-4.0	25	25	-8
Hungary	31	18	41	43	48	36	33	3	33	5.1	49	-2.7	31	31	-2
Iceland	31	80*	34	45	27	43	47	-4	43	5.6	44	1.5	82	44	1
Ireland	30	23	26	51	53	37	32	5	32	9.5	5	-4.1	24	5	-27
Italy	27	22	27	45	39	32	30	2	30	5.5	45	-4.3	23	23	-7
Latvia	38	27	57	62	56	48	46	2	46	3.7	63	-0.2	56	56	10
Lithuania	32	35	52	59	53	46	44	2	44	4.8	52	-1.7	36	36	-8
Luxembourg	31	14	8	54	15	24	27	-3	24	6.1	39	-4.6	22	22	-2
Macedonia, FYR	34	60*	43	33	50	44	42	2	42	3.2	68	-2.5	32	32	-10
Malta	15	0	2	48	3	14	16	-2	14	--	--	--	--	--	--
Moldova	14	0	68	59	72	43	35	8	35	2.5	75	-1.1	39	39	4
Netherlands	34	18	0	45	11	22	24	-2	22	6.0	40	-4.4	23	23	1
Norway	55	54	14	49	43	43	43	0	43	6.1	39	-0.8	44	39	-4
Poland	30	4	29	57	52	34	30	4	30	5.4	46	-3.8	26	26	-4
Portugal	26	21	46	31	51	35	31	4	31	5.0	50	-3.4	28	28	-3
Romania	30	12	36	43	56	35	30	5	30	3.5	65	-1.6	37	37	7
Slovakia	46	18	37	60	59	44	40	4	40	3.9	61	-2.5	32	32	-8
Slovenia	32	33	34	40	46	37	35	2	35	5.4	46	-3.5	27	27	-8
Spain	31	14	23	14	53	27	20	7	20	5.5	45	-3.7	26	26	6
Sweden	50	51	43	55	46	49	50	-1	49	7.5	25	-0.5	50	25	-24
Switzerland	45	32	42	62	32	43	45	-2	43	6.6	34	-5.2	19	19	-24
Ukraine	14	20	35	35	53	31	26	5	26	4.8	52	-3.1	29	29	3
United Kingdom	38	21	30	41	20	30	32	-2	30	6.3	37	-5.3	18	18	-12
Yugoslavia	25	60*	38	27	61	42	37	5	37	3.9	61	-2.4	33	33	-4
RUSSIAN FEDERATION	58	48	27	37	54	45	42	3	42	5.4	46	-2.0	35	35	-7
ASIA															
Afghanistan	27	42	80	45	72	53	48	5	48	0.6	94	-0.3	54	54	6
Armenia	49	52	80	38	75	59	55	4	55	1.2	88	-0.6	48	48	-7
Azerbaijan	35	0	51	27	57	34	28	6	28	2.2	78	-1.8	36	36	8
Bahrain	23	0	0	56	8	17	20	-3	17	--	--	--	--	--	--
Bangladesh	9	50	80*	45	51	47	46	1	46	0.6	94	-0.6	48	48	2
Bhutan	70	80*	80	37	77	69	67	2	67	0.8	92	1.7	83	83	16

182

Country	Land	Water	Air	Spp & genes	Res use	EWI + RU	EWI - RU	RU diff	EWI	Foot ha/p	Foot score	Ebal ha/p	Ebal score	EF score	EF diff
Brunei Darussalam	35	80*	10	59	28	42	46	-4	42	--	--	--	--	--	--
Cambodia	36	80*	80	31	80	61	57	4	57	0.8	92	2.2	86	86	29
China	37	23	22	31	64	35	28	7	28	1.8	82	-1.2	39	39	11
Cyprus	45	47	13	51	36	38	39	-1	38	--	--	--	--	--	--
Georgia	36	19	80*	31	71	47	41	6	41	1.1	89	-0.1	58	58	17
India	24	21	25	40	59	34	27	7	27	1.1	89	-0.5	50	50	23
Indonesia	61	2	80*	50	72	53	48	5	48	1.5	85	1.5	82	82	34
Iran	33	23	33	40	53	36	32	4	32	2.5	75	-2.0	35	35	3
Iraq	18	13	51	41	58	36	31	5	31	1.7	83	-1.6	37	37	6
Israel	37	18	0	54	18	25	27	-2	25	5.4	46	-5.4	18	18	-7
Japan	34	27	29	11	27	26	25	1	25	5.9	41	-5.8	16	16	-9
Jordan	29	5	20	58	56	34	28	6	28	1.7	83	-1.7	36	36	8
Kazakhstan	38	9	34	47	62	38	32	6	32	4.4	56	-3.0	30	30	-2
Korea, DPR	37	59	23	65	41	45	46	-1	45	1.9	81	-1.5	37	37	-8
Korea, R	33	27	7	43	27	27	27	0	27	5.6	44	-5.6	17	17	-10
Kuwait	44	0	0	70	11	25	28	-3	25	10.3	0	-11.1	0	0	-25
Kyrgyzstan	36	0	80	54	83	51	42	9	42	1.9	81	-0.6	48	48	6
Lao PDR	46	80*	80*	45	88	68	63	5	63	0.9	91	6.3	100	91	28
Lebanon	17	55	22	57	33	37	38	-1	37	3.2	68	-2.9	30	30	-7
Malaysia	47	0	35	50	59	38	33	5	33	3.7	63	-0.2	56	56	23
Maldives	27	60*	80*	20	48	47	47	0	47	--	--	--	--	--	--
Mongolia	58	80*	59	44	68	62	60	2	60	4.3	57	0.8	76	57	-3
Myanmar	28	36	80*	52	82	56	49	7	49	1.1	89	1.5	82	82	33
Nepal	50	71	80*	56	75	66	64	2	64	1.0	90	-0.2	56	56	-8
Oman	25	15	20	52	40	30	28	2	28	3.4	66	-3.1	29	29	1
Pakistan	26	13	80*	57	59	47	44	3	44	1.1	89	-0.6	48	48	4
Philippines	29	29	39	30	66	39	32	7	32	1.4	86	-0.7	46	46	14
Qatar	37	0	0	66	19	24	26	-2	24	--	--	--	--	--	--
Saudi Arabia	30	0	17	46	23	23	23	0	23	6.1	39	-6.6	12	12	-11
Singapore	32	52	0	71	7	32	39	-7	32	12.3	0	-13.8	0	0	-32
Sri Lanka	43	61	80*	43	63	58	57	1	57	1.0	90	-0.6	48	48	-9
Syrian Arab R	18	0	22	62	63	33	25	8	25	2.6	74	-1.8	36	36	11
Tajikistan	40	0	80	36	76	46	39	7	39	0.9	91	-0.6	48	48	9
Thailand	18	2	39	33	60	30	23	7	23	2.7	73	-1.7	36	36	13
Turkey	22	0	51	39	71	37	28	9	28	2.7	73	-1.6	37	37	9
Turkmenistan	43	0	35	44	51	35	30	5	30	3.6	64	-3.1	29	29	-1
United Arab Emirates	26	0	0	42	14	16	17	-1	16	16.0	0	-17.5	0	0	-16
Uzbekistan	33	0	50	36	60	36	30	6	30	2.7	73	-2.1	34	34	4
Viet Nam	28	37	80*	50	72	53	49	4	49	1.0	90	-0.4	52	52	3
Yemen	41	31	80	53	65	54	51	3	51	0.7	93	-0.5	50	50	-1
PACIFIC															
Australia	55	21	11	25	42	31	28	3	28	8.5	15	-0.2	56	15	-13
Fiji	36	45	80*	25	72	52	46	6	46	--	--	--	--	--	--
New Zealand	59	39	32	23	50	41	38	3	38	9.6	4	5.0	100	4	-34
Papua New Guinea	53	43	80*	35	69	56	53	3	53	1.4	86	30.0	100	86	33
Samoa	30	60*	77	32	67	53	50	3	50	--	--	--	--	--	--
Solomon Is	40	80*	80*	43	76	64	61	3	61	--	--	--	--	--	--
Tonga	9	--	80	0	59	37	30	7	30	--	--	--	--	--	--
Vanuatu	34	--	80	36	80	57	50	7	50	--	--	--	--	--	--

Notes

The Ecosystem Wellbeing Index (EWI) is the lower of the EWI including resource use (EWI + RU) and the EWI excluding resource use (EWI - RU). The former is the unweighted average of indices of land, water, air, species and genes, and resource use. The latter is the unweighted average of indices of land, water, air, and species and genes. Taking the lower version of the EWI prevents resource use (a set of indicators of human pressure on the ecosystem) from offsetting poor performance in the other ecosystem dimensions (primarily sets of indicators of the state of the ecosystem).

    Land = land index (Table 10).

    Water = water (inland waters) index (Table 14).

    Air = air index (Table 17).

    Spp & genes = species and genes index (Table 19).

    Res use = resource use index (Table 22).

    EWI + RU = EWI including resource use.

    EWI - RU = EWI excluding resource use.

    RU diff = resource use difference = difference in points between the EWI excluding resource use and the EWI including resource use (minus means that inclusion of resource use lowers the EWI).

    Foot ha/p = ecological footprint in hectares per person. Data are for 1996 and are from Wackernagel *et al.* (2000). The footprint is the estimated amount of productive land and sea a country requires to produce the renewable resources it consumes and absorb its emissions of carbon dioxide from fossil fuels, divided by the country's population. Productivity is based on an average for the world, not an estimate of actual productivity in the country.

    Foot score = ecological footprint score. The performance criteria are shown in Table 9a. I have set the top of fair at a little below the world average ecological footprint of 2.2 hectares/person.

Ebal ha/p = ecological balance in hectares per person. The ecological balance is the difference between a country's footprint and its national productive area. A positive number indicates a surplus: the footprint is smaller than the country's productive capacity. A negative number indicates a deficit: the footprint is bigger than the country's productive capacity. Data are for 1996 and are from Wackernagel *et al.* (2000).

Ebal score = ecological balance score. The performance criteria are shown in Table 9a. I have set the top of medium at 0 and the top of fair at 1, so that a surplus of 0.1-1.0 gets a fair score, a surplus greater than 1.0 gets a good score, and a deficit gets a medium, poor or bad score depending on its size.

EF score = Ecological Footprint score, the lower of the ecological footprint score and the ecological balance score.

EF diff = difference between the EF score and the EWI. A positive number is the amount by which the EF score is higher than the EWI. A negative number is the amount by which it is lower.

Correlations between the EWI, its main components (dimensions and elements) and income are shown in Table 9b.

band	top point on scale	ecological footprint (ha/person)	ecological balance (ha/person)
good	100	0	5
fair	80	2	1
medium	60	4	0
poor	40	6	-1
bad	20	8	-5
base	0	10	-9

Table 9a. Performance criteria for the Ecological Footprint .

	EWI	income	land div	land quality	Land	Water	global atmos	local air	Air	wild div	domes div	Species & genes	energy	res sectors	Res use
EWI	1														
income	-0.537	1													
land diversity	0.334	0.012	1												
land quality	0.164	0.215	0.029	1											
Land	0.423	0.066	*0.712*	0.540	1										
Water	*0.775*	-0.302	0.218	-0.005	0.172	1									
global atmosphere	*0.730*	*-0.751*	0.047	-0.029	0.088	0.393	1								
local air quality	0.196	0.556	0.046	0.503	0.326	-0.070	-0.451	1							
Air	*0.758*	*-0.711*	0.027	0.023	0.089	0.382	**0.933**	0.103	1						
wild diversity	0.325	0.007	0.065	0.013	0.052	0.084	0.037	0.253	0.043	1					
domesticated diversity	0.188	-0.129	-0.100	0.139	-0.070	0.014	0.040	0.234	0.075	0.292	1				
Species & genes	0.323	-0.017	0.048	0.074	0.055	0.065	0.018	0.278	0.027	**0.935**	0.635	1			
energy	*0.644*	**-0.817**	0.116	-0.130	0.080	0.355	**0.843**	-0.543	*0.793*	0.010	0.024	-0.013	1		
resource sectors	0.370	-0.369	0.261	0.154	0.321	0.221	0.372	-0.174	0.310	-0.085	-0.122	-0.100	0.448	1	
Resource use	*0.628*	*-0.754*	0.198	-0.030	0.197	0.352	*0.775*	-0.454	*0.712*	-0.030	-0.035	-0.052	**0.921**	*0.760*	1

Table 9b. Correlations between the EWI, ecosystem dimensions and elements, and income (GDP per person). Correlations of 0.8 (or -0.8) and above are shown in **bold**; those between 0.6 and 0.8 (or -0.6 and -0.8) are shown in *italic*.

* A score with an asterisk has been reduced in accordance with the insufficient data rule. To prevent high scores resulting merely from lack of data, a good score is allowed only if it is based on all applicable components (data in an indicator, indicators in an index), and a fair score only if it is based on at least half the components. Good and fair scores (100-61) based on fewer than half the applicable components have been reduced to 60. Good scores (100-81) based on more than half but not all the applicable components have been reduced to 80.

Table 10. Land Index; Basic Data; Native Forest Change

Country	Total area 000 ha	Land area 000 ha	1995 ha/p	2000 ha/p	Forest note	Native forest 80 000 ha	Native forest 95 000 ha	Ch 80-95 %/yr	Fch score	Conv score	Nat score	LMC score	LP score	LD score	LQ score	Land index
AMERICAS																
Antigua & Barbuda	44	44	0.7	0.6		10.0	8.7	-0.9	40	75	11	42	80*	55	--	55
Argentina	278040	273669	7.9	7.4		36135.6	33394.5	-0.5	50	84	55	63	28	51	54	51
Bahamas	1388	1001	3.6	3.3		238.1	158.3	-2.7	19	94	45	53	45	50	100	50
Barbados	43	43	0.2	0.2		0	0	--	--	42	9	25	0	17	--	17
Belize	2296	2280	10.7	9.5		2046.5	1959.5	-0.3	55	95	19	56	90	67	72	67
Bolivia	109858	108438	14.6	13.0		55450.5	48281.7	-0.9	40	96	53	63	70	65	52	52
Brazil	854740	845651	5.3	5.0		591496.9	546239.0	-0.5	50	88	54	64	48	59	48	48
Canada	997061	922097	31.1	29.6	t 80/94	244571	244571	0.0	80	94	69	81	57	73	96	73
Chile	75663	74880	5.3	4.9		7616.5	6876.6	-0.7	45	93	50	63	77	68	59	59
Colombia	113891	103870	2.7	2.5		57733.8	52861.5	-0.6	48	90	61	66	69	67	57	57
Costa Rica	5110	5106	1.4	1.3		1925.4	1220.0	-3.0	17	81	24	41	85	56	10	10
Cuba	11086	10982	1.0	1.0		1972.9	1596.7	-1.4	34	50	4	29	55	38	52	38
Dominica	75	75	1.1	1.1		45.5	45.5	0.0	80	75	43	66	80*	71	--	71
Dominican R	4873	4838	0.6	0.6		1424.0	1574.9	0.7	98	55	4	57	90	65	57	57
Ecuador	28356	27684	2.4	2.2		14169.9	11091.6	-1.6	31	85	56	57	79	64	65	64
El Salvador	2104	2072	0.4	0.3		154.6	101.1	-2.8	18	49	2	23	2	16	13	13
Grenada	34	34	0.4	0.4		3.6	3.6	0.0	80	59	41	60	0	40	--	40
Guatemala	10889	10843	1.1	1.0		5037.8	3813.4	-1.8	29	75	35	46	79	57	26	26
Guyana	21497	19685	23.7	22.9	#	18651.9	18569.2	0.0	70	97	92	86	2	61	30	30
Haiti	2775	2756	0.4	0.3		38.0	12.5	-7.1	0	56	0	19	3	14	2	2
Honduras	11209	11189	2.0	1.7		5693.4	4111.6	-2.1	25	78	28	44	51	46	27	27
Jamaica	1099	1083	0.4	0.4		507.4	159.5	-7.4	0	64	11	25	35	28	53	28
Mexico	195820	190869	2.1	1.9		63564.8	55278.3	-0.9	40	79	36	52	35	46	43	43
Nicaragua	13000	12140	2.7	2.4		7251.4	5545.9	-1.8	29	71	25	42	60	48	41	41
Panama	7552	7443	2.8	2.6		3746.3	2794.4	-1.9	28	87	36	50	89	63	20	20
Paraguay	40675	39730	8.2	7.2		16899.6	11518.2	-2.5	20	88	52	53	35	47	59	47
Peru	128522	128000	5.4	5.0		70609.9	67378.3	-0.3	55	94	71	73	46	64	38	38
St Kitts & Nevis	26	26	0.6	0.7		11.2	11.2	0.0	80	65	35	60	59	60	--	60
St Lucia	62	61	0.4	0.4		7.4	4.6	-3.1	16	65	34	38	63	46	--	46
St Vincent & Grenadines	39	39	0.4	0.3		12.5	10.5	-1.2	36	64	28	43	41	42	--	42
Suriname	16326	15600	38.1	37.4		14848.7	14712.9	-0.1	60	99	94	84	21	63	45	45
Trinidad & Tobago	513	513	0.4	0.4		191.8	148.3	-1.7	30	66	51	49	13	37	15	15
United States	936352	915912	3.4	3.3	t 92	--	203646	--	--	64	25	44	65	51	70	51
Uruguay	17741	17481	5.4	5.2		667.4	658.0	-0.1	60	83	50	64	3	44	86	44
Venezuela	91205	88205	4.0	3.6		51720.7	43742.1	-1.1	38	92	44	58	98	71	72	71
AFRICA																
Algeria	238174	238174	8.5	7.6		1974.1	1376.4	-2.4	21	94	83	66	55	62	31	31
Angola	124670	124670	11.4	9.7		25245.0	22079.6	-0.9	40	94	53	62	52	59	56	56
Benin	11262	11062	2.1	1.8		5649.9	4611.2	-1.3	35	83	13	44	74	54	69	54
Botswana	58173	56673	38.4	34.9		15011.7	13915.6	-0.5	50	99	44	64	81	70	65	65
Burkina Faso	27400	27360	2.6	2.3		4735.0	4251.2	-0.7	45	83	12	47	63	52	31	31
Burundi	2783	2568	0.4	0.4		246.7	225.3	-0.6	48	42	0	30	18	26	23	23
Cameroon	47544	46540	3.5	3.1		21667.5	19581.6	-0.7	45	83	15	48	43	46	50	46
Cape Verde	403	403	1.1	0.9		6.4	6.4	0.0	80	74	0	51	0	34	10	10
Central African R	62298	62298	18.9	17.2		31851.2	29923.6	-0.4	53	96	44	64	68	65	91	65
Chad	128400	125920	18.8	16.5		12319.6	11021.1	-0.7	45	94	54	64	34	54	53	53
Comoros	223	223	0.4	0.3		16.5	9.0	-4.0	11	38	0	16	0	11	50	11
Congo, DR	234486	226705	5.0	4.4		120681.2	109203.1	-0.7	45	95	45	62	63	62	82	62
Congo, R	34200	34150	13.3	11.6		20091.5	19500.0	-0.2	58	98	51	69	29	56	87	56
Côte d'Ivoire	32246	31800	2.4	2.2		7144.2	5403.1	-1.8	29	70	21	40	63	48	87	48
Djibouti	2320	2318	3.9	3.6		22.4	22.4	0.0	80	99	7	62	4	43	70	43
Egypt	100145	99545	1.6	1.5		0.0	0.0	--	--	93	79	80*	2	54	63	54
Equatorial Guinea	2805	2805	7.0	6.2		1893.9	1778.1	-0.4	53	91	49	64	0	43	97	43
Eritrea	11760	10100	3.2	2.6		233.0	233.0	0.0	80	90	2	57	18	44	42	42
Ethiopia	110430	100000	1.8	1.6		14338.6	13439.2	-0.4	53	85	5	47	63	52	46	46
Gabon	26767	25767	23.9	21.0		19398.3	17838.0	-0.6	48	96	65	69	13	50	76	50
Gambia	1129	1000	0.9	0.8		104.5	89.9	-1.0	39	72	11	41	20	34	75	34
Ghana	23854	22754	1.3	1.1		10929.7	8969.3	-1.3	35	72	2	36	48	40	71	40
Guinea	24586	24572	3.4	3.3		7563.1	6363.1	-1.1	38	88	30	52	12	39	89	39
Guinea-Bissau	3612	2812	2.6	2.3		2452.3	2307.9	-0.4	53	85	1	46	0	31	71	31
Kenya	58037	56914	2.1	1.9		1255.4	1173.8	-0.3	55	86	43	61	67	63	54	54
Lesotho	3035	3035	1.6	1.4		0.0	0.0	--	--	79	1	40	16	32	32	32
Liberia	11137	9632	4.6	3.1		4887.1	4501.3	-0.5	50	93	13	52	14	39	93	39
Libyan Arab J	175954	175954	35.4	31.4		190.0	190.0	0.0	80	98	82	87	1	58	22	22
Madagascar	58704	58154	4.2	3.6		17088.6	14889.1	-0.9	40	89	15	48	18	38	37	37

Country	Total area 000 ha	Land area 000 ha	1995 ha/p	2000 ha/p	Forest note	Native forest 80 000 ha	Native forest 95 000 ha	Ch 80-95 %/yr	Fch score	Conv score	Nat score	LMC score	LP score	*LD score*	*LQ score*	Land index
Malawi	11848	9408	1.0	0.9		4168.9	3212.9	-1.7	30	73	4	36	69	47	84	47
Mali	124019	122019	12.3	10.9		13224.2	11571.0	-0.9	40	93	67	67	21	52	32	32
Mauritania	102552	102522	44.0	38.4		554.0	554.0	0.0	80	99	84	88	19	65	22	22
Mauritius	204	203	0.2	0.2		2.8	2.8	0.0	80	26	0	35	52	41	90	41
Morocco	44655	44630	1.7	1.6		3787.2	3514.4	-0.5	50	70	1	40	5	28	76	28
Mozambique	80159	78409	4.5	4.0		18321.1	16833.9	-0.6	48	91	35	58	33	50	82	50
Namibia	82429	82329	53.3	47.7		13000.0	12374.1	-0.3	55	98	54	69	80	73	68	68
Niger	126700	126670	13.8	11.8		2550.0	2550.0	0.0	80	95	69	81	45	69	21	21
Nigeria	92377	91077	0.9	0.8		15636.4	13629.2	-0.9	40	56	3	33	41	36	40	36
Rwanda	2634	2467	0.5	0.3		167.8	162.4	-0.2	58	40	0	32	78	47	24	24
São Tomé & Principe	96	96	0.7	0.7		56.0	56.0	0.0	80	50	1	44	0	29	91	29
Senegal	19672	19253	2.3	2.0		8091.0	7269.2	-0.7	45	82	1	43	59	48	46	46
Seychelles	45	45	0.6	0.6		3.3	3.3	0.0	80	73	2	52	73	59	--	59
Sierra Leone	7174	7162	1.7	1.5		1919.1	1303.0	-2.5	20	86	3	36	9	27	64	27
Somalia	63766	62734	7.6	6.2		781.5	749.8	-0.3	55	96	32	61	2	41	58	41
South Africa	122104	122104	3.3	3.0		7420.7	7203.8	-0.2	58	77	27	54	48	52	33	33
Sudan	250581	237600	8.9	8.1		47695.8	41410.0	-0.9	40	88	30	53	45	50	50	50
Swaziland	1736	1720	2.0	1.7		74.0	74.0	0.0	80	76	0	52	16	40	91	40
Tanzania	94509	88359	3.0	2.6		38102.5	32356.2	-1.1	38	90	41	56	78	63	60	60
Togo	5678	5439	1.3	1.2		1562.9	1223.7	-1.6	31	51	1	28	59	38	46	38
Tunisia	16361	15536	1.7	1.6		429.2	353.9	-1.3	35	62	18	38	6	27	37	27
Uganda	24104	19965	1.1	0.9		6991.1	6083.5	-0.9	40	60	22	41	75	52	41	41
Zambia	75261	74339	9.1	8.1		35854.2	31354.6	-0.9	40	88	71	66	80	71	52	52
Zimbabwe	39076	38685	3.6	3.3		9524.4	8625.8	-0.7	45	86	18	50	67	56	73	56
EUROPE																
Albania	2875	2740	0.9	0.9	t 57/95	1196	928	-0.5	50	61	3	38	17	31	17	17
Austria	8386	8273	1.0	1.0	t 90/96	3794	3840	0.2	85	76	1	52	70	59	57	57
Belarus	20760	20748	2.0	2.0	t 97	--	7670	--	--	65	1	33	34	33	77	33
Belgium	3052	3028	0.3	0.3	t 82/97	362	352	-0.2	58	42	0	33	23	30	57	30
Bosnia & Herzegovina	5113	5100	1.5	1.3	t	--	22219	--	--	80	0	40	6	29	21	21
Bulgaria	11091	11055	1.3	1.3	t	--	2621	--	--	42	2	22	44	29	46	29
Croatia	5654	5592	1.2	1.3	t 96	--	1728	--	--	67	1	34	49	39	24	24
Czech R	7886	7728	0.7	0.8	t 86/95	2625	2630	0.0	80	49	0	43	66	51	49	49
Denmark	4309	4243	0.8	0.8	t 90	--	104	--	--	29	1	15	57	29	93	29
Estonia	4510	4227	2.8	3.0	t 96	--	1711	--	--	63	1	32	57	40	86	40
Finland	33814	30459	6.0	5.9	t 89/96	21812	21720	-0.1	60	90	13	54	47	52	84	52
France	55150	55010	0.9	0.9	t 97	--	14195	--	--	55	0	27	50	35	83	35
Germany	35698	34927	0.4	0.4	t 61/87	10162	10740	0.2	85	52	0	46	70	54	68	54
Greece	13196	12890	1.2	1.2	t 92	--	3239	--	--	61	0	30	10	23	57	23
Hungary	9303	9234	0.9	0.9	t 96	--	1675	--	--	37	0	18	58	31	51	31
Iceland	10300	10025	37.4	35.7	t 98	--	18	--	--	98	40	69	50	63	31	31
Ireland	7028	6889	1.9	1.8	t 96	--	1	--	--	64	1	32	25	30	98	30
Italy	30127	29406	0.5	0.5	t	--	9724	--	--	48	1	24	33	27	59	27
Latvia	6460	6205	2.4	2.6	t 97	--	2741	--	--	65	0	32	51	38	61	38
Lithuania	6520	6480	1.7	1.8	t 96	--	1694	--	--	46	0	23	51	32	77	32
Luxembourg	257	257	0.6	0.6	t 97	--	47	--	--	47	0	23	47	31	66	31
Macedonia, FYR	2571	2543	1.3	1.3	t	--	876	--	--	66	0	33	64	43	34	34
Malta	32	32	0.1	0.1	t 96	--	0	--	--	44	0	22	0	15	--	15
Moldova	3370	3297	0.8	0.8	t 97	--	323	--	--	26	0	13	17	14	49	14
Netherlands	4084	3392	0.2	0.2	t 96	--	239	--	--	50	0	25	53	34	80	34
Norway	32388	30683	7.1	6.9	t 96	--	8410	--	--	94	30	62	41	55	93	55
Poland	32325	30442	0.8	0.8	t 96	--	8903	--	--	43	1	22	46	30	42	30
Portugal	9198	9150	0.9	0.9	t	--	2549	--	--	43	1	22	35	26	52	26
Romania	23839	23034	1.0	1.0	t 97	--	6210	--	--	50	1	25	41	30	39	30
Slovakia	4901	4808	0.9	0.9	t 96	--	2001	--	--	62	0	31	76	46	54	46
Slovenia	2025	2012	1.0	1.0	t 96	--	1098	--	--	81	2	41	57	46	32	32
Spain	50599	49944	1.3	1.3	t 90	--	11605	--	--	52	0	26	40	31	66	31
Sweden	44996	41162	4.7	4.6	t 96	--	26695	--	--	89	21	55	41	50	64	50
Switzerland	4129	3955	0.6	0.5	t 97	--	1169	--	--	79	0	39	57	45	82	45
Ukraine	60370	57935	1.1	1.1	t 96	--	5033	--	--	28	0	14	15	14	37	14
United Kingdom	24410	24160	0.4	0.4	t	--	1069	--	--	51	0	25	64	38	78	38
Yugoslavia	10217	10200	1.0	1.0	t	--	2855	--	--	53	0	26	22	25	28	25
RUSSIAN FEDERATION	1707540	1688850	11.4	11.5	t 88/93	804529	799198	-0.1	60	90	66	72	31	58	76	58
ASIA																
Afghanistan	65209	65209	3.3	2.9		1984.7	1390.1	-2.3	23	81	17	40	2	27	68	27
Armenia	2980	2820	0.8	0.8	t 96	--	321	--	--	70	13	41	66	49	88	49
Azerbaijan	8660	8660	1.1	1.1	t 88	--	916	--	--	70	6	38	29	35	77	35
Bahrain	69	69	0.1	0.1		0.0	0.0	--	--	68	0	34	0	23	--	23

Country	Total area 000 ha	Land area 000 ha	1995 ha/p	2000 ha/p	Forest note	Native forest 80 000 ha	Native forest 95 000 ha	Ch 80-95 %/yr	Fch score	Conv score	Nat score	LMC score	LP score	LD score	LQ score	Land index
Bangladesh	14400	13017	0.1	0.1		1117.5	699.7	-3.1	16	24	0	13	2	9	23	9
Bhutan	4700	4700	2.5	2.2		2974.2	2748.0	-0.5	50	94	29	58	94	70	91	70
Brunei Darussalam	576	527	1.8	1.6		482.7	433.9	-0.7	45	96	59	67	96	77	35	35
Cambodia	18103	17652	1.8	1.6		12025.3	9822.8	-1.3	35	75	22	44	67	52	36	36
China	959805	932742	0.8	0.7		105907.0	99522.5	-0.4	53	71	22	48	56	51	37	37
Cyprus	925	924	1.2	1.2	t 96	--	90	--	--	77	3	40	56	45	57	45
Georgia	6970	6970	1.3	1.4	t	--	2788	--	--	75	8	41	27	36	93	36
India	328759	297319	0.3	0.3		55081.6	50384.8	-0.6	48	28	2	26	20	24	40	24
Indonesia	190457	181157	0.9	0.9		121815.0	103665.7	-1.1	38	73	51	54	76	61	86	61
Iran	163319	162200	2.6	2.4		1975.9	1464.5	-2.0	26	83	6	38	37	38	33	33
Iraq	43832	43737	2.2	1.9		69.0	69.0	0.0	80	84	25	63	0	42	18	18
Israel	2106	2062	0.4	0.3	t 97	--	31	--	--	60	1	30	50	37	95	37
Japan	37780	37652	0.3	0.3	t	--	13382	--	--	43	8	25	53	34	98	34
Jordan	8921	8893	1.6	1.3		35.0	22.4	-2.9	18	91	50	53	13	40	29	29
Kazakhstan	271730	267073	16.2	16.5	t 93	--	10499	--	--	81	7	44	26	38	41	38
Korea, DPR	12054	12041	0.5	0.5		4700.0	4700.0	0.0	80	62	1	48	14	37	79	37
Korea, R	9926	9873	0.2	0.2		6304.0	6226.0	-0.1	60	63	0	41	17	33	98	33
Kuwait	1782	1782	1.1	0.9		0.0	0.0	--	--	94	33	63	7	44	66	44
Kyrgyzstan	19850	19180	4.2	4.1	t 88	--	672	--	--	86	7	46	17	36	94	36
Lao PDR	23680	23080	4.8	4.2		14467.1	12430.7	-1.0	39	95	17	50	38	46	79	46
Lebanon	1040	1023	0.3	0.3		65.3	39.0	-3.4	14	59	1	25	2	17	86	17
Malaysia	32975	32855	1.6	1.5		21704.1	15371.1	-2.3	23	73	41	45	56	49	47	47
Maldives	30	30	0.1	0.1		0.0	0.0	--	--	80	0	40	0	27	--	27
Mongolia	156650	156650	63.9	58.8		9406.0	9406.0	0.0	80	98	60	79	78	79	58	58
Myanmar	67658	65755	1.5	1.4		32890.2	26875.0	-1.3	35	81	7	41	3	28	80	28
Nepal	14718	14300	0.7	0.6		5565.6	4766.1	-1.0	39	70	21	43	64	50	76	50
Oman	21246	21246	9.9	8.4		0.0	0.0	--	--	99	77	80*	80*	80	25	26
Pakistan	79609	77088	0.6	0.5		2608.8	1580.3	-3.3	15	62	5	27	23	26	28	26
Philippines	30000	29817	0.4	0.4		10815.5	6562.8	-3.3	15	60	9	28	39	32	29	29
Qatar	1100	1100	2.0	1.8		0.0	0.0	--	--	95	16	55	1	37	73	37
Saudi Arabia	214969	214969	11.8	9.9		262.0	220.9	-1.1	38	96	69	67	80*	71	30	30
Singapore	62	61	0.0	0.0		4.7	4.0	-1.1	38	44	0	27	42	32	61	32
Sri Lanka	6561	6463	0.4	0.3		2009.3	1657.1	-1.3	35	60	0	32	66	43	74	43
Syrian Arab R	18518	18378	1.3	1.1		162.9	92.2	-3.7	13	61	9	27	0	18	46	18
Tajikistan	14310	14060	2.4	2.3	t	--	390	--	--	89	10	49	22	40	94	40
Thailand	51311	51089	0.9	0.8		17858.5	11100.8	-3.1	16	53	8	26	72	41	18	18
Turkey	77482	76963	1.3	1.2	t 96	--	8100	--	--	54	2	28	10	22	34	22
Turkmenistan	48810	46993	11.5	10.5	t	--	3742	--	--	92	12	52	24	43	93	43
United Arab Emirates	8360	8360	3.8	3.4		0.0	0.0	--	--	94	77	80*	0	53	26	26
Uzbekistan	44740	41424	1.8	1.7	t 88	--	1609	--	--	80	2	41	18	33	70	33
Viet Nam	33169	32549	0.4	0.4		9658.2	7646.8	-1.5	33	66	2	33	19	28	51	28
Yemen	52797	52797	3.5	2.9		9.0	9.0	0.0	80	93	14	62	0	41	55	41
PACIFIC																
Australia	774122	768230	42.8	40.7	t 94	--	155835	--	--	92	12	52	60	55	85	55
Fiji	1827	1827	2.4	2.2		811.0	757.0	-0.5	50	77	4	44	20	36	100	36
New Zealand	27053	26799	7.3	6.9	t 96	--	6398	--	--	75	9	42	92	59	79	59
Papua New Guinea	46284	45286	10.5	9.4		38558.4	36908.5	-0.3	55	98	63	72	14	53	98	53
Samoa	284	283	1.7	1.6		151.0	127.0	-1.1	38	51	1	30	30	30	--	30
Solomon Is	2890	2799	7.4	6.3		2439.6	2370.6	-0.2	58	96	26	60	0	40	75	40
Tonga	75	72	0.7	0.7		0.0	0.0	--	--	26	0	13	0	9	--	9
Vanuatu	1219	1219	7.2	6.4		1007.0	893.0	-0.8	43	89	20	50	1	34	100	34

Notes

The **Land index** is the lower of a land diversity index (**LD score**) and a land quality index (**LQ score**).

The land diversity index is the average of two weighted indicators (column heading in parentheses) [weight in brackets]:

Land modification and conversion (LMC score) [2].

Land protection (LP score) [1]. See Table 12 for data.

Protected area coverage was given a lower weight because it measures a policy response, not the actual state of land diversity.

Land modification and conversion is the average of three unweighted indicators:

Converted land as % of total land (Conv score). The converted land area comprises cultivated land and built land. See Table 11 for data.

Natural land as % of total land (Nat score). See Table 11 for data.

% annual change in native forest area (Fch score). Ideally, forests would be differentiated within the converted land and natural land indicators, and changes in the area of native forest would be shown by changes within those indicators. This cannot be done with available data. See this table for data.

Total area is the total surface area (land + inland waters) in thousands of hectares. Data refer to 1997 and are from FAO (1999), except for Belgium and Luxembourg which are from OECD (1999). China includes Hong Kong and Macao.

Land area is in thousands of hectares. Data refer to 1997 and are from FAO (1999), except for Belgium and Luxembourg which are from OECD (1999). China includes Hong Kong and Macao.

1995 ha/p = land hectares per person in 1995, on the basis of population data from United Nations Population Division (1998b).

2000 ha/p = land hectares per person in 2000, on the basis of population data from United Nations Population Division (1998b).

Forest note = see Native forest below. # indicates a score for a decline of less than 0.05%.

Native forest = forest composed of tree species known to be indigenous to the area, or non-plantation forest. Areas are in thousand hectares (000 ha). Data are for 1980 and 1995, except where a different year is indicated in the Forest note column. If two years are given (e.g., 88/93), the first is instead of 1980, the second instead of 1995. All data are from FAO (1997a), except where indicated by the letter t in the Forest note column, which are from UNECE & FAO (2000).

Ch 80-95 %/yr = average annual percentage change in native forest area between 1980 and 1995 (or the applicable years).

Fch score = score for % annual change in native forest area. The performance criteria are shown in Table 10a. The tops of the fair and medium bands have been set so that an increase in forest area gets a good score, a decline of 0.1% or more a medium score or worse, and zero change (stability) a fair score. If the forest area is reported to be exactly the same size at the end of the reporting period as at the beginning (exactly 0.0 change), the score is 80. If there is a decline of less than 0.05%, the score is reduced to 70—indicated by # (Guyana is the only case).

Conv score = score for converted land as % of total land. The performance criteria are shown in Table 10a. The top of the medium band is based on the landscape pattern theory that habitat becomes dissected into isolated patches below 60% coverage (see Nat score below).

Nat score = score for natural land as % of total land. The performance criteria are shown in Table 10a. Fair performance is defined as better than 60, on the basis of landscape pattern theory, which suggests that if habitat coverage is reduced to less than 59.28% the landscape becomes dissected into isolated patches (O'Neill *et al.* 1995), which in turn leads to a loss of species.

LMC score = land modification and conversion score, the average of the above three scores.

LP score = land protection score. See Table 12 for data and performance criteria.

LD score = land diversity index, the weighted average of the land modification score and the land protection score.

LQ score = land quality index. See Table 13 for data and performance criteria.

band	top point on scale	converted land as % of total land	natural land as % of total land	% annual change in forest area
good	100	0	100	0.8
fair	80	20	80	0.0
medium	60	40	60	-0.1
poor	40	60	40	-0.9
bad	20	80	20	-2.5
base	0	100	0	-5.7

Table 10a. Performance criteria for indicators of land modification and conversion.

* A score with an asterisk has been reduced in accordance with the insufficient data rule. To prevent high scores resulting merely from lack of data, a good score is allowed only if it is based on all applicable components (data in an indicator, indicators in an index), and a fair score only if it is based on at least half the components. Good and fair scores (100-61) based on fewer than half the applicable components have been reduced to 60. Good scores (100-81) based on more than half but not all the applicable components have been reduced to 80.

Table 11. Natural, Modified, Cultivated, and Built Land

Country	Natural note	Cultivated [Built] notes	Natural 000 ha	Nat %	Mod 000 ha	Mod %	Cult 000 ha	Cult %	Built 000 ha	Built %	Nat score	Conv score
AMERICAS												
Antigua & Barbuda	d	C8+F0+P0	5	11.4	28	63.6	8	18.2	3	6.8	11	75
Argentina	d	C27200+F547+ P14200	149970	54.8	79639	29.1	41947	15.3	2113	0.8	55	84
Bahamas	d	C10+F0+P0	452	45.2	493	49.3	10	1.0	46	4.6	45	94
Barbados	d	C17+F0+P0	4	9.3	14	32.6	17	39.5	8	18.6	9	42
Belize	d	C89+F2+P5	440	19.3	1731	75.9	96	4.2	13	0.6	19	95
Bolivia	d	C2100+F28+ P2100	57037	52.6	46717	43.1	4228	3.9	456	0.4	53	96
Brazil	d	C65300+F4900+P18500	460666	54.5	286593	33.9	88700	10.5	9692	1.1	54	88
Canada	r	C45700+Ft0+ Pe2688 [u86]	640558	69.5	226653	24.6	48388	5.2	6498	0.7	69	94
Chile	d	C2297+F1015+P1290	37421	50.0	31992	42.7	4602	6.1	865	1.2	50	93
Colombia	d	C4430+F126+ P4008	63024	60.7	30318	29.2	8564	8.2	1964	1.9	61	90
Costa Rica	d	C505+F28+ P234	1251	24.5	2905	56.9	767	15.0	183	3.6	24	81
Cuba	d	C4450+F245+ P217	462	4.2	5057	46.0	4912	44.7	551	5.0	4	50
Dominica	d	C15+F0+P0	32	42.7	24	32.0	15	20.0	4	5.3	43	75
Dominican R	d	C1500+F45+ P209	179	3.7	2507	51.8	1754	36.3	398	8.2	4	55
Ecuador	d	C3001+F45+ P509	15613	56.4	7931	28.6	3555	12.8	585	2.1	56	85
El Salvador	d321a	C816+F4+P59	45	2.2	974	47.0	879	42.4	174	8.4	2	49
Grenada	d	C11+F0+P0	14	41.2	6	17.6	11	32.4	3	8.8	41	59
Guatemala	d	C1905+F28+ P260	3779	34.9	4359	40.2	2193	20.2	512	4.7	35	75
Guyana	d	C496+F8+P#56	18111	92.0	964	4.9	560	2.8	50	0.3	92	97
Haiti	d102a	C910+F8+P50	0	0.0	1557	56.5	968	35.1	231	8.4	0	56
Honduras	d	C2045+F3+ P154	3106	27.8	5590	50.0	2202	19.7	291	2.6	28	78
Jamaica	d	C274+F15+P26	119	11.0	574	53.0	315	29.1	75	6.9	11	64
Mexico	d	C27300+F109+Pe7950	69396	36.4	81478	42.7	35359	18.5	4636	2.4	36	79
Nicaragua	d	C2746+F14+ P482	3028	24.9	5642	46.5	3242	26.7	228	1.9	25	71
Panama	d	C655+F6+P147	2668	35.8	3833	51.5	808	10.9	134	1.8	36	87
Paraguay	d	C2285+F9+ P2170	20659	52.0	14310	36.0	4464	11.2	297	0.7	52	88
Peru	d	C4200+F184+ P2712	91136	71.2	28571	22.3	7096	5.5	1197	0.9	71	94
St Kitts & Nevis	d	C7+F0+P0	9	34.6	8	30.8	7	26.9	2	7.7	35	65
St Lucia	d	C17+F0+P0	21	34.4	19	31.1	17	27.9	4	6.6	34	65
St Vincent & Grenadines	d	C11+F0+P0	11	28.2	14	35.9	11	28.2	3	7.7	28	64
Suriname	d	C67+F8+P2	14657	94.0	841	5.4	77	0.5	25	0.2	94	99
Trinidad & Tobago	d295a	C122+F13+P1	264	51.5	75	14.6	136	26.5	38	7.4	51	66
United States	r	C179000+ Ft13687+ Pe23925 [u87]	230838	25.2	359070	39.2	216612	23.6	109392	11.9	25	64
Uruguay	d	C1307+F156+ P1307	8740	50.0	5776	33.0	2770	15.8	195	1.1	50	83
Venezuela	d	C3490+F253+P1824	38700	43.9	42599	48.3	5567	6.3	1339	1.5	44	92
AFRICA												
Algeria	c	C8040+F485+ P3163	197680	83.0	27083	11.4	11688	4.9	1723	0.7	83	94
Angola	c	C3500+F120+ P3500	66070	53.0	50913	40.8	7120	5.7	567	0.5	53	94
Benin	c	C1595+F14+ P44	1440	13.0	7695	69.6	1653	14.9	274	2.5	13	83
Botswana	m	C346+F1+P346	24940	44.0	30949	54.6	693	1.2	91	0.2	44	99
Burkina Faso	c	C3440+F20+ P600	3280	12.0	19485	71.2	4060	14.8	535	2.0	12	83
Burundi	c	C1100+F92+ P#96	0	0.0	1092	42.5	1288	50.2	188	7.3	0	42
Cameroon	c	C7160+F16+ P200	6980	15.0	31507	67.7	7376	15.8	677	1.5	15	83
Cape Verde	s	C41+F40+P3	0	0.0	300	74.4	84	20.8	19	4.7	0	74
Central African R	m	C2020+F6+ P300	27410	44.0	32394	52.0	2326	3.7	168	0.3	44	96
Chad	c	C3256+F4+ P3256	68000	54.0	51059	40.5	6516	5.2	345	0.3	54	94
Comoros	F0+R1	C118+F0+P2	1	0.4	83	37.2	120	53.8	19	8.5	0	38
Congo, DR	c	C7880+F42+ P1500	102020	45.0	112924	49.8	9422	4.2	2339	1.0	45	95
Congo, R	m	C185+F37+ P185	17420	51.0	16191	47.4	407	1.2	132	0.4	51	98
Côte d'Ivoire	m	C7350+F66+ P1300	6680	21.0	15713	49.4	8716	27.4	691	2.2	21	70
Djibouti	F0+R154	0	154	6.6	2133	92.0	0	0.0	31	1.3	7	99
Egypt	c	C3300+F34+P0	78640	79.0	14396	14.5	3334	3.3	3175	3.2	79	93
Equatorial Guinea	m	C230+F3+P10	1375	49.0	1166	41.6	243	8.7	21	0.7	49	91
Eritrea	F0+R161	C393+F49+ P393	161	1.6	8939	88.5	835	8.3	165	1.6	2	90
Ethiopia	F134+R4777	C10500+F140+P2000	4911	4.9	79610	79.6	12640	12.6	2839	2.8	5	85
Gabon	m	C495+F21+ P470	16750	65.0	7965	30.9	986	3.8	66	0.3	65	96
Gambia	m	C200+F1+P20	110	11.0	611	61.1	221	22.1	58	5.8	11	72
Ghana	c	C4550+F53+ P840	460	2.0	15943	70.1	5443	23.9	908	4.0	2	72
Guinea	m	C1485+F4+ P1070	7370	30.0	14279	58.1	2559	10.4	364	1.5	30	88
Guinea-Bissau	F23+R0	C350+F1+P#10	23	0.8	2372	84.4	361	12.8	56	2.0	1	85
Kenya	c	C4520+F118+ P2130	24470	43.0	24283	42.7	6768	11.9	1393	2.4	43	86
Lesotho	F0+R18	C325+F6+P200	18	0.6	2387	78.6	531	17.5	99	3.3	1	79
Liberia	m	C327+F6+P200	1250	13.0	7739	80.3	533	5.5	110	1.1	13	93
Libyan Arab J	c158360a	C2115+F210+ P1330	144544	82.1	27450	15.6	3655	2.1	305	0.2	82	98
Madagascar	c	C3108+F217+ P2400	8720	15.0	43000	73.9	5725	9.8	709	1.2	15	89

Country	Natural note	Cultivated [Built] notes	Natural 000 ha	Nat %	Mod 000 ha	Mod %	Cult 000 ha	Cult %	Built 000 ha	Built %	Nat score	Conv score
Malawi	c	C1710+F126+ P184	380	4.0	6516	69.3	2020	21.5	492	5.2	4	73
Mali	c	C4650+F14+ P3000	81750	67.0	32096	26.3	7664	6.3	509	0.4	67	93
Mauritania	c93300a	C502+F2+P500	85857	83.7	15541	15.2	1004	1.0	120	0.1	84	99
Mauritius	F0+R0	C106+F9+P1	0	0.0	53	26.1	116	57.1	34	16.7	0	26
Morocco	c	C9595+F321+ P2100	450	1.0	30843	69.1	12016	26.9	1321	3.0	1	70
Mozambique	c	C3180+F28+ P3180	27440	35.0	43683	55.7	6388	8.1	898	1.1	35	91
Namibia	m	C820+F0+P820	44460	54.0	36134	43.9	1640	2.0	95	0.1	54	98
Niger	c95000a	C5000+F12+ P1044	87948	69.4	32193	25.4	6056	4.8	473	0.4	69	95
Nigeria	c	C30738+F151+P4000	2730	3.0	48387	53.1	34889	38.3	5071	5.6	3	56
Rwanda	c	C1150+F88+ P70	0	0.0	995	40.3	1308	53.0	164	6.6	0	40
São Tomé & Principe	F1+R0	C41+F0+P#0	1	1.0	47	49.0	41	42.7	7	7.3	1	50
Senegal	c	C2266+F112+ P570	190	1.0	15688	81.5	2948	15.3	427	2.2	1	82
Seychelles	F0+R1	C7+F1+P0	1	2.2	32	71.1	8	17.8	4	8.9	2	73
Sierra Leone	F13+R203	C546+F6+P220	216	3.0	5960	83.2	772	10.8	214	3.0	3	86
Somalia	c	C1061+F4+ P1061	20070	32.0	40115	63.9	2126	3.4	423	0.7	32	96
South Africa	c	C16300+F1295+P8150	32970	27.0	61483	50.4	25745	21.1	1906	1.6	27	77
Sudan	m	C16900+F203+ P11000	71280	30.0	136859	57.6	28103	11.8	1358	0.6	30	88
Swaziland	F0+R4	C180+F72+ P115	4	0.2	1304	75.8	367	21.3	45	2.6	0	76
Tanzania	c	C4000+F154+ P3500	36230	41.0	42940	48.6	7654	8.7	1535	1.7	41	90
Togo	F12+R41	C2430+F21+ P20	53	1.0	2706	49.8	2471	45.4	209	3.8	1	51
Tunisia	c	C4900+F201+ P310	2800	18.0	6871	44.2	5411	34.8	454	2.9	18	62
Uganda	m	C6810+F20+ P180	4390	22.0	7592	38.0	7010	35.1	973	4.9	22	60
Zambia	m	C5265+F44+ P3000	52780	71.0	12831	17.3	8309	11.2	419	0.6	71	88
Zimbabwe	c	C3210+F84+ P1720	6960	18.0	26159	67.6	5014	13.0	552	1.4	18	86
EUROPE												
Albania	F85+W0+R4	C702+Ft102+ P42 [ea90]	89	3.2	1578	57.6	846	30.9	227	8.3	3	61
Austria	F34+W84+R7	C1479+Ft0+ Pe194 [e90]	125	1.5	6193	74.9	1681	20.3	274	3.3	1	76
Belarus	F43+W0+R92	C6319+Ft195+ P297	135	0.7	13283	64.0	6811	32.8	519	2.5	1	65
Belgium	F0+W0+R0	C870+Ft294+ Pe55 [e95]	0	0.0	1273	42.0	1219	40.3	536	17.7	0	42
Bosnia & Herzegovina	F0+W0+R16	C650+Ft57+ P120	16	0.3	4086	80.1	827	16.2	171	3.4	0	80
Bulgaria	F256+W0+R0	C4411+Ft969+ P180 [e94]	256	2.3	4403	39.8	5560	50.3	836	7.6	2	42
Croatia	F2+W33+R20	C1442+Ft47+ P109	55	1.0	3715	66.4	1598	28.6	224	4.0	1	67
Czech R	F0+W0+R0	C3331+Ft0+ Pe95	0	0.0	3786	49.0	3426	44.3	516	6.7	0	49
Denmark	F0+W10+R16	C2373+Ft341+ Pe32	26	0.6	1209	28.5	2746	64.7	262	6.2	1	29
Estonia	F2+W0+R34	C1143+Ft305+ P31	36	0.9	2639	62.4	1479	35.0	73	1.7	1	63
Finland	F1263+W408+R2388	C2129+Ft0+ Pe10 [e90]	4059	13.3	23322	76.6	2139	7.0	939	3.1	13	90
France	F30+W0+R53	C19468+Ft961+Pe1208 [e95]	83	0.2	30335	55.1	21637	39.3	2955	5.4	0	55
Germany	F0+W0+R0	C12060+Ft0+ Pe527	0	0.0	18245	52.2	12587	36.0	4095	11.7	0	52
Greece	F0+W0+R0	C3915+Ft120+ Pe#508 [ea80]	0	0.0	7810	60.6	4543	35.2	537	4.2	0	61
Hungary	F0+W0+R7	C5047+Ft136+ Pe115	7	0.1	3419	37.0	5298	57.4	510	5.5	0	37
Iceland	F0+W0+ R4043	C6+Ft12+Pe6 [e95]	4043	40.3	5823	58.1	24	0.2	135	1.3	40	98
Ireland	F1+W0+R38	C1346+Ft590+ Pe352	39	0.6	4380	63.6	2288	33.2	182	2.6	1	64
Italy	F6+W197+R0	C10927+Ft133+Pe#454 [e90]	203	0.7	13802	46.9	11514	39.2	3887	13.2	1	48
Latvia	F4+W0+R11	C1830+Ft143+ P80	15	0.2	4012	64.7	2053	33.1	125	2.0	0	65
Lithuania	F12+W0+R16	C3006+Ft284+ P50 [ea95]	28	0.4	2936	45.3	3340	51.5	176	2.7	0	46
Luxembourg	F0+W0+R0	C67+Ft39+Pe8	0	0.0	122	47.5	114	44.4	21	8.2	0	47
Macedonia, FYR	F0+W0+R2	C658+Ft30+P64	2	0.1	1690	66.5	752	29.6	99	3.9	0	66
Malta	F0+W0+R0	C11+Ft0+P0 [e95]	0	0.0	14	43.8	11	34.4	7	21.9	0	44
Moldova	F0+W0+R0	C2183+Ft1+P37	0	0.0	857	26.0	2221	67.4	219	6.6	0	26
Netherlands	F0+W0+R0	C935+Ft100+ Pe103 [e93]	0	0.0	1693	49.9	1138	33.5	561	16.5	0	50
Norway	F250+W329+ R8533	C902+Ft300+ Pe14	9112	29.7	19655	64.1	1216	4.0	700	2.3	30	94
Poland	F198+W0+R0	C14424+Ft39+ Pe409 [e95]	198	0.7	13063	42.9	14872	48.9	2309	7.6	1	43
Portugal	F55+W44+R0	C2900+Ft834+ Pe100 [e90]	99	1.1	3803	41.6	3834	41.9	1414	15.5	1	43
Romania	F233+W0+R0	C9900+Ft91+ P487	233	1.0	11191	48.6	10478	45.5	1132	4.9	1	50
Slovakia	F20+W0+R0	C1605+Ft15+ Pe84 [e95]	20	0.4	2955	61.5	1704	35.4	129	2.7	0	62
Slovenia	F50+W0+R0	C285+Ft1+P50 [e95]	50	2.5	1577	78.4	336	16.7	49	2.4	2	81
Spain	F5+W3+R0	C19164+Ft1904+Pe1069 [e90]	8	0.0	25870	51.8	22137	44.3	1929	3.9	0	52
Sweden	F5177+ W2854+R455	C2799+Ft569+ Pe58 [e90]	8486	20.6	28078	68.2	3426	8.3	1172	2.8	21	89
Switzerland	F7+W0+R9	C444+Ft4+ Pe111 [ba80]	16	0.4	3099	78.4	559	14.1	281	7.1	0	79
Ukraine	F59+W6+R43	C34081+Ft4425+P750	108	0.2	16008	27.6	39256	67.8	2563	4.4	0	28
United Kingdom	F0+W0+R0	C6425+Ft1400+Pe1101	0	0.0	12312	51.0	8926	36.9	2922	12.1	0	51
Yugoslavia	F4+W12+R6	C4058+Ft39+ P212	22	0.2	5339	52.3	4309	42.2	530	5.2	0	53
RUSSIAN FEDERATION	F749198+ W70000+ R288669	C127962+ Ft17340+ Pe8814	1107867	65.6	417994	24.8	154116	9.1	8873	0.5	66	90
ASIA												
Afghanistan	c	C8054+F8+ P3000	11090	17.0	42039	64.5	11062	17.0	1018	1.6	17	81

Country	Natural note	Cultivated [Built] notes	Natural 000 ha	Nat %	Mod 000 ha	Mod %	Cult 000 ha	Cult %	Built 000 ha	Built %	Nat score	Conv score
Armenia	F284+W41+ R30	C559+Ft13+P69 [e95]	355	12.6	1631	57.8	641	22.7	193	6.8	13	70
Azerbaijan	F400+W15+ R128	C1935+Ft20+ P220	543	6.3	5562	64.2	2175	25.1	380	4.4	6	70
Bahrain	F0+R0	C5+F0+P0	0	0.0	47	68.1	5	7.2	17	24.6	0	68
Bangladesh	c	C8241+F310+ P60	0	0.0	3200	24.6	8611	66.2	1206	9.3	0	24
Bhutan	c	C160+F8+P27	1365	29.0	3045	64.8	195	4.1	95	2.0	29	94
Brunei Darussalam	i	C7+F0+P1	310	58.8	194	36.8	8	1.5	15	2.8	59	96
Cambodia	c	C3807+F7+ P150	3880	22.0	9296	52.7	3964	22.5	512	2.9	22	75
China	c	C135371+ F33800+ P40000	205200	22.0	456408	48.9	209171	22.4	61963	6.6	22	71
Cyprus	F0+W0+R28	C145+Ft27+P0 [e95]	28	3.0	684	74.0	172	18.6	40	4.3	3	77
Georgia	F550+W0+R8	C1066+Ft200+ P189	558	8.0	4698	67.4	1455	20.9	259	3.7	8	75
India	c	C169850+ F14620+ P1130	5950	2.0	77269	26.0	185600	62.4	28500	9.6	2	28
Indonesia	m	C30987+F6125+P1195	93150	51.4	39638	21.9	38307	21.1	10062	5.6	51	73
Iran	c	C19400+F79+ P4400	9730	6.0	125418	77.3	23879	14.7	3173	2.0	6	83
Iraq	c	C5540+F14+ P400	10930	25.0	25814	59.0	5954	13.6	1039	2.4	25	84
Israel	F0+W0+R21	C437+Ft91+P15	21	1.0	1212	58.8	543	26.3	286	13.9	1	60
Japan	F3061+W0+ R0	C4295+Ft10682+Pe65	3061	8.1	13261	35.2	15042	40.0	6288	16.7	8	43
Jordan	c	C390+F23+P79	4450	50.0	3654	41.1	492	5.5	297	3.3	50	91
Kazakhstan	F0+W0+ R19312	C30135+Ft5+ P18682	19312	7.2	197953	74.1	48822	18.3	986	0.4	7	81
Korea, DPR	F47+R27	C2000+F1470+P5	74	0.6	7362	61.1	3475	28.9	1130	9.4	1	62
Korea, R	c	C1924+F†363+Pe#0	0	0.0	6226	63.1	2287	23.2	1360	13.8	0	63
Kuwait	c	C7+F5+P7	588	33.0	1091	61.2	19	1.1	84	4.7	33	94
Kyrgyzstan	F100+W0+ R1325	C1425+Ft57+ P900	1425	7.4	15143	79.0	2382	12.4	230	1.2	7	86
Lao PDR	i	C852+F4+P80	3830	16.6	18069	78.3	936	4.1	245	1.1	17	95
Lebanon	F0+R11	C308+F13+P2	11	1.1	597	58.4	323	31.6	92	9.0	1	59
Malaysia	c	C7605+F99+ P28	13470	41.0	10626	32.3	7732	23.5	1027	3.1	41	73
Maldives	F0+R0	C3+F0+P0	0	0.0	24	80.0	3	10.0	3	10.0	0	80
Mongolia	c	C1320+F0+ P1320	93990	60.0	59870	38.2	2640	1.7	150	0.1	60	98
Myanmar	c	C10151+F276+P35	4600	7.0	48523	73.8	10462	15.9	2170	3.3	7	81
Nepal	c	C2968+F56+ P176	3000	21.0	7010	49.0	3200	22.4	1090	7.6	21	70
Oman	c	C63+F0+P63	16360	77.0	4626	21.8	126	0.6	134	0.6	77	99
Pakistan	c	C21600+F168+P500	3850	5.0	43967	57.0	22268	28.9	7003	9.1	5	62
Philippines	i	C9520+F203+ P128	2590	8.7	15279	51.2	9851	33.0	2097	7.0	9	60
Qatar	F0+R181	C17+F0+P5	181	16.5	869	79.0	22	2.0	28	2.5	16	95
Saudi Arabia	c178420a	C3830+F1+ P3830	149301	69.5	56877	26.5	7661	3.6	1130	0.5	69	96
Singapore	F0+R0	C1+F0+P0 [i]	0	0.0	27	44.3	1	1.6	33	54.1	0	44
Sri Lanka	F0+R18	C1888+F139+ P44	18	0.3	3831	59.3	2071	32.0	543	8.4	0	60
Syrian Arab R	c	C5521+F127+ P830	1650	9.0	9521	51.8	6478	35.2	729	4.0	9	61
Tajikistan	F21+W18+ R1337	C890+Ft10+ P355	1376	9.8	11137	79.2	1255	8.9	292	2.1	10	89
Thailand	c	C20445+F529+P80	4090	8.0	22986	45.0	21054	41.2	2959	5.8	8	53
Turkey	F186+W144+ R888	C29162+Ft1854+Pe1238	1218	1.6	40374	52.5	32254	41.9	3117	4.0	2	54
Turkmenistan	F0+W0+ R5668	C1695+Ft12+ P1695	5668	12.1	37715	80.3	3402	7.2	208	0.4	12	92
United Arab Emirates	c7440a	C81+F60+P29	6474	77.4	1354	16.2	170	2.0	362	4.3	77	94
Uzbekistan	F200+W0+ R636	C4850+Ft300+ P2080	836	2.0	32216	77.8	7230	17.5	1142	2.8	2	80
Viet Nam	c	C7202+F1470+P33	650	2.0	20939	64.3	8705	26.7	2255	6.9	2	66
Yemen	F0+R7564	C1555+F0+ P1555	7564	14.3	41339	78.3	3110	5.9	784	1.5	14	93
PACIFIC												
Australia	F18836+ W29472+ R40538	C26100+ Ft1043+ Pe30000	88846	11.6	618250	80.5	57143	7.4	3991	0.5	12	92
Fiji	F38+R36	C285+F78+P17	74	4.1	1334	73.0	380	20.8	39	2.1	4	77
New Zealand	F1599+W0+ R907	C3280+Ft1542+Pe1317	2506	9.4	17559	65.5	6139	22.9	595	2.2	9	75
Papua New Guinea	c	C670+F30+P9	28530	63.0	15827	34.9	709	1.6	220	0.5	63	98
Samoa	F4+R0	C122+F9+P0	4	1.4	140	49.5	131	46.3	8	2.8	1	51
Solomon Is	F711+R20	C60+F18+P4	731	26.1	1966	70.2	82	2.9	20	0.7	26	96
Tonga	F0+R0	C48+F0+P0	0	0.0	19	26.4	48	66.7	5	6.9	0	26
Vanuatu	F232+R16	C120+F7+P3	248	20.3	832	68.3	130	10.7	9	0.7	20	89

Notes

The land modification and conversion indicator measures the converted and natural proportions of a country's land area. All data are in thousand hectares (000 ha), and all percentages are in terms of land area (Table 10).

Natural note = sources of data in the natural land column. A single lower-case letter (c, d, i, m, r, or s) indicates a source. If it is followed by a number and a lower-case letter a (e.g., d321a), it means that the estimate of natural land has been adjusted to avoid excessive conflict with the estimates of degraded land in Table 13. The original estimate is the number between the source letter and the a. ("Excessive conflict" arises when the area of degraded land exceeds the combined area of cultivated and modified land, in which case the area of natural land was adjusted so as to increase the area of modified land until the combined area of cultivated and modified land equals 100% of the area of degraded land.) Combinations of upper-case letters and numbers show the estimated area of natural land that is forest (F), other woodland (W), and remaining unconverted land (R). For more explanation, see Natural land below.

Cultivated [Built] notes = sources of data in the cultivated and built columns. For explanation, see Cultivated land and Built land below.

Natural/Nat = natural land = land that is negligibly to lightly human-influenced. Estimates of natural land area are extremely rough and different sources often differ greatly. The sources are given in the Natural note column:

Americas (except Canada and United States): Dinerstein, Olson, Graham *et al.* (1995), indicated by the letter d.

Canada and USA: Ricketts, Dinerstein, Olson *et al.* (1998), indicated by the letter r.

Africa (except Cape Verde, Comoros, Djibouti, Eritrea, Ethiopia, Guinea-Bissau, Lesotho, Mauritius, São Tomé & Principe, Seychelles, Sierra Leone, Swaziland, Togo): Conservation International (1996), indicated by the letter c; or MacKinnon & MacKinnon (1986a), indicated by the letter m. In the event of a conflict between these sources, the lower estimate was chosen.

Cape Verde: Stuart & Adams (1990), indicated by the letter s.

Europe: UNECE & FAO (2000), indicated by the F+W+R figures. F = the reported area of native forest that is undisturbed. W = the reported area of other woodland that is undisturbed. R = a *Wellbeing of Nations* (WoN) estimate of the area of remaining unconverted land that is natural.

Asia (except Armenia, Azerbaijan, Bahrain, Cyprus, Georgia, Israel, Japan, Kazakhstan, DPR Korea, Kyrgyzstan, Lebanon, Maldives, Qatar, Singapore, Sri Lanka, Tajikistan, Turkey, Turkmenistan, Uzbekistan, Yemen): Conservation International (1996), indicated by the letter c; Asian Bureau for Conservation & World Conservation Monitoring Centre (1997), indicated by the letter i; or MacKinnon & MacKinnon (1986b), indicated by the letter m. In the event of a conflict among these sources, the lowest estimate was chosen, except in the cases of Brunei Darussalam, Lao PDR, and Philippines. For these countries, Asian Bureau for Conservation & World Conservation Monitoring Centre (1997) was chosen as the source, because it provided more detailed assessment that clearly distinguished between natural and modified components of remaining original habitat.

Russian Federation, Armenia, Azerbaijan, Cyprus, Georgia, Israel, Japan, Kazakhstan, Kyrgyzstan, Tajikistan, Turkey, Turkmenistan, Uzbekistan: UNECE & FAO (2000), indicated by the F+W+R figures. F = the reported area of native forest that is undisturbed. W = the reported area of other woodland that is undisturbed. R = a WoN estimate of the area of remaining unconverted land that is natural.

Australia and New Zealand: UNECE & FAO (2000), indicated by the F+W+R figures. F = the reported area of native forest that is undisturbed. W = the reported area of other woodland that is undisturbed. R = a WoN estimate of the area of remaining unconverted land that is natural.

Papua New Guinea: Conservation International (1996), indicated by the letter c.

All other countries: WoN estimates, indicated by F+R figures (as for UNECE & FAO [2000] but without the W figure). F = the estimated area of natural forest that is natural. R = the estimated area of remaining unconverted land that is natural.

Dinerstein, Olson, Graham *et al.* (1995) used satellite imagery, maps and assessments by regional experts to define and map Latin American and Caribbean ecoregions and estimate habitat loss and fragmentation for each ecoregion. Table 11a shows my interpretations of their estimates to determine the percentage of each ecoregion that is intact or natural. Dinerstein, Olson, Graham *et al.* (1995) did not provide country-by-country estimates of habitat loss and fragmention. To do this, WoN overlaid their ecoregion maps with national boundaries to allocate ecoregions to countries. For ecoregions shared by more than one country, this implies that the percentage of intact habitat is evenly distributed throughout the ecoregion. This may not be true: an ecoregion estimated to be 50% intact and shared equally by two countries could be 75% intact in one country and 25% intact in the other. WoN's interpretations of the method of Dinerstein, Olson, Graham *et al.* (1995) produced some apparent overestimates of natural land area (for example, Trinidad & Tobago) but no obvious underestimate.

Ricketts, Dinerstein, Olson *et al.* (1998) used satellite imagery and assessments by national experts to define and map North American ecoregions and estimate the intact percentage of each. WoN overlaid their ecoregion map with national boundaries to allocate ecoregions to Canada or the United States, and estimate how much of the land area of each country is natural (= intact).

Conservation International (1996) was a global-scale analysis that used maps and satellite imagery to obtain country-by-country estimates of areas that were undisturbed, partially disturbed, or human dominated. The method is described in Hannah *et al.* (1994) and Hannah, Carr & Lankerani (1995). The smallest area mapped was 40,000 ha, and the smallest area recognized as undisturbed was 100,000 ha. The method tended to overestimate the undisturbed percentage in large, sparsely populated countries, and to underestimate it in small, densely populated countries. WoN interpreted undisturbed as equivalent to natural.

MacKinnon & MacKinnon (1986a &1986b) used maps and satellite imagery to estimate the percentage of original habitat remaining in subSaharan African countries (MacKinnon & MacKinnon 1986a) and South and Southeast Asian countries (MacKinnon & MacKinnon 1986b). Asian Bureau for Conservation & World Conservation Monitoring Centre (1997) used the same approach to update MacKinnon & MacKinnon (1986b). The term "original habitat remaining" is misleading, implying that the habitat is natural although some or much of it may be modified.

Stuart & Adams (1990) reported of Cape Verde: "Original vegetation unknown, and in any case long since destroyed through over-grazing and erosion."

The *Temperate and Boreal Forest Resources Assessment 2000* (UNECE & FAO 2000) contains national estimates by countries in North America, Europe and Asia-Pacific of the percentages of their native forest and other woodland that are undisturbed. WoN interpreted undisturbed as equivalent to natural.

WoN estimates assumed: 1% of native forest land (F) for each 0.2 ha F per person (up to 20 ha F per person) + 1% of remaining unconverted land (R) for each 0.1 ha R per person (up to 10 ha R per person). Exceptionally, for Finland, Iceland, Norway, Russia, Kazakhstan, Turkmenistan, Australia, and New Zealand—countries with low population densities (more than 5.0 ha/person) and natural forest and woodland data from UNECE & FAO (2000)—WoN assumed 50% of R was natural. WoN estimates were made in any of the following circumstances: (a) no other estimate was available; (b) to supplement UNECE & FAO (2000), which covers only forests and other woodland; (c) a Conservation International (1996) estimate of 0% seemed too low.

Mod = modified land = land that is moderately to heavily human-influenced, but not cultivated or built. Uncultivated permanent pasture is counted as modified. Otherwise this category is a residual obtained as follows: total land - natural land - cultivated land - built land = modified land.

Cult = cultivated land = cropland + plantation forest + cultivated pasture. The areas of cropland (C), plantation forest (F) and cultivated pasture (P) are given in the Cultivated [Built] notes column.

Cropland (C) = land under permanent or temporary agricultural crops, including temporary meadows for mowing or pasture, land under market and kitchen gardens, and land temporarily fallow (under five years). Data are for 1997 and are from FAO (1999a), except for Belgium and Luxembourg which are from Organisation for Economic Co-operation and Development (1999).

Plantation forest (F) = forests that have been established artificially, usually consisting of non-indigenous species or stocks. Data are for 1995 and are from FAO (1997a), except where indicated by the letter t which are for different years (given in the forest note column of Table 10) and are from UNECE & FAO (2000). † indicates a conflict between the reported area of forest and other reported areas in R Korea, resolved by reducing the area of plantation forest (in 000 ha) from 1,400 to 363.

Cultivated pasture (P) = sown (not wild) meadows and pastures. Except for Australia, data are WoN estimates, and are either 10% of the area of permanent pasture (land used for five years or more for wild or cultivated herbaceous forage crops) or the same area as cropland, whichever is smaller. Permanent pasture data are for 1994—the last year for which FAO has compiled pasture data—and are from FAO (1999a), except where indicated by the letter e which are for 1997 and are from Organisation for Economic Co-operation and Development (1999). In the case of Australia, FAO and OECD figures for arable land include 30 million ha of cultivated grassland. This has been subtracted from cropland and recorded separately as cultivated pasture. The FAO and OECD figures for permanent pasture are assumed to be all uncultivated. # indicates a conflict between the reported area of permanent pasture and other reported areas—resolved by reducing the area of permanent pasture as follows (in 000 ha): Guyana from 1230 to 562; Burundi from 1,090 to 963; Guinea-Bissau from 1,080 to 107; São Tomé & Principe from 1 to 0; Greece from 5217 to 5079; Italy from 4558 to 4538; R Korea from 90 to 0.

Built = built land = land occupied by buildings, transport infrastructure (roads, railways, docks, airports, etc.) and other human structures, including mines and quarries, waste tips, derelict land, and urban and suburban parks and gardens. Data are WoN estimates for 1996 except where indicated by a note in brackets (e.g., [u86]) in the Cultivated [Built] notes column as follows:

b Beeler (1992).

e Eurostat, European Commission, & the European Environment Agency (1998).

i Asian Bureau for Conservation & World Conservation Monitoring Centre (1997).

u United Nations Statistical Commission & Economic Commission for Europe (1992).

The applicable year is indicated in brackets. Data for years before 1990 have been adjusted to 1996 (indicated by the letter a) on the basis of population. Data for 1990 onwards have not been adjusted. Lithuania's built area, reported as an exceptionally low 17,600 ha, has been adjusted to 176,000 ha.

WoN estimates of built land draw on the data from the above sources to derive an average of 0.05 ha built land per person, except as follows:

Countries with a population density of 0.0-0.2 ha per person and a real Gross Domestic Product (GDP) of purchasing power parity (PPP) $0-PPP$5,000 (Bangladesh, Maldives): 0.01 ha built land per person.

Countries with a population density of 0.0-0.2 ha per person and a real GDP of PPP$10,200-PPP$20,000 (Barbados, Mauritius, Bahrain, R Korea): 0.03 ha built land per person.

Countries with a population density of 3.3-6.4 ha per person and a real GDP of PPP$5,100-PPP$10,000 (Brazil, Chile, Uruguay, Venezuela): 0.06 ha built land per person.

Countries with a population density of 3.3-6.4 ha per person and a real GDP of PPP$10,200-PPP$20,000 (Bahamas, United Arab Emirates): 0.16 ha built land per person.

Countries with a population density of 6.5-102.4 ha per person and a real GDP of PPP$2,500-PPP$10,000 (Argentina, Belize, Bolivia, Guyana, Paraguay, Suriname, Algeria, Botswana, Gabon, Libyan Arab J, Namibia, Russian Federation, Kazakhstan, Mongolia, Oman, Saudi Arabia): 0.06 ha built land per person.

Countries with a population density of 6.5-12.8 ha per person and a real GDP of PPP$10,200-PPP$20,000 (New Zealand): 0.16 ha built land per person.

Countries with a population density of 25.7-102.4 ha per person and a real GDP of PPP$10,200-PPP$20,000 (Australia): 0.22 ha built land per person.

Nat score = score for natural land as % of total land. See Table 10a for performance criteria.
Conv score = score for converted (cultivated + built) land as % of total land. See Table 10a for performance criteria.

Categories of Dinerstein, Olson, Graham et al. (1995)			WoN interpretations
habitat loss	habitat block size	habitat fragmentation	
0-10% lost	very large	relatively contiguous	95% intact
0-10% lost	all others	all others	90% intact
10-24% lost	very large	relatively contiguous	85% intact
10-24% lost	large or very large	low fragmentation	80% intact
10-24% lost	all others	all others	75% intact
24-49% lost	very large	relatively contiguous	70% intact
24-49% lost	large or very large	low fragmentation	60% intact
24-49% lost	all others	all others	50% intact
50-89% lost	very large	relatively contiguous	40% intact
50-89% lost	large or very large	low fragmentation	25% intact
50-89% lost	all others	all others	10% intact
more than 90% lost	all	all	0% intact
no data	all	all	0% intact

Table 11a. Intact percentages of ecoregions of Latin America and the Caribbean. *Wellbeing of Nations* (WoN) interpretations of Dinerstein and colleagues' categories of habitat loss, habitat block size, and habitat fragmentation.

Table 12. Land Protection

Country	Total area 000 ha	MTP 000 ha	MTP %	ITP 000 ha	ITP %	LTP 000 ha	LTP %	KTP 000 ha	KTP %	PP 000 ha	PP %	Wtd tot %	Size score	No & type unit	Ave % TP	Ave % PP	Ave % totP	Wtd %	Div score	LP score
AMERICAS																				
Antigua & Barbuda	44	0	0	0	0	0	0	4	9.1	0	0	22.7	83	--	--	--	--	--	--	80*
Argentina	278040	0	0	1793	0.6	1235	0.4	145	0.1	5939	2.1	2.9	23	12 ft	--	--	6.3	4.7	38	28
Bahamas	1388	0	0	0	0	95	6.8	3	0.2	1	0.1	14.0	68	5 mez	0.0	0.0	0.0	0.0	0	45
Barbados	43	0	0	0	0	0	0	0	0	0	0	0	0	2 ft	--	--	0.0	0.0	0	0
Belize	2296	0	0	108	4.7	69	3.0	21	0.9	630	27.4	32.9	93	3 mez	11.8	26.7	38.5	25.1	85	90
Bolivia	109858	8060	7.3	1895	1.7	189	0.2	0	0	7674	7.0	25.5	86	14 ez	2.9	3.8	6.7	4.8	38	70
Brazil	854740	7415	0.9	12202	1.4	2229	0.3	320	0	30296	3.5	7.3	49	18 ez	3.1	6.7	9.8	6.4	46	48
Canada	997061	22293	2.2	16022	1.6	3847	0.4	816	0.1	51789	5.2	12.0	64	8 ft	--	--	7.6	5.7	43	57
Chile	75663	6728	8.9	1429	1.9	510	0.7	54	0.1	5406	7.1	30.7	91	4 ft	--	--	9.6	7.2	49	77
Colombia	113891	2372	2.1	5858	5.1	751	0.7	31	0	349	0.3	16.7	73	17 ez	6.3	8.3	14.6	10.4	61	69
Costa Rica	5110	0	0	194	3.8	336	6.6	51	1.0	617	12.1	30.3	90	5 mez	12.9	7.2	20.1	16.5	73	85
Cuba	11086	0	0	0	0	116	1.0	33	0.3	1750	15.8	9.7	59	5 mez	4.6	5.2	9.8	7.2	49	55
Dominica	75	0	0	0	0	0	0	7	9.3	9	12.0	29.2	89	--	--	--	--	--	--	80*
Dominican R	4873	0	0	694	14.2	249	5.1	6	0.1	299	6.1	48.9	100	4 mez	14.5	0.8	15.3	14.9	70	90
Ecuador	28356	0	0	3642	12.8	261	0.9	0	0	3645	12.9	33.4	93	13 ez	6.7	1.0	7.7	7.2	49	79
El Salvador	2104	0	0	0	0	0	0	3	0.1	2	0.1	0.3	2	3 mez	0.2	0.2	0.4	0.3	2	2
Grenada	34	0	0	0	0	0	0	0	0	0	0	0	0	--	--	--	--	--	--	0
Guatemala	10889	0	0	1267	11.6	527	4.8	27	0.2	344	3.2	32.2	92	6 mez	8.1	0.7	8.8	8.4	54	79
Guyana	21497	0	0	0	0	59	0.3	0	0	0	0	0.4	3	5 ez	0.0	0.0	0.0	0.0	0	2
Haiti	2775	0	0	0	0	0	0	7	0.3	2	0.1	0.5	4	5 mez	0.1	0.0	0.1	0.1	1	3
Honduras	11209	0	0	332	3.0	327	2.9	21	0.2	449	4.0	12.5	65	5 mez	1.2	3.2	4.4	2.8	22	51
Jamaica	1099	0	0	0	0	0	0	0	0	82	7.5	3.8	30	5 mez	0.0	11.4	11.4	5.7	43	35
Mexico	195820	0	0	1338	0.7	543	0.3	64	0	12635	6.5	5.1	40	9 mez	1.8	2.9	4.7	3.2	26	35
Nicaragua	13000	0	0	295	2.3	34	0.3	10	0.1	1244	9.6	9.9	60	4 mez	5.5	10.9	16.4	10.9	62	60
Panama	7552	0	0	1185	15.7	145	1.9	22	0.3	181	2.4	44.7	100	4 mez	10.5	7.4	17.9	14.2	68	89
Paraguay	40675	0	0	1160	2.9	196	0.5	9	0	35	0.1	6.7	47	5 ez	1.4	0.4	1.8	1.6	13	35
Peru	128522	1533	1.2	1274	1.0	171	0.1	22	0	3760	2.9	6.7	47	16 ez	4.8	2.2	7.0	5.9	44	46
St Kitts & Nevis	26	0	0	0	0	0	0	3	11.5	0	0	28.7	89	1 ft	--	--	0.0	0.0	0	59
St Lucia	62	0	0	0	0	0	0	1	1.6	6	9.7	8.8	55	5 ft	--	--	25.7	19.3	79	63
St Vincent & Grenadines	39	0	0	0	0	0	0	0	0	4	10.3	5.2	41	--	--	--	--	--	--	41
Suriname	16326	0	0	0	0	0	0	8	0	796	4.9	2.5	20	3 ez	0.3	5.1	5.4	2.8	22	21
Trinidad & Tobago	513	0	0	0	0	0	0	2	0.4	17	3.3	2.4	19	2 mez	0.1	0.0	0.1	0.1	1	13
United States	936352	31542	3.4	29443	3.1	8127	0.9	1742	0.2	59548	6.4	19.5	79	8 ft	--	--	6.6	4.8	38	65
Uruguay	17741	0	0	0	0	14	0.1	1	0	31	0.2	0.3	2	4 ft	--	--	1.0	0.7	6	3
Venezuela	91205	10650	11.7	7425	8.1	1128	1.2	53	0.1	36781	40.3	67.5	100	16 ez	23.8	20.9	44.7	34.2	94	98
AFRICA																				
Algeria	238174	5640	2.4	0	0	98	0	24	0	129	0.1	6.1	44	4 ft	--	--	23.6	17.7	75	55
Angola	124670	2960	2.4	2400	1.9	63	0.1	0	0	2758	2.2	11.1	62	9 ez	0.2	7.4	7.6	3.9	31	52
Benin	11262	0	0	777	6.9	0	0	0	0	485	4.3	16.0	72	4 ez	13.1	10.6	23.7	18.4	77	74
Botswana	58173	3823	6.6	728	1.3	0	0	0	0	5945	10.2	24.2	84	5 ez	17.1	1.5	18.6	17.8	76	81
Burkina Faso	27400	0	0	478	1.7	57	0.2	0	0	2321	8.5	8.0	52	4 ez	1.1	33.3	34.4	25.8	86	63
Burundi	2783	0	0	0	0	0	0	0	9	144	5.2	2.6	21	3 ez	0.0	2.9	2.9	1.4	11	18
Cameroon	47544	0	0	1026	2.2	0	0	6	0	1066	2.2	5.5	42	8 ez	5.0	2.2	7.2	6.1	44	43
Cape Verde	403	0	0	0	0	0	0	0	0	0	0	0	0	--	--	--	--	--	--	0
Central African R	62298	2810	4.5	292	0.5	86	0.1	0	0	2258	3.6	14.3	69	5 ez	5.3	15.7	21.0	13.1	66	68
Chad	128400	0	0	414	0.3	0	0	0	0	11080	8.6	4.9	39	7 ez	0.4	5.3	5.7	3.0	24	34
Comoros	223	0	0	0	0	0	0	0	0	0	0	0	0	--	--	--	--	--	--	0
Congo, DR	234486	7285	3.1	2632	1.1	0	0	0	0	0	0	9.9	60	10 ez	13.5	1.2	14.7	14.1	68	63
Congo, R	34200	0	0	513	1.5	0	0	0	0	1187	3.5	4.8	38	2 ez	0.2	1.9	2.1	1.1	9	29
Côte d'Ivoire	32246	1150	3.6	574	1.8	158	0.5	8	0	102	0.3	13.4	67	3 ez	7.9	1.5	9.4	8.6	54	63
Djibouti	2320	0	0	0	0	10	0.4	0	0	0	0	0.8	6	2 ft	--	--	0.0	0.0	0	4
Egypt	100145	0	0	0	0	30	0	7	0	695	0.7	0.3	2	2 ft	--	--	0.0	0.0	0	2
Equatorial Guinea	2805	0	0	0	0	0	0	0	0	0	0	0	0	3 ez	0.0	0.0	0.0	0.0	0	0
Eritrea	11760	0	0	0	0	0	0	0	0	501	4.3	2.2	18	8 ez	0.0	4.6	4.6	2.3	18	18
Ethiopia	110430	0	0	2797	2.5	233	0.2	5	0	15664	14.2	12.4	65	11 ez	2.7	14.7	17.4	10.0	60	63
Gabon	26767	0	0	0	0	15	0.1	0	0	708	2.6	1.5	12	2 ez	0.0	3.7	3.7	1.8	14	13
Gambia	1129	0	0	0	0	11	1.0	7	0.6	3	0.3	3.1	25	2 ez	0.9	0.7	1.6	1.2	10	20
Ghana	23854	0	0	1014	4.3	75	0.3	8	0	171	0.7	9.3	57	3 ez	3.2	1.1	4.3	3.7	30	48
Guinea	24586	0	0	112	0.5	51	0.2	0	0	0	0	1.3	10	5 ez	0.5	3.0	3.5	2.0	16	12

194

Country	Total area 000 ha	MTP 000 ha	MTP %	ITP 000 ha	ITP %	LTP 000 ha	LTP %	KTP 000 ha	KTP %	PP 000 ha	PP %	Wtd tot %	Size score	No & type unit	Ave % TP	Ave % PP	Ave % totP	Wtd %	Div score	LP score
Guinea-Bissau	3612	0	0	0	0	0	0	0	0	0	0	0	0	3 ez	0.0	0.0	0.0	0.0	0	0
Kenya	58037	1175	2.0	1658	2.9	589	1.0	22	0	1013	1.7	13.2	66	13 ez	10.3	7.9	18.2	14.2	68	67
Lesotho	3035	0	0	0	0	0	0	0	0	7	0.2	0.1	1	1 ft	--	--	8.7	6.5	46	16
Liberia	11137	0	0	129	1.2	0	0	0	0	0	0	2.4	19	3 ez	0.4	0.0	0.4	0.4	3	14
Libyan Arab J	175954	0	0	0	0	50	0	1	0	122	0.1	0.1	1	1 ft	--	--	0.0	0.0	0	1
Madagascar	58704	0	0	152	0.3	589	1.0	3	0	486	0.8	2.5	20	9 ez	1.5	0.4	1.9	1.7	14	18
Malawi	11848	0	0	545	4.6	142	1.2	9	0.1	362	3.1	12.6	65	3 ez	11.4	13.3	24.7	18.0	76	69
Mali	124019	0	0	750	0.6	0	0	0	0	3782	3.0	2.7	22	5 ez	0.8	3.0	3.8	2.3	18	21
Mauritania	102552	1173	1.1	310	0.3	13	0	0	0	250	0.2	3.4	27	3 ez	0.3	0.0	0.3	0.3	2	19
Mauritius	204	0	0	0	0	0	0	7	3.4	5	2.5	8.1	52	--	--	--	--	--	--	52
Morocco	44655	0	0	0	0	0	0	9	0	307	0.7	0.3	2	3 ft	--	--	1.6	1.2	10	5
Mozambique	80159	0	0	1575	2.0	0	0	0	0	5012	6.3	7.2	49	7 ez	0.0	0.0	0.0	0.0	0	33
Namibia	82429	8843	10.7	831	1.0	97	0.1	4	0	1435	1.7	29.9	90	4 ez	8.9	2.7	11.6	10.2	60	80
Niger	126700	1280	1.0	220	0.2	0	0	0	0	8194	6.5	6.2	45	4 ez	4.2	3.6	7.8	6.0	44	45
Nigeria	92377	0	0	2226	2.4	49	0.1	0	0	745	0.8	5.4	42	8 ez	5.0	0.7	5.7	5.3	41	41
Rwanda	2634	0	0	250	9.5	14	0.5	0	0	132	5.0	27.3	87	3 ez	8.1	3.4	11.5	9.8	59	78
São Tomé & Principe	96	0	0	0	0	0	0	0	0	0	0	0	0	2 ft	--	--	0.0	0.0	0	0
Senegal	19672	0	0	913	4.6	92	0.5	7	0	1228	6.2	13.1	66	5 ez	4.1	3.4	7.5	5.8	43	59
Seychelles	45	0	0	0	0	0	0	3	6.7	0	0	16.7	73	--	--	--	--	--	--	73
Sierra Leone	7174	0	0	0	0	0	0	0	0	153	2.1	1.0	8	4 ez	0.0	3.1	3.1	1.5	12	9
Somalia	63766	0	0	0	0	0	0	0	0	524	0.8	0.4	3	6 ez	0.0	0.1	0.1	0.0	0	2
South Africa	122104	1962	1.6	1738	1.4	528	0.4	34	0	2135	1.7	8.3	53	16 ez	2.9	3.9	6.8	4.8	38	48
Sudan	250581	7480	3.0	890	0.4	103	0	0	0	3750	1.5	9.1	56	16 ez	2.1	1.4	3.5	2.8	22	45
Swaziland	1736	0	0	0	0	0	0	0	0	60	3.5	1.8	14	1 ft	--	--	3.2	2.4	19	16
Tanzania	94509	2771	2.9	1156	1.2	167	0.2	5	0	22162	23.4	21.7	82	10 ez	10.0	11.5	21.5	15.7	71	78
Togo	5678	0	0	356	6.3	0	0	2	0	71	1.3	16.4	73	3 ez	3.1	2.0	5.1	4.1	33	59
Tunisia	16361	0	0	0	0	29	0.2	15	0.1	0	0	0.4	3	3 ft	--	--	2.1	1.6	13	6
Uganda	24104	0	0	716	3.0	157	0.7	3	0	4036	16.7	15.4	71	9 ez	4.9	34.3	39.2	22.0	82	75
Zambia	75261	2240	3.0	3781	5.0	322	0.4	20	0	16283	21.6	28.9	89	4 ez	5.3	12.3	17.6	11.4	63	80
Zimbabwe	39076	1465	3.7	1057	2.7	180	0.5	2	0	2289	5.9	18.5	77	4 ez	4.8	3.8	8.6	6.7	47	67
EUROPE																				
Albania	2875	0	0	0	0	0	0	38	1.3	56	1.9	2.9	23	2 ft	--	--	0.9	0.7	6	17
Austria	8386	0	0	0	0	27	0.3	8	0.1	2344	28.0	14.8	70	2 ft	--	--	20.6	15.4	71	70
Belarus	20760	0	0	0	0	304	1.5	0	0	561	2.7	3.7	30	2 ft	--	--	7.2	5.4	42	34
Belgium	3052	0	0	0	0	0	0	0	0	78	2.6	1.3	10	2 ft	--	--	9.0	6.7	47	23
Bosnia & Herzegovina	5113	0	0	0	0	17	0.3	0	0	8	0.2	0.7	6	2 ft	--	--	0.9	0.7	6	6
Bulgaria	11091	0	0	108	1.0	126	1.1	57	0.5	200	1.8	5.0	40	2 ft	--	--	10.6	7.9	52	44
Croatia	5654	0	0	0	0	56	1.0	32	0.6	288	5.1	5.4	42	2 ft	--	--	15.0	11.2	62	49
Czech R	7886	0	0	0	0	69	0.9	17	0.2	1137	14.4	9.3	57	2 ft	--	--	32.6	24.4	84	66
Denmark	4309	0	0	0	0	10	0.2	20	0.5	1335	31.0	16.7	73	2 ft	--	--	4.2	3.1	25	57
Estonia	4510	0	0	112	2.5	66	1.5	0	0	330	7.3	13.0	66	2 ft	--	--	6.3	4.7	38	57
Finland	33814	0	0	801	2.4	169	0.5	95	0.3	1710	5.1	8.4	54	1 ft	--	--	5.8	4.3	34	47
France	55150	0	0	0	0	272	0.5	12	0	5084	9.2	5.4	42	3 ft	--	--	17.2	12.9	66	50
Germany	35698	0	0	0	0	34	0.1	3	0	8843	24.8	12.6	65	2 ft	--	--	27.9	20.9	81	70
Greece	13196	0	0	0	0	47	0.4	36	0.3	149	1.1	1.5	12	4 ft	--	--	1.2	0.9	7	10
Hungary	9303	0	0	0	0	159	1.7	0	0	470	5.1	5.9	44	2 ft	--	--	35.1	26.3	86	58
Iceland	10300	0	0	160	1.6	28	0.3	16	0.2	769	7.5	7.6	50	--	--	--	--	--	--	50
Ireland	7028	0	0	0	0	43	0.6	5	0.1	13	0.2	1.5	12	1 ft	--	--	10.8	8.1	52	25
Italy	30127	0	0	0	0	356	1.2	13	0	1768	5.9	4.8	38	4 ft	--	--	3.9	2.9	23	33
Latvia	6460	0	0	0	0	45	0.7	7	0.1	736	11.4	7.3	49	2 ft	--	--	11.1	8.3	53	51
Lithuania	6520	0	0	0	0	143	2.2	29	0.4	474	7.3	8.7	55	2 ft	--	--	7.5	5.6	42	51
Luxembourg	257	0	0	0	0	0	0	0	0	36	14.0	7.0	48	2 ft	--	--	8.6	6.4	46	47
Macedonia, FYR	2571	0	0	0	0	149	5.8	14	0.5	17	0.7	12.7	65	2 ft	--	--	13.8	10.3	61	64
Malta	32	0	0	0	0	0	0	0	0	0	0	0	0	--	--	--	--	--	--	0
Moldova	3370	0	0	0	0	0	0	19	0.6	21	0.6	1.2	10	1 ft	--	--	5.4	4.0	32	17
Netherlands	4084	0	0	0	0	0	0	74	1.8	404	9.9	7.6	50	2 ft	--	--	12.6	9.4	58	53
Norway	32388	0	0	1041	3.2	385	1.2	159	0.5	490	1.5	9.5	58	2 ft	--	--	1.0	0.7	6	41
Poland	32325	0	0	0	0	101	0.3	65	0.2	2746	8.5	4.9	39	2 ft	--	--	13.8	10.3	61	46
Portugal	9198	0	0	0	0	70	0.8	13	0.1	512	5.6	4.6	37	6 ft	--	--	5.4	4.0	32	35
Romania	23839	0	0	580	2.4	421	1.8	37	0.2	35	0.1	7.8	51	2 ft	--	--	3.4	2.5	20	41
Slovakia	4901	0	0	0	0	198	4.0	5	0.1	844	17.2	16.8	74	2 ft	--	--	29.6	22.2	82	76
Slovenia	2025	0	0	0	0	84	4.1	0	0	31	1.5	9.0	56	2 ft	--	--	12.5	9.4	58	57
Spain	50599	0	0	0	0	195	0.4	29	0.1	3991	7.9	4.7	38	6 ft	--	--	7.9	5.9	44	40
Sweden	44996	0	0	1061	2.4	800	1.8	174	0.4	1585	3.5	9.7	59	2 ft	--	--	0.9	0.7	6	41

Country	Total area 000 ha	MTP 000 ha	MTP %	ITP 000 ha	ITP %	LTP 000 ha	LTP %	KTP 000 ha	KTP %	PP 000 ha	PP %	Wtd tot %	Size score	No & type unit	Ave % TP	Ave % PP	Ave % totP	Wtd %	Div score	LP score
Switzerland	4129	0	0	0	0	17	0.4	0	0	696	16.9	9.2	57	4 ft	--	--	12.9	9.7	59	57
Ukraine	60370	0	0	261	0.4	479	0.8	25	0	173	0.3	2.2	18	2 ft	--	--	1.6	1.2	10	15
United Kingdom	24410	0	0	0	0	0	0	0	0	4943	20.2	10.1	60	2 ft	--	--	22.0	16.5	73	64
Yugoslavia	10217	0	0	0	0	130	1.3	14	0.1	183	1.8	3.0	24	2 ft	--	--	3.0	2.2	18	22
RUSSIAN FED.	1707540	19028	1.1	14833	0.9	2616	0.2	41	0	14264	0.8	5.3	41	4 ft	--	--	1.7	1.3	10	31
ASIA																				
Afghanistan	65209	0	0	0	0	41	0.1	0	0	177	0.3	0.4	3	2 ft	--	--	0.0	0.0	0	2
Armenia	2980	0	0	150	5.0	63	2.1	0	0	0	0	16.7	73	1 ft	--	--	10.0	7.5	50	66
Azerbaijan	8660	0	0	0	0	151	1.7	41	0.5	284	3.3	5.8	43	1 ft	--	--	0.0	0.0	0	29
Bahrain	69	0	0	0	0	0	0	0	0	0	0	0	0	--	--	--	--	--	--	0
Bangladesh	14400	0	0	0	0	0	0	0	0	98	0.7	0.3	2	3 ez	0.0	0.0	0.0	0.0	0	2
Bhutan	4700	0	0	520	11.1	237	5.0	0	0	241	5.1	40.3	100	4 ez	19.3	7.0	26.3	22.8	83	94
Brunei Darussalam	576	0	0	0	0	85	14.8	30	5.2	0	0	47.4	100	6 H	24.7	7.1	31.8	28.2	88	96
Cambodia	18103	0	0	644	3.6	87	0.5	5	0	2531	14.0	15.0	70	6 ez	4.4	11.3	15.7	10.0	60	67
China	959805	45037	4.7	3516	0.4	930	0.1	81	0	18653	1.9	13.7	67	6 ft	--	--	5.3	4.0	32	56
Cyprus	925	0	0	0	0	0	0	9	1.0	66	7.1	5.5	42	1 ft	--	--	33.4	25.0	85	56
Georgia	6970	0	0	0	0	143	2.1	52	0.7	0	0	5.2	41	2 ft	--	--	0.0	0.0	0	27
India	328759	0	0	1720	0.5	1595	0.5	87	0	10811	3.3	3.4	27	26 ez	0.4	0.9	1.3	0.8	6	20
Indonesia	190457	6687	3.5	6152	3.2	1420	0.7	168	0.1	19133	10.0	21.3	81	17 ez	11.2	2.6	13.8	12.5	65	76
Iran	163319	0	0	884	0.5	182	0.1	16	0	7218	4.4	3.4	27	1 ft	--	--	12.0	9.0	56	37
Iraq	43832	0	0	0	0	0	0	0	0	0	0	0	0	--	--	--	--	--	--	0
Israel	2106	0	0	0	0	0	0	3	0.1	305	14.5	7.5	50	--	--	--	--	--	--	50
Japan	37780	0	0	777	2.1	527	1.4	17	0	1230	3.3	7.9	52	2 ft	--	--	12.1	9.1	56	53
Jordan	8921	0	0	0	0	0	0	1	0	297	3.3	1.6	13	--	--	--	--	--	--	13
Kazakhstan	271730	0	0	801	0.3	467	0.2	0	0	6069	2.2	2.0	16	3 ft	--	--	8.3	6.2	45	26
Korea, DPR	12054	0	0	0	0	124	1.0	37	0.3	154	1.3	2.4	19	3 ft	--	--	0.7	0.5	4	14
Korea, R	9926	0	0	0	0	0	0	0	0	364	3.7	1.9	15	1 ft	--	--	3.4	2.5	20	17
Kuwait	1782	0	0	0	0	0	0	2	0.1	25	1.4	0.9	7	--	--	--	--	--	--	7
Kyrgyzstan	19850	0	0	0	0	272	1.4	27	0.1	389	2.0	3.2	26	2 ft	--	--	0.1	0.1	1	17
Lao PDR	23680	0	0	0	0	0	0	0	0	2756	11.6	5.8	43	5 ez	0.0	7.3	7.3	3.6	29	38
Lebanon	1040	0	0	0	0	0	0	3	0.3	0	0	0.4	3	1 ft	--	--	0.0	0.0	0	2
Malaysia	32975	0	0	574	1.7	225	0.7	105	0.3	601	1.8	5.6	42	6 ez	13.9	19.7	33.6	23.7	84	56
Maldives	30	0	0	0	0	0	0	0	0	0	0	0	0	--	--	--	--	--	--	0
Mongolia	156650	10407	6.6	4957	3.2	696	0.4	19	0	50	0	23.5	84	2 ft	--	--	18.2	13.6	67	78
Myanmar	67658	0	0	161	0.2	0	0	0	0	13	0	0.4	3	10 ez	0.2	0.0	0.2	0.2	2	3
Nepal	14718	0	0	791	5.4	226	1.5	0	0	253	1.7	14.0	68	12 ez	6.5	4.6	11.1	8.8	55	64
Oman	21246	3400	16.0	0	0	0	0	0	0	28	0.1	40.1	100	--	--	--	--	--	--	80*
Pakistan	79609	0	0	868	1.1	0	0	14	0	2857	3.6	4.0	32	12 ez	0.3	0.9	1.2	0.7	6	23
Philippines	30000	0	0	320	1.1	117	0.4	0	0	775	2.6	4.1	33	5 ez	0.9	13.6	14.5	7.7	51	39
Qatar	1100	0	0	0	0	0	0	0	0	2	0.2	0.1	1	--	--	--	--	--	--	1
Saudi Arabia	214969	1220	0.6	1327	0.6	60	0	0	0	79714	37.1	21.2	81	--	--	--	--	--	--	80*
Singapore	62	0	0	0	0	0	0	0	0	3	4.8	2.4	19	3 H	24.2	4.1	28.3	26.2	86	42
Sri Lanka	6561	0	0	0	0	445	6.8	85	1.3	298	4.5	17.9	76	5 ez	4.7	4.5	9.2	6.9	48	66
Syrian Arab R	18518	0	0	0	0	0	0	0	0	0	0	0	0	1 ft	--	--	0.0	0.0	0	0
Tajikistan	14310	0	0	0	0	86	0.6	1	0	500	3.5	2.7	22	--	--	--	--	--	--	22
Thailand	51311	0	0	1668	3.3	2545	5.0	119	0.2	2741	5.3	17.0	74	6 ez	10.2	6.8	17.0	13.6	67	72
Turkey	77482	0	0	0	0	377	0.5	40	0.1	866	1.1	1.5	12	1 ft	--	--	1.2	0.9	7	10
Turkmenistan	48810	0	0	545	1.1	274	0.6	2	0	1156	2.4	4.3	34	2 ft	--	--	0.4	0.3	2	24
United Arab Emirates	8360	0	0	0	0	0	0	0	0	0	0	0	0	--	--	--	--	--	--	0
Uzbekistan	44740	0	0	575	1.3	230	0.5	14	0	0	0	3.4	27	2 ft	--	--	0.0	0.0	0	18
Viet Nam	33169	0	0	0	0	188	0.6	15	0	792	2.4	2.1	17	8 ez	0.7	4.2	4.9	2.8	22	19
Yemen	52797	0	0	0	0	0	0	0	0	0	0	0	0	--	--	--	--	--	--	0
PACIFIC																				
Australia	774122	14597	1.9	22903	3.0	7092	0.9	1962	0.3	12276	1.6	13.2	66	11 ft	--	--	9.2	6.9	48	60
Fiji	1827	0	0	0	0	11	0.6	8	0.4	0	0	1.8	14	4 ft	--	--	5.2	3.9	31	20
New Zealand	27053	1257	4.6	1656	6.1	764	2.8	304	1.1	1578	5.8	31.9	92	1 ft	--	--	43.8	32.8	93	92
Papua New Guinea	46284	0	0	0	0	0	0	7	0	1026	2.2	1.1	9	6 ez	0.1	5.9	6.0	3.0	24	14
Samoa	284	0	0	0	0	0	0	3	1.1	9	3.2	3.8	30	--	--	--	--	--	--	30
Solomon Is	2890	0	0	0	0	0	0	0	0	0	0	0	0	2 ft	--	--	0.0	0.0	0	0
Tonga	75	0	0	0	0	0	0	0	0	0	0	0	0	--	--	--	--	--	--	0
Vanuatu	1219	0	0	0	0	0	0	0	0	3	0.2	0.1	1	--	--	--	--	--	--	1

Notes

Land protection is the average of two weighted indicators (column heading in parentheses) [weights in brackets]:

Protected area size (Size score) [2]—protected area as % of total area, weighted for size.

Protected area diversity (Div score) [1]—protected area as % of total area, weighted for diversity.

Protected area diversity was given a lower weight than protected area size because the data are less reliable.

The protected area size indicator measures how much of a country's land and inland water area is protected, weighted according to degree of protection and size of the protected areas. All data are in thousand hectares (000 ha), and all percentages are in terms of total (land + inland water) area. Data are for 1997 and are from the *United Nations list of protected areas 1997* (IUCN World Commission on Protected Areas & World Conservation Monitoring Centre 1998). Marine protected areas were excluded because information on them is weak and incomplete.

TP = totally protected areas: IUCN Category I, Strict Nature Reserve/Wilderness Area; Category II, National Park; and Category III, Natural Monument (IUCN CNPPA 1994). Totally protected areas have been grouped into four size classes:

MTP = 1 million hectares and above
ITP = 100,000-999,999 hectares
LTP = 10,000-99,999 hectares
KTP = 1,000-9,999 hectares, or entire islands less than 1,000 hectares

PP = partially protected areas: IUCN Category IV, Habitat/Species Management Area; Category V, Protected Landscape/Seascape; and Category VI, Managed Resource Protected Area (IUCN CNPPA 1994).

As defined by IUCN - World Conservation Union, totally protected areas are maintained in a natural state and are closed to extractive uses. Partially protected areas are managed for specific uses (e.g., recreation) or to provide optimum conditions for certain species or ecological communities. Totally protected areas are more likely to protect a wide range of natural ecological communities. For such communities to persist and evolve "naturally", buffered as far as possible against human activities, the areas need to be large. The bigger the area, the more protective it will be (Reid & Miller 1989).

Wtd tot % = weighted total percentage. Protected areas qualify as large on a sliding scale, which recognizes that it is as great an achievement for a country of 80,000 ha to protect 8,000 ha as it is for a country of 80 million ha to protect 8 million ha. Each 1% of protected area (as a percentage of total area) was multiplied by one of the factors in Table 12a. The factors vary depending on whether the areas are totally or partially protected, their size, and the size of the country.

Size score = protected area size score. The performance criteria are shown in Table 12b. The top of the medium band is set at 10% because international targets are for full protection of 10% of each major ecological region (IUCN/UNEP/WWF 1991) or 10% of each biome (Recommendation 16 of the IVth World Congress on National Parks and Protected Areas [McNeely 1993]).

The protected area diversity indicator (Div score) is intended to measure how much of each major ecosystem type occurs within protected areas. Ideally, it would use a classification of major ecosystem types that distinguished either the main vegetation types or the main groups of ecological communities. The classification needs to be consistent across countries and regions and at a scale that would provide adequate detail for small countries but not unmanageable detail for large countries. World Wildlife Fund has developed such a classification for the Americas (Dinerstein, Olson, Graham *et al.* 1995; Ricketts, Dinerstein, Olson *et al.* 1998) and has used it to assess protected area coverage of ecosystem diversity. However, the assessment was by ecoregion only, not by country and ecoregion, and so could not be used here. Asian Bureau for Conservation & World Conservation Monitoring Centre (1997) cover Southern Asia and Papua New Guinea thoroughly but in a non-standard way, particularly their treatment of totally and partially protected areas. The two assessments used here (World Conservation Monitoring Centre [1997] and Iremonger, Ravilious, & Quinton [1997]) reviewed coverage of ecosystem diversity by country and ecosystem type. World Conservation Monitoring Centre's ecofloristic zone classification is not as detailed as World Wildlife Fund's ecoregion classification. However, the detail is adequate, except for Central America and the Caribbean where only major ecofloristic zones are identifed. The forest type classification covers a narrower array of ecosystem types, and the types are crudely defined. In many countries remarkably few types are recognized (for example, only one in New Zealand). The ecofloristic zone assessment distinguishes between totally and partially protected areas; the forest type assessment does not.

No & type unit = the number of ecosystem units identified by the assessment of the country concerned, and the type of ecosystem classification used:

ez = ecofloristic zone; mez = major ecofloristic zone. Data are from World Conservation Monitoring Centre (1997)

ft = forest type. Data are from Iremonger, Ravilious, & Quinton (1997)

Ave % TP = the average percentage of the ecosystem type that is totally protected = the totally protected area of each ecosystem unit as a percentage of the total area of that unit, added together and divided by the number of units.

Ave % PP = the average percentage of the ecosystem type that is partially protected = the partially protected area of each ecosystem unit as a percentage of the total area of that unit, added together and divided by the number of units.

Ave % totP = the average percentage of the ecosystem type that is protected. In the case of ecofloristic zones (and major ecofloristic zones), this is the sum of totally and partially protected percentages. In the case of forest types, all degrees of protection are lumped together.

Wtd % = weighted total percentage, obtained by multiplying the totally protected percentage by 1, the partially protected percentage by 0.5, and adding them together. When only a total percentage was available (forest types), it was multiplied by 0.75.

Div score = protected area diversity score. The performance criteria are the same as for protected area size (Table 12b).

area category	country 10 million+ ha	country 1 million+ ha	country 100,000+ ha	country 10,000+ ha
MTP (1 million+ ha)	2.5	--	--	--
ITP (100,000+ ha)	2.0	2.5	--	--
LTP (10,000+ ha)	1.5	2.0	2.5	--
KTP (1,000+ ha)	1.0	1.5	2.0	2.5
PP	0.5	0.5	0.5	0.5

Table 12a. Factors for multiplying each 1% of protected area (as a percentage of total area), depending on whether the areas are totally protected (TP) or partially protected (PP), their size (M, I, L, or K), and the size of the country.

band	top point on scale	protected area as % of total area
good	100	40
fair	80	20
medium	60	10
poor	40	5
bad	20	2.5
base	0	0

Table 12b. Performance criteria for indicators of land protection.

Table 13. Land Quality

Country	Cultivated 000 ha	Modified 000 ha	Total 000 ha	Light 000 ha	L %	Moderate 000 ha	M %	Strong 000 ha	S %	Extreme 000 ha	E %	Weighted total %	LQ score
AMERICAS													
Antigua & Barbuda	8	28	36	--	--	--	--	--	--	--	--	--	--
Argentina	41947	79639	121586	44482	36.6	8528	7.0	197	0.2	0	0	25.6	54
Bahamas	10	493	503	0	0	0	0	0	0	0	0	0	100
Barbados	17	14	31	--	--	--	--	--	--	--	--	--	--
Belize	96	1731	1827	0	0	253	13.8	0	0	0	0	13.8	72
Bolivia	4228	46717	50945	1386	2.7	9004	17.7	3068	6.0	0	0	28.1	52
Brazil	88700	286593	375293	43181	11.5	75101	20.0	16445	4.4	0	0	32.3	48
Canada	48388	226653	275041	4472	1.6	2956	1.1	0	0	0	0	1.9	96
Chile	4602	31992	36594	3486	9.5	2630	7.2	2139	5.8	0	0	20.6	59
Colombia	8564	30318	38882	7775	20.0	4991	12.8	0	0	0	0	22.8	57
Costa Rica	767	2905	3672	0	0	917	25.0	2284	62.2	0	0	118.3	10
Cuba	4912	5057	9969	991	9.9	2245	22.5	0	0	0	0	27.5	52
Dominica	15	24	39	--	--	--	--	--	--	--	--	--	--
Dominican R	1754	2507	4261	53	1.2	929	21.8	19	0.4	0	0	23.0	57
Ecuador	3555	7931	11486	1120	9.8	887	7.7	369	3.2	0	0	17.4	65
El Salvador	879	974	1853	2	0.1	1493	80.6	358	19.3	0	0	109.6	13
Grenada	11	6	17	--	--	--	--	--	--	--	--	--	--
Guatemala	2193	4359	6552	21	0.3	3966	60.5	324	4.9	0	0	68.0	26
Guyana	560	964	1524	907	59.5	464	30.4	0	0	0	0	60.2	30
Haiti	968	1557	2525	0	0	0	0	2525	100	0	0	150.0	2
Honduras	2202	5590	7792	34	0.4	4191	53.8	638	8.2	0	0	66.3	27
Jamaica	315	574	889	87	9.8	195	21.9	0	0	0	0	26.8	53
Mexico	35359	81478	116837	575	0.5	17449	14.9	16584	14.2	0	0	36.5	43
Nicaragua	3242	5642	8884	237	2.7	3293	37.1	24	0.3	0	0	38.9	41
Panama	808	3833	4641	197	4.2	895	19.3	1841	39.7	0	0	80.9	20
Paraguay	4464	14310	18774	102	0.5	2266	12.1	1101	5.9	0	0	21.2	59
Peru	7096	28571	35667	1892	5.3	12774	35.8	1407	3.9	0	0	44.3	38
St Kitts & Nevis	7	8	15	--	--	--	--	--	--	--	--	--	--
St Lucia	17	19	36	--	--	--	--	--	--	--	--	--	--
St Vincent & Grenadines	11	14	25	--	--	--	--	--	--	--	--	--	--
Suriname	77	841	918	198	21.6	218	23.7	0	0	0	0	34.5	45
Trinidad & Tobago	136	75	211	9	4.3	202	95.7	0	0	0	0	97.8	15
United States	216612	359070	575682	12171	2.1	79244	13.8	1254	0.2	0	0	15.2	70
Uruguay	2770	5776	8546	400	4.7	402	4.7	0	0	0	0	7.0	86
Venezuela	5567	42599	48166	3401	7.1	4206	8.7	515	1.1	0	0	13.9	72
AFRICA													
Algeria	11688	27083	38771	11633	30.0	13083	33.7	2508	6.5	0	0	58.5	31
Angola	7120	50913	58033	2473	4.3	939	1.6	7654	13.2	0	0	23.5	56
Benin	1653	7695	9348	691	7.4	1058	11.3	25	0.3	0	0	15.4	69
Botswana	693	30949	31642	761	2.4	2568	8.1	1761	5.6	0	0	17.7	65
Burkina Faso	4060	19485	23545	2767	11.8	2757	11.7	6316	26.8	0	0	57.8	31
Burundi	1288	1092	2380	56	2.4	1734	72.9	0	0	0	0	74.1	23
Cameroon	7376	31507	38883	3767	9.7	1284	3.3	5673	14.6	0	0	30.0	50
Cape Verde	84	300	384	0	0	0	0	302	78.6	0	0	117.9	10
Central African R	2326	32394	34720	998	2.9	719	2.1	232	0.7	0	0	4.6	91
Chad	6516	51059	57575	15361	26.7	7011	12.2	317	0.6	0	0	26.5	53
Comoros	120	83	203	0	0	0	0	40	19.7	0	0	29.5	50
Congo, DR	9422	112924	122346	8294	6.8	3252	2.7	2171	1.8	0	0	8.8	82
Congo, R	407	16191	16598	1351	8.1	25	0.2	234	1.4	0	0	6.3	87
Côte d'Ivoire	8716	15713	24429	1827	7.5	0	0	461	1.9	0	0	6.6	87
Djibouti	0	2133	2133	418	19.6	0	0	70	3.3	0	0	14.8	70
Egypt	3334	14396	17730	473	2.7	3004	16.9	0	0	0	0	18.3	63
Equatorial Guinea	243	1166	1409	47	3.3	0	0	0	0	0	0	1.6	97
Eritrea	835	8939	9774	963	9.9	154	1.6	1145	11.7	672	6.9	37.9	42
Ethiopia	12640	79610	92250	6758	7.3	9773	10.6	8512	9.2	2642	2.9	33.9	46
Gabon	986	7965	8951	633	7.1	733	8.2	0	0	0	0	11.8	76
Gambia	221	611	832	154	18.5	28	3.4	0	0	0	0	12.7	75
Ghana	5443	15943	21386	618	2.9	1264	5.9	1043	4.9	0	0	14.7	71
Guinea	2559	14279	16838	1351	8.0	280	1.7	0	0	0	0	5.7	89
Guinea-Bissau	361	2372	2733	423	15.5	188	6.9	0	0	0	0	14.7	71
Kenya	6768	24283	31051	2127	6.9	2683	8.6	2914	9.4	10	0	26.2	54
Lesotho	531	2387	2918	0	0	413	14.2	795	27.2	0	0	55.0	32
Liberia	533	7739	8272	211	2.6	193	2.3	0	0	0	0	3.6	93
Libyan Arab J	3655	27450	31105	14870	47.8	16235	52.2	0	0	0	0	76.1	22
Madagascar	5725	43000	48725	372	0.8	7511	15.4	8896	18.3	454	0.9	45.0	37
Malawi	2020	6516	8536	1310	15.3	6	0.1	8	0.1	0	0	7.9	84

Country	Cultivated 000 ha	Modified 000 ha	Total 000 ha	Light 000 ha	L %	Moderate 000 ha	M %	Strong 000 ha	S %	Extreme 000 ha	E %	Weighted total %	LQ score
Mali	7664	32096	39760	11456	28.8	14905	37.5	856	2.2	0	0	55.2	32
Mauritania	1004	15541	16545	9367	56.6	5590	33.8	1588	9.6	0	0	76.5	22
Mauritius	116	53	169	16	9.5	0	0	0	0	0	0	4.8	90
Morocco	12016	30843	42859	1733	4.0	2357	5.5	1262	2.9	0	0	11.9	76
Mozambique	6388	43683	50071	7839	15.7	395	0.8	128	0.3	0	0	9.1	82
Namibia	1640	36134	37774	2348	6.2	4098	10.8	517	1.4	0	0	16.0	68
Niger	6056	32193	38249	17972	47.0	18947	49.5	1330	3.5	0	0	78.3	21
Nigeria	34889	48387	83276	1666	2.0	9645	11.6	15539	18.7	0	0	40.7	40
Rwanda	1308	995	2303	47	2.0	1626	70.6	0	0	0	0	71.6	24
São Tomé & Principe	41	47	88	8	9.1	0	0	0	0	0	0	4.6	91
Senegal	2948	15688	18636	2676	14.4	963	5.2	2704	14.5	0	0	34.2	46
Seychelles	8	32	40	--	--	--	--	--	--	--	--	--	--
Sierra Leone	772	5960	6732	268	4.0	1069	15.9	0	0	0	0	17.9	64
Somalia	2126	40115	42241	10206	24.2	804	1.9	830	2.0	1033	2.4	21.8	58
South Africa	25745	61483	87228	334	0.4	6893	7.9	27151	31.1	0	0	54.8	33
Sudan	28103	136859	164962	17155	10.4	36282	22.0	3446	2.1	0	0	30.4	50
Swaziland	367	1304	1671	0	0	0	0	52	3.1	0	0	4.7	91
Tanzania	7654	42940	50594	4960	9.8	4770	9.4	1653	3.3	136	0.3	19.9	60
Togo	2471	2706	5177	36	0.7	1062	20.5	433	8.4	0	0	33.5	46
Tunisia	5411	6871	12282	7767	63.2	1867	15.2	0	0	0	0	46.8	37
Uganda	7010	7592	14602	248	1.7	3167	21.7	1269	8.7	242	1.7	39.0	41
Zambia	8309	12831	21140	4622	21.9	2721	12.9	537	2.5	0	0	27.6	52
Zimbabwe	5014	26159	31173	95	0.3	3700	11.9	352	1.1	0	0	13.7	73
EUROPE													
Albania	846	1578	2424	48	2.0	906	37.4	835	34.4	0	0	90.0	17
Austria	1681	6193	7874	199	2.5	1714	21.8	0	0	0	0	23.0	57
Belarus	6811	13283	20094	3254	16.2	634	3.2	0	0	0	0	11.3	77
Belgium	1219	1273	2492	434	17.4	182	7.3	123	4.9	0	0	23.4	57
Bosnia & Herzogovina	827	4086	4913	73	1.5	1132	23.0	1789	36.4	0	0	78.3	21
Bulgaria	5560	4403	9963	181	1.8	3275	32.9	17	0.2	0	0	34.1	46
Croatia	1598	3715	5313	536	10.1	1909	35.9	1085	20.4	0	0	71.6	24
Czech R	3426	3786	7212	48	0.7	2231	30.9	0	0	0	0	31.3	49
Denmark	2746	1209	3955	275	7.0	0	0	0	0	0	0	3.5	93
Estonia	1479	2639	4118	522	12.7	20	0.5	0	0	0	0	6.8	86
Finland	2139	23322	25461	2922	11.5	623	2.4	0	0	0	0	8.2	84
France	21637	30335	51972	6351	12.2	1255	2.4	17	0	0	0	8.5	83
Germany	12587	18245	30832	6432	20.9	1334	4.3	245	0.8	0	0	15.9	68
Greece	4543	7810	12353	2954	23.9	1213	9.8	65	0.5	0	0	22.5	57
Hungary	5298	3419	8717	1270	14.6	1724	19.8	109	1.3	0	0	29.1	51
Iceland	24	5823	5847	1159	19.8	2777	47.5	0	0	0	0	57.4	31
Ireland	2288	4380	6668	0	0	76	1.1	0	0	0	0	1.1	98
Italy	11514	13802	25316	2952	11.7	2872	11.3	591	2.3	58	0.2	21.0	59
Latvia	2053	4012	6065	743	12.3	820	13.5	0	0	0	0	19.6	61
Lithuania	3340	2936	6276	776	12.4	341	5.4	0	0	0	0	11.6	77
Luxembourg	114	122	236	19	8.1	31	13.1	0	0	0	0	17.2	66
Macedonia, FYR	752	1690	2442	106	4.3	555	22.7	443	18.1	0	0	52.0	34
Malta	11	14	25	--	--	--	--	--	--	--	--	--	--
Moldova	2221	857	3078	31	1.0	930	30.2	7	0.2	0	0	31.0	49
Netherlands	1138	1693	2831	471	16.6	0	0	32	1.1	0	0	9.9	80
Norway	1216	19655	20871	326	1.6	535	2.6	0	0	0	0	3.4	93
Poland	14872	13063	27935	4442	15.9	8267	29.6	0	0	0	0	37.5	42
Portugal	3834	3803	7637	974	12.8	1659	21.7	0	0	0	0	28.1	52
Romania	10478	11191	21669	323	1.5	6822	31.5	1485	6.9	0	0	42.6	39
Slovakia	1704	2955	4659	94	2.0	1158	24.9	0	0	0	0	25.9	54
Slovenia	336	1577	1913	29	1.5	424	22.2	425	22.2	0	0	56.3	32
Spain	22137	25870	48007	3733	7.8	5192	10.8	755	1.6	0	0	17.1	66
Sweden	3426	28078	31504	1863	5.9	4753	15.1	0	0	0	0	18.1	64
Switzerland	559	3099	3658	219	6.0	206	5.6	2	0.1	0	0	8.8	82
Ukraine	39256	16008	55264	5002	9.1	18875	34.2	174	0.3	1750	3.2	45.6	37
United Kingdom	8926	12312	21238	742	3.5	1880	8.9	69	0.3	0	0	11.1	78
Yugoslavia	4309	5339	9648	498	5.2	2074	21.5	2573	26.7	0	0	64.2	28
RUSSIAN FEDERATION	154116	417994	572110	20062	3.5	56561	9.9	62	0	830	0.1	11.8	76
ASIA													
Afghanistan	11062	42039	53101	11800	22.2	2600	4.9	0	0	0	0	16.0	68
Armenia	641	1631	2272	56	2.5	104	4.6	0	0	0	0	5.8	88
Azerbaijan	2175	5562	7737	115	1.5	829	10.7	0	0	0	0	11.4	77
Bahrain	5	47	52	--	--	--	--	--	--	--	--	--	--
Bangladesh	8611	3200	11811	10317	87.4	1157	9.8	1494	12.6	48	0.4	73.2	23
Bhutan	195	3045	3240	301	9.3	0	0	0	0	0	0	4.7	91

Country	Cultivated 000 ha	Modified 000 ha	Total 000 ha	Light 000 ha	L %	Moderate 000 ha	M %	Strong 000 ha	S %	Extreme 000 ha	E %	Weighted total %	LQ score
Brunei Darussalam	8	194	202	0	0	52	25.7	32	15.8	0	0	49.4	35
Cambodia	3964	9296	13260	10199	76.9	1079	8.1	49	0.4	0	0	47.2	36
China	209171	456408	665579	236264	35.5	58203	8.7	82548	12.4	280	0	45.1	37
Cyprus	172	684	856	0	0	194	22.7	0	0	0	0	22.7	57
Georgia	1455	4698	6153	145	2.4	142	2.3	0	0	0	0	3.5	93
India	185600	77269	262869	61872	23.5	52536	20.0	9812	3.7	3925	1.5	40.3	40
Indonesia	38307	39638	77945	5753	7.4	2064	2.6	292	0.4	0	0	6.9	86
Iran	23879	125418	149297	38369	25.7	51555	34.5	7039	4.7	0	0	54.4	33
Iraq	5954	25814	31768	904	2.8	11843	37.3	10649	33.5	0	0	89.0	18
Israel	543	1212	1755	4	0.2	39	2.2	0	0	0	0	2.3	95
Japan	15042	13261	28303	559	2.0	0	0	0	0	0	0	1.0	98
Jordan	492	3654	4146	2057	49.6	1525	36.8	0	0	0	0	61.6	29
Kazakhstan	48822	197953	246775	39650	16.1	39650	16.1	24800	10.0	0	0	39.2	41
Korea, DPR	3475	7362	10837	2289	21.1	0	0	0	0	0	0	10.6	79
Korea, R	2287	6226	8513	205	2.4	0	0	0	0	0	0	1.2	98
Kuwait	19	1091	1110	374	33.7	0	0	0	0	0	0	16.9	66
Kyrgyzstan	2382	15143	17525	64	0.4	481	2.7	0	0	0	0	2.9	94
Lao PDR	936	18069	19005	1655	8.7	1103	5.8	51	0.3	0	0	10.6	79
Lebanon	323	597	920	0	0	63	6.8	0	0	0	0	6.8	86
Malaysia	7732	10626	18358	5296	28.8	3335	18.2	99	0.5	0	0	33.4	47
Maldives	3	24	27	--	--	--	--	--	--	--	--	--	--
Mongolia	2640	59870	62510	7702	12.3	10057	16.1	0	0	0	0	22.3	58
Myanmar	10462	48523	58985	5576	9.5	2959	5.0	0	0	0	0	9.8	80
Nepal	3200	7010	10210	1361	13.3	389	3.8	49	0.5	49	0.5	12.2	76
Oman	126	4626	4752	2515	52.9	2073	43.6	0	0	0	0	70.1	25
Pakistan	22268	43967	66235	26734	40.4	17036	25.7	7462	11.3	0	0	62.9	28
Philippines	9851	15279	25130	3298	13.1	4197	16.7	3748	14.9	1999	8.0	61.6	29
Qatar	22	869	891	198	22.2	21	2.4	0	0	0	0	13.5	73
Saudi Arabia	7661	56877	64538	52532	81.4	12006	18.6	0	0	0	0	59.3	30
Singapore	1	27	28	5	17.9	0	0	2	7.1	0	0	19.6	61
Sri Lanka	2071	3831	5902	1541	26.1	0	0	0	0	0	0	13.1	74
Syrian Arab R	6478	9521	15999	512	3.2	4928	30.8	150	0.9	0	0	33.7	46
Tajikistan	1255	11137	12392	465	3.8	132	1.1	0	0	0	0	3.0	94
Thailand	21054	22986	44040	2682	6.1	34393	78.1	0	0	996	2.3	85.8	18
Turkey	32254	40374	72628	331	0.5	17745	24.4	12827	17.7	0	0	51.2	34
Turkmenistan	3402	37715	41117	339	0.8	1184	2.9	0	0	0	0	3.3	93
United Arab Emirates	170	1354	1524	1005	65.9	519	34.1	0	0	0	0	67.1	26
Uzbekistan	7230	32216	39446	362	0.9	5786	14.7	0	0	0	0	15.1	70
Viet Nam	8705	20939	29644	6829	23.0	4257	14.4	547	1.8	0	0	28.6	51
Yemen	3110	41339	44449	11698	26.3	5104	11.5	0	0	0	0	24.6	55
PACIFIC													
Australia	57143	618250	675393	88016	13.0	3027	0.4	2743	0.4	0	0	7.5	85
Fiji	380	1334	1714	0	0	0	0	0	0	0	0	0	100
New Zealand	6139	17559	23698	3965	16.7	456	1.9	0	0	0	0	10.3	79
Papua New Guinea	709	15827	16536	314	1.9	25	0.2	0	0	0	0	1.1	98
Samoa	131	140	271	--	--	--	--	--	--	--	--	--	--
Solomon Is	82	1966	2048	504	24.6	0	0	0	0	0	0	12.3	75
Tonga	48	19	67	--	--	--	--	--	--	--	--	--	--
Vanuatu	130	832	962	0	0	0	0	0	0	0	0	0	100

Notes

The land quality index (*LQ score*) consists of one indicator: the area of degraded land as a percentage of the area of cultivated + modified land, weighted according to severity of degradation. All data are in thousand hectares (000 ha), and all percentages are in terms of the combined cultivated and modified land area.

Cultivated = cultivated land area. Data are for 1997 and are from Table 11.

Modified = modified land area. Data are for 1990-1998 and are from Table 11. Note that the estimated area of modified land is a residual, derived from estimates of cultivated, built, and natural land. The reliability of these estimates is uncertain.

Total = total area of cultivated + modified land.

Light (L); Moderate (M); Strong (S); Extreme (E) = areas affected by degrees of soil degradation as defined in Table 13a. Data are for 1990 and are from GLASOD—the Global Assessment of the Status of Human-induced Soil Degradation (Oldeman 1993; Oldeman, Hakkeling, & Sombroek 1991; UNEP/ISRIC 1990)—except for: Iran, which are from FAO, UNDP & UNEP (1994); Kazakhstan, which are for the mid-1990s and are from Baitullin & Bekturova (1997); and Bangladesh, Bhutan, Cambodia, China, India, Indonesia, Korea DPR, Korea R, Lao PDR, Malaysia, Myanmar, Nepal, Pakistan, Philippines, Sri Lanka, Thailand, and Viet Nam, which are for the mid-1990s and are from ASSOD—the Assessment of the Status of Human-induced Soil Degradation in South and Southeast Asia (van Lynden & Oldeman 1997).

Weighted total % = the percentages of light, moderate, strong, and extreme degradation multiplied by the factors given in the points column of Table 13a. Percentages of light + modified + strong + extreme degradation may total more than 100% due to estimation problems discussed below and because estimates of cultivated area, modified area, and degraded area come from different sources. The weighted total percentages of Costa Rica, El Salvador, Haiti and Cape Verde also exceed 100% due to the effect of the weights.

LQ score = land quality index (degraded land score). The performance criteria are shown in Table 13c. The top of the good band is 0%, the background rate of human-induced soil degradation on natural land.

The data from ASSOD and for Iran were expressed as areas or percentages of the land areas of the countries concerned. These data were used directly without change. The data for Kazakhstan were given as area of "strong desertification" and area of "other desertification". The area of "strong desertification" was adopted as the area of strong land degradation. The area of "other desertification" was divided into equal areas of low and moderate degradation.

GLASOD's *World Map on Status of Human-induced Soil Degradation* distinguished the four degrees of soil degradation defined in Table 13a, and five extents of soil degradation defined in Table 13b. To produce the GLASOD map, groups of soil scientists gave their expert opinion on the types, degree and extent of soil degradation in 21 regions. They classified map units by type of degradation (if any) and by degree and extent of each type. A map unit may be affected by more than one type of degradation. For example, one part of the unit may be compacted while another part may have lost soil to water erosion.

As a regional assessment, GLASOD was not intended for use at country level. However, some regions consist of one or two countries (Argentina, Paraguay, Mexico, United States, Canada, China, Japan, the two Koreas) and many countries are as big as (or bigger than) the smallest region (Uruguay). Although inaccurate for small countries, GLASOD provides a good idea of the extent and severity of land degradation in countries of 10 million hectares and above.

To obtain country data, *The Wellbeing of Nations* (WoN) superimposed national boundaries on the GLASOD map using Map Maker, which then calculated the percentages of each map unit in each country. These percentages were used to estimate how much of each country is affected by each degree of degradation. GLASOD's ranges were converted to averages, as shown in the WoN average column of Table 13b. Where two types of land degradation affect a map unit, it was assumed that they do not overlap. In such cases, the percentages may exaggerate the area affected by degradation, particularly if both types of degradation are very frequent or dominant in extent.

The main problem with all the sources is that their information comes from expert opinion rather than from monitoring representative conditions on the ground. Kazakhstan illustrates the difference between one expert opinion and another. Using GLASOD's estimates, Kazakhstan's weighted total percentage of degraded land is 7.6%, similar to those of Kyrgyzstan (2.9%), Tajikistan (3.0%), Turkmenistan (3.3%) and Uzbekistan (15.1%). Using estimates by national scientists (Baitullin & Bekturova 1997), Kazakhstan's weighted total percentage is much higher: 39.2%.

The main problem with WoN's interpretation of the sources is that the estimates of soil degradation are denominated in terms of the cultivated + modified land area. As noted above, there is great uncertainty about the estimates of modified land. If they are too high, the weighted total percentage will be lower than it should be, and vice versa. One alternative would be to use the total land area as the denominator. However, this would favor countries with large areas of little used land, such as Canada and Russia. It would also detract from an important function of the indicator, which is to show the condition of the land that supports the essential resource sectors of agriculture and timber production. The other alternative is to use the cultivated area alone as the denominator, since this is better known and more reliable than the modified area. However, in many countries large areas of uncultivated land are degraded by grazing (and to a lesser extent timber production). Consequently, the degraded land area is often larger than the cultivated land area. The ideal would be to show degradation of cultivated land and of modified land separately, but this is not yet possible. Since the ideal is out of reach, none of the alternatives is satisfactory, and cultivated and modified land are both important, I chose to keep the focus on both.

degree	definition	points
Light	Land with somewhat reduced agricultural suitability; restoration to full productivity possible by modifying management; original biotic functions still largely intact.	$\% \times 0.5$
Moderate	Land with greatly reduced agricultural suitability; major improvements required to restore productivity; original biotic functions partly destroyed.	$\% \times 1.0$
Strong	Land non-reclaimable at farm level; major engineering works required for restoration; original biotic functions destroyed.	$\% \times 1.5$
Extreme	Land unreclaimable and beyond restoration; original biotic functions fully destroyed.	$\% \times 2.0$

Table 13a. Degrees of soil degradation. The percentage of each type was multiplied by the factor in the points column to obtain the weighted total percentage.

extent of map unit affected		
	GLASOD range (%)	WoN average (%)
1. infrequent	1-5	3
2. common	6-10	8
3. frequent	11-25	18
4. very frequent	26-50	38
5. dominant	>50	75

Table 13b. Extents of soil degradation. GLASOD's estimated ranges of the extent of degraded land were converted to the average percentages shown in the WoN average column.

band	top point on scale	degraded land as weighted % of cultivated + modified land
good	100	0
fair	80	10
medium	60	20
poor	40	40
bad	20	80
base	0	160

Table 13c. Performance criteria for land quality.

Table 14. Water Index; River Conversion; Water Withdrawal

Country	Note	Gross cap GWh/y	Used cap GWh/y	Used %G	Tot supply km³/y	Dam cap km³	Dam %TS	RC score	Int supply km³/y	WW km³/y	WW %IS	WW score	WQ score	IW score
AMERICAS														
Antigua & Barbuda	ff90	--	--	--	0.05	--	--	--	0.05	0.005	10.0	80	--	60*
Argentina	ff95	535000	30576	5.7	814.00	--	--	89	276.00	28.58	10.4	79	38	38
Bahamas	--	--	--	--	--	--	--	--	--	--	--	--	--	--
Barbados	ff96	--	--	--	0.08	--	--	--	0.08	0.08	100.0	20	--	20
Belize	ff93	2000	--	--	18.55	--	--	--	16.00	0.10	0.6	99	--	60*
Bolivia	fs90	178000	1760	1.0	622.53	--	--	98	303.53	1.38	0.5	99	--	80*
Brazil	ff92	3020000	311073	10.3	8233.0	--	--	79	5418.0	54.87	1.0	98	23	23
Canada	ss90	1332000	353618	26.5	3460.0	--	--	53	3290.0	51.20	1.6	97	50	50
Chile	fs90	227000	16676	7.3	922.00	--	--	85	884.00	21.40	2.4	95	21	21
Colombia	ff96	1000000	34650	3.5	2132.0	--	--	93	2112.0	8.94	0.4	99	10	10
Costa Rica	ff97	223000	3375	1.5	112.40	--	--	97	112.40	5.77	5.1	90	--	80*
Cuba	ff95	2000	104	5.2	38.12	--	--	90	38.12	5.21	13.7	73	60*	60
Dominica	f96	200	17	8.5	--	--	--	83	--	0.02	--	--	--	60*
Dominican R	ff94	50000	790	1.6	20.99	--	--	97	20.99	8.34	39.7	47	--	47
Ecuador	ff97	115000	5560	4.8	432.00	--	--	90	432.00	16.99	3.9	92	--	80*
El Salvador	ff92	7000	2280	32.6	25.25	--	--	47	17.77	0.73	4.1	92	--	47
Grenada	--	38	18	47.4	--	--	--	33	--	--	--	--	--	33
Guatemala	ff92	95000	2275	2.4	111.27	--	--	95	109.20	1.16	1.1	98	--	80*
Guyana	ff92	8000	5	0.1	241.00	--	--	100	241.00	1.46	0.6	99	--	80*
Haiti	ff91	4000	160	4.0	14.02	--	--	92	13.01	0.98	7.5	85	--	80*
Honduras	ff92	16000	2230	13.9	95.93	--	--	72	95.93	1.52	1.6	97	--	72
Jamaica	ff93	450	100	22.2	9.40	--	--	58	9.40	0.90	9.6	81	--	58
Mexico	ff98	155000	31442	20.3	457.22	--	--	60	409.00	77.81	19.0	62	5	5
	mm95				475.26				426.34	73.50	17.2			
Nicaragua	ff98	33000	375	1.1	196.69	--	--	98	189.74	1.29	0.7	99	--	80*
Panama	ff90	26000	2975	11.4	147.98	--	--	77	147.42	1.64	1.1	98	--	77
Paraguay	ff87	111000	51680	46.6	336.00	--	--	33	94.00	0.43	0.5	99	--	33
Peru	ss90	1812000	14400	0.8	1913.0	--	--	98	1616.0	18.97	1.2	97	--	80*
St Kitts & Nevis	f	--	--	--	0.02	--	--	--	0.02	--	--	--	--	--
St Lucia	f97	--	--	--	--	--	--	--	--	0.01	--	--	--	--
St Vincent & Grenadines	f95	--	20	--	--	--	--	--	--	0.01	--	--	--	--
Suriname	fs90	12840	1435	11.2	128.00	--	--	78	88.00	0.49	0.6	99	--	78
Trinidad & Tobago	ff97	--	--	--	3.84	--	--	--	3.84	0.30	7.8	84	--	60*
United States	ss90	4485000	354946	7.9	2956.0	--	--	84	2810.0	489.00	17.4	65	46	46
Uruguay	fs90	32000	5767	18.0	139.00	--	--	64	59.00	4.2	7.1	86	--	64
Venezuela	ff70	345000	82169	23.8	1233.2	--	--	56	722.45	4.1	0.6	99	--	56
AFRICA														
Algeria	ff90 f92	12000	135	1.1	14.33	4.30	30.0	50	13.90	4.50	32.4	52	--	50
Angola	ff87	150000	940	0.6	184.00	--	--	99	184.00	0.48	0.3	99	--	80*
Benin	ff94 f94	2500	--	--	25.80	0.03	0.1	100	10.30	0.15	1.5	97	--	80*
Botswana	ff92 f92	--	--	--	14.70	0.40	2.7	95	2.90	0.11	3.8	92	--	80*
Burkina Faso	ff92 f94	800	84	10.5	17.50	4.30	24.6	55	17.50	0.38	2.2	96	--	55
Burundi	ff87	6000	98	1.6	3.60	--	--	97	3.60	0.10	2.8	94	--	80*
Cameroon	ff87	294000	2645	0.9	268.00	--	--	98	268.00	0.40	0.1	100	--	80*
Cape Verde	ff90	--	--	--	0.30	--	--	--	0.30	0.03	10.0	80	--	60*
Central African R	ff87	--	76	--	141.00	--	--	--	141.00	0.07	0.0	100	--	60*
Chad	fs90	150	--	--	43.00	--	--	--	15.00	0.19	1.3	97	--	60*
Comoros	f	--	2	--	1.02	--	--	--	1.02	--	--	--	--	--
Congo, DR	ff90	1397000	5420	0.4	1019.0	--	--	99	935.00	0.36	0.0	100	--	80*
Congo, R	ff87	50000	435	0.9	832.00	--	--	98	222.00	0.04	0.0	100	--	80*
Côte d'Ivoire	ff87 f93	46000	1190	2.6	77.70	38.10	49.0	31	76.70	0.71	0.9	98	--	31
Djibouti	ff85	--	--	--	2.30	--	--	--	0.30	0.01	3.3	93	--	60*
Egypt	ff93 f94	50000	11564	23.1	68.50	169.0	246.7	0	1.80	53.10	2950	0	--	0
Equatorial Guinea	ff87	--	2	--	30.00	--	--	--	30.00	0.01	0.0	100	--	60*
Eritrea	ff87# f93	--	--	--	8.80	0.03	0.3	99	2.80	0.13	4.6	91	--	80*
Ethiopia	ff87#	650000	1981	0.3	110.00	--	--	99	110.00	2.07	1.9	96	--	80*
Gabon	ff87	80000	720	0.9	164.00	--	--	98	164.00	0.06	0.0	100	--	80*
Gambia	fs90	--	--	--	8.00	--	--	--	3.00	0.03	1.0	98	--	60*
Ghana	ff70 f94	13000	6040	46.5	53.20	148.5	279.1	0	30.30	0.30	1.0	98	6	0
Guinea	ff87	26000	185	0.7	226.00	--	--	99	226.00	0.74	0.3	99	--	80*
Guinea-Bissau	ff91 f94	300	--	--	27.00	0.00	0.0	100	16.00	0.02	0.1	100	--	80*
Kenya	ff90 f92	9000	3183	35.4	30.20	4.10	13.6	73	20.20	2.05	10.1	80	36	36
Lesotho	ff87 f94	2000	6	0.3	5.23	0.01	0.2	100	5.23	0.05	1.0	98	--	80*
Liberia	ff87	11000	180	1.6	232.00	--	--	97	200.00	0.13	0.1	100	--	80*
Libyan Arab J	ff94 f92	--	--	--	0.60	0.39	65.0	17	0.60	4.60	766.7	0	--	0
Madagascar	fs90	321000	350	0.1	337.00	--	--	100	337.00	19.70	5.8	88	--	80*
Malawi	ff94 f94	6000	890	14.8	18.68	0.10	0.5	70	17.54	0.94	5.4	89	--	70

Country	Note	Gross cap GWh/y	Used cap GWh/y	Used %G	Tot supply km³/y	Dam cap km³	Dam %TS	RC score	Int supply km³/y	WW km³/y	WW %IS	WW score	WQ score	*IW score*
Mali	fs90 f92	5000	210	4.2	100.00	11.00	11.0	78	60.00	1.49	2.5	95	10	10
Mauritania	fs90 f94	--	25	--	11.40	0.90	7.9	84	0.40	1.63	407.5	0	--	0
Mauritius	ff74 f94	150	145	96.7	2.21	0.07	3.2	94	2.21	0.36	16.3	67	--	67
Morocco	ff91 f92	4700	2338	49.7	30.00	11.00	36.7	43	30.00	11.05	36.8	49	4	4
Mozambique	ff92 f87	72000	579	0.8	208.00	44.60	21.4	59	97.00	0.61	0.6	99	--	59
Namibia	ff91 f92	9000	815	9.1	45.50	0.90	2.0	96	6.20	0.25	4.0	92	18	18
Niger	fs90 f90	1330	--	--	32.50	0.10	0.3	99	3.50	0.50	14.3	71	--	71
Nigeria	fs90 f93	91000	5450	6.0	280.00	30.3	10.8	78	221.00	4.00	1.8	96	--	78
Rwanda	ff93	3000	175	5.8	6.30	--	--	88	6.30	0.77	12.2	76	--	76
São Tomé & Principe	f f80	--	8	--	2.18	0.04	1.8	96	2.18	--	--	--	--	60*
Senegal	fs90 f94	4000	1000	25.0	39.40	1.60	4.1	92	26.40	1.50	5.7	89	31	31
Seychelles	--	--	--	--	--	--	--	--	--	--	--	--	--	--
Sierra Leone	ff87	6800	10	0.1	160.00	--	--	100	160.00	0.37	0.2	100	--	80*
Somalia	ff87	600	16	2.7	13.50	--	--	95	6.00	0.81	13.5	73	--	73
South Africa	ff90 f90	--	529	--	50.00	26.90	53.8	26	44.80	13.31	29.7	53	18	18
Sudan	ff95 f95	19000	935	4.9	154.00	8.80	5.7	89	35.00	17.80	50.9	40	0	0
Swaziland	ff80 f89	3800	120	3.2	4.51	0.20	4.4	91	2.64	0.66	25.0	57	--	57
Tanzania	ff94	190000	1730	0.9	89.00	--	--	98	80.00	1.17	1.5	97	60*	60
Togo	ff87 f94	1700	5	0.3	12.00	1.50	12.5	75	11.50	0.09	0.8	98	--	75
Tunisia	ff90 f91	1000	45	4.5	3.94	1.50	38.1	42	3.52	3.08	87.5	25	--	25
Uganda	ff70	13000	985	7.6	66.00	--	--	85	39.00	0.20	0.5	99	19	19
Zambia	ff94 f94	28750	7116	24.8	116.00	200.0	172.4	0	80.20	1.71	2.1	96	--	0
Zimbabwe	ff87	18500	2275	12.3	20.00	--	--	75	14.10	1.22	8.7	83	--	75
EUROPE														
Albania	ss90	13000	5573	42.9	23.80	--	--	37	18.60	0.34	1.8	96	60*	37
Austria	oo93	75000	36890	49.2	84.00	--	--	31	55.00	2.25	4.1	92	23	23
Belarus	ff90 f91	7600	19	0.3	58.00	3.08	5.3	89	37.20	2.73	7.3	85	--	80*
Belgium	oo94	1750	234	13.4	17.00	--	--	73	12.00	7.01	58.4	37	5	5
Bosnia & Herzegovina	--	28000	1240	4.4	--	--	--	91	--	--	--	--	--	60*
Bulgaria	re88	26400	1840	7.0	205.00	--	--	86	18.00	11.00	61.1	36	29	29
Croatia	re90	20000	7153	35.8	--	--	--	44	61.40	0.56	0.9	98	13	13
Czech R	oo97	13100	1969	15.0	16.00	--	--	70	15.00	2.49	16.6	67	17	17
Denmark	oo96	120	16	13.3	6.00	--	--	73	6.00	0.96	16.0	68	22	22
Estonia	ff95 f95	2000	2	0.1	12.81	0.00	0.0	100	12.71	0.16	1.3	97	19	19
Finland	oo94	46000	11785	25.6	110.00	--	--	54	107.00	2.44	2.3	95	45	45
France	so94	200000	62800	31.4	183.00	--	--	49	168.00	40.67	24.2	57	12	12
Germany	oo95	120000	18207	15.2	178.00	--	--	70	107.00	43.37	40.5	46	17	17
Greece	oo97	80000	4300	5.4	72.00	--	--	89	60.00	8.70	14.5	71	43	43
Hungary	oo96	7000	156	2.2	120.00	--	--	96	76.00	6.01	7.9	84	18	18
Iceland	oo97	184000	5564	3.0	170.00	--	--	94	170.00	0.16	0.1	100	--	80*
Ireland	oo94	1400	727	51.9	46.00	--	--	28	43.00	1.18	2.7	95	23	23
Italy	ss90	340000	44880	13.2	185.00	--	--	74	185.00	54.60	29.5	54	22	22
Latvia	ff94 f88	6000	1862	31.0	35.45	1.05	3.0	94	16.74	0.29	1.7	97	27	27
Lithuania	ff95 f91	5000	373	7.5	24.90	1.82	7.3	85	15.56	0.25	1.6	97	35	35
Luxembourg	oo95	125	64	51.2	1.60	--	--	29	0.90	0.06	6.7	87	14	14
Macedonia, FYR	--	9000	740	8.2	--	--	--	84	--	--	--	--	--	60*
Malta	ff95 f93	--	--	--	0.02	0.00	1.0	98	0.02	0.06	300.0	0	--	0
Moldova	ff92 f94	2100	285	13.6	11.65	2.02	17.3	65	1.00	2.96	296.0	0	18	0
Netherlands	oo96	1000	80	8.0	91.00	--	--	84	11.00	4.43	40.3	46	18	18
Norway	oo94	600000	104067	17.3	393.00	--	--	65	382.00	2.59	0.7	99	54	54
Poland	so97	23000	2062	9.0	56.20	--	--	82	49.50	11.80	23.8	57	4	4
Portugal	so91	33000	13740	41.6	53.00	--	--	38	18.50	8.60	46.5	42	21	21
Romania	rr94	70000	18950	27.1	208.00	--	--	53	37.00	26.00	70.3	32	12	12
Slovakia	oo97	8000	4912	61.4	83.00	--	--	19	13.00	1.31	10.1	80	18	18
Slovenia	ee90	12500	3758	30.1	18.70	--	--	50	--	0.50	2.7	95	33	33
Spain	so97	138000	41041	29.7	108.00	--	--	50	108.00	40.86	37.8	48	14	14
Sweden	so95	176000	51000	29.0	176.20	--	--	51	164.00	2.71	1.7	97	57	51
Switzerland	oo94	144000	28219	19.6	53.00	--	--	61	40.00	2.60	6.5	87	32	32
Ukraine	ff92	45000	8611	19.1	139.55	--	--	62	53.10	25.99	48.9	41	20	20
United Kingdom	oe94	8000	3317	41.5	147.00	--	--	38	145.00	14.24	9.8	80	21	21
Yugoslavia	--	118000	14526	12.3	--	--	--	75	--	--	--	--	--	60*
RUSSIAN FEDERATION	fo97 f92	2400000	191412	8.0	4498.2	360.0	8.0	84	4312.7	87.37	2.0	96	48	48
ASIA														
Afghanistan	ff87	--	455	--	65.00	--	--	--	55.00	26.11	47.5	42	--	42
Armenia	ff94 f93	21800	3450	15.8	10.53	1.16	11.0	78	9.07	2.93	32.3	52	--	52
Azerbaijan	ff95 f91	43500	2300	5.3	30.27	21.45	70.9	14	8.11	16.53	203.8	0	--	0
Bahrain	ff91	--	--	--	0.12	--	--	--	0.004	0.24	6000	0	--	0
Bangladesh	ff90 f91	1000	740	74.0	1210.6	20.30	1.7	97	105.00	14.64	13.9	72	50	50
Bhutan	ff87	70000	1685	2.4	95.00	--	--	95	95.00	0.02	0.0	100	--	80*

203

Country	Note	Gross cap GWh/y	Used cap GWh/y	Used % G	Tot supply km³/y	Dam cap km³	Dam % TS	RC score	Int supply km³/y	WW km³/y	WW % IS	WW score	WQ score	*IW score*
Brunei Darussalam	ff94 *f95*	--	--	--	8.50	0.05	0.6	99	8.50	0.09	1.1	98	--	80*
Cambodia	ff87	83000	74	0.1	476.11	--	--	100	120.57	0.52	0.4	99	--	80*
China	ff93 *f95*	5922000	186900	3.2	2829.6	480.0	17.0	66	2812.4	525.5	18.7	63	23	23
Cyprus	ff93 *f94*	23500	1	0.0	0.90	0.30	33.3	47	0.90	0.21	23.3	58	--	47
Georgia	ff90 *f96*	139000	6010	4.3	63.33	3.18	5.0	90	58.13	3.47	6.0	88	19	19
India	ff90 *f96*	2638000	69070	2.6	1907.8	250.0	13.1	74	1260.5	500.0	39.7	47	21	21
Indonesia	ff90 *f95*	2147000	21400	1.0	2838.0	15.80	0.6	99	2838.0	74.35	2.6	95	2	2
Iran	ff93 *f93*	176000	7376	4.2	137.51	39.20	28.5	51	128.50	70.03	54.5	38	23	23
Iraq	ff90 *f92*	90000	690	0.8	75.42	50.20	66.6	17	35.20	42.80	121.6	16	13	13
Israel	rr89	--	9	--	2.20	--	--	--	1.70	1.85	108.8	18	--	18
Japan	ff92 *f93*	718000	81668	11.4	430.00	28.98	6.7	87	430.00	91.40	21.3	59	27	27
Jordan	ff93 *f93*	100	22	22.0	0.88	0.14	15.9	68	0.68	0.98	144.1	11	5	5
Kazakhstan	ff93 *f94*	110000	9200	8.4	109.61	88.75	81.0	9	75.42	33.67	44.6	44	13	9
Korea, DPR	ff87	--	23760	--	77.13	--	--	--	67.00	14.16	21.1	59	--	59
Korea, R	fo97 *f94*	72000	2424	3.4	69.70	16.20	23.2	57	64.85	24.80	38.2	48	27	27
Kuwait	ff94	--	--	--	0.02	--	--	--	0.00	0.54	54000	0	--	0
Kyrgyzstan	ff94 *f94*	163000	12660	7.8	20.58	21.50	104.5	0	46.45	10.09	21.7	59	--	0
Lao PDR	ff87 *f95*	232000	1040	0.4	331.55	7.30	2.2	96	190.42	0.99	0.5	99	--	80*
Lebanon	ff94 *f95*	1000	890	89.0	4.41	0.25	5.7	89	4.80	1.29	26.9	55	--	55
Malaysia	ff95	230000	6770	2.9	580.00	--	--	94	580.00	12.73	2.2	96	0	0
Maldives	ff87	--	--	--	0.03	--	--	--	0.03	0.003	10.0	80	--	60*
Mongolia	ff93	6000	1	0.0	34.80	--	--	100	34.80	0.43	1.2	98	--	80*
Myanmar	ff87	366000	1615	0.4	1045.6	--	--	99	880.60	3.96	0.4	99	36	36
Nepal	ff94 *f95*	727000	2828	0.4	210.20	0.09	0.0	100	198.20	28.95	14.6	71	--	71
Oman	ff91 *f96*	--	--	--	0.98	0.06	6.1	88	0.98	1.22	124.5	15	--	15
Pakistan	ff91	262000	24540	9.4	418.27	--	--	81	248.00	155.6	62.7	35	13	13
Philippines	ff95 *f95*	46800	5699	12.2	479.00	4.75	1.0	98	479.00	55.42	11.6	77	29	29
Qatar	ff94	--	--	--	0.05	--	--	--	0.05	0.28	560.0	0	--	0
Saudi Arabia	ff92 *f93*	--	--	--	2.40	0.48	20.0	60	2.40	17.02	709.2	0	--	0
Singapore	rr75	--	--	--	0.60	--	--	--	0.60	0.19	31.7	52	--	52
Sri Lanka	ff90 *f96*	7000	4540	64.9	50.00	5.94	11.9	76	50.00	9.77	19.5	61	--	61
Syrian Arab R	ff93 *f94*	5000	3496	69.9	26.26	15.80	60.2	20	7.00	14.41	205.9	0	--	0
Tajikistan	ff94 *f94*	527000	16120	3.1	15.98	28.97	181.3	0	66.30	11.87	17.9	64	--	0
Thailand	ff90 *f95*	55500	8366	15.1	409.94	85.00	20.7	59	210.00	33.13	15.8	68	2	2
Turkey	fo97 *f92*	433000	49575	11.4	183.76	206.0	112.1	0	196.00	35.55	18.1	64	15	0
Turkmenistan	ff94 *f95*	23900	5	--	24.72	2.89	11.7	77	1.36	23.78	1749	0	--	0
United Arab Emirates	ff95 *f95*	--	--	--	0.15	0.08	53.3	27	0.15	2.11	1407	0	--	0
Uzbekistan	ff94 *f94*	88000	6900	7.8	50.41	19.00	37.7	42	16.34	58.05	355.3	0	0	0
Viet Nam	ff90	300000	10900	3.6	891.21	--	--	93	366.50	54.33	14.8	70	37	37
Yemen	ff90 *f95*	--	--	--	4.10	0.18	4.4	91	4.10	2.93	71.5	31	--	31
PACIFIC														
Australia	so94	264000	15212	5.8	352.00	--	--	88	352.00	15.06	4.3	91	21	21
Fiji	rr87	1090	385	35.3	28.60	--	--	45	28.60	0.03	0.1	100	--	45
New Zealand	so93	152000	26395	17.4	313.00	--	--	65	313.00	2.00	0.6	99	39	39
Papua New Guinea	ff87	175000	570	0.3	801.00	--	--	99	801.00	0.10	0.0	100	43	43
Samoa	--	140	25	17.9	--	--	--	64	--	--	--	--	--	60*
Solomon Is	rr87	1000	46	4.6	44.70	--	--	91	44.70	0.00	0.0	100	--	80*
Tonga	--	--	--	--	--	--	--	--	--	--	--	--	--	--
Vanuatu	--	--	--	--	--	--	--	--	--	--	--	--	--	--

Notes

In the absence of adequate data on marine waters, the water index is an inland waters index (*IW score*)—the lowest score of three sub-elements (column heading in parentheses): inland water diversity (RC score) and water withdrawal (WW score), covered in this table; and inland water quality (WQ score), covered in Tables 15 and 16.

Inland water diversity is represented by river conversion by dams, measured by dam capacity as % of total water supply or, if unavailable, river flow dammed for hydropower as a percentage of dammable flow. Hydropower includes large (more than 10 megawatts) and small (under 10 megawatts) schemes. Hydropower data are for the end of 1996 and are from World Energy Council (1999).

Note = sources of data on water supply and water withdrawal (in regular type), and dam capacity (*in italics*). In an entry in regular type (e.g., ff90), the first letter indicates the source for water supply (both total supply and internal supply), the second letter the source for water withdrawal, and the number the year to which the water withdrawal data refer. In an entry in italics (e.g., *f95*), the letter indicates the source for dam capacity, the number the applicable year. The sources are:

    e   Eurostat, European Commission & the European Environment Agency (1998)

    f   Food and Agriculture Organization of the United Nations (1995a, 1997b, 1997c, 1997d, 1999c, 2000b)

    m   Instituto Nacional de Estadística, Geografía e Informática (1998)

    o   Organisation for Economic Co-operation and Development (1999)

    r   World Resources Institute *et al.* (1998)

    s   Shiklomanov (1997)

Eritrea's and Ethiopia's shares of the former Ethiopia's withdrawal were estimated on the basis of population

Gross cap = gross theoretical hydropower capability, measured in gigawatt hours per year (GWh/y). This is the annual energy potentially available in a country if all natural flows were harnessed with 100% efficiency by turbines down to sea level or to the water level at the border with neighboring countries. It is the maximum river flow that is potentially dammable for hydropower, and is usually estimated on the basis of precipitation and run-off. If gross theoretical capability is not known, the technically exploitable capability (the amount of energy potentially available within the limits of current technology) was used instead.

Used cap = electrical energy in gigawatt hours per year (GWh/y) generated by operational hydropower schemes plus the probable amount to be generated by schemes under construction.

Used % G = used capacity as a percentage of gross capacity.

Tot supply = total renewable water resources in cubic kilometers per year (km³/y) = water available to a country from precipitation within its borders plus river flows from neighboring countries. *In North Africa (Algeria, Djibouti, Egypt, Libya, Mauritania, Morocco, Somalia, Sudan, Tunisia), Malta, and much of West Asia (Afghanistan, Bahrain, Cyprus, Iran, Iraq, Jordan, Kuwait, Kyrgyzstan, Lebanon, Oman, Pakistan, Qatar, Saudi Arabia, Syria, Tajikistan, Turkey, Turkmenistan, United Arab Emirates, Yemen), the data are for* <u>actual</u> *renewable water resources = total renewable water resources minus the quantity of flows reserved to upstream and downstream countries through formal or informal agreements or treaties.*

Dam cap = dam capacity = the total cumulative capacity of all dams in cubic kilometres (km³).

Dam % TS = dam capacity as % of total supply.

RC score = river conversion score. The performance criteria are shown in Table 14a. They are intended to reflect the objective of maintaining all major riverine ecosystems in large units.

Int supply = internal renewable supply in cubic kilometers per year (km³/y) = water available to a country from precipitation within its borders (excluding river flows from neighboring countries).

WW = water withdrawal = annual withdrawals of ground and surface water for domestic, agricultural and industrial uses, in cubic kilometers per year (km³/y).

WW % IS = water withdrawal as a percentage of internal renewable supply. The indicator takes no account of annual or seasonal shortages which can be marked.

WW score = water withdrawal score. The performance criteria are shown in Table 14a. The top of bad (100%) matches a point that is clearly unsustainable.

band	top point on scale	flow dammed for hydropower as % of dammable flow	dam capacity as % of total water supply	water withdrawal as % of internal renewable supply
good	100	0	0	0
fair	80	10	10	10
medium	60	20	20	20
poor	40	40	40	50
bad	20	60	60	100
base	0	100	100	200

Table 14a. Performance criteria for river conversion and water withdrawal indicators.

* A score with an asterisk has been reduced in accordance with the insufficient data rule. To prevent high scores resulting merely from lack of data, a good score is allowed only if it is based on all applicable components (data in an indicator, indicators in an index), and a fair score only if it is based on at least half the components. Good and fair scores (100-61) based on fewer than half the applicable components have been reduced to 60. Good scores (100-81) based on more than half but not all the applicable components have been reduced to 80.

Table 15. Inland Water Quality: Score, Oxygen Balance, Nutrients, and Acidification

Country	Basin	Station	Sources & years	Score	Based on	DO mg/l	BOD mg/l	COD mg/l	N mg/l	P mg/l	Alk. mg/l	pH
AMERICAS												
Argentina	La Plata	R Paraná at Puerto Libertad	g 94	19	HM: Cu	9.9	--	--	0.45	0.073	18.2	7.3
		R Paraná at Corrientes	g 94	20	F coli	7.8	--	--	0.14	0.031	20.5	7.4
		R Paraná at Rosario	g 94	32	HM: Hg	7.3	1.0	8.0	0.05	--	34.4	7.4
		average		24								
	N Mar Argentino	L Nahuel Huapi at Bariloche	g 94	53	Acid	10.6	--	--	0.02	0.002	12.7	6.7
	country average			38								
	not covered: Argentine interior, Subpolar SE Pacific, Chubut, S Mar Argentino; Groundwater											
Brazil	Amazon	R Amazon mouth	a 90	60*	P	--	--	--	0.17	0.020	--	--
		R Tocantins mouth	a 90	60*	SS	--	--	--	0.02	0.003	--	--
		average		60								
	São Francisco	R Capibaribe	g 88-90	0	F coli; HM: Cd	5.5	6.0	--	--	--	86.6	7.1
		R São Francisco at Petrolandia	g 88-90	0	HM: Cd, Pb	8.4	3.0	--	--	--	38.5	6.6
		average		0								
	L tropical W Atlantic	R Paraguaçu at Pedra do Cavalo	g 88-90	8	HM: Cr	5.5	2.0	--	0.60	0.058	53.9	6.7
		R Paraiba do Sul at Barra Mansa	g 88-90	29	HM: Pb	7.5	2.0	26.0	0.80	0.084	15.3	7.0
		average		18								
	La Plata	B Guarapiranga	g 88-90	16	HM: Cd, Cu	7.9	3.0	10.0	0.70	0.031	16.1	6.9
	country average			23								
	not covered: Guianan tropical W Atlantic, Intertropical W Atlantic, Parnaíba; Groundwater											
Canada	Mackenzie	R Mackenzie mouth	o 94-96	29	P	--	--	--	--	0.090	--	--
		R Great Bear	g 91-92	60	HM: Pb	--	--	--	0.16	--	--	7.8
		average		44								
	L subpolar NE Pacific	R Skeena	g 91	42	HM: Hg	--	--	--	0.13	0.016	--	7.9
	U temperate NE Pacific	R Fraser at Hope	g 91	19	P	--	--	--	0.12	0.171	--	8.0
	Columbia	R Columbia df	o 95-97	60	HM: Cd	--	--	--	0.10	0.010	--	--
	Churchill	R Churchill	g 94-96	80	HM: Cu	11.0	--	--	--	0.008	--	7.5
	Nelson	R Nelson at Gillam	g 94-96	60	HM: Cr	--	--	--	--	0.017	--	7.8
		R Saskatchewan mouth	o 94-96	47	P	9.5	--	--	0.13	0.041	--	--
		R Roseau	g 94-96	37	P	7.4	--	--	--	0.063	--	7.8
		average		48								
	St Lawrence	L Ontario mid lake	g 94-96	60*	Acid	12.3	--	--	--	--	--	8.4
		L Superior mid lake	g 96	80*	Acid	13.3	--	--	--	0.003	--	7.2
		average		70								
	Fundy & Maine	R St John mouth	o 93-95	35	HM: Cd	--	--	--	0.20	0.021	--	--
	country average			50								
	not covered: Arctic—W Beaufort Sea, E Beaufort Sea, Arctic Archipelagic Seas, Lincoln Sea & Nares Strait, W Baffin Bay; Pacific—E Bering Sea, Gulf of Alaska; Atlantic—Foxe Basin, NW Hudson Bay, S Hudson Bay, James Bay, E Hudson Bay, Hudson Strait & Ungava Bay, Labrador Sea, U temperate NW Atlantic; Groundwater											
Chile	Subtropical SE Pacific	R Maipo at El Manzano	g 88	34	F coli	11.0	1.0	4.0	0.19	0.000	75.0	8.3
	Groundwater	G pozo Panamericana 1377	g 88	9	N	4.4	0	--	12.52	0.000	219.0	7.3
	country average			21								
	not covered: Titicaca/Poopó/Atacama, Temperate SE Pacific, Subpolar SE Pacific, S Mar Argentino											
Colombia	Magdalena	R Magdalena mouth	a 90	21	P	--	--	--	0.25	0.120	--	--
		R Cauca at Juanchito	g 88	0	F coli	5.5	1.0	20.0	0.60	0.010	20.3	6.8
	country average			10								
	not covered: L tropical E Pacific, Intertropical E Pacific, W Caribbean, S Caribbean, Orinoco, Amazon; Groundwater											
Cuba	N Caribbean	B Damuji	g 94	61	N	7.7	--	--	0.72	0.004	--	8.2
		B Hanabanilla	g 94-95	58	P	8.5	--	2.0	0.53	0.028	--	7.5
		average		59								
	Groundwater	G Aguada del Cura	g 94	80*	Acid	--	--	--	0.05	--	--	7.0
	country average			60*								
	not covered: E Gulf of Mexico, U tropical W Atlantic, S Caribbean											
Mexico	Colorado	R Colorado	g 94-96	0	F strep	8.4	2.0	19.0	0.40	0.067	191.4	7.9
	Grande de Santiago	L de Chapala	g 94-96	8	F coli	6.7	2.0	32.0	6.03	0.567	296.4	8.7
		R Lerma	g 94-96	0	P; F coli	1.3	23.0	107.0	5.64	1.383	8.0	7.0
		average		4								
	U tropical E Pacific	R Balsas at Balsas	g 94-96	0	F coli	6.4	38.0	76.0	0.09	0.219	144.5	7.4

Country	Basin	Station	Sources & years	Score	Based on	DO mg/l	BOD mg/l	COD mg/l	N mg/l	P mg/l	Alk. mg/l	pH
	Bravo del Norte (Grande)	R Bravo at Matamoros	g 94-96	5	HM: Cu	7.7	4.0	34.0	0.50	0.160	164.0	8.1
		R Bravo at Presa de la Amistad	g 94-96	22	N	8.3	12.0	33.0	2.39	--	125.3	6.9
		R Conchos at Ojinaga	g 94-96	6	F coli	8.3	5.0	17.0	3.11	0.254	264.8	6.0
		average		11								
	SW Gulf of Mexico	R Pánuco	g 94-96	10	HM: Cu	7.6	1.0	27.0	0.30	0.066	165.4	7.9
		R Coatzacoalcos	g 94-96	0	F coli	6.1	2.0	59.0	0.83	0.110	62.3	7.0
		average		5								
	SE Gulf of Mexico	R Grijalva	g 94-96	0	F coli	5.4	4.0	18.0	2.80	0.104	110.2	7.9
		R Usumacinta	g 94-96	9	F coli	7.6	3.0	16.0	1.85	0.063	138.2	8.2
		average		4								
	Groundwater	G pozo Aguascalientes	g 94-96	16	N	--	1.0	--	3.00	0.020	365.7	7.0
		G pozo Hacienda Tahdzibichen	g 94-96	9	F coli	4.8	3.0	17.0	6.98	0.016	336.9	7.1
		average		12								
	country average			5								
	not covered: Mexican interior, U subtropical NE Pacific, W Gulf of California, E Gulf of California, W Caribbean											
United States	E Bering Sea	R Yukon at Pilot Station	g 94-95	26	P	10.1	--	--	0.15	0.102	88.0	7.8
	Gulf of Alaska	R Talkeetna at Talkeetna	g 94-96	49	P	11.3	--	--	0.28	0.039	38.1	7.8
	Columbia	R Columbia at Bonneville	g 94	60	P	10.0	--	--	0.17	0.025	--	8.1
	U subtropical NE Pacific	R Sacramento at Sacramento	g 94-96	44	P	9.2	--	--	0.13	0.045	0.0	7.6
	Colorado	R Colorado at Hoover Dam	g 94-96	58	HM: Cr	7.2	--	--	0.36	0.012	--	7.9
	St Lawrence	R St Lawrence df	g 94	76	Acid	8.8	--	--	0.33	0.010	92.0	7.9
		R Niagara at L Ontario	g 94	58	HM: Cr	12.0	--	--	0.69	0.010	--	8.0
		average		67								
	L temperate NW Atlantic	R Hudson at Troy	g 94	34	F coli	11.8	--	--	0.88	0.045	76.0	8.1
		R Delaware at Trenton	g 94-96	34	P	10.4	2.0	--	0.95	0.074	30.2	7.8
		average		34								
	Chesapeake Bay	R Susquehanna at Harrisburg	g 94-95	39	P	10.0	--	--	0.95	0.053	29.8	7.5
		R Potomac at Washington	g 94-96	25	P	10.1	--	--	1.37	0.106	--	7.8
		average		32								
	NE Gulf of Mexico	R Apalachicola at Chattahoochee	g 94-95	52	F coli	9.8	--	--	0.44	0.033	--	7.7
	Mississippi	R Mississippi mouth	o 93-95	19	P	9.0	1.5	--	1.43	0.200	--	--
		R Arkansas at Little Rock	g 94-96	32	P	8.7	--	--	0.36	0.081	--	7.8
		R Missouri at Hermann	g 94-96	17	P	9.3	--	--	1.25	0.269	154.1	7.9
		R Ohio at New Grand Chain	g 94-95	24	P	8.1	--	--	0.92	0.111	--	7.6
		average		23								
	Bravo del Norte (Grande)	R Grande at Brownsville	g 94-96	20	P	7.4	4.0	--	0.10	0.131	--	8.2
	country average			46								
	not covered: US interior, E Chukchi Sea, W Beaufort Sea, L subpolar NE Pacific, U temperate NE Pacific, Oceanic NE Pacific, Fundy & Maine, Subtropical NW Atlantic, Brazos, Texas Colorado; Groundwater											
AFRICA												
Ghana	W Gulf of Guinea	R Pra at Daboase	g 94 DO g 91-93	0	HM: As, Cd	7.7	--	--	3.00	--	53.7	7.1
	Volta	R Volta at B Kpong	g 94-95	12	HM: Cu, Zn	5.2	4.0	--	0.25	--	38.0	7.0
		R White Volta at Nawuni	g 94-95	13	HM: Zn	7.2	3.0	--	1.32	--	41.5	7.0
		average		12								
	country average			6								
	not covered: Groundwater											
Kenya	U intertropical W Indian	R Tana	g 88	32	P	--	--	--	0.01	0.080	74.0	7.5
	Shebelli-Juba	L Naivasha	g 88	40	P	--	--	--	--	0.050	188.0	8.8
	country average			36								
	not covered: Rift Valley; Groundwater											
Mali	Niger	R Niger at Bamako	g 94-96	15	P	8.5	--	--	0.50	0.405	19.2	6.9
		R Niger at Koulikoro (06)	g 94-96	7	P	8.1	--	--	0.53	0.833	19.2	7.2
		average		11								
	Groundwater	G forage Bamako (05)	g 94-96	4	P	--	--	--	0.44	1.050	51.0	5.9
		G forage Nossombougou (8)	g 96	15	P	--	--	--	0.72	0.400	161.0	7.7
		average		9								
	country average			10								
	not covered: Sahara, Senegal, Volta											
Morocco	SW Mediterranean	R Moulouya	g 94-96	0	HM: Hg, Pb	8.3	2.0	2.0	0.06	0.380	227.5	7.8
	U subtropical NE Atlantic	R Sebou at Kenitra	g 94-96	0	F coli	4.9	19.0	87.0	0.83	0.340	176.7	8.1
		R Bou Regreg at Barrage Sidi Mohamed Ben Abdella	g 94-96	14	N	5.8	2.0	--	8.98	0.204	117.4	8.1
		R er Rbia at Sidi Daoui	g 94-96	0	F coli	8.3	3.0	20.0	0.23	0.200	161.7	8.3

Country	Basin	Station	Sources & years	Score	Based on	DO mg/l	BOD mg/l	COD mg/l	N mg/l	P mg/l	Alk. mg/l	pH
		average		5								
	Groundwater	G puits artesien Ire 4/125	g 94-96	14	O	2.4	--	--	2.16	--	218.1	7.2
		G puits Mamora Ire 442/13	g 94-96	0	N	5.7	--	--	25.62	--	312.9	7.2
		average		7								
	country average			4								
	not covered: Sahara											
Namibia	Orange	R Orange mouth	a 90	18		--	--	--	0.72	--	--	--
	not covered: Etosha, Okavango, Cunene, L Subtropical SE Atlantic; Groundwater											
Senegal	Senegal	R Senegal at St Louis	g 95 COD g 91-93	0	O	--	--	185.0	1.06	--	90.0	7.2
		R Senegal at Podor	g 95	18	F coli	--	--	--	0.19	--	60.0	8.0
		average		9								
	Groundwater	G forage 2 Fatick	g 93	60*	N	--	--	--	0.18	--	400.0	8.0
		G forage 3 Ziguinchor bis	g 93	47	N	--	--	--	1.24	--	320.0	7.8
		average		53								
	country average			31								
	not covered: L subtropical NE Atlantic											
South Africa	Orange	R Orange mouth	a 90	18		--	--	--	0.72	--	--	--
	not covered: L Subtropical SE Atlantic, L subtropical W Indian, U subtropical W Indian; Groundwater											
Sudan	Nile	R Blue Nile at Khartoum	g 91-92	0	P	7.6	4.0	--	1.02	1.418	114.7	7.7
		R White Nile at Jebel Aulia	g 91-92	0	P	8.1	5.0	--	0.44	2.085	104.7	8.2
	country average			0								
	not covered: Sahara, Rift Valley, W Red Sea; Groundwater			0								
Tanzania	Nile	R Kagera at Nyakanyasi	g 91	69	Acid	--	--	--	0.12	--	42.0	7.8
		L Victoria at South Port	g 91-92	60*	O	6.0	4.0	--	--	--	67.3	7.5
		average		67								
	U intertropical W Indian	R Ruvu at Mlandizi	g 92-93	63	F coli	8.5	--	--	--	--	74.5	8.0
	Groundwater	G Makutopora Basin at Dodoma	g 91-93	60*	Acid	--	--	--	--	--	244.7	8.4
		G Sakina borehole	g 91-92	60*	Acid	--	--	--	--	--	148.0	8.7
		average		60								
	country average			60*								
	not covered: Rift Valley, Congo, Zambezi, Ruvuma, Rufiji											
Uganda	Nile	L Albert	a 90	19	P	--	--	--	0.02	0.160	--	--
	not covered: Rift Valley; Groundwater											
EUROPE												
Albania	Adriatic	R Semani at Mbrostar	e 90	60*	N	6.6	3.4	3.3	0.50	0.000	--	--
	not covered: Ionian; Groundwater											
Austria	Danube	R Danube df	o 95-97	21	N	11.0	3.1	--	2.45	0.092	--	--
		R Inn df	o 95-97	26	P	11.3	2.5	--	1.52	0.101	--	--
	country average			23								
	not covered: German Bight (Elbe), Rhine; Groundwater											
Belgium	Rhine	R Meuse df 94-96	o 94-96	10	P	10.5	2.2	--	2.57	0.707	--	--
		R Meuse at Lanaye/ Ternaaien 91-92	g 91-92	0	F coli	8.1	4.0	21.0	3.31	0.566	140.1	7.6
		latest		10								
	SE North Sea	R Schelde (Escaut) df 94-96	o 94-96	0	P	7.4	4.2	--	9.19	1.320	--	--
		R Schelde at Doel 91	g 91	12	P	4.0	2.0	68.0	6.13	0.569	167.7	7.5
		latest		0								
	country average			5								
	not covered: Groundwater											
Bulgaria	Aegean	R Arda df	oc 93	59	N	7.8	--	--	0.77	--	--	--
		R Maritza at Svilengrad	e 91	17	N	7.2	4.5	--	6.10	--	--	--
		average		38								
	Danube	R Jantra mouth	oc 93	20	N	8.1	--	--	2.81	--	--	--
		R Osam mouth	oc 93	20	N	9.8	--	--	2.88	--	--	--
		average		20								
	country average			29								
	not covered: W Black Sea; Groundwater											
Croatia	Danube	R Danube at Borovo	e 90	17	P	10.3	1.8	3.9	2.70	0.300	--	--
		R Sava at Zupanja	e 90	10	P	7.6	3.3	28.2	3.60	0.700	--	--
	country average			13								
	not covered: Adriatic; Groundwater											
Czech R	Oder	R Oder (Odra) df	o 95-97	15	P	9.4	5.4	--	5.03	0.430	--	--
	German Bight	R Elbe (Labe) df	o 95-97	18	N	10.3	3.7	--	4.99	0.186	--	--
	Danube	R Morava df	o 95-97	18	N, P	11.3	4.9	--	4.23	0.264	--	--
	country average			17								
	not covered: Groundwater											

Country	Basin	Station	Sources & years	Score	Based on	DO mg/l	BOD mg/l	COD mg/l	N mg/l	P mg/l	Alk. mg/l	pH
Denmark	SW Baltic	R Sus mouth	o 95-97	17	P	--	2.1	--	1.93	0.278	--	--
		R Odense mouth	o 95-97	19	N	--	1.9	--	3.86	0.134	--	--
		average		18								
	S Skagerrak & W Kattegat	R Guden mouth	o 95-97	27	P	--	2.6	--	1.44	0.098	--	--
	NE North Sea	R Skjern mouth	o 95-97	20	N	10.0	1.7	--	2.61	0.064	--	--
	country average			22								
	not covered: N Baltic; Groundwater											
Estonia	S Gulf of Finland	R Narva 10 km from mouth	e 85-90	19	N	10.4	2.1	27.0	3.90	0.100	--	--
		R Narva at L Vörtsjäry	e 91	22	N	--	--	--	2.40	0.043	--	7.8
		average		20								
	SE Baltic	R Pärnu 1 km from mouth	e 85-90	18	N	11.9	1.7	33.9	4.30	0.200	--	--
	country average			19								
	not covered: Groundwater											
Finland	W Barents Sea	L Inari (151)	g 94-96	51	Acid	11.7	--	--	0.01	0.003	8.1	7.1
	Gulf of Bothnia	R Tornionjoki (14100)	g 94-96	56	Acid	11.8	--	--	0.01	0.018	14.0	7.0
		L Yli-Kitka (144)	g 94-96	56	Acid	9.9	--	--	0.01	0.006	13.0	7.1
		R Kokernaenjoki mouth	o 95-97	15	HM: Cu	10.7	--	--	0.66	0.048	--	--
		average		42								
	N Gulf of Finland	R Kalkkinen (4800)	g 94-96	40	HM: Hg	11.4	--	--	0.01	0.006	9.4	7.1
		R Kymijoki (5610)	g 94-96	42	HM: Hg	11.2	--	--	0.03	0.022	11.5	6.9
		average		41								
	country average			45								
	not covered: Groundwater											
France	La Manche	R Seine mouth 94-96	o 94-96	4	P	5.7	4.5	--	6.51	1.003	--	--
		R Seine at Paris 91-93	g 91-93	0	F coli	8.9	4.0	24.0	19.28	0.573	--	7.8
		latest		4								
	Loire	R Loire mouth	o 94-96	17	P	10.0	5.0	--	2.67	0.282	--	--
		R Loire at Ingrandes	g 94	2	N	10.8	5.0	34.0	22.62	0.314	--	8.0
		average		9								
	Bay of Biscay	R Garonne mouth	o 94-96	22	P	9.8	1.4	--	2.15	0.119	--	--
		R Garonne at Valence d'Agen	g 94-95	14	N	10.0	2.0	8.0	9.36	0.136	--	8.1
		average		18								
	N Mediterranean	R Rhone mouth	o 94-96	19	P	10.1	2.0	--	1.55	0.179	--	--
		R Rhone at St Vallier	g 94	14	F coli	10.1	1.0	35.0	6.88	0.122	--	8.1
		average		16								
	country average			12								
	not covered: Rhine, SE North Sea, Ligurian & Tyrrhenian Seas; Groundwater											
Germany	German Bight	R Elbe mouth 95-97	o 95-97	18	N, P	11.2	--	--	4.46	0.220	--	--
		R Elbe at Geesthacht 88-90	g 88-90	5	HM: Cd	8.8	5.0	38.0	4.15	0.399	2.0	7.6
		R Weser mouth 95-97	o 95-97	18	N,P	10.2	3.3	--	4.78	0.210	--	--
		R Weser at Intschede 88-90	g 88-90	16	P	9.1	5.0	17.0	3.86	0.325	--	7.8
		average (latest)		18								
	Rhine	R Rhine df	o 95-97	19	N	9.9	--	--	3.41	0.137	--	--
		R Rhine at Kleve/Bimmen	g 88-90	0	HM: Zn	9.6	3.0	14.0	3.23	0.718	262.8	7.6
		R Rhine at Koblenz	g 88-90	16	P	9.0	2.0	15.0	2.70	0.326	332.7	7.8
		R Moselle at Koblenz	g 88-90	15	P	9.4	2.0	15.0	3.17	0.420	278.2	7.8
		average		12								
	Danube	R Danube df 95-97	o 95-97	21	N	11.1	2.4	--	2.43	0.096	--	--
		R Danube at Jochenstein 88-90	g 88-90	20	P	10.9	3.0	15.0	1.57	0.137	--	7.9
		latest		21								
	country average			17								
	not covered: Oder, SW Baltic; Groundwater											
Greece	Adriatic	L Mikri Prespa	o 92	59	N	--	--	--	0.10	0.026	--	--
	Ionian	R Akeloos mouth	o 93-95	56	HM: Cd	11.3	--	--	--	--	--	--
	Aegean	R Axios mouth	o 93-95	9	P	11.5	--	--	2.11	0.764	--	--
		R Strimonas mouth	o 93-95	20	P	11.0	--	--	1.62	0.131	--	--
		average		14								
	country average			43								
	not covered: Groundwater											
Hungary	Danube	R Danube df	o 93-95	19	HM: Cu	9.5	2.4	--	2.53	0.126	--	--
		R Danube at Budapest	g 91-92	15	F coli	11.0	5.0	24.0	2.56	0.211	156.7	7.8
		R Tisza at Szolnok	g 91-92	15	P	8.4	3.0	--	2.15	0.402	2.5	7.9
		R Tisza df	o 93-95 P o 95	17	P	11.9	2.0	--	1.16	0.310	--	--
		average		16								
	Groundwater	G deep well Pest County	g 91	20	N	--	--	--	2.74	--	12.1	--
	country average			18								
	not covered: none											
Ireland	Celtic Sea	R Blackwater mouth	o 95-97	20	N, P	10.6	1.9	--	2.68	0.138	--	--

Country	Basin	Station	Sources & years	Score	Based on	DO mg/l	BOD mg/l	COD mg/l	N mg/l	P mg/l	Alk. mg/l	pH
		R Barrow mouth	o 95-97	18	N	11.2	2.2	--	4.62	0.118	--	--
		average		19								
	Irish Sea	R Boyne mouth	o 95-97	19	N	11.0	1.8	--	3.15	0.113	--	--
	Scottish & Irish Atlantic	R Clare mouth	o 95-97	31	P	10.6	1.5	--	1.77	0.082	--	--
	country average			23								
	not covered: Groundwater											
Italy	Ligurian & Tyrrhenian	R Arno mouth	o 93-95	19	N	8.4	--	--	3.17	0.143	--	--
	Adriatic	R Adige mouth	o 94-96	33	P	10.9	9.7	--	1.78	0.075	--	--
		R Po mouth	o 94-96	19	P	6.9	3.4	--	2.73	0.180	--	--
		average		26								
	country average			22								
	not covered: N Mediterranean, Ionian, SE Mediterranean, Danube; Groundwater											
Latvia	SE Baltic	R Gauja at Sigulda	e 91	27	P	12.8	1.6	31.0	1.20	0.100	--	--
		R Daugava at Jekabpils	e 91	27	P	8.7	2.1	36.5	1.30	0.100	--	--
	country average			27								
	not covered: S Gulf of Finland; Groundwater											
Lithuania	SE Baltic	R Nemunas	e 91	60*	O	10.4	3.9	--	--	--	--	--
	Groundwater	G Juodkrante	g 94-96	18	P	6.9	2.0	18.0	1.01	0.222	132.5	7.0
		G Marijanpole	g 94-96	11	HM: Zn	2.1	2.0	17.0	2.57	0.053	386.7	7.2
		G Panevezys	g 94-96	0	HM: Zn	3.6	1.0	10.0	0.69	0.014	272.2	7.5
		G Varena	g 94-96	16	N	2.7	2.0	2.0	6.60	0.052	167.5	7.5
		average		11								
	country average			35								
	not covered: none											
Luxembourg	Rhine	R Sûre df	o 93-95	14	P	10.4	3.5	--	5.08	0.449	--	--
	not covered: Groundwater											
Moldova	Danube	R Prut at Ungheni	e 91	19	P	11.8	1.9	24.0	1.70	0.200	--	--
	N Black Sea	R Dnestr at Bender	e 91	18	N	10.1	2.5	22.2	4.30	0.200	--	--
	country average			18								
	not covered: Groundwater											
Netherlands	Rhine	L Ijsselmeer	g 94-95 BOD & COD g 91-93	19	P	12.2	3.0	28.0	2.25	0.156	--	8.7
		R Rhine Ijssel arm	g 94-95 BOD & COD g 91-93	17	P	8.6	2.0	21.0	4.34	0.304	--	8.1
		R Rhine Ijssel-Kampen	o 94-96	17	P	9.0	--	--	4.10	0.273	--	--
		R Rijn/Maas delta	o 94-96	19	N, P	11.2	--	--	3.29	0.208	--	--
	country average			18								
	not covered: German Bight, SE North Sea; Groundwater											
Norway	Norwegian Sea	R Altaelva at Alta	g 91-93	60	HM: Cu	--	--	--	--	0.011	--	--
		R Vefsna at Mosjøen	g 91-93	60	HM: Cu	--	--	--	--	0.005	--	--
		R Orkla at Vormstad	g 91-93	19	HM: Cu	--	--	--	--	0.005	--	--
		R Suldalslaagen at Sand	g 91-93	60*	HM: Hg	--	--	--	--	0.004	--	--
		average		50								
	N Skagerrak & E Kattegat	R Otra mouth	o 95-97	60*	HM: Pb	--	--	--	0.17	0.004	--	--
		R Skienselva mouth	o 95-97	70	HM: Cu	--	0.4	--	0.23	0.004	--	--
		R Numedalslaagen at Bommestad	g 91-93	47	HM: Cu	--	--	--	--	0.010	--	--
		R Drammenselva mouth	o 95-97	60*	HM: Pb	--	--	--	0.30	0.006	--	--
		R Glåma mouth	o 95-97	59	HM: Cu	--	--	--	0.41	0.025	--	--
		average		59								
	country average			54								
	not covered: W Barents Sea; Groundwater											
Poland	Wisla	R Wisla mouth	o 95-97	19	P	10.6	4.2	--	1.88	0.194	--	--
		R Wisla at Kiezmark	g 94-95	0	F coli	10.8	4.0	26.0	3.58	0.226	159.5	8.2
		R Wisla at Warszawa	g 94-95	9	F coli	10.8	7.0	38.0	4.35	0.238	--	8.4
		R Wisla at Krakow	g 94-95	0	F coli, HM: Zn	8.2	8.0	33.0	8.70	0.592	--	7.6
		average		7								
	Oder	R Oder mouth	o 95-97	17	P	10.0	4.4	--	2.55	0.318	--	--
		R Oder (Odra) at Krajnik	g 94-95	0	F coli	10.6	5.0	44.0	4.39	0.311	140.9	8.2
		R Oder (Odra) at Wroclaw	g 94-95	0	F coli	10.0	7.0	25.0	5.88	0.313	2.2	7.9
		R Oder (Odra) at Chalupki	g 94-95	0	F coli	8.7	8.0	25.0	8.12	0.429	2.1	7.5
		average		4								
	Groundwater	G Pomeranian Lake District	g 94-95	1	HM: Zn	--	--	--	12.44	0.300	--	7.5
	country average			4								

Country	Basin	Station	Sources & years	Score	Based on	DO mg/l	BOD mg/l	COD mg/l	N mg/l	P mg/l	Alk. mg/l	pH
	not covered: German Bight (Elbe)											
Portugal	L temperate NE Atlantic	R Douro mouth	o 92-93	32	P	9.7	2.3	--	0.90	0.080	--	--
		R Tejo at Santarem	g 91-92	18	P	7.4	2.0	18.0	1.00	0.256	142.5	7.4
		average		25								
	U subtropical NE Atlantic	R Guadiana mouth	o 92-93	18	P	7.7	4.9	--	1.02	0.242	--	--
	country average			21								
	not covered: Groundwater											
Romania	Danube	R Danube at Bazias	e 91	15	N, P	10.0	4.4	30.9	7.60	0.400	--	--
		R Oltul at Isbiceni	e 91	10	P	10.3	--	54.1	3.60	0.700	--	--
		R Muresul at Nadlac	e 91	12	N	8.8	6.1	7.4	11.00	0.100	--	--
	country average			12								
	not covered: Groundwater											
Slovakia	Danube	R Maly Dunaj (Danube) df	o 95-97	17	P	9.7	3.1	--	2.66	0.274	--	--
		R Hornad df	o 95-97	18	P	9.7	5.9	--	3.64	0.222	--	--
		R Hron mouth	o 95-97	19	P	10.7	3.4	--	2.15	0.194	--	--
		R Vah mouth	o 95-97	19	P	10.0	3.8	--	2.88	0.201	--	--
	country average			18								
	not covered: Wisla; Groundwater											
Slovenia	Danube	R Sava at Brezice	e 90	19	P	9.2	6.3	35.0	1.70	0.200	--	--
		R Drava at Ormoz	e 91	48	N	10.2	2.5	9.7	1.20	0.000	--	--
	country average			33								
	not covered: Adriatic; Groundwater											
Spain	L temperate NE Atlantic	R Duero df	o 95-97	15	P	7.3	3.5	--	1.85	0.392	--	--
	U subtropical NE Atlantic	R Guadiana mouth	o 95-97	17	P	9.9	4.1	--	1.94	0.316	--	--
		R Guadalquivir mouth	o 94-96	7	P	6.5	22.4	--	2.19	0.838	--	--
		average		12								
	NW Mediterranean	R Ebro mouth	o 95-97	14	P	9.7	8.1	--	3.32	0.444	--	--
	country average			14								
	not covered: Bay of Biscay, N Mediterranean; Groundwater											
Sweden	N Skagerrak & E Kattegat	L Vanern	o 95-97 pH e 90	58	N	--	--	--	0.83	0.007	--	7.4
	N Baltic	R Mörrumsan mouth	o 95-97	60*	P	--	--	--	0.18	0.020	--	--
		R Ronneaan mouth	o 95-97	38	N	--	--	--	1.62	0.037	--	--
		L Vattern	o 95-97 pH e 90	59	N	--	--	--	0.77	0.005	--	7.5
		average		52								
	Gulf of Bothnia	R Dalalven mouth	o 95-97	60*	P	--	--	--	0.14	0.017	--	--
		R Rane mouth	o 95-97	60*	P	--	--	--	0.05	0.016	--	--
		average		60								
	country average			57								
	not covered: Groundwater											
Switzerland	Rhine	R Rhine at Basel	g 94-96	37	P	10.7	--	--	1.60	0.060	137.4	8.1
		R Rhine at Diepoldsau	g 94-96	10	HM: Cr	11.4	--	--	0.57	0.083	98.1	8.2
		R Aare at Brugg	g 94-96	31	N	10.5	--	--	1.95	0.066	153.6	8.0
		average		26								
	N Mediterranean	R Rhone at Chancy	g 94-96	13	HM: Cr	10.8	--	--	0.60	0.074	98.7	8.2
		R Rhone at Porte du Scex	g 94-96	23	P	11.3	--	--	0.60	0.113	74.0	8.2
		average		18								
	Adriatic	R Ticino at Riazzino	g 91	52	P	11.5	--	--	1.01	0.035	52.2	7.9
	country average			32								
	not covered: Danube; Groundwater											
Ukraine	N Black Sea	R Dnestr at Mogiliv-Podilskiy	e 89-91	19	P	12.8	3.1	23.5	2.30	0.200	--	--
	Dnepr	R Dnepr at Kherson	e 89-91	27	P	9.6	3.0	32.3	0.50	0.100	--	--
	Don	R Severskiy Donez at Krujilivka	e 91	14	P	3.4	1.5	--	1.00	0.400	--	--
	country average			20								
	not covered: Wisla, Danube, Azov Sea; Groundwater											
United Kingdom	W North Sea	R Leven	g 94-96	40	HM: Pb	10.9	2.0	--	0.43	--	12.1	7.0
		R Tweed above Galafoot	g 94-96	51	N	11.3	2.0	--	1.10	--	--	7.8
		R Trent at Nottingham	g 94-96	14	N	10.6	3.0	--	9.34	--	161.1	8.0
		R Thames at London	g 94-96	15	N	10.2	2.0	--	7.85	--	187.1	8.1
		average		30								
	English Channel	R Exe at Exeter	g 94-96	20	N	11.1	2.0	--	2.82	--	39.6	7.8
	Celtic Sea	R Severn mouth	o 94-96	7	P	10.7	2.2	--	6.59	0.832	--	--
		R Avon at Bristol	g 94-96	15	N	9.6	3.0	--	7.96	--	219.9	8.1
		average		11								
	Irish Sea	R Dee	g 94-96	20	N	10.5	1.0	--	2.52	--	--	7.6
		R Mersey	g 94-96	15	N	7.7	4.0	--	8.10	--	102.9	7.4
		R Clyde mouth	o 94-96	11	N	8.4	3.7	--	3.06	0.621	--	--
		average		15								
	Scottish & Irish Atlantic	R Carron	g 94-96	35	HM: Cd	11.3	1.0	--	0.06	--	--	6.5

Country	Basin	Station	Sources & years	Score	Based on	DO mg/l	BOD mg/l	COD mg/l	N mg/l	P mg/l	Alk. mg/l	pH
		Lower Bann mouth	o 95-97	19	P	9.2	3.4	--	1.12	0.161	--	--
		average		27								
		country average		21								
		not covered: Groundwater										
RUSSIAN FEDERATION	Volga	R Volga at Narimanov	g 94	64	N	9.7	2.0	--	0.66	--	115.5	8.0
		R Volga at B Cheboksarskoye (201)	g 94	19	P	10.4	3.0	--	2.20	0.168	192.8	7.6
		R Belaya at Ufa (203)	g 94	34	P	11.4	2.0	--	1.37	0.074	129.6	7.9
		average		39								
	Severnaya Dvina	R Severnaya Dvina at Ust-Pinega (213)	g 94	58	P	8.3	2.0	--	0.18	0.027	105.4	7.8
	White Sea	R Mezen at Borovo	g 94	60	P	8.0	2.0	--	0.05	0.025	60.7	7.1
	E Barents Sea	R Pechora at Nar'jan-Mar	g 94	47	P	8.2	2.0	--	0.16	0.041	60.3	7.2
	Ob	R Ob at Salehard (011)	g 94	57	N	7.9	2.0	--	0.85	--	81.0	7.1
		R Tom at Tomsk (204)	g 94	39	HM: Hg	8.5	2.0	--	1.13	--	79.8	7.5
		R Irtysh at Krasnyi Jar (205)	g 94	18	P	9.7	3.0	--	0.65	0.235	53.2	7.7
		average		38								
	Yenisey	R Yenisei at Igarka (210)	g 94	20	HM: Zn	8.6	1.0	--	0.00	0.021	88.1	7.4
		L Baikal mid-lake (024)	g 91-93	40	HM: Hg	11.1	1.0	--	0.11	0.021	60.9	7.8
		R Selenga mouth	g 94	60	HM: Pb	9.7	2.0	--	0.07	0.015	110.6	7.5
		average		40								
	Lena	R Lena delta (028)	g 94	59	P	11.1	1.0	--	0.07	0.026	61.7	7.5
	Kolyma	R Kolyma at Kolymskoe	g 94	63	Acid	9.7	2.0	--	0.06	0.021	25.5	7.1
	Neva	L Onezhskoye (Onega)	g 94	59	Acid	10.3	2.0	--	0.28	0.014	16.5	7.0
	Don	R Don at Bagaevskij	g 94	30	P	15.5	4.0	--	0.07	0.087	202.3	6.9
	Azov Sea	R Kuban mouth	g 94	17	N	10.9	2.0	--	5.83	0.066	124.7	7.8
	Amur	R Amur mouth	g 94	61	N	10.2	4.0	--	0.73	--	31.2	7.2
		country average		48								
	not covered: Interior—N Caspian; Arctic—W Barents Sea, W Kara Sea, Pyasina, Taimyr, Khatanga, Anabar, Olenek, Yana, Indigirka, W Chukchi Sea; Atlantic—N Gulf of Finland, S Gulf of Finland, SE Baltic, Dnepr, E Black Sea; Pacific—W Bering Sea, U temperate NW Pacific, Sea of Okhotsk; Groundwater											
ASIA												
Bangladesh	Ganges	R Meghna at Ashuganj	g 94-95	16	P	6.6	2.0	--	4.89	0.376	82.6	7.3
		R Padma at Bheramara	g 94-95	46	F coli	7.3	3.0	--	--	--	60.1	7.3
		R Brahmaputra at Fulchhari	g 94-95	49	F coli	7.1	2.0	--	--	--	88.9	7.2
		average		37								
	NE Bay of Bengal	R Karnaphuli at Rangunia	g 95	38	N	6.6	1.0	16.0	1.61	--	75.6	7.4
		L Kaptai at Kaptai	g 94-95	41	N	6.8	1.0	9.0	1.48	--	40.2	7.4
		average		39								
	Groundwater	G tube well (07)	g 94-95	77	O, Acid	6.2	1.0	--	--	--	130.2	7.3
		G tube well (09)	g 94-95	71	Acid	6.3	0.0	--	--	--	79.7	7.2
		average		74								
	country average		50									
	not covered: none											
China	Bo Hai	R Huang (Yellow) at Jinan	g 94-96	0	SS, F coli	8.9	3.0	3.0	3.40	0.833	177.1	8.0
	Chang	R Chang (Yangtze) at Wuhan	g 94-96	20	HM: Cd	8.3	2.0	3.0	1.07	0.115	109.2	7.9
		L Tai	g 94-96	27	P	9.5	2.0	4.0	1.16	0.100	50.0	8.1
		average		23								
	Xi	R Xi (Pearl) at Zhaoqing	g 94-96	28	F coli	7.7	1.0	3.0	1.04	0.092	90.8	7.9
	Chinese South China Sea	L Plover Cove (19), Hong Kong	g 94-96	40	N	8.0	--	--	1.50	0.016	23.2	7.9
	country average		23									
	not covered: E Asian interior, Balkhash, Tarim, Indus, Ganges, Irrawaddy, Salween, Amur, W Sea of Japan, E Yellow Sea, Liaodong Wan, SW Yellow Sea, East China Sea, Gulf of Tonkin, Mekong; Groundwater											
Georgia	S Caspian	R Kura at Rustavi	e 89	19	N	9.3	2.9	14.2	3.10	--	--	--
	E Black Sea	R Rioni at Poti	e 89	20	N	9.5	2.4	7.9	2.60	0.100	--	--
	country average		19									
	not covered: Groundwater											
India	Gulfs of Kachchh & Khambhat	R Sabarmati at Ahmedabad	g 95-96	0	O, N, F coli	1.1	78.0	220.0	32.80	1.067	429.8	7.6
		R Mahi at Vasad	g 95-96	18	P	9.6	2.0	10.0	3.41	0.216	181.9	8.3
		R Narmada near Garudeshwar	g 95-96	18	N	8.1	3.0	10.0	4.86	0.119	168.4	8.1
		R Tapti near Burhanpur	g 95-96	17	P	7.5	2.0	28.0	1.57	0.320	197.1	7.6
		average		13								
	Malabar Coast	R Chaliyar at Kalpalli	g 95-96	19	F coli	6.6	1.0	10.0	0.43	--	28.0	7.0
		R Periyar near Alwaye	g 95-96	20	F coli	7.2	1.0	10.0	1.91	--	8.4	6.7

Country	Basin	Station	Sources & years	Score	Based on	DO mg/l	BOD mg/l	COD mg/l	N mg/l	P mg/l	Alk. mg/l	pH
		R Kallada at Panamthottam	g 95-96	17	F coli	8.0	1.0	8.0	1.03	--	11.9	7.2
		average		19								
	Coromandel Coast	R Cauvery near Musiri	g 95-96	17	F coli	6.8	1.0	17.0	3.49	--	166.2	7.6
		R Pennar near Nellore	g 95-96	42	P	6.1	3.0	15.0	0.45	0.047	223.0	8.0
		average		29								
	Krishna	R Krishna near Vijayawada	g 95-96	28	P	7.4	2.0	9.0	1.16	0.096	141.5	8.0
		R Krishna at Gadwal	g 95-96	26	N	7.2	2.0	11.0	2.21	0.022	134.8	7.7
		R Tungabhadra at Ullanuru	g 95-96	18	N	7.2	1.0	29.0	5.10	0.047	154.5	8.5
		R Bhima near Takali	g 95-96	19	P	6.2	5.0	27.0	2.10	0.173	172.6	8.1
		average		23								
	Godavari	R Godavari near Polavaram	g 95-96	50	P	7.2	1.0	9.0	0.43	0.037	84.8	7.4
		R Godavari near Mancheral	g 95-96	19	P	7.7	2.0	12.0	0.52	0.198	182.3	8.0
		R Wainganga near Ashti	g 95-96	19	N, P	6.1	5.0	23.0	3.23	0.177	186.6	8.1
		average		29								
	NW Bay of Bengal	R Mahanadi mouth	a 90	24	SS	--	--	--	--	--	--	--
		R Subarnarekha at Jamshedpur	g 95-96	26	F coli	6.4	3.0	40.0	0.50	--	63.4	7.7
		average		25								
	Ganges	R Ganga df	a 90	17	SS	--	--	--	0.86	0.075	--	--
	Groundwater	G well Ahmedabad	g 95-96	17	N	5.7	1.0	7.0	5.98	0.055	406.2	7.9
		G well Baroda	g 95	19	N	7.5	1.0	9.0	4.02	0.048	417.6	8.0
		G well Kalpalli	g 95-96	19	F coli	5.7	0.0	4.0	2.16	--	31.2	6.8
		G well Eluru (Alwaye)	g 95-96	20	N	4.8	1.0	9.0	2.78	--	13.5	7.0
		G well Musiri	g 95-96	19	N	4.6	1.0	16.0	3.10	--	202.5	7.5
		G well Vijayawada	g 95-96	0	N	4.2	3.0	13.0	50.96	0.655	345.3	7.5
		average		16								
	country average			21								
	not covered: Rajasthan, Indus, Maharashtra Coast, Lakshadweep Sea, Mannar, NE Bay of Bengal, Irrawaddy, Andaman Sea											
Indonesia	U intertropical E Indian (Java)	R Garang 91-93	g 91-93	0	F coli	6.2	4.0	12.0	1.23	0.112	107.0	7.6
		R Garang 94	g 94	17	HM: Cu	4.6	--	14.0	0.32	0.180	88.0	7.8
		lower		0								
	Java Sea & Karimata Strait (Sumatra)	R Musi at Palembang	g 91-93	5	HM: Zn	4.6	4.0	22.0	0.41	0.129	26.7	6.7
	Java Sea (Java)	R Banjir Kanal 91-93	g 91-93	0	F coli	1.4	14.0	26.0	2.75	0.243	58.6	6.9
		R Banjir Kanal 94	g 94	1	HM: Zn	2.6	7.0	8.0	1.39	0.409	45.1	6.7
		R Sunter 91-93	g 91-93	0	F coli, HM: Pb, Zn	0.8	24.0	48.0	6.13	0.546	98.8	7.1
		R Sunter 94	g 94	6	HM: Cd	1.8	9.0	37.0	0.96	0.263	54.3	6.7
		R Citarum 91-93	g 91-93	0	F coli, HM: Pb	1.3	18.0	44.0	3.70	0.415	84.7	7.5
		R Citarum 94	g 94	0	HM: Cd	3.1	8.0	12.0	0.30	1.347	39.0	7.3
		R Surabaya 91-93	g 91-93	0	F coli, HM: Pb	2.9	18.0	51.0	1.84	0.185	142.6	7.4
		B Saguling 91-93	g 91-93	0	F coli, HM: Pb	6.6	4.0	14.0	1.52	0.196	65.9	8.2
		B Saguling 94	g 94	11	P	4.5	5.0	13.0	0.00	0.649	48.0	7.6
		average 91-93		0								
	Groundwater (Java)	G well Senayan Jakarta	g 91-93	11	HM: Zn	0.0	--	6.0	0.33	0.198	179.4	8.3
		G well Pulogadung Jakarta	g 91-93	0	HM: Zn	0.0	--	6.0	0.22	0.598	202.4	7.3
		G well Cibeureum	g 91-93	0	HM: Pb	3.7	1.0	3.0	0.99	0.136	122.6	7.5
		average		4								
	country average			2								
	not covered: Strait of Malacca, W Sumatra, U intertropical E Indian (Bali-Alor), N Timor & Arafura Seas, Sulu & Celebes Seas, Makassar Strait, Java Sea & Karimata Strait (Kalimantan), Bali & Flores Seas, Molucca & Halmahera Seas, Ceram & Banda Seas, New Guinea tropical, New Guinea intertropical, Bismarck & Solomon Seas, N Coral Sea											
Iran	Shatt-al-Arab	Shatt-al-Arab mouth	a 90	13	SS	--	--	--	--	0.010	--	--
	Groundwater	G well 7 Tabriz	g 91-92	33	P	10.5	1.0	7.0	0.30	0.000	136.6	7.1
	country average			23								
	not covered: S Caspian, Iranian interior, Helmand, Hari Rud & Murgab, Baluchistan, N Persian Gulf & Gulf of Oman, Makran Coast											
Iraq	Shatt-al-Arab	Shatt-al-Arab mouth	a 90	13	SS	--	--	--	--	0.010	--	--
	not covered: Groundwater											
Japan	L temperate NW Pacific (Honshu)	R Kyu-Kitakami at Kanomata	g 92-93	29	P	9.8	2.0	4.0	0.53	0.090	26.2	6.8
		R Tone at Tone-Ozeki	g 94-96	16	HM: Cd	9.8	2.0	3.0	2.40	0.135	31.0	7.2
		R Sagami at Samukawa	g 94-96	20	F coli	9.0	2.0	2.0	1.98	0.063	53.5	7.7

213

Country	Basin	Station	Sources & years	Score	Based on	DO mg/l	BOD mg/l	COD mg/l	N mg/l	P mg/l	Alk. mg/l	pH
		R Kiso at Inuyama	g 94-96	37	F coli	10.4	1.0	--	0.68	0.029	18.5	7.3
		average		25								
	U subtropical NW Pacific (Honshu)	L Biwa south center	g 94-96	65	P	10.1	1.0	--	0.15	0.021	--	8.1
		R Yodo at Hirakata Bridge	g 91-92	16	P	8.9	2.0	--	1.34	0.356	30.8	7.4
		average		40								
	U subtropical NW Pacific (Shikoku)	R Yoshino at Takase	g 94-96	19	N	9.4	1.0	--	3.51	0.016	32.3	7.4
	U subtropical NW Pacific (Kyushu)	R Chikugo at Senoshita	g 94-96	29	P	9.8	2.0	--	1.19	0.093	--	7.7
		R Kuma at Yokoishi	g 94-95	40	F coli	9.6	1.0	--	0.86	0.030	34.6	7.9
		average		34								
	E Sea of Japan (Honshu)	R Shinano at Kyuzogoya	g 94-95	37	HM: Pb	10.1	1.0	--	0.88	--	23.1	7.2
	E Sea of Japan (Hokkaido)	R Ishikari at Ishikari	g 94-96	22	F coli	11.3	1.0	--	0.79	0.068	37.1	7.3
	Groundwater (Honshu)	G Suginami filtration plant	g 94-96	15	N	7.3	1.0	--	8.47	--	41.2	6.2
	country average			27								
	not covered: Sea of Okhotsk, L temperate NW Pacific (Hokkaido), U subtropical NW Pacific (Ryukyu Is)											
Jordan	Rift Valley	R Zarqua at King Talal Dam	g 94-96	0	O, N, HM: Pb	--	74.0	165.0	45.85	--	--	7.5
	Groundwater	G Awajan well 23	g 96	0	N	--	--	--	63.74	--	--	7.0
		G Azraq well 2	g 95-96	20	N	10.5	--	--	2.82	--	--	7.5
		G Rahme well Wadi Araba	g 94-96	13	N	--	--	--	9.85	--	--	7.2
		average		11								
	country average			5								
	not covered: Arabian interior, E Red Sea											
Kazakhstan	Aral Sea	R Syr Darya mouth	a 90	13	SS	--	--	--	--	--	--	--
	not covered: N Caspian, Balkhash, Turgay, E Asian interior, Ob; Groundwater											
Korea, R	Korea Strait	R NakDong	o 95-97	25	N	9.1	1.1	--	2.26	0.047	--	--
		R YoungSan	o 95-97	20	P	11.3	1.5	--	1.76	0.127	--	--
		average		22								
	E Yellow Sea	R Han mouth OECD 95-97	o 95-97	--	--	10.6	1.4	--	1.76	0.039	--	--
		R Han GEMS 94-96	g 94-96	21	HM: Cu	10.3	1.0	--	0.23	--	43.4	7.7
		R Keum	o 95-97	45	N	9.2	1.3	--	1.33	0.033	--	--
		average		33								
	country average			27								
	not covered: W Sea of Japan; Groundwater											
Malaysia	Strait of Malacca	R Klang	g 92	0	F coli	4.7	4.0	43.0	3.99	0.297	--	7.1
		R Linggi	g 92	0	F coli	4.3	2.0	53.0	1.66	--	--	6.3
		R Sekudai	g 92	0	F coli, HM: Cu	4.6	1.0	28.0	1.92	0.016	--	6.4
	country average			0								
	not covered: Malay/Thai South China Sea, Borneo South China Sea, Sulu & Celebes Seas; Groundwater											
Myanmar	Irrawaddy	R Irrawaddy	a 90	36	SS	--	--	--	--	--	--	--
	not covered: NE Bay of Bengal, Salween, Andaman Sea, Mekong; Groundwater											
Pakistan	Indus	R Indus at Kotri	g 94-96	0	SS, HM: Cr, Cu	5.3	6.0	17.0	5.99	0.436	133.9	7.4
		R Ravi below Lahore	g 94-96	0	F coli	7.4	3.0	37.0	6.33	0.234	144.6	7.8
		R Ravi above Lahore	g 94-96	0	F coli	7.0	2.0	27.0	7.06	0.140	127.7	7.8
		R Chenab Gujra branch	g 94-96	0	F coli	7.2	2.0	27.0	5.49	0.023	123.1	7.8
		average		0								
	Groundwater	G Lahore	g 94-96	27	P	--	--	8.0	0.36	0.100	242.5	7.6
	country average			13								
	not covered: Baluchistan, Makran Coast											
Philippines	Philippine South China Sea (Luzon)	B La Mesa	g 94-95	28	F coli	8.4	1.0	--	--	--	64.5	7.5
	L subtropical NW Pacific	R Cagayan	g 94-96	30	F coli	8.1	3.0	--	--	--	49.7	7.8
	country average			29								
	not covered: U tropical W Pacific, Sulu & Celebes Seas; Groundwater											
Thailand	Chao Phraya	R Chao Phraya at Bangkok	g 91-93	0	F coli	1.7	5.0	--	1.56	0.320	120.3	7.4
		R Chao Phraya below Nakhon Sawan	g 91-93	0	F coli	3.7	1.0	--	0.12	0.227	70.9	7.9
		R Prasak at Kaeng Khoi	g 91-92	0	F coli	4.1	1.0	--	0.12	0.075	145.3	7.7
		average		0								
	E Gulf of Thailand	R Bang at Pa Kong	g 91-93	0	F coli, HM: Pb	3.8	2.0	--	0.41	0.351	60.5	7.1
	Mekong	R Mun at Ubon Ratchathani	g 91-93	7	P	0.0	2.0	--	1.10	0.837	45.0	7.3
	country average			2								

Country	Basin	Station	Sources & years	Score	Based on	DO mg/l	BOD mg/l	COD mg/l	N mg/l	P mg/l	Alk. mg/l	pH
	not covered: Salween, Andaman Sea, Strait of Malacca, Malay/Thai South China Sea, W Gulf of Thailand; Groundwater											
Turkey	S Black Sea	R Yesilirmak mouth	o 95-97	17	P	9.8	1.8	--	2.91	0.270	--	--
		R Sakarya mouth	o 95-97	12	P	9.0	3.7	--	1.70	0.490	--	--
		average		14								
	Aegean	R Gediz mouth	o 95-97	17	P	4.5	11.7	--	0.87	0.287	--	--
	country average			15								
	not covered: Turkish interior, S Caspian, W Black Sea, E Black Sea, E Mediterranean, Shatt-al-Arab; Groundwater											
Uzbekistan	Aral Sea	R Amu Darya mouth	a 90	0	SS	--	--	--	--	--	--	--
	not covered: Groundwater											
Viet Nam	Gulf of Tonkin	R Hong (Red) mouth	a 90	19	SS	--	--	--	--	--	--	--
	Mekong	R Mekong mouth	a 90	56	SS	--	--	--	--	--	--	--
	country average			37								
	not covered: Vietnamese South China Sea; Groundwater											
PACIFIC												
Australia	Murray-Darling	R Murray-Darling mouth Atlas	a 90	0	SS	--	--	--	0.03	0.100	--	--
		R Murray-Darling mouth OECD	o 92	31	P	--	--	--	0.01	0.085	--	--
		lower		0								
	W Coral Sea	R Burdekin mouth	a 90	52	SS	--	--	--	--	--	--	--
	Subpolar SW Pacific	R Derwent mouth	o 93	10	N	--	--	--	13.30	0.006	--	--
	country average			21								
	not covered: Gulf of Carpentaria, S Arafura & Timor Seas, L intertropical E Indian, W Australian subtropical, U temperate E Indian, L temperate E Indian, Subpolar E Indian, W Tasman Sea, Bass Strait; Groundwater											
New Zealand	E Tasman Sea (South I)	R Oreti at Riverton highway bridge	g 94-96	56	N	11.2	0	--	0.91	0.025	--	7.6
		R Waiau at Tuatapere	g 94-96	72	P	11.4	0	--	0.24	0.016	--	7.7
		R Haast at Roaring Billy	g 94-96	28	P	11.6	0	--	0.07	0.096	--	7.7
		R Grey at Dobson	g 94-96	65	P	10.9	0	--	0.16	0.021	--	7.3
		R Buller at Te Huha	g 94-96	59	P	11.1	0	--	0.11	0.026	--	7.6
		R Motueka at Woodstock	g 94-96	59	P	11.2	0	--	0.18	0.026	--	8.0
		average		56								
	E Tasman Sea (North I)	R Manawatu at Opiki bridge	g 94-96	19	P	10.5	2.0	--	1.00	0.161	--	7.7
		R Rangitikei at Kakariki	g 94-96	28	P	10.8	1.0	--	0.27	0.096	--	8.0
		R Wanganui at Paetawa	g 94-96	19	P	10.3	1.0	--	0.46	0.158	--	7.6
		R Waingongoro at SH45	g 94-96	20	P	10.8	1.0	--	2.00	0.128	--	7.9
		R Waitara at Bertrand road	g 94-96	19	P	10.6	1.0	--	0.60	0.168	--	7.6
		R Waikato at Rangiriri	g 94-96	36	P	9.3	1.0	--	0.70	0.065	--	7.5
		R Hoteo at Gubbs	g 94-96	34	P	8.9	1.0	--	0.80	0.072	--	7.3
		average		25								
	Temperate SW Pacific (North I)	R Waitangi at Wakelins	g 94-96	63	P	9.7	0	--	0.44	0.023	--	7.5
		R Waihou at Te Aroha bridge	g 94-96	24	P	9.3	1.0	--	1.34	0.109	--	7.2
		R Tarawera at Awakaponga	g 94-96	21	P	6.9	2.0	--	0.49	0.122	--	7.2
		R Rangitaiki at Te Teko	g 94-96	49	P	10.7	1.0	--	0.41	0.039	--	7.1
		R Motu at Houpoto	g 94-96	24	P	10.5	0	--	0.12	0.111	--	7.7
		R Mohaka at Raupunga	g 94-96	19	P	10.9	1.0	--	0.17	0.156	--	8.3
		R Ngaruroro at Chesterhope	g 94-96	46	P	10.7	0	--	0.13	0.042	--	8.2
		R Tukituki at Red bridge	g 94-96	54	P	11.7	1.0	--	0.84	0.033	--	8.6
		R Ruamahanga at Waiaenga	g 94-96	31	P	10.6	1.0	--	0.68	0.082	--	7.6
		R Hutt at Boulcott	g 94-96	71	P	10.9	0	--	0.34	0.017	--	7.3
		average		40								
	Temperate SW Pacific (South I)	R Wairau at Tuamarina	g 94-96	26	P	10.7	0	--	0.14	0.104	--	7.7
		R Hurunui at Shi bridge	g 94-96	30	P	10.9	0	--	0.32	0.089	--	7.9
		R Waimakariri above old highway bridge	g 94-96	19	P	10.5	0	--	0.13	0.178	--	7.8
		R Opihi at Waipopo	g 94-96	36	P	11.1	0	--	0.68	0.064	--	7.6
		R Waitaki at Shi bridge	g 94-96	40	P	11.0	0	--	0.14	0.050	--	7.6
		R Taieri at Outram	g 94-96	51	P	11.6	1.0	--	0.30	0.036	--	7.6
		R Clutha at Balclutha	g 94-96	53	P	11.0	0	--	0.15	0.034	--	7.7
		R Mataura at Seaward Downs	g 94-96	39	P	10.8	1.0	--	1.14	0.054	--	7.2
		average		37								
	country average			39								
	not covered: Groundwater											
Papua New Guinea	Bismarck & Solomon Seas	R Sepik mouth	a 90	60*	SS	--	--	--	--	--	--	--
	N Coral Sea	R Fly mouth	a 90	27	SS	--	--	--	--	--	--	--
	country average			43								
	not covered: New Guinea intertropical; Groundwater											

Notes

The inland water quality score is the average score of drainage basins in each country. Each basin score is the lowest score of six indicators: oxygen balance, nutrients, acidification, suspended solids, microbial pollution, and arsenic and heavy metals. This table gives the basin and country scores, the indicator that determines each basin score, and data on oxygen balance, nutrients, and acidification. Table 16 gives data on suspended solids, microbial pollution, and arsenic and heavy metals.

Countries use different methods for measuring pollutants, so the data are not strictly comparable. All data are annual mean values at the location indicated in the Station column. Data are for the years and from the sources indicated in the Sources & years column.

Basin = drainage basin. Surface water basins are defined in Appendix 6. Groundwater is treated as if it were a single basin. Basins and groundwater not covered are noted at the end of each country section. Parts of basin names are abbreviated as follows: E = east; L = lower; N = north; S = south; U = upper; W = west.

Station = monitoring station (the point where the data are collected). Stations were chosen to meet the following criteria:

At least one station per country basin (portion of a basin in a country) near the mouth or downstream frontier (df).

In long coastal basins drained by many short rivers, additional stations to represent groups of rivers along the coast.

In large (100,000 km^2 or more) river basins, additional stations to represent sub-basins, preferably near the confluence with the main river or at or below major centers of population.

If the flow is interrupted by a large lake or reservoir, an additional station near the entrance to the lake or reservoir.

Groundwater stations at intervals throughout the country.

It was seldom possible to met these criteria in full. Four types of station are identified by a letter before the name of the water body concerned: B = built reservoir; G = groundwater; L = lake; R = river.

Sources & years = data sources, applicable years, and exceptions. Sources are indicated as follows:

a   National Water Research Institute (1996)

e   Eurostat et al. (1995)

g   Global Environmental Monitoring System (GEMS)/WATER data summaries and database (UNEP & WHO GEMS/Water Collaborating Centre 1988-1990, 1991-1993, 1999)

o   Organisation for Economic Co-operation and Development (1997 & 1999)

oc   OECD Centre for Co-operation with the Economies in Transition (1996)

When a single year is given, all data are for that year (unless otherwise noted in the Sources column). When a period is given (e.g., 94-96), all data are annual averages for that period (unless otherwise noted in the Sources column). If data for one of the indicators are for a different year, the indicator, source and year are noted after the indicator code. For example—o 95-97; pH e 90—means that data are from OECD and are for 1995-1997, except for acidity (pH) which are from Eurostat et al. and are for 1990. The codes used are: BOD = biochemical oxygen demand; COD = chemical oxygen demand; DO = dissolved oxygen; N = total nitrogen; P = total phosphorus.

Score = water quality score, the lowest score of the six indicators. Country scores are the average of basin scores (with groundwater treated as a single basin), which are the average of station scores.

Based on = the indicator that determines the station score (the indicator with the lowest score):

Acid = acidification, the average score of of alkalinity and acidity (pH) (this table)

F coli = fecal coliforms (microbial pollution) (Table 16)

HM = arsenic and heavy metals, the lowest score of arsenic (As), zinc (Zn), chromium (Cr), copper (Cu), nickel (Ni), lead (Pb), cadmium (Cd) and mercury (Hg) (Table 16)

N = total nitrogen (this table)

O = oxygen balance, the average of scores for dissolved oxygen, biochemical oxygen demand and chemical oxygen demand (this table)

P = total phosphorus (this table)

SS = total suspended solids (Table 16)

When two or more indicators are listed, their scores are the same.

The performance criteria are shown in Tables 15a and 15b. For convenience, the same criteria have been used for flowing surface waters (rivers), still surface waters (lakes), and groundwater, although ideally they should be different since natural conditions differ among them. For example, dissolved oxygen is naturally higher in rivers than in lakes, and concentrations of heavy metals are naturally higher in groundwater than in surface waters.

For dissolved oxygen (DO), the tops of the good and fair bands correspond to the range of 9-12 mg/l (depending on temperature) for 100% oxygen saturation of natural running waters (National Water Research Institute 1996). The tops of the medium, poor and bad bands match the draft quality classes of the United Nations Economic Commission for Europe (1990).

For biochemical oxygen demand (BOD), chemical oxygen demand (COD), total nitrogen (N), total phosphorus (P), alkalinity, acidity (pH) and microbial pollution (fecal coliforms), the tops of the fair, medium, poor and bad bands match the draft quality classes of the United Nations Economic Commission for Europe (1990): the good band corresponds to Class I (excellent), the fair band to Class II (good), the medium band to Class III (fair), the poor band to Class IV (poor), the bad band to Class V (bad).

For total suspended solids (TSS), the top of the bad band (1000 mg/l) is the point at which suspended solids start to limit light penetration and may shorten the life of reservoirs through sedimentation (National Water Research Institute 1996).

For arsenic and heavy metals, the tops of medium, poor and bad match the draft quality classes of the United Nations Economic Commission for Europe (1990): the good band corresponds to Class I (excellent), the fair band to Class II (good), the medium band to Class III (fair), the poor band to Class IV (poor), the bad band to Class V (bad).

DO = dissolved oxygen in milligrams of oxygen per liter (mg/l).

BOD = biochemical oxygen demand in milligrams of oxygen per liter (mg/l).

COD = chemical oxygen demand in milligrams of oxygen per liter (mg/l).

N = total nitrogen in milligrams of nitrogen per liter (mg/l). Few countries report total nitrogen. Most entries are various combinations of organic nitrogen, ammonia (NH_3), nitrates (NO_3) and nitrites (NO_2), one or more of which may be missing. Hence, nitrogen levels are usually understated, which is why the score for nutrients is the lower of the N score and P score.

P = total phosphorus in milligrams of phosphorus per liter (mg/l), but sometimes only phosphate (PO_4).

Alk. = alkalinity, measured as milligrams of calcium carbonate ($CaCO_3$) per liter (mg/l).

Ph = acidity in Ph units. The pH scale is logarithmic: 7.0 is neutral and each whole unit of the scale represents a multiplication factor of 10 (so 6.0 is 10 times more acid than 7.0, and 5.0 is 100 times more acid).

band	top point on scale	DO mg O$_2$/l	BOD mg O$_2$/l	COD mg O$_2$/l	N mg/l	P mg/l	alkalinity mg CaCO$_3$/l	pH	TSS mg/l	no. fecal coliforms/ 100 ml
good	100	12	0	0	0	0	400	8.5	0	0
fair	80	9	3	3	0.30	0.010	200	6.5	125	10
medium	60	6	5	10	0.75	0.025	100	6.3	250	30
poor	40	4	9	20	1.50	0.050	20	6.0	500	100
bad	20	3	15	30	2.50	0.125	10	5.3	1000	1000
base	0	1	30	60	25.00	1.250	0	4.5	2000	10000

Table 15a. Performance criteria for dissolved oxygen (DO), biochemical oxygen demand (BOD), chemical oxygen demand (COD), total nitrogen (N), total phosphorus (P), alkalinity, acidity (pH), total suspended solids (TSS), and microbial pollution (fecal coliforms).

band	top point on scale	As µg/l	Zn µg/l	Cr µg/l	Cu µg/l	Ni µg/l	Pb µg/l	Cd µg/l	Hg µg/l
good	100	0	0	0	0	0	0	0	0
fair	80	5	22	0.5	1.0	7.5	0.05	0.03	0.002
medium	60	10	45	1.0	2.0	15.0	0.10	0.07	0.003
poor	40	50	59	11.0	6.5	88.0	1.30	0.70	0.012
bad	20	100	65	16.0	9.2	790.0	34.00	1.80	2.400
base	0	200	260	80.0	92.0	800.0	68.00	18.00	2.500

Table 15b. Performance criteria for arsenic and heavy metals.

* A score with an asterisk has been reduced in accordance with the insufficient data rule. To prevent high scores resulting merely from lack of data, a good score is allowed only if it is based on all applicable components (in this case, all indicators in a station score, all stations in a basin score, all basins in a country score), and a fair score only if it is based on at least half the components. Good and fair scores (100-61) based on fewer than half the applicable components have been reduced to 60. Good scores (100-81) based on more than half but not all the applicable components have been reduced to 80.

Table 16. Inland Water Quality: Suspended Solids, Microbial Pollution, and Arsenic and Heavy Metals

Country	Basin	Station	Sources & years	TSS mg/l	F coli/ 100 ml	As µg/l	Zn µg/l	Cr µg/l	Cu µg/l	Ni µg/l	Pb µg/l	Cd µg/l	Hg µg/l
AMERICAS													
Argentina	La Plata	R Paraná at Puerto Libertad	g 94	--	250	10.0	42	5.0	15.0	--	6.0	1.00	--
		R Paraná at Corrientes	g 94	39	1204	--	--	--	--	--	--	--	--
		R Paraná at Rosario	g 94	--	246	--	--	--	2.0	--	--	--	1.020
Brazil	Amazon	R Amazon mouth	a 90	186	--	--	--	--	--	--	--	--	--
		R Tocantins mouth	a 90	202	--	--	--	--	--	--	--	--	--
	São Francisco	R Capibaribe	g 88-90	44	21000	--	55	--	14.0	--	48.0	37.00	0.748
		R São Francisco at Petrolandia	g 88-90	10	1000	--	55	--	10.0	--	76.0	28.00	0.030
	L tropical W Atlantic	R Paraguaçu at Pedra do Cavalo	g 88-90	8	295	--	151	56.0	45.0	--	--	--	--
		R Paraiba do Sul at Barra Mansa	g 88-90	25	12	--	11	--	7.0	--	20.0	--	0.076
	La Plata	B Guarapiranga	g 88-90	4	95	--	78	--	26.0	--	--	5.00	--
Canada	Mackenzie	R Mackenzie mouth	o 94-96	--	--	--	--	1.5	3.9	--	1.5	0.25	--
		R Great Bear	g 91-92	1	--	--	1	--	1.0	1.0	1.0	--	--
	L subpolar NE Pacific	R Skeena	g 91	--	--	--	--	--	--	--	--	--	0.011
	U temperate NE Pacific	R Fraser at Hope	g 91	--	--	--	--	--	--	--	--	--	0.010
	Columbia	R Columbia df	o 95-97	--	--	--	--	0.3	1.6	--	0.9	0.08	--
	Churchill	R Churchill	g 94-96	3	--	--	3	--	1.0	--	--	--	--
	Nelson	R Nelson at Gillam	g 94-96	9	--	--	2	1.0	2.0	1.0	--	--	--
		R Saskatchewan mouth	o 94-96	--	--	--	--	1.1	2.7	--	0.7	0.32	--
		R Roseau	g 94-96	40	37	1.0	5	--	3.0	1.0	1.0	--	--
	Fundy & Maine	R St John mouth	o 93-95	--	--	--	--	--	2.0	--	2.0	1.00	--
Chile	Subtropical SE Pacific	R Maipo at El Manzano	g 88	430	380	26.0	--	--	3.0	--	--	--	--
	Groundwater	G pozo Panamericana 1377	g 88	7	2	--	--	--	25.0	--	--	--	--
Colombia	Magdalena	R Magdalena mouth	a 90	928	--	--	--	--	--	--	--	--	--
		R Cauca at Juanchito	g 88	118	130000	--	99	--	77.0	--	--	--	--
Cuba	Groundwater	G Aguada del Cura	g 94	--	2	--	--	--	--	--	--	--	--
Mexico	Colorado	R Colorado	g 94-96	30	82000	--	--	--	--	--	--	--	--
	Grande de Santiago	L de Chapala	g 94-96	31	6601	--	--	--	--	--	--	--	--
		R Lerma	g 94-96	90	1100000	--	--	--	--	--	--	--	--
	U tropical E Pacific	R Balsas at Balsas	g 94-96	1334	110000	--	--	--	--	--	--	--	--
	Bravo del Norte (Grande)	R Bravo at Matamoros	g 94-96	80	--	--	95	--	70.0	--	--	--	--
		R Bravo at Presa de la Amistad	g 94-96	16	34	--	--	--	--	--	--	--	--
		R Conchos at Ojinaga	g 94-96	105	7300	--	--	--	--	--	--	--	--
	SW Gulf of Mexico	R Pánuco	g 94-96	133	303	--	20	--	50.0	--	--	--	--
		R Coatzacoalcos	g 94-96	42	23000	--	--	--	--	--	--	--	--
	SE Gulf of Mexico	R Grijalva	g 94-96	45	33000	--	--	--	--	--	--	--	--
		R Usumacinta	g 94-96	77	5960	--	--	--	--	--	--	--	--
	Groundwater	G pozo Aguascalientes	g 94-96	6	3	--	--	--	--	--	--	--	--
		G pozo Hacienda Tahdzibichen	g 94-96	3	6118	--	--	--	--	--	--	--	--
United States	E Bering Sea	R Yukon at Pilot Station	g 94-95	--	3	--	--	--	--	2.0	--	--	--
	Gulf of Alaska	R Talkeetna at Talkeetna	g 94-96	--	11	--	--	--	--	--	--	--	--
	Columbia	R Columbia at Bonneville	g 94	--	2	1.0	3	1.0	2.0	1.0	--	--	--
	U subtropical NE Pacific	R Sacramento at Sacramento	g 94-96	--	80	1.0	1	1.0	1.0	1.0	--	--	--
	Colorado	R Colorado at Hoover Dam	g 94-96	--	1	2.0	2	2.0	2.0	2.0	--	--	--
	St Lawrence	R St Lawrence df	g 94	--	2	--	--	--	--	--	--	--	--
		R Niagara at L Ontario	g 94	--	17	--	--	2.0	--	--	--	--	--
	L temperate NW Atlantic	R Hudson at Troy	g 94	--	389	--	--	--	--	--	--	--	--
		R Delaware at Trenton	g 94-96	--	92	1.0	21	--	2.0	1.0	2.0	--	--
	Chesapeake Bay	R Susquehanna at Harrisburg	g 94-95	--	53	--	--	--	--	5.0	--	--	--
		R Potomac at Washington	g 94-96	--	37	--	2	2.0	2.0	1.0	--	--	--
	NE Gulf of Mexico	R Apalachicola at Chattahoochee	g 94-95	--	58	--	--	--	--	--	--	--	--
	Mississippi	R Mississippi mouth	o 93-95	--	--	--	--	2.1	9.8	--	5.9	1.00	--
		R Arkansas at Little Rock	g 94-96	--	79	1.0	3	2.0	2.0	2.0	--	1.00	--
		R Missouri at Hermann	g 94-96	--	939	2.0	2	2.0	2.0	3.0	--	--	--

Country	Basin	Station	Sources & years	TSS mg/l	F coli/ 100 ml	As µg/l	Zn µg/l	Cr µg/l	Cu µg/l	Ni µg/l	Pb µg/l	Cd µg/l	Hg µg/l
		R Ohio at New Grand Chain	g 94-95	--	252	--	--	--	--	2.0	--	--	--
	Bravo del Norte (Grande)	R Grande at Brownsville	g 94-96	--	388	4.0	3	2.0	2.0	2.0	--	--	--
AFRICA													
Ghana	W Gulf of Guinea	R Pra at Daboase	g 94 TSS & HM g 91-93	66	12	428.0	55	--	--	--	--	37.00	--
	Volta	R Volta at B Kpong	g 94-95 HM g 91-93	5	0	--	143	--	43.0	--	--	--	--
		R White Volta at Nawuni	g 94-95 HM g 91-93	185	16	--	133	--	--	--	--	--	--
Mali	Niger	R Niger at Bamako	g 94-96	--	40	--	--	--	--	--	--	--	--
		R Niger at Koulikoro (06)	g 94-96	--	24	--	--	--	--	--	--	--	--
	Groundwater	G forage Bamako (05)	g 94-96	--	1	--	--	--	--	--	--	--	--
		G forage Nossombougou (8)	g 96	--	10	--	--	--	--	--	--	--	--
Morocco	SW Mediterranean	R Moulouya	g 94-96	25	5967	--	18	6.0	9.0	89.0	72.0	1.00	5.426
	U subtropical NE Atlantic	R Sebou at Kenitra	g 94-96	200	19000	6.0	55	4.0	16.0	129.0	62.0	2.00	0.208
		R Bou Regreg at Barrage Sidi Mohamed Ben Abdella	g 94-96	21	259	7.0	27	2.0	11.0	--	9.0	1.00	--
		R er Rbia at Sidi Daoui	g 94-96	50	81000	5.0	37	5.0	11.0	54.0	51.0	2.00	0.619
	Groundwater	G puits artesien Ire 4/125	g 94-96	--	0	--	63	2.0	--	--	--	--	--
		G puits Mamora Ire 442/13	g 94-96	--	0	1.0	24	1.0	4.0	--	3.0	1.00	--
Namibia	Orange	R Orange mouth	a 90	1111	--	--	--	--	--	--	--	--	--
Senegal	Senegal	R Senegal at St Louis	g 95 Fcoli = Fstrep	--	200	--	--	--	--	--	--	--	--
		R Senegal at Podor	g 95	--	1800	--	--	--	--	--	--	--	--
South Africa	Orange	R Orange mouth	a 90	1111	--	--	--	--	--	--	--	--	--
Sudan	Nile	R Blue Nile at Khartoum	g 91-92	1106	--	--	--	--	--	--	--	--	--
		R White Nile at Jebel Aulia	g 91-92	77	--	--	--	--	--	--	--	--	--
Tanzania	U intertropical W Indian	R Ruvu at Mlandizi	g 92-93	--	17	--	--	--	--	--	--	--	--
EUROPE													
Austria	Danube	R Danube df	o 95-97	--	--	--	--	0.4	2.4	--	1.0	0.01	--
		R Inn df	o 95-97	--	--	--	--	0.8	2.6	--	1.3	0.01	--
Belgium	Rhine	R Meuse df 94-96	o 94-96	--	--	--	--	--	2.1	--	3.2	--	--
		R Meuse at Lanaye/Ternaaien	g 91-92	10	14023	3.0	77	8.0	18.0	6.0	7.0	1.00	0.045
	SE North Sea	R Schelde (Escaut) df	o 94-96	--	--	--	--	2.4	12.0	--	7.2	0.39	--
		R Schelde at Doel	g 91	52	1069	7.0	68	10.0	16.0	8.0	6.0	1.00	0.000
Czech R	Oder	R Oder (Odra) df	o 95-97	--	--	--	--	7.3	8.3	--	14.1	2.55	--
	German Bight	R Elbe (Labe) df	o 95-97	--	--	--	--	2.6	9.5	--	2.4	0.27	--
	Danube	R Morava df	o 95-97	--	--	--	--	3.2	3.9	--	3.4	2.09	--
Finland	Gulf of Bothnia	R Tornionjoki (14100)	g 94-96	4	--								
		R Kokernaenjoki mouth	o 95-97	--	--	--	--	1.8	28.4	--	1.0	0.10	--
	N Gulf of Finland	R Kalkkinen (4800)	g 94-96	1	--	--	--	--	--	--	--	--	0.013
		R Kymijoki (5610)	g 94-96	5	--	--	--	--	--	--	--	--	0.011
France	La Manche	R Seine at Paris	g 91-93	39	140000	5.0	96	3.0	11.0	5.0	6.0	1.00	0.200
	Loire	R Loire mouth	o 94-96	--	--	--	--	--	--	--	--	0.40	--
		R Loire at Ingrandes	g 94 Fcoli g 91-93	41	4012	5.0	64	3.0	13.0	--	3.0	318.00	0.246
	Bay of Biscay	R Garonne mouth	o 94-96	--	--	--	--	2.9	5.3	--	1.5	0.27	--
		R Garonne at Valence d'Agen	g 94-95	27	--	--	14	1.0	12.0	--	2.0	--	0.000
	N Mediterranean	R Rhône mouth	a 90 HM o 94	626	--	--	--	--	10.0	--	--	0.14	--
		R Rhône at St Vallier	g 94 Fcoli g 91-93	19	3785	10.0	50	10.0	10.0	10.0	10.0	144.00	0.083
Germany	German Bight	R Elbe mouth	a 90 HM o 95	37	--	--	--	1.0	2.1	--	--	0.39	--
		R Elbe at Geesthacht	g 88-90	21	1953	--	--	--	--	--	--	14.00	0.465
		R Weser mouth	o 95-97 TSS a 90	31	--	--	--	2.0	4.9	--	4.3	0.20	--

Country	Basin	Station	Sources & years	TSS mg/l	F coli/ 100 ml	As µg/l	Zn µg/l	Cr µg/l	Cu µg/l	Ni µg/l	Pb µg/l	Cd µg/l	Hg µg/l
		R Weser at Intschede	g 88-90 Fcoli = tot coli ÷ 10	--	1205	--	--	--	--	--	--	1.00	0.041
	Rhine	R Rhine df	o 95-97	--	--	--	--	3.2	7.7	--	3.2	0.20	--
		R Rhine at Kleve/Bimmen	g 88-90	--	3592	2.0	1154	9.0	11.0	7.0	8.0	--	0.130
		R Rhine at Koblenz	g 88-90	--	--	2.0	--	4.0	7.0	5.0	6.0	--	0.968
		R Moselle at Koblenz	g 88-90	--	--	2.0	34	4.0	5.0	5.0	7.0	--	0.251
	Danube	R Danube df	o 95-97	--	--	--	--	1.0	3.4	--	1.4	--	--
		R Danube at Jochenstein	g 88-90	--	769	--	--	--	--	--	--	--	0.176
Greece	Ionian	R Akeloos mouth	o 93-95	--	--	--	--	--	--	--	--	0.20	--
	Aegean	R Axios mouth	o 93-95	--	--	--	--	--	--	--	--	0.23	--
		R Strimonas mouth	o 93-95	--	--	--	--	--	--	--	--	0.23	--
Hungary	Danube	R Danube df	o 93-95 HM o 95	--	--	--	--	8.6	14.7	--	12.0	2.00	--
		R Danube at Budapest	g 91-92	--	3346	--	--	5.0	--	--	14.0	1.00	--
		R Tisza at Szolnok	g 91-92	42	47	--	77	--	22.0	--	10.0	--	0.357
	Groundwater	G deep well Pest County	g 91	--	0								
Italy	Ligurian & Tyrrhenian	R Arno mouth	o 93-95 HM o 92-94	--	--	--	--	--	--	--	--	0.32	--
	Adriatic	R Adige mouth	o 94-96 HM o 92-94	--	--	--	--	--	--	--	--	1.00	--
		R Po mouth	a 90	278	--	--	--	--	--	--	--	--	--
Lithuania	Groundwater	G Juodkrante	g 94-96	--	--	--	78	--	2.0	1.0	1.0		--
		G Marijanpole	g 94-96	--	--	--	154	--	19.0	1.0	2.0	--	--
		G Panevezys	g 94-96	--	--	--	467	--	1.0	1.0	1.0	--	--
		G Varena	g 94-96	--	--	--	56	--	3.0	1.0	1.0	--	--
Luxembourg	Rhine	R Sûre df	o 93-95 Pb o 95	--	--	--	--	1.3	3.0	--	6.0	0.12	--
Netherlands	Rhine	L Ijsselmeer	g 94-95 Fcoli g 91-93	34	16	--	16	3.0	3.0	3.0	2.0	--	0.020
		R Rhine Ijssel arm	g 94-95 Fcoli g 91-93	25	111	--	39	3.0	5.0	3.0	3.0	--	0.026
		R Rhine Ijssel-Kampen	o 94-96	--	--	--	--	2.8	5.3	--	3.0	0.09	--
		R Rijn/Maas delta	o 94-96	--	--	--	--	2.9	3.4	--	2.4	0.23	--
Norway	Norwegian Sea	R Altaelva at Alta	g 91-93	--	--	--	2	--	2.0	--	--	--	0.002
		R Vefsna at Mosjøen	g 91-93	--	--	--	4	--	2.0	--	--	--	0.002
		R Orkla at Vormstad	g 91-93	--	--	--	27	--	12.0	--	--	--	0.002
		R Suldalslaagen at Sand	g 91-93	--	--	--	3	--	--	--	--	--	0.002
	N Skagerrak & E Kattegat	R Otra mouth	o 95-97	--	--	--	--	0.5	0.6		0.3	0.03	--
		R Skienselva mouth	o 95-97	--	--	--	--	0.5	1.5		0.1	0.03	--
		R Numedalslaagen at Bommestad	g 91-93	--	--	--	18	--	5.0	--	1.0	--	0.002
		R Drammenselva mouth	o 95-97	--	--	--	--	0.5	1.0		0.2	0.02	--
		R Glåma mouth	o 95-97	--	--	--	--	0.5	2.3		0.7	0.05	--
Poland	Wisla	R Wisla mouth	o 95-97 TSS a 90	79	--	--	--	0.3	1.4	--	0.9	0.09	--
		R Wisla at Kiezmark	g 94-95	21	17000	--	12	1.0	2.0	2.0	2.0	--	0.154
		R Wisla at Warszawa	g 94-95	33	6000	--	68	3.0	8.0	6.0	8.0	1.00	0.400
		R Wisla at Krakow	g 94-95	28	34000	--	305	5.0	24.0	41.0	34.0	7.00	0.699
	Oder	R Oder mouth	o 95-97	--	--	--	--	0.4	3.0	--	1.7	0.11	--
		R Oder (Odra) at Krajnik	g 94-95	23	32000	--	23	1.0	4.0	3.0	3.0	--	0.200
		R Oder (Odra) at Wroclaw	g 94-95	26	50000	--	102	7.0	5.0	15.0	10.0	4.00	0.358
		R Oder (Odra) at Chalupki	g 94-95	22	110000	--	234	7.0	6.0	15.0	7.0	4.00	0.356
	Groundwater	G Pomeranian Lake District	g 94-95	--		--	255	--	--		--	--	--
Portugal	L temperate NE Atlantic	R Tejo at Santarem	g 91-92	12	1258	26.0	29	8.0	13.0	--	--	--	0.139
	U subtropical NE Atlantic	R Guadiana mouth	o 92-93	--	--	--	--	--	--	--	--	1.90	--
Slovakia	Danube	R Maly Dunaj (Danube) df	o 95-97	--	--	--	--	0.6	7.8	--	1.8	0.03	--
		R Hornad df	o 95-97	--	--	--	--	3.1	--	--	9.7	1.54	--
		R Vah mouth	o 95-97	--	--	--	--	0.7	2.1	--	0.9	0.08	--
Spain	L temperate NE Atlantic	R Duero df	o 95-97	--	--	--	--	0.0	0.2	--	--	0.70	--
	U subtropical NE Atlantic	R Guadalquivir mouth	o 94-96	--	--	--	--	4.5	4.4	--	2.6	1.40	--

Country	Basin	Station	Sources & years	TSS mg/l	F coli/ 100 ml	As µg/l	Zn µg/l	Cr µg/l	Cu µg/l	Ni µg/l	Pb µg/l	Cd µg/l	Hg µg/l
	NW Mediterranean	R Ebro mouth	o 95-97 TSS a 90	86	--	--	--	0.6	1.8	--	0.6	0.11	--
Sweden	N Baltic	R Mörrumsan mouth	o 95-97	--	--	--	--	0.4	1.5	--	0.4	0.01	--
		R Ronneaan mouth	o 95-97	--	--	--	--	0.6	1.4	--	0.3	0.02	--
	Gulf of Bothnia	R Dalalven mouth	o 95-97	--	--	--	--	0.3	1.4	--	0.4	0.02	--
		R Rane mouth	o 95-97	--	--	--	--	0.1	1.4	--	0.2	0.01	--
Switzerland	Rhine	R Rhine at Basel	g 94-96	17	--	--	6	1.0	1.0	1.0	1.0	--	0.012
		R Rhine at Diepoldsau	g 94-96 HM g 91-93	119	--	--	--	49.0	--	--	--	--	--
		R Aare at Brugg	g 94-96 HM g 91-93	19	--	--	8	--	2.0	--	1.0	--	--
	N Mediterranean	R Rhone at Chancy	g 94-96 HM g 91-93	29	--	--	--	38.0	--	--	--	--	--
		R Rhone at Porte du Scex	g 94-96	119	--	--	11	--	3.0	--	3.0	--	0.019
United Kingdom	W North Sea	R Leven	g 94-96	3	--	--	4	1.0	1.0	1.0	2.0	--	--
		R Tweed above Galafoot	g 94-96	5	--	--	2	1.0	4.0	1.0	1.0	--	--
		R Trent at Nottingham	g 94-96	18	--	2.0	47	4.0	10.0	27.0	7.0	--	0.035
		R Thames at London	g 94-96	14	--	1.0	22	2.0	6.0	5.0	3.0	--	0.016
	English Channel	R Exe at Exeter	g 94-96	10	--	1.0	8	1.0	2.0	4.0	1.0	--	0.016
	Celtic Sea	R Severn mouth	o 94-96	--	--	--	--	2.1	5.3	--	4.3	0.13	--
		R Avon at Bristol	g 94-96	21	--	--	28	2.0	5.0	7.0	8.0	1.00	0.036
	Irish Sea	R Dee	g 94-96	11	--	2.0	16	2.0	2.0	4.0	3.0	--	0.013
		R Mersey	g 94-96	11	--	2.0	27	5.0	7.0	8.0	5.0	--	0.088
		R Clyde mouth	o 94-96	--	--	--	--	17.0	6.1	--	7.3	0.50	--
	Scottish & Irish Atlantic	R Carron	g 94-96	1	--	--	4	1.0	1.0	2.0	2.0	1.00	0.030
		Lower Bann mouth	o 95-97	--	--	--	--	1.0	3.3	--	0.5	0.10	--
RUSSIAN FEDERATION	Volga	R Volga at Narimanov	g 94	18	--	--	36	--	--	--	--	--	--
		R Volga at B Cheboksarskoye (201)	g 94	14	--	--	14	--	--	--	--	--	--
		R Belaya at Ufa (203)	g 94	80	--	--	8	--	--	--	--	--	0.008
	Severnaya Dvina	R Severnaya Dvina at Ust-Pinega (213)	g 94	8	--	--	8	--	--	--	--	--	--
	White Sea	R Mezen at Borovo	g 94	4	--	--	8	--	--	--	--	--	--
	E Barents Sea	R Pechora at Nar'jan-Mar	g 94	6	--	--	10	--	--	--	--	--	--
	Ob	R Ob at Salehard (011)	g 94	9	--	--	41	--	--	--	--	--	--
		R Tom at Tomsk (204)	g 94	18	--	--	--	--	--	--	--	--	0.104
		R Irtysh at Krasnyi Jar (205)	g 94	16	--	--	21	--	--	--	--	--	--
	Yenisey	R Yenisei at Igarka (210)	g 94	2	--	--	65	--	--	--	--	--	--
		L Baikal mid-lake (024)	g 91-93	0	--	--	9	--	--	--	--	--	0.018
		R Selenga mouth	g 94	33	--	--	2	--	--	--	1.0	--	--
	Lena	R Lena delta (028)	g 94	35	--	--	7	--	--	--	--	--	--
	Kolyma	R Kolyma at Kolymskoe	g 94	21	--	--	9	--	--	--	--	--	--
	Neva	L Onezhskoye (Onega)	g 94	0	--	--	14	--	--	--	1.0	--	--
	Don	R Don at Bagaevskij	g 94	137	--	--	9	--	--	--	--	--	--
	Azov Sea	R Kuban mouth	g 94	44	--	--	10	--	--	--	--	--	--
	Amur	R Amur mouth	g 94	18	--	--	13	--	--	--	--	--	--
ASIA													
Bangladesh	Ganges	R Meghna at Ashuganj	g 94-95 Fcoli = tot coli. ÷ 10	39	76	--	--	--	--	--	--	--	--
		R Padma at Bheramara	g 94-95 Fcoli = tot coli ÷ 10	212	80	--	--	--	--	--	--	--	--
		R Brahmaputra at Fulchhari	g 94-95 Fcoli = tot coli ÷ 10	34	67	--	--	--	--	--	--	--	--
	NE Bay of Bengal	R Karnaphuli at Rangunia	g 95	54	--	--	--	--	--	--	--	--	--
		L Kaptai at Kaptai	g 94-95 Fcoli = tot coli ÷ 10	25	56	--	--	--	--	--	--	--	--
	Groundwater	G tube well (07)	g 94-95	56	0	--	--	--	--	--	--	--	--
		G tube well (09)	g 94-95	21	0								
China	Bo Hai	R Huang (Yellow) at Jinan	g 94-96	8470	45000	9.0	50	6.0	1.0	--	1.0	--	--
	Chang	R Chang (Yangtze) at Wuhan	g 94-96	140	161	--	25	--	4.0	--	19.0	2.00	--
		L Tai	g 94-96	--	6	2.0	31	8.0	3.0	--	1.0	--	--
	Xi	R Xi (Pearl) at Zhaoqing	g 94-96	65	650	9.0	42	1.0	8.0	--	2.0	--	0.078

221

Country	Basin	Station	Sources & years	TSS mg/l	F coli/ 100 ml	As µg/l	Zn µg/l	Cr µg/l	Cu µg/l	Ni µg/l	Pb µg/l	Cd µg/l	Hg µg/l
	Chinese South China Sea	L Plover Cove (19), Hong Kong	g 94-96	--	5	--	--	--	--	--	--	--	--
India	Gulfs of Kachchh & Khambhat	R Sabarmati at Ahmedabad	g 95-96	--	380000	--	--	--	--	--	--	--	--
		R Mahi at Vasad	g 95-96	--	82	--	--	--	--	--	--	--	--
		R Narmada near Garudeshwar	g 95-96	--	177	--	--	--	--	--	--	--	--
		R Tapti near Burhanpur	g 95-96	0	20	--	--	--	--	--	--	--	--
	Malabar Coast	R Chaliyar at Kalpalli	g 95-96	--	1239	--	--	--	--	--	--	--	--
		R Periyar near Alwaye	g 95-96	--	1062	--	--	--	--	--	--	--	--
		R Kallada at Panamthottam	g 95-96	--	2331	--	--	--	--	--	--	--	--
	Coromandel Coast	R Cauvery near Musiri	g 95-96	0	2535	--	--	--	--	--	--	--	--
		R Pennar near Nellore	g 95-96	0	--	--	--	--	--	--	--	--	--
	Krishna	R Krishna near Vijayawada	g 95-96	0	89	--	--	--	--	--	--	--	--
		R Krishna at Gadwal	g 95-96	0	0	--	--	--	--	--	--	--	--
		R Tungabhadra at Ullanuru	g 95-96	0	918	--	--	--	--	--	--	--	--
		R Bhima near Takali	g 95-96	--	11	--	--	--	--	--	--	--	--
	Godavari	R Godavari near Polavaram	g 95-96	0	0	--	--	--	--	--	--	--	--
		R Godavari near Mancheral	g 95-96	0	0	--	--	--	--	--	--	--	--
		R Wainganga near Ashti	g 95-96	--	7	--	--	--	--	--	--	--	--
	NW Bay of Bengal	R Mahanadi mouth	a 90	909	--	--	--	--	--	--	--	--	--
		R Subarnarekha at Jamshedpur	g 95-96	--	708	--	--	--	--	--	--	--	--
	Ganges	R Ganga df	a 90	1130	--	--	--	--	--	--	--	--	--
	Groundwater	G well Ahmedabad	g 95-96	--	3	--	--	--	--	--	--	--	--
		G well Baroda	g 95	--	3	--	--	--	--	--	--	--	--
		G well Kalpalli	g 95-96	--	1379	--	--	--	--	--	--	--	--
		G well Eluru (Alwaye)	g 95-96	--	526	--	--	--	--	--	--	--	--
		G well Musiri	g 95-96	0	815	--	--	--	--	--	--	--	--
		G well Vijayawada	g 95-96	--	97	--	--	--	--	--	--	--	--
Indonesia	U intertropical E Indian (Java)	R Garang	g 91-93	97	280000	--	67	48.0	--	15.0	--	--	--
		R Garang	g 94	--	--	--	--	--	20.0	--	--	--	--
	Java Sea & Karimata Strait (Sumatra)	R Musi at Palembang	g 91-93	77	4327	--	211	30.0	22.0	--	--	10.00	--
	Java Sea (Java)	R Banjir Kanal	g 91-93	105	740000	--	154	30.0	22.0	--	66.0	6.00	--
		R Banjir Kanal	g 94	58	--	--	253	--	31.0	11.0	--	--	--
		R Sunter	g 91-93	125	850000	--	295	31.0	27.0	16.0	74.0	10.00	--
		R Sunter	g 94	288	--	--	202	--	43.0	112.0	--	13.00	--
		R Citarum	g 91-93	215	570000	--	113	28.0	46.0	35.0	128.0	12.00	--
		R Citarum	g 94	236	--	--	3	50.0	--	--	--	18.00	--
		R Surabaya	g 91-93	297	78000	--	87	--	29.0	--	99.0	8.00	--
		B Saguling	g 91-93	54	12000	--	135	28.0	25.0	--	112.0	9.00	--
		B Saguling	g 94	282	--	--	--	--	--	--	--	--	--
	Groundwater (Java)	G well Senayan Jakarta	g 91-93	23	--	--	156	--	--	--	--	--	--
		G well Pulogadung Jakarta	g 91-93	13	--	--	504	--	--	--	--	--	--
		G well Cibeureum	g 91-93	5	0	--	194	--	18.0	--	194.0	11.00	--
Iran	Shatt-al-Arab	Shatt-al-Arab mouth	a 90	1364	--	--	--	--	--	--	--	--	--
	Groundwater	G well 7 Tabriz	g 91-92	0	0	--	--	--	--	--	--	--	--
Iraq	Shatt-al-Arab	Shatt-al-Arab mouth	a 90	1364	--	--	--	--	--	--	--	--	--
Japan	L temperate NW Pacific (Honshu)	R Kyu-Kitakami at Kanomata	g 92-93	19	91	--	15	4.0	--	10.0	--	--	--
		R Tone at Tone-Ozeki	g 94-96	21	1993	4.0	21	--	6.0	8.0	5.0	5.00	--
		R Sagami at Samukawa	g 94-96	145	1086	--	5	--	--	--	--	--	0.000
		R Kiso at Inuyama	g 94-96	4	225	1.0	9	1.0	1.0	1.0	1.0	--	--
	U subtropical NW Pacific (Honshu)	L Biwa south center	g 94-96	10	1	--	--	--	--	--	--	--	--
		R Yodo at Hirakata Bridge	g 91-92 Fcoli = tot coli ÷ 10	19	2279	--	13	--	10.0	--	--	--	--
	U subtropical NW Pacific (Shikoku)	R Yoshino at Takase	g 94-96	3	54	--	5	--	--	--	--	--	--
	U subtropical NW Pacific (Kyushu)	R Chikugo at Senoshita	g 94-96	11	217								
		R Kuma at Yokoishi	g 94-95	5	103	--	8	--	--	--	--	--	--
	E Sea of Japan (Honshu)	R Shinano at Kyuzogoya	g 94-95	26	200	--	10	1.0	4.0	--	6.0	--	--

Country	Basin	Station	Sources & years	TSS mg/l	F coli/ 100 ml	As µg/l	Zn µg/l	Cr µg/l	Cu µg/l	Ni µg/l	Pb µg/l	Cd µg/l	Hg µg/l
	E Sea of Japan (Hokkaido)	R Ishikari at Ishikari	g 94-96 Fcoli = tot coli ÷ 10	34	904	1.0	6	551.0	--	--	1.0	--	--
	Groundwater (Honshu)	G Suginami filtration plant	g 94-96	1	1	--	6	--	--	--	--	--	--
Jordan	Rift Valley	R Zarqua at King Talal Dam	g 94-96	60	1858	--	24	26.0	13.0	7.0	87.0	14.00	--
	Groundwater	G Awajan well 23	g 96	--	1	--	18	17.0	8.0	--	1.0	--	--
		G Azraq well 2	g 95-96	--	2	--	4	1.0	--	29.0	6.0	--	--
		G Rahme well Wadi Araba	g 94-96	120	2	--	65	16.0	7.0	--	2.0	--	--
Kazakhstan	Aral Sea	R Syr Darya mouth	a 90	1364	--	--	--	--	--	--	--	--	--
Korea, R	E Yellow Sea	R Han GEMS	g 94-96	5	260	--	9	--	9.0	--	--	--	--
Malaysia	Strait of Malacca	R Klang	g 92	311	430000	24.0	41	17.0	--	--	28.0	10.00	0.002
		R Linggi	g 92	420	160000	12.0	24	36.0	--	--	41.0	10.00	0.002
		R Sekudai	g 92	163	120000	1.0	91	--	214.0	--	60.0	--	0.001
Myanmar	Irrawaddy	R Irrawaddy	a 90	607	--	--	--	--	--	--	--	--	--
Pakistan	Indus	R Indus at Kotri	g 94-96	3417	2216	--	--	257.0	167.0	--	--	--	--
		R Ravi below Lahore	g 94-96	304	12144	--	--	--	--	--	--	--	--
		R Ravi above Lahore	g 94-96	348	19000	--	--	13.0	--	--	--	--	--
		R Chenab Gujra branch	g 94-96	467	16000	--	--	--	--	--	--	--	--
	Groundwater	G Lahore	g 94-96	1	0	--	--	--	--	--	--	--	--
Philippines	Philippine South China Sea (Luzon)	B La Mesa	g 94-95	7	659	--	--	--	--	--	--	--	--
	L subtropical NW Pacific	R Cagayan	g 94-96 Fcoli = tot coli ÷ 10	68	540	--	--	--	--	--	--	--	--
Thailand	Chao Phraya	R Chao Phraya at Bangkok	g 91-93	--	230000	--	175	38.0	23.0	--	53.0	4.00	0.416
		R Chao Phraya below Nakhon Sawan	g 91-93	--	54000	--	157	8.0	5.0	--	16.0	1.00	0.217
		R Prasak at Kaeng Khoi	g 91-92	--	12980	--	152	9.0	10.0	--	25.0	1.00	0.000
	E Gulf of Thailand	R Bang at Pa Kong	g 91-93	--	18000	--	206	67.0	23.0	--	115.0	10.00	0.192
	Mekong	R Mun at Ubon Ratchathani	g 91-93	--	2067	--	92	3.0	13.0	--	20.0	--	0.400
Turkey	S Black Sea	R Yesilirmak mouth	o 95-97 HM o 95	--	--	--	--	--	7.0	--	--	--	--
		R Sakarya mouth	o 95-97	--	--	--	--	3.3	12.3	--	10.3	3.33	--
	Aegean	R Gediz mouth	o 95-97 HM o 95	--	--	--	--	5.0	--	--	12.0	--	--
Uzbekistan	Aral Sea	R Amu Darya mouth	a 90	3275	--	--	--	--	--	--	--	--	--
Viet Nam	Gulf of Tonkin	R Hong (Red) mouth	a 90	1057	--	--	--	--	--	--	--	--	--
	Mekong	R Mekong mouth	a 90	294	--	--	--	--	--	--	--	--	--
PACIFIC													
Australia	Murray-Darling	R Murray-Darling mouth Atlas	a 90	3797	--	--	--	--	5.0	6.3	--	2.5	--
	W Coral Sea	R Burdekin mouth	a 90	355	--	--	--	--	--	--	--	--	--
Papua New Guinea	Bismarck & Solomon Seas	R Sepik mouth	a 90	68	--	--	--	--	--	--	--	--	--
	N Coral Sea	R Fly mouth	a 90	816	--	--	--	--	--	--	--	--	--

Notes

This table gives data on suspended solids, microbial pollution, and arsenic and heavy metals. Countries use different methods for measuring pollutants, so the data are not strictly comparable. All data are annual mean values at the location indicated in the Station column. Data are for the years indicated in the Sources & years column.

Basin = drainage basin. Surface water basins are defined in Appendix 6. Groundwater is treated as if it were a single basin. Parts of basin names are abbreviated as follows: E = east; L = lower; N = north; S = south; U = upper; W = west.

Station = monitoring station (the point where the data are collected).

Sources & years = data sources, applicable years, and exceptions. Sources are indicated as follows:

a   National Water Research Institute (1996)

e   Eurostat *et al.* (1995)

g   Global Environmental Monitoring System (GEMS)/WATER data summaries and database (UNEP & WHO GEMS/Water Collaborating Centre 1988-1990, 1991-1993, 1999)

o   Organisation for Economic Co-operation and Development (1997 & 1999)

oc   OECD Centre for Co-operation with the Economies in Transition (1996)

When a single year is given, all data are for that year (unless otherwise noted in the Sources column). When a period is given (e.g., 94-96), all data are annual averages for that period (unless otherwise noted in the Sources column). If data for one of the indicators are for a different year, the indicator, source and year are noted after the indicator code. For example—o 95-97 TSS a 90—means that data are from OECD and are for 1995-1997, except for total suspended solids (TSS) which are from National Water Research Institute and are for 1990. The codes used are: F coli = fecal coliforms; HM = arsenic and heavy metals; Pb = lead; TSS = total suspended solids.

TSS = total suspended solids in milligrams per liter (mg/l).

F coli = microbial pollution, measured by the mean number of fecal coliforms per 100 milliliters (ml). Where fecal streptococci are measured instead (indicated in the Sources & years column), they are treated as equivalent to fecal coliforms. Where total coliforms are measured instead (also indicated in the Sources & years column), the number has been divided by 10 to approximate an equivalent level of fecal coliforms.

As = arsenic in micrograms per liter (μg/l).

Zn = zinc in micrograms per liter (μg/l).

Cr = chromium in micrograms per liter (μg/l).

Cu = copper in micrograms per liter (μg/l).

Ni = nickel in micrograms per liter (μg/l).

Pb = lead in micrograms per liter (μg/l).

Cd = cadmium in micrograms per liter (μg/l).

Hg = mercury in micrograms per liter (μg/l).

GEMS/WATER data on arsenic and on heavy metals except mercury, originally recorded in milligrams, were converted to micrograms. Since data recorded as 0.000 mg may mask quite high levels in micrograms (e.g., 0.5 μg of cadmium), they were treated as null values (--).

Cadmium values for the Loire in France reported to GEMS/WATER are much higher than for other stations in France, and much higher than the values reported to OECD. They have been excluded from the score for the Loire (Table 15).

Table 17. Air Index; Global Atmosphere

Country	CO₂ 000 mt C	CO₂/ha kg C	CO₂/p kg C	GG score	ODS year	ODS mt odp	ODS/ha g odp	ODS/p g odp	ODS score	*GA score*	*LA score*	Air index
AMERICAS												
Antigua & Barbuda	92	2091	1384	45	98	27	613.6	403.9	0	0	--	0
Argentina	37629	135	1055	54	98	1894	6.8	52.4	59	54	47	47
Bahamas	475	342	1633	40	98	60	43.2	202.6	20	20	--	20
Barbados	245	5698	918	57	98	25	581.4	93.2	43	43	--	43
Belize	106	46	473	76	97	5	2.2	22.3	82	76	--	76
Bolivia	2952	27	380	81	97	47	0.4	6	95	81	--	80*
Brazil	78666	92	481	76	97	10315	12.1	63	55	55	51	51
Canada	133890	134	4425	12	98	989	1	32.4	74	12	65	12
Chile	15884	210	1086	53	98	1090	14.4	73.5	51	51	23	23
Colombia	18551	163	463	77	98	1262	11.1	30.9	75	75	--	75
Costa Rica	1355	265	362	82	98	344	67.3	89.5	44	44	40	40
Cuba	6854	618	619	69	97	685	61.8	61.9	55	55	60	55
Dominica	22	293	311	84	97	2	26.7	28.2	77	77	--	77
Dominican R	3609	741	446	78	98	509	104.5	61.8	55	55	--	55
Ecuador	5549	196	465	77	98	369	13	30.3	76	76	47	47
El Salvador	1489	708	252	87	98	199	94.6	33	74	74	--	74
Grenada	50	1471	539	73	--	--	--	--	--	73	--	73
Guatemala	2097	193	199	90	97	382	35.1	36.3	71	71	33	33
Guyana	279	13	331	83	98	30	1.4	35.3	72	72	--	72
Haiti	379	137	48	98	--	--	--	--	--	80*	--	80
Honduras	1129	101	189	90	98	116	10.3	18.9	85	85	35	35
Jamaica	2928	2664	1164	51	98	222	202	87.5	45	45	--	45
Mexico	99893	510	1060	53	P98	5491	28	57.3	57	53	17	17
Nicaragua	831	64	178	91	98	41	3.2	8.5	93	91	18	18
Panama	2089	277	767	62	98	361	47.8	130.5	34	34	25	25
Paraguay	1041	26	205	90	98	113	2.8	21.6	83	83	--	80*
Peru	7818	61	321	84	98	337	2.6	13.6	89	84	--	80*
St Kitts & Nevis	28	1077	712	64	97	4	153.8	101.7	40	40	--	40
St Lucia	54	871	364	82	98	6	96.8	39.9	68	68	--	68
St Vincent & Grenadines	36	923	323	84	98	2	51.3	17.8	86	84	--	80*
Suriname	576	35	1398	45	--	--	--	--	--	45	--	45
Trinidad & Tobago	5995	11686	4695	11	98	215	419.1	167.6	26	11	--	11
United States	1480881	1582	5449	6	P98	32228	34.4	117.6	36	6	53	6
Uruguay	1469	83	450	77	98	218	12.3	66.3	53	53	--	53
Venezuela	51144	561	2245	32	P97	5752	63.1	252.5	15	15	--	15
AFRICA												
Algeria	25974	109	884	58	98	1785	7.5	59.3	56	56	--	56
Angola	1409	11	120	94	--	--	--	--	--	80*	--	80
Benin	203	18	36	98	97	14	1.2	2.5	98	98	--	80*
Botswana	916	16	595	70	97	16	0.3	10.4	92	70	--	70
Burkina Faso	265	10	24	99	98	37	1.4	3.3	97	97	--	80*
Burundi	61	22	10	99	98	64	23	9.9	92	92	--	80*
Cameroon	647	14	46	98	97	286	6	20.5	84	84	--	80*
Cape Verde	33	82	83	96	--	--	--	--	--	80*	--	80
Central African R	66	1	19	99	97	0	0	0	100	99	--	80*
Chad	30	0	4	100	98	38	0.3	5.2	96	96	--	80*
Comoros	18	81	28	99	98	4	17.9	6.1	95	95	--	80*
Congo, DR	637	3	13	99	--	--	--	--	--	80*	--	80
Congo, R	496	15	183	91	95	15	0.4	5.9	95	91	--	80*
Côte d'Ivoire	3568	111	254	87	97	158	4.9	11.2	91	87	--	80*
Djibouti	100	43	162	92	--	--	--	--	--	80*	--	80
Egypt	29829	298	461	77	98	2816	28.1	42.7	66	66	--	66
Equatorial Guinea	167	60	397	80	--	--	--	--	--	80	--	80
Eritrea	--	--	--	--	--	--	--	--	--	--	--	--
Ethiopia	930	8	16	99	98	62	0.6	1	99	99	--	80*
Gabon	909	34	799	60	98	14	0.5	12	90	60	--	60
Gambia	59	52	50	97	98	11	9.7	9	93	93	--	80*
Ghana	1106	46	59	97	98	54	2.3	2.8	98	97	49	49
Guinea	298	12	41	98	98	42	1.7	5.7	95	95	--	80*
Guinea-Bissau	63	17	55	97	--	--	--	--	--	80*	--	80
Kenya	1813	31	64	97	97	534	9.2	18.8	85	85	--	80*
Lesotho	--	--	--	--	98	3	1	1.5	99	80*	--	80
Liberia	91	8	38	98	--	--	--	--	--	80*	--	80
Libyan Arab J	11386	65	2185	33	97	1234	7	236.8	16	16	--	16
Madagascar	328	6	22	99	97	132	2.2	9	93	93	--	80*
Malawi	198	17	20	99	98	184	15.5	17.8	86	86	--	80*
Mali	131	1	13	99	97	115	0.9	11	91	91	--	80*

Country	CO$_2$ 000 mt C	CO$_2$/ha kg C	CO$_2$/p kg C	GG score	ODS year	ODS mt odp	ODS/ha g odp	ODS/p g odp	ODS score	GA score	LA score	Air index
Mauritania	805	8	327	84	97	7	0.1	2.8	98	84	--	80*
Mauritius	465	2279	410	79	98	45	220.6	39.4	68	68	--	68
Morocco	8702	195	324	84	97	1295	29	48.2	61	61	--	61
Mozambique	303	4	16	99	96	43	0.5	2.4	98	98	--	80*
Namibia	--	--	--	--	97	33	0.4	20.3	84	80*	--	80
Niger	302	2	31	98	97	61	0.5	6.2	95	95	--	80*
Nigeria	22435	243	216	89	98	5476	59.3	51.5	59	59	--	59
Rwanda	135	51	23	99	--	--	--	--	--	80*	--	80
São Tomé & Principe	21	219	152	92	--	--	--	--	--	80*	--	80
Senegal	855	43	97	95	98	138	7	15.3	88	88	--	80*
Seychelles	54	1200	720	64	97	2	44.4	26.7	79	64	--	64
Sierra Leone	127	18	29	99	--	--	--	--	--	80*	--	80
Somalia	4	0	0	100	--	--	--	--	--	80*	--	80
South Africa	86532	709	2232	32	98	1022	8.4	26	79	32	42	32
Sudan	988	4	36	98	97	315	1.3	11.4	91	91	--	80*
Swaziland	109	63	118	94	97	18	10.4	19.5	84	84	--	80*
Tanzania	673	7	21	99	97	225	2.4	7.2	94	94	--	80*
Togo	219	39	51	97	95	50	8.8	12.3	90	90	--	80*
Tunisia	4541	278	493	75	98	974	59.5	104.3	39	39	--	39
Uganda	297	12	15	99	98	14	0.6	0.7	99	99	--	80*
Zambia	670	9	78	96	97	63	0.8	7.3	94	94	--	80*
Zimbabwe	4968	127	443	78	97	1051	26.9	93.7	42	42	--	42
EUROPE												
Albania	432	150	138	93	--	--	--	--	--	80*	--	80
Austria	16557	1974	2044	34	98	454	54.1	55.8	58	34	66	34
Belarus	16757	807	1619	40	98	268	12.9	26	79	40	58	40
Belgium	28127	9216	2778	25	98	565	185.1	55.7	58	25	58	25
Bosnia & Herzegovina	1211	237	344	83	91	145	28.4	33.1	73	73	--	73
Bulgaria	13452	1213	1603	40	98	39	3.5	4.7	96	40	28	28
Croatia	5190	918	1157	51	97	121	21.4	27	78	51	59	51
Czech R	33495	4247	3252	20	97	19	2.4	1.8	99	20	58	20
Denmark	15380	3569	2926	23	98	294	68.2	55.8	58	23	62	23
Estonia	5151	1142	3559	18	98	57	12.6	39.9	68	18	--	18
Finland	15307	453	2977	23	98	287	8.5	55.7	58	23	66	23
France	92878	1684	1588	40	P98	9184	166.5	156.5	29	29	55	29
Germany	227364	6369	2771	25	98	4573	128.1	55.7	58	25	61	25
Greece	22027	1669	2084	34	P98	1277	96.8	120.5	36	34	43	34
Hungary	15874	1706	1563	41	98	123	13.2	12.2	90	41	59	41
Iceland	572	56	2091	34	98	7	0.7	25.4	80	34	69	34
Ireland	9936	1414	2717	26	98	205	29.2	55.7	58	26	60	26
Italy	111323	3695	1940	36	P97	8004	265.7	139.5	32	32	27	27
Latvia	2224	344	904	57	97	43	6.7	17.5	86	57	--	57
Lithuania	4027	618	1087	53	98	111	17	30.1	76	53	52	52
Luxembourg	2154	8381	5164	8	98	23	89.5	54.5	58	8	60	8
Macedonia, FYR	2917	1135	1468	43	98	80	31.1	40	68	43	--	43
Malta	480	15000	1259	48	98	144	4500	375.3	2	2	--	2
Moldova	2835	841	648	68	98	40	11.9	9.1	93	68	--	68
Netherlands	44256	10836	2834	25	P98	17082	4182.7	1089.5	0	0	57	0
Norway	18470	570	4202	14	98	52	1.6	11.8	91	14	58	14
Poland	95413	2952	2466	29	97	443	13.7	11.4	91	29	63	29
Portugal	13522	1470	1371	46	98	550	59.8	55.7	58	46	50	46
Romania	29390	1233	1303	47	98	2670	112	118.8	36	36	43	36
Slovakia	10046	2050	1870	37	97	10	2	1.9	98	37	65	37
Slovenia	4109	2029	2059	34	97	9	4.4	4.5	96	34	--	34
Spain	66584	1316	1681	39	P97	7354	145.3	185.6	23	23	51	23
Sweden	12945	288	1462	43	98	495	11	55.8	58	43	73	43
Switzerland	11102	2689	1531	42	97	8	1.9	1.1	99	42	63	42
Ukraine	100427	1664	1967	35	98	3949	65.4	77.6	49	35	--	35
United Kingdom	142096	5821	2427	30	P98	4630	189.7	78.9	48	30	55	30
Yugoslavia	13416	1313	1262	48	91	1142	111.8	108.8	38	38	--	38
RUSSIAN FEDERATION	390616	229	2645	27	P97	15848	9.3	107.3	38	27	48	27
ASIA												
Afghanistan	299	5	14	99	--	--	--	--	--	80*	--	80
Armenia	758	254	213	89	--	--	--	--	--	80*	--	80
Azerbaijan	8693	1004	1138	51	97	228	26.3	29.8	76	51	--	51
Bahrain	4052	58725	6956	0	98	22	318.8	37	70	0	--	0
Bangladesh	6683	464	54	97	97	841	58.4	6.9	94	94	--	80*
Bhutan	107	23	55	97	--	--	--	--	--	80*	--	80
Brunei Darussalam	1475	2561	4783	10	98	65	112.8	206.3	19	10	--	10
Cambodia	140	8	13	99	--	--	--	--	--	80*	--	80

226

Country	CO₂ 000 mt C	CO₂/ha kg C	CO₂/p kg C	GG score	ODS year	ODS mt odp	ODS/ha g odp	ODS/p g odp	ODS score	*GA score*	*LA score*	Air index
China	917997	956	734	63	P97	98053	102.2	78.4	49	49	22	22
Cyprus	1489	1610	1951	36	98	207	223.8	268.4	13	13	--	13
Georgia	1205	173	235	88	98	27	3.9	5.3	96	88	--	80*
India	279899	851	290	85	P97	31855	96.9	33	74	74	25	25
Indonesia	65103	342	320	84	98	4484	23.5	21.7	83	83	--	80*
Iran	78585	481	1216	50	98	8938	54.7	135.9	33	33	--	33
Iraq	24916	568	1176	51	--	--	--	--	--	51	--	51
Israel	15581	7398	2659	27	P97	14138	6713.2	2412.6	0	0	--	0
Japan	316164	8369	2508	29	P97	8414	222.7	66.8	53	29	55	29
Jordan	3831	429	625	69	97	1239	138.9	202.3	20	20	--	20
Kazakhstan	33471	123	2044	34	--	--	--	--	--	34	--	34
Korea, DPR	68794	5707	2994	23	97	509	42.2	22.1	82	23	--	23
Korea, R	116701	11757	2552	28	97	15273	1538.7	334	7	7	53	7
Kuwait	13653	7662	7882	0	97	616	345.7	355.6	4	0	38	0
Kyrgyzstan	1776	89	384	81	--	--	--	--	--	80*	--	80
Lao PDR	96	4	19	99	92	4	0.2	0.9	99	99	--	80*
Lebanon	4300	4135	1368	46	98	602	578.8	188.6	22	22	--	22
Malaysia	35710	1083	1702	39	98	2639	80	123.3	35	35	--	35
Maldives	83	2767	315	84	98	1	33.3	3.7	97	84	--	80*
Mongolia	2103	13	829	59	98	20	0.1	7.8	94	59	--	59
Myanmar	2318	34	53	97	98	52	0.8	1.2	99	97	--	80*
Nepal	553	38	25	99	97	31	2.1	1.4	99	99	--	80*
Oman	4850	228	2104	34	94	414	19.5	199.4	20	20	--	20
Pakistan	25588	321	178	91	97	2089	26.2	14.5	88	88	--	80*
Philippines	20249	675	283	86	97	2991	99.7	41.9	66	66	39	39
Qatar	10348	9407	18197	0	98	135	122.7	233.1	17	0	--	0
Saudi Arabia	72616	338	3728	17	96	3440	16	182.7	23	17	--	17
Singapore	21909	353371	6393	0	98	123	1983.9	35.4	72	0	--	0
Sri Lanka	2096	319	115	94	98	314	47.9	17	86	86	--	80*
Syrian Arab R	13011	703	870	58	97	2805	151.5	187.6	22	22	--	22
Tajikistan	1519	106	256	87	--	--	--	--	--	80*	--	80
Thailand	56992	1111	954	56	98	4593	89.5	76.2	49	49	39	39
Turkey	54042	697	852	59	97	4656	60.1	73.4	51	51	52	51
Turkmenistan	8397	172	1984	35	96	31	0.6	7.5	94	35	--	35
United Arab Emirates	21697	2595	9404	0	97	693	82.9	300.4	10	0	--	0
Uzbekistan	27936	624	1204	50	97	58	1.3	2.5	98	50	--	50
Viet Nam	11595	350	152	92	97	792	23.9	10.4	92	92	--	80*
Yemen	4411	84	271	86	97	416	7.9	25.5	80	80	--	80
PACIFIC												
Australia	86336	112	4709	11	98	26	0	1.4	99	11	66	11
Fiji	206	113	262	87	97	14	7.7	17.8	86	86	--	80*
New Zealand	8492	314	2258	32	97	83	3.1	22.1	82	32	80	32
Papua New Guinea	659	14	146	93	97	39	0.8	8.7	93	93	--	80*
Samoa	36	127	209	90	97	5	17.6	29.1	77	77	--	77
Solomon Is	44	15	109	94	97	2	0.7	4.9	96	94	--	80*
Tonga	33	440	338	83	--	--	--	--	--	80*	--	80
Vanuatu	17	14	96	95	--	--	--	--	--	80*	--	80

Notes

The **Air index** is the lower of a global atmosphere index (*GA score*), covered in this table, and a local air quality index (*LA score*), covered in Table 18

The global atmosphere index is the lower score of two indicators (column heading in parentheses):

Greenhouse gases, represented by carbon dioxide emissions per person (GG score).

Use—production or consumption, whichever is higher—of ozone depleting substances per person (ODS score).

CO₂ = total carbon dioxide emissions from fossil-fuel burning, cement manufacture, and gas flaring, in thousands of metric tons of carbon (000 mt C). Data are for 1997—except for R Congo which are for 1996 (because the 1997 figure of 72,000 mt is much lower than previous years)—and are from the Carbon Dioxide Information Analysis Center (CDIAC) (Marland *et al.* 2000). CDIAC derives its estimates from the energy statistics of the United Nations Statistical Division (supplemented with gas flaring data from the US Department of Energy's Energy Information Administration) and cement production estimates compiled by the US Department of Interior's Bureau of Mines.

CO₂/ha = carbon dioxide emissions per hectare of total (land + inland waters) area, in kilograms of carbon (kg C).

CO₂/p = carbon dioxide emissions per person, in kilograms of carbon (kg C).

GG score = the score for carbon dioxide emissions per person. The performance criteria are shown in Table 17a. The top of the fair band matches the point below which carbon emissions per person must fall to keep atmospheric concentrations at less than double the pre-industrial level. Dangerous climate change could occur above this level (Corner House 1997). To stay below it, global emissions would have to be cut from 6.6 billion metric tons of carbon in 1997 to between 3.7 and 4.9 billion metric tons. If the intermediate amount of 4.3 billion were shared equally by the world population of 10.8 billion projected for 2050 (UN's "medium variant" projection [United Nations Population Division 1998c]), each person would have an emissions allowance of just under 400 kilograms.

ODS year = the applicable year of the data on ozone depleting substances (ODS). The letter P before the year indicates that the data for that country refer to production. Data for all other countries refer to consumption. Production was chosen whenever it was higher than consumption, as it better reflects the reliance on ODS of the countries concerned. Consumption means net consumption, after subtracting amounts that were destroyed.

227

Consumption by members of the European Community (EC), which is reported for the EC as a whole and not for individual countries, was allocated to those countries (Austria, Belgium, Denmark, Finland, France, Germany, Greece, Ireland, Italy, Luxembourg, Netherlands, Portugal, Spain, Sweden, United Kingdom) on the basis of population. Production data are reported for individual countries.

ODS = annual use of ozone depleting substances (ODS) in metric tons of ozone depleting potential (mt odp). ODS include chlorofluorocarbons (CFCs), halons, other fully halogenated CFCs, carbon tetrachloride, methyl chloroform, HCFCs, and methyl bromide. These substances are used in automobile and truck air conditioning units, domestic and commercial refrigeration and air conditioning/heat pump equipment, aerosol products, portable fire extinguishers, pre-polymers, and insulation boards, panels and pipe covers (Ozone Secretariat, United Nations Environment Programme 1997). Data are from Ozone Secretariat, United Nations Environment Programme (1999) and United Nations Environment Programme (1998).

ODS/ha = use of ozone depleting substances per hectare of total (land + inland waters) area in grams of ozone depleting potential (g odp).

ODS/p = use of ozone depleting substances per person in grams of ozone depleting potential (g odp).

ODS score = the score for use of ozone depleting substances per person. The performance criteria are shown in Table 17a. The top of the good band (zero consumption/production) corresponds to international agreements to eliminate ODS.

band	top point on scale	CO_2 emissions per person (kilograms carbon)	use of ozone depleting substances per person (grams)
good	100	0	0
fair	80	400	25
medium	60	800	50
poor	40	1600	100
bad	20	3200	200
base	0	6400	400

Table 17a Performance criteria for carbon dioxide emissions and use (consumption or production) of ozone depleting substances.

* A score with an asterisk has been reduced in accordance with the insufficient data rule. To prevent high scores resulting merely from lack of data, a good score is allowed only if it is based on all applicable components (data in an indicator, indicators in an index), and a fair score only if it is based on at least half the components. Good and fair scores (100-61) based on fewer than half the applicable components have been reduced to 60. Good scores (100-81) based on more than half but not all the applicable components have been reduced to 80.

Table 18. Local Air Quality

Country	City	Site	Year	SO₂ mean	SO₂ days	NO₂ mean	NO₂ days	O₃ days	CO days	SPM mean	PM10 mean	Pb mean	*LA* score	Based on
AMERICAS														
Argentina	Córdoba	1I	91	--	--	102	70	--	--	324	--	--	24	SPM
		2B	91	--	--	93	--	--	--	128	--	--	37	NO₂
		3R	91	--	--	97	90	--	--	101	--	--	28	NO₂
		ave											30	
	Mendoza	1I	94	2.6	--	22.6	--	--	--	--	--	0.2	77	NO₂
		2C	94	2.6	--	84.6	--	--	--	--	--	0.4	39	NO₂
		3R	94	2.6	--	20.7	--	--	--	--	--	0.2	79	NO₂
		ave											65	
	average												47	
Brazil	Osasco	1M	95	23	--	--	--	--	--	131	95	--	42	PM10
	Porto Alegre	1I	96	40	--	--	--	--	--	110.4	--	--	55	SPM
		2B	96	30.5	--	--	--	--	--	81.2	--	--	60*	SPM
		ave											57	
	Rio de Janeiro	1I	96	--	--	--	--	--	--	274	--	--	30	SPM
		2C	96	--	--	--	--	--	--	136	--	--	50	SPM
		3BR	96	--	--	--	--	--	--	82	--	--	60*	SPM
		ave											47	
	São Paulo	1M	95	17	19	--	--	--	1	--	90	--	44	PM10
		2C	95	34	24	--	--	--	50	116	89	--	44	PM10
		3BR	95	16	2	--	--	--	28	--	61	--	56	PM10
		ave											48	
	Vitória	2C	96	18	--	--	--	--	--	66	--	--	71	SPM
		3C	96	12	--	--	--	--	--	67	--	--	70	SPM
		4C	96	20	--	--	--	--	--	154	--	--	46	SPM
		ave											62	
	average												51	
Canada	Hamilton	0	95o	21.0	--	36.3	--	--	--	65.6	--	0.03	64	NO₂
	Montréal	0	95o	10.1	--	34.6	--	--	--	34.1	--	0.025	65	NO₂
	Vancouver	0	95o	10.6	--	34.7	--	--	--	24.2	--	0.01	65	NO₂
	average												65	
Chile	Santiago	1C	95	34	3	75	96	14	21	--	95	--	26	NO₂
		2C	95	23	0	86	104	0	20	--	91	--	23	NO₂
		3R	95	--	--	--	--	114	--	--	73	--	20	O₃
	average												23	
Costa Rica	Heredia	1C	96	55.2	5	28	0	0	5	--	76.5	--	49	PM10
	San José	2C	96	40.4	2	41	0	0	6	271.7	97.3	--	30	SPM
		3C	96	24.6	2	40	0	0	5	246.7	54.2	--	33	SPM
		4C	96	40	2	52	0	0	17	242	55	0.38	33	SPM
		ave											32	
	average												40	
Cuba	Habana	1C	94	0.6	--	4.9	--	--	--	--	--	--	60*	NO₂
Ecuador	Guayaquil	1C	95	--	--	--	--	--	--	127.3	--	--	52	SPM
	Quito	1I	95	39.6	0	--	--	--	--	196	--	--	38	SPM
		2B	95	22.3	0	--	--	--	--	154	56.9	--	46	SPM
		ave											42	
	average												47	
Guatemala	Guatemala	1I	97	--	--	87	--	--	--	370	111	0.1	19	SPM
		2C	96	--	--	52	0	0	--	322	94	0.08	24	SPM
		3R	97	--	--	45	--	--	--	110	40	0.22	56	SPM
	average												33	
Honduras	Tegucigalpa	1C	97	--	--	48	--	--	--	495	124	0.11	12	SPM
		2R	96	--	--	14	0	30	--	--	22	--	59	O₃
	average												35	
Mexico	Guadalajara	0	97o[S96]	27.5	--	210.3	--	--	--	--	107.7	--	14	NO₂
	México	0	97o	41.1	--	239.8	--	--	--	--	148.0	--	10	NO₂
		2I	96	55.1	20	73.4	81	154	0	365	126.4	0.455	12	O₃
		3B	96	52.5	23	80.9	132	254	5	180	60.6	0.236	0	O₃
		5R	96	36.7	0	79	107	246	3	227	56.7	0.173	0	O₃
	average of 2I, 3B, 5R												4	
	Monterrey	0	97o	21.9	--	103.9	--	--	--	--	67.2	--	34	NO₂
	average												17	
Nicaragua	Managua	1C	97	--	--	42	--	--	--	393	79	--	18	SPM
		2R	96	--	--	27	0	120	--	--	44	0	19	O₃
	average												18	
Panama	Panamá	1I	97	--	--	40	--	--	--	70	--	1.2	36	Pb
		2C	96	--	--	59	0	--	--	--	99	2.7	13	Pb

Country	City	Site	Year	SO$_2$ mean	SO$_2$ days	NO$_2$ mean	NO$_2$ days	O$_3$ days	CO days	SPM mean	PM10 mean	Pb mean	*LA score*	Based on
		3R	97	--	--	46	--	--	--	--	67	1.7	26	Pb
	average												25	
United States	Chicago	0	97o	12.1	--	52.0	--	--	--	--	25.9	0.053	54	NO$_2$
	Denver	0	97o	13.0	--	54.3	--	--	--	--	20.9	--	53	NO$_2$
	Los Angeles	0	97o	6.0	--	63.6	--	--	--	--	38.0	0.034	48	NO$_2$
	New York	0	97o	17.0	--	55.9	--	--	--	--	27.9	0.045	52	NO$_2$
	Washington-Baltimore	0	97o	--	--	43.2	--	--	--	--	22.0	0.009	58	NO$_2$
	average												53	
Venezuela	Caracas	1I	95	--	--	56	--	--	--	53	--	0.8	48	Pb
		2B	95	--	--	79	--	--	--	63	--	1.7	26	Pb
		3R	95	--	--	37	--	--	--	43	--	0.7	52	Pb
	average												42	
AFRICA														
Ghana	Accra	1I	90	--	--	--	--	--	--	149	--	--	47	SPM
		2R	90	--	--	--	--	--	--	130	--	--	51	SPM
	average												49	
South Africa	Cape Town	2C	95	--	--	72	160	22	--	--	27	--	11	NO$_2$
	Durban	1I	95	53	--	--	--	--	--	--	--	--	59	SO$_2$
		2B	94	26	--	--	--	--	--	--	--	0.61	56	Pb
		3R	95	10	--	--	--	--	--	--	--	--	60*	SO$_2$
	ave												58	
	Johannesburg	1C	94	--	--	39	0	0	0	--	--	0.42	61	NO$_2$
		2B	95	21.5	--	39.7	--	--	--	106.3	--	1.28	34	Pb
		3R	95	17.2	--	23.2	--	14	--	62.7	--	0.27	72	SPM
	ave												56	
	average												42	
EUROPE														
Austria	Graz	0	97o	10.9	--	34.0	--	--	--	46.0	--	--	66	NO$_2$
	Linz	0	97o	6.9	--	27.0	--	--	--	36.2	--	--	73	NO$_2$
	Wien [score based on 0; 1I, 2C, 3R shown here for comparison]	0	97o[N96]	14.0	--	42.0	--	--	--	43.9	--	--	59	NO$_2$
		1I	96	17	1	32	0	--	0	--	--	--	68	NO^2
		2C	96	17	0	--	--	14	0	--	36	--	71	PM10
		3R	96	19	1	33	0	27	0	--	36	--	61	O$_3$
	average												66	
Belarus	Minsk	1I	95	--	--	30	--	--	--	50	--	--	60*	NO$_2$
		3C	95	--	--	26	--	--	--	--	--	--	60*	NO$_2$
		5R	95	--	--	54	--	--	--	21	--	--	53	NO$_2$
	average												58	
Belgium	Antwerpen	0	97o[P95]	23.1	--	52.9	--	--	--	75.5	--	0.06	54	NO$_2$
	Brussel/Bruxelles	0	97o[P95]	12.1	--	47.8	--	--	--	78.2	--	0.099	56	NO$_2$
	Liège	0	97o[P95]	12.0	--	37.2	--	--	--	82.3	--	0.11	63	NO$_2$
	average												58	
Bulgaria	Plovdiv	1I	96	79	--	48	--	--	--	155.8	--	0.2	45	SPM
		2C	96	111.4	--	72.1	--	--	--	352.3	--	0.51	21	SPM
		3R	96	100.8	--	44.3	--	--	--	156.7	--	0.225	40	SO$_2$
	ave												35	
	Sofija	1I	96	32.1	--	144.5	--	--	--	188.3	--	0.175	24	NO$_2$
		2C	96	38.7	--	207.8	--	--	--	307.5	--	0.45	14	NO$_2$
		3R	96	26.2	--	125.7	--	--	--	185	--	0.125	29	NO$_2$
	ave												22	
	average												28	
Croatia	Zagreb	1I	95	40	3	--	--	--	--	--	--	--	60*	SO$_2$
		2C	95	30	0	--	--	--	--	78	--	0.52	59	Pb
		3R	95	24	0	--	--	--	--	63	--	0.52	59	Pb
	average												59	
Czech R	Brno	0	97 [P95]	12.8	--	26.9	--	--	--	50.2	--	0.06	73	NO$_2$
	Hradec Králove	0	97o[P94]	15.8	--	36.0	--	--	--	30.2	--	0.051	64	NO$_2$
	Olomouc	0	97o [P95]	34.0	--	53.9	--	--	--	39.3	--	0.043	53	NO$_2$
	Ostrava	0	97o[P95]	26.9	--	44.2	--	--	--	65.5	--	0.068	58	NO$_2$
	Praha	0	97o[P95]	23.8	--	79.3	--	--	--	58.8	--	0.059	40	NO$_2$
	Ustí nad Labem	0	97o[P95]	24.0	--	38.7	--	--	--	53.2	--	0.029	61	NO$_2$
	average												58	
Denmark	Ålborg	0	97o	2.8	--	34.0	--	--	--	53.9	--	0.013	66	NO$_2$
	Köbenhavn	0	97o	4.6	--	42.9	--	--	--	46.6	--	0.016	59	NO$_2$
	average												62	
Finland	Helsinki	0	97o	4.1	--	32.0	--	--	--	40.9	--	0.01	68	NO$_2$
	Oulu	0	97o	2.0	--	22.9	--	--	--	--	16.0	--	77	NO$_2$
	Tampere	0	97o	2.0	--	--	--	--	--	85.4	--	--	60*	SPM

230

Country	City	Site	Year	SO₂ mean	SO₂ days	NO₂ mean	NO₂ days	O₃ days	CO days	SPM mean	PM10 mean	Pb mean	*LA* score	Based on
	Turku	0	97o	6.0	--	36.1	--	--	--	--	--	--	60*	NO₂
	average												66	
France	Aix-en-Provence	1C	95	22	--	53	--	--	--	--	--	--	53	NO₂
	Marseille	1C	96	19	--	66	--	--	--	--	--	--	47	NO₂
		2C	96	25	--	69	--	--	--	--	--	--	45	NO₂
		3C	96	30	--	82	--	--	--	--	--	--	39	NO₂
		ave											44	
	Nantes	0	95o[P93]	8.0	--	37.1	--	--	--	16.9	--	--	63	NO₂
	Paris	1	96	22	--	62	--	--	--	17	--	--	49	NO₂
		2	96	18	--	49	--	--	--	21	--	--	55	NO₂
		3	96	15	--	51	--	--	--	30	--	--	54	NO₂
		ave											53	
	Rouen	0	95o	25.2	--	38.7	--	--	--	21.0	--	--	61	NO₂
	Strasbourg	1C	96	20	0	46	0	21	--	--	29	--	57	NO₂
	average												55	
Germany	Berlin	0	97o	10.7	--	29.8	--	--	--	43.4	--	--	70	NO₂
	Dortmund	1M	96	14	0	38	0	5	0	56	--	--	62	NO₂
		2IR	96	15	0	38	1	--	0	55	--	--	62	NO₂
		ave											62	
	Duisburg	1IR	96	22	2	38	0	--	0	42	--	--	62	NO₂
		2C	96	22	2	40	1	--	0	63	--	--	60	NO₂
		4R	96	20	0	38	0	--	0	53	--	--	62	NO₂
		ave											61	
	Frankfurt	0	97o	11.0	--	52.0	--	--	--	37.8	--	--	54	NO₂
	Freiburg	0	97o	6.9	--	27.2	--	--	--	13.0	--	0.02	73	NO₂
	Gelsenkirchen	0	97o	14.8	--	39.2	--	--	--	57.0	--	0.041	61	NO₂
	Köln	1BR	96	14	0	40	0	2	0	43	--	--	60	NO₂
		2R	96	13	0	38	0	6	0	52	--	--	62	NO₂
		ave											61	
	Leipzig	0	97o	11.3	--	53.1	--	--	--	56.5	--	--	53	NO₂
	München	0	97o	7.0	--	47.9	--	--	--	50.9	--	--	56	NO₂
	average												61	
Greece	Athína	0	97o	27.3	--	55.8	--	--	--	--	--	0.218	52	NO₂
		1I	95	22	0	50	26	66	1	--	--	--	36	O₃
		2C	95	44	3	95	54	0	44	--	--	--	36	NO₂
		3R	95	36	7	48	12	30	1	--	--	--	56	NO₂
	average of 1I, 2C, 3R												43	
Hungary	Budapest	0	97o[Pb94]	19.9	--	36.2	--	--	--	--	63.1	0.211	55	PM10
		1I	96	46	2	25	--	--	--	79	--	--	63	SO₂
		2R	96	34	0	35	--	--	--	55	--	--	65	NO₂
		3C	96	60	13	99	--	--	--	65	--	--	35	NO₂
	average of 1I, 2R, 3C												54	
	Debrecen	0	97o[Pb94]	11.7	--	30.3	--	--	--	--	--	0.342	70	NO₂
	Győr	0	97o[Pb94]	11.1	--	78.3	--	--	--	23.4	--	0.06	41	NO₂
	Miskolc	0	97o[P96]	25.5	--	30.1	--	--	--	--	43.7	--	65	PM10
	Pécs	0	97o[Pb94]	7.2	--	33.2	--	--	--	21.1	--	0.342	67	NO₂
	average												59	
Iceland	Reykjavík	0	97o[Pb96]	3.9	--	30.5	--	--	--	--	27.1	0.028	69	NO₂
Ireland	Cork	0	93o	12.0	--	--	--	--	--	--	--	--	60*	SO₂
	Dublin	0	93o	19.6	--	--	--	--	--	--	--	--	60*	SO₂
	average												60	
Italy	Milano	0	93o [N92]	30.9	--	248.4	--	--	--	77.3	--	--	9	NO₂
	Torino	0	93o	--	--	--	--	--	--	151.1	--	--	46	SPM
	average												27	
Lithuania	Kaunas	1I	96	1	--	30	--	--	--	100	--	0.017	58	SPM
		2C	96	1	--	40	--	--	--	200	--	--	38	SPM
		3R	96	0.9	--	20	--	--	--	100	--	--	58	SPM
		ave											51	
	Klaipėda	1I	96	8	--	30	--	--	--	100	--	--	58	SPM
		2C	96	2	--	20	--	--	--	99	--	0.015	58	SPM
		3R	96	2	--	20	--	--	--	99	--	--	58	SPM
		ave											58	
	Šiauliai	1C	96	2	--	50	--	--	--	200	--	--	38	SPM
		2R	96	3	--	20	--	--	--	100	--	--	58	SPM
		ave											48	
	Vilnius	1I	96	3	--	40	--	--	--	200	--	--	38	SPM
		2C	96	4	--	40	--	--	--	100	--	0.012	58	SPM
		3R	96	2	--	30	--	--	--	100	--	0.023	58	SPM
		ave											51	

Country	City	Site	Year	SO_2 mean	SO_2 days	NO_2 mean	NO_2 days	O_3 days	CO days	SPM mean	PM10 mean	Pb mean	*LA* score	Based on
	average												52	
Luxembourg	Esch-sur-Alzette	0	97o	11.0	--	34.1	--	--	--	--	28.0	0.12	66	NO_2
	Luxembourg	0	97o	16.5	--	52.2	--	--	--	--	26.0	0.079	54	NO_2
	average												60	
Netherlands	Den Haag	0	97o	8.9	--	41.0	--	--	--	--	42.0	--	59	NO_2
	Rotterdam	0	97o	10.9	--	47.9	--	--	--	--	43.9	--	56	NO_2
	Vlaardingen	0	97o	15.1	--	45.9	--	--	--	--	47.1	0.02	57	NO_2
	average												57	
Norway	Bergen	0	97o[Pb92]	--	--	40.0	--	--	--	--	--	0.029	60	NO_2
	Drammen	0	97o[Pb92]	--	--	45.0	--	--	--	--	--	0.23	57	NO_2
	Oslo	0	97o[Pb92]	--	--	43.2	--	--	--	22.8	--	0.108	58	NO_2
	average												58	
Poland	Kraków	0	97o	30.0	--	30.3	--	--	--	--	37.5	--	70	NO_2
	Łódź	0	97o	14.0	--	41.9	--	--	--	--	--	0.112	59	NO_2
	Warszawa	0	97o	11.9	--	30.2	--	--	--	--	--	--	60*	NO_2
	average												63	
Portugal	Barreiro	0	96o	11.9	--	25.9	--	--	--	--	86.5	--	45	PM10
	Lisboa	0	96o	10.1	--	50.0	--	--	--	--	41.8	--	55	NO_2
	average												50	
Romania	Bucureşti	1I	96	6	--	--	--	--	--	16	--	0.75	50	Pb
		2C	95	17	--	79	48	--	--	87	--	1.36	33	Pb
		3R	96	3.7	--	69.3	--	--	--	70.7	81	--	45	NO_2
	average												43	
Slovakia	Banská Bystrica	0	97o	26.2	--	49.0	--	--	--	--	--	--	55	NO_2
	Bratislava	0	97o	21.9	--	33.8	--	--	--	38.2	--	--	66	NO_2
	Košice	0	97o	23.0	--	9.1	--	--	--	58.2	--	--	74	SPM
	average												65	
Spain	Barcelona	1	96	--	--	66.7	--	--	--	--	--	--	47	NO_2
		2	96	12.2	--	45	--	--	--	--	--	--	57	NO_2
		3	96	12.5	--	50.3	--	--	--	--	--	--	55	NO_2
		ave											53	
	Madrid	0	97o	15.7	--	66.2	--	--	--	--	32.8	--	47	NO_2
	Valladolid	0	97o	--	--	55.3	--	--	--	--	--	--	52	NO_2
	average												51	
Sweden	Göteborg	0	96o	4.5	--	30.1	--	--	--	--	7.0	--	70	NO_2
	Stockholm	0	96o	4.0	--	23.0	--	--	--	--	4.0	--	77	NO_2
	average												73	
Switzerland	Basel	0	96o	6.8	--	26.8	--	--	--	36.0	--	0.05	73	NO_2
	Genève	1C	95	13	0	58	0	0	0	--	--	--	51	NO_2
	Zürich	0	96o	10.0	--	36.0	--	--	--	34.0	--	0.041	64	NO_2
	average												63	
United Kingdom	Birmingham	1C	95	18	4	45	5	10	0	--	23	--	57	NO_2
	Edinburgh	1C	95	21	0	49	2	1	0	--	20	--	55	NO_2
	Glasgow	0	97o	--	--	50.2	--	--	--	--	--	0.041	55	NO_2
	Liverpool	1C	95	24	4	49	0	7	0	--	27	--	55	NO_2
	London	0	97o[S96]	28.1	--	61.0	--	--	--	--	--	0.09	49	NO_2
	Manchester	0	97o	--	--	52.3	--	--	--	--	--	--	54	NO_2
	Newcastle	0	97o [S96]	22.0	--	40.0	--	--	--	--	--	--	60	NO_2
	Sheffield	1I	95	--	--	49	1	--	0	--	--	--	55	NO_2
	average												55	
RUSSIAN FEDERATION	Moskva	0	92o	1.0	--	79.8	--	--	--	100.5	--	--	40	NO_2
	Novosibirsk	0	93o	5.0	--	50.1	--	--	--	111.0	--	--	55	NO_2
	Omsk	0	93o	10.0	--	30.0	--	--	--	99.4	--	--	58	SPM
	S Peterburg	0	93o	9.9	--	80.0	--	--	--	100.0	--	--	40	NO_2
	average												48	
ASIA														
China	Beijing	1I	94	115	--	--	--	--	--	485	--	--	13	SPM
		2B	94	89.9	--	--	--	--	--	343	--	--	22	SPM
		3R	94	110	--	--	--	--	--	322	--	--	24	SPM
		ave											20	
	Chongqing	1	94	330	--	60	--	--	--	340	--	--	7	SO_2
	Guangzhou	1I	94	66.7	--	--	--	--	--	400	--	--	18	SPM
		2B	94	75.4	--	--	--	--	--	359	--	--	20	SPM
		3R	94	62.4	--	--	--	--	--	339	--	--	22	SPM
		ave											20	
	Hong Kong	1I	96	19	0	65	9	--	--	99	59	0.078	47	NO_2
		2C	96	18	0	62	7	--	--	101	59	0.083	49	NO_2
		3R	96	15	0	47	1	5	--	87	52	0.083	56	NO_2
		ave											51	

Country	City	Site	Year	SO₂ mean	SO₂ days	NO₂ mean	NO₂ days	O₃ days	CO days	SPM mean	PM10 mean	Pb mean	*LA score*	Based on
	Shanghai	1I	94	67	--	--	--	--	--	232	--	--	34	SPM
		2B	94	79.2	--	--	--	--	--	289	--	--	28	SPM
		3R	94	62.4	--	--	--	--	--	235	--	--	34	SPM
		ave											32	
	Shenyang	1I	94	256	--	--	--	--	--	539	--	--	10	SPM
		2B	94	98	--	--	--	--	--	449	--	--	15	SPM
		3R	94	64	--	--	--	--	--	428	--	--	16	SPM
		ave											14	
	Xi'an	1I	94	63	--	--	--	--	--	459	--	--	14	SPM
		2B	94	79.7	--	--	--	--	--	503	--	--	12	SPM
		3R	94	44.9	--	--	--	--	--	482	--	--	13	SPM
		ave											13	
	average												22	
India	Ahmadabad	1I	96	31	--	13	--	--	--	234	158	0.058	28	PM10
		2C	96	18	--	15	--	--	--	306	194	--	21	PM10
		3R	96	12	--	9	--	--	--	187	92	--	39	SPM
		ave											29	
	Calcutta	1I	96	26	4	35	4	--	--	541	544	0.266	0	PM10
		2C	96	31	4	35	4	--	--	542	378	--	2	PM10
		3R	96	9	1	15	1	--	--	420	362	--	4	PM10
		ave											2	
	Hyderabad	1I	96	13	--	10	--	--	--	67	75	0.069	50	PM10
		2C	96	34	1	35	1	--	--	234	178	--	24	PM10
		3R	96	16	1	15	1	--	--	150	98	--	41	PM10
		ave											38	
	Jaipur	1I	96	12	1	44	8	--	--	355	315	0.078	8	PM10
		2C	96	7	--	27	7	--	--	220	184	--	23	PM10
		3R	96	7	--	20	2	--	--	226	172	--	26	PM10
		ave											19	
	Kanpur	1I	96	8	--	20	--	--	--	434	219	0.96	16	SPM
		2C	96	8	--	21	--	--	--	368	190	--	20	SPM
		3R	96	6	--	14	--	--	--	233	131	--	34	PM10
		ave											23	
	Mumbai	1I	96	25	4	32	3	--	--	244	136	0.057	33	PM10
		2B	96	18	3	54	8	--	--	194	90	--	38	SPM
		3R	96	13	1	21	2	--	--	195	111	--	38	PM10
		ave											36	
	Nagpur	1I	96	8	--	15	--	--	--	161	82	0.087	44	SPM
		2C	96	6	--	13	--	--	--	226	132	--	34	PM10
		3R	96	6	--	12	--	--	--	133	64	--	50	SPM
		ave											43	
	New Delhi	1I	96	17	--	40	--	--	--	498	216	0.332	12	SPM
		2C	96	24	2	77	7	--	--	459	246	--	14	SPM
		3R	96	11	--	46	3	--	--	299	275	--	12	PM10
		ave											13	
	average												25	
Japan	Kawasaki	0	96o	24.1	--	64.9	--	--	--	--	47.1	0.11	48	NO₂
	Matsue	0	96o	--	--	10.0	--	--	--	--	25.0	0.03	80	PM10
	Osaka	1I	94	20.9	0	65.8	--	--	0	--	46	0.06	47	NO₂
		2B	94	18.7	0	62	--	--	0	--	40	0.06	49	NO₂
		3R	94	18.3	0	60.2	--	--	--	--	47	0.06	50	NO₂
		ave											49	
	Tokyo	0	96o	18.9	--	69.0	--	--	--	--	47.9	0.09	45	NO₂
	average												55	
Korea, R	Inch'ŏn	0	97o	34.0	--	48.9	--	--	--	85.4	--	0.171	56	NO₂
	Kwangyu	0	97o	23.5	--	39.5	--	--	--	74.7	--	0.033	60	NO₂
	Pusan	0	97o	46.7	--	52.8	--	--	--	84.6	--	0.084	54	NO₂
	Sŏul	0	97o	29.3	--	60.2	--	--	--	71.3	--	0.11	50	NO₂
	Taegu	0	97o	41.9	--	45.1	--	--	--	62.7	--	0.03	57	NO₂
	Taejŏn	0	97o	28.5	--	41.4	--	--	--	66.5	--	0.181	59	NO₂
	Ulsan	1I	96	80	64	29	0	1	0	121	--	--	37	SO₂
	average												53	
Kuwait	Kuwait	1	96	44.4	9	61.5	30	61	9	--	--	--	38	O₃
Philippines	Manila	1I	95	--	--	--	--	--	--	296	--	--	27	SPM
		3B	95	--	--	--	--	--	--	210	--	--	37	SPM
		4R	95	--	--	--	--	--	--	118	--	--	54	SPM
	average												39	
Thailand	Bangkok	1I	95	--	--	--	--	--	--	385	--	0.19	19	SPM
		2B	95	--	--	--	--	--	--	138	--	0.14	49	SPM

233

Country	City	Site	Year	SO₂ mean	SO₂ days	NO₂ mean	NO₂ days	O₃ days	CO days	SPM mean	PM10 mean	Pb mean	*LA score*	Based on
		3R	95	--	--	--	--	--	--	146	--	0.08	48	SPM
	average												39	
Turkey	Ankara	0	97o	41.9	--	45.2	--	--	--	--	53.4	--	57	NO₂
	Eskişehir	0	97o [N95]	71.0	--	7.0	--	--	--	--	--	--	52	SO₂
	Istanbul	0	97o	83.2	--	--	--	--	--	--	--	--	47	SO₂
	Izmir	0	97o	64.1	--	--	--	--	--	--	--	--	54	SO₂
	average												52	
PACIFIC														
Australia	Melbourne	1I	95	1	0	22	0	1	0	--	18	0.07	78	NO₂
		2C	95	0	0	40	0	0	--	--	21	0.11	60	NO₂
		3R	95	0	0	29	0	0	0	--	17	0.1	71	NO₂
		ave											70	
	Perth	1I	95	5	0	8	0	--	--	--	--	--	60*	NO₂
		2C	95	--	--	36	0	--	2	--	24	0.26	64	NO₂
		3R	95	--	--	12	0	6	--	38	19	0.1	80*	SPM
		ave											68	
	Sydney	2B	95	--	--	--	--	--	39	70	31	0.2	52	CO
		3R	95	--	--	33	0	0	--	38	16	0.1	67	NO₂
		ave											59	
	average												66	
New Zealand	Auckland	1I	96	6.5	0	20.4	0	--	--	33	25	0.05	80	PM10
		2B	96	--	--	16.1	0	--	--	12	--	0.03	80*	NO₂
		ave											80	
	Christchurch	1BR	95	6	0	17.1	--	--	--	34	21.8	0.11	80*	NO₂
	average												80	

Notes

The local air quality index (*LA score*) is the average of city scores in each country, each city score being the lowest score of six indicators: sulfur dioxide, nitrogen dioxide, ground-level ozone, carbon monoxide, particulates, and lead.

Site = monitoring site. 0 indicates an average of several sites. 1, 2, 3, etc., indicate an individual site. The type of location is shown by a letter: B = business district; C = city center; I = industrial; M = mixed; R = residential.

Year = the year of the data. All data are from World Health Organization (1998c), unless the year is annotated with the letter o, in which case they are from Organisation for Economic Co-operation and Development (1999), supplemented by OECD Centre for Co-operation with the Economies in Transition (1996). Exceptions are indicated in brackets: N= nitrogen dioxide; P = particulates; Pb = lead; S = sulfur dioxide.

SO₂ = sulfur dioxide, recorded as annual average ambient air concentration of sulfur dioxide (SO₂ mean) in micrograms per cubic meter ($\mu g/m^3$) and as number of days per year in which ambient air concentrations of SO₂ exceeded World Health Organization (WHO) guidelines (SO₂ days).

NO₂ = nitrogen dioxide, recorded as annual average ambient air concentration of nitrogen dioxide (NO₂ mean) in micrograms per cubic meter ($\mu g/m^3$) and as number of days per year in which ambient air concentrations of NO₂ exceeded WHO guidelines (NO₂ days).

O₃ days = number of days per year in which ambient air concentrations of ground-level ozone exceeded WHO guidelines.

CO days = number of days per year in which ambient air concentrations of carbon monoxide exceeded WHO guidelines.

SPM mean = annual average ambient air concentration of suspended particulate matter in micrograms per cubic meter ($\mu g/m^3$).

PM10 mean = annual average ambient air concentration of fine particulates 10 micrometers or less in diameter in micrograms per cubic meter ($\mu g/m^3$). A micrometer is 500 times smaller than the period at the end of this sentence. The smaller the particles the more dangerous they are. The smallest particles (2.5 micrometers or less) can remain in the air for days or weeks and penetrate deep into the lungs.

Pb mean = annual average ambient air concentration of lead in micrograms per cubic meter ($\mu g/m^3$).

LA score = the local air quality index, the lowest score of the above indicators. The performance criteria are shown in Table 18a. For annual ambient air concentrations of sulfur dioxide (SO₂), nitrogen dioxide (NO₂), suspended particulate matter (SPM) and lead (Pb), the top of the medium band matches WHO guidelines (World Health Organization 1998d). WHO has issued no guidelines for fine particulates because there is no threshold for morbidity and mortality (Junker & Schwela 1998). The tops of the fair and medium bands represent 2% and 4% increases in daily mortality from PM10. For number of days per year in which ambient air concentrations of sulfur dioxide (SO₂), nitrogen dioxide (NO₂), ozone (O₃) or carbon monoxide (CO) exceeded WHO guidelines, the performance criteria reflect personal judgment.

Based on = the indicator that determines the site score (the indicator with the lowest score). Scores for SO₂ and NO₂ are for annual average ambient air concentration or for number of days per year WHO guidelines were exceeded, whichever gives the lower score.

band	top point on scale	SO₂ µg/m³	SO₂ no. days >WHO	NO₂ µg/m³	NO₂ no. days >WHO	O₃ no. days >WHO	CO no. days >WHO	SPM µg/m³	PM10 µg/m³	Pb µg/m³
good	100	0	0	0	0	0	0	0	0	0
fair	80	25	14	20	14	14	14	45	25	0.25
medium	60	50	28	40	28	28	28	90	50	0.50
poor	40	100	56	80	56	56	56	180	100	1.00
bad	20	200	112	160	112	112	112	360	200	2.00
base	0	400	224	320	224	224	224	720	400	4.00

Table 18a. Performance criteria for air pollutants. No. days >WHO = number of days when ambient air concentrations exceeded WHO guidelines.

* A score with an asterisk has been reduced in accordance with the insufficient data rule. To prevent high scores resulting merely from lack of data, a good score is allowed only if it is based on all applicable components (data in an indicator, indicators in an index), and a fair score only if it is based on at least half the components. Good and fair scores (100-61) based on fewer than half the applicable components have been reduced to 60. Good scores (100-81) based on more than half but not all the applicable components have been reduced to 80.

Table 19. Species and Genes Index; Wild Species Rank; Wild Plant Species

Country	W spp rank	Flowering plants Tot	Thr	%	Gymnosperms Tot	Thr	%	Pteridophytes Tot	Thr	%	Ave %	#G	PS score	AS score	WD score	DD score	S&G index
AMERICAS																	
Antigua & Barbuda	166=	766	3	0.4	1	--	--	33	--	--	0.4	1	60*	35	47	--	47
Argentina	18	9000	233	2.6	13	9	69.2	359	5	1.4	24.4	3	9	44	26	17	23
Bahamas	155	1065	29	2.7	3	2	66.7	43	0	0	23.1	3	11	12	11	60	27
Barbados	179	542	2	0.4	0	0	0	30	--	--	0.4	2	80*	52	66	60	64
Belize	61	2750	52	1.9	10	4	40.0	134	1	0.8	14.2	3	24	81	52	--	52
Bolivia	13	16500	222	1.4	17	4	23.5	850	1	0.1	8.3	3	39	56	47	22	39
Brazil	5	55000	1352	2.5	15	3	20.0	1200	3	0.3	7.6	3	42	25	33	1	22
Canada	51	3172	251	7.9	33	3	9.1	65	18	27.7	14.9	3	23	58	40	42	41
Chile	59	5125	285	5.6	9	9	100	150	35	23.3	43.0	3	0	23	11	33	18
Colombia	4	50000	688	1.4	20	11	55.0	1200	13	1.1	19.2	3	16	43	29	24	27
Costa Rica	23	11000	502	4.6	9	6	66.7	1110	19	1.7	24.3	3	10	57	33	--	33
Cuba	68	6004	879	14.6	23	8	34.8	495	1	0.2	16.5	3	19	11	15	57	29
Dominica	157	1027	56	5.5	1	--	--	200	1	0.5	3.0	2	70	33	51	--	51
Dominican R	78	5000	130	2.6	7	3	42.9	650	3	0.5	15.3	3	22	18	20	35	25
Ecuador	8=	18250	813	4.5	12	2	16.7	1100	9	0.8	7.3	3	43	43	43	12	33
El Salvador	62	2500	38	1.5	11	4	36.4	400	--	--	19.0	2	16	82	49	--	49
Grenada	159	919	8	0.9	1	--	--	148	--	--	0.9	1	60*	46	53	--	53
Guatemala	21=	8000	338	4.2	29	15	51.7	652	2	0.3	18.7	3	17	82	49	14	37
Guyana	36	6000	149	2.5	2	--	--	407	3	0.7	1.6	2	80*	75	77	60	71
Haiti	88=	4685	95	2.0	7	3	42.9	550	2	0.4	15.1	3	22	0	11	--	11
Honduras	30	5000	88	1.8	30	8	26.7	650	--	--	14.3	2	24	70	47	--	47
Jamaica	103	2746	737	26.8	4	3	75.0	558	4	0.7	34.2	3	0	18	9	--	9
Mexico	3	25000	1473	5.9	71	71	100	1000	14	1.4	35.8	3	0	35	17	26	20
Nicaragua	25	7000	93	1.3	14	4	28.6	576	1	0.2	10.0	3	35	80	57	--	57
Panama	17	9000	1274	14.2	15	11	73.3	900	17	1.9	29.8	3	3	51	27	--	27
Paraguay	34	7500	128	1.7	1	1	100	350	--	--	50.9	2	0	63	31	11	24
Peru	6	17121	878	5.1	24	1	4.2	1100	27	2.5	3.9	3	61	37	49	54	51
St Kitts & Nevis	171	533	4	0.8	0	0	0	126	--	--	0.8	2	80*	39	59	--	59
St Lucia	163=	909	5	0.6	--	1	--	119	--	--	0.6	1	60*	25	42	--	42
St Vincent & Grenadines	156	1000	9	0.9	1	--	--	165	--	--	0.9	1	60*	26	43	--	43
Suriname	37	4700	103	2.2	3	--	--	315	--	--	2.2	1	60*	68	64	--	64
Trinidad & Tobago	85	1982	19	1.0	1	1	100	277	1	0.4	33.8	3	0	78	39	60	46
United States	8=	18956	4539	24.0	113	46	40.7	404	84	20.8	28.5	3	4	36	20	30	23
Uruguay	115	2184	15	0.7	1	--	--	93	--	--	0.7	1	60*	51	55	30	47
Venezuela	10	20000	410	2.1	14	4	28.6	1059	12	1.1	10.6	3	33	54	43	42	43
AFRICA																	
Algeria	93	3100	138	4.5	18	3	16.7	46	--	--	10.6	2	33	39	36	50	41
Angola	28	5000	23	0.5	--	1	--	185	--	--	0.5	1	60*	61	60	43	54
Benin	83	2000	4	0.2	1	--	--	200	--	--	0.2	1	60*	80*	70	68	69
Botswana	73	2136	7	0.3	0	0	0	15	--	--	0.3	2	80*	80	80	72	77
Burkina Faso	106	1100	--	--	0	0	0	--	--	--	--	0	--	75	75	45	65
Burundi	79=	2500	--	--	--	--	--	--	--	--	--	0	--	72	72	23	56
Cameroon	31	8000	82	1.0	3	--	--	257	7	2.7	1.9	2	80*	44	62	31	52
Cape Verde	178	740	1	0.1	0	0	0	34	--	--	0.1	2	80*	0	40	--	40
Central African R	53	3600	1	0	2	--	--	--	--	--	0.0	1	60*	70	65	50	60
Chad	97=	1600	12	7.9	--	--	--	--	--	--	7.9	1	40	47	43	45	44
Comoros	162	660	4	0.6	1	--	--	60	--	--	0.6	2	60*	21	40	--	40
Congo, DR	20	11000	75	0.7	7	3	42.9	--	--	--	21.8	2	13	49	31	50	37
Congo, R	50	4350	3	0.1	7	--	--	--	--	--	0.1	1	60*	69	64	93	74
Côte d'Ivoire	43	3517	92	2.6	0	0	0	143	2	1.4	2.0	3	80	57	68	68	68
Djibouti	165	635	2	0.3	2	--	--	4	--	--	0.3	1	60*	60*	60	55	58
Egypt	118	2066	82	4.0	4	--	--	6	--	--	4.0	1	60	48	54	54	54
Equatorial Guinea	60	3000	3	0.1	0	0	0	250	8	3.2	1.7	3	83	56	69	60	66
Eritrea	84	--	--	--	--	--	--	--	--	--	--	0	--	53	53	70	59
Ethiopia	42	6500	163	2.5	3	--	--	100	--	--	2.5	1	60*	42	51	50	51
Gabon	54	6500	91	1.4	1	--	--	150	--	--	1.4	1	60*	58	59	60	59
Gambia	135=	966	1	0.1	0	0	0	8	--	--	0.1	2	80*	80*	80	66	75
Ghana	56	3600	101	2.8	1	--	--	124	2	1.6	2.2	2	78	65	71	52	65
Guinea	55	3000	37	1.2	0	0	0	--	2	--	1.2	2	80*	60	70	60	67
Guinea-Bissau	131	1000	--	--	0	0	0	--	--	--	--	0	--	80*	80	61	74
Kenya	24	6000	231	3.9	6	4	66.7	500	5	1.0	23.9	3	10	40	25	59	36
Lesotho	174	1576	21	1.3	0	0	0	15	0	0	0.7	3	93	44	68	48	61
Liberia	64	2200	25	1.1	0	0	0	--	--	--	1.1	2	80*	52	66	48	60
Libyan Arab J	140	1800	57	3.2	10	--	--	15	--	--	3.2	1	60*	48	54	72	60
Madagascar	45	9000	259	2.9	5	5	100	500	42	8.4	37.1	3	0	2	1	11	4
Malawi	44	3600	59	1.6	4	1	25.0	161	--	--	13.3	2	27	72	49	54	51
Mali	100	1741	15	0.9	0	--	--	--	--	--	0.9	1	60*	53	56	56	56

235

Country	W spp rank	Flowering plants			Gymnosperms			Pteridophytes			Ave %	#G	PS score	AS score	WD score	DD score	S&G index
		Tot	Thr	%	Tot	Thr	%	Tot	Thr	%							
Mauritania	152=	1100	3	0.3	0	0	0	--	--	--	0.3	2	80*	39	59	58	59
Mauritius	170	572	291	50.9	0	0	0	178	3	1.7	26.3	3	7	0	3	33	13
Morocco	81	3600	182	5.1	19	4	21.1	56	--	--	13.1	2	27	38	32	47	37
Mozambique	38	5500	78	1.4	10	10	100	183	2	1.1	34.2	3	0	53	26	42	31
Namibia	76	3128	74	2.4	1	--	--	45	1	2.2	2.3	2	77	53	65	27	52
Niger	125	1178	--	--	0	0	0	8	--	--	--	0	--	58	58	42	53
Nigeria	40	4614	37	0.8	1	--	--	100	--	--	0.8	1	60*	55	57	45	53
Rwanda	77	2288	--	--	2	--	--	--	--	--	--	0	--	67	67	14	49
São Tomé & Principe	158	744	2	0.3	1	--	--	150	1	0.7	0.5	2	80*	8	44	--	44
Senegal	96	2062	31	1.5	0	--	--	24	--	--	1.5	1	60*	62	61	57	60
Seychelles	160	1139	78	6.9	1	--	--	--	1	--	6.9	1	45	5	25	--	25
Sierra Leone	75	2090	29	1.4	0	0	0	--	--	--	1.4	2	80*	56	68	66	67
Somalia	71	3000	103	3.4	2	--	--	26	--	--	3.4	1	60*	48	54	--	54
South Africa	15	23000	2168	9.4	40	38	95.0	380	9	2.4	35.6	3	0	34	17	48	27
Sudan	39	3132	10	0.3	5	--	--	--	--	--	0.3	1	60*	56	58	49	55
Swaziland	82	2636	35	1.3	8	7	87.5	71	--	--	44.4	2	0	56	28	80	45
Tanzania	19	10000	429	4.3	8	5	62.5	--	2	--	33.4	2	0	39	19	9	16
Togo	74	2000	4	0.2	1	--	--	200	--	--	0.2	1	60*	77	68	83	73
Tunisia	120	2150	23	1.1	10	1	10.0	36	--	--	5.6	2	52	40	46	19	37
Uganda	29	5000	12	0.2	6	3	50.0	400	--	--	25.1	2	9	68	38	28	35
Zambia	48	4600	10	0.2	1	1	100	146	1	0.7	33.6	3	0	70	35	48	39
Zimbabwe	33	4200	95	2.3	6	3	50.0	234	2	0.9	17.7	3	18	74	46	48	47
EUROPE																	
Albania	99	2965	77	2.6	21	2	9.5	45	--	--	6.1	2	49	58	53	50	52
Austria	95	2950	22	0.8	12	--	--	66	1	1.5	1.2	2	80*	51	65	34	55
Belarus	151	--	1	--	--	--	--	--	--	--	--	0	--	54	54	40	49
Belgium	143	1400	2	0.1	2	--	--	50	--	--	0.1	1	60*	35	47	51	48
Bosnia & Herzegovina	119	--	62	--	--	1	--	--	1	--	--	0	--	25	25	43	31
Bulgaria	90	3505	105	3.0	15	1	6.7	52	--	--	4.9	2	55	35	45	22	37
Croatia	111	--	5	--	--	--	--	--	1	--	--	0	--	47	47	37	44
Czech R	130	--	--	--	--	--	--	--	--	--	--	0	--	54	54	41	50
Denmark	150	1200	2	0.2	2	--	--	50	--	--	0.2	1	60*	49	54	43	50
Estonia	132	1630	2	0.1	40	--	--	4	--	--	0.1	1	60*	58	59	65	61
Finland	144	1040	5	0.5	4	--	--	58	1	1.7	1.1	2	80*	52	66	58	63
France	70	4500	168	3.7	20	--	--	110	7	6.4	5.1	2	54	35	44	33	40
Germany	101	2600	13	0.5	10	--	--	72	1	1.4	1.0	2	80*	38	59	47	55
Greece	72	4900	565	11.5	21	3	14.3	71	3	4.2	10.0	3	35	39	37	24	33
Hungary	113	2148	30	1.4	8	--	--	58	--	--	1.4	1	60*	43	51	28	43
Iceland	173	340	1	0.3	1	--	--	36	--	--	0.3	1	60*	6	33	70	45
Ireland	161	892	--	--	2	--	--	56	1	1.8	1.8	1	60*	34	47	58	51
Italy	67	5463	306	5.6	29	2	6.9	106	3	2.8	5.1	3	54	36	45	46	45
Latvia	133	1153	--	--	4	--	--	48	--	--	--	0	--	65	65	56	62
Lithuania	154	1200	1	0.1	--	--	--	--	--	--	0.1	1	60*	58	59	58	59
Luxembourg	149	1200	1	0.1	4	--	--	42	--	--	0.1	1	60*	51	55	51	54
Macedonia, FYR	126	--	--	--	--	--	--	--	--	--	--	0	--	24	24	50	33
Malta	166=	900	14	1.6	3	1	33.3	11	--	--	17.5	2	18	46	32	80	48
Moldova	152=	--	5	--	--	--	--	--	--	--	--	0	--	57	57	63	59
Netherlands	146	1170	1	0.1	3	--	--	48	--	--	0.1	1	60*	34	47	40	45
Norway	139	1650	11	0.7	4	--	--	61	1	1.6	1.2	2	80*	36	58	30	49
Poland	105	2300	25	1.1	10	1	10.0	62	1	1.6	4.2	3	59	36	47	76	57
Portugal	107	2500	260	10.4	8	2	25.0	65	7	10.8	15.4	3	21	24	22	48	31
Romania	88=	3175	97	3.2	11	1	9.1	62	1	1.6	4.6	3	57	33	45	38	43
Slovakia	123	--	--	--	--	--	--	--	--	--	--	0	--	50	50	79	60
Slovenia	124	--	12	--	--	--	--	--	1	--	--	0	--	46	46	27	40
Spain	69	4916	970	19.7	18	6	33.3	114	9	7.9	20.3	3	15	20	17	8	14
Sweden	128	1650	12	0.7	4	--	--	60	1	1.7	1.2	2	80*	44	62	40	55
Switzerland	102	2927	29	1.0	16	--	--	87	1	1.2	1.1	2	80*	58	69	48	62
Ukraine	92	--	49	--	--	3	--	--	--	--	--	0	--	35	35	36	35
United Kingdom	141	1550	17	1.1	3	--	--	70	1	1.4	1.3	2	80*	29	54	14	41
Yugoslavia	91	--	--	--	--	--	--	--	--	--	--	0	--	28	28	26	27
RUSSIAN FEDERATION	35	--	207	--	--	5	--	--	2	--	--	0	--	33	33	44	37
ASIA																	
Afghanistan	86	3500	4	0.1	--	2	--	--	--	--	0.1	1	60*	42	51	32	45
Armenia	117	--	31	--	--	--	--	--	--	--	--	0	--	37	37	40	38
Azerbaijan	104	--	27	--	--	1	--	--	--	--	--	0	--	24	24	33	27
Bahrain	177	195	--	--	--	--	--	--	--	--	--	0	--	56	56	--	56
Bangladesh	63	5000	23	0.5	--	--	--	--	1	--	0.5	1	60*	30	45	46	45
Bhutan	57=	5446	17	0.3	22	5	22.7	--	1	--	11.5	2	31	32	31	48	37
Brunei Darussalam	57=	3000	25	0.8	--	0	--	--	--	--	0.8	1	60*	58	59	--	59
Cambodia	66	--	3	--	--	2	--	--	--	--	--	0	--	32	32	29	31

236

Country	W spp rank	Flowering plants			Gymnosperms			Pteridophytes			Ave %	#G	PS score	AS score	*WD score*	*DD score*	S&G index
		Tot	Thr	%	Tot	Thr	%	Tot	Thr	%							
China	2	30000	196	0.7	200	99	49.5	2000	17	0.9	17.0	3	19	28	23	48	31
Cyprus	147	1650	50	3.0	12	1	8.3	20	--	--	5.7	2	51	44	47	58	51
Georgia	97=	--	28	--	--	1	--	--	--	--	--	0	--	21	21	52	31
India	7	15000	1207	8.1	--	9	--	1000	30	3.0	5.6	2	52	19	35	49	40
Indonesia	1	27500	208	0.8	--	14	--	1875	42	2.2	1.5	2	80*	15	47	57	50
Iran	46=	6500	--	--	33	2	6.1	--	--	--	6.1	1	49	34	41	37	40
Iraq	112	2914	--	--	7	--	--	16	--	--	--	0	--	46	46	32	41
Israel	116	2294	32	1.4	8	--	--	15	--	--	1.4	1	60*	38	49	64	54
Japan	41	4700	617	13.1	42	15	35.7	630	75	11.9	20.2	3	15	17	16	2	11
Jordan	145	2088	9	0.4	6	--	--	6	--	--	0.4	1	60*	48	54	65	58
Kazakhstan	79=	--	71	--	--	0	--	--	--	--	--	0	--	35	35	71	47
Korea, DPR	127	2898	--	--	--	5	--	--	--	--	--	0	--	65	65	--	65
Korea, R	142	2898	63	2.2	--	2	--	--	1	--	2.2	1	60*	19	39	52	43
Kuwait	168	280	--	--	1	--	--	1	--	--	--	0	--	76	76	58	70
Kyrgyzstan	134	--	33	--	--	1	--	--	--	--	--	0	--	58	58	47	54
Lao PDR	49	--	1	--	--	1	--	--	--	--	--	0	--	37	37	62	45
Lebanon	129	2000	5	0.3	12	--	--	40	--	--	0.3	1	60*	52	56	60	57
Malaysia	16	15000	462	3.1	--	16	--	500	12	2.4	2.8	2	72	32	52	45	50
Maldives	180	260	--	--	2	--	--	15	--	--	--	0	--	0	0	60	20
Mongolia	109	2272	--	--	--	1	--	--	--	--	--	0	--	37	37	58	44
Myanmar	21=	7000	22	0.3	--	10	--	--	--	--	0.3	1	60*	38	49	57	52
Nepal	32	6500	19	0.3	23	1	4.4	450	--	--	2.4	2	76	36	56	56	56
Oman	148	1182	30	2.5	3	--	--	14	--	--	2.5	1	60*	37	48	60	52
Pakistan	46=	5309	13	0.3	21	1	4.8	137	--	--	2.6	2	74	42	58	55	57
Philippines	27	8000	313	3.9	31	6	19.4	900	41	4.6	9.3	3	37	11	24	42	30
Qatar	176	305	--	--	1	--	--	0	0	0	--	0	--	66	66	--	66
Saudi Arabia	114	1998	7	0.4	8	--	--	22	--	--	0.4	1	60*	49	54	31	46
Singapore	138	2000	28	1.4	2	--	--	166	1	0.6	1.0	2	80*	62	71	--	71
Sri Lanka	65	3000	421	14.0	--	--	--	314	34	10.8	12.4	2	29	27	28	73	43
Syrian Arab R	122	2000	7	0.4	12	1	8.3	40	--	--	4.4	2	58	63	60	67	62
Tajikistan	121	--	49	--	--	1	--	--	--	--	--	0	--	33	33	42	36
Thailand	14	11000	382	3.5	25	3	12.0	600	--	--	7.8	2	41	40	40	19	33
Turkey	52	8543	1875	22.0	22	--	--	85	1	1.2	11.6	2	31	31	31	54	39
Turkmenistan	94	--	17	--	--	--	--	--	--	--	--	0	--	28	28	75	44
United Arab Emirates	163=	340	--	--	2	--	--	5	--	--	--	0	--	42	42	--	42
Uzbekistan	108	--	40	--	--	1	--	--	--	--	--	0	--	32	32	45	36
Viet Nam	26	10500	326	3.1	--	18	--	--	14	--	3.1	1	60*	33	46	57	50
Yemen	135=	1620	148	9.1	2	--	--	28	1	3.6	6.4	2	48	54	51	57	53
PACIFIC																	
Australia	11	15148	2170	14.3	90	29	32.2	400	46	11.5	19.3	3	16	22	19	38	25
Fiji	137	1197	66	5.5	11	5	45.5	310	3	1.0	17.3	3	18	0	9	57	25
New Zealand	110	2160	202	9.4	22	2	9.1	200	7	3.5	7.3	3	43	0	21	28	23
Papua New Guinea	12	10000	26	0.3	44	5	11.4	1500	61	4.1	5.3	3	53	20	36	32	35
Samoa	169	514	18	3.5	0	0	0	223	--	--	3.5	2	65	0	32	--	32
Solomon Is	87	2780	38	1.4	22	2	9.1	370	2	0.5	3.7	3	63	7	35	60	43
Tonga	172	360	1	0.3	1	1	100	102	--	--	50.2	2	0	0	0	--	0
Vanuatu	175	870	23	2.6	--	3	--	--	--	--	2.6	1	60*	13	36	--	36

Notes

The species and genes index (**S&G index**) is the weighted average [weights in brackets] of a wild diversity index (***WD score***) [2] and a domesticated diversity index (***DD score***) [1]. Wild diversity has a higher weight because it is measured in terms of species, the extinction of which represents a greater genetic loss than the extinction of breeds and varieties, the measurement units for domesticated diversity.

The wild diversity index is the average of two unweighted indicators (column heading in parentheses):

Threatened wild plant species in a group as % of total wild plant species in that group (PS score). See this table for data.

Threatened wild animal species in a group as % of total wild animal species in that group (AS score). See Table 20 for data.

Data for the domesticated diversity index are given in Tables 20 and 21.

W spp rank = wild species rank. This is the average rank of each of the 180 countries in total numbers of wild native species in seven groups: three plant groups (flowering plants, gymnosperms, pteridophytes); and four animal groups (mammals, breeding birds, reptiles, amphibians). Countries were ranked separately for each group, and the average taken of the ranks.

The wild plant species indicator covers wild higher plants in three groups:

Flowering Plants = angiosperms
Gymnosperms = conifers, cycads, and gnetophytes
Pteridophytes = ferns, horsetails, and clubmosses

Tot = total native species.

Thr = threatened native species. Threatened means critically endangered (high risk of extinction in the immediate future), endangered (high risk of extinction in the near future) or vulnerable (high risk of extinction in the medium-term future). Full definitions are in IUCN Species Survival Commission (1994). Data are for 1998 and are from the UNEP World Conservation Monitoring Centre Threatened Plants Database (WCMC 1998a).

% = threatened native species as a percentage of total native species in the group concerned.

Ave % = the average percentage of the three groups.

#G = the number of groups covered. If all three groups are covered, then the indicator for that country is complete. If fewer than three are covered, then the result may be due to the lack of data. If the group does not exist in the country (for example, gymnosperms in Côte d'Ivoire), it is included in the number in brackets but is not counted in the calculation of the average percentage.

PS score = wild plant species score. The performance criteria are shown in Table 19a. The background extinction rate is estimated to be less than 0.01% of species per century (Reid & Miller 1989). I have assumed that the background percentage of threatened species is less than 100 times the extinction rate, or less than 1%. Therefore, the top of the good band was set at 0%, and the top of the fair band at 2%.

AS score = wild animal species score. The performance criteria are shown in Table 19a. They are identical to those for threatened plant species and have the same rationale.

band	top point on scale	threatened wild plant species in a group as % of total wild plant species in that group	threatened wild animal species in a group as % of total wild animal species in that group
good	100	0	0
fair	80	2	2
medium	60	4	4
poor	40	8	8
bad	20	16	16
base	0	32	32

Table 19a Performance criteria for wild diversity indicators.

* A score with an asterisk has been reduced in accordance with the insufficient data rule. To prevent high scores resulting merely from lack of data, a good score is allowed only if it is based on all applicable components (data in an indicator, indicators in an index), and a fair score only if it is based on at least half the components. Good and fair scores (100-61) based on fewer than half the applicable components have been reduced to 60. Good scores (100-81) based on more than half but not all the applicable components have been reduced to 80.

Table 20. Wild Animal Species; Domesticated Diversity

Country	Mammals			Birds			Reptiles			Amphibians			MB %	MB RA%	#cl	AS score	BrD mean	BrD score	Thbr mean	Thbr score	DD score
	Total	Thr	%	Total	Thr	%	Total	Thr	%	Total	Thr	%									
AMERICAS																					
Antigua & Barbuda	7	0	0.0	49	1	2.0	13	5	38.5	2	0	0.0	1.0	10.1	4	35	--	--	--	--	--
Argentina	320	32	10.0	897	37	4.1	220	6	2.7	145	5	3.4	7.1	5.1	4	44	0.1	2	0.67	33	17
Bahamas	12	5	41.7	88	3	3.4	35	5	14.3	2	0	0.0	22.5	14.9	4	12	--	--	0.00	60*	60
Barbados	6	0	0.0	24	0	0.0	9	2	22.2	1	0	0.0	0.0	5.6	4	52	--	--	0.00	60*	60
Belize	125	4	3.2	356	2	0.6	107	4	3.7	32	0	0.0	1.9	1.9	4	81	--	--	--	--	--
Bolivia	316	23	7.3	1170	27	2.3	208	2	1.0	112	1	0.9	4.8	2.9	4	56	0.6	12	0.67	33	22
Brazil	394	79	20.1	1492	112	7.5	470	22	4.7	505	6	1.2	13.8	8.4	4	25	0.1	2	2.29	0	1
Canada	193	14	7.3	426	7	1.6	41	2	4.9	41	1	2.4	4.4	4.1	4	58	4.2	55	0.75	30	42
Chile	91	21	23.1	296	19	6.4	72	0	0.0	41	3	7.3	14.8	9.2	4	23	0.8	16	0.33	51	33
Colombia	359	36	10.0	1695	76	4.5	585	13	2.2	585	0	0.0	7.3	4.2	4	43	0.3	6	0.45	43	24
Costa Rica	205	14	6.8	600	13	2.2	214	7	3.3	162	1	0.6	4.5	3.2	4	57	--	--	--	--	--
Cuba	31	11	35.5	137	14	10.2	102	7	6.9	48	0	0.0	22.9	13.1	4	11	1.7	34	0.00	80*	57
Dominica	12	1	8.3	52	3	5.8	14	4	28.6	2	0	0.0	7.1	10.7	4	33	--	--	--	--	--
Dominican R	20	5	25.0	136	14	10.3	105	10	9.5	35	1	2.9	17.6	11.9	4	18	0.5	10	0.00	60*	35
Ecuador	302	31	10.3	1388	61	4.4	374	10	2.7	402	0	0.0	7.3	4.3	4	43	0.2	4	1.00	20	12
El Salvador	135	2	1.5	251	0	0.0	73	4	5.5	23	0	0.0	0.8	1.8	4	82	--	--	--	--	--
Grenada	15	0	0.0	50	1	2.0	16	4	25.0	3	0	0.0	1.0	6.8	4	46	--	--	--	--	--
Guatemala	250	6	2.4	458	5	1.1	231	8	3.5	99	0	0.0	1.8	1.8	4	82	0.4	8	1.00	20	14
Guyana	193	9	4.7	678	2	0.3	--	6	--	--	0	--	2.5	2.5	2	75	--	--	0.00	60*	60
Haiti	4	4	100	75	13	17.3	102	7	6.9	46	1	2.2	58.7	31.6	4	0	--	--	--	--	--
Honduras	173	9	5.2	422	4	0.9	152	6	3.9	56	0	0.0	3.0	2.5	4	70	--	--	--	--	--
Jamaica	24	5	20.8	113	9	8.0	36	8	22.2	21	4	19.0	14.4	17.5	4	18	--	--	--	--	--
Mexico	450	69	15.3	769	38	4.9	687	18	2.6	285	4	1.4	10.1	6.1	4	35	0.1	2	0.33	51	26
Nicaragua	200	6	3.0	482	4	0.8	161	7	4.3	59	0	0.0	1.9	2.0	4	80	--	--	--	--	--
Panama	218	20	9.2	732	16	2.2	226	7	3.1	164	0	0.0	5.7	3.6	4	51	--	--	--	--	--
Paraguay	305	9	3.0	556	24	4.3	120	2	1.7	85	0	0.0	3.7	2.3	4	63	0.1	2	1.00	20	11
Peru	344	47	13.7	1538	71	4.6	298	6	2.0	315	1	0.3	9.1	5.2	4	37	0.4	8	1.00	100	54
St Kitts & Nevis	7	0	0.0	32	1	3.1	10	3	30.0	1	0	0.0	1.5	8.3	4	39	--	--	--	--	--
St Lucia	9	1	11.1	50	5	10.0	17	6	35.3	2	0	0.0	10.6	14.1	4	25	--	--	--	--	--
St Vincent & Grenadines	8	2	25.0	108	2	1.9	16	4	25.0	3	0	0.0	13.4	13.0	4	26	--	--	--	--	--
Suriname	180	11	6.1	603	1	0.2	151	6	4.0	95	0	0.0	3.2	2.6	4	68	--	--	--	--	--
Trinidad & Tobago	100	1	1.0	260	2	0.8	70	5	7.1	26	0	0.0	0.9	2.2	4	78	--	--	0.00	60*	60
United States	428	37	8.6	650	55	8.5	280	27	9.6	233	25	10.7	8.6	9.4	4	36	0.9	18	0.46	43	30
Uruguay	81	6	7.4	237	10	4.2	--	3	--	--	0	--	5.8	5.8	2	51	1.0	20	0.50	40	30
Venezuela	305	25	8.2	1181	24	2.0	259	12	4.6	199	0	0.0	5.1	3.7	4	54	0.2	4	0.00	80*	42
AFRICA																					
Algeria	92	13	14.1	192	5	2.6	--	2	--	--	0	--	8.4	8.4	2	39	0.5	10	0.05	90	50
Angola	276	18	6.5	765	10	1.3	--	4	--	--	0	--	3.9	3.9	2	61	1.3	26	0.00	60*	43
Benin	188	7	3.7	307	0	0.0	--	1	--	--	0	--	1.9	1.9	2	80*	1.8	36	0.00	100	68
Botswana	164	5	3.0	386	4	1.0	157	0	0.0	38	0	0.0	2.0	1.0	4	80	6.5	66	0.11	78	72
Burkina Faso	147	7	4.8	335	1	0.3	--	1	--	--	0	--	2.5	2.5	2	75	0.5	10	0.00	80*	45
Burundi	107	5	4.7	451	4	0.9	--	0	--	--	0	--	2.8	2.8	2	72	3.0	47	2.00	0	23
Cameroon	297	37	12.5	690	12	1.7	--	1	--	--	1	--	7.1	7.1	2	44	0.7	14	0.36	49	31
Cape Verde	5	3	60.0	38	2	5.3	12	0	0.0	0	0	0	32.7	21.8	4	0	--	--	--	--	--
Central African R	209	12	5.7	537	1	0.2	--	1	--	--	0	--	3.0	3.0	2	70	1.0	20	0.00	80*	50
Chad	134	17	12.7	370	1	0.3	--	1	--	--	0	--	6.5	6.5	2	47	2.0	40	0.33	51	45
Comoros	12	2	16.7	50	7	14.0	22	2	9.1	--	0	--	15.4	13.3	3	21	--	--	--	--	--
Congo, DR	415	40	9.6	929	24	2.6	--	2	--	--	0	--	6.1	6.1	2	49	3.0	47	0.30	53	50
Congo, R	200	12	6.0	449	1	0.2	--	1	--	--	0	--	3.1	3.1	2	69	13.0	86	0.00	100	93
Côte d'Ivoire	230	17	7.4	535	9	1.7	--	2	--	--	1	--	4.6	4.6	2	57	1.8	36	0.00	100	68
Djibouti	--	4	--	126	1	0.8	--	0	--	--	0	--	0.8	0.8	1	60*	3.7	51	0.00	60*	55
Egypt	98	12	12.2	153	1	0.7	83	6	7.2	6	0	0.0	6.4	5.0	4	48	1.5	30	0.11	78	54
Equatorial Guinea	184	15	8.2	273	4	1.5	--	2	--	--	0	--	4.8	4.8	2	56	--	--	0.00	60*	60
Eritrea	112	12	10.7	319	0	0.0	--	6	--	--	0	--	5.3	5.3	2	53	2.1	41	0.00	100	70
Ethiopia	255	34	13.3	626	12	1.9	--	1	--	--	0	--	7.6	7.6	2	42	0.3	6	0.03	94	50
Gabon	190	15	7.9	466	3	0.6	--	1	--	--	0	--	4.3	4.3	2	58	--	--	0.00	60*	60
Gambia	108	3	2.8	280	0	0.0	--	1	--	--	0	--	1.4	1.4	2	80*	4.0	53	0.00	80*	66
Ghana	222	13	5.9	529	6	1.1	--	2	--	--	0	--	3.5	3.5	2	65	1.3	26	0.11	78	52
Guinea	190	11	5.8	409	9	2.2	--	1	--	--	1	--	4.0	4.0	2	60	1.0	20	0.00	100	60
Guinea-Bissau	108	2	1.9	243	0	0.0	--	1	--	--	0	--	0.9	0.9	2	80*	2.5	43	0.00	80*	61
Kenya	359	51	14.2	844	18	2.1	187	5	2.7	88	0	0.0	8.1	4.8	4	40	1.6	32	0.07	86	59

239

Country	Mammals			Birds			Reptiles			Amphibians			MB %	MB RA%	#cl	AS score	BrD mean	BrD score	Thbr mean	Thbr score	DD score
	Total	Thr	%	Total	Thr	%	Total	Thr	%	Total	Thr	%	%	RA%		score	mean	score	mean	score	score
Lesotho	33	3	9.1	58	3	5.2	--	0	--	--	0	--	7.2	7.2	2	44	1.8	36	0.00	60*	48
Liberia	193	16	8.3	372	10	2.7	62	2	3.2	38	0	0.0	5.5	3.5	4	52	4.5	57	0.50	40	48
Libyan Arab J	76	9	11.8	91	1	1.1	--	3	--	--	0	--	6.4	6.4	2	48	2.6	44	0.00	100	72
Madagascar	105	50	47.6	202	27	13.4	252	18	7.1	144	2	1.4	30.5	17.4	4	2	0.1	2	1.00	20	11
Malawi	195	8	4.1	521	8	1.5	124	0	0.0	69	0	0.0	2.8	1.4	4	72	1.4	28	0.00	80*	54
Mali	137	13	9.5	397	1	0.3	16	1	6.3	--	0	--	4.9	5.4	3	53	0.6	12	0.00	100	56
Mauritania	61	10	16.4	273	1	0.4	--	2	--	--	0	--	8.4	8.4	2	39	0.8	16	0.00	100	58
Mauritius	4	4	100	27	10	37.0	11	4	36.4	0	0	0	68.5	57.8	4	0	--	--	0.67	33	33
Morocco	105	16	15.2	210	4	1.9	--	2	--	--	0	--	8.6	8.6	2	38	2.6	44	0.33	51	47
Mozambique	179	15	8.4	498	12	2.4	--	5	--	62	0	0.0	5.4	3.6	3	53	3.8	52	0.67	33	42
Namibia	154	14	9.1	469	7	1.5	--	3	--	32	1	3.1	5.3	4.6	3	53	0.7	14	0.50	40	27
Niger	131	11	8.4	299	1	0.3	--	0	--	--	0	--	4.3	4.3	2	58	1.7	34	0.33	51	42
Nigeria	274	25	9.1	681	6	0.9	>135	2	1.5	>109	0	0.0	5.0	2.9	4	55	0.2	4	0.07	86	45
Rwanda	151	8	5.3	513	6	1.2	--	0	--	--	0	--	3.3	3.3	2	67	1.4	28	2.00	0	14
São Tomé & Principe	8	3	37.5	63	9	14.3	16	1	6.3	9	0	0.0	25.9	14.5	4	8	--	--	--	--	--
Senegal	155	11	7.1	384	2	0.5	--	6	--	--	0	--	3.8	3.8	2	62	0.7	14	0.00	100	57
Seychelles	--	4	--	38	9	23.7	15	4	26.7	12	4	33.3	23.7	27.9	3	5	--	--	--	--	--
Sierra Leone	147	11	7.5	466	9	1.9	--	3	--	--	0	--	4.7	4.7	2	56	3.9	53	0.00	80*	66
Somalia	171	19	11.1	422	6	1.4	193	2	1.0	27	0	0.0	6.3	3.4	4	48	--	--	--	--	--
South Africa	247	41	16.6	596	25	4.2	299	19	6.4	95	9	9.5	10.4	9.2	4	34	0.7	14	0.09	82	48
Sudan	267	24	9.0	680	2	0.3	--	2	--	--	0	--	4.7	4.7	2	56	0.3	6	0.04	92	49
Swaziland	47	4	8.5	364	3	0.8	102	0	0.0	40	0	0.0	4.7	2.3	4	56	5.3	61	0.00	100	80
Tanzania	316	43	13.6	822	28	3.4	284	5	1.8	124	0	0.0	8.5	4.7	4	39	0.2	4	1.25	15	9
Togo	196	9	4.6	391	0	0.0	--	2	--	--	0	--	2.3	2.3	2	77	6.7	67	0.00	100	83
Tunisia	78	11	14.1	173	3	1.7	--	3	--	--	0	--	7.9	7.9	2	40	0.9	18	1.00	20	19
Uganda	338	19	5.6	830	7	0.8	149	0	0.0	50	0	0.0	3.2	1.6	4	68	0.8	16	0.50	40	28
Zambia	229	12	5.2	605	5	0.8	--	0	--	83	0	0.0	3.0	2.0	3	70	1.8	36	0.00	60*	48
Zimbabwe	270	12	4.4	532	4	0.8	153	0	0.0	120	0	0.0	2.6	1.3	4	74	2.2	41	0.28	55	48
EUROPE																					
Albania	68	3	4.4	230	1	0.4	31	4	12.9	13	0	0.0	2.4	4.4	4	58	6.3	65	0.62	35	50
Austria	83	9	10.8	213	2	0.9	14	0	0.0	20	0	0.0	5.8	2.9	4	51	3.5	50	1.12	18	34
Belarus	57	5	8.8	221	3	1.4	7	0	0.0	13	0	0.0	5.1	2.5	4	54	1.8	36	0.44	44	40
Belgium	58	11	19.0	180	1	0.6	8	0	0.0	17	0	0.0	9.8	4.9	4	35	9.5	78	0.88	25	51
Bosnia & Herzegovina	72	10	13.9	--	2	--	27	1	3.7	16	1	6.3	13.9	8.0	3	25	2.9	46	0.50	40	43
Bulgaria	81	15	18.5	240	4	1.7	33	2	6.1	17	0	0.0	10.1	6.6	4	35	1.4	28	1.17	17	22
Croatia	76	9	11.8	224	3	1.3	29	1	3.4	20	1	5.0	6.6	5.4	4	47	6.0	64	1.50	10	37
Czech R	81	8	9.9	199	1	0.5	10	0	0.0	19	0	0.0	5.2	2.6	4	54	11.3	83	2.03	0	41
Denmark	43	5	11.6	196	1	0.5	5	0	0.0	14	0	0.0	6.1	3.0	4	49	8.0	72	1.26	15	43
Estonia	65	5	7.7	213	2	0.9	5	0	0.0	11	0	0.0	4.3	2.2	4	58	6.3	65	0.17	66	65
Finland	60	6	10.0	248	3	1.2	5	0	0.0	5	0	0.0	5.6	2.8	4	52	3.6	51	0.17	66	58
France	93	18	19.4	269	2	0.7	32	3	9.4	32	1	3.1	10.1	8.1	4	35	1.8	36	0.74	30	33
Germany	76	12	15.8	239	3	1.3	12	0	0.0	20	0	0.0	8.6	4.3	4	38	2.8	45	0.36	49	47
Greece	95	14	14.7	251	2	0.8	51	6	11.8	15	1	6.7	7.8	8.5	4	39	1.0	20	0.79	28	24
Hungary	72	9	12.5	205	4	2.0	15	1	6.7	17	0	0.0	7.3	5.3	4	43	2.4	43	1.31	14	28
Iceland	11	6	54.5	88	0	0.0	0	0	0	0	0	0	27.3	27.3	4	6	2.1	41	0.00	100	70
Ireland	25	5	20.0	142	1	0.7	1	0	0.0	3	0	0.0	10.4	5.2	4	34	1.0	20	0.02	96	58
Italy	90	14	15.6	234	2	0.9	40	4	10.0	34	4	11.8	8.3	9.6	4	36	4.3	59	0.75	33	46
Latvia	83	5	6.0	217	2	0.9	7	0	0.0	13	0	0.0	3.5	1.7	4	65	6.3	65	0.39	47	56
Lithuania	68	5	7.4	202	3	1.5	7	0	0.0	13	0	0.0	4.4	2.2	4	58	9.9	80	0.58	37	58
Luxembourg	55	6	10.9	126	1	0.8	7	0	0.0	14	0	0.0	5.8	2.9	4	51	9.5	78	0.88	25	51
Macedonia, FYR	77	11	14.3	--	3	--	24	2	8.3	12	0	0.0	14.3	7.5	3	24	3.5	50	0.33	51	50
Malta	22	3	13.6	26	0	0.0	8	0	0.0	1	0	0.0	6.8	3.4	4	46	--	--	0.00	80*	80
Moldova	68	3	4.4	177	5	2.8	9	1	11.1	13	0	0.0	3.6	4.6	4	57	3.4	49	0.11	78	63
Netherlands	55	11	20.0	191	1	0.5	7	0	0.0	16	0	0.0	10.3	5.1	4	34	1.2	24	0.24	57	40
Norway	54	10	18.5	243	2	0.8	5	0	0.0	5	0	0.0	9.6	4.8	4	36	1.5	30	0.73	31	30
Poland	84	15	17.9	227	3	1.3	9	0	0.0	18	0	0.0	9.6	4.8	4	36	11.4	83	0.15	70	76
Portugal	63	17	27.0	207	4	1.9	29	0	0.0	17	1	5.9	14.4	8.7	4	24	3.1	47	0.37	49	48
Romania	84	17	20.2	247	3	1.2	25	2	8.0	19	0	0.0	10.7	7.3	4	33	0.7	14	0.19	62	38
Slovakia	85	9	10.6	209	3	1.4	14	1	7.1	18	0	0.0	6.0	4.8	4	50	4.9	59	0.00	100	79
Slovenia	69	9	13.0	207	1	0.5	21	0	0.0	20	1	5.0	6.8	4.6	4	46	4.1	54	1.94	1	27
Spain	82	24	29.3	278	6	2.2	53	6	11.3	25	3	12.0	15.8	13.7	4	20	0.8	16	1.97	1	8
Sweden	60	8	13.3	249	2	0.8	6	0	0.0	13	0	0.0	7.1	3.5	4	44	3.9	53	0.81	28	40
Switzerland	75	6	8.0	193	1	0.5	14	0	0.0	18	0	0.0	4.3	2.1	4	58	4.0	53	0.46	43	48
Ukraine	97	17	17.5	263	6	2.3	24	2	8.3	21	0	0.0	9.9	7.0	4	35	1.0	20	0.30	53	36
United Kingdom	50	12	24.0	230	1	0.4	8	0	0.0	7	0	0.0	12.2	6.1	4	29	1.1	22	1.69	6	14
Yugoslavia	86	11	12.8	--	4	--	33	1	3.0	21	0	0.0	12.8	5.3	3	28	1.3	26	0.84	26	26

Country	Mammals			Birds			Reptiles			Amphibians			MB %	MB RA%	#cl	AS score	BrD mean	BrD score	Thbr mean	Thbr score	*DD score*
	Total	Thr	%	Total	Thr	%	Total	Thr	%	Total	Thr	%									
RUSSIAN FEDERATION	269	42	15.6	628	35	5.6	58	6	10.3	23	0	0.0	10.6	7.9	4	33	2.7	45	0.46	43	44
ASIA																					
Afghanistan	123	13	10.6	235	4	1.7	103	1	1.0	6	1	16.7	6.2	7.5	4	42	0.2	4	0.00	60*	32
Armenia	77	7	9.1	--	3	--	51	5	9.8	6	0	0.0	9.1	6.3	3	37	3.5	50	0.75	30	40
Azerbaijan	91	13	14.3	--	3	--	54	5	9.3	10	0	0.0	14.3	7.9	3	24	1.4	28	0.56	38	33
Bahrain	17	1	5.9	28	1	3.6	25	0	0.0	1	0	0.0	4.8	2.4	4	56	--	--	--	--	--
Bangladesh	109	21	19.3	295	13	4.4	119	21	17.6	19	0	0.0	11.9	10.3	4	30	0.4	8	0.08	84	46
Bhutan	99	20	20.2	448	10	2.2	19	0	0.0	24	0	0.0	11.2	5.6	4	32	4.6	57	0.50	40	48
Brunei Darussalam	157	9	5.7	359	11	3.1	44	3	6.8	76	0	0.0	4.4	3.9	4	58	--	--	--	--	--
Cambodia	123	21	17.1	307	15	4.9	82	10	12.2	28	0	0.0	11.0	8.6	4	32	0.9	18	0.50	40	29
China	394	76	19.3	1100	64	5.8	340	31	9.1	263	1	0.4	12.6	8.6	4	28	0.2	4	0.04	92	48
Cyprus	21	3	14.3	79	0	0.0	23	3	13.0	4	0	0.0	7.2	6.8	4	44	6.7	60*	0.25	57	58
Georgia	89	14	15.7	--	3	--	50	7	14.0	14	1	7.1	15.7	12.3	3	21	6.1	64	0.49	41	52
India	316	86	27.2	923	56	6.1	390	25	6.4	197	3	1.5	16.6	10.3	4	19	0.3	6	0.04	92	49
Indonesia	436	140	32.1	1519	108	7.1	511	28	5.5	270	0	0.0	19.6	11.2	4	15	1.6	32	0.09	82	57
Iran	140	23	16.4	323	6	1.9	164	8	4.9	11	2	18.2	9.1	10.4	4	34	1.5	30	0.44	44	37
Iraq	81	10	12.3	172	2	1.2	81	2	2.5	6	0	0.0	6.8	4.0	4	46	0.7	14	0.33	51	32
Israel	92	14	15.2	180	4	2.2	--	4	--	--	0	--	8.7	8.7	2	38	3.3	49	0.00	80*	64
Japan	132	37	28.0	>250	20	8.0	66	11	16.7	52	10	19.2	18.0	18.0	4	17	0.2	4	3.50	0	2
Jordan	71	8	11.3	141	2	1.4	--	1	--	--	0	--	6.3	6.3	2	48	1.5	30	0.00	100	65
Kazakhstan	178	18	10.1	--	12	--	49	2	4.1	12	1	8.3	10.1	7.5	3	35	2.3	42	0.00	100	71
Korea, DPR	--	13	--	115	4	3.5	19	0	0.0	14	0	0.0	3.5	1.2	3	65	--	--	--	--	--
Korea, R	49	13	26.5	112	8	7.1	25	0	0.0	14	0	0.0	16.8	8.4	4	19	1.2	24	0.00	80*	52
Kuwait	21	1	4.8	20	0	0.0	29	1	3.4	2	0	0.0	2.4	2.1	4	76	4.5	57	0.00	60*	58
Kyrgyzstan	--	7	--	--	3	--	23	2	8.7	3	0	0.0	--	4.4	2	58	2.5	43	0.33	51	47
Lao PDR	172	27	15.7	487	13	2.7	66	12	18.2	37	0	0.0	9.2	9.1	4	37	1.2	24	0.00	100	62
Lebanon	54	6	11.1	154	0	0.0	--	1	--	--	0	--	5.6	5.6	2	52	--	--	0.00	60*	60
Malaysia	286	47	16.4	501	29	5.8	268	21	7.8	158	0	0.0	11.1	7.5	4	32	2.9	46	0.44	44	45
Maldives	3	0	0.0	23	0	0.0	2	2	100	0	0	0	0.0	33.3	4	0	--	--	0.00	60*	60
Mongolia	134	12	9.0	--	11	--	21	0	0.0	8	0	0.0	9.0	3.0	3	37	0.8	16	0.00	100	58
Myanmar	251	36	14.3	867	26	3.0	203	20	9.9	75	0	0.0	8.6	6.8	4	38	0.7	14	0.00	100	57
Nepal	167	27	16.2	611	16	2.6	80	5	6.3	36	0	0.0	9.4	6.3	4	36	0.6	12	0.00	100	56
Oman	56	9	16.1	107	2	1.9	64	4	6.3	--	0	--	9.0	8.1	3	37	6.3	60*	0.00	60*	60
Pakistan	151	18	11.9	375	12	3.2	172	9	5.2	17	0	0.0	7.6	5.1	4	42	0.5	10	0.00	100	55
Philippines	153	50	32.7	395	57	14.4	190	8	4.2	67	22	32.8	23.5	21.0	4	11	0.2	4	0.00	80*	42
Qatar	11	0	0.0	23	1	4.3	17	1	5.9	--	0	--	2.2	3.4	3	66	--	--	--	--	--
Saudi Arabia	77	7	9.1	155	5	3.2	84	2	2.4	--	0	--	6.2	4.9	3	49	0.1	2	0.00	60*	31
Singapore	45	3	6.7	118	1	0.8	--	3	--	--	0	--	3.8	3.8	2	62	--	--	--	--	--
Sri Lanka	88	20	22.7	250	9	3.6	144	8	5.6	39	0	0.0	13.1	8.0	4	27	3.1	47	0.00	100	73
Syrian Arab R	63	4	6.3	204	2	1.0	--	3	--	--	0	--	3.7	3.7	2	63	1.7	34	0.33	51	42
Tajikistan	84	9	10.7	--	5	--	44	1	2.3	2	0	0.0	10.7	4.3	3	33	1.7	34	0.33	51	42
Thailand	265	34	12.8	616	20	3.2	298	18	6.0	107	0	0.0	8.0	5.5	4	40	0.3	6	0.67	33	19
Turkey	116	17	14.7	302	7	2.3	102	12	11.8	18	3	16.7	8.5	11.4	4	31	0.4	8	0.00	100	54
Turkmenistan	103	13	12.6	--	3	--	82	2	2.4	5	0	0.0	12.6	5.0	3	28	63.5	100	0.33	51	75
United Arab Emirates	25	3	12.0	67	2	3.0	37	1	2.7	--	0	--	7.5	5.9	3	42	--	--	--	--	--
Uzbekistan	97	11	11.3	--	7	--	64	1	1.6	2	0	0.0	11.3	4.3	3	32	1.2	24	0.17	66	45
Viet Nam	213	37	17.4	535	20	3.7	180	24	13.3	80	1	1.3	10.6	8.9	4	33	0.7	14	0.00	100	57
Yemen	66	4	6.1	143	6	4.2	77	2	2.6	--	0	--	5.2	4.3	3	54	0.7	14	0.00	100	57
PACIFIC																					
Australia	252	63	25.0	649	33	5.1	748	39	5.2	205	25	12.2	15.1	11.9	4	22	1.7	34	0.46	43	38
Fiji	4	5	100	74	12	16.2	25	6	24.0	2	1	50.0	58.1	47.5	4	0	4.3	55	0.00	60*	57
New Zealand	10	8	80.0	150	62	41.3	42	11	26.2	3	1	33.3	60.7	45.2	4	0	1.2	24	0.67	33	28
Papua New Guinea	214	58	27.1	644	32	5.0	280	9	3.2	197	0	0.0	16.0	8.8	4	20	0.7	14	0.33	51	32
Samoa	3	3	100	40	6	15.0	8	1	12.5	--	0	--	57.5	42.5	3	0	--	--	--	--	--
Solomon Is	53	21	39.6	163	22	13.5	61	4	6.6	17	0	0.0	26.5	14.9	4	7	--	--	0.00	60*	60
Tonga	1	1	100	37	3	8.1	6	2	33.3	0	0	0	54.0	47.1	4	0	--	--	--	--	--
Vanuatu	12	4	33.3	76	8	10.5	20	2	10.0	0	0	0	21.9	17.9	4	13	--	--	--	--	--

Notes

The wild animal species indicator covers four higher animal classes:

Mammals (excluding oceanic mammals).

Birds. Birds include only species that breed in the country concerned, because of widely differing standards in recording vagrants, accidentals, and irregular migrants. The number of breeding bird species in Bolivia was extrapolated from the number of total bird species.

Reptiles.

Amphibians.

Total = total native species. Data are from the UNEP World Conservation Monitoring Centre Threatened Animals Database (WCMC 1998b).

Thr = threatened native species. Threatened means critically endangered (high risk of extinction in the immediate future), endangered (high risk of extinction in the near future) or vulnerable (high risk of extinction in the medium-term future). Full definitions are in IUCN Species Survival Commission (1994). Data are for 2000 and are from the IUCN Species Survival Commission (2000), except for data on threatened breeding bird species which are from BirdLife International (2000).

% = threatened native species as a percentage of total native species in the class concerned.

MB % = the average percentage of mammals and birds.

MBRA % = the average percentage of mammals, birds, reptiles and amphibians.

#cl = the number of classes covered. If all four classes are covered, then the indicator for that country is complete. If fewer than four are covered, then the result may be due to the lack of data. If the class does not exist in the country (for example, reptiles in Iceland), it is included in the number in brackets but is not counted in the calculation of the average percentage.

AS score = wild animal species score. This is based on either the average percentage of mammals and birds or the average percentage of mammals, birds, reptiles and amphibians, whichever gives the lower score. The mammal and bird data are more reliable than the data on reptiles and amphibians, and ideally the indicator would be based on these two classes alone. However, the reptile and amphibian data are no worse than the plant data, and excluding them would give misleadingly high scores to several countries, such as Barbados and Turkey. Scores are based on mammals and birds alone in 160 countries, and on the four classes in 23 countries (11 in the Americas, 2 in Africa, 4 in Europe, 6 in Asia). The performance criteria are shown in Table 19a.

The domesticated diversity index (***DD score***) is the average of two unweighted indicators (column heading in parentheses):

Breed diversity (BrD mean), represented by the number of not at risk breeds per million head of a species.

Threatened breeds (Thbr mean), represented by the ratio of threatened to not at risk breeds of a species.

Belgium and Luxembourg: in this table and Table 21, domesticated diversity entries for Belgium and Luxembourg refer to the two countries together, because FAO (2000a) does not provide data on them separately.

BrD mean = mean breed diversity = the number of not at risk breeds per million head of a species, taking the average of three domesticated mammal species: the most numerous species and the next two most numerous or best assessed species in the country concerned. Data are in Table 21. *Note: this indicator is not applied to species of fewer than 100,000 head and only one not at risk breed, to prevent such cases from inflating the score.*

BrD score = breed diversity score. The performance criteria are shown in Table 20a.

Thbr mean = mean threatened breeds = the ratio of threatened to not at risk breeds of a species, taking the average of the three species chosen for mean breed diversity. Data are in Table 21.

Thbr score = mean threatened breeds score. The performance criteria are shown in Table 20a. The tops of the poor, medium and fair bands (0.5, 0.2 and 0.1 threatened breeds per one not at risk breed) correspond to 1 threatened breed per 2, 5 and 10 not at risk breeds respectively.

band	top point on scale	number of not at risk breeds per million head of a species	ratio of threatened to not at risk breeds of a species
good	100	20	0.0
fair	80	10	0.1
medium	60	5	0.2
poor	40	2	0.5
bad	20	1	1.0
base	0	0	2.0

Table 20a Performance criteria for domesticated diversity indicators.

* A score with an asterisk has been reduced in accordance with the insufficient data rule. To prevent high scores resulting merely from lack of data, a good score is allowed only if it is based on all applicable components (data in an indicator, indicators in an index), and a fair score only if it is based on at least half the components. Good and fair scores (100-61) based on fewer than half the applicable components have been reduced to 60. Good scores (100-81) based on more than half but not all the applicable components have been reduced to 80.

Table 21. Domesticated Diversity (continued)

Country	Sp	Head 000	Br tot	Br thr	Br tm	Br ok	Br div	Thr rat	Sp	Head 000	Br tot	Br thr	Br tm	Br ok	Br div	Thr rat	Sp	Head 000	Br tot	Br thr	Br tm	Br ok	Br div	Thr rat
AMERICAS																								
Antigua & Barbuda	Bos	15.7	1	--	--	--	--	--	Cap	11.8	1	--	--	--	--	--	Ovi	12.2	0	--	--	--	--	--
Argentina	Bos	55000.0	4	1	0	1	0.0	1.00	Eqc	3300.0	2	1	0	1	0.3	1.00	Ovi	14000.0	3	0	0	2	0.1	0.00
Bahamas	Cap	14.5	0	--	--	--	--	--	Ovi	5.7	2	0	0	1	--	0.00	Sus	5.8	0	--	--	--	--	--
Barbados	Ovi	41.0	1	0	0	1	--	0.00	Bos	23.0	1	--	--	--	--	--	Sus	33.0	0	--	--	--	--	--
Belize	Bos	58.0	0	--	--	--	--	--	Eqc	5.0	0	--	--	--	--	--	Sus	23.0	1	--	--	--	--	--
Bolivia	Ovi	8574.5	1	0	0	1	0.1	0.00	Bos	6556.0	3	2	0	1	0.2	2.00	Lam	1900.0	3	0	0	3	1.6	0.00
Brazil	Bos	163470.0	27	1	3	13	0.1	0.19	Ovi	18300.0	7	2	0	3	0.2	0.67	Sus	27425.0	12	6	0	0	0.0	6.00
Canada	Bos	12981.0	14	2	1	6	0.5	0.42	Eqc	508.0	12	2	0	6	11.8	0.33	Sus	12402.7	5	3	0	2	0.2	1.50
Chile	Bos	4134.0	1	0	0	1	0.2	0.00	Eqc	590.0	1	1	0	0	1.7	1.00	Ovi	4116.0	2	0	0	2	0.5	0.00
Colombia	Bos	25614.2	10	4	1	5	0.2	0.90	Ovi	2195.6	3	0	0	1	0.5	0.00	Sus	2764.6	4	--	--	--	--	--
Costa Rica	Bos	1617.0	2	--	--	--	--	--	Eqc	114.5	0	--	--	--	--	--	Sus	290.0	1	--	--	--	--	--
Cuba	Bos	4650.0	6	0	0	1	0.2	0.00	Eqc	620.0	1	--	--	--	--	--	Ovi	310.0	1	0	0	1	3.2	0.00
Dominica	Bos	13.4	1	--	--	--	--	--	Cap	9.7	1	--	--	--	--	--	Ovi	7.6	0	--	--	--	--	--
Dominican R	Bos	1904.4	4	0	0	1	0.5	0.00	Cap	163.5	1	--	--	--	--	--	Sus	539.6	0	--	--	--	--	--
Ecuador	Bos	5534.0	2	1	0	1	0.2	1.00	Ovi	2180.2	1	--	--	--	--	--	Sus	2786.3	0	--	--	--	--	--
El Salvador	Bos	1141.5	0	--	--	--	--	--	Eqc	95.8	0	--	--	--	--	--	Sus	335.1	1	--	--	--	--	--
Grenada	Ovi	13.0	0	--	--	--	--	--	Bos	4.4	1	--	--	--	--	--	Cap	7.0	1	--	--	--	--	--
Guatemala	Bos	2300.0	2	1	0	1	0.4	1.00	Ovi	551.3	1	--	--	--	--	--	Sus	825.0	1	--	--	--	--	--
Guyana	Bos	220.0	0	--	--	--	--	--	Ovi	130.0	1	0	0	1	7.7	0.00	Sus	20.0	1	--	--	--	--	--
Haiti	Cap	1618.2	1	--	--	--	--	--	Bos	1300.0	1	--	--	--	--	--	Sus	800.0	0	--	--	--	--	--
Honduras	Bos	2060.8	1	--	--	--	--	--	Eqc	178.0	0	--	--	--	--	--	Sus	700.0	1	--	--	--	--	--
Jamaica	Cap	440.0	0	--	--	--	--	--	Bos	400.0	6	--	--	--	--	--	Sus	180.0	0	--	--	--	--	--
Mexico	Bos	30293.1	5	0	0	1	0.0	0.00	Ovi	5900.0	5	0	0	1	0.2	0.00	Sus	13854.9	3	1	0	0	0.1	1.00
Nicaragua	Bos	1693.0	1	--	--	--	--	--	Eqc	245.0	0	--	--	--	--	--	Sus	700.0	1	--	--	--	--	--
Panama	Bos	1400.0	0	--	--	--	--	--	Eqc	165.0	0	--	--	--	--	--	Sus	251.8	1	--	--	--	--	--
Paraguay	Bos	9863.0	1	1	0	0	0.1	1.00	Eqc	400.0	0	--	--	--	--	--	Sus	2500.0	0	--	--	--	--	--
Peru	Ovi	13700.0	2	0	0	2	0.1	0.00	Bos	4898.3	1	0	0	1	0.2	0.00	Lam	4147.0	4	0	0	4	1.0	0.00
St Kitts & Nevis	Cap	14.5	1	--	--	--	--	--	Bos	3.6	1	--	--	--	--	--	Ovi	8.0	0	--	--	--	--	--
St Lucia	Sus	14.8	0	--	--	--	--	--	Bos	12.4	1	--	--	--	--	--	Ovi	12.5	0	--	--	--	--	--
St Vincent & Grenadines	Ovi	13.0	0	--	--	--	--	--	Bos	6.2	1	--	--	--	--	--	Cap	6.0	1	--	--	--	--	--
Suriname	Bos	102.0	0	--	--	--	--	--	Ovi	10.6	0	--	--	--	--	--	Sus	25.0	0	--	--	--	--	--
Trinidad & Tobago	Cap	59.0	1	--	--	--	--	--	Bos	34.0	2	--	--	--	--	--	Ovi	12.0	1	0	0	1	--	0.00
United States	Bos	98521.5	34	4	0	11	0.1	0.36	Eqc	6180.0	33	6	0	16	2.6	0.38	Sus	62206.0	18	5	0	8	0.1	0.63
Uruguay	Ovi	15500.0	2	1	0	1	0.1	1.00	Bos	10700.0	0	--	--	--	--	--	Eqc	500.0	1	0	0	1	2.0	0.00
Venezuela	Bos	15992.4	6	0	0	3	0.2	0.00	Cap	4000.0	1	0	0	1	0.3	0.00	Ovi	781.0	3	--	--	--	--	--
AFRICA																								
Algeria	Ovi	18200.0	8	1	0	7	0.4	0.14	Bos	1650.0	1	0	0	1	0.6	0.00	Cap	3400.0	6	0	0	2	0.6	0.00
Angola	Bos	3900.0	7	0	0	5	1.3	0.00	Cap	2000.0	0	--	--	--	--	--	Ovi	336.0	4	--	--	--	--	--
Benin	Bos	1345.0	4	0	0	4	3.0	0.00	Cap	1087.0	2	0	0	1	0.9	0.00	Ovi	634.0	3	0	0	1	1.6	0.00
Botswana	Bos	2380.0	9	2	0	6	2.5	0.33	Cap	1835.0	2	0	0	2	1.1	0.00	Ovi	250.0	4	0	0	4	16.0	0.00
Burkina Faso	Cap	7950.0	4	--	--	--	--	--	Bos	4550.0	4	0	0	4	0.9	0.00	Ovi	6350.0	3	0	0	1	0.2	0.00
Burundi	Cap	593.7	0	--	--	--	--	--	Bos	329.0	2	2	0	0	3.0	2.00	Ovi	165.0	0	--	--	--	--	--
Cameroon	Bos	5900.0	12	5	0	7	1.2	0.71	Cap	3850.0	1	0	0	1	0.3	0.00	Ovi	3880.0	4	--	--	--	--	--
Cape Verde	Sus	636.0	0	--	--	--	--	--	Bos	22.0	0	--	--	--	--	--	Cap	112.0	1	--	--	--	--	--
Central African R	Bos	2992.1	5	0	0	5	1.7	0.00	Cap	2350.0	1	0	0	1	0.4	0.00	Sus	622.0	0	--	--	--	--	--
Chad	Bos	5582.1	4	2	0	2	0.4	1.00	Cam	700.0	3	0	0	3	4.3	0.00	Ovi	2431.6	6	0	0	3	1.2	0.00
Comoros	Cap	129.0	0	--	--	--	--	--	Bos	50.0	0	--	--	--	--	--	Ovi	20.0	0	--	--	--	--	--
Congo, DR	Cap	4500.0	4	0	0	2	0.4	0.00	Bos	900.0	10	3	0	5	5.6	0.60	Ovi	930.0	3	--	--	--	--	--
Congo, R	Cap	285.0	1	0	0	1	3.5	0.00	Bos	75.0	2	0	0	2	26.7	0.00	Ovi	115.0	1	0	0	1	8.7	0.00
Côte d'Ivoire	Ovi	1370.0	2	0	0	2	1.5	0.00	Bos	1330.0	4	0	0	4	3.0	0.00	Cap	1070.0	1	0	0	1	0.9	0.00
Djibouti	Cap	511.0	0	--	--	--	--	--	Bos	269.0	1	0	0	1	3.7	0.00	Ovi	463.0	0	--	--	--	--	--
Egypt	Ovi	4400.0	8	0	0	7	1.6	0.00	Bub	3180.0	4	1	0	3	0.9	0.33	Cap	3261.0	7	0	0	7	2.1	0.00
Equatorial Guinea	Ovi	36.0	0	--	--	--	--	--	Bos	4.8	1	--	--	--	--	--	Cap	8.1	1	0	0	1	--	0.00
Eritrea	Cap	1700.0	2	0	0	1	0.6	0.00	Bos	1550.0	4	0	0	4	2.6	0.00	Ovi	1570.0	6	0	0	5	3.2	0.00
Ethiopia	Bos	35095.2	23	1	0	12	0.4	0.00	Cap	16950.0	6	0	0	4	0.2	0.00	Ovi	22000.0	13	0	0	9	0.4	0.00
Gabon	Sus	212.0	0	--	--	--	--	--	Cap	90.0	1	0	0	1	--	0.00	Ovi	195.0	0	--	--	--	--	--
Gambia	Bos	360.0	1	0	0	1	2.8	0.00	Cap	265.0	1	--	--	--	--	--	Ovi	190.0	1	0	0	1	5.3	0.00
Ghana	Cap	2739.4	1	0	0	1	0.4	0.00	Bos	1272.9	4	1	0	3	2.4	0.33	Ovi	2516.5	4	0	0	3	1.2	0.00
Guinea	Bos	2368.0	1	0	0	1	0.4	0.00	Cap	864.0	1	0	0	1	1.2	0.00	Ovi	687.0	1	0	0	1	1.5	0.00
Guinea-Bissau	Bos	520.0	1	0	0	1	1.9	0.00	Cap	315.0	1	0	0	1	3.2	0.00	Sus	340.0	0	--	--	--	--	--

Country	Sp	Head 000	Br tot	Br thr	Br tm	Br ok	Br div	Thr rat	Sp	Head 000	Br tot	Br thr	Br tm	Br ok	Br div	Thr rat	Sp	Head 000	Br tot	Br thr	Br tm	Br ok	Br div	Thr rat
Kenya	Bos	13392.0	16	2	0	10	0.7	0.20	Cam	830.0	3	0	0	3	3.6	0.00	Cap	7600.0	4	0	0	3	0.4	0.00
Lesotho	Ovi	720.0	0	--	--	--	--	--	Bos	510.0	2	--	--	--	--	--	Cap	560.0	2	0	0	1	1.8	0.00
Liberia	Cap	220.0	1	0	0	1	4.5	0.00	Bos	36.0	2	1	0	1	--	1.00	Ovi	210.0	0	--	--	--	--	--
Libyan Arab J	Ovi	6400.0	3	0	0	1	0.2	0.00	Bos	142.0	1	0	0	1	7.0	0.00	Cap	2200.0	1	0	0	1	0.5	0.00
Madagascar	Bos	10353.0	2	1	0	1	0.1	1.00	Ovi	790.0	1	--	--	--	--	--	Sus	1700.0	0	--	--	--	--	--
Malawi	Cap	1260.0	2	0	0	2	1.6	0.00	Bos	750.0	1	0	0	1	1.3	0.00	Ovi	110.0	1	--	--	--	--	--
Mali	Cap	8524.6	3	0	0	1	0.1	0.00	Bos	6058.0	4	0	0	4	0.7	0.00	Ovi	5975.4	8	0	0	6	1.0	0.00
Mauritania	Ovi	6200.0	4	0	0	2	0.3	0.00	Cam	1185.0	2	0	0	2	1.7	0.00	Cap	4133.0	6	0	0	2	0.5	0.00
Mauritius	Cap	93.0	1	0	0	1	--	0.00	Bos	27.0	2	0	0	1	--	0.00	Ovi	7.2	3	2	0	1	--	2.00
Morocco	Ovi	16576.4	24	0	0	6	0.4	0.00	Bos	2559.8	3	0	0	2	0.8	0.00	Eqc	150.0	1	1	0	0	6.7	1.00
Mozambique	Bos	1310.0	3	1	0	1	0.8	1.00	Cap	390.0	3	1	0	1	2.6	1.00	Ovi	124.0	4	0	0	1	8.1	0.00
Namibia	Ovi	2100.0	2	0	0	2	1.0	0.00	Bos	2000.0	6	1	0	0	0.5	1.00	Cap	1700.0	2	--	--	--	--	--
Niger	Cap	6469.0	3	0	0	2	0.3	0.00	Bos	217.0	3	1	0	1	4.6	1.00	Ovi	4312.0	3	0	0	1	0.2	0.00
Nigeria	Cap	24300.0	9	0	0	2	0.1	0.00	Bos	19850.0	15	2	0	9	0.4	0.00	Ovi	20500.0	8	0	0	1	0.0	0.00
Rwanda	Bos	725.5	2	2	0	0	1.4	2.00	Cap	634.0	0	--	--	--	--	--	Ovi	290.0	0	--	--	--	--	--
São Tomé & Principe	Cap	4.8	0	--	--	--	--	--	Bos	4.0	0	--	--	--	--	--	Ovi	2.5	0	--	--	--	--	--
Senegal	Ovi	4300.0	5	0	0	4	0.9	0.00	Bos	2955.0	3	0	0	3	1.0	0.00	Cap	3595.0	1	0	0	1	0.3	0.00
Seychelles	Sus	18.2	1	--	--	--	--	--	Bos	1.4	0	--	--	--	--	--	Cap	5.2	0	--	--	--	--	--
Sierra Leone	Bos	400.0	1	0	0	1	2.5	0.00	Cap	190.0	1	0	0	1	5.3	0.00	Ovi	350.0	0	--	--	--	--	--
Somalia	Ovi	13000.0	3	--	--	--	--	--	Bos	5000.0	6	--	--	--	--	--	Cap	12000.0	8	--	--	--	--	--
South Africa	Ovi	28680.3	22	2	1	15	0.5	0.17	Bos	13565.0	16	1	1	14	1.0	0.11	Cap	6457.1	4	0	0	3	0.5	0.00
Sudan	Ovi	42500.0	14	0	0	13	0.3	0.00	Bos	35000.0	14	1	0	9	0.3	0.11	Cap	37500.0	7	0	0	6	0.2	0.00
Swaziland	Bos	652.0	4	0	0	4	6.1	0.00	Cap	438.0	2	0	0	2	4.6	0.00	Ovi	26.0	2	0	0	2	--	0.00
Tanzania	Bos	14350.0	11	7	0	4	0.3	1.75	Cap	9900.0	1	0	0	1	0.1	0.00	Ovi	4150.0	5	2	0	1	0.2	2.00
Togo	Cap	1110.0	1	0	0	1	0.9	0.00	Bos	222.8	4	0	0	4	18.0	0.00	Sus	850.0	1	0	0	1	1.2	0.00
Tunisia	Ovi	6600.0	5	0	0	4	0.6	0.00	Bos	780.0	1	1	0	0	1.3	1.00	Eqc	56.2	3	2	0	1	--	2.00
Uganda	Bos	5700.0	10	6	0	4	0.7	1.50	Cap	3650.0	3	0	0	3	0.8	0.00	Ovi	1970.0	2	0	0	2	1.0	0.00
Zambia	Bos	2273.0	4	0	0	4	1.8	0.00	Cap	1069.0	1	--	--	--	--	--	Sus	324.0	0	--	--	--	--	--
Zimbabwe	Bos	5500.0	3	1	0	2	0.4	0.50	Cap	2770.0	1	0	0	1	0.4	0.00	Ovi	525.0	4	1	0	3	5.7	0.33
EUROPE																								
Albania	Ovi	1941.0	11	2	0	9	4.6	0.22	Bos	720.0	5	3	0	2	2.8	1.50	Cap	1120.0	15	2	0	13	11.6	0.15
Austria	Sus	3810.0	0	--	--	--	--	--	Bos	2172.0	10	0	6	4	1.8	0.75	Ovi	383.7	7	1	4	2	5.2	1.50
Belarus	Bos	4515.0	5	1	0	3	0.7	0.33	Eqc	233.2	2	1	0	1	4.3	1.00	Sus	3608.0	2	0	0	1	0.3	0.00
Belgium	Sus	7632.0	3	0	0	3	0.4	0.00	Bos	3185.0	8	1	0	7	2.2	0.14	Ovi	155.0	14	10	0	4	25.8	2.50
Bosnia & Herzegovina	Bos	350.0	1	0	0	1	2.9	0.00	Eqc	50.0	1	1	0	0	--	1.00	Ovi	285.0	3	--	--	--	--	--
Bulgaria	Ovi	2774.0	9	3	0	6	2.2	0.50	Bos	671.0	2	2	0	0	1.5	2.00	Sus	1721.0	1	1	0	0	0.6	1.00
Croatia	Sus	1361.6	5	3	1	1	0.7	3.50	Bos	438.5	7	1	2	4	9.1	0.50	Ovi	488.5	6	2	0	4	8.2	0.50
Czech R	Sus	4001.0	5	2	0	3	0.7	0.67	Bos	1657.0	8	5	1	2	1.2	2.75	Ovi	93.6	11	8	0	3	32.1	2.67
Denmark	Sus	11991.0	6	1	2	3	0.3	0.67	Bos	1968.0	14	1	3	9	4.6	0.28	Ovi	156.0	14	8	1	3	19.2	2.83
Estonia	Sus	326.4	2	0	0	2	6.1	0.00	Bos	307.5	3	1	0	2	6.5	0.50	Ovi	30.8	2	0	0	2	--	0.00
Finland	Sus	1540.7	2	0	0	2	1.3	0.00	Bos	1100.6	4	0	2	2	1.8	0.50	Ovi	128.3	1	0	0	1	7.8	0.00
France	Bos	20214.0	37	1	11	25	1.2	0.26	Ovi	10240.0	51	3	6	42	4.1	0.14	Sus	16190.0	11	3	5	3	0.2	1.83
Germany	Sus	26294.0	13	2	3	8	0.3	0.44	Bos	14942.0	29	2	10	17	1.1	0.41	Ovi	2298.0	23	0	7	16	7.0	0.22
Greece	Ovi	9290.0	11	3	0	8	0.9	0.38	Bos	577.0	3	2	0	1	1.7	2.00	Cap	5520.0	2	0	0	2	0.4	0.00
Hungary	Sus	5479.0	7	4	1	2	0.4	2.25	Bos	873.0	6	3	0	3	3.4	1.00	Ovi	909.0	6	1	2	3	3.3	0.67
Iceland	Ovi	477.0	1	0	0	1	2.1	0.00	Bos	74.8	1	0	0	1	--	0.00	Eqc	79.8	1	0	0	1	--	0.00
Ireland	Bos	7093.0	9	0	1	8	1.1	0.06	Ovi	5624.0	5	0	0	5	0.9	0.00	Sus	1801.0	2	0	0	2	1.1	0.00
Italy	Ovi	10770.0	47	15	3	29	2.7	0.57	Bos	7150.0	31	0	11	20	2.8	0.28	Cap	1365.0	24	14	0	10	7.3	1.40
Latvia	Sus	403.4	4	0	1	3	7.4	0.17	Bos	375.7	4	0	2	2	5.3	0.50	Eqc	23.3	2	0	1	1	--	0.50
Lithuania	Sus	1167.7	2	0	1	1	0.9	0.50	Bos	927.7	4	0	2	2	2.2	0.50	Eqc	74.8	4	1	1	2	26.7	0.75
Luxembourg	Sus	7632.0	3	0	0	3	0.4	0.00	Bos	3185.0	8	1	0	7	2.2	0.14	Ovi	155.0	14	10	0	4	25.8	2.50
Macedonia, FYR	Ovi	1550.0	3	0	0	3	1.9	0.00	Bos	290.0	1	0	0	1	3.4	0.00	Sus	196.8	1	1	0	0	5.1	1.00
Malta	Sus	69.0	--	--	--	--	--	--	Bos	21.0	1	0	0	1	--	0.00	Ovi	16.0	1	0	0	1	--	0.00
Moldova	Ovi	940.0	2	0	0	1	1.1	0.00	Bos	525.0	4	1	0	3	5.7	0.33	Cap	95.0	1	0	0	1	--	0.00
Netherlands	Sus	13418.0	2	0	0	2	0.1	0.00	Bos	4184.0	5	0	2	3	0.7	0.33	Ovi	1465.0	7	0	3	4	2.7	0.38
Norway	Ovi	2399.0	6	1	0	5	2.1	0.20	Bos	1041.6	3	0	2	1	1.0	1.00	Sus	689.6	2	1	0	1	1.5	1.00
Poland	Sus	18537.6	9	0	3	6	0.3	0.25	Bos	6555.0	4	0	0	4	0.6	0.00	Ovi	392.1	18	0	5	13	33.2	0.19
Portugal	Ovi	5850.0	10	0	0	10	1.7	0.00	Bos	1270.0	10	1	0	9	7.1	0.11	Sus	2341.0	2	1	0	1	0.4	1.00
Romania	Ovi	8409.0	5	0	0	5	0.6	0.00	Bos	3143.0	5	0	2	3	1.0	0.33	Sus	7194.0	6	0	2	4	0.6	0.25
Slovakia	Sus	1592.6	3	0	0	2	1.3	0.00	Bos	704.8	3	0	0	3	4.3	0.00	Ovi	326.2	3	0	0	3	9.2	0.00
Slovenia	Sus	592.4	6	4	1	1	1.7	4.50	Bos	453.1	4	1	0	3	6.6	0.33	Ovi	72.4	2	1	0	1	--	1.00
Spain	Ovi	23751.0	26	4	1	18	0.8	0.25	Bos	6065.0	32	12	9	10	1.6	1.65	Sus	21600.0	12	6	4	2	0.1	4.00
Sweden	Sus	2321.0	1	0	0	1	0.4	1.00	Bos	1757.0	9	2	3	3	1.7	1.17	Ovi	420.0	5	1	0	4	9.5	0.25
Switzerland	Bos	1615.0	6	1	1	4	2.5	0.38	Ovi	490.0	9	1	4	4	8.2	0.75	Sus	1420.0	3	0	1	1	1.4	0.25
Ukraine	Bos	11722.0	10	2	0	5	0.4	0.40	Ovi	1198.0	10	0	0	3	2.5	0.00	Sus	10083.0	7	1	0	2	0.2	0.50
United Kingdom	Ovi	44656.0	56	3	9	40	0.9	0.19	Bos	11423.0	34	8	2	23	2.0	0.39	Sus	7284.0	13	9	0	2	0.3	4.50

Country	Sp	Head 000	Br tot	Br thr	Br tm	Br ok	Br div	Thr rat	Sp	Head 000	Br tot	Br thr	Br tm	Br ok	Br div	Thr rat	Sp	Head 000	Br tot	Br thr	Br tm	Br ok	Br div	Thr rat
Yugoslavia	Sus	4372.0	11	6	0	5	1.1	1.20	Bos	1831.0	7	4	0	3	1.6	1.33	Ovi	2392.0	9	0	0	3	1.3	0.00
RUSSIAN FED.	Bos	28634.0	28	5	1	17	0.6	0.32	Eqc	2000.0	35	13	1	14	7.0	0.96	Sus	17300.0	18	1	0	11	0.6	0.09
ASIA																								
Afghanistan	Ovi	14300.0	10	0	0	3	0.2	0.00	Bos	1500.0	5	--	--	--	--	--	Cap	2200.0	3	--	--	--	--	--
Armenia	Ovi	575.0	8	1	0	2	3.5	0.50	Bos	512.0	0	--	--	--	--	--	Cap	12.5	1	1	0	0	--	1.00
Azerbaijan	Ovi	5131.9	10	2	0	3	0.6	0.67	Bos	1909.8	2	0	0	2	1.0	0.00	Cap	370.9	1	1	0	0	2.7	1.00
Bahrain	Ovi	17.1	1	--	--	--	--	--	Bos	13.0	0	--	--	--	--	--	Cap	16.0	0	--	--	--	--	--
Bangladesh	Cap	33500.0	1	0	0	1	0.0	0.00	Bos	23400.0	6	1	0	4	0.2	0.25	Ovi	1110.0	1	0	0	1	0.9	0.00
Bhutan	Bos	435.0	3	1	0	2	4.6	0.50	Ovi	58.5	0	--	--	--	--	--	Sus	74.9	1	--	--	--	--	--
Brunei Darussalam	Bub	6.0	0	--	--	--	--	--	Cap	3.3	0	--	--	--	--	--	Sus	4.5	0	--	--	--	--	--
Cambodia	Bos	2820.8	2	1	0	0	0.4	1.00	Bub	693.7	2	0	0	1	1.4	0.00	Sus	2438.3	0	--	--	--	--	--
China	Sus	429211.6	114	10	0	79	0.2	0.13	Cap	141956.4	31	0	0	28	0.2	0.00	Ovi	127163.4	34	0	0	29	0.2	0.00
Cyprus	Sus	436.4	0	--	--	--	--	--	Bos	62.5	3	0	1	0	--	0.50	Cap	300.0	3	0	0	2	6.7	0.00
Georgia	Bos	1051.0	7	1	0	3	2.9	0.33	Ovi	550.0	14	1	0	7	12.7	0.14	Sus	365.9	2	1	0	1	2.7	1.00
India	Bos	214877.0	63	3	1	26	0.1	0.13	Cap	122530.0	26	0	0	11	0.1	0.00	Ovi	57600.0	57	0	0	35	0.6	0.00
Indonesia	Cap	15197.8	7	1	0	5	0.3	0.20	Bos	12239.3	16	1	0	15	1.2	0.07	Bub	3145.1	10	0	0	10	3.2	0.00
Iran	Ovi	53900.0	25	0	0	3	0.1	0.00	Bos	8047.4	9	1	0	3	0.4	0.33	Eqc	250.0	11	1	0	0	4.0	1.00
Iraq	Ovi	6000.0	8	0	0	3	0.5	0.00	Bos	1100.0	6	0	0	1	0.9	0.00	Cap	1300.0	3	1	0	1	0.8	1.00
Israel	Ovi	340.0	2	--	--	--	--	--	Bos	300.0	3	0	0	1	3.3	0.00	Cap	73.0	4	0	0	1	--	0.00
Japan	Sus	9879.0	0	--	--	--	--	--	Bos	4658.0	7	1	0	0	0.2	1.00	Eqc	27.0	8	5	2	1	--	6.00
Jordan	Ovi	2000.0	1	0	0	1	0.5	0.00	Bos	65.0	1	0	0	1	--	0.00	Cap	795.0	2	0	0	2	2.5	0.00
Kazakhstan	Ovi	9000.0	17	0	0	10	1.1	0.00	Bos	3957.9	4	0	0	3	0.8	0.00	Eqc	986.3	6	0	0	5	5.1	0.00
Korea, DPR	Sus	2970.0	1	--	--	--	--	--	Bos	565.0	0	--	--	--	--	--	Cap	1900.0	0	--	--	--	--	--
Korea, R	Sus	7863.7	0	--	--	--	--	--	Bos	2486.5	2	0	0	1	0.4	0.00	Cap	500.0	1	0	0	1	2.0	0.00
Kuwait	Ovi	445.0	3	0	0	2	4.5	0.00	Bos	20.0	0	--	--	--	--	--	Cap	150.0	0	--	--	--	--	--
Kyrgyzstan	Ovi	3400.0	5	0	0	3	0.9	0.00	Bos	825.0	4	0	0	3	3.6	0.00	Eqc	320.0	2	1	0	1	3.1	1.00
Lao PDR	Sus	1936.5	4	0	0	4	2.1	0.00	Bos	1497.0	1	0	0	1	0.7	0.00	Bub	1286.0	1	0	0	1	0.8	0.00
Lebanon	Cap	460.0	2	--	--	--	--	--	Bos	82.0	2	0	0	1	--	0.00	Ovi	162.0	1	--	--	--	--	--
Malaysia	Sus	2961.0	1	1	0	0	0.3	1.00	Bos	713.0	6	1	0	3	4.2	0.33	Cap	235.0	3	0	0	1	4.3	0.00
Maldives	Cap	--	1	0	0	1	--	0.00	--	--	--	--	--	--	--	--	--	--	--	--	--	--	--	--
Mongolia	Ovi	14694.2	16	0	0	15	1.0	0.00	Bos	3725.8	5	0	0	4	1.1	0.00	Cap	11061.9	4	0	0	4	0.4	0.00
Myanmar	Bos	10739.5	6	0	0	6	0.6	0.00	Bub	2391.0	2	0	0	2	0.8	0.00	Sus	3715.0	3	0	0	3	0.8	0.00
Nepal	Bos	7030.7	8	0	0	5	0.7	0.00	Bub	3470.6	4	0	0	3	0.9	0.00	Cap	6204.6	5	0	0	2	0.3	0.00
Oman	Cap	728.0	0	--	--	--	--	--	Bos	148.0	0	--	--	--	--	--	Ovi	160.0	1	0	0	1	6.3	0.00
Pakistan	Cap	49700.0	28	0	0	25	0.5	0.00	Bub	21300.0	4	0	0	4	0.2	0.00	Ovi	31300.0	32	0	0	29	0.9	0.00
Philippines	Sus	10390.0	2	--	--	--	--	--	Bub	3006.0	2	0	0	1	0.3	0.00	Cap	6780.0	2	0	0	1	0.1	0.00
Qatar	Ovi	207.0	0	--	--	--	--	--	Cam	47.8	0	--	--	--	--	--	Cap	177.0	0	--	--	--	--	--
Saudi Arabia	Ovi	8300.0	7	0	0	1	0.1	0.00	Cam	428.0	0	--	--	--	--	--	Cap	4500.0	4	--	--	--	--	--
Singapore	Sus	190.0	0	--	--	--	--	--	Bos	0.2	0	--	--	--	--	--	Cap	0.3	0	--	--	--	--	--
Sri Lanka	Bos	1599.0	4	0	0	2	1.3	0.00	Bub	720.7	3	0	0	3	4.2	0.00	Cap	519.3	2	0	0	2	3.9	0.00
Syrian Arab R	Ovi	15000.0	3	0	0	2	0.1	0.00	Bos	905.0	3	0	0	3	3.3	0.00	Cap	1200.0	3	0	0	2	1.7	0.00
Tajikistan	Ovi	1620.0	6	0	0	4	2.5	0.00	Bos	911.5	4	0	0	1	1.1	0.00	Cap	625.0	3	1	0	1	1.6	1.00
Thailand	Sus	7200.0	4	2	0	1	0.1	2.00	Bos	5677.0	4	0	0	3	0.5	0.00	Bub	3500.0	1	0	0	1	0.3	0.00
Turkey	Ovi	30238.0	23	0	0	13	0.4	0.00	Bos	11185.0	12	0	0	5	0.4	0.00	Cap	8376.0	7	0	0	3	0.4	0.00
Turkmenistan	Ovi	5650.0	3	0	0	1	0.2	0.00	Cap	375.0	3	1	0	1	2.7	1.00	Eqc	16.0	3	0	0	3	187.5	0.00
United Arab Emirates	Cap	1050.0	0	--	--	--	--	--	Cam	195.0	0	--	--	--	--	--	Ovi	440.0	0	--	--	--	--	--
Uzbekistan	Ovi	8000.0	8	0	0	3	0.4	0.00	Bos	5225.2	2	0	0	1	0.2	0.00	Cap	697.9	4	1	0	2	2.9	0.50
Viet Nam	Sus	18885.8	8	0	0	8	0.4	0.00	Bos	4063.6	7	0	0	6	1.5	0.00	Bub	2955.7	1	0	0	1	0.3	0.00
Yemen	Ovi	4595.1	11	0	0	1	0.2	0.00	Bos	1288.8	2	0	0	1	0.8	0.00	Cap	4150.2	7	0	0	5	1.2	0.00
PACIFIC																								
Australia	Ovi	119600.0	26	3	1	9	0.1	0.39	Bos	26710.0	17	0	0	10	0.4	0.00	Eqc	220.0	2	1	0	1	4.5	1.00
Fiji	Bos	344.6	0	--	--	--	--	--	Cap	235.0	1	0	0	1	4.3	0.00	Sus	111.7	0	--	--	--	--	--
New Zealand	Ovi	46100.0	13	0	0	3	0.1	0.00	Eqc	85.0	2	1	0	0	--	1.00	Sus	413.0	1	1	0	0	2.4	1.00
Papua New Guinea	Sus	1500.0	1	0	0	1	0.7	0.00	Bos	86.0	1	1	0	0	--	1.00	Ovi	6.0	1	0	0	1	--	0.00
Samoa	Sus	178.8	1	--	--	--	--	--	Bos	26.0	0	--	--	--	--	--	Eqa	7.0	0	--	--	--	--	--
Solomon Is	Sus	58.0	1	0	0	1	--	0.00	Bos	10.0	0	--	--	--	--	--	Eqc	0.1	0	--	--	--	--	--
Tonga	Sus	80.9	0	--	--	--	--	--	Cap	13.9	0	--	--	--	--	--	Eqc	11.4	0	--	--	--	--	--
Vanuatu	Bos	151.0	0	--	--	--	--	--	Sus	62.0	0	--	--	--	--	--	Cap	12.0	0	--	--	--	--	--

Notes

This table gives the data for the domesticated diversity index (Table 20).

Sp = the chosen species, abbreviated as follows:

Bos = cattle and kin = all domesticated forms of the genus *Bos*: cattle (*Bos primigenius*), Bali cattle (domesticated *Bos javanicus*), mithun (domesticated *Bos gaurus*) and yak (domesticated *Bos mutus*)

Bub = water buffalo (domesticated *Bubalus arnee*)

Cam = camels = both domesticated forms of the genus *Camelus*: Bactrian camel (*Camelus bactrianus* [domesticated *Camelus ferus*]) and dromedary (*Camelus dromedarius*)

Cap = goat (*Capra hircus*)

Eqa = ass (*Equus asinus*)

Eqc = horse (*Equus caballus*)

Lam = both domesticated species of the genus *Lama*: alpaca (*Lama pacos*) and llama (*Lama glama*)

Ovi = sheep (*Ovis aries*)

Sus = pig (*Sus domesticus*)

Head 000 = the estimated stock of the species, in thousands of head. Data are for 1999 and are from Food and Agriculture Organization of the United Nations (2000a).

Br tot = number of established breeds in DAD-IS = number of breeds in the Domesticated Animal Diversity Information System (DAD-IS) of the FAO Global Strategy for the Management of Farm Animal Genetic Resources, *excluding wild species, feral populations (descendants of domesticated stock, now living in the wild), and—if possible to ascertain—not yet established breeds (recent imports, experimental lines, breeds under development)*. Wild species are excluded to avoid duplication of the wild animal species indicator. Feral populations are excluded because they are often a threat to wild species and natural ecosystems. Recent imports, experimental lines and breeds under development are excluded because they are not an established part of a particular agro-ecosystem. Data are for 1998-1999 and are from FAO Initiative for Domesticated Animal Diversity (1998, 1999) and Rege (1999).

Br thr = number of established breeds that are threatened with extinction = number of African cattle breeds assessed by Rege (1999) as threatened, or number of all other breeds assessed by the FAO Initiative for Domesticated Animal Diversity (1998) as "critical" or "endangered" (excluding wild species, feral populations and not yet established breeds). FAO criteria for threatened breeds are given in Scherf (1985). A breed is "critical" if:

either total number of breeding females is less than 100

or total number of breeding males is 5 or less

or total population is slightly above 100 and decreasing, and less than 80% of females are bred pure.

A breed is "endangered" if:

either total number of breeding females is between 100 and 1000

or total number of breeding males is more than 5 but no more than 20

or total population is slightly below 1000 but increasing, and more than 80% of females are bred pure

or total population is slightly above 1000 and decreasing, and less than 80% of females are bred pure.

In the event of a conflict between Rege (1999) and FAO Initiative for Domesticated Animal Diversity (1998), I followed Rege, because his assessment of "threatened" takes account of the impact of crossbreeding and interbreeding. Because the FAO criteria do not include the degree of incrossing from other breeds (and also because they do not apply species-specific estimates of effective population size), they tend to understate the number of threatened breeds (Simon 1999).

Br tm = number of established breeds that are threatened but maintained = number of breeds assessed by the FAO Initiative for Domesticated Animal Diversity (1998) as "critical" or "endangered" (excluding wild species, feral populations and not yet established breeds) but for which active conservation programs are in place.

Br ok = number of established breeds that are not at risk of extinction = number of breeds assessed by the FAO Initiative for Domesticated Animal Diversity (1998) as "not at risk" (excluding wild species and feral populations). Breeds "not at risk" are considered by definition to be established, unless they are explicitly noted as experimental or under development, in which case they are excluded. A breed is "not at risk" if:

either total number of breeding females is more than 1000 and total number of breeding males is more than 20

or total population approaches 1000 and is increasing, and close to 100% of females are bred pure.

The difference between Br tot and Br thr + Br tm + Br ok is the number of breeds in DAD-IS that have not been assessed. For example, of Brazil's 27 cattle breeds in DAD-IS, 10 have not been assessed.

Br div = breed diversity = the number of breeds assessed as "not at risk" per million head of the species. If no breed is assessed as not at risk, it is assumed that the number of not at risk breeds is 1 (given the stock sizes concerned, it could not be less than this). For example, Malaysia has 2,961,000 pigs (Sus), but the breed columns show 1 breed in DAD-IS, 1 threatened breed, and 0 not at risk breeds. The not at risk figure is obviously incomplete, so it is assumed there is at least one not at risk breed.

Thr rat = threatened breeds ratio = the ratio of threatened (thr) and threatened but maintained (tm) breeds to not at risk breeds. In calculating the ratio, threatened but maintained breeds count as half a breed. For example, of Brazil's cattle breeds, 1 is threatened, 3 are threatened but maintained, and 13 are not at risk. The ratio is therefore $(1 + [3 \div 2]) \div 13 = 0.19$ (0.19 threatened breeds per 1 not at risk breed). If no breed is assessed as not at risk, it is assumed that the number of not at risk breeds is 1 (given the stock sizes concerned, it could not be less than this).

Note the number of established breeds in DAD-IS may be much smaller than the number that exists, and many of the breeds in DAD-IS have not been assessed. *Consequently, the indicators reflect the state of knowledge as much as of the actual level and condition of domesticated animal diversity.*

Table 22. Resource Use Index; Energy; Timber

Country	EC total	EC/ha	EC/p	E score	Timber note	Volume 000 m³	NAI 000 m³	Felling 000 m³	Prod 000 m³	Imp 000 m³	F+I % NAI	P+I % vol	Timb score	Ag score	Fish score	RS score	RU index
AMERICAS																	
Antigua & Barbuda	5	113.6	75.2	52	x90	600	--	--	0	15	--	2.5	75	12	20	36	44
Argentina	2404	8.6	67.4	66	z90	3720700	--	--	11427	397	--	0.3	97	60	60	72	69
Bahamas	24	17.3	82.5	59	x90	11600	--	--	117	101	--	1.9	81	12	74	56	57
Barbados	15	348.8	56.2	18	x90	0	--	--	5	75	--	8000	0	18	13	10	14
Belize	10	4.4	44.6	78	y90	100100	--	--	188	5	--	0.2	98	48	16	54	66
Bolivia	150	1.4	19.3	90	y90	3650500	--	--	1989	1	--	0.1	99	76	20	65	77
Brazil	6787	7.9	41.5	79	y90	65486000	--	--	197816	448	--	0.3	97	60	49	69	74
Canada	10410	10.4	344.0	18	vi94 r95	29364059	442030	214128	191178	9254	50.5	0.7	88	42	57	62	40
Chile	912	12.1	62.4	69	z90	1491100	--	--	31670	0	--	2.1	79	45	62	62	65
Colombia	1129	9.9	28.2	86	y90	6018100	--	--	18618	55	--	0.3	97	60	16	58	72
Costa Rica	113	22.1	30.1	85	y90	149100	--	--	5311	20	--	3.6	64	64	62	63	74
Cuba	444	40.1	40.1	80	y90	104400	--	--	2756	20	--	2.7	73	49	43	55	67
Dominica	1	13.3	14.1	93	x90	2700	--	--	0	15	--	0.6	94	37	14	48	70
Dominican R	209	42.9	25.8	78	x90	44200	--	--	562	374	--	2.1	79	59	6	48	63
Ecuador	355	12.5	29.7	85	y90	1310200	--	--	11340	8	--	0.9	91	69	75	78	81
El Salvador	139	66.1	23.5	67	y90	5800	--	--	5129	25	--	88.9	0	51	33	28	47
Grenada	3	88.2	32.3	58	x90	400	--	--	0	14	--	3.5	65	25	17	36	47
Guatemala	266	24.4	25.3	87	y90	416600	--	--	12995	16	--	3.1	69	62	19	50	68
Guyana	22	1.0	26.1	87	x90	3241200	--	--	442	0	--	0.0	100	70	79	83	85
Haiti	83	29.9	10.6	85	x90	1000	--	--	6397	19	--	641.6	0	52	8	20	52
Honduras	124	11.1	20.7	90	y90	345800	--	--	7176	25	--	2.1	79	58	58	65	77
Jamaica	150	136.5	59.6	46	y90	24400	--	--	343	141	--	2.0	80	48	8	45	45
Mexico	5658	28.9	60.0	70	y90	1856800	--	--	23866	1812	--	1.4	86	57	49	64	67
Nicaragua	109	8.4	23.3	88	y90	651000	--	--	4198	8	--	0.6	94	64	52	70	79
Panama	90	11.9	33.1	83	y90	440400	--	--	1098	16	--	0.3	97	58	48	68	75
Paraguay	133	3.3	26.1	87	y90	347500	--	--	8097	2	--	2.3	77	70	76	74	80
Peru	571	4.4	23.4	88	y90	10599800	--	--	9157	55	--	0.1	99	61	56	72	80
St Kitts & Nevis	2	76.9	50.8	61	x90	800	--	--	0	7	--	0.9	91	20	51	54	57
St Lucia	3	48.4	20.2	76	x90	300	--	--	0	28	--	9.3	37	17	12	22	49
St Vincent & Grenadines	2	51.3	17.9	74	x90	700	--	--	0	37	--	5.3	53	40	7	33	53
Suriname	26	1.6	63.1	68	y90	2806600	--	--	183	0	--	0.0	100	50	69	73	70
Trinidad & Tobago	375	731.0	293.7	0	y90	20800	--	--	60	69	--	0.6	94	19	60	58	29
United States	95075	101.5	349.8	18	v 92 i87-92 f92	45180000	761000	734000	490618	56638	103.9	1.2	54	42	60	52	35
Uruguay	118	6.7	36.1	82	z90	114200	--	--	6163	67	--	5.5	52	41	56	50	66
Venezuela	3277	35.9	143.9	44	y90	4923800	--	--	2038	71	--	0.0	100	51	62	71	57
AFRICA																	
Algeria	1459	6.1	49.6	75	z90	110700	--	--	2735	768	--	3.2	68	39	67	58	66
Angola	89	0.7	7.6	96	y90	861200	--	--	6472	6	--	0.8	92	64	79	78	87
Benin	65	5.8	11.5	94	y90	109800	--	--	5994	1	--	5.5	52	62	44	53	73
Botswana	134	2.3	87.0	58	x90	287400	--	--	1673	0	--	0.6	94	15	7	39	48
Burkina Faso	116	4.2	10.5	95	y90	169400	--	--	10794	0	--	6.4	48	57	18	41	68
Burundi	51	18.3	8.0	91	y90	12400	--	--	1799	0	--	14.5	24	69	62	52	71
Cameroon	185	3.9	13.3	93	y90	3867700	--	--	15172	1	--	0.4	96	65	24	62	77
Cape Verde	2	5.0	5.0	97	x90	400	--	--	0	9	--	2.3	77	21	38	45	71
Central African R	32	0.5	9.4	95	y90	3087200	--	--	3518	0	--	0.1	99	68	80*	82	88
Chad	42	0.3	5.9	97	x90	343000	--	--	1919	18	--	0.6	94	58	34	62	79
Comoros	1	4.5	1.6	98	x90	1000	--	--	0	3	--	0.3	97	41	62	67	82
Congo, DR	531	2.3	11.1	94	y90	23113100	--	--	49534	0	--	0.2	98	68	28	65	79
Congo, R	49	1.4	18.1	91	y90	4652200	--	--	4314	0	--	0.1	99	44	2	48	69
Côte d'Ivoire	216	6.7	15.4	92	y90	2079200	--	--	13283	0	--	0.6	94	60	15	56	74
Djibouti	5	2.2	8.1	96	x90	400	--	--	0	4	--	1.0	90	11	8	36	66
Egypt	1613	16.1	24.9	87	z90	3400	--	--	2829	3020	--	172.0	0	48	43	30	58
Equatorial Guinea	6	2.1	14.3	93	z90	374600	--	--	811	0	--	0.2	98	--	68	80*	86
Eritrea	29	2.5	8.4	96	--	--	--	--	2196	61	--	--	--	53	80*	66	81
Ethiopia	487	4.4	8.4	96	y90	979900	--	--	50148	24	--	5.1	54	58	60	57	76
Gabon	76	2.8	66.8	67	y90	4269600	--	--	5332	1	--	0.1	99	41	47	62	64
Gambia	14	12.4	11.8	94	x90	4700	--	--	813	3	--	17.4	18	32	63	38	66
Ghana	315	13.2	16.9	91	y90	480400	--	--	21905	1	--	4.6	57	68	39	55	73
Guinea	62	2.5	8.5	96	z90	341700	--	--	8650	9	--	2.5	75	61	78	71	83
Guinea-Bissau	7	1.9	6.2	97	x90	72800	--	--	589	0	--	0.8	92	62	58	71	84
Kenya	527	9.1	18.5	91	y90	92100	--	--	29377	4	--	31.9	0	61	65	42	66
Lesotho	175	57.7	86.8	58	z90	700	--	--	1594	0	--	227.7	0	23	0	8	33

247

Country	EC total	EC/ha	EC/p	E score	Timber note	Volume 000 m³	NAI 000 m³	Felling 000 m³	Prod 000 m³	Imp 000 m³	F+I % NAI	P+I % vol	Timb score	Ag score	Fish score	*RS* score	RU index
Liberia	52	4.7	21.6	89	y90	704800	--	--	3021	0	--	0.4	96	52	59	69	79
Libyan Arab J	547	3.1	105.0	54	z90	26000	--	--	651	167	--	3.1	69	25	63	52	53
Madagascar	115	2.0	7.9	96	y90	930400	--	--	9517	10	--	1.0	90	73	62	75	85
Malawi	105	8.9	10.4	95	y90	269000	--	--	9692	1	--	3.6	64	63	78	68	81
Mali	72	0.6	6.9	96	x90	364300	--	--	6437	1	--	1.8	82	54	63	66	81
Mauritania	40	0.4	16.3	92	z90	16800	--	--	15	1	--	0.1	99	25	25	50	71
Mauritius	36	176.5	31.8	38	y90	1300	--	--	15	91	--	8.2	39	17	28	28	33
Morocco	379	8.5	14.1	93	z90	191500	--	--	1746	964	--	1.4	86	56	35	59	76
Mozambique	186	2.3	10.1	95	y90	644200	--	--	18018	0	--	2.8	72	68	66	69	82
Namibia	141	1.7	86.9	58	x90	253300	--	--	0	0	--	0.0	100	18	66	61	59
Niger	72	0.6	7.4	96	y90	36200	--	--	6460	1	--	17.8	18	52	8	26	61
Nigeria	1570	17.0	15.1	91	y90	1017400	--	--	98514	13	--	9.7	36	66	17	40	65
Rwanda	60	22.8	10.1	89	y90	19800	--	--	3000	10	--	15.2	22	53	24	33	61
São Tomé & Principe	1	10.4	7.2	95	--	--	--	--	9	0	--	--	--	24	3	13	54
Senegal	89	4.5	10.1	95	y90	264300	--	--	4909	62	--	1.9	81	58	26	55	75
Seychelles	3	66.7	40.0	67	z90	400	--	--	0	2	--	0.5	95	11	77	61	64
Sierra Leone	36	5.0	8.1	96	y90	111700	--	--	3315	1	--	3.0	70	62	37	56	76
Somalia	94	1.5	10.7	95	x90	37700	--	--	7955	1	--	21.1	14	--	67	40	67
South Africa	3366	27.6	86.8	58	z90	809900	--	--	33171	416	--	4.1	59	54	14	42	50
Sudan	201	0.8	7.3	96	y90	1379500	--	--	9486	52	--	0.7	93	58	67	73	84
Swaziland	80	46.1	86.5	58	z90	10900	--	--	1494	0	--	13.7	26	57	--	41	49
Tanzania	394	4.2	12.5	94	y90	2155500	--	--	39022	2	--	1.8	82	67	74	74	84
Togo	32	5.6	7.5	96	y90	62700	--	--	1182	4	--	1.9	81	56	10	49	72
Tunisia	273	16.7	29.6	85	z90	33700	--	--	2807	471	--	9.7	36	56	46	46	65
Uganda	165	6.8	8.2	96	y90	255300	--	--	15649	0	--	6.1	49	73	73	65	80
Zambia	187	2.5	21.8	89	y90	813500	--	--	8042	2	--	1.0	90	61	7	53	71
Zimbabwe	302	7.7	26.9	86	y90	286300	--	--	8378	12	--	2.9	71	48	74	64	75
EUROPE																	
Albania	41	14.3	13.1	93	vif95	83455	1004	740	409	30	76.7	0.5	81	56	18	52	72
Austria	1180	140.7	145.7	44	vif92-96	1097307	27837	19821	14033	6837	95.8	1.9	65	50	1	39	41
Belarus	1040	50.1	100.5	55	vi94 f96	1201310	24960	9550	17745	29	38.4	1.5	91	40	80*	70	62
Belgium	2162	708.4	213.5	0	v97 i82-97 f86-95	141033	5176	4400	3970	5756	196.2	6.9	4	48	2	18	9
Bosnia & Herzegovina	689	134.8	195.8	35	vif95	250360	5480	1200	40	41	22.6	0.0	95	44	11	50	42
Bulgaria	824	74.3	98.2	55	vif95	467345	11972	4852	3041	39	40.9	0.7	90	47	14	50	52
Croatia	310	54.8	69.1	65	v96 if86-96	356302	7423	4600	3398	351	66.7	1.1	84	44	38	55	60
Czech R	1696	215.1	164.6	33	vif95	683806	13369	16345	13781	1240	131.5	2.2	20	49	7	25	29
Denmark	762	176.8	145.0	38	vi90 f96	55200	3200	2194	2129	3927	191.3	11.0	5	46	61	37	37
Estonia	267	59.2	184.5	37	vif96	314537	7452	4028	6061	559	61.6	2.1	85	33	29	49	43
Finland	1183	35.0	230.1	31	vif91-96	1940000	73666	54300	53670	9691	86.9	3.3	74	36	24	45	38
France	9971	180.8	170.5	37	vi97 f96	2891777	93211	60174	42770	5976	71.0	1.7	82	41	16	46	41
Germany	13819	387.1	168.4	16	v87 i95 f96	2880000	88998	46270	39052	11573	65.0	1.8	84	46	8	46	31
Greece	1130	85.6	106.9	53	vir92	151788	3813	2408	1692	1583	104.7	2.2	53	45	19	39	46
Hungary	1062	114.2	104.6	51	vif96	314667	10344	6049	4167	1390	71.9	1.8	82	51	3	45	48
Iceland	60	5.8	219.3	33	vi98 f96	800	58	0	0	119	205.2	14.9	1	14	52	22	27
Ireland	505	71.9	138.1	45	vif96	44000	3500	2330	2266	814	89.8	7.0	71	37	79	62	53
Italy	7042	233.7	122.7	31	vif95	1428742	30507	8746	9550	14210	75.2	1.7	81	48	14	48	39
Latvia	191	29.6	77.6	61	v97 if96	502000	13200	8010	10030	138	61.7	2.0	85	37	34	52	56
Lithuania	379	58.1	102.3	54	vi96 f92-96	362637	9808	5570	4879	370	60.6	1.4	85	46	29	53	53
Luxembourg	134	521.4	321.3	7	vi85-97 r92-94	20377	667	360	345	501	129.1	4.2	22	48	2	24	15
Macedonia, FYR	131	51.0	65.9	67	vif95	63420	1010	999	774	82	107.0	1.3	48	49	2	33	50
Malta	22	687.5	57.7	0	vif96	0	0	0	0	53	5300	5300	0	16	3	6	3
Moldova	198	58.8	45.2	71	vif97	41600	1035	483	406	45	51.0	1.1	87	52	80*	73	72
Netherlands	3507	858.7	224.6	0	vif91-95	54209	2328	1561	1023	5858	318.7	12.7	0	48	18	22	11
Norway	1027	31.7	233.6	31	vif94-96	771448	24391	11632	7985	4781	67.3	1.7	83	28	56	56	43
Poland	4193	129.7	108.4	48	vif92-96	1908019	42871	31617	23300	1333	76.9	1.3	81	50	40	57	52
Portugal	690	75.0	70.0	62	vif95	275760	14312	11500	8978	2436	97.4	4.1	64	40	17	40	51
Romania	1730	72.6	76.7	62	vi84 f93-97	1341465	31878	13600	11649	162	43.2	0.9	89	54	11	51	56
Slovakia	668	136.3	124.3	46	vif96	510948	13858	7400	5532	545	57.3	1.2	86	54	80*	73	59
Slovenia	262	129.4	131.3	47	vif96	310577	6339	2300	2133	545	44.9	0.9	89	43	4	45	46
Spain	3947	78.0	99.6	55	vi90 f94	594111	30092	12639	15631	5869	61.5	3.6	85	44	26	52	53
Sweden	2051	45.6	231.6	31	vif92-96	2928117	94122	66510	58100	10148	81.4	2.3	80	45	58	61	46
Switzerland	1011	244.9	139.4	29	v93-95 if85-95	394853	8848	7451	4546	1370	99.7	1.5	61	43	0	35	32
Ukraine	6506	107.8	127.4	48	vif96	1695912	30357	11300	10052	342	38.4	0.6	91	58	25	58	53
United Kingdom	9402	385.2	160.6	16	vif95	264000	13720	9000	7635	10613	143.0	6.9	17	40	17	25	20
Yugoslavia	616	60.3	58.0	70	vi95 f91-95	322313	6858	3454	1320	532	58.1	0.6	86	54	17	52	61
RUSSIAN FEDERATION	24596	14.4	166.6	39	vi93 f95	80676360	919700	150200	115600	477	16.4	0.1	96	57	58	70	54

Country	EC total	EC/ha	EC/p	E score	Timber note	Volume 000 m³	NAI 000 m³	Felling 000 m³	Prod 000 m³	Imp 000 m³	F+I % NAI	P+I % vol	Timb score	Ag score	Fish score	*RS score*	RU index
ASIA																	
Afghanistan	82	1.3	3.9	98	z90	96100	--	--	8091	3	--	8.4	39	53	--	46	72
Armenia	73	24.5	20.6	88	vif96	42740	360	200	36	0	55.6	0.1	86	32	71	63	75
Azerbaijan	465	53.7	60.8	70	vif88	127440	1440	60000	0	316	4189	0.2	0	51	80*	44	57
Bahrain	333	4826.1	571.6	0	x90	0	--	--	0	64	--	6400	0	--	32	16	8
Bangladesh	742	51.5	6.0	74	y90	78100	--	--	33058	89	--	42.4	0	42	41	28	51
Bhutan	20	4.3	10.3	95	y90	421900	--	--	1702	0	--	0.4	96	--	--	60*	77
Brunei Darussalam	101	175.3	327.5	19	x90	124600	--	--	296	38	--	0.3	97	7	7	37	28
Cambodia	75	4.1	7.2	96	z90	1484600	--	--	8008	16	--	0.5	95	63	34	64	80
China	37895	39.5	30.3	80	z90	12972000	--	--	291886	18451	--	2.4	76	41	27	48	64
Cyprus	68	73.5	89.1	58	vi80-90 f86-95	5000	90	50	35	176	251.1	4.2	0	41	2	14	36
Georgia	96	13.8	18.7	91	vif95	434000	4000	500	0	10	12.8	0.0	97	53	2	51	71
India	15026	45.7	15.6	77	y90	2998300	--	--	299490	1783	--	10.0	35	49	41	42	59
Indonesia	5379	28.2	26.4	86	y90	19752300	--	--	193218	235	--	1.0	90	54	34	59	72
Iran	4127	25.3	63.9	68	z90	141100	--	--	6793	114	--	4.9	55	46	17	39	53
Iraq	1064	24.3	50.2	75	z90	4400	--	--	177	0	--	4.0	60	39	28	42	58
Israel	660	313.4	112.6	21	vif97	6000	380	120	124	978	288.9	18.4	0	43	2	15	18
Japan	19489	515.9	154.6	8	v95 i90-95 f95	3482138	69205	29000	20093	27955	82.3	1.4	79	36	27	47	27
Jordan	172	19.3	28.1	86	z90	3400	--	--	11	250	--	7.7	41	41	0	27	56
Kazakhstan	1571	5.8	95.9	56	vif93	369810	6140	1400	315	360	28.7	0.2	93	54	57	68	62
Korea, DPR	2852	236.6	124.1	30	z90	404900	--	--	7000	14	--	1.7	83	54	22	53	41
Korea, R	6264	631.1	137.0	1	x90	460300	--	--	1822	5652	--	1.6	84	33	41	53	27
Kuwait	683	383.3	394.3	15	z90	500	--	--	0	147	--	29.4	3	5	16	8	11
Kyrgyzstan	113	5.7	24.5	88	v88	23000	--	--	42	67	--	0.5	95	58	80*	78	83
Lao PDR	53	2.2	10.5	95	y90	1686500	--	--	4591	1	--	0.3	97	67	80*	81	88
Lebanon	199	191.3	63.3	36	z90	3900	--	--	407	477	--	22.7	12	44	37	31	33
Malaysia	1871	56.7	89.2	58	y90	3774300	--	--	29297	668	--	0.8	92	59	61	59	59
Maldives	4	133.3	15.2	47	--	--	--	--	0	4	--	--	--	16	84	50	48
Mongolia	92	0.6	36.3	82	x90	344100	--	--	631	18	--	0.2	98	24	43	55	68
Myanmar	347	5.1	7.9	96	y90	4206300	--	--	22430	4	--	0.5	95	60	48	68	82
Nepal	289	19.6	13.0	90	y90	281800	--	--	21474	0	--	7.6	42	59	80*	60	75
Oman	291	13.7	126.2	48	x90	0	--	--	0	34	--	3400	0	--	64	32	40
Pakistan	2090	26.3	14.5	87	y90	170200	--	--	33044	204	--	19.5	16	45	35	32	59
Philippines	1571	52.4	22.0	74	y90	1431200	--	--	42530	907	--	3.0	70	62	42	58	66
Qatar	736	669.1	1294.2	0	x90	0	--	--	0	55	--	5500	0	--	79	39	19
Saudi Arabia	3630	16.9	186.4	37	z90	1700	--	--	0	1341	--	78.9	0	17	10	9	23
Singapore	1037	16725.8	302.6	0	x90	700	--	--	0	918	--	131.1	0	--	30	15	7
Sri Lanka	214	32.6	11.7	84	y90	96600	--	--	10414	47	--	10.8	33	45	50	43	63
Syrian Arab R	594	32.1	39.7	80	z90	18000	--	--	50	298	--	1.9	81	48	12	47	63
Tajikistan	140	9.8	23.6	88	vif95	5620	82	10	0	59	84.1	1.0	77	38	80*	65	76
Thailand	3610	70.4	60.4	65	y90	827300	--	--	36302	1292	--	4.5	57	56	56	56	60
Turkey	2590	33.4	40.8	80	vif96	1349323	36601	17606	17668	1947	53.4	1.5	87	50	49	62	71
Turkmenistan	497	10.2	117.4	51	vif95	14100	122	10	0	28	31.1	0.2	92	30	31	51	51
United Arab Emirates	1434	171.5	621.5	1	z90	600	--	--	0	850	--	141.7	0	8	73	27	14
Uzbekistan	1890	42.2	81.4	60	v88	11000	--	--	0	343	--	3.1	69	36	79	61	60
Viet Nam	849	25.6	11.1	87	y90	1049100	--	--	36232	135	--	3.5	65	43	63	57	72
Yemen	215	4.1	13.2	93	x90	100	--	--	0	186	--	186.0	0	31	80	37	65
PACIFIC																	
Australia	4415	5.7	240.8	30	vif94	15006651	339763	19560	22935	1026	6.1	0.2	99	49	16	55	42
Fiji	21	11.5	26.7	87	y90	100200	--	--	594	3	--	0.6	94	47	32	58	72
New Zealand	654	24.2	173.9	38	vif96	2553000	33700	22730	15324	54	67.6	0.6	83	25	81	63	50
Papua New Guinea	96	2.1	21.3	89	y90	6066600	--	--	8772	2	--	0.1	99	44	8	50	69
Samoa	3	10.6	17.4	91	y90	16200	--	--	131	4	--	0.8	92	31	6	43	67
Solomon Is	6	2.1	14.8	93	y90	277500	--	--	872	0	--	0.3	97	36	47	60	76
Tonga	2	26.7	20.5	87	x90	0	--	--	5	6	--	1100	0	36	60	32	59
Vanuatu	1	0.8	5.6	97	y90	99100	--	--	63	1	--	0.1	99	48	41	63	80

Notes

The resource use index (**RU index**) is the unweighted average of an energy and materials index (*E score*) and a resource sectors index (*RS score*).

The energy and materials index is limited to an energy index because of a lack of data on consumption of materials and waste generation. It is the lower score of two indicators (column heading in parentheses):

Energy consumption per hectare of total area (EC/ha).

Energy consumption per person (EC/p).

Energy consumption is production plus imports minus exports minus bunkers plus or minus stock changes of commercial energy (solid fuels, liquid fuels, gases, and electricity) and traditional fuels (such as fuelwood, charcoal, animal wastes, and plant wastes).

EC total = total energy consumption in thousands of terajoules. Data are for 1997 and are from United Nations Energy Statistics Unit (2000). Consumption by Botswana, Lesotho, Namibia, Swaziland and South Africa is lumped under the South Africa Customs Union (which consists of these five countries). I have assumed each country's share of energy consumption to be the same as its share of the combined population of these countries. Data for Eritrea and Ethiopia were also lumped together and have been separated on the basis of each country's share of their combined population.

EC/ha = energy consumption per hectare of total area in gigajoules. Data on total area are from Table 10.

EC/p = energy consumption per person in gigajoules, calculated on the basis of the population in 1997 (population data from United Nations Population Division 1998b).

E score = energy index, the lower score of energy consumption per hectare of total area and energy consumption per person. The performance criteria are shown in Table 22a. In the absence of objective standards, Portugal was used as a benchmark because it has the best combination of high human wellbeing (HWI of 72) and relatively low energy consumption per hectare (75 GJ) and per person (70 GJ). The tops of the medium and fair bands were set so that Portugal's performance would fall in the fair band.

The resource sectors index is the unweighted average of three sub-elements (column heading in parentheses):

Agriculture (Ag score). See Table 23 for data, scores and performance criteria.

Fisheries (Fish score). See Tables 23 and 24 for data and scores, and Table 24a for performance criteria.

Timber (Timb score). See this table.

Timber is represented by a single indicator: fellings + imports as a % of net annual increment; or, if that is not available, production + imports as a % of volume.

Timber note: Data on production and imports are for 1998 and are from FAO (2000a). All other data are for the year indicated in this column. If the year is marked with the letters f, i, r or v, the data come from UNECE & FAO (2000): f = fellings; i = net annual increment; r = removals; v = volume of naturally regenerated forest + plantations. If the year is marked with the letters x, y or z, the data come from FAO (1993 & 1995c) and Pandey (1995): x = volume of naturally regenerated forest only; y = volume of naturally regenerated forest + industrial plantations; z = volume of naturally regenerated forest + industrial plantations + nonindustrial plantations.

Volume = volume of growing stock of forest in thousands of cubic meters (000 m^3). Where the Notes column shows the letters v, y or z, plantations are included; where it shows the letter x, plantations are excluded.

NAI = net annual increment (including bark) in thousands of cubic meters (000 m^3).

Felling = annual fellings (including bark) in thousands of cubic meters (000 m^3). The letter r in the Notes column for Greece and Luxembourg indicates that the data refer to removals (fellings data being unavailable). The letter r in the Notes column for Canada indicates that removals data have been used instead of fellings, since the latter are reported to be 88,433,000 m^3—substantially less than the reported removals of 214,128,000 m^3, an impossibility unless a lot of wood was cut one year and removed the next.

Prod = roundwood production less bark, in thousands of cubic meters (000 m^3). Production by Belgium and Luxembourg is lumped together by FAO. It has been separated here in the same proportions as their fellings.

Imp = imports of roundwood + sawnwood + wood-based panels (but not pulp or paper products), in thousands of cubic meters (000 m^3). Imports by Belgium and Luxembourg are lumped together by FAO. They have been separated here in the same proportions as their fellings.

F+I % NAI = fellings plus imports as a percentage of net annual increment.

P+I % vol = production plus imports as a percentage of volume.

Timb score = timber score, the score of timber fellings + imports as % of net annual increment (NAI), or if unavailable, timber production + imports as % of volume. The performance criteria are shown in Table 22a. For fellings + imports as % of NAI, the top of the medium band was set to ensure that fair felling + import rates were at or below NAI. The performance criteria for production + imports as % of volume are intended to be at least as conservative as those for fellings + imports as % of NAI, but are not as well founded because the relationship between volume and net annual increment varies with forest age, species composition, productivity and environmental conditions.

band	top point on scale	energy consumption per hectare (GJ)	energy consumption per person (GJ)	fellings + imports as % of net annual increment	timber production + imports as % of volume
good	100	0	0	1	0
fair	80	40	40	81	2
medium	60	80	80	101	4
poor	40	160	160	111	8
bad	20	320	320	131	16
base	0	640	640	211	32

Table 22a. Performance criteria for energy and timber indicators.

* A score with an asterisk has been reduced in accordance with the insufficient data rule. To prevent high scores resulting merely from lack of data, a good score is allowed only if it is based on all applicable components (data in an indicator, indicators in an index), and a fair score only if it is based on at least half the components. Good and fair scores (100-61) based on fewer than half the applicable components have been reduced to 60. Good scores (100-81) based on more than half but not all the applicable components have been reduced to 80.

Table 23. Agriculture; Fish and Seafood Self-Reliance

Country	H area 000 ha	Prod 000 mt	Fert 000 mt	Prod /ha	Prod score	Fert/ 000 ha	Fert score	AP score	Cer-eals	Stch roots	Sug swtn	Oils nuts	Pulse veg	Fruit	Meat eggs	D'ry	FP % S	ASR score	Ag score	F&S P%S	FSR score
AMERICAS																					
Antigua & Barbuda	2	11	--	6.1	70	--	--	70	1	34	0	9	38	86	16	58	30	12	12	50	20
Argentina	45804	88232	840.0	1.9	38	18.3	82	60	>100	>100	>100	>100	>100	>100	>100	>100	100	100	60	100	100
Bahamas	61	111	0.4	1.8	36	6.5	93	64	1	9	79	0	57	57	28	5	29	12	12	100	100
Barbados	47	645	3.2	13.7	94	67.9	46	70	3	43	>100	17	76	15	73	26	44	18	18	33	13
Belize	69	1498	4.2	21.8	100	61.2	49	74	61	57	>100	73	79	>100	68	27	71	48	48	100	100
Bolivia	2512	9383	9.1	3.7	57	3.6	96	76	83	100	>100	>100	>100	99	>100	69	94	88	76	49	20
Brazil	237066	511451	4846.5	2.1	41	20.4	80	60	85	100	>100	>100	92	>100	>100	89	96	92	60	79	59
Canada	32248	81033	2696.4	2.5	45	83.6	39	42	>100	>100	59	>100	94	19	>100	>100	84	68	42	93	86
Chile	1897	14484	422.0	7.6	78	222.5	12	45	68	98	94	35	>100	>100	94	90	85	70	45	100	100
Colombia	24578	56694	573.0	2.3	43	23.3	77	60	50	>100	>100	88	91	>100	94	98	90	80	60	40	16
Costa Rica	1593	8542	59.7	5.4	67	37.5	62	64	18	>100	>100	88	>100	>100	>100	>100	88	76	64	100	100
Cuba	2332	47064	239.0	20.2	100	102.5	34	67	20	97	>100	30	74	>100	80	76	72	49	49	67	43
Dominica	25	133	2.7	5.3	66	108.4	33	49	2	>100	55	99	93	>100	9	48	63	37	37	34	14
Dominican R	1460	9852	102.0	6.7	73	69.9	45	59	27	>100	>100	89	>100	>100	91	60	83	66	59	15	6
Ecuador	5015	18521	94.4	3.7	57	18.8	81	69	84	>100	100	96	>100	>100	99	99	97	94	69	100	100
El Salvador	945	5931	88.0	6.3	71	93.1	37	54	63	89	>100	53	76	73	70	64	73	51	51	72	49
Grenada	21	50	--	2.4	44	--	--	44	1	84	57	86	75	>100	25	5	54	25	25	43	17
Guatemala	2876	19831	172.0	6.9	74	59.8	50	62	67	>100	>100	>100	>100	>100	88	74	91	82	62	47	19
Guyana	276	4225	15.0	15.3	98	54.4	53	75	>100	88	>100	>100	75	>100	82	32	85	70	70	100	100
Haiti	910	3676	5.0	4.0	60	--	--	60	39	100	89	38	94	>100	79	56	74	52	52	21	8
Honduras	2631	7124	78.0	2.7	47	29.6	70	58	74	96	>100	99	>100	>100	86	90	93	86	58	100	100
Jamaica	248	4106	25.0	16.6	100	100.8	35	67	1	>100	>100	82	95	>100	57	37	71	48	48	20	8
Mexico	24705	107036	1325.0	4.3	61	53.6	53	57	73	93	99	40	>100	>100	86	80	84	68	57	100	100
Nicaragua	1063	5343	39.0	5.0	65	36.7	63	64	74	88	>100	84	>100	>100	>100	93	86	64	100	100
Panama	488	3497	38.0	7.2	76	77.8	41	58	45	98	>100	35	99	>100	95	89	83	66	58	100	100
Paraguay	3694	10894	33.0	2.9	49	8.9	91	70	>100	100	100	>100	92	97	>100	86	97	94	70	88	76
Peru	3787	18825	165.0	5.0	65	43.6	58	61	45	98	98	77	>100	99	97	70	85	70	61	100	100
St Kitts & Nevis	5	231	1.1	44.2	100	211.7	13	56	0	90	>100	75	54	47	23	0	49	20	20	74	52
St Lucia	33	200	7.0	6.0	70	210	14	42	0	88	0	>100	22	>100	21	6	42	17	17	29	12
St Vincent & Grenadines	71	132	3.0	1.9	38	42.4	59	48	7	>100	85	92	95	>100	29	16	65	40	40	79	59
Suriname	90	390	7.3	4.3	61	80.8	40	50	>100	57	86	74	91	>100	58	50	77	56	50	100	100
Trinidad & Tobago	208	1746	10.0	8.4	81	48.1	56	68	4	26	>100	27	46	92	71	8	47	19	19	87	74
United States	187405	607066	20200.1	3.2	52	107.8	33	42	>100	>100	97	>100	>100	84	>100	96	97	94	42	87	74
Uruguay	1135	3291	119.0	2.9	49	104.9	34	41	>100	85	69	99	79	>100	>100	>100	91	82	41	100	100
Venezuela	3270	16161	292.0	4.9	64	89.3	38	51	54	93	95	74	85	>100	96	68	83	66	51	85	70
AFRICA																					
Algeria	5347	10507	59.0	2.0	40	11.0	89	64	52	91	0	54	93	97	90	33	64	39	39	89	78
Angola	2543	4866	10.0	1.9	38	3.9	96	67	56	100	79	88	92	99	77	66	82	64	64	93	86
Benin	2237	4692	35.0	2.1	41	15.6	84	62	81	>100	57	>100	91	100	87	58	84	68	62	75	53
Botswana	293	206	3.3	0.7	14	11.4	89	51	33	34	0	23	45	19	>100	47	38	15	15	17	7
Burkina Faso	4183	4356	24.1	1.0	20	5.8	94	57	99	99	98	99	>100	100	100	91	98	96	57	48	19
Burundi	2180	4491	6.0	2.1	41	2.8	97	69	82	100	91	95	93	100	99	88	93	86	69	94	88
Cameroon	5844	10804	34.0	1.8	36	5.8	94	65	90	>100	95	>100	99	>100	99	85	96	92	65	53	24
Cape Verde	39	67	--	1.7	34	--	--	34	13	66	52	32	75	73	62	34	51	21	21	100	100
Central African R	934	1812	1.2	1.9	38	1.3	99	68	83	100	94	98	95	100	100	99	96	92	68	95	90
Chad	2475	2458	10.5	1.0	20	4.2	96	58	91	100	96	86	100	100	>100	96	96	92	58	99	98
Comoros	84	231	0.1	2.7	47	1.2	99	73	27	100	0	>100	92	100	48	65	66	41	41	91	82
Congo, DR	9616	27937	10.0	2.9	49	1.0	99	74	79	96	96	99	95	100	90	17	84	68	68	56	28
Congo, R	449	1806	3.0	4.0	60	6.7	93	76	15	100	>100	88	89	99	47	4	68	44	44	6	2
Côte d'Ivoire	10162	14090	70.0	1.4	28	6.9	93	60	62	100	>100	>100	93	>100	95	7	82	64	60	38	15
Djibouti	4	22	--	5.2	66	--	--	66	0	0	0	0	85	7	87	35	27	11	11	21	8
Egypt	5998	53499	1194.0	8.9	82	199.1	15	48	66	>100	96	55	>100	>100	84	90	86	72	48	67	43
Equatorial Guinea	--	--	--	--	--	--	--	--	--	--	--	--	--	--	--	--	--	--	--	--	--
Eritrea	496	408	5.0	0.8	16	10.1	90	53	25	100	0	>100	90	100	100	83	75	53	53	100	100
Ethiopia	13126	18489	154.2	1.4	28	11.8	88	58	>100	>100	>100	96	>100	>100	>100	99	99	98	58	95	90
Gabon	234	1032	0.4	4.4	62	1.7	98	80	21	99	100	86	65	98	53	5	66	41	41	70	47
Gambia	261	218	0.8	0.8	16	3.1	97	56	49	80	0	>100	29	86	91	34	59	32	32	100	100
Ghana	6167	17640	13.0	2.9	49	2.1	98	73	87	>100	47	>100	97	>100	86	52	84	68	68	97	94
Guinea	3450	4334	2.8	1.2	24	0.8	99	61	68	100	81	99	95	>100	89	68	87	74	61	96	92
Guinea-Bissau	388	490	0.8	1.3	26	2.1	98	62	64	100	70	>100	91	>100	97	83	88	76	62	100	100
Kenya	3862	12813	120.0	3.3	53	31.1	69	61	75	100	99	47	>100	>100	97	100	90	80	61	100	100
Lesotho	249	419	7.1	1.7	34	28.3	72	53	56	91	0	1	55	45	85	81	52	23	23	0	0
Liberia	327	1040	--	3.2	52	--	--	--	23	100	98	99	88	99	88	17	76	55	52	80	60

251

Country	H area 000 ha	Prod 000 mt	Fert 000 mt	Prod /ha	Prod score	Fert/ 000 ha	Fert score	AP score	Cer-eals	Stch roots	Sug swtn	Oils nuts	Pulse veg	Fruit	Meat eggs	D'ry	FP % S	ASR score	Ag score	F&S P%S	FSR score
Libyan Arab J	751	1431	71.0	1.9	38	94.6	36	37	16	96	0	35	70	92	93	30	54	25	25	86	72
Madagascar	2992	8993	13.2	3.0	50	4.4	96	73	91	>100	99	77	>100	>100	100	97	95	90	73	100	100
Malawi	2486	5988	41.0	2.4	44	16.5	83	63	96	>100	>100	91	>100	100	98	71	94	88	63	96	92
Mali	3999	3423	32.0	0.8	16	8.0	92	54	91	95	89	>100	99	96	100	89	95	90	54	99	98
Mauritania	373	277	5.0	0.7	14	13.4	87	50	45	47	0	13	57	87	95	85	54	25	25	100	100
Mauritius	106	5994	34.5	56.3	100	324.2	0	50	0	45	>100	7	78	37	59	18	43	17	17	56	28
Morocco	8737	22938	298.0	2.6	46	34.1	66	56	>100	>100	89	75	>100	>100	96	86	93	86	56	100	100
Mozambique	3959	8052	11.0	2.0	40	2.8	97	68	75	100	92	>100	98	>100	91	60	89	78	68	83	66
Namibia	366	351	--	0.9	18	--	--	18	38	100	0	20	34	25	>100	100	52	23	18	100	100
Niger	10256	3613	11.0	0.3	6	1.1	99	52	89	100	85	82	>100	93	100	92	93	86	52	64	39
Nigeria	71339	122847	135.0	1.7	34	1.9	98	66	94	100	55	100	100	100	95	27	84	68	66	53	24
Rwanda	1150	4348	0.1	3.8	58	0.1	100	79	38	100	58	26	85	100	100	93	75	53	53	75	53
São Tomé & Principe	76	91	--	1.2	24	--	--	24	25	99	0	>100	91	100	82	5	63	37	24	84	68
Senegal	2791	3177	15.0	1.1	22	5.4	95	58	54	80	93	82	83	98	95	47	79	59	58	100	100
Seychelles	6	15	--	2.4	44	--	--	44	0	7	0	70	36	34	73	2	28	11	11	100	100
Sierra Leone	1134	1613	3.0	1.4	28	2.6	97	62	52	>100	71	98	95	100	93	68	85	70	62	100	100
Somalia	--	--	0.5	--	--	--	--	--	--	--	--	--	--	--	--	--	--	--	--	--	--
South Africa	11421	49835	780.0	4.4	62	68.3	46	54	>100	97	>100	85	99	>100	91	>100	96	92	54	36	14
Sudan	13039	15317	92.0	1.2	24	7.1	93	58	>100	100	>100	>100	96	>100	100	99	99	98	58	95	90
Swaziland	159	4647	6.0	29.2	100	37.9	62	81	64	51	>100	>100	54	>100	80	75	78	57	57	--	--
Tanzania	10157	19388	38.0	1.9	38	3.7	96	67	92	>100	98	>100	99	>100	96	98	98	96	67	100	100
Togo	1865	2432	17.6	1.3	26	9.4	91	58	>100	>100	0	>100	95	99	93	32	77	56	56	24	10
Tunisia	5451	7896	86.1	1.4	28	15.8	84	56	82	90	57	>100	>100	>100	99	90	90	80	56	100	100
Uganda	8189	21706	3.4	2.6	46	0.4	100	73	85	100	99	99	97	>100	95	98	97	94	73	100	100
Zambia	1384	4620	41.0	3.3	53	29.6	70	61	96	100	>100	98	>100	96	100	91	98	96	61	90	80
Zimbabwe	3195	7577	174.4	2.4	44	54.6	53	48	>100	90	>100	100	99	96	91	>100	97	94	48	87	74
EUROPE																					
Albania	424	1409	7.0	3.3	53	16.5	83	68	47	87	55	67	99	76	87	98	77	56	56	45	18
Austria	2140	11897	229.9	5.6	68	107.4	33	50	>100	87	98	68	60	65	>100	>100	85	70	50	2	1
Belarus	4360	19685	747.0	4.5	62	171.3	19	40	69	>100	75	54	98	70	>100	>100	83	66	40	100	100
Belgium	3096	16300	310.0	5.3	66	100.1	35	50	57	64	>100	25	90	32	>100	>100	71	48	48	6	2
Bosnia & Herzegovina	650	2008	16.0	3.1	51	24.6	75	63	74	97	9	50	97	72	59	84	68	44	44	28	11
Bulgaria	4011	7759	185.0	1.9	38	46.1	57	47	74	66	31	>100	98	>100	>100	>100	84	68	47	86	72
Croatia	1374	6074	186.4	4.4	62	135.7	26	44	99	99	93	73	78	75	96	79	86	72	44	100	100
Czech R	3362	17379	367.7	5.2	66	109.4	33	49	97	>100	>100	97	78	47	97	>100	89	78	49	18	7
Denmark	2587	17122	437.0	6.6	73	168.9	19	46	>100	>100	>100	42	75	14	>100	>100	79	59	46	100	100
Estonia	472	1277	22.0	2.7	47	46.7	57	52	76	94	9	24	73	26	76	>100	60	33	33	100	100
France	29584	143486	5065.0	4.8	64	171.2	19	41	>100	91	>100	>100	>100	81	>100	>100	96	92	41	41	16
Germany	21536	112382	2818.9	5.2	66	130.9	27	46	>100	>100	>100	43	46	43	87	>100	77	56	46	21	8
Greece	7787	20771	560.0	2.7	47	71.9	44	45	93	86	98	91	>100	>100	67	68	88	76	45	47	19
Hungary	5823	24239	456.6	4.2	61	78.4	41	51	>100	>100	>100	>100	>100	>100	>100	>100	100	100	51	8	3
Iceland	8	19	20.4	2.3	43	2425.7	0	21	0	40	31	1	19	0	>100	100	36	14	14	100	100
Ireland	808	5783	691.0	7.1	75	854.8	0	37	92	88	>100	13	66	7	>100	>100	71	48	37	100	100
Italy	23760	82370	1819.5	3.5	55	76.6	42	48	86	72	99	73	>100	>100	85	68	85	70	48	35	14
Latvia	698	2620	127.0	3.8	58	182.1	17	37	82	100	85	37	84	50	71	>100	76	55	37	100	100
Lithuania	1505	6289	166.0	4.2	61	110.3	32	46	9	100	99	81	>100	>100	>100	>100	86	72	46	96	92
Luxembourg	B	B	B	5.3	66	100.1	35	50	57	64	>100	25	90	32	>100	>100	71	48	48	6	2
Macedonia, FYR	583	1860	38.0	3.2	52	65.2	47	49	84	96	60	64	>100	>100	63	88	82	64	49	6	2
Malta	16	152	1.0	9.3	83	61.6	49	66	4	91	0	0	90	39	61	46	41	16	16	7	3
Moldova	2333	7105	116.0	3.0	50	49.7	55	52	95	86	>100	>100	80	>100	>100	>100	95	90	52	100	100
Netherlands	6669	25856	504.0	3.9	59	75.6	42	50	31	83	>100	22	>100	32	>100	>100	71	48	48	46	18
Norway	795	2344	203.0	2.9	49	255.2	8	28	72	82	3	16	57	21	96	>100	56	28	28	100	100
Poland	13875	84744	1634.0	6.1	70	117.8	31	50	96	>100	>100	53	>100	>100	>100	>100	94	88	50	70	47
Portugal	4845	9650	275.0	2.0	40	56.8	52	46	44	56	11	41	>100	83	87	98	65	40	40	42	17
Romania	10792	30609	428.0	2.8	48	39.7	60	54	86	99	91	>100	98	>100	>100	99	97	94	54	27	11
Slovakia	1585	7942	113.0	5.0	65	71.3	44	54	>100	92	98	>100	96	52	>100	>100	92	84	54	100	100
Slovenia	402	2185	66.2	5.4	67	164.9	19	43	53	96	82	11	61	75	99	>100	72	49	43	9	4
Spain	30748	74540	2163.9	2.4	44	70.4	45	44	99	58	99	79	>100	>100	>100	83	90	80	44	58	31
Sweden	2116	11417	304.0	5.4	67	143.7	24	45	>100	77	100	45	49	12	98	96	72	49	45	100	100
Switzerland	829	4962	116.0	6.0	70	139.9	25	47	70	81	87	28	44	45	80	>100	67	43	43	1	0
Ukraine	20988	80958	906.0	3.8	58	43.2	58	58	85	100	>100	>100	>100	100	>100	>100	98	96	58	68	44
United Kingdom	10079	58222	2221.0	5.8	69	220.4	12	40	>100	93	95	47	68	6	83	91	73	51	40	43	17
Yugoslavia	4825	16198	241.0	3.3	53	50.0	55	54	98	>100	>100	89	98	99	99	98	98	96	54	42	17
RUSSIAN FEDERATION	69599	148036	1850.0	2.1	41	26.6	73	57	93	94	85	97	91	58	79	100	87	74	57	100	100
ASIA																					
Afghanistan	8054	5007	50.0	0.6	12	6.2	94	53	96	99	39	76	>100	>100	>100	98	88	76	53	--	--

252

Country	H area 000 ha	Prod 000 mt	Fert 000 mt	Prod /ha	Prod score	Fert/ 000 ha	Fert score	AP score	Cer-eals	Stch roots	Sug swtn	Oils nuts	Pulse veg	Fruit	Meat eggs	D'ry	FP % S	ASR score	Ag score	F&S P%S	FSR score
Armenia	316	1549	8.0	4.9	64	25.3	75	69	42	100	2	4	96	95	50	87	59	32	32	100	100
Azerbaijan	1550	2973	39.0	1.9	38	25.2	75	56	62	92	2	88	98	88	60	95	73	51	51	100	100
Bahrain	--	--	0.6	--	--	--	--	--	--	--	--	--	--	--	--	--	--	--	--	--	--
Bangladesh	9193	34634	1259.4	3.8	58	137.0	26	42	89	99	>100	47	93	98	93	90	89	78	42	100	100
Bhutan	--	--	0.1	--	--	--	--	--	--	--	--	--	--	--	--	--	--	--	--	--	--
Brunei Darussalam	12	16	5.0	1.3	26	405.9	0	13	1	39	0	2	30	25	40	0	17	7	7	17	7
Cambodia	2214	3532	12.8	1.6	32	5.8	94	63	>100	100	87	79	100	100	100	51	90	80	63	100	100
China	221710	1027765	36505.0	4.6	63	164.7	19	41	94	99	98	89	>100	100	>100	92	96	92	41	87	74
Cyprus	268	923	31.0	3.4	54	115.7	31	42	19	>100	2	15	>100	>100	>100	92	66	41	41	6	2
Georgia	990	2542	37.0	2.6	46	37.4	63	54	54	99	3	51	98	>100	>100	92	75	53	53	53	24
India	296783	670289	14308.2	2.3	43	48.2	56	49	>100	>100	>100	100	>100	>100	100	100	100	100	49	100	100
Indonesia	83421	165601	2688.7	2.0	40	32.2	68	54	91	>100	99	>100	98	>100	99	54	93	86	54	100	100
Iran	14785	46709	1139.8	3.2	52	77.1	41	46	74	100	86	66	>100	>100	95	95	89	78	46	43	17
Iraq	4156	8235	349.0	2.0	40	84.0	39	39	74	79	21	22	97	>100	96	87	72	49	39	100	100
Israel	863	4156	104.0	4.8	64	120.5	30	47	7	>100	5	41	>100	>100	84	97	67	43	43	6	2
Japan	13235	49264	1563.0	3.7	57	118.1	30	43	25	79	78	20	84	60	68	80	62	36	36	55	27
Jordan	427	2063	20.0	4.8	64	46.9	56	60	6	99	0	62	>100	95	90	79	66	41	41	0	0
Kazakhstan	19034	14565	124.0	0.8	16	6.5	93	54	>100	99	55	89	>100	>100	>100	99	93	86	54	100	100
Korea, DPR	3477	11354	170.1	3.3	53	48.9	56	54	72	100	0	88	100	100	99	100	82	64	54	100	100
Korea, R	7240	24108	932.5	3.3	53	128.8	28	40	29	32	41	23	96	83	88	92	60	33	33	95	90
Kuwait	3	90	1.0	26.7	100	297.4	3	51	0	4	0	0	29	3	55	10	13	5	5	39	16
Kyrgyzstan	924	2804	31.0	3.0	50	33.6	66	58	94	>100	75	90	>100	>100	>100	98	95	90	58	100	100
Lao PDR	829	1733	6.1	2.1	41	7.4	93	67	84	100	82	>100	100	100	100	31	87	74	67	98	96
Lebanon	419	3128	50.0	7.5	77	119.3	30	53	7	>100	77	51	91	>100	75	42	68	44	44	100	100
Malaysia	94221	62403	1146.0	0.7	14	12.2	88	51	26	49	61	>100	36	>100	93	3	58	31	31	89	78
Maldives	8	56	--	7.3	76	--	--	76	0	74	0	85	76	54	22	0	39	16	16	100	100
Mongolia	298	298	4.0	1.0	20	13.4	87	53	50	82	0	0	96	1	>100	96	53	24	24	67	43
Myanmar	14607	22981	172.0	1.6	32	11.8	88	60	>100	100	>100	99	>100	>100	100	94	99	98	60	100	100
Nepal	4434	9999	103.0	2.2	42	23.2	77	59	>100	99	>100	83	>100	98	99	99	97	94	59	100	100
Oman	--	--	12.0	--	--	--	--	--	--	--	--	--	--	--	--	--	--	--	--	--	--
Pakistan	35921	89203	2409.0	2.5	45	67.1	46	45	>100	99	99	70	94	>100	97	99	95	90	45	100	100
Philippines	19490	74231	646.1	3.8	58	33.1	67	62	88	95	99	>100	98	>100	95	2	85	70	62	81	62
Qatar	--	--	0.9	--	--	--	--	--	--	--	--	--	--	--	--	--	--	--	--	--	--
Saudi Arabia	852	5683	323.0	6.7	73	379.3	0	36	18	81	0	4	77	65	67	31	43	17	17	25	10
Singapore	--	--	4.9	--	--	--	--	--	--	--	--	--	--	--	--	--	--	--	--	--	--
Sri Lanka	1874	7191	204.4	3.8	58	109.0	33	45	51	90	83	>100	79	99	90	46	80	60	45	75	53
Syrian Arab R	6558	12880	305.9	2.0	40	46.6	57	48	>100	>100	69	98	>100	>100	99	97	95	90	48	30	12
Tajikistan	917	1610	69.0	1.7	34	75.3	42	38	32	78	2	84	>100	>100	80	94	71	48	38	100	100
Thailand	27655	119871	1566.8	4.3	61	56.7	52	56	>100	>100	>100	96	>100	>100	>100	21	90	80	56	100	100
Turkey	27696	91403	1798.7	3.3	53	64.9	48	50	94	>100	>100	90	>100	>100	93	99	97	94	50	84	68
Turkmenistan	1332	1815	141.0	1.4	28	105.8	33	30	44	65	4	69	99	>100	87	95	70	47	30	100	100
United Arab Emirates	52	1064	35.0	20.6	100	679.2	0	50	1	5	0	0	65	39	46	14	21	8	8	100	100
Uzbekistan	7166	10663	530.0	1.5	30	74.0	43	36	64	86	2	>100	>100	>100	81	99	79	59	36	100	100
Viet Nam	11122	46352	1544.0	4.2	61	138.8	25	43	>100	>100	99	>100	>100	>100	99	10	88	76	43	100	100
Yemen	1081	1886	12.0	1.7	34	11.1	89	61	24	100	0	22	85	97	85	48	58	31	31	98	96
PACIFIC																					
Australia	23408	93821	1924.0	4.0	60	82.2	39	49	>100	95	>100	>100	>100	>100	>100	>100	99	98	49	41	16
Fiji	177	5197	19.0	29.4	100	107.4	33	66	11	91	>100	96	52	80	62	68	70	47	47	98	96
New Zealand	1150	3460	661.0	3.0	50	574.9	0	25	83	88	13	4	>100	>100	>100	>100	73	51	25	100	100
Papua New Guinea	2957	5472	13.0	1.8	36	4.4	96	66	1	100	99	>100	98	99	48	1	68	44	44	21	8
Samoa	--	--	--	--	--	--	--	--	0	>100	0	>100	100	>100	38	25	58	31	31	14	6
Solomon Is	293	519	--	1.8	36	--	--	36	0	100	0	>100	93	96	82	34	63	37	36	100	100
Tonga	--	--	--	--	--	--	--	--	0	>100	0	>100	100	100	29	67	62	36	36	100	100
Vanuatu	86	362	--	4.2	61	--	--	61	5	89	0	>100	>100	97	>100	78	71	48	48	66	41

Notes

Agriculture (Ag score) is the lower score of agricultural productivity (AP score) and agricultural self-reliance (ASR score). All data are for 1996, except Samoa and Tonga which are for 1992, and are from the food balance sheets and commodities database in FAO (1998a). Luxembourg is included with Belgium (B).

H area = harvested area (food crops only) in thousands of hectares (000 ha); except Haiti, Liberia, Rwanda, Bosnia & Herzegovina and Afghanistan, which is cropland area in thousands of hectares (from Table 11).

Prod = food crop production in thousands of metric tons (000 mt).

Fert = fertilizer use in thousands of metric tons (000 mt). Although the harvested area and production figures refer to the same set of food crops, the fertilizer data apply to non-food crops as well.

Prod/ha = metric tons of food crop production per harvested hectare.

Prod score = score of one of the agricultural productivity indicators: food produced per harvested hectare. The performance criteria are shown in Table 23a.

Fert/000 ha = metric tons of fertilizer used per 1000 harvested hectares.

Fert score = score of the other agricultural productivity indicator: fertilizer used per 1000 harvested hectares. The performance criteria are shown in Table 23a.

AP score = agricultural productivity score, the unweighted average score of food produced per harvested hectare (Prod score) and fertilizer used per 1000 harvested hectares (Fert score).

The remaining columns give production as a % of supply for eight categories of food: cereals; starchy roots (Stch roots); sugar crops and sweeteners (Sug swtn); oil crops, plant oils and tree nuts (Oils nuts); pulses and vegetables (Pulse veg); fruit; meat, offal, animal fats [except butter, cream, and fish oils] and eggs (Meat eggs); and dairy products [milk, butter, cream, cheese and other milk products] (D'ry). Production means total domestic production. Supply means the amount available for consumption, which is production + imports - exports ± stock changes. >100 indicates that production exceeds supply, the balance being exported.

FP % S = food production as a percentage of supply, the average of the eight groups, cereals through dairy products. >100 is counted as 100.

ASR score = agricultural self-reliance score, the score of food production as % of supply. The performance criteria are shown in Table 23a. They mirror the performance criteria for food sufficiency.

Ag score = the lower of the AP score and the ASR score.

F&SP%S = fish and seafood production as a percentage of supply. Fish and seafood include seaweeds and fish oils. Production means the domestic catch + aquaculture. Supply means the amount available for consumption, which is production + imports - exports ± stock changes. Data are for 1996 and are from the food balance sheets and commodities database in FAO (1998a).

FSR score = fish and seafood self-reliance, the score of fish and seafood production as % of supply. The performance criteria are shown in Table 24a. They are the same as for agricultural self-reliance (Table 23a).

band	top point on scale	food produced per harvested hectare (mt)	fertilizer used per 1000 harvested hectares (mt)	food production as % of supply
good	100	16	0	100
fair	80	8	20	90
medium	60	4	40	80
poor	40	2	80	65
bad	20	1	160	50
base	0	0	320	0

Table 23a. Performance criteria for agriculture indicators.

* A score with an asterisk has been reduced in accordance with the insufficient data rule. To prevent high scores resulting merely from lack of data, a good score is allowed only if it is based on all applicable components (data in an indicator, indicators in an index), and a fair score only if it is based on at least half the components. Good and fair scores (100-61) based on fewer than half the applicable components have been reduced to 60. Good scores (100-81) based on more than half but not all the applicable components have been reduced to 80.

Table 24. Fisheries

Country	Spp tot	Spp ass	O D R	O D R%	Spp score	m i b	Marine catch mt	Inland water catch mt	Total catch mt	Shelf 000 km²	S/I 000 km²	Decked vessels grt	Undeck vessels number	Fleet capacity grt	t cap/ km²	Area score	mt catch/ t cap	Catch score	FP score	FSR score	Fish score
AMERICAS																					
Antigua & Barbuda	--	--	--	--	--	m	470	0	--	35	--	--	150	450	0.01	100	1.04	21	60	20	20
Argentina	13	11	5	45	27	m	1135452	11863	--	835	--	220954	2300	227854	0.27	89	4.98	65	60	100	60
Bahamas	1	1	0	0	100	m	9557	0	--	65	--	6400	510	6910	0.11	96	1.38	28	74	100	74
Barbados	1	1	0	0	100	m	3284	0	--	1	--	2584	7750	4834	4.83	16	0.68	14	43	13	13
Belize	--	--	--	--	--	m	1229	[94] 1	--	25	--	67221	900	69921	2.80	32	0.02	0	16	100	16
Bolivia	--	--	--	--	--	--	--	5692	--	NA	--	--	--	--	--	--	--	--	--	20	20
Brazil	10	4	4	100	0	b	587600	183180	770780	905	996	84200	44000	216200	0.22	91	3.56	56	49	59	49
Canada	35	35	8	23	56	m	829878	38208	--	2875	--	596060	20470	657470	0.23	91	1.26	25	57	86	57
Chile	13	11	7	64	14	m	7433864	[94] 5	--	295	--	178618	12000	214618	0.73	71	34.64	100	62	100	62
Colombia	3	0	0	--	--	m	106926	23524	--	105	--	20950	6000	38950	0.37	85	2.75	47	66	16	16
Costa Rica	--	--	--	--	--	m	20106	1087	--	45	--	8650	2950	11600	0.26	90	1.73	35	62	100	62
Cuba	12	11	2	18	64	m	71202	2142	--	135	--	150680	--	150680	1.12	58	0.47	9	44	43	43
Dominica	--	--	--	--	--	m	838	0	--	20	--	--	895	2685	0.13	95	0.31	6	50	14	14
Dominican R	2	1	0	0	80*	b	15817	2160	17977	35	35	--	3550	10650	0.30	88	1.69	34	67	6	6
Ecuador	6	3	0	0	80*	m	505095	300	--	95	--	70200	1600	71800	0.76	70	7.03	75	75	100	75
El Salvador	--	--	--	--	--	b	10208	4325	14533	35	35	7862	10000	37862	1.08	58	0.38	8	33	49	33
Grenada	2	1	0	0	80*	m	1486	0	--	30	--	--	730	730	0.02	99	2.03	40	73	17	17
Guatemala	--	--	--	--	--	b	4228	4025	8253	25	25	4700	2900	13400	0.54	78	0.61	12	45	19	19
Guyana	1	0	0	--	--	b	43730	700	44430	35	53	4300	1600	9100	0.17	93	4.88	64	79	100	79
Haiti	1	0	0	--	--	b	5000	500	5500	35	35	280	3000	3280	0.09	96	1.68	34	65	8	8
Honduras	1	1	0	0	100	m	19626	127	--	25	--	25600	700	26300	1.05	59	0.75	15	58	100	58
Jamaica	--	--	--	--	--	b	9827	710	10537	45	45	874	7150	22324	0.50	80	0.47	9	44	8	8
Mexico	15	8	2	25	53	m	1175184	113665	--	555	--	435163	71641	650086	1.17	57	1.81	36	49	100	49
Nicaragua	--	--	--	--	--	m	10457	538	--	125	--	18100	120	21700	0.17	93	0.48	10	52	100	52
Panama	3	3	0	0	100	m	176014	130	--	95	--	267400	3000	270400	2.85	32	0.65	13	48	100	48
Paraguay	--	--	--	--	--	--	--	17810	--	NA	--	--	--	--	--	--	--	--	--	76	76
Peru	7	7	4	57	17	m	8886553	50789	--	135	--	199900	--	199900	1.48	50	44.45	100	56	100	56
St Kitts & Nevis	--	--	--	--	--	m	218	0	--	e 11	--	--	270	810	0.07	97	0.27	5	51	52	51
St Lucia	--	--	--	--	--	m	1176	0	--	1	--	--	489	1467	1.47	51	0.80	16	33	12	12
St Vincent & Grenadines	--	--	--	--	--	m	1320	0	--	8	--	41650	430	42940	5.37	13	0.03	1	7	59	7
Suriname	--	--	--	--	--	b	12860	139	12999	35	42	2300	1150	5750	0.14	94	2.26	43	69	100	69
Trinidad & Tobago	--	--	--	--	--	m	13250	0	--	15	--	2451	1450	6801	0.45	82	1.95	39	60	74	60
United States	74	59	14	24	55	m	5187877	36690	--	2325	--	1401586	72000	1617586	0.70	72	3.21	52	60	74	60
Uruguay	6	6	4	67	13	m	125597	849	--	85	--	23297	--	23297	0.27	89	5.39	67	56	100	56
Venezuela	10	7	0	0	80*	m	440065	59753	--	95	--	117002	12683	129685	1.37	53	3.39	54	62	70	62
AFRICA																					
Algeria	5	5	0	0	100	m	105872	15	--	15	--	27898	--	27898	1.86	43	3.79	58	67	78	67
Angola	2	2	0	0	100	m	87847	6000	--	85	--	24710	4200	28910	0.34	86	3.04	50	79	86	79
Benin	1	0	0	--	--	b	7000	37449	44449	15	17	668	23100	23768	1.40	52	1.87	37	44	53	44
Botswana	--	--	--	--	--	i	--	2000	--	NA	15	--	1000	3000	0.20	92	0.67	13	52	7	7
Burkina Faso	--	--	--	--	--	i	--	8000	--	NA	0	--	3000	9000	--	--	0.89	18	18	19	18
Burundi	--	--	--	--	--	i	--	21051	--	NA	2	--	1000	3000	1.50	50	7.02	75	62	88	62
Cameroon	4	3	2	67	13	b	64740	21000	85740	15	25	7900	7100	29200	1.17	57	2.94	49	40	24	24
Cape Verde	1	1	1	100	0	m	8495	0	--	35	--	3550	1250	7300	0.21	92	1.16	23	38	100	38
Central African R	--	--	--	--	--	--	--	12900	--	NA	--	--	--	--	--	--	--	--	--	90	80*
Chad	--	--	--	--	--	i	--	90000	--	NA	25	--	19100	57300	2.29	37	1.57	31	34	98	34
Comoros	2	1	0	0	80*	m	13200	0	--	35	--	--	4450	13350	0.38	85	0.99	20	62	82	62
Congo, DR	--	--	--	--	--	b	3876	154001	157877	1	79	5383	16500	54883	0.69	72	2.88	49	61	28	28
Congo, R	--	--	--	--	--	b	17000	19820	36820	15	16	8760	550	10410	0.65	74	3.54	55	64	2	2
Côte d'Ivoire	5	3	1	33	43	m	58854	11335	--	55	--	10582	3600	14182	0.26	90	4.15	61	65	15	15
Djibouti	--	--	--	--	--	--	350	0	--	4	--	--	--	--	--	--	--	--	--	8	8
Egypt	8	4	1	25	53	b	78296	171133	249429	65	71	--	36401	109203	1.54	49	2.28	43	48	43	43
Equatorial Guinea	1	0	0	--	--	b	3000	380	3380	25	25	650	1100	1750	0.07	97	1.93	39	68	--	68
Eritrea	--	--	--	--	--	--	3670	0	--	75	--	--	--	--	--	--	--	--	--	100	80*
Ethiopia	--	--	--	--	--	i	--	6325	--	NA	104	--	1835	5505	0.05	98	1.15	23	60	90	60
Gabon	1	1	1	100	0	b	32789	7606	40395	55	65	4381	1600	9181	0.01	100	4.40	62	54	47	47
Gambia	1	0	0	--	--	b	20598	2500	23098	4	5	--	1600	4800	0.96	62	4.81	64	63	100	63
Ghana	12	5	2	40	33	b	293322	60000	353322	55	66	63985	25000	138985	2.11	39	2.54	45	39	94	39
Guinea	--	--	--	--	--	b	64760	4000	68760	35	35	4516	2300	11416	0.33	87	6.02	70	78	92	78

255

Country	Spp tot	Spp ass	ODR	ODR%	Spp score	mib	Marine catch mt	Inland water catch mt	Total catch mt	Shelf 000 km²	S/I 000 km²	Decked vessels grt	Undeck vessels number	Fleet capacity grt	t cap/km²	Area score	mt catch/t cap	Catch score	FP score	FSR score	Fish score
Guinea-Bissau	1	0	0	--	--	b	6079	250	6329	55	63	2760	1150	6210	0.10	96	1.02	20	58	100	58
Kenya	1	0	0	--	--	b	5465	187241	192706	25	36	4198	10124	34570	0.96	62	5.57	68	65	100	65
Lesotho	--	--	--	--	--			26	--	NA	--									0	0
Liberia	--	--	--	--	--	m	5232	4000	--	45	--	2500	770	4810	0.11	96	1.09	22	59	60	59
Libyan Arab J	--	--	--	--	--	m	34232	0	--	35	--	12700	650	14650	0.42	83	2.34	43	63	72	63
Madagascar	2	1	0	0	80*	b	84640	30000	114640	195	201	9800	28507	95321	0.47	81	1.20	24	62	100	62
Malawi	--	--	--	--	--	i	--	53664	--	NA	24	306	2807	8727	0.36	86	6.15	71	78	92	78
Mali	--	--	--	--	--	i	--	132900	--	NA	20	--	7700	23100	1.16	57	5.75	69	63	98	63
Mauritania	4	4	4	100	0	m	84500	5500	--	25	--	38000	3500	48500	1.94	41	1.74	35	25	100	25
Mauritius	1	0	0	--	--	m	16872	[93]3	--	95	--	2663	2056	8831	0.09	96	1.91	38	67	28	28
Morocco	16	9	4	44	28	m	842791	1500	--	65	--	225377	6500	244877	3.77	22	3.44	54	35	100	35
Mozambique	3	2	0	0	80*	b	21740	5093	26833	185	203	7620	*17200*	24820	0.12	95	1.08	22	66	66	66
Namibia	10	9	2	22	57	m	290782	1195	--	125	--	67122	10	67152	0.54	78	4.33	62	66	100	66
Niger	--	--	--	--	--	i	--	3541	--	NA	0	--	3000	9000	--	--	0.39	8	8	39	8
Nigeria	9	2	2	100	0	b	231579	117903	349482	65	78	40267	77067	271468	3.48	25	1.29	26	17	24	17
Rwanda	--	--	--	--	--	i	--	3300	--	NA	2	--	1700	5100	2.55	35	0.65	13	24	53	24
São Tomé & Principe	--	--	--	--	--	m	2800	0	--	1	--	1450	2700	9550	9.55	0	0.29	6	3	68	3
Senegal	11	5	5	100	0	m	323617	35000	--	15	--	40500	10251	71253	4.75	16	4.54	63	26	100	26
Seychelles	--	--	--	--	--	m	3982	0	--	45	--	--	383	1149	0.03	99	3.46	55	77	100	77
Sierra Leone	4	2	2	100	0	b	47313	15000	62313	25	25	5850	5650	22800	0.91	64	2.73	47	37	100	37
Somalia	--	--	--	--	--	m	15200	300	--	165	--	6600	*1550*	8150	0.05	98	1.86	37	67	--	67
South Africa	12	10	2	20	60	m	573558	800	--	255	--	78430	*2600*	81030	0.32	87	7.08	75	74	14	14
Sudan	--	--	--	--	--	b	4000	40000	44000	95	225	--	7665	22995	0.10	96	1.91	38	67	90	67
Swaziland	--	--	--	--	--		--	60	--	NA	--										
Tanzania	2	1	0	0	80*	b	42771	317029	359800	65	127	2900	23550	73550	0.58	77	4.89	64	74	100	74
Togo	2	0	0	--	--	b	7203	4998	12201	1	3	449	1700	5549	1.85	43	2.20	42	42	10	10
Tunisia	10	10	4	40	33	b	82915	440	83355	55	63	3022	14450	46372	0.74	70	1.80	36	46	100	46
Uganda	--	--	--	--	--	i	--	208789	--	NA	41	--	10000	30000	0.73	71	6.96	75	73	100	73
Zambia	--	--	--	--	--	i	--	66465	--	NA	9	2200	28850	88750	9.86	0	0.75	15	7	80	7
Zimbabwe	--	--	--	--	--	i	--	16405	--	NA	4	--	840	2520	0.63	75	6.51	73	74	74	74
EUROPE																					
Albania	--	--	--	--	--	m	1160	219	--	12	--	300	--	300	0.03	99	3.87	59	79	18	18
Austria	--	--	--	--	--	i	--	400	--	NA	1	--	300	900	0.90	64	0.44	9	36	1	1
Belarus	--	--	--	--	--	--	--	256	--	NA	--	--	--	--	--	--	--	--	--	100	80*
Belgium	--	--	--	--	--	m	35088	511	--	3	--	23262	--	23262	7.75	1	1.51	30	16	2	2
Bosnia & Herzegovina	--	--	--	--	--	--	0	2500	--	5	--	--	--	--	--	--	--	--	--	11	11
Bulgaria	2	2	2	100	0	m	10444	2293	--	15	--	34373	--	34373	2.29	37	0.30	6	14	72	14
Croatia	--	--	--	--	--	b	14782	364	15146	55	56	7905	11409	42132	0.75	70	0.36	7	38	100	38
Czech R	--	--	--	--	--	--	--	3929	--	NA	--	--	--	--	--	--	--	--	--	7	7
Denmark	7	6	3	50	20	m	1998769	264	--	105	--	95208	896	97896	0.93	63	20.42	100	61	100	61
Estonia	--	--	--	--	--	m	129662	2366	--	45	--	98083	*16000*	114083	2.54	35	1.14	23	29	100	29
Finland	--	--	--	--	--	m	119048	48436	--	55	--	19994	44	20126	0.37	85	5.92	70	78	24	24
France	19	16	6	38	36	m	597195	4500	--	175	--	178807	7/21	178828	1.02	60	3.34	53	50	16	16
Germany	2	1	1	100	0	m	216864	22889	--	35	--	78779	850	81329	2.32	37	2.67	47	28	8	8
Greece	23	20	11	55	18	m	147757	17585	--	125	--	118492	1953	124351	0.99	60	1.19	24	34	19	19
Hungary	--	--	--	--	--	--	--	13506	--	NA	--	--	--	--	--	--	--	--	--	3	3
Iceland	6	5	4	80	8	m	1611809	739	--	105	--	123988	1150	127438	1.21	56	12.65	92	52	100	52
Ireland	4	3	0	0	80*	m	381595	3761	--	145	--	57884	2	57890	0.40	84	6.59	73	79	100	79
Italy	28	22	13	59	16	m	383985	10035	--	205	--	250000	1000	253000	1.23	55	1.52	30	34	14	14
Latvia	3	3	2	67	13	m	148680	514	--	35	--	62248	--	62248	1.78	44	2.39	44	34	100	34
Lithuania	3	2	0	0	80*	m	46536	1260	--	8	--	142693	--	142693	17.84	0	0.33	7	29	92	29
Luxembourg	--	--	--	--	--	--	--	0	--	NA	--	--	--	--	--	--	--	--	--	2	2
Macedonia, FYR	--	--	--	--	--	--	--	208	--	NA	--	--	--	--	--	--	--	--	--	2	2
Malta	--	--	--	--	--	m	854	0	--	8	--	19220	750	21470	2.68	33	0.04	1	17	3	3
Moldova	--	--	--	--	--	--	--	5	--	1	--	--	--	--	--	--	--	--	--	100	80*
Netherlands	3	2	1	50	20	m	433985	4107	--	65	--	180606	1	180609	2.78	32	2.40	44	32	18	18
Norway	12	11	5	45	27	m	2524665	413	--	435	--	338923	8000	362923	0.83	67	6.96	75	56	100	56
Poland	4	4	1	25	53	m	401346	24889	--	30	--	136897	870	139507	4.65	17	2.88	49	40	47	40
Portugal	9	8	3	38	36	m	260519	--	--	25	--	123279	2803	131688	5.27	14	1.98	40	30	17	17
Romania	3	3	2	67	13	m	40227	9048	--	25	--	13445	3768	24749	0.99	60	1.63	33	35	11	11
Slovakia	--	--	--	--	--	--	--	1948	--	NA	--	--	--	--	--	--	--	--	--	100	80*
Slovenia	--	--	--	--	--	m	1849	292	--	1	--	905	41	1028	1.03	59	1.80	36	48	4	4
Spain	51	46	19	41	32	m	1134331	9489	--	125	--	656216	3239	665933	5.33	13	1.70	34	26	31	26
Sweden	2	2	1	50	20	m	402643	1943	--	180	--	57000	3000	66000	0.37	85	6.10	70	58	100	58
Switzerland	--	--	--	--	--	i	--	1588	--	NA	2	--	600	1800	0.90	64	0.88	18	41	0	0

Country	Spp tot	Spp ass	ODR	ODR%	Spp score	m i b	Marine catch mt	Inland water catch mt	Total catch mt	Shelf 000 km²	S/I 000 km²	Decked vessels grt	Undeck vessels number	Fleet capacity grt	t cap/km²	Area score	mt catch/t cap	Catch score	FP score	FSR score	Fish score
Ukraine	14	13	4	31	45	m	371667	6847	--	75	--	411384	--	411384	5.49	13	0.90	18	25	44	25
United Kingdom	6	6	2	33	43	m	907756	2146	--	535	--	247407	205	248022	0.46	82	3.66	57	60	17	17
Yugoslavia	--	--	--	--	--	b	364	4766	5130	1	1	461	188	1025	1.03	59	5.00	65	62	17	17
RUSSIAN FED	41	31	4	13	74	m	4098935	212874	--	4385	--	2991912	--	2991912	0.68	73	1.37	27	58	100	58
ASIA																					
Afghanistan	--	--	--	--	--	--	--	1300	--	NA	--	--	--	--	--	--	--	--	--	--	--
Armenia	--	--	--	--	--	i	--	520	--	NA	2	101	30	191	0.10	96	2.72	47	71	100	71
Azerbaijan	--	--	--	--	--	--	--	9271	--	NA	--	--	--	--	--	--	--	--	--	100	80*
Bahrain	--	--	--	--	--	m	9388	0	--	4	--	2800	1720	7960	1.99	40	1.18	24	32	--	32
Bangladesh	3	1	0	0	60*	b	264650	586712	851362	75	89	11600	117317	363551	4.08	20	2.34	43	41	100	41
Bhutan	--	--	--	--	--	--	--	310	--	NA	--	--	--	--	--	--	--	--	--	--	--
Brunei Darussalam	--	--	--	--	--	m	4712	7	--	8	--	1132	843	3661	0.46	82	1.29	26	54	7	7
Cambodia	--	--	--	--	--	b	30500	72499	102999	60	65	--	33476	100428	1.55	49	1.02	20	34	100	34
China	14	9	4	44	28	m	11151924	1607385	--	980	--	5548449	5608	5565273	5.68	12	2.00	40	27	74	27
Cyprus	2	2	1	50	20	b	2528	65	2593	15	15	1153	491	2626	0.18	93	0.99	20	44	2	2
Georgia	--	--	--	--	--	m	2822	219	--	--	--	32870	--	32870	--	--	0.08	2	2	24	2
India	38	12	0	0	60*	m	2596205	623378	--	585	--	1078000	181505	1622515	2.77	32	1.60	32	41	100	41
Indonesia	38	16	2	13	60*	b	3174069	335358	3509427	3285	378	539505	544879	2174142	5.75	11	1.61	32	34	100	34
Iran	1	1	0	0	100	b	251000	88800	339800	105	116	60600	8700	86700	0.75	70	3.92	59	76	17	17
Iraq	--	--	--	--	--	b	2000	9900	11900	1	2	2237	1700	7337	3.67	23	1.62	32	28	100	28
Israel	1	1	1	100	0	b	2374	2715	5089	4	4	4765	210	5395	1.35	53	0.94	19	24	2	2
Japan	66	44	11	25	53	m	5875835	91455	--	775	--	1508316	25320	1584276	2.04	40	3.71	57	50	27	27
Jordan	--	--	--	--	--	b	2	350	352	1	1	--	71	213	0.21	92	1.65	33	62	0	0
Kazakhstan	--	--	--	--	--	i	--	48402	--	NA	47	26500	120	26860	0.57	77	1.80	36	57	100	57
Korea, DPR	--	--	--	--	--	m	1660550	104000	--	95	--	721000	10000	731000	7.69	2	2.27	43	22	100	22
Korea, R	35	26	7	27	51	m	2310282	9646	--	225	--	825994	--	825994	3.67	23	2.80	48	41	90	41
Kuwait	1	0	0	--	--	m	8616	0	--	10	--	11623	--	11623	1.16	57	0.74	15	36	16	16
Kyrgyzstan	--	--	--	--	--	--	--	185	--	NA	--	--	--	--	--	--	--	--	--	100	80*
Lao PDR	--	--	--	--	--	--	--	25850	--	NA	--	--	--	--	--	--	--	--	--	96	80*
Lebanon	--	--	--	--	60*	b	4065	20	4085	4	4	700	1300	4600	1.15	57	0.89	18	37	100	37
Malaysia	38	10	0	0	60*	m	1108436	3939	--	385	--	302250	12989	341067	0.89	64	3.25	52	59	78	59
Maldives	3	2	0	0	80*	m	104566	0	--	e 959	--	299	5084	15551	0.02	99	6.72	74	84	100	84
Mongolia	--	--	--	--	--	--	--	158	--	NA	--	--	--	--	--	--	--	--	--	43	43
Myanmar	1	0	0	--	--	b	606466	151748	758214	235	254	11600	110000	341600	1.34	53	2.22	42	48	100	48
Nepal	--	--	--	--	--	--	--	11230	--	NA	--	--	--	--	--	--	--	--	--	100	80*
Oman	4	1	0	0	60*	m	139864	0	--	75	--	8120	11350	42170	0.56	78	3.32	53	64	--	64
Pakistan	13	4	0	0	60*	m	405444	121405	--	55	--	189700	29193	277279	5.04	15	1.46	29	35	100	35
Philippines	24	9	2	22	57	b	1675927	186000	1861927	605	607	79100	400000	1279100	2.11	39	1.45	29	42	62	42
Qatar	--	--	--	--	--	m	4271	0	--	15	--	--	350	1050	0.07	97	4.07	60	79	--	79
Saudi Arabia	3	1	0	0	60*	m	45691	0	--	135	--	4728	7278	26562	0.20	92	1.72	34	62	10	10
Singapore	1	0	0	--	--	m	10102	[94] 23	--	1	--	4010	170	4520	4.52	17	2.23	42	30	--	30
Sri Lanka	5	2	0	0	60*	b	217500	12000	229500	55	56	12550	27269	94357	1.68	46	2.43	44	50	53	50
Syrian Arab R	--	--	--	--	--	b	1940	3560	5500	1	2	120	1250	1370	0.69	72	4.01	60	66	12	12
Tajikistan	--	--	--	--	--	i	--	260	--	NA	--	--	--	--	--	--	--	--	--	100	80*
Thailand	39	17	1	6	60*	m	3013733	188617	--	275	--	428000	39000	545000	1.98	40	5.53	68	56	100	56
Turkey	12	11	7	64	14	m	582610	47976	--	95	--	83000	2254	89762	0.94	62	6.49	72	49	68	49
Turkmenistan	--	--	--	--	--	i	--	9490	--	NA	18	22517	--	22517	1.25	55	0.42	8	31	100	31
United Arab Emirates	9	2	0	0	60*	m	105884	0	--	80	--	19000	--	19000	0.24	90	5.57	68	73	100	73
Uzbekistan	--	--	--	--	--	i	--	3611	--	NA	33	--	294	882	0.03	99	4.09	60	79	100	79
Viet Nam	3	1	0	0	60*	b	751900	136700	888600	465	471	24561	85000	279561	0.59	76	3.18	52	63	100	63
Yemen	2	0	0	--	--	m	102964	1000	--	155	--	6000	3468	9468	0.06	98	10.87	87	80*	96	80
PACIFIC																					
Australia	21	13	1	8	80*	m	203247	1724	--	2315	--	48390	2000	54390	0.02	99	3.74	57	79	16	16
Fiji	2	0	0	--	--	b	30811	3586	34397	125	125	--	42870	128610	1.03	59	0.27	5	32	96	32
New Zealand	20	17	0	0	80*	m	543128	1114	--	325	--	75300	1200	78900	0.24	90	6.88	74	81	100	81
Papua New Guinea	1	1	0	0	100	b	12500	13500	26000	595	605	3500	3100	12800	0.02	99	2.03	40	80	8	8
Samoa	--	--	--	--	--	m	1100	0	--	35	--	--	2680	8040	0.23	91	0.14	3	47	6	6
Solomon Is	--	--	--	--	--	m	70600	0	--	175	--	2900	30000	92900	0.53	79	0.76	15	47	100	47
Tonga	--	--	--	--	--	m	2596	0	--	55	--	--	780	2340	0.04	98	1.11	22	60	100	60
Vanuatu	--	--	--	--	--	m	2727	0	--	125	--	--	120	360	0.00	100	7.57	78	80*	41	41

Notes

Fisheries (Fish score) is the lower score of two indicators (column heading in parentheses):

Fishing pressure (FP score), the unweighted average score of depleted species + overexploited species as % of assessed species (Spp score), fish catching capacity per unit of fish producing area (Area score), and weight of catch per unit of fish catching capacity (Catch score).

Fish and seafood self-reliance (FSR score), represented by fish and seafood production as % of supply.

Spp tot = number of fishery species or species groups that are the subject of a major fishery, in which the country concerned is one of the main participants. All data in this and the Spp ass and ODR columns are for 1994 and are from FAO Marine Resources Service, Fishery Resources Division (1997).

Spp ass = number of the above fishery species whose status has been assessed by FAO.

ODR = number of assessed fishery species estimated to be overexploited (O), depleted (D), or depleted but recovering (R). Overexploited species are being fished at above a level that is believed to be sustainable, with a high risk of stock collapse or depletion. Catches of depleted species are well below historical levels, irrespective of the amount of fishing effort. Catches of recovering species are increasing after a collapse from a previous high. Non-ODR species are classified as underexploited or undeveloped, moderately exploited, or fully exploited. Underexploited or undeveloped species are believed to have a significant potential for expanded production. Moderately exploited species are believed to have limited potential for expanded production. Fully exploited species are being fished at or close to an optimal yield level, with no room expected for further expansion.

ODR % = overexploited species + depleted species + depleted but recovering species as a percentage of assessed species.

Spp score = species score = score for ODR %. The performance criteria are shown in Table 24a. The tops of the fair and medium bands were set at five times those for the wild species indicators (Table 19), since depleted and overexploited species are not necessarily threatened.

mib = whether the fisheries covered in the catch and area columns are marine (m), inland water (i), or both (b). Catch and area are identifiably marine or inland, but the fishing fleet may be either or both. In countries with an exclusively marine or inland fishery the fleet is obviously marine or inland. This is not so in countries with both types of fishery. In general, most decked vessels can be assumed to be marine (FAO Fishery Information, Data and Statistics Unit 1996). However, the undecked vessels may be part of either fishery. To reduce the risk of comparing fishing capacity with too small or too big a fishing area, marine coastal countries labeled m were assessed on the basis of their marine catch and area alone, and their fishing fleet was treated as entirely marine. Marine coastal countries labeled b have an inland water catch greater than their marine catch or an undecked vessel capacity greater than their decked vessel capacity, and were assessed on the basis of their total (marine + inland water) catch, with their fishing fleet treated as a combination of marine and inland water. Iran (with an inland water catch and undecked vessel capacity that do not meet these criteria) was also assessed on the basis of total catch, because the inland fishery was assumed to be entirely on the Caspian Sea. Countries labeled i are landlocked and therefore have exclusively inland fisheries.

Catch data are in metric tons (mt) and are from FAO (1998b). All data are for 1995, except where indicated otherwise in brackets. Total (marine + inland water) catch is given only for countries assessed on the basis of their combined marine and inland water catches.

Shelf = continental shelf area in thousands of square kilometers (000 km^2), except if marked with the letter e where it is the exclusive economic zone. Data are based on estimates by FAO Fishery Resources Division (1996). NA = not applicable (landlocked country).

S/I = shelf area + inland water area in thousands of square kilometers (000 km^2) if the country is assessed on both, or inland water area if the country is landlocked. The inland water area is whatever remains after subtracting the land area from the total area in Table 10.

Decked vessels/Undeck vessels: Fishing fleet capacity is in gross registered tons (grt) for decked vessels and in numbers for undecked [undeck] vessels. Data are for 1995 and are from FAO Fishery Information, Data and Statistics Unit (1998). In the undecked vessels column, numbers in regular type refer to powered vessels only; numbers in *italics*, to powered and unpowered vessels.

Fleet capacity = total of decked + undecked capacities in gross registered tons (grt). Numbers of undecked vessels were converted to tons at 3 tons per vessel (following Garcia & Newton 1994) for powered vessels only (in regular type in the undecked vessels column), and at 1 ton per vessel for fleets of powered and unpowered vessels (in *italics* in the undecked vessels column).

t cap/km^2 = tons of fishing fleet capacity per square kilometer of fish producing area (continental shelf area, inland water area or shelf + inland water area, as appropriate).

Area score = the score for weight of fish catching capacity per unit of fish producing area. The performance criteria are shown in Table 24a and are explained under Catch score below.

mt catch/t cap = metric tons of catch (marine, inland waters or both, as appropriate) per ton of fishing fleet capacity.

Catch score = the score for weight of catch per unit of fish catching capacity. The performance criteria are shown in Table 24a. The criteria for this indicator and for fish catching capacity per unit of fish producing area are based on the following calculations. Garcia and Newton (1994) estimate that the global maximum sustainable yield (MSY) of marine fisheries is 82.8 million tons taken by a world fleet of 42.0 million corrected gross registered tons (grt). Corrected grt is the actual grt of 26.2 million in 1989 multiplied by a technology coefficient of 1.59. The technology coefficient takes account of improvements in the technology of the fishing fleet. Assuming the technology coefficient continued to increase at an annual rate of 0.059 (the rate during the 1980s), it would have been 1.94 in 1995. Thus an efficient MSY fleet would have an actual grt of 21.6 million (42.0 million divided by 1.94). This would produce a global MSY average of 3.8 tons of catch per ton of capacity. Grainger and Garcia (1996) estimate the global average potential catch per km^2 of continental shelf (the main producing area of marine fisheries) to be 3.0-4.5 tons (the range is due to different methods of calculation). The mid-point figure of 3.75 tons/km^2 of shelf is convenient, being close to the figure of 3.8 tons of catch per ton of capacity. Global MSY is likely to be higher than what is sustainable in some areas, and lower than the locally sustainable level in others. Furthermore, MSY may not be sustainable in any case if the fishery's impact on the ecosystem has not been adequately taken into account. Accordingly, global MSY was used conservatively to set the top of the medium bands for both indicators. For tons of catch per ton of capacity, the top of the medium band was set at 4 tons of catch per ton of capacity, slightly higher (and therefore more conservative) than the estimated global MSY average of 3.8 tons. For tons of fishing capacity per km^2 of fish producing area, the top of the medium band was set at 1 ton of capacity per km^2 of producing area. This roughly corresponds to the 4 tons of catch per ton of capacity, since 1 ton of capacity is estimated to take 3.8 tons of catch at the global MSY average, and 3.8 tons is within the range of the global average potential catch per km^2 of continental shelf. Since the estimated potential catch per km^2 of fish producing area is based on continental shelf area, it is applicable to marine fisheries but not necessarily to inland water fisheries. Of the 157 countries covered by these indicators, 93 were rated on marine fisheries alone, 46 countries (where marine and inland water fleets could not be distinguished) were rated on marine and inland water fisheries together, and 18 landlocked countries were rated on inland water fisheries alone. The performance criteria may be less valid for the 46 countries rated on both fisheries, and may not be suitable for the 18 countries rated on inland water fisheries.

FP score = fishing pressure score, the unweighted average of the species, area and catch scores.

FSR score = fish and seafood self-reliance, the score of fish and seafood production as % of supply. See Table 23 for data. The performance criteria are shown in Table 24a. They are the same as for agricultural self-reliance (Table 23a).

band	top point on scale	depleted + overexploited species as % of assessed species	tons of fish catching capacity per km^2 of fish producing area	tons of catch per ton of fish catching capacity	fish & seafood production as % of supply
good	100	0	0.0	16	100
fair	80	10	0.5	8	90
medium	60	20	1.0	4	80
poor	40	35	2.0	2	65
bad	20	50	4.0	1	50
base	0	100	8.0	0	0

Table 24a. Performance criteria for fisheries indicators.

Table 25. Wellbeing Index and Wellbeing/Stress Index

Country	HWI	EWI	ESI	HWI - ESI	WI	WSI	WSI score	GJ/$k	Pop/ha	Spp/ha	WI rank	WSI rank	HWI rank	EWI rank
AMERICAS														
Antigua & Barbuda	49	40	60	-11	44.5	0.82	33	7.8	1.55	19.80	70	68	61=	109=
Argentina	55	40	60	-5	47.5	0.92	37	6.5	0.13	0.04	55	53=	43=	109=
Bahamas	54	32	68	-14	43.0	0.79	32	4.9	0.22	0.90	78	73=	32=	131=
Barbados	62	32	68	-6	47.0	0.91	36	4.7	6.28	14.23	59	57=	32=	131=
Belize	50	64	36	14	57.0	1.39	48	10.4	0.10	1.53	9	6	55=	13=
Bolivia	34	63	37	-3	48.5	0.92	37	6.7	0.08	0.17	50	53=	109=	17=
Brazil	45	36	64	-19	40.5	0.70	28	6.4	0.20	0.07	92	84=	72=	120=
Canada	78	43	57	21	60.5	1.37	47	15.3	0.03	0.00	7=	9=	10=	94=
Chile	55	30	70	-15	42.5	0.79	32	4.9	0.20	0.08	79	73=	43=	146=
Colombia	43	42	58	-15	42.5	0.74	30	4.1	0.37	0.48	81	79=	79=	101=
Costa Rica	56	41	59	-3	48.5	0.95	38	4.5	0.79	2.60	48	46=	41=	107=
Cuba	40	45	55	-15	42.5	0.73	29	12.9	1.01	0.62	82	82	90=	81=
Dominica	*56*	*65*	*35*	*21*	*60.5*	*1.60*	*52*	*3.3*	*0.95*	*17.44*	*6*	*1*	*41=*	*10=*
Dominican R	49	46	54	-5	47.5	0.91	36	5.4	1.74	1.22	56	57=	61=	72=
Ecuador	43	56	44	-1	49.5	0.98	39	6.0	0.45	0.77	41	40=	79=	40=
El Salvador	36	46	54	-18	41.0	0.67	27	8.2	2.98	1.61	90	90=	102=	72=
Grenada	*55*	*49*	*51*	*4*	*52.0*	*1.08*	*42*	*6.6*	*2.76*	*33.88*	*26*	*23=*	*43=*	*62=*
Guatemala	23	44	56	-33	33.5	0.41	16	6.2	1.05	0.89	148	143=	131=	85=
Guyana	51	63	37	14	57.0	1.38	48	8.1	0.04	0.34	10	7=	54	17=
Haiti	19	43	57	-38	31.0	0.33	13	8.3	2.96	1.97	166	160	145=	94=
Honduras	33	45	55	-22	39.0	0.60	24	9.3	0.58	0.58	103	104	112	81=
Jamaica	54	35	65	-11	44.5	0.83	33	17.3	2.35	3.19	68	65=	46=	122=
Mexico	45	21	79	-34	33.0	0.57	23	7.2	0.50	0.14	150	108	72=	176
Nicaragua	28	49	51	-23	38.5	0.55	22	11.7	0.39	0.65	110=	111=	118=	62=
Panama	52	37	63	-11	44.5	0.83	33	4.6	0.38	1.49	69	65=	51=	117=
Paraguay	35	46	54	-19	40.5	0.65	26	6.6	0.14	0.22	93	94=	107=	72=
Peru	44	62	38	6	53.0	1.16	43	5.0	0.20	0.16	19	16	76=	21=
St Kitts & Nevis	*52*	*53*	*47*	*5*	*52.5*	*1.11*	*42*	*6.3*	*1.46*	*27.27*	*21*	*19*	*51=*	*51=*
St Lucia	*53*	*51*	*49*	*4*	*52.0*	*1.08*	*42*	*3.7*	*2.48*	*17.84*	*25*	*23=*	*49=*	*55=*
St Vincent & Grenadines	*41*	*54*	*46*	*-5*	*47.5*	*0.89*	*36*	*4.2*	*2.92*	*33.36*	*57*	*60=*	*87=*	*46=*
Suriname	52	58	42	10	55.0	1.24	45	12.2	0.03	0.37	15	12	51=	33=
Trinidad & Tobago	53	32	68	-15	42.5	0.78	31	42.9	2.52	5.29	80	77=	49=	131=
United States	73	31	69	4	52.0	1.06	41	12.1	0.30	0.02	27	27=	18=	141=
Uruguay	61	52	48	13	56.5	1.27	45	3.9	0.19	0.15	11	11	35=	54
Venezuela	43	46	54	-11	44.5	0.80	32	16.2	0.27	0.25	73	72	79=	72=
AFRICA														
Algeria	29	44	56	-27	36.5	0.52	21	11.1	0.13	0.01	130	118=	117	85=
Angola	8	67	33	-25	37.5	0.24	10	5.3	0.10	0.05	123	171=	175	4=
Benin	27	71	29	-2	49.0	0.93	37	9.1	0.54	0.24	47	49=	124=	2
Botswana	34	68	32	2	51.0	1.06	41	11.3	0.03	0.05	35	27=	109=	3
Burkina Faso	17	58	42	-25	37.5	0.40	16	10.4	0.44	0.06	122	146=	151=	33=
Burundi	6	60	40	-34	33.0	0.15	6	12.7	2.41	1.10	156	178	177=	28=
Cameroon	15	64	36	-21	39.5	0.42	17	7.0	0.32	0.19	101	138=	157=	13=
Cape Verde	47	47	53	-6	47.0	0.89	36	1.7	1.06	2.06	60	60=	65=	70=
Central African R	16	66	34	-18	41.0	0.47	19	7.1	0.06	0.07	91	127=	153=	6=
Chad	13	59	41	-28	36.0	0.32	13	6.1	0.06	0.02	134	161=	164=	32
Comoros	20	44	56	-36	32.0	0.36	14	1.0	3.11	3.61	161	156=	141=	85=
Congo, DR	7	65	35	-28	36.0	0.20	8	12.6	0.22	0.05	135	175	176	10=
Congo, R	15	72	28	-13	43.5	0.54	22	11.2	0.09	0.15	77	114	157=	1
Côte d'Ivoire	20	57	43	-23	38.5	0.47	19	8.4	0.46	0.14	112=	127=	141=	35=
Djibouti	18	60	40	-22	39.0	0.45	18	6.4	0.28	0.28	106	133	147=	28=
Egypt	39	43	57	-18	41.0	0.68	27	8.2	0.68	0.02	89	89	94=	94=
Equatorial Guinea	15	62	38	-23	38.5	0.39	16	7.9	0.16	1.32	114	148=	157=	21=
Eritrea	10	60	40	-30	35.0	0.25	10	10.2	0.33	--	140	169=	171=	28=
Ethiopia	13	64	36	-23	38.5	0.36	14	16.5	0.57	0.07	115	156=	164=	13=
Gabon	28	62	38	-10	45.0	0.74	30	8.8	0.05	0.27	66	79=	118=	21=
Gambia	16	62	38	-22	39.0	0.42	17	8.0	1.16	1.21	107	138=	153=	21=
Ghana	22	38	62	-40	30.0	0.35	14	10.3	0.85	0.19	168	159	133=	114=
Guinea	15	66	34	-19	40.5	0.44	18	4.5	0.30	0.15	95	134=	157=	6=
Guinea-Bissau	13	66	34	-21	39.5	0.38	15	7.2	0.34	0.37	102	150=	164=	6=
Kenya	18	51	49	-31	34.5	0.37	15	15.5	0.52	0.14	143	153=	147=	55=
Lesotho	24	57	43	-19	40.5	0.56	22	46.7	0.71	0.55	94	109=	127=	35=
Liberia	*9*	*65*	*35*	*-26*	*37.0*	*0.26*	*10*	*25.6*	*0.28*	*0.26*	*126*	*168*	*174*	*10=*
Libyan Arab J	38	24	76	-38	31.0	0.50	20	15.7	0.03	0.01	164	122=	96=	169=
Madagascar	24	50	50	-26	37.0	0.48	19	8.5	0.27	0.17	124	126	127=	58=
Malawi	22	62	38	-16	42.0	0.58	23	14.6	0.92	0.39	88	106=	133=	21=

259

Country	HWI	EWI	ESI	HWI - ESI	WI	WSI	WSI score	GJ/$k	Pop/ha	Spp/ha	WI rank	WSI rank	HWI rank	EWI rank
Mali	21	44	56	-35	32.5	0.38	15	9.3	0.09	0.02	157	150=	137=	85=
Mauritania	17	40	60	-43	28.5	0.28	11	9.4	0.03	0.01	174	164=	151=	109=
Mauritius	54	44	56	-2	49.0	0.96	38	3.4	5.68	3.88	45	45	46=	85=
Morocco	36	32	68	-32	34.0	0.53	21	4.3	0.63	0.09	146	115=	102=	131=
Mozambique	11	55	45	-34	33.0	0.24	10	13.6	0.25	0.08	155	171=	169=	43=
Namibia	34	54	46	-12	44.0	0.74	30	17.3	0.02	0.05	75	79=	109=	46=
Niger	11	56	44	-33	33.5	0.25	10	8.7	0.08	0.01	149	169=	169=	40=
Nigeria	16	56	44	-28	36.0	0.36	14	16.4	1.21	0.06	133	156=	153=	40=
Rwanda	12	57	43	-31	34.5	0.28	11	15.3	2.94	1.12	144	164=	168	35=
São Tomé & Principe	*10*	*53*	*47*	*-37*	*31.5*	*0.21*	*8*	*3.9*	*1.53*	*10.32*	*163*	*174*	*171=*	*51=*
Senegal	20	54	46	-26	37.0	0.43	17	5.8	0.48	0.13	125	136=	141=	46=
Seychelles	*50*	*49*	*51*	*-1*	*49.5*	*0.98*	*39*	*4.9*	*1.71*	*25.33*	*40*	*40=*	*55=*	*62=*
Sierra Leone	6	63	37	-31	34.5	0.16	6	19.8	0.68	0.38	145	177	177=	17=
Somalia	*3*	*62*	*38*	*-35*	*32.5*	*0.08*	*3*	*15.0*	*0.16*	*0.06*	*158*	*180*	*180*	*21=*
South Africa	43	27	73	-30	35.0	0.59	24	11.8	0.33	0.20	136	105	79=	161=
Sudan	13	46	54	-41	29.5	0.24	10	4.7	0.12	0.02	171	171=	164=	72=
Swaziland	24	54	46	-22	39.0	0.52	21	25.8	0.58	1.88	104	118=	127=	46=
Tanzania	18	54	46	-28	36.0	0.39	16	21.6	0.35	0.12	132	148=	147=	46=
Togo	21	66	34	-13	43.5	0.62	25	5.0	0.82	0.49	76	103	137=	6=
Tunisia	44	32	68	-24	38.0	0.65	26	5.6	0.59	0.15	116=	94=	76=	131=
Uganda	10	44	56	-46	27.0	0.18	7	7.1	0.90	0.28	177	176	171=	85=
Zambia	16	43	57	-41	29.5	0.28	11	22.7	0.12	0.08	170	164=	153=	94=
Zimbabwe	23	55	45	-22	39.0	0.51	21	11.4	0.30	0.14	105	120=	131=	43=
EUROPE														
Albania	38	46	54	-16	42.0	0.70	28	6.2	1.08	1.17	86	84=	96=	72=
Austria	80	42	58	22	61.0	1.38	48	6.6	0.98	0.40	5	7=	4=	101=
Belarus	46	50	50	-4	48.0	0.92	37	20.7	0.49	--	53	53=	68=	58=
Belgium	80	23	77	3	51.5	1.04	41	9.4	3.33	0.56	34	31=	4=	172=
Bosnia & Herzegovina	*24*	*45*	*55*	*-31*	*34.5*	*0.44*	*18*	*113.8*	*0.78*	*--*	*141*	*134=*	*127=*	*81=*
Bulgaria	58	31	69	-11	44.5	0.84	34	24.5	0.74	0.36	67	64	39	141=
Croatia	57	33	67	-10	45.0	0.85	34	14.1	0.79	--	64	63	40	126=
Czech R	70	33	67	3	51.5	1.04	41	15.7	1.30	--	30=	31=	24=	126=
Denmark	81	31	69	12	56.0	1.17	43	6.1	1.23	0.35	13	15	2=	141=
Estonia	62	34	66	-4	48.0	0.94	38	35.2	0.31	0.44	51	48	32=	125
Finland	81	44	56	25	62.5	1.45	49	11.4	0.15	0.04	2	3	2=	85=
France	75	29	71	4	52.0	1.06	41	7.7	1.07	0.09	29	27=	16	154
Germany	77	36	64	13	56.5	1.20	44	7.9	2.30	0.08	12	13	13=	120=
Greece	70	33	67	3	51.5	1.04	41	8.5	0.81	0.41	30=	31=	24=	126=
Hungary	65	33	67	-2	49.0	0.97	39	14.5	1.08	0.27	44	43=	30=	126=
Iceland	80	43	57	23	61.5	1.40	48	9.7	0.03	0.05	4	5	4=	94=
Ireland	76	32	68	8	54.0	1.12	42	6.7	0.53	0.16	17	18	15	131=
Italy	74	30	70	4	52.0	1.06	41	6.0	1.90	0.20	28	27=	17	146=
Latvia	62	46	54	8	54.0	1.15	43	19.7	0.36	0.24	16	17	32=	72=
Lithuania	61	44	56	5	52.5	1.09	42	24.2	0.56	0.23	22	21=	35=	85=
Luxembourg	77	24	76	1	50.5	1.01	41	10.4	1.68	5.63	37	37	13=	169=
Macedonia, FYR	46	42	58	-12	44.0	0.79	32	20.5	0.79	--	74	73=	68=	101=
Malta	70	14	86	-16	42.0	0.81	33	4.4	12.16	30.34	84	69=	24=	180
Moldova	41	35	65	-24	38.0	0.63	25	30.1	1.30	--	118	99=	87=	122=
Netherlands	78	22	78	0	50.0	1.00	40	10.6	3.87	0.36	38=	38=	10=	175
Norway	82	43	57	25	62.5	1.44	49	9.6	0.14	0.06	3	4	1	94=
Poland	65	30	70	-5	47.5	0.93	37	16.6	1.20	0.08	54	49=	30=	146=
Portugal	72	31	69	3	51.5	1.04	41	4.9	1.07	0.31	32	31=	22	141=
Romania	50	30	70	-20	40.0	0.71	28	17.8	0.94	0.15	97	83	55=	146=
Slovakia	61	40	60	1	50.5	1.02	41	15.7	1.10	--	36	36	35=	109=
Slovenia	71	35	65	6	53.0	1.09	42	11.1	0.98	--	20	21=	23	122=
Spain	73	20	80	-7	46.5	0.91	36	6.3	0.78	0.11	61	57=	18=	177
Sweden	79	49	51	28	64.0	1.55	51	11.7	0.20	0.05	1	2	8=	62=
Switzerland	78	43	57	21	60.5	1.37	47	5.5	1.79	0.81	7=	9=	10=	94=
Ukraine	47	26	74	-27	36.5	0.64	26	58.2	0.84	--	128	98	65=	164
United Kingdom	73	30	70	3	51.5	1.04	41	7.7	2.41	0.08	33	31=	18=	146=
Yugoslavia	42	37	63	-21	39.5	0.67	27	25.2	1.04	--	100	90=	85=	117=
RUSSIAN FEDERATION	48	42	58	-10	45.0	0.83	33	38.1	0.09	--	65	65=	63=	101=
ASIA														
Afghanistan	*6*	*48*	*52*	*-46*	*27.0*	*0.12*	*5*	*4.9*	*0.35*	*0.06*	*178*	*179*	*177=*	*68=*
Armenia	45	55	45	0	50.0	1.00	40	8.7	1.18	--	38=	38=	72=	43=
Azerbaijan	42	28	72	-30	35.0	0.58	23	39.2	0.89	--	137	106=	85=	155=
Bahrain	*46*	*17*	*83*	*-37*	*31.5*	*0.55*	*22*	*34.6*	*8.94*	*3.86*	*162*	*111=*	*68=*	*178*
Bangladesh	27	46	54	-27	36.5	0.50	20	5.7	8.97	0.38	131	122=	124=	72=
Bhutan	14	67	33	-19	40.5	0.42	17	7.0	0.45	1.29	96	138=	163	4=

Country	HWI	EWI	ESI	HWI - ESI	WI	WSI	WSI score	GJ/$k	Pop/ha	Spp/ha	WI rank	WSI rank	HWI rank	EWI rank
Brunei Darussalam	47	42	58	-11	44.5	0.81	32	11.0	0.57	6.31	72	69=	65=	101=
Cambodia	20	57	43	-23	38.5	0.47	19	5.6	0.62	--	112=	127=	141=	35=
China	36	28	72	-36	32.0	0.50	20	9.7	1.34	0.04	160	122=	102=	155=
Cyprus	67	38	62	5	52.5	1.08	42	6.3	0.85	1.96	23	23=	27=	114=
Georgia	48	41	59	-11	44.5	0.81	32	9.5	0.71	--	71	69=	63=	107=
India	31	27	73	-42	29.0	0.42	17	9.3	3.08	0.05	172	138=	114=	161=
Indonesia	36	48	52	-16	42.0	0.69	28	7.6	1.11	0.17	138	109=	96=	131=
Iran	38	32	68	-30	35.0	0.56	22	11.0	0.41	0.04	138	109=	96=	131=
Iraq	19	31	69	-50	25.0	0.28	11	15.7	0.53	0.07	180	164=	145=	141=
Israel	59	25	75	-16	42.0	0.79	32	6.2	2.95	1.23	85	73=	38	165=
Japan	80	25	75	5	52.5	1.07	41	6.4	3.35	0.16	24	26	4=	165=
Jordan	38	28	72	-34	33.0	0.53	21	8.1	0.75	0.26	151	115=	96=	155=
Kazakhstan	43	32	68	-25	37.5	0.63	25	26.9	0.06	--	120	99=	79=	131=
Korea, DPR	*21*	*45*	*55*	*-34*	*33.0*	*0.38*	*15*	*30.6*	*1.99*	*0.24*	*153*	*150=*	*137=*	*81=*
Korea, R	67	27	73	-6	47.0	0.92	37	10.1	4.72	0.31	58	53=	27=	161=
Kuwait	50	25	75	-25	37.5	0.67	27	15.6	1.11	0.20	119	90=	55=	165=
Kyrgyzstan	38	42	58	-20	40.0	0.66	26	10.9	0.24	--	98	93	96=	101=
Lao PDR	15	63	37	-22	39.0	0.41	16	8.1	0.23	--	108	143=	157=	17=
Lebanon	40	37	63	-23	38.5	0.63	25	10.7	3.16	2.17	109	99=	90=	117=
Malaysia	46	33	67	-21	39.5	0.69	28	11.0	0.67	0.51	99	87=	68=	126=
Maldives	*22*	*47*	*53*	*-31*	*34.5*	*0.42*	*17*	*4.1*	*9.53*	*10.17*	*142*	*138=*	*133=*	*70=*
Mongolia	39	60	40	-1	49.5	0.98	39	27.7	0.02	0.01	42	40=	94=	28=
Myanmar	21	49	51	-30	35.0	0.41	16	6.6	0.67	0.12	139	143=	137=	62=
Nepal	28	64	36	-8	46.0	0.78	31	11.9	1.63	0.53	63	77=	118=	13=
Oman	31	28	72	-41	29.5	0.43	17	12.7	0.12	0.07	169	136=	114=	155=
Pakistan	18	44	56	-38	31.0	0.32	13	9.3	1.97	0.08	167	161=	147=	85=
Philippines	44	32	68	-24	38.0	0.65	26	6.3	2.53	0.32	116=	94=	76=	131=
Qatar	*40*	*24*	*76*	*-36*	*32.0*	*0.53*	*21*	*61.7*	*0.54*	*0.32*	*159*	*115=*	*90=*	*169=*
Saudi Arabia	31	23	77	-46	27.0	0.40	16	18.4	0.10	0.01	176	146=	114=	172=
Singapore	66	32	68	-2	49.0	0.97	39	10.6	57.53	37.60	43	43=	90=	131=
Sri Lanka	40	57	43	-3	48.5	0.93	37	4.7	2.87	0.58	49	49=	90=	35=
Syrian Arab R	28	25	75	-47	26.5	0.37	15	12.2	0.87	0.13	179	153=	118=	165=
Tajikistan	28	39	61	-33	33.5	0.46	18	21.0	0.43	--	147	131=	118=	113
Thailand	50	23	77	-27	36.5	0.65	26	9.0	1.20	0.25	127	94=	55=	172=
Turkey	45	28	72	-27	36.5	0.63	25	6.4	0.86	0.12	129	99=	72=	155=
Turkmenistan	32	30	70	-38	31.0	0.46	18	55.7	0.09	--	165	131=	113	146=
United Arab Emirates	41	16	84	-43	28.5	0.49	20	32.5	0.29	0.06	173	125	87=	179
Uzbekistan	36	30	70	-34	33.0	0.51	21	32.2	0.54	--	152	120=	102=	146=
Viet Nam	28	49	51	-23	38.5	0.55	22	6.8	2.41	0.35	110=	111=	118=	62=
Yemen	15	51	49	-34	33.0	0.31	12	16.3	0.34	0.04	154	163	157=	55=
PACIFIC														
Australia	79	28	72	7	53.5	1.10	42	11.9	0.02	0.02	18	20	8=	155=
Fiji	50	46	54	-4	48.0	0.93	37	6.7	0.45	0.89	52	49=	55=	72=
New Zealand	73	38	62	11	55.5	1.18	44	10.0	0.14	0.10	14	14	18=	114=
Papua New Guinea	22	53	47	-25	37.5	0.47	19	8.0	0.10	0.28	121	127=	133=	51=
Samoa	43	50	50	-7	46.5	0.86	34	4.9	0.63	2.77	62	62	79=	58=
Solomon Is	*37*	*61*	*39*	*-2*	*49.0*	*0.95*	*38*	*6.4*	*0.15*	*1.20*	*46*	*46=*	*101*	*27*
Tonga	*26*	*30*	*70*	*-44*	*28.0*	*0.37*	*15*	*9.8*	*1.32*	*6.76*	*175*	*153=*	*126*	*146=*
Vanuatu	35	50	50	-15	42.5	0.70	28	1.6	0.16	0.80	83	84=	107=	58=

Notes

The Wellbeing Index(WI) is the point on the Barometer of Sustainability where the Human Wellbeing Index (HWI) and Ecosystem Wellbeing Index (EWI) intersect. The Wellbeing/Stress Index (WSI) is the ratio of human wellbeing to ecosystem stress, calculated by dividing the HWI by the Ecosystem Stress Index (ESI).

Countries in italics were rated on less than two-thirds of the human or ecosystem sub-elements.

HWI = Human Wellbeing Index (Table 1).

EWI = Ecosystem Wellbeing Index (Table 9).

ESI = Ecosystem Stress Index = 100 minus the EWI.

HWI - ESI = Human Wellbeing Index minus Ecosystem Stress Index.

WI = Wellbeing Index (expressed as the average of the HWI and the EWI).

WSI = Wellbeing/Stress Index = the HWI divided by the ESI.

WSI score = score for Wellbeing/Stress Index. See Table 25a for performance criteria.

GJ/$k = gigajoules of energy consumed per PPP$1000 of Gross Domestic Product (GDP). Energy data are for 1997 and are from United Nations Energy Statistics Unit (2000). GDP data are also for 1997 and are from World Bank (1999a) and United Nations Development Programme (1999)

Pop/ha = population per hectare of land + inland water. Population data are estimates for 2000 and from United Nations Population Division (1998b). Area data are from FAO (1999), except for Belgium and Luxembourg which are from OECD (1999).

Spp/ha = the estimated number of wild species per hectare of land + inland water. Species are native wild species of higher plants (angiosperms, gymnosperms and pteridophytes), mammals, breeding birds, reptiles and amphibians. Species data are from the World Conservation Monitoring Centre Threatened Plants Database (WCMC 1998a) and Threatened Animals Database (WCMC 1998b). Area data are from FAO (1999), except for Belgium and Luxembourg which are from OECD (1999).

WI rank = average Wellbeing Index rank.
WSI rank = Wellbeing/Stress Index rank
HWI rank = Human Wellbeing Index rank.
EWI rank = Ecosystem Wellbeing Index rank.
Correlations between income (GDP per person) and the HWI, ESI, human elements and ecosystem elements are shown in Table 25b.
Correlations between the WSI, income (GDP per person), education, freedom and governance, and education and freedom and governance combined, are shown in Table 25c.

band	top point on scale	ratio of human wellbeing to ecosystem stress
good	100	8.0
fair	80	4.0
medium	60	2.0
poor	40	1.0
bad	20	0.5
base	0	0.0

Table 25a. Performance criteria for the Wellbeing/Stress Index.

	HWI	health	population	household wealth	national wealth	knowledge	freedom & governance	peace & order	ESI	global atmosphere	local air quality	energy
income	**0.824**	**0.902**	**0.851**	**0.895**	**0.871**	**0.948**	*0.740*	0.560	0.537	*-0.751*	0.556	**-0.817**

Table 25b. Correlations between income and the Human Wellbeing Index (HWI), human elements, the Ecosystem Stress Index (ESI) and ecosystem elements. Only correlations above 0.5 (or -0.5) are shown; those of 0.8 (or -0.8) or above are shown in **bold**; those between 0.6 and 0.8 (or -0.6 and -0.8) in *italic*.

	WSI	income	education	freedom & governance	education + freedom & governance
Wellbeing/Stress Index (WSI)	1				
income	*0.640*	1			
education	*0.766*	*0.680*	1		
freedom & governance	*0.771*	0.571	0.539	1	
education + freedom & governance	**0.883**	*0.728*	**0.887**	**0.834**	1

Table 25c. Correlations between the Wellbeing/Stress Index (WSI), income (GDP per person), education, freedom and governance, and education and freedom and governance combined. Correlations of 0.8 and above are shown in **bold**; those between 0.6 and 0.8 are shown in *italic*.

Table 26. Wellbeing Performance Groups

Group 1: fair Wellbeing Index, medium Wellbeing/Stress Index

Moderate ecosystem deficit

Country	HWI	EWI	ESI	HWI- ESI	WI	WSI	WSI score
Austria	80	42	58	22	61.0	1.38	48
Finland	81	44	56	25	62.5	1.45	49
Iceland	80	43	57	23	61.5	1.40	48
Norway	82	43	57	25	62.5	1.44	49
Sweden	79	49	51	28	64.0	1.55	51

Group 2: medium Wellbeing Index, medium Wellbeing/Stress Index

Moderate ecosystem deficit

Country	HWI	EWI	ESI	HWI- ESI	WI	WSI	WSI score
Canada	78	43	57	21	60.5	1.37	47
Latvia	62	46	54	8	54.0	1.15	43
Lithuania	61	44	56	5	52.5	1.09	42
Switzerland	78	43	57	21	60.5	1.37	47
Uruguay	61	52	48	13	56.5	1.27	45

Moderate human deficit

Country	HWI	EWI	ESI	HWI- ESI	WI	WSI	WSI score
Belize	50	64	36	14	57.0	1.39	48
Dominica	*56*	*65*	*35*	*21*	*60.5*	*1.60*	*52*
Guyana	51	63	37	14	57.0	1.38	48
Peru	44	62	38	6	53.0	1.16	43

Moderate double deficit

Country	HWI	EWI	ESI	HWI- ESI	WI	WSI	WSI score
Grenada	*55*	*49*	*51*	*4*	*52.0*	*1.08*	*42*
St Kitts & Nevis	*52*	*53*	*47*	*5*	*52.5*	*1.11*	*42*
St Lucia	*53*	*51*	*49*	*4*	*52.0*	*1.08*	*42*
Suriname	52	58	42	10	55.0	1.24	45

High ecosystem deficit

Country	HWI	EWI	ESI	HWI- ESI	WI	WSI	WSI score
Australia	79	28	72	7	53.5	1.10	42
Belgium	80	23	77	3	51.5	1.04	41
Cyprus	67	38	62	5	52.5	1.08	42
Czech R	70	33	67	3	51.5	1.04	41
Denmark	81	31	69	12	56.0	1.17	43
France	75	29	71	4	52.0	1.06	41
Germany	77	36	64	13	56.5	1.20	44
Greece	70	33	67	3	51.5	1.04	41
Ireland	76	32	68	8	54.0	1.12	42
Italy	74	30	70	4	52.0	1.06	41
Japan	80	25	75	5	52.5	1.07	41
Luxembourg	77	24	76	1	50.5	1.01	41
New Zealand	73	38	62	11	55.5	1.18	44
Portugal	72	31	69	3	51.5	1.04	41
Slovakia	61	40	60	1	50.5	1.02	41
Slovenia	71	35	65	6	53.0	1.09	42
United Kingdom	73	30	70	3	51.5	1.04	41
United States	73	31	69	4	52.0	1.06	41

High human deficit

Country	HWI	EWI	ESI	HWI- ESI	WI	WSI	WSI score
Botswana	34	68	32	2	51.0	1.06	41

Group 3: medium Wellbeing Index, poor or bad Wellbeing/Stress Index

Moderate double deficit

Country	HWI	EWI	ESI	HWI- ESI	WI	WSI	WSI score
Armenia	45	55	45	0	50.0	1.00	40
Belarus	46	50	50	-4	48.0	0.92	37
Brunei Darussalam	47	42	58	-11	44.5	0.81	32

Country	HWI	EWI	ESI	HWI- ESI	WI	WSI	WSI score
Cape Verde	47	47	53	-6	47.0	0.89	36
Colombia	43	42	58	-15	42.5	0.74	30
Costa Rica	56	41	59	-3	48.5	0.95	38
Dominican R	49	46	54	-5	47.5	0.91	36
Ecuador	43	56	44	-1	49.5	0.98	39
Fiji	50	46	54	-4	48.0	0.93	37
Georgia	48	41	59	-11	44.5	0.81	32
Macedonia, FYR	46	42	58	-12	44.0	0.79	32
Mauritius	54	44	56	-2	49.0	0.96	38
RUSSIAN FEDERATION	48	42	58	-10	45.0	0.83	33
Samoa	43	50	50	-7	46.5	0.86	34
Seychelles	*50*	*49*	*51*	*-1*	*49.5*	*0.98*	*39*
St Vincent & Grenadines	*41*	*54*	*46*	*-5*	*47.5*	*0.89*	*36*
Venezuela	43	46	54	-11	44.5	0.80	32

High ecosystem deficit

Country	HWI	EWI	ESI	HWI- ESI	WI	WSI	WSI score
Barbados	62	32	68	-6	47.0	0.91	36
Estonia	62	34	66	-4	48.0	0.94	38
Hungary	65	33	67	-2	49.0	0.97	39
Korea, R	67	27	73	-6	47.0	0.92	37
Malta	70	14	86	-16	42.0	0.81	33
Netherlands	78	22	78	0	50.0	1.00	40
Poland	65	30	70	-5	47.5	0.93	37
Singapore	66	32	68	-2	49.0	0.97	39
Spain	73	20	80	-7	46.5	0.91	36

High human deficit

Country	HWI	EWI	ESI	HWI- ESI	WI	WSI	WSI score
Benin	27	71	29	-2	49.0	0.93	37
Bolivia	34	63	37	-3	48.5	0.92	37
Central African R	16	66	34	-18	41.0	0.47	19
Congo, R	15	72	28	-13	43.5	0.54	22
Gabon	28	62	38	-10	45.0	0.74	30
Malawi	22	62	38	-16	42.0	0.58	23
Nepal	28	64	36	-8	46.0	0.78	31
Solomon Is	*37*	*61*	*39*	*-2*	*49.0*	*0.95*	*38*
Togo	21	66	34	-13	43.5	0.62	25

High double deficit, ecosystem worse

Country	HWI	EWI	ESI	HWI- ESI	WI	WSI	WSI score
Antigua & Barbuda	49	40	60	-11	44.5	0.82	33
Argentina	55	40	60	-5	47.5	0.92	37
Bahamas	54	32	68	-14	43.0	0.79	32
Bulgaria	58	31	69	-11	44.5	0.84	34
Chile	55	30	70	-15	42.5	0.79	32
Croatia	57	33	67	-10	45.0	0.85	34
Israel	59	25	75	-16	42.0	0.79	32
Jamaica	54	35	65	-11	44.5	0.83	33
Panama	52	37	63	-11	44.5	0.83	33
Trinidad & Tobago	53	32	68	-15	42.5	0.78	31

High double deficit, people worse

Country	HWI	EWI	ESI	HWI- ESI	WI	WSI	WSI score
Albania	38	46	54	-16	42.0	0.70	28
Cuba	40	45	55	-15	42.5	0.73	29
Egypt	39	43	57	-18	41.0	0.68	27
El Salvador	36	46	54	-18	41.0	0.67	27
Indonesia	36	48	52	-16	42.0	0.69	28
Mongolia	39	60	40	-1	49.5	0.98	39
Namibia	34	54	46	-12	44.0	0.74	30
Sri Lanka	40	57	43	-3	48.5	0.93	37
Vanuatu	35	50	50	-15	42.5	0.70	28

Group 4: poor Wellbeing Index, poor Wellbeing/Stress Index

High double deficit, ecosystem worse

Country	HWI	EWI	ESI	HWI- ESI	WI	WSI	WSI score
Azerbaijan	42	28	72	-30	35.0	0.58	23
Bahrain	*46*	*17*	*83*	*-37*	*31.5*	*0.55*	*22*
Brazil	45	36	64	-19	40.5	0.70	28
Kazakhstan	43	32	68	-25	37.5	0.63	25
Kuwait	50	25	75	-25	37.5	0.67	27
Malaysia	46	33	67	-21	39.5	0.69	28
Mexico	45	21	79	-34	33.0	0.57	23
Moldova	41	35	65	-24	38.0	0.63	25
Philippines	44	32	68	-24	38.0	0.65	26
Romania	50	30	70	-20	40.0	0.71	28
South Africa	43	27	73	-30	35.0	0.59	24
Thailand	50	23	77	-27	36.5	0.65	26
Tunisia	44	32	68	-24	38.0	0.65	26
Turkey	45	28	72	-27	36.5	0.63	25
Ukraine	47	26	74	-27	36.5	0.64	26
Yugoslavia	42	37	63	-21	39.5	0.67	27

High double deficit, people worse

Country	HWI	EWI	ESI	HWI- ESI	WI	WSI	WSI score
Algeria	29	44	56	-27	36.5	0.52	21
Honduras	33	45	55	-22	39.0	0.60	24
Kyrgyzstan	38	42	58	-20	40.0	0.66	26
Lesotho	24	57	43	-19	40.5	0.56	22
Nicaragua	28	49	51	-23	38.5	0.55	22
Paraguay	35	46	54	-19	40.5	0.65	26
Swaziland	24	54	46	-22	39.0	0.52	21
Viet Nam	28	49	51	-23	38.5	0.55	22
Zimbabwe	23	55	45	-22	39.0	0.51	21

Extreme double deficit

Country	HWI	EWI	ESI	HWI- ESI	WI	WSI	WSI score
Iran	38	32	68	-30	35.0	0.56	22
Jordan	38	28	72	-34	33.0	0.53	21
Lebanon	40	37	63	-23	38.5	0.63	25
Morocco	36	32	68	-32	34.0	0.53	21
Qatar	*40*	*24*	*76*	*-36*	*32.0*	*0.53*	*21*
Uzbekistan	36	30	70	-34	33.0	0.51	21

Group 5: poor Wellbeing Index, bad Wellbeing/Stress Index

High human deficit

Country	HWI	EWI	ESI	HWI- ESI	WI	WSI	WSI score
Angola	8	67	33	-25	37.5	0.24	10
Bhutan	14	67	33	-19	40.5	0.42	17
Cameroon	15	64	36	-21	39.5	0.42	17
Congo, DR	7	65	35	-28	36.0	0.20	8
Equatorial Guinea	15	62	38	-23	38.5	0.39	16
Ethiopia	13	64	36	-23	38.5	0.36	14
Gambia	16	62	38	-22	39.0	0.42	17
Guinea	15	66	34	-19	40.5	0.44	18
Guinea-Bissau	13	66	34	-21	39.5	0.38	15
Lao PDR	15	63	37	-22	39.0	0.41	16
Liberia	*9*	*65*	*35*	*-26*	*37.0*	*0.26*	*10*
Sierra Leone	6	63	37	-31	34.5	0.16	6
Somalia	*3*	*62*	*38*	*-35*	*32.5*	*0.08*	*3*

High double deficit, ecosystem worse

Country	HWI	EWI	ESI	HWI- ESI	WI	WSI	WSI score
United Arab Emirates	41	16	84	-43	28.5	0.49	20

High double deficit, people worse

Country	HWI	EWI	ESI	HWI- ESI	WI	WSI	WSI score
Afghanistan	*6*	*48*	*52*	*-46*	*27.0*	*0.12*	*5*
Bangladesh	27	46	54	-27	36.5	0.50	20
Bosnia & Herzegovina	*24*	*45*	*55*	*-31*	*34.5*	*0.44*	*18*

Country	HWI	EWI	ESI	HWI- ESI	WI	WSI	WSI score
Burkina Faso	17	58	42	-25	37.5	0.40	16
Burundi	6	60	40	-34	33.0	0.15	6
Cambodia	20	57	43	-23	38.5	0.47	19
Chad	13	59	41	-28	36.0	0.32	13
Comoros	20	44	56	-36	32.0	0.36	14
Côte d'Ivoire	20	57	43	-23	38.5	0.47	19
Djibouti	18	60	40	-22	39.0	0.45	18
Eritrea	10	60	40	-30	35.0	0.25	10
Guatemala	23	44	56	-33	33.5	0.41	16
Haiti	19	43	57	-38	31.0	0.33	13
Kenya	18	51	49	-31	34.5	0.37	15
Korea, DPR	*21*	*45*	*55*	*-34*	*33.0*	*0.38*	*15*
Madagascar	24	50	50	-26	37.0	0.48	19
Maldives	*22*	*47*	*53*	*-31*	*34.5*	*0.42*	*17*
Mali	21	44	56	-35	32.5	0.38	15
Mozambique	11	55	45	-34	33.0	0.24	10
Myanmar	21	49	51	-30	35.0	0.41	16
Niger	11	56	44	-33	33.5	0.25	10
Nigeria	16	56	44	-28	36.0	0.36	14
Pakistan	18	44	56	-38	31.0	0.32	13
Papua New Guinea	22	53	47	-25	37.5	0.47	19
Rwanda	12	57	43	-31	34.5	0.28	11
São Tomé & Principe	*10*	*53*	*47*	*-37*	*31.5*	*0.21*	*8*
Senegal	20	54	46	-26	37.0	0.43	17
Sudan	13	46	54	-41	29.5	0.24	10
Tanzania	18	54	46	-28	36.0	0.39	16
Uganda	10	44	56	-46	27.0	0.18	7
Yemen	15	51	49	-34	33.0	0.31	12
Zambia	16	43	57	-41	29.5	0.28	11

Extreme double deficit

Country	HWI	EWI	ESI	HWI- ESI	WI	WSI	WSI score
China	36	28	72	-36	32.0	0.50	20
Ghana	22	38	62	-40	30.0	0.35	14
India	31	27	73	-42	29.0	0.42	17
Iraq	19	31	69	-50	25.0	0.28	11
Libyan Arab J	38	24	76	-38	31.0	0.50	20
Mauritania	17	40	60	-43	28.5	0.28	11
Oman	31	28	72	-41	29.5	0.43	17
Saudi Arabia	31	23	77	-46	27.0	0.40	16
Syrian Arab R	28	25	75	-47	26.5	0.37	15
Tajikistan	28	39	61	-33	33.5	0.46	18
Tonga	*26*	*30*	*70*	*-44*	*28.0*	*0.37*	*15*
Turkmenistan	32	30	70	-38	31.0	0.46	18

Notes

Countries are in five groups, depending on their Wellbeing Index (WI) and Wellbeing/Stress Index (WSI). Each group is divided into up to eight sub-groups, depending on the combination of human and ecosystem wellbeing:

moderate ecosystem deficit	= HWI good or fair, EWI medium
high ecosystem deficit	= HWI fair, EWI poor or bad
moderate human deficit	= HWI medium, EWI fair
high human deficit	= HWI poor or bad, EWI fair
moderate double deficit	= HWI and EWI both medium
high double deficit, ecosystem worse	= HWI medium, EWI poor or bad
high double deficit, people worse	= HWI poor or bad, EWI medium
extreme double deficit	= HWI and EWI both poor or bad

Within each group, countries are listed by combination sub-group, and within each sub-group in alphabetical order.
Countries in italics were rated on less than two-thirds of the human or ecosystem sub-elements.
HWI = Human Wellbeing Index.
EWI = Ecosystem Wellbeing Index.
ESI = Ecosystem Stress Index = 100 minus the EWI.
HWI - ESI = Human Wellbeing Index minus Ecosystem Stress Index.
WI = Wellbeing Index (expressed as the average of the HWI and the EWI).
WSI = Wellbeing/Stress Index = the HWI divided by the ESI.
WSI score = score for Wellbeing/Stress Index. See Table 25a for performance criteria.

Table 27. Countries Ranked by Wellbeing Index

Rank	Country	HWI	EWI	ESI	WI	WSI
1	Sweden	79	49	51	64.0	1.55
2	Finland	81	44	56	62.5	1.45
3	Norway	82	43	57	62.5	1.44
4	Iceland	80	43	57	61.5	1.40
5	Austria	80	42	58	61.0	1.38
6	Dominica	56	65	35	60.5	1.60
7=	Canada	78	43	57	60.5	1.37
7=	Switzerland	78	43	57	60.5	1.37
9	Belize	50	64	36	57.0	1.39
10	Guyana	51	63	37	57.0	1.38
11	Uruguay	61	52	48	56.5	1.27
12	Germany	77	36	64	56.5	1.20
13	Denmark	81	31	69	56.0	1.17
14	New Zealand	73	38	62	55.5	1.18
15	Suriname	52	58	42	55.0	1.24
16	Latvia	62	46	54	54.0	1.15
17	Ireland	76	32	68	54.0	1.12
18	Australia	79	28	72	53.5	1.10
19	Peru	44	62	38	53.0	1.16
20	Slovenia	71	35	65	53.0	1.09
21	St Kitts & Nevis	52	53	47	52.5	1.11
22	Lithuania	61	44	56	52.5	1.09
23	Cyprus	67	38	62	52.5	1.08
24	Japan	80	25	75	52.5	1.07
25	St Lucia	53	51	49	52.0	1.08
26	Grenada	55	49	51	52.0	1.08
27	United States	73	31	69	52.0	1.06
28	Italy	74	30	70	52.0	1.06
29	France	75	29	71	52.0	1.06
30=	Czech R	70	33	67	51.5	1.04
30=	Greece	70	33	67	51.5	1.04
32	Portugal	72	31	69	51.5	1.04
33	United Kingdom	73	30	70	51.5	1.04
34	Belgium	80	23	77	51.5	1.04
35	Botswana	34	68	32	51.0	1.06
36	Slovakia	61	40	60	50.5	1.02
37	Luxembourg	77	24	76	50.5	1.01
38=	Armenia	45	55	45	50.0	1.00
38=	Netherlands	78	22	78	50.0	1.00
40	Seychelles	50	49	51	49.5	0.98
41	Ecuador	43	56	44	49.5	0.98
42	Mongolia	39	60	40	49.5	0.98
43	Singapore	66	32	68	49.0	0.97
44	Hungary	65	33	67	49.0	0.97
45	Mauritius	54	44	56	49.0	0.96
46	Solomon Is	37	61	39	49.0	0.95
47	Benin	27	71	29	49.0	0.93
48	Costa Rica	56	41	59	48.5	0.95
49	Sri Lanka	40	57	43	48.5	0.93
50	Bolivia	34	63	37	48.5	0.92
51	Estonia	62	34	66	48.0	0.94
52	Fiji	50	46	54	48.0	0.93
53	Belarus	46	50	50	48.0	0.92
54	Poland	65	30	70	47.5	0.93
55	Argentina	55	40	60	47.5	0.92
56	Dominican R	49	46	54	47.5	0.91
57	St Vincent & Grenadines	41	54	46	47.5	0.89
58	Korea, R	67	27	73	47.0	0.92
59	Barbados	62	32	68	47.0	0.91
60	Cape Verde	47	47	53	47.0	0.89
61	Spain	73	20	80	46.5	0.91
62	Samoa	43	50	50	46.5	0.86
63	Nepal	28	64	36	46.0	0.78
64	Croatia	57	33	67	45.0	0.85
65	RUSSIAN FEDERATION	48	42	58	45.0	0.83
66	Gabon	28	62	38	45.0	0.74
67	Bulgaria	58	31	69	44.5	0.84
68	Jamaica	54	35	65	44.5	0.83

Rank	Country	HWI	EWI	ESI	WI	WSI
69	Panama	52	37	63	44.5	0.83
70	Antigua & Barbuda	49	40	60	44.5	0.82
71	Georgia	48	41	59	44.5	0.81
72	Brunei Darussalam	47	42	58	44.5	0.81
73	Venezuela	43	46	54	44.5	0.80
74	Macedonia, FYR	46	42	58	44.0	0.79
75	Namibia	34	54	46	44.0	0.74
76	Togo	21	66	34	43.5	0.62
77	Congo, R	15	72	28	43.5	0.54
78	Bahamas	54	32	68	43.0	0.79
79	Chile	55	30	70	42.5	0.79
80	Trinidad & Tobago	53	32	68	42.5	0.78
81	Colombia	43	42	58	42.5	0.74
82	Cuba	40	45	55	42.5	0.73
83	Vanuatu	35	50	50	42.5	0.70
84	Malta	70	14	86	42.0	0.81
85	Israel	59	25	75	42.0	0.79
86	Albania	38	46	54	42.0	0.70
87	Indonesia	36	48	52	42.0	0.69
88	Malawi	22	62	38	42.0	0.58
89	Egypt	39	43	57	41.0	0.68
90	El Salvador	36	46	54	41.0	0.67
91	Central African R	16	66	34	41.0	0.47
92	Brazil	45	36	64	40.5	0.70
93	Paraguay	35	46	54	40.5	0.65
94	Lesotho	24	57	43	40.5	0.56
95	Guinea	15	66	34	40.5	0.44
96	Bhutan	14	67	33	40.5	0.42
97	Romania	50	30	70	40.0	0.71
98	Kyrgyzstan	38	42	58	40.0	0.66
99	Malaysia	46	33	67	39.5	0.69
100	Yugoslavia	42	37	63	39.5	0.67
101	Cameroon	15	64	36	39.5	0.42
102	Guinea-Bissau	13	66	34	39.5	0.38
103	Honduras	33	45	55	39.0	0.60
104	Swaziland	24	54	46	39.0	0.52
105	Zimbabwe	23	55	45	39.0	0.51
106	Djibouti	18	60	40	39.0	0.45
107	Gambia	16	62	38	39.0	0.42
108	Lao PDR	15	63	37	39.0	0.41
109	Lebanon	40	37	63	38.5	0.63
110=	Nicaragua	28	49	51	38.5	0.55
110=	Viet Nam	28	49	51	38.5	0.55
112=	Cambodia	20	57	43	38.5	0.47
112=	Côte d'Ivoire	20	57	43	38.5	0.47
114	Equatorial Guinea	15	62	38	38.5	0.39
115	Ethiopia	13	64	36	38.5	0.36
116=	Philippines	44	32	68	38.0	0.65
116=	Tunisia	44	32	68	38.0	0.65
118	Moldova	41	35	65	38.0	0.63
119	Kuwait	50	25	75	37.5	0.67
120	Kazakhstan	43	32	68	37.5	0.63
121	Papua New Guinea	22	53	47	37.5	0.47
122	Burkina Faso	17	58	42	37.5	0.40
123	Angola	8	67	33	37.5	0.24
124	Madagascar	24	50	50	37.0	0.48
125	Senegal	20	54	46	37.0	0.43
126	Liberia	9	65	35	37.0	0.26
127	Thailand	50	23	77	36.5	0.65
128	Ukraine	47	26	74	36.5	0.64
129	Turkey	45	28	72	36.5	0.63
130	Algeria	29	44	56	36.5	0.52
131	Bangladesh	27	46	54	36.5	0.50
132	Tanzania	18	54	46	36.0	0.39
133	Nigeria	16	56	44	36.0	0.36
134	Chad	13	59	41	36.0	0.32
135	Congo, DR	7	65	35	36.0	0.20
136	South Africa	43	27	73	35.0	0.59

Rank	Country	HWI	EWI	ESI	WI	WSI
137	Azerbaijan	42	28	72	**35.0**	0.58
138	Iran	38	32	68	**35.0**	0.56
139	Myanmar	21	49	51	**35.0**	0.41
140	Eritrea	10	60	40	**35.0**	0.25
141	*Bosnia & Herzegovina*	*24*	*45*	*55*	***34.5***	*0.44*
142	*Maldives*	*22*	*47*	*53*	***34.5***	*0.42*
143	Kenya	18	51	49	**34.5**	0.37
144	Rwanda	12	57	43	**34.5**	0.28
145	Sierra Leone	6	63	37	**34.5**	0.16
146	Morocco	36	32	68	**34.0**	0.53
147	Tajikistan	28	39	61	**33.5**	0.46
148	Guatemala	23	44	56	**33.5**	0.41
149	Niger	11	56	44	**33.5**	0.25
150	Mexico	45	21	79	**33.0**	0.57
151	Jordan	38	28	72	**33.0**	0.53
152	Uzbekistan	36	30	70	**33.0**	0.51
153	*Korea, DPR*	*21*	*45*	*55*	***33.0***	*0.38*
154	Yemen	15	51	49	**33.0**	0.31
155	Mozambique	11	55	45	**33.0**	0.24
156	Burundi	6	60	40	**33.0**	0.15
157	Mali	21	44	56	**32.5**	0.38
158	*Somalia*	*3*	*62*	*38*	***32.5***	*0.08*

Rank	Country	HWI	EWI	ESI	WI	WSI
159	*Qatar*	*40*	*24*	*76*	***32.0***	*0.53*
160	China	36	28	72	**32.0**	0.50
161	Comoros	20	44	56	**32.0**	0.36
162	*Bahrain*	*46*	*17*	*83*	***31.5***	*0.55*
163	*São Tomé & Principe*	*10*	*53*	*47*	***31.5***	*0.21*
164	Libyan Arab J	38	24	76	**31.0**	0.50
165	Turkmenistan	32	30	70	**31.0**	0.46
166	Haiti	19	43	57	**31.0**	0.33
167	Pakistan	18	44	56	**31.0**	0.32
168	Ghana	22	38	62	**30.0**	0.35
169	Oman	31	28	72	**29.5**	0.43
170	Zambia	16	43	57	**29.5**	0.28
171	Sudan	13	46	54	**29.5**	0.24
172	India	31	27	73	**29.0**	0.42
173	United Arab Emirates	41	16	84	**28.5**	0.49
174	Mauritania	17	40	60	**28.5**	0.28
175	*Tonga*	*26*	*30*	*70*	***28.0***	*0.37*
176	Saudi Arabia	31	23	77	**27.0**	0.40
177	Uganda	10	44	56	**27.0**	0.18
178	*Afghanistan*	*6*	*48*	*52*	***27.0***	*0.12*
179	Syrian Arab R	28	25	75	**26.5**	0.37
180	Iraq	19	31	69	**25.0**	0.28

Notes

Countries are ranked first by Wellbeing Index (WI) and then—among those with the same WI—by Wellbeing/Stress Index (WSI). Countries with the same three-digit WSI are differentiated by taking the WSI to four digits.

Countries in italics were rated on less than two-thirds of the human or ecosystem sub-elements.

HWI = Human Wellbeing Index.

EWI = Ecosystem Wellbeing Index.

ESI = Ecosystem Stress Index = 100 minus the EWI.

WI = Wellbeing Index (expressed as the average of the HWI and the EWI).

WSI = Wellbeing/Stress Index = the HWI divided by the ESI.

Appendix A.
Monetary and Physical Accounts

Monetary and physical accounts have indispensable but limited roles in the measurement of wellbeing and sustainability, providing detailed information on the market economy and the use of materials and energy. This appendix reviews the contributions and limitations of accounts, expanding on the summary in Chapter 1.

Counting Money: The System of National Accounts

By far the most widely used method of measuring progress is the System of National Accounts (SNA). National accounts are the records of asset changes, income, and expenditure that governments compile routinely to track the activity of their national economy, analyze its structure and performance, decide economic policies, and compare the economies of different countries.

National accounting became important during and after the Second World War to help increase production for the war effort, then to rebuild shattered economies, and eventually to guide economic development in general. Work on a standard international method of compiling national accounts began in the 1940s. The method became the SNA, codified and adopted by the United Nations in 1953 and revised in 1968 and 1993.[1]

The SNA measures the performance not of the economy as a whole but of the market economy (the production of goods and services that are owned and traded and so have a monetary value) plus some arbitrarily chosen goods and services that are not traded but for which a market value can be inferred: goods produced by farmers for their own consumption, the equivalent rental value of owner-occupied dwellings, and government services.[2] Anything without a price—from parenting and education

to forests and air—is excluded, regardless of its importance for economic welfare.

This concentration on the market economy is what makes the SNA so useful for analysis and management. Market transactions are measured in money, and market prices are the most direct and reliable way of establishing monetary values. With money as the common unit of measurement, data on a vast number of disparate activities can be combined, taken apart, and recombined, transforming the bewildering minutiae of the inventory and cash register into intelligible indicators of production, consumption, capital formation, saving, balance of trade, inflation, employment, and other factors that are vital for diagnosis. Standardization around market values and a set of widely accepted accounting conventions ensure that the many different components of the accounts are treated consistently and have the same meaning in all contexts and countries.[3]

But devotion to price has its price. It limits the applicability of the SNA to only one part of the economy. The economy is everything that has value for use or exchange. As such it consists of three other economic spheres besides the market: the nonmarket, social, and natural economies. In none of these is price the measure. The nonmarket economy includes household work, parenting, family care of children and elders, voluntary work, and reciprocal exchange of food, products, and tasks. The social economy covers education, information sharing, structures of decision making, and the norms and organizations that regulate access to resources and the conduct of economic activities. The natural economy is the ecosystem, the source of all life support, raw materials, and energy.

The market economy depends on and affects these other economies, but because the SNA excludes them it cannot account for them. It portrays the market in an imaginary world where the rest of the economy has no real substance. The ecosystem is a convenient cornucopia, a limitless supplier of resources and absorber of wastes. Human beings are consumers, abstractions with no more flesh or blood than the invisible hand.

This would not matter if the limits of the SNA were widely recognized and its leading indicators were matched by equally appealing indicators of human wellbeing and the state of the ecosystem. But this is not the case.

The presumption that the market economy is the economy and not just a part of it sets up false conflicts between "economy" and "environment" and between "economy" and "society."[4] When commentators or politicians say that an environmental or social policy is "bad for the economy" because it will reduce the growth rate of the gross domestic product, they are mistaking a part of the economy for the whole. A policy that increases the value of nonmarket services (such as work in the home) or protects the environment could very well be good for the economy even if it means a somewhat lower level of market production.[5]

Wrong Number: Gross Domestic Product

The gross domestic product (GDP) and gross national product (GNP) are much the most influential indicators derived from the national accounts. GDP measures the total value added of enterprises operating in the country concerned, regardless of whether owned by residents or nonresidents.[6] GNP measures the total value added of enterprises owned by residents of the country concerned, regardless of whether the money comes from domestic or foreign operations.[7]

Movements of these indicators are used to evaluate the overall performance of the economy and hence to judge the success or failure of economic policies pursued by governments. Politicians, analysts, bankers, investors, the business community, the media, and the public rely on them as general indicators of economic progress and even of overall wellbeing.[8]

GDP is an excellent measure of the size of the market economy, but it is a weak indicator of economic development and a completely misleading signal of welfare or wellbeing. As a measure of economic development, its main flaws (which also apply to GNP) are:[9]

- GDP does not show income distribution, so gains for the few appear as gains for all.

- GDP includes the value of depreciation of buildings, equipment, and machines instead of subtracting it.

- GDP goes up as the unpaid roles of families and communities are displaced by the paid service sector—as parenting is replaced by child care, home cooking by fast food joints, and good neighbors by alarm systems and security companies. Similarly, GDP rises in developing countries when the market displaces the nonmarket household economy as a major supplier of food, water, energy, and housing and destroys the social structure that goes with it.

- GDP takes no account of the depletion of natural resources, such as deforestation, depletion of fish stocks, reductions in fuel and mineral reserves, and losses of fertile soil.

- GDP either ignores environmental degradation or counts it as a benefit. Pollution can swell GDP several times: once when a factory produces it as a byproduct, again when industry or government spends money to clean it up, again when households or governments spend money to protect against it (buying filters or insulation, for example), and again to cope with the consequences such as medical bills for treatment of respiratory diseases. Environmental damage reduces GDP only if it directly reduces current production or increases its cost. If damage reduces future productivity or causes levels of pain and suffering that are not reflected in purchases, GDP overlooks it.

- GDP does not distinguish between costs and benefits, productive and destructive activities, or sustainable and unsustainable ones. Things most people would regard as bad—earthquakes, hurricanes, cancer, AIDS, crime, divorce—add to the GDP because dealing with them causes money to change hands. It is as if a business kept a balance sheet by merely adding up all transactions, without distinguishing between income and expenses, or between assets and liabilities.

These flaws lead GDP and GNP to exaggerate income and so encourage consumption and economic policies that cannot be sustained.[10] A country may be heading for bankruptcy—depleting its mineral reserves, destroying its forests, degrading its air and waters, and spending the proceeds on current consumption—and still be complacent about its economic performance because GDP growth looks so good.

GDP is not a measure of welfare (or even of total wealth), but it is treated as one. The common perception of GDP as a welfare indicator tilts government decisions toward expanding GDP as a major development objective, to the neglect or even at the expense of other aspects of development and the quality of life.[11]

One strategy for dealing with this problem is to remind people that GDP is simply a measure of market activity. But economists are constantly saying this. Politicians and everyone else need a general measure of progress, a clear guide through the welter of contradictory statistics. They will go on using GDP until they have something better.

Better Bookkeeping: Greening the National Accounts

Attempts at better monetary accounts are often called green accounts, a misleading term since some do not go very far to correct the SNA's environmental omissions while others try to address its main social flaws as well. Some try to replace GDP with a single number, a statement of net benefit that includes both market and nonmarket goods and services, subtracting the losses in both from the gains in both. Others recognize that GDP is a pretty good indicator of the size of the market, but people need something more—another two or three pretty good indicators of environmental and social conditions that can put the GDP in perspective.

The 1993 revision of the SNA expanded its coverage of assets to include parts of the natural environment, as long as they have a market price and someone owns or controls them: crops and livestock but not wildlife; built and cultivated land but not other land; water in reservoirs but not water in rivers or lakes; and not the sea, air, or atmosphere. A tract of timber that is under economic control (owned or licensed) is now recognized as an economic asset, but not other wood in the forest, other goods obtained from the wild such as fruit and medicines, the plants and animals for which the forest is habitat, the forest's role in the water cycle, its storage of carbon, its influence on climate, or its cultural and spiritual value. These still are excluded.[12]

Instead, the 1993 revision recommends that the majority of environmental goods and services be covered in satellite accounts that are separate from but linked to the main (or core) accounts of the SNA. This prevents the core accounts from being corrupted by nonmarket values while allowing the compilers of environmental accounts the freedom to test various ways of putting a price on nature.

The United Nations Statistical Division has developed the System of Integrated Environmental and Economic Accounting (SEEA) as a framework for environmental accounts linked to the SNA. The framework provides a home for monetary and nonmonetary accounts of the flows of resources from the ecosystem to the economy, their transformation and movements within the economy, and the flows of pollutants and wastes back to the ecosystem. The accounts include detailed breakdowns of the conventional national accounts, monetary accounts using unconventional (nonmarket) methods, and physical accounts (stocks and flows expressed, for example, in weight). They are expected to enable countries to subtract depreciation of capital, depletion of natural resources, and degradation of the environment from GDP to obtain a statement of environmentally adjusted net domestic product, or eco domestic product (EDP).[13]

Several countries are working on bits and pieces of the SEEA, some have made partial adjustments to GDP, but none has attempted a comprehensive accounting.[14] The chief constraints are inadequate data and a lack of confidence in nonmarket methods of valuation. Norway (which with France probably has the most fully developed physical accounts) has ruled out calculation of an EDP on the grounds that it would entail "a long series of subjective assessments of values".[15]

The Index of Sustainable Economic Welfare (ISEW) is even more ambitious: an attempt at an economic measure of national wellbeing.[16] ISEWs have been calculated for Australia, Denmark, Germany, Netherlands, the United Kingdom, and the United States, where it is called the Genuine Progress Indicator (GPI).[17] The GPI starts with personal consumption expenditure (taken from the national accounts and treated with some misgiving as the core contributor to wellbeing). It adjusts this figure for income distribution and then adds several benefits that national accounts omit or don't count as benefits, such as the value of household work, parenting, and volunteer work. It makes a number of other adjustments and then subtracts a series of social and environmental costs, including crime, family breakdown, loss of leisure time, underemployment, commuting, automobile accidents, noise, air and water pollution, ozone depletion, radioactive wastes, soil degradation, depletion of nonrenewable energy resources, and loss of farmland, wetlands, and forests.[18]

Marginally less ambitious are the World Bank's estimates of national wealth and genuine saving. Wealth is defined as the stock of capital that is the basis of well-being and consists of things, people, and nature. Things (or "produced assets") are machinery, equipment, buildings, infrastructure, and urban land. People (or "human resources") are labor plus investment in education plus "social capital," which is roughly the norms and organizations through which people share information, coordinate activities, and make decisions. Nature (or "natural capital") is ostensibly the ecosystem and all its benefits but in practice includes only cropland, pastures, forests, protected areas, and minerals (including fossil fuels).

National wealth calculations try to estimate the use values of things, people, and nature but in practice measure only their money-making capacity. People get the gold. Things get the silver. Nature gets the bronze. Human resources account for more than 70% of wealth in 5 out of 12 regions. Natural capital accounts for less than 10% of wealth in 7 of the regions. Except in the oil-producing Middle East (where natural capital is big because oil is big), human resources make up 60–79% of wealth, produced assets supply 15–30%, and natural capital contributes 2–21%. In the Middle East the proportions are human resources 43%, produced assets 18%, and natural capital (mostly oil) 39%.[19]

The Genuine Saving Indicator attempts to show whether the stock of national wealth is growing or shrinking. It starts with conventional measures of saving, adds investment in education, and deducts estimates of resource depletion and environmental degradation. It can help to show whether, for example, the level of government expenditure is sustainable, tax and monetary policies encourage saving, resource royalties are consumed or invested (and if invested, how), and saving is sufficient to offset any cumulative effects of pollution.[20]

Monetary accounts have to cope with incomplete and low-quality social and environmental data, just as non-monetary assessments do. But they contend with the extra problem of converting the data to monetary units. This is not a problem with things that are traded: they use the market price. It is also fairly straightforward with things that are not traded but have equivalents that are—food for subsistence, for example, or minerals in proved but undeveloped reserves—since a price can be obtained

from the equivalent. However, for everything else they must use nonmarket values. Usually these are either "contingent" values or the costs of social and environmental damage.

Contingent values are obtained by asking people how much they would pay to secure a benefit or prevent damage (willingness to pay) or how much compensation they would accept if they were deprived of the benefit or suffered the damage (willingness to accept). Genuine saving takes account of the impacts of pollution on wellbeing by estimating people's willingness to pay to avoid pain, suffering, and death from pollution-linked disease. It would value rain forests on the basis of global willingness to pay for their preservation, but who do you ask? Even if you think you know who to ask, this is a fantasy market, a bit like asking what you would do if you won the lottery. It assumes that people have sufficient information about the benefit or damage concerned—the risk of suffering and death from pollution or the benefits of rain forests—and that they have the money to pay what they say they would pay. Another basic, if unsurprising, flaw is that people are willing to accept much more than they are willing to pay (which shows that they have more sense than money).[21]

Costs are calculated from expenditures on avoiding and treating damage (such as expenditures on crime prevention or medical bills that result from pollution). Since actual expenditures are often lower than the full costs of damage, so-called maintenance costs may be estimated as well. These are hypothetical expenditures—guesses about the costs that might have been incurred to maintain social and environmental quality.[22]

If values cannot be estimated in these ways, they are assigned arbitrarily. The GPI puts the costs of greenhouse gases and radioactive wastes at $1 per barrel-equivalent of fossil fuel and nuclear energy consumption. Genuine saving sets the damage from carbon dioxide at $20 per ton of carbon emitted. National wealth assumes that nontimber benefits of forests—such as recreation, tourism, medicines, and other wild products—come from 10% of the forested area and are worth $112–$145 per hectare. Protected areas are valued at the opportunity cost (the value of benefits that could have been obtained if the area were not protected) of not using them as pasture land.[23]

The use of a single measure—money—disguises the fact that a consistent method is not being used. The grand totals (Mexico's eco domestic product of 36.4

billion pesos, the United States' GPI per person of US$4,068, India's genuine saving of 8% of GNP, Italy's national wealth of US$257,000 per person) are constructed from various combinations of market values, contingent values, actual expenditures, hypothetical expenditures, and stabs in the dark. Furthermore, the money values mask the physical data on which they are based. They overlay the assumptions and judgments embedded in the physical data with another set of assumptions and judgments.

Outside market values, economists have the choice of no numbers or wrong numbers. To their credit, they sometimes opt for no numbers. The GPI's estimate of the cost of air pollution does not include damage to health or increased mortality. Genuine saving leaves out fisheries, soil erosion, and biodiversity, and its valuation of forests ignores nonwood products and services such as carbon storage and watershed protection. National wealth excludes water and "many of the critically important ecological and life-support functions provided by natural systems, as well as existence values and the aesthetic pleasure we derive from nature."[24]

Such omissions limit the imposition of questionable money values, but they expose another problem. Monetary approaches treat the major elements of their evaluations in highly unequal ways. A core element obtained from the national accounts—whether net domestic product, personal consumption expenditures, gross domestic investment, or produced assets—is covered comprehensively. Then certain social and environmental elements—social costs, resource depletion, environmental degradation, natural capital—are covered partially, sometimes skimpily. Since accounts are built from particulars and are designed to be complete (everything should add up), these omissions create huge distortions.

A more fundamental defect lies in measuring the condition of the ecosystem only as an adjustment of a measure of human wealth. Inevitably, ecological contributions are dwarfed by those of the economy. As value added rises, resources and the environment appear to diminish in importance, even though their contribution to human wellbeing does not change. In the national wealth estimates, 74% of Western Europe's US$237,000 of total wealth per person comes from human resources, 23% from produced assets, and 2% from natural capital (the ecosystem). Since this invites the conclusion that the ecosystem no longer matters, the World Bank authors feel obliged to point out that "even though natural capital is normally third in importance as a source of wealth behind human resources and produced assets, it does form the ecological basis for life and is a fundamental building block of national wealth."[25]

The situation is analogous to the relationship between the daily food energy people must consume to exist and the nonfood energy they may consume as they go about their existence: the 2,200 kilocalories of food energy are less than 1% of the 222,500 kilocalories of other energy consumed by the average North American. If food consumption dropped to zero, it would have a negligible effect on total energy consumption, except that we'd be dead. This is one reason why we don't lump food energy with commercial energy. If something is irreplaceable and essential for us, we need to know its condition and the stresses we are placing on it independently of some measure of our own condition.

The leading argument for greening the national accounts and reforming GDP is that money is the only language that the key economic ministries in any government understand. If social and environmental problems are not translated into monetary terms, they will not be taken into account, or at best they will play second and third fiddle to "the economy."[26]

This argument fails for two reasons. First, GDP is misleading not just because it includes bad things and omits good things but because it is a monetary indicator forced into a nonmonetary role. Money is not the measure of all things. No matter how meticulous the calculation, dollars trivialize much of what we value most. Second, although money is often a deciding factor in strategies—"How much will it cost?" "What is the most cost-effective way of doing this?"—it is seldom the deciding factor when choosing national objectives, such as reducing malnutrition and mortality rates and increasing school enrollment, literacy, and access to safe water and sanitation, all of which are set instead on the basis of a consensus on performance.

GDP is a good indicator of the size of the market, and national accounts are a proven source of this and other useful information for managing the market economy. They continue to need improvement to reflect resource depletion, environmental damage, and social costs. However, they lose credibility when their scope is extended beyond what can be valued convincingly with market prices. Assessments are better suited to measuring nonmarket aspects of human wellbeing and the condition of the ecosystem.

Heavy Lifting: Physical Accounts

The nearest equivalents to national accounts in ecosystem assessment are natural resource accounts and material/energy balances. Both measure physical exchanges between the economy and the environment. Natural resource accounts record changes in the stocks of raw materials such as minerals or timber. Material/energy balances record the flows of materials and energy from the environment to the economy, through the economy, and back to the environment as pollution and wastes.[27]

Total material requirement (TMR) has been calculated for the United States, Austria, Germany, Netherlands, and Japan. It includes the natural resources that enter the economy as commodities for further processing, such as grain used in food manufacturing, petroleum sent to a refinery, minerals that go into metal products, and logs for lumber. It also includes materials that are displaced in the course of resource production or construction: for instance, soil erosion from agriculture, the rock and soil removed to reach an ore body, the portion of ore that is discarded to concentrate it, and material moved to build a highway or dredge a channel. The weight of all these materials is added up to obtain a country's TMR. For example, the TMR of the United States is 22 billion metric tons, and Japan's TMR per person is 45 metric tons.[28] Another study has calculated the total domestic output (TDO) of these countries: the amount of TMR that is returned to the national environment as pollutants of air, land, and water. For example, the TDO of the United States is 19 billion metric tons, and Japan's TDO per person is 14 metric tons.[29]

Physical accounts are highly informative but can capture only a limited set of people–ecosystem interactions. The natural world consists of countless visible and invisible parts that interact with each other at scales ranging from planetary to microscopic and are always changing. Millions of species of plants, animals, and other organisms have yet to be identified, let alone described.[30] The substances people take as resources and put back as wastes move through the system like shape-shifters, changing chemical composition and switching between solid, liquid, and gas. The small fraction of ecological goings-on that is captured by environmental statistics is recorded in a jumble of incompatible units: weight, volume, area, energy, toxicity, population numbers, and so forth. Moreover, environmental conditions are extremely patchy: this stretch of river is filthy, that stretch of river is pristine. For these reasons, physical accounts are likely to be limited to what they do best: natural resource accounts and material/energy balances.

Notes

1. Inter-Secretariat Working Group on National Accounts (1993).
2. United Nations Statistical Division (1993).
3. Hecht (n.d.).
4. Repetto et al. (1989).
5. Cobb, Halstead, & Rowe (1995a).
6. Value added is the value of the goods and services produced by an enterprise minus the value of the goods and services it buys. Total value added is the sum of the value added of all sectors of the market economy. GDP is calculated at factor cost or at market prices. GDP at factor cost is the total value added of enterprises operating in the country. GDP at market prices is GDP at factor cost plus indirect taxes minus government subsidies.
7. GNP is GDP at market prices plus (or minus) net factor income from abroad (total incomes received by residents of the country from activities carried on abroad—such as remittances from overseas workers, company profits, and interest from loans—minus any expenditure on similar items earned within the country by nonresidents). In countries where foreign debt or foreign ownership is high, GNP may be smaller than GDP.
8. Inter-Secretariat Working Group on National Accounts (1993).
9. Many economists and others have pointed out the defects of GDP and GNP. This list, which is not complete, draws mainly on Cobb, Halstead, & Rowe (1995a, 1995b); Daly & Cobb (1989); Repetto et al. (1989); Sheng (1995); Ahmad, El Sarafy, & Lutz (1989); and Lutz (1993).
10. Ahmad, El Sarafy, & Lutz (1989).
11. Sheng (1995).
12. United Nations Statistical Division (1993).
13. United Nations Statistical Division (1993).
14. For reviews, see Hamilton & Lutz (1996) and Sheng (1995).
15. Norway's Central Bureau of Statistics, quoted in Sheng (1995).
16. Daly & Cobb (1989).
17. Dieren (1995).
18. Cobb, Halstead, & Rowe (1995a).

19. Kunte et al. (1998); World Bank staff (1997).

20. Hamilton & Lutz (1996); World Bank staff (1997).

21. Munasinghe & McNeely (1995).

22. Atkinson & Hamilton (1996); Bartelmus & van Tongeren (1994); United Nations Statistical Division (1993).

23. Cobb, Halstead, & Rowe (1995a); Kunte et al. (1998); World Bank staff (1997).

24. World Bank staff (1997).

25. World Bank staff (1997).

26. United Nations Statistical Division (1993); World Bank staff (1997).

27. United Nations Statistical Division (1993).

28. Austria: Fischer-Kowalski, Haberl, & Payer (1997). United States, Germany, Netherlands, Japan: Adriaanse et al. (1997). Austrian data are for 1988. Data for the other countries are for 1994.

29. All five countries: Matthews et al. (2000). Data are for 1996 and exclude oxygen.

30. Wilson (1988); World Conservation Monitoring Centre (1992).

Appendix B.
Wellbeing Assessment

This appendix describes the Wellbeing Assessment method used in *The Wellbeing of Nations*, amplifying the summary in Chapter 1 (parts of which are repeated for completeness). It is intended to provide sufficient detail for readers to undertake their own assessments, as well as to understand how the book's findings were reached and rework them if they wish. Supplementary notes at the end of the appendix compare aspects of Wellbeing Assessment with alternatives offered by other methods.

Anyone interested in a course on the method should contact me. For a training kit, contact IUCN-The World Conservation Union.[1]

Scope and Origins of Wellbeing Assessment

Wellbeing Assessment is a method of assessing the conditions and interactions of people and the environment. It provides a systematic and transparent way of deciding the main features of human and ecosystem wellbeing to be measured, and of choosing the most representative indicators of those features. It enables the indicators to be combined into indices of each feature and ultimately into a Human Wellbeing Index, an Ecosystem Wellbeing Index, a Wellbeing Index, and a Wellbeing/Stress Index (the ratio of human wellbeing to ecosystem stress). Together, these four indices provide a measurement of sustainable development.

The method conforms with the Bellagio principles for assessing sustainable development (Supplement 1). It is designed to be used at many geographical levels, including regional, national, provincial, and municipal, but is less suitable at very small scales (below 100 km^2). Versions for local and corporate use are being developed.

Wellbeing Assessment began as a synthesis of approaches to assessment formulated by Tony Hodge, Alejandro Imbach, and Diana Lee-Smith and my Barometer of Sustainability method. These approaches were tested and improved by teams in Colombia, Zimbabwe, and India and IUCN offices in Central America, Southern Africa, and Pakistan, during the first phase (1994–1996) of an IUCN project on assessing progress toward sustainability, supported by the International Development Research Centre (IDRC).[2] I further developed the method for the second phase of the IUCN/IDRC project (1997–1999) and for this book. Wellbeing Assessment will continue to evolve as others apply it in different environmental and societal contexts.

Framework: Equal Treatment of People and Ecosystem

The underlying hypothesis of Wellbeing Assessment is that sustainable development is a combination of human wellbeing and ecosystem wellbeing. Human wellbeing is a requirement for sustainability because no rational person would want to perpetuate a low standard of living. Ecosystem wellbeing is a requirement because it is the ecosystem that supports life and makes possible any standard of living. The hypothesis is expressed in the metaphor of the Egg of Wellbeing (Figure B1). The ecosystem surrounds and supports people much as the white of an egg surrounds and supports the yolk. Just as an egg can be good only if both the yolk and white are good, so a society can be well and sustainable only if both people and the ecosystem are well.

To compare human development and ecosystem conservation and keep the focus on improving both, the wellbeing of people and the ecosystem are considered together but measured separately. Information is organized into two subsystems: people (human communities,

277

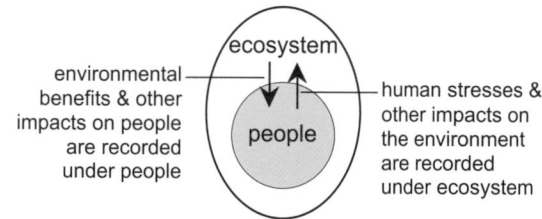

Figure B1. The Egg of Wellbeing, showing treatment of interactions between people and ecosystem.

economies, and artifacts); and ecosystem (ecological communities, processes, and resources). Interactions between the two are recorded under the receiving subsystem (Figure B1). Human stresses on the ecosystem (such as pollution and resource depletion)—as well as benefits to it from conservation—are recorded under *ecosystem*. Benefits from the ecosystem to people (from the supply of resources to spiritual comfort) are recorded under *people*, along with environmental stresses on people (such as the effects of natural disasters). For example, the impact of agriculture and fisheries on the land, water, air, and organisms is measured as part of ecosystem wellbeing; their impact on food supply, incomes, employment, health, and community stability is measured as part of human wellbeing.

Each subsystem is divided into five dimensions, pro-

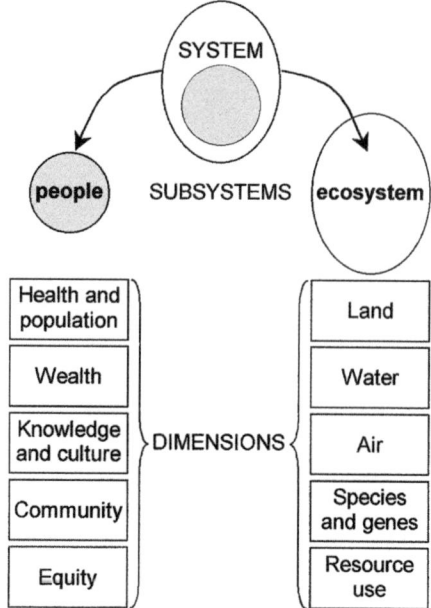

Figure B2. Wellbeing Assessment framework. Information is organized into two subsystems, each divided into five dimensions.

viding a common framework for all assessments using the Wellbeing Assessment method (Figure B2). The framework allows users to select their own indicators and produce assessments that are tailored to their conditions and needs yet broadly comparable with other well-

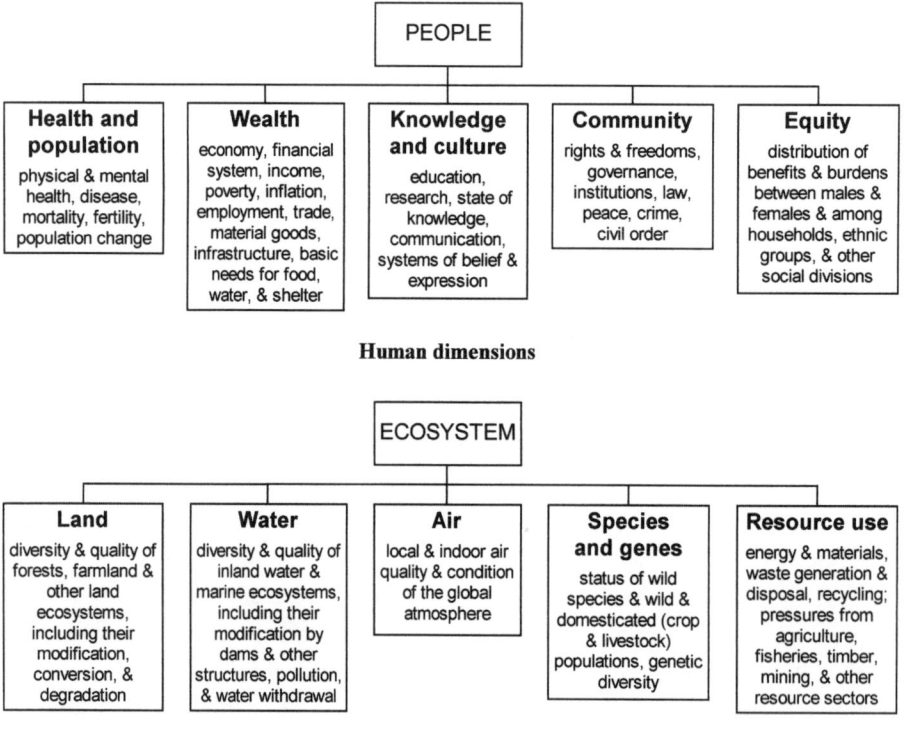

Figure B3. Illustrative list of topics covered by the dimensions.

being assessments. The dimensions are designed to combine a wide range of topics into a few major groups of roughly equal importance. They are comprehensive enough to accommodate most of the concerns of most societies: any issue regarded as significant for wellbeing and sustainable development has a place in one of them (Figure B3).

The background of the dimensions is described in Supplement 2; frameworks of other methods are discussed in Supplement 3.

Six-Stage Cycle

Because it is impossible to measure human or ecosystem wellbeing directly, assessments must select indicators of the main features of each. Knowing the essential role of indicators, it is tempting to jump right in and choose them at once. However, it is seldom clear at the start of an assessment how well a given set of indicators represents a desirable combination of human and environmental conditions, what aspects are left out, how much the indicators overlap, or how they relate to each other. Since indicators require the collection and analysis of often large amounts of data, choosing the wrong indicators can be a costly mistake.

Consequently, it is necessary first to take apart the concepts of human and ecosystem wellbeing to identify the features to be measured—and then to unpack each feature to reveal aspects that are both representative and measurable. Wellbeing Assessment does this by going down the hierarchy in Figure B4, which provides a series of increasingly specific stepping stones from system and goal to indicators and performance criteria (standards of achievement). These steps ensure that the indicators are as representative as possible of the system as a whole and of people's goals for themselves and their environment. Even so, each indicator conveys information only about the particular element or subelement it represents. To provide a picture of the entire system and of progress toward the goals, the indicators need to be combined into indices. The steps taken to select the indicators are reversed to provide a logical and transparent procedure for combining them, going back up the hierarchy from indicators to system.

Stage 1. Define the System and Goals

The system consists of the people and ecosystem of the area to be assessed. Defining it involves deciding and

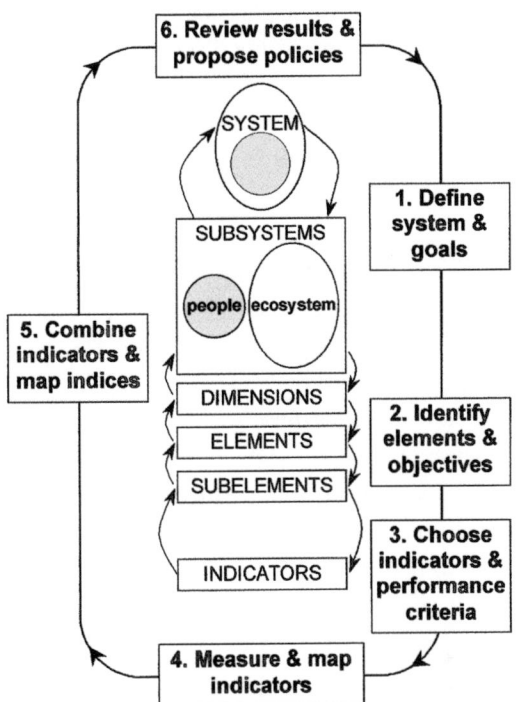

Figure B4. Six-stage assessment cycle. Starting on the right and moving clockwise, indicators are selected going down the hierarchy (center) and combined going up it.

mapping the boundaries of the assessment area and its differentiation units: the smallest units into which the area will be divided for the purposes of data collection and analysis and participation in the assessment. Differentiation units should be decision-making (administrative or political) units, such as nations, states, provinces, counties, and municipalities, because assessments are meant to aid decisions. (Because the ecosystem seldom respects political boundaries, it is also useful to divide the assessment area into ecological units, such as ecoregions or vegetation zones, and hydrological units, such as inland water and marine basins.) The finer the detail, the more the assessment will reveal local differences in human and environmental conditions but the more expensive and complicated it will be. For example, Italy consists of 20 regions, 103 provinces, and 8,102 municipalities.[3] Differentiating an Italian assessment by province would be more informative than by region and vastly more practical than by municipality.

Goals for the system and subsystems encapsulate a vision of sustainable development and provide the basis for deciding what the assessment will measure. For *The Wellbeing of Nations* (WoN), I defined the goal for the system as "sustainable and equitable combinations of human and ecosystem wellbeing," and goals for the subsystems (people and ecosystem) as "a high level of human wellbeing" and "a high level of ecosystem wellbeing." Participants in other assessments would define system and subsystem goals themselves.

Stage 2. Identify Elements and Objectives

Participants in an assessment decide which aspects of human and ecosystem wellbeing are to be measured by identifying elements and objectives. Elements are key subjects or concerns that must be considered to get an adequate sense of the state of each dimension. In WoN, I chose two for each dimension because the fewer the elements the clearer their role and the stronger their influence on the dimension index. The dimensions (Figures B2 and B3) are big conceptual boxes that accommodate concerns common to all societies (e.g., water, and knowledge and culture), without requiring them to address those of little interest to them (e.g., marine waters to Uzbekistan) or excluding those of interest to some but not all societies (e.g., the maintenance of Islamic values, which could go under knowledge and culture). Accordingly, there are many ways of dividing the dimensions into elements. Land, for example, could be divided into major ecosystems (forests, farmland, etc.). In WoN, however, I chose land diversity and land quality because these are the fundamental concerns for land management and result in fewer elements.

If an element is too broad to measure directly, it is split into subelements. If a suitable indicator can be chosen directly, the subelement level is skipped. Of the 20 elements in WoN, 2 were dropped for lack of suitable indicators, 11 were split into subelements, and 7 were not. Land quality, for example, could be measured directly by the indicator "degraded land as a percentage of cultivated + modified land." However, land diversity had to be split into two subelements—land modification and conversion and land protection—each providing a different perspective on how well the diversity of land ecosystems is maintained.

Objectives for the elements provide a logical bridge between the general goals for the system and subsystems and the specific performance criteria for the indicators. The objective "soil degradation close to background rates" translates the goal for the ecosystem ("a high level of ecosystem wellbeing") into a particular aim for land qual-ity that succinctly expresses the point of the element and provides a basis for choosing performance criteria for the indicator: the percentages of degraded land that are desirable, acceptable, or unacceptable. Objectives for dimensions and subelements may also be identified but are not necessary (and were not defined in WoN).

Once the elements are identified, the scope of the data required for indicators will be evident. At this stage, it is useful to compile a meta-database: an inventory of sources of data on each element, including when and how the data are collected, where and how stored, and how they can be obtained—essential information for the choice of indicators.

Stage 3. Choose Indicators and Performance Criteria

INDICATORS

Indicators are measurable aspects of an element. Wellbeing Assessment distinguishes between primary and secondary indicators. *Primary* indicators are the chief means of measuring the condition of elements and subelements. Performance criteria are defined for them, and they are combined into higher-level indices. Consequently, they must be chosen with great care to avoid overlap and double-counting with other primary indicators. *Secondary* indicators are supplementary sources of information, which are not combined into indices. Hence, performance criteria are not needed, and the indicators can be chosen less rigorously. If the primary indicators of health are life expectancy at birth and child and maternal mortality rates, secondary indicators might be the incidence of particular diseases, the number of doctors and hospital beds per 1,000 persons, and the percentage of children immunized against infectious diseases. (WoN used only primary indicators.) Throughout this appendix, "indicator" means "primary indicator."

Assessment participants choose one or more indicators for each element (or subelement) on the basis of how fully the indicator represents the element or subelement concerned and how reliable and feasible it is (Figure B5).

An indicator is fully *representative* if it covers the most important aspects of the element or subelement concerned and shows trends over time and differences between places and groups of people. "Life expectancy at birth" comes close to being a fully representative indicator of health because it reflects all the causes of death, and

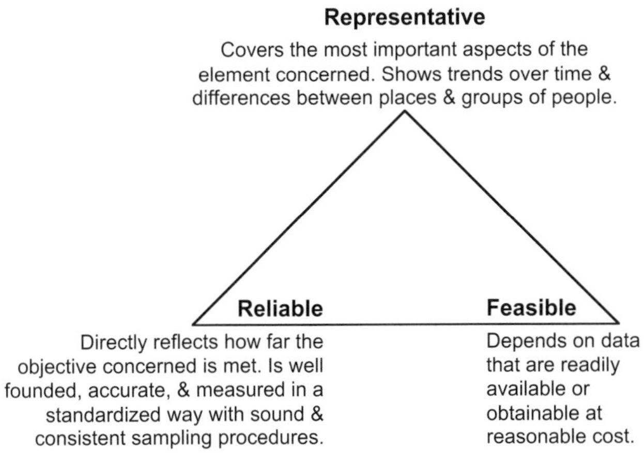

Representative

Covers the most important aspects of the element concerned. Shows trends over time & differences between places & groups of people.

Reliable

Directly reflects how far the objective concerned is met. Is well founded, accurate, & measured in a standardized way with sound & consistent sampling procedures.

Feasible

Depends on data that are readily available or obtainable at reasonable cost.

Figure B5. Basis for indicator selection. The ideal indicator is representative, reliable and feasible. Indicator selection is often a matter of balancing these qualities.

the death rates from those causes, that a typical person would be exposed to throughout life. Even so, it is incomplete since it does not measure the number of years a person can expect to live with different degrees of disability or illness. "Healthy life expectancy," by contrast, is highly representative because it subtracts the number of years likely to be lost to illness and injury.

An indicator is more likely to be *reliable* if it is accurate, is measured in a standardized way with sound and consistent sampling procedures, is well founded, and directly reflects the objective concerned. "Well founded" means that its relationship to the element it represents is well established, scientifically valid, or is a defensible and testable hypothesis. For example, stunting (low height for age) in children is a well-founded indicator of lack of food, since many studies have demonstrated the relationship. An indicator directly reflects the objective concerned if it measures its actual achievement rather than factors that advance or impede its achievement. Healthy life expectancy at birth shows how well the objective "long lives in good health" has been attained, whereas immunization rates, health expenditure, and numbers of doctors are only contributing factors.

An indicator is *feasible* if it depends on data that are readily available or obtainable at reasonable cost. The data required for an assessment will be available in a variety of forms and from a variety of sources. For the purpose of determining feasibility, the crucial distinction is between (a) data that are already collected as a matter of course and are available as maps or statistics; and (b) uncollected

Table B1. What to do with potential indicators in each of five quality classes.

Indicator Quality Class	What to Do with the Indicator
The indicator is representative, reliable and feasible.	Use it.
The indicator is reliable and feasible but not representative.	Try to find one or more additional indicators until the element or subelement is adequately represented.
The indicator is representative and feasible but not reliable.	Is it reliable enough to use if everyone is made aware of its flaws? If yes, use it and try to find one or more additional indicators that together could produce a more reliable picture. If no, drop it.
The indicator is feasible but not representative or reliable.	Drop it.
The indicator is representative and reliable but not feasible.	Can the element or subelement be represented reasonably by another indicator or set of indicators? If yes, drop it. If no, reexamine the indicator's feasibility. It may be cost-effective after all.

data. The meta-database (compiled in the previous stage) should show whether the data are collected.

Potential indicators fall into various quality classes depending on how well they meet the criteria of representativeness, reliability, and feasibility. Suggestions about what to do with indicators in each class are given in Table B1. If no indicator that adequately meets these criteria can be found, then the element or subelement should be excluded from the assessment and its exclusion clearly noted.

PERFORMANCE CRITERIA

Participants in an assessment choose performance criteria for each indicator. The criteria translate the objectives into measurable performance and enable different indicator measurements to be converted to scores so that they can be combined.

A large number of indicators is inevitable, given the broad scope of human and ecosystem wellbeing, but presents an enormous communication problem. Every indicator sends a signal. The more indicators, the more signals—

a perplexing cacophony of good, bad, and somewhere-in-between news. The problem is overcome by combining the indicators into indices. How to do this raises other obstacles, however, because a typical set of indicators is a mess of incompatible measurements: land condition in hectares, water pollution in milligrams per liter, species diversity in percentages of threatened species, health in years of life expectancy, income in money, education in school enrollment rates, freedom in the observation of rights, and so on.

Combining such different indicators mixes apples and oranges. To do this successfully requires finding a common unit that does not distort their qualities as apples or oranges ("citrus units" would favor oranges, "pome units" would favor apples). The common unit may be a physical unit, money, or a performance score. Because of the limitations of physical units and money (explained in Supplement 4), Wellbeing Assessment uses performance scores. Several scales for performance scores have been devised (described in Supplement 5). Wellbeing Assessment uses

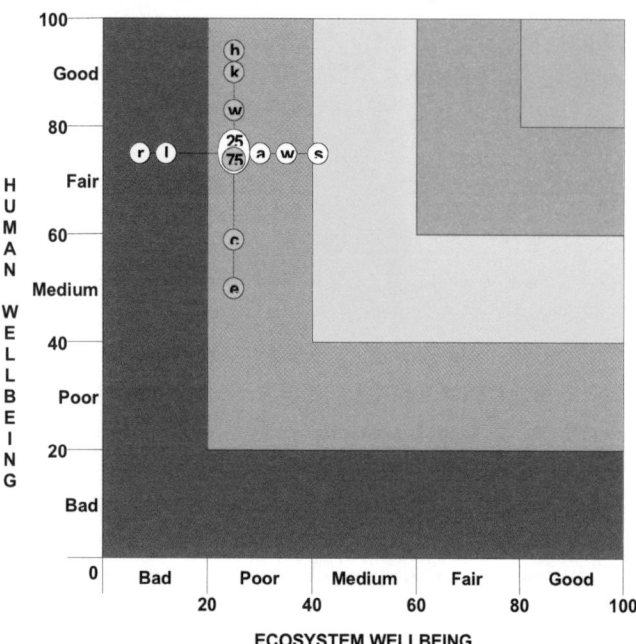

Figure B6. Barometer of Sustainability. The Wellbeing Index (WI) of a hypothetical country is shown on the Barometer. The Human Wellbeing Index (HWI) is in the yolk of the egg. The Ecosystem Wellbeing Index (EWI) is in the white. The WI is where the HWI and EWI intersect. Yellow circles (vertical axis) show the points on the scale of the human dimensions: c = community; e = equity; h = health and population; k = knowledge; w = wealth. White circles (horizontal axis) show points of the ecosystem dimenions: a = air; l = land; r = resource use; s = species and genes; w = water.

the Barometer of Sustainability (Figure B6) because it is the only performance scale designed to measure human and ecosystem wellbeing together without submerging one in the other. The Barometer's unique features are:

- Two axes: one for human wellbeing, the other for ecosystem wellbeing. This enables each set of indicators to be combined independently, keeping them separate to allow analysis of people–ecosystem interactions.

- The axis with the lower score overrides the other axis. This prevents a high score for human wellbeing from offsetting a low score for ecosystem wellbeing (or vice versa), reflecting the view that people and the ecosystem are equally important and that sustainable development must improve and maintain the wellbeing of both.

- Each axis is divided into five bands. This allows users to define not just the end points of the scale but intermediate points as well for greater flexibility and control of the scale.

Performance criteria enable an indicator measurement to be given a score by converting it to the scale of the Barometer. They define the rate of exchange between the indicator and the scale—the level of performance that is worth a given number of points (Table B2).

Choosing performance criteria involves defining the top point of each band on the basis of three factors:

- The range of performance is used to set the base and top of the scale. As a general rule, base–best (0–100) should encompass the range of performance. This may be current performance or a combination of past, current, and expected performance. For example, WoN's

Table B2. The five bands of the Barometer of Sustainability.

Band	Points Range	Top	Definition
Good	100–81	100	Desirable performance, objective fully met
Fair	80–61	80	Acceptable performance, objective almost or barely met
Medium	60–41	60	Neutral or transitional performance
Poor	40–21	40	Undesirable performance
Bad	20–1	20	Unacceptable performance
Base	0	0	Base of scale

base–best for life expectancy at birth (30–85 years) encompasses the lowest current performance of 34 years and the highest expected performance (by 2050) of 84 years. If outliers of extreme performance would make the scale unduly long, it can be cut off (at the bottom or at the top). For example, the scale for the indicator "tons of fertilizer per 1,000 harvested hectares" was cut off at 320 tons to prevent distortion by a few countries that use very much higher levels (up to 2,426 tons). In WoN, to prevent arbitrary shortening of the scale, base–best encompassed the range of performance of more than 90% of the countries in all cases except fecal coliforms.

- The objective of the element concerned guides the setting of the good band. For example, WoN's objective for the wild diversity element, "maintenance of all native wild species and reductions of extinctions to background rates," suggests that the good band of the threatened species indicators should be close to the background rate (estimated to be less than 0.01% of species per century).

- At least one of the following is used to set one or more bands:

  Estimated sustainable rate. For example, a sustainable rate of timber felling would be less than 100% of net annual increment.

  Estimated background rate ("natural" or "normal" performance). For example, the background rate of human-caused soil degradation on natural land is zero.

  Other threshold. For example, a single death represents the threshold between peace and armed conflict.

  International (or national) standard. For example, UN standards for water quality.

  International (or national) target. For example, a UN target for education is 100% primary education by 2015.

  Expert opinion. For example, Transparency International's Corruption Perceptions Index.

  Derivation from a related indicator. For example, in the absence of a UN target for secondary education, WoN used a less stringent version of the criteria for primary education.

The judgment of participants. If none of the preceding factors is available, the choice of performance criteria is entirely up to the judgment of participants. Performance criteria for 62 of WoN's 87 indicators were guided by the preceding factors; the remaining 25 were set on the basis of personal judgment.

Sustainable rates determine the top of the medium or fair band, depending on how much assessment participants want to apply the precautionary principle (that it is better to err on the side of caution). A highly precautionary approach would not allow even a slightly unsustainable rate to be considered fair (acceptable performance); a less precautionary approach might. In WoN, for instance, I took a highly precautionary approach to the indicator "timber fellings + imports as a percentage of net annual increment": fellings + imports had to be well below increment to qualify as good and not exceed it to qualify as fair. I was less precautionary in my treatment of "annual change in native forest area": the area must not decline at all to qualify as good but may shrink by up to 0.05% a year and still qualify as fair.

Background rates usually determine the top of the good band (best performance). The chief question to decide is how far from the background rate is still good (i.e., where to put the top of fair). This depends on what is at stake. In the case of the threatened species indicators (background extinction rate close to 0%), I set the top of fair at 2% because extinctions are irreparable. In the case of land degradation (background rate 0%), I set it at 10% of the cultivated and modified land area because the percentage is weighted, and 10% overall is equivalent to 20% light (easily reparable) degradation, 10% moderate (less easily reparable), 5% strong (barely reparable), or 2.5% extreme (irreparable) degradation.

The bands set by other thresholds depend on the threshold. If it is between clearly unacceptable performance on one side (armed conflict) and performance that ranges from neutral to desirable on the other (from military preparedness without conflict to complete peace), then the threshold sets the top of the poor or bad band. If it is between clearly desirable performance on one side (unfragmented habitats) and performance that ranges from neutral to unacceptable on the other (increasing fragmentation of habitats), the threshold sets the top of the medium or fair band.

Standards, targets, and expert opinion may determine several bands. The UN Economic Commission for Europe has defined five water quality classes (excellent, good, fair, poor, bad), which can be translated directly into the Barometer's good, fair, medium, poor, and bad bands. In WoN, a series of UN targets—60 years by 2000, more than 70 years by 2005, and more than 75 years by 2015—were used to set the tops of the poor, medium, and fair bands for life expectancy at birth. Single standards and targets set the top of the good, fair, or medium bands, depending on how ambitious they are. Targets such as universal primary education and elimination of ozone depleting substances cannot be bettered and form the top of the good band. The ambitiousness of less absolute targets can be judged from the range of performance: if few societies exceed them, they are put at the top of the fair band; if many exceed them, they are put at the top of the medium band. Sometimes other considerations may prevail: international targets set the top of the fair band of three of WoN's food sufficiency indicators but the top of the medium band of the fourth to aid interpretation by enabling the performance criteria of all four indicators to match.

For many indicators it is useful for the performance criteria to increase or decline exponentially (in doublings) from the best point, to reflect the increasing difficulty of improving performance as one approaches the ideal, or from the worst point, to reflect diminishing returns (Table B3). An exponential scale also accommodates a wide range of performance while keeping high standards for the good and fair bands. For example, child mortality rates range from 263 to 6 deaths per 1,000 live births. The UN target is for all countries to have rates below 45 deaths by 2015. An exponential scale from 0 to 360 accommodates the current range of performance and puts 45 at the top of the medium band, so that less than 45 is fair and half of 45 is good. A scale with bands of equal size could not do this. If it kept 45 at the top of medium, the base of the scale would be 112.5 deaths, which would exclude the performance of 44 countries. If the base of an equally divided scale were set at 265 to accommodate the current range of performance, the top of medium would rise to 106, and the top of fair (at 53) would be worse than the UN target of 45.

Choosing performance criteria is the most thought-provoking part of Wellbeing Assessment, demanding judgment throughout. This is all to the good. Pondering

Table B3. Performance criteria for two indicators.
The child mortality criteria increase exponentially from the best point, the protected land criteria from the worst point.

Band	Top Point on Scale	Child Deaths per 1,000 Live Births	Protected Land as % of Total Land
Good	100	0	40
Fair	80	22	20
Medium	60	45	10
Poor	40	90	5
Bad	20	180	2.5
Base	0	360	0

and debating the specifics of what it will take to achieve high levels of human and ecosystem wellbeing are essential for building the consensus required to develop sustainably. The criteria chosen for WoN are summarized in Appendix C.

Stage 4. Measure and Map Indicators

Having chosen the indicators, it is necessary to obtain the data for them. The assessment needs to set up its own database; make arrangements with sources of existing data to receive them regularly; and organize surveys and monitoring systems for any indicators requiring data not currently collected. The data should be linked to the base maps prepared as part of stage 1 to enable the indicators to be mapped by differentiation unit, as they are in WoN.

Data for many of the indicators will apply to the entire area of each differentiation unit. But data for some—notably water quality and local air quality—will be point data, specific to a particular measuring station. It is helpful to show the locations of these stations on maps so that users can judge the completeness of coverage. In addition, participants must decide whether to take the average of the stations or the worst measurement. If the monitoring agency is scrupulous in sampling only (or largely) those locations where air or water pollution is most likely to occur, then the average is probably the fairest reading. If it omits areas known to be polluted and includes many pristine spots, it may be more prudent to choose the worst-performing station. In WoN, I took the average of the worst pollutants at each location.

Data (indicator measurements) are given scores on the

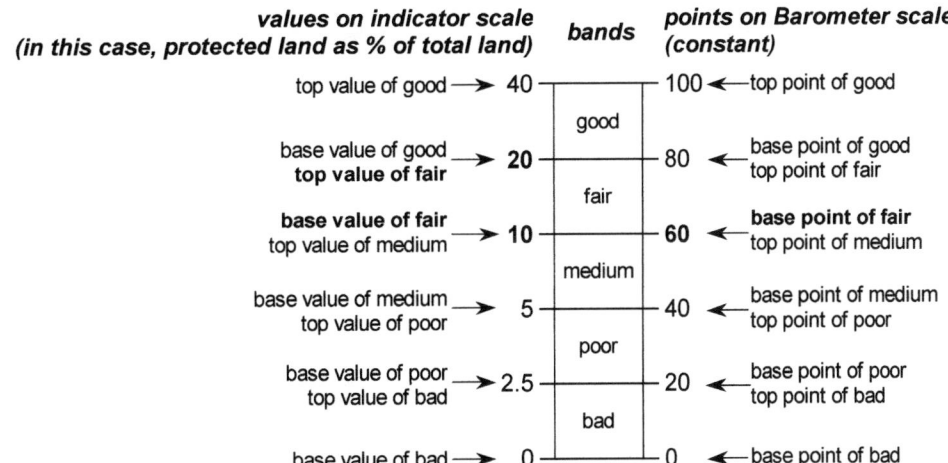

Figure B7. Correspondence of values on an indicator scale to points on the Barometer scale when best performance is the highest value and worst the lowest. The values on the indicator scale on the left—40, 20, 10, 5, 2.5, 0—are indicator specific. In this instance they define the performance bands for protected land as % of total land. The points on the Barometer scale on the right—100, 80, 60, 40, 20, 0—define the bands of the Barometer. They remain constant. See text and formula for explanation of how the values and points highlighted in bold are selected and used to calculate the score for Zimbabwe (protected land 15.8%).

basis of the performance criteria. The performance criteria define which band a given indicator measurement will go into and the indicator values that correspond to the top point and base point of that band. For example, using the performance criteria given in Table B3, Zimbabwe's protected land percentage of 18.5% would go into the fair band because it is between 20% and 10%: 20% on the indicator scale corresponds to 80 on the Barometer scale (the top point of the fair band), and 10% on the indicator scale corresponds to 60 on the Barometer scale (the base point of the fair band). Afghanistan's child mortality rate of 257 deaths per 1,000 live births would go into the bad band because it is between 180 and 360: 180 on the indicator scale corresponds to 20 on the Barometer scale (the top point of the bad band), and 360 on the indicator scale corresponds to 0 on the Barometer scale (the base point of the bad band). Note that the base point of each band on the Barometer scale is the same as the top point of the band below (Figures B7 and B8).

The indicator measurement's exact position in the band on the Barometer scale is determined by calculating its score. This is done in one of two ways, depending on whether: best performance is the highest value and worst performance is the lowest value (for example, protected land as a percentage of total land) or best performance is the lowest value and worst performance

is the highest value (for example, the child mortality rate).

When *best is the highest value and worst is the lowest*, the formula for calculating the score is:

> {[(actual indicator value – base indicator value) ÷ (top indicator value – base indicator value)] × 20} + base point of the band on the Barometer scale

The terms *top* and *base* always refer to the band in which the indicator measurement falls. The *actual indicator value* is the measurement of the indicator being scored. The *top indicator value* is the top value of the relevant band on the indicator scale, and the *base indicator value* is the base value of the band. The *base point of the band* is the base point of the relevant band on the Barometer scale (Figure B7).

Following the formula, the calculation for Zimbabwe's protected land percentage (18.5%) is:

> 18.5 (actual indicator value) – 10 (base indicator value) = 8.5
> 20 (top indicator value) – 10 (base indicator value) = 10
> 8.5 ÷ 10 = 0.85
> 0.85 × 20 = 17.0
> 17.0 + 60 (base point of band on the Barometer) = 77

When *best is the lowest value and worst is the highest*, the formula for calculating the score is:

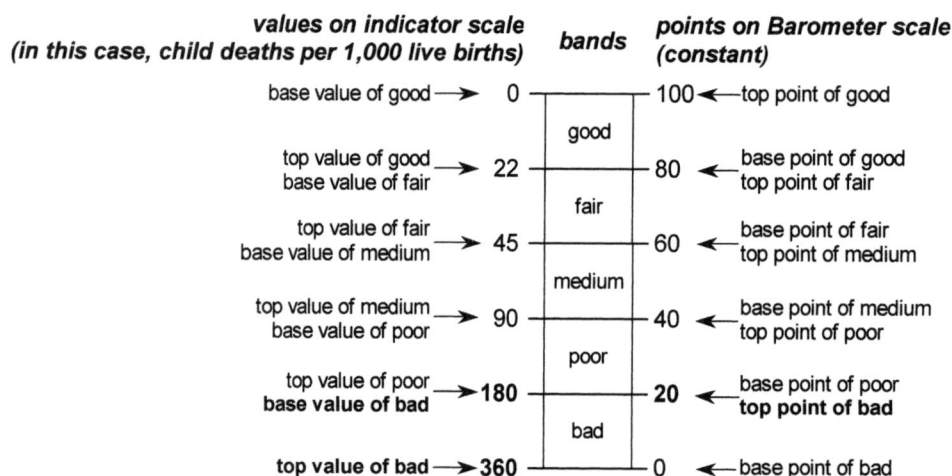

Figure B8. Correspondence of values on an indicator scale to points on the Barometer scale when best performance is the lowest value and worst the highest. The values on the indicator scale on the left—0, 22, 45, 90, 180, 360—are indicator specific. In this instance they define the performance bands for child deaths per 1,000 live births. The points on the Barometer scale on the right—100, 80, 60, 40, 20, 0—define the bands of the Barometer. They remain constant. Note that the base point of each band is still the top point of the band below. However, the base value now corresponds to the top point of the band; the top value, to the base point. See text and formula for explanation of how the values and points highlighted in bold are selected and used to calculate the score for Afghanistan (257 child deaths).

> top point of the band on the Barometer scale − {[(actual indicator value − base indicator value) ÷ (top indicator value − base indicator value)] × 20}

As before, the terms *top* and *base* always refer to the band in which the indicator measurement falls. Also as before, the *actual indicator value* is the measurement of the indicator being scored, the *top indicator value* is the top value of the band on the indicator scale, and the *base indicator value* is the base value of the band. The difference between this and the previous case is that the indicator scale goes in the opposite direction to the Barometer scale—from lowest to highest instead of from highest to lowest. Consequently, the top value of a band on the indicator scale corresponds to the *base* point of the band on the Barometer scale; and the base value of the band on the indicator scale corresponds to the *top* of the band on the Barometer scale (Figure B8). The other difference is that the final step in the calculation is to subtract from the top point of the band on the Barometer scale instead of adding to its base point.

Following the formula, the calculation for Afghanistan's child mortality rate of 257 deaths per 1,000 live births is:

> 257 (actual indicator value) − 180 (base indicator value) = 77
> 360 (top indicator value) − 180 (base indicator value) = 180
> 77 ÷ 180 = 0.428
> 0.428 × 20 = 8.56
> 20 (top point of band on the Barometer) − 8.56 = 11.44 = 11

In all cases, scores are rounded to the nearest whole point, with 0.5 rounded down.

Data availability is seldom uniform. While some differentiation units may have data on all the indicators, others may have data on only a selection of them. Such uneven coverage can seriously distort results. For example, if all units do well on water consumption and poorly on water quality, the ones that are rated only on consumption will appear to be better than they actually are. An "insufficient data rule" prevents high scores resulting merely from lack of data. A good score (81–100) is allowed only if it is based on all applicable components (e.g., data in an indicator, indicators in an element, elements in a dimension). A fair score (61–80) is allowed only if it is based on at least half the components. Potentially good scores based on more than half but not all the applicable components are reduced to 80 (the top of fair). Potentially good or fair scores based on fewer than half the applicable components are reduced to 60 (the top of medium). For example, a society with a score of 88 for water consumption but no data on water quality would have an overall water score of 80 rather than 88. If water were divided into three elements (water consumption, water quality, aquatic habitats) and data were available only for water consumption, the score would be reduced to 60.

Stage 5. Combine Indicators and Map Indices

Once the indicators have been given a score, they can be combined back up the hierarchy (Figure B4), from indicators to system: indicator scores are combined into a subelement score, subelement scores into an element index, element indices into a dimension index, and dimension indices into a subsystem index.

Components (indicators, subelements, elements, or dimensions) are combined in one of three ways:

- *Unweighted average:* The components are added and averaged. For example, if one component has a score of 70 and another has a score of 30, the combined score is 50: 70 + 30 = 100 ÷ 2 = 50.

- *Weighted average:* The components are given different weights, then added and averaged. For example, if the component with the 70 score is given a weight of 1 and the component with the 30 score is given a weight of 2, then the combined score is 43: (70 × 1) + (30 × 2) = 130 ÷ 3 = 43.3. (Scores are multiplied by their weights and then the total score is divided by the total weight. In this case a weight of 1 plus a weight of 2 makes a total weight of 3.)

- *Veto:* A lower score overrides a higher score. For example, the component with the 30 score would override the component with the 70 score, resulting in an overall score of 30.

The choice of combining procedure is a matter of judging which most closely reflects the situation in relation to the goals and objectives. The following are guidelines, not hard-and-fast rules.

An *unweighted average* is used mainly when the components are judged to be roughly equal in importance *and* in the quality and coverage of their indicators. Strong performance in all components is desirable and weak performance in any of them undesirable, but not to the extent that bad performance in one component overrides better performance in the others. For these reasons, WoN used the unweighted average to combine the peace and crime subelements, household equity and gender equity, the water quality scores of different drainage basins, the scores for threatened plants and threatened animals, and the scores for agriculture, fisheries, and timber.

The human and ecosystem dimensions are a special case. They are equally important and should be equally well represented by their indicators, but even if they are

not, the unweighted average is used to combine them into indices (the HWI and EWI) to show their roles clearly, unobscured by technical manipulation such as weighting.

The unweighted average may also be used when one component contributes to another but taking the lower score is considered too drastic. For example, WoN divided household wealth into two subelements: income and needs. Since income contributes to the provision of needs, it would be better to take the subelement with the lower score to prevent double-counting. However, needs are reported less reliably in high-income than in low-income countries, and taking the lower score would result in the misleading impression that many of the former are as poor as the latter.

Sometimes components are weighted implicitly, and no explicit weighting is necessary. An example is crime, which WoN divided into homicides and "other violent crimes" (rapes, robberies, assaults), which tend to be less consistently reported. This implicitly gave homicides a weight of 3 and the other violent crimes weights of 1 each.

A *weighted average* is used to combine components that are considered to be unequal in importance or in the quality and coverage of the indicators. The weight reflects the difference in importance or in quality and coverage. In WoN, for example, education was given twice the weight of communication because the quality of communication depends on education. Similarly, wild diversity was given twice the weight of domesticated diversity because the loss of a wild species is more significant than the loss of a livestock breed or crop variety.

A *veto* is used mainly under three circumstances. First, when good performance is essential in both components of a pair. Sometimes success in one component may be at the expense of failure in the other, and the veto ensures that only success in both is rewarded: for example, health and population, inflation and unemployment, and agricultural productivity and agricultural self-reliance. Sometimes the components are halves of a whole, and good performance in one alone does not get the job done: for example, safe water and basic sanitation, telephone accessibility and telephone reliability, land diversity and land quality, global atmosphere and local air quality.

Second, when inferior performance in one component outweighs superior performance—no matter how good—in all the others. Examples are air and water pollutants: dangerous levels of one substance are not made less dangerous by safe levels of the others.

Third, to avoid counting the same feature more than once when it is represented by more than one component. Elements and subelements may have to be represented by more than one indicator to ensure adequate coverage (see Table B1 and the section on indicators). For example, WoN had to use three indicators of food sufficiency: percentage of population with insufficient food, prevalence of stunting in children, and prevalence of low weight for age in children. These indicators measure different symptoms of the same feature: lack of food. Some countries were covered by all three, some by two, some by one. To prevent double-counting, WoN used only the lowest score.

All combining procedures used in WoN are summarized in Appendix D.

The dimensions are combined into two subsystem indices: the Human Wellbeing Index (HWI) and the Ecosystem Wellbeing Index (EWI). The HWI is the lower of *either* the unweighted average of four human dimensions (all except equity) *or* the unweighted average of all five human dimensions (including equity). Whereas the other human dimensions measure human conditions—health and population, wealth, knowledge and culture, and community—equity is a modifier, measuring how fairly those conditions are shared. When the HWI with equity is *higher* than the HWI without equity, it is a sign that human development is inadequate throughout society, and only deprivation is being shared. Hence the inclusion of equity makes conditions look rosier than they are. When the HWI with equity is *lower* than the HWI without equity, it shows that the relatively high standard of living revealed by the other dimensions is unfairly distributed. Thus the inclusion of equity gives a more realistic picture of human wellbeing overall. Accordingly, equity is included only when it does not raise the HWI.

Similarly, the EWI is the lower of *either* the unweighted average of four ecosystem dimensions (all except resource use) *or* the unweighted average of all five ecosystem dimensions (including resource use). The other ecosystem dimensions measure the state of land, water, air, and species and genes. But resource use is a modifier, measuring activities that alter the state of land, water, air, and species and genes. If the EWI with resource use is *higher* than the EWI without resource use, it is a sign that

the resource use indicators understate the impacts of these activities. Hence the inclusion of resource use makes the state of the environment look better than it is. If the EWI with resource use is *lower* than the EWI without resource use, it shows that the other ecosystem dimensions understate the impacts of resource uses. Thus the inclusion of resource use better reflects the actual state of the ecosystem. Accordingly, resource use is included only when it does not raise the EWI.

The Wellbeing Index (WI) is the point on the Barometer of Sustainability where the HWI and the EWI intersect (Figure B6). It is a graphic index, and a single number does not do it justice. Taking the lower of the HWI and EWI discounts either the state of the environment or the condition of people (whichever is higher). For example:

Society	HWI	EWI	Lower Score	Average Score
A	75	25	25	50.0
B	25	75	25	50.0
C	25	25	25	25.0

The lower number masks a crucial difference between Society A and Society B: while they have as far to go to achieve sustainability, A's priority is to improve the ecosystem, B's to improve the condition of people. Worse, the lower number suggests that Society C is in the same position as A and B, although it is much weaker, with both a depressed standard of living and an impoverished environment. While the average of the HWI and EWI also hides differences between Societies A and B, it has the merit of expressing the distance to sustainability. Although their paths will differ, A and B are equally far from sustainability. Society C, by contrast, with an average of 25.0, has much further to travel. Hence, when it is desirable to express the WI as a single number (for example, to rank performance), it is better to use the average. But bear in mind that the true WI is the juxtaposition of human and ecosystem wellbeing shown on the Barometer of Sustainability.

The Wellbeing/Stress Index (WSI) measures the ratio of human wellbeing to ecosystem stress. It is produced in two steps. First the EWI is subtracted from 100 to convert it into an Ecosystem Stress Index (ESI)—the reverse of the EWI. Then the HWI is divided by the ESI.

It is useful to know how to calculate scores and combine indicators manually, but when an assessment has to cope with many indicators and indicator combinations for many differentiation units, the work becomes extremely tedious and time-consuming. Fortunately, software called Combo is available to do it electronically. Combo calculates scores on the basis of the user's performance criteria and is a valuable tool for testing the effects of different criteria. Combo also combines indicator components on the basis of combining procedures and weights chosen by the user.[4]

Stage 6. Review Results and Propose Policies

The review links the assessment to action by:

- Analyzing the indicators and indices, the patterns of performance, and the data behind them.
- Determining the elements and areas where improvements are most needed.
- Proposing policies and actions to make the improvements.
- Planning the priority actions.
- Reviewing and revising policy, program, and project objectives and targets.

Participants examine links between indicators, patterns of performance, strengths, weaknesses, causal factors, opportunities, and obstacles. They analyze policy options for improving socioeconomic and environmental conditions, setting targets for the HWI, EWI, and WSI and for the dimensions and elements on which most progress could or should be made. They propose policies and actions (including new or revised sustainable development policies and action plans) to achieve the targets. The review also provides the diagnosis for designing programs and projects.

The Barometer of Sustainability provides a starting point, showing the HWI and EWI of each society being assessed (e.g., countries in a region, states or provinces in a country, communities in a district). By displaying each society's structure of wellbeing—the pattern of dimensions—it reveals the dimensions that most need improvement. These can be further analyzed to identify the elements and subelements requiring priority attention, how they are linked, the causes of the main problems, and what policies and actions are needed in response. The discussion in Chapter 4 illustrates the potential.

Supplement 1. Bellagio Principles for Assessing Sustainable Development

In 1996, the International Institute for Sustainable Development convened an international group of assessment specialists to draw up the Bellagio principles for assessing sustainable development.[5] The principles express a consensus on best practice for both the content and process of assessment. Their essential points are:

The content of assessment should:

1. Be guided by a clear vision of sustainable development and goals that define that vision.
2. Review the condition and trend of the whole system, its socioeconomic and ecological parts, and interactions between the parts.
3. Consider equity and disparities within the current population and between present and future generations.
4. Combine long-term and short-term views and cover distant as well as local impacts on people and ecosystems.
5. Adopt an explicit framework to link the vision and goals to indicators and focus on a limited number of issues and indicators.

The process of assessment should:

6. Use an accessible method, make the data available to all, and make explicit all judgments, assumptions, and uncertainties in data and interpretations.
7. Communicate effectively to its intended audience, using a simple structure and clear and plain language.
8. Involve key groups to ensure recognition of different values and decision makers to make the link to policies and action.
9. Be done regularly to determine trends and improve collective learning and decision making, adjusting goals, frameworks, and indicators as new insights are gained.
10. Be supported by improved local and national capacities for assessment and data collection, maintenance, and documentation.

Wellbeing Assessment satisfies principle 1 through stage 1 of the assessment cycle: define the system and goals.

It fulfills principle 2 through the framework's equal treatment of people and the ecosystem and its provision for measuring interactions between them. It accords with principle 3 through equal treatment of people and the ecosystem, which is designed to cover equity between present and future generations, and through the equity dimension, which covers equity within the current population.

Wellbeing Assessment does not oblige users to combine long-term and short-term views or cover both distant and local impacts (principle 4), but it provides ample scope for doing so. For example, WoN addresses immediate human needs and long-term requirements to maintain ecosystem diversity. It measures global and local impacts (such as global atmosphere and local air quality) and accounts for the effects of food and timber consumption on both domestic and external ecosystems.

Wellbeing Assessment meets principle 5 via the hierarchy from system and goals to indicators and performance criteria (stages 1 through 3). Although some technicalities are unavoidable, the method is designed to be as accessible as possible for people with little training in measurement and limited mathematical skills (principle 6). Throughout WoN, I have tried to make explicit all judgments, assumptions, and uncertainties. The structure of Wellbeing Assessment is simple (principle 7), and maps and the Barometer of Sustainability are designed for effective communication.

The remaining three principles are the responsibility of participants in particular assessments and the managers of national and local assessment systems. Regular global assessment of wellbeing is planned, including the production of updated and improved editions of WoN.

Supplement 2. Background of the Dimensions

The dimensions divide each subsystem into major components that meet five criteria:

- Limited in number (ideally four, certainly no more than five) because the fewer the components in an index, the stronger their effect.

- Equally important, allowing them to be combined into subsystem indices using unweighted averages (to keep the effect of each dimension on the HWI or EWI clear and simple).

- Specific enough to ensure that all assessments cover universally important aspects of human and ecosystem wellbeing.

- Broad and flexible enough to accommodate concerns common to all societies, without requiring or excluding coverage of issues that matter to some but not all.

- Easy to grasp—not dependent on a highly technical or abstract model of the human subsystem or the ecosystem—and simply expressed.

Fulfilling these criteria has been a challenge. Table B4

Table B4. Evolution of the dimensions of Wellbeing Assessment from the first draft of the Barometer of Sustainability (BoS) to the present version of *The Wellbeing of Nations* (WoN). The version is in parentheses: BoS drafts, April 1995 (BoS 95a), July 1995 (BoS 95b), 1996 (BoS 96); WoN drafts, 1997 (WoN 97), 1998 (WoN 98), 2000 (WoN 00).

Previous Dimensions	*Current Dimensions*
Human health (BoS 95a) →	Health and population (BoS 95b)
Access to resources (BoS 95a) ↓ Wealth and livelihood (BoS 96) →	Wealth (WoN 97)
Knowledge (BoS 95a) →	Knowledge and culture (WoN 98)
Institutions (BoS 95a) ↓ Behavior and institutions (BoS 95b) ↓ Freedom and order (WoN 97) →	Community (WoN 98)
Part of the other human dimensions (BoS 95a) →	Equity (BoS 96)
Part of ecosystem naturalness and ecosystem quality (BoS 95a) →	Land (BoS 96)
Part of ecosystem naturalness and ecosystem quality (BoS 95a) →	Water (BoS 96)
Part of ecosystem quality (BoS 95a) →	Air (BoS 96)
Biodiversity maintenance (BoS 95a) ↓ Biodiversity (BoS 96) ↓ Species and populations (WoN 98) →	Species and genes (WoN 00)
Resource conservation (BoS 95a) →	Resource use (BoS 96)

traces the evolution of the current set of five human and five ecosystem dimensions over the course of three drafts of the Barometer of Sustainability method (1995–1996) and three of *The Wellbeing of Nations* (1997–2000).

The four original human dimensions consisted of the three components of the Human Development Index (HDI)—human health, access to resources, and knowledge—plus institutions (not covered by the HDI).[6] Human health was soon expanded to health and population to cover both of these closely related concerns together. Access to resources was expanded to wealth and livelihood to cover all aspects of material and monetary wellbeing, later expressed more simply as wealth. Knowledge was eventually expanded to knowledge and culture to accommodate religious belief systems, societal values, the arts, and self- and community-expression—aspects neglected by assessments to date but for which undoubtedly there should be a place. Institutions was expanded to behavior and institutions to cover issues such as crime and conflict. The name was changed to freedom and order in an effort to clarify its scope. This was too limited, however, so the dimension was expanded to community to cover all aspects of governance, institutions, and community organization as well as human rights and interpersonal behavior (e.g., peace, crime). Equity was originally part of the other human dimensions but was distinguished as the fifth dimension to make it more visible.

The four original ecosystem dimensions were based on the three objectives of the *World Conservation Strategy:* maintenance of essential ecological processes and life-support systems, preservation of genetic diversity, and sustainable utilization of species and ecosystems.[7] Ecosystem naturalness and ecosystem quality corresponded to the first objective, biodiversity maintenance to the second, resource conservation to the third. This arrangement did not meet the criterion of "easy to grasp." Accordingly, ecosystem naturalness and ecosystem quality were replaced by three dimensions: land, water, and air. Biodiversity maintenance was simplified to biodiversity, and resource conservation to resource use. However, the new arrangement flouted the criterion "equally important." Putting ecosystem, species, and genetic diversity into one dimension—biodiversity—made it more important than any of the others while reducing the importance of land and water (since they could cover ecosystem quality but not the diversity of land and water ecosystems). Consequently,

biodiversity was split up by moving ecosystem diversity to land and water, and covering species and genetic diversity in a new dimension—species and populations—later renamed "species and genes" to clarify its scope.

Supplement 3. Assessment Frameworks

Methods of assessing human and environmental conditions differ chiefly in the frameworks they use to organize information (covered in this supplement) and in whether and how they combine indicators (the next supplement).

Most assessment frameworks are dual, triple, or quadruple (Figure B9). Wellbeing Assessment employs a dual framework, dividing the system into two equal subsystems: people and ecosystem. Dual frameworks are also used by the UN Environment Programme's Global Environment Outlook ("human system" and "environmental system"), the World Resources Institute's approach to measuring environmental policy performance ("human subsystem" and "environmental subsystem"), and several other methods.[8]

Triple frameworks include the World Bank's estimates of national wealth (discussed in Appendix A), which distinguish three kinds of capital: produced assets (economy), human resources (society), and natural capital (environment). Similarly, the Consultative Group on Sustainable Development Indicators divides its Dashboard of Sustainability into economic performance, social health, and environmental quality.[9]

The UN Commission on Sustainable Development uses a quadruple framework for reporting on implementation of Agenda 21, the action plan of the 1992 United Nations Conference on Environment and Development: economic aspects, social aspects, institutional aspects, and environmental aspects.[10]

These differences are not trivial: the more the human subsystem is divided, the less the weight of the environment (Figure B9). The dual framework gives people and the environment equal weight. The triple framework reduces the weight of the environment to a third; the quadruple framework reduces it to a quarter.

dual:	PEOPLE		ENVIRONMENT	
triple:	ECONOMY	SOCIETY	ENVIRONMENT	
quadruple:	ECONOMY	SOCIETY	INSTITUTIONS	ENVIRONMENT

Figure B9. Three frameworks for assessing sustainable development. The weight of the environment declines as the number of human domains increases.

Supplement 4. Common Units for Combining Indicators

Many assessment methods do not combine their indicators, preventing them from showing overall human and environmental conditions, revealing major performance patterns, or communicating results succinctly.

Those that do combine their indicators start by converting their disparate indicator measurements to a common unit. The unit is either a physical unit, money, or a performance score.

Physical units can combine only a limited range of things. Materials can be combined on the basis of their weight, but this does not account for their different impacts: a ton of arsenic is more of a problem than a ton of old lace. Pollutants with similar effects can be combined according to their potential for that effect: greenhouse gas emissions can be combined according to the contribution of each gas to global warming, and heavy metals on the basis of their toxicity. But pollutants with different effects cannot be combined in this way. Uses of energy and renewable resources can be converted into the area of productive land and sea required to supply the resources and absorb carbon dioxide from fossil fuels, but area is not a suitable unit for measuring air quality or genetic diversity.[11] No single physical unit has been found that could combine all indicators of ecosystem wellbeing, let alone of human wellbeing.

Money is standard in all economic accounts. It is also used in some environmental assessments, such as the cost of remediation (COR) index, a measure of the cost of moving from the present state of environment to a more desirable level.[12] However, it too has serious weaknesses. It reflects the market price of apples and oranges, not their taste, nutritional content, or cultural value. It can measure the value of things that are traded in the market, but it distorts the value of anything not traded. The less tradable the item, the greater the distortion. Most items in an assessment of wellbeing and sustainability have no market price, so nonmarket values must be estimated from contingent values (asking people how much they would pay for a benefit or how much compensation they would accept if deprived of the benefit) or from expenditures on avoiding and treating damage. Using these techniques together is like combining real apples (market values), fake apples (contingent values), real oranges (actual expenditures), and fake oranges (hypothetical expenditures).

Faced with the drawbacks of physical units and money, performance scores have an overwhelming advantage. They measure how good an orange is at being an orange and how good an apple is as an apple—the distance between a standard level of performance and the actual performance recorded by an indicator measurement. On a 0–100 scale, best performance is 100 and worst 0. A given apple or orange would receive a score according to how good it was in relation to best and worst. Performance criteria for apples and oranges may be very different, but since their scores are calculated in the same way on the same scale, the scores can be combined.

Performance scores allow use of whatever yardstick is most appropriate to the issue concerned: income and value added are measured in money, health in disease and death rates, employment in jobs, species diversity in percentages of threatened species, land degradation as erosion rates, and so forth. Distortion is negligible because the original units in which the indicator is measured are kept intact.

Judgment is required to decide performance criteria, but judgment is also needed when using physical units or money. When the indicators are closely related (as in the equivalent effects of pollutants or the weight of material), the judgment is not great. But when they are far apart (as in the monetary value of biodiversity, human life, security, or community harmony), the judgment required is considerable.

Supplement 5. Performance Scales

A performance scale—a scale for calculating performance scores—is set by defining *one end* of the scale (best performance), *both ends* (best and worst performance), the *midpoint* (average performance), or *bands* (both ends plus intermediate points). Definitions of these points are based either on *observed* performance (or a mixture of observed and expected performance) in a sample of societies or on *desired* performance, a specified objective (Table B5).

The Dutch Environmental Pressure index (EPI) is a *one-end* performance scale that combines compound indicators of six types of pollution (Table B6). A sustainability or no-major-effect level is defined for each type. The actual level of pollution is expressed as a percentage of the sustainability level, and the six percentages are added together to give a total index of environmental pressure. The scale goes from 0 (sustainability levels achieved for all issues) to more than 8,000 (the combined difference

Table B5. Classification of selected performance scales according to the points on the scale that are defined and on what basis.

What Is Defined → *On What Basis* ↓	*One End* (best performance)	*Both Ends* (best and worst performance)	*Midpoint* (average performance)	*Bands* (both ends + intermediate points)
Observed and expected performance		Human Development Index Environmental Sustainability Index	Development Diamond Environment Diamond	
Desired performance (objectives)	Environmental Pressure Index			Barometer of Sustainability

between the sustainability level and performance in 1985).[13]

The Human Development Index (HDI) combines indicators of longevity, education, and standard of living (income). *Both ends* of its 0–1 scale are defined. The bottom end (0) is the lowest observed performance over the past 30 years (in the HDI's sample of 174 countries) and the top end (1) is the highest expected performance in the next 30 years (Table B7). Each indicator measurement gets a score of 0 to 1 depending on where it falls in relation to the lowest and highest performance for that indicator. The indicators are combined by adding their scores and taking the average.[14]

The Environmental Sustainability Index (ESI) combines indicators of 22 factors (which are at the level of Wellbeing Assessment's elements). Like the HDI, both ends of its 0–100 scale are defined on the basis of the lowest and highest current performance for the indicator concerned.[15]

The development diamond exemplifies a scale for which the *midpoint* is defined. It has four axes, one for each indicator (Figure B10). The midpoint of each axis is defined as the average performance of a group of countries classified by income (high-income, upper-middle income, lower-middle income, low-income). The performance of a particular country is shown in relation to the average of its group. The indicators are combined visually by being displayed together but are not combined numerically. The Asian Development Bank's environment diamond is the same concept. Its four axes display compound indicators of air quality, water quality, land condition, and biodiversity. The performance of each of seven Asian countries is shown in relation to the average of the group.[16]

Polygons such as the development and environment diamonds can be effective at showing differences in performance among elements and indicators, but with one variable shown per axis (point of the polygon), they work

Table B6. Environmental Pressure Index: types of pollution and their sustainability or no-major-effect levels.

Compound Indicator: *Type of Pollution*	*Objective: Sustainability Level*
Greenhouse gases	Preindustrial levels (background rates)
Acidification	Level at which little damage occurs to vegetation on sensitive sites
Eutrophication	Soil: equilibrium fertilization (balance between nutrient addition and removal)
	Water: zero (nutrient carrying capacity already reached or exceeded)
Toxic substances	Maximum acceptable risk (national standard)
Solid waste disposal	As low as possible
Nuisance from noise and odor	As low as possible

Table B7. Human Development Index: indicators and their end points.

Element	*Indicator*	*Top End = 1*	*Bottom End = 0*
Longevity	Life expectancy at birth	85 years	25 years
Education	Adult literacy rate	100%	0%
	Combined gross enrollment rate	100%	0%
Standard of living	Real GDP per capita	PPP$40,000	PPP$100

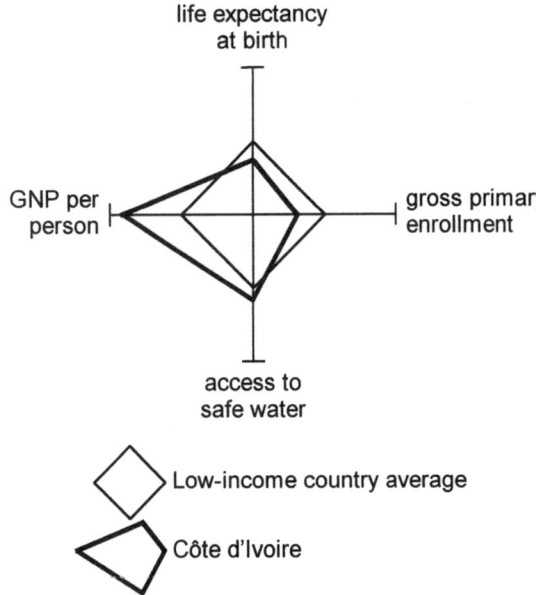

Figure B10. Example of a development diamond. Côte d'Ivoire has above average GNP per person and access to safe water, and below average life expectancy at birth and gross primary school enrollment, in relation to other low-income countries (World Bank 1995).

best when dealing with a few elements or indicators. (AMOEBA, used in the Dutch Water Management Plan, is a variable polygon with as many as 32 axes, which can be pretty confusing.)[17] Another drawback to polygons is that they are not convenient for showing change over time or the performance of more than one society per polygon.

The advantage of setting the scale on the basis of *observed* performance (as in the HDI and the development diamond) is that the range of past and present performance is a verifiable fact. The disadvantage is that the results merely show one society's performance in relation to others. It may be at the top, the bottom, or in the middle—but its rank is meaningless if everyone is doing well or badly. The Environmental Sustainability Index records where a country falls along a continuum of performance defined by the best-performing country at one end and the worst at the other; it does not show whether the best-performing country is close to sustainability or far from it.

Setting the scale on the basis of objectives or *desired* performance (as in the EPI and the Barometer of Sustainability) is more informative. The results can show not just whether a society is doing well or badly but how well or

badly—which also provides for a more meaningful comparison with other societies.

Notes

1. Requests for courses should be sent to Robert Prescott-Allen, PADATA, 627 Aquarius Road, Victoria, British Columbia, V9C 4G5, Canada; fax +1 250 474 6976; e-mail rpa@wellbeing-of-nations.ca. The training kit can be obtained from IUCN Monitoring & Evaluation Initiative, Rue Mauverney 28, Gland, 1196, Switzerland; fax +41 22 999 0025; phone +41 22 999 0001; e-mail mail@hq.iucn.org.

2. Colombia team: Natalia Ortiz and Hernando Sanchez, Monitoring and Evaluation Unit, Fundación Pro Sierra Nevada de Santa Marta. Zimbabwe teams: Sam Chimbuya and Carmel Luc-Mbizvo, IUCN Assessment Team, IUCN Regional Office for Southern Africa; Elliot Mhaka, Cephas Chidenga, Douglas Chimhande, Joseph Chizororo, Peter Gambara, Davison Haukozi, Zii Masiye, John Mbetu, Peter Mfumu, John Mupingo, Constantine Mushure, Aaaron Tshabangu, and Unity Tshabangu, District Environmental Action Plan (DEAP) Core Team, Government of Zimbabwe. India team: Ashok Kumar, Vijay Pillay, V. A. Abraham, Subash Marcus, and George Varughese, Development Alternatives.

3. Italy's regions, provinces, and municipalities: Touring Club Italiano (1993).

4. At present Combo is available only in a 16-bit version, which does not work with all 32-bit applications, although it works well with the 32-bit version of Map Maker (Appendix E). Combo can be obtained from IUCN or from me (see note 1 for contact details). Improved software, called Wellbeing Barometers, is being developed.

5. Hardi & Zdan (1977). Requests for copies of the Bellagio principles should be sent to the International Institute for Sustainable Development (IISD), 161 Portage East, 6th Floor, Winnipeg, Manitoba, R3B 0Y4, Canada; fax +1 204 958 7710; e-mail: reception@iisdpost.iisd.ca.

6. UNDP (1990, 1994).

7. IUCN/UNEP/WWF (1980).

8. UNEP GEO model: Bakkes & van Woerden (1997), Swart & Bakkes (1995). World Resources Institute (WRI) approach: Hammond et al. (1995). Other methods: Corson (1996) uses a pair of indices—environmental sustainability (ecosystem) and socioeconomic sustainability (people)—to assess the sustainability of ten industrial nations. Hodge (1995) divides his essentially dual framework (people and ecosystems) into four domains: people, interactions between people and ecosystems, ecosystems, and synthesis.

9. Consultative Group on Sustainable Development Indicators (2000).
10. United Nations (1996).
11. Equivalent effects: Adriaanse (1993). Weight: Adriaanse et al. (1997). Area and Ecological Footprint (discussed further in Chapter 3): Wackernagel & Rees (1996); Wackernagel et al. (2000).
12. Appendix A describes economic accounts. The cost of remediation index adds the estimated costs of targets for reductions in pollution, erosion, waste generation, etc.:

Harvard University Environmental Systems Program (1996).
13. Adriaanse (1993).
14. UNDP (1990, 1994, 1997, 2000).
15. Global Leaders for Environment Tomorrow Task Force (2001).
16. Development diamond: World Bank (1998). Environment diamond: Harvard University Environmental Systems Program (1996).
17. Bakkes et al. (1994).

Appendix C.
Performance Criteria Chosen for *The Wellbeing of Nations*

In Wellbeing Assessment, performance criteria are chosen for each indicator to make the indicators more operational and to enable indicator measurements to be converted to a score so that they can be combined. Choosing performance criteria involves defining the levels of performance for the indicator concerned that correspond to the base and the tops of the bands of the Barometer of Sustainability (Table C1).

This appendix describes the types of performance criteria chosen for *The Wellbeing of Nations* (WoN) and the basis for selecting them. Table C2 gives examples of each type and the number of indicators per type. Table C3 gives examples of each basis for selection and the number of indicators per basis. Tables C4 (human indicators) and C5 (ecosystem indicators) list all the performance criteria and classify them by type and basis.

Table C1. The five-band scale of the Barometer of Sustainability.
Performance criteria define levels of performance that correspond to the base of the scale and the top of each band.

Band	Range of Points	Top Point	Definition of Band
Good	100–81	100	Desirable performance, objective fully met
Fair	80–61	80	Acceptable performance, objective almost or barely met
Medium	60–41	60	Neutral or transitional performance
Poor	40–21	40	Undesirable performance
Bad	20–1	20	Unacceptable performance
Base	0	0	Base of scale

Types of Performance Criteria

Indicators can be classified in five performance groups:

1. *Best possible performance is 0, 100%, or parity.* Examples are homicide rate (0), percentage of population with safe water and basic sanitation (100%), and female share of income (parity). What must be decided here is how far from best possible good performance becomes merely fair performance and at what point fair becomes medium.

2. *No limit to best possible performance but worst possible is 0 or 100%.* Examples are income ($0) and dissolved oxygen in running waters (100% saturation). What must be decided here is how far from worst possible bad performance becomes poor performance and at what point poor becomes medium.

3. *A sustainable level can be defined, on both sides of which conditions are unsustainable.* An example is the total fertility rate (TFR, the average number of children born alive by a woman in her lifetime). In this case, the sustainable rate is the replacement rate, or 2.1 (with average sex ratios). Populations will grow if their TFRs are above this rate and will decline if they are below it.

4. *A sustainable level can be defined, on only one side of which conditions are unsustainable.* An example is timber fellings as a percentage of net annual increment. In this case, the sustainable rate is 100% or (using the precautionary principle) less than 100%. If fellings are much less than 100% no harm is done because the forest will eventually reach a natural state with a high proportion of old trees.

5. *A range of good or bad performance can be broadly
defined,* but no definite best possible, worst possible,
or sustainable level. An example is energy consumption per person.

For many indicators it is useful for the performance
criteria to increase or decline exponentially (in doublings)
from the best point to reflect the increasing difficulty of
improving performance as one approaches the ideal. An
example is the threatened species indicator. Conversely, in
a number of cases it makes sense for the performance criteria to increase or decline exponentially from the worst
point to reflect diminishing returns (for example, income
per person).

An exponential scale also accommodates a wide range
of performance while keeping high standards for the
good and fair bands. For example, child mortality rates
range from 263 to 6 deaths per 1,000 live births. The
United Nations (UN) target is for all countries to have
rates below 45 deaths by 2015. An exponential scale
from 0 to 360 accommodates the current range of performance and puts 45 at the top of the medium band, so
that less than 45 is fair and half of 45 is good. A scale
with bands of equal size could not do this. If it kept 45
at the top of medium, the base of the scale would be
112.5 deaths, which would exclude the performance of
44 countries. If the base of an equally divided scale were
set at 265 to accommodate the current range of performance, the top of medium would rise to 106, and even the
top of fair (at 53) would be worse performance than the
UN target of 45.

Because of these advantages, WoN performance
criteria are exponential except when bands are set at levels that make an exponential scale unnecessary, impractical, or excessively long. An example is life expectancy at
birth. The range of current and projected performance is
34–84 years. UN targets are for countries to achieve 60
years by 2000, over 70 years by 2005, and over 75 years
by 2015. If best is set at 85 years and the targets of 60,
70, and 75 years are used to define the tops of poor,
medium, and fair respectively, an exponential scale is
unnecessary.

In all, 10 types of performance criteria can be distinguished (Table C2), depending on which performance
group the indicator is in and whether the criteria change
exponentially.

Basis for Choosing Performance Criteria

In Wellbeing Assessment, the base of the scale and the
tops of the bands are defined on the basis of three factors:

The range of performance. As a general rule, base–best
(0–100) should encompass the range of performance.
However, if outliers of extreme performance would distort the scale, it can be cut off (at the bottom or at the
top). For example, the scale for the indicator "tons of fertilizer per 1,000 harvested hectares" was cut off at 320
tons to prevent distortion by a few countries that use very
much higher levels (up to 2,426 tons). In WoN, to prevent arbitrary shortening of the scale, base–best encompassed the range of performance of more than 90% of the
countries in all cases except fecal coliforms.

The objective of the element concerned. For example, the
objective of the peace and order element is "peaceful
communities, protected from crime and violence," implying an absence of armed conflict and low levels of military expenditure and violent crime. This guided the setting of the good and fair bands of the peace and crime
indicators.

At least one of the following:

A. *Estimated sustainable rate.* For example, a sustainable
rate of timber felling would be less than 100% of net
annual increment. In WoN, estimated sustainable
rates were usually placed at the top of the medium
band (rather than at the top of the fair band) for two
reasons. First, to comply with the precautionary principle that use levels should be well within the calculated capacity of the target population and its supporting ecosystem. Second, to ensure that if local
conditions call for a different rate, it is still likely to
be sustainable. For example, a sustainable rate of 4
tons of fish catch per ton of fishing capacity was
derived from an estimate of global maximum sustainable yield (MSY). The MSY of a national fishery
could be substantially lower or higher. Putting the
global rate at the top of medium ensured that a catch
that exceeded a lower national MSY would not
receive a good score.

B. *Estimated background rate* ("natural" or "normal" performance). For example, the background rate of
human-caused land degradation is 0. In WoN, esti-

mated background rates were usually placed at best, with the top of fair placed fairly close. In the case of land degradation, best was defined as 0% and the top of fair as 10%.

C. *Other threshold.* For example, a single death represents the threshold between peace and armed conflict.

D. *International standard.* For example, a UN standard for water quality is less than 30 milligrams of nitrogen per liter of water. In WoN, international standards were placed at best, the top of fair, or the top of medium, depending on the range of current performance. If a standard covers different levels of performance, these levels were placed at the tops of the appropriate bands. Thus the international standards for inland water quality define pollutant levels for excellent, good, fair, poor, and bad water quality classes. These were adopted to define the good, fair, medium, poor, and bad bands, respectively.

E. *International target.* For example, a UN target for education is 100% primary education by 2015. In WoN, international targets were placed at best, the top of fair, or the top of medium, depending on how ambitious they are. Targets such as universal primary education and elimination of ozone depleting substances cannot be bettered and formed the top of the good band. The ambitiousness of less absolute targets were judged from the range of performance: if few societies exceed them, they were put at the top of the fair band; if many, at the top of the medium band. Sometimes, however, other considerations prevailed: international targets set the top of the fair band of three of WoN's food sufficiency indicators but the top of the medium band of the fourth to aid interpretation by enabling the performance criteria of all four indicators to match.

F. *Expert opinion.* For example, the World Bank's classification of debt ratios and Freedom House's rating of press freedom.

G. *Derivation from a related indicator.* For example, in the absence of a specific UN target, the performance criteria for secondary education are a less stringent version of those for primary education.

H. *Personal judgment.* If none of the above factors is available, the bands are defined on the basis of personal judgment.

Table C2. WoN performance criteria by type. There are 10 types, depending on the indicator performance group and whether the scale is exponential or nonexponential.

Indicator Performance Group	1. Exponential Scale		2. Nonexponential Scale	
	No. of Indicators	Example	No. of Indicators	Example
1. Best possible performance is 0, 100%, or parity	23	Homicides per 100,000 population	29	Women's share of seats in parliament
2. Worst possible performance is 0 or 100%	4	Tertiary school enrollment	3	Dissolved oxygen in inland waters
3. Sustainable level, both sides of which are unsustainable	0	—	1	Total fertility rate
4. Sustainable level, one side of which is unsustainable	4	Annual change in native forest area	2	Timber fellings + imports as a percentage of net annual increment
5. Range of good or bad performance	6	Energy consumption per person	15	Life expectancy at birth
TOTAL	37	—	50	—

Table C3. WoN performance criteria by basis for selection (in addition to the range of performance and the objective of the element concerned).

Basis for Selection	No. of Indicators	Example
A. Estimated sustainable rate	7	Tons of catch per ton of fishing fleet capacity
B. Estimated background rate	3	Degraded land as a percentage of total cultivated + modified land
C. Other threshold	6	Deaths from armed conflict
D. International standard	21	Annual mean ambient air concentration of sulfur dioxide
E. International target	13	Life expectancy at birth
F. Expert opinion	6	Press freedom rating
G. Derivation from related indicator	6	Food production as a percentage of supply (derived from food sufficiency indicators)
H. Personal judgment	25	Ratio of richest 20%'s income share to poorest 20%'s
TOTAL	87	—

Table C4. Performance criteria for human indicators used in *The Wellbeing of Nations*.

Indicator	Unit	Base	Top of Bad	Top of Poor	Top of Medium	Top of Fair	Top of Good	Type of Performance Criteria and Basis for Selection
Life expectancy at birth	years	30	45	60	70	75	85	Type: 5.2. Basis: E. Base–best encompasses current range of 34–81 years and projected high of 84 years by 2050. Tops of poor, medium, and fair match UN targets of at least 60 years by 2000, >70 years by 2005, >75 years by 2015.
Healthy life expectancy at birth	years	24	39	54	64	69	79	Type: 5.2. Basis: G. Base–best encompasses current range of 26–75 years. Base and tops of poor, medium, fair, and good set at 6 points (or 7.1–20.0%) below the corresponding points for unadjusted life expectancy, close to the range of percentages of lifespan lost to disability (7.0–25.1%).
Child mortality rate [included for comparison but not counted as an indicator]	deaths/ 1,000 live births	360	180	90	45	22	0	Type 1.1. Basis: E. Base–best encompasses current range of 263–6 deaths. Top of medium matches UN target of <45 deaths by 2015.
Total fertility rate	children/ woman	8.2	5.0	3.4	2.6	2.2	1.2	Type: 3.2. Basis: A. Base–best encompasses current range of 7.6–1.2 children. Top of fair is a point below the replacement rate of 2.1 children.
Population with insufficient food	%	100	50	35	20	10	0	Type: 1.2. Basis: E. Base–best encompasses current range of 73–1%. Top of fair matches World Food Summit target to halve the number of hungry people by 2015.
Prevalence of stunting (low height for age) in children under 5	%	100	50	35	20	10	0	Type: 1.2. Basis: E. Base–best encompasses current range of 64–1%. Top of medium matches WHO target of <20% by 2020.
Prevalence of underweight (low weight for age) children under 5	%	100	50	35	20	10	0	Type: 1.2. Basis: E. Base–best encompasses current range of 60–1%. Top of fair matches WHO target of not more than 10%.
Prevalence of babies with low birth weight	%	100	50	35	20	10	0	Type: 1.2. Basis: E. Base–best encompasses current range of 50–2%. Top of fair matches WHO target of not more than 10%.
Population with safe water and basic sanitation	%	0	50	65	80	90	100	Type: 1.2. Basis: E. Base–best encompasses current range of 3–100%. Best matches UN target of 100%.
Gross domestic product per person	$PPP	0	2,000	5,000	10,000	20,000	40,000	Type: 2.2. Basis: C. Base–best encompasses current range of PPP$460–33,505. Bands are based on the relationship between income and health, population, knowledge, and community.
Annual inflation rate	%	60	35	10	6	3	0	Type: 5.2. Basis: E. Current range is +1,005 to –2%. Base–best encompasses performance of 91% of countries. Tops of good and fair match the range of official inflation targets. Top of poor reflects the consensus that inflation of 10% or more is harmful.

Indicator	Unit	Base	Top of Bad	Top of Poor	Top of Medium	Top of Fair	Top of Good	Type of Performance Criteria and Basis for Selection
Annual unemployment rate	%	35	25	15	10	5	0	Type: 5.2. Basis: G. Current range is 72.5–0.4%. Base–best encompasses performance of 98% of countries. The tops of fair and medium are somewhat above the equivalent points for inflation.
Present value of debt service as a percentage of exports of goods and services	%	440	220	132	66	33	0	Type: 1.2. Basis: F. Current range is 3,090–14%. Base–best encompasses performance of 91% of countries. Tops of bad and poor match the points at which the World Bank classifies a country as severely and moderately indebted, respectively.
Present value of debt service as a percentage of gross national product	%	160	80	48	24	12	0	Type: 1.2. Basis: F. Current range is 678–3%. Base–best encompasses performance of 93% of countries. Tops of bad and poor match the points at which the World Bank classifies a country as severely and moderately indebted, respectively.
Ratio of short-term debt to international reserves	ratio	8.0	4.0	2.0	1.0	0.5	0.0	Type: 1.2. Basis: C. Current range is 4,914–0. Base–best encompasses performance of 93% of countries. Top of medium is the benchmark suggested by the International Monetary Fund for the reverse indicator (ratio of international reserves to short-term debt) and in poorly regulated markets is the point above which a country is vulnerable to creditor panic.
Gross public debt (general government gross financial liabilities) as a percentage of gross domestic product	%	151	121	91	61	31	1	Type: 5.2. Basis: E. Base–best encompasses current range of 118.8–6.0%. Top of medium matches the Treaty of Maastricht's standard of no more than 60% for an acceptable ratio of public debt to GDP.
Annual central government deficit/surplus as a percentage of gross domestic product	%	–12.1	–9.1	–6.1	–3.1	–0.1	2.9	Type: 5.2. Basis: E. Current range is –15.1 to +11.7%. Base–best encompasses performance of 92% of countries. Top of medium matches the Treaty of Maastricht's standard of no more than 3% for an acceptable budget deficit.
Net primary school enrollment	% of age group	20	60	80	90	95	100	Type: 1.1. Basis: E. Current range is 13.2–99.9%. Base–best encompasses performance of 99% of countries. Best matches UN target of 100% by 2015.
Net secondary school enrollment	% of age group	0	30	60	80	90	100	Type: 1.2. Basis: G. Base–best encompasses current range of 8.0–99.9%. In the absence of a target, top of fair is set less stringently than for primary enrollment.
Tertiary school enrollment	per 10,000 population	0	35	70	140	280	560	Type: 2.1. Basis: C. Current range is 2.6–610.6 per 10,000. Base–best encompasses performance of 98% of countries. Good is set to include the lowest rates of countries with the largest proportions of highly literate adults.
Main telephone lines and cellular phones per 100 persons	%	0	6	12	25	50	100	Type: 2.1. Basis: H. Current range is 0.1–113.8%. Base–best encompasses performance of 98% of countries. Top of fair is point at which, in general, 95% of households have a main line.
Faults per 100 main telephone lines	%	200	100	50	25	12	0	Type: 1.1 Basis: H. Current range is 761.0–1.1%. Base–best encompasses performance of 97% of countries. Top of bad set at 1 fault/line/year.
Internet users	per 10,000 population	0	75	150	300	600	1,200	Type: 2.1. Basis: H. Current range is 0–3,953. Base–best encompasses performance of 92% of countries.

Indicator	Unit	Base	Top of Bad	Top of Poor	Top of Medium	Top of Fair	Top of Good	Type of Performance Criteria and Basis for Selection
Political rights rating	points	0	20	40	60	80	100	Type: 5.2. Basis: F. Base–best encompasses current range of 0–90 points. Freedom House points put on Barometer scale so that "free" = good or fair, "partly free" = medium, and "not free" = poor or bad.
Civil liberties rating	points	0	20	40	60	80	100	Type: 5.2. Basis: F. Base–best encompasses current range of 0–90 points. Freedom House points put on Barometer scale on same basis as political rights rating.
Press freedom rating	points	100	75	50	30	15	0	Type: 5.2. Basis: F. Base–best encompasses current range of 100–15. Freedom House points put on Barometer scale on same basis as political rights rating.
Corruption perceptions index	points	0	2	4	6	8	10	Type: 1.2. Basis: F. Base–best encompasses current range of 1.2–10 points. Transparency International's scale placed directly on the Barometer scale.
Deaths from armed conflicts per year	number	10,000	1,000	0	--	--	--	Type: 1.2. Basis: C. Current range is 84,100–0 deaths. Base–best encompasses performance of 90% of countries. Bands set so that any armed conflict results in at least a poor score.
Military expenditure as a percentage of gross domestic product	%	32	16	8	4	2	0	Type: 1.1. Basis: H. Current range is 35.8–0.5%. Base–best encompasses performance of 99% of countries.
Homicides	per 100,000 population	80	40	20	10	5	0	Type: 1.1. Basis: H. Current range is 142–0.4 homicides/100,000. Base–best encompasses performance of 97% of countries.
Rapes	per 100,000 population	160	80	40	20	10	0	Type: 1.1. Basis: H. Current range is 199–0 rapes/100,000. Base–best encompasses performance of 99% of countries.
Robberies	per 100,000 population	320	160	80	40	20	0	Type: 1.1. Basis: H. Current range is 688–0.1 robberies/100,000. Base–best encompasses performance of 97% of countries.
Assaults	per 100,000 population	640	320	160	80	40	0	Type: 1.1. Basis: H. Current range is 1,487–0.2/assaults per 100,000. Base–best encompasses performance of 91% of countries.
Ratio of richest 20%'s income share to poorest 20%'s	ratio	33:1	17:1	9:1	5:1	3:1	1:1	Type: 1.1. Basis: H. Base–best encompasses current range of 32.5:1–2.6:1.
Ratio of male income to female income	ratio	9:1	5:1	3:1	2:1	1.5:1	1:1	Type: 1.1. Basis: H. Base–best encompasses current range of 6.2:1–1.2:1.
Average difference between male and female school enrollment rates	%	80	40	20	10	5	0	Type: 1.1. Basis: E. Current range is 170.7–0%. Base–best encompasses performance of 98% of countries. Best matches UN target of 0% by 2005.
Women's share of seats in parliament	%	0	10	20	30	40	50	Type: 1.2. Basis: H. Base–best encompasses current range of 0–36.8%.

Table C5. Performance criteria for ecosystem indicators used in *The Wellbeing of Nations*.

Indicator	Unit	Base	Top of Bad	Top of Poor	Top of Medium	Top of Fair	Top of Good	Type of Performance Criteria and Basis for Selection
Converted land as a percentage of total land	%	100	80	60	40	20	0	Type: 5.2. Basis: C. Base–best encompasses current range of 75.5–0.7%. Top of medium is based on the landscape pattern theory that habitat becomes dissected into isolated patches below 60% coverage (= 40% converted).
Natural land as a percentage of total land	%	0	20	40	60	80	100	Type: 5.2. Basis: C. Base–best encompasses current range of 0.0–94.0%. Top of medium is set on same basis as converted land.
Annual change in native forest area	%	–5.7	–2.5	–0.9	–0.1	0.0	0.8	Type: 4.1. Basis: A. Current range is –7.4 to +0.7%. Base–best encompasses performance of 98% of countries. Tops of fair and medium have been set so that an increase in forest area gets a good score and only stability or a decline of less than 0.05% gets a fair score.
Protected land (+ inland waters) as a percentage of total land (+ inland waters)	weighted %	0	2.5	5	10	20	40	Type: 2.1. Basis: E. Current range is 0–67.5 weighted %. Base–best encompasses performance of 97% of countries. Top of medium matches international target of full protection of 10% of each major ecosystem type.
Degraded land as a percentage of cultivated + modified land	weighted %	160	80	40	20	10	0	Type: 1.1. Basis: B. Base–best encompasses current range of 0–150 weighted %. Best matches the background rate of human-induced soil degradation on natural land.
Dam capacity as a percentage of total water supply	%	100	60	40	20	10	0	Type: 1.2. Basis: H. Current range is 279–0%. Base–best encompasses performance of 91% of countries.
Flow dammed for hydropower as a percentage of dammable flow	%	100	60	40	20	10	0	Type: 1.2. Basis: H. Base–best encompasses current range of 100–0%.
Dissolved oxygen in inland waters	mg/l	1	3	4	6	9	12	Type: 2.2. Basis: B and D. Current range is 0.0–15.5 mg/l. Base–best encompasses performance at 98% of stations. Best and top of fair correspond to the range for 100% oxygen saturation of natural running waters. Tops of medium, poor, and bad match UNECE quality classes.
Biochemical oxygen demand (BOD)	mg O_2/l	30	15	9	5	3	0	Type: 1.2. Basis: D. Current range is 78.0–0.0 mg/l. Base–best encompasses performance at 99% of stations. Tops of fair, medium, poor, and bad match UNECE quality classes.
Chemical oxygen demand (COD)	mg O_2/l	60	30	20	10	3	0	Type: 1.2. Basis: D. Current range is 220.0–2.0 mg/l. Base–best encompasses performance at 94% of stations. Tops of fair, medium, poor, and bad match UNECE quality classes.
Nitrogen in inland waters	mg N/l	25.0	2.50	1.50	0.75	0.30	0	Type: 1.2. Basis: D. Current range is 63.7–0.00 mg/l. Base–best encompasses performance at 99% of stations. Tops of fair, medium, poor, and bad match UNECE quality classes.
Phosphorus in inland waters	mg P/l	1.25	0.125	0.050	0.025	0.010	0	Type: 1.2. Basis: D. Current range is 2.085–0.00 mg/l. Base–best encompasses performance at 98% of stations. Tops of fair, medium, poor, and bad match UNECE quality classes.
Alkalinity of inland waters	mg $CaCO_3$/l	0	10	20	100	200	400	Type: 2.2. Basis: D. Current range is 0.0–429.8 mg/l. Base–best encompasses performance at 98% of stations. Tops of fair, medium, poor, and bad match UNECE quality classes.
Acidity of inland waters	pH	4.5	5.3	6.0	6.3	6.5	8.5	Type: 5.2. Basis: D. Current range is 5.9–8.8. Base–best encompasses performance at 97% of stations. Best and tops of fair, medium, poor, and bad match UNECE quality classes.

Indicator	Unit	Base	Top of Bad	Top of Poor	Top of Medium	Top of Fair	Top of Good	Type of Performance Criteria and Basis for Selection
Total suspended solids in inland waters	mg/l	2,000	1,000	500	250	125	0	Type: 5.1. Basis: D. Current range is 8,470–0 mg/l. Base–best encompasses performance at 98% of stations. Top of bad is point at which water quality is seriously reduced.
Fecal coliforms in inland waters	number/ 100 ml	10,000	1,000	100	30	10	0	Type: 5.2. Basis: D. Current range is 1,100,000–0/100 ml. Base–best encompasses performance at 78% of stations. Tops of fair, medium, poor, and bad match UNECE quality classes.
Arsenic in inland waters	micrograms (µg)/l	200	100	50	10	5	0	Type: 1.2. Basis: D. Current range is 428–1 µg/l. Base–best encompasses performance at 99% of stations. Tops of medium, poor, and bad match UNECE quality classes.
Cadmium in inland waters	µg/l	18.0	1.8	0.7	0.07	0.03	0	Type: 1.2. Basis: D. Current range is 37.0–0.01 µg/l. Base–best encompasses performance at 94% of stations. Tops of medium, poor, and bad match UNECE quality classes.
Chromium in inland waters	µg/l	80	16	11	1	0.5	0	Type: 1.2. Basis: D. Current range is 551–0 µg/l. Base–best encompasses performance at 98% of stations. Tops of medium, poor, and bad match UNECE quality classes.
Copper in inland waters	µg/l	92	9.2	6.5	2	1	0	Type: 1.2. Basis: D. Current range is 214.0–0.2 µg/l. Base–best encompasses performance at 99% of stations. Tops of medium, poor, and bad match UNECE quality classes.
Lead in inland waters	µg/l	68	34	1.3	0.1	0.05	0	Type: 1.2. Basis: D. Current range is 194.0–0.1 µg/l. Base–best encompasses performance at 93% of stations. Tops of medium, poor, and bad match UNECE quality classes.
Mercury in inland waters	µg/l	2.5	2.4	0.012	0.003	0.002	0	Type: 1.2. Basis: D. Current range is 5.426–0.000 µg/l. Base–best encompasses performance at 99% of stations. Tops of medium, poor, and bad match UNECE quality classes.
Nickel in inland waters	µg/l	800	790	88	15	7.5	0	Type: 1.2. Basis: D. Base–best encompasses current range of 129–1 µg/l. Tops of medium, poor, and bad match UNECE quality classes.
Zinc in inland waters	µg/l	260	65	59	45	22	0	Type: 1.2. Basis: D. Current range is 1,154–1 µg/l. Base–best encompasses performance at 97% of stations. Tops of medium, poor, and bad match UNECE quality classes.
Water withdrawal as a percentage of internal renewable supply	%	200	100	50	20	10	0	Type: 4.2. Basis: A. Current range is 54,000–0%. Base–best encompasses performance of 91% of countries. Top of bad matches a point that is clearly unsustainable.
Carbon dioxide emissions per person	kg carbon	6,400	3,200	1,600	800	400	0	Type: 4.1. Basis: A and B. Current range is 18,197–0 kg. Base–best encompasses performance of 98% of countries. Top of fair matches the point below which carbon emissions per person must fall to keep atmospheric concentrations at less than double the preindustrial level.
Use of ozone depleting substances (ODSs) per person	g ozone depleting potential	400	200	100	50	25	0	Type: 1.1. Basis: B and E. Current range is 2,413–0 g. Base–best encompasses performance of 98% of countries. Best matches international agreements to eliminate ODSs.
Annual mean ambient air concentration of sulfur dioxide	µg/m³	400	200	100	50	25	0	Type: 1.1. Basis: D. Base–best encompasses current range of 330–0 µg/m³. Top of medium matches WHO guideline. Top of poor matches lowest observed effect level.

Indicator	Unit	Base	Top of Bad	Top of Poor	Top of Medium	Top of Fair	Top of Good	Type of Performance Criteria and Basis for Selection
Days ambient air concentration of sulfur dioxide exceeds WHO guideline	number	224	112	56	28	14	0	Type: 1.1. Basis: H. Base–best encompasses current recorded range of 64–0 days.
Annual mean ambient air concentration of nitrogen dioxide	µg/m³	320	160	80	40	20	0	Type: 1.1. Basis: D. Base–best encompasses current range of 248.4–2.3 µg/m³. Top of medium matches WHO guideline.
Days ambient air concentration of nitrogen dioxide exceeds WHO guideline	number	224	112	56	28	14	0	Type: 1.1. Basis: H. Base–best encompasses current recorded range of 160–0 days.
Days ambient air concentration of ozone exceeds WHO guideline	number	224	112	56	28	14	0	Type: 1.1. Basis: H. Current range is 309–0 days. Base–best encompasses performance at 94% of stations.
Days ambient air concentration of carbon monoxide exceeds WHO guideline	number	224	112	56	28	14	0	Type: 1.1. Basis: H. Base–best encompasses current range of 50–0 days.
Annual mean ambient air concentration of suspended particulate matter (SPM)	µg/m³	720	360	180	90	45	0	Type: 1.1. Basis: D. Base–best encompasses current range of 543–9.4 µg/m³. Top of medium matches WHO guideline.
Annual mean ambient air concentration of fine particulates 10 micrometers or less in diameter (PM10)	µg/m³	400	200	100	50	25	0	Type: 1.1. Basis: H. Current range is 544–4 µg/m³. Base–best encompasses performance at 99% of stations. Tops of fair and medium represent 2% and 4% increases in daily mortality from PM10, respectively.
Annual mean ambient air concentration of lead	µg/m³	4	2	1	0.5	0.25	0	Type: 1.1. Basis: D. Base–best encompasses current range of 2.7–0.0 µg/m³. Top of medium matches WHO guideline.
Threatened species in a group as a percentage of total species in that group: plants	%	32	16	8	4	2	0	Type: 1.1. Basis: B. Current range is 43.0–0.7%. Base–best encompasses performance of 91% of countries. Top of fair based on estimated background extinction rate of <0.01% per century.
Threatened species in a group as a percentage of total species in that group: animals	%	32	16	8	4	2	0	Type: 1.1. Basis: B. Current range is 68.5–0.8%. Base–best encompasses performance of 96% of countries. Top of fair based on estimated background extinction rate of <0.01% per century.

Indicator	Unit	Base	Top of Bad	Top of Poor	Top of Medium	Top of Fair	Top of Good	Type of Performance Criteria and Basis for Selection
Number of not-at-risk breeds per million head of a species	number	0	1	2	5	10	20	Type: 5.2. Basis: H. Current range is 0.1–63.5. Base–best encompasses performance of 99% of countries.
Ratio of threatened to not-at-risk breeds of a species	ratio	2.0	1.0	0.5	0.2	0.1	0.0	Type: 5.2. Basis: H. Current range is 3.5:1–0.0:1. Base–best encompasses performance of 98% of countries.
Energy consumption per hectare of total area	gigajoules (GJ)	640	320	160	80	40	0	Type: 5.1. Basis: H. Current range is 16,725.8–0.3 GJ. Base–best encompasses performance of 96% of countries.
Energy consumption per person	GJ	640	320	160	80	40	0	Type: 5.1. Basis: H. Current range is 1,294.2–1.6 GJ. Base–best encompasses performance of 99% of countries.
Food produced per harvested hectare	metric tons	0	1	2	4	8	16	Type: 5.1. Basis: H. Current range is 0.3–56.3 mt. Base–best encompasses performance of 95% of countries.
Fertilizer consumed per 1,000 harvested hectares	metric tons	320	160	80	40	20	0	Type: 5.1. Basis: H. Current range is 2,425.7–0.1 mt. Base–best encompasses performance of 96% of countries.
Food production as a percentage of supply	%	0	50	65	80	90	100	Type: 1.2. Basis: G. Base–best encompasses current range of 1–100%. Criteria mirror those for food sufficiency.
Depleted + overexploited fishery species as a percentage of assessed species	%	100	50	35	20	10	0	Type: 1.2. Basis: G. Base–best encompasses current range of 100–0%. Tops of fair and medium set at five times those for the threatened wild species indicators.
Tons of fishing fleet capacity per km² of continental shelf and/or inland water area	tons	8	4	2	1	0.5	0	Type: 4.1. Basis: A. Current range is 17.8–0 tons. Base–best encompasses performance of 98% of countries. Top of medium matches estimated capacity/area needed to catch estimated global maximum sustainable yield with current technology.
Tons of catch per ton of fishing fleet capacity	tons	0	1	2	4	8	16	Type: 4.1. Basis: A. Current range is 0.02–44.4 tons. Base–best encompasses performance of 98% of countries. Top of medium matches estimated global maximum sustainable yield.
Fish production as a percentage of supply	%	0	50	65	80	90	100	Type: 1.2. Basis: G. Base–best encompasses current range of 1–100%. Criteria mirror those for food sufficiency.
Timber fellings + imports as a percentage of net annual increment (NAI)	%	211	131	111	101	81	1	Type: 4.2. Basis: A. Current range is 5,300–6%. Base–best encompasses performance of 90% of countries. Top of medium ensures that only felling + import rates at or below NAI receive a fair score.
Timber production + imports as a percentage of volume	%	32	16	8	4	2	0	Type: 5.1. Basis: H. Current range is 8,000–0%. Base–best encompasses performance of 92% of countries. Bands based on a rough and possibly unrepresentative relationship between volume and NAI.

Appendix D.
Summary of Combining Procedures Used in *The Wellbeing of Nations*

Sustainability is measured by the Wellbeing Index (WI) and the Wellbeing/Stress index (WSI).

The Wellbeing Index is a graphic index shown on the Barometer of Sustainability as the intersection of the Human Wellbeing Index (HWI) and the Ecosystem Wellbeing Index (EWI).

The Wellbeing/Stress Index measures the ratio of human wellbeing to ecosystem stress. It is obtained by subtracting the EWI from 100 to provide an Ecosystem Stress Index (ESI) and dividing the HWI by the ESI.

In *The Wellbeing of Nations,* the term *index* (plural *indices*) is reserved for system, subsystem, dimension, and element scores. Scores of subelements and indicators are called simply scores. Procedures used to combine indices and scores are summarized in the text below by subsystem and dimension and in Table D1 at the end by combining procedure.

Human Wellbeing Index
The HWI is the unweighted average of five dimension indices:

> Health and population.
>
> Wealth.
>
> Knowledge and culture.
>
> Community.
>
> Equity.

Equity is included only if it lowers the HWI.

Health and Population
The health and population index is the lower of two element indices: a health index and a population index.

The health index consists of a single indicator: healthy life expectancy at birth.

The population index consists of a single indicator: total fertility rate.

Wealth
The wealth index is the unweighted average of two element indices: a household wealth index and a national wealth index.

The household wealth index is the average of two unweighted subelements:

> Needs, the lower score of two indicators: food sufficiency, represented by the percentage of the population with insufficient food, prevalence of stunting (low height for age) in children under 5 years, or prevalence of low weight for age in children under 5, whichever gives the lowest score (or, if these are not available, the percentage of babies with low birth weight); and basic services, represented by the percentage of the population with safe water or the percentage of the population with basic sanitation, whichever gives the lower score.
>
> Income, represented by gross domestic product (GDP) per person.

The national wealth index is the average of three weighted subelements [weights in brackets]:

> Size of the economy [2], represented by GDP per person.
>
> Inflation and unemployment [1], represented by the annual inflation rate or the annual unemployment rate (for the same period), whichever gives the lower score.
>
> Debt [1], represented by an external debt indicator (debt service as a percentage of exports, debt

service as a percentage of GNP, or ratio of short-term debt to international reserves, whichever gives the lowest score) or a public debt indicator (the weighted average of general government gross financial liabilities as a percentage of GDP [2] and annual central government deficit or surplus as a percentage of GDP [1]), whichever gives the lower score.

Knowledge and Culture

Because of inadequate information on culture, this dimension is limited to a knowledge element. The knowledge index is the average of two weighted subelements [weights in brackets]: education [2] and communication [1].

Education is the average of two unweighted indicators:

Primary and secondary school enrollment, the unweighted average of the net primary school enrollment rate and the net secondary school enrollment rate.

Tertiary school enrollment per 10,000 population.

Communication is the average of two unweighted indicators:

A telephone indicator, the lower score of main telephone lines + cellular phone subscribers per 100 persons and faults per 100 main telephone lines per year.

Internet users per 10,000 population.

Community

The community index is the lower of two element indices: a freedom and governance index and a peace and order index.

The freedom and governance index is the average of four unweighted indicators:

A political rights rating.

A civil liberties rating.

A press freedom rating.

A corruption perceptions index.

The peace and order index is the average of two unweighted subelements:

Peace, represented by deaths from armed conflicts per year or military expenditure as a percentage of GDP, whichever gives the lower score.

Crime, represented by the unweighted average of the homicide rate and other violent crimes (the unweighted average of the rape rate, robbery rate, and assault rate).

Equity

The equity index is the unweighted average of two element indices: a household equity index and a gender equity index.

The household equity index consists of a single indicator: the ratio of the income share of the richest fifth of the population to that of the poorest fifth.

The gender equity index is the average of three unweighted subelements:

Gender and wealth, represented by the ratio of male income to female income.

Gender and knowledge, represented by the average difference between male and female school enrollment rates.

Gender and community, represented by women's share of seats in parliament.

Ecosystem Wellbeing Index

The EWI is the unweighted average of five dimension indices:

Land.

Water.

Air.

Species and genes.

Resource use.

Resource use is included only if it lowers the EWI.

Land

The land index is the lower of two element indices: a land diversity index and a land quality index.

The land diversity index is the average of two weighted subelements [weights in brackets]:

Land modification and conversion [2], represented by the unweighted average of converted land as a percentage of total land, natural land as a percentage of total land, and percentage change in native forest area.

Land protection [1], represented by protected area as a percentage of land and inland water area (weighted according to degree of protection, size of the protected areas, and how much ecosystem diversity is protected).

The land quality index consists of a single indicator: degraded land as a percentage of cultivated + modified land, weighted according to severity of degradation [weights in brackets]: light [0.5], moderate [1.0], strong [1.5], extreme [2.0].

Water

Because of inadequate information on the sea, this dimension is limited to an inland waters element. The inland waters index is the lowest of three subelements:

Inland water diversity, represented by river conversion by dams, measured by dam capacity as a percentage of total water supply or, if that is not available, river flow dammed for hydropower as a percentage of dammable flow.

Inland water quality, the unweighted average score of drainage basins in each country, each basin score being the lowest score of six indicators: oxygen balance, nutrients, acidification, suspended solids, microbial pollution, and arsenic and heavy metals.

Water withdrawal, represented by water withdrawal as a percentage of internal renewable supply.

Air

The air index is the lower of two element indices: a global atmosphere index and a local air quality index.

The global atmosphere index is the lower score of two indicators:

Greenhouse gases, represented by carbon dioxide emissions per person.

Use (consumption or production, whichever is greater) of ozone depleting substances per person.

The local air quality index is the unweighted average of city scores in each country, each city score being the lowest score of six indicators: sulfur dioxide, nitrogen dioxide, ground-level ozone, carbon monoxide, particulates, and lead.

Species and Genes

The species and genes index is the weighted average [weights in brackets] of two element indices: a wild diversity index [2] and a domesticated diversity index [1].

The wild diversity index is the average of two unweighted subelements:

Wild plant species, represented by threatened plant species in a group as a percentage of total plant species in that group, taking the average percentage of three groups: flowering plants, gymnosperms (conifers, cycads, and gnetophytes), and ferns and allies.

Wild animal species, represented by threatened animal species in a group as a percentage of total animal species in that group, taking the average percentage of either two groups (mammals and birds) or four groups (mammals, birds, reptiles, and amphibians), whichever gives the lower score.

The domesticated diversity index is the average of two unweighted indicators:

Number of not-at-risk breeds of a species per million head of that species, taking the average of the most numerous livestock species and the two next most numerous or best-assessed livestock species.

Ratio of threatened breeds of a species to not-at-risk breeds of that species, taking the average of the most numerous livestock species and the two next most numerous or best-assessed livestock species.

Resource Use

The resource use index is the unweighted average of two element indices: an energy and materials index and a resource sectors index.

The energy and materials index covers only energy because of inadequate information on material flows. It is the lower score of two indicators: energy consumption per hectare of total area and energy consumption per person.

The resource sectors index is the unweighted average of three subelements: agriculture, fisheries, and timber.

Agriculture is the lower score of two unweighted indicators:

Agricultural productivity, the unweighted average score of tons of food crops produced per harvested hectare and tons of fertilizer used per 1,000 harvested hectares.

Agricultural self-reliance, represented by food production as a percentage of supply.

Fisheries is the lower score of two unweighted indicators:

Fishing pressure, the unweighted average score of depleted species + overexploited species as a percentage of assessed species, tons of fishing capacity per square kilometer of continental shelf (or inland waters in the case of freshwater fisheries), and tons of catch per ton of fishing capacity.

Fish and seafood self-reliance, represented by fish and seafood production as a percentage of supply.

Timber is represented by a single indicator: fellings + imports as a percentage of net annual increment or, if that is not available, production + imports as a percentage of volume.

Table D1. Summary of indices and other compound indicators by level and combining procedure (unweighted average, weighted average, or lower/lowest score). The higher level is in bold.

Level	Unweighted Average	Weighted Average	Lower/Lowest Score
Dimensions → **subsystem**	human dimensions → **HWI**		
	ecosystem dimensions → **EWI**		
Elements → **dimension**	household wealth + national wealth → **wealth**	wild diversity + domesticated diversity → **species and genes**	health + population → **health and population**
	household equity + gender equity → **equity**		freedom and governance + peace and order → **community**
	energy and materials + resource sectors → **resource use**		land diversity + land quality → **land**
			global atmosphere + local air quality → **air**
Subelements → **element**	needs + income → **household wealth**	size of the economy + inflation and unemployment + debt → **national wealth**	inland water diversity + inland water quality + water withdrawal → **inland waters**
	peace + crime → **peace and order**	education + communication → **knowledge**	
	gender and wealth + gender and knowledge + gender and community → **gender equity**	land modification and conversion + land protection → **land diversity**	
	wild plant species + wild animal species → **wild diversity**		
	agriculture + fisheries + timber → **resource sectors**		
Indicators → **subelement or element**	primary and secondary school enrollment + tertiary school enrollment → **education**	protected area as a percentage of total area weighted for size + protected area as a percentage of total area weighted for diversity → **land protection**	food sufficiency + basic services → **needs**
	telephone indicator + Internet users per 10,000 population → **communication**		annual inflation rate + annual unemployment rate → **inflation and unemployment**
	political rights rating + civil liberties rating + press freedom rating + corruption perceptions index → **freedom and governance**		external debt + public debt → **debt**

Level	Unweighted Average	Weighted Average	Lower/Lowest Score
	homicide rate + other violent crimes → **crime**		deaths from armed conflicts per year + military expenditure as a percentage of GDP → **peace**
	converted land as a percentage of total land + natural land as a percentage of total land + percentage change in native forest area → **land modification and conversion**		carbon dioxide emissions per person + use of ozone depleting substances → **global atmosphere**
	water quality of drainage basins → **inland water quality**		average percentage of threatened mammal and bird species + average percentage of threatened mammal, bird, reptile, and amphibian species → **wild animal species**
	air quality of cities → **local air quality**		agricultural productivity + agricultural self-reliance → **agriculture**
	percentage of threatened flowering plant species + percentage of threatened gymnosperm species + percentage of threatened ferns and allied species → **wild plant species**		fishing pressure + fish and seafood self-reliance → **fisheries**
	number of not-at-risk breeds of a species per million head of that species + ratio of threatened breeds of a species to not-at-risk breeds of that species → **domesticated diversity**		
Component indicators → **indicator**	net primary school enrollment rate + net secondary school enrollment rate → **primary and secondary school enrollment**	general government gross financial liabilities as a percentage of GDP + annual central government deficit/surplus as a percentage of GDP → **public debt**	percentage of population with insufficient food + prevalence of stunting in children + prevalence of low weight for age in children → **food sufficiency**
	rape rate + robbery rate + assault rate → **other violent crimes**	percentages of total area in five protected area categories → **protected area as a percentage of total area weighted for size**	percentage of population with safe water + percentage of population with basic sanitation → **basic services**
	water quality at stations → **water quality of basins**	mean percentage of totally protected ecosystem types + mean percentage of partially protected ecosystem types → **protected area as a percentage of total area weighted for diversity**	debt service as a percentage of exports + debt service as a percentage of GNP + ratio of short-term debt to international reserves → **external debt**
	air quality at sites → **air quality of cities**	lightly degraded percentage of cultivated and modified land area + moderately degraded percentage + strongly degraded percentage + extremely degraded percentage → **degraded land as a percentage of cultivated + modified land (land quality)**	main telephone lines and cellular phone subscribers per 100 persons + faults per 100 main telephone lines per year → **telephone indicator**
	percentage of threatened mammal species + percentage of threatened bird species → **average percentage of threatened mammal and bird species**		oxygen balance + nutrients + acidification + suspended solids + microbial pollution + arsenic and heavy metals → **water quality at station**

311

Level	Unweighted Average	Weighted Average	Lower/Lowest Score
	percentage of threatened mammal species + percentage of threatened bird species + percentage of threatened reptile species + percentage of threatened amphibian species → **average percentage of the four groups**		consumption of ozone depleting substances per person + production of ozone depleting substances per person → **use of ozone depleting substances**
	tons of food crops produced per harvested hectare + tons of fertilizer used per 1,000 harvested hectares → **agricultural productivity**		sulfur dioxide + nitrogen dioxide + ground-level ozone + carbon monoxide + particulates + lead → **air quality at sites**
	depleted species and overexploited species as a percentage of assessed species + tons of fishing capacity per km^2 of fish-producing area + tons of catch per ton of fishing capacity → **fishing pressure**		

Appendix E.
Map Maker Pro

The Map Processor for Windows

Downloadable from the web: www.mapmaker.com

"Map Maker Pro combines the powerful features of map making software with the user-friendliness of Windows. It has the look and feel of an image production package, with drag-and-drop facilities, a tools palette and customizable tool boxes, but it will allow you to create and manipulate professional looking maps... I would not have thought of using my PC to create a map, but found the process quite fascinating... The end results are highly rewarding and the three dimensional terrain contouring is amazing."

—*Internet magazine,* Sept. 2000,
www.vnunet.com

"Map Maker is the sort of useful program to look out for ... Map Maker is a versatile tool ..."

—*New Scientist,* Sept. 28, 1996

"An excellent and inexpensive tool for dedicated map-making... Packs a lot of specialist equipment into a small footprint."

—*Personal Computer World,* Feb. 1997

"Making a map is straightforward with Map Maker Pro ... the program is fast—screen operations and other actions reflect lean code ... An impressive set of features and capabilities at a modest price."

—*GIS World,* June 1997

Maps are vital tools for virtually any project. Whether you are designing irrigation systems, facilitating social forestry schemes, managing urban infrastructure, battling for land rights, mapping disease vectors, or rapidly laying out a refugee camp, reliable and readily updatable maps are crucial. Until recently, computer-based mapping has been expensive and complicated. *Map Maker Pro* is a simple-to-use program that has been developed in the field especially for development projects.

Map Maker users are creating the entire range of maps, from world maps (such as those in this book) to detailed plans of landmine fields and experimental horticultural plots. Map Maker enables you to:

- Make your own maps from scratch.

- Use existing data from other geographic information systems and computer-aided design programs (e.g., ArcView, ArcInfo, MapInfo, and AutoCAD).

- Prepare maps from scanned images such as paper maps and aerial photographs.

- Measure distances and areas on the screen.

- Carry out sophisticated data analyses.

- Create three-dimensional terrain models.

- Measure gradients and derive contours.

- Annotate maps with existing symbols or design your own symbols to indicate water pumps, land use patterns, health posts, and so on.

- Import entire maps or map extracts into documents written in any Windows word processor.

- Create maps in the field on a laptop using global positioning satellite (GPS) or traditional survey techniques.

- Create large-scale wall maps on multiple sheets using Map Maker's poster print option and a standard printer. (Each sheet can be updated individually.)

- Combine field measurements with existing maps by using one of a wide variety of map projections.

Map Maker Pro runs on Windows 95, 98, NT4, and 2000. Although a high-specification computer will give more impressive results, *Map Maker Pro* runs easily on a computer with a 486 processor. The program can be downloaded for a 21-day evaluation period free of charge from http://www.mapmaker.com.

Add-on modules are available from the Web site. *Rubber Map* adjusts scanned images such as aerial photographs or historical maps so that they coincide with your vector data. *Prospect* creates three-dimensional images to help assess the visual impact of forestry schemes. More modules are on the way.

Launched in September 1996, *Map Maker Pro* has been purchased by customers in 95 countries.

The Web site includes a list of independent international trainers who offer on-site training courses in Map Maker.

Map Maker Ltd, Carradale, The Pier, Kintyre, Scotland, PA28 6SQ United Kingdom; phone: +44 (0) 1583 431 358; fax: +44 (0) 1583 431 728; e-mail: info@mapmaker.com.

Appendix F.
Initial Classification of Interior, Coastal, and Ocean Basins

This preliminary classification of basins was developed to aid the selection of a representative set of water quality monitoring stations.

Inland waters are grouped into receiving basins. Drainages with no outlet to the sea form interior basins, grouped by continent. Drainages to coastal waters form coastal basins, grouped by coastal realm. Oceanic islands are assigned to ocean basins, grouped by adjacent coastal realm. Coastal realms follow the classification of Hayden, Ray, &

Dolan (1984). Interior basins are listed first; then coastal and ocean basins, roughly from west to east: North American Arctic, Eastern Pacific, Western Atlantic, Eurasian Arctic, Eastern Atlantic, Indian, and Western Pacific.

Drainages of 100,000 km² or more are identified in *italics* and their area given in square kilometers. Usually they are treated as basins in their own right, unless this would entail too fine a subdivision of the coastal body into which they flow.

Realm & Basin	Extent	Country	Station
Interior Americas			
United States interior	Great Basin complex	United States	--
Mexican interior	Casas Grandes, Nazas-Aguanaval, El Salado	Mexico	--
Titicaca/Poopó/Atacama	*Titicaca-Poopó 114,000*	Bolivia, Chile, Peru	--
Argentine interior	North-central Argentina	Argentina	--
Interior Africa			
Sahara	Sahara desert	Algeria, Chad, Egypt, Libya, Mali, Mauritania, Morocco, Niger, Sudan, Tunisia, Western Sahara	--
Lake Chad	*Lake Chad 2,381,635*	Algeria, Cameroon, Central African R, Chad, Niger, Nigeria, Sudan	--
Etosha	South-central Angola & north-central Namibia	Angola, Namibia	--
Kalahari-Makgadikgadi	Makgadikgadi pans & much of the Kalahari desert	Botswana, Namibia, Zimbabwe	--
Okavango	*Okavango 323,192*	Angola, Botswana, Namibia	--
Rift Valley	Rift Valley (Eritrea - Tanzania): Danakil; *Awash 112,030*; Central lakes; *Omo-Gibe (L Turkana) 199,952*; Southern lakes	Djibouti, Eritrea, Ethiopia, Kenya, Sudan, Tanzania, Uganda	--
Interior Asia			
Turkish interior	Burdur lakes, Akarcay, Konya, Van Lake	Turkey	--
Rift Valley	Jordan R	Jordan	R Zarqua at King Talal Dam
		Israel, Lebanon, Syria	--
Arabian	Arabian desert	Jordan, Oman, Saudi Arabia, United Arab Emirates, Yemen	--
N Caspian Sea	C Tjulenij - Volga delta -Kazakhstan/ Turkmenistan border; *Ural 270,000*	Azerbaijan, Kazakhstan, Russia	--
Volga	*Volga 1,360,000*	Russia	R Volga at Narimanov
			R Volga at B Cheboksarskoye (201)
			R Belaya at Ufa (203)
S Caspian Sea	Kazakhstan/Turkmenistan border - C Tjulenij; *Kura 225,000*	Armenia, Azerbaijan, Iran, Turkey, Turkmenistan	--
		Georgia	R Kura at Rustavi
Iranian interior	Lake Orimiye; Central plateau	Iran	--
Helmand	*Helmand 386,000*	Afghanistan, Iran	--
Hari Rud & Murgab	Hari Rud & Murgab	Afghanistan, Iran, Turkmenistan	--
Aral Sea	Aral Sea; *Amu Darya 653,000*; *Syr Darya 540,000*	Kazakhstan	R Syr Darya mouth
		Uzbekistan	R Amu Darya mouth
		Afghanistan, Kyrgyzstan, Tajikistan, Turkmenistan,	--
Balkhash Lake	*Balkhash Lake 250,000 (Ili 176,000)*	China, Kazakhstan, Kyrgyzstan	--
Tarim	Tarim desert; *Tarim 980,000*	China, Kyrgyzstan	--
Muynkum	Muynkum desert	Kazakhstan, Kyrgyzstan	--
E Asian interior	Lakes Ala, Tengiz, Aschchikol & Ghalkarteniz	China, Kazakhstan	--
Turgay	*Turgay 157,000*	Kazakhstan	--
Issyk	Lake Issyk	Kyrgyzstan	--
Gobi	Gobi desert	Mongolia	--
Baluchistan	Lake Gaz Murian - Kharan desert	Iran, Pakistan	--
W Rajasthan	W Rajasthan	India	--
Interior Pacific			
Australian interior	Australian interior	Australia	--
North American Arctic			
E Chukchi Sea	Bering Strait & C Prince of Wales - P Barrow	United States	--
W Beaufort Sea	P Barrow - Herschel I	Canada, United States	--

Realm & Basin	Extent	Country	Station
Mackenzie	Mackenzie & Kugmallit Bays (Herschel I - Warren P); *Mackenzie 1,784,580*	Canada	R Mackenzie mouth
			R Great Bear
E Beaufort Sea	Warren P - C Bathurst - C Kellett (Banks I) - C Prince Alfred (Banks I)	Canada	--
Arctic Archipelagic Seas	Amundsen Gulf, M'Clure Strait, Peary Channel & Nansen Sound - Jones Sound, Lancaster Sount & Gulf of Boothia, including intermediate waters & mainland & island drainages; *Back 106,920*	Canada	--
Lincoln Sea & Nares Strait	C Aldrich (Ellesmere I) - Nares Strait & C Brevoort - C Morris Jesup; C Brevoort - C Isabella (Ellesmere I) & C Alexander	Canada, Greenland	--
Wandel Sea	C Morris Jesup - Nordostrundingen	Greenland	--
W Baffin Bay	C Isabella (Ellesmere I) - C Dyer (Baffin I) & Davis Strait	Canada	--
E Baffin Bay	C Alexander - Kangaarsuk & Davis Strait	Greenland	--
W Greenland Sea	Nordostrundingen - Uunarteq/C Tobin	Greenland	--
W Denmark Strait	Uunarteq/C Tobin - C Wandel	Greenland	--
Northeast Pacific			
E Bering Sea	C Prince of Wales - Aleutian Is; *Yukon 836,760*	United States	R Yukon at Yukon Station
		Canada	--
Gulf of Alaska	Aleutian Is - C Fox	United States	R Talkeetna at Talkeetna
		Canada	--
Lower subpolar NE Pacific	C Fox - C Scott & C Caution	United States	--
		Canada	R Skeena
Upper temperate NE Pacific	C Scott & C Caution - C Disappointment; *Fraser 232,170*	Canada	R Fraser at Hope
		United States	--
Columbia	C Disappointment - C Lookout; *Columbia 669,410*	United States	R Columbia at Bonneville
		Canada	R Columbia df
Lower temperate NE Pacific	C Lookout - P Reyes	United States	--
Upper subtropical NE Pacific	P Reyes - C San Lucas	United States	R Sacramento at Sacramento
		Mexico	--
W Gulf of California	C San Lucas - Colorado	Mexico	--
Colorado	*Colorado 615,000*	United States	R Colorado at Hoover Dam
		Mexico	R Colorado
E Gulf of California	Colorado - Mazatlán	Mexico, United States	--
Grande de Santiago	Mazatlán - C Corrientes; *Grande de Santiago 125,000*	Mexico	L de Chapala
			R Lerma
Oceanic NE Pacific	Hawaiian Is	United States	--
Tropical East Pacific			
Upper tropical E Pacific	C Corrientes (Mexico) - P Cosigüina (Nicaragua); *Balsas 106,000*	Mexico	R Balsas at Balsas
		El Salvador, Guatemala, Honduras, Nicaragua	--
Lower tropical E Pacific	P Cosigüina - C Corrientes (Colombia)	Colombia, Costa Rica, Nicaragua, Panama	--
Intertropical E Pacific	C Corrientes - P Pariñas	Colombia, Ecuador, Peru	--
Southeast Pacific			
Subtropical SE Pacific	P Pariñas - P Toro	Peru	--
		Chile	R Maipo at El Manzano
Temperate SE Pacific	P Toro - P Tres Montes	Chile	--
Subpolar SE Pacific	P Tres Montes - C San Diego	Argentina, Chile	--
Northwest Atlantic			
Foxe Basin	C Hallowell (Baffin I) - King Charles C (Baffin I) & C Englefield (Melville Peninsula) - Seahorse P (Southampton I)	Canada	--
W Hudson Bay	Beach P (mainland) & C Munn (Southampton I) - C Churchill; *Thelon/Kazan 230,110; Churchill 280,470*	Canada	R Churchill
Nelson	C Churchill - Marsh P; *Nelson 1,129,360*	Canada	R Nelson at Gillam
			R Saskatchewan mouth
			R Roseau
		United States	--
S Hudson Bay	Marsh P - C Henrietta Maria; *Hayes 107,690; Severn 100,460*	Canada	--
James Bay	C Henrietta Maria - C Iones; *Albany 133,520; Moose 108,210*	Canada	--
E Hudson Bay	C Iones - C Wolstenholme	Canada	--
Hudson Strait & Ungava Bay	King Charles C (Baffin I) - Resolution I & C Wolstenholme - Button Is; *Koksoak 133,000*	Canada	--
Labrador Sea	C Dyer (Baffin I) - Resolution I & Button Is - North Head	Canada	--

Realm & Basin	Extent	Country	Station
Southern Greenland	Kangaarsuk & Davis Strait - Uummannarsuaq/C Farvel - C Wandel	Greenland	--
Upper temperate NW Atlantic	North Head - C Ray; C St Lawrence - C Sable	Canada	--
Gulf of St Lawrence	C Ray - C St Lawrence; *St Lawrence 1,179,980*	Canada	L Ontario mid-lake
			L Superior mid-lake
		United States	R St Lawrence df
			R Niagara at L Ontario
Bay of Fundy & Gulf of Maine	C Sable - C Cod	Canada	R St John mouth
		United States	--
Lower temperate NW Atlantic	C Cod - C Henlopen	United States	R Hudson at Troy
			R Delaware at Trenton
Chesapeake Bay	C Henlopen - C Hatteras/C Lookout	United States	R Susquehanna at Harrisburg
			R Potomac at Washington
Subtropical NW Atlantic	C Hatteras/C Lookout - Northwest Providence Channel - East C (FL)	Bahamas, United States	--
NE Gulf of Mexico	East C - Dauphin I; *Mobile/Alabama 115,000*	United States	R Apalachicola at Chattahoochee
Mississippi	Dauphin I - Texas P; *Mississippi 3,250,000*	United States	R Mississippi mouth
			R Arkansas at Little Rock
			R Missouri at Hermann
			R Ohio at New Grand Chain
		Canada	--
Brazos	Texas P - Matagorda Bay; *Brazos 114,000*	United States	--
Texas Colorado	Matagorda Bay - Port Isabel; *Colorado (Texas) 100,000*	United States	--
Bravo del Norte/Grande	Port Isabel - Playa Lauro Villar; *Bravo del Norte (Grande) 550,000*	United States	R Grande at Brownsville
		Mexico	R Bravo at Matamoros
			R Bravo at Presa de la Amistad
			R Conchos at Ojinaga
SW Gulf of Mexico	Playa Lauro Villar - Tupilco	Mexico	R Pánuco
			R Coatzacoalcos
SE Gulf of Mexico	Tupilco - C Catoche; *Grijalva/Usumacinta 120,000*	Mexico	R Grijalva
			R Usumacinta
		Guatemala	--
E Gulf of Mexico	C Corrientes - Varadero	Cuba	--
Tropical West Atlantic			
Upper tropical W Atlantic	Northwest Providence Channel & Varadero (Cuba) - P de Quemados (Cuba) - C Engaño (Dominican R) - I de Vieques (Puerto Rico)	Bahamas, Cuba, Dominican R, Haiti, Puerto Rico, Turks & Caicos Is	--
Antillean tropical W Atlantic & E Caribbean Sea	Virgin Passage (I de Vieques) - Grenada	Anguilla, Antigua & Barbuda, Barbados, British Virgin Is, Dominica, Grenada, Guadeloupe, Martinique, Montserrat, Netherlands Antilles (Saba, St Eustatius, St Maarten), St Kitts & Nevis, St Lucia, St Vincent & Grenadines, US Virgin Is	--
N Caribbean Sea	C Corrientes (Cuba) - I de Vieques (Puerto Rico)	Cuba	B Damuji
			B Hanabanilla
		Cayman Is, Dominican R, Haiti, Jamaica, Puerto Rico	--
W Caribbean Sea	C Catoche - P S Bernardo	Belize, Colombia, Costa Rica, Guatemala, Honduras, Mexico, Nicaragua, Panama	--
Magdalena	P San Bernardo - P Perret; *Magdalena 240,000*	Colombia	R Magdalena mouth
			R Cauca at Juanchito
S Caribbean Sea	P Perret - Península de Paria	Aruba, Colombia, Netherlands Antilles (Bonaire & Curaçao), Venezuela	--
Orinoco	Península de Paria -Guyana/Venezuela border; *Orinoco 966,000*	Colombia, Trinidad & Tobago, Venezuela	--
Essequibo	Guyana/Venezuela border - Georgetown; *Essequibo 147,000*	Guyana, Venezuela	--
Guianan tropical W Atlantic	Georgetown - C do Norte	Brazil, French Guiana, Guyana, Suriname	--
Amazon	C do Norte - C Gurupì; *Amazon 6,000,000*	Brazil	R Amazon mouth
			R Tocantins mouth
		Bolivia, Colombia, Ecuador, Guyana, Peru, Venezuela	--
Intertropical W Atlantic	C Gurupì - Parnaíba; Parnaíba - P Coconho;	Brazil	--
Parnaíba	*Parnaíba 325,000*	Brazil	--
São Francisco	P Coconho - P do Conselho; *São Francisco 600,000*	Brazil	R Capibaribe
			R São Francisco at Petrolandia

Realm & Basin	Extent	Country	Station
Lower tropical W Atlantic	P do Conselho - C Frio	Brazil	R Paraguaçu at Pedra do Cavalo
			R Pairaba do Sul at Barra Mansa
Southwest Atlantic			
Subtropical SW Atlantic	C Frio - P del Este	Brazil, Uruguay	--
La Plata	P del Este - P Mogotes; *la Plata/Paraná/ Uruguay 3,200,000*	Argentina	R Paraná at Puerto Libertad
			R Paraná at Corrientes
			R Paraná at Rosario
		Brazil	B Guarapiranga
		Bolivia, Paraguay, Uruguay	--
N Mar Argentino	P Mogotes - Pen. Valdés	Argentina	L Nahuel Huapi at Bariloche
Chubut	Pen. Valdés - C Tres Puntas; *Chubut 138,000*	Argentina	--
S Mar Argentino	C Tres Puntas - C San Diego	Argentina	--
Eurasian Arctic			
E Denmark Strait	Reykjanesta - Fontur (northern half of island)	Iceland	--
W Barents Sea	Nordkapp - C Orlovskij	Finland	L Inari stn 151
		Norway, Russia	
Severnaya Dvina	Dvina Gulf; *Severnaya Dvina 358,000*	Russia	R Severnaya Dvina at Ust-Pinega (213)
White Sea	C Orlovskij - Dvina Gulf - C Kanin Nos	Russia	R Mezen at Borovo
E Barents Sea	C Kanin Nos - C Zelanija; *Pechora 322,000*	Russia	R Pechora at Nar'jan-Mar
W Kara Sea	C Zelanija - C Suberta; C Sokal'skogo - C Olenij	Russia	--
Ob	Gulfs of Ob & Taz (C Suberta - C Sokal'skogo); *Ob 2,990,000; Pur 112,000; Taz 150,000*	Russia	R Ob at Salehard (011)
			R Tom at Tomsk (204)
			R Irtysh at Krasnyi Jar (205)
		China, Kazakhstan	--
Yenisey	C Olenij - Dikson I; *Yenisey 2,580,000*	Russia	R Yenisei at Igarka (210)
			L Baikal mid-lake (024)
			R Selenga mouth
		Mongolia	--
Pyasina	Dikson I - C Povorotnyi; *Pyasina 182,000*	Russia	--
Taimyr	C Povorotnyi - C Celjuskin; *Taimyr 124,000*	Russia	--
Khatanga	C Celjuskin - C Paksa; *Khatanga 422,000*	Russia	--
Anabar	C Paksa - Terpjaj-Tumsa Pen.; *Anabar 100,000*	Russia	--
Olenek	Terpjaj-Tumsa Pen. - Dzangylah I; *Olenek 219,000*	Russia	--
Lena	Dzangylah I - C Buor Haja; *Lena 2,470,000*	Russia	R Lena delta (028)
Yana	C Buor-Haja - C Svjatoj Nos & C Anisij; *Yana (Jana) 238,000*	Russia	--
Indigirka	C Svjatoj Nos & C Anisij - C Krestovskskij; *Indigirka 360,000*	Russia	--
Kolyma	C Krestovskskij - C Billingsa; *Kolyma 647,000*	Russia	R Kolyma at Kolymskoe
W Chukchi Sea	C Billingsa - Bering Strait & C Dezneva	Russia	--
Northeast Atlantic			
Icelandic Atlantic	Reykjanesta - Fontur (southern half of island)	Iceland	--
Norwegian Sea	Nordkapp - Lindesnes	Norway	R Altaelva at Alta
			R Vefsna at Mosjøen
			R Orkla at Vormstad
			R Suldalslaagen at Sand
		Faeroe Is	--
N Skagerrak & E Kattegat	Lindesnes - Helsingborg	Norway	R Otra mouth
			R Skienselva mouth
			R Numedalslaagen at Bommestad
			R Drammenselva mouth
			R Glåma mouth
		Sweden	L Vanern
N Baltic Sea	Helsingborg - Kappelskär (incl. Bornholm); Helsingør - Møns Klint	Sweden	R Mörrumsan mouth
			R Ronneaan mouth
			L Vattern
		Denmark	--
Gulf of Bothnia	Kappelskär - Hangö	Sweden	R Dalalven mouth
			R Rane mouth
		Finland	R Tornionjoki stn 14100
			L Yli-Kitka stn 144
			R Kokernaenjoki mouth
N Gulf of Finland	Hangö - Neva	Finland	R Kalkkinen stn 4800
			R Kymijoki stn 5610
		Russia	--
Neva	*Neva 281,000*	Russia	L Onezhskoye (Onega)
S Gulf of Finland	Neva - N of Riguld (Estonia)	Estonia	R Narva 10 km from mouth
			R Narva at L Vörtsjäry
		Latvia, Russia	--

Realm & Basin	Extent	Country	Station
SE Baltic Sea	N of Riguld - Gdansk Bay	Estonia	R Pärnu 1 km from mouth
		Latvia	R Gauja at Sigulda
			R Daugava at Jekabpils
		Lithuania	R Nemunas
		Russia	--
Wisla	Gdansk Bay; *Wisla (Vistula) 193,000*	Poland	R Wisla mouth
			R Wisla at Kiezmark
			R Wisla at Warszawa
			R Wisla at Krakow
		Belarus, Slovakia, Ukraine	--
Oder (S Baltic Sea)	Gdansk Bay - C Arkona; *Oder 126,000*	Poland	R Oder mouth
			R Oder (Odra) at Krajnik
			R Oder (Odra) at Wroclaw
			R Oder (Odra) at Chalupki
		Czech R	R Oder (Odra) df
		Germany	--
SW Baltic Sea	C Arkona - Samsø; Møns Klint - N of Kalundborg	Denmark	R Sus mouth
			R Odense mouth
		Germany	--
S Skagerrak & W Kattegat	Helsingør - N of Kalundborg - Hanstholm (Denmark)	Denmark	R Guden mouth
NE North Sea	Hanstholm - Sylt	Denmark	R Skjern mouth
German Bight	Sylt - Schiermonnikoog (Netherlands); *Elbe 144,500*	Germany	R Elbe mouth
			R Elbe at Geesthacht
			R Weser mouth
			R Weser at Intschede
		Czech R	R Elbe (Labe) df
		Austria, Netherlands, Poland	--
Rhine	Schiermonnikoog - Schouwen (Netherlands); *Rhine 168,757*	Netherlands	L Ijsselmeer
			R Rhine Ijssel arm
			R Rhine Ijssel-Kampen
			R Rijn/Maas delta
		Germany	R Rhine df
			R Rhine at Kleve/Bimmen
			R Rhine at Koblenz
			R Moselle at Koblenz
		Belgium	R Meuse df
			R Meuse at Lanaye/ Ternaaien
		Luxembourg	R Sûre df
		Switzerland	R Rhine at Basel
			R Rhine at Diepoldsau
			R Aare at Brugg
		Austria, France, Liechtenstein	--
SE North Sea	Schouwen - C Nez (France)	Belgium	R Schelde (Escaut) df
			R Schelde at Doel
		France, Netherlands	--
W North Sea	Duncansby Head (Scotland) - South Foreland (England)	United Kingdom	R Leven
			R Tweed above Galafoot
			R Trent at Nottingham
			R Thames at London
N English Channel	South Foreland - Land's End (England)	United Kingdom	R Exe at Exeter
Celtic Sea	Land's End - St David's Head (Wales) & Carnsore P - Mizen Head (Ireland)	United Kingdom	R Severn mouth
			R Avon at Bristol
		Ireland	R Blackwater mouth
			R Barrow mouth
Irish Sea	St David's Head - Mull of Kintyre (Scotland) & Carnsore P - Fair Head (N Ireland)	Ireland	R Boyne mouth
		United Kingdom	R Dee
			R Mersey
			R Clyde mouth
		I of Man	--
Scottish & Irish Atlantic	Shetland & Orkney Is; Duncansby Head - Mull of Kintyre; Fair Head - Mizen Head	United Kingdom	R Carron
			Lower Bann mouth
		Ireland	R Clare mouth
La Manche (S English Channel)	C Nez - I d'Ouessant	France	R Seine mouth
			R Seine at Paris
		Channel Is	--
Loire	I d'Ouessant - I de Noirmoutier; *Loire 120,000*	France	R Loire mouth
			R Loire at Ingrandes
Bay of Biscay	I de Noirmoutier - C Ortegal	France	R Garonne mouth
			R Garonne at Valence d'Agen
		Andorra, Spain	--

Realm & Basin	Extent	Country	Station
Lower temperate NE Atlantic	C Ortegal - C Espichel (Portugal)	Portugal	R Douro mouth
			R Tejo at Santarem
		Spain	R Duero df
Upper subtropical NE Atlantic	C Espichel - P Marroquí (Spain) - Jbel Musa (Morocco) - Ras Nouâdhibou (Western Sahara/Mauritania)	Portugal	R Guadiana mouth
		Spain	R Guadiana mouth
			R Guadalquivir mouth
		Morocco	R Sebou at Kenitra
			R Bou Regreg at Barrage Sidi Mohamed Ben Abdella
			R er Rbia at Sidi Daoui
		Western Sahara	--
NW Mediterranean Sea	P Marroquí - C de Creus	Spain	R Ebro mouth
		Andorra	--
N Mediterranean Sea	C de Creus - C Ferrat - C Corse & C Pertusato (Corsica) - P Falcone & C Carbonara (Sardinia)	France	R Rhone mouth
			R Rhone at St Vallier
		Switzerland	R Rhone at Chancy
			R Rhone at Porte du Scex
		Spain, Italy	--
Ligurian & Tyrrenhian Seas	C Ferrat - Scilla - P del Faro & C Boeo (Sicily) - C Carbonara - P Falcone - C Pertusato - C Corse	Italy	R Arno mouth
		France	--
Ionian Sea	C delle Correnti & P del Faro (Sicily) - Scilla - C d'Otranto & C i Gjuhes (Otranto Channel) - Akra Ténaro (Greece)	Italy, Albania	--
		Greece	R Akeloos mouth
Adriatic Sea	C d'Otranto (Italy) - C i Gjuhes (Albania)	Italy	R Adige mouth
			R Po mouth
		Switzerland	R Ticino at Riazzino
		Albania	R Semani at Mbrostar
		Greece	L Mikri Prespa
		Bosnia & Herzegovina, Croatia, Macedonia FYR, Slovenia, Yugoslavia	--
Aegean Sea (including Sea of Marmara & Sea of Crete)	Akra Ténaro - Bosporus - Kas (Turkey)	Greece	R Axios mouth
			R Strimonas mouth
		Bulgaria	R Arda df
			R Maritza at Svilengrad
		Turkey	R Gediz mouth
		Macedonia FYR, Yugoslavia	--
W Black Sea	Bosporus - C Kaliakra	Bulgaria, Turkey	--
Danube	C Kaliakra - L Sasyk; *Danube 796,250*	Romania	R Danube at Bazias
			R Oltul at Isbiceni
			R Muresul at Nadlac
		Austria	R Danube df
			R Inn df
		Bulgaria	R Jantra mouth
			R Osam mouth
		Czech R	R Morava df
		Germany	R Danube df
			R Danube at Jochenstein
		Hungary	R Danube df
			R Danube at Budapest
			R Tisza at Szolnok
			R Tisza df
		Moldova	R Prut at Ungheni
		Slovakia	R Maly Dunaj (Danube) df
			R Hornad df
			R Hron mouth
			R Vah mouth
		Italy, Switzerland, Ukraine, Yugoslavia	--
N Black Sea	L Sasyk - Dnepr; Dnepr - Kerčenska Strait	Ukraine	R Dnestr at Mogiliv-Podilskiy
		Moldova	R Dnestr at Bender
Dnepr	*Dnepr 558,000*	Ukraine	R Dnepr at Kherson
		Belarus, Russia	--
Don	*Don 422,000*	Ukraine	R Severskiy Donez at Krujilivka
		Russia	R Don at Bagaevskij
Azov Sea (except Don)	Kerčenska Strait	Russia	R Kuban mouth
		Ukraine	--
E Black Sea	Kerčenska Strait - Trabzon (Turkey)	Georgia	R Rioni at Poti
		Russia, Turkey	--
S Black Sea	Trabzon - Bosporus	Turkey	R Yesilirmak mouth
			R Sakarya mouth

Realm & Basin	Extent	Country	Station
E Mediterranean Sea	Kas (Turkey) - Port Said (Egypt)	Cyprus, Egypt, Israel, Lebanon, Syria, Turkey	--
Nile	Port Said - Alexandria; *Nile 3,112, 369*	Sudan	R Blue Nile at Khartoum
			R White Nile at Jebel Aulia
		Tanzania	R Kagera at Nyakanyasi
			L Victoria at South Port
		Uganda	L Albert
		Burundi, DR Congo, Egypt, Eritrea, Ethiopia, Kenya, Rwanda	
SE Mediterranean Sea	Alexandria - C Bon (Tunisia) + C Boeo - C delle Correnti	Egypt, Italy, Libya, Malta, Tunisia	--
SW Mediterranean Sea	C Bon - Jbel Musa	Morocco	R Moulouya
		Algeria, Tunisia	--
Senegal & Cape Verde	Ras Nouâdhibou - C Vert; *Senegal 484,181*	Senegal	R Senegal at St Louis
			R Senegal at Podor
		Cape Verde, Guinea, Mali, Mauritania	--
Lower subtropical NE Atlantic	C Vert -Guinea/Sierra Leone border	Gambia, Guinea, Guinea-Bissau, Senegal	--
Tropical East Atlantic			
Upper tropical E Atlantic	Guinea/Sierra Leone border - C Palmas (Côte d'Ivoire)	Côte d'Ivoire, Guinea, Liberia, Sierra Leone	--
W Gulf of Guinea	C Palmas - Volta; Volta - North Point (Nigeria)	Ghana	R Pra at Daboase
		Benin, Burkina Faso, Côte d'Ivoire, Guinea, Nigeria, Togo	--
Volta	*Volta 394,196*	Ghana	R Volta at B Kpong
			R White Volta at Nawuni
		Benin, Burkina Faso, Côte d'Ivoire, Mali, Togo	
Niger	North Point - West Point (Nigeria); *Niger 2,273,946*	Mali	R Niger at Bamako
			R Niger at Koulikoro
		Algeria, Benin, Burkina Faso, Cameroon, Chad, Côte d'Ivoire, Guinea, Niger, Nigeria	--
E Gulf of Guinea (Intertropical E Atlantic)	West Point - C Lopez (Gabon); *Sanaga 135,000*	Cameroon, Central African R, Equatorial Guinea, Gabon, Nigeria, São Tomé & Principe	--
Southeast Atlantic			
Upper subtropical SE Atlantic	C Lopez - Cabinda/DR Congo border; *Ogooué 220,270*	Angola, Cameroon, R Congo, Equatorial Guinea, Gabon	--
Congo	Cabinda/DR Congo border - Soyo (Angola); *Congo 3,789,053*	Angola, Burundi, Cameroon, Central African R, DR Congo, R Congo, Rwanda, Tanzania, Zambia	--
Cuanza	Soyo - Santa Maria; *Cuanza 149,000*	Angola	--
Cunene	Santa Maria - C Fria (Namibia); *Cunene 112,000*	Angola, Namibia	--
Lower subtropical SE Atlantic	C Fria - Orange; Orange - C Agulhas (South Africa)	Namibia, South Africa	--
Orange	*Orange 896,368*	Namibia	R Orange mouth
		South Africa	R Orange mouth
		Botswana, Lesotho	--
Western Indian Ocean			
Lower subtropical W Indian	C Agulhas - I Mariana (Mozambique)	Mozambique, South Africa, Swaziland	--
Upper subtropical W Indian	I Mariana - P São Sebastião; *Limpopo 401,864*	Botswana, Mozambique, South Africa, Zimbabwe	--
Madagascar subtropical	C Ankaboa - Tolanaro	Madagascar	--
Save	P São Sebastião - Marromeu (Mozambique); *Save 103,000*	Mozambique, Zimbabwe	--
Zambezi	Marromeu - I de Moçambique; *Zambezi 1,351,365*	Angola, Botswana, Malawi, Mozambique, Namibia, Zambia, Zimbabwe	--
E Mozambique Channel (Inner Madagascar tropical)	C Ankaboa - C Vilanandro	Madagascar	--
Outer Madagascar tropical	Tolanaro - C Angontsy	Madagascar, Mauritius, Réunion	--
Lower intertropical W Indian	C Angotsy - C Vilanandro (Madagascar) - I de Moçambique - C Delgado (Mozambique)	Comoros, Madagascar, Mayotte, Mozambique	--
Ruvuma	C Delgado - Songo Mnara (Tanzania); *Ruvuma 166,500*	Malawi, Mozambique, Tanzania	--
Rufiji	Songo Mnara - Buyuni; *Rufiji 178,000*	Tanzania	--
Upper intertropical W Indian	Buyuni - Kismaanyo (Somalia)	Tanzania	R Ruvu at Mlandizi
		Kenya	R Tana
		Somalia	--

321

Realm & Basin	Extent	Country	Station
Shebelli-Juba	Kismaanyo-Mogadishu; *Shebelli-Juba 810,427*	Ethiopia, Somalia	--
		Kenya	L Naivasha
Horn of Africa & S Gulf of Aden	Mogadishu - Djibouti/Eritrea border	Djibouti, Ethiopia, Somalia	--
W Red Sea	Djibouti/Eritrea border - Ra's Muhammad (Egypt)	Egypt, Eritrea, Sudan	--
E Red Sea	Ra's Muhammad - Ra's Bab al-Mandab (Yemen)	Egypt, Israel, Jordan, Saudi Arabia, Yemen	--
N Gulf of Aden & NW Arabian Sea	Ra's Bab al-Mandab - Ra's al Hadd (Oman)	Oman, United Arab Emirates, Yemen	--
S Gulf of Oman & Persian Gulf	Ra's al Hadd - al Subiya (Kuwait)	Bahrain, Kuwait, Oman, Qatar, Saudi Arabia, United Arab Emirates	--
Shatt-al-Arab	al Subiya - Ra's-e Abadan (Iran); *Shatt-al-Arab/Tigris/Euphrates 884,000*	Iran	Shatt-al-Arab mouth
		Iraq	Shatt-al-Arab mouth
		Kuwait, Syria, Turkey	--
N Persian Gulf & Gulf of Oman	Ra's-e Abadan - Ra's-e Faste	Iran	--
Makran Coast	Ra's-e Faste - Ras Muari (Pakistan)	Iran, Pakistan	--
Indus	Ras Muari - Pakistan/India border; *Indus 1,060,000*	Pakistan	R Indus at Kotri
			R Ravi below Lahore
			R Ravi above Lahore
			R Chenab Gujra branch
		Afghanistan, China, India	--
Gulfs of Kachchh & Khambhat	Pakistan/India border - Daman	India	R Sabarmati at Ahmedabad
			R Mahi at Vasad
			R Narmada near Garudeshwar
			R Tapti near Burhanpur
Maharashtra Coast	Daman - C Rama	India	--
Malabar Coast	C Rama - C Comorin	India	R Chaliyar at Kalpalli
			R Periyar near Alwaye
			R Kallada at Panamthottam
Lakshadweep Sea	Lakshadweep Is & Maldives	India, Maldives	--
Mannar	C Comorin - Matara (Sri Lanka)	India, Sri Lanka	--
Eastern Indian Ocean			
Coromandel Coast	Matara - Krishna delta (India)	India	R Cauvery near Musiri
			R Pennar near Nellore
		Sri Lanka	--
Krishna	Krsihna delta - Machilpatnam; *Krishna 258,948*	India	R Krishna near Vijayawada
			R Krishna at Gadwal
			R Tungabhadra at Ullanuru
			R Bhima near Takali
Godavari	Machilpatnam - Pondicherry; *Godavari 312,812*	India	R Godavari near Polavaram
			R Godavari near Mancheral
			R Wainganga near Ashti
NW Bay of Bengal	Pondicherry - Orissa/West Bengal border (India); *Mahanadi 141,589*	India	R Mahanadi mouth
			R Subarnarekha at Jamshedpur
Ganges	Orissa/West Bengal border - Sandwip (Bangladesh); *Ganga/Brahmaputra/Meghna 1,652,318*	India (1,096,588)	R Ganga df
		Bangladesh (121,070)	R Meghna at Ashuganj
			R Padma at Bheramara
			R Brahmaputra at Fulchhari
		Bhutan (47,000), China (240,480), Nepal (147,180)	--
NE Bay of Bengal	Sandwip - Mawdin (Myanmar)	Bangladesh,	R Karnaphuli at Rangunia
			L Kaptai at Kaptai
		India, Myanmar	--
Irrawaddy & Salween	Mawdin - Thongwa; *Irrawaddy 396,000*	Myanmar	R Irrawaddy
		China, India	--
Salween	Thongwa - Kyaikkami (Myanmar); *Salween 270,000*	Myanmar, China, Thailand	--
Andaman Sea	Kyaikkami - Phuket (Thailand) - C Ba'u (Sumatra) + Andaman & Nicobar Is	India, Indonesia, Myanmar, Thailand	--
Strait of Malacca	Phuket - Sungai Rengit (Malaysia); C Ba'u - Durian Strait (Sumatra)	Malaysia	R Klang
			R Linggi
			R Sekudai
		Indonesia, Singapore, Thailand	--
W Sumatra	C Ba'u - Sunda Strait	Indonesia	--
Upper intertropical E Indian (Java)	Sunda Strait - Bali Strait (S Java)	Indonesia	R Garang
Upper intertropical E Indian (Bali-Alor)	Bali Strait - Ombai Strait	Indonesia	--
N Timor & Arafura Seas	Timor - Tanjung Vais (New Guinea) - C Yubo (Papua New Guinea)	East Timor, Indonesia, Papua New Guinea	--
Gulf of Carpentaria	C York - C Wilberforce; *Flinders 108,000*	Australia	--

Realm & Basin	Extent	Country	Station
S Arafura & Timor Seas	C Wilberforce - C Voltaire	Australia	--
Lower intertropical E Indian	C Voltaire - North West C	Australia	--
W Australian subtropical	North West C - C Leeuwin	Australia	--
Upper temperate E Indian	C Leeuwin - C du Couedic	Australia	--
Murray-Darling	C du Couedic - C Jaffa; *Murray-Darling 1,060,000*	Australia	R Murray-Darling mouth
Lower temperate E Indian	C Jaffa - C Otway - Woolnorth P (Tasmania)	Australia	--
Subpolar E Indian	Woolnorth P - South West C (Tasmania)	Australia	--
Northwest Pacific			
W Bering Sea	C Dezneva - C Afrika; *Anadyr 191,000*	Russia	--
Upper temperate NW Pacific	C Afrika - C Lopatka	Russia	--
Sea of Okhotsk	C Lopatka - Kuril Is - Hokkaido (C Nosappu - C Soya) - E Sakhalin (C Kril'on - C Elizavety) - C Aleksandra	Japan, Russia	--
Amur & Tatarskij Strait	C Aleksandra & C Elizavety - Amgu (Russia) & C Soya (Hokkaido); *Amur 1,855,000*	Russia	R Amur mouth
		China, Mongolia	--
Lower temperate NW Pacific (Hokkaido)	C Nosappu (Hokkaido) - C Esan (Hokkaido)	Japan	--
Lower temperate NW Pacific (Honshu)	P Shiriya (Honshu) - C Shio-no (Honshu)	Japan	R Kyu-Kitakami at Kanomata
			R Tone at Tone-Ozeki
			R Sagami at Samukawa
			R Kiso at Inuyama
Upper subtropical NW Pacific (Honshu)	C Shio-no - Kanmon Strait (Honshu/Kyushu)	Japan	L Biwa south center
			R Yodo at Hirakata Bridge
Upper subtropical NW Pacific (Shikoku)	Shikoku	Japan	R Yoshino at Takase
Upper subtropical NW Pacific (Kyushu)	Kyushu	Japan	R Chikugo at Senoshita
			R Kuma at Yokoishi
Upper subtropical NW Pacific (Ryukyu Is)	Ryukyu Is	Japan	--
E Sea of Japan (Honshu)	Kanmon Strait - P Shiriya	Japan	R Shinano at Kyuzogoya
E Sea of Japan (Hokkaido)	C Esan - C Soya	Japan	R Ishikari at Ishikari
W Sea of Japan	Amgu - Pusan (R Korea)	China, DR Korea, R Korea, Russia	--
Korea Strait	Pusan - Chindo	R Korea	R NakDong
			R YoungSan
E Yellow Sea	Chindo - Lushun	R Korea	R Han mouth
			R Han
			R Keum
		China, DR Korea	--
Liaodong Wan	Lushun - Qinhuangdao; *Liao 228,960*	China	--
Bo Hai	Qinhuangdao - Penglai *Huang (Yellow) 752,443*	China	R Huang (Yellow) at Jinan
SW Yellow Sea	Penglai - Qidong	China	--
Chang	Qidong - Nanhui; *Chang (Yangtze) 2,077,783*	China	R Chang (Yangtze) at Wuhan
			L Tai
East China Sea	Nanhui - Nan'ao Dao	China	--
Chinese South China Sea	Nan'ao Dao - Xi; Xi - Sanya (Hainan)	China	L Plover Cove stn 19 Hong Kong
Xi	*Xi (Pearl) 442,100*	China	R Xi (Pearl) at Zhaoqing
		Viet Nam	--
Gulf of Tonkin	Sanya - C Doc (Viet Nam); *Hong (Red) 169,600*	Viet Nam	R Hong (Red) mouth
		China, Lao	--
Vietnamese South China Sea	C Doc - C Ky Van	Viet Nam	--
Mekong	C Ky Van - C Nai (Viet Nam/Cambodia border); *Mekong 786,000*	Viet Nam	R Mekong
		Thailand	R Mun at Ubon Ratchathani
		Cambodia, China, Lao, Myanmar	--
E Gulf of Thailand	C Nai - Chao Phraya	Cambodia	--
		Thailand	R Bang at Pa Kong
Chao Phraya	*Chao Phraya 160,000*	Thailand	R Chao Phraya at Bangkok
			R Chao Phraya below Nakhon Sawan
			R Prasak at Kaeng Khoi
W Gulf of Thailand	Chao Phraya - Ko Samui	Thailand	--
Malay/Thai South China Sea	Ko Samui - Sungai Rengit (Malaysia)	Malaysia, Thailand	--
Borneo South China Sea	C Datu (Sarawak/Kalimantan border) - Tiga Tarok (Sabah)	Brunei Darussalam, Malaysia	--
Philippine South China Sea	C Melville (Balabac) - Mayraira P (N Luzon)	Philippines	B La Mesa
Lower subtropical NW Pacific	Mayraira P - Yog P (Catanduanes)	Philippines	R Cagayan
Tropical West Pacific			
Upper tropical W Pacific	Yog P - Kalipagan (S Mindanao)	Philippines	--

Realm & Basin	Extent	Country	Station
Sulu & Celebes Seas	rest of Philippines + Sabah E of Tiga Tarok + Kalimantan N of C Mangkalihat + N Sulawesi (C Dampelas - C Pulisan)	Indonesia, Malaysia, Philippines	--
Makassar Strait	C Mangkalihat - C South (Kalimantan) & C Dampelas - Selayar I (Sulawesi)	Indonesia	--
Java Sea & Karimata Strait (Kalimantan)	C South - C Datu	Indonesia	--
Java Sea & Karimata Strait (Sumatra)	Sunda Strait - Durian Strait	Indonesia	R Musi at Palembang
Java Sea (Java)	Sunda Strait - Bali Strait (N Java)	Indonesia	R Banjir Kanal
			R Sunter
			R Citarum
			R Surabaya
			B Saguling
Bali & Flores Seas	Bali Strait - Ombai Strait	Indonesia	--
Molucca & Halmahera Seas	C Pulisan (Sulawesi) - (Sula Is) + Halmahera	Indonesia	--
Ceram & Banda Seas	C Dehekolano - Selayar I (Sulawesi) + Buru, Ambon, Seram, Tenggara Is & Aru	Indonesia	--
New Guinea tropical	C Vais - C Memori (New Guinea)	Indonesia	--
New Guinea intertropical	C Memori - C Girgir (Papua New Guinea)	Indonesia, Papua New Guinea	--
Bismarck & Solomon Seas	C Girgir - Goschen Strait (PNG) + Bismarck Archipelago & Solomon Is	Papua New Guinea	R Sepik mouth
		Indonesia, Solomon Is	--
N Coral Sea	Goschen Strait - C Yubo (PNG)	Papua New Guinea	R Fly mouth
		Indonesia	--
E Coral Sea	Vanuatu - New Caledonia	New Caledonia, Vanuatu	--
W Coral Sea	C York - Sandy C; *Burdekin 131,000; Fitzroy 143,000*	Australia	R Burdekin mouth
Oceanic tropical W Pacific	Micronesia	Guam, Kiribati, Marshall Is, Federated States of Micronesia, Nauru, Northern Mariana Is, Palau	--
Southwest Pacific			
W Tasman Sea	Sandy C - C Howe	Australia	--
Bass Strait	C Howe - C Otway; C Naturaliste - Woolnorth P (Tasmania)	Australia	--
Subpolar SW Pacific	C Naturaliste - South West C (Tasmania)	Australia	R Derwent mouth
E Tasman Sea (South I)	Southwest C - Perano Head	New Zealand	R Oreti at Riverton hwy bridge
			R Waiau at Tuatapere
			R Haast at Roaring Billy
			R Grey at Dobson
			R Buller at Te Huha
			R Motueka at Woodstock
E Tasman Sea (North I)	C Terawhiti - C Reinga	New Zealand	R Manawatu at Opiki bridge
			R Rangitikei at Kakariki
			R Wanganui at Paetawa
			R Waingongoro at SH45
			R Waitara at Bertrand road
			R Waikato at Rangiriri
			R Hoteo at Gubbs
Temperate SW Pacific (North I)	C Reinga - C Terawhiti	New Zealand	R Waitangi at Wakelins
			R Waihou at Te Aroha bridge
			R Tarawera at Awakaponga
			R Rangitaiki at Te Teko
			R Motu at Houpoto
			R Mohaka at Raupunga
			R Ngaruroro at Chesterhope
			R Tukituki at Red bridge
			R Ruamahanga at Waiaenga
			R Hutt at Boulcott
Temperate SW Pacific (South I)	Perano Head - Southwest C	New Zealand	R Wairau at Tuamarina
			R Hurunui at Shi bridge
			R Waimakariri above Old hwy bridge
			R Opihi at Waipopo
			R Waitaki at Shi bridge
			R Taieri at Outram
			R Clutha at Balclutha
			R Mataura at Seaward Downs
Oceanic SW Pacific	Fiji & Polynesia (except Hawaiian Is)	American Samoa, Cook Is, Fiji, French Polynesia, Samoa, Tokelau, Tonga, Tuvalu, Wallis & Futuna	--

B = reservoir; C = cape; df = downstream frontier; E = east; I = island; Is = islands; L = lake; N = north; NE = northeast; NW = northwest; P = point; R = river; S = south; SE = southeast; SW = southwest; W = west.

References

Accademia Italiana della Cucina. 1995. I formaggi a denominazione di origine e tipici della Sardegna. [Origin-denominated and typical cheeses of Sardinia.] In: Accademia Italiana della Cucina. 1995. *1996 guide to the restaurants of Italy.*

Adriaanse, Albert. 1993. *Environmental policy performance indicators.* Sdu Uitgeverij Koninginnegracht, The Hague.

Adriaanse, Albert, Stefan Bringezu, Allen Hammond, Yuichi Moriguchi, Eric Rodenburg, Donald Rogich, and Helmut Schütz. 1997. *Resource flows: the material basis of industrial economies.* World Resources Institute, Washington, DC.

Ahmad, Y. J., S. El Sarafy, and E. Lutz (eds.). 1989. *Environmental accounting for sustainable development.* A United Nations Environment Programme–World Bank Symposium. The World Bank, Washington, DC.

Alderson, Lawrence. 1989. *The chance to survive.* A. H. Jolly (Editorial). Yelvertoft Manor, England.

Andreae, Meinrat O., and Robert E. Dickinson. 1995. Sustainability and the changing atmosphere: assessing changes in chemical and physical climate. In: Mohan Munasinghe and Walter Shearer (eds.). 1995. *Defining and measuring sustainability: the biogeophysical foundations.* The United Nations University and the World Bank, Washington, DC.

Asian Bureau for Conservation (ABC) and World Conservation Monitoring Centre (WCMC). 1997. *Protected area systems review of the Indo-Malayan Realm.* Asian Bureau for Conservation, Hong Kong (China) and Canterbury (England).

Associazione Nazionale Allevatori Bovini Razza Valdostana. 1995. Personal communication from the director, Dr. Piero Prola, May 1995, Associazione Nazionale Allevatori Bovini Razza Valdostana, Gressan, Valle d'Aosta, Italy.

Atkinson, Giles, and Kirk Hamilton. 1996. Accounting for progress: indicators for sustainable development. *Environment* 38(7).

Baitullin, I., and G. Bekturova. 1997. National strategy to combat desertification in the Republic of Kazakhstan. *Desertification Control Bulletin* 30: 19–27.

Bakkes, J. A., G. J. van den Born, J. C. Helder, R. J. Swart, C. W. Hope, and J. D. E. Parker. 1994. *An overview of environmental indicators: state of the art and perspectives.* United Nations Environment Programme (UNEP), Nairobi, and National Institute of Public Health and Environment (RIVM), Bilthoven, Netherlands.

Bakkes, Jan, and Jaap van Woerden (eds.). 1997. *The future of the global environment: a model-based analysis supporting UNEP's first global environment outlook.* National Institute of Public Health and Environment (RIVM), Bilthoven, Netherlands, and United Nations Environment Programme (UNEP), Nairobi.

Bangladesh Bureau of Statistics. 1999. *Bangladesh compendium of environment statistics 1997.* Bangladesh Bureau of Statistics, Statistics Division, Ministry of Planning, Government of the People's Republic of Bangladesh, Dhaka.

Bartelmus, Peter, and Jan van Tongeren. 1994. *Environmental accounting: an operational perspective.* DESIPA Working Paper Series 1. United Nations, New York.

Beeler, Giuseppe L. 1992. *Prontuario dello studioso.* [*Handbook for students.*] Istituto Editoriale Ticinese, Bellinzona, Switzerland.

BirdLife International. 2000. *Threatened birds of the world.* BirdLife International, Cambridge.

BIS/IMF/OECD/World Bank 2000. *Joint BIS-IMF-OECD-World Bank statistics on external debt.* Bank for International Settlements, International Monetary Fund, Organisation for Economic Co-operation and Development and The World Bank Group. www.oecd.org/dac/debt/htm.

Bixby, Donald E., Carolyn J. Christman, Cynthia J. Ehrman, and D. Phillip Sponenberg. 1994. *Taking stock: the North American livestock census.* McDonald and Woodward, Blacksburg, Virginia.

Black, John. 1997. *A dictionary of economics.* Oxford University Press, Oxford, England.

Boltvinik, Julio, and Enrique Hernández Laos. 1999. *Pobreza y distribución del ingreso en México.* [*Poverty and income distribution in Mexico.*] Siglo Veintuno Editores, México, DF.

Bryant, Dirk, Lauretta Burke, John McManus, and Mark Spalding. 1998. *Reefs at risk: a map-based indicator of threats to the world's coral reefs.* World Resources Institute (WRI), International Center for Living Aquatic Resources Management (ICLARM), World Conservation Monitoring Centre (WCMC), United Nations Environment Programme (UNEP), Washington, DC.

Canadian Centre for Justice Statistics. 1999. *Uniform crime reporting survey.* Statistics Canada, Ottawa.

Chichilnisky, Graciela. 1997. *The knowledge revolution.* Working Paper Series 9717, Faculty of Business and Law, Deakin University, Burwood, Victoria, Australia.

Chichilnisky, Graciela. 1998. *The knowledge revolution: its impact on consumption patterns and resource use.* Paper prepared for the Human Development Report 1998. United Nations Development Programme, New York.

Cobb, Clifford, Ted Halstead, and Jonathan Rowe. 1995a. *The Genuine Progress Indicator: summary of data and methodology.* Redefining Progress, San Francisco.

Cobb, Clifford, Ted Halstead, and Jonathan Rowe. 1995b. If the GDP is up, why is America down? *The Atlantic Monthly,* October 1995.

Collar, N. J., M. J. Crosby, and A. J. Stattersfield. 1994. *Birds to watch 2: the world list of threatened birds.* BirdLife International, Cambridge, England.

Conservation International. 1996. *Database on human disturbance of world ecosystems.* Conservation International, Washington, DC.

Consultative Group on Sustainable Development Indicators. 2000. *Dashboard of sustainability,* version 1.5. International Institute for Sustainable Development, Winnipeg.

Corner House, The. 1997. *Climate and equity after Kyoto.* Briefing 3. The Corner House, Sturminster Newton, England.

Corson, Walter H. 1996. Measuring sustainability: indicators, trends, and performance. In: Dennis C. Pirages (ed.). 1996. *Building sustainable societies: a blueprint for a post-industrial world.* M.E. Sharpe.

Cunningham, E. P., and O. Syrstad. 1987. *Crossbreeding* Bos indicus *and* Bos taurus *for milk production in the tropics.* FAO Animal Production and Health Paper 68, Food and Agriculture Organization of the United Nations, Rome.

Daly, Herman E., and John B. Cobb, Jr. 1989. *For the common good: redirecting the economy toward community, the environment and a sustainable future.* Beacon Press, Boston.

Dieren, Wouter van (ed.). 1995. *Taking nature into account: toward a sustainable national income.* A report to the Club of Rome. Springer-Verlag, New York.

Dinerstein, Eric, David M. Olson, Douglas J. Graham, Avis L. Webster, Steven A. Primm, Marnie P. Bookbinder, and George Ledec. 1995. *A conservation assessment of the terrestrial ecoregions of Latin America and the Caribbean.* The World Bank, Washington, DC.

The Economist. 1997. Guide to economic indicators. 3rd edition. Profile Books, London.

The Economist. 1999. The navigators [central banks]: a survey of the world economy. *The Economist,* 25 September 1999.

Eurostat. 1997. *Indicators of sustainable development: a pilot study following the methodology of the United Nations Commission on Sustainable Development.* European Communities, Luxembourg.

Eurostat. 2000. *GDP and government finances in the EU.* Eurostat, Luxembourg.

Eurostat, European Commission, and the European Environment Agency. 1998. *Europe's environment: statistical compendium for the second assessment.* European Communities, Luxembourg.

Eurostat, European Commission, European Environment Agency Task Force, DG XI and PHARE European Commission, United Nations Economic Commission for Europe, Organisation for Economic Cooperation and Development, and World Health Organization. 1995. *Europe's environment: statistical compendium for the Dobris assessment.* Office for Official Publications of the European Community, Luxembourg.

Fairbairn, Te'o I. J., Charles E. Morrison, Richard W. Baker, and Sheree A. Groves. 1991. *The Pacific Islands: politics, economics, and international relations.* East–West Center, University of Hawaii Press, Honolulu.

FAO Fishery Information, Data and Statistics Unit. 1998. Fishery fleet statistics on diskette. Food and Agriculture Organization of the United Nations, Rome.

FAO Initiative for Domesticated Animal Diversity. 1998. *Domesticated Animal Diversity Information System (DAD-IS) 2.0.* CD-ROM. Food and Agriculture Organization of the United Nations, Rome.

FAO Initiative for Domesticated Animal Diversity. 1999. Domesticated Animal Diversity Information System (DAD-IS) online. www.fao.org/dad-is/index.htm

FAO Marine Resources Service, Fishery Resources Division. 1997. *Review of the state of world fishery resources: marine fisheries.* FAO Fisheries Circular 920. Food and Agriculture Organization of the United Nations, Rome.

FAO, UNDP, and UNEP. 1994. *Land degradation in South Asia: its severity, causes and effects upon the people.* World Soil Resources Reports 78. Food and Agriculture Organization of the United Nations, Rome.

Federal Bureau of Investigation. 1999. *Uniform crime reports:*

crime in the United States 1997. Department of Justice, Washington, DC.

Fenwick, J. 1992. *International profiles on marine scientific research*. Woods Hole Oceanographic Institution, Massachusetts.

Fischer-Kowalski, Marina, Helmut Haberl, and Harald Payer. 1997. In: Bedrich Moldan and Suzanne Billharz. 1997. *Sustainability indicators: report of the project on indicators of sustainable development*. SCOPE 58. Wiley, New York.

Food and Agriculture Organization of the United Nations (FAO). 1993. *Forest resources assessment 1990. Tropical countries*. FAO Forestry Paper 112. Food and Agriculture Organization of the United Nations, Rome.

Food and Agriculture Organization of the United Nations (FAO). 1995a. *Irrigation in Africa in figures*. Water Reports 7. Food and Agriculture Organization of the United Nations, Rome.

Food and Agriculture Organization of the United Nations (FAO). 1995b. *Water resources of African countries: a review*. Food and Agriculture Organization of the United Nations, Rome.

Food and Agriculture Organization of the United Nations (FAO). 1995c. *Forest resources assessment 1990. Global synthesis*. FAO Forestry Paper 124. Food and Agriculture Organization of the United Nations, Rome.

Food and Agriculture Organization of the United Nations (FAO). 1996a. *The Sixth World Food Survey, 1996*. Food and Agriculture Organization of the United Nations, Rome.

Food and Agriculture Organization of the United Nations (FAO). 1996b. *Global databank for farm animal genetic resources*. Domestic Animal Diversity (DAD) database. Food and Agriculture Organization of the United Nations, Rome.

Food and Agriculture Organization of the United Nations (FAO). 1997a. *Statistical estimates for forest cover, Forest Resources Assessment Programme*. Food and Agriculture Organization of the United Nations, Rome.

Food and Agriculture Organization of the United Nations (FAO). 1997b. *Irrigation in the Near East region in figures*. Water Reports 9. Food and Agriculture Organization of the United Nations, Rome.

Food and Agriculture Organization of the United Nations (FAO). 1997c. *Irrigation in the countries of the former Soviet Union in figures*. Water Reports 15. Food and Agriculture Organization of the United Nations, Rome.

Food and Agriculture Organization of the United Nations (FAO). 1997d. *Irrigation potential in Africa*. FAO Land and Water Bulletin 4. Food and Agriculture Organization of the United Nations, Rome.

Food and Agriculture Organization of the United Nations

(FAO). 1998a. FAOSTAT database. Food and Agriculture Organization of the United Nations, Rome.

Food and Agriculture Organization of the United Nations (FAO). 1998b. *FAO yearbook: fishery statistics, capture production: Vol. 82, 1996*. Food and Agriculture Organization of the United Nations, Rome.

Food and Agriculture Organization of the United Nations (FAO). 1999a. FAOSTAT database. Food and Agriculture Organization of the United Nations, Rome.

Food and Agriculture Organization of the United Nations (FAO). 1999b. *The state of food insecurity in the world*. Food and Agriculture Organization of the United Nations, Rome.

Food and Agriculture Organization of the United Nations (FAO). 1999c. *Irrigation in Asia in figures*. Water Reports 18. Food and Agriculture Organization of the United Nations, Rome.

Food and Agriculture Organization of the United Nations (FAO). 2000a. FAOSTAT database. Food and Agriculture Organization of the United Nations, Rome.

Food and Agriculture Organization of the United Nations (FAO). 2000b. *Irrigation in Latin America in figures*. Water Reports in press. Food and Agriculture Organization of the United Nations, Rome.

Freedom House. 1999a. *Freedom in the world, 1998–1999*. Freedom House, New York.

Freedom House. 1999b. *Press freedom survey, 1999*. Freedom House, New York.

Freedom House. 2000a. *Freedom in the world, 1999–2000*. Freedom House, New York.

Freedom House. 2000b. *Press freedom survey, 2000*. Freedom House, New York.

Gallopín, Gilberto Carlos. 1997. Indicators and their use: information for decision-making. Part 1: Introduction. In: Bedrich Moldan and Suzanne Billharz. 1997. *Sustainability indicators: report of the project on indicators of sustainable development*. SCOPE 58. Wiley, New York.

Garcia, S. M., and C. Newton. 1994. *Current situation, trends and prospects in world capture fisheries*. Paper presented at the Conference on Fisheries Management: Global Trends. Seattle, Washington, 14–16 June 1994. Fisheries Department, Food and Agriculture Organization of the United Nations, Rome.

Global Environmental Monitoring System (GEMS). 1988. *Assessment of freshwater quality*. United Nations Environment Programme, Nairobi, and World Health Organization, Geneva.

Global Leaders for Environment Tomorrow Task Force. 2001. *Pilot environmental sustainability index*. World Economic

Forum, in collaboration with Yale Center for Environmental Law and Policy, Yale University, and Center for International Earth Science Information Network, Columbia University, New York.

Goldsmith, Edward, Robert Allen, Michael Allaby, John Davoll, and Sam Lawrence. 1972. *Blueprint for survival.* Penguin, Harmondsworth, and Houghton Mifflin, Boston.

Grainger, R. J. R., and S. M. Garcia. 1996. *Chronicles of marine fishery landings (1950–1994). Trend analysis and fisheries potential.* FAO Fisheries Technical Paper 359. Food and Agriculture Organization of the United Nations, Rome.

Gutierrez Montes, Isabel Adriana. 1996. Aportes de un proyecto de manejo de vida silvestre a la calidad de vida de las poblaciones rurales—el caso de la Cooperativa Omar Baca, Cosigüina, Nicaragua. [*Contributions of a wildlife management project to the quality of life of rural populations—the case of the Omar Baca Cooperative, Cosigüina, Nicaragua.*] Centro Agronomico Tropical de Investigacion y Eseñanza (CATIE), Turrialba, Costa Rica.

Guveya, Emmanuel, Freddie Kachote, and Misael Kokwe. 1999. *A wellbeing assessment of Mangisai, Nyevera and Sedeya communities in Zimuto Communal Lands, Zimbabwe.* IUCN– The World Conservation Union Regional Office for Southern Africa, Harare, Zimbabwe.

Hamilton, Kirk, and Ernst Lutz. 1996. *Green national accounts: policy uses and empirical experience.* Environment Department Papers, Environmental Economics Series, Paper 39. The World Bank, Washington, DC.

Hammond, Allen, Albert Adriaanse, Eric Rodenburg, Dirk Bryant, and Richard Woodward. 1995. *Environmental indicators: a systematic approach to measuring and reporting on environmental policy performance in the context of sustainable development.* World Resources Institute, Washington, DC.

Hannah, Lee, John L. Carr, and Ali Lankerani. 1995. Human disturbance and natural habitat: a biome level analysis of a global data set. *Biodiversity and Conservation* 4: 128–155.

Hannah, Lee, David Lohse, Charles Hutchinson, John L. Carr, and Ali Lankerani. 1994. A preliminary inventory of human disturbance of world ecosystems. *Ambio* 23(4–5): 246–250.

Hardi, Peter, and Terence Zdan (eds.). 1997. *Assessing sustainable development: principles in practice.* International Institute for Sustainable Development, Winnipeg.

Harvard University Environmental Systems Program. 1996. *Measuring sustainable development in Asia: environmental quality indices.* Final Report. Asian Development Bank, Manila.

Hasnain, H. U. 1985. *Sheep and goats in Pakistan.* FAO Animal Production and Health Paper 56, Food and Agriculture Organization of the United Nations, Rome.

Hayden, Bruce P., G. Carleton Ray, and Robert Dolan. 1984. Classification of coastal and marine environments. *Environmental Conservation* 11(3): 199–207.

Hecht, Joy E. No date. *Environmental accounting: what's it all about?* IUCN Green Accounting Initiative. IUCN–The World Conservation Union, Washington, DC.

Hodge, Tony. 1995. From theory to practice: assessing progress toward sustainable development in the Great Lakes Basin. In: Tony Hodge, Susan Holtz, Cameron Smith, and Kelly Hawke Baxter (eds.). 1995. *Pathways to sustainability: assessing our progress.* National Round Table on the Environment and the Economy, Ottawa.

Hodge, R. Anthony, and Robert Prescott-Allen. 1997. *Report on British Columbia's progress toward sustainability.* Ministry of Environment, Lands and Parks, Victoria, British Columbia.

Holling, C. S. 1995. Sustainability: the cross-scale dimension. In: Mohan Munasinghe and Walter Shearer (eds.). 1995. *Defining and measuring sustainability: the biogeophysical foundations.* The United Nations University and the World Bank, Washington, DC.

Humana, Charles. 1992. *World human rights guide,* 3rd edition. Oxford University Press, New York.

Hunter, M. L. Jr., G. L. Jacobson Jr., and T. Webb. 1988. Paleoecology and the coarse-filter approach to maintaining biological diversity. *Conservation Biology* (2): 375–383.

Imbach, Alejandro. 1996. *Participatory rural assessment and mapping.* IUCN–The World Conservation Union, Gland, Switzerland.

IMF Policy Development and Review Department. 2000. Debt- and reserve-related indicators of vulnerability. International Monetary Fund, Washington, DC.

IMO/FAO/UNESCO/WMO/WHO/IAEA/UN/UNEP Joint Group of Experts on the Scientific Aspects of Marine Pollution (GESAMP). 1990. *The state of the marine environment.* Reports and Studies GESAMP 39. United Nations Environment Programme, Nairobi.

Instituto Nacional de Estadística, Geografía e Informática. 1998. *Estadísticas del medio ambiente, México, 1997.* [*Environmental Statistics, México, 1997.*] Secretaría de Medio Ambiente, Recursos Naturales y Pesca, México.

Intergovernmental Panel on Climate Change, Working Group 1. 1996. *Climate change 1995: the science of climate change.* Cambridge University Press, Cambridge, England.

International Institute for Strategic Studies. 1996. *The military balance 1996/97.* Oxford University Press for the International Institute for Strategic Studies, London.

International Institute for Strategic Studies. 1997. *The military balance 1997/98.* Oxford University Press for the International Institute for Strategic Studies, London.

International Institute for Strategic Studies. 1999a. *The military balance 1999/2000.* Oxford University Press for the International Institute for Strategic Studies, London.

International Institute for Strategic Studies. 1999b. *The 1999 chart of armed conflict.* The International Institute for Strategic Studies, London.

International Labour Office (ILO). 1999. *Key indicators of the labour market 1999.* International Labour Office, Geneva.

International Labour Office. 2000. LABORSTA: Labour Statistcs Database. http://laborsta.ilo.org/.

International Monetary Fund (IMF). 2000. *World Economic Outlook (WEO) Database September 2000.* International Monetary Fund, Washington, DC.

International Telecommunication Union. 1997. *Yearbook of statistics: telecommunication services 1986–1995.* International Telecommunication Union, Geneva.

International Telecommunication Union. 1998. *World telecommunication development report 1998.* International Telecommunication Union, Geneva.

International Telecommunication Union. 1999. *World telecommunication development report 1999.* International Telecommunication Union, Geneva.

International Telecommunication Union. 2000. Data tables on basic indicators, cellular subscribers, and Internet indicators, January 2000. Personal communication, Telecommunication Development Bureau, International Telecommunication Union, Geneva.

Inter-Parliamentary Union. 2000. *Women in national parliaments.* www.ipu.org.

Inter-Secretariat Working Group on National Accounts. 1993. *System of national accounts.* United Nations, New York.

Iremonger, S., C. Ravilious, and T. Quinton (eds.). 1997. *A global overview of forest conservation.* CD-ROM. World Conservation Monitoring Centre (WCMC) and Center for International Forestry Research (CIFOR), Cambridge, England.

IUCN CNPPA. 1994. *Guidelines for protected area management categories.* Commission on National Parks and Protected Areas (CNPPA) [now World Commission on Protected Areas], IUCN–The World Conservation Union, Gland, Switzerland, and Cambridge, England.

IUCN Species Survival Commission. 1994. *IUCN Red List categories.* IUCN–The World Conservation Union, Gland, Switzerland.

IUCN Species Survival Commission. 2000. *The 2000 IUCN Red List of Threatened Species.* IUCN–World Conservation Union, Gland, Switzerland.

IUCN/UNEP/WWF. 1980. *World conservation strategy: living resource conservation for sustainable development.* International Union for Conservation of Nature and Natural Resources (IUCN), United Nations Environment Programme (UNEP), Nairobi, and World Wildlife Fund, Gland, Switzerland.

IUCN/UNEP/WWF. 1991. *Caring for the earth: a strategy for sustainable living.* IUCN–The World Conservation Union, United Nations Environment Programme (UNEP), Nairobi, and World Wildlife Fund, Gland, Switzerland.

IUCN World Commission on Protected Areas and World Conservation Monitoring Centre. 1998. *United Nations list of protected areas 1997.* IUCN–The World Conservation Union, Gland, Switzerland, and World Conservation Monitoring Centre, Cambridge, England.

Junker, Armin, and Dietrich Schwela. 1998. *Air quality guidelines, standards and risk considerations.* Contribution to the XI World Clean Air and Environment Congress, 13–18 September 1998, Durban, South Africa.

Kumar, Ashok. 1999. *A system assessment of Dasudi Gram Panchayat.* IUCN–The World Conservation Union, Gland, Switzerland.

Kunte, Arundhati, Kirk Hamilton, John Dixon, and Michael Clemens. 1998. *Estimating national wealth: methodology and results.* Environment Department Papers, Environmental Economics Series, Paper 57. The World Bank, Washington, DC.

Landes, David. 1999. *The wealth and poverty of nations.* Abacus, London.

Leroux, Guy. 1980. *La cuisine brésilienne* [Brazilian cuisine]. Les Editions du Pacifique, Papeete, Tahiti.

Levin, Simon A. 1995. Scale and sustainability: a population and community perspective. In: Mohan Munasinghe and Walter Shearer (eds.). 1995. *Defining and measuring sustainability: the biogeophysical foundations.* The United Nations University and the World Bank, Washington, DC.

Loh, Jonathan, Jørgen Randers, Alex MacGillivray, Val Kapos, Martin Jenkins, Brian Groombridge, Neil Cox, and Ben Warren. 1999. *Living planet report 1999.* WWF International, Gland, Switzerland.

Lopez, Alan D., Joshua Salomon, Omar Ahmad, Christopher J.L. Murray, and Doris Mafat. 2000. *Life tables for 191 countries: data, methods and results.* GPE Discussion Paper 9. World Health Organization, Geneva.

Lutz, E. (ed.) 1993. *Toward improved accounting for the environment.* An UNSTAT–World Bank Symposium. The World Bank, Washington, DC.

MacKinnon, John, and Kathy MacKinnon. 1986a. *Review of the protected areas system in the Afrotropical realm.* International Union for Conservation of Nature and Natural Resources, Gland, Switzerland, and United Nations Environment Programme (UNEP), Nairobi.

MacKinnon, John, and Kathy MacKinnon. 1986b. *Review of the protected areas system in the Indo-Malayan realm.* International Union for Conservation of Nature and Natural Resources, Gland, Switzerland, and United Nations Environment Programme (UNEP), Nairobi.

Manitoba Environment. 1997. *Moving toward sustainable development reporting: state of the environment report for Manitoba 1997.* SOE Reporting, Manitoba Environment, Winnipeg, Manitoba.

Marland, Gregg, Tom Boden, and Robert J. Andres. 2000 (6 September). *National CO$_2$ emissions from fossil-fuel burning, cement manufacture, and gas flaring 1751–1997.* Carbon Dioxide Information Analysis Center, Oak Ridge National Laboratory, Oak Ridge, Tennessee.

Mathers, Colin D., Ritu Sadana, Joshua A. Salomon, Christopher J.L. Murray, and Alan D. Lopez. 2000. *Estimates of DALE for 191 countries: methods and results.* Global Programme on Evidence for Health Policy Discussion Paper 16. World Health Organization, Geneva.

Matthews, Emily, Christof Amann, Stefan Bringezu, Marina Fischer-Kowalski, Walter Hüttler, René Kleijn, Yuichi Moriguchi, Christian Ottke, Eric Rodenburg, Don Rogich, Heinz Schandl, Helmut Schütz, Ester van der Voet, and Helga Weisz. 2000. *The weight of nations: material outflows from industrial economies.* World Resources Institute, Washington, DC.

McNeely, Jeffrey (ed.). 1993. *Parks for life: report of the IVth World Congress on National Parks and Protected Areas.* IUCN–The World Conservation Union, Gland, Switzerland.

Munasinghe, Mohan, and Jeffrey McNeely. 1995. Key concepts and terminology of sustainable development. In: Mohan Munasinghe and Walter Shearer (eds.). 1995. *Defining and measuring sustainability: the biogeophysical foundations.* The United Nations University and the World Bank, Washington, DC.

National Water Research Institute. 1996. *The Annotated Digital Atlas of Global Water Quality.* World Health Organization (WHO) and United Nations Environment Programme (UNEP) Global Environment Monitoring System (GEMS), Geneva

OECD Centre for Co-operation with the Economies in Transition. 1996. *Environmental information systems in the Russian Federation: an OECD assessment.* Organisation for Economic Co-operation and Development, Paris.

Office of the UN System Support and Services. 1996. *UN conference goals and commitments inter-related to the "DAC reflection."* United Nations Development Programme, New York.

Oldeman, L. R. 1993. *An international methodology for an assessment of soil degradation and georeferenced soils and terrain database.* International Soil Reference and Information Centre, Wageningen, Netherlands.

Oldeman, L. R., R. T. A. Hakkeling, and W. G. Sombroek. 1991. *World map of the status of human-induced soil degradation: an explanatory note,* 2nd revised edition. International Soil Reference and Information Centre, Wageningen, Netherlands, and United Nations Environment Programme, Nairobi.

O'Neill, R. V., C. T. Hunsaker, D. Jones, J. M. Klopatek, V. H. Dale, M. G. Turner, R. H. Gardner, and R. Graham. 1995. Sustainability and landscape and regional scales. In: Mohan Munasinghe and Walter Shearer (eds.). 1995. *Defining and measuring sustainability: the biogeophysical foundations.* The United Nations University and the World Bank, Washington, DC.

Onis, Mercedes de, and Monika Blössner. 1997. *WHO global database on child growth and malnutrition.* World Health Organization, Geneva.

Organisation for Economic Co-operation and Development. 1994. *Environmental indicators: OECD core set.* Organisation for Economic Co-operation and Development, Paris.

Organisation for Economic Co-operation and Development. 1997. *OECD environmental data: compendium 1997.* Organisation for Economic Co-operation and Development, Paris.

Organisation for Economic Co-operation and Development. 1999. *OECD environmental data: compendium 1999.* Organisation for Economic Co-operation and Development, Paris.

Organisation for Economic Co-operation and Development, Human Resources Development Canada, and Statistics Canada. 1997. *Literacy skills for the knowledge society: further results from the International Adult Literacy Survey.* Organisation for Economic Co-operation and Development, Paris, and Human Resources Development Canada and Statistics Canada, Ottawa.

Ozone Secretariat, United Nations Environment Programme. 1997. *Production and consumption of ozone depleting substances 1986–1995.* Ozone Secretariat, UNEP, Nairobi.

Ozone Secretariat, United Nations Environment Programme. 1999. *Production and consumption of ozone depleting substances 1986–1998.* Ozone Secretariat, UNEP, Nairobi.

Pajuoja, Heikki. 1995. *The outlook for the European forest resources and roundwood supply.* UNECE/FAO Timber and Forest Discussion Papers, ETTS V Working Paper ECE/TIM/DP/4. United Nations Economic Commission for Europe and Food and Agriculture Organization of the United Nations, New York and Geneva.

Palmer, Kara, and Richard Conlin. 1997. Sustainable Seattle: the indicators of sustainable community. In: Peter Hardi and Terence Zdan. 1997. *Assessing sustainable development: princi-*

ples in practice. International Institute for Sustainable Development, Winnipeg.

Pandey, Devendra. 1995. *Forest resources assessment 1990. Tropical forest plantation resources.* FAO Forestry Paper 128. Food and Agriculture Organization of the United Nations, Rome.

Pernetta, John, and Danny Elder. 1993. *Cross-sectoral, integrated coastal area planning (CICAP): guidelines and principles for coastal area development.* IUCN–The World Conservation Union, Gland, Switzerland.

Porter, Valerie. 1991. *Cattle: a handbook to the breeds of the world.* Christopher Helm, London.

Porter, Valerie. 1993. *Pigs: a handbook to the breeds of the world.* Helm Information, Mountfield, England.

Prescott-Allen, Robert. 1995. *Barometer of sustainability: a method of assessing progress toward sustainable societies,* 3rd draft. PADATA, Victoria, BC.

Prescott-Allen, Robert. 1997. *Barometer of sustainability: measuring and communicating wellbeing and sustainable development.* An Approach to Assessing Progress Toward Sustainability: Tools and Training Series. IUCN–The World Conservation Union, Gland, Switzerland.

Ray, G. Carleton. 1996a. Biodiversity is biogeography: implications for conservation. *Oceanography* 9(1): 50–59.

Ray, G. Carleton. 1996b. Coastal–marine discontinuities and synergisms: implications for biodiversity conservation. *Biodiversity and Conservation* 5: 1095–1108.

Redefining Progress. 1999. *Footprint of Nations ranking list (1995 data).* Updated 20 October 1999. Redefining Progress, San Francisco.

Rege, J. E. O. 1999. The state of African cattle genetic resources I. Classification framework and identification of threatened and extinct breeds. *Animal Genetic Resources Information* 25: 1–25.

Rege, J. E. O., G. S. Aboagye, and C. L. Tawah. 1994. Shorthorn cattle of west and central Africa I. Origin, distribution, classification and population statistics. *World Animal Review* 78(1): 2–13.

Rege, J. E. O., and C. L. Tawah. 1999. The state of African cattle genetic resources II. Geographical distribution, characteristics and uses of present-day breeds and strains. *Animal Genetic Resources Information* 26: 1–25.

Reid, Walter V., and Kenton R. Miller. 1989. *Keeping options alive: the scientific basis for conserving biodiversity.* World Resources Institute, Washington, DC.

Repetto, R., W. Magrath, M. Wells, C. Beer, and F. Rossini. 1989. *Wasting assets: natural resources in the national income accounts.* World Resources Institute, Washington, DC.

Ricketts, Taylor, Eric Dinerstein, David Olson, Colby Loucks, William Eichbaum, Kevin Kavanagh, Prashant Hedao,

Patrick Hurley, Karen Carney, Robin Abell, and Steven Walters. 1998. *A conservation assessment of the terrestrial ecoregions of North America. Volume I: the United States and Canada* (prepublication draft). World Wildlife Fund, Washington, DC.

Sachs, Jeffrey D., and Wing Thye Woo. 1999. Executive summary: The Asian financial crisis: what happened, and what is to be done. *Asia competitiveness report 1999.* World Economic Forum, www.weforum.org.

Scherf, Beate D. (ed.). 1995. *World Watch list for domestic animal diversity,* 2nd edition. Food and Agriculture Organization of the United Nations, Rome.

Serageldin, Ismail, and Andrew Steer. 1994. Epilogue: expanding the capital stock. In: Ismail Serageldin and Andrew Steer (eds.). 1994. *Making development sustainable: from concepts to action.* Environmentally Sustainable Development Occasional Papers 2. The World Bank, Washington, DC.

Sheng, Fulai. 1995. *Real value for nature: an overview of global efforts to achieve true measures of economic progress.* World Wide Fund for Nature (WWF) International, Gland, Switzerland.

Sherman, Kenneth. 1995. Large marine ecosystems and fisheries. In: Mohan Munasinghe and Walter Shearer (eds.). 1995. *Defining and measuring sustainability: the biogeophysical foundations.* The United Nations University and the World Bank, Washington, DC.

Shiklomanov, I. A. 1997. *Comprehensive assessment of the freshwater resources of the world.* World Meteorological Organization, Geneva.

Simon, D. L. 1999. European approaches to conservation of farm animal genetic resources. *Animal Genetic Resources Information* 25: 79–99.

Smith, Adam. 1986 [1776]. *The wealth of nations. Books I–III.* Penguin Books, London.

Stuart, Simon N., and Richard J. Adams. 1990. *Biodiversity in Sub-Saharan Africa and its islands: conservation, management and sustainable use.* Occasional Papers of the IUCN Species Survival Commission 6. IUCN–The World Conservation Union, Gland, Switzerland.

Swart, Rob, and Jan Bakkes (eds.). 1995. *Scanning the global environment: a framework and methodology for integrated environmental reporting and assessment.* United Nations Environment Programme (UNEP), Nairobi, and National Institute of Public Health and Environment (RIVM), Bilthoven, Netherlands.

Third Ministerial Conference on the Protection of Forests in Europe. 1998. *Follow-up reports on the Ministerial Conferences on the Protection of Forests in Europe,* volume II. Ministry of Agriculture, Rural Development and Fisheries, Lisbon, Portugal.

Touring Club Italiano. 1993. *Annuario generale dei comuni e delle frazioni d'Italia.* [*Gazetteer of the municipalities and hamlets of Italy.*] Touring Club Italiano, Milan.

Transparency International. 1999. *1999 Corruption perceptions index.* http://www.gwdg.de/~uwvw/1999Data.html.

Transparency International. 2000. *The 2000 corruption perceptions index.* Transparency International, Berlin. www.transparancy.de/documents/cpi/2000/.

UNECE and FAO. 2000. *Temperate and boreal forest resource assessment 2000.* United Nations Economic Commission for Europe, Geneva, and Food and Agriculture Organization of the United Nations, Rome.

UNEP/ISRIC. 1990. *World map on status of human-induced soil degradation.* United Nations Environment Programme, Nairobi.

UNEP and WHO GEMS/Water Collaborating Centre. 1988–1990. *GEMS/Water data summary 1988 1990.* World Health Organization and United Nations Environment Programme. National Water Research Institute, Burlington, Ontario.

UNEP and WHO GEMS/Water Collaborating Centre. 1991–1993. *GEMS/Water data summary 1991–1993.* World Health Organization and United Nations Environment Programme. National Water Research Institute, Burlington, Ontario.

UNEP and WHO GEMS/Water Collaborating Centre. 1999. GEMS/Water database. World Health Organization and United Nations Environment Programme. National Water Research Institute, Burlington, Ontario.

UNESCO. 1999a. Illiteracy estimates and projections. Personal communication, UNESCO Institute for Statistics, United Nations Educational, Scientific and Cultural Organization, Paris.

UNESCO. 1999b. Net enrollment rates. Personal communication, UNESCO Institute for Statistics, United Nations Educational, Scientific and Cultural Organization, Paris.

UNESCO. 1999c. Number of tertiary students per 100,000 inhabitants. Personal communication, UNESCO Institute for Statistics, United Nations Educational, Scientific and Cultural Organization, Paris.

UNESCO. 1999d. *Statistical yearbook 1999.* United Nations Educational, Scientific and Cultural Organization, Paris, and Bernan Press, Lanham, MD.

UNICEF. 1999a. *The state of the world's children 1999.* Oxford University Press, Oxford, England.

UNICEF. 1999b. *The state of the world's children 2000.* www.unicef.org.

United Nations. 1992. *Agenda 21: programme of action for sustainable development.* United Nations, New York.

United Nations. 1995. *The world's women 1995: trends and statistics.* Social Statistics and Indicators Series K No. 12. United Nations, New York.

United Nations. 1996. *Indicators of sustainable development framework and methodologies.* United Nations, New York.

United Nations ACC Task Force on Basic Social Services for All. 1997. *Basic social services for all 1997.* United Nations, New York.

United Nations Crime Prevention and Criminal Justice Division. 1997. *4th UN survey of crime trends and operations of criminal justice systems.* United Nations, Vienna.

United Nations Crime Prevention and Criminal Justice Division. 1999. *5th UN survey of crime trends and operations of criminal justice systems.* United Nations, Vienna.

United Nations Development Programme. 1990. *Human development report 1990.* Oxford University Press, Oxford, England.

United Nations Development Programme. 1991. *Human development report 1991.* Oxford University Press, Oxford, England.

United Nations Development Programme. 1992. *Human development report 1992.* Oxford University Press, Oxford, England.

United Nations Development Programme. 1993. *Human development report 1993.* Oxford University Press, Oxford, England.

United Nations Development Programme. 1994. *Human development report 1994.* Oxford University Press, Oxford, England.

United Nations Development Programme. 1995. *Human development report 1995.* Oxford University Press, Oxford, England.

United Nations Development Programme. 1996. *Human development report 1996.* Oxford University Press, Oxford, England.

United Nations Development Programme. 1997. *Human development report 1997.* Oxford University Press, Oxford, England.

United Nations Development Programme. 1998. *Human development report 1998.* Oxford University Press, Oxford, England.

United Nations Development Programme. 1999. *Human development report 1999.* Oxford University Press, Oxford, England.

United Nations Development Programme. 2000. *Human development report 2000.* Oxford University Press, New York and Oxford.

United Nations Division for the Advancement of Women.

1996. *Fact sheet on women in government as at January 1996.* United Nations, New York.

United Nations Economic Commission for Europe. 1990. Draft ECE standard statistical classification of ecological freshwater quality. In: Statistical Office, Department of International Economic and Social Affairs. 1991. *Concepts and methods of environment statistics: statistics of the natural environment. A technical report.* Studies in Methods, series F, no. 57. United Nations, New York.

United Nations Economic Commission for Europe. 2000. Statistics on unemployment. www.unece.org/stats/data.htm.

United Nations Energy Statistics Unit. 2000. *1997 Energy statistics yearbook.* United Nations, New York.

United Nations Environment Programme. 1996. *Report of the Secretariat on information provided by the parties in accordance with articles 7 and 9 of the Montreal Protocol.* United Nations Environment Programme, Nairobi.

United Nations Environment Programme. 1998. *Report of the Secretariat on information provided by the parties in accordance with articles 7 and 9 of the Montreal Protocol.* United Nations Environment Programme, Nairobi.

United Nations Environment Programme. 1999. *Global environment outlook 2000.* United Nations Environment Programme, Nairobi.

United Nations Population Division. 1996. *World population prospects: the 1996 revision. Annex I: Demographic indicators.* United Nations, New York.

United Nations Population Division. 1997. *Information note: wall chart on basic social services for all, 1977.* United Nations, New York.

United Nations Population Division. 1998a. *World population prospects: the 1998 revision.* United Nations, New York.

United Nations Population Division. 1998b. *World population projections to 2150.* United Nations, New York.

United Nations Statistical Commission and Economic Commission for Europe. 1992. *The environment in Europe and North America: annotated statistics 1992.* United Nations, New York.

United Nations Statistical Division. 1993. *Integrated environmental and economic accounting: interim version. Handbook of national accounting.* Studies in Methods, Series F, 61. United Nations, New York.

United Nations Statistical Division. 1997. *Minimum national social data set (MNSDS).* Endorsed by the United Nations Statistical Commission at its 29th session, 11–14 February 1997. United Nations, New York.

United Nations Statistical Division. 1999. *Statistical yearbook.* United Nations, New York.

U.S. Bureau of the Census. 1999. *Current population survey.* U.S. Bureau of the Census, Washington, DC.

van Lynden, G. W. J., and L. R. Oldeman. 1997. *The assessment of the status of human-induced soil degradation in south and southeast Asia.* United Nations Environment Programme, Nairobi, Food and Agricultural Organization of the United Nations, Rome, and International Soil Reference and Information Centre, Wageningen, Netherlands.

Visschedjik, Jan, and Sylvère Siméant. 1998. Targets for health for all in the 21st century. *World Health Statistics Quarterly* 51(1): 56–67.

Vitousek, P. M., P. R. Ehrlich, A. H. Ehrlich, and P. A. Matson. 1986. Human appropriation of the products of photosynthesis. *BioScience* 36(6): 366–373.

Wackernagel, Mathis, Alejandro Callejas Linares, Diana Deumling, Niels B. Schulz, María Antonieta Vásquez Sánchez, Ina Susana López Falfán, and Jonathan Loh. 2000. *Ecological footprints and ecological capacities of 152 nations: the 1996 update.* Redefining Progress, San Francisco.

Wackernagel, Mathis, and William E. Rees. 1996. *Our ecological footprint: reducing human impact on the earth.* New Society Publishers, Gabriola Island, BC.

Weizsäcker, Ernst von, Amory B. Lovins, and L.Hunter Lovins. 1997. *Factor Four: doubling wealth-halving resource use.* Earthscan, London.

Welcomme, R. L. 1985. *River fisheries.* FAO Fisheries Technical Paper 262. Food and Agriculture Organization of the United Nations, Rome.

Wilson, E. O. 1988. The current state of biological diversity. In: E. O. Wilson (ed.). 1988. *Biodiversity.* National Academy Press, Washington, DC.

World Bank. 1998. *World development indicators 1998.* World development indicators on CD-ROM. The World Bank, Washington, DC.

World Bank. 1999a. *World development indicators 1999.* World development indicators on CD-ROM. The World Bank, Washington, DC.

World Bank. 1999b. *Global development finance 1999.* Global development finance on CD-ROM. The World Bank, Washington, DC.

World Bank. 2000a. *World development indicators 2000.* World development indicators on CD-ROM. The World Bank, Washington, DC.

World Bank. 2000b. *Global development finance 2000.* Global development finance on CD-ROM. The World Bank, Washington, DC.

World Bank staff. 1997. *Expanding the measure of wealth: indicators of environmentally sustainable development.* Environmentally Sustainable Development Studies and Monographs Series 17. The World Bank, Washington, DC.

World Commission on Environment and Development. 1987. *Our common future.* Oxford University Press, Oxford, England.

World Conservation Monitoring Centre. 1992. *Global biodiversity: status of the earth's living resources.* Chapman and Hall, London.

World Conservation Monitoring Centre. 1997. *Biodiversity conservation in the tropics: gaps in habitat protection and funding priorities.* WCMC Biodiversity Series 6. World Conservation Monitoring Centre, Cambridge, England.

World Conservation Monitoring Centre. 1998a. WCMC threatened plants database. World Conservation Monitoring Centre, Cambridge, England.

World Conservation Monitoring Centre. 1998b. WCMC threatened animals database. World Conservation Monitoring Centre, Cambridge, England.

World Energy Council. 1999. *Survey of energy resources.* World Energy Council, London.

World Health Organization (WHO). 1996–1998a. WHO Health-for-All database (data from WHO member states and regional offices). World Health Organization, Geneva.

World Health Organization (WHO). 1998b. *Health for all in the twenty-first century.* Document A51/5. World Health Organization, Geneva.

World Health Organization (WHO). 1998c. *Healthy cities air management information system.* AMIS 2.0, 1998. CD-ROM. World Health Organization, Geneva.

World Health Organization (WHO). 1998d. *Guidelines for air quality.* World Health Organization, Geneva.

World Health Organization (WHO). 2000. *World health report 2000.* World Health Organization, Geneva.

World Meteorological Organization. 1995. *Scientific assessment of ozone depletion: 1994.* WMO Global Ozone Research and Monitoring Project, Report 37. World Meteorological Organization, Geneva.

World Resources Institute, United Nations Environment Programme, United Nations Development Programme, and World Bank. 1998. *World Resources 1998–99.* Oxford University Press, Oxford, England.

Index